Native American Bibliography Series

Advisory Board

No. 1 *Bibliography of the Sioux,* by Jack W. Marken and Herbert T. Hoover. 1980

No. 2 *A Bibliography of Native American Writers, 1772-1924,* by Daniel F. Littlefield, Jr. and James W. Parins. 1981

No. 3 *Bibliography of the Languages of Native California,* by William Bright. 1982

No. 4 *A Guide to Cherokee Documents in Foreign Archives,* by William L. Anderson and James A. Lewis. 1983

A Guide to Cherokee Documents in Foreign Archives

by
William L. Anderson
and
James A. Lewis

Native American Bibliography Series, No. 4

The Scarecrow Press, Inc.
Metuchen, N.J., and London
1983

Library of Congress Cataloging in Publication Data

Anderson, William L., 1941-
  A guide to Cherokee documents in foreign archives.

  (Native American bibliography series ; no. 4)
  Includes index.
  1. Cherokee Indians--History--Sources--Bibliography--
Catalogs. 2. Cherokee Indians--History--Manuscripts--
Catalogs. I. Lewis, James A. (James Allen) II. Title.
III. Series.
Z1210.C46A53 1983 [E99.C5] 016.970004'97   83-4636
ISBN 0-8108-1630-X

To

Nina and Johanna

A GUIDE TO
CHEROKEE DOCUMENTS IN FOREIGN ARCHIVES

CONTENTS

CONTENTS

SPAIN

PREFACE

Our interest in A Guide to Cherokee Documents in Foreign Archives grew out of several fortuitous circumstances. As historians living in the mountains of North Carolina, we found it impossible to ignore the influence that the Cherokee Indians have had in shaping the history of this area of the United States. As scholars doing research in our areas of specialization (England and Latin America), we frequently came across large quantities of foreign materials on the Cherokees that few scholars of the American Indian have consulted or, in some cases, even knew existed. With the help of Western Carolina University, the Museum of the Cherokee Indian, and the National Endowment for the Humanities, we began a project in 1978 to collect copies of as much Cherokee material in foreign archives as possible so as to provide scholars and the tribe with access to this largely untapped reservoir of information on the Cherokee past. In the process of collecting these materials, it became apparent to us that a guide to these documents was necessary. Without some way of publicizing the existence of these materials, there was little likelihood that many people would consult them.

A Guide to Cherokee Documents in Foreign Archives could not have been completed without the assistance and labor of many people. We are extremely grateful to the Research Resources Program of the National Endowment of the Humanities for the financial aid which it has provided over the past five years. Without the support of NEH, it is safe to say that there would have been no project. Drs. William S. Coker (University of West Florida), Wilcomb E. Washburn (Smithsonian Institute), and Dwayne King (Musuem of the Cherokee Indian) provided welcome encouragement that allowed our work to continue. A number of scholars and archivists have advised and helped us in locating materials. We wish expecially to thank Drs. Eric Beerman (Madrid), John F. Bratzel (Michigan State University), Lee Kennett (University of Georgia), and Robert Cain (North Carolina State Archives) for their aid. Numerous individuals at our own university have assisted us. Dr. James Lloyd (University Archivist) has generously shared his knowledge on preparing guides. Drs. Robert Stoltz, John McCrone, and John Manock have found ways to juggle the limited resources of a medium-sized state university to support our research. Dr. Max Williams took valuable time from his own studies to read portions of our manuscript. Ms. Diana Carlson has cheerfully typed many drafts of our index. We also owe a debt to our colleagues in the history department who have tolerated our obsession with finishing a task that often meant slighting other professional obligations. Our biggest debt, however, is owed to Ms. Violet Vassian, our research assistant and typist. If any good came from the Spanish Civil War, it was her journey to the mountains of North Carolina via Spain and France in time to assist us. Long after our funds were depleted for her salary, she worked with us to finish the guide, while holding another university position, attending classes as a student, and maintaining a family. *Estamos muy agradecidos*.

INTRODUCTION

In selecting materials for inclusion in this guide, we have used the broadest approach possible. In addition to sources which directly mention the tribe, this guide also lists materials that refer to Cherokee territory and to Southern Indians in general. All documents are cited in their historical context. For example, if a letter contains attachments, or is itself an attachment, this fact is noted. Enclosures follow the covering document and are indented. Only the materials directly related to the Cherokees receive full descriptions. Entries in the guide contain the following data: (1) original archival citation and other indentifying information; (2) date; (3) geographical origin of the document; (4) title or type of document if it is something other than a letter; (5) sender and recipient; (6) whether the material is a copy or the original, if that information is stated on the document; (7) a description of the Cherokee portion of the document; (8) pages in the document; (9) language when different from the host archive; and (10) information on enclosures where pertinent. The following is an example to illustrate the above format:

(1)   (2)   (3)   (4)   (5)
Fol. 83. 12 Dec. 1765, Philadelphia. Journal of George Crog-
                         (6)   (7)
han to Ben. Franklin (duplicate). Cherokees wish to make peace
                          (8)   (9)   (10)
with the Northern Indians. 27p. *French*. [Enclosures to fol.

116b].

        Fol. 101. 18 Nov. 1765, Charleston. John Stuart to Lt.
        Gov. Bull. [Same as C.O. 5/375/73]. 3p.

For most readers of this guide, the document descriptions are the most important information in the entries. Users should note, however, that these descriptions do not purport to be exhaustive. They are only suggestive of the Cherokee information that a particular document might contain. If a letter, for example, refers to the Cherokees in passing and goes on to detail other subjects, the guide would give attention only to the information about the Cherokees. In cases where an entry is a duplicate or copy of another document cited in the guide, a cross reference takes the place of the usual description (see example above). Since some Canadian materials are modern transcripts of documents from the British Museum, these entries contain the British Museum citations as well as the Canadian ones.

A subject-name index appears at the end of the guide. The index notes all senders and recipients (except for kings and governmental agencies), geographical origins of letters when they came from Cherokee territory, and all proper nouns in the descriptive part of the entries. The subject part of the index is confined primarily to topics directly related to the Cherokees. Careful use of the index can save the researcher considerable time in tracking down specific topics.

Most of the archives mentioned in this guide have facilities to reproduce documents upon request. Reproduction policies, however, do vary from archive to archive, and individuals interested in acquiring copies of specific materials should communicate with each depository regarding their procedures on furnishing copies. In most cases, the material in the guide can be borrowed on interlibrary loan from Hunter Library at Western Carolina University.

There are certain types of documents that the guide does not include. Because maps present some unusual problems in locating and interpreting, we did not cite them unless they were attached to documents already listed. A future volume will list and duplicate most of the maps related to the Cherokees which we discovered. The guide likewise omits magazines and newspapers, like those contained in the Burney Collection in the British Musuem. Time and space forbade their systematic examination and inclusion. These types of materials only appear in cases where they happen to be enclosures to other documents. Finally, there are some foreign archives with considerable material on the Cherokees which are no longer outside the United States. The Spanish East Florida Papers (now in the Library of Congress) and the Spanish-Mexican Bexar and Nacogdoches Papers (now in Austin, Texas) are the best examples of this. The guide does not include documents from these collections.

In conclusion, a final caveat. No historian familiar with archives would ever claim to have found all the materials on a subject as broad as the Cherokees. We certainly do not. We did not, for example, examine the archives of Italy, Germany, and Russia, although there are indications that these countries have a few documents on the Cherokees. International politics prevented us from checking the holdings in the Cuban depositories. Even in the countries that we did visit, time, luck, funding, and intuition (or the lack thereof) conspired to make this guide something less than definitive. Nevertheless, if the wealth of materials that we have uncovered inspires others to use their "archival noses" to discover more documents, our work will have been successful.

ABBREVIATIONS

AC	Archive des Colonies in Archives Nationales, Paris
ADM	Admiralty
AE	Affaires Etrangères
AGI	Archivo General de Indias, Seville
AGS	Archivo General de Simancas, Valladolid
AHN	Archivo Histórico Nacional, Madrid
AM	Archive de la Marine in Archives Nationales, Paris
Anexo	Attachment
AO	Audit Office
Ap	Apartado (group of documents)
Atado	Group of documents
B (b)	Verso
Bolton	Documents cited from Herbert L. Bolton's Guide to Materials for the History of the United States in the Principal Archives of Mexico (Washington, D.C., 1913)
BM	British Museum
BN	Biblioteca Nacional, Madrid
CO	Colonial Office
CP	Correspondance Politique
Doc	Document
Encl	Enclosure
Exp	Expediente (group of documents)
FO	Foreign Office
Fol	Folio
Fr	Friar
GD	Gifts and Deposits
GM	Guerra Moderna
Libro	Bound volume of documents
M	Monsieur
MD	Memoires et Documents
MG	Manuscript Group
MPG	Maps, Plans, and Guides
MR	Map Room
Ms	Manuscript
NAF	Nouvelles Acquisitions Français
N. doc	No document number
N. fol	Not foliated
No	Number
PMG	Paymaster General
PRO	Public Record Office, London
Ramo	Archival section
RG	Record Group
Roll	Rolled document
Rollo	Microfilm role
SD	Santo Domingo
SP	State Papers
SPG	Society for the Propagation of the Gospel
Sr	Señor
Siles	Document numbers from Reyes Siles Saturnino, Documentos relativos a la independencia de Norteamérica existentes en archivos españoles (Madrid, 1980)
T	Treasury
Tramo	Volume
WO	War Office

CANADA

PUBLIC ARCHIVES OF CANADA

Ottawa

PRE-CONQUEST PAPERS
M.G. 18, M1/12   NORTHCLIFFE COLLECTION, MONCKTON PAPERS: 1758

Fol. 5. 9 July 1758, Halifax. Robt. Monckton to Gen. Amherst.
Cherokees were tired of waiting for supplies from England and
have returned home dissatisfied. 5p.

M.G. 18, M1/37   NORTHCLIFFE COLLECTION, MONCKTON PAPERS: 1760-1762

N. fol. 11 May 1760, New York. Gen. Amherst to Col. Byrd
(extract). Amherst regrets that Byrd believes his regiment will
not be sufficient to annoy the Cherokees. Byrd should attack
the Cherokees on one side and Lt. Col. Grant on the other. 2p.

N. fol. 28 May 1760, Winchester. Col. Byrd to [Gen. Amherst].
Lt. Gov. of S.C. has asked Fauquier to relieve Ft. Loudoun. 4p.

N. fol. 29 May 1760, Winchester. Col. Byrd to [Gen. Amherst].
Assembly has voted funds for 700 men to join the 300 of Byrd's
regiment to relieve Ft. Loudoun and attack the Cherokees. 2p.

N. fol. 18 July 1760, Camp at Roanoke. Col. Byrd to [Gen.
Amherst]. Byrd has been ordered to relieve Ft. Loudoun. After
Montgomery's success against the Cherokees, some 300 Creeks
joined the Cherokees who have rejected all peace offers. 2p.

M.G. 18, M1/43   NORTHCLIFFE COLLECTION, MONCKTON PAPERS: 1760

N. fol. 20 Apr. 1760, New York. [Gen. Amherst] to Lt. Gov.
Fauquier. [Same as P.R.O. W.O. 34/37/215]. 2p.

N. fol. 28 May 1760, Albany. Gen. Amherst to Gov. Dobbs.
Amherst is pleased that Dobbs will send 500 troops to the
western frontier against the Cherokees. 1p.

M.G. 18, M1/44   NORTHCLIFFE COLLECTION, MONCKTON PAPERS: 1761

N. fol. 28 Oct. 1761, Staten Island. Gen. Amherst to Lord
Rollo (copy). Amherst has learned that peace is almost settled
with the Cherokees. Grant's troops will go to Dominica. 2p.

M.G. 18, N49   HENRY FOX PAPERS: 1755-1756

Fol. 78. 13 Aug. 1756, Horton. Letter from Dunk Halifax stat-
ing that he has no knowledge about the Cherokees taking over Ft.
Duquesne. He approves Dinwiddie's treaty with the Catawbas and
Cherokees. Workmen have been sent to build a Cherokee fort. 3p.

M.G. 18, N49 (CONT'D)

> Fol. 81. 13 Aug. 1756, Horton. Letter from Dunk Halifax
> stating that the King approves the treaty with Catawbas and
> Cherokees, but Halifax reprimands Dinwiddie for not concluding
> the treaty earlier. Dinwiddie sent Glen £1,000 to build a fort
> near the Cherokees. 4p.

FUR TRADE AND INDIANS
M.G. 19 F1/1   CLAUS PAPERS: 1716-1777

> Fol. 22. 10 Mar. 1761 [1764?], Castle Cumberland. Wm. Johnson
> to Lt. Dan. Claus. Six Nations still fear that the English
> will destroy them. Six Nations are preparing an attack on the
> Cherokees, who may be joined by the Creeks. 7p.

M.G. 19 F1/2   CLAUS PAPERS: 1778-1780

> Fol. 139. 2 Nov. 1779, Detroit. Major De Peyster to Capt.
> McKee. Sasterratzee has brought belts from the Five Nations
> for the Cherokees and Choctaws. The Five Nations want these
> two tribes to continue fighting the King's enemies until further
> notice. 3p.

M.G. 19 F1/3   CLAUS PAPERS: 1781-1783

> Fol. 187. 25 Oct. 1782. Cherokee Nation. John McDonald to
> Thomas Mikin. Shawnees and some Cherokees have arrived in
> Cherokee country. To prevent the destruction of their corn,
> the Cherokees have turned over 20 white men to the rebels. 2p.

M.G. 19 F1/4   CLAUS PAPERS: 1784-1791

> Fol. 253. 12 Apr. 1791, Cherokee Nation. Geo. Welbank to Alex.
> McKee. Dragging Canoe, who strongly favors the English, is
> writing a letter to McKee. Welbank requests that McKee answer
> Dragging Canoe's letter. 2p.
>
> Fol. 313. 22 July 1791, Foot of the Miami Rapids. Alex. McKee
> to Geo. Welbank. McKee has supplied the messenger with cloth-
> ing, provisions, and ammunition for the Cherokees. He expresses
> his friendship for the Cherokees and his eagerness to provide
> assistance. McKee answers Dragging Canoe's letter by pledging
> his support. 2p.

M.G. 19 F1/5   CLAUS PAPERS: 1792-1793

> Fol. 43. 9 Oct. 1792, Glaize. Answer from Lt. Gov. Simcoe of
> Upper Canada to the General Council's speech of several Indian
> nations (including the Cherokees). Simcoe is happy that the
> Indians have proposed to make peace with the United States and
> he offers assistance. 3p.
>
> Fol. 87. 7 Feb. 1793. Speech from Confederate Nations assembled
> at the Glaize inviting the Five Nations to attend a Council

meeting at the foot of the Miami Rapids. Delegates will discuss
the peace terms before the Indians meet the American commissioners at Sandusky. Creeks, Cherokees, Southern Indians, and the
Seven Nations of Canada are expected to attend. 3p.

Fol. 227. 13 - 14 July 1793, Miami Rapids. List of Indians
Drawing Provisions. List indicates that 20 Cherokees received
provisions for 3 days. 4p.

Fol. 241. 23 July 1793, Navy Hall. John G. Simcoe to Alex.
McKee. Simcoe laments the Creek and Cherokee decision which
may adversely influence Western Indians. 2p.

M.G. 19 F1/6   CLAUS PAPERS: 1793-1794

Fol. 113. 12 Apr. 1794, Cherokee Nation. Geo. Welbank to
Alex. McKee. [Cherokee] chiefs have just returned from Walnut
Hills on the Miss. where they attended a Four Nations meeting
at the invitation of the Spaniards. American agent, Seagrove,
is visiting the Cherokees and delivering flattering talks and
goods. Welbank estimates the Creeks to number 21,000 warriors,
Choctaws 25,000, Cherokees 2,500 [?], and Chickasaws 700. 7p.

Fol. 213. 15 Sept. 1794. Return of Indians Drawing Provisions
at Swan Creek. Report includes 30 Cherokees (15 men, 5 women,
and 10 children). 1p.

Fol. 289. 4 Dec. 1794. List of Nations Who Received Presents
at Swan Creek. List includes 14 Cherokees (10 men, 2 women,
and 2 children). 1p.

Fol. 291. 4 Dec. 1794. List of Nations Who Received Presents
at Swan Creek. List includes 14 Cherokees (10 men, 2 women,
and 2 children). 1p.

Fol. 301. 4 Dec. 1794. List of the Indian Nations Receiving
Clothing. List includes 14 Cherokees (10 men, 2 women, and
2 children). 1p.

Fol. 312. [List of Indian] ... Nations ... Driven from Their
Villages and Cornfields by an American Force [and Recommended
to Receive Supplies]. List includes 30 Cherokees (15 men,
5 women, and 10 children). 1p.

Fol. 314. List of Indians. List includes 22 Cherokees (11
men, 3 women, and 8 children). 1p.

M.G. 19 F1/8   CLAUS PAPERS: 1797-1803

Fol. 89. 5 May 1799, Sandwich. Report of Joseph Jackson Sent
as a Messenger to the Mississippi by Order of the Late Deputy
Superintendent General. Large bodies of Creeks, Cherokees,
and Choctaws will join the Spanish when called upon. Most
Southern Indians have formed a confederacy to fight the Osages.
3p.

M.G. 19 F1/8 CONT'D)

Fol. 150. 15 June 1801, Amherstburg. Geo. Ironside to [Prideaux] Selby. Wathaᵢgé said that the Cherokees, Chickasaws, and deputies from other nations will have a **general** council. 1p.

M.G. 19 F16   ALEXANDER AND THOMAS MCKEE PAPERS: 1793-1809

Fol. 1. 10 Apr. 1794, Cherokees. John McDonald to Alex. McKee. McDonald refers to his previous request for a Cherokee named Nacheeah or Fool Warrior. The four Southern nations concluded a treaty with Spain (at Walnut Hills) to protect their remaining lands. McDonald has been offered a post as the Spanish commissary to the Cherokee nation but has not yet accepted. McDonald explains the cause of war between the Cherokees and the American frontiersmen. 4p.

Fol. 5. 26 Dec. 1794, Lower Cherokees. John McDonald to Alex. McKee. Creeks killed Welbank at Eufalees, the nearest Creek town to the Cherokees. Cherokees are negotiating a temporary peace with the United States. If war breaks out between the Americans and Great Britain, the Southern Indians, especially the Cherokees, will join the English. 4p.

Fol. 9. 6 Feb. 1793, Coweta Old Town, Creek Nation. G. Welbank to Alex. McKee. Welbank has forwarded a message via the Cherokees to inform McKee about the Creek plans for a general meeting at Coweta to protect Indian land. 3p.

Fol. 12. 12 Apr. 1793, Coweta Old Town. Talk from Creek Chiefs to Alex. McKee. Creeks hope that Welbank will return after accompanying Shawnees to the [Cherokee] towns. 4p.

Fol. 16. 20 May 1793, Cherokee Nation. Talk from Cherokee Chief Kahanetah (Little Turkey) to Alex. McKee. Little Turkey deplores his nation's condition and hopes to receive supplies in order to prosecute the war against the enemy. 3p.

Fol. 27. 20 Mar. 1809, Hiwassee. Speech from Black Fox (Cherokee) to Shawnee Chief Payhamaskaku [and ten Northern nations] (copy). Black Fox hopes that friendship among tribes will prevail and he desires to live in peace with the whites. 3p.

M.G. 19 F22   PAPERS OF FRANÇOIS TRINQUE: [CA. 1770-1775]

Fol. 114. Montreal. *Langue sauvage pour nommer les articles celon la coûtume des traiteurs.* List of Indian and French commercial terms sent to François Trinque. 8p. *French.*

PAPERS FROM THE BRISTISH MUSEUM
M.G. 21 B.M. ADD. MSS. 8075   PUISAYE PAPERS: 1798-1812

Fol. 111 [B.M. Fol. 107]. 20 Dec. 1810, Grand River. John Norton to Count de Puisaye. Cherokees number 6,000 - 7,000 males and 20,000 females. They have powder mills and their

M.G. 21 B.M. ADD. MSS. 8075 (CONT'D)

women manufacture cotton and woolen cloth. Norton lists the
assets and territory of the Cherokees, the most civilized of
all the Indians in the area. 4p.

M.G. 21, B.M. ADD. MSS. 21631, BOUQUET PAPERS: 1756-1757

Fol. 56 [B.M. fol. 47]. 28 July 1757, Charleston. [Bouquet]
to Capt. Paul Demeré. Governor is sending instructions
concerning Little Carpenter's report. [Bouquet] requests
intelligence on the Indians. French are using Indians as
spies. 1p. *French*.

Fol. 70 [B.M. fol. 60]. 25 Aug. 1757, Charleston. [Bouquet]
to General Webb (copy). Little Carpenter discovered a French
fort on the Ohio. Reinforcing Ft. Prince George will facilitate
communication with Ft. Loudoun. 3p. *French*.

Fol. 82 [B.M. fol. 71]. 25 Aug. 1757, Charleston. [Bouquet]
to Earl of Loudoun. Indian affairs are good. Cherokees have
shown their sincere friendship by often attacking the French.
Little Carpenter has discovered a new fort along the Ohio
sixteen days from Ft. Loudoun. Va. has built a fort only seven
miles from Ft. Loudoun. Their fort is poorly constructed--
being built only to humor the Indians. 8p.

M.G. 21, B.M. ADD. MSS. 21632, BOUQUET PAPERS: 1757-1758

Fol. 4 [B.M. fol. 1]. 10 Sept. 1757, Charleston. [Bouquet]
to Lt. Shaw. Shaw should furnish escorts to Ft. Loudoun.
[Bouquet] has done everything to see that the garrison is
properly supplied. Bogges should go to Ft. Loudoun with or
without escort. 3p.

Fol. 7 [B.M. fol. 2b]. 10 Sept. 1757. [Bouquet] to Capt.
Paul Demeré. [Bouquet] wishes Demeré success in obtaining
Indian assistance. Little Carpenter could be very helpful to
guide and locate enemy settlements. 1p.

Fol. 18 [B.M. fol. 6]. 17 Sept. 1757, Charleston. [Bouquet]
to Lt. Shaw. [Bouquet] approves any reasonable measures to
keep the Indians' friendship, but the English will be their
allies not their slaves. 4p.

Fol. 89. [8 Feb. 1758], Charleston. Bouquet to Mr. Stead.
Provisions should be sent to Fts. Prince George and Loudoun.
2p.

Fol. 115 [B.M. fol. 42b]. 24 Apr. 1757, New York. Earl of
Loudoun to Gov. Lyttleton (copy). Loudoun orders 100 Virginians
to reinforce the Va. fort located just nine miles from the S.C.
fort at Chote. The King has appointed Atkin to manage the
Southern Indians. 4p.

M.G. 21, B.M. ADD. MSS. 21634, BOUQUET PAPERS: 1759-1763

Fol. 140 [B.M. fol. 133]. 25 July 1762, New York. Gen.
Amherst to Col. Bouquet. Restraining trade has forced the
Cherokees to release all their English prisoners in S. Carolina.
Bouquet should try the same tactic at Ft. Pitt. 2p.

Fol. 146 [B.M. fol. 141]. 5 Oct. 1762, Ft. Pitt. [Bouquet]
to Gen. Amherst (draft). The Six Nations, who are fighting
the Cherokees, have become troublesome because they are no
longer getting powder, lead, and other presents. 3p.

Fol. 233 [B.M. fol. 244]. 10 May 1763, New York. Gen.
Amherst to George Croghan (copy). The King has ordered the
Southern governors to explain the peace treaty to the Indians.
3p.

Fol. 249 [B.M. fol. 257]. 19 May 1763, New York. Henry
Bouquet to Gen. Amherst (copy). Indians are uneasy about the
French land cessions in the recent treaty. An Indian meeting
would probably calm their fears. 3p.

Fol. 255 [B.M. fol. 262]. 21 May 1763, Philadelphia. [Bouquet]
to Gov. Horatio Sharpe (draft). Indians are very unhappy over
the land cessions that the French made to the English. Southern
governments have been ordered to explain the situation to the
Indians. 1p.

Fol. 285 [B.M. fol. 294]. 23 June 1763, New York. Gen.
Amherst to Col. Bouquet. Sir Wm. Johnson believes that a
Cherokee-Catawba attack on Indian insurgents would be useful.
5p.

Fol. 296 [B.M. fol. 304]. 25 June 1763, New Lancaster. Col.
Bouquet to Gen. Amherst (copy). Bouquet refuses to be under
any obligation to the Cherokees. He would rather have the
liberty to kill the savages than to always be unsure whether
they are friends or foes. 2p.

M.G. 21, B.M. ADD. MSS. 21637, BOUQUET PAPERS: 1763-1765

Fol. 65 [B.M. fol. 53]. 15 Aug. 1764, Ft. Loudoun. Col.
Bouquet to [Gen. Gage] (copy). Bouquet announces his arrival
at Ft. Loudoun. He expects Wm. Johnson's Indians to join him
when he leaves on the expedition from Pittsburg. Small Indian
parties are seen daily observing troop activity. Store houses
at the fort are in terrible condition. 2p.

M.G. 21, B.M. ADD. MSS. 21638, BOUQUET PAPERS: 1759-1765

Fol. 85 [B.M. fol. 69]. 20 Dec. 1759, Winchester. Col. Bouquet
to Gen. Stanwix (draft). Lyttleton informed Gov. Fauquier
that the Cherokees have offered to deliver the hostile Indians
but Lyttleton plans to hang the offenders in their own towns.
3p.

M.G. 21, B.M. ADD. MSS. 21638 (CONT'D)

Fol. 107 [B.M. fol. 92]. 7 June 1760, Ft. Lyttleton. [Bouquet]
to Gen. Monckton (draft). Roads to Ft. Loudoun are in poor
condition. It might be wise to disband the army until more
provisions reach Pittsburg. 1p.

Fol. 248 [B.M. fol. 196]. 12 Feb. 1761, New York. Gen.
Monckton to Col. Bouquet. Bouquet should provide ammunition
to the Indians. Croghan will certainly attack the Cherokees.
2p.

Fol. 329 [B.M. fol. 259]. 5 Oct. 1761, Ft. Pitt. [Bouquet]
to Gen. Monckton (copy). Croghan has returned from Detroit
where Wm. Johnston concluded a general treaty with the Indians.
A deserter from Ft. Chartres, who travelled from Ft. l'Assomption
to Ft. Loudoun in the Upper Cherokee territory, supplied information on conditions around the Tennessee River. 3p.

Fol. 363 [B.M. fol. 240b]. [8 Mar. 1764, New York]. [Bouquet]
to Gen. Gage (draft). Bouquet is unable to send flour and goods
to Ft. Pitt. Capt. Wm. Grant reported that an Indian party
killed a soldier and wounded another, indicating perhaps that
the savages want to continue the war. Bouquet will hold the
convoy until further notice. 1p.

Fol. 377 [B.M. fol. 304]. 2 May 1764, Carlisle. Col. Bouquet
to Gen. Gage (draft). Bad weather has delayed the six companies
ordered to Ft. Loudoun. 4p.

Fol. 423 [B.M. fol. 339]. 15 June 1764, Philadelphia. Col.
Bouquet to Gen. Gage (copy). Bouquet discusses supplies for
Ft. Loudoun. 2p.

Fol. 458 [B.M. fol. 369]. 18 Aug. 1764, New York. Gen. Gage
to Col. Bouquet. Indians attending Congress at Niagara numbered
1,600. Cherokees are preparing for war with the Creeks and
have sent out a few parties against the Shawnees. Bull hopes
that the Cherokees will intercept the French convoy going to
Ohio. 3p.

Fol. 500 [B.M. fol. 404]. 30 Dec. 1764, New York. Gen. Gage
to Col. Bouquet. Gage hopes that the problem about payment for
wagons and horses at Ft. Loudoun has been settled. 1p.

M.G. 21, B.M. ADD. MSS. 21639, BOUQUET PAPERS: 1758-1763

Fol. 7 [B.M. fol. 5]. 31 May 1758, Winchester. John St. Clair
to Col. Bouquet (copy). Cherokees have refused to join Byrd's
army because Ft. Loudoun soldiers attacked them. Blair
evidently wants to make war on the Cherokees. He requested
that St. Clair help garrison the Cherokee fort. 5p.

Fol. 11 [B.M. fol. 7]. 31 May 1758, Carlisle. [Bouquet] to
John St. Clair (copy). Capt. Bosomworth will go to Winchester
to persuade Bouquet's Indians to visit Ft. Loudoun for their
presents. 4p.

M.G. 21, B.M. ADD. MSS. 21639 (CONT'D)

Fol. 15 [B.M. fol. 9]. 3 June 1758, Carlisle. Col. Bouquet
to Sir John St. Clair (copy). In compliance with the general's
orders, Bouquet sent Capt. Bosomworth to Winchester to persuade
the Indians to visit Ft. Loudoun. Bouquet believes that a fort
in Cherokee country is nonsense. He suggests that Col. Byrd
might use his influence with the Cherokees to accompany the
tribe to Ray's Town. 5p.

Fol. 36 [B.M. fol. 26]. 22 June 1758, Carlisle. John St.
Clair to [Bouquet]. St. Clair explains the efforts to garrison
Ft. Lyttleton. Royal Americans will strengthen Ft. Loudoun.
3p.

Fol. 38 [B.M. fol. 28]. 27 June 1758, Carlisle. John St.
Clair to Col. Bouquet. St. Clair is sending the rest of his
three companies to Ft. Loudoun. 2p.

Fol. 190 [B.M. fol. 126]. 14 Oct. 1759, Carlisle. Capt. James
Sinclair to Col. Bouquet. Ft. Loudoun's hay is still unpaid
for. 2p.

M.G. 21, B.M. ADD. MSS. 21640, BOUQUET PAPERS: 1757-1759

Fol. 39 [B.M. fol. 34]. 20 May 1758, Philadelphia. Gen. Forbes
to Col. Bouquet. Cherokees are expected to defend the regiments
marching through the Allegheny Mountains and along the west
branch of the Susquehannah. Bouquet should keep the Cherokees
busy and they should be accompanied by provincials. 3p.

Fol. 42 [B.M. fol. 36]. 22 May 1758, Lancaster. Col. Bouquet
to Gen. Forbes (copy). Cherokees supposedly have brought back
some French prisoners. Bouquet will forward intelligence to
Forbes from Ray's Town. 4p.

Fol. 46 [B.M. fol. 38]. 23 May 1758, Philadelphia. Gen. Forbes
to Col. Bouquet. St. Clair writes that the Cherokees are
impatient and want to go home. Cherokees can hopefully be
persuaded to stay. 2p.

Fol. 48 [B.M. fol. 39]. 25 May 1758, Carlisle. [Bouquet] to
Gen. Forbes (draft). Bouquet expects a Cherokee party of 25
to return soon. St. Clair sent the Cherokees to Shippensburg
and ordered provisions for them. Bouquet will take responsibility for the Indians until orders arrive. 6p.

Fol. 75 [B.M. fol. 56]. 3 June 1758, Carlisle. [Bouquet] to
Gen. Forbes. [Copy of B.M. Add. Mss. 21652 fol. 46]. 6p. *French*.

Fol. 84 [B.M. fol. 59]. 10 June 1758, Philadelphia. Gen.
Forbes to Col. Bouquet. The Cherokees are a problem. Forbes
has done everything possible to please the Cherokees and has
asked Gov. Glen to urge the Cherokees to stay. 3p.

Fol. 87 [B.M. fol. 61]. 14 June 1758, Ft. Loudoun. [Col.
Bouquet] to Gen. Forbes (copy). Bouquet met with Governor

M.G. 21, B.M. ADD. MSS. 21640 (CONT'D)

Sharpe, St. Clair, and Col. Washington to plan troops' route.
Indians from Carlisle have arrived at Ft. Loudoun. Bouquet
hopes to persuade Bosomworth's Indians to join the expedition.
4p. *French.*

Fol. 91 [B.M. fol. 63]. 16 June 1758, Philadelphia. Gen.
Forbes to Col. Bouquet. Store ship has arrived and nothing
can delay the expedition except the defection of the Cherokees,
bad roads, or unsuitable wagons. Governor Glen is visiting
the Cherokees to convince them to remain with the English. 3p.

Fol. 95 [B.M. fol. 66]. 19 June 1758, Philadelphia. Gen.
Forbes to Col. Bouquet. Governor Glen will visit Carlisle to
convince Little Carpenter and the Cherokees to remain. Forbes
wishes Bouquet success with the Cherokees and agrees that it
is better to have 200 faithful Cherokees on their side than
three times the number who are wavering. 3p.

Fol. 139 [B.M. fol. 95]. 15 July 1758, [Philadelphia].
[Bouquet] to Gen. Forbes (draft). Bouquet has asked the
Cherokees to receive the Delaware who accompanied Dunlap (a
volunteer) in his expedition. The Indian will be useful in
Bouquet's negotiations with the Delawares. 3p. *French.*

Fol. 186 [B.M. fol. 126]. 8 Aug. 1758, Ray's Town. Col.
Bouquet to Gen. Forbes. Although the Indians have been very
happy since the last treaty, some 50 of them have returned home.
They have been asked to wait at Ft. Loudoun to receive presents.
Indian's desertion raises the question whether the Indians
should receive presents. 9p. *French.*

Fol. 198 [B.M. fol. 135]. 10 Aug. 1758, Carlisle. Maj. Francis
Halkett to [Col. Bouquet]. Fifty Cherokees who left for Ft.
Loudoun have revolted and demanded the presents promised to
them at end of campaign. 1p.

Fol. 202 [B.M. fol. 139]. 15 Aug. 1758, Shippensburg. Gen.
Forbes to [Bouquet]. Because of poor health, Forbes is
sending Maj. Grant to meet the Cherokees at Ft. Loudoun. Maj.
Grant can hopefully convince them to wait until Forbes' arrival.
If not, Grant should hand out the presents and let the Cherokees
return home. 4p.

Fol. 267 [B.M. fol. 173]. 23 Sept. 1758, Ray's Town. Gen.
Forbes to [Bouquet]. It does not make sense to alienate the
Indians. Although they are not dependable, they seem ready to
embrace an English alliance. Forbes has sent Mr. Basset to
Ft. Loudoun to redistribute troops. 6p.

Fol. 295 [B.M. fol. 191]. 25 Oct. 1758, Ray's Town. Gen.
Forbes to Col. Bouquet. Although Forbes persuaded Little
Carpenter and his followers to join the English, bad weather
has made the roads inaccessible. Governor of Jamaica wants
Little Carpenter to arrange peace between the Cherokees and
Virginians. If Little Carpenter leaves, the Indians probably
will not stay. Catawbas are marching with some Cherokees. 4p.

M.G. 21, B.M. ADD. MSS. 21640 (CONT'D)

> Fol. 316 [B.M. fol. 207]. 4 Jan. 1759, Ft. Loudoun. Maj.
> Halkett to Col. Bouquet. Halkett reports on supplies and troops
> at Ft. Loudoun. 2p.

M.G. 21, B.M. ADD. MSS. 21641, BOUQUET PAPERS: 1758

> Fol. 15 [B.M. fol. 13]. 16 July 1758, Ft. Cumberland. Col.
> Washington to [Bouquet]. Three parties have left for enemy
> country, the largest consisting of an officer and 18 Cherokees.
> Washington will send another party of Cherokees and white men
> tomorrow. Indian parties are more effective than whites, but
> Washington is troubled by the Indians' bad behavior. 3p.

> Fol. 58 [B.M. fol. 46]. 19 Aug. 1758, Ft. Cumberland. Col.
> Washington to [Bouquet]. Capt. McKenzie's party returned with-
> out encountering the enemy. His troops almost killed three
> Cherokees who were returning from Ft. Duquesne after collecting
> intelligence. 2p.

M.G. 21, B.M. ADD. MSS. 21642, BOUQUET PAPERS: 1758-1764

> Fol. 1 [B.M. fol. 1]. 19 June 1758, Ft. Loudoun. Lt. Ourry
> to Col. Bouquet. Ourry attaches the expense account (£1052.7.8)
> for supplies to Ft. Loudoun and the Indians. 2p.

> Fol. 3 [B.M. fol. 4]. 4 July 1758, Ft. Loudoun. Lt. Ourry to
> [Col. Bouquet]. Ft. Loudoun is a troublesome post. It lacks
> workmen and tools and the roads need repair. 3p.

> Fol. 7 [B.M. fol. 7]. 8 July 1758, Ft. Loudoun. Lt. Ourry to
> Col. Bouquet. The three companies of Royal Americans are in
> good health and spirits and they want to join Bouquet. 1p.

> Fol. 8 [B.M. fol. 9]. 12 July 1758, Ft. Loudoun. Lt. Ourry to
> Col. Bouquet. Deserter has been captured. 1p.

> Fol. 9 [B.M. fol. 11]. 13 July 1758, Ft. Loudoun. Lt. Ourry
> to Col. Bouquet. Ourry has requested wagons to transport corn
> to Ray's Town. He has made ready for the general the house
> where Bouquet talked with the Indians. 2p.

> Fol. 11 [B.M. fol. 13]. 19 July 1758, Ft. Loudoun. Lt. Ourry
> to Col. Bouquet. Ourry is sending 35 wagons (5 of Indian corn
> and 30 of flour) to Ray's Town. 2p.

> Fol. 13 [B.M. fol. 15]. 21 July 1758, Ft. Loudoun. Lt. Ourry
> to Col. Bouquet. Hatchets and axes will arrive with the wagon
> of corn tomorrow. Maj. Waddle of N.C. and Maj. Wells of Penn.
> have arrived with their companies. 2p.

> Fol. 15 [B.M. fol. 17]. 6 Aug. 1758, Ft. Loudoun. Lt. Ourry to
> Col. Bouquet. Ourry needs reinforcements. 2p.

> Fol. 17 [B.M. fol. 19]. 11 Aug. 1758, Ft. Loudoun. Lt. Ourry
> to Col. Bouquet. Indians have arrived to receive their presents.

M.G. 21, B.M. ADD. MSS. 21642 (CONT'D)

Yellow Bird and another chief gave a friendly talk. Maj. Grant
will arrive soon with instructions for delivering the Indian
goods. 2p.

Fol. 19 [B.M. fol. 21]. 10 Aug. 1758, Ft. Loudoun. Lt. Ourry
to Col. Bouquet. Ourry has just received Bouquet's letter
about the arrival of 50 Indians. He is troubled because supplies are too low. Capt. Sharp has employed Mr. Crawford, who
should be very useful because he speaks Cherokee. 2p. *French.*

Fol. 126 [B.M. fol. 106]. 11 Feb. 1760, Philadelphia. Lt.
Ourry to Col. Bouquet. Col. Byrd plans to lead an expedition
against the Cherokees. 2p.

Fol. 149 [B.M. fol. 128]. 11 July 1760, Ft. Bedford. Lt.
Ourry to Col. Bouquet. Ourry agrees that Maj. Grant greatly
aided in the punishment of the Cherokees. 1p.

Fol. 158 [B.M. fol. 138]. 29 Sept. 1760, Ft. Bedford. Lt.
Ourry to Col. Bouquet. Cherokees attacked the Ft. Loudoun
garrison on its march to Ft. Prince George. They killed 25
soldiers and enslaved 200 more. All the officers were killed
except Capt. Stuart whom the Cherokees plan to use to correspond
with Ft. Prince George (their next target). Little Carpenter
saved Capt. Stuart and returned him to Col. Byrd. The attack
will probably be blamed on the evacuation of the King's troops
from the Cherokee country and S. Carolina. 2p.

Fol. 360 [B.M. fol. 320]. 3 May 1762, Ft. Bedford. Lt. Ourry
to Col. Bouquet. Loss of Charleston will cause the Cherokees
and other tribes to become insolent. 2p.

Fol. 481 [B.M. fol. 428]. [ca. 22 Apr. 1763], [Ft. Bedford?]
Lt. Ourry to Col. Bouquet. Northern Indians fear the Cherokees and have sought refuge in the fort. 2p.

Fol. 483 [B.M. fol. 429]. 10 May 1763, Ft. Bedford. Lt. Ourry
to Col. Bouquet. At Col. Croghan's request a party of 100 Six
Nations Indians were provided supplies and ammunition on their
way to fight the Cherokees. 2p.

M.G. 21, B.M. ADD. MSS. 21643, BOUQUET PAPERS: 1754-1759

Fol. 76 [B.M. fol. 58]. 21 Feb. 1758, Ft. Loudoun. Capt. Paul
Demeré to [Col. Bouquet]. Little Carpenter and the Great
Warrior of Chote arrived with two French and one female
Twightwee prisoners. Cherokees plan to attack the French
and their Indian allies. About 130 Cherokees have gone to
assist the Virginians. The Tellico people have reformed. 4p.

Fol. 146 [B.M. fol. 106]. 6 June 1758, Ft. Loudoun. Col.
Adam Stephen to [Bouquet]. Stephen is busy with the Cherokees.
1p.

M.G. 21, B.M. ADD. MSS. 21643 (CONT'D)

    Fol. 147 [B.M. fol. 108]. 7 June 1758, Ft. Loudoun. Col.
Adam Stephen to Col. Bouquet. Indians are in better spirits.
Wahutchy [Wawhatchee?] is the troublemaker. Indian party
returning from Winchester reported that the French are rebuilding the fort at Presque Isle. Indians complain about the lack
of food. 2p.

    Fol. 178 [B.M. fol. 132]. 28 June 1758, Ft. Loudoun. Lt. John
Billings to Col. Bouquet. Soldier was killed when he refused
to march to Ft. Loudoun. Capt. Sharp took the rest of company
to Ft. Loudoun. 1p.

    Fol. 200 [B.M. fol. 158]. 25 July 1758, Ft. Loudoun. Col.
Armstrong to Col. Bouquet. Roads to Ray's Town and Lyttleton
are being repaired. Maj. Wells and two companies will leave
before the artillery does to examine and repair difficult
passages. 2p.

M.G. 21, B.M. ADD. MSS. 21644, BOUQUET PAPERS: 1759

    Fol. 12 [B.M. fol. 7]. 6 Jan. 1759. Ft. Bedford. Capt. Alex.
McKenzer to Col. Bouquet. Maj. Halkett ordered Maj. Campbell
at Ft. Loudoun to send 200 men. 3p.

    Fol. 408 [B.M. fol. 305]. 13 Aug. 1759, Ft. Bedford. Col.
Bouquet to Lt. Col. Wall (copy). Bouquet requests an exact
count of all troops, including the two companies that will be
stationed at Ft. Loudoun. 2p.

    Fol. 458 [B.M. 347]. 30 Aug. 1759, Winchester. Lt. Col.
Mercer to Col. Bouquet. A party of thirteen Catawbas and two
Cherokees has just arrived in response to a request made last
year. The two Cherokees have lived with the Catawbas for some
time and see no reason not to respond to the request also.
Mercer has no orders to give them presents and does not know
what to do with the presents on hand. 7p.

M.G. 21, B.M. ADD. MSS. 21645, BOUQUET PAPERS: 1760

    Fol. 85. 4 Mar. 1760, Pittsburg. Maj. Tulleken to Bouquet.
Lyttleton's peace with the [Cherokees] was brief. Indians
scalped almost 40 frontier settlers as soon as Lyttleton returned to Charleston. 4p.

    Fol. 137 [B.M. fol. 114]. 10 May 1760, Winchester. Col. Byrd
to [Col. Bouquet]. Byrd awaits orders. Byrd would send as
many men as possible to stop Cherokee hostility along the
southwestern frontiers. 2p.

    Fol. 153 [B.M. fol. 130]. 2 June 1760, Virginia. Thomas Walker
to Col. Bouquet. Expedition against the Cherokees forces
Walker to remain in southern Virginia. He will return as soon
as his mission is completed. 2p.

M.G. 21, B.M. ADD. MSS. 21645 (CONT'D)

Fol. 216 [B.M. fol. 187]. 23 Aug. 1760, Virginia. Thomas
Walker to Col. Bouquet. Col. Montgomery's retreat from the
Cherokee country makes it impossible for Virginians to do
more than clear part of the road and establish posts to facilitate Gen. Amherst's attempt next year. 2p.

M.G. 21, B.M. ADD. MSS. 21646, BOUQUET PAPERS: 1761

Fol. 81 [B.M. fol. 92]. 19 Mar. 1761, Ft. Byrd. [John?] Read
to Col. Bouquet. Indian guides are uneasy about the Cherokee
stone tomahawk found near Ft. Byrd. 1p.

Fol. 96 [B.M. fol. 111]. 1 Apr. 1761, Winchester. Col. Adam
Stephen to Col. Bouquet. Stephen requested that Amherst send
him reinforcements to wage war in the Cherokee country. 2p.

Fol. 181 [B.M. fol. 199]. 12 May 1761, Winchester. Col. Adam
Stephen to [Col. Bouquet]. Northern Indians reportedly attacked
200 Cherokees near Ft. Chiswell leaving six Cherokees dead and
many wounded. 1p.

Fol. 219 [B.M. fol. 247]. 1 June 1761, Detroit. Capt. Don
Campbell to [Col. Bouquet]. Indian nations want to attack the
Cherokees. Campbell has supplied Indians with ammunition and
encouraged them to fight the Cherokees. 3p.

M.G. 21, B.M. ADD. MSS. 21647, BOUQUET PAPERS: 1761

Fol. 10 [B.M. fol. 11]. 7 July 1761, Detroit. Capt. Campbell
to Col. Bouquet. Six Nations council agreed to stop their
hostility against the Cherokees. Six Nations admitted plan to
seek assistance from the Shawnees and Southern Indians in
retaking Indian land from the English. 6p.

Fol. 33. 20 July 1761. Mr. Hoops to Bouquet. Byrd was to
make forced marches to draw the [Cherokees] away from Grant.
N. Carolina's troops have not yet joined Byrd. 2p.

Fol. 47 [B.M. fol. 42]. 25 July 1761, Winchester. Geo. Mercer
to [Bouquet]. Col. Byrd reports the presence of Frenchmen from
Ft. l'Assomption near the Cherokees. 3p.

Fol. 206 [B.M. fol. 183]. 30 Sept. 1761, Lake Sandusky. Lt.
Meyer to Col. Bouquet. Sandusky Indian returning from Carolina
reportedly lost a fight with the Cherokees. 3p. *French.*

M.G. 21, B.M. ADD. MSS. 21648, BOUQUET PAPERS: 1762

Fol. 1 [B.M. fol. 1]. 7 Jan. 1762, Ft. Chiswell. Col. Adam
Stephen to [Bouquet]. The King and Governor of the Cherokees
and 500 chiefs and warriors came out to meet Stephen with a
flag of truce as he approached their towns. Cherokees have
signed the peace proposals. Northern Indians have fought with
the Cherokees. 2p.

M.G. 21, B.M. ADD. MSS. 21648 (CONT'D)

Fol. 81. 16 Mar. 1762, Sandusky. Ensign Pauli to Col. Bouquet. Indians advised the Wyandotts not to attack the Southern Indians. The Six Nations have joined the Southern Indians against the English and want the Wyandotts to join also. 2p.

Fol. 252 [B.M. fol. 219]. 13 June 1762, Ft. Cumberland. James Livingston to Col. Bouquet. Cherokees took all of Capt. Christy's goods when he was returning from their country. 1p.

M.G. 21, B.M. ADD. MSS. 21649, BOUQUET PAPERS: 1763

Fol. 101 [B.M. fol. 89]. 19 Mar. 1763, Ft. Pitt. Geo. Croghan to [Col. Bouquet]. Although the Cherokees are enemies and have been forced by the Western Indians to go to war, they have desired peace with the English for the last two years. Croghan fears that Cherokee friendship may be more troublesome than he expected. 2p.

Fol. 456 [B.M. fol. 373]. 7 Sept. 1763, Canagogick. Christian F. Post to [Bouquet]. Post plans to travel through N. and S. Carolina preaching the gospel to the heathens. Indians have robbed him of all his belongings amounting to £60. 4p.

Fol. 551 [B.M. fol. 451]. 7 Nov. 1763, Winchester. Col. Stephen to [Col. Bouquet]. Cherokees refused to go to Augusta for the treaty. Creeks have encouraged the Cherokees to join them in a game of ball they want to play with the English. 3p.

Fol. 569 [B.M. fol. 467]. 13 Nov. 1763, Bedford. Capt. Ecuyer to Col. Bouquet. Cherokees have refused the English presents and an alliance. 4p. *French.*

M.G. 21, B.M. ADD. MSS. 21650, BOUQUET PAPERS: 1764

Fol. 84 [B.M. fol. 106]. 27 Mar. 1764, Pensborough. Robert Callender to Col. Bouquet. Convoy loaded with supplies has left Loudoun in good order but poorly escorted. Only a few soldiers remain at Ft. Loudoun to protect 2,000 flour casks. 2p.

Fol. 90 [B.M. fol. 113]. 31 Mar. 1764, Philadelphia. Plumsted and Franks to Bouquet. Convoy of supplies from Ft. Loudoun escorted by provincial troops may be in danger from the Indians. 2p.

Fol. 215 [B.M. fol. 252]. 9 June 1764, Carlisle. Col. John Armstrong to Col. Bouquet. Armstrong is outraged at the murders committed by the Indians near Ft. Loudoun. 1p.

Fol. 256 [B.M. fol. 305]. 30 June 1764, Camp near Ft. Loudoun. Capt. Schlösser to Col. Bouquet. Schlösser received notice of a pardon for deserters who voluntarily return. He does not expect many to do so. 2p.

M.G. 21, B.M. ADD. MSS. 21650 (CONT'D)

Fol. 306. 22 July 1764, Charleston. Capt. Cochrane to Bouquet.
S. Carolina has not yet decided if Ft. Prince George is to be
rebuilt. 2p.

Fol. 327 [B.M. fol. 384]. 2 Aug. 1764, Winchester. Thos.
Rutherford to Col. Bouquet. Rutherford is sending troops to
join Bouquet. It should be easy to enlist many Cherokees
since they are at war with the Shawnees and want to join the
English. 2p.

Fol. 426. 15 Sept. 1764, Charleston. Capt. Cochrane to Bouquet.
[Geo.] Price, commander at Ft. Prince George, refuses to allow
any interference with the Indians who, he maintains, are under
his jurisdiction. 4p.

M.G. 21, B.M. ADD. MSS. 21651, BOUQUET PAPERS: 1764-1765

Fol. 235 [B.M. fol. 204]. 7 Mar. 1765, Bedford. Nathaniel
McCulloch to [Bouquet]. Convoy carring Indian goods was
attacked near Ft. Loudoun. 2p.

Fol. 238 [B.M. fol. 206]. 9 Mar. 1765. Ft. Loudoun. Lt.
Charles Grant to Col. Bouquet. Frontiersmen destroyed goods
intended for the Indians five miles from Ft. Loudoun. 2p.

M.G. 21, B.M. ADD. MSS. 21652, BOUQUET PAPERS: 1758-1760

Fol. 17 [B.M. fol. 12]. 25 May 1758, Carlisle. Col. Bouquet
to Gen. Forbes (draft). Armstrong and Byrd will march to Fts.
Loudoun and Lyttleton. Cherokees are in good spirits but will
not leave until the rest of their party returns. Cherokees
from Shippensburg are ill-behaved. Cherokees are expected to
protect Bouquet's party, which will work near Ray's Town. 10p.
French.

Fol. 38 [B.M. fol. 20]. 30 May 1758, Carlisle. Col. Bouquet
to Gen. Forbes (draft). Cherokees are en route to Ft. Duquesne
with orders from Vohobacken not to return without prisoners or
scalps. 3p. *French.*

Fol. 46 [B.M. fol. 25]. 3 June 1758. Col. Bouquet to Gen.
Forbes. There are problems managing the Indians. Bouquet
hopes that Bosomworth will bring the Cherokees to Ft. Loudoun
or Ray's Town. Catawbas will not abandon the Cherokees nor
Wahatchee, whom they respect very much. A new supply of
presents and the arrival of Little Carpenter with 200 warriors
should encourage the other Cherokees to stay. 11p. *French.*

Fol. 61 [B.M. fol. 32]. 7 June 1758, Carlisle. Col. Bouquet
to [Gen. Forbes] (draft). Bouquet describes the poor conduct
of the Cherokees and their attitude toward the English. The
tribe might join the French. Cherokees refused to attend the
council meeting at Ft. Loudoun. 11p. *French.*

M.G. 21, B.M. ADD. MSS. 21652 (CONT'D)

Fol. 88 [B.M. fol. 42]. 16 June 1758, Ft. Loudoun. Col.
Bouquet to John St. Clair (draft). A party of 100 Cherokees
and 27 Catawbas are ready to go to war. Bouquet promised
them presents. 2p.

Fol. 90 [B.M. fol. 44]. 16 June 1758, Ft. Loudoun. Col.
Bouquet to Gen. Forbes (draft). Bouquet has 27 Catawbas and
99 Cherokees ready for war. He has supplied the Cherokees
who promise to meet him at Ft. Lyttleton. 5p. *French.*

Fol. 101 [B.M. fol. 49]. 28 June 1758, Camp near Ray's Town.
Col. Bouquet to [Gen. Forbes]. Cherokees are behaving well,
but the enemy has not yet made an appearance. Two parties
of 15 Cherokees and 15 soldiers (under Capts. Clayton and
Ward) left to scout the roads through the Alleghenies. 6p.
French

Fol. 107 [B.M. fol. 51]. 30 June 1758, Camp near Ray's Town.
Col. Bouquet to Sir John St. Clair (draft). Cherokees are
still dependable. They are even helping to build the ware-
houses, something they never did before. 4p. *French.*

Fol. 111 [B.M. fol. 53]. 11 July 1758, Camp near Ray's Town.
Col. Bouquet to Gen. Forbes. Cherokees are gathering intelligence around the Ohio River. 9p. *French.*

Fol. 120 [B.M. fol. 57]. 15 July 1758, Camp near Ray's Town.
Col. Bouquet to Gen. Forbes (draft). Bouquet has persuaded
the Cherokees to accept the Anibas (Delawares) who accompanied
Dunlap on the Ohio. Anibas could be useful with the [Shawnee]
negotiations. Cherokees are asked to identify themselves as
allies by wearing a yellow band on their forehead and arms.
6p. *French.*

Fol. 126 [B.M. fol. 60]. 4 Sept. 1758. [Bouquet] to Gen.
[Forbes] (draft). Supplies are needed. Delays have caused
the army to get restless. Troops are being sent to replace
those at Fts. Loudoun and Lyttleton. 8p. *French.*

Fol. 155 [B.M. fol. 71]. 24 Sept. 1758, Loyal Hannon.
[Bouquet] to the governor of Ft. Duquesne (draft). Cherokees
have refused to release Belestre, even though Va. and Carolina
offered a considerable ransom and presents, because the tribe
lost a chief in battle. 2p.

M.G. 21, B.M. ADD. MSS. 21653, BOUQUET PAPERS: 1760-1765

Fol. 277 [B.M. fol. 195]. 21 July 1763, Ft. Lyttleton.
[Bouquet] to John McDowell (copy). The people at Ft. Loudoun
will not furnish horses except by force. Their lack of cooperation will be remembered when they need help. 2p.

Fol. 373 [B.M. fol. 262]. 8 Mar. 1764, New York. Col. Bouquet
to Plumsted and Franks (copy). Convoy will continue from Ft.
Loudoun to Ft. Pitt. 1p.

M.G. 21, B.M. ADD. MSS. 21653 (CONT'D)

Fol. 373 [B.M. fol. 262b]. 8 Mar. 1764, New York. Col.
Bouquet to Capt. Robt. Callender (copy). Renewed hostilities
at Ft. Pitt does not alter Bouquet's plan. Convoy at Ft.
Loudoun should be ready to proceed at Capt. Schlösser's call.
2p.

Fol. 377 [B.M. fol. 264]. 8 Mar. 1764, New York. Col.
Bouquet to Capt. Schlösser (draft). Schlösser should march
with three companies of the Royal Americans to Ft. Loudoun.
Enemy hostility is not expected. 3p.

Fol. 389 [B.M. fol. 276]. 27 Apr. 1764, Carlisle. [Col.
Bouquet] to Capt. David Hay (copy). Several companies of
the Royal Americans have orders to march from Philadelphia
to Ft. Loudoun. 2p.

Fol. 400 [B.M. fol. 284]. 3 May 1764, Carlisle. Col.
Bouquet to Capt. Wm. Grant (copy). Three Royal American
companies and three companies under Grant are ordered to
march to Ft. Loudoun and wait for results of the Penn.
assembly. 5p.

Fol. 412 [B.M. fol. 292]. 4 June 1764, Philadelphia. Col.
Bouquet to the Governor and Commissioners (draft). All
troops enlisted through next December are hopefully equipped
and ready. Bouquet wants them to assemble at Ft. Loudoun.
3p.

M.G. 21, B.M. ADD. MSS. 21655, BOUQUET PAPERS: 1758-1765

Fol. 1 [B.M. fol. 1]. 11 May 1758, Ft. Lyttleton. Capt.
Edward Ward. The Cherokees Account. List of supplies for
the Cherokees amounting to £75.1.6. 1p.

Fol. 2 [B.M. fol. 2]. 30 May 1758, Shippensburg. Capt. Bosomworth to Bouquet. Indians might go to Ft. Loudoun. 1p.

Fol. 3 [B.M. fol. 4]. 5 and 6 June 1758, Ft. Loudoun. Capt.
Trent to Bouquet. Cherokees refuse to wait for Bouquet's
arrival and threaten to join the Creeks against the English
if they are not given many presents. 4p.

Fol. 7 [B.M. fol. 6]. 7 June 1758, Ft. Loudoun. Capt.
William Trent to Col. Bouquet (copy). Cherokee party arrived
from Ft. Lyttleton and claimed to have lost a man fighting
the enemy at the little French fort. Trent gave presents to
Wawhatchee and his men with the condition that they stay.
Wawhatchee and ten [Cherokees] are going to Winchester and
the rest will remain at Ft. Loudoun. It is difficult to
know the Indians' real intentions. 1p.

Fol. 11 [B.M. fol. 9]. 16 June 1758, Ft. Loudoun. Capt.
Bosomworth to Col. Bouquet. March to Ft. Lyttleton has been

M.G. 21, B.M. ADD. MSS. 21655 (CONT'D)

delayed by difficulties in equipping the Indians. To insure
their loyalty, the Indians will not be given presents until
after the campaign. 2p.

Fol. 13 [B.M. fol. 11]. 18 June 1758, Ft. Loudoun. Capt.
Bosomworth to Col. Bouquet. Two parties of warriors from
Winchester will join Bouquet at Lyttleton. The Carlisle
parties will leave with McKee. To insure loyalty, presents
will be stored until the Indians return. 1p.

Fol. 14 [B.M. fol. 13]. 14 July 1758, Camp at Cumberland.
Capt. Bosomworth to Col. Bouquet. There are no Catawbas at
Winchester nor any sign of Little Carpenter. 1p.

Fol. 15 [B.M. fol. 15]. 23 July 1758, Camp at Ray's Town.
Capt. Bosomworth. Calculation for the Expense of Indian
Warriors for their Service during the Campaign. 1p.

Fol. 17 [B.M. fol. 17]. 10 Sept. 1758, Camp at Ray's Town.
Capt. Bosomworth to Col. Bouquet. Bosomworth will march
tomorrow with the Cherokee and Ohio Indians to the advanced
posts. Three of Mr. Glen's favorite Indians have left for
home. 2p.

Fol. 138 [B.M. fol. 138]. 10 Apr. 1761, Ft. Pitt. Geo. Croghan
to Col. Bouquet. Delaware George has kept his nation from going
to war against the Cherokees. 1p.

M.G. 21, B.M. ADD. MSS. 21661, HALDIMAND PAPERS: 1758-1777

Fol. 355 [B.M. fol. 352]. 9 July 1774, New York. [Gen.
Haldimand] to Amherst (draft). Misunderstandings with the Ga.
Indians have been settled, but the Virginians and frontiersmen
are doing everything possible to incite the Ohio Indians to go
to war. 3p. *French.*

M.G. 21, B.M. ADD. MSS. 21664, HALDIMAND PAPERS: 1769-1771

Fol. 93 [B.M. fol. 102]. 20 Jan. 1770, Charleston. John Stuart
to Brig. Gen. Fred. Haldimand. Southern District Indians are
friendly. Nevertheless, it is hard to tell how long the present
tranquility will last since the Virginians continue encroaching
on Cherokee land. 1p.

Fol. 94 [B.M. fol. 104]. 4 Aug. 1769, Charleston. John Stuart
to Brig. Gen. Haldimand. New boundary line between Va. and
the Cherokees will be negotiated if Va. pays the expenses. 2p.

Fol. 96 [B.M. fol. 106]. 24 Apr. 1769, Charleston. John Stuart
to Brig. Gen. Haldimand (duplicate). Stuart met with the Cherokees and Creeks along the N.C. and Ga. frontiers. Stuart is
pleased that Haldimand approves his sentiments concerning
quarrels among the Indians. 2p.

M.G. 21, B.M. ADD. MSS. 21665, HALDIMAND PAPERS: 1771-1777

Fol. 175 [B.M. fol. 161]. 6 Aug. 1773, New York. [Gen. Haldimand]. to Gen. Gage (draft). Southern affairs remain the same. Congress at Augusta has determined how much land the Creeks and Cherokees will cede. Little Carpenter reports that the confederation will make the Western Indians come to reason. 2p. *French.*

Fol. 182 [B.M. fol. 168]. 31 Aug. 1773, New York. [Gen. Haldimand] to Gen. Gage (draft). Ga. frontiersman murdered two young Cherokees who were sons of chiefs. Murderer was captured but escaped, resulting in rumors of Indian hostility. 2p. *French.*

Fol. 287 [B.M. fol. 269]. 14 July [1774], New York. [Gen. Haldimand] to Gen. Gage (draft). [Haldimand] sends Stuart's letter on Southern Indian affairs. 2p. *French.*

Fol. 305 [B.M. fol. 291]. 6 Aug. 1774, New York. Gen. Haldimand to Gen. Gage (draft). Haldimand is concerned over the sale of Indian land by [Gov.] Wright. 1p. *French.*

M.G. 21, B.M. ADD. MSS. 21666, HALDIMAND PAPERS: 1756-1775

Fol. 65 [B.M. fol. 64]. [ca. Oct. - Dec. 1758]. James Robertson to Brig. Gen. Haldimand. Cherokees are not expected at Winchester until mid-April. 5p.

M.G. 21, B.M. ADD. MSS. 21669, HALDIMAND PAPERS: 1760-1765

Fol. 85 [B.M. fol. 116]. 17 July 1764, Three Rivers. Haldimand to Col. Burton (draft). Haldimand hopes for peace with the Southern Indians but doubts whether the Shawnees and Delawares will remain peaceful. 2p. *French.*

M.G. 21, B.M. ADD. MSS. 21670, HALDIMAND PAPERS: 1759-1774

Fol. 103 [B.M. fol. 60]. 28 June 1773, Pittsburg. Speech from Shawnees (from Scioto) to McKee and Kiashuta and their reply. Shawnees question Virginia's right to settle on their land just because the land was sold by the Six Nations and Cherokees. 2p.

M.G. 21, B.M. ADD. MSS. 21671, HALDIMAND PAPERS: 1765-1769

Fol. 256 [B.M. fol. 188]. 14 Mar. 1767, Mobile. Charles Stuart to Brig. Gen. Taylor. Six Cherokee ambassadors are concluding peace with the Chickasaws. Cherokees are expected to join the Chickasaws against the Creeks. 3p.

Fol. 262 [B.M. fol. 192]. 14 Mar. 1767, Mobile, Charles Stuart to [Brig. Gen. Taylor]. Cherokees have offered to join the Chickasaws against the Creeks. 3p.

M.G. 21, B.M. ADD. MSS. 21671 (CONT'D)

Fol. 281 [B.M. fol. 212]. 7 June 1767, Augusta. John Stuart to [Brig. Gen. Haldimand] (copy). Stuart met with the principal Cherokee chiefs and S.C. traders to regulate the price of goods and hear complaints. Cameron and the Cherokees will run the boundary line with N.C. and Virginia. 3p.

Fol. 293 [B.M. fol. 217]. 25 June 1767, Charleston. John Stuart to Brig. Gen. Haldimand. Cherokees are friendly. Cherokee representatives and Cameron, the commissary of the Cherokee nation, are running the N.C. boundary line. 3p.

Fol. 302 [B.M. fol. 222]. 22 July 1767, Charleston. John Stuart to Brig. Gen. Haldimand. Indian affairs have improved. Cherokee boundary line with N.C. satisfies Gov. Tryon. 2p.

Fol. 380 [B.M. fol. 277]. 24 Mar. 1768, Charleston. John Stuart to Brig. Gen. Haldimand (copy). Stuart is pleased that Haldimand agrees with him about Indian presents being sent to the governors. Cherokee deputies have not returned from the peace negotiations with the Northern Indians. 4p.

M.G. 21, B.M. ADD. MSS. 21672, HALDIMAND PAPERS: 1770-1774

Fol. 7 [B.M. fol. 7]. 26 Aug. 1770, Charleston. John Stuart to Brig. Gen. Haldimand. Stuart will meet with the principal Cherokee chiefs in October to confirm the Va. boundary line. Shawnees and Northern tribes are tampering with the Southern Indians. 2p.

Fol. 10 [B.M. fol. 10]. 23 Jan. 1771, Charleston. John Stuart to Brig. Gen. Haldimand. Shawnees are probably trying to persuade the Southern Indians to form a confederacy with the Northern and Western Indians. Cherokees and Chickasaws favor the Six Nations. Va. boundary line has been settled with the Cherokees. 3p.

Fol. 69 [B.M. fol. 38]. [1772], [Charleston]. John Stuart to [Brig. Gen. Haldimand]. Stuart has no complaints about the Indians' behavior at the Congress. 3p.

Fol. 79 [B.M. fol. 47]. 21 June 1772, Charleston. John Stuart to Brig. Gen. Haldimand. Cherokees are peaceful and the Cherokee chief wishes to visit Stuart. 3p.

Fol. 92 [B.M. fol. 51]. 13 Sept. 1772. John Stuart to Brig. Gen. Haldimand. Cherokees killed some immigrants on their way to the Miss. River. Traders purchasing Cherokee land are likely to create problems with the Creeks. 3p.

Fol. 101 [B.M. fol. 65]. 8 Jan. 1773, Charleston. John Stuart to Maj. Gen. Haldimand. Creeks are upset by the frequent English requests for land. Stuart will meet the Cherokees and Creeks to settle the exchange of land for payment of debts owed to the traders. 2p.

M.G. 21, B.M. ADD. MSS. 21672 (CONT'D)

Fol. 136 [B.M. fol. 87]. 1 June 1773, Pensacola. Copy of
description of Creek and Cherokee boundary line. 2p.

Fol. 145 [B.M. fol. 97]. 5 July 1773, Charleston. John Stuart
to Gen. Gage. Creeks refuse to give up land, which forces the
Cherokees to move their boundary nearer to Cherokee towns.
There is disagreement over debts since most traders burned
their account book when the Cherokees agreed to cede land. 3p.

Fol. 151 [B.M. fol. 101]. 5 July 1773, Seneca. Talk from Big
Sawny (Carotutoy) to Alex. Cameron. [Same as P.R.O. C.O. 5/74/
155]. 3p.

Fol. 156 [B.M. fol. 105]. 6 July 1773, Settico in the Overhill
Cherokees. Talk from Oconostota, Willinawa, Judd's Friend, and
Cold Weather to Alex. Cameron. [Same as P.R.O. C.O. 5/74/163].
2p.

Fol. 158 [B.M. fol. 107]. 15 July 1773, Keowee. Talk from
Lower Cherokees (Attakullakulla, Ecuij, and Chinisto) to Alex.
Cameron. [Same as P.R.O. C.O. 5/74/165]. 2p.

Fol. 160 [B.M. fol. 109]. 21 July 1773, Cherokee Nation. Alex.
Cameron to John Stuart. [Same as P.R.O. C.O. 5/74/161]. 2p.

Fol. 167 [B.M. fol. 115]. 6 Aug. 1773, New York. [Gen.
Haldimand] to John Stuart (copy). Stuart should obtain satisfaction soon for the Cherokee murder of Va. immigrants last
year. Little Carpenter's reports are hopefully true and the
league and their Northern confederacies will really punish the
Western Indians. 2p.

Fol. 170 [B.M. fol. 119]. 10 Aug. 1773, Charleston. John
Stuart to Gen. Haldimand. Deputies from the Northern tribes,
Creeks, and Chickasaws will meet at Chote in Cherokee country.
The murderer of two Cherokees killed along the Ga. frontier
was apprehended but escaped. 3p.

Fol. 172 [B.M. fol. 121]. 12 Aug. 1773, New York. [Maj. Gen.
Haldimand] to John Stuart (copy). Haldimand regrets the murder
of the young Cherokees and will request that a reward be offered
for the apprehension of the murderer. He suggests that presents
be given to the victim's family. 2p.

Fol. 176 [B.M. fol. 125]. 20 Aug. 1773, Charleston. John
Stuart to Maj. Gen. Haldimand. Stuart is continuing the prosecution against Richard Pearis who illegally bought [Cherokee]
land. Stuart has employed a surveyor to run the boundary for
N.C., S.C., and Georgia. 2p.

Fol. 187 [B.M. fol. 133]. 11 Oct. 1773. Alex. Cameron to
[John Stuart]. [Same as P.R.O. C.O. 5/75/9]. 5p.

M.G. 21, B.M. ADD. MSS. 21672 (CONT'D)

Fol. 194 [B.M. fol. 137]. 17 Oct. 1773, Charleston. John
Stuart to Maj. Gen. Haldimand. Stuart has sent Cameron an
extract of Haldimand's instructions concerning Collins [guilty
of murdering two Cherokees]. He expects to receive information
from Cameron about the Cherokees' meeting at Chote. Action
will be taken against Richard Pearis. 3p.

Fol. 203 [B.M. fol. 144]. 22 Nov. 1773, Charleston. John
Stuart to Maj. Gen. Haldimand. Stuart is sending an abstract
of Cameron's letter concerning the Cherokees. Indian affairs
are peaceful. 3p.

Fol. 206 [B.M. fol. 146]. 14 Dec. 1773, Virginia. Arthur
Campbell to Earl of Dunmore (copy). Cherokees supposedly
killed Wm. Russell's son and five others. 2p.

Fol. 208 [B.M. fol. 147]. 20 Dec. 1773, Virginia. Earl of
Dunmore to John Stuart. Dunmore will take every step to
secure the murderers [who are supposedly Cherokees]. 2p.

Fol. 218 [B.M. fol. 156]. 5 Jan. 1774, Charleston. John
Stuart to Maj. Gen. Haldimand (copy). Pearis is obligated to
relinquish his claim [to Cherokee land]. Oconostota assured
Stuart about the Cherokees' pacific intentions. Objective of
the proposed meeting at Chote is to form a confederacy that
will force the Western tribes to come to reason. 3p.

Fol. 228 [B.M. fol. 112]. 17 and 22 Jan. 1774, Charleston.
Charles Stuart to Maj. Gen. Haldimand. Cherokees murdered
five whites and a negro [Wm. Russell's party]. 5p.

Fol. 254 [B.M. fol. 172]. 28 Jan. 1774, Savannah. John Stuart
to Alex. Cameron. [Same as P.R.O. C.O. 5/75/53]. 2p.

Fol. 261 [B.M. fol. 178]. 3 Feb. 1774, Charleston. John
Stuart to Maj. Gen. Haldimand. Cherokees are suspected of
murdering whites in Virginia. Although Stuart believes that
the Cherokees are not guilty, they cannot be trusted. 8p.

Fol. 280 [B.M. fol. 188]. 4 Feb. 1774, Keowee. Talk from
Chinisto of Sugar Town for Headmen and Warriors of Lower
Cherokees to Alex. Cameron. [Same as P.R.O. C.O. 5/75/83].
1p.

Fol. 281 [B.M. fol. 190]. 4 Feb. 1774. Talk from Chinisto of
Sugar Town for Headmen and Warriors of Lower Cherokees to
Alex. Cameron. [Same as P.R.O. C.O. 5/75/83]. 1p.

Fol. 282 [B.M. fol. 192]. 4 Feb. 1774, Lochaber. Alex.
Cameron to [John Stuart]. [Same as P.R.O. C.O. 5/75/57]. 3p.

Fol. 285 [B.M. fol. 194]. 9 Feb. 1774, Lochaber. Alex.
Cameron to [John Stuart]. [Same as P.R.O. C.O. 5/75/77]. 2p.

Fol. 287 [B.M. fol. 196]. 10 Feb. 1774, Charleston. John
Stuart to Gen. Haldimand. Cherokees accompanied the Creeks who
attacked the Georgia militia. Terror has spread throughout
the southern provinces. Stuart told Cameron to use all possible
means to keep the Cherokees on the English side. 4p.

Fol. 309 [B.M. fol. 206]. 21 Feb. 1774, Sugartown. Talk from
Wolf of Seneca and Chinisto of Sugartown on behalf of the Middle
and Lower Cherokee Warriors and Headmen. [Same as P.R.O.
C.O. 5/75/85]. 2p.

Fol. 318 [B.M. fol. 53]. 31 July 1772, Mobile. Charles Stuart
to Gen. Halidmand. Cherokees and Chickasaws encouraged the
Talapooses and Choctaws to seek peace. 3p. *French*

Fol. 320 [B.M. fol. 215]. 25 Feb. 1774, Keowee. Report of a
meeting by Cameron with the Headmen of the Middle and Lower
Cherokee Towns. [Same as P.R.O. C.O. 5/75/87].

Fol. 325 [B.M. fol. 219]. March 1774, Keowee. Alex. Cameron
to [John Stuart]. [Same as P.R.O C.O. 5/75/79]. 7p.

Fol. 359 [B.M. fol. 246]. 12 Apr. 1774, Keowee. Alex. Cameron
to John Stuart (copy). All is well around Keowee. Ball play
is a weekly event. Two traders in the Cherokee and Chickasaw
nations killed a Creek outside Tugaloo. Indians were informed
how much Stuart relies on their promise to observe the treaties.
8p.

Fol. 372 [B.M. fol. 255]. 23 Apr. 1774, Savannah. John Stuart
to Gen. Haldimand. Emistisiguo does not know the reason for
the frequent meetings at Chote, but the Cherokees have inflamed
the Creeks by encouraging jealousy and spreading false rumors.
3p.

Fol. 382 [B.M. fol. 265]. 14 May 1774, Charleston. John
McIntosh to John Stuart (copy). Cherokees should receive a
limited amount of ammunition to prevent them from supplying
the Creeks. Emistisiguo's warning that the Cherokees would
like to see a war between the Creeks and English is correct.
3p.

Fol. 385 [B.M. fol. 267]. 17 June 1774, Chickasaws. John
McIntosh to Charles Stuart (extract). Terrapin and some Cherokees and Chickasaws killed seven whites and one negro near
the Illinois. The Cherokee who was shot by an Englishman vows
to take revenge. 1p.

Fol. 392 [B.M. fol. 274]. 13 Sept. 1774, Charleston. Letter
from John Stuart stating that the Shawnees, Delawares, and
Mingoes are fighting the Virginians and have asked for aid from
the Upper Cherokees. Stuart is afraid that the Cherokees will
comply. Payemingo reported that the Cherokees have been
involved in a lot of mischief. 3p.

M.G. 21, B.M. ADD. MSS. 21672 (CONT'D)

Fol. 397 [B.M. fol. 278]. 20 Nov. 1774, Charleston. John Stuart to Gen. Haldimand. Cameron has received satisfaction from the Cherokees for their involvement with the Shawnees in the Va. murder. Cherokees executed one murderer and another fled to the Chickasaws. 4p.

M.G. 21, B.M. ADD. MSS. 21673, HALDIMAND PAPERS: 1765-1774

Fol. 152 [B.M. fol. 190]. 28 July 1773, Charleston. John Stuart to Gov. Martin (extract). Cameron reported the murder of two young Cherokees in Ga. by John Collins. Steps have been taken to stop the Cherokees from taking revenge and the proper persons have been assigned to capture the murderer. 2p.

Fol. 155 [B.M. fol. 194]. 12 Aug. 1773, New York. Gen. Haldimand to Gov. Martin (copy). Haldimand sends extract of a letter from [John Stuart] suggesting a reward for the apprehension of John Collins, who murdered two Cherokees. 1p.

M.G. 21, B.M. ADD. MSS. 21687, HALDIMAND PAPERS: 1756-1776

Fol. 303 [B.M. fol. 192]. 31 Mar. 1774. Gen. Haldimand to Thomas Barrow (copy). Haldimand orders the payment of expenses incurred at Augusta for the congress between the Creeks and Cherokees to negotiate the land cession. 2p.

M.G. 21, B.M. ADD. MSS. 21695, HALDIMAND PAPERS: 1773-1775

Fol. 21 [B.M. fol. 23]. 4 Aug. 1773, New York. [Gen. Haldimand] to Earl of Dartmouth (copy). Boundary of lands ceded by the Creeks and Cherokees has been settled at Augusta. Creeks are trying to convince the Cherokees to join them against the Chickasaws. 5p.

Fol. 31 [B.M. fol. 32]. 31 Aug. 1773, New York. [Gen. Haldimand] to Earl of Dartmouth. John Collins killed two young Cherokees. Reward is offered for his apprehension. 4p.

M.G. 21, B.M. ADD. MSS. 21731, HALDIMAND PAPERS: 1774-1777

Fol. 329 [B.M. fol. 326]. 30 June 1777, St. Augustine. Maj. Prevost to [Gen. Haldimand]. Cherokees have signed an advantageous peace treaty, relinquishing much of their land and promising to remain neutral. 8p. *French*

M.G. 21, B.M. ADD. MSS. 21761, HALDIMAND PAPERS: 1781

Fol. 125 [B.M. fol. 134]. 30 July 1781, Savannah. Charles Shaw to Maj. De Peyster (copy). Delaware chief delivered a talk from the Northern to Southern Indians in the presence of several Creeks and Cherokee chiefs. In general the Cherokees are faithful, although poverty has induced some of them to temporize with the rebels. Delaware families who came South will be incorporated with the Cherokees. 3p.

M.G. 21, B.M. ADD. MSS. 21761 (CONT'D)

Fol. 154 [B.M. fol. 171]. 26 Sept. 1781, Upper Shawnee Village.
Capt. Alex. McKee to Maj. De Peyster (copy). Messengers from
the Southern Indians report they are still fighting the enemy.
6p.

M.G. 21, B.M. ADD. MSS. 21763, HALDIMAND PAPERS: 1783-1784

Fol. 43 [B.M. fol. 25]. 5 Mar. 1783, Detroit. Maj. De Peyster
to Brig. Gen. McLean (copy). A party of 50 Cherokees arrived
at Wakatomakee, 27 of which have come to Detroit with letters
for McKee. 2p.

Fol. 304 [B.M. fol. 216]. 1 Aug. 1783, Detroit. Col. De
Peyster to Brig. Gen. McLean. Cherokees must have taken the
prisoners mentioned on Douglas's list. 4p.

Fol. 318 [B.M. fol. 225]. 8 Aug. 1783, Niagara. Brig. Gen.
McLean to Brig. Gen. Haldimand. Forty chiefs and warriors of
the Six Nations are going with the Creeks and Cherokees to
Detroit. 4p.

M.G. 21, B.M. ADD. MSS. 21775, HALDIMAND PAPERS: 1782-1784

Fol. 138 [B.M. fol. 152]. 11 Aug. 1783, Montreal. Brig. Gen.
John Johnson to Gen. Haldimand. Johnson transmits proceedings
[not included] of several meetings with the Six Nations at
Niagara. Deputies from the Six Nations and Col. Butler are
going to Detroit to inform the Cherokees, Creeks, Western
and other Indians about the meetings at Niagara. 2p.

M.G. 21, B.M. ADD. MSS. 21777, HALDIMAND PAPERS: 1777-1783

Fol. 79 [B.M. fol. 93]. 9 Apr. 1779, Pensacola. Commissioners
of Indian Affairs to Lt. Gov. Hamilton (duplicate). Capt.
Cameron's Loyal Refugee Company is being sent to collect the
Cherokees and march them to Ga. or Carolina. Cherokees continue
to be faithful to the government. 7p.

Fol. 131 [B.M. fol. 143]. 15 July 1779, Coosawitchie. Alex.
Cameron to Lt. Gov. Hamilton. Virginians have invaded and
burned the Cherokee settlements, but the Cherokees continue
to fight on the Va., S.C., and Ga. frontiers. 5p.

Fol. 157. 26 Oct. 1779, Coosawitchie. Talk from the Cherokees
to tribes along the Wabash. Cherokees urge other tribes to
remain loyal to the English and against the Virginians. 2p.

M.G. 21, B.M. ADD. MSS. 21779, HALDIMAND PAPERS: 1778-1784

Fol. 240 [B.M. fol. 143]. 2, 4, and 6 Oct. 1783, Niagara.
Meetings Held ... by the Six Nations and a Deputation from
Shawnees, Delawares, and Cherokees (copy). Indians are
reconciled to peace with the Americans but are alarmed by the
rumors that the King has given their land to the Americans.
Ft. Stanwix Treaty (1768) gave the King the only land he could
claim. 6p.

M.G. 21, B.M. ADD. MSS. 21779 (CONT'D)

Fol. 275 [B.M. fol. 167]. 5 Sept. 1784, Buckungehelas Town.
George Girty to Alex. McKee (copy). Cherokees and Shawnees
have gone to look for horses. Spaniards from New Orleans sent
a speech to the Indians informing them that the English and
Americans are united. 1p.

M.G. 21, B.M. ADD. MSS. 21781, HALDIMAND PAPERS: 1776-1783

Fol. 32. 26 Aug. 1778, Montreal. Guy Carleton to Lt. Gov.
Hamilton. Hamilton should tell Stuart to secure the Southern
Indians. 5p.

Fol. 40. 8 Apr. 1779, Quebec. Guy Carleton to Lt. Gov.
Hamilton. Reduction of Georgia will probably stimulate the
Southern Indians. 3p.

M.G. 21, B.M. ADD. MSS. 21782, HALDIMAND PAPERS: 1772-1784

Fol. 128 [B.M. fol. 82]. 26 Aug. 1778, Montreal. Gen.
Haldimand to Lt. Gov. Hamilton. Communications should be
maintained with Stuart and the Cherokees. The Southern
Indians might help obtain success. 4p.

Fol. 235 [B.M. fol. 156]. 28 Dec. 1778, Vincennes. Lt. Gov.
Hamilton to Gen. Haldimand. Letter has been sent to Stuart
with belts for the Chickasaws and Cherokees. Southern Indians
are preparing for war. 4p.

Fol. 266 [B.M. fol. 179]. 24 Jan. 1779, Vincennes. Lt. Gov.
Hamilton to Gen. Haldimand. Southern Indians plan to attack
the rebels. Volunteer party has been sent to the Cherokee
River Indians. 6p.

M.G. 21, B.M. ADD. MSS. 21783, HALDIMAND PAPERS: 1772-1784

Fol. 18 [B.M. fol. 18]. 5 April 1781. Copy of report of
Council held at Detroit with deputation of principal chiefs
of the Shawnees, Delawares, and Cherokees. Indians request
assistance. The Swan (Cherokee chief) stated that he had
adhered to the agreement with Gov. Hamilton and sent such
agreement to the Southern Nations who commenced hostilities
against the enemy. 5p.

Fol. 129 [B.M. fol. 89]. 26 Sept. 1781, Upper Shawnee Village.
Alex. McKee to Maj. De Peyster. [Same as M.G. 21, Add. Mss.
21761, fol. 154]. 6p.

Fol. 390 [B.M. fol. 319]. 28 June 1783, Detroit. Major de
Peyster to Gen. Haldimand. De Peyster invited four deputies
from each nation to attend the meeting. Whole villages,
however, started out before his message could reach them.
Indians are impatient to know what will become of their land
and nations. Delawares, Shawnees, and Wyandotts will not
attend until they consult with the Cherokees and Six Nations.
2p.

M.G. 21, ADD. MSS. 24322, PAPERS RELATING TO AMERICAN AFFAIRS: 1718-1796

Fol. 71 [B.M. fol. 2]. 9 and 16 Sept. 1730. Order to pay Robert Johnson £400, which added to the £300 already received will defray the expenses of seven Cherokees. 2p.

Fol. 212 [B.M. fol. 112]. 18 May 1785, Wakitumikee. Minutes of Council attended by chiefs from the Shawnees, Mingoes, Delawares, and Cherokees and by James Shirlock and four other Americans. Indian chiefs complain about white encroachments on their territory. 4p.

LATE EIGHTEENTH CENTURY PAPERS
M.G. 23 A 4/11   SHELBURNE MSS.: 1763-1766

Fol. 103. Observations Relating to the Boundaries of Carolina (copy). The greatest expense in the governments annual budget is presents for the Creeks, Cherokees, and Chickasaws. 14p.

M.G. 23 A 4/15   SHELBURNE MSS.: 1766-1767

Fol. 2. 10 May 1766 , Ft. Prince George. Alex. Cameron to Mr. Stuart (extract). Wilkinson was appointed commissioner to run the boundary beginning at Dewises Corner and continuing 50 miles southwest to the Savannah River. Cherokees propose running a straight line from Reedy R. to Chiswell's Mines, giving up a portion of their land to avoid arguments. 3p.

RECORDS RELATING TO INDIAN AFFAIRS, SERIES II
R.G. 10 C1220/2   MINUTES OF THE COMMISSION FOR INDIAN AFFAIRS AT
ALBANY: 1732-1748

Fol. 137. 26 July 1738, Albany. Minutes containing a report from Lawrence Claase to Commissioners of Indian Affairs. Senecas, Cayugas, and Oneidas are going to war against the Catawbas and Cherokees. Cherokees or Catawbas murdered a Cayuga Indian near Philadelphia. 3p.

Fol. 140a. 25 Aug. 1738, Albany. Minutes containing a letter from Commissioners of Indian Affairs to Lt. Gov. of [New York]. Although the time has now passed when the Six Nations delegates were to meet with the Southern Indians, the commissioners still hope a lasting peace with the Southern Indians can be arranged. 3p.

Fol. 227. 14 May 1742, Albany. Minutes containing a speech from Senecas to Commissioners for Indian Affairs. Tribe looks forward to confirmation of peace with the Southern Indians. 1p.

Fol. 227a. 14 June 1742, Albany. Minutes of a meeting of Six Nations and Gov. Clark. Six Nations told the Cherokees that they would be glad to meet in the spring to exchange prisoners and negotiate peace. Gov. Clark praised the Six Nations for not joining the Cherokees in a war against the Catawbas. 3p.

Fol. 229. 15 June 1742, Albany. Minutes containing a speech from Gov. Geo. Clark to the Six Nations. Six Nations will hopefully join the rest of the tribes under His Majesty's protection. 3p.

R.G. 10 C1220/2 (CONT'D)

Fol. 230a. 16 June 1742, Albany. Minutes containing an answer
from Six Nations to Gov. Clark's speech. Cherokees will meet
with the Six Nations in the spring to negotiate peace. The
Six Nations made the Cherokee, responsible for arranging the
future meeting, a sachem. 4p.

Fol. 251a. 29 June 1743, Albany. Minutes containing Bd. of
Commissioners' reply to Henry Barclay's letter. Cherokees have
evidently released the five Senecas that they held prisoner. 1p.

R.G. 10 C1221/4   MINUTES OF INDIAN AFFAIRS UNDER WM. JOHNSON: 1755-
        1757

Fol. 355. 17-23 Nov. 1756, Ft. Johnson. Minutes of a meeting
between Johnson and the Six Nations. English have built two
forts in the Cherokee country as barrier against the French.
Six Nations will accept any assistance from the Southern Indians.
Six Nations warriors going through Cherokee nation must carry
a pass signed by Johnson. The seven Cherokee towns north of
mountains are friendly (as are the Creeks, Chickasaws, and
Catawbas), but the lower three Cherokee towns favor the French.
39p.

R.G. 10 C1221/5   MINUTES OF INDIAN AFFAIRS UNDER WM. JOHNSON: 1757-
        1759

Fol. 19. [ca. 10-13 Apr. 1757]. Minutes containing extract of
a letter from George Croghan to Sir Wm. Johnson (14 Mar. 1757).
Croghan encloses extracts from his old journals. Under Gov.
Morris's orders, Croghan took the 50 Indians to meet Gen.
Braddock at Ft. Cumberland. Braddock was disappointed since
he had expected 400 Indians. Although the Cherokees had been
sent for, their arrival could not be guaranteed. 11p.

Fol. 91. 22 May 1757, Ft. Johnson. Minutes containing letter
from Johnson (7 May 1757). Reportedly 100 Cherokees from the
Maryland and Va. frontier are leaving to fight the French in
Ohio. 2p.

Fol. 104. 7 June 1757. Minutes containing a letter from
George Croghan to Wm. Johnson [24 May 1757). Indians are happy
about the way they have been treated. A party of Cherokee
warriors (62) killed four Ohio Indians and took two prisoners.
There have been 300-400 Southern Indians at Ft. Cumberland this
spring. 3p.

Fol. 114. 23 April 1757. Minutes recording that six Onondaga
Indians requested permission to visit Ft. Cumberland to join
the Southern Indians leaving to fight the [French] along the
Ohio. 1p.

Fol. 118. 9 May 1757. Minutes recording that the Ohio Indians
fear more Southern Indian attacks after the three that took
place in the spring. 4p.

Fol. 134. 19 May 1757, Lancaster. Minutes of a meeting reporting that the Shawnees traveling through Carolina to attack their
enemy were taken prisoners. 6p.

Fol. 139. 20 May [1757], Lancaster. Minutes of a meeting
reporting that Johnson informed the [Northern] Indian chiefs
that a small present would be given those Cherokees who joined
the English. 5p.

Fol. 189. 26-31 July 1757. Minutes recording that three Cherokees and several Mohawks came to meet Johnson. Johnson is
pleased that the Cherokees have joined the English against the
French. Cherokee chief indicated that only death could separate
his tribe from the English. Johnson and the Six Nation Indians
performed the condolence ceremony for the Cherokees. 7p.

Fol. 211. 12 Sept. 1757, Ft. Johnson. Minutes of a meeting of
three Mohawk chiefs, two Seneca sachems, and two Cherokee
Indians with Johnson. Indians confirm their desire to fight
the French. Two Cherokees have been killed, one a chief
warrior, and the tribe is determined to get revenge. 3p.

Fol. 217. 16-20 Sept. 1757, Ft. Johnson. Minutes of a meeting
of Oneida, Mohawk, Seneca, and Cherokee chiefs with Wm. Johnson.
Johnson recommends that the Six Nations strengthen their alliance with the Cherokees. The Six Nations will ask for a
meeting with Cherokees, who should also be encouraged to
continue fighting the French. River Indians hope that the
Cherokees will accept the proposed meeting. 20p.

Fol. 254. 27 June 1758, Ft. Johnson. Minutes of a meeting of
two Mohawks with Wm. Johnson. Chief Sachem of the Bear Tribe
is surprised that Johnson wants them to go to war on such short
notice. They wish to wait for the Southern Indians who are
expected to arrive soon. Johnson indicates that he is forced
to obey the general's orders. 4p.

Fol. 263. 19 July 1758, Ft. Johnson. Minutes of a meeting of
Wm. Johnson with Cherokee warriors, Six Nations chiefs, and
Susquehannah Indians. Indians performed condolence ceremony
for the Cherokees, during which that tribe was given a scalp
in compensation for the great Cherokee killed last year at the
Ohio. 1p.

Fol. 264. 21 July 1758, Ft. Johnson. Minutes containing a
speech from Wm. Johnson to the Delawares. Cherokees, who fought
the French in Ohio, want the Delawares to leave the area so they
will not get killed by mistake. 3p.

Fol. 268. 21 July 1758, Ft. Johnson. Minutes containing a
speech from a Cherokee chief to Wm. Johnson, Mohawks, Senecas,
Oneidas, and Tuscaroras. Cherokees have joined the English to
fight the French. Cherokees hope that friendship can be maintained with the Six Nations. They also hope that other Indians
will be as zealous as the Cherokees in fighting the French.
Cherokee women implore their Six Nations sisters to take care
of their men during the war and they promise to reciprocate. 7p.

R.G. 10 C1221/5 (CONT'D)

Fol. 277. 24 July 1758, Ft. Johnson. Minutes containing a
speech from Thomas, Chief Sachem and Warrior of Aughguaga, on
behalf of Johnson and the Six Nations to the Cherokees. Johnson
agrees to maintain contact between the tribes and thanks the
Cherokees for their eagerness in fighting the French. Six
Nations performed a ceremony greeting the Cherokees. 8p.

R.G. 10 C1222/6   MINUTES OF INDIAN AFFAIRS UNDER WM. JOHNSON: 1761-
*   1763*

Fol. 207. 22 Apr. - 2 May 1762, Johnson Hall. Proceedings at
a Conference and Treaty ... with the Six Nations and Wm. Johnson.
The Chenussio chief reported that Kinderuntie and 50 men had
British approval from Ft. Pitt when they fought against the
Cherokees last fall. 25p.

Fol. 319. 4 Apr. - 24 Sept. 1762. Thomas Hutchins's Journal
and Report of His Transactions with Several Western Indian
Nations [to Geo. Croghan]. Army deserter is believed to have
sought refuge in a Shawnee town near the place where the Cherokees killed and scalped two Shawnees and took a young Delaware
prisoner. 9p.

Fol. 327. 12 Oct. - 27 Nov. 1762. Alexander McKee's Journal
of Transactions with the Shawnees. McKee met a returning war
party of Six Nations warriors (20) with a Cherokee prisoner and
a scalp. Man who committed the murder along the Carolina
frontiers is dead. The young boys (believed to be half-breed
Cherokees) also involved in murder will not be prosecuted. 7p.

Fol. 333. 21 Nov. 1762, Johnson Hall. Minutes containing
instructions from Wm. Johnson to Lt. Guy Johnson, attending a
meeting of the Six Nations at Onondaga. Guy Johnson should
deliver the response of the Lt. Gov. of Va. to the Six Nations'
request concerning a war with the Cherokees and free passage
through his colony. 2p.

Fol. 334. 30 Nov. - 8 Dec. 1762, Upper Oneida Castle. Minutes
of a meeting of Lt. Guy Johnson with the Oneidas. Indian chief
reported that many young men were preparing for war against the
Southern Indians. Lt. Johnson explained Lt. Gov. Fauquier's
message concerning the right of free passage through his colony
to fight against the [Cherokees]. 13p.

Fol. 347. [ca. Sept. - Nov. 1762]. Minutes containing a speech
from Lt. Gov. Fauquier to Six Nations. Peace has been concluded
with the Cherokees, and the Six Nations should stop warring
against them. If the Six Nations are determined to continue the
Cherokee war, however, Va. will not interfere. 2p.

Fol. 444. [ca. July 1763]. Minutes containing letter from
Gen. Amherst to Wm. Johnson (26 June 1763). The Southern
Indians will certainly follow Johnson's orders. 2p.

R.G. 10 C1222/6 (CONT'D)

Fol. 446. [ca. July 1763]. Minutes containing a letter from
Geo. Croghan to Wm. Johnson (2 July 1763). Croghan fears that
the Southern Indians will join the Northern Indians against the
English. 2p.

Fol. 448. 7 July 1763, Johnson Hall. Minutes of a meeting
between the principal Mohawks and Sir Wm. Johnson. Canadagaria,
Chief Sachem of the Mohawks, informed Johnson that several
Western and Southern nations went to New Orleans where they
were given ammunition and arms and urged to fight the English.
2p.

Fol. 450. 8 July 1763, Johnson Hall. Minutes containing a
letter from Wm. Johnson to Gen. Amherst. French have been
instrumental in the present disturbances. Johnson fears that
any removal of troops from the South could induce the Cherokees
to assist the French. 2p.

Fol. 472. 24 July 1763, Johnson Hall. Minutes containing a
letter from Wm. Johnson to Gen. Amherst. The English cut off
the Cayugas returning from their war against the Cherokees. 5p.

Fol. 493. [ca. Aug. 1763]. Minutes containing an extract of
a letter from Gen. Amherst to Wm. Johnson (14 Aug. 1763).
Stuart reports everything is quiet among the Southern Indians.
Shawnees and Mohawks, not the Cherokees, captured the Catawba
women. 2p.

Fol. 495. [ca. Aug. - Sept. 1763]. Minutes containing information from Capt. Thomas Baugh reporting the arrival of a
party of 78 Indians at Green Briar and Jackson's River where
they were well received. Indians claimed that they were going
to war against the Cherokees. 2p.

Fol. 497. [ca. Aug. - Sept. 1763. Minutes containing an
extract of a letter from Wm. Johnson to Gen. Amherst (20 Aug.
1763). Gov. Fauquier reports that the marauding Indians
along the frontiers are evidently Northern Indians returning
from a campaign against the Cherokees. 2p.

Fol. 498. [ca. Aug. - Sept. 1763]. Minutes containing a
letter from Wm. Johnson to Gen. Amherst (25 Aug. 1763). Since
the capture of Canada, the Six Nations and Western Indians
have been busy attacking the Cherokees, sending numerous
parties through the frontiers of the English provinces. The
Senecas persuaded some of these war parties to attack the
English. 3p.

R.G. 10 C1222/7   MINUTES OF INDIAN AFFAIRS UNDER WM. JOHNSON: 1763-
                  1768

Fol. 12. 10 - 15 Nov. 1763, Albany. Minutes recording that
an Onondaga Indian plans to seek revenge for the murder of his
nephew who was killed while returning from the Cherokee country
by the Hurons. 3p.

R.G. 10 C1222/7 (CONT'D)

Fol. 15. [Nov. 1763]. Minutes containing a letter from John Blair to Gov. of New York (22 Oct. 1763). Andrew Lewis reported that a party of 94 Indians which passed through the Va. frontiers last spring supposedly on their way to fight the Cherokees was the group who massacred the frontiersmen. It is believed that they were Northern Indians who had solicited the Cherokees' aid, not attacked them. 1p.

Fol. 21. 14 - 22 Dec. 1763, Johnson Hall. Minutes of meetings between Wm. Johnson and Six Nations. Cayagas reported that their sachems did not attend the congress because they were fighting the Cherokees. 7p.

Fol. 128. [June 1764]. Minutes containing an extract of a letter from Col. Bouquet to Wm. Johnson (31 May 1764). Indians should have something (to distinguish them from the enemy) as the Cherokees did by wearing a yellow cloth on their heads. 1p.

Fol. 255. 30 Dec. 1764, Johnson Hall. Minutes recording information from a Seneca chief that the Delawares will keep the peace, but half of the Shawnees are against it. Pontiac, a man of great influence among all the Western and Southern nations, is also against the peace treaty. 7p.

Fol. 273. [ca. Mar. - Apr. 1765]. Minutes containing a letter from the Bd. of Trade to Wm. Johnson (10 July 1764). Bd. sends a plan concerning the future management of Indian affairs throughout North America. 4p. [Enclosures to fol. 284].

> Fol. 276. 10 July 1764. Plan for the Future Management of Indian Affairs. Plan describes the boundary lines between Southern and Northern Districts. Indians in the Southern District shall appoint a deputy from each tribe who will attend the meetings and secure Indian welfare. Plan lists Indian tribes in Southern District, including the Cherokees. 7p.

> Fol. 282. 10 July 1764, Whitehall. Bd. of Trade to John Stuart (extract). Bd. explains reasons for the boundary line location dividing the Northern and Southern Indian Districts. 3p.

Fol. 352. [ca. Aug. - Sept. 1765]. Minutes containing a letter from Lt. Gov. Fauquier to Wm. Johnson (22 July 1765). Cherokees have requested mediation. Five Northern Indians, now in Cherokee country, will visit Johnson to request the same. 1p.

Fol. 352. [Sept. 1765]. Minutes containing a letter from Gov. Fauquier (17 Sept. 1765). Johnson will recommend that the Six Nations seek peace with the Southern tribes. 1p.

Fol. 359. [Sept. 1765]. Minutes containing a letter from Stuart (17 Sept. 1765). Johnson will advise the Six Nations to establish peace with the Cherokees, although there are benefits in allowing the war to continue. 1p.

R.G. 10 C1222/7 (CONT'D)

Fol. 359. [ca. Apr. - May 1766]. Minutes containing a letter from Johnson (30 Mar. 1766). At Stuart's direction, a Cherokee party surrounded the Illinois Indians so the latter could not block the passage of English troops. War has reduced the Cherokees to two-thirds their size ten years ago. 3p.

Fol. 384. [Oct. 1766]. Minutes containing letter from John Stuart to Wm. Johnson (June 1766). Stuart sends a copy of a talk from the Cherokees indicating harassment by the Northern Indians. Stuart is not certain (like Johnson) that peace should be made between the Cherokees and Northern Indians. Cherokees have not received any satisfaction for the murder of some of their tribe by inhabitants of Augusta County, Virginia. 2p. [Enclosures to fol. 388.]

> Fol. 385. 10 May 1766, Ft. Prince George. Alex. Cameron to John Stuart (extract). Cameron describes running the Cherokee boundary lines. Northern Indians killed some Cherokees who were hunting. Creeks offered to aid the Cherokees seek revenge in Virginia. Ecuij, Old Warrior of Estatoe, saved two white hunters from being killed by the Creeks. Attakullakulla ordered the execution of the Northern Indian who attacked the Cherokees. 2p.

> Fol. 387. 8 May 1766, Ft. Prince George. Congress attended by Alex. Cameron, Ensign Price, and Cherokee Chiefs (copy). Kittagusta (Prince of Chote) requests that the N.C. and Va. boundaries be run. He also requests that Stuart arrange a peace with the Northern Indians to stop the attacks on the Cherokees. 2p.

Fol. 441. 17 June 1767, Johnson Hall. Minutes recording that the Onondagas lost four men to a Cherokee attack. Onondagas agreed to wait for the arrival of Cherokee deputies before seeking revenge. 1p.

Fol. 442. 14 July 1767, Johnson Hall. Minutes recording that some Senecas met a Cherokee party (150) which claimed to be sent against the Six Nations by the English. 1p.

Fol. 453. 17 Oct. 1767, Johnson Hall. Minutes recording that the Cherokees want to know the intentions of the Six Nations. 1p.

Fol. 453. 4 Nov. 1767, Johnson Hall. Minutes recording that Wm. Johnson sent a message to the Six Nations announcing a general meeting in the spring and explaining the Prince of Chote's speech to John Stuart. 2p.

Fol. 456. 2 Dec. 1767, Johnson Hall. Minutes recording that Johnson sent a message to the Six Nations requesting a reply to the Cherokee peace proposals. 1p.

Fol. 456. 23 Dec. 1767, Johnson Hall. Minutes recording that Cherokee deputies had arrived in New York and would soon leave for Johnson Hall to establish peace with the Six Nations. 1p.

R.G. 10 C1222/8   MINUTES OF INDIAN AFFAIRS UNDER WM. JOHNSON: 1768

Fol. 1. 29 - 30 Dec. 1767, Johnson Hall. Minutes recording
the reception by Johnson of Little Carpenter, Oconostota,
Corrinah (the Raven King), and six other Cherokees. Cherokees
want peace. Johnson answers that he has been trying for over
a year to persuade the Six Nations to reach a peace treaty with
the Cherokees. He has also taken great pains to prevent the
Six Nations from sending war parties against them. 3p.

Fol. 4. 1 Jan. 1768, Johnson Hall. Minutes recording that
Johnson announced a meeting with the Six Nations around 10 Feb.
and asked that the Six Nations inform all nations to make peace
with the Cherokees. 1p.

Fol. 4. 3 [Feb.] 1768, Johnson Hall. Minutes recording that
the Six Nations sent a message explaining their delay and
requesting that the Cherokees not be introduced until all the
tribes assembled. 2p.

Fol. 5. 29 Feb. 1768, Johnson Hall. Minutes recording that
Johnson accepted the Six Nations' request concerning the
Cherokees. 1p.

Fol. 5. 2 Mar. 1768, Johnson Hall. Minutes recording that
the Onondaga and Seneca Indians agreed with Johnson's order
forbidding the sale of liquor during the Congress, especially
since the Cherokees would attend. Attakullakulla embraced
Taghtaghquisera, a Caughnawaga chief with whom he had formerly
lived as an adopted brother. 3p.

Fol. 7. 3 Mar. 1768, Johnson Hall. Minutes recording that
Johnson welcomed various Indian tribes and told them to make
peace with the Cherokees. 2p.

Fol. 9. 4 - 12 Mar. 1768, Johnson Hall. Proceedings of a
General Congress of the Six Nations, the Chiefs of the
Cognawagey and the Seven Confederate Nations of Canada, and
the Deputies Sent from the Cherokee Nation. Northern Indians
do not want to be surrounded by a boundary line such as the
Cherokees have. Treaty beween the Six Nations, the Seven
Confederate Nations of Canada, and the Cherokees was concluded.
Indians assured everyone that peace with the Cherokees will be
observed. 33p.

Fol. 115. 24 Oct. - 6 Nov. 1768, Ft. Stanwix. Proceedings of
a treaty with the Six Nations, Shawnees, Delawares, and Senecas.
Six Nations ceded land to the English beginning at the mouth
of the Cherokee River. 47p.

Fol. 162. 12 Nov. 1768. Minutes recording a meeting of
Shawnee, Delaware, and Mingo Indians with Wm. Johnson. Indians
have informed all the Indians (including the Southern tribes)
what Johnson told them three years ago. 5p.

Fol. 169. 20 Jan. 1769. Minutes recording that Thomas
Wildman, a Cognawagey chief, asked Johnson if any word was
received yet from the tribal members who had accompanied the
Cherokees home. 1p.

Fol. 169. 21 Jan. 1769. Minutes recording that Johnson received a letter from Stuart reporting the arrival of Attakulla-
Kulla [with some Cognawageys]. Attakullakulla indicated that
he expected the Chickasaws and Creeks to come and negotiate a
peace. 3p.

Fol. 177. 7 Mar. 1768. Minutes containing a report from the
Bd. of Trade to the King (copy). Bd. of Trade's report has
been sent to Wm. Johnson. Bd. also sent copies of the treaties
establishing boundaries with the Creeks, Cherokees, and Choctaws.
Six Nations claim land occupied by the Cherokees. Southern
District Indians consist of the Choctaws, Creeks, Cherokees,
a few Chickasaws, and the Catawbas. Ga., the Carolinas, and
Virginia are the provinces which deal with the Creeks and
Cherokees. 19p. [Enclosures to fol. 206.]

> Fol. 197. 10 Nov. 1763, Augusta. Congress with Chickasaws,
> Upper and Lower Creeks, Choctaws, Cherokees, and Catawbas
> describing the Creek boundary with the English settlements.
> 2p.
>
> Fol. 198. 19 Oct. 1765, Ft. Prince George. A Cession of
> Lands by the Cherokees to the Province of South Carolina
> (extract). 2p.
>
> Fol. 199. 10 May 1766, Ft. Prince George. Alex Cameron
> to John Stuart (extract). Cameron describes the Cherokee
> boundary with N. Carolina. Cherokee line runs straight
> from Reedy R. to Chiswell's Mines. Cherokees are willing
> to give up part of their hunting ground in N.C. to avoid
> disputes with the whites. 2p.
>
> Fol. 200. 15 July 1767, N. Carolina. Gov. Tryon to Bd.
> of Trade (extract). Tryon describes the boundary between
> N. C. and the Cherokees. 1p.
>
> Fol. 201. 1 Feb. 1766, Charleston. John Stuart to
> Headmen of the Cherokees (extract). Stuart has settled
> the Ga. and Fla. boundary with the Creeks and Cherokees.
> There should be no more Indian land disputes. 1p.
>
> Fol. 201. 2 - 6 May 1765, Johnson Hall. Extract from
> minutes of a conference with Six Nations, Delawares, and
> Sir William Johnson regarding boundary lines. Indians
> agreed to cede land, including that extending down the
> Ohio to the Cherokee River, if their warriors will always
> be allowed free passage through that country. 6p.

Fol. 207. 5 Nov. 1768, Ft. Stanwix. Minutes containing Deed
of Cession from the Six Nations to the King. Land ceded includes territory bordering with the Southern Indians. 4p.

R.G. 10 C1223/9 SIR WM. JOHNSON, CORRESPONDENCE: 1756-1772

Fol. 19. 29 Apr. - 11 May 1765, Johnson Hall. Minutes of a
Conference with Six Nations and Delawares concerning boundaries
which extend down the Ohio to the Cherokee River. 37p.

Fol. 91. 25 Dec. 1765 [?], Johnson Hall. Minutes recording
that the Six Nations renewed their treaty with the Cherokees.
4p.

Fol. 117. 3 Dec. [1770?], Johnson Hall. Minutes recording
that Johnson praised the Northern Indians for selecting able
men to inform the Southern Indians about joining the war. 3p.

Fol. 187. 24 Mar. 1764, Johnson Hall. Minutes of conference
with the Six Nations containing news that several Cayugas were
killed while returning from Cherokee country. Cayuga sachems
would not let the tribe seek satisfaction. 15p.

Fol. 214. 10 May 1762, Ft. Pitt. Geo. Croghan to [Wm. Johnson]
(copy). A large number of Six Nation Indians pass by Ft. Pitt
in their war against the Southern Indians. A party passed
Ft. Pitt a few days ago with two Cherokee prisoners and eight
scalps. 3p.

Fol. 242. 28 and 30 Sept. 1762. Intelligence transmitted by
Geo. Croghan to Gen. Amherst and Wm. Johnson. French told a
Ouatanon [Wea] party going to fight the Cherokees that the
English had designs against the Western Indians. 4p.

Fol. 299. 14 Aug. 1763, New York. Information from Captain
Thomas Baugh. [Same as C1223/6/495]. 3p.

Fol. 376. 6 Oct. 1763, [Johnson Hall]. Minutes recording that
a war party returning from the Cherokee country with scalps
and prisoners reported that the Ottawas asked the Delawares to
fight the English. 2p.

Fol. 387. 14 Nov. 1763, [Johnson Hall]. Minutes recording
that the Hurons killed several Onondagas returning from the
Cherokee country. 2p.

Fol. 411. 31 Aug. 1763, Johnson Hall. [Wm. Johnson] to Gen.
Amherst. Fauquier has no proof that the Six Nations committed
hostilities along Va. frontiers. Both the Northern and Western
Indians are the Cherokees' enemies. 4p.

Fol. 415. 14 Aug. 1763, New York. Gen. Amherst to Wm. Johnson.
[Same as P.R.O. C.O. 5/63/275]. 5p.

Fol. 436. 8 July 1763, Johnson Hall. Wm. Johnson to Gen.
Amherst. Cherokees might be persuaded to assist the Southern
troops if they were told that English have prevented attacks
on them from the Western Indians. 2p.

Fol. 461. 19 June 1763, Albany. [Wm. Johnson] to Gen. Amherst.
Johnson believes that Misesajas [Missisaugas?], Chippewas, and
Delawares might be stopped by turning their inveterate enemies
(the Cherokees and Catawbas) against them. 2p.

R.G. 10 C1223/10   MINUTES OF THE COUNCIL WITH PONTIAC: 1766

Fol. 5. 22 - 30 July 1766, Lake Ontario. Proceedings of a
Congress with Pontiac and Chiefs of the Ottawas, the Chiefs of
Potawattamis, Hurons, and Chippewas. An Onondaga Indian, with
a Cherokee scalp, replied to Pontiac's speech about withdrawing the bad belts. 25p.

Fol. 32. 12 May 1766. Minutes containing a speech to the Six
Nations indicating why the Cherokee war began. 4p.

*R.G. 10 C1223/11   MINUTES OF INDIAN AFFAIRS UNDER GUY JOHNSON: 1774-
                    1775*

Fol. 22. 1 - 3 Dec. 1774, [Guy Park]. Minutes of a meeting
of Guy Johnson with Six Nations. The Six Nations have decided
not to participate in the Southern Indians' war plans. 10p.

Fol. 32. 8 Dec. 1774, [Guy Park]. Minutes recording that the
Onondaga deputies left with their message to the [Southern
Indians?]. 1p.

Fol. 37. 20 - 28 Jan. 1775, Guy Park. Minutes of a meeting
of [Guy Johnson] with Six Nations. Southern messenger
describes the battle at Kanawha. 19p.

*R.G. 10 C1223/12   MINUTES OF INDIAN AFFAIRS UNDER GUY JOHNSON: 1779-
                    1780*

Fol. 55. 3 Nov. 1779, [Niagara]. Minutes of a meeting of Col.
Guy Johnson and Six Nations. Rebels have destroyed the Six
Nations villages and corn fields. Six Nations request assist-
ance from the Western and Southern nations. 7p.

Fol. 62. 7 Nov. 1779, [Niagara]. Minutes recording that
letters indicate that the Cherokees and other nations constantly
fought against the southern frontier settlements. A speech
from the Cherokees to the Wabash Indians was read explaining
their hostility against the Virginians. 5p.

Fol. 225. 28 Mar. - 3 [Apr.] 1780, Niagara. Minutes of a
general meeting of Col. Johnson with Shawnees, Delawares,
Nanticokes, and Six Nations. Col. Johnson gave the Indians
a road belt for the Seven Nations of Canada and the Western
and Southern allies. 15p.

Fol. 240. 31 Mar. and 1 Apr. 1780, [Niagara?]. Minutes recording that the Seneca deputies arrived to begin the journey to
the Western and Southern nations. 5p.

Fol. 248. 5 Apr. 1780, [Niagara?]. Minutes recording that
Johnson explained to the [Seneca] deputies the message they
are to carry to the Six Nations, Shawnees, Delawares, and the
Western and Southern confederates. 5p.

R.G. 10 C1223 (CONT'D)

Fol. 254. 8 Apr. 1780. [Niagara?]. Minutes recording that
Col. Johnson received a report about McKee's meeting at
Wakitomikee with the Six Nations, Hurons, Delawares, Shawnees,
Miamis, Cherokees of Kisinguen's party, and the Cherokees of
Chote. Report includes a speech by Pecanguelis (Delaware)
to the Raven of Chote concerning a rebel hatchet taken from
the Chote Cherokees. Raven replied to the speech. 4p.

R.G. 10 C1223/13   MINUTES OF DETROIT COUNCIL: 1781-1790

Fol. 134. 15 June 1782, Detroit. Minutes of a meeting of
De Peyster with Cherokees from Chote. Speech from Tha-is-Kin
regarding the rebels seizure of their land and requesting
supplies to continue to fight. Tha-is-Kin also delivers a
speech from the Cherokee women deploring the war. 4p.

Fol. 138. 6 July 1782, Detroit. Minutes of a meeting of
De Peyster with Cherokees, Shawnees, and Six Nations. Capt.
Dick, a Cherokee chief, confirms his tribe's alliance with the
Six Nations and requests clothing and arms. Major De Peyster
promises to meet the Cherokees' needs. 8p.

Fol. 198. 7 Mar. 1783, Detroit. Minutes of a meeting of De
Peyster with Band of Cherokees and Hurons (copy). Cherokees
request supplies so that they can continue the war. De
Peyster is grateful for their assistance and loyalty. Although
he cannot presently furnish supplies, he promised to do the
best he can in the future. 2p.

Fol. 200. 24 Apr. 1783, Detroit. Minutes of a meeting of
De Peyster with Shawnees, Cherokees (a deputation to the
Western Indians), Hurons, Ottawas, Chippewas, and Pottawattamis.
De Peyster wants the Indians to remain quiet while a peace
treaty is being negotiated. He regrets the attacks upon their
villages and hopes they will be prevented in the future.
De Peyster will deliver the presents soon. 5p.

Fol. 221. 16 and 18 July 1783, Detroit. Minutes of a meeting
of De Peyster with Cherokees, Creeks, Shawnees, Delawares,
and others (copy). Capt. Logan, a Mingo, delayed his arrival
so he could accompany the Cherokees to Detroit. De Peyster
informed the Indians that peace has been concluded. Fourteen
Creek and Cherokee women requested assistance and De Peyster
promised to aid them. 8p.

Fol. 239. 6 - 9 Sept. 1783, Lower Sandusky. Minutes of a
meeting of Alex. McKee with Hurons, Shawnees, Delawares,
Mingoes, Cherokees, and Creeks (copy). Peace has been concluded. New boundary is not intended to deprive the Indians
of any land. McKee urges the Indians to advise their young
men to refrain from all hostile acts. Capt. Brant (Six Nations)
told the Cherokees and other Indian nations that the Six
Nations intend to remain at peace. Tribes have agreed to
free their prisoners. 22p.

R.G. 10 C1223/14   PAPERS RELATING TO INDIAN AFFAIRS IN THE PROVINCE
OF QUEBEC AND LOWER CANADA: 1717-1842

Fol. 8.   10 July 1764. *Plan pour le maniement futur des*
affaires des sauvages (translation). Plan includes provisions
for Northern and Southern Indian Districts. 14p. *French.*

R.G. 10 C10999/8   SIR JOHN JOHNSON'S CORRESPONDENCE: 1791-1794

Fol. 8305.   16 Jan. 1793, Creek Nation. Geo. Welbank to Capt.
Alex. McKee. Spanish have had little success in turning the
Creeks against the Americans, except for some Upper Creeks whose
hunting ground (along with the Cherokees) is being threatened.
Some Shawnee and Cherokee chiefs and two Creeks were lost in
an attack on a Cumberland fort. 6p.

Fol. 8488.   28 June 1793, Detroit. M. Elliot to Col. McKee.
Col. England is anxious to hear about a Cherokee horse that
was to be purchased for him. 3p.

Fol. 8537.   13 Aug. 1793, Miami Rapids. Message from Wyandots,
Seven Nations of Canada, Delawares, Shawnees, Miamis, Chippewas,
Senecas, Potowatomis, Conoys, Munsees, Nanticokes, Mohicans,
Creeks, and Cherokees to United States Commissioners (copy).
Indians discuss signing land cession deeds. 6p.

Fol. 8544.   14 Aug. 1793, Capt. Elliot's at the mouth of the
Detroit River. U.S. Commissioners to chiefs and warriors
assembled at Miami Rapids (copy). Commissioners discuss
questions of peace and boundary lines. 2p.

Fol. 8547.   16 Aug. 1793, Capt. Elliot's at the mouth of the
Detroit River. U.S. Commissioners to chiefs and warriors
assembled at Miami Rapids (copy). Commissioners regret that
the Indians want Ohio to serve as a boundary. This cannot be
granted and the negotiations are ended. 1p.

Fol. 8549.   22 Aug. 1793, Foot of the Rapids. Alex. McKee to
Gov. Simcoe (copy). Hopes for peace between the Americans and
Indians vanished after the Indians insisted on using Ohio as
a boundary. 3p.

R.G. 10 C10999/9   SIR JOHN JOHNSON'S CORRESPONDENCE: 1795-1796

Fol. 8857.   14 Feb. 1795, Swan Creek. Geo. Ironside to Col.
Alex. McKee. Creeks, Cherokees, Choctaws, and Chickasaws
have formed a league and have committed hostile acts. 4p.

Fol. 8877.   27 Feb. 1795, Swan Creek. Geo. Ironside to Col.
Alex. McKee. Cherokees returned home two months ago. 1p.

Fol. 8880.   2 Mar. 1795, Greenville. Message from Maj. Gen.
Anthony Wayne to the Cherokees settled at the head waters of the
Sciota. Wayne advises all peaceful Indians to withdraw from
hostile Indian territory. 3p.

R.G. 10 C11000/10   SIR JOHN JOHNSON'S CORRESPONDENCE: 1797-1805

> Fol. 9368. 25 Mar. 1798 - 30 Apr. 1803. List of Chippewas,
> Pottawatamis, Ottawas, Wyandotts, Shawnees, Munsees, Six
> Nations, Sauks, Delawares, Foxes, Cherokees, and Catawbas at
> Amherstburg. 2p.

R.G. 10 C11000/11   SIR JOHN JOHNSON'S CORRESPONDENCE: 1806-1812

> Doc. 10019. 15 June 1809, Washington. Speech from Two-Chale,
> Sky-Oque, and Seed (Cherokee Chiefs) to Shawnees, Wyandotts,
> Potawatomis, Chippewas, and **Ottawas** (copy). Indians should
> not interfere in the American quarrels with foreign powers.
> Cherokees have become more civilized and are now farming and
> making their own clothes. 2p.

> Doc. 10040. 28 June 1809, Amherstburg. Capt. Elliot to Col.
> Blair. American agents living with the Cherokees influence
> tribe's opinions. 3p.

ARCHIVES DU MINISTÈRE DES AFFAIRES ETRANGÈRES

Paris

CORRESPONDANCE POLITIQUE, ANGLETERRE
C.P. ANGLETERRE/443: JAN.-JULY 1761

>Fol. 358. July 1761. *La Louisianne.* Report lists French
>forts and garrisons. Cherokee R. marks the boundary between
>the French and English territory. Shawnee, Alibamo, and Chero-
>kee territory extends to the Appalachian Mountains. 3p.

C.P. ANGLETERRE/444: JULY-DEC.: 1761

>Fol. 202. 25 Aug. 1761, London. Bussy to le Duc de Choiseul.
>France and England have long disputed the ownership of Ohio.
>English claim that the Six Nations sold them Ohio and the
>Cherokee territory in 1729. 15p.

C.P. ANGLETERRE/585, SUPPLÉMENT: 1792

>Fol. 218. 1792. *État des notes données à M. de Montmorin en*
>*1791.* The reputed six Cherokees visiting London were not
>Indians but English and Spaniards who were making plans against
>Santo Domingo. 4p.

CORRESPONDANCE POLITIQUE, ESPAGNE.
C.P. ESPAGNE/594: MAY-JULY 1779

>Fol. 132. [May?] 1779, London. *Déclaration faite à Londres*
>*par Mr. le Marquis d'Almodovar et envoyée a cet ambassadeur*
>*par un courrier espagnol.* Anglo-Spanish war results from many
>grievances, chief of which is the English attempts to encourage
>the Choctaws, Cherokees, and Chickasaws to war on Louisiana.
>7p.

CORRESPONDANCE POLITIQUE, ÉTATS-UNIS
C.P. ÉTATS-UNIS/29: JAN.-MAY 1785

>Fol. 99. 9 Mar. 1785, Pennsylvania. Extract of letter from
>Bedford expressing hope that the practice of naming new dis-
>tricts after famous patriots continues. Western territory in
>N. C. is called the State of Franklin. 4p.

>Fol. 207. 30 Apr. 1785, Richmond. Le Maire to le Comte de
>Vergennes. Encloses memoir on Kentucky. 2p. [Enclosures to
>fol. 212].

C.P. ÉTATS-UNIS/29 (CONT'D)

Fol. 208. 30 Apr. 1785. *Mémoire* from Le Maire describing geographical, demographical, geological, and other information about the American states. The Carolinas and Ga. are separated from the Miss. R. by the Cherokees and the Chickasaws, two of the most feared tribes. The Green R. in Va. belongs to the Cherokees who refuse to allow Virginians to settle there. 10p.

Fol. 297. 18 May 1785, New York. Barbé Marbois to [Vergennes]. Marbois expresses concern over states wanting to keep their independence. Franklin, which was part of N.C., is determined to remain independent. 10p.

C.P. ÉTATS-UNIS/30: JUNE-DEC.: 1785

Fol. 253. 29 Aug. 1785, New York. Barbé Marbois to Vergennes. Congress is close to recognizing Vermont's independence. Maine, Kentucky, Franklin, and other districts are already requesting to become states. 10p.

Fol. 265. 31 Aug. 1785, New York. *État de Frankland.* Resolution from the residents of Franklin concerning election to the Franklin assembly. 3p.

C.P. ÉTATS-UNIS/32: JULY 1786 -DEC. 1787

Fol. 99. 15 Oct. 1786, New York. Guillaume Otto to Vergennes. Congress has limited ability to control states such as Maine, Kentucky, Franklin, and Vermont. 4p.

Fol. 207. 5 Mar. 1787, New York. Guillaume Otto to [Montmorin]. Franklin and Kentucky not only insist upon the right to use the Miss. R. but threaten war against La. unless Spain renounces her right to exclusive navigation. 6p. [Enclosures to fol. 211b].

Fol. 210. *Note communiquée par le géographe des États Unis à son retour de l'Ohio.* Residents west of the Alleghenies will take reprisals if they are not granted navigation rights on the Miss. River. 3p.

Fol. 304. 15 July 1787, New York. [Guillaume] Otto to le Comte de Montmorin. Otto fears that Franklin and Ky. might turn to the English for aid to secure navigation rights on the Mississippi. 5p.

Fol. 411. 15 Dec. 1787, New York. [Guillaume] Otto to le Comte de Montmorin. Georgians are forming four regiments of 750 men each to fight the Creeks. About 1500 citizens from Franklin will join the Georgians, who have asked Spain not to aid Georgia's enemies. 8p.

C.P. ÉTATS-UNIS/34: 1789

Fol. 19. 4 Feb. 1789, New York. Le Comte de Moustier to le Comte de Montmorin. S.C. remains neutral in the war between Georgia and the Creeks. The Creek leader, McGillivray, has incited the Cherokees to fight against Franklin, which is allied to Georgia. 7p.

C.P. ÉTATS-UNIS/41: MAY-SEPT. 1794

Fol. 108. 9 Prairial II [28 May 1794], Philadelphia. Fauchet, Pétry, and LaForest to Minister of Foreign Affairs (duplicate). Spain is interested in keeping friendly relations with the United States in order to maintain peace with their turbulent neighbors on the Ohio. Spain fears the Cherokees and Creeks. 5p.

C.P. ÉTATS-UNIS/42: OCT.-DEC. 1794

Fol. 446. 7 Nivose III [27 Dec. 1794], Philadelphia. Fauchet, LaForest, and Pétry to Commissioner of Foreign Relations (duplicate). Wayne's successes have diminished Indian hostility but the Cherokees continue their hostility along the frontiers of the Carolinas, Ga., and the Tenn. R. in spite of the new treaty with neighboring tribes. 8p.

C.P. ÉTATS-UNIS, SUPPLÉMENT 4: 1776-1789

Fol. 62. 28 Nov. 1784, Charleston. LaForest to [Vergennes]. N.C. has conditionally ceded its western lands to Congress. This will affect S.C. and Georgia. 8p.

Fol. 70. 20 Dec. 1784. Extract of a letter written by a settler on N. Carolina's western lands. Settler opposes the manner in which Indian land at the big bend of the Tenn. R. is purchased. He hopes that future land purchases can be postponed until the American commissioners arrive next spring. 2p.

Fol. 82. 27 Feb. 1785, Danbury, N. Carolina. Gov. Alex. Martin to Brig. Gen. Sevier (translation). Martin wants more details on Franklin's plans to withdraw from N.C. and information regarding usurpation of Indian land. Martin warns that Indian goods will be suspended until safe delivery can be guaranteed. 1p. [Enclosures to fol. 85].

 Fol. 83. [Mar. 1785], [Jonesboro]. Reply from State of Franklin's General Assembly to Martin's letter. Assembly explains their state's determination to remain independent. Assembly also expresses attitude of the western settlers toward Indian goods. 5p.

Fol. 86. 28 Feb. 1785, Wilmington, N. Carolina. Pétry to le Marquis de Castries. Settlers west of the Appalachians want their independence and have elected a governor who plans to seize Indian land unless the Indians can prove ownership. 3p.

C.P. ÉTATS-UNIS, SUPPLÉMENT 4 (CONT'D)

Fol. 88. 16 Mar. 1785, Charleston. LaForest to [Vergennes].
LaForest discusses the boundary disputes between the Carolinas
and Georgia. Settlers west of the Appalachians have declared
themselves independent from N.Carolina. Nashville is being
settled rapidly. 4p.

Fol. 106. 1 June 1785, Wilmington, N. Carolina. Pétry to le
Marquis de Castries (duplicate). Pétry explains the motives
behind the formation of Franklin and describes their government
and laws. 4p.

Fol. 108. 10 June 1785, Charleston. LaForest to Vergennes.
Conduct of Ga. and western N.C. settlers has caused Congress
to appoint peace commissioners to deal with the Cherokees and
other Indian nations. Upper Cherokees resent the loss of their
land to Franklin. Creeks, who have suffered invasions by
Georgians, have invited the Cherokees to defend their lands
together. LaForest fears that the Choctaws and Chickasaws
will also join in their fight. The United States offered
protection to the Cherokees, Creeks, Choctaws, and Chickasaws.
LaForest describes character of various Indian nations,
including the Cherokees. 12p.

Fol. 116. 1 May 1786, Charleston. Chateaufort to [Vergennes].
Chateaufort encloses a translation of the peace treaty between
the Americans and the Cherokees. This treaty guarantees the
same limits as the 1777 treaty of Dewit's [Dewise's] Corner,
subject to revision from the Mar. 1784 law authorizing land
cessions. Cherokees and Creeks are natural enemies of the
American allies because of their geographical location. 11p.
[Enclosures at fol. 118].

    Fol. 118. 28 Nov. 1785, Hopewell on the Keowee.
    Traduction du traité fait avec les Indiens. Treaty
    contains a description of the Cherokee boundaries. 4p.

Fol. 210. 10 Nov. 1786, Williamsburg. Oster to Castries.
Cherokees have joined the Shawnees, Potawatomis, Chippewas,
Ottawas, Mingoes, and Twightwees in their hostility against
the Americans. Congress ordered the states to replenish their
militias in order to defend the frontiers against the Indians.
It is rumored that the English have incited Indians against
the Americans. 4p.

Fol. 221. Feb. 1787. Thomas Hutchins. *Rapport sur les
dispositions des habitants des districts occidenteaux.* Report
estimates population of western settlements at 15,000. Ky.
and Franklin threaten to withhold taxes if they are not
granted navigation rights on the Miss. River. 2p.

Fol. 281. July - Sept. 1787, Portsmouth, New Hampshire.
*Journal du Newhampshire contenant également quelques détails
sur le Massachussets et les autres etats de l'union.* Journal
includes a translated letter to Don Diego de Guardoqui, Spanish
Minister, stating that a professional soldier offered to help

C.P. ÉTATS UNIS,SUPPLÉMENT 4 (CONT'D)

the Spanish defend their monopoly over the Miss. River. Franklin
and other states are preparing to fight for their navigation
rights. A second letter mentions that Franklin sent an
American soldier to purchase arms and ammunition for an
expedition against New Orleans. 24p.

Fol. 318. 26 Dec. 1787, Charleston. Pétry to le Comte de
Montmorin. Franklin has considerable influence among the settlements west of the Appalachians. Ga. gov. sent a commissioner
to keep Franklin informed about the measures taken against the
Indians. 6p.

Fol. 322. 26 Jan. 1788, New York. LaForest to [Montmorin].
LaForest lists the population of each American state, except
Kentucky, Franklin, and Ohio whose combined population is
about 2,900,000. 3p.

Fol. 400. 31 Dec. 1788, Wilmington. Ducher to [Montmorin].
Franklin is composed of new immigrants from Europe, adventurers,
rebels, and others who will not pay their taxes or debts.
Franklin also has legislative problems. 4p.

Fol. 403. 28 Apr. 1789, Wilmington. Ducher to [Montmorin].
Sevier, the gov. of Franklin, defeated the Cherokees and Creeks.
Commissioners from both the Carolinas and Ga. sent a peace
message and presents to the Cherokees in an effort to stop
hostilities. Ducher fears, however, that Franklin will not
stop fighting against the Cherokees and Creeks. 6p.

C.P. ÉTATS-UNIS, SUPPLÉMENT 26: 1772-1792

Fol. 377. 22 Feb. 1788, Charleston. Pétry to [Moustier].
Franklin wants independence and has offered assistance to Ga.
against the Creeks. Ga. appointed a commissioner to keep the
peace with the Southern Indians. S.C. is preparing to defend
its borders against hostile tribes. 11p.

MÉMOIRES ET DOCUMENTS, AMÉRIQUE
M.D. AMÉRIQUE/1: 1712-1725

Fol. 112. [ca. 1718-1721.] *Ce qu'on estime nécessaire pour*
l'utilité et la conservation de la colonie de la Louisianne.
Report describes the location of Indian settlements. The
Margot R. is near the Cherokees and Chickasaws. Cherokees
travel via the Wabash R. when they are fighting against the
Illinois. 35p.

M.D. AMÉRIQUE/11: 1713-1771

Fol. 199. 29 Mar. 1765, Mobile. Monberaut to his son.
Monberaut urges his son to find the Mortar and ask him to see
[John] Stuart in Pensacola before Stuart leaves for Charleston
to handle the affairs of the Cherokees, Katapas [Catawbas?],
and other Indian nations in his district. 4p.

M.D. AMÉRIQUE/11 (CONT'D)

Fol. 290. 17 Nov. 1766, Mobile. *Mémoire* from Montault de
Monberaut responding to Gov. Johnstone's charges of misconduct
and misappropriation of Indian presents. At a conference with
Johnstone, Stuart, and the Indians, the Mortar demanded that
prices set by traders among the Talapooses, Cowetas, Abekas,
and Alibamos be the same as those among the Cherokees. The
Mortar had just arrived from the Cherokees and could not be
deceived. Monberaut includes copies of letters from Johnstone
and Stuart. 96p.

M.D. AMÉRIQUE/21: 1632-1766

Fol. 50. 26 Sept. 1761. Letter from Thiton de Siligne. 1p.
[Enclosures to fol. 95].

Fol. 51. 1761. *Mémoire sur le Canada et la Louisianne.*
It is important for France to retain Canada and Louisiana.
English claims to the Indians and their territory are
unjustified. 7p.

Fol. 70. 1761. *Injustice des Anglais dans leurs
prétentions sur les possessions des Français dans
l'Amérique Septentrionale.* English can only claim
establishments among Cherokee, Chickasaw, and Creek
nations for which they pay the tribes an annual fee.
These establishments are similar to Indian settlements
and are not permanent. 16p.

Fol. 78. [26 Sept.] 1761. [Thiton de Siligne].
*Développement du pays dont les Anglais réclament la
propriété et des peuples sauvages qu'ils prétendent
leur être soumis.* English claim the territory and
tribes living between the Old Shawnee and Cherokee
Rivers. Cherokees are unpredictable English allies.
Their nation is located northwest of the Carolina
mountains between the Cherokee R. and the Appalachian
Mountains. They have many villages along the Cherokee
R. in Tennessee and around Ft. Keowee. English have
built forts (Loudoun, Chote, and Chatuga) in Cherokee
territory. 17p.

MÉMOIRES ET DOCUMENTS, ÉTATS UNIS
M.D. ÉTATS-UNIS/7: 1781-1789

Fol. 285. Nov. 1788. [Moustier]. *Mémoire sur l'état de la
confédération américaine.* Separation of the State of Franklin
has weakened N. Carolina. S.C. remains neutral towards the
Creek-Cherokee war against Ga. and Franklin. McGillivray is
very influential in the Cherokee hostility against Franklin.
Franklin is a rebellious district and has been a center of
dissension and cruelty since its independence. Franklin,
governed by Sevier, is constantly at war with neighboring
Indians. 198p.

M.D. ÉTATS-UNIS/14: 1778-1786

Fol. 381. 26 Feb. 1786, New York. LaForest to [Castries].
Emigrants are attracted to Franklin and Kentucky. Cherokee R.
obstructs communications between those two states, N.C., and
Virginia. LaForest describes Franklin's and Kentucky's population and includes agricultural information on both states.
14p.

M.D. ÉTATS-UNIS/15: 1787-1828

Fol. 124. 19 Frimaire II [9 Dec. 1793], Paris. Létombe to
Committee of Public Safety. United States is having problems
with Spain concerning navigation of the Mississippi. Spain
has incited the Cherokees along the Ga. frontier. 4p.

M.D. ÉTATS-UNIS/18: 1787-1829

Fol. 16. 31 Dec. 1787, Portsmouth, New Hampshire. Toscan.
Mémoire sur différent objects relatif à l'état du Newhampshire
(duplicate). Report lists the American Indian nations, their
location, and number of warriors. Cherokees have 2,500 warriors
and live along the S.C. frontier. 34p.

Fol. 33. 15 Oct. 1788, New York. LaForest to [Montmorin].
LaForest describes the American settlements west of the
mountains. Recent settlements located on N.C. frontier are
called Franklin. New states like Franklin, Kentucky, and
Cumberland have frequent Indian problems. Sevier attacked the
Cherokees, resulting in numerous consequences. 25p.

ARCHIVES NATIONALES

Paris

ARCHIVES DES COLONIES
A.C. B/39   ORDERS OF THE KING AND DISPATCHES CONCERNING THE
COLONIES: 1717

Fol. 220.   26 June 1717, Paris. Minutes of Council containing the King's approval of Vaudreuil's Indian policies.
Vaudreuil must continue to do everything possible to keep
the peace. The Indians [Cherokees] evidently did not kill
the sons of Ramezay and Longueuil while returning from
Illinois, for the Kaskaskias gave them to the English.
Vaudreuil should write the N.Y. and Carolina governors to
obtain their release as soon as possible. 11p.

A.C. B/65   ORDERS OF THE KING AND DISPATCHES CONCERNING THE
COLONIES: 1737

Fol. 401.   19 Mar. 1737, Versailles. Minister to Beauharnois.
Bienville has learned that 400 Cherokee and Chickasaw braves
are settling on the Ohio and the English are believed to be
among them. These Cherokees present an extremely dangerous
situation. Minister plans to ask the Canadian tribes to help
remove the Cherokees and Chickasaws as well as the English.
3p.

Fol. 495.   19 Mar. 1737, Versailles. Minister to Bienville.
Minister requests more information about the Cherokee-
Chickasaw settlement on the Ohio. Such a settlement would
be extremely serious and all possible measures should be
taken to remove the Indians. 5p.

Fol. 506b.   19 Mar. 1737, Versailles. Minister to Salmon.
Bienville has written that some 400 Cherokees or Flatheads
have settled above the Ohio River. The English are responsible. 3p.

Fol. 522.   16 Sept. 1737, Versailles. Minister to Salmon.
Bienville has sent reports about the Illinois and Wabash
posts and about Indian tribes including the Osages, Cherokees,
and Sioux. 4p.

Fol. 529.   16 Sept. 1737, Versailles. Minister to Bienville.
Minister has not received any additional information about
the Cherokees and Chickasaws settling on the Ohio River.
They may have left. French need to prevent similar situations
in the future. 5p.

A.C. B/66   ORDERS OF THE KING AND DISPATCHES CONCERNING THE COLONIES:
              1738

Fol. 269. 15 May 1738, Versailles. Minister to Beauharnois.
Bienville's plans to have the Kickapoos and Mascoutens destroy
the Cherokee-Chickasaw settlement on the Ohio have hopefully
been successful. 2p.

Fol. 314b. 3 Feb. 1738, Versailles. Minister to Bienville.
Kickapoos and Mascoutens have offered to destroy the Cherokee-
Chickasaw settlement along the Ohio. 2p.

Fol. 317. 24 Mar. 1738, Versailles. Minister to Bienville.
Natchez Indians left the Chickasaws to join the Cherokees.
Hopefully the Cherokee chiefs, who visited the Alibamos, will
keep their promise to remain neutral in the war. 2p.

Fol. 354. 8 Dec. 1738, Versailles. Minister to Bienville.
Cherokees and Chickasaws have decided not to settle along the
Ohio R. since they would be exposed to attacks by the Iroquois
and other nations. 2p.

Fol. 378. 21 Dec. 1738, Versailles. Minister to Bienville.
No confirmation has been made that the Cherokees settled along
the Ohio, but the English do plan to settle on the Cherokee
River. 2p.

A.C. B/72   ORDERS OF THE KING AND DISPATCHES CONCERNING THE COLONIES:
              1741

Fol. 479. 6 Oct. 1741, Versailles. Minister to Beauchamp.
Alibamos claim that the Cherokees committed the attack on the
Wabash. Minister is thankful that it was not the Chickasaws.
2p.

Fol. 481. 6 Oct. 1741, Versailles. Minister to Bienville.
Cherokees, not Chickasaws, attacked travelers on the Wabash.
French plan to build fort on the Cherokee River. 2p.

A.C. B/74   ORDERS OF THE KING AND DISPATCHES CONCERNING THE COLONIES:
              1742

Fol. 638. 22 Oct. 1742, Versailles. *Mémoire du Roy* to
Vaudreuil. The King instructs Vaudreuil concerning the Indians.
Natchez have moved to the Carolinas to join the Cherokees.
Cherokees, English allies from the Carolinas, have attacked
French travelers on the Wabash. Vaudreuil should try to prevent
future Cherokee incursions. 15p.

Fol. 660. 27 Oct. 1742, Versailles. Minister to Vaudreuil.
Cherokees presumably committed last year's attack on the French
along the Wabash. Cherokee hostility must be discouraged. The
Cherokees are powerful and could cause many disturbances for
the colony. 2p.

A.C. B/74   (CONT'D)

Fol. 667. 27 Oct. 1742, Versailles. Minister to Louboey. It
seems likely that the Cherokees were responsible for last year's
attack along the Wabash. Cherokee raids on the colony would
be unfortunate. 2p.

Fol. 670. 27 Oct. 1742, Versailles. Minister to Salmon.
Cherokees are evidently responsible for last year's attack on
the French convoy going to Illinois. Similar events must be
prevented. 2p.

Fol. 683. 15 Nov. 1742, Versailles. Minister to Vaudreuil
and Salmon. The Cherokees attacked a French convoy on its way
to Illinois last year. Bienville has proposed a new fort on the
Wabash to prevent future Cherokee attacks. 4p.

Fol. 685. 15 Nov. 1742, Versailles. Minister to Salmon.
Bonnefoy, formerly a Cherokee prisoner, confirms the Cherokee
attacks in 1740 and 1741 near the Illinois. Minister implores
Salmon to do everything possible to discourage future Cherokee
hostility. 2p.

*A.C. B/78   ORDERS OF THE KING AND DISPATCHES CONCERNING THE COLONIES:
          1744*

Fol. 298. 1 Jan. 1744, Versailles. Minister to Beauharnois.
Beauharnois should consult with Vaudreuil to end Cherokee
hostility. Cherokees want peace as soon as the Canadian tribes
stop their hostilities. 2p.

Fol. 317. 24 Mar. 1744, Versailles. Minister to Beauharnois.
Vaudreuil has written that the Chickasaws are seeking a peace
treaty. Cherokees must be included to strengthen peace, and the
Canadian tribes must stop their attack on the Chickasaws and
Cherokees. 4p.

Fol. 436. 1 Jan. 1744, Versailles. Minister to Vaudreuil.
Vaudreuil should consult with Beauharnois to stop the Cherokee
raids on La. by preventing Canadian attacks on the Cherokees.
3p.

*A.C. B/81   ORDERS OF THE KING AND DISPATCHES CONCERNING THE COLONIES:
          1745*

Fol. 279. 28 Apr. 1745, Versailles. Minister to Beauharnois.
Minister needs more information about situation in La. to help
the King decide the French action regarding the Chickasaws and
Cherokees. Vaudreuil's peace negotiations with the Chickasaws
are delayed because he lacks trading goods. Minister expects
to hear from Vaudreuil regarding the Cherokees. 2p.

*A.C. B/83   ORDERS OF THE KING AND DISPATCHES CONCERNING THE COLONIES:
          1746*

Fol. 313. 30 Apr. 1746, Versailles. Minister to Vaudreuil
and Le Normant. The proposed fort on the Wabash would insure

A.C. B/83 (CONT'D)

communication between Louisiana, Illinois, and Canada and would
prevent English settlements. Fort will also be useful against
Cherokee and Chickasaw raids. 2p.

Fol. 335. 10 Oct. 1746, Fontainebleu. Minister to Vaudreuil.
If the Shawnee peace proposals are accepted by the Choctaws
and Chickasaws, the proposed fort to protect against the
Cherokees and Chickasaws will not be necessary. 2p.

A.C. B/95   ORDERS OF THE KING AND DISPATCHES CONCERNING THE COLONIES:
1752

Fol. 229. 16 June 1752, Versailles. Minister to Duquesne.
When the Cherokees killed 18 Iroquois, Jonquière followed the
old system of trying to excite the victims to seek revenge.
English are trying to pacify both nations. 4p.

A.C. B/111   ORDERS OF THE KING AND DISPATCHES CONCERNING THE COLONIES:
1760-1761

Fol. 353. 15 Oct. 1761, Versailles. Choiseul to Kerlerec.
Choiseul is pleased that Ft. Loudoun was captured. He thinks
it will be mutually advantageous to the French and Cherokees.
Kerlerec is praised for inciting the Cherokees to fight the
English, even though the French have not been able to provide
all their needs. 1p.

A.C. B/114   ORDERS OF THE KING AND DISPATCHES CONCERNING THE COLONIES:
1762

Fol. 171. 25 Jan. 1762, Versailles. Minister to Kerlerec.
The King is happy to learn that Kerlerec continues the Cherokee
alliance. Minister is sending supplies to insure the friendship
of the Cherokees, Alibamos, Choctaws, and Illinois. 2p.

A.C. C11A/38   GENERAL CORRESPONDENCE, CANADA: 1717

Fol. 101. 12 Oct. 1717, Quebec. Vaudreuil to Council. Cherokees killed two officers (the sons of Ramezay and Longueuil)
near the Wabash. 3p.

A.C. C11A/66   GENERAL CORRESPONDENCE, CANADA: 1736

Fol. 236. 1736. *Dénombrement des nations sauvages qui ont*
rapport au gouvernement du Canada (copy). Census of Canadian
Indians. Flatheads, Chickasaws, and Cherokees are so few that
it is impossible to know the actual numbers. 22p.

Fol. 247. 1736. *Dénombrement des nations sauvages qui ont*
rapport au gouvernement du Canada. Iroqois consider the Cherokees, Chickasaws, and Flatheads as one nation, numbering about
6,000. 17p.

A.C. C11A/67   GENERAL CORRESPONDENCE, CANADA: 1737

> Fol. 162. 10 Oct. 1737, Quebec. Beauharnois to Minister
> (extract). Beauharnois has learned about the Cherokees,
> Chickasaws, and some English settling along the Ohio.
> Kickapoos and Mascoutens have offered to expel the Cherokees
> and Chickasaws. 4p.

A.C. C11A/81   GENERAL CORRESPONDENCE, CANADA: 1744

> Fol. 182. 21 Oct. 1744, Quebec. Beauharnois to Minister.
> Beauharnois will do everything possible to obtain peace with
> the Cherokees and Chickasaws. Vaudreuil is negotiating a
> peace. 6p.

A.C. C11A/85   GENERAL CORRESPONDENCE, CANADA: 1746

> Fol. 230. 3 Nov. 1746, Quebec. Beauharnois to Minister.
> Shawnees want the French to establish peace with the Cherokees
> and Chickasaws. Beauharnois thinks the Cherokees and Chicka-
> saws would influence other Indians to seek peace, thus insuring
> tranquility along the Mississippi. 10p.

A.C. C11A/97   GENERAL CORRESPONDENCE, CANADA: 1751

> Fol. 90. 27 Sept. 1751, Quebec. La Jonquière to Minister.
> The only Indians to be feared (after the Chickasaws are
> destroyed) along the Miss. R. are the Cherokees and the Flat-
> heads. Cherokee friendship, however, will not benefit the
> French because the English live among the tribe. 14p.

> Fol. 148. 29 Oct. 1751, Quebec. La Jonquière to Minister.
> The Five Nations are preparing to attack the Cherokees.
> Hopefully, these and other nations engaged by Vaudreuil will
> successfully destroy the Cherokees. Carolina officer accom-
> panied six Cherokees who visited the Five Nations to talk peace.
> They were turned down. 9p.

A.C. C11A/99   GENERAL CORRESPONDENCE, CANADA: 1753-1754

> Fol. 290. 13 Oct. 1754, Quebec. Duquesne to Minister. Chero-
> kees released a French prisoner with a message to Kerlerec
> requesting peace. Duquesne favors the request because the
> French Indians will not fight against the Cherokees. McCarty
> thinks a fort on the Cherokee R. will be necessary once the
> peace treaty is signed, but the French lack the funds to build
> a fort. 10p.

A.C. C11A/102   GENERAL CORRESPONDENCE, CANADA: 1757

> Fol. 25. 19 Apr. 1757, Montreal. Vaudreuil to Minister. A
> Canadian adopted by the Flatheads maintains that the Cherokees
> and all Indian nations are willing to unite against the English,
> who are planning to attack the Illinois. There is a need to
> build a fort on the Ohio R. to attract Cherokee settlements
> and to facilitate communication throughout the Miss. region.
> 10p.

A.C. C11A/102 (CONT'D)

Fol. 118. 26 Oct. 1757, Quebec. Vaudreuil to Minister
(duplicate). Kerlerec has negotiated a peace with the Cherokees and Flatheads. 2p.

A.C. C11A/103 GENERAL CORRESPONDENCE, CANADA: 1758

Fol. 12. 13 Feb. 1758, Montreal. Vaudreuil to Minister.
Vaudreuil is expecting a deputation from the Flatheads, but the
Cherokees who were also expected will probably accept an English
alliance. 3p.

A.C. C11A/104 GENERAL CORRESPONDENCE, CANADA: 1759

Fol. 46. 1 Apr. 1759, Montreal. Vaudreuil to Minister
(duplicate). Vaudreuil describes the arms and equipment at
Ft. Loudoun on the Cherokee River. Vaudreuil proposes a French
fort on the Cherokee R. to stop the English. 2p.

A.C. C11A/105 GENERAL CORRESPONDENCE, CANADA: 1760-1768

Fol. 77. 24 June 1760, Montreal. Vaudreuil to Minister.
English are interested in the area around the Cherokee River.
Cherokees continue to consider joining the French. French need
supplies for the Cherokees. 4p.

Fol. 356. 16 June 1762. Picoté de Belestre to Minister.
Belestre lists achievements of his son, whom the Cherokees kept
captive five years and named chief. Under his son's leadership,
the Cherokees deserted the English and joined the French.
Belestre's son later returned to the Cherokees with 50 French
soldiers to continue to fight the English. He should be
rewarded. 3p.

A.C. C11A/114 GENERAL CORRESPONDENCE, CANADA: 1740-1741

Fol. 135. [1740-1741]. Chevalier d'Arneville to Commandant
of Tombigbee (copy). Cherokees attacked the Alibamos who were
on their way to attack Tombigbee and the Choctaws. Cherokees
claim the Chickasaws attacked the Choctaws last fall. Cherokees are holding some French prisoners. 4p.

A.C. C11A/125 GENERAL CORRESPONDENCE, CANADA: 1690-1760

Fol. 538 (no. 145). 20 Dec. 1755. François Mercier. *Déposition
et rapport* (duplicate). Mercier, a Canadian, reported that the
Cherokees took him prisoner on the Miss. River. Three months
later they sold Mercier to the English who took him to Carolina.
In 1755 he escaped and joined the Alibamos (French Indians).
Mercier reports that Gen. Braddock was defeated by Canadians
and Indians. Ga. governor has tried to enlist all Indian
nations against the French with promises of presents. Ga.
governor visited the Cherokees looking for assistance against
the French and permission to build a fort on Cherokee River.
6p.

A.C. C11E/10   BOUNDARIES AND POSTS: 1686-1759

Fol. 29. 28 May 1696. *Description du pays nommé la Carolina par rapport aux productions de la terre.* Report describes location, climate, government, agriculture, and life of the Carolina Indians. Carolina, a province of North America, was previously called Florida and discovered by the Spanish. The French later took it. 8p.

Fol. 170. 24 Apr. 1757. *Extrait de l'état actuel de l'Angleterre-Virginie.* Indian friendship is very costly to the English. Moreover, the Cherokees and Catawbas are not always faithful. Cherokees have attacked the Shawnees and Delawares near Ft. Cumberland. 9p.

Fol. 176. 24 Apr. 1757. *Extrait de l'état politique actuel de l'Angleterre-Virginie.* Report describes Virginia's efforts to cultivate Cherokee and Catawba friendship. 5p.

Fol. 179. 24 Apr. 1757. *Extrait de l'état politique actuel de l'Angleterre-Virginie.* Extract of a letter dated 25 Oct. [1756] from St. James River indicating the construction of a new fort on Cherokee land. English built another fort (Ft. Loudoun) at Winchester. A party of 400 Cherokees are on their way to join the English at Ft. Cumberland. A letter dated 2 Nov. [1756] indicates that the Cherokees have abandoned the English and seized the fort recently built on Cherokee territory. 2p.

Fol. 180. 24 Apr. 1757. *Extrait de l'état politique actuel de l'Angleterre-Caroline.* Lt. Shaw returned to Charleston from Ft. Prince George with seven Indian enemy scalps. Little Carpenter and 47 warriors left Ft. Loudoun on a raid. Cherokees killed a French officer and five soldiers near the Cherokee River. Little Carpenter has agreed to peace with the Chickasaws. 4p.

Fol. 182. 24 Apr. 1757. *Extrait de l'état politique de l'Angleterre-Caroline.* An Indian party (several Cherokees, two Shawnees, and two Frenchmen) arrived at Ft. Alabama. They met Indians on the way to whom the Shawnees presented a red stick, urging them to fight the English. 1p.

Fol. 183. 24 Apr. 1757. *Extrait de l'état politique de l'Angleterre-Georgie.* Indians from the higher and lower rivers concluded a peace treaty with Georgia. Because most of those Indians were French allies, there is still apprehension. 4p.

Fol. 185. 24 Apr. 1757. *Extrait de l'état politique de l'Angleterre-Maryland.* Cherokees have taken over the new English fort on their land and have declared themselves French allies, causing anxiety among Carolina merchants. 1p.

A.C. C13A/4   GENERAL CORRESPONDENCE, LOUSIANA: 1716

Fol. 237. 29 Aug. 1716, Paris. *Arrêt du conseil de marine sur une lettre de La Mothe-Cadillac.* [*Analyse* of fol. 245]. 7p.

A.C. C13A/4 (CONT'D)

Fol. 245. 29 Aug. 1716. *Arrêt du conseil de marine sur une
lettre de La Mothe-Cadillac.* Report describes the location
and population of the Cherokees, Chickasaws, and Choctaws.
The Cherokees live in the mountains near Carolina with 72
villages and 10,000 men. Other Indian nations are contemptuous
of the Cherokees because they lack courage. After being
attacked by the Illinois, the Cherokees sought French support
and trade. 7p.

Fol. 575. Feb. 1716, Ile Dauphine. La Mothe-Cadillac to
Minister. Cherokees attacked the Illinois. 12p.

Fol. 775. 20 Jan. 1716, Ft. Louis. Bienville to Minister.
Cherokees have attacked a Kaskaskia village and killed ten to
twelve Frenchmen. 9p.

A.C. C13A/13   GENERAL CORRESPONDENCE, LOUISIANA: 1731

Fol. 42. 25 Mar. 1731, [New Orleans]. Périer to [le Comte
de Maurepas]. [Extract of fol. 46]. 7p.

Fol. 46. 25 Mar. 1731, New Orleans. Périer to le Comte de
Maurepas. English are building forts on the Cherokee River.
15p.

A.C. C13A/14   GENERAL CORRESPONDENCE, LOUISIANA: 1732

Fol. 12. 29 Mar. 1732, Alibamos. Benoist to [Crémont] (copy).
Abekas have concluded peace with the Cherokees. Col. Glover
has assembled the Coweta and Talapoose chiefs and will go to
Carolina to meet the Cherokees. Spanish have settled in
Appalachia. 4p.

Fol. 64. 14 May 1732, New Orleans. Périer to Minister. There
have been difficulties in keeping peace among the Indian nations.
Cherokees have broken the peace treaty with the Talapooses and
Alibamos. 4p.

A.C. C13A/16   GENERAL CORRESPONDENCE, LOUISIANA: 1733

Fol. 178. 25 Jan. 1733, New Orleans. Périer to le Comte de
Maurepas. French have peaceful relations with the Indian
nations, especially the Choctaws. Chickasaws and Abekas are
English allies. The Natchez have been destroyed, and the only
survivors took refuge among the Cherokees and Abekas. 22p.

Fol. 189. 25 Jan. 1733, New Orleans. M. Périer to [le Comte
de Maurepas]. [*Analyse* of fol. 178]. 12p.

Fol. 193bis. 22 Feb. 1733, [New Orleans]. Périer to [le
Comte de Maurepas]. [*Analyse* of fol. 198]. 1p.

Fol. 198. 22 Feb. 1733, New Orleans. Périer to le Comte de
Maurepas. Cherokees and Talapooses (both English allies) are
at war. 6p.

A.C. C13A/17   GENERAL CORRESPONDENCE, LOUISIANA: 1733

> Fol. 271. 1 Aug. 1733, Mobile. Crémont to Minister. Cherokees and Abekas, both English allies, have proposed to the Choctaws that the English be allowed to establish a temporary building on their territory. Choctaws have hesitated to agree because the Alibamos claimed that the English intended to kill the Choctaws. 9p.

A.C. C13A/19   GENERAL CORRESPONDENCE, LOUISIANA: 1734

> Fol. 95. 4 Nov. 1734, New Orleans. Salmon to Minister. English are trying to win over the Choctaws and Carolina Indians with presents and promises. 8p.

> Fol. 141. 8 Nov. 1734, New Orleans. Le Chevalier de Noyan to Minister. Chief Soulier Rouge [Red Shoes], whom the English sent on a mission to the Carolinas, returned dissatisfied. The English are trying to enlist the Alibamos against the Cherokees. 6p.

A.C. C13A/21   GENERAL CORRESPONDENCE, LOUISIANA: 1735-1736

> Fol. 218. 5 Sept. 1736, New Orleans. Bienville to Minister. Some 400 Cherokees and Chickasaws have settled along the Ohio River. Cherokees and Chickasaws are evidently English allies and settled there to stop French commerce between the Wabash and the Mississippi. They have attacked French voyageurs on the Ohio. Bienville hopes to enlist other Indians to combat the Cherokees. 8p.

> Fol. 305. 1 Sept. 1736, New Orleans. Salmon to Minister. Some 400 Cherokees or Flatheads have moved to the Ohio River supposedly to interfere with French commerce on the Wabash. Cherokees attacked French voyageurs on the Ohio. Natchez confirmed a Cherokee settlement on the Ohio River. Kickapoos and Mascoutens attacked the Natchez on the Cherokee River. 5p.

A.C. C13A/22   GENERAL CORRESPONDENCE, LOUISIANA: 1736-1737

> Fol. 67. 7 Sept. 1737, Mobile. De Batz. *Nations amies et ennemies des Tchikachas.* Chart illustrating Chickasaw friends and enemies, including the Toukaulou [Tugaloo?] Cherokees. These Cherokees speak a different language from the other Cherokees and live in a different village. 1p.

> Fol. 101. 21 June 1737, New Orleans. Bienville to Minister (extract). Those Cherokees and Chickasaws who planned to settle along the Ohio R. have apparently changed their mind. 12p.

> Fol. 111. 20 Dec. 1737, New Orleans. Bienville to Minister. A Canadian reportedly saw during his captivity among the Cherokees thirty Natchez families who had left the Chickasaws. Cherokees have promised to remain neutral in a French-Chickasaw war and want peace with the Alibamos. 17p.

A.C. C13A/22 (CONT'D)

Fol. 233. 24 Oct. 1737, Mobile. Diron d'Artaguiette to
Minister. Cherokees seek peace with the Alibamos. French will
not benefit from this since the Alibamos are English allies.
22p.

A.C. C13A/23 GENERAL CORRESPONDENCE, LOUISIANA: 1738

Fol. 48. 26 Apr. 1738, New Orleans. Bienville to Minister.
Cherokees and Chickasaws, fearing hostility from other Indians,
abandoned their plan to settle on Ohio River. 8p.

Fol. 52. 26 Apr. 1738, New Orleans. Bienville to Minister.
[*Analyse* of fol. 48]. 4p.

Fol. 162. 11 July 1738, New Orleans. Louboey to Minister.
Thirty Chickasaw families who had taken refuge with the Cherokees have returned to their village, undoubtedly assured that
the Cherokees will defend them if attacked. 6p.

Fol. 176. 26 Feb. 1738, Mobile. Beauchamp to Minister.
Cherokees have attacked the French, but the Iroquois avenged
the French by killing many Cherokees. 4p.

A.C. C13A/24 GENERAL CORRESPONDENCE, LOUISIANA: 1736-1739

Fol. 35. 25 Mar. 1739, New Orleans. Bienville to Minister.
Bienville lists the measures taken to defeat the journey by
the governors of Carolina and Ga. to influence the Indian
nations. Bienville, however, lacks supplies necessary to gain
Indian friendship. 18p.

Fol. 44. 25 Mar. 1739, New Orleans. Bienville to Minister.
[*Analyse* of fol. 35]. 8p.

A.C. C13A/25 GENERAL CORRESPONDENCE, LOUISIANA: 1739-1742

Fol. 104. 15 June 1740, New Orleans. Bienville to Minister.
Some Natchez evidently took refuge with the Cherokees while
others fled towards the Yazoo River. 5p.

Fol. 124. 27 June 1740, New Orleans. Bienville to Minister.
Cherokees, not the Sioux, attacked the voyageurs on the
Wabash. 2p.

Fol. 205. 4 Jan. 1741, New Orleans. Louboey to Minister.
Bertet, the commander at Tombigbee, reports the union of the
Cherokees and Chickasaws. 14p.

Fol. 236. 23 June 1740, New Orleans. Louboey to Minister.
Louboey describes an Indian attack above the Wabash on three
boats going to Illinois. Sioux or Natchez, living with the
Cherokees, are believed responsible for the attack. 7p.

Fol. 240. 29 June 1740, [New Orleans]. Louboey to Minister.
New from Illinois confirms that it was the Cherokees who
attacked the three boats on the Wabash going to Illinois.
Natchez and Chickasaws evidently accompanied the Cherokees. 4p.

A.C. C13A/25 (CONT'D)

Fol. 256. 13 Dec. 1740, [Mobile]. Beauchamp to Salmon
(extract). Abekas, Talapooses, and Alibamos confirmed the
Cherokee attack [on Wabash boats]. Chickasaws admonished the
Cherokees, who were passing through with three French prisoners,
for their attack. 1p.

A.C. C13A/26   GENERAL CORRESPONDENCE, LOUISIANA: 1740-1742

Fol. 55. 7 Mar. 1741, New Orleans. Bienville to Minister.
Bienville explains why he believes it was the Cherokees, not
the Chickasaws, who attacked the boats going to Illinois. 12p.

Fol. 81. 30 Apr. 1741, New Orleans. Bienville to Minister.
Cherokees and Flatheads attacked some Canadians at the mouth
of the Cherokee River. The French should build a fort on the
Cherokee R. to discourage future Cherokee attacks. 13p.

Fol. 88. 30 Apr. 1741, New Orleans. Bienville to Minister.
[*Analyse* of fol. 81]. 5p.

Fol. 97. 30 Sept. 1741, New Orleans. Bienville to Minister.
Natchez, who were attacked by the Upper Wabash Indians, took
refuge with the Cherokees. Chickasaws and Cherokees are allies
and the latter often travel with Chickasaw parties attacking the
French. 19p.

Fol. 170. 4 Oct. 1741. Salmon to Minister. Cherokees were
blamed for the attack on the Canadians, but a Canadian
eyewitness testified that the Chickasaws did it. 4p.

Fol. 175. 7 Mar. 1741, New Orleans. Louboey to Minister.
Alibamos and Talapooses told Bienville that the Cherokees
attacked [the boats on the Wabash]. A negro who escaped also
confirmed the Cherokee guilt, claiming that the Cherokees held
three French prisoners. 12p.

Fol. 183. 2 May 1741, New Orleans. Louboey to Minister.
[Cherokee?] Indians attacked the Canadians along the Wabash
River. 8p.

Fol. 187. 18 July 1741, New Orleans. Louboey to Minister.
Joson described a Cherokee attack on 24 Canadians along the
Wabash River. 6p.

Fol. 202. 25 Jan. 1741, Mobile. Beauchamp to Minister.
Alibamo chiefs confirmed that the Cherokees (not the Chickasaws)
attacked the Canadians along the Wabash last July. Chickasaws
saw three French prisoners with the Cherokees. Bienville has
arrived to distribute Indian presents. 8p.

Fol. 206. 25 Apr. 1741, Mobile. Beauchamp to Minister.
There is no doubt that the Cherokees, not the Chickasaws,
attacked the Canadians along Wabash. 8p.

A.C. C13A/26 (CONT'D)

Fol. 210. 18 Sept. 1741, Mobile. Beauchamp to Minister.
Chickasaws, not Cherokees, attacked two French convoys. Natchez
and Chickasaws occasionally aid the Cherokees in attacking the
French. 7p.

A.C. C13A/27   GENERAL CORRESPONDENCE, LOUISIANA: 1741-1742,1746

Fol. 36. 27 June 1742, New Orleans. Bienville to Minister.
Frenchman [Bonnefoy?] captured by Cherokees last autumn reported
that three different Cherokee attacks were wrongly blamed on
the Chickasaws. Cherokees want peace with the French but fear
aggression from the Northern Indians. 3p.

Fol. 38. 18 Feb. 1742, New Orleans. Bienville to Minister.
English urged the Cherokees to attack the French convoys along
the Miss. and Wabash. Cherokees refused because of their recent
peace treaty with most Canadian nations. However, the Cherokees
are evidently guilty of attacking the voyageurs on the Wabash.
10p.

Fol. 43. 18 Feb. and 28 Mar. 1742, New Orleans. Bienville to
Minister. [*Analyse* of fol. 38 and fol. 63]. 9p.

Fol. 63. 28 Mar. 1742, New Orleans. Bienville to Minister.
Chickasaws have separated from the Natchez, who retreated to
the Cherokees. Cherokee attack on the Wabash voyageurs indicates
the necessity of a fort on that river. 9p.

Fol. 87. 5 Aug. 1742, New Orleans. Bienville to Minister.
Alibamos and a French prisoner [who escaped from the Cherokees]
confirmed the recent Cherokee attacks on the Wabash. Natchez
have retreated to the Cherokees. French seek ways to gain peace
with the Cherokees. Cherokees will continue hostility against
the French until they obtain peace with the Canadian nations.
5p.

Fol. 91. 13 Feb. 1742. Salmon to Minister. [*Analyse* of fol.
109]. 4p.

Fol. 109. 13 Feb. 1742. Salmon to Minister. Salmon confirms
the Cherokee attack on the Wabash (previously blamed on the
Chickasaws). English encourage the Chickasaws and Cherokees
to attack the French. 4p.

Fol. 132. 12 June 1742, Mobile. Louboey to Minister. Abekas
have attacked the Cherokees and Chickasaws and are planning to
attack the Choctaws. 14p.

Fol. 139. 17 June 1742, Mobile. Louboey to Minister. Bonnefoy,
who escaped from the Cherokees, reported that the Cherokees were
responsible for several attacks falsely attributed to the
Chickasaws. 6p.

A.C. C13A/27 (CONT'D)

Fol. 176. [17-28] Aug. 1742. *Journal* of Canelle reporting
that the Cherokees have joined the Shawnees to defend the
Chickasaws. 5p.

Fol. 182. 3 Dec. 1742. *Copie de la déclaration du nommé
Coussot, prisonier échappé des Cherokquis.* Coussot describes
the Cherokee attacks since 1740. Cherokees plan to attack the
Ouyatanons [Wea]. Cherokees want peace and only attack the
French because the French Indians are hostile. English are
constantly urging the Cherokees to attack the French. Cherokees have 40 villages with over 100 men in each. 4p.

A.C. C13A/28   GENERAL CORRESPONDENCE, LOUISIANA: 1743-1745

Fol. 31. 4 Feb. 1743, New Orleans. Bienville to Minister.
Bienville recounts the experiences of a Frenchman taken prisoner
by the Cherokees while on his way to Illinois. Natchez have
found refuge among the Cherokees. 18p.

Fol. 49. 18 July 1743, New Orleans. Vaudreuil to Minister.
The Abekas and Cherokees are fighting each other. Cherokees
desire peace with the French but fear aggression from Canada.
Cherokees are trying to negotiate a peace with Canada through
the Shawnees and Hurons. If a peace is concluded, a fort will
be needed on the Cherokee R. to control the Cherokees, watch
the English, and insure safe navigation on the Wabash. 10p.

Fol. 73. 29 July 1743. Vaudreuil to Minister. Cherokees,
encouraged by the English, attacked the Abekas. Hostility
between Indian nations must be considered when planning for the
welfare of the colony. 3p.

Fol. 86. 25 Sept. 1743, New Orleans. Vaudreuil to [Minister].
Abekas have left to attack the Cherokees. Vaudreuil feels that
peace with the Cherokees depends upon peace with the Chickasaws.
10p.

Fol. 95. November 1743. *Feuille au Roi.* Report on Indian
nations indicating that the Cherokees want peace if the French
will stop Canadian aggression. English were responsible for the
Cherokee attacks. 3p.

Fol. 112. 21 July 1743, New Orleans. Salmon to Minister.
Cherokees and Chickasaws have made peace without English
encouragement. 2p.

Fol. 145. 12 June 1743, New Orleans. Louboey to Minister.
Talapooses and Cherokees are at war. French need supplies to
influence the Indians. 11p.

Fol. 160. 24 Sept. 1743, Mobile. Louboey to Minister. A
party of Abekas and Talapooses have attacked the Cherokees.
6p.

Fol. 198. 10 Feb. 1744. [*Analyse* of Vaudreuil to Minister
(25 Sept. 1743), fol. 86]. 2p.

A.C. C13A/28 (CONT'D)

Fol. 245. 6 Dec. 1744, New Orleans (triplicate). Vaudreuil to Minister. It is necessary to build a fort on the Wabash for protection against the Cherokees. Peace with the Cherokees will be useless unless the Chickasaws rid themselves of Englishmen. French need supplies to gain the Chickasaw and Cherokee friendship. 12p.

Fol. 263. 28 Dec. 1744, New Orleans. Vaudreuil to Minister (triplicate). Abekas, Cowetas, and Talapooses made peace with the Choctaws but continue their hostility against the Cherokees. 6p.

A.C. C13A/30   GENERAL CORRESPONDENCE, LOUISIANA: 1745-1747

Fol. 28. 6 Feb. 1746. Vaudreuil to Minister. Cherokees, Kickapoos, Mascoutens, Chickasaws, Abekas, Alibamos, Cowetas, and Talapooses have united to seek peace with the French at the urging of the Shawnees. Cherokees also seek peace with the Northern tribes. Vaudreuil describes the peace conditions. 11p.

Fol. 57. 12 Apr. 1746, Mobile. Vaudreuil to Minister. The Chickasaws and Cherokees are very persistent in their request for peace. Vaudreuil describes the conditions of peace offered to these tribes as well as proposals for general peace with all Indian nations. French need to meet the Indian demands in order to keep them away from the English. Peace will bring many advantages to the colony. 11p.

Fol. 71. 20 Nov. 1746, New Orleans. Vaudreuil to Minister. Goods for the Shawnees and Cherokees were poorly selected. Cherokees are anxious to obtain peace with the French. There are 47 villages among the Cherokees and Flatheads, 7 of which are located above the [Cherokee] River and 40 in the mountains near the English. 10p.

Fol. 86. 20 Nov. 1746, New Orleans. Vaudreuil to Minister. [Duplicate of fol.71]. 14p.

Fol. 242. *Mémoire sur l'état de la colonie de la Louisianne en 1746.* Most important tribes are the Choctaws (4,000 warriors), Chickasaws (600), Alibamos, Abekas, Talapooses, and the Cherokees. The English hold posts along the Cherokee R. and trade with the Chickasaws and Cherokees. French need to build forts in the Cherokee and Chickasaw territory to stop the English. Because the Cherokees are a powerful nation, it will be difficult to convince them to change their alliance. With 6,000 warriors, the Cherokees are English allies and the most powerful Indian nation in the region. 40p.

A.C. C13A/31   GENERAL CORRESPONDENCE, LOUISIANA: 1747-1748, 1751

Fol. 42. 22 Mar. 1747, New Orleans. Vaudreuil to Minister. Shawnees wish to settle near the Cherokee River. They have been sent on a mission to encourage the Cherokees to join them in fighting the English. 10p.

A.C. C13A/31 (CONT'D)

Fol. 52. 8 Apr. 1747, New Orleans. Vaudreuil to Minister.
English intention to settle near the Cherokee R. is creating
fears about French safety. French need to build a fort along
the Wabash. 8p.

A.C. C13A/32   GENERAL CORRESPONDENCE, LOUISIANA: 1748-1750

Fol. 113. 2 Nov. 1748, New Orleans. Vaudreuil to Minister.
On several occasions the Cherokees and Osages have attacked
travellers on the Miss. River. French need to keep the Indian
nations happy through supplies if they wish to keep them from
turning to the English. 18p.

A.C. C13A/33   GENERAL CORRESPONDENCE, LOUISIANA: 1749

Fol. 219. 17 Dec. 1749. Mr. le Bailly-Mesnager. *Mémoire sur
la Louisianne.* Bailly-Mesnager proposes a new colony along
the Miss. R. to counter English posts on the Cherokee River.
6p.

A.C. C13A/35   GENERAL CORRESPONDENCE, LOUISIANA: 1751

Fol. 102. 10 May 1751, New Orleans. Vaudreuil to Minister.
Cowetas are fighting the Cherokees and diverting attention
from the differences between the Abekas and Choctaws. 14p.

Fol. 167. 10 Oct. 1751, New Orleans. Vaudreuil to Minister.
Six hunters from Ft. Prud'Homme were attached by the Chickasaws
or Cherokees. Vaudreuil hopes to ascertain the guilty party
when he goes to Mobile. 11p.

Fol. 175. 10 Oct. 1751, New Orleans. Vaudreuil to Minister.
[Duplicate of fol. 167]. 13p.

A.C. C13A/36   GENERAL CORRESPONDENCE, LOUISIANA: 1750-1753

Fol. 66. 8 Apr. 1752, New Orleans. Vaudreuil to Minister.
Vaudreuil requests permission to build two forts on the
Cherokee R. (12-15 leagues from the Miss. R.) for defense
against the English, Cherokees, Flatheads, and others. 20p.

*A.C. C13A/37   GENERAL CORRESPONDENCE, LOUISIANA: 1750-1751, 1753-
                1754, 1758, 1761*

Fol. 66. 20 Aug. 1753, New Orleans. Kerlerec to Minister.
Cherokees, Chickasaws, and Shawnees occasionally attack French
boats. Cherokees took a ten year old girl prisoner and sold
her to the English. 22p.

Fol. 188. 20 May 1753, at the Illinois. McCarty to Minister.
Indians attacked a convoy on the Wabash near the Cherokee River.
Chickasaws and Cherokees are evidently the guilty party. Some
Chickasaw prisoners confirm that the Cherokees and Chickasaws
had committed all the attacks along the Miss. and Wabash R.
for the last 18 months. 6p.

A.C. C13A/38   GENERAL CORRESPONDENCE, LOUISIANA: 1754

Fol. 66. 21 June 1754, New Orleans. Kerlerec to Minister.
Shawnees take deserters to the Cherokees where they can find
English traders to translate for them. Kerlerec would like
to give amnesty to the deserters because of their knowledge
about English strategy. 3p.

Fol. 92. 18 July 1754, New Orleans. Kerlerec to Minister.
French need to build a fort on the Wabash to stop English,
Cherokee, and Chickasaw aggression. 5p.

Fol. 95. 15 Sept. 1754, New Orleans. Kerlerec to Minister.
A new fort on the Wabash would keep open communication between
Lousiana and Canada, prevent the English from building settlements, and protect the colony from the Cherokees and Chickasaws
whose war parties often use the river. Incited by English
gifts, the Cherokees, Chickasaws, and Shawnees frequently
attack the French. A Cherokee chief has proposed an alliance
with the French. 22p.

Fol. 113. 20 Sept. 1754, New Orleans. Kerlerec to Minister.
Kerlerec will leave 1 Oct. for Mobile to meet with various
Indian tribes to prevent them from becoming English allies. 3p.

Fol. 122. 18 Dec. 1754, New Orleans. Kerlerec to Minister.
Chickasaws could not withstand the Choctaws' attacks without
aid from the Cherokees and Shawnees (who often intermarry with
the tribe) and the English. 16p.

Fol. 136. 20 Dec. 1754, New Orleans. Kerlerec to Minister.
Kerlerec has received reports concerning Jean Baptiste Monteur,
who just returned to the Carolinas after being a Cherokee
prisoner. 7p.

A.C. C13A/39   GENERAL CORRESPONDENCE, LOUISIANA: 1755-1757

Fol. 35. 1 Oct. 1755, New Orleans. Kerlerec to Minister.
There is an urgent need to build a fort on the Wabash three
to four leagues below the Cherokee R. and seven to eight leagues
from the St. Louis River. 3p.

Fol. 37. 1 Oct. 1755, New Orleans. Kerlerec to Minister.
Kerlerec sends Lantagnac's memoir and requests a promotion for
Lantagnac to reward him for nine years of service among the
English and the Cherokees. 5p. [Enclosures to fol. 44b].

Fol. 40. 1 Oct. 1755. *Représentations* from Lantagnac to
Kerlerec. Lantagnac relates his experiences with the
Indians and the English from Nov. 1745, when he was
captured by the Chickasaws while hunting, until he returned
to the Alibamos. Lantagnac first lived with the English
then with the Cherokees, where he ran a trading post.
Although he could have returned to Louisiana, he remained
with the Cherokees to repay the money loaned him for his
trading post, to learn the Cherokee language, and to
discover how the English controlled their Indians. 10p.

A.C. C13A/39 (CONT'D)

Fol. 52.   5 Oct. 1755, New Orleans.   Kerlerec to Minister
(duplicate).   Indians protect French deserters.   7p.

Fol. 57.   9 Oct. 1755, New Orleans.   Kerlerec to Minister.
[Coded duplicate of fol. 60].   5p.

Fol. 60.   9 Oct. 1755, New Orleans.   Kerlerec to Minister.
Carolina and Va. governors tried to seduce Cherokee chiefs by
offering presents and promising payment for French scalps.   5p.

Fol. 149.   1 Apr. 1756, New Orleans.   Kerlerec to Minister.
English in New York, Penn., Va., and the Carolinas turn the
Indians against the French by offering them goods.   French need
the Cherokees as allies.   Shawnee chief went to Quebec to talk
to Vaudreuil about peace with the Cherokees.   If a new fort is
approved for the mouth of the Wabash, the Cherokees and Shawnees
could help protect workers building the fort.   11p.

Fol. 181.   22 July 1756, New Orleans.   Kerlerec to Minister.
Alibamo chief reported that the English were taking 600 men
to build six forts among the Cherokees.   3p.

Fol. 190.   12 Dec. 1756, New Orleans.   Kerlerec to Minister
(triplicate).   Louisiana needs supplies particularly to keep
the Indians from turning to the English.   Cherokees want peace
with the French.   3p.

Fol. 277.   21 Oct. 1757, New Orleans.   Kerlerec to Minister.
English are trying to stop French peace negotiations with the
Cherokees.   French hastily built a fort on the Wabash below the
mouth of Cherokee R. in order to fight English aggression.   6p.

Fol. 280.   21 Oct. 1757, New Orleans.   Kerlerec to Minister.
[Coded triplicate of fol. 277].   7p.

Fol. 291.   26 Oct. 1757, New Orleans.   Bobé-Descloseaux to
Minister (duplicate).   Bobé-Descloseaux requests the merchandise
and arms promised to the Cherokees for 1758.   3p.

Fol. 302.   1757.   Duplessis to Minister (duplicate).   Shawnees
have urged the Cherokees to join the French and fight the
English.   The Cherokees,who number 5,000 warriors, accept the
condition that the governor of Canada must agree to treaty
since he will have to help supply them.   3p.

Fol. 307.   13 July 1757, Montreal.   Vaudreuil to Minister.
Some Shawnees, who had been living with either the Flatheads
or Cherokees, are planning to settle along the Ohio River.
Cherokees wish to join the Shawnees and Loups in fighting the
English.   Kerlerec accepted peace with the Flatheads after they
had agreed to fight the English.   4p.

A.C. C13A/40   GENERAL CORRESPONDENCE, LOUISIANA: 1757-1759

Fol. 27. 28 Jan. 1757, New Orleans. Kerlerec to Minister
(duplicate). French lack the supplies promised the Indians.
3p.

Fol. 29. 30 Jan. 1757, New Orleans. Kerlerec to Minister
(duplicate). Kerlerec sends a copy of the preliminaries of the
peace treaty with the Cherokees. Cherokee needs are different
and greater than the Choctaws. If Vaudreuil approves the
treaty, weapons and goods will be urgently needed to insure
the Cherokee alliance. 3p.

Fol. 31. 12 and 23 Aug. 1758, New Orleans. Kerlerec to
Minister (duplicate). French need supplies and arms. Some
Cherokees have already left the French and joined the English
from lack of supplies. Alibamos and Choctaws are also joining the English. Cherokees and Chickasaws killed Grignon along
the Wabash. 6p.

Fol. 99. 25 Oct. 1758, New Orleans. Kerlerec to Minister.
[Duplicate of fol. 104.] 10p.

Fol. 104. 25 Oct. 1758, New Orleans, Kerlerec to Minister.
Peace agreement with the Cherokees has been delayed because the
recently received supplies were not sufficient for the Cherokees.
10p.

Fol. 111. 1 Dec. 1758, New Orleans. Kerlerec to Minister. A
Carolina official successfully obtained Indian permission to
build three forts in Indian territory by offering gifts. The
Indians, however, later rejected the English proposal after the
French countered with an offer of gifts. 8p.

Fol. 119. 3 Dec. 1758, New Orleans. Kerlerec to Minister.
Kerlerec discusses the administration of Indian affairs and the
distribution of goods. 16p.

Fol. 133. 12 Dec. 1758, New Orleans. Kerlerec to Minister. 4p.
[Enclosures to fol. 156].

> Fol. 135. 12 Dec. 1758, New Orleans. [Kerlerec?] *État*
> *des nations sauvages qui ont rapport à la colonie de la*
> *Louisianne.* Report describes and locates the Cherokees,
> Natchez, Choctaws, Chickasaws, Alibamos, Cowetas, Shawnees,
> Apalaches, Sioux, and others. Cherokee R. is located 40
> leagues above Ft. Chartres. Cherokees and Flatheads have
> settled at the mouth of the Cherokee River. They are
> numerous and allied to the English. Cherokees are seek-
> ing peace with the French but lack of supplies has delayed
> the peace negotiations. 42p.

A.C. C13A/41   GENERAL CORRESPONDENCE, LOUISIANA: 1759,1764

Fol. 126. 8 Oct. 1759, New Orleans. Kerlerec to Minister.
Supplies are urgently needed for the Cherokees and Choctaws.
4p.

A.C. C13A/41 (CONT'D)

Fol. 166. 5 Jan. 1759, New Orleans. Rochemore to Minister. Rochemore requests supplies to conclude the peace that Kerlerec promised the Cherokees. 3p. [Enclosures to fol. 168b].

Fol. 168. 4 Feb. 1757, New Orleans. D'Auberville to Minister (triplicate). D'Auberville forwards an inventory of merchandise that Kerlerec thinks is necessary to conclude a treaty with the Cherokees, a tribe very anxious to become a French ally. A Cherokee alliance would benefit Louisiana. 2p.

A.C. C13A/42   GENERAL CORRESPONDENCE, LOUISIANA: 1759-1764

Fol. 42. 12 June 1760, New Orleans. Kerlerec to Minister (in code). After the Cherokees were overwhelmed with gifts, they agreed to attack the English and killed 2,000 of them. Cherokees also attacked the Chickasaws. Kerlerec has requested the goods necessary to treat with the Cherokees. 12p.

Fol. 48. 12 June 1760, New Orleans. Kerlerec to Minister. [Decoded duplicate of fol. 42]. 11p.

Fol. 58. 4 Aug. 1760, New Orleans. Kerlerec to Minister. Cherokees destroyed an English army of 3,000 soldiers, only 25-30 survived. Cherokees have demanded French goods and ammunition. If their demands are not met, the Cherokees will return to the English. Cherokees and Alibamos could have 8,000 men. 6p.

Fol. 61. 24 June 1760, Mobile. *Conseil extraordinaire de guerre* (copy). French must conclude a treaty with such Indian nations as the Alibamos, Cowetas, Talapooses, and Abekas. Alibamos influenced the Cherokees to seek peace with the French. Supplies are needed for the Alibamos and Cherokees, but it will be difficult to provide goods for all. 4p.

Fol. 83. 21 Dec. 1760, New Orleans. Kerlerec to Minister. Cherokees are willing to unite with the French, but they are demanding goods and arms which Kerlerec cannot supply. 6p.

Fol. 118. 23 June 1760, New Orleans. Rochemore to Minister. Ft. l'Ascension on the Cherokee R. needs to be rebuilt. Rochemore describes the condition of other French forts. 11p.

Fol. 203. 1 Mar. 1761, New Orleans. Kerlerec to Minister. For the last two years Kerlerec has stressed the need to aid the Cherokees. French feel particularly obligated to the Cherokees now since they have captured Ft. Loudoun above the Cherokee River. Cherokees killed 50 Englishmen, took 150 prisoners, and carried 12 cannons and 2 *perriers* to their main village. 3p.

Fol. 207. 1 Mar. 1761, New Orleans. Kerlerec to Minister. English reportedly plan to attack the Illinois and Cherokees in the spring. 4p.

A.C. *C13A/42 (CONT'D)*

Fol. 217. 8 June 1761, New Orleans. Kerlerec to Minister
(triplicate). Cherokees continue to be loyal, but Kerlerec
lacks supplies and arms necessary to keep them faithful to the
French. Kerlerec maintains two Alibamo chiefs and Lantagnac
among the Cherokees to remind the tribe of their agreement. 7p.

Fol. 229. 12 and 19 July 1761, New Orleans. Kerlerec to
Minister (duplicate). Cherokee chief confirms alliance with
the French. However, the Cherokees are forced to join the
English if they are not provided with supplies. 3p.

Fol. 249. 12 Dec. 1761. Thiton de Silegne to Minister. 3p.
[Enclosures to fol. 253].

> Fol. 251. [*Mémoire*] regarding Kerlerec's faithful service
> to the King for the past 42 years. Kerlerec is credited
> with winning the Cherokees away from the English in 1756.
> Since then, the Cherokees have faithfully defended the
> French frontiers. 5p.

Fol. 267. 15 Dec. 1761, New Orleans. Kerlerec to Minister
(duplicate). Cherokees are outraged by the French failure to
keep their promise. Cherokees have been fighting the English
without sufficient arms and supplies and are now reduced to
misery. Their treaty with the French has been humiliating
and without any advantages. If powder and goods are not
received very soon, the Cherokees, Choctaws, and the Illinois
nations will turn to the English for supplies. 5p.

Fol. 280. 1741-1759. *État de ses services* [*de m. Aubry*].
In 1757 Aubry served the King by building a fort near the
Cherokee R. for protection against the English. 3p.

Fol. 286. 1761, Paris. H.P. *Mémoire concernant la population
et le commerce à la Louisianne et Cayenne*. No posts are found
between Arkansas and Illinois and no one would dare cross that
area from fear of encountering the Cherokees and Chickasaws
hunting near the Miss. River. 45p.

A.C. *C13A/43   GENERAL CORRESPONDENCE, LOUISIANA: 1762-1763*

Fol. 21b. 21 July 1762. Extract of letter from Kerlerec
stating that he is pleased that the King approves the Cherokee
alliance. 1p.

Fol. 22b. 21 July 1762. Extract of letter from Kerlerec
ordering Lantagnac to take a message to the Cherokees, who
continue to fight the English. 1p.

Fol. 25. 10 Feb. 1762, New Orleans. Kerlerec to Minister.
Cherokees have demanded that the French either abandon them
or deliver goods. Choctaws and Alibamos have made the same
demands. 2p.

A.C. C13A/43 (CONT'D)

Fol. 30.   28 Apr. 1762, New Orleans. Kerlerec to Minister.
Kerlerec has notified the Cherokees and Choctaws that goods
are coming. He also asked Chief DuLoup, who arranged the
French alliance with the Cherokees, to bring six Cherokee
chiefs to New Orleans to reinforce the alliance. Indian nations
have been asked to join the French in assisting the Spanish
against the English. 6p.

Fol. 78.   24 June 1762, New Orleans. Kerlerec to Minister
(duplicate). Kerlerec has sent word to the Cherokees, Choctaws,
Abekas, Alibamos, and other Indian nations that supplies have
arrived. Quantity and quality of merchandise received, however,
is not what Kerlerec ordered, putting him in a difficult
situation with the Indians. Kerlerec has ordered Lantagnac
to bring him six chiefs, six respected Cherokees, and War Chief
DuLoup to New Orleans to discuss ways of protecting the Illinois
by destroying all the English establishments in that area. 11p.

Fol. 90.   26 July 1762, New Orleans. Kerlerec to Minister.
Lantagnac, who has returned from his mission to the Cherokees,
will be promoted to *lieutenant reformé*, a rank he well deserves.
Cherokees continue to fight the English. Fifty to sixty Indians
plan to visit Kerlerec at the end of Sept. to show their
displeasure at not receiving promised supplies. 4p.

Fol. 196.   2 May 1763, New Orleans. Kerlerec to Minister.
Cherokees, Choctaws, and Alibamos number over 12,000 men.
Cherokees, who sacrificed themselves after being promised goods,
are very indigent. Cherokees protest that the French have
unfairly surrendered part of their land to the English.
Kerlerec expects difficulties from the Cherokees and others
when the French evacuate Illinois. 6p.

A.C. C13A/51   GENERAL CORRESPONDENCE, LOUISIANA: 1795-1802

Fol. 192.   5 Vend. XI [27 Sept. 1802], Paris. Laussat to
Minister. Laussat lists 24 Indian tribes, including the Cherokees, which could have relations with the French in Louisiana.
3p.

Fol. 194.   5 Vend. XI [27 Sept. 1802], Paris. *État d'approvi-
sionnement ... aux nations indiennes ou sauvages.* Report lists
Indian goods needed by the new French government in New Orleans.
5p.

A.C. C13C/1   LOUISIANA: 1719-1767

Fol. 117.   [1767?] *Idée générale de la manière dont le
commerce de la Louisianne peut se former.* Report describes
Louisiana's geography, commercial potential, and the military
significance of various posts. The Wabash River, which the
English and the Cherokees (English allies) have settled, is
the only river which the enemy can descend with force to the
Mississippi. 34p.

A.C. C13C/1 (CONT'D)

Fol. 346. 1767. *Exacte description de la Louisianne.* Report
describes Louisiana's ports, land, rivers, Indian nations, and
potential as a colony. Taogarias and the Cherokees settled
near the Caskinaupau [?] R. some time ago. 22p.

Fol. 358. [1767?] *État des sauvages qui habitent depuis les
Alibamons jusqu'à la Caroline.* Report gives the location and
census of the Cherokees, Abekas, Cowetas, Shawnees and other
tribes. Cherokees live near Carolina and evidently number
10,000. All Indian nations, except the Cherokees and the
Taogarias, have been to Mobile to smoke a pipe. A post in
Alibamo territory would help the French gain a Cherokee alliance
and form a barrier against the English. 5p.

A.C. C13C/2 LOUISIANA: 1699-1724

Fol. 72. 1711. John Stewart. Some Observations on American
Indians. 8p.

Fol. 76. 23 May 1711, S. Carolina. Letter from John Stewart
indicating that the French have Ft. Cartour [?] and Ft. Mobile.
They also have the Choctaws and [Chickasaws?] and are courting
the Carolina Indians. 8p.

Fol. 80. 10 Mar. 1710/11, Carolina. John Stewart to Queen
Anne. The French trade with the Choctaws, Chickasaws, and
Carolina Indians. French have 4,000 [Cherokees] and 1,000
Chickasaws on their side. 4p.

A.C. C13C/4 LOUISIANA: 1718-1719, 1741-1781

Fol. 72. 1697-1722. Beranger. *Relation de la province de la
Louisianne.* Beranger lists an Indian vocabulary that he used
during his six years in the province. 60p.

Fol. 202. [June 1739]. Report from Claude Drouet de Richarville. [Duplicate of F3/12/353]. 5p.

A.C. F3/12 CANADA: 1732-1740

Fol. 353. 10 June 1739. [Report] from Claude Drouet de
Richarville about his experiences as a Chickasaw prisoner.
Chickasaws and Cherokees are neighbors and allies. Chickasaws
want peace with the French. 6p.

A.C. F3/14 CANADA: 1750-1756

Fol. 36. 16 June 1752. Minister to Duquesne (copy). Minister
advises Duquesne on managing Indians and compares the Indian
policies of Canada and Louisiana. Minister wants the French
to protect the Indians and secure their friendship rather than
incite them to fight one another as happened in the past. La
Jonquièr was mistaken to incite the Iroquois against the
Cherokees, thus losing both nations. 4p.

A.C. F3/14 (CONT'D)

Fol. 352. 6 Oct. 1756, Quebec. Bigot to the Minister.
Cherokees and Flatheads are planning to settle along the
Cherokee River. 4p.

A.C. F3/24   LOUISIANA: 1680-1755

Fol. 25. 3 May 1699-1701, Biloxi. Sauvole. *Recueil de journal
et suite de ce qui c'est passé dans le port de Biloxi depuis le
départ du traversier pour Ft. Dominique.* Report lists location
of various Indian tribes around the Carolinas. The Cherokees
are settled near the Shawnee River. 22p.

Fol. 315. 26 Mar. 1741, St. Joseph River. Villiers to Beauharnois. Chickasaws attacked the French on the Cherokee River.
4p.

Fol. 361. [1741-1742]. *Journal* of Antoine Bonnefoy stating
the circumstances surrounding his capture by and life with the
Cherokees. Cherokees eventually adopted Bonnefoy. Cherokees
and other Indians seek peace with the French, but the English
incite them to war against the French. Of the 52 existing
Cherokee villages, only eight are French enemies. The rest
are neutral because of their remoteness and their peaceful
nature. 22p.

Fol. 373. 25 Jan. 1741, Mobile. [Journal?] of Beauchamp
reporting that the Cherokees, not the Chickasaws, attacked the
Wabash travellers last July. Chickasaws saw the Cherokees take
three French prisoners. 7p.

Fol. 422. 28 Aug. - 19 Oct. 1746, Louisiana. Journal of
Beauchamp relating his visit to the Choctaws and other tribes
to reinforce alliances with the French. Peace has been
concluded with the Indians of the Upper River as well as those
near the Wabash, Shawnee, and Cherokee Rivers. Shawnees,
Alibamos, Abekas, and Cowetas have signed a peace treaty. 49p.

A.C. F3/25   LOUISIANA: 1756-1806

Fol. 21. 21 Oct. 1757, New Orleans. Copy of letter from
Kerlerec reporting that the English are urging the Cherokees
to break off peace negotiations with the French. Cherokees
are unhappy because the French are not providing them with food
and other goods. French constructed a fort on the Wabash near
the mouth of Cherokee R. to discourage English aggression. 5p.

Fol. 29. 25 Oct. 1758, Louisiana. [Memoir] from Kerlerec
describing his original plan to unite the Indians against the
English. Kerlerec convinced the Illinois and Cherokees to
reject the English and their goods by promising the tribes
peace, an alliance, and presents. Other nations are willing to
join the French but Kerlerec desperately needs supplies to
convince them. 8p.

A.C. F3/95   COLONIES, GENERAL: 1735-1790

Fol. 22. *État des sauvages qui habitent depuis les Alibamons jusqu'à la Caroline.* Report lists villages and population of the Alibamos, Abekas, Cowetas, Appalachicolas, and Taogarias. All these tribes are friendly to the French, except for the Cherokees and Taogarias. 3p.

AFFAIRES ÉTRANGÈRES
A.E. BI/372   CONSULAR CORRESPONDENCE, CHARLESTON: 1784-1792

Fol. 258. 26 Dec. 1787, Charleston. Pétry to le Comte Montmorin (duplicate). Franklin continues to gain influence among the settlements west of the Appalachians. Franklin must be kept informed of the measures taken against the Indians. 6p.

Fol. 261. 30 Jan. 1788, Charleston. Pétry to Montmorin. Ga. has asked for government assistance against the Indians but the national government did not respond. 10p.

Fol. 272. 15 Feb. 1788, Charleston. Pétry to Montmorin. Ga. and S.C. have appointed Indian commissioners to negotiate peace. 6p.

A.E. BI/909   CONSULAR CORRESPONDENCE, NEW YORK: 1783-1787

Fol. 59. 10 July 1785, New York. Mr. de Crèvecoeur to Minister. Franklin, which is located west of the mountains and contains 19,000 residents, wants independence. 8p.

A.E. BIII/447   UNITED STATES, INDIVIDUAL AFFAIRS: 1778-1784

N. fol. 22 Nov. 1784. *Mémoire* from Philippe Dejean to Minister. Cherokees seized Dejean in the mountains of Ohio in 1757 and in 1759 the English captured him. Because of his knowledge of the English and Indian languages, he was named justice of the peace in 1767, criminal judge in 1776, and crown officer (Treasurer and Agent) of the army along the Miss. in 1777. When the Americans defeated Gen. Hamilton's army, Dejean was taken prisoner to Virginia. He requests the post of consul at Portsmouth. 4p.

SECRÉTAIRERIE D'ÉTAT IMPÉRIALE
A.F. IV   CARTON 1211 - COLONIES, MEMOIRS AND PLANS OF EXPEDITIONS:
1799-1814

Doc. 59. 25 Oct. 1801, Baltimore. *Mémoire et notes sur la Louisianne et la Florida.* Report describes location, climate, agriculture, resources, commerce, and potential of Louisiana and Florida. Florida's major product is Indian goods. The Choctaws, Chickasaws, Creeks, Cherokees, and others live in Ga. and the Carolinas. All of Florida's neighboring tribes could muster no more than 25,000 warriors. Indians will be extinct by the end of the century. 53p.

A.F. IV (CONT'D)

> Doc. 62. 29 Fructidor IX [16 Sept. 1801], Paris. Joseph
> Pontalbal. *Notes sur la Louisianne*. Pontalbal describes
> geography, population, agriculture, resources, and economic
> potential of Louisiana. The Americans have sought to take
> possession of Natchez since 1785. Americans claim to have
> peace treaties with the Alibamos, Creeks, Choctaws, and
> Chickasaws. French dispute the legality of these treaties.
> Cherokees and Creeks have been involved in territorial fights
> with the United States until 1791. Although the Americans
> try to control the Alibamos, Choctaws, Creeks, and Chickasaws,
> these Indian nations remain loyal to the French. Indians
> claim that the United States is only interested in taking
> their land. 54p.

> Doc. 67. 15 Vendémiaire XI [7 Oct. 1802], Paris. Gen. Victor
> to the First Consul. Although Spain always gave 100,000
> piastres in presents to the Indians each year, Victor believes
> the French should give about 500,000 francs worth a year. 2p.

ARCHIVES DE LA MARINE
A.M. B1/8   DELIBERATIONS OF THE COUNCIL OF THE NAVY: 1716

> Fol. 254. 28 Mar. 1716. Minutes of Council recording that
> the Carolina Indians have united with the Iroquois. 2p.

A.M. B1/9   DELIBERATIONS OF THE COUNCIL OF THE NAVY: 1716

> Fol. 270. 29 Aug. 1716. Minutes of Council recording that
> the Illinois are holding a Cherokee sent by the English. 5p.

BIBLIOTHEQUE DE L'INSTITUT DE FRANCE

Paris

FONDS CUVIER 251 (MS. 3251), LETTERS TO CUVIER: 1829

> Fol. 68. 13 Feb. 1829, Paris. David B. Warden to Cuvier,
> Sec. of Academy of Royal Sciences. Warden sends a copy of
> the *Bulletin of the Society of Geography* containing informa-
> tion about Cherokee civilization. 1p.

BIBLIOTHEQUE NATIONALE

Paris

MANUSCRITS FRANÇAIS, NOUVELLES ACQUISITIONS
N.A.F. 1307   MISCELLANEOUS PAPERS

Fol. 8. Palisot Beauvais. *Tableau des remèdes et des plantes*
employés par les Tcharlokees contre la morture des serpents.
Cherokee snake bite remedies. 2p.

DÉPÔT DES ARCHIVES DU GÉNIE

Vincennes

CARTON AMERIQUE SEPT., SECTION 2

No. 3. 1755. *Notes concernant les droits réclamés en Amerique*
par les Anglais à cause de leur alliance avec les indiens.
Report describes the course of the Miss. R. and the Indian
tribes on its banks, including the Cherokees. 21p.

GREAT BRITAIN

BRITISH MUSEUM

Greater London

ADD. MSS. 24322   MISCELLANEOUS AMERICAN PAPERS: 1718-1796

Fol. 3. 9 and 16 Sept. 1730, London. Order to pay Gov.
Johnson £400 for expenses of seven Cherokees, (Johnson's
receipts attached). 2p.

Fol. 112. 18 May 1785, Wakitumikee. Council of Shawnees,
Mingoes, Delawares, and Cherokees complaining about white
encroachment on Indian land. 4p.

Fol. 116. 1785, Detroit. George Sharpe to Gov. Hay. N.C.,
Ga., and Va. have prohibited all commerce to the Cherokee R.
until the Cherokees make peace. American officers and soldiers
intend to settle along the Cherokee River. 3p.

ADD. MSS. 25699   CHRONICLES OF THE INDIANS OF NORTH AMERICA

Fol. 1. 1836. Samuel Garner Drake. Chronicles of North
American Indians from Earliest Accounts to the Present Time.
176p.

*ADD. MSS. 35427   LETTERS FROM THOMAS HUTCHINSON TO HARDWICKE:
                   1774-1778*

Fol. 114. 26 Sept. 1776, New Bond Street. Thomas Hutchinson
to Lord Hardwicke. Ten years ago Hutchinson would have felt
sorry for Va. if the Creeks and Cherokees had attacked them.
Now, however, Virginians have caused their own distress. 2p.

ADD. MSS. 35910   HARDWICKE PAPERS: 1759-1764

Fol. 18. 15 Jan. 1760, St. James Square. Copy of letter to
Duke of Newcastle stating that it will be impossible for
England to preserve the friendship of the Cherokees, Chickasaws,
Creeks, and less important nations unless the French are
confined to the eastern bank of the Miss. River. 4p.

Fol. 108. 9 Sept. 1760, Charleston. Lt. Gov. Bull to Bd. of
Trade (copy). Cherokees have broken surrender agreement and
executed Capt. Demeré and 23 others. 3p.

Fol. 109. [1760]. Maj. Lewis to Col. Byrd (copy). Cherokees
massacred garrison of Ft. Loudoun. Little Carpenter saved
Capt. Stuart. 3p.

ADD. MSS. 35910 (CONT'D)

    Fol. 252. 1763. *Full State of Dispute between Gov. and Commons House of Assembly.* Report refers to the cost of the Cherokee war. 78p.

ADD. MSS. 38334   LIVERPOOL PAPERS: 1762

    Fol. 133. 29 June 1762. Anne Atkin to Lords of Treasury. Memorial from Edmond Atkin's widow detailing husband's expenses. 7p.

ADD. MSS. 38650   LETTERS RELATING TO NORTH AMERICA: 1775-1780

    Fol. 12b. 12 Aug. 1780, Richmond. Thomas Jefferson to Gov. Nash. Cherokees from Chickamauga towns have committed frequent murders. Jefferson has directed those towns to be destroyed. 2p.

ADD. MSS. 39311   BERKELEY PAPERS: 1768

    Fol. 226. 11 Apr. 1768, Charter House. Alex. Cuming to Dr. Berkeley. Professor Mace, who considered himself a Biblical scholar, wanted to persuade Cuming that the Book of Job and the prophecies of Isaiah were written after the time of Antiochus. Cuming believes that Mace's reasoning was so faulty that Cuming could use it to prove that a prophecy in Isaiah was not printed until after the year 1730, when the Cherokees were brought to England. 3p.

ADD. MSS. 39855   MEMOIR OF ALEXANDER CUMING

    Fol. 1. 1764. Memoir of Alex. Cuming. Cuming includes an account of his trip to Cherokee country and the Cherokee visit to Windsor. 45p.

ADD. MSS. 40760   FRANCIS PAPERS: 1756

    Fol. 232. 8 Mar. 1756, Boston. Wm. Shirley to Henry Fox (copy). Measures designed to engage the Southern Indians allied with England are being tried. Cherokees, the most formidable southern nation, have already attacked the French and have sent 130 warriors to join the Va. rangers. 4p.

    Fol. 251. 27 June 1756, Albany. Gov. Shirley to Maj. Gen. Abercromby (copy). Gov. of Va. wanted 1,000 Cherokees to assist England against the French in return for building fort in the Cherokee territory. 16p.

EGERTON MSS. 3490   LEEDS PAPERS: 1756

    Fol. 193. 8 Mar. 1756, Boston. Gov. Shirley to Henry Fox (abstract). Letters of 8 Mar. report that the Cherokees sent 130 warriors to join the Va. rangers against the Shawnees. Commissioners have visited the Cherokees and Catawbas to conclude a treaty with the former and to induce the latter to take up the hatchet. 9p.

KINGS MSS. 210   GENERAL SURVEY IN THE SOUTHERN DISTRICT

Fol. 1. Wm. DeBrahm. Report of the General Survey in the
Southern District of North America. Report includes DeBrahm's
description of his supervision of the building of Ft. Loudoun
and a compendium of the Cherokee language in English. 283p.

SLOAN MSS. 4047   LETTERS TO SIR HANS SLOANE: 1723-1724

Fol. 90. 15 Nov. 1723, Charleston. Mark Catesby to Hans
Sloane. Catesby hopes to visit the Cherokees next summer.
The tribe is a numerous nation living in the Appalachian
Mountains. 2p.

Fol. 147. 12 Mar. 1723/24, Charleston. Mark Catesby to Hans
Sloane. Catesby is setting out to visit the Cherokees, a
nation located 300 miles away. Cherokees have helped the
English by declaring war against enemy tribes. 2p.

Fol. 290. 27 Nov. 1724, Charleston. Mark Catesby to Hans
Sloane. Catesby sends a box of dried plants with an Indian
apron made from wild mulberry bark. 2p.

BRITISH MUSEUM OF NATURAL HISTORY

Greater London

MS. No. 78. 1774. Wm. Bartram's Travels in Georgia. Creeks
and Cherokees assisted surveyors. Bartram describes Indian
customs and the composition of artificial mounds near the
mountains. He mentions fishing techniques, species caught
by Indians in the Tugaloo River, and Indian crops. 102p.

MS. No. 79. 1774. Wm. Bartram's Travels in Florida. The
Creeks took possession of Florida (then controlled by the
Cherokees or Mountaineers) about the time the English colo-
nized S. Carolina. After being chased from S.C. by the
English, the Yamasees and Savannahs settled in Ga. and Fla.
where they helped the Spanish push the Cherokees back to the
mountains. 28p.

PUBLIC RECORD OFFICE

Greater London (Chancery Lane)

GIFTS AND DEPOSITS
P.R.O. 30 24/48, PART II: SHAFTESBURY PAPERS

Doc. 37. 15 Sept. 1670, Ashley River. Wm. Owen to Anthony
Ashley. Owen expects a visit from the Emperor of Tatchiqui [?]
whose country is eight days northwest. 6p.

P.R.O. 30 24/48, PART II (CONT'D)

Doc. 56.   2 Mar. 1670/71, Albermarle Point in Ashley River.
Joseph West to Anthony Ashley. Palisades built around the
houses are strong enough to defend against 1,000 Indians.   2p.

Doc. 59.   Mar. 1670/71, Albermarle Point. Stephen Bull to
Anthony Ashley. Indians are friendly and promise assistance
against the Spanish or any hostile Indian nation.   3p.

Doc. 75.   30 Aug. 1671, Ashley River. M. Mathews to Anthony
Ashley. All surrounding Indians are friendly. Mathews lists
some Indian towns, including Keyawah.   4p.

Doc. 84.   1671/72, Carolina. Abstract of letter from Wm. Owen
and J. West stating that Indians returned two runaway servants.
Emperor Cosa Chico is visiting Charleston with 100 Indians.   3p.

Doc. 114.   31 Dec. 1674, Carolina. Relation of Voyage Begun at
the Head of the Ashley River 10 October and Finished 6 November.
Author met two Indians sent by their chief to welcome him.   4p.

STATE PAPERS, DOMESTIC
S.P. 29/303   CHARLES II: FEB. - MAR. 1672

Fol. 101.   26 Feb. 1671/72, Falmouth. Thomas Holden to James
Hicks. The *William and Ralph* of London bound for Carolina has
two Carolina Indian princes who have been in London.   1p.

STATE PAPERS, DOMESTIC
S.P. 36/19   GEORGE II: 1730

Fol. 7.   15 July 1730, Windsor. Alex. Cuming to Mr. Delafay.
Cuming requests that the [Cherokee] Indian bills be paid.   2p.

STATE PAPERS, DOMESTIC
S.P. 44/127   ENTRY BOOKS: 1730-1732

Fol. 107.   23 May 1730, Charleston. A merchant in Carolina to
Alex. Cuming (copy). A new private bank wants to force their
own notes upon merchants, who cannot prevent this without
assistance from the English government or Cuming.   3p.

Fol. 112.   17 July 1730, Windsor Castle. Holles Newcastle to
Lords of Treasury (copy). His Majesty is pleased to pay the
expenses of five Cherokee chiefs and their transportation home.
1p.

Fol. 129.   31 Aug. 1730, Windsor. Holles Newcastle to Bd. of
Trade (copy). His Majesty approves negotiating a treaty with
the Cherokee chiefs.   1p.

STATE PAPERS, FOREIGN
S.P. 109/71   MISCELLANEOUS, PRECIS BOOKS: 1759-1760

> Fol. 107. 9 Jan. [1760]. Precis of a letter and enclosures
> to Amherst. Lyttleton confirms the Cherokee outrages. Ellis
> fears an eruption of war with the Creeks and Cherokees. 1p.

PUBLIC RECORD OFFICE

<u>Greater London (Kew)</u>

ADMIRALTY, SECRETARY'S DEPARTMENT: IN LETTERS
ADM. 1/506   ADMIRAL'S LETTERS, NORTH AMERICA: 1812-1815

> Fol. 343. 22 June 1811, Bermuda. Letter from Adm. Cochrane
> stating that since the American Revolution the Indians have
> been constantly subjected to local aggressions. They are now
> almost driven from their treaty lands. 2p.

> Fol. 394. 8 June 1814, H.M.S. *Orpheus* at New Providence.
> Capt. Pigot to Adm. Cochrane (copy). About 2,800 Creeks will
> fight with the English. Pigot lists supplies for the Creeks
> and other friendly tribes. 9p.

ADM. 1/4134   LETTERS FROM SEC. OF STATE: 1777

> Fol. 1. 5 July 1777, Whitehall. Wm. Knox to Philip Stephens.
> A safe delivery is needed for about 60 tons of arms, ammunition,
> and other presents for Southern Indians. 2p.

> Fol. 69. 4 Oct. 1777, Whitehall. Wm. Knox to Philip Stephens.
> Presents for Southern Indians will be shipped via the *Parnassus*
> to Jamaica since safe conveyance to Pensacola is unavailable.
> 3p.

ADMIRALTY, SECRETARY'S DEPARTMENT: OUT LETTERS
ADM. 2/88   ORDERS AND INSTRUCTIONS: 1762

> Fol. 492. 9 Aug. 1762, [Admiralty]. Lords of Admiralty to
> Capt. Blake [of *Epreuve*]. Blake is ordered to return the three
> Cherokee chiefs to Virginia. 2p.

> Fol. 535. 20 Aug. 1762, [Admiralty]. Lords of Admiralty to
> Capt. Blake. Blake is ordered to proceed with the Cherokee
> chiefs to Charleston instead of Virginia. 1p.

ADM. 2/249   LETTERS FROM LORDS OF ADMIRALTY: 1779

> Fol. 322. 18 May 1779, [Admiralty]. Lords of Admiralty to
> Navy Board. Lords request 60 tons of Indian presents for Ga.
> and the same amount for Pensacola. 2p.

ADM. 2/721   SECRETARY OF ADMIRALTY'S COMMON LETTERS: 1762

> Fol. 215. 6 Aug. 1762, [Admiralty]. Lords of Admiralty to
> Capt. Blake. Blake will be ordered to return the Cherokee
> chiefs to Virginia. 1p.

ADM. 2/722   SECRETARY OF ADMIRALTY'S COMMON LETTERS: 1763

> Fol. 307. 12 Mar. 1763. Letter to Capt. Blake reporting that
> Blake's letter of 27 Nov. describing his arrival in S.C. with
> the Cherokee chiefs has been forwarded. 1p.

ADMIRALTY, ADMIRALTY AND SECRETARIAT: LOG BOOKS
ADM. 51/313   CAPTAIN'S LOGS: 1762

> N. fol. May and June 1762, *Epreuve*. Capt. Peter Blake. Ship
> Log of *Epreuve* [which carried Timberlake and the Cherokees to
> London]. 10p.

ADM. 51/376   CAPTAIN'S LOGS: 1730

> N. fol. 9 Mar. - 12 June 1730, H.M.S. *Fox*. Thomas Arnold.
> Ship Log of H.M.S. *Fox* [which carried seven Cherokees and
> Alex. Cuming to London]. 14p.

AUDIT OFFICE
A.O. 1/1324   DECLARED ACCOUNTS

> Roll 626. 1754-1759. Declaration of the Account of Robt.
> Dinwiddie. Declaration includes the cost of building a fort
> in Cherokee country, presents for the Cherokees returning from
> Shawnee expedition in 1756, and goods furnished the Indians at
> Ft. Loudoun. 18p.

A.O. 1/1531   DECLARED ACCOUNTS

> Roll 9. 1 July 1779 - 31 Dec. 1784. Declaration of the
> Account of Lt. Col. Thomas Brown, Superintendant of Indian
> Affairs in the Atlantic Department of the Southern District.
> Declaration includes the cost for escorting 300 Cherokees
> to Savannah. 24p.

COLONIAL OFFICE: GENERAL SERIES
C.O. 1/44   JAN. - MAY 1680

> Fol. 131. 18 Mar. 1679/80, Virginia. Letter from Nicholas
> Spencer describing Col. Byrd's and the traders' mistreatment
> of the Indians. Mr. Wood will try to arrange a treaty with
> the Indians. 2p.

C.O. 1/47   JUNE - DEC. 1681

> Fol. 75. 19 July 1681, Maryland. Lord Baltimore to Earl of
> Anglesey. Savages destroyed hogs and cattle in Va. and
> Maryland. 3p.

C.O. 1/47 (CONT'D)

Fol. 258. 12 Dec. 1681. Present State of Virginia. Although
Va. is presently at peace with all Indians, the tribes cannot
be trusted. The province is at their mercy. 9p.

C.O. 1/64   JAN. - JUNE 1688

Fol. 91. 15/25 Feb. 1687/1688. Francisco Vaillant, S.J., to
Col. Dongan. Vaillant discusses the peace treaty between
England, France, and Indians. He gives a brief history of
French claims in North America. 4p.

AMERICA AND WEST INDIES
C.O. 5/4   ORIGINAL CORRESPONDENCE, SEC. OF STATE: 1711-1739

Fol. 198. 20 Aug. 1730, Whitehall. Bd. of Trade to Duke of
Newcastle. Treaty should be made with the Cherokees before
they leave London. They can bring 3,000 fighting men into the
field. 4p.

Fol. 209. 30 Sept. 1730, Whitehall. Bd. of Trade to Duke of
Newcastle. King George agrees that a treaty with the Cherokees
should be made. 3p. [Enclosures to fol. 220b].

> Fol. 211. 7 Sept. 1730, London. Articles of Friendship
> and Commerce Proposed by the Lords of Trade and Plantations
> to the Cherokee Deputies in London. 8p.

> Fol. 215. 9 Sept. 1730, London. Cherokee Deputies to
> the Bd. of Trade. Answer from Indian chiefs. 4p.

> Fol. 217. [ca. Sept. 1730]. Memorial from Alex. Cuming
> to Duke of Newcastle. Cuming suggests that gifts be
> given to the Cherokees in the King's name. He claims
> that the Lower Cherokees would have been seduced by the
> French had he not taken them to London. 1p.

> Fol. 218. 15 July 1730. J. Crowe to Alex. Cuming. Crowe
> asks Cuming to pay £41.35.4 for housing the Cherokees.
> Crowe also requests that the Indians be moved since they
> are fighting each other. 1p.

> Fol. 219. Alex. Cuming to King George. Cherokees at
> Nequisse empowered Cuming to make their homage and submis-
> sion to the King. 2p.

Fol. 222. [1730]. Memorial from Alex. Cuming to King George.
Cherokees will fight English enemies. Cuming is willing to
live among the Cherokees for 13 years to promote service to
England. 2p.

C.O. 5/5   ORIGINAL CORRESPONDENCE, SEC. OF STATE: 1733-1748

Fol. 170. 19 Nov. 1741, Admiralty. Bladen to Duke of Newcastle.
Report on proposals relating to the war in Ga. and Florida.
Gen. Oglethorpe will review and inspect monthly the real strength
of his regiment and all other forces (British as well as Indian). 10p.

C.O. 5/7   ORIGINAL CORRESPONDENCE, SEC. OF STATE: 1755-1779

Fol. 128. 1 Oct. 1766, Graves End. Geo. Campbell to Geo. Brown. Campbell requests that Brown pay Wm. Berry £35.19.7 for the Indians in London. 2p.

Fol. 129. 8 Oct. 1766. Receipt from Joseph Carpenter for £50 advanced for expenses of North American Indians. 2p.

Fol. 131. 1 Oct. 1766. Receipt from Wm. Berry of £35.19.7 for the Indian chiefs' account. 2p.

Fol. 138. 14 Jan. 1767. Receipt for goods worth £28.14.7 bought by Capt. Campbell for the Indian chiefs. 2p.

Fol. 146. 16 Jan. 1767. Receipt for goods worth £3.4 sold to the Indian chiefs by Robt. Young. 2p.

Fol. 147. [Jan. 1767]. Letter from Robt. Young sending bills for colors sold to the Indian chiefs. 2p.

Fol. 153. 5 Feb. 1767. Receipt from James McLeary totaling £1.7.4 for ribbons and silks for the Indians. 2p.

Fol. 155. Estimate of expenses for presents and transportation of three Indians to Virginia. 2p.

Fol. 156. 1751. Bills of parcels and receipts for goods purchased for the Indians in S.C. and Georgia. 35p.

Fol. 174. Sept. 1766. Receipt from Geo. Farquharson for silver arm bracelets for four Indians. 2p.

Fol. 175. Newround Court, Strand. Lt. Geo. Campbell to Geo. Brown. Campbell requests information on the Indian bills. 2p.

Fol. 176. 20 Aug. - 16 Sept. 1766. Itemized daily bills for six Indian men and three women and a receipt for £127.0.2 in full. 4p.

Fol. 178. Bills from Kingston for lodging, including board and presents for the Indians. 25p.

Fol. 192. 18 Aug. 1766. Maj. Timothy Hierlihy to Mr. Roberts. Hierlihy protests the action of Lt. Campbell, who ordered Hierlihy (Indian creditor) to have no further connection with the Indians. 2p.

Fol. 193. 20 Aug. 1766. Letter from Capt. Geo. Campbell expressing his intentions to report to Lord Shelburne on the lodging Campbell has provided for the Indians. 2p.

Fol. 194. 16 Aug. 1766. Copy of bill from Joseph Carpenter totaling £63.12.4 for bringing the Indians from Weymouth to London. 2p.

Fol. 196. Account of disbursements for the [Cherokee] Indians recently returned to America. 6p.

C.O. 5/7 (CONT'D)

Fol. 200.   18 Aug. - 30 Sept. 1766.   Lt. Campbell's bill for
Indian expenses.   2p.

Fol. 201.   4 Sept. 1766.   List of stores for Indians.   3p.

Fol. 203.   19 Sept. 1766.   James Chambers to Capt. Geo.
Campbell.   Chambers will carry the Indians to America in
spite of the refusal by many other passengers to go.   2p.

Fol. 205.   24 Dec. 1756, Whitehall.   Bd. of Trade to Wm. Pitt.
Bd. reports temper of Indians bordering S.C. and Georgia.   3p.

Fol. 208.   24 Dec. 1756, Whitehall.   Bd. of Trade to the King.
Since the Virginians have erected a fort, the Upper and Lower
Cherokees (numbering 3,000 warriors) and the Catawbas appear
steadfast in the King's favor.   The Upper Cherokees, however,
refuse to honor an agreement to protect Va. from the French.
15p.

Fol. 217.   11 Nov. 1760, Whitehall.   Bd. of Trade to Wm. Pitt.
Bd. sends letters containing an account of the surrender of
Ft. Loudoun and the massacre of the garrison by the Cherokees.
4p.   [Enclosures to fol. 229b].

> Fol. 220.   9 Sept. 1760, Charleston.   Lt. Gov. Bull to Bd.
> of Trade (copy).   Bull relates the surrender of Ft. Loudoun
> to the Cherokees, who turned the Creeks against the British
> and who have been joined by French Indians from the North.
> 5p.

> Fol. 223.   17 Sept. 1760, Williamsburg.   Lt. Gov. Fauquier
> to Bd. of Trade (copy).   Fauquier relates the massacre of
> Ft. Loudoun troops.   If the war increases, it will be
> impossible for the Carolinas to defend themselves without
> assistance from Amherst.   5p.

> Fol. 226.   7 Aug. 1760.   Articles of Capitulation of Ft.
> Loudoun (copy).   3p.

> Fol. 228.   Maj. Lewis to Col. Byrd (copy).   Indians mas-
> sacred garrison at Ft. Loudoun and Little Carpenter rescued
> John Stuart.   3p.

Fol. 230.   1 Mar. 1756, Whitehall.   Bd. of Trade to Wm. Pitt.
3p.   [Enclosures to fol. 257b].

> Fol. 236.   22 Oct. 1757.   Lt. Gov. Henry Ellis to Bd. of
> Trade (extract).   Creeks are constantly kidnapped by the
> French and the Shawnees, who seek revenge for the loss of
> three Shawnees recently killed by the English and Cherokees
> from Ft. Loudoun.   10p.

Fol. 259.   8 Jan. 1761, Whitehall.   Bd. of Trade to Wm. Pitt.
Bd. sends letters on the state of affairs with the Cherokees,
Creeks, and Choctaws.   3p.   [Enclosures to fol. 272b].

C.O. 5/7 (CONT'D)

Fol. 262. 29 Oct. 1760. Lt. Gov. Bull to Bd. of Trade (copy). While rangers were returning from the relief of Ft. Prince George, the Indians killed two men. Indians also carried away a woman and two children from a small fort 30 miles northeast of Ninety Six. 3p.

Fol. 264. 18 Nov. 1760, Charleston. Lt. Gov. Bull to Bd. of Trade (copy). Ft. Prince George reports that Lantagnac, a Frenchman who deserted Mobile 15 years ago and who became a trader in the Cherokee nation for five years, has returned to the French. He has corresponded with disaffected Cherokees through his Indian wife. Lantagnac was recently at Chote near Ft. Loudoun. 12p.

Fol. 270. 20 Oct. 1760. Gov. Ellis to Bd. of Trade (extract). Choctaws were told to warn the Creeks (as the Creeks did with the Cherokees at the commencement of the present trouble) that the Choctaws would punish the Creeks if they molested English traders. 8p.

Fol. 387. 21 Jan. 1757, Whitehall. Bd. of Trade to Wm. Pitt. Bd. reports necessity of granting aid to Va. and the Carolinas. S.C. has allocated £2,000 from money granted for defense to garrison a fort in Cherokee country and an additional £3,000 for presents to Indians who aid the Virginians. 2p.

Fol. 710. 13 May 1756, Whitehall. Bd. of Trade to Henry Fox. A person should be appointed to manage and conduct Indian affairs on the frontiers of Va., N.C., S.C., and Georgia. 2p.

Fol. 722. 9 Aug. 1787, [London]. Memorial from Sarah Stuart to Lords of Treasury. Stuart requests that her pension begin from 1783. 4p. [Enclosure of fol. 724].

Fol. 724. 5 Aug. 1787. Mr. Stuart to E. N. Stuart requests that his mother's memorial be presented to Mr. Rose or Mr. Steele. 3p.

C.O. 5/8   ORIGINAL CORRESPONDENCE, SEC. OF STATE: 1778-1783

Fol. 139. 24 Mar. 1779. Bill to pay John Stuart, Supt. of Indian Affairs on the frontiers of Va. and Carolina. 1p.

Fol. 140. [1781?] Abstract of a list of all officers and salaries in the Indian Dept. for the Eastern Division of Southern District. 2p.

Fol. 205. 23 Feb. 1782, London. Questions and Answers on Present Politics of North America and Future Expectations in Connection with France. Author recommends Indians not be used in the war. 8p.

Fol. 314. May 1782. Memorial from S.C. and Ga. merchants about lands ceded by the Creek and Cherokee Indians in 1773 to discharge their debts. 4p.

C.O. 5/12   ORIGINAL CORRESPONDENCE, SEC. OF STATE: 1720-1747

Fol. 21. 17 June - Oct. 1725. Journal of George Chicken discussing his trip to the Cherokees. 43p.

Fol. 43. May 1726. Journal of Capt. Tobias Fitch's trip to the Creeks. Creeks have no thoughts of peace with the Cherokees, since they lately killed several leading Creeks. 42p.

C.O. 5/13   ORIGINAL CORRESPONDENCE, SEC. OF STATE: 1748-1753

Fol. 143. 3 Feb. 1747/48, S. Carolina. Letter from [Gov. Glen?] stating that the Cherokees live no more than 90 miles from the Carolina settlements. Although they were a numerous nation, they do not exceed 3,000 fighting men because of their continuous wars with French Indians and losses a few years ago to smallpox. Forts should be established in the Choctaw, Cherokee, Chickasaw, and Catawba nations. 5p.

Fol. 148. Apr. 1748, S. Carolina. Gov. James Glen to Duke of Bedford (duplicate). Glen has sent an express to the Cherokee nation demanding satisfaction for an Englishman shot. If the guilty Indian is put to death, S.C. promises to build a fort in Cherokee country to keep the French out. 3p.

Fol. 225. 13 Nov. 1750, War Office. Henry Fox to Duke of Bedford. Fox discusses memorial from James Crokatt of S.C. on methods of disbursing Indian presents. Document includes Bedford's comments. 5p.

Fol. 243. July 1750, S. Carolina. Duplicate of letter from Gov. Glen stating that the French have rekindled the war between the Creeks and Cherokees. Creeks have burned two Cherokee towns, killed most of the people on the spot, and carried the rest into slavery. Nine Cherokees were killed in spite of ransom efforts. 14p.

Fol. 251. 30 Nov. 1750, Whitehall. Sec. of War to Duke of Bedford. Secretary relates James Crokatt's method of distributing Indian presents. He includes Crokatt's memorial and extract of the report of presents sent in 1748. 6p.

Fol. 255. S. Carolina. Extract of report from committee of both houses of S.C. appointed to consider distribution of Indian presents. 3p.

Fol. 259. Apr. 1748, London. J. Crokatt, J. Wright, and H. Verelst to Henry Fox. Crokatt, Wright, and Verelst suggest a scheme for disposing the money given to S.C. for Indian presents. 19p.

Fol. 273. Apr. 1748, London. Consequence of Harbor and Fort of St. Augustine and Large Tract of Land Called Florida. Report indicates influence of the French on Indian relations with Ga., Carolina, and Virginia. 13p.

C.O. 5/13 (CONT'D)

Fol. 275. Jan. 1749. Answer from James Crokatt to Mr. Verelst's memorial concerning Indian presents. 3p.

Fol. 277. 22 May 1749. W. W. to J. C. (extract). Indian presents are not suitable. 2p.

Fol. 321. 25 June 1753, S. Carolina. Gov. Glen to Earl of Holderness. S.C. is poorly populated but has more powerful Indian allies than any other province. Cherokees number nearly 3,000 gunmen, Catawbas about 400, Creeks 2,500, and Chickasaws even more. None are under French influence. 14p. [Enclosures to fol. 339b].

> Fol. 329. 23 May 1753, Williamsburg. Lt. Gov. Dinwiddie to Gov. Glen (copy). French Indians scalped the Cherokee emperor and carried the empress, her son, and some officers to Canada. 4p.

> Fol. 338. 21 June 1753, S. Carolina. Gov. Glen to Lt. Gov. Dinwiddie (copy). Emperor of Cherokees is well but was barbarously beaten by persons in Virginia. In revenge, he burnt the fine clothes and presents that Dinwiddie gave him. 4p.

C.O. 5/14   ORIGINAL CORRESPONDENCE, SEC. OF STATE: 1753-1754

Fol. 42. 29 Jan. 1754, Williamsburg. Lt. Gov. Dinwiddie to Earl of Holderness. England's right to land on the Ohio is based on the Treaty of Lancaster of 1744, which was confirmed in 1752. 4p. [Enclosures to fol. 77b].

Fol. 82. 12 Mar. 1754, Williamsburg. Lt. Gov. Dinwiddie to Earl of Holderness. Cherokees and Catawbas have offered 100[0?] men if the French should invade their hunting grounds on the Ohio. 6p. [Enclosures to fol. 86b].

Fol. 137. 30 Mar. 1754, S. Carolina. Letter from Gov. Glen indicating that it is impossible to send an entire company to Va. since troops are stationed in Ga., Ft. Prince George, and other locations. 4p. [Enclosures to 153b].

> Fol. 139. 29 Mar. 1754, Williamsburg. Lt. Gov. Dinwiddie to Gov. Glen (copy). Dinwiddie approves using Glen to pass on his correspondence with the Catawbas and Cherokees. 4p.

> Fol. 143. 5 Mar. 1754, Council Chambers. Gov. Glen to Assembly (copy). Glen was in Cherokee country building a fort when Dinwiddie's letter concerning French hostility arrived. 4p.

> Fol. 147. 14 Mar. 1754, S. Carolina. Gov. Glen to Lt. Gov. Dinwiddie (copy). Fastest and surest way to assist the Catawbas and Cherokees is through the S.C. government. 4p.

Fol. 187. 10 May 1754, Williamsburg. Letter from Lt. Gov.
Dinwiddie. 3p. [Enclosures to fol. 196b].

> Fol. 191. 25 Apr. 1754, Wills Creek. Geo. Washington to
> Lt. Gov. Dinwiddie (copy). It may be advisable to invite
> the Cherokees, Chickasaws, and Catawbas to assist the
> English since 600 Chippewas and Ottawas are marching to
> join the French. 4p.

Fol. 197. 18 June 1754, Williamsburg. Lt. Gov. Dinwiddie to
Thomas Robinson. Dinwiddie has been to Winchester to deliver
the King's presents to the chiefs of different Indian nations.
4p. [Enclosures to fol. 205b].

Fol. 233. 15 and 26 Aug. 1754, S. Carolina. Letter from
Gov. Glen refusing to blame the French for what their Indians
do. There is never a year that passes that the Cherokees do
not seize French boats on the Miss. and destroy most of the
crew. 16p. [Enclosures to fol. 253b].

> Fol. 241. 15 Apr. 1754, Williamsburg. Copy of letter
> from Lt. Gov. Dinwiddie inviting the Six Nations, Ohio R.
> tribes, Twightwees, Cherokees, Catawbas, and Chickasaws
> to meet at Winchester. 4p.

> Fol. 243. 1 June 1754, S. Carolina. Gov. Glen to Lt.
> Gov. Dinwiddie (copy). Presents should be sent to the
> Catawbas, Cherokees, Creeks, and Chickasaws. Glen asks
> that Dinwiddie not meddle with the Catawbas, Cherokees,
> and Chickasaws. 8p.

Fol. 277. 25 Oct. 1754, Williamsburg. Lt. Gov. Dinwiddie to
Thomas Robinson. A fort in Cherokee territory is necessary.
Fort built by Glen 18 months ago was so close to S.C. that it
could not stop the French or protect S.C. from invasions. 4p.
[Enclosures to fol. 281b].

C.O. 5/15   ORIGINAL CORRESPONDENCE, SEC. OF STATE: 1754-1755

Fol. 139. 12 Feb. 1755, Williamsburg. Lt. Gov. Dinwiddie to
Thomas Robinson. Fort in upper Cherokee country can probably
be built for much less than Gov. Glen estimates. 4p.

Fol. 190. 18 Oct. - 3 Nov. 1754, Camp Mt. Pleasant at Wills
Creek. Copy of an Indian treaty that includes a talk with
the Six Nations urging them to make peace with the Catawbas
and fight the French. 14p. [Enclosure of Dinwiddie's letter
of 20 Jan. 1755].

Fol. 292. 30 Apr. and 6 June 1755, Williamsburg. Lt. Gov.
Dinwiddie to Thomas Robinson (copy). Southern Indian chiefs
have gone to Charleston but hopefully a good number of them
will meet the English forces along the Ohio. 4p.

C.O. 5/16   ORIGINAL CORRESPONDENCE, SEC. OF STATE: 1755

   Fol. 278. 6 Sept. 1755, Williamsburg. Lt. Gov. Dinwiddie to
   Cherokee Messengers (copy). Dinwiddie requests that the Cherokees be sent to Holston and New Rivers to help protect their
   brothers from the French Indians and Shawnees. 2p. [Enclosure
   of Dinwiddie's letter of 1 Oct. 1755].

   Fol. 279. 5 Sept. [1755?], Williamsburg. Cherokee chiefs to
   Lt. Gov. Dinwiddie (copy). Cherokees explain why they have
   come to Virginia. 2p. [Enclosure of Dinwiddie's letter of
   1 Oct. 1755].

C.O. 5/17   ORIGINAL CORRESPONDENCE, SEC. OF STATE: 1755-1756

   Fol. 1. 24 Nov. 1755, Williamsburg. Lt. Gov. Dinwiddie to
   Thomas Robinson. Dinwiddie is upset that Glen did not inform
   Robinson of the money sent for building the Cherokee fort.
   Glen purchased land from the Cherokees. The French have at-
   tempted to draw Southern Indians and Cherokees away from
   Britain. 4p.

   Fol. 368. 9 Nov. 1756, Williamsburg. Lt. Gov. Dinwiddie to
   Sir Henry Fox. Dinwiddie has not heard from Glen concerning
   building a fort. Dinwiddie sent a commission to the Catawbas
   and Cherokees. The latter signed a treaty which called for a
   fort to be built in Upper Cherokee country. 4p. [Enclosures
   to fol. 377b].

      Fol. 370. 11 Oct. 1756, Halifax, Smith's Creek. Maj.
      Andrew Lewis to Lt. Gov. Dinwiddie. Lewis's account of
      his visit to Cherokee country. Little Carpenter and
      others prevented a large force of Cherokees from aiding
      Virginia. Cherokees have received a message from the
      Creeks to set a date to isolate and kill the English. 3p.

      Fol. 372. 23 July 1756, Chote. Old Hop to Gov. of Vir-
      ginia. Old Hop will send at least 100 men to the governor.
      In turn, he requests that the gov. send men to defend the
      fort and Cherokees. 2p.

      Fol. 373. Chote. Otassity and Skiagunsta (Warrior of
      Great Tellico) to Gov. of Virginia. Otassity and
      Skiagunsta have taken a loyalty oath to Va. and are now
      prepared to aid that state with Cherokee warriors. 2p.

      Fol. 374. Letter from [Maj. Lewis?] stating that Little
      Carpenter has evidently asked the French to build fort at
      Tellico. 3p.

      Fol. 376. 23 July 1756, Chote. Maj. Lewis to Lt. Gov.
      Dinwiddie (copy). Fort should be finished in 12-15 days.
      Had Lewis not arrived when he did, Cherokees would have
      been lost to the French. Cherokees complain about Caro-
      linians who have cheated and deceived them. 4p.

C.O. 5/18   ORIGINAL CORRESPONDENCE, SEC. OF STATE: 1757-1758

Fol. 3.   4 Jan. 1757, Williamsburg. Lt. Gov. Dinwiddie to
Henry Fox. Messenger sent to the Cherokees has not yet returned.
Sources from S.C. report that the Southern Indians remain
friendly. Dinwiddie hopes the Cherokees and Catawbas will
send some warriors in the spring. 3p.

Fol. 37.   9 Apr. 1757, Philadelphia. Wm. Denny to Sec. of
State. 4p. [Enclosures to fol. 40b].

> Fol. 39.   10 Apr. 1757, Philadelphia. Gov. Denny to
> Thomas Penn. Forts Littleton, Loudoun, Shippenburg, and
> Carlisle will be garrisoned with 100 men each so that
> ranging parties can be sent out to scout the frontier. 4p.

Fol. 65.   14 May 1757, Williamsburg. Lt. Gov. Dinwiddie to
Wm. Pitt. Nearly 400 Catawbas, Cherokees, Tuscaroras, Saponis,
and Nottaways have joined Va. forces. They have been ordered
to the frontier to accompany Virginians who plan to scalp and
scout the enemy. The French introduced scalping. 3p.

Fol. 78.   18 June 1757, Williamsburg. Lt. Gov. Dinwiddie to
Wm. Pitt. Cherokees (180) are scouting the enemy. One party
brought four scalps and a prisoner to Ft. Loudoun near Winchester.
Other Cherokees accompany Virginians searching for the enemy. 4p.

Fol. 80.   20 June 1757, Williamsburg. Lt. Gov. Dinwiddie to
Wm. Pitt. It was impossible for the garrison at Ft. Loudoun to
reinforce Ft. Cumberland. 4p.

Fol. 90.   20 July 1757, Annapolis. Gov. Sharpe to Earl of
Holderness. Cherokees returning from Ft. Duquesne assured Capt.
Dagworthy at Ft. Cumberland that the enemy does not exceed
200-300 men. 4p.

Fol. 184.   12 Sept. 1757, Williamsburg. Lt. Gov. Dinwiddie to
Wm. Pitt. Gov. Lyttleton has hopefully influenced the Cherokees and Catawbas to remain loyal to the English. 3p.

Fol. 296.   15 Jan. 1758, Boston. T. Pownall to Wm. Pitt. 4p.
[Enclosures to fol. 319b].

> Fol. 298.   1755. Memorial from T. Pownall listing all
> Indians allied to France and England. Catawbas, Cherokees,
> Chickasaws, and Creeks supposedly support the English but
> have been seduced by the French. 44p.

Fol. 446.   18 May 1758, Annapolis. Gov. Sharpe to Wm. Pitt.
Some Cherokees returning from Ft. Duquesne report that the
enemy there does not exceed 400-500. Enemy crosses the Ohio
every day and is employed about a half mile from their old fort.
4p.

Fol. 474.   29 June 1758, Williamsburg. John Blair to Wm. Pitt.
Blair has endeavored to retain a large body of Cherokees to
assist Virginia. 4p.

C.O. 5/18 (CONT'D)

Fol. 484.   27 Aug. 1758, Ft. Frederick, Maryland.   Gov. Sharpe to Wm. Pitt.   Except for three Cherokees, all Southern Indians with the English forces have returned home.   6p.

Fol. 524.   4 Nov. 1758, Charleston.   Gov. Lyttleton to Wm. Pitt (triplicate).   Lyttleton is confident that the Chickasaws will assist him and he hopes to engage some Catawbas and Cherokees also.   12p.   [Enclosures to fol. 549b].

Fol. 530.   22 Aug. 1758, Charleston.   Gov. Lyttleton to Adm. Boscawen (triplicate).   Cherokees have taken up arms against the French and many Cherokees and some Catawbas are with Gen. Forbes.   7p.

C.O. 5/19   ORIGINAL CORRESPONDENCE, SEC. OF STATE: 1759-1760

Fol. 198.   29 Dec. 1759, Ft. Prince George near Keowee.   Gov. Lyttleton to Wm. Pitt.   Cherokees attempted to cut communications between Forts Prince George and Loudoun.   English have now concluded treaty with them.   4p.   [Enclosures to fol. 201].

Fol. 200.   26 Dec. 1759.   Copy of Treaty drawn up by Lyttleton and signed by Cherokees.   3p.   [Fol. 208 is another copy of treaty].

C.O. 5/20   ORIGINAL CORRESPONDENCE, SEC. OF STATE: 1760-1761

Fol. 95.   18 Feb. 1761, Charleston.   Lt. Gov. Bull to Wm. Pitt. French Indian trade has encouraged the Cherokees to continue the war.   3p.

Fol. 121.   28 Apr. 1761, Charleston.   Lt. Gov. Bull to Wm. Pitt. Bull lists amount of troops and money already raised against Cherokees.   4p.

Fol. 125.   2-4 May 1761, Castle William in Boston.   Copies of declarations from Benedict Thomas and Francis Layton.   Cherokees captured Thomas and Layton at the surrender of Ft. Loudoun and carried them to Ft. Cherokee and later New Orleans.   8p. [Enclosure of Gov. Bernard's letter of 5 May 1761].

Fol. 135.   29 Apr. - 6 May 1761.   *South Carolina Gazette.* Report from Ft. Prince George that Capt. Mackintosh redeemed 113 people from enslavement by the Cherokees, but 50 or 60 still remain.   2p.

C.O. 5/21   ORIGINAL CORRESPONDENCE, SEC. OF STATE: 1728-1754

Fol. 73.   30 June 1748, Council Chamber at Whitehall.   Lord Justices in Council to Gov. Glen.   Order in Council directing Gov. Glen to immediately negotiate a treaty with the Cherokees for building fort to keep the French out.   2p.

Fol. 77.   30 June 1748, Council Chamber at Whitehall.   Council minutes ordering that instructions be prepared for S.C. gov. to make a treaty with the Cherokees for building a fort.   4p.

*C.O. 5/43   ORIGINAL CORRESPONDENCE, SEC. OF STATE, MISCELLANEOUS:
1743-1783*

Fol. 38. 3 June 1765, Augusta County. Col. Andrew Lewis to
Lt. Gov. Fauquier (copy). Lewis reports the arrest and subse-
quent escape of two men who murdered some Cherokees. Young
Fellow, son of Standing Turkey, was found dead. 5p.

Fol. 41. 5 June 1765, Augusta County. Col. Lewis to Lt. Gov.
Fauquier (copy). Murder of Cherokees may cause the tribe to
attack frontier inhabitants. Cherokees would otherwise live
in friendship with the English. 4p.

Fol. 43. June 1765, Augusta County. Proclamation of Augusta
Boys (copy). Col. Lewis should be arrested for giving passes
to Indians (Cherokees) who claimed to be friends. 2p.

Fol. 47. 14 June 1765, Williamsburg. Lt. Gov. Fauquier to
Col. Lewis (copy). Augusta's defiance of the government is
worse than the inhuman murdering of defenseless Indians. 3p.

Fol. 200. 18 Nov. 1768, Johnson Hall. Wm. Johnson to Earl of
Hillsborough (copy). There is no evidence that the Cherokees
claimed land west of the great mountains or north of the
Cherokee River. 5p.

Fol. 463. 11 Apr. 1783. Memorial from Merchants trading to
S.C. and Ga. to Charles James Fox. Merchants discuss land
ceded by the Creek and Cherokee Indians to repay debts owed
traders. 4p.

Fol. 465. 3 May 1783, London. Memorial from Merchants trading
to S.C. and Ga. to Earl of Shelburne (duplicate). Merchants
discuss land ceded by the Creeks and Cherokees to repay debts
owed traders. 8p.

*C.O. 5/46   ORIGINAL CORRESPONDENCE, SEC. OF STATE, MILITARY
DISPATCHES: 1755-1756*

Fol. 176. [ca. Dec. 1755]. Gen. Shirley to Western Governments.
Western governments from Pa. to S.C. will use Shirley's pro-
posals to make treaties with the Indians. 3p. [Enclosure of
Shirley's letter of 20 Dec. 1755].

Fol. 212. 23 Jan. 1756, Williamsburg. Lt. Gov. Dinwiddie to
Gen. Shirley (extract). Cherokees are already assisting
rangers against the Shawnees but Dinwiddie hopes for more
assistance from the Catawbas and Cherokees. 2p. [Enclosure
of Shirley's letter of 8 Mar. 1756].

*C.O. 5/47   ORIGINAL CORRESPONDENCE, SEC. OF STATE, MILITARY
DISPATCHES: 1756*

Fol. 209. 3 Oct. 1756, Albany. Earl of Loudoun to Henry Fox.
Since the provinces are prevented from negotiating with the
Southern Indians, England needs to consider how the Indian
trade will be conducted in the future. 31p.

*C.O. 5/48   ORIGINAL CORRESPONDENCE, SEC. OF STATE, MILITARY
            DISPATCHES: 1756-1757*

Fol. 40. 11 Oct. 1756, Halifax, Smith's Creek. Maj. Lewis
to Lt. Gov. Dinwiddie. Letter and observations on disposition of the Cherokees. 8p. [Enclosure of Loudoun's letter
of 22 Nov. 1756].

Fol. 206. 24 Dec. 1756, New York. Letter from Edmund Atkin
expressing that the Six Nations would be glad to be strength-
ened by an alliance with Southern Indians. If all Indians were
required to carry a pass, officials might prevent mischief in
the Carolinas from unknown Indians passing through Cherokee
country. 4p.

Fol. 225. 17 June 1757, on board the *Sutherland* at Sandy Hook.
Earl of Loudoun to Wm. Pitt. Virginia has not garrisoned its
fort in Cherokee country. 14p. [Enclosures to fol. 250].

> Fol. 241. 13 Dec. 1756, New Orleans. Copy of a letter
> from Mons. Kerlerec. [Same as C.O. 5/375/193]. 7p. *French.*

> Fol. 245. 23 Nov. 1756, New Orleans. *Article et condi-
> tions préliminaires de paix entre les Français et les
> Cherakis.* [Same as C.O. 5/375/187]. 8p. *French.*

> Fol. 249. 30 Jan. 1757, New Orleans. Letter from
> Kerlerec. [Same as C.O. 5/375/197]. 3p. *French.*

Fol. 338. 25 Aug. 1757, Charleston. Col. Bouquet to Earl of
Loudoun. Cherokees seem to be sincere friends and have made
the path to the French dangerous. Little Carpenter discovered
a French fort on the Ohio 16 journeys from Ft. Loudoun. Bouquet
describes conditions at Forts Prince George and Loudoun. 13p.
[Enclosure of Loudoun's letter of 17 Oct. 1757].

*C.O. 5/49   ORIGINAL CORRESPONDENCE, SEC. OF STATE, MILITARY DIS-
            PATCHES: 1758*

Fol. 1. 14 Feb. 1758, New York. Earl of Loudoun to Wm. Pitt.
Loudoun hopes to raise at least 500 Cherokees to attack Ft.
Duquesne. 26p.

*C.O. 5/50   ORIGINAL CORRESPONDENCE, SEC. OF STATE, MILITARY DIS-
            PATCHES: 1758-1759*

Fol. 7. 28 Apr. 1758, New York. Maj. Gen. Abercromby to Wm.
Pitt. In preparation for ensuing campaign, Forbes will command
operations in the South and Byrd will secure 500 or more Cherokees
to join the English at Winchester. 29p. [Enclosures to fol.
41b].

> Fol. 33. 21 Mar. 1758, Charleston. Gov. Lyttleton to
> Earl of Loudoun (extract). Assembly will raise at least
> £20,000 to outfit 500 or more Cherokees. Lt. Col. Howarth
> is traveling to the Cherokees to raise Indian forces,
> promising to compensate warriors for time lost from
> hunting. 5p.

Fol. 36. 21 Mar. 1758, Charleston. Wm. Byrd to Earl of
Loudoun (copy). Atkin's illness has delayed his trip to
the Cherokees. Col. Howarth asked the Cherokees to meet
Byrd at Keowee on 4 April. 5p.

Fol. 39. 25 Mar. and 1 Apr. 1758, Charleston. Edm. Atkin
to Earl of Loudoun (copy). Some Catawbas and all Lower
Cherokees have already gone to Virginia. Atkin has given
Byrd dispatches for Cunnicahtarky, the Cherokee governor,
and his chief men. Atkin doubts whether the Overhill
Cherokees will go to Keowee. 6p.

Fol. 106. 25 Mar. 1758, Philadelphia. Gov. Wm. Denny to Col.
Washington (copy). Teedyuscung, a Delaware chief, requests
that the Cherokees be stopped from attacking the French Indians
so that an alliance may be made with the latter. 5p. [Enclo-
sure of Abercromby's letter of 24 May 1758].

Fol. 109. 31 Mar. 1758, Ft. Loudoun. Capt. Thomas Bullitt to
Gov. Denny (copy). Bullitt explains why no peace negotiations
between Northern and Southern Indians have occurred. 4p.
[Enclosure of Abercromby's letter of 24 May 1758].

Fol. 111. 30 Mar. 1758, Ft. Loudoun. Copy of Proceedings of
a Council of Officers. Council considers peace proposal offered by Teedyuscung and other Delawares to the Cherokees.
5p. [Enclosure of Abercromby's letter of 24 May 1758].

Fol. 116. 3 Apr. 1758, Lancaster. Lt. Col. James Burd to Gov.
Denny (copy). Some 250 Cherokees left Winchester for Ft.
Duquesne and 200 more are expected very soon. Another 600
will travel to Winchester when their corn is hilled up. Va.
should pay Cherokee expenses but the Crown must handle those
of the Creeks. 3p. [Enclosure of Abercromby's letter of
24 May 1758].

Fol. 122. 13 Apr. 1758, Ft. Johnson. Wm. Johnson to Gen.
Abercromby (extract). Cherokees will join the English unless
their good will is lost through neglect or mismanagement. 2p.
[Enclosure of Abercromby's letter of 24 May 1758].

Fol. 124. 16 Apr. 1758, Philadelphia. Gov. Denny to Gen. Abercromby (extract). There are 40 Cherokees at Ft. Loudoun who
are almost naked and without arms. There are no supplies for
them. 4p. [Enclosure of Abercromby's letter of 24 May 1758].

Fol. 127. 9 Apr. 1758, Ft. Loudoun. Capt. Wm. Thompson to Lt.
Col. Armstrong (copy). Some 40 Cherokees have arrived and
130 more are expected. They want wampum and silver plates for
their arms so that they can fight like white men. 2p.
[Enclosure of Abercromby's letter of 24 May 1758].

Fol. 129. 11 Apr. 1758, Carlisle. Lt. Col. Armstrong to Gov.
Denny (copy). Cherokees are being issued provisions but are
given as little liquor as possible. They need arms and an
interpreter. 4p. [Enclosure of Abercromby's letter of 24 May
1758].

C.O. 5/50 (CONT'D)

Fol. 131. 20 Apr. 1758. Gen. Abercromby to Gov. Denny (copy). Hopefully arms and matchcoats will induce the Cherokees to stay. 2p. [Enclosure of Abercromby's letter of 24 May 1758].

Fol. 137. 28 Apr. 1758, Ft. Johnson. Wm. Johnson to Gen. Abercromby (copy). Twightwees, Tenudadies, and Delawares disagree with the Cherokees, Catawbas, and Creeks. 10p. [Enclosure of Abercromby's letter of 24 May 1758].

Fol. 246. 22 June 1758, Ft. Johnson. Wm. Johnson to Gen. Abercromby. A delegation of 23 Cherokees at Albany are evidently on their way to Ft. Johnson for a meeting. 3p. [Enclosure of Mr. Appy's letter of 2 July 1758].

Fol. 405. 1 May 1758, Philadelphia. Gen. Forbes to Wm. Pitt. It is impossible to reassign the three S.C. independent companies since they garrison forts among Ga. Indians. Cherokees and Catawbas have fulfilled their promise to come to Winchester. 8p.

Fol. 412. 19 May 1758, Philadelphia. Gen. Forbes to Wm. Pitt. Cherokees have been scouting with some success, but they are becoming homesick, complaining that the English army has not appeared. 5p.

Fol. 418. 10 July 1758, Carlisle Camp, west of the Susquehanna. Gen. Forbes to Wm. Pitt. Unable to judge time well, the Cherokees arrived too early to assist the English and lacked the patience to wait. Most Cherokees went home three weeks ago. Former Gov. Glen has gone to retrieve them. 4p.

Fol. 420. 6 Sept. 1758, Ft. Loudoun. Gen. Forbes to Wm. Pitt. After receiving their presents, most of the Southern Indians deserted and committed outrages on scattered inhabitants in northwestern Virginia. 7p.

Fol. 424. 20 Oct. 1750, Raes Town Camp. Gen. Forbes to Wm. Pitt. Cherokee and other Southern Indians have left after getting everything they could expect from the English. 4p.

C.O. 5/52   ORIGINAL CORRESPONDENCE, SEC. OF STATE: 1756-1761

Fol. 12. 1 Mar. 1756, America. Copy of intercepted letter from Duc de Mirapoix stating that the Cherokees, who are a very numerous and unconquered tribe, have offered 1000 men to go to Ohio provided they are placed on government payroll. 11p.

Fol. 24. 1 Mar. 1756, America. Letter from Duc de Mirapoix. [Extract of fol. 12]. 2p.

Fol. 34. 23 Feb. 1756, New York. Mr. Pitcher to Mr. Fox (extract). About 70 Cherokees have joined Va. forces and more are expected. Virginia plans an expedition against the Shawnees, who have infested the Southern frontiers for some time. 2p.

C.O. 5/52 (CONT'D)

Fol. 40. 31 Mar. 1756, Earl of Halifax to Gov. Charles Hardy
(duplicate). Author of intercepted letter (stating that the
Cherokees offered several hundred men and that the offer was
transmitted to Gov. Shirley) is evidently Croghan (an Irishman)
and not a Frenchman. 8p.

C.O. 5/54   ORIGINAL CORRESPONDENCE, SEC. OF STATE, MILITARY DISPATCHES:
            1758-1759

Fol. 10. 13 Dec. 1758, New York. Gen. Amherst to Wm. Johnson
and Edm. Atkin (copy). Campaign will begin as early next spring
as the weather permits. The operation needs as many Indians as
possible. 2p. [Enclosure of Amherst's letter of 18 Dec. 1758].

Fol. 55. 12 Jan. 1759, New York. Gen. Amherst to Gov. Lyttleton. Troops should march from S.C. to Chote on their way to
seize the French Fort and Ft. Prud'Homme. This would cut
Illinois off from communication with New Orleans. 4p.
[Enclosure of Amherst's letter of 18 Jan. 1759].

Fol. 258. 7 Feb. 1759, Charleston. Gov. Lyttleton to Gen.
Amherst (extract). Lyttleton explains his plans for attacking
the Alabama Fort and using the Indian nations. 4p.

C.O. 5/56   ORIGINAL CORRESPONDENCE, SEC. OF STATE, MILITARY DISPATCHES:
            JULY-OCT. 1759

Fol. 225. 23 July 1759, Ft. Loudoun. John Stanwix to Gen.
Amherst (copy). Few Overlake Indians will choose war with the
Six Nations. Col. Byrd arrived at Bedford with 500 troops.
Stanwix will try to provision Pittsburg. 3p. [Enclosure of
Amherst's letter of 22 Oct. 1759].

C.O. 5/57   ORIGINAL CORRESPONDENCE, SEC. OF STATE, MILITARY DISPATCHES:
            1759-1760

Fol. 45. 20 July 1759, Georgia. Gov. Henry Ellis to Gen.
Amherst (copy). Cherokees, who are a numerous, perfidious,
and disaffected nation living on the northwestern boundary,
have recently committed great excesses in the back country of
Carolina. They try daily to corrupt the Creeks. Ga. needs
more troops for protection. 5p. [Enclosure of Amherst's
letter of 16 Dec. 1759].

Fol. 48. 25 Oct. 1759, Camp at Crown Point. Gen. Amherst to
Gov. Ellis. Ellis is authorized to increase forces up to two
troops of rangers of 5 officers and 70 men each. 3p. [Enclo-
sure of Amherst's letter of 16 Dec. 1759].

Fol. 163. 16 Oct. 1759, Charleston. Gov. Lyttleton to Gen.
Amherst (copy). Lyttleton has received confirmation of the
Cherokee outrages and is determined to march against them with
Carolina regulars and a body of provincials. 4p. [Enclosure
of Amherst's letter of 9 Jan. 1760].

C.O. 5/57 (CONT'D)

Fol. 167. 26 Sept. 1759, Ft. Prince George. Lt. Richard
Coytmore to Gov. Lyttleton (copy). Coytmore confirms Cherokee
outrages and that open war exists in the Lower Towns. Traders
from every part of the nation have sought refuge at the fort.
3p. [Enclosure of Amherst's letter of 9 Jan. 1760].

Fol. 170. 15 Oct. 1759. Copy of General Return of Strength of
His Majesty's 3 Independent Companies in S. Carolina. 3p.
[Enclosure of Amherst's letter of 9 Jan. 1760].

Fol. 173. 23 Oct. 1759, Charleston. Gov. Lyttleton to Gen.
Amherst (copy). It would be improper and unsafe to enter into
any agreement with the headmen of the Upper and Lower Towns who
arrived Oct. 17 in Charleston. 4p. [Enclosure of Amherst's
letter of 9 Jan. 1760].

Fol. 175. 21 Dec. 1759, New York. Gen. Amherst to Gov. Lyttleton. Although he has two regiments ready to reinforce Lyttleton, Amherst hopes that S.C. alone can punish the Cherokees.
3p. [Enclosure of Amherst's letter of 9 Jan. 1760].

Fol. 179. 5 Oct. 1759, Georgia. Gov. Henry Ellis to Gen.
Amherst (copy). Cherokee and Creek mood appears very alarming.
If Lyttleton is unsuccesful in punishing the Cherokees, an
Indian war would reveal Georgia's weakness. 2p. [Enclosure of
Amherst's letter of 9 Jan. 1760].

Fol. 181. 2 Nov. 1759, Georgia. Gov. Henry Ellis to Gen.
Amherst (copy). Cherokee insolence and outrages are so great
that Lyttleton is obliged to march against them with part of
the independent companies and a large detachment of Carolina
militia. 3p. [Enclosure of Amherst's letter of 9 Jan. 1760].

Fol. 183. 21 Dec. 1759, New York. Gen. Amherst to Gov. Ellis
(copy). Amherst hopes that Lyttleton's expedition against the
Cherokees was successful either by getting satisfaction for
their repeated outrages or by chastising them--the latter
being much better. 2p. [Enclosure of Amherst's letter of 9
Jan. 1760].

Fol. 224. 23 Dec. 1759, New York. Gen. Amherst to Capt. John
Stott (copy). Gov. Lyttleton's expedition against the Cherokees might need some assistance. Amherst wants Stott to take
troops with his convoy if Lyttleton needs aid. 2p. [Enclo-
sure of Amherst's letter of 9 Jan. 1760].

Fol. 301. 27 Dec. 1759, Ft. Prince George. Gov. Lyttleton to
Gen. Amherst (copy). Lyttleton encloses a copy of the Cherokee
treaty. He has 22 principal warriors as hostages until an equal
number of Cherokees guilty of killing English subjects are
turned over. 2p. [Enclosure of Amherst's letter of 8 Mar.
1760].

C.O. 5/57 (CONT'D)

Fol. 303. 26 Dec. 1759, Ft. Prince George. Copy of Treaty of Peace and Friendship Concluded by Gov. Lyttleton with Cherokees. 4p. [Enclosure of Amherst's letter of 8 Mar. 1760].

Fol. 305. 28 Dec. 1759, Ft. Prince George. Gov. Lyttleton to Gen. Amherst (copy). Lyttleton sends copies of letters and treaty concluded with the Cherokees. He expects to leave Ft. Prince George in three or four days and will disband militia. 2p. [Enclosure of Amherst's letter of 8 Mar. 1760].

Fol. 307. 28 Dec. 1759, Ft. Prince George. Gov. Lyttleton to Gen. Amherst (copy). Lyttleton asks that Lt. Col. Probart Howarth be given command at Ft. Johnson. 2p. [Enclosure of Amherst's letter of 8 Mar. 1760].

Fol. 309. 25 Jan. 1760, Charleston. Gov. Lyttleton to Gen. Amherst (copy). Lyttleton arrived in Charleston 8 Jan. from the Cherokee nation. Cherokee expedition did not cost the Crown anything. 2p. [Enclosure of Amherst's letter of 8 Mar. 1760].

Fol. 311. 2 Feb. 1760, Charleston. Gov. Lyttleton to Gen. Amherst (copy). Cherokees have renewed hostilities. By advice of Council, Lyttleton requests His Majesty's forces for protection of S. Carolina. 3p. [Enclosure of Amherst's letter of 8 Mar. 1760].

Fol. 313. 23 Jan. 1760, Ft. Prince George. Lt. Richard Coytmore to Gov. Lyttleton (copy). Coytmore includes his daily journal of conditions at Ft. Prince George since the Cherokees violated the recent peace treaty and blockaded the fort. 6p. [Enclosure of Amherst's letter of 8 Mar. 1760].

Fol. 320. 26 Feb. 1760, New York. Gen. Amherst to Gov. Lyttleton (copy). Cherokees have broken peace again. Amherst will attempt to reduce the Cherokees by sending a 1,300 man detachment under Col. Montgomery. 4p. [Enclosure of Amherst's letter of 8 Mar. 1760].

Fol. 330. 27 Feb. 1760, New York. Gen. Amherst to Robert Leake (copy). Most practical way of feeding troops on the Cherokee expedition is by driving live cattle with them. Supply agent should be sent with the expedition. 3p. [Enclosure of Amherst's letter of 8 Mar. 1760].

Fol. 352. 24 Feb. 1760, New York. Gen. Amherst to J. Jervis (copy). Jervis should postpone his voyage to England in order to escort troops to Carolina for the Cherokee expedition. 3p. [Enclosure of Amherst's letter of 8 Mar. 1760].

Fol. 354. 5 Mar. 1760, New York. J. Jervis to Gen. Amherst (copy). Returning to New York after convoying troops to Carolina would violate orders, but Jervis will do what Amherst thinks proper. 2p. [Enclosure of Amherst's letter of 8 Mar. 1760].

C.O. 5/57 (CONT'D)

Fol. 358. 7 Mar. 1760, New York. Gen. Amherst to Capt. Stott
(copy). Amherst requests that a convoy be ready when Montgomery's detachment needs to return to New York. 2p.
[Enclosure of Amherst's letter of 8 Mar. 1760].

Fol. 360. 7 Mar. 1760, New York. Gen. Amherst to Capt.
Dudgeon (copy). With Gov. Lyttleton's consent, Dudgeon is
ordered to accompany Col. Montgomery's troops being sent to
punish the Cherokees. 2p. [Enclosure of Amherst's letter of
Mar. 1760].

Fol. 362. 24 Feb. 1760, New York. Gen. Amherst to Col. Montgomery (copy). Amherst appoints Montgomery commander of
troops being sent to Carolina. 2p. [Enclosure of Amherst's
letter of 8 Mar. 1760].

Fol. 364. 6 Mar. 1760, New York. Instructions from Gen.
Amherst to Col. Montgomery (copy). Instructions for commanding
the troops against the Cherokees. 7p. [Enclosure of Amherst's
letter of 8 Mar. 1760].

Fol. 368. 8 Mar. 1760, New York. Gen. Amherst to Maj. Grant
(copy). If Col. Montgomery becomes incapacitated, Grant should
take command and follow the instructions to Montgomery. 2p.
[Enclosure of Amherst's letter of 8 Mar. 1760].

Fol. 392. 23 Jan. 1760, New York. Gen. Amherst to Capt. Stott
(copy). Carolina newspapers indicate that troubles have been
settled with the Cherokees. Since there is no need to send
troops, Stott may pursue earlier orders. 2p. [Enclosure of
Amherst's letter of 17 Feb. 1760].

Fol. 426. 24 Dec. 1760 [1759], Pittsburgh. John Stanwix to
Gov. Hamilton (copy). Assembly's resolution disbanding troops
has upset the detachment sent from Ft. Pitt to Ft. Augusta.
These soldiers should be divided equitably between Ft. Augusta,
Ft. Loudoun, and Ft. Lyttleton. 3p. [Enclosure of Amherst's
letter of 17 Feb. 1760].

Fol. 434. 12 Jan. 1760, Georgia. Gov. Ellis to Gen. Amherst
(copy). Unlike S.C., Ga. adjoins Cherokee territory in the
northwest, Creek land in the west, and French and Spanish
possessions to the south and southwest. As a frontier province,
Ga. requests a company of men for its borders. 4p. [Enclosure
of Amherst's letter of 17 Feb. 1760].

*C.O. 5/58   ORIGINAL CORRESPONDENCE, SEC. OF STATE, MILITARY
             DISPATCHES: 1760*

Fol. 129. 18 Feb. 1760, Charleston. Gov. Lyttleton to Gen.
Amherst (copy). Assembly has voted pay for 525 calvary and
1,000 infantry to be used against the Cherokees, who have
renewed hostilities. Nevertheless, Lyttleton believes that the
levy will go very slow. 3p. [Enclosure of Amherst's letter
of 28 Apr. 1760].

Fol. 131. 1 Apr. 1760, New York. Gen. Amherst to Gov. Lyttleton (copy). Troops that the Assembly sent against the Cherokees will undoubtedly punish the savages and restore peace.
4p. [Enclosure of Amherst's letter of 28 Apr. 1760].

Fol. 133. 13 Feb. 1760, Georgia. Gov. Ellis to Gen. Amherst
(copy). Recent Cherokee incursions threaten Ga. and Amherst's
assistance is needed. Ellis will attempt to turn the Creeks
against the Cherokees. 3p. [Enclosure of Amherst's letter
of 28 Apr. 1760].

Fol. 135. 1 Apr. 1760, New York. Gen. Amherst to Gov. Ellis
(copy). The detachment sent to Carolina and the new force
raised there should soon crush the Indians. 3p. [Enclosure
of Amherst's letter of 28 Apr. 1760].

Fol. 156. 17 Apr. 1760, Charleston. Lt. Col. Grant to Gen.
Amherst (copy). Detachment sent to Carolina has encountered
difficulties procuring carriages for the Cherokee expedition.
5p. [Enclosure of Amherst's letter of 28 Apr. 1760].

Fol. 265. 21 June 1760, Schenectady. Gen. Amherst to Wm. Pitt.
Amherst accounts for events since 20 May. Montgomery will march
soon to Ft. Prince George. 23p. [Enclosures to fol. 409b].

    Fol. 376. 24 Apr. 1760, Newbern. Gov. Dobbs to Maj. Gen.
    Stanwix (copy). Dobbs will raise 500 men to act against
    Cherokees. 2p.

    Fol. 378. 22 May 1760, Philadelphia. Brig. Gen. Monckton
    to Gov. Dobbs (copy). It would be best to use the 500
    men raised by the Assembly against the Cherokees. 2p.

    Fol. 380. 29 May 1760, Albany. Amherst to Brig.
    Gen. Monckton (extract). Amherst can add nothing to
    Monckton's letter [fol. 378] to Dobbs. 2p.

    Fol. 382. 29 May 1760, Albany. Gen. Amherst to Gov. Dobbs
    (copy). Amherst approves sending the 500 men raised by
    N.C. against the Cherokees. 3p.

    Fol. 389. 8 May 1760, Charleston. Lt. Gov. Bull to Gen.
    Amherst (copy). Col. Montgomery has reached Congarees.
    Cherokees attacked Ft. Loudoun in March and have asked the
    Ottawas and other French Indians for assistance. Creeks
    seem inclined toward neutrality. 6p.

    Fol. 391. 3 June 1760, Albany. Gen. Amherst to Lt. Gov.
    Bull (copy). Amherst acknowledges Bull's information
    about Montgomery's expedition against the Cherokees.
    Amherst will not consider evacuating Ft. Prince George. 4p.

    Fol. 393. 29-31 May 1760, Charleston. Lt. Gov. Bull to
    Gen. Amherst (copy). Fauquier believes that Ft. Loudoun
    should be aided while Montgomery is attacking Keowee.
    Creeks offered the Cherokees aid. 8p.

C.O. 5/58 (CONT'D)

Fol. 397. 18 June 1760, Albany. Gen. Amherst to Lt. Gov.
Bull (copy). Troops in S.C. will pursue the best way to
punish the Cherokees and their abettors. 4p.

Fol. 399. 12 Apr. 1760, Charleston. Col. Montgomery to
Gen. Amherst (copy). Montgomery arrived in S.C. and hopes
to depart from Monk's Corner in about ten days. Indians
will give more trouble if they have abandoned the Lower
Towns as reported. 4p.

Fol. 401. 22 Apr. 1760, Monk's Corner. Col. Montgomery
to Gen. Amherst (copy). Montgomery will march for
Congarees tomorrow and wait there until carriages and
provisions can be obtained. 3p.

Fol. 403. 26 May 1760, Albany. Gen. Amherst to Col.
Montgomery (copy). Amherst is concerned with Montgomery's
delays in spite of request to the governor to prevent
them. 4p.

Fol. 405. 24 May 1760, Ninety Six. Col. Montgomery to
Gen. Amherst (copy). It appears that the Cherokees are
divided among themselves. Upper Towns refuse to assist
the Lower Towns. 6p.

Fol. 408. 18 June 1760, Albany. Gen. Amherst to Col.
Montgomery (copy). Lt. Gov. Bull has hopefully removed
any obstacles to his march. Peace should not be granted
until the Cherokees are severely punished. 4p.

*C.O. 5/59   ORIGINAL CORRESPONDENCE, SEC. OF STATE, MILITARY
             DISPATCHES: 1760*

Fol. 1. 26 Aug. 1760, Ft. William Augustus. Gen. Amherst to
Wm. Pitt. Col. Montgomery has sent an account of his success
in defeating the Cherokees and destroying their towns. 22p.
[Enclosures to fol. 104b].

Fol. 65. 12 June 1760, Charleston. Lt. Gov. Bull to Gen.
Amherst (copy). Col. Montgomery was successful in defeating the Cherokees but Bull thinks half of the militia
should remain mobilized in case affairs take an unexpected
turn. 3p.

Fol. 67. 29 June 1760, Ft. Herchheimer. Gen. Amherst to
Lt. Gov. Bull (copy). Amherst is satisfied with Montgomery's success against the Cherokees. S.C. will hopefully
now be freed from their hostility. Amherst praises Bull
for keeping half of the militia under marching orders. 3p.

Fol. 69. 24 July 1760, Camp at Oswego. Gen. Amherst to
Lt. Gov. Bull (copy). Bull is asked to forward a packet
to Montgomery who has been obliged to march further into
Cherokee country. Amherst believed that the barbarians
would sue for peace after Montgomery's first success.

Cherokee punishment will hopefully end their hostility
against S. Carolina. 2p.

Fol. 71. 4 June 1760, Camp near Ft. Prince George. Col.
Montgomery to Gen. Amherst (copy). Montgomery describes
his march through Cherokee country and his success in
destroying their towns. It is best to make peace if the
Cherokees are willing. 5p.

Fol. 74. 29 June 1760, Ft. Herchheimer. Gen. Amherst to
Col. Montgomery (copy). Montgomery's success against the
Cherokees satisfies Amherst. After the Cherokees are
punished, peace negotiations should be left to the provincial legislature. 3p.

Fol. 76. 23 June 1760, Keowee Town. Col. Montgomery to
Gen. Amherst (copy). Since the Cherokees still refuse
to negotiate, Montgomery was obliged to march further
into their country. 2p.

Fol. 78. 24 July 1760, Camp at Oswego. Gen. Amherst to
Col. Montgomery (copy). Since the Cherokees are their own
worst enemy in not accepting peace, Amherst approves
Montgomery's march further into their territory. 2p.

Fol. 101. 2 July 1760, Ft. Prince George. Col. Montgomery
to Gen. Amherst (extract). Montgomery describes his second
march into Cherokee country and his success in destroying
their towns. 5p.

Fol. 104. 2 July 1760, Ft. Prince George. Return of the
Killed and Wounded of the Royal and Highland Battallions
under Montgomery's Command (copy). Report shows 16 killed
and 66 wounded. 2p.

Fol. 289. 15 Aug. 1760, Charleston. Lt. Gov. Bull to Gen.
Amherst (copy). Montgomery has reached Echoe, a town in the
Middle Settlements, where he defeated a large body of Chero-
kees. Indians have been punished but not subdued. Bull has
taken measures to secure the frontiers. 4p. [Enclosure of
Amherst's letter of 18 Oct. 1760].

Fol. 291. 14 Oct. 1760, Lake Champlain. Gen. Amherst to Lt.
Gov. Bull (copy). Bull's measures to secure the frontiers
against any further Cherokee attacks will hopefully be successful. If not, Amherst will send assistance. Amherst does not
believe that Ft. Loudoun should have capitulated. 3p.
[Enclosure of Amherst's letter of 18 Oct. 1760].

Fol. 293. 16 Aug. 1760, Charleston. Capt. Richard Dudgeon to
Gen. Amherst (copy). Dudgeon reports the state of posts and
fortifications between Charleston and the Cherokee country.
3p. [Enclosure of Amherst's letter of 18 Oct. 1760].

Fol. 307. 7 Nov. 1760, Albany. Gen. Amherst to Wm. Pitt.
Amherst has confirmed the report about the capture of

C.O. 5/59 (CONT'D)

Ft. Loudoun and has learned about the treacherous manner in
which they have butchered Capt. Demeré and his party. 6p.
[Enclosures to fol. 335].

> Fol. 322. 2 Aug. 1760, Brunswick. Gov. Dobbs to Gen.
> Amherst (copy). If a general Southern Indian war erupts,
> Ga. will be lost and S.C. endangered. Troops are needed
> to end the Indian war and to attack Mobile and Mississippi.
> 2p.

> Fol. 324. 3 Nov. 1760, Albany. Gen. Amherst to Gov. Dobbs
> (copy). Although Ft. Loudoun is lost, neither Ga. nor
> S.C. would be threatened if the Southern provinces exerted
> themselves with spirit. 2p.

> Fol. 331. 9 Oct. 1760, Pittsburgh. Brig. Gen. Monckton
> to Gen. Amherst (copy). Monckton encloses an extract of
> Col. Byrd's letter describing the fate of Ft. Loudoun.
> Byrd probably places too much confidence in Little
> Carpenter, whose actions in Gen. Forbes's campaign demon-
> strate that he is no friend of the English. 3p.

> Fol. 333. 16 Sept. 1760, Camp 30 miles west of Kanawha
> Col. Byrd to Capt. Abercromby (extract). News of Ft.
> Loudoun's capture was brought by four men who escaped.
> Little Carpenter offers his aid. 5p.

*C.O. 5/60   ORIGINAL CORRESPONDENCE, SEC. OF STATE, MILITARY
            DISPATCHES: 1760-1761*

Fol. 64. 19, 24, 29 Oct. 1760. Charleston. Lt. Gov. Bull to
Gen. Amherst (copy). Bull describes the S.C. involvement in the
Cherokee War and the surrender of Ft. Loudoun. S.C. has raised
1,100 men to secure lasting peace. 12p. [Enclosure of
Amherst's letter of 7 Jan. 1761].

Fol. 72. 27 Nov. 1760, New York. Gen. Amherst to Lt. Gov.
Bull (copy). Amherst is pleased with the relief sent to Ft.
Prince George. Col. Grant will replace Montgomery in the
expedition against the Cherokees. 8p. [Enclosure of Amherst's
letter of 7 Jan. 1761].

Fol. 76. 18 Nov. 1760, Charleston. Lt. Gov. Bull to Gen.
Amherst (copy). Cherokee friendship is impossible because
the French persuade them with presents to continue their
hostility. More troops are needed to protect S. Carolina.
English will launch two attacks simultaneously on the Cherokees. 7p. [Enclosure of Amherst's letter of 7 Jan. 1761].

Fol. 86. 30 Nov. 1760, New York. Gen. Amherst to Maj.
Hamilton (copy). Transports left in S.C. should be dismissed
and troops brought back unless the Cherokees have made peace.
If peace is established, Hamilton is ordered to wait for further
instructions. 2p. [Enclosure of Amherst's letter of 7 Jan.
1761].

Fol. 88. 15 Nov. 1760, New York. Gen. Amherst to Lt. Col. Grant (copy). Grant is to command a large number of men to force the Cherokees to sue for peace. 13p. [Enclosure of Amherst's letter of 7 Jan. 1761].

Fol. 103. 15 Dec. 1760, New York. Gen. Amherst to Maj. Monypenny. Monypenny will take command if anything happens to Col. Grant in the Cherokee expedition. 2p. [Enclosure of Amherst's letter of 7 Jan. 1761].

Fol. 197. 17-22 Dec. 1760, Charleston. Lt. Gov. Bull to Gen. Amherst (copy). Friendly Cherokees have informed Bull that the French have a new fort eight days below Ft. Loudoun towards Ft. l'Assomption. 5p. [Enclosure of Amherst's letter of 18 Jan. 1761].

Fol. 200. 27 Dec. 1760, Charleston. Lt. Gov. Bull to Gen. Amherst (copy). Everything is ready for Grant's arrival. French Fort, eight days from Ft. Loudoun, will be no threat once the Cherokees are defeated. 5p. [Enclosure of Amherst's letter of 18 Jan. 1761].

Fol. 203. 14 Jan. 1761, New York. Gen. Amherst to Lt. Gov. Bull (copy). Amherst approves the preparations made for Grant's immediate departure. Rumors of French Fort on the Tenn. R. below Ft. Loudoun are unfounded. 5p. [Enclosure of Amherst's letter of 18 Jan. 1761].

Fol. 206. 14 Jan. 1761, New York. Gen. Amherst to Lt. Col. Grant (copy). Amherst describes Bull's measures to receive troops and hasten their march from S. Carolina. 3p. [Enclosure of Amherst's letter of 18 Jan. 1761].

Fol. 292. 13 Mar. 1761, Williamsburg. Lt. Gov. Fauquier to Gen. Amherst. House of Burgesses voted to continue the pay of 1,000 men to assist Grant against Cherokees. Col. Byrd and Amherst will discuss the peace proposals sent to the Upper Cherokee towns by Little Carpenter. 3p. [Enclosure of Amherst's letter of 6 Apr. 1761].

Fol. 294. [ca. late Jan. to early Mar. 1761], Williamsburg. Address from House of Burgesses of Va. to Gen. Amherst (copy). Burgesses requests reinforcements for the Va. regiment about to attack the Cherokees while British and S.C. troops attack tribe on the other side of mountains. 3p. [Enclosure of Amherst's letter of 6 Apr. 1761].

Fol. 296. 25 Mar. 1761, New York. Gen. Amherst to Lt. Gov. Fauquier (copy). Peace must not be granted until the Chero- kees are chastised and all Southern governors agree to terms. 2p. [Enclosure of Amherst's letter of 6 Apr. 1761].

Fol. 298. 25 Mar. 1761, New York. Gen. Amherst to John Robinson (copy). Amherst cannot spare one more man for the Cherokee operations. 4p. [Enclosure of Amherst's letter of 6 Apr. 1761].

C.O. 5/60 (CONT'D)

    Fol. 300. 2 Feb. 1761, Savannah. Lt. Gov. Wright to Gen.
Amherst (copy). Creeks are very insolent. Many want to join
the Cherokees against Carolina and Georgia. 2p. [Enclosure
of Amherst's letter of 6 Apr. 1761].

    Fol. 302. 18 Mar. 1761, New York. Gen. Amherst to Lt. Gov.
Wright (copy). Creeks are divided but the English success
against the Cherokees should dissuade the Creeks from favoring
the French. 2p. [Enclosure of Amherst's letter of 6 Apr. 1761].

C.O. 5/61   ORIGINAL CORRESPONDENCE, SEC. OF STATE, MILITARY
*   DISPATCHES: 1761*

    Fol. 1. 4 May 1761, New York. Gen. Amherst to Wm. Pitt. 11p.
[Enclosures to fol. 158b].

        Fol. 7. Lists papers referred to in Amherst's letter
        [fol. 1]. 12p.

        Fol. 13. 13 Mar. 1761, Charleston. Lt. Gov. Bull to Gen.
        Amherst (copy). Va. plans to aid the expedition against
        the Cherokees. Rangers taking provisions to Ft. Prince
        George lost 125 horses to the Indians. Creeks are not
        disposed to fight the Cherokees. 5p.

        Fol. 16. 6 Apr. 1761, New York. Gen. Amherst to Lt.
        Gov. Bull (copy). Va. forces will hopefully be ready to
        attack the Upper Cherokee towns at the same time that
        Grant attacks the Lower ones. 4p.

        Fol. 18. 16 Mar. 1761, Williamsburg. Lt. Gov. Fauquier
        to Gen. Amherst (copy). Fauquier encloses several papers
        relating to the Cherokee war and Virginia. 2p.

        Fol. 20. 17 Sept. 1760. Col. Byrd. Articles of Peace
        Proposed to the Cherokees (copy). 2p.

        Fol. 22. 16 Feb. 1761, Williamsburg. Lt. Gov. Fauquier
        to Col. Byrd (extract). There will be difficulties with
        the peace proposed to Little Carpenter. 2p.

        Fol. 24. 16 Feb. 1761, Williamsburg. Lt. Gov. Fauquier
        to Capt. Bullitt (copy). Fauquier sends Bullitt's
        instructions in case Little Carpenter returns with the
        peace terms from the Cherokees. 3p.

        Fol. 26. 21 Feb. 1761, Williamsburg. Lt. Gov. Fauquier
        to Mr. Smith, Interpreter (copy). Smith is ordered to Ft.
        Chiswell to meet with Little Carpenter. No peace can
        last without the Lower and Middle Towns joining the Upper
        ones. 3p.

        Fol. 28. 15 Apr. 1761, New York. Gen. Amherst to Lt.
        Gov. Fauquier (copy). Amherst acknowledges receipt of
        Fauquier's letters but Amherst has not changed his opinion
        on the Cherokee war. 2p.

Fol. 147. 3 Apr. 1761, Charleston. Lt. Gov. Bull to Gen. Amherst (extract). Little Carpenter has delivered 20 prisoners to Mackintosh at Ft. Prince George and promised to deliver the rest. 2p.

Fol. 149. 30 Mar. 1761, Monk's Corner. Lt. Col. Grant to Gen. Amherst (extract). Little Carpenter sent a peace talk but Grant is determined to pursue the General's instructions of chastising the Cherokees in order to secure a lasting peace. 3p.

Fol. 159. 27 Feb. 1761, New York. Gen. Amherst to Wm. Pitt (copy). Troops under Col. Grant's command arrived in Carolina on Jan. 6 and 7. 6p. [Enclosures to fol. 222b].

Fol. 164. Duplicate list of papers referred to in Amherst's letter [fol. 159]. 6p.

Fol. 171. 15 Dec. 1760, Williamsburg. Lt. Gov. Fauquier to Gen. Amherst (duplicate). Fauquier requests aid to subdue the Cherokees and suggests how the Carolina, Va., and the General's troops will be used. 3p.

Fol. 173. 21 Jan. 1761, New York. Gen. Amherst to Lt. Gov. Fauquier (duplicate). Amherst has already sent assistance to S.C. and hopes that Va. will maintain the old regiment at 1,000 men in case they are needed. 4p.

Fol. 175. 13 Feb. 1761, New York. Gen. Amherst to Lt. Gov. Fauquier (extract). Troops have arrived in Charleston. Col. Grant will take the field in Mar. and reach Ft. Prince George by 1 May. By then he wishes the Va. forces to be at Chote to act in concert with the King's troops. 2p.

Fol. 181. 24 Jan. 1761, Charleston. Lt. Gov. Bull to Gen. Amherst (duplicate). Great Warrior returned from the French with men and presents. Creeks offered provisions and protection to the Cherokees near Ft. Prince George. 4p.

Fol. 187. 17 Jan. 1761, Charleston. James Grant to Gen. Amherst (duplicate). Lt. Gov. asked the rangers to serve in the Cherokee war. Cherokees were told that the English might seek meetings with the headmen in order to put them to death. It is impossible to proceed until the spring when the grass will be available for cattle. 7p.

Fol. 197. 13 Feb. 1761, New York. Gen. Amherst to James Grant (duplicate). Amherst is satisfied with Grant's reasons for not proceeding until spring. 6p.

Fol. 210. 10 Dec. 1760. Copy of intelligence from a Shaway Indian reporting a Cherokee complaint to the Miss. Gov. about English mistreatment. Cherokees have declared war on the English. Choctaws promise to send 2,000 men in the spring to help the Cherokees. Cherokees are enemies of the Illinois Indians. 3p.

C.O. 5/61 (CONT'D)

Fol. 223. 15 May 1761, New York. Gen. Amherst to Wm. Pitt. Grant executed three deserters. 6p. [Enclosures to fol. 262b].

Fol. 226. List of papers referred to in Amherst's letter [fol. 223]. 4p.

Fol. 228. 7 May 1761, New York. Gen. Amherst to Lt. Gov. Bull (copy). Amherst is pleased that many prisoners have been recovered from the barbarians. Bull must be prepared to chastise the Cherokees without assistance from the Six Nations. 2p.

Fol. 230. 20 Apr. 1761, Charleston. Lt. Gov. Bull to Gen. Amherst (copy). Bull will ask the Assembly to requisition troops. Fauquier gives no hope for assistance from Va. against the Cherokees. 3p.

Fol. 232. 26 Apr. 1761, Charleston. Lt. Gov. Bull to Gen. Amherst (copy). Assembly will comply as much as possible with the King's request. 4p.

Fol. 234. 30 Apr. 1761, Charleston. Lt. Gov. Bull to Gen. Amherst (extract). Col. Grant is moving the army which should reach Ninety Six by 3 May. Grant's entrance into Cherokee country will contribute to a lasting peace. 2p.

Fol. 236. 17 Apr. 1761, Williamsburg. Lt. Gov. Fauquier to Gen. Amherst (copy). Part of the regiment from Ft. Pitt is now resting at Winchester. Regiment has orders to join Byrd's division on the southwestern frontiers as soon as supplies arrive. Fauquier awaits Amherst's orders. 4p.

Fol. 238. Apr. 1761. Copy of address from House of Burgesses to Lt. Gov. Fauquier. Request for troops cannot be met before the end of summer. 3p.

Fol. 240. 17 Apr. 1761, Williamsburg. Instructions [from Lt. Gov. Fauquier] to Commissioners Appointed to Purchase Prisoners Brought in by the Cherokee Indians (copy). 3p.

Fol. 242. 22 Apr. 1761, Williamsburg. Lt. Gov. Fauquier to Gen. Amherst (copy). Gov. Dobbs is certain the Assembly will not grant any men without orders from Amherst. Attack on the Upper Cherokees will depend on the Va. regiment alone. 2p.

Fol. 244. 11 May 1761, New York. Gen. Amherst to Lt. Gov. Fauquier (copy). Va. regiment is probably sufficient to attack the Cherokees on the Va. side. Amherst cannot believe that N.C. will refuse aid. 3p.

Fol. 262. 1 Apr. 1761, Ft. Prince George. Talk from Young Warrior of Estatoe to Mr. Mackintosh (copy). Young Warrior protests his innocence of charges of mischief. 2p.

C.O. 5/61 (CONT'D)

Fol. 263. 13 Aug. 1761, Albany. Gen. Amherst to Wm. Pitt. Grant's expedition against the Cherokees was successful. 12p. [Enclosures to fol. 398b].

Fol. 269. Lists papers referred to in Amherst's letter [fol. 263]. 12p.

Fol. 277. 15 Apr. 1761, Charleston. Lt. Gov. Bull to Gen. Amherst (copy). Although Capt. Mackintosh has received 67 English prisoners and expects 25 more, 100 prisoners still remain in the nation. Bull fears that Cherokees will kill the rest because of Col. Grant's advance. 4p.

Fol. 279. 12 and 18 May 1761, New York. Gen. Amherst to Lt. Gov. Bull (extract). When the Cherokees see the English superiority, they are more likely to give up rather than kill their prisoners. 3p.

Fol. 281. 6 June 1761, Charleston. Lt. Gov. Bull to Gen. Amherst (copy). Bull informed Fauquier about his intentions to conclude peace with the Cherokees at the proper time. Bull asked the Va. governor to propose terms. 4p.

Fol. 283. 2 July 1761, Albany. Gen. Amherst to Lt. Gov. Bull (copy). Grant's expedition has hopefully forced the Cherokees to seek peace. Governors of Va. and the Carolinas should arrange peace terms. 2p.

Fol. 285. 17 June 1761, Charleston. Lt. Gov. Bull to Gen. Amherst (copy). Bull forwards Grant's letters. 4p.

Fol. 287. 13 July 1761, Albany. Gen. Amherst to Lt. Gov. Bull (copy). Grant plans to move against the Cherokees in June. Bull may already be involved in peace negotiations before receiving this letter. 2p.

Fol. 289. 16 July 1761, Charleston. Lt. Gov. Bull to Gen. Amherst (extract). Bull congratulates Amherst on the Cherokee expedition under Grant. Destruction of Cherokee towns and cornfields will hopefully turn the tribe towards a genuine peace. 2p.

Fol. 290. 1 Aug. 1761, Albany. Gen. Amherst to Lt. Gov. Bull (extract). Grant's punishment of the savages will hopefully compel them to sue for peace. Grant praises the behavior of the Upper Chickasaws. 3p.

Fol. 292. 24 Apr. 1761, Wilmington. Gov. Dobbs to Gen. Amherst (copy). Assembly voted to place a 500 man regiment under Amherst's direction. 4p.

Fol. 294. [April 1761]. Copy of speech from Gov. Dobbs to Assembly. Dobbs thanks the Assembly for granting troops. 2p.

C.O. 5/61 (CONT'D)

Fol. 296. 29 May 1761, Albany. Gen. Amherst to Gov. Dobbs (copy). Troops should join Col. Byrd's forces as soon as possible. 2p.

Fol. 297. 30 Apr. 1761, Williamsburg. Lt. Gov. Fauquier to Gen. Amherst (copy). Fauquier encloses a copy of the instructions to Byrd. Council believes that Fauquier has no power to raise more men for the campaign. 2p.

Fol. 299. 30 Aug. 1761. Lt. Gov. Fauquier to Col. Byrd (copy). Fauquier instructs Col. Byrd on how to conduct the expedition against the Upper Cherokee Towns. Big Island is 130 miles from Chote. 3p.

Fol. 301. 28 May 1761, Albany. Gen. Amherst to Lt. Gov. Fauquier (copy). Va. regiment is capable of serving whenever ordered. 2p.

Fol. 303. 6 May 1761, Williamsburg. Lt. Gov. Fauquier to Gen. Amherst (copy). Fauquier asks that the 500 men raised by N.C. be ordered to join the Va. regiment. 2p.

Fol. 305. 3 June 1761, Albany. Gen. Amherst to Lt. Gov. Fauquier (copy). Amherst has requested that N.C. troops join the Va. regiment. 2p.

Fol. 377. 10 July 1761, Camp near Ft. Prince George. Lt. Col. Grant to Gen. Amherst (extract). Grant sends a journal of the operations against the Cherokees and praises behavior of his troops. Cherokees must certainly starve or come to terms. 3p.

Fol. 379. 1 June - 9 July 1761. Copy of [Col. Grant's] Journal of the March ... against the Cherokees. 12p.

Fol. 385. June-July 1761. Copy of List of ... the Towns in the Middle and Back Settlements Burnt [by Grant]. 2p.

Fol. 387. 10 June 1761. Copy of Return of the Killed and Wounded [in action against the Cherokees] on 10 June 1761. 2p.

Fol. 389. 1 Aug. 1761, Albany. Gen. Amherst to Lt. Col. Grant (extract). Amherst is satisfied with Grant's actions and instructs him not to leave until peace is concluded. 4p.

Fol. 399. 5 Oct. 1761, Staten Island. Gen. Amherst to Wm. Pitt. Cherokees have humbly sued for peace. 6p. [Enclosures to fol. 464b].

Fol. 402. Lists papers referred to in Amherst's letter [fol. 399]. 5p.

Fol. 405. 17 Aug. 1761, Charleston. Lt. Gov. Bull to Gen. Amherst (copy). At Grant's recommendation, Bull rewarded the Upper Chickasaws who joined the Cherokee expedition. 3p.

C.O. 5/61 (CONT'D)

Fol. 407. 1 Sept. 1761, Staten Island. Gen. Amherst to
Lt. Gov. Bull (copy). Amherst appreciates that Bull
rewarded the Chickasaws at Grant's recommendations and
that he showed concern for the soldiers' families.
Amherst is surprised that N.C. troops remained inactive
until 10 August. 3p.

Fol. 409. 15 Aug. 1761, Williamsburg. Lt. Gov. Fauquier
to Lt. Gov. Bull (copy). Unsuccessful expeditions against
the Cherokees persuaded Bull not to request any men for
the coming winter. 2p.

Fol. 410. 6 Sept. 1761, Staten Island. Gen. Amherst to
Lt. Gov. Fauquier (copy). Assembly should maintain the
Va. regiment after peace is concluded with the Cherokees
and until Va. is free from Indian hostility. 3p.

Fol. 455. 3 Sept. 1761, Camp near Ft. Prince George.
Lt. Col. Grant to Gen. Amherst (extract). Grant encloses
a copy of a conference with the Cherokees to aid Amherst
in evaluating the peace prospects with that tribe. 3p.

Fol. 457. 29-31 Aug. 1761. Copy of journal of conference
with the Cherokee deputies. 8p.

Fol. 461. 2 Oct. 1761, Staten Island. Gen. Amherst to
Lt. Col. Grant (extract). After conference with the
Cherokees, Amherst is hopeful that peace will be settled
soon. Amherst would not consider withdrawing troops until
peace is concluded. 3p.

Fol. 482. 27 Nov. 1761, New York. Gen. Amherst to Wm. Pitt.
Amherst orders Grant's troops to Dominica as soon as Bull and
the Indians conclude peace. 8p. [Enclosures to fol. 537b].

Fol. 486. Lists papers referred to in Amherst's letter
[fol. 482]. 4p.

Fol. 525. 24 Sept. 1761, Charleston. Lt. Gov. Bull to
Gen. Amherst (copy). Assembly approved the peace treaty
with the Cherokees. Bull now awaits Little Carpenter's
final decision on the treaty. 5p.

Fol. 528. 23 Oct. 1761, Staten Island. Gen. Amherst to
Lt. Gov. Bull (copy). Peace is hopefully settled with
the Cherokees in Carolina. Grant and his troops are
ordered to embark for their new destination. 2p.

*C.O. 5/62   ORIGINAL CORRESPONDENCE, SEC. OF STATE, MILITARY
                 DISPATCHES: 1762*

Fol. 11. 25 Mar. 1762, Charleston. Gov. Thomas Boone to Gen.
Amherst (copy). Assembly has continued the use of rangers to
intimidate the Indians and to keep open communications with
Ft. Prince George. 3p. [Enclosure of Amherst's letter of
12 May 1762].

C.O. 5/62 (CONT'D)

Fol. 13. 2 Apr. 1762, Charleston. Gov. Boone to Gen. Amherst
(copy). Cherokee War cost S.C. £100,000 sterling. 3p.
[Enclosure of Amherst's letter of 12 May 1762].

Fol. 23. 7 Apr. 1762, Williamsburg. Lt. Gov. Fauquier to Gen.
Amherst (copy). Capt. Bullit sent geographical data covering
the area from Va.'s back settlements to the Overhill Cherokee
towns. Timberlake found Holston R. navigable. 2p. [Enclosure
of Amherst's letter of 12 May 1762].

Fol. 197. 25 June 1762, Charleston. Gov. Boone to Gen. Amherst
(copy). Cherokees delivered most, if not all, remaining
prisoners to the commanding officer on June 13 at Ft. Prince
George. 3p. [Enclosure of Amherst's letter of 20 July 1762].

Fol. 201. 8 July 1762, New York. Gen. Amherst to Gov. Boone.
Amherst is pleased to learn that the Cherokees delivered the
prisoners. 3p. [Enclosure of Amherst's letter of 20 July
1762].

*C.O. 5/63 ORIGINAL CORRESPONDENCE, SEC. OF STATE, MILITARY
         DISPATCHES: 1763*

Fol. 53. 4 May 1763, New York. Gen. Amherst to Govs. of Va.,
N. and S. Carolina, Ga., and J. Stuart (copy). In concert with
Stuart, the governors should meet with the Southern Indians to
explain the peace treaty. 3p. [Enclosure of Amherst's letter
of 14 May 1763].

Fol. 59. March–June 1763. Extracts of letters regarding
hostility of Western Indians. Miamis request supplies to go
to war against the Cherokees. 11p. [Enclosure of Amherst's
letter of 11 June 1763].

Fol. 113. 19 June 1763, Albany. Wm. Johnson to Gen. Amherst
(copy). Johnson suggests setting the Cherokees, Catawbas, and
other tribes against the unfriendly Indians. 3p. [Enclosure
of Amherst's letter of 27 June 1763].

Fol. 141. 31 May 1763, Charelston. Gov. Thomas Boone to Gen.
Amherst (copy). Boone proposes that the governors and
Southern Indians meet Sept. 15 at Augusta. 2p. [Enclosure of
Amherst's letter of 27 June 1763].

Fol. 143. 15 June 1763, New York. Gen. Amherst to Gov. Boone
(copy). Amherst wishes that the Indian meeting could be held
sooner than mid-September. He suggests two methods to provision the Indians. 3p. [Enclosure of Amherst's letter of 27
June 1763].

Fol. 145. 31 May 1763, Charleston. John Stuart to Gen.
Amherst (copy). Amherst acknowledges receipt of letters
regarding the Indian meeting. Stuart will do his utmost to
prevent fraud in the Indian trade but he has no jurisdiction
over traders. 3p. [Enclosure of Amherst's letter of 27 June
1763].

C.O. 5/63 (CONT'D)

Fol. 147.   15 June 1763, New York.   Gen. Amherst to John Stuart
(copy).   Amherst approves preparations for the Indian meeting.
Stuart should warn Southern Indians to ignore messages from
misguided Northern tribes.   3p.   [Enclosures of Amherst's
letter of 27 June 1763].

Fol. 149.   23 July 1763, New York.   Gen. Amherst to Earl of
Egremont.   Indian disturbances in the back settlements make it
impossible to obey orders to disband and reduce troops.   8p.

Fol. 261.   2 Aug. 1763, Williamsburg.   Lt. Gov. Fauquier to
Gen. Amherst (copy).   Indian devastation along the frontier
from the Potomac to the Carolina line is evidently the work of
Northern Indians returning from attacking the Cherokees.   3p.
[Enclosure of Amherst's letter of 3 Sept. 1763].

Fol. 263.   21 Aug. 1763, New York.   Gen. Amherst to Lt. Gov.
Fauquier (copy).   Amherst commends raising the militia.
Amherst will inform Wm. Johnson that the Northern Indians
devastated the Va. frontiers.   3p.   [Enclosure of Amherst's
letter of 3 Sept. 1763].

Fol. 267.   17 Aug. 1763, Ft. Bedford.   Capt. Ourry to Gen.
Amherst (extract).   Ourry describes the action of Col. Stephen
and the Va. volunteers against the Indians near Ft. Cumberland.
2p.   [Enclosure of Amherst's letter of 3 Sept. 1763].

Fol. 269.   25 Aug. 1763, New York.   Gen. Amherst to Capt. Ourry
(extract).   Amherst praises the Virginians.   He would like the
volunteers under Col. Stephen's command to escort supplies to
Ft. Pitt.   2p.   [Enclosure of Amherst's letter of 3 Sept. 1763].

Fol. 271.   25 Aug. 1763, New York.   Gen. Amherst to Col. Stephen
(copy).   Amherst would like the volunteers under Stephen's
command to escort supplies to Ft. Pitt.   Va. will hopefully
drive the enemy from its own settlements and also help protect
defenseless neighbors.   3p.   [Enclosure of Amherst's letter
of 3 Sept. 1763].

Fol. 273.   30 July 1763, Johnson Hall.   Wm. Johnson to Gen.
Amherst (copy).   Johnson is apprehensive about the Western
Indians' attempt to isolate him.   4p.   [Enclosure of Amherst's
letter of 3 Sept. 1763].

Fol. 275.   14 Aug. 1763, New York.   Gen. Amherst to Wm. Johnson
(copy).   Catawbas complain about Cherokees seizing Catawba
women.   One female captive escaped and blamed the Shawnees and
Mohawks, not Cherokees, for her capture.   6p.   [Enclosure of
Amherst's letter of 3 Sept. 1763].

Fol. 282.   20 Aug. 1763, New York.   Gen. Amherst to Wm. Johnson
(copy).   Capt. Baugh's report confirms Virginia's belief that
the hostile Indians along their frontiers are Northern Indians
returning from attacking the Cherokees.   3p.   [Enclosure of
Amherst's letter of 3 Sept. 1763].

C.O. 5/63 (CONT'D)

Fol. 293. 29 July 1763, Charleston. Gov. Boone to Gen. Amherst
(copy). Troops are ordered to occupy St. Augustine, Pensacola,
and Mobile which the Southern Indians will undoubtedly visit.
3p. [Enclosure of Amherst's letter of 3 Sept. 1763].

Fol. 297. 30 July 1763, Charleston. John Stuart to Gen.
Amherst. It is necessary to regulate the Indian trade in captured territory. Cherokees were not involved in the abduction
of Catawba women. 6p. [Enclosure of Amherst's letter of 3
Sept. 1763].

*C.O. 5/65/PART I   ORIGINAL CORRESPONDENCE, SEC. OF STATE, INDIAN
AFFAIRS: 1760-1763*

Fol. 1. 25 July 1760, Birchin Lane, Cornhill. Merchants trading to S.C. and Ga. to Robert Wood. 2p. [Enclosures to fol.
2b].

Fol. 2. [1760?] Memorial from merchants trading with
S.C. and Ga. to Wm. Pitt. Merchants warn that the Creeks
seem determined to join the Cherokees in destroying inhabitants of S.C. and Georgia. 2p.

Fol. 53. 1 June 1763, Charleston. John Stuart to Earl of
Egremont. Stuart has written the governors of Va., the Caro-
linas, and Ga. about holding a congress with the Creeks,
Choctaws, Cherokees, Chickasaws, and Catawbas. 7p.

Fol. 57. 8 June 1763, Whitehall. Bd. of Trade to Earl of
Egremont. 2p. [Enclosures to fol. 78].

Fol. 70a. 1763. Eman Bowen. An Accurate Map of North
America. Map shows British, Spanish, and French posses-
sions according to the Treaty of Paris and includes
Indian tribes and some Cherokee towns. 1p. [M.R. 26].

*C.O. 5/65/PART II   ORIGINAL CORRESPONDENCE, SEC. OF STATE, INDIAN
AFFAIRS: 1760-1763*

Fol. 18. 14 July 1763, Whitehall. Earl of Egremont to Bd. of
Trade (draft). Indian country should be under some civil
jurisdiction. 11p.

Fol. 24. 19 Sept. 1763, St. James. Dunk Halifax to Bd. of
Trade (draft). The King agrees not to place Indian lands
under Canada or any established colonial government. 9p.

Fol. 29. 4 Oct. 1763. Bd. of Trade to Earl of Halifax. 4p.
[Enclosures to fol. 41b].

Fol. 31. 4 Oct. 1763. Draft of proclamation from King
George declaring that friendly tribes under English protection should not be disturbed in the land set aside for
them. 21p.

C.O. 5/65 PART II (CONT'D)

Fol. 57. 10 Nov. 1763, Augusta. Letter from Govs. of Ga., the Carolinas, Va., and John Stuart concerning meeting with chiefs of the Chickasaws, Creeks, Choctaws, Cherokees, and Catawbas. 4p.

Fol. 69. 5 Dec. 1763, Charleston. John Stuart to Earl of Egremont. Cherokees are unwilling to visit Augusta for fear of being attacked by the Creeks. Little Carpenter and Great Warrior wish to go to England. 15p. [Enclosures to fol. 74b].

Fol. 74. 19 Nov. 1763, Ft. Augusta. John Stuart. Distribution of Presents to the Indians at the Congress [at Ft. Augusta]. 1p.

Fol. 99. 26 Jan. 1764, St. James. Dunk Halifax to Bd. of Trade. Halifax forwards a journal of the Southern Indian's congress and an extract of Gov. Boone's letter explaining his refusal to send traders to the Cherokees. 3p.

Fol. 107. 11 Feb. 1764, St. James. Dunk Halifax to John Stuart. Halifax has learned that Attakullakulla and Oconostota want to go to England. Stuart should prepare them to accept a refusal of their request. 3p.

C.O. 5/65 PART III   ORIGINAL CORRESPONDENCE, SEC. OF STATE, INDIAN AFFAIRS: 1760-1764

Fol. 13. 27 Feb. 1764, Charleston. Thomas Boone to Earl of Halifax. Boone sends copies of the journal of the congress at Augusta. 2p. [Enclosures to fol. 70b].

Fol. 16. 22 Feb. 1764, Charleston. List of miscellaneous costs of congress at Augusta. 1p.

Fol. 17. 1 Oct. - 21 Nov. 1763, Augusta. Copy of Journal of the Proceedings of the Southern Congress at Augusta [with the Chickasaw, Choctaw, Creek, Cherokee, and Catawba Indians]. 106p.

Fol. 85. 12 May 1764, St. James. Earl of Halifax to John Stuart (draft). Stuart is ordered to St. Augustine or Pensacola to assist in distributing presents and negotiating with the Indians. 4p.

Fol. 91. 6 May 1763, Charleston. John Stuart to Earl of Halifax. Stuart will try to explain to Attakullakulla and Oconostota the King's refusal to permit their visit to England. He will discourage such applications in the future. 8p.

Fol. 123. Plan for Future Management of Indian Affairs. Plan includes list of Indian tribes in the Northern and Southern Districts. 26p.

C.O. 5/66   ORIGINAL CORRESPONDENCE, SEC. OF STATE, INDIAN AFFAIRS:
         1765-1766

Fol. 25.   6 Mar. 1765, Whitehall. Bd. of Trade to Earl of
Halifax. 2p. [Enclosures to fol. 28b].

> Fol. 27.   6 Mar. 1765. Extract of minutes of House of
> Lords stating that bringing Indians from America may have
> dangerous consequences. 2p.

Fol. 70.   24 Aug. 1765, Charleston. John Stuart to Earl of
Halifax. Virginia's frontier inhabitants attacked a party of
Overhill Cherokees. Encroachments on Cherokee land has con-
cerned all Indian nations in the Southern District. 14p.

Fol. 83.   12 Dec. 1765, Philadelphia. Geo. Croghan to Ben.
Franklin. 7p. [Enclosures to fol. 111b].

> Fol. 87.   28 Feb. - 25 Sept. 1765. Journal from Col.
> Croghan to Wm. Johnson. French told the Illinois Indians
> that the English were going to seize the Illinois country
> and turn it over to the Cherokees to settle. 50p.

Fol. 114.   27 Dec. 1765, Philadelphia. Col. Croghan to Wm.
Johnson (copy). British should establish a government in the
Illinois territory so that the Southern Indians could settle
one side of Carolina's frontiers and the Western nations the
other side. The Six Nations and Northern tribes would settle
closer to the Ohio. 4p.

Fol. 143.   13 Sept. 1766, Whitehall. Circular letter from the
Earl of Shelburne stating that atrocities against Indians must
be prevented and that Indian boundaries must be protected. 5p.

Fol. 201.   May 1765, Johnson Hall. Wm. Johnson to Bd. of Trade
(copy). 30p. [Enclosures to fol. 267b].

> Fol. 235.   Apr. - May 1765, Johnson Hall. Copy of confer-
> ence with the Six Nations and Delawares. Six Nations
> approved the boundary line beginning at Shamokin (or Ft.
> Augusta) and running to the Cherokee River. 68p.

Fol. 295.   16 Nov. 1765, Johnson Hall. Wm. Johnson to Bd. of
Trade (copy). Fauquier reported the Cherokees' losses during
the past and present war with the Six Nations and Western
Indians. Peace between the Indians will not be easy to achieve.
17p. [Enclosures to fol. 322b].

Fol. 342.   24 Jan. 1764, Mobile. John Stuart to John Pownall
(copy). Stuart sent the Cherokees and Chickasaws to guard the
Wabash and Ohio Rivers and to seize French traders involved
in illicit trade with hostile tribes. 11p.

Fol. 356.   24 Aug. 1765, Charleston. John Stuart to John
Pownall (copy). Cherokees complain that encroachment of their
land is contrary to 1763 agreement at the Augusta congress.
Stuart reports arrest of Terrapin. 32p.

Fol. 372. 19 Oct. 1765 - 10 Jan. 1766, Ft. Prince George.
Copy of Cherokee land cession to S.C. between Dewises Corner
and Long Canes. 4p.

Fol. 374. 10 May 1766, Ft. Prince George. Copy of certificate
from Cherokee chiefs who assisted in marking the boundary line
between S.C. and the Cherokees. 3p.

Fol. 376. 5 Feb. 1766, Charleston. John Stuart to Gov. Tryon
(copy). Gov. Bull's proposed boundary with the Cherokees will
settle complaints about encroachment. 5p.

Fol. 380. 9 Apr. and 5 May 1766, Brunswick. Gov. Tryon to
John Stuart (copy). Tryon has sent his opinion to England
about the boundary between N. and S. Carolina. 6p.

Fol. 384. 28 May 1766, Charleston. John Stuart to Gov. Tryon
(copy). Running the boundary line cannot be delayed past
September. Creeks have offered to support the Cherokees in
seeking revenge for mistreatment. 7p.

Fol. 388. 10 Feb. 1766, Charleston. John Stuart to Lt. Gov.
Fauquier (copy). Stuart reports the murder of Cherokees in
Augusta County, Virginia. Carolina has encroached on the
Cherokee's hunting grounds. Cameron will be present when the
boundary line is run in the early spring. 6p.

Fol. 392. 17 June 1766, Brunswick. Gov. Tryon to John Stuart
(copy). If the Cherokee boundary is run directly from Reedy R.
to Chiswell's Lead Mines as the tribe requests, part of
Mecklenburg and Rowan Counties will be west of the line. 4p.

Fol. 394. 3 June 1766, Ft. Prince George. Extract of letter
from Ensign George Price reporting that an Indian party led
by White Owl has supposedly murdered Mr. Boyd and three men.
Virginians can build a factory at the Lead Mines but not at
the Great Island on the Holston River. 3p.

Fol. 396. 9 Apr. 1766, Ft. Prince George. Copy of letter from
Alex. Cameron noting that he is waiting for Judd's Friend
before marking the boundary. Good Warrior of Estatoe is planning to attack the Northern Indians with the Cherokees and
Creeks. 4p.

Fol. 398. 10 May 1766, Ft. Prince George. Alex. Cameron to
John Stuart (copy). There are problems over the boundary line.
Creeks have attempted to stop English friendship with the
Cherokees. Great Warrior and Attakullakulla want to go to
England. 14p.

Fol. 406. 1 June 1766, Toqueh. Copy of letter from Alex.
Cameron reporting that the Cherokees deny murdering Boyd and
friends. Traders have mistreated the Cherokees. 5p.

Fol. 410. 7 May 1766, Ft. Prince George. Extract of letter
from Ensign Geo. Price reporting complaints by Overhill traders
about Indian insolence. Creeks are moving rapidly into Cherokee territory. 3p.

C.O. 5/66 (CONT'D)

Fol. 412. 11 July 1766, Toqueh. Talk from Oconostota and other
Cherokee Chiefs to Lt. Gov. Bull (copy). Tribe requests that
the whites be stopped from settling Cherokee land. 5p.

Fol. 416. 20 Oct. 1765, Ft. Prince George. Copy of talk from
Cherokee headmen and warriors asking that running the boundary
line be delayed until spring. They also request better rates
on trade goods. 8p.

C.O. 5/67   ORIGINAL CORRESPONDENCE, SEC. OF STATE, INDIAN AFFAIRS:
1766-1767

Fol. 1. 1 Feb. 1766, Charleston. John Stuart to Cherokees
(copy). Stuart will ask the N.C. Gov. to settle the boundary
line as the Cherokees proposed. 5p.

Fol. 5. 8 May 1766, Ft. Prince George. Copy of talk from
Cherokees reporting an agreement with S.C. over the boundary
line. Tribe renews request for a boundary agreement with N.C.
and Virginia. 7p.

Fol. 9. 17 Sept. 1765, Johnson Hall. Wm. Johnson to John
Stuart (copy). Lt. Gov. of Va. has requested that Johnson
bring about a peace between the Six Nations and Cherokees.
Johnson believes that England would benefit from a war between
the Six Nations and Cherokees. 6p.

Fol. 13. 1 June 1766, Charleston. John Stuart to Lt. Gov.
Bull (copy). Stuart doubts whether peace between the Cherokees and their northern enemies would benefit the English
provinces. Yet the Cherokees should not become too weak. 4p.

Fol. 15. 16 May 1766, Oakeyhoys. Letter from Upper Creeks
answering Gov. Johnson's talk (copy). A party of Cherokees
have gone to England. Creeks complain about ammunition sent
to the Cherokees for use against the Creeks. 12p.

Fol. 23. 19 May 1766, Pensacola. Copy of letter from Gov.
Johnson encouraging war between the Creeks and Choctaws and
between the Cherokees and Creeks. 4p.

Fol. 33. 16 Dec. 1765, Ft. Cavendish, Illinois. Copy of letter
from Maj. Farmar reporting that the Cherokees killed some
Frenchmen and kidnapped an Illinois Indian woman. If the
Cherokees continue to fight along the Ohio, English interests
will suffer. 6p.

Fol. 39. 10 July 1766, Savannah. Gov. Wright to John Stuart
(extract). Creeks can hopefully be prevented from uniting with
the Cherokees. 4p.

Fol. 45. 10 July 1766, Charleston. John Stuart to Bd. of Trade
(copy). Cherokees object to Lt. Gov. Bull's proposed boundary
line. Stuart proposes going in person to N.C. to get the line

run. No one has punished the murderers of the Cherokees in
Virginia. 25p. [Enclosure of a letter from the Bd. of Trade
of 3 Sept. 1766].

Fol. 102. 8 Aug. 1766, Charleston. Letter from John Stuart
reporting that the Virginians who murdered the Cherokees have
not been punished. It is not the proper time to consider peace
between the Cherokees and Northern Indians. Cherokees,
Chickasaws, and Choctaws each furnished 100 warriors for the
expedition taking the Illinois territory. Cherokees request
that the boundary line be run with Va. and N. Carolina. 10p.

Fol. 114. 30 Aug. 1766, New York. Gen. Gage to [John Stuart]
(extract). Cherokees are pleased with S.C. boundary line.
Gage hopes the same can be done in N.C. and Virginia. Stuart
should mediate with the tribe's northern enemies only if the
Cherokees declare war against the Creeks. 4p.

Fol. 116. 16 Nov. 1766, Charleston. John Stuart to Bd. of
Trade (copy). Stuart will instruct commissaries residing in
Cherokee, Chickasaw, and Choctaw nations to persuade the
Indians to join the English against the Creeks. 4p.

Fol. 199. 2 Dec. 1766, Charleston. John Stuart to Bd. of
Trade (copy). Because of illness and the approaching hunting
season, Cherokees have postponed until April running the
boundary line with N. Carolina. Cherokees are upset that
Fauquier has not answered their request to continue the
boundary line with Virginia. 10p. [Enclosure of Mr. Pownall's
letter of 2 Feb. 1767].

Fol. 205. 1 Oct. 1766, Pensacola. Charles Stuart to John
Stuart (copy). Can the English trust the Indians? What should
the British do if the Chickasaws and Cherokees choose to remain
neutral or join the Creeks? 5p. [Enclosures to Mr. Pownall's
letter of 2 Feb. 1767].

Fol. 212. 24 Nov. 1766, Charleston. John Stuart to Lt. Gov.
Fauquier (copy). Stuart requests an answer to an earlier letter
proposing a boundary line to separate Cherokee hunting grounds
from the Va. settlements. 10p. [Enclosure of Mr. Pownall's
letter of 2 Feb. 1767].

Fol. 218. 27 Aug. 1766, Toqueh. Abstract of letter from
Alex. Cameron reaffirming Little Carpenter's friendship and
Testenenea's control of his town. Cherokee traders are cor-
rupt. 3p. [Enclosure of Mr. Pownall's letter of 2 Feb. 1767].

Fol. 220. 6 Nov. 1766, Ft. Prince George. Abstract of letter
from Ensign Geo. Price with news from the Middle Settlements
that the Chickasaws and Choctaws have isolated two or three
large Upper Creek towns and killed the Mortar. 2p.

Fol. 240. 22 Sept. 1766. Talk from Cherokee Chiefs to [John
Stuart]. Cherokees will be at Reedy R. with Cameron by Apr. 10

C.O. 5/67 (CONT'D)

to run the boundary line. Gov. of Va. will hopefully agree to
settle his boundary line. 6p. [Enclosure of Mr. Pownall's
letter of 2 Feb. 1767].

Fol. 244. 22 Aug. 1766, Charleston. Talk from Upper Cherokees
to John Stuart (copy). Cherokees ask that peace be arranged
with their northern enemies and that N.C. and Va. agree to run
the boundary. Murderers of their people have not been punished.
Cherokees are at war with the Nottowegas, Savamigas, Twightwees,
Tawaws, Yachtanues, and Kickapoos. 4p. [Enclosure of Mr.
Pownall's letter of 2 Feb. 1767].

Fol. 246. 1766, Chote. Talk of Attakullakulla to John Stuart
(copy). Young men from Chilhowie and Great Island have returned
from the war in Illinois with a scalp. 3p. [Enclosure of Mr.
Pownall's letter of 2 Feb. 1767].

C.O. 5/68   ORIGINAL CORRESPONDENCE, SEC. OF STATE, INDIAN AFFAIRS:
*   1767*

Fol. 87. 1 Apr. 1767, Charleston. Letter from John Stuart
reporting that the Cherokees face extermination because of
constant harassment by their northern enemies. Cherokees
deny killing seven Virginians in Indian country. Price is still
suspicious that Boyd was murdered by the Cherokees. With Gage's
approval, Stuart proposes to send Cherokee deputies to N.Y. to
treat with the Northern Indians. 3p. [Enclosures to fol. 107b].

Fol. 99. 21 Jan. 1767, Ft. Prince George. Abstract of
letter from Ensign Geo. Price reporting that seven
Virginians have been killed on their way to the Overhill
Towns. 2p.

Fol. 100. 5 Feb. 1767. Talk to Kittagusta, Headmen, and
Warriors of Cherokee nation complaining that the Cherokees
killed 17 white men when Virginians had murdered only 9
of their people. 4p.

Fol. 102. 5 Mar. 1767, Toqueh. Talk from Overhill Cherokee Chiefs to John Stuart. Cherokees deny killing Mr. Ross
and six other Virginians. Tribe claims that they killed
only one white man along the Mississippi. 3p.

Fol. 104. 5 Mar. 1767, Toqueh. Talk from Oconostota and
Overhill Cherokees to John Stuart. Cherokees deny killing
Mr. Boyd, Mr. Ross, and their companions. 3p.

Fol. 106. 16 Mar. 1767, Ft. Prince George. Talk from
Lower Cherokees to [John Stuart]. Lower Cherokees defend
the Seven Towns against charges of murdering white men. 3p.

Fol. 108. 1 Apr. 1767, Charleston. Letter from John Stuart
containing his decision to meet the Cherokee traders and Indians
at Long Canes on May 8 to talk about trade regulations. He will
also meet with the Cherokees on May 16 to continue the N.C.
boundary. There is still no word from Fauquier about the boundary with Virginia. 4p. [Enclosures to fol. 113b].

C.O. 5/68 (CONT'D)

Fol. 110. [1767]. *Regulations for the Better Carrying on of Trade with the Indian Tribes in the Southern District.* 4p.

Fol. 119. 11 Apr. 1767, Port Royal. Letter from John Stuart discussing the boundary line. Stuart proposes sending Cherokee deputies to New York to negotiate peace with their northern enemies. Stuart has requested a recall of all general trade licenses for all nations. 3p. [Enclosures to fol. 124b].

Fol. 121. 11 Apr. 1767, Charleston. John Stuart to Lt. Gov. Fauquier (copy). Stuart requests Fauquier's consent to run the boundary line between Va. and Indian land. Stuart also requests satisfaction or compensation for relatives of Cherokees murdered in Augusta County, Va., in May, 1765. There is no truth to report that the Indians murdered seven whites. 3p.

Fol. 125. 11 Apr. 1767, Port Royal. John Stuart to [Earl of Shelburne]. Estimate of annual expenses for Southern District amounts to £336.2.3 if all positions were filled. If prices of Indian goods are not lowered, Stuart suggests imposing a small duty on exported peltry and furs to cover expenses of the Indian Department. 4p. [Enclosures to fol. 129b].

Fol. 127. Estimate of Annual Expenses for Officer's Salaries and Other Contingencies in the Southern Department of Indian Affairs. 6p.

Fol. 132. 30 May 1767, Johnson Hall. Wm. Johnson to Earl of Shelburne. Johnson persuaded the Six Nations to agree to peace with the Cherokees, a task which many thought difficult and impractical. 6p.

Fol. 136. 28 July 1767, Charleston. John Stuart to [Earl of Shelburne]. Lt. Gov. Fauquier is unable to regulate the Indian traders or mark the boundary line without the King's orders. 5p. [Enclosures to fol. 151b].

Fol. 139. 1767. Schedule of papers enclosed in Stuart's letter [fol. 136]. 2p.

Fol. 140. 21 May 1767, Camp near Whitehall. Memorial from S.C. Traders to John Stuart. Traders to S.C. protest the Cherokees' request for lower prices on trading goods. 3p.

Fol. 144. [1767]. *Regulations to Be Observed in Carrying on the Trade with the Indians in the Southern District.* Regulations include a price list for trading goods. 4p.

Fol. 151. 21 May 1767, Hard Labor. Copy of affidavit from John Bowie with a warrant to apprehend Jacob Williams, a mulatto living in Chote. 2p.

C.O. 5/68 (CONT'D)

Fol. 162. 3 Oct. 1767, Charleston. John Stuart to Earl of
Shelburne. Lord Montague, Gov. Wright, and Lt. Gov. Brown
have promised assistance in enforcing trade regulations with
the Indians. 4p.

Fol. 168. 14 Aug. 1767, Johnson Hall. Wm. Johnson to Earl of
Shelburne. War between the Northern and Southern Indians has
hurt the Southern Indians the most. 6p.

Fol. 172. [ca. Aug. - Sept. 1767]. Wm. Johnson to Earl of
Shelburne. 6p. [Enclosures to fol. 213b].

    Fol. 176. Review of the Progressive State of Trade,
    Politics, and Proceedings of the Indians in the Northern
    District. 74p.

Fol. 220. 23 Dec. 1767, Whitehall. Bd. of Trade to Earl of
Shelburne. Six Nations claim land that the Cherokees occupy
as hunting ground. 6p.

C.O. 5/69   ORIGINAL CORRESPONDENCE, SEC. OF STATE, INDIAN AFFAIRS:
          1767-1768

Fol. 3. 5 Jan. 1768, Whitehall. Earl of Shelburne to Wm.
Johnson (draft). Boundary line between the provinces and
various Indian tribes should be completed as soon as possible.
2p.

Fol. 5. [Rec. 19 Jan. 1768]. Wm. Johnson to Earl of Shelburne.
Indians wish to know the status of the intended boundary line.
4p.

Fol. 46. 24 Feb. 1768, Whitehall. Earl of Hillsborough to Wm.
de Brahm (draft). Appropriations to cover the cost of surveying
in the Southern District are the same as last year's. 4p.

Fol. 48. 3 Dec. 1767, Johnson Hall. Wm. Johnson to Earl of
Shelburne. Johnson denies that exceptions made for Northern
tribes can be applied to Southern nations. 12p.

Fol. 60. 7 Mar. 1768, Whitehall. Bd. of Trade to King George.
Treaties have established boundaries with the Creeks, Cherokees,
and Choctaws in N. and S. Carolina. Cherokees and other tribes
use hunting grounds south of the Ohio more than the Six Nations
do. Creeks and Cherokees confine their trade to Ga., N.C.,
S.C., and Virginia. 50p. [Enclosures to fol. 111b].

    Fol. 87. Map of eastern U.S. and Canada showing Cherokee
    territory and Keowee. 1p.

    Fol. 92. 10 Nov. 1763, Augusta. Report about the Creeks,
    Chickasaws, Choctaws, Cherokees, and Catawbas attending a
    congress at Augusta to discuss land grants. 2p.

    Fol. 94. 19 Oct. 1765, Ft. Prince George. Extract of
    report on Cherokee land cessions to S. Carolina. 2p.

Fol. 96. 10 May 1766, Ft. Prince George. Alex. Cameron to John Stuart (extract). Cameron describes the line dividing the Cherokees from N. Carolina. 3p.

Fol. 98. 15 July 1767, N. Carolina. Gov. Tryon to Bd. of Trade (extract). Tryon describes boundary line between N.C. and the Cherokees. 1p.

Fol. 100. 1 Feb. 1766, Charleston. John Stuart to Headmen of the Cherokees (extract). English have settled boundaries with Creeks and Choctaws to avoid future disputes regarding land. 1p.

Fol. 102. 2-6 May 1765, Johnson Hall. Extract of minutes from conference with the Six Nations and Delawares stating that their boundaries extend along the Ohio to the Cherokee River. 16p.

Fol. 112. 12 Mar. 1768, Whitehall. Earl of Hillsborough to Wm. Johnson (draft). English will settle the boundary line proposed by Bd. of Trade with the Six Nations in conformity with the agreement at the Indian Congress of 1765. They will also settle borders with the Choctaws, Creeks, and Cherokees. 5p.

Fol. 128. 10 Feb. 1768, Charleston. John Stuart to [Earl of Shelburne]. Great Warrior, Little Carpenter, and the Raven of Nucasse have gone to Johnson Hall to make peace with the Six Nations. Fauquier has compensated relatives of the murdered Cherokees with trading goods. 6p. [Enclosures to fol. 136b].

Fol. 131. 21 Nov. 1767, Williamsburg. Lt. Gov. Fauquier to John Stuart (copy). Since it is impossible to bring the murderers to justice, Va. has purchased goods to satisfy the relatives of nine Cherokees slain in Augusta County, Virginia. 2p.

Fol. 133. 17 Sept. 1767, Williamsburg. Lt. Gov. Fauquier to John Stuart (copy). Fauquier has not received authorization to run the Cherokee boundary line. Va. will purchase goods to compensate the tribe for the murder of its braves. 3p.

Fol. 157. 12 May 1768, Whitehall. Earl of Hillsborough to John Stuart (draft). Hillsborough is surprised that Fauquier forgot about receiving a copy of the Proclamation of 1763. Hillsborough has a letter from Fauquier acknowledging receipt of the Proclamation. 3p.

Fol. 163. 14 Mar. 1768, Johnson Hall. Wm. Johnson to Earl of Shelburne. Johnson describes the peace negotiations between the Cherokees and the Six Nations. 4p. [Enclosures to fol. 180b].

Fol. 165. 4-12 Mar. 1768, Johnson Hall. Proceedings of a General Congress of the Six Nations, the Chiefs of

C.O. 5/69 (CONT'D)

Coghnawagey, and of the Seven Confederate Nations of
Canada, and the Deputys Sent from the Cherokee Nation to
Treat of Peace. 32p.

Fol. 193. 7 May 1768, Charleston. John Stuart to Earl of
Shelburne. Cherokees have concluded peace with the Six Nations
and the Seven Confederate Nations of Canada. Attakullakulla
has gone to Ft. Pitt to meet the Shawnee, Delaware, Mingo, and
Susquehanna deputies. Wabash Indians continue to harass the
Overhill Villages. Creeks seek Cherokee aid against the
Choctaws and Chickasaws. Stuart discusses the Va. Indian
boundary line. 6p.

Fol. 204. 12 July 1768, Whitehall. Earl of Hillsborough to
John Stuart (draft). The King is pleased to learn about peace
between the Northern Indians and the Cherokees. The superintendents will hopefully now arrange a peace between the
Cherokees and Western Indians. 4p.

Fol. 212. 20 June 1768, Guy Park near Johnson Hall. Guy
Johnson to Earl of Hillsborough. Wm. Johnson is ill after attending the congress with the Northern Indians and Cherokees. 3p.

Fol. 214. 14 July 1768, Charleston. John Stuart to Earl of
Hillsborough. The Bd. of Trade's management plan for Indian
affairs has served as Stuart's guide. 3p.

Fol. 216. 14 July 1768, Charleston. John Stuart to Earl of
Hillsborough. Cherokee deputies have set 25 Oct. to meet Va.
commissioners to mark the boundary line. The proposed line
reserves more territory to the Cherokees than they need. If
the line is approved, the English can easily obtain additional
land between the Kanawha and Cherokee Rivers. 4p. [Enclosures
to fol. 219b].

Fol. 218. 7 May 1768, Charleston. John Stuart to Earl of
Shelburne. [Duplicate of fol. 193]. 4p.

Fol. 226. 15 Sept. 1768, Whitehall. Earl of Hillsborough to
John Stuart (draft). The King is pleased that the Cherokees
are willing to surrender lands south of Ohio as far as the
Catawba River. The colonies will not need to extend their
western limits beyond the Proclamation of 1763 for a long time.
3p.

Fol. 230. 20 July 1768, Johnson Hall. Wm. Johnson to Earl of
Hillsborough. Since the Northern Department has always been
considered more important than the Southern Department, should
both receive equal allowance? 12p.

Fol. 258. 15 Sept. 1768, Charleston. John Stuart to [Earl of
Hillsborough]. Regulation of Indian trade will be left to the
colonies. 3p.

Fol. 260. 15 Sept. 1768, Charleston. John Stuart to [Earl of
Hillsborough]. Cherokees are upset with the evacuation of Ft.
Prince George, and Saluy (Young Warrior of Estatoe) has come

to inquire about it. Stuart will meet with the Cherokees on
3 Oct. to ratify the land cession and boundary line. 4p.
[Enclosures to fol. 273b].

Fol. 262. 25 June 1768, New York. Gen. Gage to John
Stuart (copy). Cherokees should be notified about plans
to evacuate Ft. Prince George. 2p.

Fol. 264. 13 Aug. 1768, Charleston. John Stuart to Gen.
Gage (copy). Fuser sent orders to evacuate Ft. Prince
George before the Cherokees could be notified. 3p.

Fol. 266. 20 May 1768, Toqueh. Abstract of letter from
Alex. Cameron stating that Mr. Waters's store, located
above Ft. Charlotte to trade with the Lower Towns and
Tugaloo Indians, might cause problems. 2p.

Fol. 268. 23 July 1768, Savannah. John Stuart to Capt.
Louis Valentine Fuser (copy). Since the Great Council of
the Cherokees is meeting at Chote, Stuart believes evacuation of Ft. Prince George should be postponed until
the Cherokees can be notified. 2p.

Fol. 270. 1 Aug. 1768, [Savannah]. Talk from John Stuart
to Oconostota, Attakullakulla, Ostenaco, Willinawa, and
other Headmen and Warriors of Upper and Lower Cherokee
Nations (copy). Stuart discusses evacuation of Ft. Prince
George. 3p.

Fol. 272. 1 Aug. 1768, Savannah. John Stuart to Alex.
Cameron (copy). Stuart promises to try to prevent trouble
over the evacuation of Ft. Prince George. 3p.

Fol. 280. 16 Aug. 1768, Charleston. John Stuart to [Earl of
Hillsborough]. Description of land cession by the Cherokees
should be corrected to read all land between the "Connahway
and Catawba Rivers" rather than "Connahway and Cherokee Rivers."
Va. commissioners will meet the Cherokees at Chiswell's Mine on
10 Nov. concerning the boundary line. 4p.

Fol. 292. 15 Nov. 1768, Whitehall. Earl of Hillsborough to
John Stuart (draft). Commanding officer was at fault in alarming the Indians when Ft. Prince George was evacuated. 3p.

Fol. 298. 15 Sept. 1768, Charleston. John Stuart to [Earl of
Hillsborough]. Two deputies should be regularly employed to
manage the affairs of the Choctaws, Chickasaws, the smaller
nations along the Miss., and to assist the superintendent with
the Cherokees, Creeks, and Catawbas. 4p. [Enclosures to fol.
301b].

Fol. 300. 15 Sept. 1768, Charleston. John Stuart to
Governors of the Southern Colonies (copy). Stuart will
ratify the boundary line dividing the provinces from Indian
lands. He will also attempt to reconcile the differences
between the Cherokees and other tribes and discuss the surrender of Indian land within the limits of any province. 4p.

C.O. 5/69 (CONT'D)

Fol. 302. 10 Dec. 1768, Whitehall. Earl of Hillsborough to
John Stuart (draft). It is difficult to determine whether
Stuart's recommendation for Indian affairs is appropriate. 2p.

Fol. 306. 23 Oct. 1768, Ft. Stanwix. Wm. Johnson to Earl of
Hillsborough. Johnson apologizes for delaying an account of
the boundary line settlement with the Indians. 6p.

Fol. 310. 18 Nov. 1768, Johnson Hall. Wm. Johnson to Earl of
Hillsborough. Six Nations have ceded their rights to lands as
far south as the Cherokee River. Johnson has never seen any
Cherokee claim to the land west of the great mountains or north
of the Cherokee River. 5p. [Enclosures to fol. 348b].

> Fol. 314. Oct. and Nov. 1768, Ft. Stanwix. Proceedings
> at a Treaty Held by Wm. Johnson with Six Nations, Shawnees,
> Delawares, Senecas of Ohio, and Other Dependent Tribes.
> Report contains Northern Indian's claim to the Cherokee
> River. 61p.

> Fol. 346. Copy of the Six Nations land cession as far
> south as the Cherokee River. 6p.

C.O. 5/70   ORIGINAL CORRESPONDENCE, SEC. OF STATE, INDIAN AFFAIRS:
*   1768-1769*

Fol. 1. 4 Jan. 1769, Whitehall. Earl of Hillsborough to Wm.
Johnson. Boundary line established with the Six Nations will
probably displease the Cherokees. 5p.

Fol. 51. 1 Mar. 1769, Whitehall. Earl of Hillsborough to
John Stuart (draft). Johnson's deviation from instructions in
settling boundary line with the Northern Indians has caused
Virginians to object to continuing the line between Va. and
Cherokee territory. 3p.

Fol. 55. 28 Dec. 1768, Charleston. John Stuart to [Earl] of
Hillsborough]. Stuart sends journals and copies of Cherokee
and Creek treaties ratifying land cessions. Attakullakulla
has returned from his northern visit with one of the Six
Nations' principal warriors, who is now at Chote proposing
peace with the Creeks and Chickasaws. 7p. [Enclosures to
fol. 104b].

> Fol. 68. 6 Nov. 1768, Williamsburg. Gov. Botetourt to
> John Stuart (copy). Botetourt postponed meeting the
> Cherokees at Chiswell's Mine until 10 May. Goods to
> compensate relatives of the murdered Cherokees have been
> sent to Bedford. 2p.

> Fol. 76. 8-17 Oct. 1768. Journal of John Stuart regarding
> Cherokee and Creek land cessions and boundary line. 37p.

> Fol. 95. 14 Oct. 1768, Hard Labor. Copy of treaty with
> the Cherokees concerning land cessions. 6p.

Fol. 99. 12 Nov. 1768, Augusta. Treaty with the Creeks
ordering the tribe to observe peace and friendship with
England as established in 1763 between Southern District
governors and the principal chiefs and warriors of the
Creeks, Cherokees, Chickasaws, Choctaws, and Catawbas.
6p.

Fol. 105. 3 Jan. 1769, Charleston. John Stuart to Earl of
Hillsborough. Cherokees have problems with settlers near the
boundary line. 4p. [Enclosures to fol. 109b].

Fol. 107. 10 Nov. 1768, Horse Creek. Jacob Sommerhall
to John Stuart. Lawrence Rambo believes that Stuart is
an old Cherokee agent who should be reprimanded for allowing Indians to kill the backwoods people. 2p.

Fol. 110. 3 Jan. 1769, Charleston. John Stuart to Earl of
Hillsborough. Stuart faces frequent difficulties in executing
his office of Superintendent of Indian Affairs. 3p.

Fol. 124. 12 Feb. 1769, Charleston. John Stuart to [Earl of
Hillsborough]. If Johnson allows people to purchase Northern
Indian land south of the Kanawha, the Cherokees will lose all
their hunting grounds beyond the mountains. Cherokees have
never admitted to being conquered by the Six Nations. 7p.
[Enclosures to fol. 172b].

Fol. 130. 10 Feb. 1766, Charleston. John Stuart to Lt.
Gov. Fauquier (copy). Stuart is disturbed by Cherokee
discontent over the murder of their tribesmen in Augusta
County and over the extension of Va. and Carolina settlements into their hunting ground. 4p.

Fol. 132. 24 Nov. 1766, Charleston. John Stuart to Lt.
Gov. Fauquier (abstract). Fauquier has not replied to
letters concerning the Cherokee boundary line or the woman
supposedly kidnapped by the Nottaways. 3 p.

Fol. 134. 2 Mar. 1766, Charleston. John Stuart to Lt.
Gov. Fauquier (abstract). Boundary line cannot be continued beyond N.C. until Stuart receives Fauquier's advice.
2p.

Fol. 136. 6 May 1767, Williamsburg. Lt. Gov. Fauquier
to John Stuart (abstract). Fauquier denies knowledge of
the Proclamation of 1763. 3p.

Fol. 138. 21 July 1767, Charleston. John Stuart to Lt.
Gov. Fauquier (abstract). Stuart sends abstracts of the
King's instructions of 1761 and the Proclamation of 1763.
Future land cession will not interfere with the Cherokee's
hunting grounds. 3p.

Fol. 140. 17 Sept. 1767, Williamsburg. Lt. Gov. Fauquier
to John Stuart (abstract). Fauquier is not authorized to

C.O. 5/70 (CONT'D)

run the boundary line and he would not know where to run it if he were. 2p.

Fol. 142. 27 Jan. 1768, Williamsburg. Lt. Gov. Fauquier to John Stuart (abstract). Fauquier cannot run the boundary line with the Cherokees without the King's order. 3p.

Fol. 144. 12 Mar. 1768, Williamsburg. John Blair to John Stuart (copy). Fauquier has died and Blair does not know where to run the boundary line. 3p.

Fol. 146. 4 Apr. 1768, Charleston. John Stuart to John Blair (copy). Stuart will notify the Cherokees to meet with commissioners to complete the boundary line. 4p.

Fol. 148. 10 June 1768, Williamsburg. John Blair to John Stuart (copy). Cherokees use land claimed by the Six Nations for hunting grounds. 4p.

Fol. 150. 7 July 1768, Charleston. John Stuart to John Blair (copy). Stuart outlines agreement dividing N.C. and Va. from Cherokee land. 3p.

Fol. 152. 3 Aug. 1768, Williamsburg. John Blair to John Stuart (copy). Blair questioned the Cherokee line stopping at Chiswell's Mine until he learned that the mines were located on a branch of the Kanawha River. 3p.

Fol. 154. 19 Aug. 1768, Charleston. John Stuart to John Blair (copy). Provinces should pay expenses for marking the boundary line and furnish provisions in their territory. 4p.

Fol. 156. 19 Aug. 1768, Charleston. John Stuart to John Blair (copy). The colonies will manage the Indian trade. The office of commissary will cease. 2p.

Fol. 158. 6 Nov. 1768, Williamsburg. Gov. Botetourt to John Stuart (copy). Botetourt sent goods to compensate relatives of the murdered Cherokees to Bedford. 2p.

Fol. 160. 7 Dec. 1768, Charleston. John Stuart to Gov. Botetourt (copy). Cherokees have already taken satisfaction for the slain tribesmen by murdering five persons. Goods intended for compensation might be used as presents to the chiefs who will mark the boundary line. 3p.

Fol. 162. 20 Dec. 1768, Williamsburg. Gov. Botetourt to John Stuart (copy). Stuart's proposed boundary between the Cherokees and Va. will give a large tract of land to the Cherokees that has already been purchased by Johnson at Ft. Stanwix from the Northern Indians. 3p.

Fol. 164. 19 Jan. 1769, Charleston. John Stuart to Gov. Botetourt (copy). Boundary line resulted from negotia-

tions begun in 1765 between the Cherokees and Fauquier.
Although Fauquier was constantly asked for his opinion
regarding the boundary line, he never replied. 6p.

Fol. 167. 10 Jan. 1769, Charleston. Col. Lewis and Dr.
Walker to John Stuart (copy). Proposed line would be a
great disservice to Great Britain. 4p.

Fol. 169. 20 Oct. 1765. Abstract of talk from Cherokee
Headmen concerning the boundary line. 3p.

Fol. 171. 19 Jan. 1769. Talk from John Stuart to Head
Beloved Man of Chote, Attakullakulla, Oconostota, and
Principal Chiefs. Ostenaco believes that the Cherokees
would not object to the running of the boundary line as
long as it secures possession of land between Holston and
Kanawha Rivers. 4p.

Fol. 173. 24 Mar. 1769, Whitehall. Earl of Hillsborough to
Wm. Johnson (draft). Bd. of Trade has not yet issued its
report on Johnson's proceedings with the Six Nations and their
allies nor on Stuart's negotiations with the Southern Indians.
2p.

Fol. 177. 24 Mar. 1769, Whitehall. Earl of Hillsborough to
John Stuart (draft). Bd. of Trade has not issued its report
on Stuart's or Johnson's proceedings on the boundary line
settlements. 3p.

Fol. 181. 15 Feb. 1769, Johnson Hall. Wm. Johnson to [Earl
of Hillsborough]. Boundary line arrangements with Indians
are difficult because considerable time has elapsed between
the original proposals and a final settlement. 7p.

Fol. 187. 25 Apr. 1769, Whitehall. Bd. of Trade to King
George. There is a conflict over land ceded by the Six Nations
and land claimed by the Cherokees. 23p.

Fol. 203. 13 May 1769, Whitehall. Earl of Hillsborough to
John Stuart (draft). The King consents to altering the boundary
line between the Cherokees and Virginia. 3p.

Fol. 205. 12 Feb. 1769. Letter from John Stuart proposing
altering the boundary line between Va. and the Cherokees. 2p.

Fol. 206. 13 May 1769, Whitehall. Earl of Hillsborough to
Wm. Johnson (draft). The King does not want his subjects to
settle beyond the Kanawha R., the western boundary of Virginia.
4p.

Fol. 208. 26 Mar. 1769, Charleston. John Stuart to [Earl of
Hillsborough]. Evacuation of Ft. Prince George should not
disturb the Indians. 3p.

C.O. 5/70 (CONT'D)

Fol. 210. 14 Arp. 1769, Charleston. John Stuart to Earl of
Hillsborough. Stuart sends an estimate of the annual expenses
for officials in the Southern Department. 3p. [Enclosures to
fol. 221b].

> Fol. 212. 14 Apr. 1769, Charleston. John Stuart to Earl
> of Hillsborough. Estimate of expenses for the Southern
> Department of Indian Affairs. 2p.

Fol. 230. 15 July 1769, Whitehall. Earl of Hillsborough to
John Stuart (draft). Hillsborough sends Stuart the King's
orders regarding the boundary line between the Cherokees and
Virginia. Stuart's estimate of annual expenses for the
Southern Department is reasonable. 3p.

Fol. 234. 26 June 1769, Johnson Hall. Wm. Johnson to Earl of
Hillsborough. Ownership of land extending to the Cherokee R.
is disputed by the Six Nations and the Southern Indians. 5p.

Fol. 243. 25 July 1769, Charleston. John Stuart to Earl of
Hillsborough. Cherokee chiefs assembled at Chote have indicated
that they expect to be well paid for additional land ceded
within Virginia. 4p. [Enclosures to fol. 263b].

> Fol. 246. 29 Mar. 1769, Toqueh. Talk from Oconostota to
> John Stuart. Cherokees will not give up land unless they
> are well paid for it. Tribe wishes to stay as far away
> as possible from the Virginians since the Cherokees
> consider them bad men. 4p.

> Fol. 248. 3 May 1769, Chehaw Square. Escotchaby (Young
> Lieutenant of Cowetas) to John Stuart. S.C. Governor
> told a Cherokee called Saluy that Va. was going to war
> against the Creeks and had asked the Cherokees for
> assistance. 3p.

> Fol. 250. 19 July 1769. John Stuart to Escotchaby (Young
> Lieutenant of Cowetas). Saluy's message that Va. planned
> to attack the Creeks and request Cherokee assistance is
> false. 4p.

> Fol. 254. 20 May 1769, Creek Nation. The Mortar to John
> Stuart. Some Cowetas have killed a few Cherokees. The
> Mortar, the Abekas, and the Talapooses ask Stuart to tell
> Chote to take revenge on Coweta if they wish. 3p.

> Fol. 256. 31 May 1769, Augusta. Geo. Munro to John Stuart
> (abstract). The Creeks reportedly killed three Cherokees
> last spring. 3p.

Fol. 264. 30 July 1769, Charleston. John Stuart to Earl of
Hillsborough. Stuart is pleased that the King approved his
actions concerning boundary lines. Stuart will send a new map
of the boundaries as soon as possible. Stuart has problems

C.O. 5/70 (CONT'D)

with the superintendency because he does not hold military
rank. 4p. [Enclosures to fol. 269b].

Fol. 270. 21 Aug. 1769, Johnson Hall. Wm. Johnson to Earl of
Hillsborough. Johnson explains the proceedings of the Treaty
of Stanwix resulting in a new boundary line. 8p.

Fol. 274. 26 Aug. 1769, Johnson Hall. Wm. Johnson to Earl of
Hillsborough. The Six Nations report that some tribes insist
on continuing the war. Johnson fears that the Cherokees and
other allied tribes might be influenced by the warlike Indians.
9p. [Enclosures to fol. 282b].

Fol. 289. 3 Oct. 1769, Charleston. John Stuart to Earl of
Hillsborough. Stuart wrote Botetourt about resuming boundary
line negotiations with the Cherokees. Cherokees are extremely
alarmed at Virginia's encroachments on their hunting grounds
as a result of the Treaty of Stanwix. 4p. [Enclosures to fol.
298b].

> Fol. 291. 3 Aug. 1769, Charleston. John Stuart to Gov.
> Botetourt (copy). Stuart describes boundary alterations
> according to the King's orders. If Va. will not defray
> expenses, Stuart will ratify the earlier treaty with the
> Cherokees (14 Oct. 1768). 3p.

> Fol. 293. 22 Aug. 1769, Williamsburg. Gov. Botetourt to
> John Stuart (copy). Botetourt will ask the Assembly to
> approve the King's requisitions [concerning the boundary
> line] when it meets in November. 2p.

> Fol. 295. 29 July 1769, Toqueh. Talk from Headmen and
> Warriors of the Cherokee to John Stuart (copy). Chero-
> kees will no longer attempt to stop the Six Nations from
> attacking the Catawbas. Virginia's governor should order
> whites not to hunt on Cherokee land. Signatories include
> Oconostota, Little Carpenter, Otacite, Willinawa, Okiyoulah
> [Ugy Uyley?], and Scotteloske. 3p.

Fol. 299. 3 Oct. 1769, Charleston. John Stuart to [Earl of
Hillsborough]. Stuart is pleased that his estimate of annual
expenses of the Indian Department appears reasonable. 3p.

Fol. 331. 9 Dec. 1769, Whitehall. Earl of Hillsborough to
Wm. Johnson (draft). Since Johnson has not told the Indians
about the King's wish to refuse cession of land below the
Kanawha, he should declare the Treaty of Stanwix ratified. 4p.

*C.O. 5/71 PART I   ORIGINAL CORRESPONDENCE, SEC. OF STATE, INDIAN
                 AFFAIRS: 1769-1770*

Fol. 9. 2 Dec. 1769, Charleston. John Stuart to Earl of
Hillsborough. Stuart met with the Upper Creek and Cherokee
chiefs on 20 October. Young Warrior of Estatoy (Saluy) denied
saying that Va. intended to march against the Creeks and had
asked Cherokees for assistance. 5p. [Enclosures to fol. 13b].

C.O. 5/71 PART I (CONT'D)

Fol. 52.   20 Jan. 1770, Charleston.   John Stuart to Earl of Hillsborough.   Stuart sends a copy of the Va. Assembly's address.   Extending Virginia's territory would place settlements beyond the reach of government and revive Indian apprehension. 3p.   [Enclosures to fol. 66b].

   Fol. 54.   18 Dec. 1769, Williamsburg.   Gov. Botetourt to John Stuart (copy).   House of Burgesses has agreed to the King's requisition but wants more land than Stuart has recommended.   2p.

   Fol. 56.   [ca. Nov. - Dec. 1769], Virginia.   Address from House of Burgesses to Gov. Botetourt (copy).   Boundary line with the Cherokees should be extended.   3p.

   Fol. 59.   [ca. Nov. - Dec. 1769], Virginia.   Memorial from House of Burgesses to Gov. Botetourt (copy).   Boundary line with the Cherokees should be extended.   5p.

   Fol. 61.   13 Jan. 1770, Charleston.   John Stuart to Gov. Botetourt (copy).   Cherokees will never agree to give up territory requested by Virginia's Assembly.   4p.

   Fol. 63.   29 July 1769, Toqueh.   Talk from Headmen and Warriors of the Cherokees to John Stuart.   [Abstract of C.O. 5/70/295].   3p.

   Fol. 65.   20 Dec. 1768, Williamsburg.   David Ross to Alex. Cameron (copy).   Ross wishes to purchase land that the Cherokees will turn over to the English.   Ross cannot acquire land, however, unless he can get it from the Indians first and has it mentioned in land cession.   4p.

Fol. 69.   27 Jan. 1770, Charleston.   John Stuart to Earl of Hillsborough.   Indians (especially Creeks) are angry over land encroachments.   3p.

Fol. 73.   10 Feb. 1770, Johnson Hall.   Wm. Johnson to Earl of Hillsborough.   Johnson reports on the congress of the Cherokees, Six Nations, and Canada Confederates at Onondaga. Cherokee discontent still exists.   Cherokees want the Six Nations to join them in attacking their common enemies among the Southern and Western tribes.   4p.

Fol. 75.   14 Apr. 1770, Whitehall.   Earl of Hillsborough to John Stuart (draft).   Stuart is right to be concerned over Virginia's desire to alter the proposed boundary line.   3p.

Fol. 81.   14 Apr. 1770, Whitehall.   Earl of Hillsborough to Wm. Johnson (draft).   Cherokee proposal to the Six Nations Confederacy is very important.   Their answer to the Cherokees will depend upon Johnson's opinion.   4p.

Fol. 105.   2 May 1770, Charleston.   John Stuart to Earl of Hillsborough.   Stuart sends minutes of the Apr. 10 congress held

C.O. 5/71 PART I (CONT'D)

with the Cherokees. There are problems in extending Virginia's
boundary line. Some Shawnees and Delawares have visited the
Cherokees and Creeks suggesting a confederacy with the Western
Indians to prevent encroachments on land. Cherokees refused
to discuss the matter. 4p. [Enclosures to fol. 126b].

> Fol. 107. 10-12 Apr. 1770, Congarees. Letter from John
> Stuart on the congress with the Cherokees regarding the
> boundary line. Shawnees are traveling through the Chero-
> kee nation to attack the Choctaws. 16p.

Fol. 127. 12 June 1770, Whitehall. Earl of Hillsborough to
John Stuart (draft). Creek and Cherokee decision to ignore
the Shawnee and Delaware proposal is fortunate. This proof of
Cherokee friendship reinforces the need to conclude a final
settlement of their boundary line with Virginia. 2p.

*C.O. 5/71 PART II   ORIGINAL CORRESPONDENCE, SEC. OF STATE, INDIAN
AFFAIRS: 1769-1770*

Fol. 3. 8 June 1770, Charleston. John Stuart to Earl of
Hillsborough. Chickasaw and Cherokee are friendly nations.
4p. [Enclosures to fol. 6b].

Fol. 9. 31 July 1770, Whitehall. Earl of Hillsborough to Mr.
Francis (draft). Hillsborough cannot determine anything about
Monberaut's complaints until a full inquiry has been made. 2p.

Fol. 11. 31 July 1770, Whitehall. Earl of Hillsborough to
John Stuart. Monberaut accuses Gov. Johnstone and John Stuart
of failing to honor certain agreements. 3p. [Enclosures to
fol. 18b].

> Fol. 13. Memoir from Montault de Monberaut complaining
> about Gov. Johnstone and John Stuart. 8p. *French.*

Fol. 21. 5 July 1770, Charleston. John Stuart to Earl of
Hillsborough. Virginia's interest dictates that it should
accept the boundary line ordered in the King's instructions to
Stuart. 3p.

Fol. 23. 16 July 1770, Charleston. John Stuart to Earl of
Hillsborough. Stuart sent Cameron to convene the Cherokees on
Oct. 5 to obtain a land cession for Virginia. 3p. [Enclosures
to fol. 40b].

> Fol. 31. 27 June 1770, Ninety Six. Alex. Cameron to
> John Stuart (abstract). Richard Pearis and Hite visited
> the Lower Towns to get some land titles. Pearis promised
> to take the Young Warrior with him to England. 3p.

> Fol. 33. 17 May 1770, Keowee. John Watts (Cherokee
> interpreter) to John Stuart. Pearis has tried to obtain
> Cherokee land and Stuart should expel him from Cherokee
> territory. 3p.

C.O. 5/71 PART II (CONT'D)

> Fol. 37. 21 June 1770. Gov. Botetourt to John Stuart
> (copy). Botetourt asks that Stuart immediately negotiate
> a treaty with the Cherokees for land cessions approved by
> the King. 3p.

Fol. 41. 12 July 1770, Johnson Hall. Wm. Johnson to Earl of
Hillsborough. Cherokees deny encouraging Northern Indians to
go to war. Johnson proposes convincing the Six Nations that
he has no desire for more Indian land. 4p.

Fol. 59. 3 Oct. 1770, Whitehall. Earl of Hillsborough to John
Stuart (draft). Settling the Va. line is important and should
not be delayed. Nevertheless, Indian affairs in West Fla.
should take priority. 4p.

Fol. 61. 3 Oct. 1770, Whitehall. Earl of Hillsborough to
De Brahm (draft). The King denies De Brahm's request to visit
England for 6 months. The Crown wants a quick general survey
of the Southern District. 2p.

Fol. 63. 3 Oct. 1770, Whitehall. Earl of Hillsborough to
Wm. Johnson (draft). Union between the Northern and Southern
Indians should be prevented at all costs. 3p.

Fol. 87. 15 Nov. 1770, Whitehall. Earl of Hillsborough to
Wm. Johnson (draft). The last Indian congress attempted to
prevent the Six Nations from warring with the Western Indians
and from uniting with the Southern Indians. 3p.

Fol. 93. 14 Aug. 1770, Johnson Hall. Wm. Johnson to Earl of
Hillsborough. Johnson urged some Six Nations chiefs to stop
their hostilities against the Southern Indians. Treaty of Ft.
Stanwix is ratified. 8p. [Enclosures to fol. 118b].

> Fol. 99. 15-22 July 1770, near German Flats. Copy of
> the Proceedings at a Treaty with the Six Nations,
> Indians of Canada, and the Deputies from the Cherokee
> Nation. 40p.

C.O. 5/72   ORIGINAL CORRESPONDENCE, SEC. OF STATE, INDIAN AFFAIRS:
1770-1771

Fol. 16. 1 Dec. 1770, Charleston. John Thomas to Earl of
Hillsborough. Stuart has four deputies for his district, but
the Spanish have a superintendent and three deputies (all
French) for Miss. alone. 2p.

Fol. 20. 28 Nov. 1770, Charleston. John Stuart to Earl of
Hillsborough. Stuart submits a journal of the proceedings with
the Cherokees at Lochaber. He was unable to obtain all the
territory asked for in the instructions. 4p. [Enclosures to
fol. 42b].

> Fol. 22. 18-20 Oct. 1770, Lochaber. Copy of the Report
> of the General Meeting of the Principal Chiefs and War-
> riors of the Cherokee Nation with John Stuart. 14p.

C.O. 5/72 (CONT'D)

Fol. 29. 18 Oct. 1770, Lochaber. Treaty ceding Cherokee
land to Va. and further proceedings of the Indian congress.
11p.

Fol. 35. 17 Aug. 1770. Copy of the minutes of the Council
of Va. containing letter from Oconostota (14 June) concerning land granted to Richard Pearis and Jacob Hite.
Minutes also contain Col. Lewis's letter complaining
about Stuart. 8p.

Fol. 39. 18 Aug. 1770. Gov. Botetourt to Oconostota
(copy). Botetourt lacks authority to approve giving land
to Richard Pearis. 3p.

Fol. 39b. 18 Aug. 1770, Williamsburg. Gov. Botetourt to
Col. Andrew Lewis. Stuart plans to meet with the Cherokee chiefs. 1p.

Fol. 41. 16 Oct. 1770, New York. Gen. Gage to John
Stuart (copy). All Western tribes and the Wabash Indians
have agreed to peace with the Cherokees. It was wise to
refuse permission to Va. to extend their line. 4p.

Fol. 43. 29 Nov. 1770, Charleston. John Stuart to Earl of
Hillsborough. Stuart answers Monberaut's complaints. His
reply was delayed because Stuart was settling the Va. boundary
line. 12p. [Enclosures to fol. 80b].

Fol. 49. 31 Mar. 1764, New York. Gen. Gage to John
Stuart (abstract). Gage recommends Monberaut. 1p.

Fol. 50. 3 Jan. 1765, Mobile. John Stuart to Gen. Gage
(abstract). Monberaut will handle Indian affairs in
Stuart's absence. 1p.

Fol. 51. 24 Jan. 1765, Mobile. John Stuart to John
Pownall (abstract). Monberaut successfully employed the
Mortar Warrior to seduce the Cherokees. 2p.

Fol. 52. Instructions from John Stuart to Monberaut
(copy). Monberaut will run Indian affairs in Stuart's
absence. 3p.

Fol. 81. 2 Dec. 1770, Charleston. John Stuart to Earl of
Hillsborough. Peace between the Cherokees and Northern Indians
has been more effective in confirming the tribe's friendship
than anything tried previously. Cherokee decision to join the
Six Nations in opposing a western confederacy will bring
favorable results. All Indians in Stuart's district have asked
for restraints on traders. 8p. [Enclosures to fol. 114b].

Fol. 89. 26 Aug. 1770, Mobile. Charles Stuart to John
Stuart (abstract). Captured French letters reveal that
a Frenchman was taken prisoner by the Chickasaws or
Cherokees. He does not live with the Chickasaws. 5p.

C.O. 5/72 (CONT'D)

Fol. 93. 27 Sept. 1770, Pensacola. Charles Stuart to
John Stuart (abstract). Stuart has not heard more about
the reported meeting between the Creeks, Cherokees, and
the Western nations. 3p.

Fol. 99. Sept. 1770. Talk from Creeks to Charles Stuart
(abstract). Western Indians have reportedly made peace
with the Cherokees. 4p.

Fol. 105. 25 Nov. 1770, Charleston. Talk from John
Stuart to Headwarriors of the Upper Creeks (copy).
Stuart received the Creek messages while settling the
boundary line with the Cherokees in Virginia. He will
have no more discussions with the Cherokees concerning
land. 4p.

Fol. 131. 11 Feb. 1771, Whitehall. Earl of Hillsborough to
John Stuart (draft). The King approves the final boundary
line between Va. and the Cherokees. 4p.

Fol. 165. 5 Mar. 1771, Charleston. John Stuart to [Earl of
Hillsborough]. Cherokees met with a number of strange Indians.
Two Cherokees acting as spies among the Creeks confirm that
the Spanish invited the Creeks to Havana. 4p. [Enclosures
to fol. 182b].

Fol. 169. 23 Feb. 1771, Charleston. John Stuart to
Alex. Cameron (copy). Stuart wishes Cameron success in
stopping the Cherokees and their allies from attacking
the Chickasaws. It would have been better if the Cherokees
had chosen to attack the Creeks instead. 4p.

Fol. 171. 8 Feb. 1771, Ft. Prince George. Alex. Cameron
to John Stuart (copy). Northern Indians' mission to the
Cherokees proposed an attack on the whites and Creeks.
Cherokees dissuaded the visitors from this project but
agreed to attack the Chickasaws. 3p.

Fol. 173. 1 Feb. 1771, Long Canes. Richard King to John
Caldwell (abstract). There are rumors of a meeting
between the Northern Indians, Creeks, and Cherokees.
Such meeting would determine questions of war or peace.
4p.

Fol. 177. 23 Jan. 1771, Long Canes. Alex. Cameron to
[John Stuart] (abstract). Tuckassie reports that
Spaniards have visited the Upper Creeks and invited their
chiefs to New Orleans. Nottaways and Shawnees are visiting the Overhill Cherokees. 2p.

Fol. 179. 26 Dec. 1771. Pensacola. Charles Stuart to
John Stuart (copy). Chickasaw Leader refused to talk
with Mortar. Mortar is now believed to be going to the
Cherokees. 8p.

C.O. 5/72 (CONT'D)

Fol. 183. 18 Feb. 1771, Johnson Hall. Wm. Johnson to Earl of
Hillsborough. Johnson is apprehensive about an alliance between
the Northern and Southern Indians. 4p.

Fol. 210. 27 Apr. 1771, Charleston. John Stuart to Earl of
Hillsborough. Western Indian dissatisfaction with the land
cession made at Ft. Stanwix has induced the tribes to seek an
alliance with the Southern Indians. Cherokees have offered
to give up considerable tracts of land (claimed by Creeks) to
satisfy their debts. 6p. [Enclosures to fol. 229b].

Fol. 213. 11 Dec. 1770, Charleston. John Stuart to Alex.
Cameron (abstract). Indian land given to Cameron has
caused Stuart to be criticized. 2p.

Fol. 215. 23 Jan. 1771, Lochaber. Alex. Cameron to
John Stuart (extract). Cameron explains why Cherokees
gave land to Cameron's son. 3p.

Fol. 217. 4 Mar. 1771, Toqueh. Alex. Cameron to John
Stuart (copy). Young Cherokees want war against the
Western or Southern Indians, particularly the Choctaws or
Chickasaws. Cameron has been assured that the Cherokees
will never unanimously consent to attack their English
neighbors unless compelled by a superior force of Indians.
4p.

Fol. 219. 19 Mar. 1771, Toqueh. Alex. Cameron to John
Stuart (copy). Young Cherokees are upset with the land
cession at the congress and want the boundary run to
Chiswell's Mines as originally agreed upon. 4p.

Fol. 221. 12 Feb. 1771, Keowee. Talk from Headmen of
Lower Towns to Headmen of the Overhill Towns (copy).
Lower Towns have lived in peace with Southern tribes for
many years and do not wish to attack them without provocation. Even then, the Lower Cherokees would first consult
their Father. 2p.

Fol. 223. 12 Feb. 1771, Toqueh. Talk from Oconostota to
John Stuart (copy). Cherokees want to stop Northern
Indians passing through Cherokee country from warring
against the Choctaws. Northern Indians claim that Gen.
Johnson gave them permission to attack the Choctaws. 2p.

Fol. 225. 28 Feb. 1771, Toqueh. Talk from Cameron to
Overhill Cherokees (copy). Cameron is upset that the
Cherokees ceded land to the traders. Cherokees have
recently held conferences with the Shawnees, Delawares,
Mingos, and Nontoogahs [?]--all dangerous tribes. 3p.

Fol. 227. 3 Mar. 1770, Toqueh. Headmen and Warriors of
the Cherokee to Alex. Cameron (copy). Letter contains
report on speeches by the Great Warrior, Judd's Friend,
the Prince, and Corn Tassel. Cherokees have not agreed

C.O. 5/72 (CONT'D)

> with the Northern Indians to attack the Southern tribes.
> Cherokees expect an answer soon to proposed friendship
> with westerners. 4p.

> Fol. 229. 22 Feb. 1771, Chote. Copy of land grants from
> the Cherokees to the traders. 2p.

Fol. 230. 27 Apr. 1771, Charleston. John Stuart to Earl of
Hillsborough. Stuart requests a leave of absence to visit
England for relief of his gout. 2p.

Fol. 240. 3 July 1771, Whitehall. Earl of Hillsborough to
John Stuart (draft). Stuart should supply a map with the new
Choctaw, Creek, and Cherokee boundaries. Hillsborough disap-
proves the Indian land granted to traders. 5p.

Fol. 243. 3 July 1771, Whitehall. Earl of Hillsborough to
John Stuart (draft). Hillsborough denies Stuart's request for
a leave of absence but he may visit a northern colony. 2p.

Fol. 326. 23 Sept. 1771, Pensacola. John Stuart to Earl of
Hillsborough. Cherokees have angered the Creeks, who claim
the land that the Cherokees ceded to pay debts. 4p.
[Enclosures to fol. 333b].

> Fol. 328. 4 June 1771, Ft. Charlotte, Augusta. Edward
> Keating to Andrew McLean (extract). Cherokees are of-
> fended by Creek claim to the ceded land. 4p.

> Fol. 330. 8 June 1771, Charlotte. Copy of report con-
> cerning a meeting between the Cherokees and their traders
> to discuss land cessions. 4p.

> Fol. 332. 21 June 1771, Augusta. Abstract of letter
> from Andrew McLean stating that Creeks would rather give
> their land away than let the Cherokees dispose of it. 2p.

Fol. 334. 24 Sept. 1771, Pensacola. John Stuart to Earl of
Hillsborough. Indians are accompanying the surveying of
boundary lines in Virginia. 6p. [Enclosures to fol. 365b].

> Fol. 337. 1771. Sketch of Cherokee Boundaries with the
> Province of Virginia. 1p. [M.P.G. 348].

> Fol. 340. 3 Aug. 1771, Council Chambers, Pensacola.
> Extracts from the minutes of the Council of West Florida
> noting that reports of whites attacking a large party of
> Indians are false. It was the Cherokees who attacked the
> Indian party. 10p.

> Fol. 346. 1 May 1771, Oakchoy. Talk from Emistisiguo
> to John Stuart (copy). Upper Creeks are waiting for con-
> firmation that the Cherokees turned over Creek land in
> payment for debts. Cherokees report that whites have sent
> cattle to the head of the Coosa River. 4p.

C.O. 5/72 (CONT'D)

Fol. 348. 15 July 1771, Tallassee. Talk from Upper Creek Headmen and Warriors to John Stuart (copy). Creeks have no information from Stuart about the Cherokee land cession. Stuart had said earlier that the English would not ask for nor accept more land if offered. 3p.

Fol. 350. 30 Aug. 1771, Pensacola. John Stuart to Gov. Peter Chester (copy). Land cession from the Six Nations includes the hunting grounds of the Choctaws and many western tribes. Creeks claim that land ceded to the traders by the Cherokees. 4p.

Fol. 364. 10 Aug. 1771, Pensacola. Talk from John Stuart to Emistisiguo and Upper Creek Chiefs (copy). Stuart is unaware of an agreement between the Cherokees and traders. 3p.

C.O. 5/73 ORIGINAL CORRESPONDENCE, SEC. OF STATE, INDIAN AFFAIRS: 1771-1772

Fol. 1. 11 Jan. 1772, Whitehall. Earl of Hillsborough to John Stuart (draft). It is not appropriate that the Cherokees cede land to the traders, but the Bd. of Trade will accept the Cherokee land cession to pay off debts if the Creeks approve it. 5p.

Fol. 22. 29 Dec. 1771, Mobile. John Stuart to Earl of Hillsborough (copy). Stuart is pleased at obtaining permission to go to N.Y. or one of the northern colonies to recover his health. 1p.

Fol. 24. 29 Dec. 1771, Mobile. John Stuart to Earl of Hillsborough. 3p. [Enclosures to fol. 37b].

Fol. 26. 29 Oct. - 2 Nov. 1771, Pensacola. Copy of report on the Congress of Upper Creeks stating that Cherokees cannot cede land to traders without permission from the superintendent. 24p.

Fol. 46. 6 Feb. 1772, Mobile. John Stuart to Earl of Hillsborough. Shawnee messengers told the Creeks that the Western Confederacy wants all Southern tribes to be at peace. Mortar Warrior has gone to visit the Cherokees, and the Creek leader (Handsome Fellow) has gone to the Chickasaws on private matters. 10p. [Enclosures to fol. 60b].

Fol. 55. 20 Jan. 1772, Mobile. Talk from John Stuart to Upper Creek Chiefs (copy). Cherokees ceded land to the traders without Stuart's knowledge and the King's permission. 4p.

Fol. 95. 9 Feb. 1772, Mobile. John Stuart to Earl of Hillsborough. Stuart ordered Cameron to publish a warning against the unauthorized Cherokee land cession to the traders. Stuart forwards a memorial of those involved in the Cherokee cession. Cherokee land ceded to the traders is claimed by the Creeks.

C.O. 5/73 (CONT'D)

Cameron was wrong in accepting land from an Indian woman for
his son. 4p. [Enclosures to fol. 108].

Fol. 97. 30 Oct. 1772, Savannah. John Jamieson, Geo.
Baillie, and Thomas Netherclift to John Stuart (copy).
Traders are willing to compensate the Creeks for contested
land ceded by the Cherokees. 2p.

Fol. 99. 13 Nov. 1771, Augusta. Geo. Galphin, Robt.
McKay, James Jackson, and Andrew McLean to John Stuart
(copy). Cherokees have ceded land to the traders in
payment for debts. 3p.

Fol. 101. 4 Jan. 1772, Mobile. John Stuart to John
Jamieson, Geo. Baillie, and Thomas Netherclift (copy)
Everyone involved in the cession of Cherokee land to the
traders must relinquish their claims. 2p.

Fol. 103. 20 Jan. 1772, Mobile. John Stuart to Geo.
Galphin et al. (copy). Cherokee cession to the traders
displeases the King and is contrary to the proclamation
of 1763. 2p.

Fol. 105. 10 Sept. 1771. Memorial from principal Creek
and Cherokee traders to John Stuart (copy). Traders
explain the Cherokee land cession in payment for debts. 3p.

Fol. 107. 11 Dec. 1770. John Stuart to Alex. Cameron
(abstract). Gift of Cherokee land to Cameron's son has
caused Stuart to be heavily criticized. 2p.

Fol. 150. 4 Apr. 1772, Johnson Hall. Wm. Johnson to Earl of
Hillsborough. Cherokees thank the Six Nations and Johnson for
the peace of 1768. 7p.

Fol. 154. 1 July 1772, Whitehall. Earl of Hillsborough to
Wm. Johnson (draft). Hillsborough is surprised that the
Shawnees are dissatisfied with the cessions [Treaty of Ft.
Stanwix] of land in Va. and southwest of the Allegheny Mountains.
Other tribes deny the right of the Six Nations to cede this
land. 4p.

Fol. 156. 13 June 1772, Charleston. John Stuart to Earl of
Hillsborough. Ga. and S.C. traders have tried to persuade the
Creeks to agree to the Cherokee land cessions. 5p. [Enclosures
to fol. 160b].

Fol. 161. Map of Creek and Cherokee Country. Map shows lands
granted by Cherokees to traders. 1p. [M.R. 18]. [Enclosure
of fol. 162].

Fol. 162. 12 June 1772, Charleston. John Stuart to Earl of
Hillsborough. Traders should avoid negotiating land cessions
from the Cherokees to repay debts. Most land ceded by the
Cherokees belonged to the Creeks. John Thomas agreed with the
Spanish proposal to form confederacies with the Arkansas, Chero-
kees, Chickasaws, and Shawnees. 12p. [Enclosures to fol. 231b].

Fol. 176. 3 Oct. 1767, Charleston. John Stuart to Gov.
Grant (copy). Stuart discusses Indian trade regulations.
7p.

Fol. 180. Nov. 1768, Augusta. John Stuart to Gov. Wright
(copy). N.C., S.C., and Va. have provided for expenses of
running boundary line in their provinces since the costs do
not belong to the Indian department. 7p.

Fol. 206. 5 Oct. 1771, New Orleans. John Thomas to John
Stuart (copy). French tried to persuade the Arkansas
Indians to join the Kickapoos against the English. Thomas
may join the Arkansas, Chickasaws, and the Cherokees
against the Kickapoos. 3p.

Fol. 208. 19 Feb. 1772, Mobile. John Stuart to John
Thomas (copy). Thomas had no claim to more pay than
officers at Natchez, Tombigbee, and Ft. Prince George.
He may, however, be compensated for the losses he sustained
when Ft. Bute was robbed. 6p.

Fol. 214. 11 Mar. 1772, Ft. Bute. John Thomas to John
Stuart (copy). Arkansas Indians have promised to war
against the Osages in conjunction with the Chickasaws,
Shawnees, and Cherokees. 3p.

Fol. 215. 21 Feb. 1772, Ft. Bute. Copy of letter from
Henry Le Fleur confirming that the Arkansas Indians have
promised to war on the Osages and Kickapoos with the aid
of the Chickasaws, Shawnees, and Cherokees. 1p.

Fol. 223. 10 Apr. 1772. Copy of charges by John Stuart
against John Thomas. Thomas had no authority to negotiate
with the Spanish governor to engage the Cherokees,
Chickasaws, and Shawnees against the Osages and Kickapoos.
2p.

Fol. 226. 10 Apr. 1772, Pensacola. John Stuart to John
Thomas (copy). Because Thomas had no authority to form a
confederacy with the Arkansas in Spanish territory nor the
legal power to set the Cherokees, Chickasaws, and Shawnees
to war upon the Osages and Kickapoos, Stuart suspended him
from office. 3p.

Fol. 234. 7 Aug. 1772, Whitehall. Earl of Hillsborough to
John Stuart (draft). Hillsborough does not wish to interfere
with Stuart's decision to remove Thomas from office. 3p.

Fol. 249. 2 Sept. 1772, Whitehall. Earl of Dartmouth to John
Stuart (draft). Proper attention has been shown to the details
of the Cherokee treaty of 18 Oct. 1770. 3p.

Fol. 257. 19 July 1772, Charleston. John Stuart to Earl of
Hillsborough. 4p. [Enclosures to fol. 393b].

C.O. 5/73 (CONT'D)

Fol. 259. 16 Mar. 1772, Tuckabatchee. David Taitt to [John Stuart] (copy). Augusta merchants have sent talks to the Upper and Lower Towns about Cherokee land given to the traders. 7p.

Fol. 263. 4 May 1772, Geehaws. David Taitt to John Stuart (copy). Emistisiguo reports that the Northern Indians have sent a white skin with red borders into Cherokee country signaling their support for war. Emistisiguo did not believe their talk. 3p.

Fol. 272. 19 Apr. 1772, Oakchoys. Talk from Emistisiguo to John Stuart (copy). Emistisiguo discusses the boundary line and false rumors of English settlements along the Cherokee River. 4p.

Fol. 290. 30 Jan. - 20 Apr. 1772, Upper Creek Nation. Journal of Taitt's Journey to and through Upper Creek Nation. Augusta merchants have sent the Creeks a talk requesting confirmation of land grant by the Cherokees. 39p.

Fol. 397. 27 Sept. 1772, Whitehall. Earl of Dartmouth to John Stuart (draft). Dartmouth has not received a map of America with Indian boundaries. Indian congresses should be held only when necessary. 1p.

Fol. 403. 23 Sept. 1772, Charleston. John Stuart to Earl of Hillsborough. The Cherokee leader guilty of murder has long been an enemy of the whites and was responsible for the last war. Cherokee chiefs were alarmed at his return with so many scalps and refused to admit him. 5p. [Enclosures to fol. 423b].

Fol. 414. 7 July 1772, Mobile. Charles Stuart to John Stuart (copy). Paya Mingo Euluxy will probably attempt to recapture his wife taken by the Cherokees. Cherokees have returned with white scalps that they claimed were French. Scalps really belonged to people coming to settle along the Mississippi. 4p.

Fol. 416. 21 July 1772, Cherokee Nation. Copy of talk from Oconostota, Judds' Friend, Willinawa, and Old Tassel denying that the Cherokees will join the Northern Indians against the whites. 2p.

Fol. 420. 9 Aug. 1772, Lochaber. Alex. Cameron to John Stuart (copy). Mankiller and his followers have attacked whites. Mankiller and his brother Kennititah are guilty of many violations since the peace. Northern Indians and the Cherokees got drunk and chased the traders. 4p.

Fol. 424. 24 Sept. 1772, Charleston. John Stuart to Earl of Hillsborough. 3p. [Enclosures to 451b].

Fol. 445. [1772]. Copies of letters from John Stuart and John Thomas containing Stuart's charges against John Thomas

C.O. 5/73 (CONT'D)

for agreeing with the Spanish gov. to engage the Cherokees,
Chickasaws, Shawnees, and the Arkansas in a war against the
Osages and Kickapoos. Thomas replies to the charges. 14p.

Fol. 454. 9 Dec. 1772, Whitehall. Earl of Dartmouth to John
Stuart (draft). Creeks and Cherokees have ceded land. Stuart
and Gage must handle the murders committed by the Cherokees.
7p.

Fol. 458. 9 Dec. 1772, Whitehall. Earl of Dartmouth to John
Stuart (draft). Circumstances will dictate the propriety of
demanding satisfaction for murders committed by the Cherokee
leader. 4p.

C.O. 5/74   ORIGINAL CORRESPONDENCE, SEC. OF STATE, INDIAN AFFAIRS:
*   1772-1773*

Fol. 5. 4 Nov. 1772, Johnson Hall. Wm. Johnson to Earl of
Dartmouth. Wabash, Kickapoos, and Piankashaws did not attend
the Congress at Scioto because some of their people had been
killed last year by a party of the Six Nations and Cherokees.
Cherokees stopped the circulation of belts of the Seneca chief.
7p.

Fol. 22. 4 Jan. 1773, Charleston. John Stuart to Earl of
Dartmouth. Frequent petitions to extend boundaries have caused
the Cherokees and other Southern tribes to distrust the English.
Cherokees and Lower Creeks dispute ownership of land ceded by
the Cherokees to traders. 8p. [Enclosures to fol. 31b].

    Fol. 26. 3 Sept. 1772, Chickasaw Nation. John McIntosh
    to Charles Stuart (copy). Eleuxy visited the Cherokees
    instead of the Creeks. Northern Indians are coming to make
    peace with the Chickasaws, Creeks, and Cherokees. Chero-
    kees will soon be at war with whites. 4p.

    Fol. 28. 21 Sept. 1772, Pallachicola. David Taitt to
    [John Stuart] (abstract). Creeks are certain the Chero-
    kees will not claim land the Creeks intend to cede. Land
    between the forks of the Savannah is Creek but the tribe
    is giving it to the Cherokees to repay their debts. 3p.

Fol. 32. 3 Mar. 1773, Whitehall. Earl of Dartmouth to John
Stuart (draft). Cherokees will hopefully be reasonable in
forthcoming negotiations concerning the Ohio. Dartmouth is
surprised that the Creeks refused to join the cession proposed
by the Cherokees. 5p.

Fol. 35. 8 Jan. 1773, Charleston. John Stuart to Earl of
Dartmouth. Cherokees wish to give Wilkinson land in payment
for debts. In 1768, the Cherokees gave Cameron's Indian son 12
square miles of land. Richard Pearis and Jacob Hite have sold
land obtained from the Cherokees to emigrants from the northern
colonies. 5p. [Enclosures to fol. 50b].

C.O. 5/74 (CONT'D)

Fol. [38]. 8 Dec. 1770. Map of land along the Broad and
Saludy Rivers ceded by Cherokees to Edward Wilkinson in
payment for debts. 1p.

Fol. 39. 15 Oct. 1768, Hard Labor. Minutes of Congress
Held at Hard Labor (abstract). Minutes concern land given
to Cameron's son by a Cherokee woman. 3p.

Fol. 41. 11-12 Apr. 1771, Keowee. Memorial from Edward
Wilkinson to John Stuart (copy). Wilkinson requests that
S.C. either accept land ceded him by the Cherokees, pay
him for the land, or accept it for taxes and 10 years
quitrent. 6p.

Fol. 43. 7 Nov. 1770, Keowee. Oconostota to John Stuart
(copy). Oconostota requests permission to cede land to
Wilkinson. 2p.

Fol. 45. 11 Apr. 1771, Keowee. Edward Wilkinson to John
Stuart (copy). Wilkinson wants Stuart to recommend that
the King accept the Cherokee land cession. 1p.

Fol. 47. 12 Apr. 1771, Keowee. David McDonald to John
Stuart (copy). McDonald sends Oconostota's talk and a
chart of the land. 2p.

Fol. 49. 4 June 1771, Charleston. John Ward to John
Stuart. Ward forwards a memorial and letter from Wilkinson
and a talk from a Cherokee chief [Oconostota] regarding
land ceded to Wilkinson. 2p.

Fol. 51. 26 Dec. 1772, Johnson Hall. Wm. Johnson to [Earl of
Dartmouth] (copy). Several Southern Indian nations have proposed an attack on the Six Nations. 6p.

Fol. 58. 10 Apr. 1773, Whitehall. Earl of Dartmouth to John
Stuart (draft). Wilkinson should have a share, in common with
other traders, from the sale of lands ceded by the Creeks and
Cherokees. 2p.

Fol. 60. 17 Feb. 1773, Charleston. John Stuart to Earl of
Dartmouth. Stuart has begun negotiations with the Creeks and
Cherokees to obtain a land cession for the King. Creek and
Cherokee chiefs will meet with Gov. Wright in Augusta on 25
May. 3p.

Fol. 62. 25 Feb. 1770, Charleston. John Stuart to Earl of
Dartmouth. The May Indian meeting will give Stuart an opportunity to confer with the Cherokees about the western murders
committed by their tribe. 4p. [Enclosures to fol. 65b].

Fol. 64. 22 Nov. 1772, Little Tallassee. David Taitt to
John Stuart (copy). Northern Indians will reportedly come
South to make peace with the Creeks, Chickasaws, Cherokees,
and Choctaws in the spring. Cherokees killed five whites
whom they thought to be French. 4p.

Fol. 70. 27 Feb. 1773, Charleston. John Stuart to Earl of
Dartmouth. Stuart justifies the dismissal of John Thomas. 3p.
[Enclosures to fol. 95b].

Fol. 96. 5 May 1773, Whitehall. Earl of Dartmouth to John
Stuart (draft). Cherokees have happily chosen a natural northern boundary which will prevent future disputes. 5p.

Fol. 99. 8 Apr. 1773, Charleston. John Stuart to Earl of
Dartmouth. Cherokee and Creek chiefs will convene on 25 May
to negotiate land cessions between the Savannah and Broad
Rivers. 2p. [Enclosures to fol. 111b].

Fol. 123. 7-10 Apr. 1773, Johnson Hall. Congress of Six
Nations. Six Nations have sent belts to the Cherokees
advising them to be ready for war. 14p.

Fol. 144. 16 June 1773, Savannah. John Stuart to Earl of
Dartmouth. At the Augusta Congress with the Cherokees and
Creeks, Stuart explained the proposal to prohibit settlement
along the Ohio and Cherokee boundaries. 4p.

Fol. 146. 21 June 1773, Savannah. John Stuart to Earl of
Dartmouth. Oconostota sent Otacite Ousteneka to represent the
Cherokees at the Congress, while he remained at Chote to receive
the Shawnees and other Northern tribes. According to Little
Carpenter, the Weyaughtenous, Piankashaws, Kickapoos, and other
Western tribes have rejected Cherokee friendship. 7p.

Fol. 150. 30 June 1773, Charleston. John Stuart to Earl of
Dartmouth. Creeks never consented to the cession proposed by
Cherokees. Cherokees have granted additional land to the
English to compensate for that which the Creeks claim. This
new cession brings the English boundary very near to the
Cherokee villages. 4p.

Fol. 152. 5 Aug. 1773, Charleston. John Stuart to Earl of
Dartmouth. John and Hezekiah Collins murdered two Cherokees
who were sent to mark the boundary line agreed upon at Augusta.
5p. [Enclosures to fol. 158b].

> Fol. 155. 5 July 1773, Seneca. Big Sawny (Carotutoy)
> to Alex. Cameron (copy). Big Sawny complains about the
> murdered Cherokees but he will give Cameron time to find
> the guilty party. 3p.

> Fol. 157. 5 July 1773, Seneca. Ecuij (Good Warrior) to
> Alex. Cameron (copy). Murder of the two Cherokees spoiled
> talks at Savannah. 3p.

Fol. 159. 24 Aug. 1773, Charleston. John Stuart to Earl of
Dartmouth. Hezekiah Collins, murderer of two Cherokee youths,
was captured but escaped. Stuart sends a message from the
Overhill Cherokees inquiring about the murder of white men.
3p. [Enclosures to fol. 166b].

C.O. 5/74 (CONT'D)

    Fol. 161. 21 July 1773. Alex. Cameron to [John Stuart] (abstract). Cameron describes a murder committed by the Second Man of Chote. 3p.

    Fol. 163. 6 July 1773, Settico in the Overhill Cherokee. Talk from Oconostota, Willinawa, Judd's Friend, and Cold Weather to Alex. Cameron (copy). Overhill Cherokees give an account of a murder of a white by the Second Man of Chote. 3p.

    Fol. 165. 15 July 1773, Keowee. Talk from Little Carpenter, Ecuij, and Chinisto to Alex. Cameron. Lower Cherokees have promised not to take revenge for two Cherokees killed but there is no news on how the white man was killed in the Overhill area. 3p.

Fol. 167. 28 Oct. 1773, Whitehall. Earl of Dartmouth to John Stuart (draft). Dartmouth praises Stuart's success in handling difficulties in the Creek and Cherokee cession. Murderer of the Cherokees on Broad R. has escaped 4p.

Fol. 171. 22 Sept. 1773, Johnson Hall. Wm. Johnson to Earl of Dartmouth. Indians at Scioto have proposed a conference with the Wabash and Cherokee Indians in July. 4p. [Enclosures to fol. 174b].

    Fol. 173. 28 June 1773, Pittsburgh. Talk from Shawnees to Alex. McKee (copy). Shawnees were told that English settlements would be made along the Ohio to Big Bones since the Six Nations and Cherokees sold that country. 3p.

Fol. 179. 1 Dec. 1773, Whitehall. Earl of Dartmouth to Wm. Johnson (draft). Indian affairs are tense because of the unrestrained English settlements and because of the French and Spanish promises to the savages along the Mississippi. 4p.

C.O. 5/75   ORIGINAL CORRESPONDENCE, SEC. OF STATE, INDIAN AFFAIRS: 1773-1774

Fol. 6. 21 Dec. 1773, Charleston. John Stuart to Earl of Dartmouth. Hezekiah Collins murdered two Cherokees. Richard Pearis and Jacob Hite have relinquished their claim to the Indian lands ceded them. Great Warrior of Chote wants a confederacy to force peace on the Western tribes. 5p. [Enclosures to fol. 22b].

    Fol. 9. 11 Oct. 1773. Alex. Cameron to John Stuart (abstract). Great Warrior only seeks peace with tribes presently at war. Cold Weather might exchange talks with the Northern Indians. Little Carpenter has gone to hunt his enemies the Yachtanues, Kickapoos, Piankashaws, and Twightwees. 7p.

    Fol. 15. 9 Sept. 1773, Woositchie. David Taitt to John Stuart (abstract). The Mortar returned from the Cherokees unhappy about the recent land cession. 4p.

Fol. 19. 8 Nov. 1773, Great Oakchoys, Upper Creek Nation.
Talk from Cherokees to the Mortar and Creeks. Hiwassee,
Toqueh, and Chote request a general meeting with the
Nottaways and Shawnees. 3p.

Fol. 23. 5 Feb. 1774, Whitehall. Earl of Dartmouth to John
Stuart (draft). Dartmouth is glad that there is no reason to
be apprehensive concerning Indian alliances prejudicial to the
King's interests. 3p.

Fol. 42. 13 Feb. 1774, Charleston. John Stuart to Earl of
Dartmouth. Arms and presents were sent to West Fla. for the
Choctaws and Chickasaws. Cameron has been sent more presents
for the Cherokees. 6p. [Enclosures to fol. 58b].

Fol. 49. 22 Jan. 1774, Little Tallassee. David Taitt to
John Stuart (copy). Howmatcha (thought to be a witch) and
others committed the murders near Ogeechee in revenge for
the murder by the Cowetas who reside among the Cherokees.
4p.

Fol. 53. 28 Jan. 1774, Savannah. John Stuart to Alex.
Cameron (copy). Cameron's presence among the Cherokees
is necessary to prevent them from joining the Creeks.
Cameron should not go past Ft. Prince George, but he
should find out the intentions of the Great Warrior. 3p.

Fol. 55. 27 Jan. 1774, Savannah. Gov. Wright to John
Stuart (copy). Choctaws should be assisted in their war
with the Creeks. Stuart should try to engage Cherokee
and Chickasaw aid if war erupts between the English and
the Creeks. 2p.

Fol. 57. 4 Feb. 1774. Alex. Cameron to John Stuart
(abstract). Cameron expects an attack from the Cherokees.
He is building a fort at Lochaber and will visit the
Cherokees in two or three days. 3p.

Fol. 63. 23 Mar. 1774, Charleston. John Stuart to Earl of
Dartmouth. There has been no success in punishing the murderer
of the young Cherokees along the Broad River. Stuart has no
reason to expect any Cherokee disturbance. The tribe shows no
inclination to join the Creeks. 4p. [Enclosures to fol. 88b].

Fol. 77. 9 Feb. 1774, Lochaber. Alex. Cameron to John
Stuart (copy). Cameron would like instructions about
turning the Cherokees against the Creeks. If Cherokee
assistance is requested, the tribe's respect for whites
will diminish since the English boast of needing no help.
3p.

Fol. 79. 1 Mar. 1774, Keowee. Alex. Cameron to John
Stuart (copy). Cherokees do not want a quarrel with the
whites or Creeks. Tribe has heard that the Raven and some
young warriors from Tugaloo have joined the Creeks.
Delawares and Senecas, not Cherokees, were probably responsible for murdering the Virginians. 7p.

C.O. 5/75 (CONT'D)

Fol. 83.   4 Feb. 1774, Keowee.   Talk from Chinisto of
Sugar Town and Lower Cherokees to Alex. Cameron (copy).
Cherokees will not war against the whites.   2p.

Fol. 85.   21 Feb. 1774, Sugar Town.   Copy of talk from
Wolf of Seneca and Chinisto on behalf of the Middle and
Lower Cherokee settlements rejecting the Coweta offer.   4p.

Fol. 87.   25 Feb. 1774, Keowee.   Copy of report of a
meeting by Cameron with the headmen of the Middle and
Lower Cherokee towns.   Chinisto of Sugar Town reports
the rejection of the Coweta overtures.   3p.

Fol. 89.   24 Mar. 1774, Charleston.   John Stuart to Earl of
Dartmouth.   Stuart was forced to supply the Creeks and Cherokees at the congress from provisions for the Southern Department
in return for land cession.   3p.   [Enclosures to fol. 92b].

Fol. 91.   26 Feb. 1774, Savannah.   Gov. Wright to John
Stuart (copy).   It is not clear when the sale of Creek
and Cherokee lands will   produce enough revenue to pay for
the goods furnished by Stuart at the congress.   2p.

Fol. 95.   4 May 1774, Whitehall.   Earl of Dartmouth to John
Stuart (draft).   Money advanced for purchase of lands [from
the Cherokees and Creeks] should be replaced.   4p.

Fol. 117.   6 May 1774, Charleston.   John Stuart to Earl of
Dartmouth (duplicate).   Cherokees persuaded the Creeks not to
go to Savannah.   Cherokees would like the Creeks to war against
the English.   Emistisiguo wanted to know reason for the numerous
meetings between the Cherokees and the Creeks, Chickasaws,
Arkansaws, Shawnees, Delawares, and Illinois.   4p.   [Enclosures
to fol. 132b].

Fol. 119.   Report of Conference between Gov. Wright and
Upper Creeks (copy).   Some whites killed the Elk, a Creek
Indian, in Cherokee country.   12p.

Fol. 127.   2 Mar. 1774, Chote.   Talk from Oconostota to
Mr. Carter or Parker of Virginia (copy).   Oconostota will
not join the Cowetas in a war against the whites.   3p.

Fol. 129.   1774.   Report on the murders of Great Elk and
Mad Turkey by whites near Tugaloo.   2p.

Fol. 133.   6 July 1774, Whitehall.   Earl of Dartmouth to John
Stuart (draft).   It is unfortunate that the Cherokees persuaded
most Creek chiefs not to accompany Taitt to Savannah.   3p.

Fol. 139.   20 June 1774, Johnson Hall.   Wm. Johnson to Earl of
Dartmouth.   Settlements below the Great Kanawha R. disturb the
Indians.   5p.   [Enclosures to fol. 148b].

Fol. 147. 1774. Intelligence from Shawnees Living with
Creeks. Meeting at Scioto with the Western and Southern
nations will plan a time to attack the English. 3p.

Fol. 151. 26 July 1774, Johnson Hall. Guy Johnson to Earl of
Dartmouth (copy). Wm. Johnson's sudden death terminated the
congress with the Six Nations. Indian embassy was sent to the
Southern tribes. 3p. [Enclosures to fol. 162b].

Fol. 165. 2 Aug. 1774, Charleston. John Stuart to Earl of
Dartmouth. Murder of the young Indian along the Holston R.
makes the Cherokees uneasy. Stuart is suspicious of those
Cherokees who have been closely connected with the Shawnees
and other Western tribes and who have continued trying to unite
all the tribes. There are now 30 Cherokee deputies at Scioto.
5p. [Enclosures to fol. 195b].

  Fol. 168. 20 Feb. 1774, Fincastle County. Copy of affidavit from Thomas Sharp accusing Elk Warrior and another
  Cherokee of murdering Wm. Russell and two other whites.
  1p.

  Fol. 169. 12 Feb. 1774, Fincastle County. Copy of affidavit from Isaac Thomas (Cherokee trader) concerning the
  murder of Wm. Russell and others in which Elk Warrior
  evidenly participated. 2p.

  Fol. 170. 5 Apr. 1774, Williamsburg. Gov. Dunmore to
  John Stuart (copy). Dunmore demands the punishment of
  the murderers of Wm. Russell and party. Cameron should
  stop the purchasing of Indian land south and west of the
  boundary line. 3p.

  Fol. 174. 3 June 1774, Keowee. Alex. Cameron to [John
  Stuart] (copy). Cameron reports the Cherokee mood.
  Cherokees will not surrender the Elk although he was one
  of the murderers of Wm. Russell and his party. 8p.

  Fol. 178. June 1774. Great Warrior of Overhill Cherokees
  to Alex. Cameron (copy). Whites killed a young Cherokee
  at Watauga. Cherokees returning from the north report
  that Wm. Johnson told the Mohawks to war against the
  Cherokees. 3p.

  Fol. 182. 26 June 1774, Keowee. Edward Wilkinson to Alex.
  Cameron (copy). The Second Man of the Great Island's son
  was murdered at Watauga, but some whites saved Kittagiskee.
  Shawnees have asked the Overhill Towns to join them against
  the whites. 3p.

  Fol. 186. 4 July 1774, Cherokee Nation. Alex. Cameron to
  [John Stuart] (abstract). Most Cherokee headmen would
  like to see the Creeks humbled. Although Oconostota has
  not been faithful, Cameron believes he is now sincere.
  Whites killed the Indian at Watauga most likely in revenge
  for Russell's murder. 8p.

C.O. 5/75 (CONT'D)

Fol. 192. 18 July 1774, Augusta. David Taitt to John
Stuart (copy). Cherokee was shot at a horse race in
Virginia. Cherokees released two white men rather than
kill them but they want Stuart to punish those guilty of
murder. 3p.

Fol. 194. 21 July 1774, New Bern. Gov. Martin to [John
Stuart] (abstract). Martin prohibits trespassing on
Cherokee territory. Gov. Dunmore believes the Cherokees,
Creeks, and other tribes will join the Shawnees. 2p.

Fol. 196. 5 Oct. 1774, Whitehall. Earl of Dartmouth to John
Stuart (draft). Cherokee peace can hopefully be preserved so
that the tribe will not assist the Choctaws. 3p.

Fol. 200. 3 Sept. 1774, Charleston. John Stuart to Earl of
Dartmouth. Virginians have invited Great Warrior and the
principal Cherokee chiefs to meet along the Holston to discuss
land purchase. Stuart ordered Cameron to prevent the Cherokees
from concluding any such agreement. 3p. [Enclosures to fol.
219b].

Fol. 202. 9 June 1774, Botetourt County. Talk from Col.
Andrew Lewis to Oconostota (copy). Lewis expresses regret
over murder of the Cherokee at Watauga. Cherokees, however,
are believed responsible for death of five whites on the
Ohio River. 4p.

Fol. 204. 11 June 1774, Fincastle County. Wm. Preston
to Cherokees (copy). Virginians will attempt to punish the
murderers of Cherokees at Watauga. Cherokees should also
punish their people guilty of robbery or murder. 4p.

Fol. 206. 20 June 1774, Fincastle, Virginia. Arthur
Campbell to Alex. Cameron (copy). Crabtree, murderer of
the Cherokee at Watauga, has eluded capture. Nothing has
been done about the Cherokee murderers of Wm. Russell and
party along the Ohio. 4p.

Fol. 208. 18 July 1774, Chote. Oconostota to Alex.
Cameron (copy). Virginians want to meet the Cherokees at
Long Island. 2p.

Fol. 210. 15 Aug. 1774, Lochaber. Alex. Cameron to [John
Stuart] (copy). Cherokees are not responsible for the
murder of Russell and party since there were only two of
them with the guilty group of Delawares. Virginians have
no claim to land at Watauga. 4p.

Fol. 212. 23 Aug. 1774, Augusta. Talk from Cujesse Mico
and Creeks to John Stuart and Gov. Wright (copy).
Emistisiguo is hunting near Cherokee R. but Hillibees,
Oakfuskees, Caligies, Upper Eufalees, Abekas, Tallapooses,
and Alibamos want peace and have nothing to say to the
Cowetas. 4p.

C.O. 5/75 (CONT'D)

      Fol. 218. 20 Sept. 1773, Toqueh. Pass from Cameron to
      Ugayoolah, warrior and headman of the Tennessee. 2p.

Fol. 220. 12 Sept. 1774, Charleston. John Stuart to Earl of
Dartmouth. Cameron will hopefully disprove the reported murders
committed by the Overhill Indians. Stuart wants to know the
objective of the Northern tribe's embassy at Chote. Gov. Martin
and Earl of Dunmore should be careful if the Cherokees desert
the English. 3p. [Enclosures to fol. 223b].

      Fol. 222. 25 Aug. 1774, Lochaber. Alex. Cameron to John
      Stuart. Cherokees murdered some whites. Northern Indians
      have arrived at Chote but their intentions and number are
      not known. 3p.

Fol. 228. 10 Sept. 1774, Guy Park. Guy Johnson to Earl of
Dartmouth. Southern Indians have formed an alliance and have
approached the Six Nations. 4p.

Fol. 230. 6 Oct. 1774, Savannah. John Stuart to Earl of
Dartmouth. Creeks will execute two more murderers if they
return from the Cherokees. Stuart suspects that the Cherokees
have joined the Creeks in breaking with the English. 3p.

C.O. 5/76 *ORIGINAL CORRESPONDENCE, SEC. OF STATE, INDIAN AFFAIRS:*
          1774-1775

Fol. 3. 15 Dec. 1774, Charleston. John Stuart to Earl of
Dartmouth. Cameron persuaded the Cherokees to give satisfaction
for Capt. Russell's murder. This illustrates the Cherokee's
friendship towards the English. Cameron found that the young
Cherokees are ready to join the Shawnees and Western tribes.
6p. [Enclosures to fol. 9b].

      Fol. 8. 15 Sept. 1774, Mobile. Charles Stuart to [John
      Stuart] (abstract). Chickasaws scalped a French Negro
      near the Cherokee River. 3p.

Fol. 10. 14 Dec. 1774, Guy Park. Col. Guy Johnson to Earl of
Dartmouth. Indians have asked for information regarding a
peace agreement with one of the Southern tribes since the
Shawnees at Kanawha ceded land to Virginia. 11p. [Enclosures
to fol. 25b].

Fol. 28. 1 Feb. 1775, Whitehall. Earl of Dartmouth to John
Stuart (draft). Chickasaws have committed excesses similar to
other Indian tribes in the Southern Department. New trade
regulations will hopefully restrain traders from provoking the
Indians. 3p.

Fol. 30. 3 Jan. 1775, Charleston. John Stuart to Earl of
Dartmouth. Some North Carolinians were negotiating for land
purchases from the Cherokees. 6p. [Enclosures to fol. 40b].

      Fol. 39. 17 Dec. 1774. Alex. Cameron to [John Stuart]
      (abstract). Richard Henderson and other North Carolinians

C.O. 5/76 (CONT'D)

　　　　visited Cherokee territory to buy land. Little Carpenter
　　　　returned with them. 2p.

Fol. 59. 3 Mar. 1775, Whitehall. Earl of Dartmouth to John
Stuart (draft). Only S.C. has laws against settlements on
Indian land. Stuart should prevent any contact between the
Southern Indians and foreigners. 4p.

Fol. 89. 28 Mar. 1775, Charleston. John Stuart to Earl of
Dartmouth (copy). Stuart complains that the constant attempts
to defraud Indians of their land will disturb the tribes. He
forwards Mr. Henderson's proceedings on the Cherokee land
cession. 2p. [Enclosures to fol. 94b].

　　　　Fol. 91. 23 Feb. 1775, Lochaber. Alex. Cameron to John
　　　　Stuart (copy). The Great Warrior and Overhill chiefs will
　　　　meet Little Carpenter at Long Island to receive presents.
　　　　Richard Pearis is surveying his land grant. Chilhowie
　　　　will support the Elk. 4p.

　　　　Fol. 93. 2 Mar. 1775, Lochaber. Alex. Cameron to John
　　　　Stuart (copy). Richard Henderson sent presents to Long
　　　　Island and received a large tract of land in return.
　　　　Henderson claims that the King's Proclamation cannot bar
　　　　anyone from purchasing Indian land. 4p.

Fol. 120. 20 May 1775, Charleston. John Stuart to Earl of
Dartmouth. Choctaws, Chickasaws, and Cherokees are friendly
to His Majesty's interest. 3p.

Fol. 150. 21 July 1775, St. Augustine. John Stuart to Earl of
Dartmouth. Suspicions concerning Stuart's influence over the
Cherokee and Catawba Indians have made Charleston dangerous for
him. Two persons carrying letters from Va. were killed near
the Cherokee towns. Creek party has left for Cherokee territory
to punish some escaped murderers. 5p. [Enclosures to fol. 168b].

　　　　Fol. 153. 18 July 1775, St. Augustine. John Stuart to
　　　　Committee of Charleston (copy). Stuart denies receiving
　　　　orders to have the Indians attack frontier inhabitants.
　　　　Nor has Stuart taken part in the dispute between Great
　　　　Britain and her colonies. 7p.

　　　　Fol. 157. 21 June 1775, Charleston. Committee of
　　　　Charleston to John Stuart (copy). Committee will hold
　　　　Stuart's estate in bond for the good behavior of Southern
　　　　Department Indians. 4p.

　　　　Fol. 163. 18 July 1775, St. Augustine. John Stuart to
　　　　W.H. Drayton (copy). Stuart denies encouraging the Chero-
　　　　kees, Catawbas, and others to attack local inhabitants. 4p.

　　　　Fol. 167. 6 July 1775, Savannah. Gov. James Wright to
　　　　John Stuart (copy). Carolina committee has appointed three
　　　　persons each to manage the Creek and Cherokee affairs. Taitt
　　　　reports that five Creeks set out for the Cherokee territory
　　　　to put murderers to death. 3p.

C.O. 5/76 (CONT'D)

Fol. 172. 17 Sept. 1775, St. Augustine. John Stuart to Earl of Dartmouth. Stuart informed the Creeks, Cherokees, and others about the lack of ammunition. He asked the Creek and Cherokee deputies to resist American attempts to win them over. 6p. [Enclosures to fol. 182b].

> Fol. 177. 1 Aug. 1775, Little Tallassee. David Taitt to John Stuart (copy). S.C. Committee has appointed Geo. Galphin, Leroy Hammond, and David Zubly as superintendents for Creek affairs. Committee appointed three others for the Cherokees. 4p.

> Fol. 179. 30 Aug. 1775, St. Augustine. John Stuart to Great Warrior, Attakullakulla, Ostenaco, Ecuij, Prince of Chote, and all Cherokee chiefs (copy). Savannah residents seized gun powder intended for the Cherokees. Cherokees were admonished for murdering whites in their nation. The differences between England and America should not concern the Cherokees. 4p.

Fol. 183. 25 Oct. 1775, St. Augustine. John Stuart to Earl of Dartmouth. If peace can be arranged between the Creeks and Choctaws, then those tribes and the Chickasaws and Cherokees could cooperate in attacking the rebels. 6p. [Enclosures to fol. 190b].

> Fol. 187. 12 Sept. 1775, Boston. Lt. Gen. Gage to John Stuart (copy). Stuart should order the Indians to fight against His Majesty's enemies. 3p.

> Fol. 189. 24 Oct. 1775, St. Augustine. John Stuart to Henry Stuart (copy). Henry Stuart should persuade the Upper Creeks, Cherokees, and others to act against the King's enemies. John McIntosh should approach the Chickasaws. 4p.

C.O. 5/77   ORIGINAL CORRESPONDENCE, SEC. OF STATE, INDIAN AFFAIRS: 1776

Fol. 22. 17 Dec. 1775, St. Augustine. John Stuart to Earl of Dartmouth. Stuart attaches instructions sent to deputies among the Creeks and Cherokees. Indians were told to join His Majesty's faithful subjects. Galphin, Wilkinson, and Rae (traders from Augusta) have been appointed to supervise Indian affairs in the Southern District. 4p. [Enclosures to fol. 31b].

> Fol. 28. 16 Dec. 1775, St. Augustine. John Stuart to Alex. Cameron (copy). Stuart instructs Cameron to persuade the Cherokees to cooperate with other Indians against the rebels. Continental Congress has appointed Edward Wilkinson, Geo. Galphin, and Mr. Rae to supervise Indian affairs in the Southern District. 4p.

C.O. 5/77 (CONT'D)

> Fol. 30. 15 Dec. 1775, St. Augustine. John Stuart to
> David Taitt (copy). Stuart received instructions to
> employ Southern District Indians against the rebels. 3p.

Fol. 36. 10 Feb. 1776, St. Augustine. John Stuart to Earl of
Dartmouth. Stuart submits a map of Southern District Indian
boundaries requested by Lord Hillsborough. 4p.

Fol. 38. 19 Jan. 1776, St. Augustine. John Stuart to Earl of
Dartmouth. Cherokees visited Stuart at St. Augustine. Henry
Stuart has about 5,000 lbs. of gun powder and 1,000 balls to
distribute to the Creeks and Cherokees. 4p.

Fol. 40. 6 Jan. 1776, St. Augustine. John Stuart to Earl of
Dartmouth. American superintendents of Indian affairs have
called for a Cherokee meeting at Ft. Charlotte in April and
one for Creeks at Augusta in May. 3p. [Enclosures to fol.
49b].

> Fol. 42. 4 Dec. 1775, Savannah. Gov. Wright to John
> Stuart (copy). American superintendents have called for
> meetings with the Cherokees and Creeks. 3p.

Fol. 52. 24 Oct. 1775, St. Augustine. John Stuart to Gen.
Gage. Henry Stuart was granted credit in Pensacola for the
Indian supplies that he may need [for the Creeks and Cherokees].
3p.

Fol. 63. 24 Oct. 1775, St. Augustine. John Stuart to Henry
Stuart (duplicate). [Same as C.O. 5/76/189]. 4p.

Fol. 67. 8-11 Jan. 1776, St. Augustine. John Stuart to Earl
of Dartmouth. Cameron reports that 62 Cherokees have arrived
at St. Augustine for a visit. Cherokees stand firm in their
attachment to His Majesty in spite of trying circumstances.
Richard Pearis has been taken prisoner by Cunningham's party.
2p. [Enclosures to fol. 88b].

> Fol. 69. 27 June 1775, Charleston. John Lewis Gervais
> to Alex. Cameron (abstract). Gervais reprimands Cameron
> for encouraging the Cherokees to attack S. Carolina. 3p.

> Fol. 71. 21 July 1775, Keowee. Alex. Cameron to John
> Stuart (copy). Charges against Stuart in S.C. were false.
> Indians took up arms upon learning that a party was coming
> from S.C. to kill or capture Cameron. 4p.

> Fol. 73. 21 Aug. 1775, S. Carolina. Talk from Wm. Henry
> Drayton to Cherokees (copy). Cameron has not been told
> the truth. S. Carolinians do not plan war against the
> Cherokees if the tribe remains peaceful. Drayton invites
> the Cherokees to join Mr. Pearis and himself for talks. 3p.

> Fol. 75. 26 Sept. 1775, S.C. Congress. Wm. Henry Drayton
> to Alex. Cameron (copy). Drayton requests that Cameron
> leave the Cherokees so he cannot influence them. 4p.

Fol. 77. 16 Oct. 1775, Keowee. Alex. Cameron to Wm. Henry
Drayton (copy). Cameron refuses to leave the Cherokees. 4p.

Fol. 79. 29 Oct. 1775, Charleston. Henry Lawrence
[Laurens] to Edward Wilkinson (copy). Wilkinson is ordered
to counterbalance Cameron's influence upon the Cherokees. 3p.

Fol. 81. 8 Nov. 1775. Copy of letter from Alex. Cameron
explaining that Drayton had authorized Pearis to have
Cameron killed or taken prisoner. Cameron was present at
Sugar Town when Pearis met the Cherokees. 7p.

Fol. 85. 8 Nov. 1775. Speech from Lower Cherokees to a
party setting off for East Florida (copy). Stuart should
be informed that the Cherokees have no clothes to wear or
meat to eat. 3p.

Fol. 87. 9 Nov. 1775, Keowee. Alex. Cameron to John
Stuart (copy). Indians would be uncontrollable if they
entered the dispute between Great Britain and the colonies.
Cameron could not lead the Indians against friends,
neighbors, and fellow subjects (especially women and
children). 3p.

Fol. 93. 20 May 1776, Cockspur, Georgia. John Stuart to Geo.
Germain. Although American agents have met with the Creeks,
the Cherokees, and others to obtain promises of neutrality,
Stuart believes that the tribes will aid the King. 3p.

Fol. 101. 5 Sept. 1776, Whitehall. Geo. Germain to John Stuart
(draft). Stuart's agents have permission to send ammunition to
the Indians. Should Gen. Howe operate in the Southern colonies
during the winter, Indian assistance will be very important. 8p.

Fol. 105. 6 June 1776, St. Augustine. John Stuart to Geo.
Germain. Indian agents have sent letters confirming their
tribe's friendship. 4p. [Enclosures to fol. 112b].

Fol. 107. 15 Mar. 1776. John Stuart to Maj. Gen. Clinton
(copy). Taitt has more influence with the Creeks than
Wilkinson, who was formerly a trader with the Cherokees.
Indian expenses will greatly increase because of rebel
competition. 8p.

Fol. 111. 9 May 1776, Cape Fear River. Copy of letter
from John Stuart ordering that new instructions be sent
to Mr. Cameron, Henry Stuart, and Mr. Browne. If Indians
are to be useful, officers working with the Indians should
hold some military rank. 4p.

Fol. 121. 6 Nov. 1776, Whitehall. Geo. Germain to John Stuart
(draft). Germain sent Indian goods to Pensacola. Creeks and
Choctaws will hopefully join the Cherokees against the rebels.
S.C. has offered rewards for Cherokee scalps and has declared
that Cherokee children taken prisoners will become the captors'
slaves. 6p.

C.O. 5/77 (CONT'D)

Fol. 126. 23 Aug. 1776, Pensacola. John Stuart to Geo. Germain. Henry Stuart has completed his mission to the Choctaws, Chickasaws, and Cherokees. Cherokees have attacked the frontiers, but the Creeks have refused to join them. Settlements have begun on lands supposedly purchased by Henderson. 8p. [Enclosures to fol. 199b].

>Fol. 130. 23 Mar. 1776, Cussitas. Lower Creeks to John Stuart (copy). Creeks will permit a new path for the Cherokees to Pensacola through Creek territory. Creeks want ammunition, mediation with the Choctaws, and peace with the whites. 4p.

>Fol. 132. 2 Mar. 1776, Little Tallassee. Emistisiguo and Niahahlucko to John Stuart (copy). Stuart is responsible for supplying the Upper and Lower Creeks and the Cherokees. Creeks promise friendship. 5p.

>Fol. 137. 3 May 1776. Robert Rae to Samuel Thomas, Interpreter (copy). Rae wants the Indians to be neutral. Cherokees (600) at Ft. Charlotte gave assurances that they would not fight. 3p.

>Fol. 139. 7 May 1776, Toqueh. Alex. Cameron to John Stuart (copy). Ecuij went to the American meeting at Ft. Charlotte. Other chiefs promised to listen only to the King's talks. The Terrapin, the Wolf, the Bear, and Kenatita promised to oppose American attempts to rebuild the old fort at Keowee. 6p.

>Fol. 143. 7 May 1776, Toqueh. Henry Stuart and Alex. Cameron to the inhabitants of Watauga and Nolichucky (copy). Residents are warned about Indian danger and advised to move to West Florida. 3p.

>Fol. 145. 7 May 1776, Toqueh. Henry Stuart to John Stuart (copy). Cherokees remain friendly. Some Cherokees went to Ft. Charlotte for ammunition. New settlements at the Holston R. and Watauga and the inhabitants of Carolina and Ga. have hemmed in the Cherokees. Some Cherokees have gone to talk to the Creeks. 8p.

>Fol. 149. 13 May 1776, [Watauga]. John Carter to Henry Stuart and Alex. Cameron (copy). People of Watauga and Nolichucky want peace with the Cherokees. Some inhabitants are determined to support the King. 4p.

>Fol. 151. 23 May 1776, Toqueh. Henry Stuart and Alex. Cameron to Mason Pinson and the inhabitants of Nolichucky (copy). All inhabitants, loyalist or rebel, must heed the warning about Cherokee hostilities. Residents should move to West Florida. 4p.

C.O. 5/77 (CONT'D)

Fol. 153. 23 May 1776, Toqueh. H. Stuart and Alex.
Cameron to John Carter and the inhabitants of Watauga
(extract). Young Cherokees are determined to recover
Watauga and Nolichucky. 2p.

Fol. 154. 7 June 1776, Sinnake, Cherokee Nation. Hugh
Hamilton to John Stuart (copy). All Lower Town Cherokees
are attached to the King. Rebels are building forts along
the frontier from the Savannah R. to N. Carolina. Rebels
have told Indians that they do not intend to disturb them.
3p.

Fol. 156. 28 June 1776, Toqueh. Henry Stuart to Edward
Wilkinson (copy). Stuart wants the villains who seek an
Indian war with settlements of Va. and N.C. punished.
There have been some efforts to stop attacks on Watauga
and Nolichucky. 4p.

Fol. 158. 4 July 1776, Cane Creek. Hugh Hamilton to
Alex. Cameron (copy). Without seeking Hamilton's advice,
the Cherokees attacked frontier settlements, killing about
100 and taking many women and children prisoners. 4p.

Fol. 162. 5 July 1776, Cane Creek Camp. Hugh Hamilton to
Alex. Cameron (copy). The Turkey will send Robin of
Cheowee for Cameron's clothes. The Turkey wishes Cameron's
advice in further action against the rebels. 2p.

Fol. 163a. 7-10 July 1776, Little Tallassee. David Taitt
to John Stuart (copy). Cameron informed Taitt that the
Shawnees, Delawares, and Mohawks talked with the Cherokees
and planned to visit the Creeks. Back settlements could
be supplied from Pensacola via Great Tallassee, and then
through the Lower and Middle Cherokee Settlements. 8p.

Fol. 167. 9 July 1776, Toqueh. Alex. Cameron to John
Stuart (copy). Dragging Canoe has turned the Cherokees
against Watauga and Nolichucky settlements. Northern
Indians have encouraged the Cherokees to act against white
encroachments. Cherokees expect goods and ammunition. 4p.

Fol. 169. 25 Aug. 1776, Pensacola. Henry Stuart to John
Stuart (copy). Henry Stuart describes his mission to the
Cherokees. 42p.

Fol. 193. [1776]. Talk from Committee of Fincastle County,
Va., to Oconostota and the Cherokees (copy). Committee
seeks Cherokee friendship. 4p.

Fol. 200. 23 Aug. 1776, Pensacola. John Stuart to Geo. Germain.
Gen. Clinton's plan will be costly. It involves assembling the
Creeks, supporting additional officers, and supplying the Chero-
kees. 4p. [Enclosures to fol. 203b].

Fol. 203. 1776. John Stuart. Estimate of Indian Expenses
in Southern District in 1775 and 1776. 3p.

*C.O. 5/78   ORIGINAL CORRESPONDENCE, SEC. OF STATE, INDIAN AFFAIRS:
             1776-1777*

Fol. 3.   7 Feb. 1777, Whitehall. Geo. Germain to John Stuart
(draft). Peace is arranged between the Creeks and Choctaws.
Creeks will now hopefully assist the Cherokees. 9p.

Fol. 15. 26 Oct. 1776, Pensacola. John Stuart to Geo. Germain.
Cameron's letter explains the Cherokees' distress. Stuart hopes
the Cherokees will be able to hold out a little longer since
he is sending ammunition and the Upper Creeks will soon assist
them. 10p. [Enclosures to fol. 54b].

Fol. 20. 28 Aug. 1776. Geo. Galphin to John Burgess
(copy). Indians should remain neutral or face the threat
that they will be driven from their lands and have their
towns and crops destroyed as the Cherokees experienced.
There are about 8,000 men attacking the Cherokees. 3p.

Fol. 22. 31 Aug. 1776, Toqueh. Alex. Cameron to John
Stuart (copy). Dragging Canoe and the young braves have
influenced the Cherokee chiefs to fight for the King. In
order to suppress the rebellion, Cameron hopes Stuart will
order the Creeks to join the Cherokees. 8p.

Fol. 26. 1 Sept. 1776, Savannah. Talk from Jonathan
Bryan to Creek Headmen and Warriors (copy). Bryan wants
to talk with the Creeks, to renew friendships, and to tell
the tribe about the unhappiness the Cherokees brought upon
themselves. 3p.

Fol. 30. 19 Sept. 1776, Cussita. Samuel Thomas to John
Stuart (copy). Creeks have been warned to recall their
warriors or face the same fate as the Cherokees. 4p.

Fol. 32. 26 Sept. 1776, Cussita. David Holmes to John
Stuart (copy). A general meeting with the Creeks failed
to persuade them to send any assistance to East Fla. or to
the Cherokees until they have seen Stuart. 3p.

Fol. 34. 29 Sept. 1776, Chehaws and Euchees. Thomas
Brown to John Stuart (copy). Mr. Grierson's letter
explains the Cherokee situation. Oakfuskees claim that
there was not a warrior left among the Cherokees. 10p.

Fol. 39. [Fall 1776]. Daniel McMurphy to John Burgess
(copy). If they interfere in the war, Indians risk suffering the fate of the Cherokees whose corn crop has been
destroyed by 6,000 men now in their nation. 2p.

Fol. 41. [Fall 1776]. Talk from Geo. Galphin to the
Creeks (copy). Creeks are wise to avoid the path of the
Cherokees who joined the King's side. Cherokees have seen
their towns burned, their corn cut down, and their people
driven into the woods to perish. If there are Creeks at
St. Augustine, they should be sent home. 2p.

Fol. 45. 23 Sept. 1776, Toqueh. Alex. Cameron to John
Stuart (copy). Indian relief parties were defeated. The
Valley Indians will not assist in defending their country,
and the Cherokees are divided. 7p.

Fol. 49. [Fall 1776]. Talk from Daniel McMurphy to
Sinittahaugey and Headmen at the Forks (copy). Three
great armies of 6,000 men are now in Cherokee territory.
Creeks should not join the King's troops. 2p.

Fol. 51. 18 and 22 Aug. 1776, Ogeechee. Geo. Galphin to
Timothy Barnard (copy). Americans threatened the Creeks
if they did not leave. Lower Cherokees have been driven
off their land and their towns destroyed. Cameron is
afraid of being killed by the Indians. Galphin describes
a battle with the Cherokees. 4p.

Fol. 63. 2 Apr. 1777, Whitehall. Geo. Germain to John Stuart
(draft). The King has approved Stuart's negotiations to obtain
peace between the Creeks and Choctaws. The King also approves
engaging the Creeks to assist the Cherokees. Lt. Gov. Hamilton
at Detroit will use the Indians to create a diversion along
the frontiers of Va. and Pa. which should help the Cherokees.
5p.

Fol. 72. 24 Nov. 1776, Pensacola. John Stuart to Geo. Germain.
A large body of Virginians has arrived in the Overhill Cherokee
towns. The 4,000 rebels so intimidated the Cherokees that they
fled with their families into the woods, destroying their houses
and crops to prevent utilization by the Virginians. 7p.

Fol. 76. 23 Jan. 1777, Pensacola. John Stuart to Geo. Germain.
Cherokee fate has dampened the Creek spirit. Some 200 destitute
Cherokees have taken refuge in Pensacola. 5p. [Enclosures to
fol. 82b].

Fol. 81. 19 Nov. 1776, Little Tallassee. Talk from
Emistisiguo to John Stuart (copy). Scotchie [Cameron]
and the Cherokees were obliged to run because the Virginians were so near. 3p.

Fol. 83. 24 Jan. 1777, Pensacola. John Stuart to Geo. Germain
Cherokees and Creeks are now entirely dependent upon the King's
bounty since they can no longer hunt and trade. 5p. [Enclosures
to fol. 86b].

Fol. 86. 24 Jan. 1777, Pensacola. John Stuart. General
Account of Expenses Incurred in the Southern District of
Indian Affairs from 1 Jan. 1775 - 31 Dec. 1776. Cherokee
expenses of Henry Stuart, John Stuart, and John McGillivray
totaled £5433. 3p.

Fol. 105. 10 Mar. 1777, Pensacola. John Stuart to Geo. Germain.
Most Cherokees want help. Principal chief of the Upper Creeks
set out with 300-400 men to assist the Cherokees. Virginians
plan to attack Mobile via Tombigbee. Troops from the Carolinas

C.O. 5/78 (CONT'D)

and Ga. will assist the attack by passing through the country
between the Upper Creeks and Cherokees. 4p. [Enclosures to
fol. 115b].

> Fol. 107. 19 Feb. 1777, Little Tallassee. David Taitt
> to John Stuart (extract). Emistisiguo and the Creeks went
> to aid the Cherokees because 200 rebels left Seneca to
> intercept the traders with Cherokee goods. 2p.

> Fol. 109. 23 Dec. 1776, Savannah. Talk from Gen. McIntosh
> to the Creeks (copy). British have cheated the Cherokees,
> who were foolish to believe them. Only the Americans can
> furnish goods. 6p.

> Fol. 113. 9 Feb. 1777, Pensacola. John Stuart to Capts.
> Daniel Wirdner, James MacDonald, and Cressian Reynard
> (copy). Rebels have not yet encroached upon Cherokee
> land. 6p.

Fol. 116. 10 Mar. 1777, Pensacola. John Stuart to Wm. Knox.
Supplies will hopefully arrive in time to convince the Choctaws
and Chickasaws to join a general confederacy with the Creeks and
Cherokees. Another large party of Creeks has joined the Cherokees. Nevertheless, Indians might make peace with the rebels
as some Cherokees have. 4p.

Fol. 124. 14 Apr. 1777, Pensacola. John Stuart to Geo.
Germain. Granting refuge to every person who seems loyal has
allowed rebel emissaries to approach all Indian nations. 4p.
[Enclosures to fol. 132b].

> Fol. 128. 8 Apr. 1777, Mobile. Charles Stuart to John
> Stuart (copy). Large party of Cherokees has settled
> where John Stuart's brother was attacked. 4p.

Fol. 143. 14 June 1777, Pensacola. John Stuart to Geo.
Germain. Cherokee fate is known to other Indians and dampens
their spirits. Cherokee distress is considerable and Stuart
has not been able to relieve it. Many Cherokees have stopped
fighting and others have fled to the Creeks. 8p. [Enclosures
to fol. 163b].

> Fol. 147. 19 Jan. 1777, Ft. Patrick Henry. Talk from
> Wm. Christian to the Raven, Cherokee Chief (copy). Since
> [Dragging] Canoe began the war, Christian burnt his town.
> Chilhowee was also burnt because the town refused to send
> hostages. Cherokees should make peace in Williamsburg
> and let whites settle their own dispute. 7p.

> Fol. 153. 14 May 1777, Mobile. Talk from John Stuart to
> Choctaws and Chickasaws (copy). Because rebels want Indian
> land, tribes must be vigilant to preserve their territory.
> Cherokees could not protect their hunting ground, which
> induced the tribe to go to war. Choctaws and Chickasaws
> should unite with other Southern nations to oppose the
> King's enemies. 7p.

C.O. 5/78 (CONT'D)

Fol. 157. 5 June 1777, Little Tallassee. David Taitt to John Stuart (copy). Upper Creeks plan to attack Ga. after the Green Corn Dance. Some Cherokees advised the Cowetas to attack the fort at the head of the Little R. near Buffalo Lick. 6p.

Fol. 160. 3 Mar. 1777. Talk from Patrick Henry, Jr. to Oconostota. Henry expects Oconostota and other Cherokees to meet Cols. Christian, Preston, and Shelly to confirm peace. Va. will protect the Cherokees unless they violate the peace. 4p.

Fol. 162. 28 Mar. 1777, Great Island Fort. Talk from Nathaniel Gist to Oconostota, Raven, Dragging Canoe, and Tassel (copy). Delawares and Shawnees have made peace with Virginia. English wrote Washington begging for peace since the French and Spanish have entered the war. English ships must now go home to defend England. This year will be worse than the last if the Cherokees do not make peace. 4p.

Fol. 175. 11 Oct. 1777, Whitehall. Geo. Germain to John Stuart (draft). Germain will send Stuart a commission as colonel, but it will be limited to the command of the Indians. The loss of vessels with Indian goods to S.C. privateers will probably cause Stuart some trouble, but Germain promises more presents. 6p.

Fol. 180. 5 Nov. 1777, Whitehall. Geo. Germain to John Stuart (draft). Germain sends Stuart a commission as colonel of the Indian nations within the Southern District. 2p.

Fol. 182. 24 Nov. 1777, on board the *Queen Indiaman* at Gravesend. Narrative of Wm. Grant, former sergeant in the rebel army, about the Cherokee war in 1776. 6p.

Fol. 186. 22 Aug. 1777, Pensacola. John Stuart to Geo. Germain. Stuart has been forced to send considerable presents to his deputies among the Indians since the warriors cannot hunt while employed against the rebels. Cherokees' lack of provisions made it impossible for them to fight the rebels. A Creek party has offered assistance to the Cherokees, but hunger forced the Creeks to return home after an excursion to the Va. frontier. 6p. [Enclosures to fol. 217b].

Fol. 191. 14 June 1777, St. Augustine. Brig. Gen. Prevost to John Stuart (copy). Stuart should use Indians to help Great Britain and have the tribes declare their determination to force the rebels to return to their British allegiance. Prevost suggests Stuart call an Indian congress in East Florida. 4p.

Fol. 195. 11 July 1777, Pensacola. John Stuart to Alex. Cameron (copy). Stuart opposes Cameron's idea of putting some Cherokees on the payroll. Cameron may reward their service with presents but he should remind Cherokees that defense of their lands is one of the causes of the war. 4p.

C.O. 5/78 (CONT'D)

Fol. 199. 13 July 1777, Little Tallassee. Alex. Cameron
to John Stuart (extract). Va. wanted 20 Cherokee hostages
to insure peace, but the Cherokees plan to resume war with
or without assistance as soon as they can get some corn.
More presents and provisions are needed. 4p.

Fol. 203. 14 July 1777, Pensacola. John Stuart to David
Taitt (copy). Taitt should consult with Cameron about
employing Indians against the rebels. 2p.

Fol. 205. 24 July 1777, Pensacola. John Stuart to Brig.
Gen. Prevost (copy). St. Augustine is too far away for
Choctaws, Chickasaws, Cherokees, and Upper Creeks to
attend meeting. Taitt and Cameron are going along with
the Cherokees and Upper Creeks on an expedition against
the rebel provinces. 8p.

Fol. 211. 13 Aug. 1777, Little Tallassee. David Taitt
to John Stuart (copy). Galphin promised the Creeks trade
and forgiveness if they remain neutral. Stuart has written
Cameron about employing Cherokees against the rebels. 4p.

Fol. 218. 26 July 1777, Pensacola. John Stuart to Wm. Knox.
Shawnees have attacked Henderson's settlements between the
Cumberland and Luisa Rivers. Although compelled to come to
terms with the rebels, Cherokees have informed Cameron that
they are ready to join the Creeks in attacking rebel provinces.
4p.

Fol. 220. 26 Aug. 1777, Pensacola. John Stuart to Wm. Knox.
Indians found most of the presents acceptable. Deputies took
them to the different nations. 3p.

*C.O. 5/79 ORIGINAL CORRESPONDENCE, SEC. OF STATE, INDIAN AFFAIRS:
           1777-1778*

Fol. 7. 15 Sept. 1777, Pensacola. John Stuart to Geo. Germain.
Stuart submits David Taitt's case involving a law suit concerning the return of runaway slaves. The Governors of Va., the two
Carolinas, Ga., and the Indian tribes of the Southern District
agreed in the 1763 treaty at Ft. Augusta on how to handle
fugitive slaves. 4p. [Enclosures to fol. 28b].

Fol. 9. 7 Aug. 1777. Case of David Taitt. 13p.

Fol. 16. 13 July 1777, Pensacola. David Taitt to John
Stuart (copy). Alex. Macullagh's part in Taitt's case. 4p.

Fol. 18. 3 July 1777, Pensacola. Certificate from Gov.
Peter Chester indicating that William Clifton, who decided
the case against Taitt, is Chief Justice of West Florida.
2p.

Fol. 19. July 1777, Pensacola. Proceedings in Court of
Pleas of Taitt v. Macullagh. 11p.

Fol. 25. July 1777, Pensacola. Further proceeding of
Taitt's case. 3p.

Fol. 27. 21 Aug. 1777. Statement from David Hodge and
other jurors charging irregularities in Taitt's case by
Chief Justice Clifton. 3p.

Fol. 29. 6 Oct. 1777, Pensacola. John Stuart to Geo. Germain.
After being entertained by rebels at Charleston, Creeks stopped
raid planned by Cameron and Taitt against Georgia. Cameron
(with his company of refugees and about 150 Cherokees) and
Taitt (with traders, Capt. Jackson's company, and some other
refugees) were planning to lead the Creeks. 7p. [Enclosures
to fol. 38b].

Fol. 33. 21 Sept. 1777, Little Tallassee. Alex. McGillivray to John Stuart (copy). Galphin has successfully
stopped the Lower Creeks from attacking Georgia. 4p.

Fol. 53. 10 Mar. 1778, Whitehall. Geo. Germain to John Stuart
(draft). Stuart should prevent the Spanish in New Orleans from
influencing or trading with the Indians. 4p.

Fol. 64. 23 Jan. 1778, Pensacola. John Stuart to Geo. Germain
(duplicate). About 400 Cherokees and 70 Choctaws attended
Stuart's conference with the Creeks. Cherokees criticized the
Creeks for not assisting them. Despite severe losses, the
Cherokees are ready to fight whenever called upon. 8p.

Fol. 68. 15 May 1778, Whitehall. Geo. Germain to John Stuart
(draft). Germain is pleased that the Creeks have returned to
their former loyalty and that all nations in Stuart's department
are content. 3p.

Fol. 81. 13 Apr. 1778, Pensacola. John Stuart to Geo. Germain.
Stuart refused Gov. Chester's request that Capt. Cameron and 23
Cherokee traders from his company be sent to Natchez with the
Choctaws. Cameron and his men are now serving at Mobile. 8p.
[Enclosures to fol. 106b].

Fol. 109. 1 July 1778, Whitehall. Geo. Germain to John Stuart
(draft). The newly arrived King's troops in West Fla. should
bolster Indian loyalty and encourage them to defend their
country. It should also convince rebels that attempts to settle
along Miss. R. will end in their destruction. 5p.

Fol. 112. 5 Mar. 1778, Pensacola. John Stuart to Geo. Germain
(duplicate). Cherokees have returned to their villages and are
still attached to His Majesty. Scarcity of provisions and other
disasters at home induced them to prolong their stay in Pensacola.
They will be ready to serve the King after their corn is planted.
8p. [Enclosures to fol. 124b].

Fol. 122. 10 Jan. 1778, Pensacola. Copy of Proclamation
from Peter Chester forbidding rum trade with Indians in
the Southern District. 6p.

C.O. 5/79 (CONT'D)

Fol. 125.   24 Mar. 1778, Pensacola. John Stuart to Wm. Knox.
Arms, ammunition, and other Indian presents have arrived
without damage. 3p.

Fol. 127.   16 Sept. 1776, Pensacola. John Stuart to Geo.
Germain (duplicate). Stuart awaits word about rebel forces in
Cherokee country. Chickasaws will guard the passage through
their country and at the juncture of the Cherokee and Ohio
Rivers. Little Carpenter will station himself along the Ohio
with a strong party to stop rebels there. 6p.

Fol. 132.   16 Sept. 1776, Pensacola. John Stuart to Geo.
Germain (duplicate). Stuart is sending news about the Creeks
and Cherokees. 2p.

Fol. 134.   5 Mar. 1778, Pensacola. John Stuart to Geo. Germain.
Stuart thanks Germain for the commission as colonel of the
several Indian nations within the Southern District. 3p.

Fol. 136.   2 May 1778, Pensacola. John Stuart to Geo. Germain
(duplicate). Peace with the Creeks has been hard to secure.
Fate of the Cherokees has depressed loyalist enthusiasm in the
South and has frightened the Southern Indians so much that
Stuart's influence has diminished. 8p. [Enclosures to fol.
155b].

> Fol. 140.   20 Feb. 1778, Chote, Cherokee Nation. Joseph
> Martin to John Stuart (copy). Martin is loyal and requests
> that the Cherokee trade be reopened. 2p.

> Fol. 152.   7 Apr. 1778, Little Tallassee. David Taitt to
> John Stuart (copy). Messenger with news about the success-
> ful meeting of the Abekas and Tallapooses is a Natchez
> chief warrior. He traveled beyond the Cherokee boundaries
> last year. 3p.

Fol. 156.   18 May 1778, Pensacola. John Stuart to Wm. Knox.
Stuart acknowledges notification that Indian goods have been
sent to St. Augustine. 3p.

Fol. 158.   18 May 1778, Pensacola. John Stuart to Wm. Knox.
Cherokee defeats and punishment have affected other Southern
Indians and encouraged the Cherokees to be neutral in the war.
Most of the Cherokees, nevertheless, can still be depended
upon. 3p.

Fol. 166.   5 Aug. 1778, Whitehall. Geo. Germain to John Stuart
(draft). Since war with France is imminent, Stuart should
prevent Frenchmen from trading with and visiting Indian nations
east of the Miss. R. without first taking an oath of allegiance
to His Majesty. 5p.

Fol. 173.   3 June 1778, Pensacola. John Stuart to Geo. Germain
(duplicate). Nothing will prevent Stuart from employing the
Indians and refugees to protect faithful subjects and to harrass
enemies. 6p. [Enclosures to fol. 183b].

C.O. 5/79 *(CONT'D)

Fol. 184. 10 Aug. 1778, Pensacola. John Stuart to Geo. Germain. Indians will not attack back settlements of Ga. and S.C. until the ceremony of the Busk or Green Corn Feast is over. Cherokee party is guarding the juncture of the Ohio and Cherokee Rivers in order to intercept rebel supplies from New Orleans. Cherokees intend to annoy the rebels as much as possible once harvest is over. 16p. [Enclosures to fol. 213b].

Fol. 231. 2 Dec. 1778, Whitehall. Geo. Germain to Col. John Stuart (draft). Stuart should exert his influence over the Indians to organize numerous attacks against Georgia. Germain intends to employ Wabash Indians to recover the Illinois country. Cherokees and Chickasaws will hopefully cooperate with the Wabash. 7p.

C.O. 5/80   ORIGINAL CORRESPONDENCE, SEC. OF STATE, INDIAN AFFAIRS: 1778-1779

Fol. 3. 9 Oct. and 26 Nov. 1778, Pensacola. John Stuart to Wm. Knox. Friendship with neighboring Indians will prevent a rebel attack from Ga. or Carolina. Creek chief would not want to be driven from his home as the Cherokees have, but he saw no English forces ready to help the Creeks. 12p. [Enclosures to fol. 13b].

Fol. 12. 26 Nov. 1778, Pensacola. John Stuart. List of Presents Needed for Indians in Southern District. 3p.

Fol. 18. 3 Mar. 1779, Whitehall. Geo. Germain to John Stuart (draft). A specially appointed officer will command Stuart's parties designed to work with the Indians. 3p.

Fol. 20. 4 Dec. 1778, Pensacola. John Stuart to Geo. Germain. Southern District Indians are well disposed towards His Majesty. But Cherokees are divided—many have made peace with the rebels and returned home while a greater number have moved 100 miles down the river and built a large town. Although threatened, the latter remain loyal to His Majesty. 18p. [Enclosures to fol. 62b].

Fol. 31. 8 Sept. 1778, St. Augustine. Gov. Tonyn to John Stuart (copy). Tonyn wants more Indians for Florida. 4p.

Fol. 49. 20 Nov. 1778, Little Tallassee. Alex. McGillivray to John Stuart (copy). McGillivray depends chiefly upon the Cherokees for intelligence about what the rebels think of the Creeks. Emistisiguo wanted to talk with the Cherokees and was displeased that McDonald did not visit when passing through. 3p.

Fol. 67. 31 Mar. 1779, Whitehall. Geo. Germain to John Stuart (draft). Stuart's expenses for the Southern Department have risen so much that the public and parliament have debated them. Stuart must keep within his budget, and the military must pay for and authorize his extraordinary expenses. The conquest of Ga. and arrival of Gen. Campbell will hopefully impress the Indians. 5p.

C.O. 5/80 (CONT'D)

Fol. 75. 11 Jan. 1779, Pensacola. John Stuart to Geo. Germain. Indian expenses have greatly increased because bribery is the only method of securing Indian assistance. 9p.

Fol. 88. 2 June 1779, Whitehall. Geo. Germain to John Stuart (draft). Stuart's last bills have not been accepted. Indian services do not justify wasting public funds and Stuart's deputies have been spending vast sums for their own use. 6p.

Fol. 109. 26 Mar. 1779, Pensacola. Alex. Cameron and Charles Stuart to Geo. Germain. John Stuart died 21 March. As senior deputies, Cameron and Charles Stuart will carry on until further orders. 4p.

Fol. 115. 16 June 1779, London. Paper from the Spanish Ambassador to Lord Viscount Weymouth (translation). English sent the Choctaws, Cherokees, and Chickasaws against the innocent inhabitants of Louisiana, who would have been destroyed if the Choctaws had not decided against it. 8p.

Fol. 123. 25 June 1779, Whitehall. Geo. Germain to Alex. Cameron and Lt. Col. Thomas Browne (draft). Cameron is now superintendent of the Choctaws, Chickasaws, and other nations in the western division of the Southern District. Brown will be superintendent of the Creeks, Cherokees, Catawbas, and other nations in the eastern division of the Southern District. 6p. [Enclosures to fol. 129b].

Fol. 126. 25 June 1779. Estimate of Ordinary Expenses in the Atlantic Department of the Southern District of Indian Affairs. Expenses total £1955. 2p.

Fol. 128. 25 June 1779. Estimate of Ordinary Expenses in the Mississippi Department of the Southern District of Indian Affairs. Expenses total £1955. 2p.

Fol. 142. 10 Apr. 1779, Pensacola. Alex. Cameron and Charles Stuart to Geo. Germain. Although commissioners appointed by Gov. Chester to act as superintendents are ignorant of Indian affairs, Cameron and Stuart will cooperate with them. Creeks, Choctaws, Chickasaws, and Cherokees are friendly. Cherokees in Pensacola joined the Creeks last winter in going to war. Lt. Scott in the Cherokee Nation has been ordered to get as many Indians as possible to join the soldiers and traders marching against the frontiers of Ga. and Carolina. 6p. [Enclosures to fol. 166b].

Fol. 145. 25 Mar. 1779, Pensacola. Brig. Gen. John Campbell to Charles Stuart and Alex. Cameron (copy). Campbell wants an opinion on the emergency caused by John Stuart's death. 2p.

Fol. 147. 26 Mar. 1779, Pensacola. Charles Stuart and Alex. Cameron to Brig. Gen. John Campbell (duplicate). Gov. Chester's commissioners are not qualified to be superintendents of Indian affairs in the Southern Department. 7p.

Fol. 151. 27 Mar. 1779, Pensacola. Brig. Gen. Campbell
to Alex. Cameron and Charles Stuart (copy). Cameron and
Stuart should avoid disputes with Chester's commissioners. 3p.

Fol. 153. 29 Mar. 1779, Pensacola. Alex. Cameron and
Charles Stuart to Brig. Gen. Campbell (copy). Cameron and
Stuart cannot surrender control over the Indian Department,
but they will do all they can for the King's service. 3p.

Fol. 155. 26 Mar. 1779, Pensacola. Gov. Peter Chester to
Charles Stuart (copy). Chester will appoint commissioners,
including Charles Stuart, to perform the function of the
superintendent's office. 2p.

Fol. 157. 26 Mar. 1779, Pensacola. Charles Stuart to Gov.
Peter Chester (copy). Stuart declines Chester's commission.
2p.

Fol. 159. 31 Mar. 1779, Pensacola. Circular from the
Commissioners for Indian Affairs to Charles Stuart (copy).
Commissioners request that Charles Stuart continue as
Deputy Superintendent of Indian Affairs. 2p.

Fol. 161. 31 Mar. 1779, Pensacola. Charles Stuart to
Commissioners for Indian Affairs (copy). Stuart agrees
to continue as deputy. 2p.

Fol. 163. 25 Dec. 1778, Ft. Sackville, Post Vincennes. Lt.
Gov. Hamilton to John Stuart (copy). Hamilton will send a
belt to the Chickasaws and Cherokees requesting an attack
on Va. to coincide with an English attack from the north.
6p.

Fol. 167. 6 May 1779, Mobile. Charles Stuart to Geo. Germain.
Lack of presents restricts Indian activity. There is no news
about the rebel officers who were recruiting along the Holston
River last January. 4p. [Enclosures to fol. 170b].

Fol. 171. 10 May 1779, Pensacola. Alex. Cameron to Geo.
Germain. Cameron encloses letters and talks from the Cherokees.
Rebels captured Mr. Scott, who escaped to the Cherokees. Warrior
of Cowee has been wounded three times since the rebellion began.
Edward Wilkinson, a rebel commissioner, lived among the Cherokees.
Rebels captured John Ramsay, who accompanied Cameron from the
Upper Cherokees and promised him his life if he would guide the
rebels against the Cherokees. 8p. [Enclosures to fol. 184b].

Fol. 175. Talk from Cowee Warrior to John Stuart (copy).
Cowee Warrior is loyal. 3p.

Fol. 177. 9 Apr. 1779, Ustanaula. Robert Dewes to Alex.
Cameron (extract). Dewes names Cherokee leaders (the
Raven, Young Turkey, Terrapin, and Cowee Warrior) and
towns that supplied men for Scott's expedition. Cherokees
seem unanimous against the rebels. Raven and Old Tassel
have visited McDonald. 4p.

C.O. 5/80 (CONT'D)

Fol. 179. 27 Mar. 1779, Celaquoe. Walter Scott to Alex.
Cameron (copy). Cherokees who met Scott at Celaquoe
promised to bear arms but their departure has been postponed three days at the request of Little Turkey. 7p.

Fol. 183. 2 Mar. 1779, Seneca. Edward Wilkinson to John
Ramsay (copy). Ramsay is ordered to send headman and
warriors from each Valley Town. Although Upper Town
warriors have been asked to come, they may not. 4p.

Fol. 187. 10 May 1779, Pensacola. Commissioners for Indian
Affairs to Geo. Germain. Cherokees are friendly. Walter Scott
has gone to Ga. and Carolina frontiers with 300 Cherokees.
Parties from almost every Cherokee town are joining the war,
even some from towns friendly to the rebels. Some 300 rebels
from Watauga on the Holston R. intend to attack the Cherokees
at Chickamauga. 13p. [Enclosures to fol. 231b].

Fol. 194. 16-28 Apr. 1779, Pensacola (copy). Minutes of
the Board of Commissioners for Indian Affairs recording
that Cameron and loyal refugees accompanied some Cherokees
on an expedition against Ga. and S. Carolina. Cherokees
are determined to join Gen. Prevost and Col. Campbell.
Robert Dewes was appointed assistant commissary of Indian
Affairs for the Cherokee Nation. 19p.

Fol. 210. 27 Mar. 1779, Celaquoe. Walter Scott to Alex.
Cameron. [Same as fol. 179]. 6p.

Fol. 213. 9 Apr. 1779, Ustanalla. Robert Dewes to Alex.
Cameron. [Same as fol. 177]. 4p.

Fol. 215. Talk from Tuwekee (Cowee Warrior) to John Stuart.
[Same as fol. 175]. 4p.

Fol. 217. 2 Mar. 1779, Seneca. Edward Wilkinson to John
Ramsay. [Same as fol. 183]. 3p.

Fol. 219. 15 Apr. 1779, Natchez. Mr. Alston to Hardy
Perry (extract). Some 300 rebels threaten to descend the
Holston R. and attack the Chickamaugas. 2p.

Fol. 220. 27 Apr. 1779. Copy of affidavit from Capt.
Michael Jackson stating that Americans along the Holston
River are preparing to attack Gov. Hamilton in Illinois. 2p.

Fol. 221. 21 Apr. 1779, Pensacola. Commissioners for
Indian Affairs to Charles Stuart (copy). Stuart is ordered
to continue supplying presents to visiting Indians. 4p.

Fol. 223. 3 May 1779, Pensacola. Commissioners for Indian
Affairs to Charles Stuart (copy). Commissioners recommend
economy and stricter accounting in the distribution of
supplies by Stuart. 4p.

C.O. 5/80 (CONT'D)

Fol. 232. 5 Aug. 1779, Whitehall. Geo. Germain to Alex.
Cameron (draft). Cameron is the new Superintendent of Indian
Affairs for the Miss. District. Stuart's bills will no longer
be paid. 4p.

Fol. 234. 6 Aug. 1779, Savannah. David Taitt to Geo. Germain.
In 1777 Galphin led a party of Upper Creeks to kill Cameron,
who had fled from the rebels and disaffected Cherokees. In
the fall and winter of 1778, Creeks and Cherokees were constantly at Pensacola. Hundred of Cherokees remained during
the winter in order to be supported. 12p. [Enclosures to
fol. 251b].

> Fol. 242. 30 May 1779, Pensacola. Commissioners for
> Indian Affairs to David Taitt (copy). Commissioners
> dismiss Taitt from managing Indian affairs in the Southern
> District. 3p.

> Fol. 246. 14 Mar. 1779, Headquarters. Maj. Gen. Prevost
> to David Taitt (copy). All Cherokees should be sent to
> Prevost. Taitt needs help in restraining Indians from
> wanton cruelty. 4p.

> Fol. 250. 24 May 1779, Creek Nation. Robert Grierson to
> David Taitt (extract). A rebel party came down the Chero-
> kee R. to Chickamauga and scared the women and children
> while the warriors were away. Rebels burnt Chickamauga.
> 2p.

Fol. 260. 7 Aug. 1779, Savannah. Charles Shaw to Geo. Germain.
Indian expenses have been unavoidable since the Cherokees were
driven from their settlements and their corn crops failed for
two years. Gov. Tonyn's promise to the Creeks and Seminoles
that they would be compensated for their losses in return for
immediate assistance has also been expensive. 7p. [Enclo-
sures to fol. 265b].

Fol. 271. 25 Oct. 1779, Whitehall. Wm. Knox to David Taitt
(draft). Germain has no objection to Cameron or Col. Brown
employing Taitt. 4p.

*C.O. 5/81 ORIGINAL CORRESPONDENCE, SEC. OF STATE, INDIAN AFFAIRS:
1779-1780*

Fol. 12. 18 Feb. 1780, Whitehall. Wm. Knox to Richard
Cumberland (copy). Germain thinks that £1,000 is too much for
West Florida's Indian expenses since there are no longer as
many tribes to deal with as in the past. 7p.

Fol. 37. 18 Dec. 1779, Pensacola. Alex. Cameron to Geo.
Germain. Cameron visited the Cherokees in May to incite them
to attack the frontiers. While their warriors were absent,
Virginians on the Holston R. destroyed Chickamauga. Virginians
want Great Warrior to mediate Cherokee neutrality. General
Williamson's expedition against the Cherokees prevented Savannah
from being infested by the rebels. Cherokees are dejected that
Cameron no longer works with them. 10p.

C.O. 5/81 (CONT'D)

Fol. 42.   20 Dec. 1779, Pensacola.   Alex. Cameron to Geo.
Germain.   Cameron acknowledges his appointment as Superintend-
ent of Indian Affairs for the western division of the Southern
District.   9p.   [Enclosures to fol. 70b].

> Fol. 51.   15 Dec. 1779, Pensacola.   Alex. Cameron to Gen.
> Henry Clinton (copy).   Cameron will need time and money
> before he can become as well acquainted with the Indians
> now under his care as he was with the Creeks and Cherokees.
> 8p.

> Fol. 61b.   10-15 Dec. 1779.   List of bills drawn on the
> treasury by Alex. Cameron, including Cherokee expenses.
> 3p.

Fol. 71.   1 June 1779, Pensacola.   Commissioners for Indian
Affairs to Geo. Germain.   Capt. Alex. Cameron and his company
of loyalists have been sent to recruit Cherokees for an attack
on the rebel frontier in Ga. or the Carolinas.   4p.

Fol. 73.   12 July 1779, Pensacola.   Commissioners for Indian
Affairs to Geo. Germain (quadruplicate).   Rebels have destroyed
the Chickamauga settlement, but Cameron will hopefully be able to
lead the Cherokees in seeking revenge.   Commissioners instructed
officials among the Chickasaws, Cherokees, and Choctaws to watch
the rebels along the Ohio River.   13p.   [Enclosures to fol. 93b].

> Fol. 80.   30 May 1779, Pensacola.   Commissioners for Indian
> Affairs to David Taitt and Wm. McIntosh.   Commissioners
> order Taitt and McIntosh to refrain from interfering in
> the Indian affairs of the Southern District.   3p.

> Fol. 82.   30 May 1779, Pensacola.   Commissioners for Indian
> Affairs to David Holms (copy).   Southern Indians must
> support the King.   Holms should recruit a party of Creeks
> and go to Augusta.   6p.

> Fol. 87.   20 May 1779, Pensacola.   Commissioners for Indian
> Affairs to Alex. Cameron (copy).   Cameron and his company
> should assemble a large party of Cherokees to attack the
> frontiers of Ga. or Carolina and to join the King's troops.
> Indians must be restrained from committing atrocities
> against the loyalists.   5p.

> Fol. 92.   25 May 1779, Chickasaw Nation.   Copy of letter
> from James Colbert reporting that the rebels attacked some
> Cherokees, who escaped to the Chickasaws.   Mr. Hazel
> promised to stay with the Cherokees at the mouth of Bar
> Creek.   4p.

Fol. 105.   5 Apr. 1780, Whitehall.   Geo. Germain to Alex.
Cameron (draft).   Germain was aware of Cameron's influence over
the Cherokees when Cameron was recommended for the Miss. District.
Plan for the Cherokees and the Chickasaws to cooperate with
the Wabash Indians was not carried out.   Cameron is not prohib-

ited from dealing with the Cherokees and he should form a
Chickasaw, Cherokee, and Creek alliance to counteract the
Spanish and to defend Mobile. 17p.

Fol. 151. 31 Dec. 1779, Savannah. Thomas Brown to Geo.
Germain (duplicate). Brown acknowledges his appointment as
Superintendent of Indian Affairs for the Atlantic District.
At the request of Generals Prevost and Leslie, Brown will meet
with the Creeks and Cherokees at a congress in Savannah. 4p.
[Enclosure at fol. 194].

Fol. 153. 10 Mar. 1780, Savannah. Thomas Brown. Estimate of
the Number of Officers and Expenses ... Necessary for Managing
and Conducting of the Creek and Cherokee Indians During the
War. 3p. [Enclosure of fol. 155].

Fol. 155. 10 Mar. 1780, Savannah. Thomas Brown to Geo.
Germain (duplicate). Brown notified the Creeks and Cherokees
about the Savannah congress. Some 300 Cherokees, including
traders and white men from villages destroyed by Gen. Williamson,
are camped nine miles away and will accompany Brown on an expedition under Gen. Patterson. Rebels have attempted to undermine
Creek and Cherokee loyalty. 12p. [Enclosure at fol. 153].

Fol. 161. 18 Mar. 1780, Savannah. Thomas Brown to Geo.
Germain. Cherokees have gone home from fear of a smallpox
epidemic, which cost them 2500 men earlier. A military post
is needed near Augusta to profit from Indian and loyalist help.
8p.

Fol. 171. 5 July 1780, Whitehall. Geo. Germain to Thomas
Brown (draft). Germain is confident that Brown will persuade
many Cherokees to meet Lord Cornwallis in his march through
Carolina. 7p.

Fol. 188. 25 May 1780, Savannah. Thomas Brown to Geo. Germain.
Clinton ordered Brown to march towards Augusta and add a
considerable body of Creek and Cherokee Indians to his troops
if necessary. 3p. [Enclosures to fol. 191b].

Fol. 194. 27 Dec. 1779, Savannah. Talk from Brown to Creek
Chiefs (copy). Brown, newly appointed superintendent, asks for
the Creek's support. [Cherokees received a similar talk]. 4p.
[Enclosure of fol. 151].

Fol. 204. 1 May 1780, Pensacola. Alex. Cameron to Geo. Germain
(duplicate). Commissioners' complaints astonished Cameron.
McKinnon had to purchase a supply of goods for the Cherokees
since none were available. 4p.

Fol. 206. 18 July 1780, Pensacola. Alex. Cameron to Geo.
Germain. Opaymataha (Chickasaw Leader) sent a talk to the
Choctaws threatening them with Cherokee and Shawnee attacks
if they did not return to the English interest. Some Shawnees
have settled along the Cherokee R. between the Cherokee and
Chickasaw settlements. 19p. [Enclosures to fol. 235b].

C.O. 5/81 (CONT'D)

  Fol. 218. Talk from Opaymataha (Chickasaw Leader) to
  Cameron (copy). Spanish want the Chickasaws to be friendly
  with the Choctaws, Cherokees, Delawares, and Creeks. 3p.

  Fol. 220. 17 Dec. 1779, New Orleans. Talk from Gov.
  Gálvez to Opaymataha. Chickasaws, Abemaquis [Abekas or
  Abnaki], Talapooses, Cowetas, Alibamos, Cherokees, and
  other Indians will hopefully live in friendship with Spain.
  3p. *French.*

  Fol. 230. 30 June 1780, Pensacola. Alex. Cameron to Maj.
  Gen. Campbell (copy). Cameron proposes to raise cavalry to
  accompany the Indians as Brown did in the East Division. 4p.

  Fol. 234. 25 June 1780, Pensacola. Alex. Cameron to Thomas
  Brown (copy). Campbell has prohibited further presents and
  provisions for visiting Indians from Brown's department
  except when Indian aid is absolutely required. Cameron
  wants a refund for presents and provisions given to the
  Creeks at Pensacola. 4p.

Fol. 248. 1 July 1779, Pensacola. Commissioners for Indian
Affairs to Geo. Germain (quintuplicate). 2p. [Enclosures to
fol. 281b].

  Fol. 250. 2 May – 28 June 1779, Pensacola. Minutes of
  Meeting of Commissioners for Indian Affairs (quintuplicate).
  Because Capt. Colbert was a stranger, he could not convince
  the Chickasaws and Cherokees to accompany him. Cherokees
  are determined to revenge the attack on Chickamauga. 58p.

Fol. 282. 23 Oct. 1779, Pensacola. Commissioners for Indian
Affairs to Geo. Germain (triplicate). Commissioners have closed
their accounts since Indian superintendents have been appointed.
4p. [Enclosures to fol. 313b].

  Fol. 284. 5 July – 30 Sept. 1779, Pensacola. Minutes of
  Meeting of Commissioners for Indian Affairs (copy).
  Cameron will have jurisdiction over the Choctaws, Chickasaws,
  and other Indians in Miss. district. Brown will handle the
  Creeks and Cherokees. 34p.

  Fol. 303. 1 Apr. – 30 Sept. 1779. General Account of
  Goods Purchased by the Commissioners of Indian Affairs. 2p.

  Fol. 305. 1 Apr. – 30 Sept. 1779. General Account of
  Goods Issued. 2p.

  Fol. 307. May 1779. Return of Presents Supplied to
  Alex. Cameron for the Cherokees in May 1779. 2p.

Fol. 316. 25 Aug. 1780, Savannah. Charles Shaw to Geo. Germain
(duplicate). Col. Brown has ordered presents for a general
meeting with the Creeks and Cherokees next month at Augusta to
end hostilities against Ga. and S.C. frontiers. 4p.

C.O. 5/81 (CONT'D)

Fol. 318. 18 Sept. 1780, Savannah. Charles Shaw to Geo.
Germain. Shaw has already sent a considerable supply of arms,
ammunition, and Indian goods for Brown's Indian meeting at
Augusta. Shaw hopes that the Cherokees do not meet the rebels
who attacked Augusta. 4p.

Fol. 320. Aug. 1780, Pensacola. Alex. Cameron to Geo. Germain.
Cameron's influence with the Cherokees was the principal reason
that he was appointed to handle the Choctaws and Chickasaws.
Cameron hoped that he will be equally successful with these
new tribes. Cameron was aware of John Stuart's instructions
to have Cherokees and Chickasaws cooperate with the Wabash
Indians. 12p. [Enclosures to fol. 327b].

C.O. 5/82   ORIGINAL CORRESPONDENCE, SEC. OF STATE, INDIAN AFFAIRS:
            1780-1784

Fol. 88. 20 Sept. 1780, Pensacola. Alex. Cameron to Geo.
Germain. Cameron will be very frugal but influence over Indians
without presents, provisions, and ammunition will be impossible.
4p. [Enclosures from fols. 92-108].

Fol. 90. 22 Sept. 1780, Pensacola. Alex. Cameron to Geo.
Germain. Cameron has been ordered to visit Indian nations
without proper support. Indian supplies should be consigned
only to Cameron or the superintendent. 3p.

Fol. 100. 14 Sept. 1780, Headquarters, Pensacola. Brig. Maj.
James Campbell to Alex. Cameron (copy). Cameron should person-
ally visit the Indians. Campbell will furnish ammunition. 2p.
[Enclosure of fol. 88].

Fol. 102. 18 Sept. 1780, Pensacola. Alex. Cameron to Maj. Gen.
Campbell (copy). Cameron will visit the Indians as soon as
horses are procured. He wants permission to raise a cavalry
escort and act with the Indians according to earlier plan. 6p.
[Enclosure of fol. 88].

Fol. 105. 18 Sept. 1780, Headquarters, Pensacola. Maj. Gen.
John Campbell to Alex. Cameron (copy). In the future, Indians
should furnish horses and an escort to carry ammunition given
them. 3p. [Enclosure of fol. 88].

Fol. 107. 19 Sept. 1780, Pensacola. Alex. Cameron to Maj. Gen.
Campbell (copy). Cameron requests permission to hire 50 horses
at £3 each to carry ammunition and supplies to the Indians. 4p.
[Enclosure of fol. 88].

Fol. 111. 31 Oct. 1780, Pensacola. Alex. Cameron to Geo.
Germain (duplicate). Choctaws expect their own congress since
the Creeks and Cherokees will hold one at Augusta. More money
is needed for Indians. Cameron wants to resign his post. 12p.

Fol. 117. 30 Nov. 1780, Pensacola. Alex. Cameron to Geo.
Germain (duplicate). Supplying Creeks in Pensacola increases

Cameron's expenses. Chickasaws are constantly scouting the
Miss. and Cherokee Rivers for Virginians, French, and Spanish.
13p. [Enclosures to fol. 129b].

> Fol. 128. 8 Nov. 1780, Pensacola. Alex. Cameron to Gen.
> Campbell (duplicate). Witholding Indians' presents will
> hurt the King's cause. Indians want to receive ammunition
> at the Tombigbee River. 4p.

Fol. 130. 10 Feb. 1781, Pensacola. Alex. Cameron to Geo.
Germain (duplicate). Indians fought well in attacking a village,
but the English troops were repulsed. Cameron could have recruited all the tribes for England, but he did not do so because
of expense involved. Cameron has exceeded his budget because
Gen. Campbell refused to pay for services he ordered. 9p.
[Enclosures to fol. 144b].

> Fol. 135. 27 Jan. 1781, Pensacola. Alex. Cameron to Maj.
> of Brigade James Campbell (duplicate). If Gen. Campbell
> does not pay the bill, Cameron will ask Col. Brown to do
> so. 11p.

Fol. 155. 18 Feb. 1781, Pensacola. David Taitt to Wm. Knox.
Cameron and Taitt are threatened with suits. Taitt assumed
Cameron was authorized to settle accounts in the eastern
division before Col. Brown took over. 5p. [Enclosures to fol.
162b].

> Fol. 158. 1 Feb. 1779, Pensacola. John Stuart to David
> Taitt (copy). Taitt should take a party of Indians to
> Augusta. England should provide the Cherokees with suffi-
> cient provisions to eliminate any excuse for visiting the
> Creeks. 4p.

> Fol. 160. 1 Jan. - 30 June. List of David Taitt's ex-
> penses, including payment to Robert Grierson for provisions
> supplied to the Cherokees joining the army in Georgia. 2p.

Fol. 163. 24 Sept. 1780, Savannah. Charles Shaw to Geo.
Germain (duplicate). Col. Brown defeated the rebels at Augusta.
Indians behaved with uncommon bravery and the Cherokees merit
the highest praise. Creeks and Cherokees supposedly lost many
men. 3p. [Enclosures to fol. 165b].

> Fol. 165. 23 Sept. 1780, Savannah. Printed untitled
> account of Col. Brown and Indians' battle with the rebels
> at Augusta. 2p.

Fol. 166. 14 Feb. 1781, Savannah. Charles Shaw to Geo. Germain.
Since the recapture of S.C., Cherokees have unanimously supported
the King. Many Cherokees are now operating along the frontiers
of N.C. and Va. to prevent frontier inhabitants from opposing
Cornwallis. Cherokees have destroyed settlements along the
Watauga and Holston Rivers. 4p.

C.O. 5/82 (CONT'D)

Fol. 168. 14 Feb. 1781, Pensacola. Late Commissioners for
Indian Affairs to Geo. Germain. Commissioners sent presents
and ammunition to insure Cherokee and Chickasaw friendship when
the rebels attacked those nations in the summer of 1779. 4p.
[Enclosures to fol. 173b].

Fol. 176. 6 June 1781, Whitehall. Wm. Knox to Charles Shaw
(draft). Col. Brown is directed to have the Cherokees cooperate
with Canadian Indians in attacking southern provinces and in
preventing the rebels from opposing Cornwallis. 3p.

Fol. 211. 9 Mar. 1781, Augusta. Col. Brown to Geo. Germain
(duplicate). Creeks and Cherokees have humanely confined their
attacks to enemy soldiers, something contrary to past Indian
practice. 5p. [Enclosure at fol. 450].

Fol. 218. 1 Sept. 1781, Whitehall. Wm. Knox to Col. Brown
(draft). James Wright has received many Indian presents for
the extraordinary expenses in the Indian Department. Indians
should be ready to aid St. Augustine if the Spanish attack. 4p.

Fol. 252. 9 Aug. 1781, Charleston. Col. Brown to Geo. Germain
(duplicate). Creeks arrived at Hogechee on the day that the
English capitulated. Rebels prevented the Cherokees and Creeks
from uniting. Cherokees have suffered from rebel banditti. 9p.

Fol. 277. 6 Apr. 1782, Savannah. Col. Thomas Brown to Geo.
Germain. Cherokees have been fighting everywhere with varying
success. Numerous banditti from Ohio have repeatedly attacked
Cherokee towns. In return, the Cherokees have obliged all
inhabitants over the mountains to live in blockhouses for their
security. Brown sends talk from the Raven of Chote. 7p.
[Enclosures to fol. 288b].

> Fol. 281. 10 Oct. 1781, Savannah. Col. Alured Clarke to
> Col. Thomas Brown (copy). Clarke wants Brown to employ
> Indians against the rebels along the frontier and for
> Savannah's defense. 4p.

> Fol. 283. 28 Dec. 1781, Savannah. Col. Brown to Henry
> Clinton (copy). Cherokees have suffered losses and are now
> incapable of hunting or securing needed clothing. They
> must receive supplies soon. Cherokees are following
> Cornwallis's orders. 8p.

> Fol. 287. 1 Sept. 1781, Savannah. Copy of talk from
> Raven of Chote stating that the Cherokees need ammunition
> and supplies to fight. Oconostota visited Va. to make
> rebels believe the nation wanted peace, but the purpose
> of the trip was to save corn and towns from being burnt.
> 4p.

Fol. 289. 28 Jan. 1782, Charleston. Farquhar Bethune to Geo.
Germain. Lt. Gov. Graham has been appointed superintendent,
which became vacant with Cameron's death. 6p. [Enclosures to
fol. 293b].

C.O. 5/82 (CONT'D)

Fol. 343. 25 Sept. 1782, Ft. Picolata on St. John's River.
Lt. Col. Brown to Earl of Shelburne (duplicate). Since the
evacuation of Savannah, Creeks and Cherokees have remained
loyal to the King. In the course of the war, the Cherokees
have shown uncommon fidelity and attachment. 6p.

Fol. 347. 12 Jan. 1783, St. Augustine. Lt. Col. Thomas Brown
to Thomas Townshend. Cherokees and Northern Indians at Picolata
have asked for help. Northern Indians' deputies arrived in
St. Augustine with 1,200 Cherokees to establish a confederacy
among the English tribes. They have sent emissaries to the
Choctaws and Chickasaws. Cherokees, numbering 3,000 warriors,
have decided to move to the Ohio and Tenn. Rivers. 16p.

Fol. 355. 25 Feb. 1783, St. Augustine. Lt. Col. Brown to
Thomas Townshend (duplicate). Cherokees and Creeks who left
St. Augustine last month returned home satisfied. 8p.

Fol. 367. 1 June 1783, St. Augustine. Lt. Col. Brown to
Thomas Townshend. Officers, interpreters, and traders in the
Cherokee and Creek country are ordered to withdraw. 8p.
[Enclosures to fol. 379b].

Fol. 390. 5 July 1783, St. Augustine. John Douglas to Lord
North. Douglas was appointed Indian affairs' deputy for the
western division of the Southern District in the absence of
Superintendent Graham. 4p.

Fol. 392. 30 July 1783, St. Augustine. Lt. Col. Thomas Brown
to Lord North. Brown has ordered officers, interpreters, and
traders to withdraw from Creek and Cherokee country. Those
Indians believe that England will not abandon them and have
refused to meet the rebels. Cherokees will probably have to
relinquish part of their hunting ground in Va. and the Carolinas
in order to keep the rest. 4p. [Enclosures to fol. 394b].

Fol. 395. 31 July 1783, St. Augustine. Lt. Col. Brown to Lord
North (duplicate). Bills for Brown's department have been
drawn on the treasury. Guy Carleton has ordered extraordinary
expenses paid. 2p.

Fol. 397. 15 Sept. 1783, St. Augustine. Lt. Col. Brown to
Lord North. Brown will remain at St. Augustine as superintendent until the troops are removed. Many Indians wish to accompany him to the Bahamas. 4p.

Fol. 403. 24 Oct. 1783, St. Augustine. Lt. Col. Brown to Lord
North. A party from each Creek and Cherokee town plans to visit
Brown after the Green-Corn Festival because they do not believe
that the King has divided Indian land between Va. and Spain.
4p. [Enclosures to fol. 410b].

Fol. 407. [2] Oct. 1783, St. Augustine. Lt. Col. Brown
to Brig. Gen. McArthur (copy). Supplies will be necessary

C.O. 5/82 (CONT'D)

for the many Indians expected here after the Green-Corn
Festival because they want to learn whether their English
friends will abandon them. 4p.

Fol. 409. 3 Oct. 1783, St. Augustine. Brig. Gen. McArthur
to Lt. Col. Brown. It is important to keep the good will of
Indians coming here after the Green-Corn Festival. 3p.

Fol. 418. 24 Oct. 1783, St. Augustine. Thomas Brown to Lord
North. [Duplicate of fol. 403]. 7p. [Enclosures to fol. 429b].

Fol. 422. 12 Sept. 1783, St. Augustine. Thomas Brown to
Guy Carleton. Presents will be needed to satisfy Indians
coming here after the Green-Corn Festival to learn whether
the English are forsaking them. 4p.

Fol. 424. 2 Oct. 1783. Thomas Brown to Brig. Gen.
McArthur. [Same as fol. 407]. 4p.

Fol. 426. 3 Oct. 1783, St. Augustine. Brig. Gen. McArthur
to Thomas Brown. [Copy of fol. 409]. 3p.

Fol. 430. 5 Feb. 1784, St. Augustine. John Douglas to Lord
North. Indians continue their frequent visits and do not believe
that the English will leave them to the mercy of the Spanish
and rebels. Douglas requests payment for expenses of the western
division of the Southern Department. 4p.

Fol. 432. 8 June 1784, St. Augustine. Lt. Col. Brown to Lord
North. Brown has learned that 500-600 Indians and families will
visit St. Augustine to offer refuge to their English friends.
Presents and provisions will be needed to send them away happy.
4p. [Enclosures to fol. 435b].

Fol. 434. [June 1784]. Estimate of the Expense ... for
600 Indian Gunmen and their Families. Expenses total
£3558. 2p.

Fol. 436. 15 Feb. 1784, St. Augustine. Lt. Col. Brown to Lord
North. Brown sends copies of Cherokee and Creek talks. 4p.
[Enclosures to fol. 447b].

Fol. 438. 12 Sept. 1783, St. Augustine. Lt. Col. Brown
to Guy Carleton. [Copy of fol. 422]. 4p.

Fol. 440. 4 Oct. 1783, New York. Guy Carleton to Lt. Col.
Brown (copy). Brown should dissuade the Indians from
leaving East Florida. Indian departure would destroy the
tribes and embarrass the King. 2p.

Fol. 442. 3 Oct. 1783, St. Augustine. Brig. Gen. McArthur
to Lt. Col. Brown. [Copy of fol. 409]. 3p.

Fol. 444. St. Augustine. Lt. Col. Brown to Gov. Tonyn and
Brig. Gen. McArthur (copy). Indians should be sent away
satisfied. 2p.

C.O. 5/82 (CONT'D)

Fol. 445. Gov. Tonyn and Brig. Gen. McArthur to Lt. Col. Brown. Brown's estimate for presents is barely sufficient. 2p.

Fol. 446. 17 Nov. 1783, Cherokee River. Talk from Little Turkey and Overhill Cherokees to Thomas Brown. Cherokees would rather die than forsake the English. 4p.

C.O. 5/83   ORIGINAL CORRESPONDENCE, SEC. OF STATE, MILITARY
           DISPATCHES: 1763-1765

Fol. 52. 11 Feb. 1764, New York. Maj. Gen. Gage to Earl of Halifax. Creek deserters, who had been living among the Cherokees for four to five years, were the murderers of some Carolina backsettlers. Creeks and Cherokees try to make the English suspicious of the other. 6p.

Fol. 167. 13 July 1764, New York. Maj. Gen. Gage to Earl of Halifax. Maj. Loftus can hopefully use the Cherokees and Chickasaws as mediators in taking possession of Illinois. 6p.

Fol. 172. 10 Aug. 1764, New York. Maj. Gen. Gage to Earl of Halifax. Cherokees complain about settlers on their land. Creeks and Cherokees have committed some hostilities against each other, and the Cherokees have tried to turn the English against the Creeks. Cherokees killed five Frenchmen by mistake. 6p.

Fol. 175. 13 Oct. 1764, St. James. Earl of Halifax to Maj. Gen. Gage (draft). There should be an inquiry into the Cherokee murder of five Frenchmen along the Mississippi. 3p.

Fol. 219. 13 Dec. 1764, New York. Maj. Gen. Gage to Earl of Halifax. Report that the Cherokees killed some Frenchmen is probably false since the raiding party has returned from war against the Wabash, Twightwee or Miami, Shawnee, and Delaware Indians. A Cherokee prisoner was reportedly taken to Illinois. 9p.

Fol. 285. 13 Apr. 1765, New York. Maj. Gen. Gage to Earl of Halifax. Cherokee war party on the Ohio has taken some French prisoners. Capt. Cochrane has been informed in order to obtain their release. 7p.

Fol. 306. 27 Apr. 1765, New York. Maj. Gen. Gage to Earl of Halifax. Ft. Moore will be replaced by a brick fort. Gov. Bull has sent for the two Frenchmen taken by the Cherokees. In June, Bull intends to fix the boundary between S.C. and the Cherokees to prevent disputes. 8p.

Fol. 411. 1 June 1765, New York. Maj. Gen. Gage to Earl of Halifax. Gage warns Mons. Aubry that the Cherokees and Chickasaws cannot ignore large quantities of ammunition going to their enemies. 7p.

C.O. 5/83 (CONT'D)

Fol. 455. 24 Sept. 1765, New York. Gen. Gage. General Distribution of His Majesty's Forces in North America. Ft. Prince George had 1 ensign, 1 sergeant, 1 drummer, and 22 soldiers. 1p.

C.O. 5/84   ORIGINAL CORRESPONDENCE, SEC. OF STATE, MILITARY DISPATCHES: 1765-1766

Fol. 1. 1756-1764. Amount of Bills Drawn by Gen. Gage and Others. Lists Stuart's bills for Indian presents. 7p.

Fol. 83. 28 Mar. 1766, New York. Gen. Gage to Sec. Conway. 10p. [Enclosures to fol. 113b].

Fol. 88. 29 Mar. 1766, New York. Gen. Gage. General Distribution of His Majesty's Forces in North America. Report lists Ft. Prince George in Cherokee country. 2p.

Fol. 114. 10 May 1766. Report about the Proclamation of 1763 stating that Ft. Augusta near the Creeks and Cherokees should be maintained. 28p.

Fol. 157. 24 June 1766, New York. Maj. Gen. Thomas Gage to Sec. Conway. Several Indian nations assembled at Ft. Pitt have complained about murders of their people and about new settlers. 8p. [Enclosures to fol. 166b].

Fol. 188. 26 Aug. 1766, New York. Gen. Gage to Duke of Richmond. Gage sends an estimate of expenses from the Cherokee meeting. 8p. [Enclosures to fol. 195b].

Fol. 192. 8 Aug. 1766, Charleston. John Stuart to Gen. Gage (extract). Friendship with the Cherokees and Choctaws is necessary. When the boundary line is surveyed in N.C., Cherokee leaders should be made Medal Chiefs to counteract the insinuations of the Creeks and to prepare them for service if war breaks out with the Creeks. 3p.

Fol. 194. Copy of an Estimate of Expenses in Convening the Chiefs of the Cherokee Nation at Ninety Six. Estimate totals £10,450 in S.C. currency. 2p.

Fol. 216. 10 Oct. 1766, New York. Gen. Gage to Earl of Shelburne. 7p. [Enclosures to fol. 224b].

Fol. 220. 10 Oct. 1766. Gen. Gage. General Distribution of His Majesty's Forces in North America. Report lists Ft. Prince George in Cherokee country. 2p.

Fol. 235. 21 Nov. 1766, War Office. Lord Barrington to Earl of Shelburne. 2p. [Enclosures to fol. 240b].

Fol. 237. 11 Oct. 1766, New York. Estimated budget from Gen. Gage to the Sec. of War (abstract). Budget lists expenses of transporting provisions to Fts. Wm. Augusta, Prince George, and Charlotte. 3p.

C.O. 5/84 (CONT'D)

Fol. 239. 11 Oct. 1766, New York. Gen. Gage to Lord
Barrington (copy). Northern and Southern Indian superintendents should list their employees and annual pay. 4p.

Fol. 243. 9 Dec. 1766, War Office. Lord Barrington to Earl of
Shelburne. 2p. [Enclosures to fol. 252b].

Fol. 245. 20 Oct. 1766, New York. Gen. Gage to Lord
Barrington (copy). Gage sends a list of the superintendent's staff for Indian affairs in the Northern District
and will forward Stuart's list for the Southern District
as soon as possible. 4p.

Fol. 253. 11 Dec. 1766, Whitehall. Earl of Shelburne to Gen.
Gage (draft). It is doubtful that any method of managing the
Indians is better than leaving trade to the care of local of-
ficials and providing them with some general rules. Southern
Indians are not managed as well as they could be 14p.

Fol. 260. 12 Nov. 1766, New York. Gen. Gage to Earl of
Shelburne. Only way to prevent the Indians from being cheated
is to confine trade to forts, but the Indians want goods to be
sent into their nations. Traders with Spanish licenses are
reportedly selling merchandise to the Indians cheaper. 8p.

Fol. 264. 23 Dec. 1766, War Office. Lord Barrington to Earl of
Shelburne. 2p. [Enclosures to fol. 266b].

Fol. 266. Robert Leake. An Estimate of the Expense of
Provisions for His Majesty's Troops (copy). Report lists
Ft. Loudoun. 2p.

*C.O. 5/85 ORIGINAL CORRESPONDENCE, SEC. OF STATE, MILITARY
            DISPATCHES: 1766-1767*

Fol. 9. 23 Dec. 1766, New York. Thomas Gage to Earl of
Shelburne. Best way to end a threatened Creek war is to attack
the tribe from all sides with every Indian nation available and
with troops from S.C. and Georgia. 10p. [Enclosures to fol.
19b].

Fol. 45. 1767. Abstract of Contingent Charges in North America
for 1767. Report includes an estimate of the cost of Southern
Indian relations. 4p.

Fol. 47. 20 Feb. 1767, New York. Thomas Gage to Earl of
Shelburne. Cherokees are distressed by their losses from
disease and from the war with Northern Indians. They have
asked the superintendent to mediate peace. Setting Indians
against one another is detrimental to the King's interest. 4p.
[Enclosures to fol. 56b].

Fol. 57. 22 Feb. 1767, New York. Thomas Gage to Earl of
Shelburne. There is no better plan for managing Indians than
the present one. Restricting Indian trade to posts cannot be
successful. 10p. [Enclosures to fol. 71b].

Fol. 62. June-Dec. 1766. Journal of Capt. Harry Gordon.
French garrisoned Ft. Massaic to contain Cherokee parties
harassing French traders among the Wabash and Shawnees.
A new fort along the Ohio will prevent the French from
visiting the Wabash Indians and will equalize the strength
between the Cherokee and the Wabash. 18p.

Fol. 72. 3 Apr. 1767, New York. Thomas Gage to Earl of
Shelburne. Fts. Prince George and Charlotte are not useful
for trade but can be helpful in case of an Indian war. 14p.
[Enclosures to fol. 82b].

Fol. 83. 4 Apr. 1767, New York. Thomas Gage to Earl of
Shelburne. There are many reasons for the recent increase in
the expense of the Northern and Southern Indian Departments.
6p.

Fol. 91. 7 Apr. 1767, New York. Thomas Gage to Earl of
Shelburne. Because of Northern Indian hostility, the Cherokees
supposedly murdered the Virginians in revenge for the unpunished
murder of Cherokees two years ago. 8p. [Enclosures to fol.
98b].

Fol. 107. 29 Apr. 1767, New York. Thomas Gage to Earl of
Shelburne. Cherokees have not answered charges concerning the
murder of seven Va. traders. If this can be settled, Stuart
wants to send Cherokee deputies to New York to negotiate peace
with their northern enemies. 6p. [Enclosures to fol. 112b].

Fol. 117. 27 May 1767, New York. Thomas Gage to Earl of
Shelburne. Cherokees did not murder seven Va. traders. Northern
Indians at war with the Cherokees evidently killed Mr. Boyd.
Cherokees will send deputies to negotiate peace with the
Northern Indians. Northern tribes, however, will evidently
consent to peace only if the Cherokees acknowledge themselves
as conquered. 8p. [Enclosures to fol. 125b].

Fol. 145. 20 Aug. 1767, New York. Thomas Gage to Earl of
Shelburne. Too many licensed traders from various provinces
have created disorder in Indian country. 6p. [Enclosures to
fol. 154b].

Fol. 148. 21 July 1767, Charleston. John Stuart to Gen.
Gage (extract). Sending Indian presents to the various
governors to distribute increases expenses of the Indian
department. 3p.

Fol. 150. May 1767. Speeches from Saluy (Cherokee)
and other Indian chiefs to John Stuart (extract). Indians
discuss trade. 4p.

Fol. 155. 24 Aug. 1767, New York. Thomas Gage to Earl of
Shelburne. Stuart has sent good news about the Indian meetings
at Hard Labor and Augusta. Traders have agreed to lower their
prices. Indians complained about ill treatment suffered in
traveling during the war against the Southern tribes. 11p.
[Enclosures to fol. 162b].

C.O. 5/85 (CONT'D)

Fol. 201. 14 Nov. 1767, Whitehall. Earl of Shelburne to Gen. Gage (draft). Bd. of Trade is considering whether or not to eliminate forts and to entrust Indian affairs to the respective colonies. Shelburne has instructed the Lt. Gov. of Va. to complete the boundary with the Western Indians. 8p.

Fol. 205. 10 Oct. 1767, New York. Thomas Gage to Earl of Shelburne. Lt. Gov. Fauquier has done everything possible to punish the murderers of the [Cherokees], but frontiersmen rescued them from jail. 9p.

C.O. 5/86   ORIGINAL CORRESPONDENCE, SEC. OF STATE, MILITARY DISPATCHES: 1768

Fol. 9.   22 Jan. 1768, New York. Gen. Gage to Earl of Shelburne. Gage sent to Wm. Johnson the Cherokee deputies who arrived to make peace with the Northern Indians. Cherokees said that the Creeks killed two whites along the St. Mary's R. in East Florida. 10p.

Fol. 30. 12 Mar. 1768, Whitehall. Earl of Hillsborough to Maj. Gen. Gage (draft). Hillsborough is sending a map which indicates the Indian line already settled with the Choctaws, Creeks, Cherokees, and the proposed settlement with the Six Nations. 8p.

Fol. 59. 14 May 1768, Whitehall. Earl of Hillsborough to Maj. Gen. Gage (draft). Hillsborough instructs Gage on dealing with the Indians. 3p.

Fol. 76. 25 Apr. 1768, New York. Gen. Gage to Earl of Shelburne. Letter intended for Johnson concerning the Indian boundary will probably reach him before the Indians attending a congress with the Cherokees have returned home. 3p.

Fol. 113. 18 June 1768, New York. Gen. Gage to Earl of Hillsborough. Gage received a report from Ft. Prince George concerning Creek hostility. Some Creeks have incited the Cherokees against the English. 6p.

Fol. 140. 20 June 1768. Copy of the *Massachusetts Gazette* announcing the death of Kittagusta, Prince of Chote. Miss. and Ohio Indians continue to harass Upper Cherokees, and renegade Creeks have given inflammatory speeches to the Cherokees. 1p.

Fol. 145. 17 Aug. 1768, New York. Maj. Gen. Gage to Earl of Hillsborough. Cherokees will meet the Va. commission at Col. Chiswell's Mine to run the boundary line. Cherokees are satisfied with the boundary and with the new peace with the Northern Indians. 10p.

Fol. 170. 9 Sept. 1768, New York. Maj. Gen. Gage to Earl of Hillsborough. Lt. Gov. Bull has sent individuals to watch over Fts. Prince George and Charlotte. 7p.

C.O. 5/86 (CONT'D)

Fol. 196. 9 Oct. 1768, New York. Maj. Gen. Gage to Earl of
Hillsborough. A Cherokee interpreter blames hunters for the
recent massacre. Cherokee chiefs asked Stuart to explain why
troops have departed from Ft. Prince George. 4p.

C.O. 5/87   ORIGINAL CORRESPONDENCE, SEC. OF STATE, MILITARY
*   DISPATCHES: 1769*

Fol. 60. 7 Jan. 1769, New York. Maj. Gen. Gage to Earl of
Hillsborough. Season is too advanced to finish line between
Va. and the Cherokees, but the Indians will meet next spring
to complete unmarked part. Cherokees claim country below the
Kanawha River. 3p.

Fol. 72. 24 Mar. 1769, Whitehall. Earl of Hillsborough to
Maj. Gen. Gage (draft). The King approves Stuart's boundary
settlement with the Southern Indians, but the Cherokee line
must be delayed until the value of the land is determined. 10p.

Fol. 84. 13 May 1769, Whitehall. Earl of Hillsborough to Maj.
Gen. Gage (draft). Hillsborough sends copies of the King's
speech to Parliament, circular letter to the governors, and
letters to Johnson and Stuart regarding the boundary line. 4p.

Fol. 86. 1 Apr. 1769, New York. Maj. Gen. Gage to Earl of
Hillsborough. Va. objects to the Cherokee boundary. Col. Lewis
and Doctor Walker will confer with Stuart about the line.
Cherokees complain that hunters from Va. and N.C. trespass on
their hunting grounds. 7p.

Fol. 101. 10 June 1769, New York. Maj. Gen. Gage to Earl of
Hillsborough. Stuart delayed a new boundary treaty between Va.
and the Cherokees until the King's orders were received. 8p.

Fol. 119. 15 July 1769, Whitehall. Earl of Hillsborough to
Maj. Gen. Gage (draft). Government has left the management and
expense of Indian commerce to the colonies, and the King intends
to limit annual Indian expenses to £5,000 for the Northern
District and £4,000 for the Southern. 4p.

Fol. 144. 20 Dec. 1768, Williamsburg. David Ross to Alex.
Cameron. [Extract of C.O. 5/71/65]. 2p.

Fol. 157. 9 Sept. 1769, New York. Maj. Gen. Gage to Earl of
Hillsborough. There are illegal designs to obtain Indian land
at the negotiations for the Va. boundary treaty. Johnson hopes
to influence the Indian council at Onondaga. 8p. [Enclosures
to fol. 162b].

   Fol. 161. 8 Aug. 1769, Carlisle. John Armstrong to
   Joseph Shippen, Sec. to John Penn (copy). Cherokees
   mistreated Va. frontiersmen while returning home from the
   peace treaty with the Western and Northern tribes. 5p.

C.O. 5/88   ORIGINAL CORRESPONDENCE, SEC. OF STATE, MILITARY
            DISPATCHES: 1769-1770

Fol. 26.   6 Jan. 1770, New York. Maj. Gen. Gage to Earl of
Hillsborough. Onondaga Congress between the Six Nations and
Cherokees has forced the English to choose between permitting
the tribes to war with each other or trying to unite them. The
latter choice would be dangerous. 8p. [Enclosures to fol. 31b].

> Fol. 30.   8 Dec. 1769, Johnson Hall. Sir Wm. Johnson to
> Gen. Gage (copy). Cherokees want the Six Nations and
> Caughnawagas to unite against common enemies among the
> Western and Southern Indians. 4p.

Fol. 44.   1 Jan. 1770, Philadelphia. Geo. Croghan to Gen. Gage
(copy). Hurons, Chippewas, Ottawas, and Potawatomis will
confirm a peace with the Cherokees. This peace will be detrimental to the public interest. 4p.

Fol. 62.   24 Apr. 1770, New York. Lt. Gen. Gage to Earl of
Hillsborough. Stuart objects to the extension of the boundary
between Va. and the Cherokees. Gage points out difficulties
if the Northern Indian boundary is extended. 7p. [Enclosures
to fol. 69b].

Fol. 72.   12 June 1770, Whitehall. Earl of Hillsborough to Lt.
Gen. Gage (draft). Indian boundary line has produced the same
evils that it was supposed to remedy. 8p.

Fol. 76.   14 May 1770, New York. Lt. Gen. Gage to Earl of
Hillsborough. Cherokees are determined to continue the war with
the Western Nations. This pressure may prevent the Wabash Indians from disturbing the English in Illinois. Cherokees
complain about traders and boundary line. 7p. [Enclosures to fol.
81b].

> Fol. 80.   27 Jan. 1770, New Orleans. Gen. Alex. O'Reilly
> to Commanding Officers of Spanish posts on the Mississippi
> (translation). Lt. Gov. must prevent Spanish Indians from
> harassing the English and he should encourage the tribes
> to live in peace with the English and other Indians. 3p.

Fol. 92.   2 June 1770, New York. Lt. Gen. Gage to Earl of
Hillsborough. The meeting between the Six Nations and Cherokees cannot be postponed much longer. Shawnees have already
met the visiting Cherokees. 5p.

Fol. 122.   18 Aug. 1770, New York. Lt. Gen. Gage to Earl of
Hillsborough. Shawnees and Delawares are reportedly planning a
general confederation of Northern, Southern, and Western Indians.
8p. [Enclosures to fol. 136b].

Fol. 139.   28 Sept. 1770, Whitehall. Earl of Hillsborough to
Lt. Gen. Gage (draft). Although a Northern and Southern Indian
confederation would be dangerous, Hillsborough fears that peace
between the Creeks and Choctaws may threaten West Florida. Indian affairs are unstable because of Stuart's inattention. 6p.

C.O. 5/88 (CONT'D)

Fol. 146. 8 Sept. 1770, New York. Lt. Gen. Gage to Earl of
Hillsborough. Johnson has stopped the Western Indian's plan
to form a confederation. Virginia's Assembly has appropriated
money to help pay for marking the boundary with the Cherokees.
7p. [Enclosures to fol. 151b].

Fol. 160. 15 Nov. 1770, Whitehall. Earl of Hillsborough to
Lt. Gen. Gage (draft). Johnson has temporarily averted a
dangerous confederacy between the Northern and Southern
Indians. 4p.

Fol. 164. 10 Nov. 1770, New York. Lt. Gen. Gage to Earl of
Hillsborough. Gage points out some of the Indian trade
problems in the Northern and Southern Districts. 18p.

Fol. 174. 12 Nov. 1770, New York. Lt. Gen. Gage to Earl of
Hillsborough. The Western nations and the Wabash have agreed
to make peace with the Cherokees. The Six Nations promise to
war against any people the Cherokees desire. It is fortunate
that Virginia was prevented from extending their boundary
farther than the Cherokees wanted. 5p. [Enclosures to
fol. 262b].

*C.O. 5/89   ORIGINAL CORRESPONDENCE, SEC. OF STATE, MILITARY
             DISPATCHES: 1770-1771*

Fol. 11. 7 Dec. 1770, New York. Lt. Gen. Gage to Earl of
Hillsborough. A Six Nations party has returned with four
Choctaw scalps given to them by the Cherokees. The Six Nations
are not sure how long the Cherokees will continue the war
against the Choctaws. 6p. [Enclosures to fol. 19b].

Fol. 33. 16 Jan. 1771, New York. Lt. Gen. Gage to Earl of
Hillsborough. Stuart will send information about the Cherokee
boundary treaty with Virginia. Western Indians continue to
raid Cherokee country. 5p. [Enclosures to fol. 65b].

Fol. 80. 2 Apr. 1771, New York. Lt. Gen. Gage to Earl of
Hillsborough. Stuart believes that the Shawnees have influenced
the Cherokees to misbehave. 7p. [Enclosures to fol. 91b].

Fol. 84. 7 Mar. 1771, Ft. Pitt. Copy of Intelligence
from Ft. Pitt. As directed by the Six Nations, the
Shawnees and Delawares are seeking peace with the Western
and Southern Indians to free themselves to attack in the
north. Cherokees and Southern nations, meanwhile, will
strike at the frontiers of the Carolinas and Virginia. 4p.

Fol. 86. [ca. Mar. 1771], Ft. Pitt. Copy of Intelligence
from Ft. Pitt. Six Nations told the Shawnees to talk with
the Western and Southern nations. If all unite, they
could drive the English out within four years since the
whites own no land in their territory. 4p.

Fol. 99. 7 May 1771, New York. Lt. Gen. Gage to Earl of
Hillsborough. The numerous Northern Indians who visited the

C.O. 5/89 (CONT'D)

Cherokees have frightened the S. Carolinians. Northern warriors wanted to attack the whites, but the Cherokees refused. They did agree to attack the Chickasaws. 8p.

Fol. 170. 1 Oct. 1771, New York. Lt. Gen. Gage to Earl of Hillsborough. If necessary, Gage will talk with Stuart about obtaining aid from the Cherokees and Chickasaws. 8p. [Enclosures to fol. 177b].

C.O. 5/90   ORIGINAL CORRESPONDENCE, SEC. OF STATE, MILITARY DISPATCHES: 1772-1773

Fol. 3. 4 Dec. 1771, New York. Lt. Gen. Gage to Earl of Hillsborough. 4p. [Enclosures to fol. 6b].

Fol. 5. Speech from the Delawares, Munsees, and Mohegans to the Governors of Pennsylvania, Maryland, and Virginia (copy). Six Nations sold to the English all the lands east of the Ohio R. and south to the Cherokee River. Now there is encroachment west of the Alleghanies. Cherokees and the Six Nations are forced to meet frequently because the tribes believe that the English are plotting against Indians living in the Ohio territory. 4p.

Fol. 15. 5 Feb. 1772, New York. Lt. Gen. Gage to Earl of Hillsborough. Those Wabash and other Indians who killed the English in Illinois and captured English boats on the Ohio R. attacked the Cherokees. 5p.

Fol. 77. 7 Oct. 1772, New York. Lt. Gen. Gage to Earl of Hillsborough. Cherokees intend to make peace with Northern and Western Indians. Creeks claim the lands that the Cherokees gave to traders in repayment for debt. Cherokees killed seven Virginians and a Negro. There are new settlers on Cherokee land. 6p.

Fol. 80. 4 Nov. 1772, New York. Lt. Gen. Gage to Earl of Dartmouth. Creeks have conferred with the Cherokees and Six Nations about a war against the English. 4p. [Enclosures to fol. 83b].

Fol. 86. 9 Dec. 1772, Whitehall. Earl of Dartmouth to Lt. Gen. Gage (draft). Western and Southern Indians' refusal to meet the Six Nations at Scioto is troublesome. 3p.

Fol. 102. 6 Jan. 1773, New York. Lt. Gen. Gage to Earl of Dartmouth. Ohio Indians sent belts to the Southern Nations and held meetings. These activities were probably in response to a plan for a general confederacy formed three years ago between Western and Southern nations. 6p. [Enclosures to fol. 106b].

Fol. 114. 8 Feb. 1773, New York. Lt. Gen. Gage to Earl of Dartmouth. Stuart is still negotiating with the Southern tribes but thinks that the Cherokees will not act independently from the Six Nations. Cherokees are grateful for the English mediation in making peace with the Six Nations. 4p. [Enclosures to fol. 117b].

C.O. 5/90 (CONT'D)

Fol. 178. 4 Aug. 1773, New York. Maj. Gen. Frederick Haldimand
to Earl of Dartmouth. Boundary line for lands ceded by Creeks
and Cherokees has been settled at Augusta. Creeks want to involve the Chickasaws and Cherokees in their quarrel against the
Choctaws. 6p. [Enclosures to fol. 182b].

Fol. 183. 31 Aug. 1773, New York. Maj. Gen. Haldimand to Earl
of Dartmouth. John Collins murdered two Cherokee warriors.
Haldimand promised justice to the friends of the deceased. 6p.
[Enclosures to fol. 187b].

> Fol. 186. 28 June 1773, Pittsburgh. Talk from Shawnees
> to Keashuta and Alex. McKee (copy). Six Nations and
> Cherokees have sold Shawnee land. 3p.

*C.O. 5/91 ORIGINAL CORRESPONDENCE, SEC. OF STATE, MILITARY DISPATCHES:
1774*

Fol. 14. 5 Jan. 1774, New York. Maj. Gen. Haldimand to Earl
of Dartmouth. Haldimand does not expect Indian problems in the
Northern and Southern Departments. 4p. [Enclosures to fol. 17b].

Fol. 113. 2 Mar. 1774, New York. Maj. Gen. Haldimand to Earl
of Dartmouth. 8p. [Enclosures to fol. 130b].

> Fol. 117. 3 Feb. 1774, Charleston. John Stuart to Maj.
> Gen. Haldimand (copy). Creeks have murdered whites in the
> newly ceded lands. Cherokees continue to be friendly but
> are suspected of murdering a Virginian. Cameron will
> reside at Keowee. 8p.

> Fol. 121. 20 Dec. 1773, [Williamsburg]. Gov. Earl of
> Dunmore to John Stuart (abstract). There should be an
> inquiry into the reported murder of a Virginian by Cherokees.
> 1p.

> Fol. 122. 14 Dec. 1773, Virginia. Arthur Campbell to
> Earl of Dunmore (copy). Cherokees supposedly murdered
> Mr. Russell, 4 whites, and 1 Negro. 2p.

> Fol. 127. 28 Jan. 1774, Savannah. John Stuart to Alex.
> Cameron (copy). Cherokees are the principal concern of
> Cameron's superintendency. If the Cherokees attempt to
> join the Creeks, Cameron must send for Great Warrior. 3p.

> Fol. 129. 27 Jan. 1774, Savannah. James Wright to John
> Stuart (copy). Choctaws should be encouraged in their war
> against the Creeks. Stuart should cultivate Cherokee and
> Chickasaw friendship in case their assistance is needed
> against the Creeks. 3p.

Fol. 133. 5 Apr. 1774, New York. Maj. Gen. Haldimand to Earl
of Dartmouth. Wm. Johnson believes that the Six Nations might
prevent the Cherokees from joining the Creeks against English.
Last year's Creek and Cherokee congress cost £1750. 4p.
[Enclosures to fol. 135b].

C.O. 5/91 (CONT'D)

Fol. 135. 27 Jan. 1774, Little Tallassee. David Taitt to [John Stuart] (extract). Cowetas living with the Cherokees murdered the six people at the head of the Ogeechee River. 3p.

C.O. 5/94 ORIGINAL CORRESPONDENCE, SEC. OF STATE, MILITARY DISPATCHES: 1776-1777

Fol. 34. 17 Jan. 1777, New York. Gen. Howe to Geo. Germain 2p. [Enclosures to fol. 97b].

Fol. 39. 30 Aug. 1776, Pensacola. John Stuart to Gov. Tonyn (copy). Encouraged by the Northern Indians, some 2,000 Cherokees attacked the settlements. Creeks will not join the Cherokees. 3p.

Fol. 43. 30 Aug. 1776, Pensacola. John Stuart to Gen. Howe (copy). Cherokees attacking the frontier inhabitants are upset by encroachment on their hunting grounds. Six Nations, Shawnee, Delaware, and Western Confederacy deputies claim that their situation is the same. Virginian settlers on Watauga and Holston Rivers have refused the Cherokee request to leave. 8p.

Fol. 47. 10 June 1776, Charleston. Robert Millar and Richard King to Alex. Cameron (copy). Lower Town Indians would be peaceful if left alone. 10p.

Fol. 52. 13 May 1776. John Carter for the people at Watauga to Henry Stuart and Alex. Cameron. [Same as C.O. 5/77/149]. 3p.

Fol. 54. 5 July 1776, Cane Creek Camp. Hugh Hamilton to Alex. Cameron. [Same as C.O. 5/77/162]. 2p.

Fol. 58. 2 Mar. 1776, Little Tallassee. Talk from Emistisiguo to John Stuart. [Same as C.O. 5/77/132]. 4p.

Fol. 62. 4 July 1776, Cane Creek. Hugh Hamilton to Alex. Cameron. [Same as C.O. 5/77/158]. 4p.

Fol. 64. 7 June 1776, Sinnake in Cherokee Nation. Hugh Hamilton to John Stuart. [Same as C.O. 5/77/154]. 3p.

Fol. 68. 28 June 1776, Toqueh. Henry Stuart to Edward Wilkinson. [Same as C.O. 5/77/156]. 3p.

Fol. 70. 23 March 1776. Talk from Lower Creeks to John Stuart. [Same as C.O. 5/77/130]. 3p.

Fol. 76. 8 May 1776. Robert Rae to Thomas Graham (copy). Capt. Stuart's brother arrived in the Overhill Cherokee towns with 20 whites to lead the Indians against the settlements. Cherokees (600) were present at congress held Apr. 1. 4p.

Fol. 78. 3 May 1776. Robert Rae to Samuel Thomas, Interpreter. [Same as C.O. 5/77/137]. 3p.

C.O. 5/94 (CONT'D)

Fol. 80. 13 Jan. 1777, New York. Gen. Howe to John Stuart
(copy). If the Cherokees are already at war, Stuart should
urge neighboring tribes to join them. 6p.

Fol. 87. 30 Aug. 1776, Pensacola. Gov. Chester to Gen.
Howe (copy). Little Carpenter reports that 1,000 Cherokees have attacked settlers from Carolina and Va. living
on Indian land. 4p.

Fol. 153. 4 Apr. 1777, New York. Gen. Howe to Geo. Germain.
3p. [Enclosures to fol. 162b].

Fol. 155. 22 Dec. 1776, Pensacola. John Stuart to Gen.
Howe (copy). Creeks favor the English but are cautious
because of what happened to the Cherokees. Cherokee
attack on settlements of N.C. and Va. forced Virginians
to retreat from the Cherokee land. 3p.

Fol. 157. 14 Nov. 1776, Attowa Hatchie. Talk from
Dragging Canoe to Alex. Cameron (copy). Virginians refused
to talk with Little Carpenter but want Cherokees to join
them against the King. 7p.

Fol. 161. 19 Nov. 1776, Little Tallassee. Talk of
Emistisiguo to John Stuart. Virginians have forced the
Cherokees to flee and are now advancing towards the Creeks.
3p.

Fol. 213. 5 June 1777, New York. Gen. Howe to Geo. Germain.
Stuart's talk to the Southern Indians and other factors will
probably help protect the Floridas. 3p. [Enclosures to fol.
236b].

Fol. 219. 28 Apr. 1777, St. Augustine. Gov. Tonyn to Gen.
Wm. Howe (extract). Stuart's deputies are ordered to send
the Upper Creeks to middle Ga. and Savannah if possible.
Cherokees will invade Carolina. 3p.

Fol. 227. [May-June 1777]. Talk from Howe to the Cherokees, Creeks, Choctaws, and Chickasaws (copy). Howe
praises the Indians for their fidelity to the King and
willingness to help subdue disloyal whites. 4p.

Fol. 269. 15 July 1777, New York. Gen. Howe to Geo. Germain.
England is losing the friendship of Southern Indians because
unreliable traders have been licensed and because the Indians
received too much liquor. 4p. [Enclosures to fol. 289b].

Fol. 271. 12 July 1777, New York. Gen. Howe to Gov.
Chester (copy). Indian provisions and presents have been
sent to Stuart by ship. Rum should be kept from the
Indians. 4p.

Fol. 273. 10 Apr. 1777, Pensacola. Copy of conference
report between Gov. Chester, Lt. Col. Stiell, and John
Stuart. Stuart should encourage the formation of a
Southern Indian confederacy for mutual protection and to

C.O. 5/94 (CONT'D)

support the King. English should provide the Cherokees
with supplies, ammunition, and arms and encourage the Creeks
and other Indians to assist the Cherokees. 4p.

Fol. 279. 4 Mar. 1777, Pensacola. John Stuart to Gen.
Howe (copy). Although the Cherokees have been severely
chastised by the rebels, they are determined to continue
the war. Some Upper Creeks will assist the Cherokees under
Cameron's direction. 6p.

Fol. 282. 13 Apr. 1777, Pensacola. John Stuart to Gen.
Howe (copy). Emistisiguo has not been heard from since
going to assist the Cherokees. There will be no difficulty
in getting Indians to help the King's forces. 4p.

Fol. 299. 3 Sept. 1777, Whitehall. Geo. Germain to Gen. Howe
(draft). 3p. [Enclosures to fol. 302b].

Fol. 301. [June–July 1777]. Memorial from Gov. Campbell
et al. to Geo. Germain. The attack on the Southern colonies should not be delayed. Indians are impatient. 4p.

*C.O. 5/95   ORIGINAL CORRESPONDENCE, SEC. OF STATE, MILITARY
              DISPATCHES: 1777-1778*

Fol. 35. 8 Mar. 1778, Whitehall. Geo. Germain to Henry Clinton
(draft). Ga. and S.C. should be conquered. Fla. rangers and
Indians under Provost will attack Southern frontiers while
Stuart moves a large body of Indians toward Augusta. 27p.

*C.O. 5/97   ORIGINAL CORRESPONDENCE, SEC. OF STATE, MILITARY
              DISPATCHES: 1778-1779*

Fol. 233. 3 May 1779, New York. Gen. Henry Clinton to Geo.
Germain. John Stuart has died. Cameron will assume the
superintendency of Indian affairs until further orders. 4p.
[Enclosures to fol. 236b].

Fol. 235. 13 Jan. 1779, Vincennes. Lt. Gov. Henry
Hamilton to Commandant at Natchez. The Southern tribes
(Chickasaws, Cherokees, Shawnees, Delawares, and others),
the Northern tribes (Mingoes, Miamis, Wyandats, and
Senecas), and the Great Lakes tribes (Potawatomis, Ottawas,
Chippewas, and Hurons) will undertake an expedition against
Va. in the spring. Many Southern Indians are assembling
on the Cherokee River. 3p.

Fol. 333. 25 June 1779, Whitehall. Geo. Germain to Gen. Henry
Clinton (draft). Southern District will be divided. Alex.
Cameron and Col. Brown will serve as superintendents. 9p.

*C.O. 5/100   ORIGINAL CORRESPONDENCE, SEC. OF STATE, MILITARY
               DISPATCHES: 1780*

Fol. 334. 12 Nov. 1780, New York. Gen. Clinton to Geo. Germain.
3p. [Enclosures to fol. 342b].

C.O. 5/100 (CONT'D)

Fol. 338. 24 Oct. 1780, Camp near Indian lands west of
the Catawba River, S. Carolina. Col. Rawdon to Maj. Gen.
Leslie (copy). Maj. Ferguson and 800 militia from Ninety
Six marched to Tryon County to protect friends. A large
army from Nolichucky and elsewhere appeared on the frontier.
Cornwallis's fears for the safety of Ninety Six are unfounded. 9p.

*C.O. 5/114   ORIGINAL CORRESPONDENCE, SEC. OF STATE, PETITIONS: 1768-
1771*

Fol. 257. 22 Oct. 1771. Petition from Wm. Turner to the King.
Turner discovered gold and silver mines while living among the
Cherokees for eight years. 3p. [Enclosures to fol. 262b].

Fol. 259. 10 Mar. 1771, Cowee. Talk from Towecke (Chief
of the Middle Settlements) to the King. Towecke offers
gold and silver to the English. He includes an assay of the
gold and silver and a recommendation for Turner. 7p.

C.O. 5/121   ORIGINAL CORRESPONDENCE, SEC. OF STATE, ADMIRALTY: 1775

Fol. 332. 22 Aug. 1775, Admiralty. Lords of Admiralty to Earl
of Dartmouth. 2p. [Enclosures to fol. 337b].

Fol. 336. 18 June 1775, Saint John, Georgia. Lt. Wm.
Grant to Vice-Admiral Samuel Gravis (copy). Members of
the Charleston provincial congress told Georgians that
John Stuart had influenced the Cherokees and Catawbas to
attack inhabitants. 4p.

C.O. 5/148   ORIGINAL CORRESPONDENCE, SEC. OF STATE, CUSTOMS: 1776

Fol. 337. 19 Dec. 1776, Custom House, London. Edward Stanley
to Wm. Knox. 2p. [Enclosures to fol. 340b].

Fol. 339. 18 Dec. 1776, Custom House, Portsmouth. Wm.
Stiles and Robert Earl to Commissioners of Customs (copy).
Back settlement Indians in the Southern provinces unexpect-
edly attacked Gen. Lee's army and killed 9,000 soldiers. 3p.

*C.O. 5/149   ORIGINAL CORRESPONDENCE, SEC. OF STATE, TREASURY AND
CUSTOMS: 1777*

Fol. 26. 26 Feb. 1777, Whitehall. Wm. Knox. to John Robinson
(draft). Indian presents should be sent to St. Augustine. 3p.
[Enclosures to fol. 29b].

Fol. 28. 8 Nov. 1776. John Stuart to Graham and Johnson,
Stuart's Agents in London (extract). Creek parties will
assist the Cherokees and Gov. Tonyn. 2p.

Fol. 42. 3 Mar. 1777, Treasury. John Robinson to Wm. Knox.
Robinson asks for instructions on handling money for Stuart's
Indian presents. 2p. [Enclosure to fol. 47b].

C.O. 5/149 (CONT'D)

>   Fol. 43. 20 Feb. 1777, James Graham to [John Robinson]
>   (copy). Stuart's bills cannot be paid unless the Treasury
>   pays them. 2p.
>
>   Fol. 45. 23 Aug. 1776, Pensacola. John Stuart to Lords
>   of Treasury. Stuart requests money to pay bills. 3p.

Fol. 58. 8 Mar. 1777, Treasury. John Robinson to Wm. Knox.
3p. [Enclosures to fol. 63b].

>   Fol. 62. 25 Nov. 1776. Extract of letter from Guy Carleton
>   complaining that Indian presents were so badly chosen that
>   they were almost useless. Carleton has ordered more
>   presents. 3p.

Fol. 68. 8 Mar. 1777, Treasury. John Robinson to Wm. Knox.
Treasury has agreed to pay Stuart's bills drawn on Mr. Graham.
2p.

Fol. 149. 19 May 1777, Whitehall. Wm. Knox to John Robinson
(draft). Knox wants permission to send Stuart more appropriate
presents for the Indians. 3p.

Fol. 170. 31 May 1777, Whitehall. Wm. Knox to John Robinson
(draft). Knox sends a list of suitable presents for the Southern
Indians. 2p. [Enclosures to fol. 173b].

>   Fol. 172. Indent of Supply of Goods Suitable for Presents
>   to the Indians in the Southern District. 2p.

Fol. 362. 22 Dec. 1777, Treasury. John Robinson to Wm. Knox.
Should Stuart's bills for officers' salaries and expenses
(£8,410) and for the Indian congress in Mobile (£6,564) be paid?
2p.

Fol. 366. 23 Dec. 1777, Treasury. John Robinson to Wm. Knox.
2p. [Enclosures to fol. 371b].

>   Fol. 368. Memorial from John Graham to Commissioners of
>   Treasury. Graham wants reimbursement for money spent on
>   troops which were formerly supported by the sale of ceded
>   Creek and Cherokee land. 2p.

*C.O. 5/150   ORIGINAL CORRESPONDENCE, SEC. OF STATE, TREASURY AND
                CUSTOMS: 1778*

Fol. 145. 18 July 1778, Treasury. John Robinson to Wm. Knox.
Germain believes that another supply of suitable Indian presents
and pork should be sent to Stuart. 2p.

Fol. 165. 6 Aug. 1778, Treasury. John Robinson to Wm. Knox.
Should Stuart's bill for £3,000 be paid? 2p.

C.O. 5/151   ORIGINAL CORRESPONDENCE, SEC. OF STATE, TREASURY AND
*   CUSTOMS: 1778-1779*

Fol. 24.   21 January 1779, Treasury. John Robinson to Wm. Knox.
Treasury approves presents for Indians in Southern District.
2p.

Fol. 81.   17 Mar. 1779, Treasury Chambers. Grey Cooper to Wm.
Knox. Should John Stuart's bills amounting to £16,711 be paid?
2p.

Fol. 186. 27 Apr. 1779, Whitehall. Wm. Knox to Grey Cooper
(draft). Propriety of Stuart's bills cannot be determined
until expenditures are examined closely. Stuart was instructed
to help the Cherokees. 16p.

Fol. 213. 12 June 1779, Treasury. John Robinson to Wm. Knox.
Robinson is forwarding information on Stuart's bills. 2p.

Fol. 266. 31 July 1779, Treasury Chambers. John Robinson to
Wm. Knox. Germain should determine whether bills of the Southern
Dept. totaling £1,946 should be paid. 2p.

Fol. 306. 20 Aug. 1779, Treasury Chambers. John Robinson to
Wm. Knox. Germain approves the instructions and expense
estimates sent to Alex. Cameron and Thomas Brown. 2p.

Fol. 343. 31 Oct. 1779, Treasury. John Robinson to Wm. Knox.
Robinson is forwarding list of bills and vouchers for Southern
Department expenses. 2p.

C.O. 5/152   ORIGINAL CORRESPONDENCE, SEC. OF STATE, TREASURY: 1780

Fol. 62.   6 Apr. 1780, Treasury Chambers. John Robinson to Wm.
Knox. Robinson forwards letters concerning Indian expenses
for Germain to consider. 2p.

Fol. 75.   13 Apr. 1780, Whitehall. Wm. Knox to John Robinson
(draft). Knox indicates which bills for the Southern District
of Indian Affairs should be paid. 9p.

Fol. 178. 20 July 1780, Treasury. John Robinson to Wm. Knox.
What should be done with bills from the commissioners of the
Superintendent of Indian Affairs in Southern District? 1p.

Fol. 312. 18 Nov. 1780, Treasury. John Robinson to Wm. Knox.
What should be done about bills from Maj. Gen. Campbell for
the Southern Department totaling £688 and £7,966? 2p.

Fol. 316. 22 Nov. 1780, Treasury. John Robinson to Wm. Knox.
What should be done about the bill (£1,036) from Thomas Brown
for Indian affairs in the Atlantic Division? 2p.

Fol. 330. 14 Dec. 1780, Treasury. Grey Cooper to Wm. Knox.
What should be done about bills from Alex. Cameron, Superin-
tendent of Indian Affairs in the Mississippi Division? 2p.
[Enclosures to fol. 333b].

C.O. 5/152 (CONT'D)

> Fol. 331.   23 July 1780, Pensacola.   Alex. Cameron to John
> Robinson.   Cameron reports bills for the Miss. Division.   3p.

> Fol. 333.   28 June 1780, Pensacola.   Alex. Cameron to John
> Robinson.   Cameron reports bills for the Miss. Division.   2p.

Fol. 334.   14 Dec. 1780, Treasury.   Grey Cooper to Wm. Knox.
What should be done about bills drawn by the commissioners for
Indian affairs in the Southern Department?   2p.

C.O. 5/153   ORIGINAL CORRESPONDENCE, SEC. OF STATE, TREASURY: 1781

Fol. 35.   27 Feb. 1781, Treasury.   John Robinson to Wm. Knox.
Robinson forwards material on Sarah Stuart's request for bills
(£36,671) from John Stuart.   2p.

Fol. 81.   9 Apr. 1781, Treasury.   Grey Cooper to Wm. Knox.
Cooper sends extracts from the commander in chief's quarterly accounts to help determine financial status of Stuart's office.
2p.   [Enclosures to fol. 84b].

Fol. 103.   11 May 1781, Treasury, Grey Cooper to Wm. Knox.
What should be done about bills (£2,091) from Cameron for extra
expenses in his department?   2p.

Fol. 128.   22 June 1781, Treasury.   John Robinson to Wm. Knox.
Robinson forwards memorial from Donald MacPherson, Commissary
of Provisions to the loyal refugees and Indians in West Fla.,
requesting payment.   2p.

Fol. 140.   7 July 1781, Treasury.   John Robinson to Wm. Knox.
What should be done about Maj. Gen. Campbell's bills (£4,729)
for extra Indian expenses?   2p.

C.O. 5/158   ORIGINAL CORRESPONDENCE, SEC. OF STATE, MISCELLANEOUS:
          1781

Fol. 196.   4 June 1781, Northumberland Street.   Sarah Stuart
to Geo. Germain.   Stuart sends a memorial to the King.   2p.
[Enclosures to fol. 199b].

> Fol. 198.   Memorial from Sarah Stuart to King George.
> Rebels imprisoned Sarah Stuart for two years and confiscated
> her family's property.   She seeks aid.   4p.

C.O. 5/176   ORIGINAL CORRESPONDENCE, SEC. OF STATE, N. CAROLINA,
          S. CAROLINA, AND GEORGIA: 1778-1783

Fol. 123.   1 Dec. 1780, Savannah.   Gov. Wright to Geo. Germain.
3p.   [Enclosures to fol. 128b].

> Fol. 125.   25 Nov. 1780, Savannah.   Address from Georgia
> Council to Gov. Wright.   Forces left in Ga. are barely
> sufficient to garrison Savannah.   Yet the government has
> ordered part of them to Augusta and Ninety Six.   6p.

C.O. 5/178   ORIGINAL CORRESPONDENCE, SEC. OF STATE: 1779-1782

Fol. 56. 13 Aug. 1780, Charleston. James Simpson to [Geo. Germain]. Col. Turnbull has repulsed one attack at Ninety Six, and Brown's Corps and Bryan's N.C. militia under Col. Pattison have turned back another. 7p.

Fol. 154. 4 July 1781, Sandy Hook. Vice-Admiral Arbuthnot to [Geo. Germain]. Reinforcements sent to Charleston have enabled Ninety Six to be relieved. 7p.

*C.O. 5/182   ORIGINAL CORRESPONDENCE, SEC. OF STATE, MILITARY
              DISPATCHES AND MISCELLANEOUS: 1778-1780*

Fol. 102. 14 Apr. 1779, Savannah. Lt. Col. Prevost to Geo. Germain. Creeks now support the rebels after being discouraged by the lack of support given the Cherokees in the joint attack on S. Carolina. 10p. [Enclosures to fol. 114b].

Fol. 205. 8 Nov. 1779, Savannah. Maj. Gen. Prevost to Geo. Germain. 3p. [Enclosures to fol. 212b].

> Fol. 207. 15 Oct. 1779, Little Tallassee. Alex. Cameron to Maj. Gen. Prevost (copy). Gen. Williamson has attacked the Cherokees and burned their corn. Cherokees will probably favor the rebels once Cameron is removed from managing their affairs. 7p.

C.O. 5/211   ENTRY BOOK OF LETTERS AND DISPATCHES: 1753-1755

Fol. 8. 28 Aug. 1753, Whitehall. Earl of Holderness to Governors in America (draft). Indian allies of England's enemies will probably commit hostilities, but the King is determined not to be the aggressor. 6p.

Fol. 126. 25 Nov. 1754, St. James. Instructions from King George to Maj. Gen. Braddock. Braddock should assign someone agreeable to the Southern Indians to cultivate their friendship. 26p.

Fol. 262. 29 Aug. 1755. Letter to Gov. Lyttleton recommending that the mountains passes to the Cherokee Middle and Lower Settlements be secured to stop the French. 3p.

Fol. 264. 29 Aug. 1755, Whitehall. Thomas Robinson to Lt. Gov. Dinwiddie. Robinson informed Gov. Lyttleton about money that Dinwiddie advanced to Gov. Glen for building a fort and for giving presents to the Southern Indians. 3p.

C.O. 5/212   ENTRY BOOK OF LETTERS AND DISPATCHES: 1756-1757

Fol. 127. 14 Aug. 1756, Whitehall. Henry Fox to Lt. Gov. Dinwiddie (draft). The King is pleased with the Catawba and Cherokee treaties. The July 1754 order to advance money to secure the Cherokees and to build a fort in their country should not be delayed. 8p.

C.O. 5/214   ENTRY BOOK OF LETTERS AND DISPATCHES: 1759-1763

Fol. 53. 23 Jan. 1759, Whitehall. Wm. Pitt to Brig. Gen.
Forbes (duplicate). Pitt is confident that Forbes has taken
every step to maintain undisputed possession of the Ohio River,
thus cutting trade and communication between Canada and the
Western and Southern Indians. 7p.

Fol. 57. 23 Jan. 1759, Whitehall. Wm. Pitt to Governors of
Virginia, Maryland, and Pennsylvania (draft). Forbes is supposed
to control the Ohio territory and to cut off trade and communication between Canada and the Western and Southern Indians. 5p.

Fol. 280. 23 July 1762, Whitehall. Earl of Egremont to Jeffrey
Amherst (draft). When a vacancy occurs, Ensign Timberlake will
be promoted to lieutenant as a reward for escorting some Cherokee chiefs to London. 3p.

Fol. 288. 7 Aug. 1762, Whitehall. Earl of Egremont to Gov.
Boone (draft). Capt. Blake is returning with three Cherokee
chiefs from London. Their interpreter has died. 4p.

C.O. 5/223   ENTRY BOOK OF LETTERS TO BD. OF TRADE: 1766-1768

Fol. 1. 16 Aug. 1766, Whitehall. Earl of Shelburne to Bd. of
Trade. Wappingers came to England (to petition recovery of land)
without the King's consent. They should be sent back as the three
Cherokees who made an unauthorized visit to England were. 2p.

Fol. 12. 5 Oct. 1767, Whitehall. Earl of Shelburne to Bd. of
Trade. There should be ways to reduce Indian expenses. 12p.

*C.O. 5/225   ENTRY BOOK OF LETTERS FROM SEC. OF STATE ON INDIAN AFFAIRS:
              1766-1768*

Fol. 4. 13 Sept. 1766, Whitehall. Earl of Shelburne to John
Stuart. The King is displeased at the violations of the Proclamation of 1763 which prohibited deception of the Indians. 2p.

Fol. 7. 11 Dec. 1766, Whitehall. Earl of Shelburne to Wm.
Johnson. Shelburne is pleased that the Cherokees are satisfied
with the S.C. boundary. Hopefully the N.C. and Va. boundaries
will achieve the same results. 7p.

Fol. 14. 11 Dec. 1766, Whitehall. Earl of Shelburne to John
Stuart. It is good news that the Cherokees are content with
the boundary. Shelburne is sorry that Va. made no reparation for
the murder of nine Cherokees. Cherokees should be reprimanded for
killing Mr. Boyd. 5p.

Fol. 21. 19 Feb. 1767, Whitehall. Earl of Shelburne to John
Stuart. Shelburne is displeased that the Gov. of West Fla. is
at war with the Creeks, and he has written the Southern governors
to restore peace between the Indians and provinces. 3p.

C.O. 5/226   ENTRY BOOK OF LETTERS, SEC. OF STATE: 1766-1768

Fol. 2. 16 Nov. 1766, Charleston. John Stuart to Bd. of Trade.
[Entry letter of C.O. 5/67/116]. 3p. [Enclosures to fol. 5].

Fol. 4. 1 Oct. 1766, Pensacola. Charles Stuart to John
Stuart. [Entry letter of C.O. 5/67/205]. 2p.

Fol. 4b. 30 Aug. 1766, New York. Gen. Gage to John Stuart.
[Entry letter of C.O. 5/67/114]. 2p.

Fol. 5. 19 Feb. 1767. Letter to Sir Wm. Johnson asking for his
assistance in terminating hostilities among the Indian tribes. The
King has given Stuart permission to hold an Indian congress if
absolutely necessary. 2p.

Fol. 5b. 19 Feb. 1767. Letter to John Stuart reporting His
Majesty's displeasure with any measure interrupting harmony
between the Southern Indians and the King's subjects. The King
has requested that the governors of East Fla., Ga., and S.C.
restore peace with the Indians. 3p.

Fol. 8. 1 Apr. 1767, Charleston. Letter from John Stuart.
[Entry letter of C.O. 5/68/87]. 3p.

Fol. 9. 1 Apr. 1767, Charleston. Letter from John Stuart.
[Entry letter of C.O. 5/68/108]. 4p.

Fol. 13. 11 Apr. 1767, Port Royal. Letter from John Stuart.
[Entry letter of C.O. 5/68/119]. 2p. [Enclosures to fol. 13b].

Fol. 13b. 11 Apr. 1767, [Charleston]. John Stuart to
Lt. Gov. Fauquier. [Entry letter of C.O. 5/68/121]. 1p.

Fol. 14. 11 Apr. 1767, Port Royal. Letter from John Stuart.
[Entry letter of C.O. 5/68/125]. 4p.

Fol. 15b. 30 May 1767, Johnson Hall. Wm. Johnson to [Earl of
Shelburne]. [Entry letter of C.O. 5/68/132]. 4p.

Fol. 17. 28 July 1767, Charleston. Letter from John Stuart.
[Entry letter of C.O. 5/68/136]. 5p.

Fol. 22b. 3 Oct. 1767, Charleston. Letter from John Stuart.
[Entry letter of C.O. 5/68/162]. 2p.

Fol. 23b. 19 Dec. 1767. [Earl of Shelburne] to Wm. Johnson.
It is essential to complete boundary between the provinces and
Indian hunting grounds. 1p.

Fol. 24. Rec. 19 Jan. 1768. Wm. Johnston to [Earl of Shelburne].
[Entry letter of C.O. 5/69/5]. 5p.

Fol. 51. 7 Mar. 1768, Whitehall. Thomas Robinson et al. to the
King. [Entry letter of C.O. 5/69/60]. 46p. [Enclosures to
fol. 87b].

C.O. 5/226 (CONT'D)

Fol. 76. 10 Nov. 1763, Augusta. Congress at Augusta
attended by the Creeks, Chickasaws, Choctaws, Cherokees,
and Catawbas. [Entry of C.O. 5/69/92]. 2p.

Fol. 77. 19 Oct. 1765, Ft. Prince George. Cherokee land
cession to S. Carolina. [Entry of C.O. 5/69/94]. 2p.

Fol. 77b. 10 May 1766, Ft. Prince George. Alex. Cameron
to John Stuart. [Entry letter of C.O. 5/69/96]. 3p.

Fol. 78b. 15 July 1767. Gov. Wm. Tryon to Bd. of Trade.
[Entry letter of C.O. 5/69/98]. 2p.

Fol. 79. 1 Feb. 1766, Charleston. John Stuart to Headmen
of Cherokees. [Entry letter of C.O. 5/69/100]. 2p.

Fol. 79b. 2-6 May 1765, Johnson Hall. Minutes of Conference with the Six Nations and Delawares. [Entry of C.O.
5/69/102]. 17p.

Fol. 87b. 10 Feb. 1768, Charleston. Letter from John Stuart.
[Entry letter of C.O. 5/69/128]. 6p. [Enclosures to fol. 93].

Fol. 90. 17 Sept. 1767, Williamsburg. Lt. Gov. Fauquier
to John Stuart. [Entry letter of C.O. 5/69/133]. 4p.

Fol. 91b. 21 Nov. 1767, Williamsburg. Lt. Gov. Fauquier
to John Stuart. [Entry letter of C.O. 5/69/131]. 2p.

Fol. 99b. 14 Mar. 1768, Johnson Hall. Wm. Johnson to Earl of
Shelburne. [Entry letter of C.O. 5/69/163]. 6p.

Fol. 102. 7 May 1768, Charleston. John Stuart to Earl of
Shelburne. [Entry letter of C.O. 5/69/193]. 6p.

Fol. 117. 14 July 1768, Charleston. John Stuart to [Earl of
Hillsborough]. [Entry letter of C.O. 5/69/214]. 3p.

Fol. 118. 14 July 1768, Charleston. John Stuart to [Earl of
Hillsborough]. [Entry letter of C.O. 5/69/216]. 3p.

Fol. 119b. 20 July 1768, Johnson Hall. Wm. Johnson to [Earl
of Hillsborough]. [Entry letter of C.O. 5/69/230]. 13p.

C.O. 5/227   ENTRY BOOK OF LETTERS TO SEC. OF STATE: 1768-1771

Fol. 2. 15 Sept. 1768, Charleston. John Stuart to [Earl of
Hillsborough]. [Entry letter of C.O. 5/69/258]. 3p.

Fol. 3. 15 Sept. 1768, Charleston. John Stuart to [Earl of
Hillsborough[. [Entry letter of C.O. 5/69/260]. 5p.

Fol. 5b. 16 Aug. 1768, Charleston. John Stuart to [Earl of
Hillsborough]. [Entry letter of C.O. 5/69/280]. 2p.

C.O. 5/227 (CONT'D)

Fol. 6b. 15 Sept. 1768, Charleston. John Stuart to [Earl of Hillsborough]. [Entry letter of C.O. 5/69/298]. 4p. [Enclosures to fol. 10].

   Fol. 8b. 15 Sept. 1768. John Stuart to Governors of Southern Provinces. [Entry letter of C.O. 5/69/300]. 4p.

Fol. 11. 23 Oct. 1768, Ft. Stanwix. Wm. Johnson to [Earl of Hillsborough]. [Entry letter of C.O. 5/69/306]. 7p.

Fol. 14. 18 Nov. 1768, Johnson Hall. Wm. Johnson to [Earl of Hillsborough]. [Entry letter of C.O. 5/69/310]. 6p.

Fol. 25. 28 Dec. 1768, Charleston. John Stuart to [Earl of Hillsborough]. [Entry letter of C.O. 5/70/55]. 10p.

Fol. 28b. 3 Jan. 1769, Charleston. John Stuart to [Earl of Hillsborough]. [Entry letter of C.O. 5/70/105]. 4p.

Fol. 30. 3 Jan. 1769, Charleston. John Stuart to [Earl of Hillsborough]. [Entry letter of C.O. 5/70/110]. 2p.

Fol. 38. 15 Feb. 1769, Johnson Hall. Wm. Johnson to [Earl of Hillsborough]. [Entry letter of C.O. 5/70/181]. 14p.

Fol. 45b. 12 Feb. 1769. John Stuart to [Earl of Hillsborough]. [Entry letter of C.O. 5/70/124]. 14p.

Fol. 49b. 25 Apr. 1769, Whitehall. Bd. of Trade of the King. [Entry letter of C.O. 5/70/187]. 21p.

Fol. 60. 26 Mar. 1769, Charleston. John Stuart to [Earl of Hillsborough]. [Entry letter of C.O. 5/70/208]. 2p.

Fol. 60b. 14 Apr. 1769, Charleston. John Stuart to [Earl of Hillsborough]. [Entry letter of C.O. 5/70/210]. 4p. [Enclosures to fol. 62].

   Fol. 62. 14 Apr. 1769. John Stuart to [Earl of Hillsborough]. [Entry of C.O. 5/70/212]. 1p.

Fol. 67b. 26 June 1769, Johnson Hall. Wm. Johnson to [Earl of Hillsborough]. [Entry letter of C.O. 5/70/234]. 6p.

Fol. 75. 30 July 1769, Charleston. John Stuart to [Earl of Hillsborough]. [Entry letter of C.O. 5/70/264]. 5p.

Fol. 78b. 25 July 1769, Charleston. John Stuart to [Earl of Hillsborough]. [Entry letter of C.O. 5/70/243]. 5p.

Fol. 80b. 21 Aug. 1769, Johnson Hall. Wm. Johnson to [Earl of Hillsborough]. [Entry letter of C.O. 5/70/270]. 11p.

Fol. 86. 26 Aug. 1769, Johnson Hall. Wm. Johnson to [Earl of Hillsborough]. [Entry letter of C.O. 5/70/274]. 14p.

C.O. 5/227 (CONT'D)

Fol. 95. [3 Oct. 1769], Charleston. John Stuart to [Earl of Hillsborough]. [Entry letter of C.O. 5/70/289]. 3p.

Fol. 96. 3 Oct. 1769, Charleston. John Stuart to [Earl of Hillsborough]. [Entry letter of C.O. 5/70/299]. 3p.

Fol. 104. 2 Dec. 1769, Charleston. John Stuart to [Earl of Hillsborough]. [Entry letter of C.O. 5/71/9 Part I]. 6p.

Fol. 111. 20 Jan. 1770, Charleston. John Stuart to [Earl of Hillsborough]. [Entry letter of C.O. 5/71/52 Part I]. 2p.

Fol. 115. 10 Feb. 1770, Johnson Hall. Wm. Johnson to [Earl of Hillsborough]. [Entry letter of C.O. 5/71/73 Part I]. 4p.

Fol. 117b. 2 May 1770, Charleston. John Stuart to [Earl of Hillsborough]. [Entry letter of C.O. 5/71/105 Part I]. 5p.

Fol. 121. 8 June 1770, Charleston. John Stuart to [Earl of Hillsborough]. [Entry letter of C.O. 5/71/3 Part II]. 3p.

Fol. 125b. 5 July 1770, Charleston. John Stuart to [Earl of Hillsborough]. [Entry letter of C.O. 5/71/21 Part II]. 3p.

Fol. 126b. 16 July 1770, Charleston. John Stuart to [Earl of Hillsborough]. [Entry letter of C.O. 5/71/23 Part II]. 4p.

Fol. 129. 12 July 1770, Johnson Hall. Wm. Johnson to [Earl of Hillsborough]. [Entry letter of C.O. 5/71/41 Part II]. 6p.

Fol. 137. 14 Aug. 1770, Johnson Hall. Wm. Johnson to Earl of Hillsborough. [Entry letter of C.O. 5/71/93 Part II]. 13p.

C.O. 5/228   ENTRY BOOK OF LETTERS TO SEC. OF STATE: 1770-1784

Fol. 1. 28 Nov. 1770, Charleston. John Stuart to Earl of Hillsborough. [Entry letter of C.O. 5/72/20]. 5p.

Fol. 6. 29 Nov. 1770, Charleston. John Stuart to [Earl of Hillsborough]. [Entry letter of C.O. 5/72/43]. 15p.

Fol. 21. 2 Dec. 1770, Charleston. John Stuart to [Earl of Hillsborough]. [Entry letter of C.O. 5/72/81]. 12p.

Fol. 43. 18 Feb. 1771, Johnson Hall. Wm. Johnson to [Earl of Hillsborough]. [Entry letter of C.O. 5/72/183]. 7p.

Fol. 50. 5 Mar. 1771, Charleston. John Stuart to [Earl of Hillsborough]. [Entry letter of C.O. 5/72/165]. 4p.

Fol. 62. 27 Apr. 1771, Charleston. John Stuart to [Earl of Hillsborough]. [Entry letter of C.O. 5/72/210]. 6p.

Fol. 68. 27 Apr. 1771, Charleston. John Stuart to [Earl of Hillsborough]. [Entry letter of C.O. 5/72/230]. 1p.

Fol. 84. 23 Sept. 1771, Pensacola. John Stuart to [Earl of Hillsborough]. [Entry letter of C.O. 5/72/326]. 5p.

Fol. 89. 24 Sept. 1771, Pensacola. John Stuart to [Earl of Hillsborough]. [Entry letter of C.O. 5/72/334]. 10p.

Fol. 107. 29 Dec. 1771, Mobile. John Stuart to [Earl of Hillsborough]. [Entry letter of C.O. 5/73/22]. 1p.

Fol. 111. 6 Feb. 1772, Mobile. John Stuart to [Earl of Hillsborough]. [Entry letter of C.O. 5/73/46]. 9p.

Fol. 129. 9 Feb. 1772, Mobile. John Stuart to [Earl of Hillsborough]. [Entry letter of C.O. 5/73/95]. 4p.

Fol. 145. 4 Apr. 1772, Johnson Hall. Wm. Johnson to [Earl of Hillsborough]. [Entry letter of C.O. 5/73/150]. 9p.

Fol. 154. 13 June 1772, Charleston. John Stuart to [Earl of Hillsborough]. [Entry letter of C.O. 5/73/156]. 4p.

Fol. 158. 12 June 1772, Charleston. John Stuart to [Earl of Hillsborough]. [Entry letter of C.O. 5/73/162]. 18p.

Fol. 191. 23 Sept. 1772, Charleston. John Stuart to [Earl of Hillsborough]. [Entry letter of C.O. 5/73/403]. 6p.

Fol. 202. 4 Jan. 1772, Charleston. John Stuart to [Earl of Dartmouth]. [Entry letter of C.O. 5/74/22]. 10p.

Fol. 211. 8 Jan. 1772, Charleston. John Stuart to [Earl of Dartmouth]. [Entry letter of C.O. 5/74/35]. 5p.

Fol. 216. [18 Mar. 1772]. Edward Wilkinson to Earl of Dartmouth. [Entry letter to C.O. 5/395/13]. 5p.

Fol. 220. 26 Dec. 1772, Johnson Hall. Wm. Johnson to [Earl of Dartmouth]. [Entry letter of C.O. 5/74/51]. 6p.

Fol. 225. 17 Feb. 1773, Charleston. John Stuart to [Earl of Dartmouth]. [Entry letter of C.O. 5/74/60]. 4p.

Fol. 228. 25 Feb. 1773, Charleston. John Stuart to [Earl of Dartmouth]. [Entry letter of C.O. 5/74/62]. 4p.

Fol. 237. 8 Apr. 1773, Charleston. John Stuart to [Earl of Dartmouth]. [Entry letter of C.O. 5/74/99]. 2p.

Fol. 251. 14 June 1773, Savannah. Gov. Wright and John Stuart to [Earl of Dartmouth]. [Entry letter of C.O. 5/662/51]. 2p.

Fol. 252. 16 June 1773, Savannah. John Stuart to [Earl of Darmouth]. [Entry letter of C.O. 5/74/144]. 2p.

Fol. 254. 21 June 1773, Savannah. John Stuart to [Earl of Dartmouth]. [Entry letter of C.O. 5/74/146]. 6p.

C.O. 5/228 (CONT'D)

Fol. 259. 30 June 1773, Charleston. John Stuart to [Earl of Dartmouth]. [Entry letter of C.O. 5/74/150]. 4p.

Fol. 262. 5 Aug. 1773, Charleston. John Stuart to [Earl of Dartmouth]. [Entry letter of C.O. 5/74/152]. 4p.

Fol. 265. 24 Aug. 1773, Charleston. John Stuart to [Earl of Dartmouth]. [Entry letter of C.O. 5/74/159]. 4p.

Fol. 271. 22 Sept. 1773, Johnson Hall. Wm. Johnson to [Earl of Dartmouth]. [Entry letter of C.O. 5/74/171]. 4p.

Fol. 292. 21 Dec. 1773, Charleston. John Stuart to [Earl of Dartmouth]. [Entry letter of C.O. 5/75/6]. 5p.

Fol. 302. 13 Feb. 1774, Charleston. John Stuart to [Earl of Dartmouth]. [Entry letter of C.O. 5/75/42]. 6p.

Fol. 307. 23 Mar. 1774, Charleston. John Stuart to [Earl of Dartmouth]. [Entry letter of C.O. 5/75/63]. 7p.

Fol. 313. 24 Mar. 1774, Charleston. John Stuart to [Earl of Dartmouth]. [Entry letter of C.O. 5/75/89]. 3p.

Fol. 340. 6 May 1774, Charleston. John Stuart to [Earl of Dartmouth]. [Entry letter of C.O. 5/75/117]. 5p.

Fol. 344. 20 June 1774, Johnson Hall. Wm. Johnson to [Earl of Dartmouth]. [Entry letter of C.O. 5/75/139]. 7p.

Fol. 356. 26 July 1774, Johnson Hall. Guy Johnson to [Earl of Dartmouth]. [Entry letter of C.O. 5/75/151]. 4p.

Fol. 360. 2 Aug. 1774, Charleston. John Stuart to [Earl of Dartmouth]. [Entry letter of C.O. 5/75/165]. 5p.

C.O. 5/229   ENTRY BOOK OF LETTERS TO SEC. OF STATE: 1774-1778

Fol. 1. 3 Sept. 1774, Charleston. John Stuart to [Earl of Dartmouth]. [Entry letter of C.O. 5/75/200]. 3p.

Fol. 2. 12 Sept. 1774, Charleston. John Stuart to [Earl of Dartmouth]. [Entry letter of C.O. 5/75/220]. 3p.

Fol. 3. 10 Sept. 1774, Guy Johnson to [Earl of Dartmouth]. [Entry letter of C.O. 5/75/228]. 7p.

Fol. 6. 6 Oct. 1774, Savannah. John Stuart to [Earl of Dartmouth]. [Entry letter of C.O. 5/75/230]. 4p.

Fol. 10b. 14 Dec. 1775 [1774], Guy Park. Col. Guy Johnson to [Earl of Dartmouth]. [Entry letter of C.O. 5/76/10]. 11p.

Fol. 16. 15 Dec. 1774, Charleston. John Stuart to [Earl of Dartmouth]. [Entry letter of C.O. 5/76/3]. 5p.

Fol. 18b. 3 Jan. 1775, Charleston. John Stuart to [Earl of Dartmouth]. [Entry letter of C.O. 5/76/30]. 6p.

C.O. 5/229 (CONT'D)

Fol. 24.   28 Mar. 1775, Charleston. John Stuart to [Earl of Dartmouth]. [Entry letter of C.O. 5/76/89]. 5p.

Fol. 29.   20 May 1775, Charleston. John Stuart to [Earl of Dartmouth]. [Entry letter of C.O. 5/76/120]. 3p.

Fol. 38.   21 July 1775, St. Augustine. John Stuart to [Earl of Dartmouth]. [Entry letter of C.O. 5/76/150]. 6p.

Fol. 44b.   17 Sept. 1775, St. Augustine. John Stuart to [Earl of Dartmouth]. [Entry letter of C.O. 5/76/172]. 6p.

Fol. 47b.   25 Oct. 1775, St. Augustine. John Stuart to Earl of Dartmouth. [Entry letter of C.O. 5/76/183]. 5p.

Fol. 57b.   17 Dec. 1775, St. Augustine. John Stuart to Earl of Dartmouth. [Entry letter of C.O. 5/77/32]. 5p.

Fol. 60.   10 Feb. 1776, St. Augustine. John Stuart to [Earl of Dartmouth]. [Entry letter of C.O. 5/77/36]. 2p.

Fol. 61.   19 Jan. 1776, St. Augustine. John Stuart to [Earl of Dartmouth]. [Entry letter of C.O. 5/77/38]. 3p.

Fol. 62b.   6 Jan. 1776, St. Augustine. John Stuart to [Earl of Dartmouth]. [Entry letter of C.O. 5/77/40]. 2p.

Fol. 63b.   8 and 11 Jan. 1776, St. Augustine. John Stuart to [Earl of Dartmouth]. [Entry letter of C.O. 5/77/67]. 2p.

Fol. 65b.   20 May 1776, Cockspur, Georgia. John Stuart to [Geo. Germain]. [Entry letter of C.O. 5/77/93]. 2p.

Fol. 68.   6 June 1776, St. Augustine. John Stuart to [Geo. Germain]. [Entry letter of C.O. 5/77/105]. 4p.

Fol. 80.   23 Aug. 1776, Pensacola. John Stuart to [Geo. Germain]. [Entry letter of C.O. 5/77/126]. 13p.

Fol. 86.   23 Aug. 1776, Pensacola. John Stuart to [Geo. Germain]. [Entry letter of C.O. 5/77/200]. 4p.

Fol. 94.   26 Oct. 1776, Pensacola. John Stuart to [Geo. Germain]. [Entry letter of C.O. 5/78/15]. 11p.

Fol. 104.   24 Nov. 1776, Pensacola. John Stuart to [Geo. Germain]. [Entry letter of C.O. 5/78/72]. 6p.

Fol. 107.   23 Jan. 1777, Pensacola. John Stuart to [Geo. Germain]. [Entry letter of C.O. 5/78/76]. 10p.

Fol. 112.   24 Jan. 1777, Pensacola. John Stuart to [Geo. Germain]. [Entry letter of C.O. 5/78/83]. 5p.

Fol. 117b.   10 Mar. 1777, Pensacola. John Stuart to [Geo. Germain]. [Entry letter of C.O. 5/78/105]. 8p.

C.O. 5/229 (CONT'D)

Fol. 121b. 10 Mar. 1777, Pensacola. John Stuart to [Wm. Knox].
[Entry letter of C.O. 5/78/116]. 7p.

Fol. 124b. 14 Apr. 1777, Pensacola. John Stuart to [Geo.
Germain]. [Entry letter of C.O. 5/78/124]. 4p.

Fol. 131. 14 June 1777, Pensacola. John Stuart to [Geo.
Germain]. [Entry letter of C.O. 5/78/143]. 13p.

Fol. 137. 22 Aug. 1777, Pensacola. John Stuart to [Geo.
Germain]. [Entry letter of C.O. 5/78/186]. 9p.

Fol. 141. 26 July 1777, Pensacola. John Stuart to Wm. Knox.
[Entry letter of C.O. 5/78/218]. 5p.

Fol. 161b. 23 Jan. 1778, Pensacola. John Stuart to [Geo.
Germain]. [Entry letter of C.O. 5/79/64]. 8p.

Fol. 176. 13 June 1778, Pensacola. John Stuart to [Geo.
Germain]. [Entry letter of C.O. 5/79/81]. 12p.

Fol. 182. 5 Mar. 1778, Pensacola. John Stuart to [Geo.
Germain]. [Entry letter of C.O. 5/79/112]. 7p.

Fol. 185. 24 Mar. 1778, Pensacola. John Stuart to Wm. Knox.
[Entry letter of C.O. 5/79/125]. 1p.

C.O. 5/230   ENTRY BOOK OF LETTERS TO SEC. OF STATE: 1778-1781

Fol. 1b. 16 Sept. 1776, Pensacola. John Stuart to [Geo.
Germain]. [Entry letter of C.O. 5/79/127]. 4p.

Fol. 4. 5 Mar. 1778, Pensacola. John Stuart to [Geo.
Germain]. [Entry letter of C.O. 5/79/134]. 1p.

Fol. 4. 2 May 1778, Pensacola. John Stuart to [Geo. Germain].
[Entry letter of C.O. 5/79/136]. 8p.

Fol. 9b. 18 May 1778, Pensacola. John Stuart to Wm. Knox.
[Entry letter of C.O. 5/79/158]. 2p.

Fol. 12. 10 Aug. 1778, Pensacola. John Stuart to [Geo.
Germain]. [Entry letter of C.O. 5/79/184]. 11p.

Fol. 20. 9 Oct. and 26 Nov. 1778, Pensacola. John Stuart to
Wm. Knox. [Entry letter of C.O. 5/80/3]. 11p.

Fol. 25b. 4 Dec. 1778, Pensacola. John Stuart to [Geo.
Germain]. [Entry letter of C.O. 5/80/20]. 16p.

Fol. 39b. 26 Mar. 1779, Pensacola. Alex. Cameron and Charles
Stuart to [Geo. Germain]. [Entry letter of C.O. 5/80/109]. 2p.

Fol. 40b. 10 Apr. 1779, Pensacola. Alex. Cameron and Charles
Stuart to [Geo. Germain]. [Entry letter of C.O. 5/80/142]. 5p.

Fol. 43. 6 May 1779, Pensacola. Charles Stuart to [Geo. Germain]. [Entry letter of C.O. 5/80/167]. 3p.

Fol. 44. 10 May 1779, Pensacola. Alex. Cameron to [Geo. Germain]. [Entry letter of C.O. 5/80/171]. 6p.

Fol. 46b. 10 May 1779, Pensacola. Commissioners for Indian Affairs to [Geo. Germain]. [Entry letter of C.O. 5/80/187]. 14p.

Fol. 53. 6 Aug. 1779, Savannah. David Taitt to [Geo. Germain]. [Entry letter of C.O. 5/80/234]. 13p.

Fol. 59b. 7 Aug. 1779, Savannah. Charles Shaw to [Geo. Germain]. [Entry letter of C.O. 5/80/260]. 7p.

Fol. 68. 18 Dec. 1779, Pensacola. Alex. Cameron to [Geo. Germain]. [Entry letter of C.O. 5/81/37]. 9p.

Fol. 75b. 1 June 1779, Pensacola. Commissioners for Indian Affairs to [Geo. Germain]. [Entry letter of C.O. 5/81/71]. 3p.

Fol. 76b. 12 July 1779, Pensacola. Commissioners for Indian Affairs to [Geo. Germain]. [Entry letter of C.O. 5/81/73]. 11p.

Fol. 90. 31 Dec. 1779, Savannah. Thomas Brown to [Geo. Germain]. [Entry letter of C.O. 5/81/151]. 2p.

Fol. 91. 10 Mar. 1780, Savannah. Col. Thomas Brown to [Geo. Germain]. [Entry letter of C.O. 5/81/155]. 9p.

Fol. 95. 18 Mar. 1780, Savannah. Col. Brown to [Geo. Germain]. [Entry letter of C.O. 5/81/161]. 5p.

Fol. 100. 25 May 1780, Savannah. Thomas Brown to [Geo. Germain]. [Entry letter of C.O. 5/81/188]. 2p.

Fol. 102b. 31 Dec. 1779, Savannah. Thomas Brown to [Geo. Germain]. [Entry letter of C.O. 5/81/151]. 2p.

Fol. 103b. 1 May 1780, Pensacola. Alex. Cameron to [Geo. Germain]. [Entry letter of C.O. 5/81/204]. 2p.

Fol. 104b. 18 July 1780, Pensacola. Alex. Cameron to [Geo. Germain]. [Entry letter of C.O. 5/81/206]. 12p.

Fol. 110b. 13 Aug. 1780, Charleston. James Simpson to [Geo. Germain]. [Entry letter of C.O. 5/178/56]. 7p.

Fol. 116b. 25 Aug. 1780, Savannah. Charles Shaw to [Geo. Germain]. [Entry letter of C.O. 5/81/316]. 2p.

Fol. 118. 18 Sept. 1780, Savannah. Charles Shaw to [Geo. Germain]. [Entry letter of C.O. 5/81/318]. 3p.

C.O. 5/230 (CONT'D)

Fol. 120b. Aug. 1780, Pensacola. Alex. Cameron to [Geo. Germain]. [Entry letter of C.O. 5/81/320]. 10p.

Fol. 125b. 23 Oct. 1779, Pensacola. Commissioners for Indian Affairs to [Geo. Germain]. [Entry letter of C.O. 5/81/282]. 4p.

Fol. 131. 22 Sept. 1780, Pensacola. Alex. Cameron to [Geo. Germain]. [Entry letter of C.O. 5/82/90]. 1p.

Fol. 144b. 30 Nov. 1780, Pensacola. Alex. Cameron to [Geo. Germain]. [Entry letter of C.O. 5/82/117]. 9p.

Fol. 153b. 31 Oct. 1780, Pensacola. Alex. Cameron to [Geo. Germain]. [Entry of C.O. 5/82/111]. 9p.

Fol. 158. 24 Sept. 1780, Savannah. Charles Shaw to [Geo. Germain]. [Entry letter of C.O. 5/82/163]. 1p.

Fol. 158b. 14 Feb. 1781, Savannah. Charles Shaw to [Geo. Germain]. [Entry letter of C.O. 5/82/166]. 3p.

Fol. 161. 24 Feb. 1781, Pensacola. A. Rainsford and the late Commissioners for Indian Affairs to [Geo. Germain]. [Entry letter of C.O. 5/82/168 which was dated 14 Feb. 1781]. 4p.

Fol. 167. 9 Mar. 1781, Augusta. Col. Brown to [Geo. Germain]. [Entry letter of C.O. 5/82/211]. 3p.

Fol. 170. 4 Aug. 1781, Sandy Hook. Vice Admiral Arbuthnot to [Geo. Germain]. [Entry letter of C.O. 5/178/154]. 5p.

C.O. 5/231   ENTRY BOOK OF LETTERS TO SEC. OF STATE: 1781-1782

Fol. 16. 9 Aug. 1781, Charleston. Col. Brown to [Geo. Germain]. [Entry letter of C.O. 5/82/252]. 6p.

C.O. 5/232   ENTRY BOOK, PRECIS OF DOCUMENTS RELATING TO AMERICAN REVOLT: 1768-1775

Fol. 174. Proposition for the Establishment of a Colony and Government upon the Lands West of the Alleghany Mountains Ceded by the Indians at Ft. Stanwix in 1769. 25p.

C.O. 5/233   ENTRY BOOK OF LETTERS, MILITARY DISPATCHES: 1768-1769

Fol. 1b. 22 Jan. 1768, New York. Letter from Maj. Gen. Gage. [Entry letter of C.O. 5/86/9]. 9p.

Fol. 22. 24 Apr. 1768, New York. Maj. Gen. Gage to Earl of Shelburne. Indian affairs in the Southern District are peaceful but Stuart expects a new war between the Creeks and Cherokees. 10p.

Fol. 30. 25 Apr. 1768, New York. Maj. Gen. Gage to Earl of Shelburne. [Entry letter of C.O. 5/86/76]. 2p.

C.O. 5/233 (CONT'D)

Fol. 43b. 18 June 1768, New York. Maj. Gen. Gage to Earl of
Hillsborough. [Entry letter of C.O. 5/86/113]. 6p.

Fol. 48b. 17 Aug. 1768, New York. Maj. Gen. Gage to Earl of
Hillsborough. [Entry letter of C.O. 5/86/145]. 10p.

Fol. 60. 9 Sept. 1768, New York. Maj. Gen. Gage to Earl of
Hillsborough. [Entry letter of C.O. 5/86/170]. 7p.

Fol. 72b. 9 Oct. 1768, New York. Maj. Gen. Gage to Earl of
Hillsborough. [Entry letter of C.O. 5/86/196]. 5p.

Fol. 88. 5 Jan. 1769, New York. Maj. Gen. Gage to Earl of
Hillsborough. Boundary line now extends down the Ohio to the
Cherokee River. If Southern provinces try to claim lands below
the Kanawha by virtue of the Six Nations' cession, a quarrel
will probably erupt with the Southern Indians. 7p.

Fol. 95b. 7 Jan. 1769, New York. Maj. Gen. Gage to Earl of
Hillsborough. [Entry letter of C.O. 5/87/60]. 2p.

Fol. 105b. 1 Apr. 1769, New York. Maj. Gen. Gage to Earl of
Hillsborough. [Entry letter of C.O. 5/87/86]. 7p.

Fol. 112. 10 June 1769, New York. Maj. Gen. Gage to Earl of
Hillsborough. [Entry letter of C.O. 5/87/101]. 11p.

Fol. 121b. 22 July 1769, New York. Maj. Gen. Gage to Earl of
Hillsborough. Virginia's new line will terminate at the
juncture of the Kanawha and Ohio Rivers. Private land grants
in the treaty of Ft. Stanwix will not be confirmed. 4p.

Fol. 126. 9 Sept. 1769, New York. Maj. Gen. Gage to Earl of
Hillsborough. [Entry letter of C.O. 5/87/157]. 9p.

C.O. 5/234   ENTRY BOOK OF LETTERS, MILITARY DISPATCHES: 1769-1771

Fol. 1. 4 Dec. 1769, New York. Maj. Gen. Gage to Earl of
Hillsborough. Cherokee and Six Nations' meeting will help preserve the fidelity of these nations. 9p.

Fol. 14b. 6 Jan. 1770, New York. Maj. Gen. Gage to Earl of
Hillsborough. [Entry letter of C.O. 5/88/26]. 9p. [Enclosures
to fol. 20b].

    Fol. 18b. 8 Dec. 1769, Johnson Hall. Wm. Johnson to Maj.
    Gen. Gage. [Entry letter of C.O. 5/88/30]. 5p.

Fol. 20b. 21 Feb. 1770, New York. Maj. Gen. Gage to Earl of
Hillsborough. [Enclosures to fol. 26b]. 8p.

    Fol. 24b. 1 Jan. 1770, Philadelphia. Geo. Croghan to Maj.
    Gen. Gage. [Entry letter of C.O. 5/88/44]. 3p.

Fol. 34. 24 Apr. 1770, New York. Lt. Gen. Gage to Earl of
Hillsborough. [Entry letter of C.O. 5/88/62]. 8p.

C.O. 5/234 (CONT'D)

Fol. 38b. 14 May 1770, New York. Lt. Gen. Gage to Earl of
Hillsborough. [Entry letter of C.O. 5/88/76]. 8p.

Fol. 42. 2 June 1770, New York. Lt. Gen. Gage to Earl of
Hillsborough. [Entry letter of C.O. 5/88/92]. 6p.

Fol. 52. 18 Aug. 1770, New York. Lt. Gen. Gage to Earl of
Hillsborough. [Entry letter of C.O. 5/88/122]. 11p.

Fol. 57b. 8 Sept. 1770, New York. Lt. Gen. Gage to Earl of
Hillsborough. [Entry letter of C.O. 5/88/146]. 6p.

Fol. 66b. 10 Nov. 1770, New York. Lt. Gen. Gage to Earl of
Hillsborough. [Entry letter of C.O. 5/88/164]. 25p.

Fol. 78b. 12 Nov. 1770, New York. Lt. Gen. Gage to Earl of
Hillsborough. [Entry letter of C.O. 5/88/174]. 6p.

Fol. 82. 7 Dec. 1770, New York. Lt. Gen. Gage to Earl of
Hillsborough. [Entry letter of C.O. 5/89/11]. 9p.

Fol. 87. 16 Jan. 1771, New York. Lt. Gen. Gage to Earl of
Hillsborough. [Entry letter of C.O. 5/89/33]. 5p.

Fol. 92. 2 Apr. 1771, New York. Lt. Gen. Gage to Earl of
Hillsborough. [Entry letter of C.O. 5/89/80]. 8p. [Enclosures
to fol. 98b].

 Fol. 95b. 7 Mar. 1771, Fort Pitt. Intelligence from
 Ft. Pitt. [Entry letter of C.O. 5/89/84]. 7p.

Fol. 101b. 7 May 1771, New York. Lt. Gen. Gage to Earl of
Hillsborough. [Entry letter of C.O. 5/89/99]. 8p.

Fol. 120b. 1 Oct. 1771, New York. Lt. Gen. Gage to Earl of
Hillsborough. [Entry letter of C.O. 5/89/170]. 9p.

C.O. 5/241   ENTRY BOOK OF LETTERS, DISPATCHES TO GOVERNORS: 1768-1774

Fol. 10. 12 Mar. 1768, Whitehall. Earl of Hillsborough to Wm.
Johnson. [Entry letter of C.O. 5/69/112]. 2p.

Fol. 11. 12 Mar. 1768, Whitehall. Earl of Hillsborough to Gen.
Gage. [Entry letter of C.O. 5/86/30]. 6p.

Fol. 44. 12 July 1768, Whitehall. Earl of Hillsborough to John
Stuart. [Entry letter of C.O. 5/69/204]. 3p.

Fol. 53. 15 Sept. 1768, Whitehall. Earl of Hillsborough to John
Stuart. [Entry letter of C.O. 5/69/226]. 2p.

Fol. 57. 12 Oct. 1768, Whitehall. Earl of Hillsborough to Gen.
Gage. Stuart's prestige will hopefully allow England to arbi-
trate differences among the Southern Indians once treaty negotiations end. 7p.

C.O. 5/241 (CONT'D)

Fol. 65. 15 Nov. 1768, Whitehall. Earl of Hillsborough to
John Stuart. [Entry letter of C.O. 5/69/292]. 2p.

Fol. 85b. 1 Mar. 1769, Whitehall. Earl of Hillsborough to
John Stuart. [Entry letter of C.O. 5/70/51]. 2p.

Fol. 88. 24 Mar. 1769, Whitehall. Earl of Hillsborough to
Gen. Gage. [Entry letter of C.O. 5/87/72]. 8p.

Fol. 91b. 24 Mar. 1769, Whitehall. Earl of Hillsborough to
Wm. Johnson. [Entry letter of C.O. 5/70/173]. 1p.

Fol. 95b. 13 May 1769, Whitehall. Earl of Hillsborough to
Wm. Johnson. [Entry letter of C.O. 5/70/206]. 3p.

Fol. 96b. 13 May 1769, Whitehall. Earl of Hillsborough to
John Stuart. [Entry letter of C.O. 5/70/203]. 3p.

Fol. 100b. 27 May 1769, Whitehall. Earl of Hillsborough to
Gen. Gage. Hillsborough has nothing to add to the dispatch
with the King's resolutions on the Indian boundary line. 2p.

Fol. 105. 15 July 1769, Whitehall. Earl of Hillsborough to
Gen. Gage. [Entry letter of C.O. 5/87/119]. 3p.

Fol. 106b. 15 July 1769, Whitehall. Earl of Hillsborough to
John Stuart. [Entry letter of C.O. 5/70/230]. 3p.

Fol. 116b. 9 Dec. 1769, Whitehall. Earl of Hillsborough to
Wm. Johnson. [Entry letter of C.O. 5/70/331]. 3p.

Fol. 136. 14 Apr. 1770, Whitehall. Earl of Hillsborough to
Wm. Johnson. [Entry letter of C.O. 5/71/81 Part I]. 4p.

Fol. 138. 14 Apr. 1770, Whitehall. Earl of Hillsborough to
John Stuart. [Entry letter of C.O. 5/71/77 Part I]. 3p.

Fol. 139b. 16 Mar. 1770, Whitehall. Bd. of Trade to Gov.
Botetourt. [Entry letter of C.O. 5/1336/162]. 3p.

Fol. 149. 12 June 1770, Whitehall. Earl of Hillsborough to
John Stuart. [Entry letter of C.O. 5/71/127 Part I]. 2p.

Fol. 150. 12 June 1770, Whitehall. Earl of Hillsborough to
Lt. Gen. Gage. [Entry letter of C.O. 5/88/72]. 7p.

Fol. 161b. 31 July 1770, Whitehall. Earl of Hillsborough to
John Stuart. [Entry letter of C.O. 5/71/11 Part II]. 2p.

Fol. 166. 28 Sept. 1770, Whitehall. Earl of Hillsborough to
Lt. Gen. Gage. [Entry letter of C.O. 5/88/139]. 7p.

Fol. 171b. 3 Oct. 1770, Whitehall. Earl of Hillsborough to
John Stuart. [Entry letter of C.O. 5/71/59 Part II]. 3p.

Fol. 173. 3 Oct. 1770, Whitehall. Earl of Hillsborough to
Wm. Johnson. [Entry letter of C.O. 5/71/63 Part II]. 3p.

C.O. 5/241 (CONT'D)

Fol. 176. 15 Nov. 1770, Whitehall. Earl of Hillsborough to Lt. Gen. Gage. [Entry letter of C.O. 5/88/160]. 3p.

Fol. 177. 15 Nov. 1770, Whitehall. Earl of Hillsborough to Wm. Johnson. [Entry letter of C.O. 5/71/87 Part II]. 2p.

Fol. 184b. 11 Feb. 1771, Whitehall. Earl of Hillsborough to John Stuart. [Entry letter of C.O. 5/72/131]. 3p.

Fol. 189. 4 May 1771, Whitehall. Earl of Hillsborough to John Stuart. Generally, the English should avoid interfering in quarrels between tribes. 3p.

Fol. 192b. 3 July 1771, Whitehall. Earl of Hillsborough to John Stuart. [Entry letter of C.O. 5/72/240]. 3p.

Fol. 194. 3 July 1771, Whitehall. Earl of Hillsborough to John Stuart. [Entry letter of C.O. 5/72/243]. 1p.

Fol. 199. 11 Jan. 1772, Whitehall. Earl of Hillsborough to John Stuart. [Entry letter of C.O. 5/73/1]. 4p.

Fol. 211. 1 July 1772, Whitehall. Earl of Hillsborough to Wm. Johnson. [Entry letter of C.O. 5/73/154]. 3p.

Fol. 212. 7 Aug. 1772, Whitehall. Earl of Hillsborough to John Stuart. [Entry letter of C.O. 5/73/234]. 2p.

Fol. 214b. 2 Sept. 1772, Whitehall. Earl of Dartmouth to John Stuart. [Entry letter of C.O. 5/73/249]. 3p.

Fol. 217. 27 Sept. 1772, Whitehall. Earl of Dartmouth to John Stuart. [Entry letter of C.O. 5/73/397]. 1p.

Fol. 219. 9 Dec. 1772, Whitehall. Earl of Dartmouth to John Stuart. [Entry letter of C.O. 5/73/458]. 3p.

Fol. 220. 9 Dec. 1772, Whitehall. Earl of Dartmouth to John Stuart. [Entry letter of C.O. 5/73/454]. 4p.

Fol. 230b. 3 Mar. 1773, Whitehall. Earl of Dartmouth to John Stuart. [Entry letter of C.O. 5/74/32]. 3p.

Fol. 236. 10 Apr. 1773, Whitehall. Earl of Dartmouth to John Stuart. [Entry letter of C.O. 5/74/58]. 1p.

Fol. 236b. 5 May 1773, Whitehall. Earl of Dartmouth to John Stuart. [Entry letter of C.O. 5/74/96]. 2p.

Fol. 244b. 28 Oct. 1773, Whitehall. Earl of Dartmouth to John Stuart. [Entry letter of C.O. 5/74/167]. 3p.

C.O. 5/242   ENTRY BOOK OF LETTERS, DISPATCHES TO GOVERNORS: 1774-1790

Fol. 1b.   1774.   Estimate of the Expense Attending the General
Surveys of His Majesty's Dominions in North America in 1774.   2p.

Fol. 6b.   6 July 1774, Whitehall.   Earl of Dartmouth to John
Stuart.   [Entry letter of C.O. 5/75/133].   2p.

Fol. 9b.   5 Oct. 1774, Whitehall.   Earl of Dartmouth to John
Stuart.   [Entry letter of C.O. 5/75/196].   1p.

Fol. 10b.   2 Nov. 1774, Whitehall.   Earl of Dartmouth to John
Stuart (draft).   Dartmouth is unable to instruct Stuart because
of the uncertainty of disputes with the Creek Indians and the
disturbances on the back of Va. and Carolina.   2p.

Fol. 27b.   1 Feb. 1775, Whitehall.   Earl of Dartmouth of John
Stuart.   [Entry letter of C.O. 5/76/28].   2p.

Fol. 37.   3 Mar. 1775, Whitehall.   Earl of Dartmouth to John
Stuart.   [Entry letter of C.O. 5/76/59].   3p.

Fol. 58b.   5 Sept. 1776, Whitehall.   Geo. Germain to John Stuart.
[Entry letter of C.O. 5/77/101].   6p.

Fol. 63.   6 Nov. 1776, Whitehall.   Geo. Germain to John Stuart.
[Entry letter of C.O. 5/77/121].   3p.

Fol. 74b.   7 Feb. 1777, Whitehall.   Geo. Germain to John Stuart.
[Entry letter of C.O. 5/78/3].   6p.

Fol. 78.   2 Apr. 1777, Whitehall.   Geo. Germain to John Stuart.
[Entry letter of C.O. 5/78/63].   14p.

Fol. 86.   11 Oct. 1777, Whitehall.   Geo. Germain to John Stuart.
[Entry letter of C.O. 5/78/175].   3p.

Fol. 88.   5 Nov. 1777, Whitehall.   Geo. Germain to John Stuart.
[Entry letter of C.O. 5/78/180].   1p.

Fol. 107.   10 Mar. 1778, Whitehall.   Geo. Germain to John Stuart.
[Entry letter of C.O. 5/79/53].   4p.

Fol. 115b.   15 May 1778, Whitehall.   Geo. Germain to John Stuart.
[Entry letter of C.O. 5/79/68].   1p.

Fol. 118b.   1 July 1778, Whitehall.   Geo. Germain to John Stuart.
[Entry letter of C.O. 5/79/109].   4p.

Fol. 121.   5 Aug. 1778, Whitehall.   Geo. Germain to John Stuart.
[Entry letter of C.O. 5/79/166].   3p.

Fol. 124.   26 Sept. 1778, Whitehall.   Wm. Knox to John Stuart.
Lords of Treasury have ordered suitable presents this autumn
for Southern Department Indians.   2p.

C.O. 5/242 (CONT'D)

Fol. 125. 14 Oct. 1778, Whitehall. Wm. Knox to John Stuart.
Knox sends invoice for Indian presents. Supplies will hopefully
enable Stuart to preserve Indian attachment to the King. 1p.

Fol. 128b. 2 Dec. 1778, Whitehall. Geo. Germain to John Stuart.
[Entry letter of C.O. 5/79/231]. 5p.

Fol. 134b. 3 Mar. 1779, Whitehall. Geo. Germain to John Stuart.
[Entry letter of C.O. 5/80/18]. 1p.

Fol. 142. 31 Mar. 1779, Whitehall. Geo. Germain to John Stuart.
[Entry letter of C.O. 5/80/67]. 4p.

Fol. 144. 2 June 1779, Whitehall. Geo. Germain to John Stuart.
[Entry letter of C.O. 5/80/88]. 4p.

Fol. 149b. 25 June 1779, Whitehall. Geo. Germain to Alex.
Cameron. [Entry letter of C.O. 5/80/123]. 4p.

Fol. 151. 25 June 1779, Whitehall. Geo. Germain to Col. Brown
[Entry letter of C.O. 5/80/123]. 4p.

Fol. 153. 5 Aug. 1779, Whitehall. Geo. Germain to Alex.
Cameron. [Entry letter of C.O. 5/80/232]. 3p.

Fol. 159b. 5 Apr. 1780, Whitehall. Geo. Germain to Alex.
Cameron. [Entry letter of C.O. 5/81/105]. 10p.

Fol. 182. 6 June 1781, Whitehall. Wm. Knox to Charles Shaw.
[Entry letter of C.O. 5/82/176]. 2p.

Fol. 190. 1 Sept. 1781, Whitehall. Wm. Knox to Lt. Col. Brown.
[Entry letter of C.O. 5/82/218]. 2p.

C.O. 5/258   ENTRY BOOK OF LETTERS FROM TREASURY: 1776-1781

Fol. 16b. 3 Mar. 1777, Treasury. John Robinson to Wm. Knox.
[Entry letter of C.O. 5/149/42]. 1p.

Fol. 18b. 8 Mar. 1777, Treasury. John Robinson to Wm. Knox.
[Entry letter of C.O. 5/149/68]. 2p.

Fol. 42b. 22 Dec. 1777, Treasury. John Robinson to Wm. Knox.
Entry letter of C.O. 5/149/362]. 2p.

Fol. 54. 18 July 1778, Treasury. John Robinson to Wm. Knox.
[Entry letter of C.O. 5/150/145]. 1p.

Fol. 55. 6 Aug. 1778, Treasury. John Robinson to Wm. Knox.
[Entry of C.O. 5/150/165]. 2p.

Fol. 67. 21 January 1779, Treasury. John Robinson to Wm. Knox.
[Entry letter of C.O. 5/151/24]. 2p.

Fol. 90. 12 June 1779, Treasury. John Robinson to Wm. Knox.
[Entry letter of C.O. 5/151/213]. 1p.

C.O. 5/258 (CONT'D)

Fol. 90. 16 July 1779, Treasury. John Robinson to Wm. Knox.
What should be done with bills (£9,015) for Southern Department
expenses? 1p.

Fol. 103. 31 Oct. 1779, Treasury. John Robinson to Wm. Knox.
[Entry letter of C.O. 5/151/343]. 1p.

Fol. 121b. 20 July 1780, Treasury. John Robinson to Wm. Knox.
[Entry letter of C.O. 5/152/178]. 1p.

Fol. 133. 18 Nov. 1780, Treasury. John Robinson to Wm. Knox.
[Entry letter of C.O. 5/152/312]. 2p.

Fol. 134. 22 Nov. 1780, Treasury. John Robinson to Wm. Knox.
[Entry letter of C.O. 5/152/316]. 1p.

Fol. 135b. 14 Dec. 1780, Treasury. Grey Cooper to Wm. Knox.
[Entry letter of C.O. 5/152/330]. 2p.

Fol. 136. 14 Dec. 1780, Treasury. Grey Cooper to Wm. Knox.
[Entry letter of C.O. 5/152/334]. 2p.

Fol. 139. 27 Feb. 1781, Treasury. John Robinson to Wm. Knox.
[Entry letter of C.O. 5/153/35]. 2p.

Fol. 146. 9 Apr. 1781, Treasury. Grey Cooper to Wm. Knox.
[Entry letter of C.O. 5/153/81]. 1p.

Fol. 146b. 11 May 1781, Treasury. Grey Cooper to Wm. Knox.
[Entry letter of C.O. 5/153/103]. 2p.

Fol. 152. 22 June 1781, Treasury. John Robinson to Wm. Knox.
[Entry letter of C.O. 5/153/128]. 1p.

Fol. 155b. 7 July 1781, Treasury. John Robinson to Wm. Knox.
[Entry letter of C.O. 5/153/140]. 1p.

C.O. 5/263 ENTRY BOOK OF LETTERS, SECRET DISPATCHES: 1778-1783

Fol. 1. 8 Mar. 1778, Whitehall. Geo. Germain to Henry Clinton.
[Entry letter of C.O. 5/95/35]. 11p.

*C.O. 5/283 OBSERVATIONS ON THE RIGHT OF GREAT BRITAIN TO NORTH
          AMERICA: 1739*

Fol. 1. 16 Apr. 1739. Harmon Verelst. Some Observations on
the Right of the Crown of Great Britain to the Northwest Continent
of America (copy). England has purchased the land from the
Indians. 17p. [Enclosures to fol. 53].

Fol. 11. Documents Supporting the British Claim to America
and the Carolinas (copy). The French have been trying to
turn the Five Nations against the English and the Western
and Southern Indians. These latter tribes are a barrier
between Carolina and the French and Spanish settlements.
47p.

C.O. 5/283 (CONT'D)

> Fol. 42b. 16 Apr. 1704. Col. Moore to Nathaniel Johnson
> (copy). Whether Moore will reach home by mid-March is
> dependent on whether his horses are able to carry him to
> the Cherokees before then. 3p.

> Fol. 44b. 16 Jan. 1737/38, New York. Copy of letter from
> Geo. Clark, Gov. of New York, stating that the French plan
> an expedition against the Carolina Indians. 2p.

C.O. 5/284   MEMOIR ON AMERICAN INDIANS: 1730-1765

Fol. 1. [ca. 1760]. [Peter Wraxall]. Some Thoughts on the
British Indian Interest in North America (copy). British need
Indian allies against the French. They also need superintendents
for the Northern and Southern Indians. 45p.

*C.O. 5/286.   CAROLINA PROPRIETY, ENTRY BOOK OF COMMISSIONS, INSTRUC-
TIONS: 1663-1697*

Fol. 3. 23 May 1663. A Relation and Proposal to All That Will
Plant in Carolina. Settlers need to propagate Christian faith
among the Indians. 3p.

Fol. 18. Copy of instructions to Joseph West, a storekeeper
who is ordered to deliver presents to the Indians. 2p.

Fol. 24. 27 July 1669. Copy of instructions to Carolina
Government and Council stating that no one is permitted to
settle within two and one half miles of any Indian town. 4p.

Fol. 33b. 10 May 1671, Whitehall. Instructions from Carolina
Proprietors stating that the value of beads should be maintained
since this is the currency used to buy Indian goods. 4p.

Fol. 65b. 10 Apr. 1677. Carolina Proprietors to Government and
Council. Indian complaints about English encroachments on their
land has hopefully been settled to the Indians' satisfaction. 4p.

Fol. 74b. 19 May 1679, Whitehall. Capt. John Comins to
Government and Council. Mr. Percevall and Maurice Mathews have
received Indian goods to purchase Indian land around Edisto
(Colleton) R. and the surrounding area. 2p.

Fol. 76b. 17 May 1680. Carolina Proprietors to Government
and Council. A judge has been appointed to insure proper
treatment of the Indians. 3p.

Fol. 77b. 17 May 1680. Carolina Proprietors to Col. Joseph
West. Carolinians are ordered to maintain peace with the
Indians. 2p. [Enclosures to fol. 79].

> Fol. 78. Instructions for the Commission Appointed to Hear
> and Determine Differences Between the Christians and
> Indians. Any Indian living within 200 miles of English
> settlements cannot be enslaved. 3p.

C.O. 5/286 (CONT'D)

Fol. 79b. 21 Feb. 1680 [1681], Whitehall. Carolina Proprietors to Government and Council. If the Westoes's friendship had been preserved, neighboring Indians would not have dared offend Carolina. 2p. [Enclosures to fol. 81].

Fol. 80. 21 Feb. 1680/81. Instructions from Carolina Proprietors to Andrew Percevall. English must grant the Westoes an honorable peace so that the other Indians have no reason to despise England. 3p.

Fol. 85. 9 Mar. 1680/81. Instructions from Carolina Proprietors to Andrew Percevall and Maurice Mathews. Beaver trade should be reestablished with the Indians. 2p.

Fol. 86. 7 Mar. 1680/81, Whitehall. Carolina Proprietors to Government and Council. Carolina has attracted the friendship of the warlike Westoes and has intimidated other Indians. Yet, the government should consider whether another nation ought to replace the Westoes in being supplied with arms and ammunition. 4p.

Fol. 95b. 10 May 1682, [Whitehall]. Instructions from Carolina Proprietors to Joseph Moreton. No Indian living within 400 miles of Charleston and under English protection should be enslaved. 11p.

Fol. 101. 5 June 1682, Whitehall. Carolina Proprietors to [Government of Carolina]. Indians are useful to settlers by returning runaway slaves and selling food. 1p.

Fol. 110b. 16 June 1694, Mr. Thornburgh's house on Tower Hill. Meeting of Carolina Proprietors asking for the Governor and Council's opinion on confirming lost deeds for land purchased from the Indians. 2p.

C.O. 5/287 CAROLINA PROPRIETY, ENTRY BOOK OF COMMISSIONS, INSTRUC-
*   TIONS: 1674-1685*

Fol. 1. 10 May 1682. Carolina Proprietors to Joseph Moreton. [Duplicate of C.O. 5/286/95b]. 14p.

Fol. 12. Fundamental Constitutions of Carolina. Constitution includes provisions for making war and peace with neighboring Indians. 20p.

Fol. 24. Fundamental Constitutions of Carolina. [Same as fol. 12]. 18p.

Fol. 37b. 30 Sept. 1683, Whitehall. Carolina Proprietors to Governor and Deputies. Some proprietors dealing with Indians are more concerned with profit than public benefit. 6p.

Fol. 58b. 12 Mar. 1684. Instructions from Carolina Proprietors to Joseph West. No Indians living within 400 miles of Charleston and under English protection should be enslaved and sent away from Carolina as long as they are peaceful. 10p.

C.O. 5/288   CAROLINA PROPRIETY ENTRY BOOK OF COMMISSIONS, INSTRUC-
                TIONS, ETC.: 1682-1698

Fol. 8b. 30 Sept. 1683, Whitehall. Carolina Proprietors to
Governor and Deputies. [Duplicate of C.O. 5/287/37b]. 5p.

Fol. 10b. 6 Nov. 1683, Whitehall. Carolina Proprietors to Seth
Sothell. Maurice Mathews and James Moore have unjustly warred
on Indians to enslave them. 2p.

Fol. 15b. 3 June 1684, Whitehall. [Carolina Proprietors] to
Richard Kyrle. Do not allow the purchase of Indian slaves from
other Indians. 2p.

Fol. 22b. 12 Mar. 1684. Carolina Proprietors to Gov. Joseph
West. [Duplicate of C.O. 5/287/58b]. 6p.

Fol. 30b. 5 May 1684, Whitehall. Carolina Proprietors to Gov.
Joseph West. Parliament can grant permission to sell abroad
Indians captured in war. 1p.

Fol. 34. 10 Sept. 1685. Carolina Proprietors to Gov. Joseph
Moreton and Deputies. Maurice Mathews and John Boone will be
dismissed as deputies because they have continued to ship Indians
away. 2p.

Fol. 49b. 2 Nov. 1686, [Whitehall]. Carolina Proprietors to
James Colleton and Joseph West. Maurice Mathews will be given
1,000 acres of land as compensation for land purchased from the
Indians. 1p.

Fol. 52. 3 Mar. 1686, [Whitehall]. Instructions from Carolina
Proprietor to James Colleton. Is Bernard Skenking, who has
opposed enslaving Indians, guilty of any misdeameanor that would
cause his removal as sheriff of Berklay County? 3p.

Fol. 60b. [July 1686]. [George] Muschamp has seized a ship
from Scotland or Ireland involved in illegal trade with Carolina.
It contained only a few skins purchased from the Indians. 1p.

Fol. 61. 10 Oct. 1687, Whitehall. Carolina Proprietors to
[James Colleton]. The King can rest assured that those who
favor pirates, oppress people, and sell Indians are no longer
in office. 3p.

Fol. 63. 17 Oct. 1687, Whitehall. Carolina Proprietors to
Paul Grimball. Grimball is the new Secretary and Receiver to
the Proprietors in Carolina because of his integrity and opposition to receiving pirates and shipping Indians away. 1p.

Fol. 86b. 13 May 1691. Carolina Proprietors to Grand Council
of Carolina. James Colleton has been accused of declaring martial
law in order to monopolize Indian trade. 1p.

Fol. 89. 13 May 1691. Carolina Proprietors to Seth Sothell et
al. There should be an investigation of report that the
Carolinians have attacked the Cherokees. 1p.

C.O. 5/288 (CONT'D)

Fol. 91. 13 May 1691, London. Carolina Proprietors to Grand
Council of Carolina. Proprietors request a draft of law to
regulate Indian trade. 2p.

Fol. 94b. 8 Nov. 1691. Instructions from Carolina Proprietors
to Gov. Philip Ludwell. No Indian living within 400 miles of
Charleston can be shipped away from Carolina. 6p.

Fol. 98. 8 Nov. 1691. Carolina Proprietors to Gov. Philp
Ludwell. Proprietors will investigate charges that James
Colleton declared martial law to monopolize Indian trade and
that Carolina inhabitants have killed several Indians. 3p.

Fol. 111. 7 Apr. 1693. Carolina Proprietors to Gov. Philip
Ludwell. Proprietors should see and approve all new laws before
they are applied except those where delay will expose inhabitants
to attack by a foreign enemy or hostile Indians. 1p.

*C.O. 5/290   CAROLINA PROPRIETY, ENTRY BOOK OF COMMISSIONS AND
              INSTRUCTIONS: 1710-1726*

Fol. 92. 3 Mar. 1715/16, St. James. Carteret et al. to Governor
and Council of S. Carolina. Peace with the Cherokees is good
and their assistance should help end the Yammasee War. 1p.

*C.O. 5/291   CAROLINA PROPRIETY, ENTRY BOOK OF COMMISSIONS AND
              INSTRUCTIONS: 1713-1723*

Fol. 12. 1713. Instructions to Gov. Charles Eden to investigate
reasons for Indian war. 4p.

*C.O. 5/295   NORTH CAROLINA, ORIGINAL CORRESPONDENCE, BOARD OF TRADE:
              1736-1740*

Fol. 16. 1736. Mr. Crimble has proposed settlements in N.C.
at the heads of the Pee Dee and Cape Fear Rivers, two places
where the Cherokees and Catawbas can invade N. Carolina. 4p.

Fol. 87. 19 May 1737, St. James. Copy of Order in Council to
lay out 1,200,000 acres at the heads of Pee Dee, Cape Fear, and
Neuse Rivers for settlement. 7p.

*C.O. 5/297   NORTH CAROLINA, ORIGINAL CORRESPONDENCE, BOARD OF TRADE:
              1750-1757*

Fol. 87. 15 Feb. 1750/51, Edenton. Gov. Johnson to Secretary
Hill. 3p. [Enclosure at C.O. 5/297/91].

Fol. 91. Draft of Boundary Line between Provinces of North
Carolina and Virginia from Peter's Creek to Steep Rock Creek.
2p. [M.P.G. 361].

Fol. 169. Dec. 1754, Newbern, North Carolina. Speech from Dobbs
to Council and Assembly. It is important to extend trade to the
territory beyond the mountains and elsewhere. Indian traders

C.O. 5/297 (CONT'D)

should be regulated, and friendship with Indian neighbors should
be promoted. 12p. [Enclosures to fol. 178b].

>   Fol. 177. 16 Dec. 1754, Newbern. Address of the General
>   Assembly stressing the importance of keeping Indians
>   friendly with N.C. in order to secure their trade and
>   friendship. 4p.

Fol. 185. 8 Feb. 1755, Newbern. Gov. Dobbs to Bd. of Trade.
Dobbs proposes building a fort in the mountains to protect the
frontier and Indian allies. 5p. [Enclosures to fol. 188b].

Fol. 195. Copy of Proposal for Altering and Fixing the Boundary
Line between North and South Carolina. Boundary should go no
further than the Cherokee mountains. Gov. Glen claims that the
Catawbas and Cherokees are S.C. subjects and that no other
colony has right to trade with them. 14p.

Fol. 210. 1755. List of Indian Nations in North Carolina.
Cherokees in Anson County, along the Savannah and Miss. Rivers,
and in the Upper, Lower, and Valley settlements total 2,590
warriors. 2p.

Fol. 227. 4 Jan. 1755, Newbern. Gov. Dobbs to Bd. of Trade.
8p. [Enclosures to fol. 278b].

>   Fol. 233. N. Carolina. Gov. Dobbs to Gov. Glenn (copy).
>   Dobbs has sent suggestions to the Bd. of Trade concerning
>   the boundary between N. and S. Carolina, and he asks Glen
>   to do the same. Glen will hopefully aid Va. in repelling
>   the French and in securing Indian territory beyond the
>   mountains. 3p.

>   Fol. 240. 12 Mar. 1755, Newbern. Gov. Dobbs to Gov. Glen
>   (copy). Assembly approved only a 50 man company to defend
>   the frontier, back settlers, and Indian allies against the
>   French Indians. 8p.

>   Fol. 244. [ca. 1755], [N. Carolina]. Report on the progress
>   of the boundary line between N. and S. Carolina. Boundary
>   will not be run further than the Cherokee mountains. Glen
>   claims that the Catawbas and Cherokees are S.C. subjects.
>   9p.

>   Fol. 264. 13-23 Dec. 1754, N. Carolina. Journal of the
>   House of Burgesses of North Carolina. It is important to
>   extend trade beyond the mountains. Indian traders should
>   be regulated. 12p.

Fol. 279. 24 Aug. 1755, Newbern. Gov. Dobbs to Bd. of Trade.
Dobbs discusses boundary between N. and S.C. and Glen's dealings
with the Catawbas and Cherokees. 12p.

Fol. 296a. 28 Oct. 1755, Newbern. Gov. Dobbs to Bd. of Trade
(duplicate). 4p. [Enclosures to fol. 307b].

C.O. 5/297 (CONT'D)

      Fol. 298. 25 Sept. 1755, Newbern. Speech from Gov. Dobbs
to Council and Assembly. French are attempting to win
over all Indians and intimidate those who remain English
allies. 4p.

Fol. 312. 26 Dec. 1755, Newbern. Gov. Dobbs to Bd. of Trade.
Cherokees and the Six Nations claim the same land. English
also claim land through purchases made from the Cherokees. 23p.

Fol. 326. 15 Mar. 1756, Newbern. Gov. Dobbs to Bd. of Trade.
Dobbs discusses boundary line between N. and S. Carolina. 7p.
[Enclosures to fol. 331b].

Fol. 338. 14 June 1756, Newbern. Gov. Dobbs to Bd. of Trade.
Actions of those Cherokees returning from attacking the Shawnees
caused the Catawbas to meet with Chief Justice Henley. 3p.
[Enclosures to fol. 343b].

      Fol. 340. 26 May 1756, Salisbury. Copy of report describing
conference held between Chief Justice Henley and the king and
warriors of the Catawbas. Cherokees told the Catawbas that
the Cherokees will ally with the French. A white woman
taken by the Catawbas from the Cherokees was compelled by
the Cherokees to [plunder frontier settlements]. 7p.

Fol. 369. 31 Oct. 1756, Newbern. Gov. Dobbs to Bd. of Trade.
Dobbs is alarmed that Va. sent Maj. Lewis to build a fort among
the Cherokees. N.C. will pay to build a fort to secure the
Catawbas. Southern provinces will have enough expenses in
keeping Cherokee, Chickasaw, Creek, and Choctaw friendship. 13p.
[Enclosures to fol. 386b].

      Fol. 375. 30 Sept. 1756, Rowan, N. Carolina. Maj. Lewis
to Gov. Lyttleton (copy). Lewis was treated kindly by Old
Hop and Little Carpenter while building a fort in Cherokee
country. Cherokees explained why they did not send warriors
to assist Virginia. Lewis thinks that an understanding
exists between the French and Cherokees. 10p.

      Fol. 383. 14 Oct. 1756. Address from N.C. Assembly to the
King. Cherokees are leaning towards the French, which
explains their outrages along the N.C. frontier. 5p.

C.O. 5/298   NORTH CAROLINA, ORIGINAL CORRESPONDENCE, BD. OF TRADE:
         1757-1759

Fol. 44. 12 Dec. 1757. John Rutherford to Gov. Dobbs (copy).
Rutherford discusses unsettled situation of back settlers because
of Indian threats and conflict over boundary between the two
Carolinas. 7p. [Enclosure of Dobb's letter of 27 Dec. 1757].

Fol. 62. 1757, N. Carolina. Speech from Gov. Dobbs to Council
and Assembly. French are turning all Indians against England.
5p. [Enclosure of Dobb's letter of 27 Dec. 1757].

C.O. 5/298 (CONT'D)

Fol. 99. 20 Dec. 1758, Edenton. Gov. Dobbs to Bd. of Trade.
When English troops approach, the Indians quit the French and
want to become English allies. 3p. [Enclosures to fol. 101b].

Fol. 101. Dec. 1758. Speech from Dobbs to Council and
Assembly. English need to protect western frontiers from
the French. 3p.

Fol. 126. 27 Nov. 1758, Edenton. Reports of the Committee of
Public Claims. There are numerous claims for compensation for
supplying Indian provisions. 30p. [Enclosure of Dobb's letter
of 22 Jan. 1759].

*C.O. 5/299 PART I   NORTH CAROLINA, ORIGINAL CORRESPONDENCE, BOARD OF
TRADE: 1760-1766*

Fol. 1. 19 Jan. 1760, Brunswick. Gov. Dobbs to Bd. of Trade.
Smallpox has killed many Cherokees and Catawbas. Cherokees talk
about joining the Creeks if they do not number enough to make a
nation. 5p. [Enclosures to fol. 64b].

Fol. 5. Speech from Dobbs to Council and Assembly (copy).
Dobbs wants two companies to be continued against the French
and in case war breaks out with the Cherokees. 3p.

Fol. 7. Address from Council Replying to Dobbs' Speech
(copy). Measures taken by N.C. and adjoining provinces
will hopefully prevent rupture with the Cherokees. 3p.

Fol. 9. 28 Nov. 1759. Address from Assembly Replying to
Dobbs' Speech (copy). Assembly believes that vigorous
prosecution of murders committed by Cherokees along the
frontier will have desired effect. 4p.

Fol. 11. Speech from Dobbs to Council and Assembly (copy).
Dobbs is grateful for supplies to defend N.C. against the
Cherokees. 4p.

Fol. 13. 6 Dec. 1759, Wilmington. Reports from Committee
of Public Claims indicating that Jacob Lash, John Peters,
and Col. Geo. Smith were paid for provisions given the
Cherokees. 20p.

Fol. 73. 28 May 1760, New Bern. Gov. Dobbs to Bd. of Trade. 11p.
[Enclosures from fols. 64-72b and 79-113b].

Fol. 111. Gov. Dobbs to Council and Assembly. Aid bill
was not passed because it was no longer useful for the war
against the Cherokees. Peace will probably be concluded
before troops could be raised. 4p.

Fol. 112. 9 Feb. 1764. Address from the Assembly to Dobbs.
Now that Indians are happy with their claims and boundaries,
peace may be lasting. Assembly would like to know the terms
of the Indian treaty. 4p.

Fol. 114. 21 July 1760, Brunswick. Gov. Dobbs to Bd. of Trade.
Letters from Charleston indicate that a general Indian war is
likely. 4p. [Enclosures to fol. 127b].

> Fol. 116. Speech from Dobbs to Council and Assembly. Col.
> Montgomery's punishment of the Cherokees will hopefully
> bring peace and prevent a general Indian war. 4p.

> Fol. 118. 2 July 1760, Council Chamber. Address from the
> Council to Gov. Dobbs. Alliance of powerful Western tribes
> threatens destruction of the southern frontier settlements.
> 2p.

> Fol. 125. Act for Granting an Aid to His Majesty. Chero-
> kees, Creeks, and other Indians are encouraged by the French
> to murder and capture inhabitants. 6p.

Fol. 147. 3 Aug. 1760. Gov. Dobbs to Bd. of Trade (duplicate).
4p. [Enclosures to fol. 162b].

> Fol. 149. Answers from Dobbs to Resolutions of an Assembly
> Committee [concerning distressed state of N. Carolina]
> (duplicate). Capt. Waddell acted courageously against the
> Cherokees. 24p.

Fol. 163. 9 Feb. 1761, Brunswick. Gov. Dobbs to John Pownall.
Troops being raised for use against the Cherokees will not be
ready before May. Assembly will meet in March, giving enough
time to raise troops for a summer campaign against the Cherokees
or the French in Mississippi. 3p.

C.O. 5/299 PART II   NORTH CAROLINA, ORIGINAL CORRESPONDENCE, BOARD
OF TRADE: 1760-1766

Fol. 3. 12 Dec. 1760, Brunswick. Gov. Dobbs to Bd. of Trade
(duplicate). Dobbs explains his rejection of the aid bill which
provided troops against the Cherokees. 5p.

Fol. 23. Dec. 1760, Brunswick. Gov. Dobbs to Bd. of Trade
(duplicate). Since peace with the Cherokees has not been ratified, Assembly had to meet to decide whether militia should be
disbanded or not. 7p. [Enclosures to fol. 36b].

> Fol. 27. Answer to Queries Sent by the Bd. of Trade.
> Cherokees live in and beyond the western mountains.
> Although formerly numbering 3,000 warriors, the tribe now
> has only 2,000 braves because of war, sickness, and
> famine. 19p.

Fol. 41. 17 May 1762, Brunswick. Gov. Dobbs to Bd. of Trade.
Patentee associates have not received payment from the settlers
allowed to occupy land without titles because of the confusion
caused by the Cherokee war and uncertain boundaries. 5p.

C.O. 5/299 PART II (CONT'D)

Fol. 52. 30 Apr. 1762, Wilmington. Gov. Dobbs to Bd. of Trade (duplicate). Dobbs recommends the appointment of Hugh Waddell, who behaved courageously in the Cherokee expedition, as councilor. 4p.

Fol. 92. 16 Sept. 1763. Representation of Cuchet Jouvencel in answer to Dobbs' Complaints against the Lower House. Assembly granted Proclamation Money for 300 men to defend the province against the Cherokees and other Indians. 10p.

Fol. 106. 29 Mar. 1764. Gov. Dobbs to Bd. of Trade. 4p. [Enclosures to fol. 113b].

> Fol. 108. Speech from Dobbs to Council and Assembly (copy). Dobbs attended the Indian congress at Augusta where a treaty was made with the Chickasaws, Choctaws, Upper and Lower Creeks, Cherokees, and Catawbas. This treaty settled claims and boundaries with Va., the Carolinas, and Georgia. 3p.

> Fol. 110. 9 Feb. 1764. Address from the Council to Dobbs. Dobbs's efforts to conclude peace with the Indians at Augusta will hopefully add to security of the Southern colonies. 3p.

Fol. 146. 27 Jan. 1766, Brunswick. Gov. Tryon to Bd. of Trade. Tryon discusses the temporary boundary line between N. and S. Carolina. 8p.

Fol. 154. 30 Apr. 1766, Brunswick. Gov. Tryon to Bd. of Trade. Ft. Dobbs is no longer useful against the Indians since N.C. settlements are more than 70 miles west of the fort. 4p.

Fol. 182. 2 Aug. 1766, Brunswick. Gov. Tryon to Bd. of Trade. The number of back country settlers has greatly increased. These inhabitants differ in health and complexion from the residents of the maritime parts of N.C. as much as the sturdy Briton differs from the puny Spaniard. 4p. [Enclosures to fol. 193b].

> Fol. 188. 26 Mar. - 28 June 1766. Minutes of Council. Governor should direct the Surveyor General to run a boundary line between N.C. and the Cherokee hunting grounds. 12p.

C.O. 5/300   NORTH CAROLINA, ORIGINAL CORRESPONDENCE, BD. OF TRADE:
1767-1768

Fol. 39. 28 Apr. 1767, Wilmington. Gov. Tryon to Bd. of Trade. Tryon will be present at the running of the temporary boundary line between N.C. and the Cherokees. 2p.

Fol. 79. 15 July 1767, Brunswick. Gov. Tryon to Bd. of Trade. Tryon describes the boundary line between N.C. and the Cherokees. 3p.

C.O. 5/300 (CONT'D)

Fol. 135b. Estimate of Expense for Running the Cherokee
Boundary Line. 3p. [Enclosure of Tryon's letter of 5 Mar.
1768].

Fol. 139. 7 Mar. 1760, Brunswick. Gov. Tryon to Bd. of Trade
(duplicate). Observation on Several Acts Passed by the
Assembly. Assembly passed an act to build a public road to
connect the western frontiers with Brunswick County. 8p.

*C.O. 5/301   NORTH CAROLINA, ORIGINAL CORRESPONDENCE, BD. OF TRADE:
1768-1771*

Fol. 26. 12 Dec. 1768. Brunswick. Gov. Tryon to Earl of
Hillsborough (duplicate). Boundary between N. and S.C. should
be completed. 3p. [Enclosures to fol. 31b].

> Fol. 28. 29 Nov. 1768. Lord Montague to Gov. Tryon
> (extract). Tryon should accept boundary line as Montague
> wants it. 3p.

> Fol. 30. Sketch of Montague's proposed boundary line. 2p.

> Fol. 31. 11 Dec. 1768, Brunswick. Gov. Tryon to Lord
> Montague (copy). Montague's proposed boundary would be
> injurious to N. Carolina. 3p.

Fol. 38. 26 Dec. 1768, Brunswick. Gov. Tryon to Earl of
Hillsborough (duplicate). Tryon lists pay for troops assembled
to preserve peace and to run western boundary. 2p.

Fol. 146. 7 June 1770, Newbern. Gov. Tryon to Earl of Hillsborough (duplicate). Disorders near the Cherokee and Catawba
lands make it necessary to complete boundary line. 3p.

*C.O. 5/305   NORTH CAROLINA, ORIGINAL CORRESPONDENCE, BD. OF TRADE.
1765-1775*

Fol. 58. 29 May 1771, Whitehall. Bd. of Trade to Committee of
Council for Plantation Affairs. 1p. [Enclosures to fol. 61b].

> Fol. 59. 29 May 1771, Whitehall. Additional Instructions
> from the King to Charles Montague (draft). The King
> describes how to run the boundary between the two Carolinas
> until it reaches the Cherokee line. 5p.

*C.O. 5/306   NORTH CAROLINA, ORIGINAL CORRESPONDENCE, SEC. OF STATE:
1702-1748*

Fol. 3. 22 Dec. 1702 and 8 Feb. 1703, Carolina. Mr. Blathwate
to Mitchell Cole. Blathwate will increase trade with Indians.
2p.

Fol. 10. 28 July 1708, Carolina. Letter to Thomas Nairne
reporting that English traders are setting the Indians against
each other. 3p.

C.O. 5/306 (CONT'D)

>   Fol. 17. 1 Jan. 1721/22. Petition from Capt. Thomas Ekines
>   to Government of N. Carolina. Ekines requests the governship
>   of N.C. where the Indians are difficult to govern. 2p.

>   Fol. 47. 21 June 1732. Bd. of Trade to Duke of Newcastle.
>   S.C. Indians are preparing to attack N.C. tribes. 3p.
>   [Enclosures to fol. 49b].

>>   Fol. 49. 4 Sept. 1731, N. Carolina. Gov. Burrington to
>>   to Bd. of Trade (extract). S.C. Indians will attack N.C.
>>   Indians. 2p.

*C.O. 5/307   NORTH CAROLINA ORIGINAL CORRESPONDENCE, SEC. OF STATE:
               1749-1783*

>   Fol. 38. 28 Sept. 1749, New Bern. Petition from Cornelius
>   Lynch to resurvey land belonging to Capt. Thomas Pollock, who
>   lived among the Indians. 7p.

*C.O. 5/308   NORTH CAROLINA, ORIGINAL CORRESPONDENCE, SEC. OF STATE:
               1717-1733*

>   Fol. 26. 8 July 1731, N. Carolina. Geo. Burrington to Duke of
>   Newcastle. Cherokees and Catawbas threaten war against the
>   Tuscaroras, who now live in peace with Virginia. 24p.

*C.O. 5/309   NORTH CAROLINA, ORIGINAL CORRESPONDENCE, SEC. OF STATE:
               1734-1746*

>   Fol. 71. 23-24 Apr. 1735, New Hanover. Copy of minutes of
>   Council stating that any Cherokee or Catawba land taken by the
>   new western boundary should be placed under S.C. jurisdiction.
>   4p.

>   Fol. 103. 23-24 Apr. 1735, New Hanover. Minutes of Council
>   stating that N.C. will make certain in the new boundary that S.C.
>   Indians will remain under S.C. jurisdiction. 4p.

>   Fol. 104. 23 Apr. 1735. Minutes of Commissioners for the
>   Boundary Line stating that the Cherokees and Catawbas will remain
>   under S.C. jurisdiction regardless of the new boundary. 4p.

*C.O. 5/310   NORTH CAROLINA, ORIGINAL CORRESPONDENCE, SEC. OF STATE:
               1761-1767*

>   Fol. 1. Dec. 1761, Brunswick. Gov. Dobbs to Earl of Egremont.
>   Before being disbanded, the new regiment and Virginians entered
>   Cherokee country just as the Cherokees were signing peace. This
>   action forced the headmen to hasten to Charleston for the
>   ratification. 4p.

>   Fol. 25. 15 July 1763, Brunswick. Gov. Dobbs to Earl of Egre-
>   mont. Presents for the Indian Congress at Augusta have not
>   arrived. 2p.

C.O. 5/310 (CONT'D)

Fol. 27. 17 July 1763, Brunswick. Gov. Dobbs to Earl of Egremont (duplicate). Dobbs will attend the Indian meeting if his
health permits. Indians would prefer to hold meeting in·
Charleston. 3p.

Fol. 32. 26 Feb. 1765, Brunswick. Gov. Dobbs to Earl of Halifax.
Peace has been made with all Indian enemies. 4p.

Fol. 88. 1 Aug. 1766, Brunswick. Gov. Tryon to Bd. of Trade
(copy). It may be necessary to move the swivel guns at Salisbury
to some temporary fort for use against the Indians. 5p.

Fol. 113. 19 Feb. 1767, Whitehall. Earl of Shelburne to Gov.
Tryon (draft). Superintendent of Indian Affairs will restore
peace between the Indians and the King's subjects. 5p.

Fol. 142. 2 Feb. 1767, Brunswick. Gov. Tryon to Earl of
Shelburne. Tryon plans to attend the boundary running between
the Cherokee hunting grounds and western settlements. 3p.

Fol. 175. 20 June 1767, Whitehall. Earl of Shelburne to Gov.
Tryon (draft). During the boundary running between N.C. and the
Cherokee hunting grounds, the Cherokees must be convinced that
England plans to protect those lands necessary for their sub-
sistence. 4p.

Fol. 219. 8 July 1767, Brunswick. Gov. Tryon to Earl of
Shelburne. Tryon sends materials about the [Cherokee] boundary
line. Tryon is disappointed that Stuart told the Indians to
meet at Reedy R. instead of Salisbury. 4p. [Enclosures to fol.
258b].

> Fol. 221. 1 June 1767, Tiger River Camp. Talk from Tryon
> to Cherokees (copy). Tryon discusses the boundary line.
> Lack of supplies will force Tryon to return to Salisbury.
> 4p.

> Fol. 223. 2 June 1767, Tiger River Camp. Talk from Judd's
> Friend to Gov. Tryon. Boundary line should be run straight
> from S. Carolina. Whites pay little for land--a shirt or
> a match coat (which will soon wear out)--but the land lasts
> forever. 4p.

> Fol. 225. 13 July 1767, N. Carolina. Certificate from
> Gov. Tryon that the talk of Judd's Friend and other papers
> are true copies. 2p.

> Fol. 227. 16 Feb. 1767, Brunswick. Gov. Tryon to John
> Stuart (copy). Tryon wants Stuart to schedule an Indian
> meeting at Salisbury on May 16. Tryon plans to attend the
> boundary running to insure that Indians receive justice. 3p.

> Fol. 229. 2 Mar. 1767, Charleston. John Stuart to Gov.
> Tryon (duplicate). Stuart sends the Cherokee's reply about
> the boundary. Traders living near Cowee were probably killed

by the relatives of Cherokees who were murdered in Augusta
County, Virginia. Northern Indians warring against the
Cherokees were probably the ones who committed violence in
the Cherokee hunting grounds. 3p.

Fol. 231. 31 Mar. 1767, Charleston. John Stuart to Gov.
Tryon (copy). Stuart will meet with the Cherokee deputies
at Long Canes to settle matters about the traders. There
has been no word from Fauquier about the boundary line. 2p.

Fol. 233. 1 May 1767, Brunswick. Gov. Tryon to John
Rutherford, Robert Palmer, and John Frohock (copy). Tryon
orders these three men to meet him at Salisbury to run a
temporary line with the Cherokees. 1p.

Fol. 235. 20 May 1767, Salisbury. Gov. Tryon to John
Stuart (copy). Tryon is expected to meet the Cherokees and
Stuart at Salisbury, and he is now proceeding to Reedy
River. 1p.

Fol. 237. 14 May 1767, Hard Labor. John Stuart to Gov.
Tryon (copy). Cherokee deputies will not go to Salisbury
because of its distance from Reedy R. (where the line will
be run) and because the Northern Indians threaten to attack
them. 2p.

Fol. 239. 23 May 1767, Capt. Fifer's, Mecklenburg County
(copy). Gov. Tryon to Alex. Cameron. Tryon wants the
Cherokees to meet him at one day's march from Reedy River.
Since there will be over 20 Indians, they must provide for
themselves. 1p.

Fol. 241. 4 June 1767, Reedy River Camp. Gov. Tryon to
John Rutherford, Robert Palmer, and John Frohock (copy).
Tryon orders these three men to meet with Cherokee chiefs and
Cameron in order to run the boundary agreed upon with the
Prince of Chote, Judd's Friend, and the Lower Town warriors
at Ft. Prince George in 1765. 1p.

Fol. 243. 6 June 1767, Reedy River Camp. Gov. Tryon to
John Rutherford, Robert Palmer, and John Frohock (copy).
Tryon sends directions for running Cherokee boundary. 1p.

Fol. 245. 6 June 1767, Reedy River Camp. Gov. Tryon to
Alex. Cameron (copy). Tryon wants Cameron's cooperation
in running boundary line. 1p.

Fol. 246. 19 May – 12 June 1767, Salisbury. Orders from
Gov. Tryon to his escort (copy). Tryon instructs his
escort on how to greet the Cherokees and on how to distribute
the rations. 15p.

Fol. 255. 21 May – 13 June 1767. Journal of Tryon from
Salisbury to the Western Frontiers to Meet the Cherokee
Indians and the Escort's Return. 7p.

C.O. 5/310 (CONT'D)

Fol. 259. 14 July 1767, Brunswick. Gov. Tryon to Earl of
Shelburne. Commissioners gave Tryon's name to the mountain
where the rivers drained west into the Miss., indicating the
province's desire to expand west. Cherokees named Tryon, Ohaiah
Equah (Great Wolf). 3p. [Enclosures to fol. 275b].

Fol. 261. 13 July 1767. Certification that enclosed
papers relating to Cherokee boundary are true copies. 1p.

Fol. 263. 13 June 1767. Copy of agreement concerning the
Cherokee boundary line, including as signatories Ustenecah
Ottassatie (Judd's Friend), Ecuij (Good Warrior of Estatoe),
Saluy (Young Warrior of Estatoe), Tiftoe (Keowee Warrior),
Wolf of Keowee, and Chinisto of Sugar Town. 1p.

Fol. 264. 4-18 June 1767. A copy of the Journals Kept by
the Commissioners ... to Run the Dividing Line [between
North Carolina and the Cherokee Hunting Grounds]. 7p.

Fol. 268. 13 June 1767, Col. Clark's house on Pacolet.
Talk from Judd's Friend and Saluy to Commissioners for the
Boundary Line (duplicate). English will hopefully build
on Cherokee lands. 4p.

Fol. 270. 13 June 1767, Col. Clark's house on Pacolet.
Commissioners for the Boundary Line to Judd's Friend and
Saluy (duplicate). Commissioners will recommend that
the governor revoke the proclamation forbidding settlement
on the Cherokee land. 4p.

Fol. 272. 23 June 1767, Salisbury. Robert Palmer and
John Frohock to Gov. Tryon (copy). Rutherford will deliver
to Tryon their journals and papers relating to running the
boundary line. 1p.

Fol. 274. 14 June 1767, Pacolet River. Alex. Cameron to
Gov. Tryon (copy). Harmony existed between the commissioners
and Indians during the expedition. 2p.

Fol. 294. 18 July 1767, Brunswick. Gov. Tryon to Earl of
Shelburne. 2p. [Enclosures to fol. 305].

Fol. 296. 15-27 Apr. 1767. Copy of minutes of Council
indicating that Tryon's attendance at boundary running would
be very helpful. 12p.

Fol. 302. 11-16 July 1767. Copy of minutes of Council
which includes Tryon's proclamation defining the Cherokee's
boundary and forbidding settlement on Cherokee land. 6p.

Fol. 306. 15 July 1767, Brunswick. Gov. Tryon to Earl of
Shelburne. Indians have been left alone since the Augusta Congress
in 1763 except for one of the Young Warrior of Estatoe's men who
was whipped by a settler. 3p.

C.O. 5/310 (CONT'D)

Fol. 308. 14 Nov. 1767, Whitehall. Earl of Shelburne to Gov.
Tryon (draft). The new Cherokee boundary will be useful in
determining the exact limits of N. Carolina. 4p.

C.O. 5/311   NORTH CAROLINA, ORIGINAL CORRESPONDENCE, SEC. OF STATE:
*   1768*

Fol. 40. 5 Mar. 1768, Brunswick. Gov. Tryon to Earl of
Shelburne. Tryon sends an estimate of the expenses in running
the boundary. 3p. [Enclosures to fol. 43b].

   Fol. 43. Estimate of the Expense of Running the Dividing
   Line between the Western Frontiers of the Province and
   the Cherokee Hunting Ground. 2p.

Fol. 75. 5 Dec. 1767, Newburn. *Speech of ... William Tryon ...*
to the General Assembly of North Carolina. Tryon discusses
running the boundaries between N.C. and the Cherokee hunting
grounds. 4p. [Enclosure of Tryon's letter of 11 Dec. 1767].

Fol. 77. [Dec. 1767], Newburn. *To William Tryon ... the Address*
of ... His Majesty's Council. Council replies to Tryon's speech
on running dividing line between N.C. and the Cherokee hunting
grounds. 4p. [Enclosure of Tryon's letter of 11 Dec. 1767].

C.O. 5/312   NORTH CAROLINA, ORIGINAL CORRESPONDENCE, SEC. OF STATE:
*   1768-1769*

Fol. 3. 27 Oct. 1768, Brunswick. Gov. Tryon to Earl of Hillsborough. Churton's map of N. Carolina, which contains the
Cherokee boundaries, is inaccurate. 4p.

Fol. 9. 12 Dec. 1768, Brunswick. Gov. Tryon to Earl of Hillsborough. Churton's map is inaccurate. Officials should complete
boundary line of the Carolinas. 4p. [Enclosures to fol. 13b].

   Fol. 11. 29 Nov. 1768, Charleston. Charles Montague to
   Gov. Tryon (extract). Montague sends his proposal for
   the boundary between N. and S. Carolina. 3p.

   Fol. 13. 11 Dec. 1768, Brunswick. Gov. Tryon to Charles
   Montague (copy). Montague's proposal would injure N.
   Carolina. 3p.

C.O. 5/313   NORTH CAROLINA, ORIGINAL CORRESPONDENCE, SEC. OF STATE:
*   1769-1770*

Fol. 8. 23 Oct. 1769, Newbern. *Speech of ... William Tryon*
to the General Assembly. The King is leaving the regulation
of Indian Affairs to the colonies. 4p.

Fol. 87. 7 June 1770, Newbern. Gov. Tryon to Earl of Hillsborough. 3p. [Same as C.O. 5/301/146].

Fol. 93. 2 July 1770, Newbern. Gov. Tryon to Earl of Hillsborough. 4p. [Enclosures to fol. 97b].

C.O. 5/313 (CONT'D)

>   Fol. 95. Estimate of Monies Emitted and Raised in ... North
>   Carolina from the Year 1748. Estimate includes expenses for
>   two Cherokee expeditions. 3p.

C.O. 5/315   NORTH CAROLINA, ORIGINAL CORRESPONDENCE, SEC. OF STATE:
*   1771-1772*

Fol. 105. 17 Dec. 1771. Minutes of the N.C. House stating that
the Governors of the two Carolinas will appoint a commissioner
to extend the boundary to the Cherokee line. 4p.

C.O. 5/318   NORTH CAROLINA, ORIGINAL CORRESPONDENCE, SEC. OF STATE:
*   1774-1777*

Fol. 30. 10 Mar. 1775, Newbern. Gov. Martin to Earl of
Dartmouth. Henderson, an attorney, is persuading people that
land purchases from the Indians are legal. His actions threaten
the peace. 10p.

Fol. 70. 23 Mar. 1775, Newbern. Gov. Martin to Earl of
Dartmouth. In spite of Stuart's opposition, settlers continue
to buy and lease Indian land. Henderson has leased 400 square
miles from Cherokees for 999 years. 6p. [Enclosures to fol.
84b].

Fol. 102. 4 May 1775, Newbern. Gov. Martin to Earl of
Dartmouth. Henderson is attempting to settle on Indian lands.
10p. [Enclosures to fol. 109b].

>   Fol. 107. 22 Feb. 1775. Proposals for the Encouragement
>   of Settling the Lands Purchased by Richard Henderson ... on
>   the Branches of the Mississippi River from the Cherokee
>   Tribe of Indians. 4p.

Fol. 198. 12 Sept. 1775, on board the *Cruizer*, Cape Fear River.
Gov. Martin to Earl of Dartmouth. Henderson has purchased 35
million acres of land and has already attracted 1,000 settlers
from Va. and N. Carolina. 8p. [Enclosures to fol. 213b].

Fol. 216. 16 Oct. 1775, on board the *Cruizer*, Cape Fear River.
Gov. Martin to Earl of Dartmouth. Martin has heard nothing
about the success of rebel meetings with the Cherokees. 36p.

Fol. 236. 12 Nov. 1775, on board the *Cruizer*, Cape Fear River.
Gov. Martin to Earl of Dartmouth. Land purchased by Henderson
from the Cherokees, called Transylvania, probably belongs to Lord
Granville. Richard Carswell is attempting to purchase Indian
land west of Henderson's. 16p.

C.O. 5/323   NORTH CAROLINA, ENTRY BOOK OF INSTRUCTIONS: 1730-1754

Fol. 19. 14 Dec. 1730, St. James. Instructions from the King
to Geo. Burrington. The King gives instructions concerning the
N.C. trade with the Indians. 91p.

C.O. 5/323 (CONT'D)

>   Fol. 64b.   18 July 1733.   Instructions from the King to Gabriel
>   Johnson.   Johnson is ordered to send a map of N.C., including its
>   provincial fortifications and bordering Indian settlements.   82p.

C.O. 5/325   NORTH CAROLINA, ENTRY BOOK OF INSTRUCTIONS: 1760-1770

>   Fol. 32.   30 June 1761, St. James.   Instructions from the King
>   to Gov. Dobbs.   Dobbs is ordered to maintain good relations with
>   the Indians.   101p.

>   Fol. 128.   24 Dec. 1765, St. James.   Instructions from the King
>   to Gov. Tryon.   Tryon is ordered to protect Indian land.   83p.

C.O. 5/326   NORTH CAROLINA, ENTRY BOOK OF INSTRUCTIONS: 1771-1775

>   Fol. 2b.   30 Jan. 1771.   Instructions from the King to Gov.
>   Martin.   Martin is to protect the Indians from traders.   178p.

>   Fol. 90b.   29 May 1771.   Additional Instructions from the King
>   to Gov. Martin.   [Entry letter of C.O. 5/305/58].   3p.

C.O. 5/327   NORTH CAROLINA, ENTRY BOOK OF LETTERS, INSTRUCTIONS,
*   ABSTRACTS OF LETTERS TO BD. OF TRADE: 1728-1753*

>   Fol. 3b.   [ca. 1731-1732].   Gov. Burrington to Bd. of Trade
>   (abstract).   Cherokees threaten war.   17p.

>   Fol. 11b.   4 Sept. 1731.   Gov. Burrington to Bd. of Trade
>   (abstract).   N.C. Indians expect to be attacked by S.C. tribes.
>   N.C. Indians are allied with the Five Nations.   9p.

>   Fol. 20.   2 Dec. 1732.   Gov. Burrington to Bd. of Trade (abstract).
>   Indian Affairs continue the direction that Burrington gave them.
>   Indians are hostile to one another.   2p.

C.O. 5/328   NORTH CAROLINA, ENTRY BOOK OF LETTERS TO SEC. OF STATE:
*   1766-1771*

>   Fol. 6.   10 July 1767.   Letter to Gov. Tryon discussing the
>   boundary between N.C. and the Cherokee hunting grounds and
>   mentioning the proclamation requiring all settlers to leave land
>   beyond the line.   2p.

>   Fol. 9b.   8 July 1767, Brunswick.   Gov. Tryon to [Earl of
>   Shelburne].   [Entry letter of C.O. 5/310/219].   1p.

>   Fol. 10.   14 July 1767, Brunswick.   Gov. Tryon to [Earl of
>   Shelburne].   [Entry letter of C.O. 5/310/259].   1p.

>   Fol. 10b.   15 July 1767, Brunswick.   Gov. Tryon to [Earl of
>   Shelburne].   [Entry letter of C.O. 5/310/306].   1p.

>   Fol. 10b.   16 July 1767.   Letter from Gov. Tryon discussing the
>   boundary between N.C. and the Cherokees.   2p.

C.O. 5/328 (CONT'D)

Fol. 13. 31 Oct. 1767, Brunswick. Letter from Gov. Tryon enclosing a letter sent to Bd. of Trade about running line between N.C. and the Cherokees. 5p.

Fol. 42b. 27 Oct. 1768. Gov. Tryon to [Earl of Hillsborough]. [Entry letter of C.O. 5/312/3]. 7p.

Fol. 48b. 12 Dec. 1768. Gov. Tryon to [Earl of Hillsborough]. [Entry letter of C.O. 5/312/9]. 4p.

C.O. 5/330   NORTH CAROLINA, ENTRY BOOK OF LETTERS TO SEC. OF STATE:
1774-1780

Fol. 14. 10 Mar. 1775, Newbern. Gov. Martin to [Earl of Dartmouth]. [Entry letter of C.O. 5/318/30]. 15p.

Fol. 21. 23 Mar. 1775, Newbern. Gov. Martin to [Earl of Dartmouth]. [Entry letter of C.O. 5/318/70]. 9p.

Fol. 39b. 4 May 1775, Newbern. Gov. Martin to [Earl of Dartmouth]. [Entry letter of C.O. 5/318/102]. 11p.

Fol. 84. 12 Sept. 1775, on board the *Cruizer*, Cape Fear River. Gov. Martin to [Earl of Dartmouth]. [Entry letter of C.O. 5/318/198]. 7p.

Fol. 87b. 16 Oct. 1775, on board the *Cruizer*, Cape Fear River. Gov. Martin to [Earl of Dartmouth]. [Entry letter of C.O. 5/318/216]. 43p.

Fol. 109. 12 Nov. 1775, on board the *Cruizer*, Cape Fear River. Gov. Martin to [Earl of Dartmouth]. [Entry letter of C.O. 5/318/236]. 20p.

C.O. 5/332   NORTH CAROLINA, ENTRY BOOK OF LETTERS FROM SEC. OF STATE:
1768-1782

Fol. 87. 10 June 1771, St. James. Additional Instructions from the King to Gov. Martin. The King discusses the boundary between the Cherokees and the Carolinas. 2p.

C.O. 5/348   NORTH CAROLINA, SESSIONAL PAPERS, JOURNAL OF ASSEMBLY:
1756-1760

Fol. 1. 30 Sept. 1756, Newbern. Address from Assembly to Governor. French are hemming in the colonies, securing the Indian trade, and turning all the Indians against the English. 4p. [Enclosure of Dobbs's letter of 27 Jan. 1757].

Fol. 11. 14 Oct. 1756, Newbern. Address to the King warning that the Cherokees are wavering in their friendship. Their hostility towards the frontier inhabitants shows that they have allied with the French. 4p. [Enclosure of Dobbs's letter of 27 Jan. 1757].

C.O. 5/348 (CONT'D)

Fol. 15. 18 Oct. 1756, Newbern. Journal of Assembly that a bill
is ready for erecting a fort and raising two companies to defend
the western frontier. 4p. [Enclosure of Dobbs's letter of 27
Jan. 1757].

Fol. 16b. 19 Oct. 1756, Newbern. Journal of Assembly reporting
that Capt. Hugh Wadell left to join Va. Commissioners who will
confirm alliances with the Cherokees and Catawbas. 3p.
[Enclosure of Dobbs's letter of 20 Jan. 1757].

Fol. 22b. 25 Oct. 1756, Newbern. Speech from Dobbs expressing
his appreciation for the supplies granted to defend the frontier.
This help was particularly important because of the loss of
Oswego and the fear of losing the Cherokees to the French. 5p.
[Enclosed in Dobbs's letter of 20 Jan. 1757].

Fol. 38. 27 May 1757, Newbern. Journal of Assembly noting that
Capt. Wadell will be paid £30 for his negotiations with the
Cherokees and Catawbas. 3p.

Fol. 57. 10 Dec. 1757, Newbern. Message from Dobbs requesting
a bill authorizing Superintendent Atkin to regulate the Indian
trade. This would unify all Indian allies of England. 5p.

Fol. 97. 10 May 1759, Newbern. Message from Dobbs reporting
that the Cherokees murdered some frontier inhabitants. 4p.
[Enclosure of Dobbs's letter of 11 Sept. 1759].

Fol. 110. 27 Nov. 1759, Newbern. Message from Dobbs concerning
the militia's refusal to march against the Cherokees because
the trip would extend beyond N. Carolina. 3p.

Fol. 111. 28 Nov. 1759, Newbern. Message to Dobbs stating that
Assembly's measures to obtain satisfaction for Cherokee murders
should have desired effect. Dobbs reported that Wadell asked
for £1,500 to pay for the milita against the Cherokees. 8p.

Fol. 114b. 29 Nov. 1757, Newbern. Message to Dobbs offering
partial payment to Wadell. 4p.

Fol. 161. 12 Nov. 1760, Newbern. Speech from Dobbs stating that
he offered peace to the Cherokees. He proposes raising more
forces until the treaty is confirmed. 6p.

Fol. 165. 14 Nov. 1760. Address to Dobbs stating that N.C. will
assist Va. and S.C. as much as possible since the Cherokees may
not sign the treaty. 5p.

Fol. 167. 17 Nov. 1760. Answer from Dobbs thanking Assembly for
supplies sent to secure peace with the Cherokees. 3p.

Fol. 187b. 3 Dec. 1760. Journal of Assembly reporting the need
for aid against the Cherokees who are evidently encouraged by
the French. Because the French lost Canada, they may attack the
Southern colonies. 7p.

*C.O. 5/349   NORTH CAROLINA, SESSIONAL PAPERS, COUNCIL & COUNCIL IN
              ASSEMBLY: 1756-1760*

Fol. 1.   12 Mar. - 25 Oct. 1756, Newbern. Minutes of Council
reporting that Va. and S.C. are supposed to build a fort to
defend the Cherokees. 19p.

Fol. 34.   30 Sept. - 25 Oct. 1756, Newbern. Minutes recommending
a law for Indian allies. Cherokees are suspected of allying with
the French. French John, who has lived among the Cherokees for
a considerable time, has been sent to the Alabama Fort and to the
Savannahs. 42p. [Enclosure of Dobbs's letter of 2 Jan. 1757].

Fol. 56.   16-28 May 1757, Newbern. Minutes reporting that Capt.
Hugh Wadell will join Va. commission in negotiating with the
Cherokees and Catawbas. 20p.

Fol. 66.   22 Nov. - 14 Dec. 1757, Newbern. Minutes requesting
that a bill be passed authorizing Edmund Atkin to regulate Indian
trade since he is the Superintendent of Indian Affairs. 28p.

Fol. 102.   23 Nov. 1759-9 Jan. 1760, Newbern. Minutes expressing hope that a future war with the Cherokees can be prevented.
37p. [Enclosure of Dobbs's letter of 19 Jan. 1760].

Fol. 149.   30 June - 14 July 1760, Newbern. Minutes stating that
Col. Montgomery's defeat of the Cherokees will bring peace and
may prevent a general Indian war with the Creeks. 10p.

C.O. 5/350   NORTH CAROLINA, SESSIONAL PAPERS, COUNCIL: 1760-1768

Fol. 76.   15-27 Apr. 1767, Wilmington. Minutes of Council noting
that Stuart will be present when line is run between N.C. and
the Cherokee hunting ground. 13p. [Enclosure of Gov. Dobbs's
letter of 18 July 1767].

Fol. 82.   11 July 1767, Brunswick. Minutes of Council describing the line between N.C. and the Cherokee hunting ground. 7p.
[Enclosure of Dobbs's letter of 18 July 1767].

*C.O. 5/351   NORTH CAROLINA, SESSIONAL PAPERS, JOURNAL OF LOWER HOUSE
              OF ASSEMBLY: 1761-1768*

Fol. 162.   3 Nov. - 2 Dec. 1766, Newbern. Journal of Lower House
asking that the Gov. appoint commissioners to run the line between
N.C. and the Cherokees. A fixed line is necessary for peace until
His Majesty obtains further land grants from the Indians. 109p.

Fol. 207.   5 Dec. 1767 - 16 Jan. 1768, Newbern. Journal of
Lower House reporting that the boundary between N.C. and the
Cherokee hunting grounds has been run. Cherokee chiefs have
strictly fulfilled their obligations and will probably aid N.C.
in future Indian wars. They will bring Indian trade to N.
Carolina. 96p. [Enclosure of Dobbs's letter of 5 Mar. 1768].

Fol. 256.   5 Dec. 1767 - 16 Jan. 1768, Newbern. Journal of
Lower House. [Same as fol. 207]. 86p.

C.O. 358   SOUTH CAROLINA, ORIGINAL CORRESPONDENCE, BD. OF TRADE:
           1720-1723

Fol. 7. 24 June 1720, Carolina. Abstract of a letter to Joseph
Boone noting that the continuation of the Creek and Cherokee war
is desirable. 4p.

Fol. 14. Boone and Col. Barnwell's Answers to Several Queries
Relating to Carolina. Cherokees, who number 3,800 men, are now
fighting the French. If the French secure Cherokee friendship,
Va. and Carolina will be in danger. 10p.

Fol. 20. Boone and Barnwell's List of Proper Places Fit for
Garrisons in Carolina. A fort at the Hogologee R. would inter-
rupt communication between the French in Miss. and Canada.
It would also curtail French efforts to win over the Cherokees.
4p.

Fol. 22. Boone and Barnwell's Account of the Distances from
Charleston to Seven Settlements. There are three roads leading
to the Hogologee R., including one via the Congarees and
Cherokee territory. 2p.

Fol. 27. 15 Sept. 1720. Francis Nicholson to Charles DeLafay
Col. Barnwell sent Nicholson the Indian trade financial records.
1p. [Enclosures to fol. 39b].

   Fol. 30. 1720. Account of Several Things Proper ... [for]
   Presents to the Headmen of the Indians in Carolina. 1p.

   Fol. 31. Invoice of ... Indian Trading Goods. 1p.

   Fol. 34. Memorandum listing necessities for newly built
   forts and orders concerning Indian trade and presents. 2p.

   Fol. 35. Memorandum concerning Indian trade of Va. and
   Carolina. Competition for Indian trade between the provinces
   must be worked out or the French will gain control of the
   Indians. 3p.

Fol. 47. Memorial from Several Merchants Trading to Carolina for
Improving the ... Indian Trade. 3p.

Fol. 87. 13 July 1721, Carolina. Francis Nicholson and the
Carolina Council to Bd. of Trade. Nicholson and the Council
have made treaties with the Creeks and Cherokees. 4p. [Enclo-
sures to fol. 100b].

Fol. 101. 19 July 1721, Charleston. Francis Nicholson to Bd.
of Trade. Nicholson wants to settle Indian affairs. 3p. [En-
closures to fol. 103b].

Fol. 114. 24 Jan. 1721 [1722], London. John Lloyd to Wm. Popple.
2p. [Enclosures to fol. 118b].

   Fol. 116b. Lists of Acts and Ordinances of Carolina. List
   includes the Act for Better Regulation of Indian Trade and
   to Settle Indian Boundary. 5p.

C.O. 5/358 (CONT'D)

Fol. 125. 9 May 1722, London. Letter from John Lloyd. 3p.
[Enclosures to fol. 133b].

Fol. 127. Copy of instructions to Francis Young and John
Lloyd warning about the consequences if the French and Spanish
win over such Indians as the Creeks and the Cherokees. 11p.

Fol. 133. Memorial from John Lloyd to Carteret (copy).
French and Spanish are encroaching on the frontiers and
endeavoring to win over the Creeks and Cherokees. 4p.

Fol. 366. 10 July 1723, London. Francis Young to Alured
Popple. Young sends a list of acts being presented to Bd. of
Trade, including one amending the act regulating Indian trade.
2p.

C.O. 5/359   SOUTH CAROLINA, ORIGINAL CORRESPONDENCE, BD. OF TRADE:
1723-1725

Fol. 49. 10 Oct. 1723, Charleston. Francis Nicholson to Bd. of
Trade (duplicate). Nicholson sends a copy of the document
showing how the French and Spanish try to turn the Indians
against the English. 4p.

Fol. 55. 12 Oct. 1723, Charleston. Francis Nicholson to Bd. of
Trade (duplicate). Nicholson sends a copy of proceedings with
the Indians. 3p. [Enclosures to fol. 81b].

Fol. 57. List of papers sent with Nicholson's letter of
12 Oct. 1723, including Council resolutions on Indian
Affairs. 2p.

Fol. 58. 2 Oct. 1723. Duplicate of speech from Gov. to
Assembly recommending that the Indian trade be given serious
attention because it is very difficult to manage. 6p.

Fol. 61. 17 Sept. 1723, Edisto. Jn. Barnwell to Gov.
Nicholson (copy). A Yamasee Indian visited several Pala-
chocolas who formerly belonged to the Cherokeeleechee gang
that killed Duall and his company. 2p.

Fol. 63b. 24 Sept. 1723, Ft. Moore. Copy of a letter from
Gerrard Monger reporting that the Lower Creeks tried to
prevent the Yamasees from falsely reporting that the Cherokees were discovered nearby. 3p.

Fol. 67. 30 July 1723, Ocheese River. John Woort to John
Bee (copy). Woort found two escaped Indian slaves from
Carolina who were starving. 4p.

Fol. 72. 2 Oct. 1723. Speech from Gov. to Assembly.
[Extract of fol. 58]. 2p.

Fol. 79. 24 Apr. 1723. Extract of Journal of Council
reporting that Cherokeeleechee's people can trade freely
with Carolina if they come in peace. 2p.

C.O. 5/359 (CONT'D)

Fol. 80. 14 Mar. - 17 July 1723. Resolutions of Gov. and Council on Indian affairs concerning Indian trade. 3p.

Fol. 105. 4 Dec. 1723, Charleston. Gov. Nicholson to Bd. of Trade. Nicholson sends copies of proceedings with the Indians. 4p. [Enclosures to fol. 124b].

Fol. 115. 2 Nov. 1723, Charleston. Copy of speeches from Outassatah (King of the Lower Cherokees), Kureeroskee (Lord Chancellor) and Skiagunsta (from Tennessee in the Upper Cherokees) requesting standard prices, weights, and measures on goods. 2p.

Fol. 116. 8 Nov. 1723. Report from the Committee on Indian Affairs requesting that the Gov. arrest unlicensed traders in Cherokee territory and have the Frenchman among the Cherokees sent to Charleston. 5p.

Fol. 122b. 9 Oct. 1723, Cussita. Col. Hasting to Gov. [Nicholson] (copy). Some Cussitas tried to convince the Tallapooses to join them against the Yamasees. Tallapooses, however, want to war against the Cherokees. 3p.

Fol. 125. 14 Dec. 1723, Charleston. Gov. Nicholson to Bd. of Trade. Assembly's time is so monopolized by the currency problem that Nicholson has not yet introduced the question of Indian trade. 3p. [Enclosures to fol. 131b].

Fol. 127. 14 Dec. 1723. List of papers enclosed with Nicholson's letter of 14 December, including a speech from Outassatah [see fol. 115]. 2p.

Fol. 132. 17 Feb. 1723/24, Charleston. Gov. Nicholson to Bd. of Trade. Nicholson expects an account [about trade?] from the Upper and Lower Cherokees and the Upper and Lower Creeks. 4p. [Enclosures to fol. 136b].

Fol. 137. 10 Mar. 1723, Charleston. Gov. Nicholson to Bd. of Trade (duplicate). 4p. [Enclosures to fol. 163b].

Fol. 151. 27 Feb. 1723, Charleston. Gov. Nicholson to Gov. of St. Augustine (copy). Nicholson complains that Cherokeeleechee came to S.C. and carried off a Negro slave, which he gave to Gov. of St. Augustine. 2p.

Fol. 190. 5 May 1724, Charleston. Gov. Nicholson to Bd. of Trade. Act to regulate Indian Affairs will hopefully have a good effect. Col. Geo. Chicken succeeds Col. Moore as the Commissioner for Indian Affairs. 4p. [Enclosures to fol. 197b].

Fol. 203. 26 July 1724, Charleston. Gov. Nicholson to Bd. of Trade. 3p. [Enclosures to fol. 213b].

Fol. 209. 17 July 1724, Charleston. Gov. Nicholson to Arthur Middleton, Ralph Izard and B. Schenckingh (copy).

C.O. 5/359 (CONT'D)

Col. Chicken will hopefully describe accurately the
state of the Indian trade with Great Britain. 1p.

Fol. 259. 5 Dec. 1724, S. Carolina. Gov. Nicholson to Bd. of
Trade. Nicholson sends letter from Capt. Hatton in Cherokee
territory. 3p. [Enclosures to fol. 268b].

Fol. 265. 12 Nov. 1724, Nayowee. John Sharp to Gov.
Nicholson (copy). Creeks attacked Sharp's house [in
Cherokee territory] while the Cherokees remained in their
forts. 2p.

Fol. 266. 14 and 18 Nov. 1724, Cherokee. W. Hatton to
Gov. Nicholson (copy). Hatton describes the Creek expedition against Tugaloo and Nayowee, two towns separated by
a river, where they attacked Sharp's house. Cherokees and
Catawbas should be kept friendly if possible. 5p.

Fol. 269. 16 Dec. 1724, S. Carolina. Gov. Nicholson to Bd. of
Trade. Nicholson will send an account of Indian affairs. 2p.

Fol. 284. 27 Feb. 1724, Charleston. Gov. Nicholson to Bd. of
Trade. 2p. [Enclosures to fol. 295b].

Fol. 291. Speech from Nicholson to Lower House (copy).
Col. Geo. Chicken can elaborate on Indian affairs and the
need for a garrison. 3p.

Fol. 304. 30 Apr. 1725, Charleston. Gov. Nicholson to Bd. of
Trade. 3p. [Enclosures to fol. 309b].

Fol. 306. List of Laws Passed by Present Assembly. List
included one for the regulation of Indian trade. 3p.

*C.O. 5/361 SOUTH CAROLINA, ORIGINAL CORRESPONDENCE, BD. OF TRADE:
1729-1730*

Fol. 34. 19 Dec. 1729. Robert Johnson to Secretary. Johnson
requests that £200 be given to those Cherokees who sent a talk
and presents to the King. 4p.

Fol. 139. 16 July 1730, Windsor Castle. T. Delafray to Mr.
Popple. Delafray encloses Alex. Cuming's memorial concerning the
Cherokees. 2p. [Enclosures to fol. 140].

Fol. 140. [ca. July 1730]. Memorial from Alex. Cuming
volunteering to live among the Cherokees for three years to
promote the King's interest. 1p.

Fol. 164. 31 Aug. 1730, Windsor Castle. Duke of Newcastle to
Bd. of Trade. King approves the new Cherokee treaty. 2p.

Fol. 166. [July-Sept. 1730]. Memorial from Alex. Cuming to Bd.
of Trade. Cherokees want Cuming to be their director. Cuming
seeks the King's approval for this. 2p.

C.O. 5/361 (CONT'D)

Fol. 168. 30 Sept. 1730, London. Alex..Cuming to Alured Popple.
One Indian chief desires to remain with Cuming. 2p.

*C.O. 5/362   SOUTH CAROLINA, ORIGINAL CORRESPONDENCE, BD. OF TRADE:
            1730-1733*

Fol. 18. 27 Dec. 1730, Charleston. Robert Johnson to Bd. of
Trade. Seven Cherokees in Johnson's care have arrived in good
health and are satisfied with His Majesty's presents. 3p.

Fol. 20. 27 Dec. 1730, Charleston. Robert Johnson to Bd. of
Trade. [Abstract of fol. 18]. 1p.

Fol. 38. 13 Aug. 1731, Charleston. Letter from Robert Johnson
concerning legal summons. People are often summoned to court
while away (for example, at the Cherokee Mountains) and thus
cannot defend themselves. 3p.

*C.O. 5/363   SOUTH CAROLINA, ORIGINAL CORRESPONDENCE, BD. OF TRADE:
            1733-1734*

Fol. 101. 23 July 1734, S. Carolina. Memorial from Governor's
Council and Assembly to the King. French, Creeks, and Choctaws
may overrun S. Carolina. If the Creeks turn against S. Carolina,
the Cherokees will also probably desert. Cherokees are presently
troublesome, probably because of French activities. It is
necessary to build forts among the Cherokees to keep their
friendship. 14p.

Fol. 195. 9 Nov. 1734, S. Carolina. Gov. Johnson to Bd. of
Trade. Cherokees have become unruly and threaten traders if
they do not lower prices. Because the Cherokees have seized a
store of goods, S.C. has prohibited trade with them until restitution is made. Virginians are underselling S.C. traders. 16p.

*C.O. 5/364   SOUTH CAROLINA, ORIGINAL CORRESPONDENCE, BD. OF TRADE:
            1731-1735*

Fol. 172. 10 May 1731. Copy of Capt. Wattis's Journal containing his threat to send the Cherokees and Catawbas against the
Tuscaroras if they did not pay for their damages and return
slaves. 8p. [Enclosure of fol. 180].

Fol. 180. 11 May 1731, N. Carolina. Letter from Geo. Burrington
noting that the Tuscaroras refuse to give satisfaction. 1p.
[Enclosure at fol. 172].

*C.O. 5/365   SOUTH CAROLINA, ORIGINAL CORRESPONDENCE, BD. OF TRADE:
            1735-1737*

Fol. 134. 6 Aug. 1736, [Charleston]. Lt. Gov. Broughton to Bd.
of Trade. [Abstract of fol. 139]. 10p.

Fol. 139. 6 Aug. 1736, Charleston. Lt. Gov. Broughton to Bd.
of Trade. Ga. is giving S.C. trouble with the Indian trade.

C.O. 5/365 (CONT'D)

Queen Anne disallowed the S.C. law obliging Virginians to get a
S.C. license before trading with the Cherokees. 18p.

Fol. 154. 17 July 1736, [Charleston]. Petition from S.C.
Council and Assembly to the King. The King's law was hopefully
intended to regulate Ga. residents and not to prevent S.
Carolinians from trading with the Creek, Cherokee, and other
friendly nations. The King has already ordered Carolinians to
trade with the Cherokees and to erect settlements from Charleston
towards the Cherokee towns. 15p.

C.O. 5/366   SOUTH CAROLINA, ORIGINAL CORRESPONDENCE, BD. OF TRADE:
1737-1738

Fol. 5. 5 Aug. 1737, [London]. Francis Fane to Bd. of Trade.
Fane has no objection to S.C. ordinance setting up free trade
with the Creeks, Cherokees, and other friendly Indians. 2p.

Fol. 70. 25 May 1738, Kensington. Order in Council directing
the Bd. of Trade to prepare instructions for S.C. and Ga. to
settle differences over Indian trade and to reject S. Carolina's
act establishing free trade with the Creeks, Cherokees, and
other Indian nations. 6p.

Fol. 120. 20 July 1738, Charleston. Col. Wm. Bull to Bd. of
Trade. Choctaws, numbering 46 towns and 16,000 men, seek English
friendship and commerce. If the French win over the Choctaws,
French influence could extend to the Cherokees, who are presently
at peace with the Choctaws. 6p.

C.O. 5/367   SOUTH CAROLINA, ORIGINAL CORRESPONDENCE, BD. OF TRADE:
1739-1740

Fol. 112. 5 Oct. 1739, Charleston. Col. Wm. Bull to Bd. of
Trade. [Abstract of fol. 114]. 3p.

Fol. 114. 5 Oct. 1739, Charleston. Col. Wm. Bull to Bd. of
Trade. Priber has convinced the Cherokees to make peace with
the French. This peace might result in a French fort in Cherokee country. 4p.

C.O. 5/368   SOUTH CAROLINA, ORIGINAL CORRESPONDENCE, BD. OF TRADE:
1740-1742

Fol. 13. 10 May 1740, Oakfuskee. A. Willy to Capt. Croft
(copy). French met with the Upper and Lower Creeks and the
Cherokees (or Stinking Lenguas). 6p.

Fol. 47. 10 Nov. 1740, Georgia. Trustees of Georgia to Bd. of
Trade. Cherokees live northwest of Augusta and number about
5,000 warriors, not including the 1,000 lost to smallpox and rum.
If the French win over the Cherokees, Carolina will need many
troops to survive. 18p.

C.O. 5/368 (CONT'D)

Fol. 56.   20 Mar. 1740/41, S. Carolina. Lt. Gov. Bull to Bd.
of Trade. Bull asks for assistance to defend the Cherokees
against a French army marching to attack them this summer. 2p.

Fol. 156. 15 June 1742, Charleston. Lt. Gov. Bull to Bd. of
Trade. The Cherokees are S. Carolina's most numerous Indian
ally with about 3,000 men. French usually employ other Indians
against the Cherokees and Chickasaws. 5p. [Enclosures to fol.
160b].

Fol. 159. 3 June 1742. Petition from S.C. Assembly to the
King. The united opposition of the French and Spanish can
be dangerous. Assembly seeks aid for the Cherokees against
French and Indian army now only a few days' march from
Cherokee country. 4p.

C.O. 5/370   SOUTH CAROLINA, ORIGINAL CORRESPONDENCE, BD. OF TRADE:
1743-1744

Fol. 6.   23 Jan. 1743/44, Georgia Office. Caveat from Mr.
Martyn, Sec. to the Ga. Trustees, opposing the petition for a
silver mine grant since the mine is in Ga. and on Cherokee land.
2p.

Fol. 64.   1744. Copy of Minutes from Upper and Lower Houses
of Assembly and Council relating to the discovery of a silver
mine among the Cherokees. 35p.

Fol. 145. 24 Apr. 1744, Whitehall. Letter from Lords of
Committee of Council for Plantation Affairs referring to the Bd.
of Trade papers on the silver mine discovery [among the Chero-
kees]. 1p. [Enclosures to fol. 153b].

Fol. 146. 14 Oct. 1743. Copy of Address and Petition from
Assembly of S.C. against private control over the silver
mine discovered among the [Cherokees]. 5p.

Fol. 149. 8 Oct. 1743. Copy of Testimony from Wm. Wright,
refiner, who will visit this spring the supposed Cherokee
silver mine. 1p.

Fol. 150. 11 Oct. 1743. Copy of testimony from Michael
Rowe indicating that men have already left to work in the
Cherokees' silver mine. 1p.

Fol. 151. 11 Oct. 1743. Copy of testimony from Thomas
Murray who has talked with people who supposedly saw silver
brought from a Cherokee mine and who interviewed others
going to mine ore. 2p.

Fol. 152. Message from the Upper House to the Lower House
of S. Carolina (copy). Why did a Lower House committee begin
an independent rather than a joint inquiry into the silver
mine? 4p.

C.O. 5/370 (CONT'D)

Fol. 155.   19 June 1744, Council Chamber, Whitehall.   Order from
Lords of Committee of Council concerning petition from James
Maxwell and Cornelius Doharty requesting title confirmation to
a 30,000 acre grant bought from Cherokees.   3p.

Fol. 157.   Petition from James Maxwell and Cornelius Doharty
requesting confirmation of a land grant bought from the
Cherokees.   6p.

Fol. 161.   19 June 1744.   Order from Lords of Committee of
Council that Ga. Trustees' petition be heard before any grant is
awarded to Maxwell and Doharty.   3p.

Fol. 163.   Petition from Trustees for Establishing Ga. to King's
Council.   Cherokee land purchased by Maxwell and Doharty
containing iron, tin, lead, copper, and silver is land that the
King already granted to the trustees.   2p.

*C.O. 5/371   SOUTH CAROLINA, ORIGINAL CORRESPONDENCE, BD. OF TRADE:
            1722-1747*

Fol. 2.   2 Feb. 1744/45.   Gov. James Glen to Bd. of Trade.   4p.
[Enclosures to fol. 12b].

    Fol. 6.   10 Oct. 1744.   Emperor of the Cherokees to Gov.
    Glen.   Emperor has not visited Glen because he was busy
    hunting to pay back traders and because the Cherokees heard
    rumors that the English were at war with the French and
    Spanish.   4p.

    Fol. 10   3 Dec. 1744, Charleston.   Message from Glen to
    House of Commons in the *Supplement to the South Carolina
    Gazette*.   Chickasaws, Catawbas, Creeks, and the Emperor of
    the Cherokees have expressed their desire for lasting ties
    to the British.   3p.

Fol. 14.   25 Oct. 1722, Carolina.   Richard West to Bd. of Trade.
West discusses act regulating the Indian trade and other bills.
10p.

Fol. 18.   22 Mar. 1722/23, London.   Memorial from Francis Yonge
to Bd. of Trade.   Yonge discusses West's report on Indian trading
law.   6p.

Fol. 26.   11 Jan. 1727/28.   Francis Fane to Bd. of Trade.   Fane
reports on eight S.C. acts passed from 1723-1725, including one
for regulating Indian trade.   2p.

Fol. 28.   4 June 1728, S. Carolina.   Francis Fane to Bd. of Trade.
Fane reports on several acts passed in 1727, including one providing for several expeditions against the Indians and for
appointing an Indian affairs commissioner.   2p.

Fol. 30.   6 Oct. 1730, S. Carolina.   Francis Fane to Bd. of Trade.
Fane reports on six acts passed in 1726, including one regulating
the Indian trade.   2p.

C.O. 5/371 (CONT'D)

Fol. 42. 13 Oct. 1735, S. Carolina. Francis Fane to Bd. of Trade. Fane reports on ten acts passed in 1733, including several providing for better security against the Indians and regulating the Indian trade. 3p.

Fol. 44. 25 May 1736, S. Carolina. Francis Fane to Bd. of Trade. Fane reports on eight acts passed in 1735, including one raising funds to regulate the Indian trade. 4p.

Fol. 48. 24 Dec. 1737, S. Carolina. Francis Fane to Bd. of Trade. Fane reports on 16 acts passed in 1736 and 1737, including one eliminating certain duties on the Indian trade and releasing Indian traders from certain penalties. 5p.

Fol. 54. 15 Jan. 1741/42, S. Carolina. Francis Fane to Bd. of Trade. Fane reports on acts passed from 1738-1741, including one preserving peace and regulating trade with Indians friendly to S. Carolina. 6p.

Fol. 61. Representation from John Fenwick to Bd. of Trade. French power is growing over all the Indians between the Hudson Bay and the Gulf of Mexico, except for the Senecas, Creeks, Chickasaws, and Cherokees. If the Creeks and Cherokees had been led by the French in 1715, all S.C. would have fallen. 6p.

Fol. 101. 2 May 1746, Saluda. Gov. Glen to Bd. of Trade (duplicate). Emperor of the Cherokees informed Glen that the French sent peace proposals and requested permission to build a fort in Cherokee country. French will return next winter for an answer. 5p.

Fol. 104. 29 Sept. 1746, S. Carolina. Gov. Glen to Bd. of Trade. French threat will turn the Cherokees towards them. Although Glen proposed a fort in the Overhill Towns, the Cherokees did not readily agree to it. Creeks are less numerous than the Cherokees, numbering only 2,500 gunmen, and are the only barrier against French Louisiana. 6p.

Fol. 133. 28 Apr. 1747, S. Carolina. Gov. Glen to Bd. of Trade. Although the Cherokees are being courted by the French, the tribe is attached to England and has offered assistance in building a fort in their country to keep the French out. 5p.

Fol. 140. 30 July 1747, Whitehall. Duke of Newcastle to Bd. of Trade. Should England build a fort among the Cherokees to keep the French out? 2p.

C.O. 5/372   SOUTH CAROLINA, ORIGINAL CORRESPONDENCE, BD. OF TRADE: 1748-1751

Fol. 27. 20 May 1748, Whitehall. Committee of Council for Plantation Affairs to Bd. of Trade. Bd. should prepare instructions for Gov. Glen to make a treaty with the Cherokees acquiring land to build a fort. 3p.

C.O. 5/372 (CONT'D)

Fol. 34. Feb. 1747/48, S. Carolina. Gov. Glen to Bd. of Trade. Glen lists the Indian tribes and the number of warriors. Cherokees live no more than 90 miles from the English settlements and have about 3,000 fighting men. 8p.

Fol. 38. 14 Apr. 1748, S. Carolina. Gov. Glen to Bd. of Trade. Assembly wants Glen to promise the Cherokees to build a fort in their country if they put to death the murderer of an Englishman. 4p.

Fol. 42. 23 Apr. 1748, S. Carolina. Gov. Glen to Bd. of Trade. Glen's journey among S.C. Indian neighbors had more influence upon them than £10,000 worth of presents in Charleston could buy. 3p.

Fol. 52. 30 June 1748, Whitehall. Copy of Order in Council approving the additional instructions concerning Glen's negotiations with the Cherokees to build a fort in their country. 3p.

Fol. 67. 26 July 1748, S. Carolina. Gov. Glen to Bd. of Trade. Indians have so terrified traders that they even fear the Cherokees. Cherokees have executed the Indian guilty of murdering an Englishman. Forts should be built in the Cherokee and Choctaw nations, between the Catawbas and Cherokees, and between the Chickasaws and Creeks. 4p.

Fol. 76. 10 Oct. 1748, S. Carolina. Gov. Glen to Bd. of Trade. Glen will tell Cherokees that they will no longer be rewarded for warring against French. Glen is pleased that Bd. approves building a fort in Cherokee country. 6p.

Fol. 80. 10 Oct. 1748, S. Carolina. Gov. Glen to Bd. of Trade. Glen is pleased that the Government will appropriate £1,500 sterling annually in London to purchase presents for Indians near S. Carolina. 15p. [Enclosures to fol. 95b].

Fol. 88. Governor Glen's Observations upon the Acts of Assembly ... of South Carolina [for 1747-1748]. Maj. Wm. Pinckney was appointed Commissioner of Indian Trade. 14p.

Fol. 120. 19 July 1749, S. Carolina. Gov. Glen to Bd. of Trade. 3p. [Enclosures to fol. 155b].

Fol. 122. [1749], S. Carolina. Answers from Gov. Glen to Queries from the Bd. of Trade. Glen lists neighboring Indians and warriors. Cherokees have about 3,000 gunmen and are friendly to the English. Catawbas have 300 gunmen, the Chickasaws 2,500, and the Choctaws many thousands. 60p.

Fol. 158. 12 Aug. 1749, S. Carolina. Gov. Glen to Bd. of Trade. A general meeting of the Cherokee, Creek, and Catawba headmen will be held in August to conclude peace between the Creeks and Cherokees, who have been at war many years. French have previously prevented this peace. 8p.

C.O. 5/372 (CONT'D)

Fol. 168. 23 Dec. 1749, S. Carolina. Gov. Glen to Bd. of Trade.
French in the Alabama Fort and Mobile have tried to stop the
Indians from attending a peace conference for the Creeks and
Cherokees. French Indians have attacked Cherokee towns and
many Cherokees, including Half Breed Johnie, died on the way.
The Cherokee Emperor was not expected to live. 11p. [Enclosures
to fol. 196b].

> Fol. 190. S. Carolina. Gov. Glen to Monsieur Vaudreuil,
> Gov. of Louisiana (copy). Many Indians are free and
> independent, having never been conquered. They have the
> right to make treaties and trade with whomever they
> please. 4p.

Fol. 226. 15 July and 16 Sept. 1750, S. Carolina. Gov. Glen
to Bd. of Trade. French have rekindled the Creek-Cherokee war.
Creeks burned two Cherokee towns, killed most of the inhabitants,
and carried off the rest as slaves. Neighboring Cherokee towns
have moved further north. Glen has purchased land from the
Cherokees to build a fort. 28p.

Fol. 252. 2 Oct. 1750, S. Carolina. [Gov. Glen] to Bd. of
Trade. French Indians have killed many Cherokees. Glen hopes
that he has reconciled the Creeks and Cherokees. 19p.

Fol. 282. Feb. 1750 [1751]. Gov. Glen to Bd. of Trade. Glen
describes S.C. boundaries and foreigner encroachments. S. Carolina's last land purchase was from the Cherokees and it lies
about 240 miles northwest of Charleston. Catawbas, Cherokees,
Creeks, and Chickasaws possess great countries. Many traders
have built houses, gardens, and small plantations among these
tribes. 46p.

C.O. 5/373   SOUTH CAROLINA, ORIGINAL CORRESPONDENCE, BD. OF TRADE:
1746-1752

Fol. 7. 6 June 1750. Andrew Rutledge to James Crokatt (extract).
One argument in favor of annexing Ga. to Carolina is that the
Creek and Cherokee trade might be better regulated. Georgians
cause the confusion in the Cherokee trade. 3p.

Fol. 12. 6 Feb. 1752, Treasury Chambers. Lords of Treasury to
Bd. of Trade. Treasury forwards Crokatt's memorial requesting
£3,000 worth of presents for tribes bordering S.C. and Georgia.
2p. [Enclosures to fol. 14b].

> Fol. 13. 22 Jan. 1752. Memorial from Crokatt to Lords of
> Treasury. S.C. and Ga. need £3,000 worth of presents for
> neighboring Indian allies. Presents are needed to counteract
> French encroachments. 2p.

Fol. 65. 19 June 1752. Trustees for Establishing Ga. to Bd.
of Trade. 23p. [Enclosures to fol. 111b].

C.O. 5/373 (CONT'D)

Fol. 99. 28 May 1752, Oakchoys Square. Talk from Patrick Graham to the Upper and Lower Creeks and their Reply. [French?] are responsible for the differences between the Creeks and Cherokees. 7p.

Fol. 175. Dec. 1751, S. Carolina. Gov. Glen to Bd. of Trade. Instead of the English losing the Catawbas, Cherokees, Creeks, and Chickasaws to the French, they have won the favor of many hostile Indians. The French know that the Cherokee country is the key to Carolina. The Creeks and Cherokees have agreed to peace. 29p. [Enclosures to fol. 196b].

Fol. 192. 1746. Extracts of ... an Account of the Commotions in the Township of Saxagotha ... Occasioned by ... the French and Indians ... by Stephen Crell. French have made peace with the Cherokees. 4p.

Fol. 194. 1746. Extract of journal of Col. Francis Lejeau reporting that Glen requested a meeting with the Catawbas at Congarees, the Cherokees at Ninety Six, and the Creeks and Chickasaws at New Windsor to counteract French attempts to seduce the Cherokees. 2p.

Fol. 195. Indian Traders to Gov., Council, and Assembly. Remonstrance of the Present State of the Indian Trade of the Cherokee Nation. Troops are needed in the Lower Towns to convince the Cherokees that Carolina and Ga. are their masters as well as friends. 2p.

Fol. 197a. 29 Jan. 1752. Gov. Glen to Bd. of Trade. 3p. [Enclosures to fol. 205b].

Fol. 200. 12 Feb. 1746. Copy of the Deed of Sale by the Cherokee Indians. 4p.

C.O. 5/374   SOUTH CAROLINA, ORIGINAL CORRESPONDENCE, BD. OF TRADE:
1752-1754

Fol. 12. 27 July 1752, S. Carolina. Gov. Glen to Bd. of Trade. A garrisoned fort in the Overhill Towns would eventually bring that country into the King's fold. 6p.

Fol. 20. 10 Nov. 1752, London. James Crokatt to Bd. of Trade Crokatt sends a memorial concerning Indian presents. 2p. [Enclosures to fol. 29b].

Fol. 22. Memorial from James Crokatt on Indian presents. Expenses of distributing Indian presents are too much. It cost £300 to send agents and 20 men to the Cherokees in 1746 to distribute £100 worth of presents. 4p.

Fol. 24. 9 Nov. 1749, London. Memorial from James Crokatt to Duke of Bedford (copy). Crokatt discusses distribution of Indian presents. 4p.

C.O. 5/374 (CONT'D)

       Fol. 26.   22 Oct. 1750, London.   Second Memorial from James
       Crokatt to Duke of Bedford (copy).   Indian presents have
       not been purchased.   4p.

       Fol. 28.   13-19 Nov. 1750, War Office.   Henry Fox, Sec.
       of War, to the Duke of Bedford (copy).   Report of Fox
       includes Bedford's comments on Indian presents.   4p.

Fol. 69.   16 Dec. 1752, S. Carolina.   Gov. Glen to Bd. of Trade.
Glen has again stopped a French inspired war between the Cherokees and Creeks.   The Cherokees had suffered the most and were
overjoyed at the news of the proposed peace.   8p.

Fol. 150.   25 June 1753, S. Carolina.   Gov. Glen to Bd. of
Trade.   Indian parties have passed through Cherokee country to
war against the Creeks.   Some 400 Cherokees went to assist the
Chickasaws.   8p.   [Enclosures to fol. 186b].

       Fol. 157.   30 May - 4 June 1753.   A Treaty Between the
       Government of South Carolina and the Creek Nation.   Treaty
       includes peace between the Creeks and Cherokees.   51p.

Fol. 187.   30 July 1753, S. Carolina.   Gov. Glen to Bd. of Trade.
When S.C. purchased Cherokee land, the government negotiated
only with the Lower Towns.   Overhill leaders do not recognize
this purchase.   Cherokees have agreed to peace with the Creeks
and have pressed for a fort near the Lower Towns.   7p.
[Enclosures to fol. 223b].

       Fol. 191.   July 1749 - Nov. 1752.   An Account of Presents
       for the Indians [Allied with and near S.C. and Georgia].
       Report indicates presents given to each tribe.   48p.

Fol. 225.   25 Oct. 1753, en route to Cherokee nation.   Gov.
Glen to Bd. of Trade (copy).   Va. traders in Tellico and the
Overhill Towns are reportedly endeavoring to create confusion.
All traders in the Overhill Towns oppose the new fort because
it may cause the Indians to resettle the Lower Towns.   5p.
[Enclosures to fol. 229b].

       Fol. 228.   11 Sept. 1753, Richmond.   Charles Pinckney to
       Mr. Pownall.   A new fort among the Cherokees is important
       for the peace and safety of the province.   3p.

Fol. 233.   9 Apr. 1754.   Extract of letter from Wm. Pinckney
with information from the Cherokees indicating that the French
Indians have tried to make peace and obtain permission to build
a French fort among the Cherokees.   Old Hop would not answer
the French until he had heard from S. Carolina.   1p.

Fol. 234.   1 June 1754.   Representation from Charles Pinckney
to Bd. of Trade.   French should be prevented from building a
fort among the Upper Cherokees.   4p.

C.O. 5/375   SOUTH CAROLINA, ORIGINAL CORRESPONDENCE, BD. OF TRADE:
*   1754-1757*

Fol. 3.   27 June 1754.   Representation from Charles Pinckney to
Bd. of Trade.   Pickney discusses the French plan to build a
fort among the Upper Cherokees.   5p.

Fol. 7.   26 Aug. 1754, S. Carolina.   Gov. Glen to Bd. of Trade.
An account of Glen's journey to the Cherokees to build a fort
near the Lower Towns.   10p.   [Enclosures to fol. 21b].

> Fol. 12.   [ca. July - August 1754].   Address from an inhab-
> itant of Saxagotha to Gov. Glen (copy).   Glen should be
> praised for quieting the Cherokees, for procuring a general
> peace between neighboring Indians, and for building a fort
> in the Cherokee country.   4p.

> Fol. 15.   15 - 22 Jan. 1754, Charleston.   Speech from Glen
> to General Assembly in the *South Carolina Gazette*.   Fort in
> Cherokee country is completed.   5p.

Fol. 26.   29 June 1754.   Representation from Charles Pinckney
to Bd. of Trade.   Pinckney discusses boundary between N. and
S. Carolina.   3p.   [Enclosure of fol. 28].

Fol. 28.   5 July 1754, Craven Street.   Letter from Charles
Pinckney enclosing paper on boundary between N. and S. Carolina.
2p.   [Enclosure at fol. 26].

Fol. 49.   29 May 1755, S. Carolina.   Gov. Glen to Bd. of Trade.
The Cherokee King has sent some tribesmen to request a meeting
halfway between Charleston and Chote.   French and Northern
Indians have reportedly concluded a peace treaty with the Cherokees.   Cherokees have avoided speaking about the Overhill fort.
13p.   [Enclosures to fol. 70b].

> Fol. 57.   21 Nov. 1754.   Speech from Gov. Glen to General
> Assembly in the *South Carolina Gazette*.   French are endeav-
> oring to win over the English Indians.   7p.

> Fol. 61.   Speech from Glen to King Hagler (Catawba King),
> Headmen, and Warriors (copy).   Glen wants the Catawbas'
> assistance along the Ohio.   He requested the same from the
> Cherokees and Creeks.   6p.

> Fol. 65.   Gov. Glen to the Six Nations.   Mohawks who were
> sent to assist the Catawbas, Creeks, and Cherokees along
> the Ohio were killed by mistake.   Cherokees have complained
> about the Six Nations warriors.   4p.

> Fol. 67.   Jan. 1755.   Gov. Glen to Lt. Gov. Dinwiddie.
> Glen asks for the promised aid to build a fort among the
> Upper Cherokees.   Shawnees and Tawaws have harassed the
> Cherokees ever since the Cherokees refused to join them in
> war against Carolina.   Glen itemizes the estimated cost
> for the fort.   7p.

C.O. 5/375 (CONT'D)

Fol. 77. 23 Jan. 1756, Office of Ordnance. Mr. Bogdani to John Pownall. What is the Bd. of Trade's opinion on the request for 179 barrels of gunpowder for the Indian trade in S. Carolina? 3p.

Fol. 85. 4 Feb. 1756. Representation from Charles Pinckney to Bd. of Trade. Pinckney discusses Cherokee complaints and the building of a fort among the Upper Cherokees. 4p.

Fol. 93. 1 May 1756, Office of Ordnance. Mr. Bogdani to John Pownall. What is the Bd. of Trade's opinion on the request to export 17,200 pounds of gunpowder to S.C. for the Indian trade? 2p.

Fol. 95. 25 June 1756, Office of Ordnance. John Boddington to John Pownall. What is the Bd. of Trade's opinion on the request to export 12,650 pounds of gunpowder, 702 small arms, and 19 pairs of pistols to S.C. for the Indian trade? 2p.

Fol. 97. 14 Apr. 1756, S. Carolina. Gov. Glen to Bd. of Trade. Glen has added 16-18,000 people and 40 million acres of land to His Majesty's control by meeting with the Cherokees. Glen is certain that the Cherokees and Creeks would have abandoned England upon news of Braddock's defeat if he had not met them. 20p. [Enclosures to fol. 127b].

> Fol. 109. 24-31 July 1755, S. Carolina. *South Carolina Gazette*. Account of Glen's meeting with the Cherokees resulting in the tribe giving all its land to the King. 4p.

> Fol. 111. [June 1755], Saluda. Copy of report of Gov. Glen's meeting with the Cherokees resulting in the tribe giving all its land to the King. 4p.

> Fol. 113. 12 Jan. 1756. Historical Relation of Facts Delivered by Ludovick Grant ... to ... Governor [Glen]. Grant reports on the surrender of Cherokee land. 11p.

> Fol. 124. 12 Jan. 1756. A Conversation between ... the Governor of South Carolina and Chuconunto [Little Carpenter], Headman of the Cherokees. The two men discuss [Little Carpenter's] trip to England. 4p.

Fol. 132. 19 July 1756, Charleston. Gov. Lyttleton to Bd. of Trade (duplicate). Assembly only granted the King a £14,000 loan to build a fort among the Upper Cherokees. 7p.

Fol. 136. 19 June 1756, Charleston. Gov. Lyttleton to Bd. of Trade. If the Assembly were dissolved, it would be impossible to proceed with building the Cherokee fort this summer. Glen was directed to ask Gen. Braddock for money for building the fort among the Cherokees. 12p.

Fol. 142. 11 Aug. 1756, Charleston. Gov. Lyttleton to Bd. of
Trade. Lyttleton approved a tax bill providing £4,000 sterling
for building a fort among the Upper Cherokees. At the Cherokees'
request, Va. has begun a fort in a different spot. Lyttleton
asked Little Carpenter and Old Hop to aid the Virginians with
as many warriors as possible. 7p.

Fol. 146. 14 Aug. 1756, Charleston. Gov. Lyttleton to Bd. of
Trade. Ft. Prince George has been repaired. 3p.

Fol. 148. 2 Dec. 1756. Representation from Charles Pinckney
to Bd. of Trade. Creeks have not responded to the invitations
to meet with the Cherokees and the S.C. Governor. Creeks have
received many presents from the French. 6p.

Fol. 152. 2 Dec. 1756. Charles Pinckney. The Strength of the
Province of South Carolina and a Scheme for its Defense and
Security Against the French. There are two forts (one about
460 and the other about 500 miles from Charleston) being built
in the Cherokee country. 5p.

Fol. 155. 17 Oct. 1756, Charleston. Gov. Lyttleton to Bd. of
Trade. About 190 Lower Cherokees left Charleston after promising to fight the French. Maj. Lewis, who supervised the
building of Virginia's fort among the Upper Cherokees, complained
about Little Carpenter's excuses for not sending any men to
Virginia. 9p.

Fol. 163. 25 Dec. 1756, Charleston. Gov. Lyttleton to Bd. of
Trade (duplicate). Capt. Demeré writes that the Cherokees who
visited the Alabama Fort are the same Tellico Indians who tried
unsuccessfully to turn the Creeks against the English. 7p.
[Enclosures to fol. 170b].

Fol. 171. 31 Dec. 1756, Charleston. Gov. Lyttleton to Bd. of
Trade. Capt. Demeré writes that the French are preparing to
invade the Cherokee nation. Lyttleton has ordered reinforcements
for Capt. Demeré. Little Carpenter has assured Demeré that he
is coming to Charleston. 4p. [Enclosures to fol. 177b].

   Fol. 173. 25 Nov. 1756, English Camp [in Cherokee country].
   Intelligence from Capt. R. Demeré with news that Old Warrior
   of Tomotley heard that some Tellico Cherokees visited the
   Alabama Fort and met with some Choctaws. Lantagnac and
   Brown will bring goods to the Cherokees. 4p.

   Fol. 175. 2 Dec. 1756, English Camp. Intelligence from
   Capt. R. Demeré with news that Tellico Cherokees went to
   Mobile intending to go on to New Orleans and eventually
   France. French have invited Cherokees to a meeting at Cold
   Springs. French plan to proceed to Hiwassee Old Town and
   erect a fort. 2p.

   Fol. 176. 13 Dec. 1756, English Camp. Intelligence from
   Capt. R. Demeré with news that Judd's Friend does not know
   whether all the Overhill Towns will join the French. He
   expects to ask the governor for men very soon. 4p.

C.O. 5/375 (CONT'D)

Fol. 180. 22 Apr. 1757, Charleston. Gov. Lyttleton to Bd. of
Trade. Captured French documents reveal that preliminary articles of peace and friendship exist between Kerlerec, Governor
of La., and the Cherokee deputies from Tellico. English have
been in danger of losing the Cherokees for years. Lyttleton
describes talk with Little Carpenter and plans for a fort in
the Cherokee country. 9p. [Enclosures to fol. 202b].

> Fol. 187. 23 Nov. 1756, New Orleans. *Articles et condi-*
> *tions préliminaires de paix entre les Français et la nation*
> *cherakis* (copy). 8p. *French.*
>
> Fol. 193. 13 Dec. 1756, New Orleans. Copy of letter from
> Mons. de Kerlerec discussing the Cherokees, numbering
> 3,500 warriors, and their decision to conclude a peace
> treaty with the French. Cherokee desire for peace has
> intensified during the last three years, but Kerlerec will
> withhold ratification of the treaty until Cherokees prove
> their sincerity by warring on the English. 8p. *French.*
> [Translated extract at W.O. 34/38/12].
>
> Fol. 197. 30 Jan. 1757, New Orleans. Copy of letter from
> Mons. de Kerlerec who forwards copies of the peace treaty
> with the Cherokees. If Vaudreuil agrees to the treaty, he
> will have to supply the Cherokees with their needs, espe-
> cially ammunition. Supplies for the Choctaws should be
> doubled. 4p. *French.* [Translated extract at W.O. 34/
> 38/14].

Fol. 203. 24 May 1757, Charleston. Gov. Lyttleton to Bd. of
Trade. Assembly has enabled Lyttleton to help garrison the new
Cherokee fort with a provincial company. Assembly has also
helped raise another 50 man company to garrison Ft. Prince George
at Keowee. Old Hop has sent runners to all towns asking for a
general war against the French. 11p. [Enclosures to fol. 211b].

> Fol. 209. Report from both Houses of Assembly concerning
> the boundary line between N. and S. Carolina. Since S.C.
> has built Ft. Prince George and Ft. Loudoun among the
> Cherokees, the northern boundary should include the area
> where the forts exist. 5p.

Fol. 212. 11 June 1757, Charleston. Gov. Lyttleton to Bd. of
Trade. Indian affairs are much improved. Many Cherokee parties
have gone to war and 140 Catawbas have marched to Virginia. 6p.

Fol. 217. 12 July 1757, Charleston. Gov. Lyttleton to Bd. of
Trade. S.C. has taken measures to reimburse the expenses of
soldiers at Ft. Loudoun. Lyttleton sends the plan of Ft.
Loudoun [not enclosed]. 5p.

Fol. 228. 24 Nov. 1757, Council Chamber, Whitehall. Order in
Council forwarding to the Bd. of Trade a memorial requesting
money for fortifications. 1p. [Enclosures to fol. 232b].

C.O. 5/375 (CONT'D)

Fol. 229. 22 Nov. 1757. Memorial from James Wright
reporting that S.C. has built and repaired forts among the
Upper and Lower Cherokees. Yet more money is needed for
fortifications. 3p.

C.O. 5/376 SOUTH CAROLINA, ORIGINAL CORRESPONDENCE, BD. OF TRADE:
        1757-1760

Fol. 1. 15 Sept. 1757, Charleston. Gov. Lyttleton to Bd. of
Trade (duplicate). Col. Montgomery's Highland Battalion
arrived in Charleston on Sept. 1. 7p. [Enclosures to fol. 14b].

Fol. 13b. 7 Jan. 1757. Copy of General Account of
Ordnance Stores. Report includes Ft. Prince George at
Keowee. 4p.

Fol. 15. 3 Nov. 1757, Charleston. Gov. Lyttleton to Bd. of
Trade. Ft. Prince George at Keowee is better prepared than
when it was first built. Capt. Demeré's brother has taken
command at Ft. Loudoun. Little Carpenter has gone to war
[against the French?] with about 40 warriors. 4p.

Fol. 17. 30 Nov. 1757, Charleston. Gov. Lyttleton to Bd. of
Trade. Unless S. Carolina's boundary includes the Cherokees
and Catawbas, the present trade regulations will not work and
there will be no restraints on traders after they pass the
boundary. S.C. has spent a great deal of money building two
forts among the Cherokees. 9p.

Fol. 31. 6 Dec. 1757, Court at St. James. Copy of Order in
Council proposing that a skillful engineer be sent to S.C. to
supervise fortifications, including the two Cherokee forts. 3p.

Fol. 35. 6 Dec. 1758. Memorial from James Wright to Bd. of
Trade. Wright has purchased presents for several tribes bordering S. Carolina. 1p. [Enclosures to fol. 38b].

Fol. 36. 6 Dec. 1758. James Wright. Account of Goods
Shipped to Gov. Lyttleton for the Indians. 5p.

Fol. 41. 7 Aug. 1758, Charleston. Gov. Lyttleton to Bd. of
Trade (duplicate). Lord Loudoun had planned to have many
Cherokees for his offensive operations along the Ohio. After
returning from an expedition to the French Fort, Little Carpenter
is trying to collect as many warriors as he can. S.C. has two
forts among the Cherokees but none among the Creeks, Catawbas,
or Chickasaws. 18p. [Enclosures to fol. 54b].

Fol. 51. 3 June 1758, Ft. Prince George. Little Carpenter
to Gov. Lyttleton (copy). Little Carpenter promises to
fight the King's enemies in Virginia. He hopes that
Lyttleton will forget the Cherokees rogues from the Lower
Towns. 3p.

C.O. 5/376 (CONT'D)

Fol. 53. 2 July 1758, Ft. Prince George. Geo. Turner to
Gov. Lyttleton (extract). Turner delivered presents to the
Cherokees. Little Carpenter said that conjurers warned
the Cherokees against going to Virginia. 4p.

Fol. 55. 2 Oct. 1758, Charleston. Gov. Lyttleton to Bd. of
Trade (duplicate). Lt. Gov. Fauquier requested that the Cherokees be restrained from revenging Va. murders. Gen. Forbes
reports that his Cherokees have returned home. 6p. [Enclosures
to fol. 64b].

Fol. 59. 7 Aug. 1758, Ft. Prince George. Talk from Tistoe,
the Wolf, and other Headmen of the Lower Towns to Gov.
Lyttleton (copy). Lower Cherokees are uneasy about recent
misunderstanding. They will fight for England as soon as
they receive ammunition and other necessities. 2p.

Fol. 60. 28 July 1758, Chote. Talk from Old Hop and
Headmen of the Upper Cherokees to Gov. Lyttleton (copy).
Upper Cherokees are ashamed and sad over the conduct of
their young warriors. Tribe wishes to live in peace with
England. 2p.

Fol. 61. 26 Sept. 1758, Charleston. Talk from Gov.
Lyttleton to Headmen and Warriors of the Middle and Lower
Cherokee Settlements (copy). Cherokees should not seek
revenge on Virginians. English will give presents to
compensate the relatives of the slain Cherokees. 3p.

Fol. 63. 29 July 1758, Ft. Loudoun. Little Carpenter to
Gov. Lyttleton (copy). Cherokees were the aggressors in
Virginia. Willinawa, who had a relative killed by the
Virginians, seeks no revenge. 3p.

Fol. 65. 1 Dec. 1758. Gov. Lyttleton to Bd. of Trade. Gov.
of Va. has thanked Lyttleton for preventing a Cherokee war
against Virginia. Lyttleton sends the minutes of his November
conferences with the Cherokees. 2p. [Enclosures to fol. 70b].

Fol. 67. 8 - 16 Nov. 1758, Council Chamber. Minutes of the
Conferences Between Gov. Lyttleton and the Cherokee Deputies
(copy). Lyttleton attempts to settle the differences between
the tribe and Virginia. 7p.

Fol. 71. 2 Dec. 1758, Charleston. Gov. Lyttleton to Bd. of
Trade. Assembly consented to using £20,000 to outfit the Cherokees for the expedition against Ft. Duquesne. 7p. [Enclosures
to fol. 76b].

Fol. 77. 18 Feb. 1758 [1759], Charleston. Gov. Lyttleton to
Bd. of Trade (triplicate). Capt. Demeré writes that Little
Carpenter is coming to Ft. Loudoun with prisoners from his
expedition against the French. 3p.

C.O. 5/376 (CONT'D)

Fol. 79. 21 Feb. 1759, Charleston. Gov. Lyttleton to Bd. of
Trade. Gen. Forbes wrote that Little Carpenter and nine other
Cherokees deserted two days before the fall of Ft. Duquesne.
Cherokees were pursued, disarmed, and conducted to Williamsburg.
3p.

Fol. 81. 14 Apr. 1759, Charleston. Gov. Lyttleton to Bd. of
Trade. Capt. Demeré wrote that the Upper Cherokees have sent
runners to the Northern Indians and French asking for peace.
Keowee Indians killed a Catawba woman in revenge for a Cherokee female killed by the Catawbas. French commander at Mobile
plans an expedition against Ft. Loudoun. 10p. [Enclosures to
fol. 95b].

Fol. 98. 8 May 1759, Charleston. Gov. Lyttleton to Bd. of
Trade. Since Little Carpenter deserted Gen. Forbes, Lyttleton
treated the chief coldly. Lyttleton, however, gave Little
Carpenter some gifts because the Cherokees have promised that
Little Carpenter will oppose the French in his nation. 5p.

Fol. 105. 1 Sept. 1759, Charleston. Gov. Lyttleton to Bd. of
Trade (duplicate). Settico Cherokees have scalped 19 people
along the Yadkin and Catawba Rivers. Wawhatchee, a Lower Cherokee, denies that the Cherokees and Creeks had agreed to war
against England. 8p. [Enclosures to fol. 129b].

> Fol. 109. 22 May 1759. Talk from Gov. Lyttleton to the
> Emperor Old Hop and Little Carpenter (copy). Lyttleton
> wants satisfaction for the 19 whites scalped by Moytoy of
> Settico and others. 3p.
>
> Fol. 111. 27 June 1759, Ft. Loudoun. Old Hop and Little
> Carpenter to Gov. Lyttleton (copy). Little Carpenter has
> talked to the people guilty of [scalping 19 whites] and was
> assured they would not do it again. Willinawa, warrior
> from Toqueh, agrees to maintain peace. 3p.
>
> Fol. 113. 10 July 1759, Ft. Loudoun. Capt. Paul Demeré
> to Gov. Lyttleton (copy). Little Carpenter is afraid to
> turn over any of those guilty of scalping whites because
> their leader is related to the Great Warrior who would
> never consent to it. 4p.
>
> Fol. 115. 22 July 1759, Ft. Loudoun. Capt. Paul Demeré
> to Gov. Lyttleton (extract). In spite of promises to
> remain home, Little Carpenter will attack the French. Corn
> Tassel of Toqueh said that there were bad talks at Settico
> and Tellico again. 2p.
>
> Fol. 117. 3 Aug. 1759, Ft. Prince George. Lt. Coytmore
> to Gov. Lyttleton (extract). Creeks have a talk from the
> French to the Cherokees. Creeks are determined to war
> against England if the Cherokees will join them. Old Hop
> has sent messenger to the Northern Indians. Upper Creeks
> and a few French will assist the Overhill Towns in cutting
> off Ft. Loudoun. 4p.

C.O. 5/376 (CONT'D)

Fol. 119. 1 May 1759, Chickasaw nation. John Buckells to
Jerome Courtonne (copy). Letter contains the journal of
Buckells (a Chickasaw trader) stating that the Chickasaws
have attacked the new French fort at the forks of the Wabash
and Cherokee Rivers. 5p.

Fol. 126. Message from Lyttleton to Assembly (copy).
Cherokees have raided this province and slaughtered some
of its inhabitants. French are endeavoring to turn the
tribe against England. 3p.

Fol. 130. 10 Sept. 1759, Charleston. Gov. Lyttleton to Bd. of
Trade. 4p. [Enclosures to fol. 133b].

Fol. 132. 6 June 1759, Council Chamber. Copy of minutes
of Council reporting the interrogation of Maximillian More
and his half-breed son, who came to Ft. Loudoun with news
about the French and Creek treaty. 4p.

Fol. 134. 16 Oct. 1759. Gov. Lyttleton to Bd. of Trade.
Lyttleton has requested the Chickasaws and Catawbas to attack
the Cherokees. He asked Atkin to cause a diversion by having
the Breed Camp, Upper Chickasaw, and Creek Indians fall upon
the Cherokees. 7p. [Enclosures to fol. 157b].

Fol. 138. 12 Sept. 1759, Ft. Loudoun. Maurice Anderson
to Lt. Coytmore (copy). Settico Cherokees have attempted
to surprise the fort. Supplies are low and the roads
blocked. Settico and Tellico are only towns openly hostile.
2p.

Fol. 140. 13 Sept. 1759, Ft. Loudoun. Capt. Paul Demeré
to Gov. Lyttleton (copy). Indians were peaceful at Ft.
Loudoun until Demeré stopped supplying them ammunition.
A messenger sent by Old Hop and Standing Turkey to the
Alabama Fort said that the time had come for England to
cut the Indians off. Little Carpenter will hopefully
straighten out everything when he returns. 3p.

Fol. 142. 26 Sept. 1759, Ft. Prince George. Lt. Richard
Coytmore to Gov. Lyttleton (copy). A crisis has developed.
The Lower Towns, except for Kewohee which appears to be
neutral, are at war. It is impossible to supply Ft. Loudoun.
3p.

Fol. 144. 26 Sept. 1759, Ft. Prince George. John Stuart
to Gov. Lyttleton (copy). All communications with Ft.
Loudoun are cut off. War will happen regardless of whether
the Indian demand for ammunition is granted. Stuart will
help defend the fort until reinforcements arrive. 2p.

Fol. 146. Message from Lyttleton to Assembly (copy).
Lyttleton will delay declaring war against the Cherokees,
but the Assembly must help repress Cherokee hostility by
granting supplies. 2p.

Fol. 148. Speech from Lyttleton to Assembly. Lyttleton adjourns the assembly so he can join the Cherokee expedition. 2p.

Fol. 150. 6 Oct. 1759, Commons House of Assembly. Message from Assembly to Lyttleton (copy). Assembly requests an estimate of how many men will be needed to repel the Cherokees and to obtain satisfaction. 2p.

Fol. 152. 11 Oct. 1759, Commons House of Assembly. Message from Assembly to Lyttleton (copy). Could the governor delay declaring war against the Cherokees until all peaceful means of obtaining satisfaction are exhausted? 2p.

Fol. 154. Message from Lyttleton to Assembly (copy). Cherokee expedition will need 1,500 men. 2p.

Fol. 156. Speech from Lyttleton to Assembly (copy). Vigorous and speedy measures are needed to stop the Cherokees. Gov. is soliciting aid from the Catawbas and Chickasaws. He has written the Creeks, the Breed Camp, and the Chickasaws to fall upon Cherokee towns to create a diversion. 4p.

Fol. 158. 23 Oct. 1759, Charleston. Gov. Lyttleton to Bd. of Trade (duplicate). Lyttleton has taken a variety of measures against the Cherokees, including holding peaceful conferences with the tribe. He has decided, however, to send a force against them to seek satisfaction. 5p. [Enclosures to fol. 166b].

Fol. 162. 18 - 22 Oct. 1759, Council Chamber. Minutes of the conferences between Gov. Lyttleton and some Headmen of the Cherokees. Lyttleton met with the Great Warrior of Chote, the Black Dog of Hiwassee, Tistoe of Keowee, and others. He gave them the English terms for peace. 9p.

Fol. 167. 27 Oct. - 14 Dec. 1759. Speaker of Assembly to Mr. Wright (extract). Little Carpenter has returned from the French Fort with prisoners and scalps. Some people question the necessity of an expedition against the Cherokees. Governor will meet the Cherokees at Ft. Prince George. 3p.

Fol. 169. 29 Dec. 1759, Ft. Prince George. Gov. Lyttleton to Bd. of Trade. Lyttleton has concluded peace with the Cherokees and holds 21 principal warriors as hostages for the delivery of an equal number of those guilty of murdering the King's subjects. 3p. [Enclosures to fol. 172b].

Fol. 171. 26 Dec. 1759, Ft. Prince George. Copy of Treaty of Peace and Friendship Concluded by ... Lyttleton ... with Attacullaculla ... and Other [Cherokees]. 4p.

Fol. 173. 10 Dec. 1759, Ft. Prince George. Gov. Lyttleton to Bd. of Trade. Lyttleton describes his Cherokee expedition. 3p.

C.O. 5/376 (CONT'D)

Fol. 175. 21 Jan. 1760, Charleston. Gov. Lyttleton to Bd. of Trade. Lyttleton summoned the Assembly to defray the cost of the [Cherokee] expedition. Gov. sent supplies to Ft. Loudoun and Ft. Prince George. 3p.

Fol. 177. 8 Mar. 1760, Charleston. Gov. Lyttleton to Bd. of Trade. Lt. Coytmore was seriously wounded at Ft. Prince George and the hostages were put to death. 3p. [Enclosures to fol. 180b].

> Fol. 179. 24 Feb. 1760, Ft. Prince George. Alex. Miln to Gov. Lyttleton (extract). Cherokees shot Lt. Coytmore and the garrison executed the hostages. 4p.

Fol. 181. 22 Feb. 1760, Charleston. Gov. Lyttleton to Bd. of Trade (triplicate). Lyttleton has asked Amherst and Va. for troops to reinforce Ft. Loudoun. Upper Cherokees are quiet except for Settico. Little Carpenter blames the French for the Lower Towns' conduct. 8p. [Enclosures to fol. 188b].

> Fol. 186. 7 Feb. 1760. Speech form Lyttleton to General Assembly. Lyttleton reports on Cherokee hostility. 2p.

> Fol. 186b. 14 Feb. 1760. Message from Lyttleton to Assembly. Lyttleton is pleased that the Assembly is sending 1,000 men to relieve Ft. Prince George and to chastise the Cherokees. 3p.

> Fol. 187. 7 - 13 Feb. 1760. Two addresses from Assembly to Lyttleton. Assembly will grant supplies and pay for a 1,000 man regiment to relieve Ft. Prince George and to chastise the Cherokees. 2p.

Fol. 195. 7 Apr. 1759, St. James. Copy of Order in Council to send a small detachment of artillerymen to aid S.C. which has recently built and repaired several forts. 3p.

Fol. 197. 7 Apr. 1759, St. James. Copy of Order in Council to send cannon to S.C. which has recently built and repaired several forts. 3p.

Fol. 205. 30 June 1760, Charleston. Lt. Gov. Bull to Bd. of Trade. Overhill Towns, except for Little Carpenter's village, oppose peace. Middle Settlements favor it but are afraid to act alone. Bull describes Col. Montgomery's activities in the Cherokee country. 4p.

Fol. 207. 20 July 1760, Charleston. Lt. Gov. Bull to Bd. of Trade. Bull describes Montgomery's operations against the Cherokees and explains why Montgomery plans to go to New York. 5p. [Enclosures to fol. 214b].

> Fol. 211. 12 July 1760, Charleston. Lt. Gov. Bull to Col. Montgomery (copy). Bull realizes that Montgomery has orders to join the main army, but the Cherokees and French are still dangerous. 5p.

*C.O. 5/377   SOUTH CAROLINA, ORIGINAL CORRESPONDENCE, BD. OF TRADE:
              1760-1764*

Fol. 1. 9 Sept. 1760, Charleston. Lt. Gov. Bull to Bd. of
Trade. Ft. Loudoun surrendered and Capt. Demeré and 23 others
were murdered. 3p. [Enclosures to fol. 4b].

> Fol. 3. Maj. Lewis to Col. Byrd (copy). Garrison
> evacuating Ft. Loudoun was attacked 15 miles away from the
> fort. All officers were killed except for Capt. Stuart,
> who was saved by Little Carpenter. 2p.

Fol. 5. 11 Nov. 1760. Thomas Pownall to Bd. of Trade. Critical
state of S.C. requires immediate attention. 2p.

Fol. 7. 6 May 1760, Charleston. Lt. Gov. Bull to Bd. of Trade.
Bull describes the measures taken against the Cherokees,
including Montgomery's expedition and the diversions by the
Chickasaws and Creeks. Bull asked Va. to relieve Ft. Loudoun.
5p.

Fol. 11. 8 May 1760, Charleston. Lt. Gov. Bull to Bd. of
Trade. Bull gives further information on the Cherokee war and
some reflections on how to end it. 4p.

Fol. 13. 14 May 1760, Charleston. Lt. Gov. Bull to Bd. of
Trade. Upper and Lower Creeks are divided into one party
favoring the French and Cherokees and another supporting
England. 4p.

Fol. 17. 29 and 31 May 1760, Charleston. Lt. Gov. Bull to Bd.
of Trade (duplicate). Upper Creek and Cherokee war has caused
great distress. Cherokees have about 2,000 men, the Creeks
2,000, and the Choctaws over 5,000. Little Carpenter hopes that
Montgomery will chastise the Lower Cherokees severely. 6p.

Fol. 21. 17 June 1760, Charleston. Lt. Gov. Bull to Bd. of
Trade. Montgomery has been successful against the Cherokees.
After the Cherokees are subdued, the Creeks will be next. Va.
voted assistance for the Cherokee war. 4p. [Enclosures to
fol. 23].

> Fol. 23. 7 - 10 June 1760, S. Carolina. James Grant to
> Lt. Gov. Bull in the *South Carolina Gazette*. Account
> details Montgomery's campaign against the Cherokees.
> 1p.

Fol. 26. 31 Aug. 1760, Charleston. Lt. Gov. Bull to Bd. of
Trade (duplicate). Bull describes Ft. Loudoun's surrender, the
difficulty of waging war in Cherokee country, and Virginia's
assistance. 5p.

Fol. 29. 15 Aug. 1760, Charleston. Lt. Gov. Bull to Bd. of
Trade (duplicate). Bull describes Montgomery's expedition and
Bull's measures taken after Montgomery's retreat. Va. troops
have not marched yet. 4p.

C.O. 5/377 (CONT'D)

Fol. 31. 21 and 24 Oct. 1760, Charleston. Lt. Gov. Bull to
Bd. of Trade. Bull's message and a talk from the French
stopped the Cherokees from attacking Ft. Prince George via Ft.
Loudoun. Prisoners will be exchanged at Ft. Ninety Six. Bull
includes the proposed peace with the Cherokees. 8p.

Fol. 35. 21, 24, and 29 Oct. 1760, Charleston. Lt. Gov. Bull
to Bd. of Trade (duplicate). While Rangers returned from
relieving Ft. Prince George, the Indians killed two white males
and took a woman and two children captive near a small fort
30 miles northeast of Ft. Ninety Six. [Same as fol. 31 except
for the postscript dated 29 Oct.]. 9p.

Fol. 41. 18 Nov. 1760, Charleston. Lt. Gov. Bull to Bd. of
Trade. French attempted to prevent the Cherokees from making
peace. Lantagnac offered men and cannon to help the Cherokees
take Ft. Prince George. Bull describes the English plan for an
offensive. 5p.

Fol. 44. 17 Dec. 1760, Charleston. Lt. Gov. Bull to Bd. of
Trade. Ft. Prince George relieved. French have built a fort
on the Cherokee R. ten days march below Ft. Loudoun and nearly
midway between Ft. Loudoun and Ft. l'Assomption. French have
long considered a Cherokee fort to secure passage along the
Mississippi River. 3p.

Fol. 50. 29 Jan. 1761, Charleston. Lt. Gov. Bull to Bd. of
Trade. Bull has taken measures to supply 1,200 troops under Col.
Grant to war against the Cherokees. Gov. has requested aid from
Va. and N. Carolina. Creeks have invited the Lower Cherokees
to visit their towns. 7p. [Enclosures to fol. 55b].

Fol. 56. 17 Feb. 1761, Charleston. Lt. Gov. Bull to Bd. of
Trade. Mohawk hostility towards the Cherokees testifies to the
Mohawk friendship with England. Creeks do not wish the same
punishment dealt the Cherokees and will not join them. 4p.

Fol. 71. 6 June 1761, Lincoln's Inn. Matthew Lamb to Bd. of
Trade. Lamb reports on several S.C. acts, including one for
defraying expense of recent expedition against the Cherokees.
3p.

Fol. 73. 30 Apr. 1761, Charleston. Lt. Gov. Bull to Bd. of
Trade. Bull gives progress of the troops mobilized to fight
the Cherokees. War preparations against the Cherokees may discourage the Creeks and cause the French to lose ground. 4p.

Fol. 75. 16 May 1761, Charleston. Lt. Gov. Bull to Bd. of
Trade. Amherst believes 1,000 Virginian troops sufficient to
attack the Upper Cherokees. Bull describes progress of Grant.
3p. [Enclosures to fol. 78b].

>   Fol. 76. 29 Apr. - 6 May 1761. *South Carolina Weekly
>   Gazette*. Grant expresses satisfaction with Col. Middleton's
>   regiment. Capt. Colbert and his Chickasaws delivered two
>   Cherokee scalps at Ninety Six. 4p.

Fol. 79.   28 May 1761, Charleston. Lt. Gov. Bull to Bd. of
Trade. Col. Grant's army, now at Keowee, numbers 2,250 soldiers,
281 provision wagons, and 40-50 Negroes serving as pioneers. 3p.

Fol. 81.   19 June 1761, Charleston. Lt. Gov. Bull to Bd. of
Trade. Little Carpenter asked Grant to remain at Ft. Prince
George until he could consult with his tribe and return. Some
60 or 70 Cherokees under Grant's protection have been permitted
to settle east of Ft. Prince George and have been given corn and
peas to plant. Creeks have been urged to attack the northwestern
Cherokees. 4p.

Fol. 83.   17 July 1761, Charleston. Lt. Gov. Bull to Bd. of
Trade. Grant defeated the Cherokees, burning 15 towns and all
the plantations. He destroyed over 1,400 acres of corn and beans.
Middle, Lower, and back settlement Indians have been driven into
the mountains. Grant intends to invite Little Carpenter and
Great Warrior to treat for peace. 3p.

Fol. 85.   23 Sept. 1761, Charleston. Lt. Gov. Bull to Bd. of
Trade (duplicate). Preliminary treaty with the Cherokees has
been reached. Creeks have concluded a treaty with the French
and Choctaws. They invited the Cherokees to help destroy the
Chickasaws. 6p. [Enclosures to fol. 88b].

> Fol. 88.   [23 Sept. 1761]. Terms of Peace to be Granted
> to the Cherokee Indians (copy). Signatories include
> Attakullakulla. 2p.

Fol. 89.   5 Dec. 1761, Charleston. Lt. Gov. Bull to Bd. of Trade.
Bull has disbanded the regiment raised for the Cherokee war.
Quarrel has arisen between Little Carpenter and several of the
headmen who have returned home. 3p.

Fol. 93.   28 Feb. 1762, Charleston. Gov. Thomas Boone to Bd.
of Trade. Cherokee treaty has had good effects and there have
been efforts to reestablish Cherokee trade. 4p.

Fol. 95.   3 Mar. 1762, Treasury Chambers. Mr. West to Bd. of
Trade. West transmits memorial from Gov. Glen. 2p. [Enclosures
to fol. 143b].

> Fol. 97. Memorial from James Glen to Lords of Treasury.
> Glen requests reimbursement for expenses while governor.
> He cites his work with the Cherokees. 4p.

> Fol. 100.   27 Apr. 1761. Memorial from Glen to House of
> Commons. S. Carolina's influence and authority with the
> Indians was never greater than during Glen's administration.
> 4p.

> Fol. 102.   23 Apr. 1761, S. Carolina. An Account of Monies
> Paid for the Public by James Glen. Glen paid £750 for the
> Saluda meeting, Cherokee treaty, and other Indian expenses.
> 11p.

C.O. 5/377 (CONT'D)

>Fol. 108. 29 Apr. 1761, S. Carolina. Oath of Dr. Alex.
>Garden who accompanied Glen to meet the Cherokees. He
>describes the 1755 meeting. 4p.
>
>Fol. 110. 6 Apr. 1761. Oath of Chevillette who accompa-
>nied Glen to meet with the Cherokees at Saluda in 1755. He
>describes the meeting and estimates the expenses involved.
>4p.
>
>Fol. 112. 21 Apr. 1761, Beaver Creek. Declaration from
>James Beamer describing the Saluda meeting with the Chero-
>kees in 1755. 7p.
>
>Fol. 124. Copy of an account of Glen's meeting with
>Connacaughte and other Cherokees at Saluda. 8p.
>
>Fol. 130. Historical Relation of Facts Delivered by
>Ludovick Grant ... to ... Governor [Glen]. [Same as C.O.
>5/375/113]. 20p.
>
>Fol. 140. Conversation between Governor [Glen] and
>Chuconunto [Little Carpenter], Headman of Cherokees.
>[Same as C.O. 5/375/124]. 7p.

Fol. 144. Nov. 1762, Inner Temple. Memorial from Charles Garth
to Bd. of Trade. Garth discusses the Indian trade. Cherokees
could not have fought very long if the tribe had not been
supplied with goods from Va. and Georgia. 4p.

Fol. 146. [Nov. 1762], Inner Temple. Memorial from Charles
Garth to Bd. of Trade. No decision on the N.C. and S.C.
boundary could be enacted until peace was established again
with the Cherokees. 4p.

Fol. 148. 29 May 1762. An Act to Regulate the Trade with the
Cherokees (copy). 10p.

Fol. 153. [1762]. Copy of report from S.C. Assembly regarding
the boundary line with N. Carolina. Northern boundary should
include Ft. Prince George and Ft. Loudoun in Cherokee country.
6p.

Fol. 177. 23 Nov. 1762, Commons House of Assembly. Address
from House of Commons to Boone. Attention paid to the Cherokee
chiefs recently in England was due to the importance of their
friendship to S. Carolina. 3p.

Fol. 179. 23 Nov. 1762, Upper House of Assembly. Address from
Council to Boone. Splendor of the British Court will awe the
Cherokees and secure their friendship. 3p.

Fol. 221. 17 June 1763, Charleston. Gov. Boone to Bd. of Trade.
There is no record of Indian complaints about the S.C. surveys.
3p.

C.O. 5/377 (CONT'D)

Fol. 233. 15 Sept. 1763, Charleston. Gov. Boone to Bd. of
Trade. 7p. [Enclosures to fol. 258b].

    Fol. 239. 3 - 13 Sept. 1763. Message from Gov. Boone to
    Assembly (copy). The Mortar killed the traders because he
    had been told by the Cherokees that the whites planned to
    encourage the Choctaws and Chickasaws to fight the Creeks.
    13p.

Fol. 259. 27 Sept. 1763, S. Carolina. Gov. Boone to Bd. of
Trade. 3p. [Enclosures to fol. 268b].

    Fol. 261. 28 May 1762, Commons House. Message from
    Commons House to Council (copy). Funding changes in the
    Indian Trading Bill were unintentional. 2p.

    Fol. 263. 29 May 1762, Commons House. Message from
    Commons House to Council. The House agrees with the
    amendments to the Indian Trading Bill. 2p.

Fol. 271. 26 Jan. 1764, St. James. Dunk Halifax to Bd. of
Trade. Halifax forwards a copy of the journal of a congress
with the Southern Indians and Gov. Boone's letter explaining
his refusal to send traders to the Cherokees. 2p. [Enclosures
to fol. 333b].

    Fol. 273. A Rough Sketch of a Plan for the Management of
    Indians and the Conducting of the Necessary Commerce with
    Them. (copy). 10p.

    Fol. 278. 24 Nov. 1763, Charleston. Gov. Boone to Sec.
    of State [Dunk Halifax] (extract). S.C. refused the
    Cherokee petition for traders because regulations prohibit
    approval. 3p.

    Fol. 280. 1 Oct. - 21 Nov. 1763. Journal of the Proceed-
    ings of the Southern Congress Held with the Southern
    Indians at Augusta (copy). Cherokees proposed Saluda Old
    Town for congress because other sites were too dangerous
    since two Cherokees were killed by Creeks. Journal lists
    attending Cherokees and describes the talks. 104p.

Fol. 334. 7 Apr. 1764, Charleston. Gov. Boone to Bd. of Trade.
S.C. will gladly stop giving frequent presents to the Cherokees,
Creeks, and Catawbas. 9p. [Enclosures to fol. 354b].

    Fol. 340. 1764. Copy of minutes of Council concerning
    John Stuart's claims. Several Cherokees from Chote are
    going home with the Creeks. 28p.

Fol. 357. Jan. and Apr. 1764. Extract of Journal of Commons
House stating that the Indians who killed the whites have been
living among the Cherokees for four or five years. 13p.

C.O. 5/377 (CONT'D)

Fol. 417. 9 Jan. 1764, Charleston. Gov. Boone to Bd. of Trade.
11p. [Enclosures to fol. 426b].

Fol. 423. [4 Jan. 1764]. Speech from Boone to Assembly
(copy). Forts Augusta, Moore, and Prince George are in
disrepair and lack supplies. 5p.

C.O. 5/378   SOUTH CAROLINA, ORIGINAL CORRESPONDENCE, BD. OF TRADE:
1764-1768

Fol. 1. 20 Aug. 1764, Charleston. Lt. Gov. Bull to Bd. of
Trade. Young Warrior of Estatoe arrested two Creeks for
murdering the white man at Long Canes. Act of Assembly for
placing Cherokee trade in public hands is contrary to the
King's proclamation. 4p.

Fol. 5. 8 Oct. 1764, Charleston. Lt. Gov. Bull to Bd. of
Trade. Bull has agreed to repeal the Cherokee trade act. S.C.
has destroyed the paper bills of credit which were issued during
the Cherokee war. 4p.

Fol. 18. 8 Sept. 1765, Charleston. Lt. Gov. Bull to Bd. of
Trade. Bull has appointed a gentleman who is well-liked by the
Cherokees as commissioner for running the boundary line. He is
instructed to be fair to the Indians. 6p.

Fol. 41. 10 Dec. 1764, Charleston. Lt. Gov. Bull to Bd. of
Trade. Cherokees and Northern Indians have harassed the Catawbas.
The Cherokee treaty of 1761 set the boundary 40 miles east of
Ft. Prince George. 6p.

Fol. 47. 15 Mar. 1765, Charleston. Lt. Gov. Bull to Bd. of
Trade. N. Carolinians are encroaching on the Cherokee's chief
hunting ground. Judd's Friend has been rewarded for his
assistance against the French. 5p.

Fol. 52. 5 June 1765, Charleston. Gov. Bull to Bd. of Trade.
Stuart has sent the Indian trade regulations. The Frenchman
captured by Judd's Friend last winter near Ft. l'Assomption
while carrying ammunition to the Shawnees and Delawares appears
to be a *coureur de bois*. He will be sent to New Orleans. 4p.

Fol. 54. 25 Jan. 1766, Charleston. Gov. Bull to Bd. of Trade.
Unlike other forts, the woods at Ft. Prince George are not
private property and can be cut as wanted. 4p.

Fol. 56. 20 Nov. 1765, Lincoln's Inn. Mathew Lamb to Bd. of
Trade. Lamb reports on S.C. acts passed during Aug. 1764,
including an ordinance to repeal part of the Cherokee trade act.
3p.

Fol. 93. 9 June 1766, Charleston. Gov. Bull to Bd. of Trade.
Bull describes new line run between the Cherokees and S. Carolina.
2p. [Enclosure at fol. 126].

C.O. 5/378 (CONT'D)

Fol. 95.   29 June 1766, Charleston.   Gov. Montague to Bd. of
Trade.   Montague sends plan for boundary between S.C. and the
Cherokees.   3p.

Fol. 126.   2 - 9 June 1766, *South Carolina Gazette*.   Proclamation
of Gov. Bull requiring persons north of boundary between S.C.
and the Cherokees to leave the area.   4p.   [Enclosure of fol. 93].

Fol. 239.   10 Mar. 1767, Lincoln's Inn.   Mathew Lamb to Bd. of
Trade.   Lamb reports on five S.C. acts passed during March and
July 1766, including an act restraining the exportation of
Indian corn and peas.   3p.

Fol. 241.   14 Apr. 1767, Charleston.   Gov. Montague to Bd. of
Trade.   Montague transmits papers on better trade regulations
for the Indians.   2p.   [Enclosures to fol. 245b].

> Fol. 243.   Regulations for the Better Carrying on the Trade
> with the Indian Tribes in the Southern District.   5p.

*C.O. 5/379   SOUTH CAROLINA, ORIGINAL CORRESPONDENCE, BD. OF TRADE:
         1768-1770*

Fol. 22.   [Rec. 1 June 1769].   Memorial from Thomas Crowley to
the Earl of Hillsborough.   Crowley represents John D. Hammerer,
who went to teach the Cherokee youth at Long Canes and now
requests aid.   3p.

Fol. 52.   21 Dec. 1769, Whitehall.   Lords of Committee of Council
to Bd. of Trade.   What is the commissioners' opinion on the N.C.
and S.C. boundaries?   1p.   [Enclosures to fol. 65b].

> Fol. 53.   19 Apr. 1769, Charleston.   Gov. Charles Montague
> to Earl of Hillsborough (copy).   Gov. Tryon's plan for N.C.
> boundary would be injurious to S. Carolina.   1p.

> Fol. 54.   [ca. Apr. 1769].   Committee report on boundary
> line between the Carolinas and the Cherokees.   13p.

> Fol. 61.   15 Dec. 1765, [Charleston].   Lt. Gov. Bull to Bd.
> of Trade (extract).   Boundary must stop a few miles north
> of the road from Ninety Six to Ft. Prince George.   1p.

> Fol. 62.   12 Dec. 1768, Brunswick.   Gov. Tryon to Gov.
> Montague (copy).   Tryon discusses the boundary between the
> two Carolinas.   3p.

> Fol. 64.   29 Nov. 1768, Charleston (extract).   Gov. Montague
> to Gov. Tryon.   Montague discusses the boundary between the
> two Carolinas.   2p.

> Fol. 65.   11 Dec. 1768.   Gov. Tryon to Gov. Montague (copy).
> Tryon discusses the boundary between the two Carolinas.   3p.

C.O. 5/379 (CONT'D)

Fol. 84. Letter to Gov. Nicholson reporting that Capts. Chicken and Hitch are returning to the Creeks and Cherokees to settle Indian affairs. 1p.

Fol. 99. 6 Dec. 1769, Charleston. Lt. Gov. Bull to Earl of Hillsborough (duplicate). Cherokees and Creeks have invited the Catawbas to join them. 4p.

Fol. 117. 7 June 1770, Charleston. Lt. Gov. Bull to Earl of Hillsborough. 7p. [Duplicate of C.O. 5/393/64].

C.O. 5/380   SOUTH CAROLINA, ORIGINAL CORRESPONDENCE, BD. OF TRADE: 1770-1775

Fol. 9. [Rec. 2 Apr. 1770]. Memorial from Mr. Garth (Agent for S. Carolina) to Bd. of Trade. Garth discusses the boundary between N. and S. Carolina. S.C. built and maintained Ft. Loudoun and Ft. Prince George in Cherokee country. 9p.

C.O. 5/381   SOUTH CAROLINA, ORIGINAL CORRESPONDENCE, BD. OF TRADE: 1720-1774

Fol. 5. 30 Aug. 1720, Whitehall. Bd. of Trade to Lord Justices (draft). Report contains instructions for S.C. governor on defending his province. Since the warlike Cherokees favor England and oppose France, small forts should be built among them. 18p.

Fol. 74. 30 Sept. 1730, Whitehall. Bd. of Trade to Duke of Newcastle. There have been two meetings with the Cherokee chiefs. Those Indians seem fully satisfied with the agreements and their treatment since arriving in England. 3p.

Fol. 81. 2 Apr. 1731, Whitehall. Bd. of Trade to Gov. Johnson. Bd. is pleased that the seven Cherokee chiefs are satisfied with their treatment in England. They will be the means for a lasting peace with S. Carolina's Indian nations. 4p.

Fol. 260. 17 Feb. 1737/38, Whitehall. Bd. of Trade to the King. Bd. has no objections to the ordinance asserting S. Carolina's right to free trade with the Creeks, Cherokees, and other friendly nations. 2p.

C.O. 5/382   SOUTH CAROLINA, ORIGINAL CORRESPONDENCE, SEC. OF STATE: 1699-1724

Fol. 24. 10 July 1708, S. Carolina. Letter from Thomas Nairne stating that the Cherokees are situated to keep any Illinois or French Indians from raiding Carolina. Cherokees are S. Carolina's only frontier defense, but they face harassment by the Iroquois. 5p.

Fol. 34. [ca. July 1715], Carolina. Carolina Proprietors to the King. Carolina needs aid against a general revolt of 8-10,000 Indians. 3p. *French.*

C.O. 5/383   SOUTH CAROLINA, ORIGINAL CORRESPONDENCE, SEC. OF STATE:
               1715-1736

Fol. 84. 7 June 1726, [South Carolina]. A. Middleton to Gov.
Nicholson (copy). More Creeks and Cherokees will be attending
Middleton's talks with the Creeks. It will be difficult to
keep the Indians peaceful. A rupture will be expensive and
dangerous to Carolina frontier settlements. 4p.

Fol. 140. 18 Apr. 1729, Geneva. John Savy to Duke of Newcastle.
Mr. Wyat has delivered presents from the Cherokee headmen.
Savy intends to continue trading with the Cherokees. 3p.

Fol. 197. [ca. Apr. 1731], S. Carolina. Memorial from Robert
Johnson to the Queen. Johnson helped the Bd. of Trade make its
friendship treaty with the Cherokees in London. He now wants
assistance. 3p.

C.O. 5/384   SOUTH CAROLINA, ORIGINAL CORRESPONDENCE, SEC. OF STATE:
               1737-1743

Fol. 11. 6 June 1738, Whitehall. Bd. of Trade to Duke of
Newcastle. 2p. [Enclosures to fol. 36b].

> Fol. 14. 20 Apr. 1738, Council Chamber. Lt. Gov. Bull to
> Bd. of Trade (copy). The Spanish are manning the fort at
> the Apalachee Old Towns which the Carolinians and friendly
> Indians conquered in 1702-1703. 2p.

Fol. 44. 5 Oct. 1738, Whitehall. Bd. of Trade to Duke of
Newcastle. 2p. [Enclosures to fol. 51b].

> Fol. 47. 20 July 1738, Charleston. Lt. Gov. Bull to Bd.
> of Trade (copy). The Choctaws, whose 16,000 men outnumber
> all the tribes friendly to S.C. and who have favored the
> French, have proposed a friendship and commerce treaty with
> the English. 9p.

Fol. 65. 13 Dec. 1739, Whitehall. Bd. of Trade to Duke of
Newcastle. 3p. [Enclosures to fol. 71b].

> Fol. 68. 5 Oct. 1739, Charleston. Lt. Gov. Bull to Bd.
> of Trade. [Copy of C.O. 5/388/164 Part I]. 7p.

Fol. 83. 19 Aug. 1740, Whitehall. Bd. of Trade to Duke of
Newcastle (duplicate). 3p. [Enclosures to fol. 87b].

> Fol. 86. 3 June 1740, Charleston. Lt. Gov. Bull to Bd.
> of Trade (extract). Indians are expected to assist
> Oglethorpe. Trade and commerce are the easiest means to
> keep peace with the Indians. 4p.

Fol. 102. 20 Mar. 1740/41, S. Carolina. Lt. Gov. Bull to Duke
of Newcastle (duplicate). Cherokees are apprehensive about
French plans to attack them this summer. Bull asks for assistance to support the Cherokees. 3p.

C.O. 5/384 (CONT'D)

Fol. 110. 28 May 1741, Whitehall. Bd. of Trade to Duke of Newcastle. Bd. sends extract of letter about the Cherokees fearing a French attack this summer. 2p. [Enclosures to fol. 115b].

> Fol. 111. 20 Mar. 1740/41, S. Carolina. Lt. Gov. Bull to Bd. of Trade. [Extract of fol. 102]. 3p.

Fol. 138. 14 Feb. 1742/43, Whitehall. Bd. of Trade to Duke of Newcastle. 1p. [Enclosures to fol. 148].

> Fol. 139. 20 Oct. 1742. Extract of representation from Governor and Council of S. Carolina reporting that Oglethorpe, the Chickasaws, and other Indians repulsed the Spanish attack against Frederica. 17p.

Fol. 149. [May 1743]. Representation from S.C. Agents noting that the French Indians have attacked the Southern tribes along the Carolina and Ga. frontiers. 2p.

Fol. 153. 31 May 1743, Whitehall. Bd. of Trade to Duke of Newcastle. 2p. [Enclosures to fol. 159b].

> Fol. 156. 2 Mar. 1742/43, Frederica. Francis Moore to Lt. Gov. Bull (copy). Spanish have driven back the last Indian that Oglethorpe sent against Florida. 2p.

Fol. 160. 8 June 1743, Whitehall. Bd. of Trade to Duke of Newcastle. 3p. [Enclosures to fol. 189b].

> Fol. 164. 4 Mar. 1742/43, Charleston. Lt. Gov. Bull to Bd. of Trade (copy). Bull asks for protection for S.C., which has endured considerable expense in repairing forts, maintaining men, and giving presents to the Indians. 2p.

> Fol. 167. 15 Dec. 1742, New York. Geo. Clark to Lt. Gov. Bull (copy). A French and Indian party is marching southward. Bull hopefully will have time to alert all Indian nations. 2p.

> Fol. 183. 1 Mar. 1742/43. Copy of deposition from John Raven Bedon stating that the Spaniards captured eight Indians from Oglethorpe, but they all escaped. 2p.

C.O. 5/385   SOUTH CAROLINA, ORIGINAL CORRESPONDENCE, SEC. OF STATE:
          1744-1753

Fol. 1. 14 Nov. 1751. Memorial from James Crokatt to Earl of Holderness. Crokatt requests £3,000 to purchase Indian presents for S.C. tribes since the French are making encroachments daily. 4p.

Fol. 3. 9 Oct. 1749 - 4 Apr. 1752, on board the *Dolphin*. Invoices of goods bought by Harmon Verelst for Indians allied with S.C. and Georgia. 6p.

C.O. 5/385 (CONT'D)

Fol. 7.   Oct. 1749 - Nov. 1753, S. Carolina. Account from
Harmon Verelst, who is authorized to purchase presents for
Indians allied with S.C. and Georgia. 12p.

Fol. 15.   2 Feb. 1750, S. Carolina. Jermyn Wright to Harmon
Verelst (copy). Receipt for guns on board the *Dolphin*. 2p.

Fol. 17.   10 Dec. 1750, Whitehall. Bd. of Trade to Duke of
Bedford. Bd. sends an extract of Glen's letter on Indian
affairs and his proposal for building a fort among the Cherokees.
3p. [Enclosures to fol. 28b].

    Fol. 19.   15 July and 16 Sept. 1750, S. Carolina. Gov.
    Glen to Bd. of Trade. [Extract of C.O. 5/372/226]. 18p.

Fol. 37.   2 Oct. 1750 - 27 Dec. 1750. Account of Indian Presents
Purchased by Jermyn Wright [and] Shipped ... to South Carolina.
40p.

Fol. 91.   10 Nov. 1749, Whitehall. Bd. of Trade to Duke of
Bedford. 2p. [Enclosures to fol. 95b].

    Fol. 93.   12 Aug. 1749. Gov. Glen to Bd. of Trade.
    [Extract of C.O. 5/372/158]. 5p.

Fol. 103.   1749. Answers from Glen to Queries from the Bd. of
Trade. [Extract of C.O. 5/372/122]. 8p.

Fol. 107.   1 Nov. 1749, Whitehall. Bd. of Trade to Duke of
Bedford. 1p. [Enclosure at fol. 103].

Fol. 118.   20 Oct. 1748, [Whitehall]. Bd. of Trade to Duke of
Bedford. Bd. sends a copy of Glen's letter on Indian affairs
and his proposal for new forts among the S.C. frontier Indians.
2p. [Enclosures to fol. 123b].

    Fol. 120.   26 July 1748, S. Carolina. Gov. Glen to Bd. of
    Trade. [Copy of C.O. 5/372/67]. 8p.

Fol. 132.   21 July 1748, Whitehall. Bd. of Trade to Duke of
Bedford. 2p. [Enclosures to fol. 137b].

    Fol. 134.   14 Apr. 1748, S. Carolina. Gov. Glen to Bd. of
    Trade. [Copy of C.O. 5/372/38]. 6p.

Fol. 139.   6 Dec. 1748, Whitehall. Bd. of Trade to Duke of
Bedford. 3p. [Enclosures to fol. 163b].

    Fol. 141.   Feb. 1747/48, S. Carolina. Gov. Glen to Bd.
    of Trade. [Copy of C.O. 5/372/34]. 12p.

    Fol. 147.   14 Apr. 1748, S. Carolina. Gov. Glen to Bd. of
    Trade. [Copy of C.O. 5/372/38]. 6p.

    Fol. 150.   26 July 1748, S. Carolina. Glen to Bd. of
    Trade. [Copy of C.O. 5/372/67]. 11p.

C.O. 5/385 (CONT'D)

      Fol. 156. 10 Oct. 1748, S. Carolina. Gov. Glen to Bd. of
      Trade. [Copy of C.O. 5/372/76]. 9p.

    Fol. 164. 2 May 1746, Saluda. Gov. Glen to Duke of Newcastle.
    [Duplicate of C.O. 5/388/158]. 4p.

    Fol. 172. 14 Nov. 1751. Memorial from James Crockatt to Earl
    of Holderness. [Same as fol. 1]. 2p.

    Fol. 211. 22 Apr. 1751, Whitehall. Bd. of Trade to Duke of
    Bedford. 2p. [Enclosures to fol. 220b].

      Fol. 213. 2 Oct. 1750, S. Carolina. Gov. Glen to Bd. of
      Trade. [Extract of C.O. 5/372/252]. 15p.

C.O. 5/386   SOUTH CAROLINA, ORIGINAL CORRESPONDENCE, SEC. OF STATE:
           1754-1776

    Fol. 1. 11 Feb. 1761, Whitehall. Bd. of Trade to Wm. Pitt.
    French have reportedly built a fort on the Cherokee R. midway
    between Ft. Loudoun and Ft. l'Assomption. 2p. [Enclosures
    to fol. 5b].

      Fol. 4 . 17 Dec. 1760, [Charleston]. Lt. Gov. Bull to Bd.
      of Trade. [Extract of C.O. 5/377/44]. 2p.

    Fol. 12. 11 Dec. 1761, Whitehall. Bd. of Trade to Earl of
    Egremont. Bd. sends a copy of the preliminary peace with the
    Cherokees signed by Bull and Attakullakulla. 4p. [Enclosures
    to fol. 22b].

      Fol. 15. 23 Sept. 1761, [Charleston]. Lt. Gov. Bull to
      Bd. of Trade. [Extract of C.O. 5/377/85]. 8p.

      Fol. 19. 23 Sept. 1761. Terms of Peace to be Granted to
      the Cherokees. [Same as C.O. 5/377/88]. 7p.

    Fol. 47. 20 June 1754, Whitehall. Bd. of Trade to Thomas
    Robinson. French intend to build a fort in Cherokee country.
    Cherokees requested an English fort in their country in 1747
    and land was purchased for that purpose in 1750. 7p.
    [Enclosures to fol. 59b].

      Fol. 52. 1 June 1754. Representation from Charles
      Pinckney to Bd. of Trade. [Copy of C.O. 5/374/234]. 7p.

      Fol. 58. 9 Apr. 1754, S. Carolina. Extract of letter
      from Wm. Pinckney. [Same as C.O. 5/374/233]. 2p.

    Fol. 68. 9 Mar. 1757, Whitehall. Bd. of Trade to Wm. Pitt.
    4p. [Enclosures to fol. 96b].

      Fol. 71. 25 Dec. 1756, Charleston. Gov. Lyttleton to Bd.
      of Trade. [Copy of C.O. 5/375/163]. 9p.

Fol. 85.   25 Nov. 1756, English Camp. Intelligence from
Capt. Raymond Demeré. [Same as C.O. 5/375/173]. 6p.

Fol. 87.   2 Dec. 1756, English Camp. Intelligence from
Capt. Demeré. [Same as C.O. 5/375/175]. 3p.

Fol. 91.   31 Dec. 1756, Charleston. Gov. Lyttleton to Bd.
of Trade. [Same as C.O. 5/375/171]. 8p.

Fol. 95.   13 Dec. 1756, English Camp. Intelligence from
Capt. Raymond Demeré. [Same as C.O. 5/375/176]. 4p.

Fol. 104.   6 Feb. 1760, Whitehall. Bd. of Trade to Wm. Pitt.
On advice of the King's council, 1,500 militia marched into
Cherokee country to stop Indian raids. 4p. [Enclosures to
fol. 175b].

Fol. 110.   1 Sept. 1759, Charleston. Gov. Lyttleton to
Bd. of Trade. [Same as C.O. 5/376/105]. 9p.

Fol. 115.   22 May 1759, Charleston. Talk from Lyttleton
to the Emperor Old Hop and Little Carpenter. [Same as
C.O. 5/376/109]. 5p.

Fol. 118.   27 June 1759, Ft. Loudoun. Talk from Old Hop
and Little Carpenter to Gov. Lyttleton. [Same as C.O.
5/376/111]. 5p.

Fol. 121.   10 July 1759, Ft. Loudoun. Capt. Paul Demeré
to Gov. Lyttleton. [Same as C.O. 5/376/113]. 9p.

Fol. 125.   22 July 1759, Ft. Loudoun. Capt. Paul Demeré
to Gov. Lyttleton. [Same as C.O. 5/376/115]. 3p.

Fol. 127.   3 Aug. 1759, Ft. Prince George. Lt. Coytmore
to Gov. Lyttleton. [Same as C.O. 5/376/117]. 10p.

Fol. 133.   1 May 1759, Chickasaw nation. John Buckells
(a Chickasaw trader) to Jerome Courtonne. [Same as C.O.
5/376/119]. 14p.

Fol. 141.   16 Oct. 1759, Charleston. Gov. Lyttleton to Bd.
of Trade. [Duplicate of C.O. 5/376/134]. 8p.

Fol. 145.   26 Sept. 1759, Ft. Prince George. Lt. Richard
Coytmore to Gov. Lyttleton. [Same as C.O. 5/376/142]. 3p.

Fol. 147a.   13 Sept. 1759, Ft. Loudoun. Capt. Paul Demeré
to Gov. Lyttleton. [Same as C.O. 5/376/140]. 3p.

Fol. 148.   12 Sept. 1759, Ft. Loudoun. Maurice Anderson
to Lt. Coytmore. [Same as C.O. 5/376/138]. 3p.

C.O. 5/386 (CONT'D)

> Fol. 150. 26 Sept. 1759, Ft. Prince George. John Stuart
> to Gov. Lyttleton. [Same as C.O. 5/376/144]. 3p.
>
> Fol. 152. [5 Oct. 1759]. Speech from Lyttleton to Assembly
> (copy). Cherokees are so strong that vigorous and speedy
> measures are needed to repress them. Catawbas and Chickasaws
> are being solicited to join the English forces. 4p.
>
> Fol. 154. 6 Oct. 1759. Message from Assembly to Lyttleton.
> [Same as C.O. 5/376/150]. 3p.
>
> Fol. 156. [ca. 6 Oct. 1759]. Message from Lyttleton to
> Assembly (copy). Lyttleton hopes that the Assembly will
> pay for the 1,500 militia. 2p.
>
> Fol. 158. 11 Oct. 1759. Message from Assembly to Lyttleton.
> [Same as C.O. 5/376/152]. 2p.
>
> Fol. 160. Message from Lyttleton to Assembly. [Same as
> C.O. 5/376/146]. 3p.
>
> Fol. 162. Speech from Lyttleton to House of Assembly.
> [Same as C.O. 5/376/148]. 3p.
>
> Fol. 164. 23 Oct. 1759, Charleston. Gov. Lyttleton to
> Bd. of Trade. [Same as C.O. 5/376/158]. 9p.
>
> Fol. 169. 18 - 22 Oct. 1759, Council Chamber. Minutes of
> the Conferences between Gov. Lyttleton and Some Headmen
> of the Cherokees. [Same as C.O. 5/376/162]. 11p.
>
> Fol. 174. 27 Oct. - 14 Dec. 1759. Speaker of the House
> to Mr. Wright. [Same as C.O. 5/376/167]. 4p.

Fol. 176. 21 Feb. 1760, Whitehall. Bd. of Trade to Wm. Pitt.
Bd. sends a copy of Lyttleton's letter on ending the Cherokee
war and the subsequent peace treaty. 3p. [Enclosures to fol.
184].

> Fol. 178. 29 Dec. 1759, Ft. Prince George. Gov. Lyttleton
> to Bd. of Trade. [Same as C.O. 5/376/169]. 3p.
>
> Fol. 180. 26 Dec. 1759, Ft. Prince George. Treaty of
> Peace and Friendship Concluded by ... Lyttleton ... with
> Attacullaculla ... and Other [Cherokees]. [Same as C.O.
> 5/376/171]. 7p.

Fol. 185. 23 Sept. 1760, Whitehall. Edward Sedgwick to Robert
Wood. Sedgwick requests that Bull's letter concerning Col.
Montgomery's engagements with the Cherokees and his reasons
for retreating be shown to Pitt. 3p. [Enclosures to fol. 192b].

> Fol. 187. 20 July 1760, Charleston. Lt. Gov. Bull to
> Bd. of Trade. [Same as C.O. 5/376/207]. 4p.

C.O. 5/386 (CONT'D)

     Fol. 189.   12 July 1760, Charleston.   Lt. Gov. Bull to Col.
Montgomery.   [Same as C.O. 5/376/211].   4p.

     Fol. 191.   10 [Aug. - Sept.] 1760.   Mr. Pownall to Robert
Wood.   Cherokees massacred Ft. Loudoun garrison.   Capt.
Demeré and all the officers, except one, have lost their
lives.   2p.

Fol. 197.   19 Dec. 1760, Whitehall.   Bd. of Trade to Wm. Pitt.
Bd. encloses a copy of Bull's letter describing relations with
the Cherokees since the tribe's violation of the capitulation
at Ft. Loudoun.   3p.

     Fol. 200.   21 and 24 Oct. 1760, Charleston.   Lt. Gov. Bull
to Bd. of Trade.   [Copy of C.O. 5/377/31].   20p.

C.O. 5/387   SOUTH CAROLINA, ORIGINAL CORRESPONDENCE, SEC. OF STATE:
              1715-1729

Fol. 15.   8 May 1715, Charleston.   Letter from Geo. Rodd
stating that the Cherokees are friendly to England and will
join them in battle.   4p.

Fol. 121.   12 Mar. 1723/24, Charleston.   Gov. Nicholson to
Carteret.   3p.   [Enclosures to fol. 132b].

     Fol. 131.   11 May 1723, Charles City.   Report from
Committee of the King's Council to Gov. Nicholson (copy).
It is dangerous to give up the Altamaha R. since it is
the source of communication between all the Southern and
Western Indians friendly to the Carolinas.   4p.

Fol. 237.   24 - 25 Jan. 1726/27, Council Chamber, Charleston.
Discourse with the Long Warrior of Tunisee and with the Lower
Creeks.   Lower Creeks claim that the Cherokees are afraid of
them.   Creeks can live with French and Spanish trade alone.
Yamasees speak the same language as the Lower Cherokees, but
they picked up a different language when driven out of the
Carolinas.   If Cherokees make peace, the Creeks will have to
look elsewhere for slaves.   21p.

Fol. 245.   26 Jan. 1726/27.   General Conference between Headmen
of the Cherokee and Lower Creek Indians in the Presence of Both
Houses of Assembly Relating to the Peace Now Mediating between
Them.   8p.

Fol. 288.   13 June 1728, Charleston.   Letter from Arthur
Middleton.   6p.   [Enclosures to fol. 330b].

     Fol. 292.   30 Sept. 1727, Council Chamber, Charleston.
An Act for Carrying on Several Expeditions Against Our
Indian and Other Enemies (copy).   Act includes permission
to ask the Cherokees for assistance in the expedition
against the Lower Creeks.   4p.

C.O. 5/387 (CONT'D)

>   Fol. 294. 13 Sept. 1727 - 24 May 1728. Journal of Col.
>   Glover containing messages from Long Warrior and Elizar
>   Wiggan in Cherokee country. 34p.

*C.O. 5/388 PART I   SOUTH CAROLINA, ORIGINAL CORRESPONDENCE, SEC. OF
STATE: 1730-1746*

Fol. 25. 27 Dec. 1730, Charleston. Gov. Johnson to Duke of
Newcastle. The seven Cherokees under Johnson's care arrived
safely. They are pleased with the King's rewards. 2p.

Fol. 34. 15 Nov. 1731, Charleston. Gov. Johnson to Duke of
Newcastle. Johnson approves of a bill to better regulate the
Indian trade. 4p.

Fol. 45. 15 Dec. 1732, Charleston. Gov. Johnson to Duke of
Newcastle. There is little reason to suspect that S.C. Indians
will disturb Indians under Gov. Burrington's jurisdiction. 3p.

Fol. 125. 6 Feb. 1736/37, Charleston. Lt. Gov. Broughton to
Duke of Newcastle. Broughton is sending for some Cherokees
to intimidate the Negroes, who are more dangerous to Carolina's
safety than the Spanish. 3p.

Fol. 139. 6 Apr. 1737, Whitehall. Duke of Newcastle to Lt.
Gov. Broughton (draft). If the Spanish violate existing
peace, English agents will ask the Creeks and other friendly
Indians to enforce the treaty. 5p.

Fol. 157. 20 July 1738, Charleston. Lt. Gov. Bull to Duke of
Newcastle. S.C. and Ga. will always be threatened as long as
the French have any influence over the Choctaws and Cherokees.
6p.

Fol. 164. 5 Oct. 1739, Charleston. Lt. Gov. Bull to [Duke of
Newcastle]. French expedition from Montreal will pass near the
Cherokees and will probably try to get their consent to build
a fort there. This will give the French as much influence over
the Cherokees as they already have over the Creeks. 4p.

Fol. 174. 28 Feb. 1739/40, Charleston. Lt. Gov. Bull to Duke
of Newcastle. French have stopped S. Carolina's trade with the
Choctaws and interrupted the same trade with the Chickasaws.
Bull asks for assistance to continue trade with friendly Indians
to prevent their seduction by the French. 4p.

Fol. 175. 3 June 1740, Charleston. Lt. Gov. Bull to Duke of
Newcastle. Arms and presents have been sent for the Indians
assisting Oglethorpe in the siege of St. Augustine. 4p.
[Enclosures to fol. 183b].

>   Fol. 177. 22 May 1740, New Windsor. Mr. Wood to [Lt.
>   Gov. Bull?] (copy). Capt. Kent intends to send eight
>   Chickasaws and eleven Cherokees to the general. 4p.

C.O. 5/388 PART I (CONT'D)

> Fol. 179. 10 May 1740, Oakfuskee. A. Willy to Capt. Croft
> (copy). The Upper and Lower Creeks and the Cherokees
> (or Stinking Lenguas) met with the French. 7p.

Fol. 184. 28 July 1740, Charleston. Lt. Gov. Bull to Duke of
Newcastle. 2p. [Enclosures to fol. 186b].

> Fol. 185. 26 July 1740, S. Carolina. Petition from S.C.
> Council and Assembly to the King. S.C. asks for assistance
> since that province and Ga. have no protection against the
> French except for a few small Indian nations. 2p.

Fol. 193. 20 Mar. 1740/41, S. Carolina. Lt. Gov. Bull to
Duke of Newcastle. [Same as C.O. 5/384/102]. 4p.

C.O. 5/388 PART II   SOUTH CAROLINA, ORIGINAL CORRESPONDENCE, SEC.
OF STATE: 1730-1746

Fol. 2. 14 Oct. 1741, Charleston. Lt. Gov. Bull to Duke of
Newcastle. Indians are peaceful. Frequent treaties, presents,
and agents have prevented the tribes from joining the Spanish.
The French, however, are the greatest danger. 4p.

Fol. 39. 15 June 1742, Charleston. Lt. Gov. Bull to Duke of
Newcastle. Safety of the province depends on the Indian allies,
the Cherokees being the most numerous. The Cherokees consist
of about 3,000 men settled at the head of Savannah R. and along
the branches of the Miss. River. Cherokees and Catawbas have
often been attacked by the Senecas or the Six Nations from Albany.
French frequently employ Indians to attack the Cherokees and
Chickasaws. 4p.

Fol. 67. 23 Feb. 1742/43. Committee Report recommending that
the Indian allies be warned about Spanish designs and French
activities. 6p.

Fol. 72. 4 Mar. 1742/43. Lt. Gov. Bull to Duke of Newcastle.
Bull requests protection from French and Spanish designs since
S.C. has exhausted its treasury building and repairing forts
and buying Indian presents. 2p. [Enclosures to fol. 90b].

> Fol. 80. 13 Dec. 1742, New York. Gov. Geo. Clark to Lt.
> Gov. Bull (copy). French and Indians are marching south.
> Bull will hopefully have time to warn all Indian nations.
> 2p.

> Fol. 81. 1 Mar. 1742/43. Deposition from John Raven Bedon.
> [Same as C.O. 5/384/183]. 2p.

> Fol. 85. 17 Feb. 1742/43. Copy of deposition from Charles
> Hicks reporting that two Indian parties visited the governor
> of St. Augustine and received numerous presents. Later
> those Indians reportedly killed some Spaniards traveling to
> St. Augustine. 5p.

C.O. 5/388 PART II (CONT'D)

Fol. 89. Copy of deposition from Edmond Gale reporting Spanish complaints that the woods between St. Simons and Frederica were impassable because of hostile Indians. 4p.

Fol. 91. 17 Mar. 1742/43, Charleston. Lt. Gov. Bull to Duke of Newcastle. 2p. [Enclosures to fol. 92b].

Fol. 92. 2 Mar. 1742/43, Frederica. Francis Moore to Lt. Gov. Bull. [Same as C.O. 5/384/156]. 2p.

Fol. 103. 12 July 1743. Representation of Proceedings of the Governor, Council and Assembly of South Carolina. Carolina frontiers (which have not been exposed to Indian attacks for many years) are in danger. 18p.

Fol. 112. 22 Nov. 1743, Charleston. Lt. Gov. Bull to Duke of Newcastle. Bull is sending information on the prisoner exchange with the Spaniards and on the reported silver mine in Cherokee country. 2p.

Fol. 135. 2 Feb. 1744 [1745], S. Carolina. Letter to Duke of Newcastle with information on the present state of affairs and a letter from the Emperor of the Cherokees. 3p. [Enclosures to fol. 143b].

Fol. 141. [Dec. 1744]. Speech of Glen to Assembly in *Supplement to the South Carolina Gazette*. Glen forwards a letter from the Emperor of the Cherokees professing attachment to the English. Glen reports similar news from the Creeks, Chickasaws, and Catawbas. 2p.

Fol. 142. 10 Oct. 1744. Emperor of the Cherokees to Gov. Glen (copy). Cherokees offer assistance to the English who are at war with the French and Spanish. 3p.

Fol. 147. 28 May 1745, S. Carolina. Gov. Glen to [Duke of Newcastle] (duplicate). Glen will send the Emperor of the Cherokees' crown to England by the next ship so that it may be laid at His Majesty's feet. 4p.

Fol. 150. 15 Feb. 1745/46, S. Carolina. Gov. Glen to Duke of Newcastle (duplicate). Indian affairs have never been better. The Emperor of the Cherokees with 120 headmen and the Catawba King with 18 headmen have visited Charleston and returned home well satisfied. 6p.

Fol. 158. 2 May 1746, Saluda. Gov. Glen to Duke of Newcastle (duplicate). The Emperor of the Cherokees said that the French have offered peace proposals and requested permission to build a small fort among the Cherokees. Glen plans to meet with the Catawbas, Cherokees, Creeks, and Chickasaws. 4p.

Fol. 160. 3 May 1746, Saluda. Gov. Glen to [Duke of Newcastle]. [Same as fol. 158 except for date]. 6p.

C.O. 5/388 PART II (CONT'D)

Fol. 163. 29 Sept. 1746, S. Carolina. Gov. Glen to [Duke of
Newcastle]. Glen met the Emperor of the Cherokees, who
indicated that French threats on some Cherokee towns have forced
those towns to favor the French. Glen proposed building a fort
in Cherokee country for the tribe's security and to keep the
French away. 4p.

Fol. 165. 4 Oct. 1746, S. Carolina. Gov. Glen to Duke of
Newcastle. Glen sends more letters about the Indian situation.
4p.

Fol. 166. 14 Oct. 1746, S. Carolina. Gov. Glen to Duke of
Newcastle. [Duplicate of fol. 165 but dated 14 Oct.]. 4p.

*C.O. 5/389   SOUTH CAROLINA, ORIGINAL CORRESPONDENCE, SEC. OF STATE:
              1748-1751*

Fol. 1b. 1748. Account from Harmon Verelst, who will receive
£3,000 for purchasing Indian goods for friendly S.C. and Ga.
tribes. 10p.

Fol. 7. 25 Aug. 1748. Warrant from the Lords Justices to
John Hume, Jermyn Wright, and Harmon Verelst (copy). Warrant
grants permission to purchase £3,000 worth of Indian presents.
4p.

Fol. 9. 4 Jan. 1748 [1749]. Invoice of goods bought by Harmon
Verelst for Indian presents. 14p.

Fol. 17. 4 Jan. 1748 [1749]. Bill of lading for S.C. goods
shipped by Harmon Verelst. 2p.

Fol. 18. Oct. 1748 - Jan. 1748 [1749]. Invoices and receipts
for goods purchased by Harmon Verelst. 38p.

Fol. 42. 3 Feb. 1747, S. Carolina. Gov. Glen to [Duke of
Newcastle]. Cherokees are not more than 96 miles from some
Carolina outsettlements. Although formerly numerous, the
Cherokees do not now exceed 3,000 fighting men because of losses
from smallpox and wars. Forts are needed among the Choctaws,
Upper Cherokees, Chickasaws, and Catawbas. 9p.

Fol. 52. 30 Jan. 1747, S. Carolina. Representation and
petition from Governor, Council, and Assembly of S.C. to the
King. S.C. has spent about £1,500 annually for treaties and
presents to the Choctaws, Creeks, Cherokees, Catawbas, and
Chickasaws to counteract French and Spanish influence. 2p.

Fol. 53. [3] Feb. 1747, S. Carolina. Gov. Glen to Duke of
Newcastle. [Duplicate of fol. 42]. 8p.

Fol. 58. 14 Apr. 1748. Gov. Glen to [Duke of Newcastle].
Glen demanded satisfaction from the Cherokees for the murder
of an Englishman. If the Cherokees punish the murderer, S.C.
will build a fort in their country to protect them from the
French. 4p.

C.O. 5/389 (CONT'D)

Fol. 62.   4 June 1748, London. Abraham Bosomworth to Duke of
Bedford. Trustees have recommended that Bosomworth be replaced
as Indian agent for Georgia. 2p.

Fol. 66.   27 July 1748, S. Carolina. Gov. Glen to Duke of
Bedford. Traders are scared of the Cherokees. Cherokees have
executed the murderer of the Englishman. Catawbas complain that
the Cherokees allow the French to cross Cherokee territory to
attack the Catawbas. Fort is needed in Cherokee country. 6p.

Fol. 72.   25 Aug. 1748. Invoices and bill of lading for Indian
presents shipped to Jermyn Wright. 11p.

Fol. 77.   15 Nov. – 5 Dec. 1748. Invoices and bills for Indian
presents shipped to Jermyn Wright. 18p.

Fol. 94.   Sept. – Dec. 1748. Account of Indian Presents ...
[Purchased for Indians Allied with S.C. and Georgia]. 8p.

Fol. 99.   [27 July 1748], S. Carolina. Gov. Glen to Duke of
Bedford. [Same as fol. 66]. 5p.

Fol. 103. 10 Oct. 1748, S. Carolina. Gov. Glen to [Duke of
Bedford?]. Glen will tell the Cherokees they can no longer be
rewarded for warring against the French. Glen supports building
forts in surrounding Indian nations, but one in Cherokee
territory is the most important. 10p.

Fol. 126. Jermyn Wright to Duke of Bedford. Wright discusses
Crokatt's scheme for purchasing Indian presents. 3p.

Fol. 128. 1 June 1749. Copy of petition from Journal of
Assembly concerning the unsuitablility of some Indian goods.
2p.

Fol. 130. 12 Aug. 1749, S. Carolina. Gov. Glen to [Duke of
Bedford]. Glen will meet with the headmen of the Cherokees,
Creeks, and Catawbas on Aug. 25 to establish peace between the
Creeks and Cherokees. 4p.

Fol. 142. 23 Dec. 1749, S. Carolina. Gov. Glen to Duke of
Bedford. Glen transmits papers on present Indian affairs. 2p.
[Enclosures to fol. 163b].

> Fol. 146. Gov. Glen to Mons. Vaudreuil. [Same as C.O.
> 5/372/190]. 4p.

> Fol. 158. 23 Apr. 1748, S. Carolina. Gov. Glen to Bd. of
> Trade. [Copy of C.O. 5/372/42]. 3p.

> Fol. 160. 23 Dec. 1748. S. Carolina. Gov. Glen to Bd.
> of Trade. [Letter continues at fol. 154; copy of C.O.
> 5/372/168]. 10p.

C.O. 5/389 (CONT'D)

Fol. 177. 27 May 1749 - 24 Feb. 1750. An Account of the Distribution of Presents to the Indians [Allied with South Carolina
and Georgia]. Report lists Indian presents and towns. 14p.

Fol. 193. 18 Sept. 1750, London. Abraham Bosomworth to Mr.
Aldworth. Bosomworth requests reimbursement for personal
money spent distributing Indian presents. 4p.

Fol. 195. Memorial from Abraham Bosomworth to Duke of Bedford.
Bosomworth requests reimbursement for money spent distributing
Indian presents. 2p.

Fol. 197. 23 May 1750, S. Carolina. Certification from Glen
that he appointed Bosomworth Indian agent. 2p.

Fol. 199. 12 July 174[9], S. Carolina. Instructions from
Glen to Abraham Bosomworth. Directions for distributing
Indian presents. 4p.

Fol. 201. 21 May 1750, Charleston. Geo. Saxby to Abraham
Bosomworth. Bosomworth will visit England to apply for a
salary as Indian agent. 2p.

Fol. 203. 9 June 1748, Whitehall. Duke of Bedford to Gov.
of S. Carolina (copy). Bedford requests Bosomworth's appointment as Indian agent to distribute presents to friendly S.C.
and Ga. tribes. 2p.

Fol. 205. 15 July and 16 Sept. 1750, S. Carolina. Gov. Glen
to Duke of Bedford (duplicate). Creeks have burned two Cherokee towns, killed most of the inhabitants, and carried the rest
into slavery. Neighboring Cherokee towns have moved further
north. Creeks and Catawbas complain that the Cherokees favor
northern and French enemies. A fort is necessary in Cherokee
country. 15p.

Fol. 213. 2 Oct. 1750, S. Carolina. Gov. Glen to Duke of
Bedford. The French have renewed the war between the Creeks
and Cherokees, and the French Indians have killed many Cherokees. 14p.

Fol. 221. 10 Nov. 1750. Abraham Bosomworth to Duke of Bedford.
Bosomworth requests compensation for expenses as Indian agent
in distributing Indian goods. 4p.

Fol. 223. Memorial from Bosomworth to Duke of Bedford. [Copy
of fol. 195]. 2p.

Fol. 225. 19 Nov. 1750, Queens Square, Westminster. Harmon
Verelst to Richard Aldworth. Complaints about Indian presents
are unjustified. 2p.

Fol. 231. 14 Dec. 1750. Jermyn Wright and Harmon Verelst to
Richard Aldworth. It is not possible to act contrary to
treasury warrant in matters concerning the S.C. and Ga. Indian
presents. 2p.

C.O. 5/389 (CONT'D)

Fol. 235. Feb. 1751. Gov. Glen to Bd. of Trade. [Copy of
C.O. 5/372/282]. 41p.

Fol. 257. 12 Mar. 1750/51. Statement from Glen regarding the
services of Abraham Bosomworth. Bosomworth distributed Indian
presents to tribes allied with S.C. and Ga. and led large Indian
parties against the Spaniards in Florida. 4p.

*C.O. 5/390   SOUTH CAROLINA, ORIGINAL CORRESPONDENCE, SEC. OF STATE:
              1762-1767*

Fol. 1. 11 Nov. 1762, Charleston. Gov. Thomas Boone to Earl
of Egremont. Three Cherokees arrived safely on the *Epreuve*.
Boone sends a copy of his talk with Judd's Friend. 3p.
[Enclosures to fol. 5].

  Fol. 3. 3 Nov. 1762, Council Chambers, Charleston. Talk
  between Judd's Friend and Gov. Boone. Judd's Friend
  describes his trip to England. 5p.

Fol. 6. 27 Nov. 1762, Charleston. Capt. Peter Blake to Earl
of Egremont. Cherokees received proper care and attention on
their return voyage from England. English schooner trading
with the French was taken and some goods were given to the
Indians. 3p.

Fol. 10. 21 Apr. 1763, Charleston. Gov. Boone to Earl of
Egremont. Boone is sending Baron des Jonnes, a Frenchman
captured in Cherokee country, to England. 3p.

Fol. 12. 1 June 1763, Charleston. Gov. Boone to Earl of
Egremont. Indian conference was held at Augusta. Choctaws
and Creeks are warring with the Chickasaws. Cherokees and
Choctaws are almost always at war. 3p.

Fol. 22. 24 Nov. 1763, Charleston. Gov. Boone to Sec. of
State for the Southern Department. Trade act forced Boone to
refuse Cherokee request for traders. Little Carpenter and
Oconostota wish to go to England. 4p. [Enclosures to fol. 27b].

  Fol. 24. [ca. Nov. 1763]. A Scheme for the Management
  of Indians. 9p.

Fol. 32. 11 Feb. 1764, St. James. Earl of Halifax to Gov.
Boone. Boone should refuse request of Little Carpenter and
Oconostota to visit England because such trips are non-productive
and expensive. 4p.

Fol. 42. 13 Sept. 1764, Charleston. Lt. Gov. Bull to Earl of
Halifax. Ft. Prince George will be repaired. 3p.

Fol. 62. 8 Sept. 1765, Charleston. Lt. Gov. Bull to Earl of
Halifax. Repairs on Ft. Prince George cost as much as rebuilding the fort. 3p.

C.O. 5/390 (CONT'D)

Fol. 74. 27 May 1762, Whitehall. Sandys et al. to Lords of
Treasury (copy). Account of James Glen's expenses during the
Saluda conference to conclude a treaty with the Cherokees in
June 1755. 7p.

Fol. 78. 14 Apr. 1756, Charleston. Gov. Glen to Bd. of Trade
(extract). French are present in Cherokee territory. Although
the Cherokees have been promised a fort, no money is available
except for what Gov. Dinwiddie sent. 9p.

Fol. 84. [ca. June 1755]. Copy of account of Glen's meeting
with the Cherokees at Saluda. 8p.

Fol. 88. 20 Mar. 1756 [1757]. Message from Gov. Glen to
Speaker and Assembly (copy). Glen asks for money to pay for
the Indian presents given at Saluda. 4p.

Fol. 90. 22 Mar. 1757. Committee report noting the agreement
before Glen's meeting with the Cherokees that the tribe would
receive presents, not to exceed £500 sterling, if they surrendered all their lands. 4p.

Fol. 92. 29 June 1766, Charleston. Charles Montague to Bd.
of Trade (copy). Montague sends plan of the boundary between
S.C. and the Cherokees. 3p.

Fol. 170. S. Carolina. Charles Montague to Earl of Shelburne.
Montague issued a proclamation detailing Indian complaints
against whites. 2p.

Fol. 172. 5 Mar. 1767, Charleston. Gov. Montague to Earl of
Shelburne. Indian disturbances continue and are probably
caused by traders' misbehavior. 3p.

*C.O. 5/391   SOUTH CAROLINA, ORIGINAL CORRESPONDENCE, SEC. OF STATE:
            1767-1768*

Fol. 33. 18 July 1768, Charleston. Lt. Gov. Bull to Earl of
Hillsborough. Bull discusses boundary line between N. and S.
Carolina. 7p.

Fol. 47. 16 Aug. 1768, Charleston. Lt. Gov. Bull to Earl of
Hillsborough. Capt. Fuser, who is well liked by the Cherokees,
was made Capt. of Ft. Prince George. He will explain the
withdrawal of troops to the Cherokees. 3p.

*C.O. 5/392   SOUTH CAROLINA, ORIGINAL CORRESPONDENC, SEC. OF STATE:
            1768-1769*

Fol. 15. 10 Apr. 1769, Charleston. Copy of report from
Committee Council of S. Carolina arguing against the boundary
between N. and S.C. as proposed by Gov. Tryon. 10p. [Enclosure
of Montague's letter of 19 Apr. 1769].

C.O. 5/392 (CONT'D)

> Fol. 52.   4 Oct. 1769, Charleston.   Lt. Gov. Bull to Earl of
> Hillsborough.   Mr. Hammerer, who planned to teach Cherokee
> children, has retired due to lack of financial support.
> Assembly will consider additional support.   4p.

C.O. 5/393   SOUTH CAROLINA, ORIGINAL CORRESPONDENCE, SEC. OF STATE:
           1769-1770

> Fol. 5.   6 Dec. 1769, Charleston.   Lt. Gov. Bull to Earl of
> Hillsborough.   The Catawbas, for whom the state reserved
> 150,000 acres, have been invited to live with the Cherokees
> and Creeks.   4p.

> Fol. 64.   7 June 1770, Charleston.   Lt. Gov. Bull to Earl of
> Hillsborough.   Bull discusses boundary line, troops, and the
> western settlements.   8p.

C.O. 5/394   SOUTH CAROLINA, ORIGINAL CORRESPONDENCE, SEC. OF STATE:
           1770-1772

> Fol. 5.   30 Nov. 1770, Charleston.   Lt. Gov. Bull to Earl of
> Hillsborough.   Cherokees serve as a barrier against the Ohio
> and Illinois Indians and act as a counterbalance to the Creeks.
> Cheroke women might be useful in spinning silk since they place
> no great value on their time.   When planters use all present
> farm land, Cherokee territory west to Keowee might be purchased.
> 31p.

C.O. 5/395   SOUTH CAROLINA, ORIGINAL CORRESPONDENCE, SEC. OF STATE:
           1773

> Fol. 13.   18 Mar. 1773.   Petition from Edward Wilkinson
> (commissioner and storekeeper of public trade with the Cherokees)
> to Earl of Dartmouth.   Cherokees wish to pay off their debt by
> ceding land.   1p.

C.O. 5/396   SOUTH CAROLINA, ORIGINAL CORRESPONDENCE, SEC. OF STATE:
           1773-1777

> Fol. 7.   11 Feb. 1774, Charleston.   Lt. Gov. Bull to Earl of
> Dartmouth.   Creeks murdered some settlers and precautions have
> been taken to prevent flight from the western frontier.   Men
> are scouting the banks of the Savannah R. and the Cherokee
> boundary line.   4p.   [Enclosures to fol. 10b].

> Fol. 14.   24 Mar. 1774, Charleston.   Lt. Gov. Bull to Earl of
> Dartmouth.   Inactivity may encourage the Creeks and Cherokees
> to fight for England, especially since they can easily acquire
> plunder and glory.   3p.   [Enclosures to fol. 21b].

> Fol. 50.   3 Aug. 1774, Charleston.   Lt. Gov. Bull to Earl of
> Dartmouth.   Council met without Bull's consent to request the
> purchase of small arms for the Irish and other frontiersmen.
> Bull discusses S. Carolina's preparedness in case of an Indian
> war.   4p.   [Enclosures to fol. 53b].

C.O. 5/396 (CONT'D)

Fol. 151. 2 July 1775, Charleston. Wm. Campbell to Earl of
Dartmouth. Stuart is suspected of arousing the Indians and he
has gone to St. Augustine. Many Indians are ready to take up
arms if Stuart will lead them. 8p. [Enclosures to fol. 167b].

Fol. 225. 31 Aug. 1775, Charleston. Wm. Campbell to [Earl of
Dartmouth]. Stuart denies the charges against him. 11p.
[Enclosures to fol. 237b].

Fol. 304. 8 July 1776, on board the *Bristol* near Charleston.
Wm. Campbell to Geo. Germain. Stuart and his deputies have been
successful in keeping rebels from gaining ground among the
Indians. 7p.

C.O. 5/400   SOUTH CAROLINA, ENTRY BOOK OF LETTERS AND INSTRUCTIONS:
*   1720-1730*

Fol. 31. 30 Aug. 1720, Whitehall. Copy of representation to
the governor of Carolina stating that the Cherokees, a warlike
tribe living in the Appalachian Mountains, are British allies
and France's enemy. Small forts should be built among the
Cherokees to keep their loyalty and provide English security.
10p.

Fol. 41. 30 Aug. 1720, Whitehall. Copy of instructions to
Francis Nicholson stating that it is essential for Carolina
to regain the affection of the Indians who were formerly loyal
and to preserve good relations with those who remained faithful,
especially the Cherokees. 51p.

Fol. 291. 10 June 1730, St. James. Instruction to Robert
Johnson, newly appointed governor of S.C., stating that it is
essential for Carolina to regain the affection of those Indians
formerly loyal and to preserve good relations with those who
remained faithful, especially the Cherokees. 88p.

Fol. 384. 20 Aug. 1730, Whitehall. Bd. of Trade to Duke of
Newcastle. England should have a treaty with the Cherokees
since the nation can field 3,000 fighting men. 3p.

Fol. 387. 8 Sept. 1730, Whitehall. Alured Popple to Richard
Arnold, Deputy Sec. of War. Bd. of Trade needs guards because
of the Cherokee's visit. 1p.

Fol. 388. 9 Sept. 1730. Articles of Friendship and Trade
Proposed by the Board of Trade to the Deputies of the Cherokee
Nation in South Carolina. 7p.

C.O. 5/401   SOUTH CAROLINA, ENTRY BOOK OF LETTERS AND INSTRUCTIONS:
*   1730-1739*

Fol. 1. 30 Sept. 1730, Whitehall. Alured Popple to Alex.
Cuming. Popple denies Cuming's request to keep an Indian
chief with him. 2p.

C.O. 5/401 (CONT'D)

Fol. 2. 30 Sept. 1730, Whitehall. Bd. of Trade to Duke of
Newcastle. Bd. sends copies of proposals made to the Cherokees
and the Indian's answers. 2p.

Fol. 17. 2 Apr. 1731, Whitehall. Bd. of Trade to Gov. Johnson.
Bd. is happy that the Cherokee chiefs are satisfied with their
treatment in England. It will help maintain lasting peace with
the S.C. frontier Indians. 2p.

Fol. 32. 26 May 1732, Whitehall. Bd. of Trade to Lords of
Committee of Council. Settling S.C. is necessary since it is
a barrier against the Spanish, French, and many Indian nations.
9p.

Fol. 45. 21 June 1732, Whitehall. Bd. of Trade to Gov. Johnson.
Johnson should try to prevent S.C. Indians from attacking tribes
in N. Carolina. 1p.

Fol. 199. 1 Feb. 1736/37, Whitehall. Alured Popple to Mr. Fane.
Popple wants an opinion on S.C. acts passed in 1736, including
an ordinance for maintaining free trade with the Creeks, Cherokees, and other Indian nations. 4p.

Fol. 219. 21 June 1737, Whitehall. Alured Popple to Dudley
Ryder and John Strange. Popple requests an opinion on whether
any colony can grant a monopoly over the Indian trade in their
province. 3p.

Fol. 224. 14 Sept. 1737, Whitehall. Bd. of Trade to Lords of
Committee of Council. Bd. discusses the dispute between S.C.
and Ga. over the Indian trade. 10p.

Fol. 251. 17 Feb. 1737/38, Whitehall. Representation from Bd.
of Trade to the King. Ordinance passed in S.C. permits free
trade with the Creeks, Cherokees, and other friendly Indians.
2p.

Fol. 265. 21 June 1738, Whitehall. Bd. of Trade to the King.
Bd. has prepared instructions for Ga. Trustees to settle the
Indian trade dispute between Ga. and S. Carolina. 5p.

Fol. 269. 21 June 1738, Whitehall. Bd. of Trade to the King.
Bd. has prepared instructions for S. Carolina's governor to
settle the Indian trade dispute between S.C. and Georgia. 4p.

Fol. 337. 19 July 1739, Whitehall. Instructions from Bd. of
Trade to Gov. Glen. Gov. must maintain friendship with the
Indians, especially the Cherokees. 83p.

C.O. 5/402   SOUTH CAROLINA, ENTRY BOOK OF LETTERS AND INSTRUCTIONS:
*   1739-1755.*

Fol. 31. 28 May 1741, Whitehall. Bd. of Trade to Duke of
Newcastle. Bd. sends extract of Bull's letter about the
Cherokees' fear of a French attack. 1p.

C.O. 5/402 (CONT'D)

Fol. 37. 19 Aug. 1741, Whitehall. Bd. of Trade to Lt. Gov.
Bull. Bull must prevent the French from building a fort or
making settlements among the Cherokees. 4p.

Fol. 56. 3 Aug. 1742, Whitehall. Bd. of Trade to Duke of
Newcastle. Bd. sends an extract of Glen's letter about the
Cherokee desire to have a fort to keep the French out. 1p.

Fol. 131. 22 July 1747, Whitehall. Bd. of Trade to Duke of
Newcastle. Bd. sends an extract of Glen's letter about the
Cherokee desire to have a fort to keep the French out. 1p.

Fol. 133. 13 Aug. 1747, Whitehall. Bd. of Trade to Duke of
Newcastle. Bd. sends a representation concerning the Cherokee
desire to have a fort built in their country. 1p.

Fol. 134. 13 Aug. 1747, Whitehall. Representation from Bd.
of Trade to Duke of Newcastle. The Cherokees are the most
powerful nation on S. Carolina's border and they desire a fort.
Glen should negotiate a treaty for land to build the fort. 2p.

Fol. 147. 9 June 1748, Whitehall. Bd. of Trade to Lords of
Committee of Council. Bd. sends draft of Glen's instructions
concerning building a fort in Cherokee country. 2p.

Fol. 149. 9 June 1748, Whitehall. Additional instructions
from Bd. of Trade to Gov. Glen. Glen should immediately
negotiate a treaty for land to build a fort in Cherokee country.
He should then send the agreement, plans, and estimate of
expenses to England. 2p.

Fol. 163. 22 July 1748, Whitehall. Bd. of Trade to Gov. Glen.
Bd. is sending the King's directions on building a fort in
Cherokee country. Bd. will also consider proposals for building
forts elsewhere. 4p.

Fol. 170. 20 Oct. 1748, Whitehall. Bd. of Trade to Duke of
Bedford. Bd. sends copy of Glen's letter relating to Indian
affairs and his proposal for erecting forts among neighboring
Indian nations. 1p.

Fol. 179. 6 Dec. 1748, Whitehall. Bd. of Trade to Duke of
Bedford. Bd. sends copies of Glen's letter on proposals to
stop the French and Spanish from winning over the Indians. 2p.

Fol. 184. 20 Dec. 1748, Whitehall. Bd. of Trade to Gov. Glen.
Indian presents were mishandled and did not reach the tribes. 6p.

Fol. 233. 15 Nov. 1750, Whitehall. Bd. of Trade to Gov. Glen.
Indians did not receive the presents given to the traders.
Catawbas and the Six Nations need to be reconciled because all
English Indians should be friendly to each other. 38p.

Fol. 273. 10 Dec. 1750, Whitehall. Bd. of Trade to Duke of
Bedford. Bd. sends Glen's proposal to build a fort in Cherokee country and recommends that he be given discretionary
orders to begin construction. 2p.

C.O. 5/402 (CONT'D)

Fol. 427.   12 July 1753, Whitehall.   Bd. of Trade to Lords of
Treasury.   Bd. is considering Crokatt's memorial requesting
that England pay for the presents given to Indians bordering
S.C. and Georgia.   4p.

Fol. 439.   20 June 1754, Whitehall.   Bd. of Trade to Thomas
Robinson.   Bd. sends a copy of Pinckney's request to build a
fort in Cherokee country.   French also plan a fort there.   6p.

*C.O.   5/403   SOUTH CAROLINA, ENTRY BOOK OF LETTERS AND INSTRUCTIONS:
         1755-1760*

Fol. 16.   4 Nov. 1755, Whitehall.   Bd. of Trade to the King.
Bd. sends drafts of the instructions for Gov. Lyttleton.   4p.

Fol. 20.   4 Nov. 1755, St. James.   Instructions from the King
to Gov. Lyttleton (draft).   Gov. will maintain friendship with
faithful Indians, especially the Cherokees.   132p.

Fol. 165.   19 Nov. 1756.   Bd. of Trade to Gov. Lyttleton.
Lyttleton should thank the Assembly for provisions to build a
fort in Cherokee country.   Lyttleton's predecessor mistakenly
assured the assembly that no claims would be made on them for
building a Cherokee fort.   10p.

Fol. 175.   24 Dec. 1756, Whitehall.   Bd. of Trade to Wm. Pitt.
Bd. sends letters from the governors of Ga. and S.C. on the
frontier Indian situation.   2p.

Fol. 177.   24 Dec. 1756, Whitehall.   Bd. of Trade to the King.
Lyttleton writes that the Lower Cherokees and Catawbas remain
friendly.   Upper Cherokees have refused to honor the agreement
to protect Va. borders once a fort was built in their country.
Could the Cherokees (about 2,000 warriors) and Catawbas (300)
be used against the Creeks if hostilities begin?   16p.

Fol. 193.   10 Feb. 1757, Whitehall.   Bd. of Trade to Gov.
Lyttleton.   Lyttleton's measures have hopefully prevented
Creek and Upper Cherokee retaliation.   5p.

Fol. 200.   9 Nov. 1757, Whitehall.   Bd. of Trade to Gov.
Lyttleton.   Bd. approves Lyttleton's measures to reconcile the
Indians and counteract the French.   9p.

Fol. 209.   9 Nov. 1757, Whitehall.   Bd. of Trade to King George.
Lyttleton has established such influence over the Assembly that
he has been able to garrison two new forts in Cherokee country.
4p.

Fol. 222.   27 Jan. 1758, Whitehall.   Bd. of Trade to Lords of
the Committee of Council.   Bd. reports on James Wright's
memorial referring to S. Carolina's expense in building two
forts among the Cherokees and in paying for other military
projects.   Wright requests supplies.   13p.

C.O. 5/403 (CONT'D)

Fol. 245. 29 June 1758, Whitehall. Bd. of Trade to Lords of
Treasury. Bd. recommends Wright's request for money for
Indian presents. 3p.

Fol. 255. 24 July 1758, Whitehall. Bd. of Trade to Gov.
Lyttleton. Bd. approves Lyttleton's measures to prevent the
Cherokees from attacking Virginia. 6p.

Fol. 270. 6 Feb. 1760, Whitehall. Bd. of Trade to Wm. Pitt.
Bd. sends Lyttleton's papers regarding Cherokee hostility. 2p.

Fol. 272. 21 Feb. 1760, Whitehall. Bd. of Trade to Wm. Pitt.
Bd. sends Lyttleton's letter and a copy of the Cherokee peace.
Three Indian hostages have already been delivered and 20 more
are promised in exchange for the Indian hostages now being held.
2p.

Fol. 274. 25 Apr. 1760, Whitehall. Bd. of Trade to Wm. Pitt.
Bd. sends Gov. Ellis' letter relating to the broken treaty by
the Cherokees and the renewed hostilities. 2p.

Fol. 278. 24 Sept. 1760, Whitehall. Edward Sedgwick to Robert
Wood. Sedgwick sends Bull's letter on Col. Montgomery's
expedition against the Cherokees and the reasons Montgomery
left. 2p.

Fol. 280. 11 Nov. 1760, Whitehall. Bd. of Trade to Wm. Pitt.
Bd. sends letters from the Lt. Governors of S.C. and Va. on the
massacre of Ft. Loudoun's garrison. 1p.

*C.O. 5/404   SOUTH CAROLINA, ENTRY BOOK OF LETTERS AND INSTRUCTIONS:
            1760-1774*

Fol. 1. 11 Nov. 1760, Whitehall. Bd. of Trade to Wm. Pitt.
Bd. sends Bull's letter on the surrender and massacre of Ft.
Loudoun's garrison. 2p.

Fol. 3. 19 Dec. 1760, Whitehall. Bd. of Trade to Wm. Pitt.
Bd. sends Bull's letter on Cherokee hostilities since their
breach of the Ft. Loudoun capitulation. 1p.

Fol. 4. 8 Jan. 1761, Whitehall. Bd. of Trade to Wm. Pitt.
Bd. sends Ellis's and Bull's letters on the Cherokee, Creek, and
Choctaw affairs. 1p.

Fol. 5. 11 Feb. 1761, Whitehall. Bd. of Trade to Wm. Pitt.
Bd. sends extract of Bull's letter concerning the new French
fort on the Cherokee R. between Ft. Loudoun and Ft. l'Assomption
on the Ohio. 1p.

Fol. 66. 21 Sept. 1761, Whitehall. Bd. of Trade to the King.
Bd. sends draft of instructions for Gov. Boone. 4p.

Fol. 70. 11 Nov. 1761, St. James. Instructions from the King
to Gov. Boone. Boone must regain the affections of the frontier
Indians, especially the Cherokees. 95p.

C.O. 5/404 (CONT'D)

Fol. 162.   11 Dec. 1761, Whitehall. Bd. of Trade to Earl of
Egremont. Bd. sends extract of Bull's letter reporting that
a general peace has been signed with Attakullakulla. 1p.

Fol. 163.   27 May 1762, Whitehall. Bd. of Trade to Lords of
Treasury. Bd. supports Glen's request for travel reimbursement
for his trip to Saluda in June 1755 to conclude peace with the
Cherokees. 8p.

Fol. 171.   3 June 1762, Whitehall. Bd. of Trade to Gov. Boone.
Hopefully nothing will disturb the new peace with the Cherokees.
Jealousy and discontent among Indians have caused conflicting
regulations on Indian trade. 2p.

Fol. 195.   5 Aug. 1763. Bd. of Trade to John Stuart. Indian
agents should write the Bd. of Trade in all official matters.
4p.

Fol. 235.   24 Dec. 1765. Bd. of Trade to the King. Bd. sends
draft of instructions for Gov. Montague. 6p.

Fol. 240.   19 Feb. 1766, St. James. Instructions from the King
to Gov. Montague. Montague must protect Indian possessions and
regain their affections, especially the Cherokees. 121p.

Fol. 443.   24 Apr. 1771, Whitehall. Bd. of Trade to Lords of
Committee of Council. Boundary between N. and S.C. should
extend to the Cherokees. 4p.

Fol. 448.   29 May 1771, Whitehall. Bd. of Trade to Lords of
the Committee of Council. Bd. sends draft of additional
instructions to Montague. 1p.

Fol. 449.   29 May 1771. Additional instructions from Bd. of
Trade to Gov. Montague. Boundary between N. and S.C. should
extend to the line agreed upon with the Cherokees. 6p.

C.O. 5/405   SOUTH CAROLINA, ENTRY BOOK OF LETTERS AND INSTRUCTIONS:
*   1774-1775*

Fol. 1.   20 June 1774. Bd. of Trade to the King. Bd. sends
draft of instructions for Gov. Campbell. Campbell must
maintain good relations with the S.C. frontier Indians, especially the Cherokees. 99p.

C.O. 5/406   SOUTH CAROLINA, ENTRY BOOK OF ABSTRACTS OF CAROLINA
*   LETTERS TO BD. OF TRADE: 1721-1756*

Fol. 2.   19 July 1721. Col. Nicholson to [Bd. of Trade]
(abstract). Nicholson hopes to settle Indian affairs. 1p.

Fol. 7b.   17 Feb. 1723/24. Gen. Nicholson to [Bd. of Trade]
(abstract). Indian traders will hopefully arrive in time for
the Assembly session. 2p.

C.O. 5/406 (CONT'D)

Fol. 10.   14 Dec. 1723. Gen. Nicholson to [Bd. of Trade]
(abstract). Indian trade question cannot be presented to the
Assembly yet. 1p.

Fol. 12b. 16 Dec. 1724. Gen. Nicholson to [Bd. of Trade]
(abstract). Nicholson promises an account of the session
concerning Indians. 1p.

Fol. 14b. 27 Dec. 1730. Gov. Johnson to [Bd. of Trade]
(abstract). All seven Cherokees arrived [from England]
healthy and satisfied. 1p.

Fol. 18b. 6 Aug. 1736. Lt. Gov. Broughton to Bd. of Trade
(abstract). Broughton will continue cooperation with Ga. and
will not claim exclusive trading rights for Indians within
S. Carolina boundaries. 6p.

Fol. 22.   5 Oct. 1739. Col. Bull to [Bd. of Trade] (abstract).
Bull is apprehensive that the French may build their long
desired fort among the Cherokees. Priber, a Saxon, has influenced
the Cherokees to make peace with the French. Cherokee country
is included in [S. Carolina's] proprietary charter. 2p.

Fol. 24.   20 Mar. 1740/41. Col. Bull to [Bd. of Trade]
(abstract). French threaten the Cherokees. 1p.

Fol. 31.   4 June 1745, Charleston. Gov. Glen to Bd. of Trade
(abstract). Glen will send the crown of the Emperor of the
Cherokees to England and give an account of neighboring Indians,
French, and Spanish. 3p.

Fol. 32.   11 Feb. 1745. Gov. Glen to Bd. of Trade (abstract).
Glen has entertained the Cherokees and Catawbas and given them
presents. 2p.

Fol. 33.   2 May 1746, Saluda. Gov. Glen to Bd. of Trade.
[Abstract of C.O. 5/371/101]. 1p.

Fol. 33.   29 Sept. 1746, Charleston. Gov. Glen to Bd. of
Trade. [Abstract of C.O. 5/371/104]. 1p.

Fol. 33b. 28 Apr. 1747, [S. Carolina]. Gov. Glen to Bd. of
Trade. [Abstract of C.O. 5/371/133]. 2p.

Fol. 35b. 26 July 1748, [S. Carolina]. Gov. Glen to Bd. of
Trade. [Abstract of C.O. 5/372/67]. 2p.

Fol. 40b. 15 July 1750, [S. Carolina]. Gov. Glen to Bd. of
Trade. [Abstract of C.O. 5/372/226]. 3p.

Fol. 42.   2 Oct. 1750, [S. Carolina]. Gov. Glen to Bd. of
Trade. [Abstract of C.O. 5/372/252]. 2p.

Fol. 45.   27 July 1752, [S. Carolina]. Gov. Glen to Bd. of
Trade. [Abstract of C.O. 5/374/12]. 1p.

Fol. 45b. 16 Dec. 1752, [S. Carolina]. Gov. Glen to Bd. of
Trade. [Abstract of C.O. 5/374/69]. 1p.

C.O. 5/406 (CONT'D)

Fol. 46. 30 July 1753, [S. Carolina]. Gov. Glen to Bd. of Trade. [Abstract of C.O. 5/374/187]. 2p.

Fol. 46b. 25 Oct. 1753, [en route to the Cherokee nation]. Gov. Glen to Bd. of Trade. [Abstract of C.O. 5/374/225]. 2p.

Fol. 47. 26 Aug. 1754, [S. Carolina]. Gov. Glen to Bd. of Trade. [Abstract of C.O. 5/375/7]. 2p.

Fol. 48. 29 May 1755, [S. Carolina]. Gov. Glen to Bd. of Trade. [Abstract of C.O. 5/375/49]. 4p.

Fol. 49b. 14 Apr. 1756, [S. Carolina]. Gov. Glen to Bd. of Trade. [Abstract of C.O. 5/375/97]. 4p.

Fol. 51b. 19 July 1756, [Charleston]. Gov. Lyttleton to Bd. of Trade. [Abstract of C.O. 5/375/132]. 1p.

Fol. 52. 19 June 1756, [Charleston]. Gov. Lyttleton to Bd. of Trade. [Abstract of C.O. 5/375/136]. 2p.

Fol. 52b. 11 Aug. 1756, [Charleston]. Gov. Lyttleton to Bd. of Trade. [Abstract of C.O. 5/375/142]. 2p.

Fol. 53. 14 Aug. 1756, [Charleston]. Gov. Lyttleton to Bd. of Trade. [Abstract of C.O. 5/375/146]. 2p.

Fol. 53b. 17 Oct. 1756, [Charleston]. Gov. Lyttleton to Bd. of Trade. [Abstract of C.O. 5/375/155]. 3p.

C.O. 5/407   SOUTH CAROLINA, ENTRY BOOK OF LETTERS FROM SEC. OF STATE: 1766-1767

N. fol. 25 Oct. 1766, Whitehall. Earl of Shelburne to Charles Montague. Southern provinces are fearful about Indian disturbances. Indian traders have caused most of the trouble. 3p.

Fol. 2. 19 Feb. 1767, Whitehall. Earl of Shelburne to Charles Montague. Nothing can retard the growth of the Southern colonies more than Indian disturbances. 3p.

C.O. 5/408   SOUTH CAROLINA, ENTRY BOOK OF LETTERS FROM SEC. OF STATE: 1768-1782

Fol. 66. 10 June 1771, St. James. Additional instructions from George III to Charles Montague. Boundary line should be run from Salisbury Road to the line agreed upon with the Cherokees. 2p.

Fol. 71. 4 Dec. 1771, Whitehall. Earl of Hillsborough to Charles Montague. Hillsborough discusses the final settlement of the N.C. boundary line. 6p.

Fol. 73. 11 Jan. 1772, Whitehall. Earl of Hillsborough to Charles Montague. Hillsborough discusses Carolina's boundary. 4p.

C.O. 5/409   SOUTH CAROLINA, ENTRY BOOK OF LETTERS TO SEC. OF STATE:
1767-1772

Fol. 55b.   7 June 1770, Charleston.   Lt. Gov. Bull to Earl of
Hillsborough.   [Entry letter of C.O. 5/393/64].   9p.

Fol. 82.   30 Nov. 1770, Charleston.   Lt. Gov. Bull to Earl of
Hillsborough.   [Entry letter of C.O. 5/394/5].   44p.

C.O. 5/410   SOUTH CAROLINA, ENTRY BOOK OF LETTERS TO SEC. OF STATE:
1772-1781

Fol. 32.   11 Feb. 1774, Charleston.   Lt. Gov. Bull to Earl of
Dartmouth.   [Entry letter of C.O. 5/396/7].   4p.

Fol. 35b.   24 Mar. 1774, Charleston.   Lt. Gov. Bull to Earl of
Dartmouth.   [Entry letter of C.O. 5/396/14].   5p.

Fol. 44b.   3 Aug. 1774, Charleston.   Lt. Gov. Bull to Earl of
Dartmouth.   [Entry letter of C.O. 5/396/50].   5p.

Fol. 81b.   2 July 1775, Charleston.   Wm. Campbell to Earl of
Dartmouth.   [Entry letter of C.O. 5/396/151].   5p.

Fol. 103b.   31 Aug. 1775, Charleston.   Wm. Campbell to Earl of
Dartmouth.   [Entry letter of C.O. 5/396/225].   18p.

Fol. 134b.   8 July 1776, on board the *Bristol* near Charleston.
Wm. Campbell to Geo. Germain.   [Entry letter of C.O. 5/396/304].
6p.

C.O. 5/443   SOUTH CAROLINA, JOURNAL OF UPPER HOUSE OF ASSEMBLY:
18 MAY 1742 - 18 FEB. 1743

Fol. 2.   19 May 1742, Upper House.   Minutes containing message
from Bull arguing that it is prudent to honor the Cherokee
request for arms and ammunition to protect themselves from the
French.   3p.

Fol. 4.   20 May 1742, Upper House.   Minutes containing message
from Bull stating that the Cherokees may be forced to become
enemies of S.C. if they are attacked by the French.   10p.

Fol. 10b.   22 May 1742, Upper House.   Minutes containing report
of Commons disapproving public expenses without the prior consent
of the Assembly.   Great expense has resulted from traders indis-
criminately inviting Indians to visit Charleston.   7p.

Fol. 14b.   25 May 1742, Upper House.   Minutes containing committee report stating that a petition should be sent to the
King requesting three companies of troops to protect the Cherokees from the French.   5p.

Fol. 16b.   26 May 1742, Upper House.   Minutes containing message
to Commons concurring with the committee report that a petition
be sent to His Majesty [requesting three companies of troops to
protect the Cherokees from the French].   1p.

C.O. 5/443 (CONT'D)

Fol. 19b. 1 June 1742, Upper House. Minutes containing message from Commons reporting that they have amended resolution limiting additional pay for the officers and troops of the three companies [to protect the Cherokees]. 4p.

Fol. 21b. 2 June 1742, Upper House. Minutes containing petition to the King requesting three independent companies to protect the Cherokees from the French and proposing a new fort at Congarees or somewhere near the Cherokees. 8p.

Fol. 25. 3 June 1742, Upper House. Minutes containing resolution of Commons that Wm. McCarty will be paid £300 for carrying arms and ammunition to the Cherokees. 3p.

Fol. 33. 7 June 1742, Upper House. Minutes containing committee report recommending raising a company of rangers and as many Indians as necessary to protect the frontier. 6p.

Fol. 35. 8 July 1742, Upper House. Minutes containing a Plan of Defense ... [for South Carolina] in Case of Invasion. Friendly Indians will have a place to rendezvous where English officers will form them into separate companies. 12p.

C.O. 5/449   SOUTH CAROLINA, JOURNAL OF UPPER HOUSE OF ASSEMBLY: 1744

Fol. 21. 28 Feb. 1743/44, Upper House. Minutes containing memorial from James Abercromby reporting that the French are courting the Chickasaws and Creeks who are the only barrier for S.C. and Ga. against attack from the southwest and west. The French recently attempted to destroy the Cherokees, the colonies only barrier against the French and Canadian Indians. 8p.

*C.O. 5/455   SOUTH CAROLINA, JOURNAL OF MINUTES OF COUNCIL:
             JAN. 1745/46 - MAY 1747*

Fol. 2b. 9 Jan. 1745/46, Council Chamber. Minutes containing petition from John Turk and Michael Taylor to settle Ninety Six. Indians will readily relinquish their right to that land if the governor supports the plan. 3p.

Fol. 4. 10 Jan. 1745/46, Council Chamber. Minutes containing location of lands at Ninety Six settled by Turk and Taylor. Several hundred families would settle there if exempted from taxes. 3p.

Fol. 5. 11 Jan. 1745/46, Council Chamber. Minutes containing message from Glen to Commons. Newcomers from the Northern provinces will be exempt from taxes for 15 years. They should be encouraged to settle close to the Carolina settlements instead of at Ninety Six to promote the security of South Carolina. 3p.

Fol. 6. 14 Jan. 1745/46, Council Chamber. Minutes containing resolution that the government will satisfy the Indians concerning new settlements. 2p.

Fol. 12b. 22 Jan. 1745/46, Council Chamber. Minutes containing message from Glen to Commons. Glen requests reimbursement for buying land at Ninety Six. 3p.

Fol. 17b. 25 Jan. 1745/46, Council Chamber. Minutes containing
letter from McGillivray to Glen. Creeks fear that the Cherokees
might start a war because of false rumors spread by whites. 3p.

Fol. 30b. 13 Mar. 1745/46, Council Chamber. Minutes containing
petition from the Cherokees in the name of their Emperor and
seven Upper Towns requesting arms and ammunition to defend
themselves from the French. 3p.

Fol. 37. 27 Mar. 1746, Council Chamber. Minutes containing
letter from Skiagusta and Conontocheskoi (Lower Cherokees) to
Glen. Some Frenchmen and French Indians have arrived at Chote.
Lower Cherokees want assistance against the French and Indians.
Ludovick Grant writes that some Northern Indians are visiting
the Cherokees to negotiate a general peace. 10p.

Fol. 41b. 11 Apr. 1746, Council Chamber. Minutes containing
letters from Beamer to Glen and Capt. Richard Kent to Martin
Campbell. French wish to make peace with the Tugaloo Indians.
Capt. Richard Kent writes that Keowhee, Hywaee [Little Hiwassee],
and Oconee have made peace with the French. 7p.

Fol. 44b. 13 Apr. 1746, Council Chamber. Minutes containing
letter from C. Dougharty to Glen. The Indians, especially the
Overhill Towns, need ammunition to protect themselves from
their enemies. French are trying to seduce these Indians.
Ludovick Grant reports that the French made a peace proposal to
the Cherokees and Chickasaws. Glen should prevail on the
Cherokees to make peace with the Catawbas. 4p.

Fol. 46b. 17 Apr. 1746, Council Chamber. Minutes containing
forthcoming talk of Glen to the Cherokees and a letter from
James Paris to Richard Kent. Glen will tell the Cherokees that
the French lie. He also lists the rewards for each French
captive that the Cherokees bring Glen. James Paris writes that
the French and Indians marched into Tannisee under a flag of
truce. 12p.

Fol. 58b. 4 June 1746, Council Chamber. Minutes containing
affidavit from John Taylor and James Brannon, who escaped from
the French only to be recaptured by the Nottoways. Tellico
Indians finally set the two men free. French plan to trade with
the Cherokees. 2p.

Fol. 66b. 13 June 1746, Council Chamber. Minutes containing
message from Glen stating that the French have visited Indians
allied to England. Indians are so important to the fate of
[S.C.] that attention must always be paid to their affairs.
French influence must be stopped. 2p.

Fol. 83b. 18 Sept. 1746, Council Chamber. Minutes containing
message from Commons to Glen. Cherokee friendship is very
precarious. 2p.

Fol. 84b. 21 Oct. 1746, Council Chamber. Minutes containing
a letter from Robert Bunning to Glen. Eleven Cherokee towns

C.O. 5/455 (CONT'D)

have signed a peace with the French. Cherokees want forts in Chote, Tennessee, and Great Tellico to defend themselves against their enemies. Council supports the purchase of land at Ninety Six. 3p.

Fol. 85b. 21 Oct. 1746, Council Chamber. Minutes containing an examination of Mr. Kelley, who was asked about the French and English influence among the Cherokees. 5p.

Fol. 121. 7 Mar. 1746 [1747], Council Chamber. Minutes reporting that the Bd. received a deed of conveyance signed by 32 Cherokee chiefs for land at Ninety Six. 2p.

Fol. 131. 7 Apr. 1746/47, Council Chamber. Minutes recording that the Council read letters from Col. Pawley (S.C. agent in Cherokee nation) and Geo. Haig to Glen. 2p.

Fol. 135b. 15 Apr. 1747, Council Chamber. Minutes containing message from Glen to Commons. Cherokees are united in desiring a fort. 6p.

Fol. 138. 15 Apr. 1747, Council Chamber. Minutes containing message from Commons to Glen. There is no need to continue Col. Pawley as a Cherokee agent. 1p.

Fol. 148b. 22 May 1747, Council Chamber. Minutes containing message from Gov. to Commons. Governor sends an expense account (totaling £3,843) for Col. Pawley's agency among the Cherokees and an account (£975) for lands purchased at Ninety Six. 3p.

Fol. 149b. 22 May 1747, Council Chamber. Minutes containing message from Commons to Glen. Commons wants to know the total expense for the purchase of lands at Ninety Six. 1p.

Fol. 149b. 23 May 1747, Council Chamber. Minutes containing message from Glen to Commons. Powder and bullets still must be paid for lands at Ninety Six. Glen lists several talks and letters from the Raven and other Cherokees. 2p.

Fol. 150b. 26 May 1747, Council Chamber. Minutes containing message from Assembly to Glen. S.C. needs to send an agent to the Cherokees to counteract the French. 2p.

Fol. 151. 28 May 1744 [1747], Council Chamber. Minutes containing message from Glen to Commons. Delaying Col. Pawley's return to Cherokee country has caused no harm. 2p.

C.O. 5/455   SOUTH CAROLINA, JOURNAL OF UPPER HOUSE OF ASSEMBLY:
         20 NOV. 1746 - 29 JUNE 1748

Fol. 180. 14 Apr. 1746, Upper House of Assembly. Minutes containing message from Commons to Upper House. Upper House committee should join the Lower House committee on Indian Affairs. 3p.

Fol. 181. 15 Apr. 1746, Upper House of Assembly. Minutes containing message from Commons to Upper House. Commons agrees that fort should be built in Cherokee country. Cherokees should

C.O. 5/455 (CONT'D)

punish those guilty of recent hostile actions and no longer
assist Northern or French Indians against the Catawbas.   4p.

Fol. 187b.   22 May 1746, Upper House of Assembly. Minutes
recording the appointment of a committee to consider a report
from Lower House about building a fort among the Creeks
[Cherokees?]   2p.

Fol. 202b.   6 June 1747, Upper House of Assembly. Minutes
recording the reading of a committee report. Last spring some
French and their Indians visited Chote, the mother town of the
Upper Cherokees, and met with the Chickasaws, Creeks, and the
Savannahs, proposing a general peace with France. Catawbas
refused to attend. 10p.

Fol. 209b.   10 June 1747, Upper House of Assembly. Minutes
containing message from Commons stating the desirability of
building forts in Creek and Cherokee territory. Committee has
been appointed to suggest ways to defray the estimated expenses
of £10,000 for each fort. 9p.

Fol. 214.   11 June 1747, Upper House of Assembly. Minutes
containing message to Commons disagreeing with the need to
build two forts among the Cherokees and Creeks. Money should
be used to expand trade to the Choctaws instead. 3p.

Fol. 216b.   12 June 1747, Upper House of Assembly. Minutes
containing resolution to pay Geo. Haig for delivering powder
and bullets to the Cherokees in payment for land purchase at
Ninety Six. 3p.

C.O. 5/455   SOUTH CAROLINA, JOURNAL OF MINUTES OF COUNCIL: 4 JUNE -
17 NOV. 1747

Fol. 226b.   9 June 1747, Council Chamber. Minutes containing
information from the Governor that a famous Cherokee doctor
refused to care for a Frenchman shot by a French Indian. Cherokees request a fort. 3p.

Fol. 230.   23 July 1747, Council Chamber. Minutes recording
information from the Governor that the Cherokees request permission to come to Charleston. 2p.

Fol. 239b.   10 Nov. 1747, Council Chamber. Minutes recording
the granting of John Scott's petition for land around Ninety
Six or Saluda. 4p.

C.O. 5/455   SOUTH CAROLINA, JOURNAL OF UPPER HOUSE OF ASSEMBLY:
22 JAN. - 29 JUNE 1748

Fol. 253.   22 Jan. 1747 [1748], Upper House. Minutes containing
speech from Gov. Glen stating that S.C. has a good relationship
with all neighboring Indians. 2p.

C.O. 5/455 (CONT'D)

Fol. 255. 30 Jan. 1747 [1748], Upper House. Minutes containing
petition from Governor, Council, and Assembly to the King. S.C.
complains about the heavy expenses involved in securing friendship of the Choctaws, Creeks, Cherokees, Catawbas, and Chickasaws.
8p.

Fol. 270. 8 Apr. 1748, Upper House. Minutes containing message
from Commons regarding the expenses resulting from the Cherokees
murdering Edward Carrol. Cherokees have mistreated James Butler,
a trader among the tribe. If the murderer is shot, S.C. will
build a fort among the Overhill Towns. 3p.

Fol. 276b. 4 May 1748, Upper House. Minutes containing message
from Commons reporting the postponement of building a fort in
Cherokee country. Gov. should invite eight to ten Cherokee
headmen to visit Charleston. Fort should be built near the
Lower Towns to keep the French out. 3p.

Fol. 290b. 11 June 1748, Upper House. Minutes containing messages to the Lower House and Upper House. The Cherokees traders
now in town should be questioned about Indian affairs. Several
Cherokee chiefs who are guilty of misconduct are planning to
visit Charleston. 2p.

Fol. 296b. 20 June 1748, Upper House. Minutes containing a
report on Indian Affairs stating that the Upper and Middle
Cherokees should be brought to Charleston without talking to
the Lower Cherokees. Keowee people should be punished for their
misbehavior. 2p.

Fol. 298. 21 June 1748, Upper House. Minutes containing a
recommendation for the content of talk the Governor will give
to the Cherokees. 8p.

Fol. 304. 25 June 1748, Upper House. Minutes containing message
from Commons and a report on Indian Affairs. Commons will pay
up to £1,500 to build a fort and barracks among the Cherokees.
Half Breed Johnny should have presents equal to those of the
Squirrel King. If the son of the Warrior of Estatoe is not
educated among the English, Capt. Taylor should be appointed
his guardian. 7p.

Fol. 307. 27 June 1748, Upper House. Minutes containing message
from Lower House reporting a resolution approving the building
of a fort among the Upper Cherokees whenever the governor and
council direct it. 2p.

Fol. 314. 29 June 1748, Upper House. Minutes containing report
on Indian Affairs stating that Half Breed Johnny and Tugaloo
Warrior should be informed that the Cherokee trade will be
stopped unless Keowee, Estatoe, and Hoostinaree pay for their
misconduct towards Mr. Haig. Abraham Smith should be paid
£100 for carrying expresses to the Cherokees. 5p.

C.O. 5/459   SOUTH CAROLINA, MINUTES OF COUNCIL: 24 APR. - 15 DEC. 1749

Fol. 7b.   4 May 1749, Council Chamber. Minutes containing letter
from Duke of Bedford to Gov. Glen. Bedford recommends Abraham
Bosomworth's appointment as distributor of S.C. and Ga. Indian
presents. 3p.

Fol. 8b.   5 May 1749, Council Chamber. Minutes containing
message from Glen to Commons. Assembly will hopefully thank the
King for help towards the expense of Indian presents. 2p.

Fol. 10b.   10 May 1749, Council Chamber. Minutes containing
message from Glen to Commons. Glen has received letters from
Bedford relating to the King's presents to S.C. to ease Indian
expenses. 1p.

Fol. 20.   17 May 1749, Council Chamber. Minutes containing
memorial from Wm. Pinckney (Com. for Indian Affairs) complaining about unlicensed Indian traders. 5p.

Fol. 26.   23 May 1749, Council Chamber. Minutes containing a
letter from Wm. Sludders and Thomas Devall describing a meeting
between the Creeks and Cherokees. Creeks will agree to peace
if the Cherokees will drive away all the Nottaways and other
Northern Indians. 6p.

Fol. 33.   27 May 1749, Council Chamber. Minutes recording Glen's
hope that the Council will accept Bedford's recommendation to
appoint Bosomworth as Indian agent to distribute Indian presents
in S.C. and Georgia. Since Glen cannot go to Savannah or appoint
a delegate to make peace between the Creeks and Cherokees, the
Indians must come to Charleston. 2p.

Fol. 59b.   1 June 1749, Council Chamber. Minutes containing an
application from Pat Graham and message from Glen to Commons.
Graham applied to Glen for half of the Indian presents. Glen
agreed to omit the word "strict" in describing the Cherokees
as "strict allies." 13p.

Fol. 65b.   2 June 1749, Council Chamber. Minutes containing
intelligence from Mr. Brown that the Creeks wait impatiently
for the conclusion of peace with the Cherokees. 6p.

Fol. 76b.   23 June 1749, Council Chamber. Minutes containing
Glen's request that Bosomworth be given instructions for distributing Indian presents. 6p.

Fol. 98b.   13 July 1749, Council Chamber. Minutes containing
instructions to Bosomworth for distributing Indian presents. 14p.

Fol. 122b.   4 Aug. 1749, Council Chamber. Minutes containing a
list of Indian presents from England held by the Commissary
General. 3p.

Fol. 130.   1 Sept. 1749, Council Chamber. Minutes containing
Glen's request for the Board's opinion on how to receive the
Cherokees and Catawbas coming to Charleston. 2p.

C.O. 5/459 (CONT'D)

Fol. 130b. 4 Sept. 1749, Council Chamber. Minutes containing
letters from Thomas Ross and Thomas Devall to Glen and from
Anthony Dean to the traders in the Creek nation. Thomas Ross
writes that Chickilly (a Creek headman) only went to war after
the Cherokees killed several Upper Creeks. Creeks want peace.
Thomas Devall writes that the French will frustrate peace
between the Cherokees and Creeks to appease their own Indians.
Anthony Dean writes from the seven Overhill Towns that the
Cherokees have agreed to peace with the Creeks. Nottoways,
Senecas, and other Northern Indians will be prohibited from
passing through Cherokee country to attack the Creeks. 15p.

Fol. 137b. 5 Sept. 1749, Council Chamber. Minutes containing
a petition from Charleston merchants and recording a talk
between Glen and five Cherokee chiefs. Merchants complain about
the Creek and Cherokees during recent war between those nations.
Glen talked with the Emperor, Tasitee, Johnie, Tugaloo Warrior,
and Yellow Bird. 5p.

Fol. 139b. 6 Sept. 1749, Council Chamber. Minutes containing a
list of Cherokee and Creek headmen and warriors visiting
Charleston. The Emperor from Great Tellico, Tacito, the Raven
of Euphorsee and Hiwassie (two towns now one), Johnnie, Headman
of Tennessee, Conontotche Skyo of Tugaloo, and Tchisqua Tellone
(the Yellowbird of Keowee) were among those attending a meeting
in Charleston. 29p.

Fol. 153b. 7 Sept. 1749, Council Chamber. Minutes containing
a letter from James Beamer to Wm. Pinckney. James Beamer
complains about unlicensed traders in the Cherokee nation and
the quality of hides. Creeks and Cherokees have made peace.
Cherokees, Creeks, and Catawbas have received presents. 7p.

Fol. 156b. 11 Sept. 1749, Council Chamber. Minutes containing
information from Glen that the Cherokees and Creeks should be
approached about protecting the Catawbas from the Northern
Indians. Sick Cherokees returned home. Glen has talked with the
Cherokees about building a fort in their nation. Commissary
General distributed presents to the Cherokees, Creeks, and
Catawbas. 4p.

Fol. 222b. 9 Dec. 1749, Council Chamber. Minutes containing
petition from Luke Gibson whose warrant for 150 acres of land
expired before he returned from the Cherokees. 6p.

C.O. 5/465   SOUTH CAROLINA, JOURNAL OF UPPER HOUSE OF ASSEMBLY:
MAR. 1751 - AUG. 1753

Fol. 13. 27 Apr. 1751, Upper House. Minutes containing message
from Commons that traders should stop trading with the Cherokees
who are supplying visiting Northern Indians. Cherokee fort
would check the Northern Indians and prevent the French from
building a fort there. 7p.

Fol. 23.   9 May 1751, Upper House. Minutes containing petition
from inhabitants of the south branches of the Santee R. reporting news from the Cherokee nation that four traders have been
killed. 6p.

Fol. 27.   11 May 1751, Upper House. Minutes containing message
from Commons who have resolved to raise troops since the Cherokees are expected to attack the frontier settlers soon. 3p.

Fol. 28.   13 May 1751, Upper House. Minutes containing message
to Commons stating that troops should march toward the Cherokees
to prevent any attacks on the settlements. 2p.

Fol. 39.   12 June 1751, Upper House. Minutes containing message
from Commons noting that the Committee on Indian Affairs should
be revived to handle the Cherokees. 5p.

Fol. 41.   14 June 1751, Upper House. Minutes containing report
from the Committee on Indian Affairs stating that the Cherokees
have conducted themselves contrary to their promises. Little
Carpenter is chiefly responsible by giving bad talks in the
Overhill Towns of Tennessee, Chote, and Toqueh. Forts in
Cherokee country would secure the Cherokees for the British.
10p.

Fol. 45b.   15 June 1751, Upper House. Minutes containing
report from the Committee on Indian Affairs proposing to raise
an army to punish the Cherokees. 3p.

Fol. 47.   30 Aug. 1751, Upper House. Minutes containing a report
from the Committee of Conference stating that a fort should be
built near the Lower Cherokees to secure traders and enforce
regulations. French may persuade the Cherokees to allow a
French fort. 5p.

Fol. 51.   21 Nov. 1751, Upper House. Minutes containing speech
from Governor to Assembly. Governor asks advice on treating
with the Cherokees now in town. 3p.

Fol. 52.   22 Nov. 1751, Upper House. Minutes containing address
to Governor promising to give close attention to Cherokee
affairs. 3p.

Fol. 61.   25 Jan. 1752, Upper House. Minutes recording that
the Upper House read a bill for preserving peace with friendly
Indians and for regulating S.C. Indian trade. 5p.

Fol. 73.   7 Mar. 1752, Upper House. Minutes containing message
from Commons hoping that the Committee determining the northern
and southern boundaries will also decide if a fort proposed for
the Lower Cherokees would be within S. Carolina's border. 3p.

Fol. 76b.   11 Mar. 1752, Upper House. Minutes containing message to Commons about bill concerning Indian peace and trade.
4p.

C.O. 5/465 (CONT'D)

Fol. 78b. 16 Mar. 1752, Upper House. Minutes containing
petition from Robert Bunning requesting pay for escorting the
Cherokees from Charleston to the Cherokee border. 5p.

Fol. 80b. 17 Mar. 1752, Upper House. Minutes containing
message to Commons stating that a committee of both houses
will discuss amending the Indian peace and trade bill. 8p.

Fol. 81b. 18 Apr. 1752, Upper House. Minutes containing
report from the committee on amendments to the Indian peace
bill. 8p.

Fol. 86. 23 Apr. 1752, Upper House. Minutes recording further
discussion on the Indian peace bill. 7p.

Fol. 90b. 29 Apr. 1752, Upper House. Minutes containing list
of Indian goods on hand. 4p.

Fol. 94b. 2 May 1752, Upper House. Minutes containing message from Commons reporting that Commons sent a list of
unsuitable Indian presents which should be sold to the public.
4p.

Fol. 96. 5 May 1752, Upper House. Minutes containing message
from Commons reporting news from Patrick Brown (an Indian
trader) that the Lower Cherokees are warring against the
Northern Indians and the Creeks. 5p.

Fol. 98. 6 May 1752, Upper House. Minutes containing report
from Upper House Committee on Indian Affairs which lists
reasons why the Creeks and Cherokees should be at peace.
Cherokees and Creeks are a good barrier against the French. 9p.

Fol. 105b. 9 May 1752, Upper House. Minutes containing
message from Commons who agree that the government should not
interfere in the Creek-Cherokee war. 6p.

Fol. 113b. 16 May 1752, Upper House. Minutes recording
Glen's approval of Indian peace and trade act. 6p.

Fol. 151b. 3 Mar. 1753, Upper House. Minutes indicating the
Upper House read a bill to rectify ommissions in the Indian
Trade Act. 5p.

Fol. 154. 5 Mar. 1753, Upper House. Minutes indicating the
Upper House read a bill to rectify ommissions in the Indian
Trade Act. 4p.

Fol. 170b. 17 Apr. 1753, Upper House. Minutes containing
message to Lower House indicating what presents should be
given to the Creeks and Cherokees at Ft. Moore. 4p.

Fol. 172b. 18 Apr. 1753, Upper House. Minutes containing
report from the Committee of Conference recommending the
presents to be distributed to the Creeks and Cherokees. 6p.

C.O. 5/467   SOUTH CAROLINA, JOURNAL OF COUNCIL: FEB. 1752 - NOV. 1752

Fol. 11.   7 Feb. 1752, Council Chamber. Minutes containing
letters from Lachlan McGillivray to Wm. Pinckney. War has
erupted between the Upper Creeks and Cherokees. Cherokees
started the conflict by killing some Oakfuskees. Cherokees
also stole some horses and goods from Moses Thompson and others
in Amelia township. Raven of Hiwassee reports that the Creeks
have killed some Cherokees. 9p.

Fol. 15b.   3 Mar. 1752, Council Chamber. Minutes containing
letter from Capt. Fairchild to Glen. Some 50 Northern Indians
visited the Cherokees. 30p.

Fol. 30.   6 Mar. 1752. Minutes containing resolution to advise
the Cherokees that the Northern Indians must obtain a pass from
the Congree Fort or be treated as enemies. 10p.

Fol. 34b.   7 Mar. 1752. Minutes containing order to the Clerk
to select relevant Indian Affairs' papers since the beginning
of the Cherokee treaty for Commons to examine. 3p.

Fol. 35b.   10 Mar. 1752. Minutes containing message from Glen
to Commons containing a list of papers relating to Indian affairs
since the last Cherokee treaty. 3p.

Fol. 37.   11 Mar. 1752, Council Chamber. Minutes containing
message from Commons to Glen. Commons request the prevention
of future hostilities by the Cherokees and Nottoways. Commons
desire complete information about all Indians near S. Carolina.
2p.

Fol. 41.   14 Mar. 1752, Council Chamber. Minutes containing
letters of Robert Bunning and James Beamer. Dan Murphy and
60 Cherokees have gone to settle a new place. Murphy promised
them cheaper goods from Va. or N. York. Tomotley, Chewee,
Ellijay, and two other towns do not have copies of the peace
between the Cherokees and S. Carolina. Little Carpenter is
reportedly visiting the French to make peace. Cherokees want
a fort in the Lower Towns, not in the Overhill Towns. 9p.

Fol. 45.   16 Mar. 1752, Council Chamber. Minutes containing
message from Glen to Commons. Glen forwards letters from
Bunning and Beamer, who live among the Cherokees. 2p.

Fol. 45b.   17 Mar. 1752, Council Chamber. Minutes containing
letter from Glen to Creeks. Creeks should end their war with
the Cherokees and their Northern Indian allies. Cherokee
friendship will help shield the Creeks from attacks by the Six
Nations. 9p.

Fol. 52.   24 Mar. 1752, Council Chamber. Minutes containing
letter from Ludvick Grant to Glen. Grant reports that the
Cherokees are returning home from Charleston. Little Carpenter
has gone north, but his French companion has returned to Chote.
Warrior of Settico (Small Pox Conjurer) expects a large number
of Senecas to visit the Overhill Towns on their way to war
against the Cowetas. 7p.

C.O. 5/467 (CONT'D)

Fol. 55. 31 Mar. 1752, Council Chamber. Minutes containing a
talk between Glen and Acorn Whistler (an Upper Creek). Creeks
have made many treaties with the Cherokees, but the Cherokees
always break them. 7p.

Fol. 58. 1 Apr. 1752, Council Chamber. Minutes containing a
talk between Glen and Cherokees from Estatoe. Creeks drove
the Cherokees to Charleston. All the Cherokees that went to
England, except Tehnganunto (Little Carpenter), are dead. Glen
states that the Cherokees were killed by Creeks after the
Cherokees left town. 6p.

Fol. 60b. 2 Apr. 1752, Council Chamber. Minutes recording that
Glen sent soldiers after the Creek murderers. Upper Creeks
claim that the Lower Creeks killed the Cherokees. 6p.

Fol. 63. 3 Apr. 1752, Council Chamber. Minutes containing
letter from Maj. Luttrell to Glen. A Cherokee who escaped [from
the Creeks?] is being brought to Charleston. 2p.

Fol. 65b. 5 Apr. 1752, Council Chamber. Minutes containing
resolution to send a letter to the Cherokees by the Lower Creeks.
3p.

Fol. 66b. 6 Apr. 1752, Council Chamber. Minutes recording
information from Henry Defanson that the Lower Creeks who
murdered the Cherokees offered to sell a Cherokee prisoner for
two gals. of rum. Militia will bring those Creeks to Charleston.
7p.

Fol. 69b. 7 Apr. 1752, Council Chamber. Minutes containing
petition from Anson County settlers along the N.C. frontier
complaining about the Cherokees. John Anderson is supplying
the Cherokees with ammunition. 14p.

Fol. 76. 16 Apr. 1752, Council Chamber. Minutes recording
that Glen sent letters to the Creeks and Cherokees about the
Lower Creek's murder of several Cherokees. 5p.

Fol. 79. 21 Apr. 1752, Council Chamber. Minutes containing
talks from Judd's Friend and the Raven indicating that they told
the Cherokees to return goods stolen from whites. Glen should
let the Cherokees and Creeks settle their own differences.
Creeks raided Cherokee country and killed the Raven's brother
and others. 5p.

Fol. 81. 23 Apr. 1752, Council Chamber. Minutes containing
paper from James Graeme with information on the number of
Creek, Cherokee, Chickasaw, and Catawba warriors. Paper also
lists Indian treaties, names and character of headmen, and
Indian relations with the French. 5p.

Fol. 83. 24 Apr. 1752, Council Chamber. Minutes containing
Glen's request for advice about handling the Lower Creeks who
murdered the Cherokees. 3p.

C.O. 5/467 (CONT'D)

Fol. 84.   28 Apr. 1752, Council Chamber. Minutes containing
letter from Glen to Upper and Lower Creeks. Glen asks for
punishment for the murderers of the Cherokees. 10p.

Fol. 88b.   29 Apr. 1752, Council Chamber. Minutes containing
message from Glen to Assembly. Creeks destroyed two Cherokee
towns and killed nine Cherokees. 5p.

Fol. 91b.   1 May 1752, Council Chamber. Minutes containing
a report from a committee of Commons expressing surprise at
Glen for thinking that the Cherokee murders are important. If
the Creeks are punished, it might begin a war between the English
and the Creeks. Cherokees have not given satisfaction for
robbing and killing S. Carolinians. 3p.

Fol. 95b.   5 May 1752, Council Chamber. Minutes containing
talk from Skiagunsta of Keowee and Good Warrior of Estatoe to
Glen. War with the Creeks and Northern Indians have forced
most Lower Towns to move. Cherokees request ammunition and
guns so they will not have to move. 25p.

Fol. 107b.   7 May 1752, Council Chamber. Minutes containing
message from Glen stating that the Governor, Council, and
Assembly view the Creek murder of Cherokees as an insult
against the government. Satisfaction should be demanded.
Commons will hopefully allocate money for building a fort among
the Lower Cherokees. 4p.

Fol. 118.   15 May 1752, Council Chamber. Minutes containing
report from Commons arguing that S.C. should not interfere in
the Creek-Cherokee dispute. Fort should be built only after
the Cherokees sell all the land between Long Canes and Keowee
to the English. 8p.

Fol. 124b.   25 May 1752, Council Chamber. Minutes containing
letter from James Beamer and Richard Smith to Glen and talks
from Old Hop and the Prince of Tanasee. The Creeks have
plundered English traders in Cherokee country. Nottoways are
also at war with the Cherokees. Caneecatee (Old Hop) and
Kittegunsta (Prince of Tanasee) describe trouble in Cherokee
country. 14p.

Fol. 131.   27 May 1752, Council Chamber. Minutes containing
Glen's recommendation that Mrs. Bosomworth, a Creek by birth,
is an ideal person to win away Malatchi from the French so
peace may be established between the Creeks and Cherokees. 3p.

Fol. 132.   2 June 1752, Council Chamber. Minutes containing
letter from Mary Bosomworth to Glen. Mary Bosomworth offers
to persuade the Creeks to give satisfaction for robbing traders
among the Lower Cherokees and to establish peace with the
Cherokees. 12p.

Fol. 138.   4 June 1752, Council Chamber. Minutes containing
letter from Thomas Bosomworth to Glen. Bosomworth requests
information about the government's need for his wife. 4p.

C.O. 5/467 (CONT'D)

Fol. 139b. 11 June 1752, Council Chamber. Minutes containing
letter from Mary Bosomworth to Glen. Mary Bosomworth asks that
her husband be authorized to assist her. Creek agent believes
the tribe would never give up the murderers of the Cherokees.
6p.

Fol. 142. 15 June 1752, Council Chamber. Minutes containing
list of presents given to Tasitee (a Cherokee) and information
that John Dart's list of presents given to Raven, Capt. Caesar,
Skiagunsta, Moetoe (Raven's son), and others do not agree with
other records. 9p.

Fol. 146. 16 June 1752, Council Chamber. Minutes recording
information that the Council obtained from Dart about Indian
presents. Creek agent should insist that the Cherokee murderers
be executed in the presence of the Carolina traders. Creeks
should make immediate restitution to those traders whom they
robbed in the Cherokee nation. 3p.

Fol. 147. 24 June 1752, Council Chamber. Minutes containing
instructions from Glen to Bosomworth and letters from James
Beamer to Glen. Bosomworth is to be the agent for the Creeks.
Creeks should turn over the Cherokee prisoner and execute the
murderers of the Cherokees. Beamer reports that the Cherokees
desire the governor to help them make peace with the Creeks.
10p.

Fol. 165. 18 July 1752, Council Chamber. Minutes recording
Council decision to support the building of a fort among the
Lower Cherokees. 7p.

Fol. 187b. 1 Sept. 1752, Council Chamber. Minutes containing
representation from Glen to Bd. of Trade. It is necessary to
build forts among the Indians, especially the Cherokees. One
should be built in the Overhill Towns. 8p.

Fol. 236b. 31 Oct. 1752, Council Chamber. Minutes containing
letter from Thomas Bosomworth to Glen. Acorn Whistler has been
executed [for murdering the Cherokees]. Cherokee horses have
been returned. Creeks have agreed to meet the Cherokee headmen.
68p.

C.O. 5/468   SOUTH CAROLINA, JOURNAL OF COUNCIL: NOV. 1752 - FEB. 1753

Fol. 4. 15 Nov. 1752, Council Chamber. Minutes containing
letter from the Governor to the Creek headmen. Acorn Whistler,
the Creek ringleader guilty of killing the Cherokees, has been
executed. Governor is pleased that Creeks accepted the Cherokee peace proposal. Catawbas are warned not to provoke the
Cherokees. 11p.

Fol. 11. 25 Nov. 1752, Council Chamber. Minutes containing
letter from James Beamer, Cherokee trader, to Glen. Cherokees
complain about the Catawbas murdering several Cherokees. Tosale
and Chuchee, two Cherokee headmen, have expressed their friendship and request supplies. 3p.

C.O. 5/468 (CONT'D)

Fol. 66. 16 Dec. 1752, Council Chamber. Minutes containing letter from Tasitee of Hiwassee to Glen. Tasitee will acquaint the Cherokee Emperor about the Creek peace proposal. 9p.

Fol. 71. 2 Jan. 1753, Council Chamber. Minutes containing letter from Catawba King to Glen. Catawbas have sent peace proposals to the Cherokees. 20p.

Fol. 80b. 11 Jan. 1753, Council Chamber. Minutes containing letter from John Buckles to Glen. Chickasaws have asked for Cherokee assistance against the French. 7p.

Fol. 84. 16 Jan. 1753, Council Chamber. Minutes containing journal of Bosomworth reporting Malatchi's decision to cease hostilities against the Cherokees until peace can be concluded. Red Coat King also approved the peace with the Cherokees. 28p.

Fol. 98. 31 Jan. 1753, Council Chamber. Minutes containing appendix to Bosomworth's journal describing Acorn Whistler's execution for killing the Cherokees. 26p.

C.O. 5/474   SOUTH CAROLINA, JOURNAL OF COUNCIL: JULY 1759 - JUNE 1760

Fol. 8. 13 Aug. 1759, Council Chamber. Minutes containing decision of Council to postpone consideration of Cherokee letters and talks to the following day. 2p.

Fol. 8b. 14 Aug. 1759, Council Chamber. Minutes recording information from Mr. Nutt that Ft. Loudoun and Ft. Prince George lack supplies. French are responsible for Cherokee dissatisfaction with the English. Cherokees should not receive more ammunition. Government examined the number of troops at Fts. Loudoun and Prince George. 3p.

Fol. 10. 28 Aug. 1759, Council Chamber. Minutes recording that the Council read a copy of a talk from Wawhatchee (Lower Cherokee headman) to the Ga. Governor. Council decided to tell Cherokee headmen to send their complaints to S.C., not Georgia. 2p.

Fol. 12. 17 Sept. 1759, Council Chamber. Minutes recording that Lt. Coytmore requested instructions concerning those unauthorized Cherokees near Ft. Prince George. Council decided that Coytmore should prevent a rupture with the Cherokees but be ready to repel any attack. 2p.

Fol. 13. 1 Oct. 1759, Council Chamber. Minutes containing information from letters from Capt. Paul Demeré and Lt. Coytmore about recent murders by the Cherokees. Council decided that the Governor should ask Atkin to divert the Cherokees by encouraging the Upper Chickasaws and Creeks to attack Upper Cherokee towns. Va. will be requested to send troops and supplies to Ft. Loudoun. 2p.

Fol. 14b. 4 Oct. 1759, Council Chamber. Minutes containing decision of the Governor to accompany the army against the Cherokees. 2p.

C.O. 5/474 (CONT'D)

Fol. 15b. 6 Oct. 1759, Council Chamber. Minutes containing decision that S.C. should declare war against the Cherokees. 2p.

Fol. 16. 7 Oct. 1759, Council Chamber. Minutes containing decision of Council to intercept Cherokee goods and ammunition in route from Virginia. 2p.

Fol. 16b. 11 Oct. 1759, Council Chamber. Minutes containing decision of Council that the Governor has the discretion to declare war against the Cherokees when he sees fit. 2p.

Fol. 18b. 14 Oct. 1759, Council Chamber. Minutes containing decision of Council that the Governor should inform Fauquier that Va. goods for the Cherokees were stopped in Salisbury, N. Carolina. 1p.

Fol. 19. 15 Oct. 1759, Council Chamber. Minutes containing decision of Council that Cherokees visiting Charleston should be housed properly but not receive the usual marks of friendship. Headman of Middle Settlements named Round O and his followers have always been friendly to the English. 2p.

Fol. 19b. 18 Oct. 1759, Council Chamber. Minutes containing talk between Great Warrior of Chote and the Governor. Great Warrior wants to delay talk since he has no gifts to demonstrate his friendship. 2p.

Fol. 20b. 19 Oct. 1759, Council Chamber. Minutes containing talks from Great Warrior of Chote, Tistoe of Keowee, Head Warrior of Estatoe, and Killianaca (Black Dog) of Hiwassee. Old Hop of Chote stated that the killing of a white man near Ft. Loudoun was encouraged by another white man. Toucolussor of Settico ordered the killing at Tellico. Great Warrior wants peace. 4p.

Fol. 22. 20 Oct. 1759. Council Chamber. Minutes containing discussion of Council on how many Cherokees must be executed for the tribe's murders and how many hostages the English need. 2p.

Fol. 22b. 21 Oct. 1759, Council Chamber. Minutes containing continued discussion of how many Cherokees must be executed and how many hostages must be kept. 1p.

Fol. 23. 22 Oct. 1759, Council Chamber. Minutes containing discussion on whether to plan an expedition to the Cherokees to demand satisfaction or to keep hostages until Cherokees make satisfaction. 4p.

Fol. 25. 29 Oct. 1759, Council Chamber. Minutes recording information that a gunner from H.M.S. *Trent* was ordered to join the Cherokee expedition. 1p.

Fol. 26b. 10 Nov. 1759, Council Chamber. Minutes containing letter from Gov. Lyttleton to John Cleland. Lyttleton requested 500 more men. Little Carpenter has returned to the Upper Nation with two French prisoners. Troops from N.C. have been authorized to cooperate with S.C. or Va. forces against the Cherokees. 2p.

Fol. 27b. 24 Nov. 1759, Council Chamber. Minutes containing letter from Gov. Lyttleton to John Cleland. Lyttleton writes from Saluda Old Town requesting 500 men. Cherokees that split from Round O's gang at Congarees have been very disruptive. Cherokees informed Lyttleton that the tribe sent a painted tomahawk to the Creeks asking for their assistance. 4p.

Fol. 31. 26 Nov. 1759, Council Chamber. Minutes recording that the Council unanimously agreed that Lyttleton's request for troops was impossible. 1p.

Fol. 34. 7 Jan. 1760, Council Chamber. Minutes containing letter from Gov. Lyttleton to John Cleland. Peace is concluded with the Cherokees. Cherokees left 21 hostages until others are sent to replace them. Smallpox has broken out in the army. 2p.

Fol. 35. 9 Jan. 1760, Council Chamber. Minutes containing reply from Lyttleton to the Board's address. Lyttleton is pleased that the Cherokee treaty was approved. 1p.

Fol. 35b. 11 Jan. 1760, Council Chamber. Minutes containing Treaty of Peace and Friendship Concluded ... at Ft. Prince George 26 Dec. 1759. Cherokee hostages are named. Signatories include Attakullakulla, Oconostota, Otassite, Kittagusta, Okoneca, and Keliamnoteh. 4p.

Fol. 37. 16 Jan. 1760, Council Chamber. Minutes recording that since the Cherokee expedition terminated sooner than expected, the General Assembly will meet in Feb. rather than in March. 1p.

Fol. 37b. 1 Feb. 1760, Council Chamber. Minutes containing testimony of Thomas Beamer who describes the attempt by Young Warrior of Estatoe to exchange two prisoners for the release of the hostages. Cherokees killed Mr. Elliot, ten whites, and took two prisoners. 4p.

Fol. 39b. 2 Feb. 1760, Council Chamber. Minutes containing report from Aaron Price with information from an Indian woman. Young Warrior Scaroroski of Estatoe and Round O encouraged the Cherokees to kill the 24 whites. Round O was upset because his two sons were hostages. 3p.

Fol. 40b. 7 Feb. 1760, Council Chamber. Minutes recording that the Governor has received letters concerning the recent murders by Cherokees. 2p.

C.O. 5/474 (CONT'D)

Fol. 41. 11 Feb. 1760, Council Chamber. Minutes recording that the Governor has received more news concerning murders by the Cherokees. S.C. will raise troops to protect the back settlements and prevent additional murders. 4p.

Fol. 43. 12 Feb. 1760, Council Chamber. Minutes containing procedures to raise the militia. 1p.

Fol. 43b. 14 Feb. 1760, Council Chamber. Minutes containing information that since Overhill Towns were not involved in recent murders by the Lower Towns Little Carpenter will be allowed to free hostages from the Overhill Towns in exchange for the Cherokee offenders or for the two Englishmen recently captured. 3p.

Fol. 45b. 26 Feb. 1760, Council Chamber. Minutes containing the Governor's questions on plans to relieve Ft. Prince George. Amherst asked for troops. 1p.

Fol. 46. 29 Feb. 1760, Council Chamber. Minutes recording that the Council considered plans to relieve Ft. Prince George. 3p.

Fol. 47. 3 Mar. 1760, Council Chamber. Minutes recording that the Council continued to consider plans to relieve Ft. Prince George. 2p.

Fol. 48b. 6 Mar. 1760, Council Chamber. Minutes containing instructions to Col. Richard Richardson commanding the relief for Ft. Prince George. 4p.

Fol. 50. 15 Mar. 1760, Council Chamber. Minutes containing Council's decision to send reinforcements to Ft. Ninety Six. 1p.

Fol. 51. 21 Mar. 1760, Council Chamber. Minutes containing Council's decision to make Jacob Brooks commander of Rhall's Fort and to inform him that when the King's troops arrive, they will immediately march to relieve the back settlers against the Indians. 2p.

Fol. 51b. 27 Mar. 1760, Council Chamber. Minutes containing Council's decision on measures to protect the back settlements from the Cherokees. 3p.

Fol. 54. 7 Apr. 1760, Council Chamber. Minutes containing information that Lt. Col. Grant arrived in Charleston. Inhabitants built forts at Steven's Creek and at the head of the Ashpoo River for protection against the Cherokees. Brown of Breed Camp was appointed to lead the Chickasaws against the Cherokees. Edmund Atkin writes that some Creeks will join the attack against the Cherokees. 4p.

Fol. 55b. 9 Apr. 1760, Council Chamber. Minutes containing information that the rangers will drive cattle for the troops. Capt. Paul Demeré at Ft. Loudoun will be informed when the troops arrive for the Cherokee expedition. 1p.

C.O. 5/474 (CONT'D)

Fol. 56. 12 Apr. 1760, Council Chamber. Minutes containing
Council's decision to ask troops to fight the Cherokees and to
relieve Ft. Loudoun. 2p.

Fol. 57. 15 Apr. 1760, Council Chamber. Minutes containing
information on the problems in getting wagons to carry supplies
for the expedition against the Cherokees. 1p.

Fol. 57. 16 Apr. 1760, Council Chamber. Minutes containing
Council's decision to give Col. Andrew Richardson at Ninety Six
discretionary power to march against the Cherokees. 2p.

Fol. 57b. 22 Apr. 1760, Council Chamber. Minutes containing
information that the Assembly agreed to raise scalp money to
£35. Catawbas asked for a secure place to keep their women and
children while they war against the Cherokees. Individuals
visiting the Upper and Lower Creeks and the Upper and Lower
Chickasaws carry commissions permitting attacks on the Cherokees.
3p.

Fol. 58b. 26 Apr. 1760, Council Chamber. Minutes containing
Council's recommendation that a fund be established at Augusta
to pay for Cherokee scalps and for presents to the Creeks
fighting against the Cherokees. 1p.

Fol. 58b. 27 Apr. 1760, Council Chamber. Minutes containing
Council's decision to grant request from the Ft. Ninety Six
garrison not to be sent elsewhere. 2p.

Fol. 59. 30 Apr. 1760, Council Chamber. Minutes containing
Council's decision to reinforce two forts built by Enoree
residents among the Lower Cherokees. 2p.

Fol. 60. 5 May 1760, Council Chamber. Minutes containing talk
from Red Tick (Touksecay), a Catawba headman, stating that his
nation is determined to war against the Cherokees. 3p.

Fol. 61. 6 May 1760, Council Chamber. Minutes containing talk
from Bull to Red Tick. S.C. will give arms to the Catawbas
fighting the Cherokees and clothing to their women and children.
Bull will try to help the Catawbas against those settlers who
have seized their land. 3p.

Fol. 63. 20 May 1760, Council Chamber. Minutes containing
Council's decision that Col. Richardson at Ninety Six should
reinforce Ft. Pennington and several other nearby forts.
Montgomery will soon reach Ft. Prince George. 2p.

Fol. 63b. 23 May 1760, Council Chamber. Minutes containing
Council's decision to supply fort near Saluda with ammunition
and salt. 2p.

Fol. 64. 24 May 1760, Council Chamber. Minutes containing list
of stipulations before any treaty can be concluded with the
Cherokees. 2p.

C.O. 5/474 (CONT'D)

Fol. 66.   2 June 1760, Council Chamber.   Minutes containing
information from Bull that Abraham, a Negro, has returned from
Ft. Loudoun with letter from Paul Demeré and a talk from Little
Carpenter pleading for the English to restore friendship with
the Overhill Cherokees.   Since S.C. fears a Creek war, Little
Carpenter might be instrumental in establishing general peace.
3p.

Fol. 67b.   5 June 1760. Council Chamber.   Minutes containing
information from Bull that the Upper Creeks who murdered the
English traders belonged to the French and Cherokee party.   2p.

Fol. 68.   9 June 1760, Council Chamber.   Minutes containing
Council's decision to supply Brook's Fort between the Broad and
Saluda Rivers and to pay that fort's garrison.   2p.

Fol. 68b.   10 June 1760, Council Chamber.   Minutes containing
letter from Lt. Col. Grant to Bull.   Grant reports encounters
with the Cherokees at Little Keowee, Estatoe, and Sugar Town
(the latter two having at least 100 houses).   It is virtually
impossible to pass over the mountains but Grant believes the
Cherokees will come to terms.   4p.

Fol. 70b.   11 June 1760, Council Chamber.   Minutes containing
Council's decision to pay arrears to garrison of Ft. Prince
George and to provision the fort.   2p.

Fol. 71.   18 June 1760, Council Chamber.   Minutes containing
Council's opinion that Bull should inform the Assembly about
Ft. Wm. Henry Lyttleton on the Enoree R. and other forts in
S. Carolina.   2p.

Fol. 71b.   19 June 1760, Council Chamber.   Minutes containing
information that Bull requested provisions from the Assembly for
Ft. Wm. Henry Lyttleton on the Enoree River.   2p.

Fol. 72.   20 June 1760, Council Chamber.   Minutes containing
letters from some Indian traders reporting that the Chickasaws
proposed to supply themselves with ammunition from Ft. Loudoun.
Two Cherokee prisoners in Charleston reported that the war began
because the traders, Coytmore, and Bell at Ft. Keowee mistreated
the tribe.   6p.

Fol. 75b.   30 June 1760, Council Chamber.   Minutes containing
letters from Col. Montgomery to Bull and Capt. Paul Demeré to
Montgomery.   Montgomery reports that Old Warrior and Tistoe
failed to bring peace.   Only Little Carpenter's people among the
Upper Towns want peace.   Middle Settlements desire peace but are
afraid of fellow tribesmen.   Only Va. can supply Ft. Loudoun.
Demeré writes that Little Carpenter reports an attack will soon
be made on Ft. Loudoun.   4p.

C.O. 5/474   SOUTH CAROLINA, JOURNAL OF GENERAL ASSEMBLY: OCT. 1757-
            MAY 1758

Fol. 93b. 18 Nov. 1757. Minutes containing committee report
recommending that S.C. not reduce allowances for persons who
supply provisions and liquor to Indians traveling the road to
Charleston. 2p.

Fol. 103. 18 Jan. 1758. Minutes recording the reading of several accounts about supplies for Fts. Loudoun and Prince George
and entertaining Indians. 3p.

Fol. 104. 19 Jan. 1758. Minutes recording the reading of several accounts for supplying Fts. Loudoun and Prince George. 3p.

Fol. 105. 24 Jan. 1758. Minutes recording the reading of several accounts for supplying Fts. Loudoun and Prince George. 3p.

Fol. 106. 25 Jan. 1758. Minutes recording the reading of several accounts for supplying Fts. Loudoun and Prince George. 2p.

Fol. 107. 27 Jan. 1758. Minutes containing order that John
Chevillette's accounts concerning Ft. Loudoun be resubmitted.
3p.

Fol. 108. 28 Jan. 1758. Minutes recording the reading of several
accounts for supplying Ft. Loudoun, including rum provisions for
the Lower Cherokees and the Indian interpreters at the fort. 3p.

Fol. 109b. 1 Feb. 1758. Minutes recording the reading of
several accounts concerning Ft. Loudoun. 4p.

Fol. 111. 2 Feb. 1758. Minutes recording that Daniel Cannon's
certificate for Ft. Loudoun was resubmitted. 3p.

Fol. 112. 7 Feb. 1758. Minutes recording the reading of several
accounts concerning Fts. Loudoun and Prince George. 4p.

Fol. 113b. 8 Feb. 1758. Minutes recording the approval of only
£25 of £75 bill for building four large stone chimneys at Ft.
Loudoun. John Elliot (Indian trader) submitted his bill for
board and entertainment of two French prisoners redeemed from
the Cherokees. John Stuart petitioned to be reimbursed for
supplies given to Little Carpenter and other Cherokee headmen.
12p.

Fol. 119. 9 Feb. 1758. Minutes containing message from Lyttleton
reporting that he is sending accounts about Ft. Prince George.
5p.

Fol. 121. 10 Feb. 1758. Minutes recording the reading of several accounts concerning Ft. Loudoun. 2p.

Fol. 126b. 8 Mar. 1758. Minutes recording the reading of several accounts concerning Fts. Prince George and Loudoun. 5p.

C.O. 5/474 (CONT'D)

Fol. 128b.   9 Mar. 1758.   Minutes recording the reading of several accounts concerning Fts. Prince George and Loudoun.   4p.

Fol. 131.   14 Mar. 1758.   Minutes recording the reading of several accounts concerning Ft. Loudoun.   3p.

Fol. 133.   17 Mar. 1758.   Minutes containing message from
Lyttleton noting that the Earl of Loudoun received reports from
Va. and Penn. on the great service done by the Cherokees.   Loudoun
has sent Col. Byrd to bring the Cherokees to a meeting at
Winchester.   Lt. Col. Howarth should have the Cherokees assemble
at Keowee for Col. Byrd to lead to Winchester.   3p.

Fol. 134.   18 Mar. 1758.   Minutes containing report of committee
considering Lyttleton's message.   Committee is willing to use
£20,000 to outfit Cherokees joining the King's forces.   5p.

Fol. 136b.   19 Apr. 1758.   Minutes recording the reading of
several accounts concerning Fts. Prince George and Loudoun.   3p.

Fol. 138.   21 Apr. 1758.   Minutes recording that the Assembly
approved payment for several bills concerning Fts. Prince George
and Loudoun.   It also approved payment for rum for those Indians
who fought with Little Carpenter and the Great Warrior.   20p.

Fol. 160.   12 May 1758.   Minutes containing the Schedule of the
Charges ... [of S.C. from 25 Mar. 1757 to 25 Mar. 1758].   Schedule
lists expenses for Fts. Loudoun and Prince George.   12p.

Fol. 166b.   19 May 1758.   Minutes containing message from
Lyttleton and an audit report.   Lyttleton reports appointment of
Edmond Atkin as Agent and Superintendent of Affairs of the
Southern Indians.   An audit report notes that expense accounts,
including some for Fts. Prince George and Loudoun, are not listed
in their proper places.   10p.

C.O. 5/474   SOUTH CAROLINA, JOURNAL OF UPPER HOUSE OF ASSEMBLY:
NOV. 1758 - MAR. 1760

Fol. 208.   13 Oct. 1759, Upper House.   Minutes containing
resolution from Commons and speech from Lyttleton to the Assembly.
Commons resolved that the Treasurer should pay £4,000 for expenses
of the intended expedition against the Cherokees.   Lyttleton
complains about the insufficient supplies voted for the Cherokee
expedition.   2p.

Fol. 209.   7 Jan. 1760, Upper House.   Minutes containing speech
from Lyttleton to the Assembly.   Lyttleton describes the treaty
concluded with the Cherokees on 26 Dec. at Ft. Prince George.
He also discusses the recent hostilities of the Cherokee and
S. Carolina's request to Amherst for troops.   3p.

Fol. 210.   8 Feb. 1760, Upper House.   Minutes containing address
from Council to Lyttleton.   Council will do its best to repel
the Cherokees.   2p.

C.O. 5/474 (CONT'D)

Fol. 213b. 11 Mar. 1760, Upper House. Minutes containing speech from Lyttleton informing the Assembly that the King's forces have arrived in Charleston. Lyttleton expects additional aid from neighboring provinces [against the Cherokees]. 3p.

C.O. 5/475   SOUTH CAROLINA, JOURNAL OF COMMONS: OCT. 1758 - APR. 1759

Fol. 21. 19 Jan. 1759. Minutes recording the reading of several accounts concerning supplying Ft. Loudoun, determining a place for Upper Cherokee fort, and the expenses of Little Carpenter and followers returning home. 18p.

Fol. 29b. 23 Jan. 1759. Minutes containing message from Lyttleton supporting Capt. Raymond Demeré's expenses while commanding in the Cherokee nation. 3p.

Fol. 33b. 30 Jan. 1759. Minutes containing report from the Committee on the Treasurer's accounts indicating that carrying provisions to Fts. Loudoun and Prince George had cost over £4,100 and was paid from 30 Apr. 1758 - 18 Jan. 1759. 2p.

Fol. 38. 3 Feb. 1759. Minutes recording the reading of several accounts about entertainment of the Cherokees, work and provisions for Ft. Loudoun, and carrying the Indian presents to Ft. Prince George. 22p.

Fol. 64b. 14 Mar. 1759. Minutes recording the reading of accounts about presents and pay to soldiers employed at Ft. Loudoun. 4p.

Fol. 72b. 21 Mar. 1759. Minutes containing message from Lyttleton about the salaries of a gunner at Ft. Loudoun and an interpreter at Ft. Prince George. 3p.

Fol. 73b. 22 Mar. 1759. Minutes containing message to Lyttleton that Commons will not fix the salaries of gunner at Ft. Loudoun or an interpreter at Ft. Prince George. Commons will provide £15 from last October's allowance for the interpreter. 4p.

Fol. 76. 27 Mar. 1759. Minutes containing report from the Committee on the Treasurer's Accounts indicating that S.C. has paid £15,178 to purchase Cherokee presents to persuade the tribe to aid Col. Byrd against Ft. Duquesne. 7p.

Fol. 85b. 4 Apr. 1759. Minutes containing A Schedule of The Charges ... [of S.C.] from 25 Mar. - 31 Dec. 1758. Schedule lists expenses for Fts. Prince George and Loudoun. 19b.

C.O. 5/481   SOUTH CAROLINA, JOURNAL OF COUNCIL: DEC. 1763 - DEC. 1764

Fol. 2b. 30 Dec. 1763, Council Chamber. Minutes containing advice of Council to Gov. Boone and an affidavit from Edward McGarry. Council advised Boone to send ammunition to the militia near Ninety Six. Edward McGarry mistook some Creeks as Cherokees who were stealing horses. Moytoy of Hiwassee said that the Creeks visiting the Cherokees gave the death hoop and raised some white scalps on a pole. 7p.

C.O. 5/481 (CONT'D)

Fol. 7b. 13 Jan. 1764. Council Chamber. Minutes containing
talk from Young Twin (Creek) stating that the seven Creek
murderers lived with the Cherokees for several years and have
helped that tribe fight the whites. 5p.

Fol. 24b. 7 Mar. 1764, Council Chamber. Minutes containing
letter from Maj. Robert Farmer and a talk from the Cowetas.
Farmer writes from Mobile that the Creeks aided the Cherokees in
murdering 130 back-settlers. Cowetas report that the renegade
Creeks living among the Cherokees have caused the Cowetas to
spill much blood. 9p.

Fol. 28b. 2 Apr. 1764, Council Chamber. Minutes containing
letter from Ensign Charles Taylor to Gov. Boone. A Coweta and an
Oakfuskee were in Tugaloo with 16 other Creeks. Several Cherokees
from Old Chota will join the Creeks. Seroue and others are going
to Estatoe to prevent the Cherokees from joining the Creeks. 9p.

Fol. 34. 4 Apr. 1764, Council Chamber. Minutes containing letter
from Capt. Prevost to Gov. Boone. Fts. Prince George and Moore
lack provisions. 7p.

Fol. 37. 6 Apr. 1764, Council Chamber. Minutes containing
letter from Gov. Boone to Capt. Prevost. Ft. Prince George will
not be deserted since it is a barrier against the Cherokees and
provides security for the local Indian trading post. 7p.

Fol. 40. 9 Apr. 1764, Council Chamber. Minutes containing
letter from Geo. Galphin to Gov. Boone. Creeks have driven away
the Indian murderers and their families. It is not known whether
the criminals have gone to join the Cherokees or the Mortar. 5p.

Fol. 56b. 18 May 1764, Council Chamber. Minutes containing
letter from Lazarus Brown to Col. Middleton. Brown describes
Henry Benfield's murder by two Creeks claiming to be Cherokees.
Cherokees have reportedly joined the Creeks, and Little Carpenter
seems to be England's greatest enemy. 5p.

Fol. 59. 28 May 1764, Council Chamber. Minutes containing a
talk from Young Warrior of Estatoe and a letter from Ensign
Price relating to the murder of Benfield. 3p.

Fol. 65b. 14 June 1764, Council Chamber. Minutes containing
letter from Capt. Gavin Cochran to Bull. Capt. Mason reports
from Ninety Six that James Thomson was fired upon by two Indians
at Long Canes. 4p.

Fol. 74. 12 July 1764, Council Chamber. Minutes containing a
talk from Great Warrior (Oconostota) and Prince of Chote that
they had been fighting the Twelftways [Twightwees?], Youtenews
[Yachtanues?], Tawaws [Ottawas], and the Savannahs. Ensign
Bryce [Price] reports that two families have settled on branches
of the Keowee River. 4p.

Fol. 84b. 10 Aug. 1764, Council Chamber. Minutes containing a
talk from two Creek chiefs stating that the Mortar was persuaded
to forgo his Cherokee visit since the Cherokees were now at peace
with the English. 2p.

C.O. 5/481 (CONT'D)

Fol. 85b.   24 Aug. 1764, Council Chamber. Minutes containing
information from Gen. Gage that he has asked the Cherokees to
stop supplies sent along the Miss. R. to the Illinois and other
nations at war with the English. 2p.

Fol. 87b.   28 Aug. 1764, Council Chamber. Minutes containing
information from Bull that since Commons refused to increase the
government debt, [John] Watts among the Overhill Towns had to
promise future rewards if the Cherokees stop supplies from going
to the Northern Indians at war with the English. 4p.

Fol. 93b.   8 Oct. 1764, Council Chamber. Minutes containing
letter from John Watts who writes from Tomotly that Little
Carpenter and the Overhill warriors say that they cannot [stop
the supplies] until spring. The nephew of Judd's Friend just
escaped from imprisonment in Illinois, where the Indians were
told to kill all Englishmen and Cherokees. Cherokees visited
Ft. l'Assomption last spring. 4p.

*C.O. 5/482   SOUTH CAROLINA, JOURNAL OF GENERAL ASSEMBLY: JAN. -
            OCT. 1764*

Fol. 1b.   4 Jan. 1764. Minutes containing speech from Boone
stating that the frontier forts (Augusta, Moore and Prince George)
need repair and provisions. Crown no longer pays for troop
provisions. Creeks murdered 14 people at Long Canes. 3p.

Fol. 3b.   14 Jan. 1764. Minutes containing talk from Young Twin
[a Creek] stating that the Creek murderers have lived among
Cherokees for four to five years and helped them fight the whites.
2p.

Fol. 10.   25 May 1764. Minutes recording the reading of several
accounts for entertaining the Indians, buying a steer for Little
Carpenter and others, purchasing wine and sangree for Cherokees,
and provisioning Fts. Prince George and Loudoun. 20p.

Fol. 20.   29 May 1764. Minutes containing message from Bull
concerning the two Creeks who murdered Beddingfield and then
lived in Tugaloo for two years with Cherokee wives. Young Warrior
of Estatoe seized the Creeks as proof of his friendship with the
English. 5p.

Fol. 23.   31 May 1764. Minutes containing report of the committee
on the Creek murderers which recommends that presents for the
Young Warrior of Estatoe not exceed £700. 3p.

Fol. 26b.   5 June 1764. Minutes containing message from Bull
restating the House resolution that presents for Young Warrior
of Estatoe not exceed £700. 6p.

Fol. 29.   27 June 1764. Minutes containing message from Bull
stating that Ft. Prince George's storehouse needs to be enlarged.
Fts. Prince George and Moore need repairs. 8p.

C.O. 5/482 (CONT'D)

Fol. 35. 29 June 1764. Minutes containing committee report claiming that Ft. Prince George's storehouses built by Col. Grant are sufficient. Fort does need other repairs, however. 3p.

Fol. 37b. 3 July 1764. Minutes containing message from Bull and petition from Capt. John Dargan. Bull forwards the committee recommendations on Fts. Moore and Prince George. Dargan petitioned the Assembly for his back pay and the pay owed to his company for Grant's expedition against the Cherokees. Assembly approved bills concerning Little Carpenter, Keowee, Ft. Prince George, and the Cherokees. 31p.

Fol. 60. 11 July 1764. Minutes containing petition from Thomas Sumter requesting an allowance for accompanying Judd's Friend and two other Cherokees from Va. to England. 9p.

Fol. 65b. 13 July 1764. Minutes containing committee report stating that Thomas Sumter has no claim [for accompanying the Cherokees to London] since he was not employed by S. Carolina. 5p.

Fol. 67b. 16 July 1764. Minutes recording that the Assembly appointed a committee to examine the Cherokee trade commission accounts. Assembly approved a bill for maintaining the Cherokees who were returning home. 14p.

Fol. 75. 18 July 1764. Minutes containing letter from the director of Cherokee Indian Trade and a message from Bull. The director of Cherokee Indian Trade describes the state of Indian commerce. Bull relates the needed repairs at Ft. Prince George. 5p.

Fol. 77. 19 July 1764. Minutes containing report from the committee to examine Cherokee trade accounts which recommends that trade be continued following the present plan. 3p.

Fol. 85b. 28 July 1764. Minutes containing report from committee recommending that repairs be made at Ft. Prince George. 4p.

Fol. 87. 31 July 1764. Minutes containing report from Committee on Public Accounts describing Lyttleton's expedition and other expenses during the recent Cherokee war. 22p.

Fol. 97b. 1 Aug. 1764. Minutes recording that the Assembly postponed consideration of the committee report concerning repairs at Ft. Prince George. 3p.

Fol. 100. 3 Aug. 1764. Minutes containing petition from Wm. Shackleford and Wm. Lupton to be reimbursed for goods supplied to troops marching against the Cherokees. 6p.

Fol. 103b. 7 Aug. 1764. Minutes recording information that the Assembly will send a message with a copy of the report on the Ft. Prince George repairs. 6p.

C.O. 5/482 (CONT'D)

Fol. 106. 8 Aug. 1764. Minutes containing A Schedule of the
Charges of ... [S.C. from 1 Jan. 1762 - 31 Dec. 1763]. Schedule
includes expenses for the Cherokees and Fts. Prince George and
Loudoun. 22p.

Fol. 131b. 24 Aug. 1764. Minutes containing message from Bull
forwarding Gage's request for the Cherokees to assist His
Majesty's troops. Bull believes that the Chickasaws are better
able to attack post in Illinois. 3p.

Fol. 132b. 25 Aug. 1764. Minutes containing report from a
committee recommending against buying provisions to persuade
the Cherokees and Chickasaws to intercept French supplies for
·the Shawnees, Delawares, and Detroit Indians. 5p.

Fol. 144. 6 Oct. 1764. Minutes containing message to Bull
suggesting that he request a garrison for Ft. Johnson. There was
always a garrison there until it was withdrawn for the expedition
against the Cherokees. 6p.

C.O. 5/483 SOUTH CAROLINA, JOURNAL OF COMMONS: JAN. - AUG. 1765

Fol. 2. 10 Jan. 1765. Minutes containing message from Bull
noting the Cherokee request to send someone to help mark boundaries between the tribe and the English. 6p.

Fol. 4b. 11 Jan. 1765. Minutes containing address to Bull
stating that the Cherokee request for assistance in marking
the boundaries will be considered. 4p.

Fol. 6. 15 Jan. 1765. Minutes recording the reading of accounts
about supplies sent to Ft. Prince George and about rum supplied
to the Indians at Ft. Loudoun in 1757. 10p.

Fol. 17b. 31 Jan. 1765. Minutes containing report from a
committee stating that no more than £500 will be granted to
defray expenses for marking boundaries between the English and
the Cherokees. 3p.

Fol. 20b. 12 Feb. 1765. Minutes containing resolution of
Commons that no more than £500 be used to pay for marking
boundary between the English and the Cherokees. 2p.

Fol. 24. 5 Mar. 1765. Minutes recording the reading of several
accounts including some concerning Ft. Prince George. 9p.

Fol. 28. 6 Mar. 1765. Minutes containing two messages from
Bull about repairs of Ft. Prince George and about rewarding
Judd's Friend and the Cherokees for intercepting a convoy sent
to the Delawares and Shawnees. 10p.

Fol. 32b. 7 Mar. 1765. Minutes recording the reading of several
accounts including some for provisions taken to Ft. Prince
George. 4p.

C.O. 5/483 (CONT'D)

Fol. 36. 13 Mar. 1765. Minutes containing report from a committee recommending that soldiers repairing Ft. Prince George be paid. Committee also recommends giving goods worth £900 to Judd's Friend and other Cherokees who captured some French. 8p.

Fol. 39b. 14 Mar. 1765. Minutes recording that Commons considered a report for repairing Ft. Prince George and for rewarding Judd's Friend and other Cherokees. 6p.

Fol. 42. 15 Mar. 1765. Minutes containing message to Bull approving the House committee's report on Ft. Prince George and on rewarding Judd's Friend and the Cherokees. 5p.

Fol. 52b. 1 Apr. 1765. Minutes recording that officials in the Secretary's office could not find a copy of the act passed in 1739 to prevent land purchases from the Indians. 7p.

Fol. 55b. 2 Apr. 1765. Minutes containing report of committee to audit accounts that the ranger's pay (£611.17) for the Cherokee expedition exceeded the allocation. 6p.

C.O. 5/485   SOUTH CAROLINA, JOURNAL OF COUNCIL: 1765

Fol. 18. 25 Jan. 1765. Council Chamber. Minutes recording that magistrate John Tinkler acted too hastily in arresting Terrapin, a Cherokee warrior. Glen has requested money to mark the boundary with the Cherokees. 3p.

Fol. 97. 19 Mar. 1765, Council Chamber. Minutes recording the reading of a petition from settlers near Cherokee towns who complain about Indian hostility. Cherokees have taken three settlers to Ft. Prince George. 6p.

Fol. 103. 20 Mar. 1765, Council Chamber. Minutes recording the opinion of the attorney general that the men brought to Ft. Prince George [by the Cherokees] are not within the S.C. jurisdiction and cannot be legally prosecuted for their crimes. 2p.

Fol. 128. 23 Apr. 1765, Council Chamber. Minutes recording that Mr. Wyley is satisfied that the Catawbas were not involved in the murder of the Cherokees. 5p.

Fol. 168. 25 May 1765, Council Chamber. Minutes containing letter from John Stuart to Bull. Stuart discusses regulations for the Southern District Indian trade, including prices for goods. 14p.

Fol. 196. 21 June 1765, Council Chamber. Minutes containing instructions to Edward Wilkinson for running the boundary between S.C. and the Cherokees. 15p.

C.O. 5/556   EAST FLORIDA, ORIGINAL CORRESPONDENCE, SEC. OF STATE:
1775-1776

Fol. 92. 11 Jan. 1776, St. Augustine. Gov. Tonyn to Earl of
Dartmouth. Stuart will inform Tonyn about the rebel plan to
kill Cherokee agents residing with the tribe. 3p. [Enclosures
to fol. 95b].

Fol. 94. 30 Dec. 1775, E. Florida. Copy of affidavit from
Thomas Grey of Ga. regarding his trip to E. Florida. Grey
denies taking an Indian party along for protection. 3p.

Fol. 308. 10 June 1776, St. Augustine. Gov. Tonyn to Geo.
Germain. If Tonyn had known about Gage's plan, he would not
have invited the Creeks to a congress on St. Johns R. since the
Cherokees were apparently also invited. 6p. [Enclosures to
fol. 343b].

Fol. 314. 20 Apr. 1776, St. Augustine. Gov. Tonyn to David
Taitt (copy). Thomas Grey, a half-breed, is accompanying
some Creeks to persuade the Indians to join the rebels.
Mr. Buchanan, who has lived with the Creeks and Cherokees,
says that those tribes are waiting for instructions to support
the King. 5p.

Fol. 322. 2 May 1776, Chehaws, Lower Creeks. Thomas Brown
to Gov. Tonyn (copy). Lower Cherokees cannot act against the
rebels until Cameron decides to remove Mr. Wilkinson from
their midst. 4p.

Fol. 324. 8 May 1776, Chehaws, Lower Creeks. Thomas Brown
to Gov. Tonyn (copy). Why has Wilkinson at Keowee not been
ordered to leave the Cherokees? Cherokees seem indifferent
about giving assistance. 8p.

Fol. 328. [ca. May 1776], St. Augustine. Thomas Brown to
Gov. Tonyn (copy). Stuart and the Indians could help open a
passage to Ninety Six to obtain ammunition. 15p.

Fol. 336. 12 Sept. 1775, Boston. Gen. Gage to John Stuart.
Gov. Tonyn expects to keep the Indians friendly by supplying
them with ammunition. 3p.

Fol. 338. 21 May 1776, St. Augustine. Gov. Tonyn to Gen.
Clinton. Getting Indian assistance could have been easy. It
is easy to recognize loyal subjects. 3p.

Fol. 340. 10 June 1776, St. Augustine. Gov. Tonyn to Gen.
Clinton (copy). Creeks and Cherokees, who were willing to
help a few months ago, have now lost interest. 7p.

Fol. 346. 6 Nov. 1776, Whitehall. Geo. Germain to Gov. Tonyn
(draft). Hostilities between the Cherokees and rebels have
already begun. Cherokees have voluntarily sided with the loyalists. 8p.

C.O. 5/557   EAST FLORIDA, ORIGINAL CORRESPONDENCE, SEC. OF STATE:
            1776-1777

Fol. 11.   30 Oct. 1776, St. Augustine.   Gov. Tonyn to Geo. Germain.
Gen. Lee's scheme was frustrated by news that the Cherokees backed
the government and some 2,000 of them had already begun war
against the back settlements.   5p.

Fol. 45.   7 Jan. 1777, St. Augustine.   Gov. Tonyn to Geo. Germain.
3p.   [Enclosures to fol. 50b].

> Fol. 49.   8 Nov. 1776, Chehaws.   Thomas Brown to Gov. Tonyn.
> Indians will become disorderly if not used soon.   4p.

Fol. 273.   18 Sept. 1777, St. Augustine.   Gov. Tonyn to Geo.
Germain.   Rangers are ready to join the Indians and the King's
troops to attack Georgia.   Indians presents have arrived.   8p.
[Enclosures to fol. 367b].

> Fol. 277.   29 June 1777, St. Augustine.   Brig. Gen. Prevost
> to Gov. Tonyn (copy).   Local inhabitants benefited most from
> Col. Fuser's expedition.   The Indians kept the plunder, the
> Rangers the cattle, and the soldiers the trouble.   3p.

> Fol. 289.   30 June 1777, St. Augustine.   General Account of
> Sundry Expenses Incurred for Indians from 25 June 1776 to
> 24 June 1777 (copy).   4p.

> Fol. 297.   15 Apr. 1777, St. Augustine.   Gov. Tonyn to John
> Stuart (copy).   Best way to prevent attack from the Holston
> R. on West Fla. would be to encourage all the Indians to
> strike at the Southern frontiers.   4p.

> Fol. 299.   23 May 1777, Upper Creek Nation.   David Taitt to
> Gov. Tonyn (copy).   Cherokee defeat has scared the Creeks.
> Cherokee chiefs have gone to make peace with the rebels.
> Oconostota, Little Carpenter, and others went from Long
> Island to Williamsburg.   Lower Towns have gone to Duet's
> Corner on the S.C. frontier.   7p.

> Fol. 303.   29 May 1777, Lower Creek Nation.   Wm. McIntosh to
> Gov. Tonyn (copy).   Galphin has received goods from the French
> to give to the Indians.   All the Lower Creek chiefs, except the
> Cussita's, have been persuaded to stay home.   4p.

> Fol. 305.   23 May 1777, Little Tallassee, Upper Creeks.   David
> Taitt to Thomas Brown (copy).   Cherokees have made peace with
> the rebels.   Those still resisting are useless from lack of
> provisions.   4p.

> Fol. 307.   12 June 1777, St. Augustine.   Gov. Tonyn to David
> Taitt (copy).   Galphin's nephew is permitted to supply Indian
> traders with goods.   3p.

> Fol. 311.   16 June 1777, St. Augustine.   Gov. Tonyn to John
> Stuart (copy).   Holmes, Galphin's nephew, supplies goods to
> all those traders who will also deliver Galphin's talks to the
> tribes.   10p.

C.O. 5/557 (CONT'D)

Fol. 321. 21 July 1777, Pensacola. John Stuart to Gov.
Tonyn (copy). Although forced to make temporary peace with
rebels, the Cherokees are ready to strike again when the
opportunity presents itself. Cherokees will soon have
enough corn to subsist. 15p.

Fol. 329. 2 June 1777. Copy of intelligence from Chickasaw
nation stating that the Cherokees met with the rebels, who
now want peace. 4p.

Fol. 331. 12 July 1777, Pensacola. David Taitt to John
Stuart. Ga. can be attacked successfully only from St.
Augustine. Upper and Lower Creeks will not go as far as
St. Augustine since it would now leave their country exposed
to the rebels. 4p.

Fol. 333. 2 June 1777, Chickasaw Nation. James Colbert to
Charles Stuart (copy). Cherokees have visited Holston R.
and Long Island. 3p.

Fol. 335. 13 July 1777, Little Tallassee. Alex. Cameron
to John Stuart. [Same as C.O. 5/78/199]. 4p.

Fol. 337. 1 June 1777, Chickasaw Nation. James Colbert to
David Taitt (copy). Two Cherokees and a Chickasaw met with
many whites at the Holston River. Rebels have partly paid
their debt to the Cherokees. 4p.

Fol. 341. 2 June 1777, Chickasaw Nation. Copy of letter from
James Colbert reporting that he left 10 horses with the Creeks
and lost 2 from the band of 55 horses that he had for the
Cherokees. 3p.

Fol. 343. 28 July 1777, Pensacola. John Stuart to Gov.
Tonyn (copy). Holmes has faithfully performed his duties.
Indians will harrass the S.C., Ga., N.C., and Va. frontiers.
4p.

Fol. 345. 28 July 1777, Pensacola. David Holmes to John
Stuart (copy). Holmes denies encouraging the Indians to turn
against the government. 3p.

Fol. 347. 15 Aug. 1777, Upper Creek Nation. David Taitt to
Gov. Tonyn (copy). Because the Indians can never stand alone
against the whites, the Tuckabatchees will require assistance
from both Floridas or share the fate of the Cherokees. 4p.

Fol. 364. 13 Aug. 1777, Augusta. Talk from Col. Elbert to
Creeks (copy). If the Creeks follow the King's advice, they
will be deceived as the Cherokees were. 6p.

*C.O. 5/566   EAST FLORIDA, ENTRY BOOK OF LETTERS FROM SEC. OF STATE:
              1768-1783*

Fol. 61. 6 Nov. 1776, Whitehall. Earl of Dartmouth to Gov.
Tonyn. [Entry letter of C.O. 5/556/346]. 5p.

C.O. 5/568   EAST FLORIDA, ENTRY BOOK OF LETTERS TO SEC. OF STATE:
            1774-1777

Fol. 89b. 11 Jan. 1776, St. Augustine. Gov. Tonyn to Earl of
Dartmouth. [Entry letter of C.O. 5/556/92]. 3p.

Fol. 134. 10 June 1776, St. Augustine. Gov. Tonyn to Earl of
Dartmouth. [Entry letter of C.O. 5/556/308]. 11p.

Fol. 150. 30 Oct. 1776, St. Augustine. Gov. Tonyn to Geo.
Germain. [Entry letter of C.O. 5/557/11]. 6p.

C.O. 5/569   EAST FLORIDA, ENTRY BOOK OF LETTERS TO SEC. OF STATE:
            1777-1781.

Fol. 12. 18 Sept. 1777, St. Augustine. Gov. Tonyn to Geo.
Germain. [Entry letter of C.O. 5/557/273]. 5p.

C.O. 5/588   WEST FLORIDA, ORIGINAL CORRESPONDENCE, SEC. OF STATE:
            1770-1771

Fol. 9. 26 Sept. 1770, Pensacola. Gov. Chester to Earl of
Hillsborough. Natchez formerly belonged to the Natchez Indians,
whom the French almost annihilated. The Creeks and Cherokees as-
similated the remaining 100 Natchez. 14p. [Enclosures to fol.30].

Fol. 103. 9 Mar. 1771, Pensacola. Gov. Chester to Earl of
Hillsborough. 7p. [Enclosures to fol. 114].

    Fol. 111. [ca. 1771], Pensacola. Copy of deposition from
    Wm. Smith and Wm. Gregory regarding Creek disturbances. The
    Mortar is going north to kill whites because he lost two or
    three of his people during the Cherokee war. 3p.

Fol. 173. 13 Apr. 1771, Pensacola. Gov. Chester to Earl of
Hillsborough. 4p. [Enclosures to fol. 200].

    Fol. 177. [ca. Jan. - Mar. 1771]. Charles Stuart to Gov.
    Chester (copy). Stuart describes the grievances of the
    Chickasaws, Choctaws, and Creeks. The Mortar will not
    succeed in his schemes with the Cherokees. 6p.

Fol. 201. 3 July 1771, Whitehall. Earl of Hillsborough to Gov.
Chester (draft). The question of colonial regulation of Indian
trade will be reconsidered when those colonies dealing with the
Southern Indians reach an agreement. 7p.

Fol. 237. 21 June 1771, Pensacola. Gov. Chester to Earl of
Hillsborough. 2p. [Enclosures to fol. 278].

    Fol. 241. 11 Feb. - 8 Apr. 1771, W. Florida. Copy of minutes
    of Council noting that the Chickasaw complaints about
    encroachments on their land and the trade in liquor could
    also be made by other Southern tribes. The Mortar will not
    succeed in his schemes with the Cherokees. 37p.

C.O. 5/590   WEST FLORIDA, ORIGINAL CORRESPONDENCE, SEC. OF STATE:
*   1772-1773*

Fol. 15. 16 Nov. 1772, Pensacola. Gov. Chester to Earl of
Hillsborough. Terrapin led the Chickasaw party which committed
hostilities in Illinois last summer. Northern Indians are trying
to form a dangerous confederacy with the Southern tribes. 4p.
[Enclosures to fol. 22].

> Fol. 19. 3 Sept. 1772, Chickasaw Nation. John McIntosh to
> Charles Stuart. Northern Indians are coming to make peace
> with the Chickasaws, Creeks, and Cherokees. Cherokees will
> probably soon be at war since they have already killed
> several whites along the Holston River. 4p.

C.O. 5/591 WEST FLORIDA, ORIGINAL CORRESPONDENCE, SEC. OF STATE:
*   1773-1774*

Fol. 136. 7 Mar. 1774, Pensacola. Gov. Chester to Earl of
Dartmouth. 5p. [Enclosures to fol. 148].

> Fol. 141. 27 Jan. 1774, Creek Nation. David Taitt to Gov.
> Chester (extract). Four Creek renegades living with the
> Cherokees have killed a Coweta Indian for being a witch. The
> victim's brother and six other Indians followed the murderers'
> tracks to a white man's house and killed all the inhabitants.
> 2p.

Fol. 265. 8 June 1774, Pensacola. Gov. Chester to Earl of
Dartmouth. 2p. [Enclosures to fol. 308].

> Fol. 266. 22 Dec. 1773 - 28 Mar. 1774, Pensacola. Copy of
> minutes of Council containing extracts of Taitt's letters
> concerning the Creek renegades living with the Cherokees and
> containing measures to improve Florida's defenses against the
> Indians. 38p.

C.O. 5/592   WEST FLORIDA, ORIGINAL CORRESPONDENCE, SEC. OF STATE:
*   1774-1776*

Fol. 141. 17 Nov. 1775, Pensacola. Gov. Chester to Earl of
Dartmouth (duplicate). 4p. [Enclosures to fol. 160].

> Fol. 145. 30 Sept. 1775, Pensacola. Extract of minutes of
> Council of West Fla. stating that the Liberty Folks have
> seized all the ammunition belonging to the merchants and plan
> to give 2,000 weights each to the Creeks and Cherokees. Gov.
> Wright has appointed three persons to manage the Creek affairs
> and three more for the Cherokees. 8p.

Fol. 355. 2 July 1776, Pensacola. Gov. Chester to Geo. Germain.
Some friendly Cherokees recently visited Pensacola. 4p.
[Enclosures to fol. 370].

> Fol. 363. 17 June 1776, Pensacola. Talk from Chenoue
> (Slave Catcher) to Gov. Chester (copy). A path to West
> Fla. is now opened to carry supplies. Cherokees are ready
> to fight for the King. 4p.

C.O. 5/592 (CONT'D)

> Fol. 367. [ca. 17 June 1776], Pensacola. Answer from Gov.
> Chester to Cherokee Talk (copy). King George will supply
> the Cherokees via the new path through the Creeks. Chero-
> kees should only follow the advice of John Stuart, Charles
> Stuart, or the Great Warrior (Col. Steele). 4p.

Fol. 395. 1 Sept. 1776, Pensacola. Gov. Chester to Geo.
Germain. Little Carpenter reports that the Cherokees have
joined the Northern nations to war on the frontier settlements.
About 1,800 Cherokee warriors have set out to attack the Va. and
Carolina frontiers. 7p.

C.O. 5/593   WEST FLORIDA, ORIGINAL CORRESPONDENCE, SEC. OF STATE:
             1776-1777

Fol. 1. 14 Sept. 1776, Pensacola. Gov. Chester to Geo. Germain
(duplicate). 4p. [Enclosures to fol. 40].

> Fol. 9. 4-7 Sept. 1776, Pensacola. Copy of minutes of West
> Florida Council reporting the departure of 7,000 men to
> attack the Cherokees. Rebels have destroyed the Lower
> Cherokee Towns. Carolinians have attacked the Cherokees
> near the Broad River. 30p.

Fol. 61. 7 Feb. 1777, Whitehall. Geo. Germain to Gov. Chester
(draft). Peace between the Creeks and Choctaws left the latter
responsible for watching the Mississippi. Chickasaws have
always been faithful and the Cherokees have demonstrated their
hatred of the rebels. 8p.

Fol. 77. 25 Oct. 1776, Pensacola. Gov. Chester to Geo. Germain.
Stuart has arranged a peace between the Creeks and the Choctaws
and persuaded both to support the Cherokees against usurpers of
Cherokee land. 4p.

Fol. 105. 26 and 28 Dec. 1776, Pensacola. Gov. Chester to Geo.
Germain. All British vessels supplying New Orleans should be
forced to leave their cargoes at Pensacola and post assurances
that the goods will only go to loyalists and allied Indians. 8p.
[Enclosures to fol. 120].

> Fol. 117. 27 Dec. 1776, Pensacola. Extract of examination
> of Wm. Tracy, a rebel deserter from the army which marched
> against the Cherokees, reporting that he saw 600 canoes on the
> Holston R. preparing to attack Mobile and Pensacola in the
> spring. 2p.

Fol. 181. 24 Jan. 1777, Pensacola. Gov. Chester to Geo. Germain.
Alex. Cameron, commissary for the Cherokees, confirmed Tracy's
information about boats being built on the Holston R. for a
spring attack. 2p.

Fol. 277. 2 July 1777, Whitehall. Geo. Germain to Gov. Chester
(draft). Abundant goods and credit will hopefully enable Stuart
to secure the Indians' friendship so that the rebels will not
attempt an invasion. 5p.

C.O. 5/593 (CONT'D)

Fol. 375. 12 June 1777, Pensacola. Gov. Chester to Geo.
Germain. Stuart's conference with the Choctaws and Chickasaws
was successful. Chester was unable to send Tonyn all the Indians
because 400 are attacking the Ga. and Carolina frontiers.
Virginians might attack the Chickasaws. 4p. [Enclosures to
fol. 398].

> Fol. 383. 3 May 1777, Mobile. John Stuart to Gov. Chester
> (extract). Virginians plan to attack the Chickasaws. Lack
> of supplies forced the Cherokees to make peace with rebels.
> 3p.

> Fol. 387. 20 Apr. 1777, St. Augustine. Gov. Tonyn to
> David Taitt (copy). Tonyn requests Creek assistance and
> that the Cherokees invade S.C. or Georgia. 3p.

> Fol. 391. 23 May 1777, Little Tallassee. David Taitt to
> Gov. Tonyn. [Same as C.O. 5/557/299]. 4p.

> Fol. 395. 23 May 1777, Little Tallassee. David Taitt to
> John Stuart (copy). Northern Indians seek peace with the
> Cherokees. Great Warrior and Little Carpenter have gone
> to Williamsburg. 4p.

*C.O. 5/594   WEST FLORIDA, ORIGINAL CORRESPONDENCE, SEC. OF STATE:
        1777-1778*

Fol. 253. 10 Mar. 1778, Whitehall. Geo. Germain to Gov. Chester
(draft). Chester and Stuart ordered to frustrate any Spanish
attempts to win over the Indians. 4p.

Fol. 263. 16 Jan. 1778, Pensacola. Gov. Chester to Geo. Germain
(duplicate). Keeping Southern Indians friendly requires constant
attention. 4p.

Fol. 341. 25 Mar. 1778, Pensacola. Gov. Chester to Geo. Germain
(duplicate). Rebels have invaded W. Florida. Cameron reports
that the Indians are unwilling to fight unless led by troops.
10p. [Enclosures to fol. 356].

*C.O. 5/597   WEST FLORIDA, ORIGINAL CORRESPONDENCE, SEC. OF STATE,
        MILITARY PAPERS: 1778-1779*

Fol. 9. 22 Mar. 1779, Pensacola. Brig. Gen. John Campbell to
Geo. Germain. 12p. [Enclosures to fol. 64b].

> Fol. 61. 25 Dec. 1778, Ft. Sackville, Vincennes. Lt. Gov.
> Henry Hamilton to John Stuart (copy). Hamilton is sending
> a belt to the Chickasaws and Cherokees requesting that they
> attack Va. and the Northern enemy. 4p.

C.O. 5/597 (CONT'D)

Fol. 63. 13 Jan. 1779, Vincennes. Lt. Gov. Hamilton to Commandant at the Natchez (copy). A spring expedition against Va. is planned by four Southern tribes (the Chickasaws, Cherokees, Shawnees, and Delawares), by four Northern tribes (the Mingos, Miamis, Wyandots, and Senecas), and by four tribes from Kaskaskia (the Potawotamies, Ottawas, Chippewas, and Hurons). 3p.

Fol. 65. 24 June 1779, Whitehall. Geo. Germain to Brig. Gen. Campbell (draft). Indian superintendency in the Southern District will be split into a Mississippi and an Atlantic division. 7p.

Fol. 115. 15 Dec. 1779, Pensacola. Maj. Gen. Campbell to Geo. Germain (duplicate). Campbell does not consider Cameron capable of being superintendent because he lacks education and is in poor health. He recommends Wm. Ogilvy. 23p. [Enclosures to fol. 141b].

Fol. 148. 4 Apr. 1780, Whitehall. Geo. Germain to Maj. Gen. Campbell (draft). Choctaw threat will be eliminated if the Chickasaws join the Cherokees and Creeks to support the English. Present superintendents are subordinate to district military commanders. 14p.

Fol. 203. 15 May 1780, Pensacola. Maj. Gen. Campbell to Geo. Germain. 9p. [Enclosures to fol. 216b].

Fol. 209. 20 Apr. 1780, Pensacola. Maj. Gen. Campbell to Gov. Gálvez (copy). Campbell rejects Gálvez's proposal to prohibit the use of Indians in national quarrels. 8p.

Fol. 235. 1 Nov. 1780, Whitehall. Geo. Germain to Maj. Gen. Campbell (draft). Loss of the Choctaws means the loss of communications with the Mississippi Indians. It may be wise to place the Chickasaws and Creeks under Cameron and leave the Cherokees and Catawbas to Col. Brown. 12p.

C.O. 5/619 WEST FLORIDA, ENTRY BOOK OF LETTERS FROM SEC. OF STATE: 1768-1781

Fol. 41b. 3 July 1771, Whitehall. Earl of Hillsborough to Gov. Chester. [Entry letter of C.O. 5/588/201]. 7p.

Fol. 75. 7 Feb. 1777, Whitehall. Geo. Germain to Gov. Chester. [Entry letter of C.O. 5/593/61]. 6p.

Fol. 81. 2 July 1777, Whitehall. Geo. Germain to Gov. Chester. [Entry letter of C.O. 5/593/277]. 3p.

Fol. 84b. 10 Mar. 1778, Whitehall. Geo. Germain to Gov. Chester. [Entry letter of C.O. 5/594/253]. 2p.

C.O. 5/621   WEST FLORIDA, ENTRY BOOK OF LETTERS TO SEC. OF STATE: 1770-1776

Fol. 2.   26 Sept. 1770, Pensacola. Gov. Chester to Earl of Hillsborough. [Entry letter of C.O. 5/588/9]. 18p.

Fol. 87b. 16 Nov. 1772, Pensacola. Gov. Chester to Geo. Germain. [Entry letter of C.O. 5/590/15]. 3p.

Fol. 166. 2 July 1776, Pensacola. Gov. Chester to Geo. Germain. [Entry letter of C.O. 5/592/355]. 4p.

Fol. 170. 1 Sept. 1776, Pensacola. Gov. Chester to Geo. Germain. [Entry letter of C.O. 5/592/395]. 8p.

Fol. 179. 25 Oct. 1776, Pensacola. Gov. Chester to Geo. Germain. [Entry letter of C.O. 5/593/77]. 7p.

C.O. 5/622   WEST FLORIDA, ENTRY BOOK OF LETTERS TO SEC. OF STATE: 1776-1781

Fol. 1.   26 and 28 Dec. 1776, Pensacola. Gov. Chester to Geo. Germain. [Entry letter of C.O. 5/593/105]. 6p.

Fol. 4.   24 Jan. 1777, Pensacola. Gov. Chester to Geo. Germain. [Entry letter of C.O. 5/593/181]. 2p.

Fol. 13b. 12 June 1777, Pensacola. Gov. Chester to Geo. Germain. [Entry letter of C.O. 5/593/375]. 4p.

Fol. 21b. 16 Jan. 1778, Pensacola. Gov. Chester to Geo. Germain. [Entry letter of C.O. 5/594/263]. 4p.

Fol. 24b. 25 Mar. 1778, Pensacola. Gov. Chester to Geo. Germain. [Entry letter of C.O. 5/594/341]. 10p.

C.O. 5/631   WEST FLORIDA, MINUTES OF COUNCIL: 1776-1778

Fol. 66b. 4 Sept. 1776, Council Chamber. Minutes containing extracts of letters from David Taitt and Thomas Brown to John Stuart. Galphin informed the Creeks that 7,000 men have gone to destroy the Cherokees. Creeks are warned not to assist the Cherokees. Brown reports that the rebels destroyed the Lower Cherokee Towns. 10p.

Fol. 124. 26 Mar. 1777, Council Chamber. Minutes containing petitions from Cameron and others who lost their possessions or fought against the rebels in Cherokee country. 15p.

Fol. 138. 20-29 Aug. 1777, Council Chamber. Minutes containing petition from Wm. Woodward, whom the rebels forced to abandon his settlement in Cherokee territory. 15p.

Fol. 225. 10 Jan. 1778, Council Chamber. Minutes containing proclamation of Gov. Chester (12 July 1777) stopping trade with the Southern Indians. 8p.

C.O. 5/636　GEORGIA, ORIGINAL CORRESPONDENCE, BD. OF TRADE: 1734-1735

Fol. 27.　6 Sept. 1734, Charleston.　Jenys Baker to James Oglethorpe.　Trading with the Cherokees is forbidden since they have not made any submission to the government for insulting English traders.　Cherokees will probably soon request supplies and trade since they lack ammunition and are being attacked by enemies.　3p.

Fol. 66.　20 Nov. 1734, S. Carolina.　Letter from Sam Eveleigh stating that six Indian traders decided not to obtain licenses in S.C. but planned to get their goods at Savannah for trading with the Cherokees.　3p.

Fol. 133.　17 Jan. and 8 Feb. 1734/35, S. Carolina.　Sam Eveleigh to Benjamin Martin.　The richest gold mines of New Mexico lie at $36°-37°$ latitude opposite California.　Since the Cherokee Mountains are at the same latitude, they probably contain the same ore.　4p.

Fol. 166.　28 Jan. 1734/35, Charleston.　Robert Johnson to James Oglethorpe.　General Assembly passed a duty act charging Indian traders for building a fort and maintaining a garrison in Cherokee country.　Johnson believes some traders will move to Ga. to avoid the charges.　4p.

C.O. 5/638　GEORGIA, ORIGINAL CORRESPONDENCE, BD. OF TRADE: 1735-1736

Fol. 379.　13 Oct. 1736, S. Carolina.　Sam Eveleigh to Harman Verelst.　Oglethorpe delayed his trip to London until the return of two agents sent to the Cherokees and Creeks.　1p.

Fol. 382.　16 Oct. 1736, Carolina.　Sam Eveleigh to Harman Verelst.　Cherokees have killed four Frenchmen and captured one.　3p.

Fol. 400.　24 July 1736, Savannah.　Gen. Oglethorpe to [Bd. of Trustees].　Oglethorpe hopes to keep the Cherokees and Creeks from warring against the English.　Ga. is spending £7,000 to provide two Indian agents with presents and supplies.　1p.

C.O. 5/639　GEORGIA, ORIGINAL CORRESPONDENCE, BD. OF TRADE: 1735-1737

Fol. 20.　26 Nov. 1736, Savannah.　Letter from Thomas Causton reporting that Mr. Brown (a Cherokee trader) and Barnard have gone to visit the Cherokees.　2p.

Fol. 156.　4 Feb. 1736/37, Council Chamber, Charleston.　Thomas Broughton to Thomas Causton.　Broughton requested that the Creeks and Cherokees help defend Ga. and Carolina.　2p.

Fol. 260.　25 Apr. 1737, Savannah.　Thomas Causton to Georgia Trustees.　Mr. Lawry will deliver a message to the Cherokees.　3p.

Fol. 294.　23 May 1737, S. Carolina.　Sam Eveleigh to Harman Verelst.　An Upper Cherokee trader reports that 175 Upper Cherokees have gone to the Miss. R. to intercept the French.　2p.

C.O. 5/640   GEORGIA, ORIGINAL CORRESPONDENCE, BD. OF TRADE: 1737-1741

Fol. 381.   5 Oct. 1739, Savannah.   Gen. Oglethorpe to Georgia
Trustees.   Oglethorpe reports his return from Indian country.
Tooanahowi and 200 men have gone to war against the Spanish.
Cherokees are raising 600 men and the Creeks 400 to join
Oglethorpe against the Spanish.   3p.

Fol. 399.   19 Oct. 1739, Savannah.   Gen. Oglethorpe to Harmon
Verelst (duplicate).   Cherokees blame the traders for the 1,000
deaths caused by too much liquor and smallpox.   Cherokees are
threatening revenge and requesting French assistance.   Oglethorpe
has ordered corn to be given the Cherokees.   8p.

Fol. 403.   11 Oct. 1739, Savannah.   Gen. Oglethorpe to Georgia
Trustees.   Because of the rupture with Spain and because of
Cherokee and Creek discontent with the Carolina traders,
Oglethorpe has sent Mr. Eyres to the Cherokees to act as Indian
agent.   4p.

Fol. 405.   20 Oct. 1739, Savannah.   Gen. Oglethorpe to Georgia
Trustees.   Oglethorpe maintains one agent among the Creeks and
one among the Cherokees.   He needs money to raise a troop of
rangers and to pay officers leading the Indians.   Without
assistance, Ga. will be exposed to Spanish and Indian insults.
7p.

Fol. 429.   29 Dec. 1739, Frederica.   Gen. Oglethorpe to Georgia
Trustees.   Oglethorpe has asked his Indian allies for assistance
against the Spanish.   He will supply the Indians with food and
arms and grant a salary to their leaders and interpreters.   The
Creeks, Cherokees, Chickasaws, Yuchis, and Yamacraws are receiving the same provisions.   8p.

Fol. 449.   1 Feb. 1739/40, Frederica.   Gen. Oglethorpe to Col.
Stephens.   Oglethorpe describes his expedition with the Indians
against Florida.   8p.

C.O. 5/641   GEORGIA, ORIGINAL CORRESPONDENCE, BD. OF TRADE: 1741-1746

Fol. 97.   3 Mar. 1741/42, Frederica.   Gen. Oglethorpe to Ga.
Trustees.   Oglethorpe has concluded peace between the Chickasaws,
Cherokees, and Creeks.   Cherokees will furnish 2,000 men if the
tribe can be protected from its enemies.   Cherokee Emperor Moy
Toy was recently killed.   3p.

C.O. 5/643   GEORGIA, ORIGINAL CORRESPONDENCE, BD. OF TRADE: 1750-1752

Fol. 36.   25 July 1750, Savannah.   President and Assistants of
Georgia to Benj. Martyn.   Creeks and Yuchis have attacked Ga.
settlements after taking refuge around Darien under the pretense
of fleeing from the Cherokees and Nottoways.   2p.

Fol. 60.   Oct. 1750, S. Carolina.   Gov. Glen to President and
Assistants of Georgia (copy).   Cherokees have approximately
3,000 fighting men.   French have successfully maintained a war
between the Creeks and Cherokees.   4p.

C.O. 5/643 (CONT'D)

Fol. 172. 28 Feb. 1750/51, Savannah. President and Assistants
to Benj. Martyn. Only the Trustees should have the power to
license traders. Trade with the Creeks, Chickasaws, and other
Southern and Western nations should be confined to Georgia.
Trade with the Cherokees, Catawbas, and northwestern nations
should be under Carolina's control. 4p.

Fol. 199. 16 Apr. 1751, Georgia. Henry Parker to Gov. Glen
(copy). Neither the Choctaws nor the Cherokees have visited
Ga. in large numbers since Gen. Oglethorpe's departure. 3p.

C.O. 5/644   GEORGIA, ORIGINAL CORRESPONDENCE, BD. OF TRADE: 1752-1754

Fol. 40. 28 July 1752, Georgia. Assistants in Ga. to Benj.
Martyn (extract). Mr. and Mrs. Bosomworth are evidently on
their way to the Creeks to demand punishment of the murderers
of the Cherokees. Creeks believe that the English either favor
or fear the Cherokees. 6p.

Fol. 76. 26 June 1752, Savannah. Mr. Habersham to Benj.
Martyn (extract). Although once numerous, the Cherokees
presently number only 2,000 gunmen in the Upper and Lower Towns.
The majority of Cherokees live within boundaries of Georgia.
Habersham describes the location and size of other Indian tribes.
4p.

C.O. 5/645   GEORGIA, ORIGINAL CORRESPONDENCE, BD. OF TRADE: 1756-1757

Fol. 70. 5 Jan. 1756, Georgia. Gov. Reynolds to Bd. of Trade.
Reynolds describes the present situation in Ga. and states that
peace and friendship with the Indians has been renewed. 8p.

Fol. 172b. 4 Dec. 1746, at the Forks on the Altamaha. Talk
from Chickilli Tuskeestonduah Mico (a Creek King) to Maj. Wm.
Horton. From the 12 kegs of wine demanded by the Creeks in
compensation for injuries, Santachee carried two to the Cherokees.
4p.

Fol. 213. [Mar. 1746]. Wm. Horton to Thomas Bosomworth.
Cherokees, Creeks, and Chickasaws are determined to declare war
against the English. Because of this danger, Gov. Glen changed
his plans about visiting the Cherokees. 2p.

C.O. 5/646   GEORGIA, ORIGINAL CORRESPONDENCE, BD. OF TRADE: 1757-1759

Fol. 5. 5 May 1757, Savannah. Lt. Gov. Henry Ellis to Bd. of
Trade. Because the government has changed, the Indians visit
weekly expecting presents. 30p.

Fol. 33. 1 Aug. 1757, Georgia. Lt. Gov. Ellis to Bd. of Trade.
10p. [Enclosures to fol. 39b].

Fol. 38. 28 July 1757. Address from Upper House and Commons
to Lt. Gov. Ellis. Ga. is important since it serves as
barrier against the French, Spanish, and numerous Indian
nations. 4p.

C.O. 5/646 (CONT'D)

Fol. 57.   20 Sept. 1757, Savannah. Lt. Gov. Ellis to Bd. of
Trade (duplicate). Ellis agrees with Lyttleton that S.C.
should be in charge of Indian negotiations. 5p.

Fol. 60.   22 Oct. 1757, Georgia. Lt. Gov. Ellis to Bd. of Trade.
Creeks are constantly courted by the French and Shawnees.
Shawnees seek revenge for the murder of three individuals killed
by the English and Cherokees near Ft. Loudoun. 8p.

Fol. 67.   [Rec. 2 Mar. 1758]. Certificate from David Douglas
and Edward Barnard confirming the fair distribution of Indian
presents. 2p.

Fol. 69.   20 Nov. 1756, Savannah. Testimony from Indian traders
that the Indian presents were justly distributed. 2p.

Fol. 71.   Savannah. A General Account of Indian Presents
Distributed ... from 16 Dec. 1755 to 15 Feb. 1757. Account lists
dates and presents given to the Cherokees. 4p.

Fol. 85.   25 Oct. 1757, Savannah. Minutes of Council reporting
that the French, Shawnees, and Cherokees have been hostile
against Georgia. Shawnees seek revenge for tribal members
murdered by soldiers from Ft. Loudoun. 2p.

Fol. 95.   11 Mar. 1757, Savannah. Lt. Gov. Ellis to Bd. of
Trade (quintuplicate). Frontiersmen and traders cause Indian
troubles. 25p.

Fol. 133.   18 Feb. 1758, Georgia. Lt. Gov. Ellis to Bd. of
Trade. Major reason for convening the Assembly was to enforce
law preventing unlicensed trade with the Indians. 9p.

Fol. 168.   31 Mar. 1758, Georgia. Lt. Gov. Ellis to Bd. of
Trade (quadruplicate). Ellis requests funds for presents and
expenses for the Indians who constantly visit Savannah. 5p.

Fol. 179.   20 July 1758, Georgia. Gov. Ellis to Bd. of Trade
(triplicate). Upper Creeks plan to attack the French fort on
the Cherokee River. 8p.

Fol. 199.   9 Nov. 1758, Georgia. Gov. Ellis to Bd. of Trade
(triplicate). Cherokees were unable to get the Creeks and
Chickasaws to attack Virginia. Creeks killed two Cherokees. 4p.

Fol. 201.   28 Jan. 1759, Georgia. Gov. Ellis to Bd. of Trade
(duplicate). Although Ga. is close to the French settlements
and numerous Indian tribes, the province has never had a
sufficient defense. 12p.

Fol. 234.   24 Apr. 1759, Georgia. Gov. Ellis to Bd. of Trade.
Shawnees have moved from Creek territory to the French fort on
the Cherokee R. for safety. 27p.

C.O. 5/646 (CONT'D)

Fol. 250. 26 July 1759, Georgia. Gov. Ellis to Bd. of Trade. Creek neutrality has been the greatest check upon the Cherokees. Cherokees are upset with the treatment received in North. Gen. Forbes was ill-advised to treat the Indians so rudely. 12p.

Fol. 262. 6 Sept. 1759, Georgia. Gov. Ellis to Bd. of Trade (quadruplicate). Cherokees committed the recent murders and had planned (along with the discontented Creeks) to attack the traders. Cherokees asked Ellis to settle their differences with S. Carolina. 5p.

C.O. 5/647   GEORGIA, ORIGINAL CORRESPONDENCE, BD. OF TRADE: 1759-1760

Fol. 3. 6 Jan. 1760, Georgia. Gov. Ellis to Bd. of Trade. Lyttleton has concluded a peace with the Cherokees. Atkin is not suitable for position as Indian agent. One agent cannot manage Indian nations in South. 4p.

Fol. 5. 15 Feb. 1760, Georgia. Gov. Ellis to Bd. of Trade (duplicate). Lyttleton's treaty with the Cherokees is too severe. Ellis has requested Creek assistance against the Cherokees and offered £5 sterling for every Cherokee scalp. 4p.

Fol. 10. 5 Mar. 1760, Georgia. Gov. Ellis to Bd. of Trade. Cherokees continue to attack the S.C. frontier. Ga. has not been attacked probably because of its friendship with the Creeks. 3p.

Fol. 12. 15 Mar. 1760, Georgia. Gov. Ellis to Bd. of Trade (duplicate). No Cherokee hostility reported in Georgia. The Bosomworths have encouraged the Creeks to fight against the enemy. 4p.

C.O. 5/648   GEORGIA, ORIGINAL CORRESPONDENCE, BD. OF TRADE: 1760-1764

Fol. 1. 16 Apr. 1760, Georgia. Gov. Ellis to Bd. of Trade. Because of French and Cherokee influence over the Creeks, Ellis will need presents to obtain Creek assistance against the Cherokees. No Cherokee hostility has been reported in Ga. since Ellis's last letter. 4p.

Fol. 3. 15 May 1760, Georgia. Gov. Ellis to Bd. of Trade. Rangers and Indians have prevented Cherokee hostility in Georgia. Some Chickasaws and Creeks have brought in scalps and burned Estatoe and Keowee. Creeks still remain neutral. 3p.

Fol. 5. 7 June 1760, Georgia. Gov. Ellis to Bd. of Trade (triplicate). The French and Cherokees have evidently encouraged some Creek hostility but most Creeks have not defected. 5p.

Fol. 8. 10 and 15 July 1760, Georgia. Gov. Ellis to Bd. of Trade (duplicate). French at the Alabama Fort have tried to persuade the Creeks to abandon the English and join the Cherokees. 5p.

Fol. 11. 25 Aug. 1760, Georgia. Gov. Ellis to Bd. of Trade.
Indian affairs have not changed since Ellis's letter of 10 July.
5p.

Fol. 14. 5 Sept. 1760, Georgia. Gov. Ellis to Bd. of Trade.
Ga. is not affected by Montgomery's retreat or by the surrender
of Ft. Loudoun. French have tried to counter English efforts
to persuade the Creeks to fight the Cherokees. 5p.

Fol. 19. 20 Oct. 1760, Georgia. Gov. Ellis to Bd. of Trade.
Choctaws have told the Creeks (as the Creeks earlier told the
Cherokees) that they would not tolerate Creek interference with
traders bringing goods to the Choctaws. 5p.

Fol. 24. 27 June 1760, Savannah. Gov. Ellis to Bd. of Trade.
Cherokee war has delayed sale of ceded Creek lands. 7p.
[Enclosures to fol. 55b].

Fol. 58. 23 Dec. 1760, Savannah. James Wright to Bd. of Trade.
French and Cherokees have tried to persuade the Creeks to join the
war against the English. Several Creek leaders with Cherokee
wives have helped divide the nation between the English and the
French and Cherokees. 11p. [Enclosures to fol. 65b].

Fol. 74. 20 Feb. 1761, Savannah. Gov. James Wright to Bd. of
Trade (copy). Some Creeks have joined the Cherokees in their
massacres. Creeks killed a soldier near Ft. Prince George. 7p.

Fol. 84. 15 Apr. 1761, Savannah. Gov. Wright to Bd. of Trade.
Indian affairs continue unchanged. The Upper Creeks have
promised friendship to the English. 10p.

Fol. 130. 28 Dec. 1761, Savannah. Gov. Wright to Bd. of Trade.
Wright is unhappy with Carolina-Cherokee peace and doubts it will
last. 5p.

Fol. 133. 20 Feb. 1762, Savannah. Gov. Wright to Bd. of Trade.
Creeks will hopefully remain peaceful if Cherokee hostility
should erupt again. 7p.

Fol. 137. 26 Apr. 1762, Savannah. Gov. Wright to Bd. of Trade.
Good news will hopefully continue from Indian country. 5p.

Fol. 140. 10 June 1762, Savannah. Gov. Wright to Bd. of Trade.
Louisiana governor invited the Cherokees and Creeks to visit
New Orleans. 8p. [Enclosures to fol. 144b].

Fol. 189. 22 Feb. 1763, Savannah. Gov. Wright to Bd. of Trade.
Creeks are disturbed that S.C. provides Cherokees with cheaper
goods. 4p.

Fol. 212. 22 June 1763, Savannah. Gov. Wright to Bd. of Trade.
No one in Ga. has obtained land privately from the Indians or
even applied for a license, except for Bosomworth. 3p.

C.O. 5/648   (CONT'D)

Fol. 222. 17 Jan. 1764, Old Palace Yard, Westminister.
Memorial from Denys Rolle to Bd. of Trade. Rolle proposes a
settlement on the Altamaha and Appalachicola Rivers to aid the
Creek trade. Augusta is more convenient for the Cherokee trade.
3p.

Fol. 236. 23 Dec. 1763, Savannah. Gov. Wright to Bd. of Trade.
4p. [Enclosures to fol. 241b].

    Fol. 238. 10 Nov. 1763, Ft. Augusta. Treaty of Peace
    between George III and the Chickasaws, Upper and Lower
    Creeks, Choctaws, Cherokees, and Catawbas (copy). Signa-
    tories include Attakullakulla, Kittagusta Chotis, Skiagunsta,
    Ousteneka, Willinawaw, and Ecuij. 7p.

Fol. 282. 17 Jan. 1764, Savannah. Gov. Wright to Bd. of Trade.
Creek murderers of S. Carolinians are evidently living among
the Cherokees. 4p. [Enclosures to fol. 286b].

    Fol. 284. 28 Dec. 1763, Augusta. Copy of Affidavit from
    Arthur Coodey stating that a Cherokee named Moy Toy told
    him about the Creek murderers. 4p.

    Fol. 286. [8 Jan. 1764], [Silver Bluff]. Copy of talk from
    Tugulkee (Young Twin) stating that the murderers of the Long
    Canes settlers have lived with the Cherokees for four or
    five years. 2p.

C.O. 5/651   GEORGIA, ORIGINAL CORRESPONDENCE, BD. OF TRADE: 1769-1772

Fol. 5. 8 Nov. 1769, Savannah. Gov. Wright to Earl of Hillsborough (duplicate). 2p. [Enclosures to fol. 13b].

    Fol. 7. [Oct. - Nov. 1769]. Message from Wright to Lower
    House (copy). Wright recommends a bill to prevent encroach-
    ments on Indian land. 4p.

    Fol. 9. [Oct. - Nov. 1769]. Address from Upper House to
    Wright (copy). Upper House agrees that a law to prevent
    encroachments on Indian land is needed. 3p.

    Fol. 11. 2 Nov. 1769. Extract from Journal of Commons
    containing message from Commons to Wright. Commons will
    draft a bill to prevent encroachments on Indian land. 4p.

Fol. 26. 11 May 1770, Savannah. Gov. Wright to Earl of Hillsborough (duplicate). Bill for regulating Indian affairs cannot
work without the cooperation of neighboring provinces. 7p.
[Enclosures to fol. 37b].

Fol. 40. 20 July 1770, Savannah. Gov. Wright to Earl of
Hillsborough (duplicate). 5p. [Enclosures to fol. 44b].

C.O. 5/651 (CONT'D)

Fol. 43. 11-18 July 1770. *South Carolina and American General Gazette.* Virginia's General Assembly voted £2,500 to pay for running the boundary between Va. and the Indian hunting grounds. 4p.

Fol. 66. 8 Dec. 1770. Gov. Wright to Earl of Hillsborough. [Duplicate of C.O. 5/661/1]. 4p. [Enclosures to fol. 71b].

Fol. 68. 2 Oct. 1770, Savannah. Talk from Gov. Wright to Lieutenant of Cowetas, Selichee, and Lower Creeks. [Same as C.O. 5/661/3]. 4p.

Fol. 78. 28 Feb. and 2 Mar. 1771, Savannah. Gov. Wright to Earl of Hillsborough. [Duplicate of C.O. 5/661/25]. 6p. [Enclosures to fol. 89b].

Fol. 90. [12 Dec. 1771]. Memorial from Gov. Wright to Earl of Hillsborough. Cherokees wish to cede land between the Ga. boundary and the Broad and Oconee Rivers in payment for their debt. Money from sale of this land would help the defense of Georgia. 16p. [Enclosures to fol. 128b].

Fol. 106. List of papers relating to Wright's memorial. 4p.

Fol. 108. 22 Feb. 1771, Chote. Deed of sales from Chero- kees for land on the Broad River. Signatories include Oconostota of Chote, Willinawaw of Toqueh, Judd's Friend of Island Town, Willanota of Settico, Kenatita of Great Tellico, Hienttylisky [?] of Chilhowee, Scahylosky of Chilhowee, and Ugy Yuley of Tenasse. 2p.

Fol. 109. 7 Mar. 1771, Tugaloo. Speech from Judd's Friend to Scotchie at the Convention of Overhill Cherokee Chiefs (copy). Alex. Cameron asserts the Cherokees' right to dispose of their lands as they please. 3p.

Fol. 111. 3 May 1771, Chote. Talk from Cherokee Headmen, Warriors, and Beloved Men to Gov. Wright. Cherokees offer 60 sq. miles of land to the King in payment for their debt to the traders. Signatories include Oconostota, Willinawaw, Judd's Friend, and Attakullakulla. 3p.

Fol. 113. 23 May 1771, Savannah. Answer from Gov. Wright to Oconostota, Willinawaw, Judd's Friend, and Attakullakulla (copy). Wright will seek the King's approval on suggested land cession. 3p.

Fol. 115. 6 June 1771, Augusta. Philemon Kemp to Gov. Wright (copy). Kemp includes a talk from Emistisiguo and other Upper Creek chiefs in which the Creeks indicate that they were informed of the land cession by the Cherokees. 7p.

Fol. 121. 25 June 1771. Talk from Gov. Wright to Emisti- siguo and Gun Merchant (copy). Cherokees must settle their conflicting claims with the Creeks over land the Cherokees want to cede. 3p.

C.O. 5/651 (CONT'D)

> Fol. 123. 8 June 1771, near Ft. Charlotte. Speeches
> from Judd's Friend and Oconostota at a meeting of the
> Cherokees and traders (copy). Creeks have no claim to the
> land that the Cherokees propose to cede. 4p.

> Fol. 127. [1771]. Memorial from the Principal Traders to
> the Creek and Cherokee Nations to Gov. Wright. Traders
> explain the history surrounding the proposed land cession
> and the reasons to accept the proposal. 2p.

Fol. 143. 26 Sept. 1771, Savannah. Pres. Habersham to Earl of
Hillsborough. [Duplicate of C.O. 5/661/75]. 5p. [Enclosures
to fol. 147b].

> Fol. 146. 20 Aug. 1771, Cussita, Lower Creeks. Talk from
> Emistisiguo to Gov. Wright, John Stuart, and Geo. Galphin.
> [Same as C.O. 5/661/78]. 3p.

Fol. 152. [25 Mar. 1772]. Memorial from Merchants trading
with Ga. to Bd. of Trade. Merchants want the Bd. to approve
Wright's plan concerning the proposed Indian land cession. 2p.

Fol. 157. 31 Oct. 1771, Savannah. Pres. Habersham to Earl of
Hillsborough. [Duplicate of C.O. 5/661/84]. 7p. [Enclosures
to fol. 164b].

Fol. 167. 30 Dec. 1771, Savannah. Pres. Habersham to Earl of
Hillsborough. [Duplicate of C.O. 5/661/97]. 4p. [Enclosures
to fol. 171b].

Fol. 174. 30 Mar. 1772, Savannah. Pres. Habersham to Earl of
Hillsborough. [Duplicate of C.O. 5/661/111]. 3p.

Fol. 176. 24 Apr. 1772, Savannah. Pres. Habersham to Earl of
Hillsborough. [Duplicate of C.O. 5/661/115]. 7p. [Enclosures
to fol. 184b].

> Fol. 182. 16 Apr. 1772, Savannah. James Spalding et al.
> (Indian traders) to Pres. Habersham. [Same as C.O. 5/661/
> 121]. 5p.

Fol. 197. 15 June 1772, Savannah. Pres. Habersham to Earl of
Hillsborough. [Duplicate of C.O. 5/661/151]. 3p.

C.O. 5/654   GEORGIA, ORIGINAL CORRESPONDENCE, SEC. OF STATE: 1735-1741

Fol. 18. 7 Oct. 1735. Trustees for Establishing Ga. to Duke
of Newcastle. Trustees request that Newcastle inform the Lt.
Gov. of S.C. that His Majesty in Council has ratified *An Act for
Maintaining the Peace with the Indians in the Province of Georgia.*
2p.

Fol. 20. 3 Apr. 1735. *An Act for Maintaining the Peace with
the Indians in the Province of Georgia. 11p.*

C.O. 5/654 (CONT'D)

Fol. 32.   6 Feb. 1735/36. Extract of a letter from Carolina
reporting that the Creeks will attack the two Floridas. Cherokees must be kept ready in case they are needed against the
Spanish. 3p.

Fol. 34.   16 Feb. 1735/36, Tybee Road. James Oglethorpe to Duke
of Newcastle. A Carolina agent had confused the Ga. Indians
by telling them that the King lacks authority to make Indian
treaties. Oglethorpe believes that he prevented a general
Indian war. 3p.

Fol. 58.   18 May 1736, Frederica. James Oglethorpe to Ga.
Trustees (copy). Charlestonians are angry about the Indian
trade. Private individuals have turned the Indians against the
Spanish and Georgia. 4p.

Fol. 60.   17 Apr. 1736, Frederica. James Oglethorpe to [Duke
of Newcastle]. Spanish fear that the Ga. Indians might attack
them. Oglethorpe will try to prevent an attack. 4p.

Fol. 66.   18 Oct. 1736, St. Augustine. A treaty between Mr.
Oglethorpe and the Gov. of St. Augustine. [Translation of fol.
70]. 6p.

Fol. 70.   18 Oct. 1736, St. Augustine. A treaty between Mr.
Oglethorpe and the Gov. of St. Augustine. Oglethorpe and the
Spanish governor agree to prevent attacks (including Indian)
upon each other. 7p. *Spanish.*

Fol. 74.   3 July 1736, Savannah. James Oglethorpe to Mr. Stone.
If the act for maintaining peace with the Indians is carried
out, it will destroy French and Spanish influence among the
Indians. 2p.

Fol. 76.   20 Oct. 1736, Ga. Office [Westminister]. Benj. Martyn
to Duke of Newcastle. Martyn requests that the memorial from
Ga. Trustees be given to the Queen. 2p. [Enclosures to fol.
80b].

> Fol. 78.   20 Oct. 1736. Memorial from Ga. Trustees to the
> Queen (copy). Trustees will continue to avoid disputes
> with friendly Indian neighbors. 4p.

Fol. 81.   24 Dec. 1736, Ga. Office [Westminister]. Benj. Martyn
to Duke of Newcastle. If the Chickasaws are not aided, all
Indians along the frontier will join the French. 2p. [Enclo-
sures to fol. 86b].

> Fol. 83.   [12]-13 July 1736, Savannah. Talk from Chicka-
> saws to Oglethorpe. Since the Cherokees are the Chickasaws'
> only friends, the Chickasaws request Oglethorpe's assistance
> against the French. Tannasee and Great Tellico were the
> friendliest Cherokee towns until the Creeks killed their
> chief warrior. 8p.

C.O. 5/654 (CONT'D)

Fol. 95.   9 Feb. 1736/37, Charleston.   Mr. Thorpe to his brother in London (extract).   Capt. Chilleroft has been sent to the Creeks and Col. Butler to the Cherokees to get their assistance against the Spanish.   3p.

Fol. 101.   Apr. 1737.   James Oglethorpe to Duke of Newcastle. Government should reprimand the Lt. Gov. of S.C. for encouraging the Creeks to attack the Spanish.   He should be forbidden to interfere with the Creeks, Cherokees, or any other Ga. Indians. 3p.

Fol. 107.   [Rec. 7 Apr. 1737].   Letter from James Oglethorpe reporting that His Majesty forbade anyone from visiting the Creeks, Cherokees, and other Ga. Indians without a license from the Ga. Trustees.   Lt. Gov. of S.C. encouraged the Creeks to attack the Floridas.   3p.

Fol. 109.   22 June 1737, Ga. Office, Westminister.   Ga. Trustees to Robert Walpole.   It is necessary to raise £7,000 yearly to defray governmental expenses in Georgia, including support for the Indians.   3p.

Fol. 131.   2 Apr. 1738.   James Oglethorpe to Duke of Newcastle. Fts. Moore, Prince George, Johnson, Argyle, and others have been demolished.   4p.

Fol. 133.   8 May 1738, St. James.   Instructions from George [II] to James Oglethorpe (draft).   Oglethorpe should prevent the English Indians from committing hostilities against the Spanish and their Indian allies.   8p.

Fol. 170.   8 Oct. 1738, Frederica.   James Oglethorpe to Duke of Newcastle.   Indians report some Spanish encroachment on the frontier of Carolina.   4p.   [Enclosures to fol. 173b].

Fol. 199.   18 Mar. 1738/39, Charleston.   James Oglethorpe to Duke of Newcastle.   Gov. of St. Augustine complains that the Yuchis and Cherokees murdered two Spanish soldiers at Poopa. These were Carolina Indians and the murders occurred before Oglethorpe arrived.   3p.   [Enclosures to fol. 202b].

> Fol. 201.   13 Mar. 1738/39, St. Augustine.   Gov. Manuel de Montiano to James Oglethorpe (translation).   Montiano complains about the Yuchis and Cherokees murdering two cavalry men at Poopa in June 1738.   4p.

Fol. 217.   28 Aug. 1739, Ga. Office, Westminister.   Benj. Martyn to Duke of Newcastle.   Martyn asks that he be reimbursed for buying Indian presents since the gifts were given to help protect English colonists.   3p.   [Enclosures to fol. 220b].

Fol. 223.   8 Oct. 1739, Savannah.   James Oglethorpe to Duke of Newcastle.   As ordered, Oglethorpe asked for 1,000 allied Indians to annoy the Spanish.   3p.

C.O. 5/654 (CONT'D)

Fol. 225.   9 Oct. 1739, Whitehall. Duke of Newcastle to James
Oglethorpe (draft). 4p. [Enclosures to fol. 231b].

    Fol. 229.   9 Oct. 1739, Kensington. Instructions from
    George [II] to Oglethorpe (draft). Oglethorpe should obtain
    troops from S.C. and as many Indians as possible for attack
    on St. Augustine. 5p.

Fol. 238.   5 Dec. 1739, Ga. Office, Westminister. Benj. Martyn
to Duke of Newcastle. S.C. and Ga. were supposed to prepare
laws for settling the Indian trade. Ga. has already done this
and asks that S.C. do the same. 4p. [Enclosures to fol. 241b].

Fol. 242.   29 Dec. 1739, Frederica. James Oglethorpe to Ga.
Trustees. [Extract of C.O. 5/640/429]. 4p. [Enclosures to
fol. 248b].

    Fol. 246.   Allowances for a Company of [Cherokee] Indians
    Commanded by Capt. Samuel Brown. 2p.

Fol. 249.   31 Dec. 1739, Frederica. James Oglethorpe to Duke
of Newcastle. Oglethorpe describes his attack on Florida
using soldiers and Indians. 3p.

Fol. 251.   22 Jan. 1739/1740, Frederica. James Oglethorpe to
[Duke of Newcastle]. Oglethorpe gives further details about
his attack on Florida. 8p.

Fol. 255.   12 Mar. 1739/1740, Ga. Office. Benj. Martyn to
Andrew Stone. 2p. [Enclosures to fol. 261b].

    Fol. 257.   20 Oct. 1739. Gen. Oglethorpe to Ga. Trustees.
    [Extract of C.O. 5/640/405]. 1p.

    Fol. 257.   16 Nov. 1739, Frederica. Gen. Oglethorpe to Ga.
    Trustees (extract). French have attacked the Carolina
    Indians and Spanish have invaded Georgia. 4p.

    Fol. 260.   Allowances for a Company of Cherokee Indians
    Commanded by Capt. Samuel Brown. 2p.

Fol. 264.   1 Apr. 1740, Charleston. James Oglethorpe to Duke
of Newcastle. Oglethorpe expects assistance from the Cherokees,
Creeks, and Chickasaws. Some 500 Cherokees are reportedly
already on their way and more will follow. 4p. [Enclosures to
fol. 267b].

    Fol. 266.   Report from Committee of Conference Appointed to
    Consult Oglethorpe in Relation to the Siege of St. Augustine
    (copy). Report details money and provisions for soldiers
    and Indians. 3p.

Fol. 268.   2 Apr. 1740, Charleston. James Oglethorpe to Duke
of Newcastle. [Duplicate of fol. 264 but dated 2 Apr. 1740].
4p.

C.O. 5/654 (CONT'D)

Fol. 270. 30 Apr. 1740, Frederica. James Oglethorpe to Duke of Newcastle (duplicate). Although 100 Indians have already joined him, Oglethorpe expects at least a 1,000. Cost of Indian presents and food for 4 months will total £7 sterling per person. 4p. [Enclosures to fol. 278b].

Fol. 276. List of troops and people who will pay them for their attack on St. Augustine. Indians cost £7 sterling per person. Number of Indians will not exceed 1,000. 2p.

Fol. 291. 15 May 1740, Florida. James Oglethorpe to Duke of Newcastle. Indians behaved commendably in the capture of San Diego. 3p. [Enclosures to fol. 294b].

Fol. 295. Account of Necessities for Defense of Georgia and Carolina. Account includes provisions for the Cherokee company commanded by Capt. Samuel Brown. 2p.

Fol. 303. May 1740. An Account of General Oglethorpe's [and the Indians'] Proceedings in Florida. 4p.

Fol. 322. 15 Apr. 1741. Benj. Martyn to Duke of Newcastle. 1p. [Enclosures to fol. 333b].

Fol. 323. State of the Province of Georgia in the Year 1740. Creeks inhabit the eastern and southern parts of the province; and the Cherokees and Chickasaws live in the northern parts. The Choctaws, Blew Mouths, and other Indians reside in the western parts. Cherokees number about 4,000 warriors, having lost 1,000 men to smallpox and rum. 18p.

Fol. 334. 30 Apr. 1741. Gen. Oglethorpe to Mr. Verelst (copy). Oglethorpe sent Capt. Dunbar with funds to raise 1,000 Indians. 2p.

Fol. 338. 12 May 1741, Frederica. James Oglethorpe to Duke of Newcastle. Oglethorpe sent Capt. Dunbar to raise Indian troops 4p. [Enclosures to fol. 340b].

Fol. 359. 5 Oct. 1741, Queen Square, Westminister. Harmon Verelst to Andrew Stone. Verelst sends a list of services, including Indian expenses that Oglethorpe believes is necessary to defend S.C. and Georgia. 3p. [Enclosures to fol. 364b].

Fol. 363. June 1741. Proposals Relating to the War in Georgia and Florida. If war erupts with France, it will be necessary to raise and arm the Creeks, Chickasaws, and Cherokees. 3p.

Fol. 397. 7 Dec. 1741. Gen. Oglethorpe to Chancellor of the Exchequer (copy). Oglethorpe has employed Indians to contain the Spanish at St. Augustine. 4p. [Enclosure of fol. 399].

Fol. 399. 7 Dec. 1741, Frederica. Gen. Oglethorpe to [Harmon] Verelst (extract). Although expensive, Indians are absolutely necessary. 2p. [Enclosures at fol. 397].

C.O. 5/661   GEORGIA, ORIGINAL CORRESPONDENCE, SEC. OF STATE: 1770-1772

Fol. 1.   8 Dec. 1770, Savannah.   Gov. Wright to Earl of Hillsborough.   Creeks who murdered the two whites at the Oconees have fled to the Cherokees.   Trade with the Creeks cannot be stopped because so many other provinces trade with the Creeks, Choctaws, Chickasaws, and Cherokees.   4p.   [Enclosures to fol. 6b].

> Fol. 3.   2 Oct. 1770, Savannah.   Talk from Gov. Wright to Lieutenant of Cowetas, Selichee, and Lower Creeks (copy).   Wright demands satisfaction (in accordance with the Treaty of Augusta signed by the Upper and Lower Creeks, Cherokees, Chickasaws, and Catawbas) for the murder of two whites.   4p.

Fol. 25.   28 Feb. and 2 Mar. 1771, Savannah.   Gov. Wright to Earl of Hillsborough.   Some Northern and Creek Indians are visiting the Cherokees.   Wright fears these Indians might unite. Northern and Western Indians are urging the Cherokees to join against the whites.   6p.   [Enclosures to fol. 38b].

Fol. 75.   26 Sept. 1771, Savannah.   Pres. James Habersham to Earl of Hillsborough.   Habersham sends a talk from a Lower Creek headman concerning the old Cherokee proposal to give up land for debts to the traders.   Since the Creeks also claim those lands, the Cherokees were asked to persuade Creeks to agree to surrender the land.   5p.   [Enclosures to fol. 79b].

> Fol. 78.   20 Aug. 1771, Cussita, Lower Creeks.   Talk from Emistisiguo to Gov. Wright, Capt. Stuart, and Geo. Galphin (copy).   Cherokees claim Creek land.   3p.

Fol. 84.   31 Oct. 1771, Savannah.   Pres. Habersham to Earl of Hillsborough.   A military post on the Oconee R., which would keep peace among Creeks and settlers, is only possible if the Creeks and Cherokees jointly surrender the land.   7p.   [Enclosures to fol. 91b].

Fol. 92.   11 Jan. 1772, Whitehall.   Earl of Hillsborough to Pres. Habersham (draft).   Negotiations with the Cherokees for land cession will be difficult as long as the Creeks claim the same land.   6p.

Fol. 97.   30 Dec. 1771, Savannah.   Pres. Habersham to Earl of Hillsborough.   Trade with the Creeks can be stopped only if all Southern colonies agree and only if trade with the Cherokees, Chickasaws, and Choctaws is also curtailed.   4p.   [Enclosures to fol. 102b].

Fol. 111.   30 Mar. 1772, Savannah.   Pres. Habersham to Earl of Hillsborough.   Merchants will only negotiate the Cherokee land cession through John Stuart.   If Stuart takes charge, Habersham has little doubt that the Creeks will join the Cherokees in the land cession.   4p.

Fol. 113.   6 June 1772, Whitehall.   Earl of Hillsborough to Pres. Habersham (draft).   Bd. of Trade has not yet reported on the Cherokee land cession.   2p.

C.O. 5/661 (CONT'D)

Fol. 115. 24 Apr. 1772, Savannah. Pres. Habersham to Earl of
Hillsborough. Cherokee land suggested for the cession is good
for raising silk, indigo, hemp, and tobacco. 7p. [Enclosures
to fol. 122b].

    Fol. 121. 16 Apr. 1772, Savannah. James Spalding et al.
    (Indian traders) to Pres. Habersham (copy). Traders outline
    the background (from Dec. 1770) of the proposed Cherokee
    land cession to pay Indian debts. 4p.

Fol. 151. 15 June 1772, Savannah. Pres. Habersham to Earl of
Hillsborough. Silk production will become very important in
the back country if the Indians cede land. 3p.

Fol. 157. 7 Aug. 1772, Whitehall. Earl of Hillsborough to
Pres. Habersham (draft). Hillsborough supports Gov. Wright's
plan concerning the proposed Indian land cession. 3p.

Fol. 159. 12 Aug. 1772, Savannah. Pres. Habersham to Earl of
Hillsborough. Intruders, including N.C. Regulators, are settling on land proposed to be ceded by the Cherokees. Habersham
has ordered their removal. 4p. [Enclosures to fol. 163b].

    Fol. 161. 4 Aug. 1772, Savannah. James Habersham.
    A Proclamation. Habersham orders all settlers to leave
    Indian land. 2p.

    Fol. 162. 12 Aug. 1772, Savannah. Pres. Habersham to
    Edward Barnard. Barnard is ordered to distribute copies
    of Habersham's proclamation [ordering the removal of people
    settled on Indian land]. 2p.

Fol. 164. 4 Nov. 1772, Whitehall. Earl of Dartmouth to Pres.
Habersham (draft). Dartmouth approves Habersham's conduct
concerning the usurpations of Cherokee land to be ceded. 3p.

Fol. 166. 9 Nov. 1772, Whitehall. Bd. of Trade to the King.
Bd. recommends that the Creeks and Cherokees meet at Augusta
to settle the proposed land cession. 16p. [Enclosures to fol.
222b].

    Fol. 174. List of papers enclosed in the Bd. of Trade's
    letter of 9 Nov. 1772. 3p.

    Fol. 176. [12 Dec. 1771]. Memorial from Gov. Wright to
    Hillsborough. [Copy of C.O. 5/651/90]. 22p.

    Fol. 188. List of papers relating to Wright's memorial.
    [Copy of C.O. 5/651/106]. 5p.

    Fol. 192. 22 Feb. 1771, Chote. Deed of sale from the
    Cherokees for land on the Broad River. [Copy of C.O. 5/651/
    108]. 2p.

C.O. 5/661 (CONT'D)

Fol. 194. 7 Mar. 1771, Tugaloo. Speech from Judd's Friend
to Scotchie. [Same as C.O. 5/651/109]. 3p.

Fol. 196. 3 May 1771, Chote. Talk from Cherokee Headmen,
Warriors, and Beloved Men to Gov. Wright . [Copy of C.O. 5/
651/111]. 4p.

Fol. 198. 23 May 1771, Savannah. Answer from Gov. Wright
to Oconostota, Willinawa, Judd's Friend, and Attakullakulla.
[Same as C.O. 5/651/113]. 3p.

Fol. 200. 6 June 1771, Augusta. Philemon Kemp to Gov.
Wright. [Same as C.O. 5/651/115]. 14p.

Fol. 208. 25 June 1771. Talk from Gov. Wright to Emistisiguo and Gun Merchant. [Same as C.O. 5/651/121]. 5p.

Fol. 211. 8 June 1771, near Ft. Charlotte. Speeches from
Judd's Friend and Oconostota at a meeting of the Cherokees
and Indian traders. [Same as C.O. 5/651/123]. 4p.

Fol. 213. [1771]. Memorial from the Principal Traders to
the Creek and Cherokee Nations to Gov. Wright. [Copy of
C.O. 5/651/127]. 9p.

Fol. 219. [25 Mar. 1772]. Memorial from Merchants Trading
with Georgia to Bd. of Trade. [Copy of C.O. 5/651/152].
3p.

Fol. 221. Map of Ga. and frontiers showing the proposed
Cherokee land cession. 1p. [M.P.G. 20].

Fol. 223. 12 Dec. 1772, Whitehall. Earl of Dartmouth to Gov.
Wright (draft). Government has accepted Wright's plans for
obtaining and disposing of the ceded Creek and Cherokee land. 8p.

C.O. 5/662 GEORGIA, ORIGINAL CORRESPONDENCE, SEC. OF STATE: 1773

Fol. 1. 6 Jan. 1773, Whitehall. Earl of Dartmouth to Gov.
Wright (draft). The King has agreed to remit quitrents for ten
years to individuals who buy the lands ceded by Creeks and
Cherokees. 3p.

Fol. 3. 12 Jan. 1773, Savannah. Pres. Habersham to Earl of
Dartmouth. Indian land cession will bring in settlers and
contribute greatly to the peace and security of Georgia. 3p.
[Enclosures to fol. 6b].

Fol. 9. 24 Mar. 1773, Savannah. Gov. Wright to Earl of
Dartmouth. Indian Congress will be held in May to settle the
Creek and Cherokee land cession. 4p. [Enclosures to fol. 36b].

Fol. 11. 1-13 Mar. 1773. Copy of Journal of Upper House
containing speech from Wright to the Assembly. Wright will
try to bring in more settlers after the Cherokee-Creek land
cession. 16p.

C.O. 5/662 (CONT'D)

Fol. 19. 1-13 Mar. 1773. Copy of Minutes of Commons containing a message from Wright to Commons and an address of Commons to Wright. Wright and Stuart have agreed to hold a congress with the Creeks and Cherokees to obtain a joint cession of land. 36p.

Fol. 37. 10 Apr. 1773, Whitehall. Earl of Dartmouth to Gov. Wright (draft). Edward Wilkinson claims that the Cherokees have offered to cede land to pay their debt of £8436. Tribe cannot legally cede land to Wilkinson but he should be reimbursed from the sale of Creek and Cherokee lands. 3p.

Fol. 39. 8 Apr. 1773, Savannah. Gov. Wright to Earl of Dartmouth. Creeks will be informed that the Cherokees propose an Augusta meeting on 25 May. 4p.

Fol. 41. 10 June 1773, Whitehall. Earl of Dartmouth to Gov. Wright (draft). Wright will undoubtedly conclude the Cherokee and Creek land cession satisfactorily. 3p.

Fol. 47. 16 June 1773. Two proclamations from Wright in the *Georgia Gazette* concerning Creek and Cherokee land cessions. 4p. [Enclosure of fol. 49].

Fol. 49. 17 June 1773, Savannah. Gov. Wright to Earl of Dartmouth. Congress with [the Creeks and Cherokees] has been satisfactorily concluded. Western Indians and the Creeks are now in Chote. Indians probably still desire a confederacy. 4p.

Fol. 51. 14 June 1773, Savannah. Gov. Wright and John Stuart to Earl of Dartmouth. Wright sends copy of the treaty of Cherokee and Creek land cession. 2p. [Enclosures to fol. 58b].

Fol. 53. 1 June 1773, Augusta. Copy of treaty of the Cherokee and Creek land cession. 3p.

Fol. 55. 1 June 1773, Augusta. Copy of release from debts to the traders owed by the Cherokees and Creeks (copy). 3p.

Fol. 57. 1 June 1773, Augusta. Copy of a declaration from the traders accepting the terms of the Cherokee and Creek land cession and releasing all claims that the traders might have on the Crown or province. 4p.

Fol. 61. 10 Aug. 1773, Savannah. Gov. Wright to Earl of Dartmouth. Ceded Indian lands may exceed two million acres. After the Indian Congress, Hezekiah Collins murdered two Cherokees who were returning home. 4p. [Enclosures to fol. 67b].

Fol. 63. 22 July 1773. James Wright. *A Proclamation.* Wright offers a reward for the arrest and conviction of Hezekiah Collins, who murdered two Cherokees. 2p.

Fol. 64. 21 June 1773. Address from Upper House to Gov. Wright (copy). Upper House thanks Wright for his efforts in the Cherokee and Creek land cession. Wright replies to the Upper House on 22 June. 3p.

C.O. 5/662 (CONT'D)

> Fol. 66. 30 June 1773, Address from Commons to Gov.
> Wright (copy). Commons congratulates Wright on the Chero-
> kee-Creek land cession. Wright replies. 2p.

> Fol. 67. 1773. Philip Younge. A Map of the Lands Ceded
> ... by the Creek and Cherokee Indians. Map describes the
> agricultural produce and soil. 1p. [M.P.G. 2].

Fol. 68. 16 Aug. 1773, Savannah. Gov. Wright to Earl of
Dartmouth. [Hezekiah] Collins was arrested in S.C. for murdering the Cherokees, but he escaped. 3p.

Fol. 70. 28 Oct. 1773, Whitehall. Earl of Dartmouth to Gov.
Wright (draft). Dartmouth congratulates Wright on the Cherokee-Creek land cession. [H. Collins] will hopefully be caught
and punished. 4p.

C.O. 5/663   GEORGIA, ORIGINAL CORRESPONDENCE, SEC. OF STATE: 1773-1774

Fol. 3. 30 Oct. 1773, Savannah. Gov. Wright to Earl of
Dartmouth. Wright will personally meet the people who come to
purchase the ceded lands. 3p.

Fol. 5. 5 Feb. 1774, Whitehall. Earl of Dartmouth to Gov.
Wright (draft). Dartmouth will be glad to hear that Wright
successfully carried out the plans for the ceded lands. 4p.

Fol. 7. 20 Dec. 1773, Savannah. Gov. Wright to Earl of
Dartmouth. 2p. [Enclosures to fol. 37b].

> Fol. 9. 20 Dec. 1773, Savannah. James Wright. Answers
> to the Heads of Inquiry Relative to the Present State and
> Condition of the Province of Georgia. Cherokees have
> 3,000 gunmen, the Creeks 4,000, and the Chickasaws 450.
> Cherokees are much more civilized than the Creeks. 24p.

Fol. 38. 27 Dec. 1773, Savannah. Gov. Wright to Earl of
Dartmouth. Ceded lands are very satisfactory. Wright changed
the name of the Broad R. to the Dart R. and ordered that the
town of Dartmouth be laid out. 4p.

Fol. 40. 4 Jan. 1774, Savannah. Gov. Wright to Earl of
Dartmouth. The rumored murders of whites by the Creeks might
discourage people from settling [the newly ceded lands]. 2p.

Fol. 42. 2 Mar. 1774, Whitehall. Earl of Dartmouth to Gov.
Wright (draft). Settling the ceded lands can hopefully be
successful even though the first family there was murdered. 3p.

Fol. 44. 31 Jan. 1774, Savannah. Gov. Wright to [Earl of
Dartmouth]. The murder of two families will stop the sale of
ceded lands. 8p. [Enclosures to fol. 52b].

> Fol. 48. Talk from Gov. Wright to Upper Creeks (copy).
> Although Wright recently met with the Creeks and Cherokees
> to accept the ceded lands, the Creeks murdered several
> settlers. 4p.

C.O. 5/663 (CONT'D)

Fol. 53. 2 Mar. 1774, Savannah. Gov. Wright to Earl of
Dartmouth. Collins, who murdered two Cherokees, has not been
apprehended. Had it not been for the Creeks murdering some
whites, over 10,000 people would have settled the newly ceded
lands by next January. 3p.

Fol. 57. 12 Mar. 1774, Savannah. Gov. Wright to Earl of
Dartmouth. Wright requests troops to punish the Creeks guilty
of murdering whites on the ceded lands since the King assisted
S.C. in its war against the Cherokees. 8p. [Enclosures to
fol. 70b].

> Fol. 61. 9 Mar. 1774. Address from Council of Ga. to the
> King. Council thanks the King for consenting to the Creek
> and Cherokee land cession. 3p.

> Fol. 63. 8 Mar. 1774. Address from Commons to the King.
> Commons thanks the King for consenting to the Creek and
> Cherokee land cession. 2p.

> Fol. 66. 9 Mar. 1774. Message from Wright to Upper House
> (copy). Recently ceded land will attract enough settlers
> to secure Ga. from future attacks by the savages. 3p.

Fol. 88. 4 May 1774, Whitehall. Earl of Dartmouth to Gov.
Wright (draft). Commons' address on the Indian land cession will
be acceptable to the King. 4p.

Fol. 90. 21 Mar. 1774, Savannah. Gov. Wright to Earl of
Dartmouth. Two whites in Cherokee country killed the leader of
the Creek party guilty of murdering several settlers. 3p.
[Enclosures to fol. 93b].

Fol. 96. 18 Apr. 1774, Savannah. Gov. Wright to Earl of
Dartmouth. Creeks were reluctant to visit Savannah for a talk
because they feared imprisonment as Gov. Lyttleton did to the
Cherokees in 1759. 6p. [Enclosures to fol. 108b].

> Fol. 101. [Apr. 1774], [Savannah]. Report of conference
> between Gov. Wright and Upper Creeks (copy). Creeks
> (Elk in Cherokee country and Mad Turkey in Augusta) as well
> as whites have been murdered. War should be averted. 10p.

Fol. 114. 4 May 1774, Savannah. Gov. Wright to Earl of
Dartmouth. Creek murders have stopped settlement of the
ceded lands. 4p.

Fol. 120. 18 May 1774, Savannah. Gov. Wright to Earl of
Dartmouth. Wright recommends that settlers choose and survey
their own land. 4p. [Enclosures to fol. 125b].

> Fol. 122. 3 and 17 May 1774. Copy of minutes of Council
> of Georgia reporting that the ceded land has many large
> 5,000 acre tracts suitable for cultivation. 6p.

C.O. 5/663 (CONT'D)

Fol. 126. 24 May 1774, Savannah. Gov. Wright to Earl of
Dartmouth. Thomas Fee, guilty of murdering [Mad Turkey] at
Augusta, was arrested at Ninety Six, but he was later freed by
country people. 3p.

Fol. 128. 3 Aug. 1774, Whitehall. Earl of Dartmouth to Gov.
Wright (draft). Wright should not expect that local problems
will change the Crown's plan for settling the [recently ceded]
lands. 3p.

Fol. 130. 28 June 1774, Savannah. Gov. Wright to Earl of
Dartmouth. Settlers will be afraid to purchase newly ceded
lands unless troops are sent to maintain order. 3p.

Fol. 132. 25 July 1774, Savannah. Gov. Wright to Earl of
Dartmouth. News from the North report rumors of an Indian
confederacy and hostility. 4p. [Enclosures to fol. 139b].

Fol. 182. 10 Dec. 1774, Whitehall. Earl of Dartmouth to Gov.
Wright (draft). Dartmouth's letter [fol. 128] was not intended
to censure Wright. There will be many problems if the general
scheme for land grants is altered because of local circumstances.
3p.

*C.O. 5/664   GEORGIA, ORIGINAL CORRESPONDENCE, SEC. OF STATE: 1774-
              1775.*

Fol. 1. 13 Oct. 1774, Savannah. Gov. Wright to Earl of
Dartmouth. 2p. [Enclosures to fol. 10b].

　　Fol. 3. 14 Sept. 1774. *Georgia Gazette*. Cherokees brought
　　nine scalps from Virginia. 4p.

Fol. 11. 21 Oct. 1774, Savannah. Gov. Wright and John Stuart
to Earl of Dartmouth (duplicate). 2p. [Enclosures to fol. 13b].

　　Fol. 12b. 20 Oct. 1774, Savannah. Copy of a treaty with
　　the Upper and Lower Creeks. Congress with the Creeks,
　　Chickasaws, Choctaws, Cherokees, and Catawbas in Nov. 1763
　　established a general peace and friendship. 4p.

Fol. 20. 16 Nov. 1774, Savannah. Gov. Wright to Earl of
Dartmouth. 4p. [Enclosures to fol. 25b].

　　Fol. 22. 2 Nov. 1774. Proclamation from Geo. Wright in
　　Georgia Gazette concerning the Creek and Cherokee land
　　cession. 4p.

Fol. 39. 20 Dec. 1774, Savannah. Gov. Wright to Earl of
Dartmouth. Cherokees are trying to persuade the Creeks to break
with the English. 4p.

Fol. 45. 1 Feb. 1775, Savannah. Gov. Wright to Earl of
Dartmouth. 5p. [Enclosures to fol. 59b].

C.O. 5/664 (CONT'D)

        Fol. 58. 25 Jan. 1775. *Georgia Gazette*. Creeks and
Cherokees have ceded land. Any one with claims against the
Indians should attend the Council Chamber meeting. 4p.

Fol. 140. 20 June 1775, Savannah. Gov. Wright to Earl of
Dartmouth. Rebels feel justified in raising troops because they
claim that Mr. Stuart has asked the Cherokees to attack them.
4p. [Enclosures to fol. 143b].

Fol. 146. 8 July 1775, Savannah. Gov. Wright to Earl of
Dartmouth. Council of Safety in Charleston has appointed two
sets of three Indian Affairs' superintendents for the Creeks
and Cherokees. 4p. [Enclosures to fol. 156b].

Fol. 225. 23 Sept. 1775, Savannah. Gov. Wright to Earl of
Dartmouth. Cherokees told the Council of Safety that the tribe
will side with the colonies if the Cherokees should enter the
dispute between Great Britain and the provinces. 4p. [Enclo-
sures to fol. 237b].

*C.O. 5/665   GEORGIA, ORIGINAL CORRESPONDENCE, SEC. OF STATE: 1775-
1780*

Fol. 1. 14 Oct. 1775, Savannah. Gov. Wright to Earl of
Dartmouth. At the direction of the Continental Congress, the
Council of Safety is sending peace talks to the Indians to
prevent the superintendent's deputies from inciting the Indians.
6p. [Enclosures to fol. 11b].

Fol. 12. 1 Nov. 1775, Savannah. Gov. Wright to Earl of
Dartmouth. It is impossible to restrain the Creeks and Cherokees
unless trade and ammunition are provided. 4p. [Enclosures to
fol. 16b].

Fol. 24. 9 Dec. 1775, Savannah. Gov. Wright to Earl of Dartmouth.
Mr. Cunningham seized the powder and bullets intended for the
Cherokees or the rebels. 6p. [Enclosures to fol. 39b].

Fol. 77. 27 Mar. 1776, on board the *Scarborough* at Cockspur.
Gov. Wright to Geo. Germain. Only presents and trade can
influence the Indians. 3p. [Enclosures to fol. 81b].

        Fol. 79. 23 Mar. 1776, Cockspur. James Jackson to Gov.
Wright (copy). Firms trading with the Creeks and Cherokees
hold commissions from the Continental Congress to transact
business with those Indians. 3p.

        Fol. 81. 21 Mar. 1776, Cockspur. Memorial from James
Jackson and Andrew McLean to Gov. Wright. Jackson and
McLean ask for exclusive trading rights with the Cherokees
and Creeks. 2p.

Fol. 99. 8 Oct. 1777, Somerset St., London. Gov. Wright to
Geo. Germain. Stuart can inform Graham about the Indians and
others that he has ready for an expedition into Ga. or S. Carolina.
4p.

C.O. 5/665 (CONT'D)

Fol. 137. 9 July 1779, Whitehall. Geo. Germain to Gov. Wright
(draft). Cameron is the new Superintendent of the Miss. District,
handling the Choctaws, Chickasaws, and others. Col. Brown has
been appointed Superintendent of Atlantic District dealing with
the Creeks, Cherokees, Catawbas, and others. 8p.

Fol. 205. 20 Jan. 1780, Savannah. Gov. Wright to Geo. Germain
(duplicate). A Cherokee party of 230 men and 18 to 20 women
and children have expressed their strong dislike of the rebels.
Cherokees may be useful in the expedition against Carolina. 4p.

Fol. 207. 10 Feb. 1780, Savannah. Gov. Wright to Geo. Germain.
Col. Brown, newly appointed Superintendent for the Creeks and
Cherokees, is now in Savannah. 4p. [Enclosures to fol. 210b].

Fol. 326. 18 Sept. 1780, Savannah. Gov. Wright to Geo. Germain.
3p. [Enclosures to fol. 331b].

> Fol. 328. 27 July 1780, Ninety Six. Col. Nisbet Balfour
> to Gov. Wright (copy). Balfour requests Gov. Graham's
> assistance in settling disturbances over the ceded lands.
> 2p.

> Fol. 328b. 19 Aug. 1780, Savannah. Gov. Wright to Col.
> Balfour (copy). Wright will send Lt. Gov. Graham, if
> necessary, to settle disturbances over the ceded land.
> Col. Brown, however, reports everything is peaceful. 4p.

> Fol. 330. 18 Sept. 1780, Savannah. Gov. Wright to Col.
> Balfour. Settlers on the ceded lands and others from
> Carolina have defeated Col. Brown and his Indians at
> Augusta. 4p.

C.O. 5/674   GEORGIA, ENTRY BOOK OF LETTERS FROM BOARD OF TRADE: 1761-
          1781

Fol. 55. 9 Dec. 1775, Savannah. Gov. Wright to Earl of
Dartmouth. [Entry letter of C.O. 5/665/24]. 8p.

C.O. 5/677   GEORGIA, ENTRY BOOK OF LETTERS FROM SEC. OF STATE: 1768-
          1782

Fol. 31. 11 Jan. 1772, Whitehall. Earl of Hillsborough to Pres.
Habersham. [Entry letter of C.O. 5/661/92]. 6p.

Fol. 37b. 6 June 1772, Whitehall. Earl of Hillsborough to Pres.
Habersham. [Entry letter of C.O. 5/661/113]. 1p.

Fol. 38. 7 Aug. 1772, Whitehall. Earl of Hillsborough to Pres.
Habersham. [Entry letter of C.O. 5/661/157]. 2p.

Fol. 38b. 4 Nov. 1772, Whitehall. Earl of Dartmouth to Pres.
Habersham. [Entry letter of C.O. 5/661/164]. 1p.

C.O. 5/677 (CONT'D)

Fol. 40. 12 Dec. 1772, Whitehall. Earl of Dartmouth to Gov.
Wright. [Entry letter of C.O. 5/661/223]. 5p.

Fol. 42b. 6 Jan. 1773, Whitehall. Earl of Dartmouth to Gov.
Wright. [Entry letter of C.O. 5/662/1]. 2p.

Fol. 44. 10 Apr. 1773, Whitehall. Earl of Dartmouth to Gov.
Wright. [Entry letter of C.O. 5/662/37]. 2p.

Fol. 45b. 28 Oct. 1773, Whitehall. Earl of Dartmouth to Gov.
Wright. [Entry letter of C.O. 5/662/70]. 3p.

Fol. 47. 5 Feb. 1774, Whitehall. Earl of Dartmouth to Gov.
Wright. [Entry letter of C.O. 5/663/5]. 2p.

Fol. 47b. 2 Mar. 1774, Whitehall. Earl of Dartmouth to Gov.
Wright. [Entry letters of C.O. 5/663/42]. 2p.

Fol. 48b. 4 May 1774, Whitehall. Earl of Dartmouth to Gov.
Wright. [Entry letter of C.O. 5/663/88]. 3p.

Fol. 51b. 3 Aug. 1774, Whitehall. Earl of Dartmouth to Gov.
Wright. [Entry letter of C.O. 5/663/128]. 1p.

Fol. 53. 10 Dec. 1774, Whitehall. Earl of Dartmouth to Gov.
Wright. [Entry letter of C.O. 5/663/182]. 2p.

Fol. 74. 9 July 1779, Whitehall. Earl of Dartmouth to Gov.
Wright. [Entry letter of C.O. 5/665/137]. 5p.

*C.O. 5/678   GEORGIA, ENTRY BOOK OF LETTERS TO THE SEC. OF STATE: 1767-
1772*

Fol. 89. 11 May 1770, Savannah. Gov. Wright to Earl of Hillsborough. [Entry letter of C.O. 5/651/26]. 9p.

Fol. 102b. 8 Dec. 1770, Savannah. Gov. Wright to Earl of
Hillsborough. [Entry letter of C.O. 5/661/1]. 4p.

Fol. 110b. 28 Feb. and 2 Mar. 1771, Savannah. Gov. Wright to
Earl of Hillsborough. [Entry letter of C.O. 5/661/25]. 10p.

Fol. 120. 26 Sept. 1771, Savannah. Gov. Wright to Earl of
Hillsborough. [Entry letter of C.O. 5/661/75]. 5p.

Fol. 124b. 31 Oct. 1771, Savannah. Pres. Habersham to Earl of
Hillsborough. [Entry letter of C.O. 5/661/84]. 6p.

Fol. 129. 30 Dec. 1771, Savannah. Pres. Habersham to Earl of
Hillsborough. [Entry letter of C.O. 5/661/97]. 4p.

Fol. 131b. 30 Mar. 1772, Savannah. Pres. Habersham to Earl of
Hillsborough. [Entry letter of C.O. 5/661/111]. 3p.

*C.O. 5/679   GEORGIA, ENTRY BOOK OF LETTERS TO SEC. OF STATE: 1772-
              1780*

Fol. 1. 24 Apr. 1772, Savannah. Pres. Habersham to Earl of
Hillsborough. [Entry letter of C.O. 5/661/115]. 6p.

Fol. 11. 15 June 1772, Savannah. Pres. Habersham to Earl of
Hillsborough. [Entry letter of C.O. 5/661/151]. 3p.

Fol. 12b. 12 Aug. 1772, Savannah. Pres. Habersham to Earl of
Hillsborough. [Entry letter of C.O. 5/661/159]. 5p.

Fol. 14b. 9 Nov. 1772, Whitehall. Bd. of Trade to the King.
[Entry letter of C.O. 5/661/166]. 13p.

Fol. 21. 12 Jan. 1773, Savannah. Pres. Habersham to Earl of
Dartmouth. [Entry letter of C.O. 5/662/3]. 2p.

Fol. 21b. 24 Mar. 1773, Savannah. Gov. Wright to Earl of
Dartmouth. [Entry letter of C.O. 5/662/9]. 4p.

Fol. 23. 8 Apr. 1773, Savannah. Gov. Wright to Earl of
Dartmouth. [Entry letter of C.O. 5/662/39]. 2p.

Fol. 25. 17 June 1773, Savannah. Gov. Wright to Earl of
Dartmouth. [Entry letter of C.O. 5/662/47]. 6p.

Fol. 28. 10 Aug. 1773, Savannah. Gov. Wright to Earl of
Dartmouth. [Entry letter of C.O. 5/662/61]. 6p.

Fol. 31. 16 Aug. 1773, Savannah. Gov. Wright to Earl of
Dartmouth. [Entry letter of C.O. 5/662/68]. 2p.

Fol. 33. 30 Oct. 1773, Savannah. Gov. Wright to Earl of
Dartmouth. [Entry letter of C.O. 5/663/3]. 2p.

Fol. 34. 27 Dec. 1773, Savannah. Gov. Wright to Earl of
Dartmouth. [Entry letter of C.O. 5/663/38]. 4p.

Fol. 36. 4 Jan. 1774, Savannah. Gov. Wright to Earl of
Dartmouth. [Entry letter of C.O. 5/663/40]. 1p.

Fol. 36b. 31 Jan. 1774, Savannah. Gov. Wright to Earl of
Dartmouth. [Entry letter of C.O. 5/663/44]. 9p.

Fol. 40b. 2 Mar. 1774, Savannah. Gov. Wright to Earl of
Dartmouth. [Entry letter of C.O. 5/663/53]. 2p.

Fol. 41b. 12 Mar. 1774, Savannah. Gov. Wright to Earl of
Dartmouth. [Entry letter of C.O. 5/663/57]. 7p.

Fol. 46b. 21 Mar. 1774, Savannah. Gov. Wright to Earl of
Dartmouth. [Entry letter of C.O. 5/663/90]. 2p.

Fol. 47b. 18 Apr. 1774, Savannah. Gov. Wright to Earl of
Dartmouth. [Entry letter of C.O. 5/663/96]. 5p.

C.O. 5/679 (CONT'D)

Fol. 52. 4 May 1774, Savannah. Gov. Wright ot Earl of
Dartmouth. [Entry letter of C.O. 5/663/114]. 4p.

Fol. 54. 18 May 1774, Savannah. Gov. Wright to Earl of
Dartmouth. [Entry letter of C.O. 5/663/120]. 3p.

Fol. 55. 24 May 1774, Savannah. Gov. Wright to Earl of
Dartmouth. [Entry letter of C.O. 5/663/126]. 2p.

Fol. 56. 28 June 1774, Savannah. Gov. Wright to Earl of
Dartmouth. [Entry letter of C.O. 5/663/130]. 3p.

Fol. 57. 25 July 1774, Savannah. Gov. Wright to Earl of
Dartmouth. [Entry letter of C.O. 5/663/132]. 4p.

Fol. 72b. 20 Dec. 1774, Savannah. Gov. Wright to Earl of
Dartmouth. [Entry letter of C.O. 5/664/39]. 4p.

Fol. 96. 20 June 1775, Savannah. Gov. Wright to Earl of
Dartmouth. [Entry letter of C.O. 5/664/140]. 4p.

Fol. 98. 8 July 1775, Savannah. Gov. Wright to Earl of
Dartmouth. [Entry letter of C.O. 5/664/146]. 5p.

Fol. 115. 23 Sept. 1775, Savannah. Gov. Wright to Earl of
Dartmouth. [Entry letter of C.O. 5/664/225]. 5p.

Fol. 126. 14 Oct. 1775, Savannah. Gov. Wright to Earl of
Dartmouth. [Entry letter of C.O. 5/665/1]. 7p.

Fol. 129. 1 Nov. 1775, Savannah. Gov. Wright to Earl of
Dartmouth. [Entry letter of C.O. 5/665/12]. 6p.

Fol. 141. 27 Mar. 1776, on board the *Scarborough* at Cockspur.
Gov. Wright to Geo. Germain. [Entry of C.O. 5/665/77]. 2p.

Fol. 154. 20 Jan. 1780, Savannah. Gov. Wright to Earl of
Dartmouth. [Entry letter of C.O. 5/665/205]. 4p.

Fol. 155b. 10 Feb. 1780, Savannah. Gov. Wright to Earl of
Dartmouth. [Entry letter of C.O. 5/665/207]. 4p.

C.O. 5/707   GEORGIA, SESSIONAL PAPERS, COUNCIL: 1772-1773

Fol. 194. 8 and 20 July 1773, Council Chamber, Savannah.
Minutes containing petition from some S.C. inhabitants requesting
land north of Savannah R. that was recently ceded by the Creeks
and Cherokees. 4p.

Fol. 196b. 22 July 1773, Council Chamber, Savannah. Minutes
containing Council's decision that a reward should be offered
for the capture of the murderer of the two Cherokees. 1p.

Fol. 200. 7 Dec. 1773, Council Chamber, Savannah. Minutes
containing resolution to make John Stuart and Hugh Middleton
judges with jurisdiction in lands ceded by the Creeks and
Cherokees. 1p.

C.O. 5/1059   NEW YORK, ORIGINAL CORRESPONDENCE, BD. OF TRADE: 1737-
              1742

Fol. 154a.   30 Nov. 1740.   Lt. Gov. Clark to Bd. of Trade.   The
Six Nations have agreed to be friendly with all Indians under
the King's protection in the west and south.   2p.

Fol. 216.   15 Dec. 1741, New York.   Lt. Gov. Clark to Bd. of
Trade.   4p.   [Enclosures to fol. 219].

> Fol. 218.   June 1741, Charleston.   Lt. Gov. Bull to Lt.
> Gov. Clark (copy).   Bull attaches a description of his
> conference with the Cherokees and Catawbas.   Cherokees
> are an important barrier against the French.   1p.

> Fol. 218.   23 May 1741.   Conference with the Cherokee and
> Catawba Indians (copy).   Governor of New York arranged the
> peace agreement between the Six Nations and the Southern
> Indians.   3p.

Fol. 220.   12 July 1741, Frederica.   Gen. James Oglethorpe to
Lt. Gov. Clark (copy).   Oglethorpe informed the Creeks about a
general meeting of all British Indians to make peace.   Creeks
have already made peace with the Cherokees.   Creeks and Cherokees are the most powerful of all the Southern Indians.   2p.

Fol. 235.   15 June 1742, Albany.   Speech from Lt. Gov. Clark to
the Six Nations (copy).   Six Nations should renew their friendship and peace with the Southern Indians.   4p.   [Enclosure of
Clark's letter of 24 Aug. 1742].

Fol. 237.   16 June 1742, Albany.   Answer from the Six Nations to
Clark's speech (copy).   A Cherokee told them that the Six Nations
may travel freely to and from the South.   Six Nations made that
Cherokee a sachem.   4p.   [Enclosure of Clark's letter of 24 Aug.
1742].

C.O. 5/1067   NEW YORK, ORIGINAL CORRESPONDENCE, BD. OF TRADE: 1755-
              1757

Fol. 371.   21 Nov. 1756, Ft. Johnson.   A Conference with the
Six Nations (copy).   Mr. Atkin requests that the Six Nations
join with the Southern Indians against the French.   5p.   [Enclo-
sure of Atkin's letter of 27 Dec. 1756 to the Bd. of Trade].

Fol. 373b.   23 Nov. 1756, Ft. Johnson.   Conference with the Six
Nations.   Mr. Atkin requests that the Six Nations carry a pass
in Cherokee country to distinguish them from French Indians.
5p.   [Enclosure of Atkin's letter of 27 Dec. 1756 to the Bd.
of Trade].

C.O. 5/1125   NEW YORK, ENTRY BOOK OF LETTERS FROM BD. OF TRADE: 1727-
              1734

Fol. 148.   29 June 1732.   Bd. of Trade to Col. Cosby.   N.C.
governor believes that S.C. Indians plan to attack N.C. Indians.
The latter hope for support from the Five Nations.   1p.

C.O. 5/1126   NEW YORK, ENTRY BOOK OF LETTERS FROM BD. OF TRADE: 1735-
1748

Fol. 40b. 6 Dec. 1738, Whitehall. Bd. of Trade to Lt. Gov.
Clark. Lt. Gov. of Va. had made progress in establishing good
relations between the Five Nations and the Cherokees and
Catawbas until the Five Nations broke off negotiations and
attacked the Catawbas. 3p.

C.O. 5/1259   PROPRIETIES, ORIGINAL CORRESPONDENCE, BD. OF TRADE: 1699

Fol. 457. [Rec. 16 Nov. 1699]. Dr. Cox to Bd. of Trade. A
Demonstration of the Just Pretentions of ... the King of
England unto the Province of Carolana, Alias Florida and of
the Present Proprietary under His Majesty. Report discusses the
Carolina Indian trade. 8p.

C.O. 5/1260   PROPRIETIES, ORIGINAL CORRESPONDENCE, BD. OF TRADE:
1699-1701

Fol. 363. [Rec. 25 July 1700]. Memorial from John Smith to
Bd. of Trade. Smith discusses how to discover silver mines
in Carolina and requests that money be given to Edward Loughton
and Richard Tranter for Indian presents. 3p. [Enclosures to
fol. 367].

Fol. 365. [Mar. 1700]. Memorial from Edward Loughton
and Richard Tranter to Bd. of Trade. Loughton and Tranter
need money for Indian presents to pay for their search
for gold and silver beyond the Appalachian Mountains. 3p.

Fol. 367. 22 Mar. 1699/1700. Jean Collture to Bd. of
Trade. Collture is willing to guide Loughton to the
Carolina mines. 1p.

N. fol., (G-17). 27 Dec. 1700, Carolina. James Moore to
Thomas Cutler. Silver ore was discovered somewhere along the
Savannah River. 3p.

C.O. 5/1264   PROPRIETIES, ORIGINAL CORRESPONDENCE, BD. OF TRADE:
1707-1715

Fol. 152. 17 Sept. 1708, Carolina. Governor R. Johnson and
the Council of Carolina to Proprietors. Cherokees number
5,000 men and are settled in 60 towns along a mountain ridge.
They are lazy and are only average hunters, making trade with
the tribe inconsiderable. 11p.

Fol. 293. 27 May 1715, Virginia. Col. Spotswood to Sec.
Stanhope (copy). There is a general revolt of Indians bordering
S. Carolina. 2p.

Fol. 295. 23 May 1715, S. Carolina. Letter from Gov. Charles
Craven discussing the Indian war. 3p.

C.O. 5/1264 (CONT'D)

Fol. 297. 8 July 1715, St. James. Lords Proprietors of
Carolina to Bd. of Trade.   S.C. needs provisions for defense
against the Indians. 4p.

Fol. 299. 15 July 1715, St. James. Lords Proprietors of
Carolina to Bd. of Trade. Proprietors discuss steps taken to
defend S.C. and request financial assistance. 4p.

*C.O. 5/1265 PROPRIETIES, ORIGINAL CORRESPONDENCE, BD. OF TRADE: 1715-
1720*

Fol. 2. 30 July 1715, Carolina. David Crawley to Wm. Byrd.
Indians are revolting in Carolina. 2p.

Fol. 11. Sept. 1716. Memorial from Abel Kelleby and the
merchants trading with Carolina to Bd. of Trade. Enemy Indians
might obtain guns through Virginia's Indian trade. 2p.

Fol. 34. 19 July 1715. Charleston. Letter to [Joseph] Boone
and [Richard] Beresford reporting that the Cherokees have gone
home with plans to return with an even greater force and plans
to make further alliances. 5p. [Enclosures to fol. 41b].

Fol. 46. 1715. Address from the Assembly of S.C. to King
George. [Copy of fol. 52]. 2p.

Fol. 48. 15 Mar. 1715/16, Charleston. Assembly of S.C. to
S.C. Agents. Cherokees visited Charleston to make peace. Col.
Moore tried unsuccessfully to persuade the Cherokees to join
in attack on the Creeks. Although the tribe is determined to
make peace with all Indians hostile to the English, the Cherokees killed those Creeks and Yamasees who were trying to
persuade them to eliminate white men living among their tribe.
4p.

Fol. 50. 12 June 1716, Whitehall. Sec. Stanhope to Bd. of
Trade. 2p. [Enclosures to fol. 52b].

Fol. 52. 1715. Address from Assembly of South Carolina
to the King. Assembly requests protection from the Indians.
3p.

Fol. 53. [1716]. Account Showing the Quantity of Skins and
Furs Imported from Carolina from Christmas 1698 to Christmas
1715. 2p.

Fol. 58. 1716. Memorial from Richard Beresford to Bd. of
Trade. Beresford discusses S.C. and the Indian war. 7p.

Fol. 63. 28 Apr. 1716, S. Carolina. Duplicate of address from
the House of Assembly reporting that the Creeks have moved
closer to the French since the Cherokees murdered some Creek
headmen. 4p.

C.O. 5/1265 (CONT'D)

Fol. 65. 1716. Reply from House of Assembly to Gov. [Craven's] speech. Indians will continue to be dangerous unless God and the King interfere. 2p.

Fol. 66. 1716. Speech from Gov. Craven to House of Assembly. Indian threat is over. 2p.

Fol. 84. 1716. Memorial from Joseph Boone and Richard Beresford to Bd. of Trade. Virgininas are interfering with the Carolina Indian trade. 4p. [Enclosures to fol. 95b].

> Fol. 86. 6 Aug. 1716. Committee of Assembly of Carolina to Joseph Boone and Richard Beresford. Although the Cherokees have not warred against the Creeks, Yuchis, and other English enemies, they have forced the Catawbas and other smaller nations to make peace with Carolina. Cherokees have promised to turn over Wateree Jack, thought to be the source of most Indian mischief. 4p.

> Fol. 89. 1715-1716, S. Carolina. Paragraphs from letters reporting that the Virginians evidently want S.C. to fight the Southern Indians so Va. can monopolize trade with the Northern Indians. 3p.

> Fol. 91. 1715-1716, S. Carolina. Paragraphs from letters reporting that Va. traders have promised the Indians cheaper supplies than have the Carolina traders. 4p.

> Fol. 94. 18 Aug. 1716. Affidavits from James Cochran and Geo. Duckett stating that the Spanish encouraged the Yamasees and other nations to attack S. Carolina. 2p.

Fol. 114. 25 Jan. 1716-17, St. James. *An Humble Address from the Representatives of the Inhabitants ... of South Carolina.* Representatives request aid because savage Indians kill and capture S. Carolinians daily. 3p.

Fol. 123. [1717]. *La très humble représentation des habitants de la Caroline méridionale.* S.C. residents ask the King for protection from the Indians. 3p. *French.*

Fol. 125. [Rec. 8 May 1717]. *The Case of the Colony of South Carolina.* S.C. requests aid against the Indians, French, and Spanish. 2p.

Fol. 127. 27 July 1716, St. James. Lords Proprietors of Carolina to Bd. of Trade. Carolina has established peace with the Cherokees and other Indians because of the arms that Carolina received from England and because the Cherokees attacked the Yamasees and Creeks. 3p.

Fol. 129. 26 Jan. 1716/17, Carolina. Governor and Council to Lords Proprietors of Carolina. The only important Carolina Indian allies are the Cherokees. Their demands are so unreasonable, however, that Carolina has become their tributary. 3p.

C.O. 5/1265 (CONT'D)

Fol. 138. 4 July 1716, Chowan, N. Carolina. Abstract of
letter reporting the Va. discovery of a mountain pass to the
Cherokees and other great Indian nations. If Virginians begin
to supply the Cherokees with goods, S.C. will suffer. 4p.

Fol. 140. 25 Apr. 1717, Charleston. Letter from Gov. Boone
complaining that the Cherokees have made S.C. their tributary.
The only way to end this is to encourage a war between the
Creeks and Cherokees without offending either. 2p.

Fol. 142. 29 Mar. - 27 Apr. 1717, S. Carolina. Abstracts of
letters from S.C. stating that peace with the Creeks might
make the Cherokees jealous. 2p.

Fol. 144. 24 and 25 Apr. 1717, [S. Carolina]. Abstract of
letter from Joseph Boone stating that the Indians will destroy
the country if the King does not help. 1p.

Fol. 145. 6 Feb., 22 Mar., and 8 Apr. 1717, S. Carolina.
Abstracts of letters from S.C. reporting that the Creeks will
not make peace with the Cherokees. 1p.

Fol. 167. 8 June 1717, S. Carolina. Copy of letter to Joseph
Boone reporting that the Senecas have joined the Creeks in
planning an attack on the Cherokees and Catawbas. Creeks have
indicated that the English should not assist the Cherokees or
Catawbas. 3p.

Fol. 193. 24 Sept. 1717, Pennsylvania. W. Smith to Bd. of
Trade. 2p. [Enclosures to fol. 201b].

   Fol. 195. 19 July 1717, Conostoga. Minutes of Council
   in which Indians were informed that the Indian allies of
   England must be friendly to each other. 6p.

Fol. 217. 20 Mar. 1717 [1718], Custom House, London. Charles
Carkesse to Wm. Popple. 2p. [Enclosures to fol. 218b].

   Fol. 218. 31 Dec. 1717, S. Carolina. Col. Wm. Rhett to
   Commissioner of Customs (extract). S.C. passed a duty
   on goods imported from England to pay off the Indian war
   debts. 2p.

Fol. 226. 15 Feb. 1717, Charleston. Gov. Johnson to Mr. Shelton
(extract). St. Augustine reports that the [Creeks?] made peace
with the Cherokees. Creeks have also offered peace to Carolina.
1p. [Enclosure of fol. 227].

Fol. 227. 24 Apr. 1718. Richard Shelton to Wm. Popple.
Shelton forwards a letter from the Gov. of Bermuda about an
intended Indian invasion of Carolina. He also includes an
extract of Johnson's letter in response. 2p. [Enclosure at
fol. 226].

C.O. 5/1265 (CONT'D)

Fol. 229. 8 Mar. 1717/18, Carolina. Committee of Assembly to
Joseph Boone. Although the Cherokees and Catawbas concluded
peace with Carolina, they have not been heard from. Some
Carolina Indians, encouraged by the French and Spanish, are
probably planning to attack the Cherokees and Catawbas. 4p.

Fol. 233. 13 May 1718. Memorial from Joseph Boone to Bd. of
Trade. Carolina is in a miserable state because of war with
neighboring Indians who are encouraged by the French and
Spanish. 2p. [Enclosures to fol. 237b].

> Fol. 235. 8 Mar. 1717 [1718], Carolina. Committee of
> Assembly to Joseph Boone. [Copy of fol. 229]. 3p.

> Fol. 237. Address from the Representatives and Inhabit-
> ants of South Carolina to the King. S.C. is in a miserable
> condition due to the Indian war. 2p.

Fol. 247. 17 Dec. 1717 and 13 June 1718, S. Carolina. Extract
of several letters reporting that the Indian trade act will
cause the Indians to turn to the French. 6p.

Fol. 313. 16 Feb. 1718/19, Philadelphia. Gov. Keith to Wm.
Popple. [Enclosures to fol. 329b]. 3p.

> Fol. 316. [1719], Philadelphia. Report from Gov. Wm.
> Keith to Bd. of Trade. French have been active among
> the Indians. Iroquois have achieved a great influence
> over the Carolina Indians. 28p.

Fol. 366. 6 Nov. 1719, Charleston. Governor and Council to
Bd. of Trade. Carolina is suffering from the Spanish hostility,
Indian war, and severe taxes. 3p. [Enclosures to fol. 371].

Fol. 376. 27 Dec. 1719. Col. Robt. Johnson to Bd. of Trade.
French and Spanish threats, the danger of another Indian war,
and the differences between the Lords Proprietors and the
people have led the population to depose Johnson. 3p.
[Enclosures to fol. 379].

Fol. 380. 12 Jan. 1719/20, Charleston. Col. Johnson to Bd.
of Trade. [Abstract of fol. 381]. 2p.

Fol. 381. 12 Jan. 1719/20, Charleston. Col. Johnson to Bd.
of Trade. Johnson describes the Indians, their towns, and how
far they live from Charleston. Cherokees have 60 towns and
about 10,000 people. 16p.

Fol. 393. 1720. *A True State of the Case Between the Inhabitants of South Carolina and the Lords Proprietors*. S.C. is
forced to request the King's assistance because of the Indian
war, pirates, the Spanish threat, fortification expenses, and
the presents the colony must give the Indians to keep them
loyal. 4p.

C.O. 5/1265 (CONT'D)

Fol. 399. 29 Jan. 1719 [1720], S. Carolina. Temporary
Government of S.C. to Bd. of Trade. 2p. [Enclosures to fol.
402b].

> Fol. 400. An Answer to the Queries ... Relating to the
> State of South Carolina. There are 11,500 Cherokees,
> including 3,800 men. Cherokees are English allies but the
> French are trying to win them over. 5p.

C.O. 5/1268   PROPRIETIES, ORIGINAL CORRESPONDENCE, BD. OF TRADE:
1730-1737

Fol. 100. 1718, Pennsylvania. Copy of a paper from Mr. Logan
describing French trade, Indians, and routes from St. Lawrence
to the Miss. River. 7p.

C.O. 5/1287   PROPRIETIES, ENTRY BOOK OF LETTERS: 1695-1699

Fol. 218. 22 Mar. 1698/99, Charleston. Edward Randolph to
Earl of Bridgewater. If the King approves, Mr. More will
search for the mines taking along 50 white men and 100 Cherokees
as guards. 7p.

C.O. 5/1293   PROPRIETIES, ENTRY BOOK OF LETTERS: 1716-1727

Fol. 11b. 5 July and 17 Aug. 1716, Whitehall. Bd. of Trade to
Lords Proprietors of Carolina. Bd. requests a report on Carolina
and the measures taken to suppress Indian war. Bd. mentions a
letter charging Carolina with failure to provide assistance
against the Indians. 2p.

Fol. 21b. 5 Dec. 1716. Joseph Boone and Richard Beresford
to Lords Proprietors of Carolina. Boone and Beresford complain
about Virginia's Indian traders and about Virginia's lack of
assistance in the Indian wars. 11p.

Fol. 46. 27 July 1716, St. James. Lords Proprietors of Carolina
to Bd. of Trade. [Entry letter of C.O. 5/1265/127]. 3p.

Fol. 49b. 17 June 1717, St. James. Lords Proprietors of
Carolina to Bd. of Trade. Peace will be established with all
Indians. 5p.

Fol. 52. 27 June 1717, Whitehall. Bd. of Trade to Lords
Proprietors of Carolina. Lt. Gov. Spotswood has complained
about the treatment given troops sent to assist Carolina in
the Indian war. 1p.

Fol. 72b. 3 Apr. 1718, Whitehall. Wm. Popple to Richard
Shelton. Gov. of Bermuda fears another Indian invasion of
Carolina. 1p.

Fol. 74. 24 Apr. 1718. Richard Shelton to Wm. Popple.
[Entry letter of C.O. 5/1265/227]. 1p.

C.O. 5/1293 (CONT'D)

Fol. 76. [13 May] 1718. Memorial from Joseph Boone to Bd. of Trade. [Entry of C.O. 5/1265/233]. 1p.

Fol. 85b. 29 Apr. 1718. Queries to Col. Johnson. Johnson is to report the strength of Carolina's Indians and whether the Indians favor the English, French, or Spanish. 2p.

Fol. 91. 16 Feb. 1718/19, Philadelphia. Gov. Wm. Keith to Wm. Popple. 2p. [Enclosures to fol. 102].

Fol. 91b. [1719], Philadelphia. Report from Gov. Wm. Keith to Bd. of Trade. [Entry of C.O. 5/1265/316]. 22p.

*C.O. 5/1309   VIRGINIA, ORIGINAL CORRESPONDENCE, BD. OF TRADE: 1695-
1699*

Fol. 66. July 1697, Virginia. Andros to Bd. of Trade. There are several Indian nations living 100 to 400 miles from the settlements. The English trade with them, but they have made no attempt to Christianize the Indians. 4p.

Fol. 214. 12 Nov. 1698. Earl of Bellomont to Gov. Nicholson. Nicholson will obtain trade from the new Indian nations settled along the Va. and Carolina frontier. 1p.

Fol. 234. Feb. 1699, James City, Virginia. Gov. Nicholson to Bd. of Trade. Nicholson will submit a proclamation in April to the Assembly regarding the N.C. boundary and establishing trade with foreign Indians. 4p.

C.O. 5/1310   VIRGINIA, ORIGINAL CORRESPONDENCE, BD. OF TRADE: 1699

Fol. 12b. 1 July 1699, James City. Col. Francis Nicholson to Bd. of Trade. Gov. Blakiston will join Nicholson in helping to solve the Indian problem. 19p. [Enclosures to fol. 188].

Fol. 146. 6 May 1699, New York. Earl of Bellomont to Col. Nicholson (extract). England will benefit from the Indian trade along the frontiers of Va., Carolina, and areas further west. 3p.

Fol. 147a. 16 Jan. 1698/99. Col. Cadwallader Jones. An Essay [on] Louisiana and Virginia. Jones discusses the Indian trade and includes a sketch of Louisiana that includes 60 Cherokee towns. 8p.

Fol. 154. 24 June 1692, James City. Copy of minutes of Council recording dangers involved in the Indian trade and recommending that the Indian trade be managed in Va. as it has been in New York. 2p.

C.O. 5/1312   VIRGINIA, ORIGINAL CORRESPONDENCE, BD. OF TRADE:
1700-1702

Fol. 17. 8 June 1700, Virginia. Robert Collson to Gov.
Nicholson (copy). Emperor of Piscataway and vassals have seen
some strange Indians from the mountains called Towittowos [?],
who are hired by the French to raid other Indians and the British.
2p. [Enclosure of Nicholson's letter of 1 Aug. 1700].

Fol. 19. 13 July 1700, Jamestown. Gov. Nicholson to Lt. Col.
Mason (copy). Nicholson encloses the Council's order for
managing Indian affairs. 1p. [Enclosure of Nicholson's letter
of 1 Aug. 1700].

Fol. 19. 13 July 1700, Stafford County, Virginia. G. Mason
to Gov. Nicholson (copy). Mason reports the measures taken to
guard the frontiers. 2p. [Enclosure of Nicholson's letter of
1 Aug. 1700].

Fol. 20. 20 July 1700, Virginia. G. Mason to Gov. Nicholson
(copy). Indian affairs are unchanged. 2p. [Enclosure of
Nicholson's letter of 1 Aug. 1700].

Fol. 32. 12 Nov. 1698, New York. Earl of Bellomont to Gov.
Nicholson. Nicholson must establish trade with the Dowaganhas
[?] and other Indians west of Va. and Carolina. 1p. [Enclo-
sure of Nicholson's letter of 1 Aug. 1700].

Fol. 32. 14 Jan. and 4 Mar. 1698/99, James City, Virginia.
Gov. Nicholson to Earl of Bellomont. Council and Assembly will
discuss the Indian trade. 2p. [Enclosure of Nicholson's
letter of 1 Aug. 1700].

Fol. 32b. 6 May 1699, N. York. Earl of Bellomont to Gov.
Nicholson. Trade should be established with the Indians
settled west of Va. and Carolina. 2p. [Enclosure of Nicholson's
letter of 1 Aug. 1700].

Fol. 33. 29 Oct. 1699, Jamestown. Gov. Nicholson to Earl of
Bellomont. Nicholson will try to pass a law concerning the
Indian trade. 1p. [Enclosure of Nicholson's letter of 1 Aug.
1700].

C.O. 5/1316   VIRGINIA, ORIGINAL CORRESPONDENCE, BD. OF TRADE: 1708-
1715

Fol. 12. 2 Nov. 1708, Whitehall. Earl of Sunderland to
Council of Trade. Sunderland sends extract of letter complaining about S. Carolinians interfering with Virginia's trade with
the Western Indians. 1p. [Enclosures to fol. 16b].

Fol. 15. 24 June 1709, Virginia. Col. Jennings to Earl
of Sunderland (extract). S.C. seized the goods that
Indian traders from Va. were carrying to the Western
Indians. Virginia's Indian trade will be non-existent if
S.C. monopolizes the Western Indian trade. 3p.

C.O. 5/1316 (CONT'D)

Fol. 60. 28 May 1708. Memorial from College of William and
Mary to Col. Edmund Jennings (copy). The college complains
about S.C. interrupting Virginia's trade with Southern and
Western Indians. The college receives money from all skins
and furs exported from Virginia. 4p. [Enclosure of Col.
Jennings' letter of 27 Nov. 1708].

Fol. 78. Map and description of the Potomac R. and the Va.
mountains. 2p. *French.*

Fol. 97. 26 Sept. 1709, Windsor. Copy of Order in Council
forbidding the S.C. Governor to impose a duty on goods traded
with the Western Indians. 3p.

Fol. 113. 8 Oct. 1709, Virginia. Col. Jennings to Bd. of
Trade. Surveyors have been asked to estimate the cost of
running the Carolina boundary line. The King will hopefully
stop S.C. from further encroachments on Virginia's trade with
the Western Indians. 5p. [Enclosures to fol. 122].

> Fol. 115. 8 Oct. 1709, Virginia. Col. Jennings to Bd.
> of Trade. [Abstract of fol. 113]. 3p.

> Fol. 118. 22 Apr. 1708, Virginia. Col. Jennings to
> Nathaniel Johnson (copy). Johnson should inquire into
> the seizure of Va. goods being traded with the Western
> Indians. 2p.

> Fol. 119. 22 July 1708, S. Carolina Council Chamber.
> Nathaniel Johnson to Col. Jennings (extract). Johnson
> justifies the seizure of the traders' goods from Virginia.
> 2p.

> Fol. 120. 2 Nov. 1708. [Col. Jennings] to Nathaniel
> Johnson (extract). [Jennings] will submit to the Queen
> the question of trade with the Western Indians. 1p.

> Fol. 120. 19 Feb. 1708/09. Depositions from Robert Hix,
> David Crawley, and Nathaniel Urven about the Indian traders'
> goods being seized. 5p.

Fol. 141. 24 Apr. 1710, Virginia. Col. Jennings to Bd. of
Trade. Jennings has received the Queen's order to settle the
border dispute between Carolina and Va. and to stop Carolina's
interference with the Va. Indian trade. 3p.

Fol. 233. 15 Dec. 1710, Virginia. Lt. Gov. Spotswood to Bd.
of Trade. [Abstract of fol. 235]. 3p.

Fol. 235. 15 Dec. 1710, Virginia. Lt. Gov. Spotswood to Bd.
of Trade. Spotswood gives a partial answer to the Bd.'s letter
regarding the Carolina boundaries and the Indian traders. There
are additional complaints about the Indian traders. 8p.

C.O. 5/1316 (CONT'D)

Fol. 295. 15 Oct. 1711, Virginia. Lt. Gov. Spotswood to Bd. of Trade. Spotswood has sent the militia to prevent the Va. Indians from joining the Tuscaroras. He has called a meeting of tributary and neighboring Indians. 6p.

Fol. 314. 8 Feb. 1711, [Virginia]. Lt. Gov. Spotswood to Earl of Dartmouth. [Extract of fol. 341]. 2p.

Fol. 325. 5 Sept. 1711, Virginia. Lt. Gov. Spotswood to Bd. of Trade. [Abstract of fol. 326]. 1p.

Fol. 326. 5 Sept. 1711, Virginia. Lt. Gov. Spotswood to Bd. of Trade. Spotswood informed Hyde in N.C. about the boundary line. S.C. has passed a law contradicting the Queen's orders permitting Va. traders to trade with the Western Indians. 4p.

Fol. 330. 8 June 1711. Copy of act passed in Carolina requiring traders from Va. and other colonies to acquire licenses in Charleston. 5p.

Fol. 341. 8 Feb. 1711, [Virginia]. Lt. Gov. Spotswood to Earl of Dartmouth. Senecas are trying to unite all the Indians along the Va. and neighboring frontiers against the English. Spotswood thinks that he can halt the Senecas' dangerous plan unless the French supply the Indians with arms and ammunition. 4p.

Fol. 349. 8 May 1712, Virginia. Lt. Gov. Spotswood to Bd. of Trade. [Abstract of fol. 350]. 2p.

Fol. 350. 8 May 1712, Virginia. Lt. Gov. Spotswood to Bd. of Trade. There is no progress in settling the boundaries with Carolina. S.C. is sending 700 Indians to assist N.C. against the Tuscaroras. 6p.

Fol. 383. 15 Oct. 1712, Virginia. Lt. Gov. Spotswood to Bd. of Trade. [Abstract of fol. 384]. 1p.

Fol. 384. 15 Oct. 1712, Virginia. Lt. Gov. Spotswood to Bd. of Trade. Indians continue their incursions into N. Carolina. 3p.

Fol. 390. 11 Feb. 1712 [1713], Virginia. Lt. Gov. Spotswood to Bd. of Trade. If N.C. had done its part, the S.C. forces (850 Indians and 33 whites) would have reduced the enemy. S.C. Indians are made up of many different nations and led by one person. The Indians would immediately disperse should their leader fail . 10p.

Fol. 425. 14 Sept. 1713, Virginia. Col. Spotswood to Bd. of Trade. [Abstract of fol. 426]. 2p.

Fol. 426. 14 Sept. 1713, Virginia. Col. Spotswood to Bd. of Trade. Since the S.C. Indians scattered the Tuscaroras, the latter have settled near Va. frontiers where some Northern

C.O. 5/1316 (CONT'D)

Indians have reportedly joined them. Spotswood plans to send an expedition of 200 militia and tributary Indians to force the Tuscaroras to seek peace or to drive them away. 6p.

C.O. 5/1317   VIRGINIA, ORIGINAL CORRESPONDENCE, BD. OF TRADE: 1715-1717

Fol. 185. 9 May 1716, Virginia. Lt. Gov. Spotswood to Bd. of Trade. S.C. has forced Virginians to stop trading with foreign Indians. Catawbas joined the Cherokees in assisting S.C. against the Creeks. 8p.

C.O. 5/1318   VIRGINIA, ORIGINAL CORRESPONDENCE, BD. OF TRADE: 1717-1720

Fol. 3. 1717. Memorial from several Va. merchants about acts preventing fraud in tobacco payment and about furthering the Indian trade. 11p.

Fol. 16. 16 Apr. 1717, Virginia. Lt. Gov. Spotswood to Secretary. Spotswood discusses the Indian trade problems between Va. and S. Carolina. 8p.

Fol. 20. 2 May 1717, Virginia. Council of Va. to Bd. of Trade. Council answers objections to Indian trade act. 4p.

Fol. 22. 19 June 1717. Report from solicitor general on three Va. acts relating to the tobacco and Indian trade. 2p.

Fol. 24. 1717. Memorial from Francis Kennedy to Bd. of Trade. Kennedy asks to be reimbursed for assistance to S.C. during the Indian war. 2p.

Fol. 26. 30 Apr. 1717, Virginia. Lt. Gov. Spotswood to Bd. of Trade. S.C. has not compensated the Va. forces sent against the Indians. 5p.

Fol. 31b. Abstract of the Export of Skins and Furs from the Upper District of the James River [from 1712-1716]. 1p.

Fol. 32. 24 Apr. 1717. Memorial from Virginia Indian Company to Bd. of Trade. The Indian company answers complaints against the act regulating the Indian trade. 32p.

Fol. 48. 10 July 1717, Treasury Chambers. Wm. Lowndes to Wm. Popple. Lowndes sends a memorial from Francis Kennedy. 2p. [Enclosures to fol. 51b].

> Fol. 49. 10 July 1717. Memorial from Francis Kennedy to Lords of Treasury. Kennedy asks for compensation for his service to S.C. during the Indian insurrection of 1715-1716. 2p.

Fol. 79. 16 Jan. 1716/17, Virginia. Lt. Gov. Spotswood to Wm. Popple. 4p. [Enclosures to fol. 104b].

C.O. 5/1318 (CONT'D)

Fol. 81. [ca. Jan. 1717]. The Answer of Lt. Governor
Spotswood to the Queries and Letters. Lt. Gov. Spotswood
refers to the troops sent to aid S.C. in the Indian war.
20p.

Fol. 105. [ca. Jan. 1717]. Lt. Gov. Spotswood to Bd. of Trade.
Frontiersmen dealing with the Indians are deceitful. 8p.
[Enclosures to fol. 110b].

Fol. 138. 29 Aug. 1717, Virginia. Lt. Gov. Spotswood to Bd.
of Trade. Lt. Gov. Spotswood issued a proclamation prohibiting
clandestine trade with the Indians. Indian trade will be continued under the present regulations. 7p. [Enclosures to fol.
147b].

Fol. 216. 14 Aug. 1718, Virginia. Lt. Gov. Spotswood to Bd.
of Trade. French are expanding and attempting to establish
contact with the Western Indians. 16p. [Enclosures to fol.
252b].

Fol. 230. 13 Nov. 1718, Williamsburg. Proclamation from
Lt. Gov. Spotswood asking for the repeal of acts designed
to prevent tobacco fraud and to regulate Indian trade. 2p.

Fol. 264. 27 Sept. 1718, Virginia. Lt. Gov. Spotswood to Bd.
of Trade. Lt. Gov. Spotswood explains why the act to regulate
Indian trade should be repealed. 7p.

Fol. 293. 22 Dec. 1718, Virginia. Lt. Gov. Spotswood to Bd.
of Trade. Cherokees who came to Va. with some traders are
unaware of French designs against the tribe. Cherokees number
more than 4,000 men and would be able to repel the few hostile
French marching against them. 14p. [Enclosures to fol. 308b].

Fol. 409. 11 Aug. 1719, Virginia. Lt. Gov. Spotswood to Bd.
of Trade. Good relations with neighboring tribes are necessary
for protection against the Northern Indians. 11p.

Fol. 428. 1 Feb. 1719/20, Virginia. Lt. Gov. Spotswood to Bd.
of Trade. Lt. Gov. Spotswood fears that the French are now
trading with Coosatees [Cussitas?] settled near the Cherokees.
The French will soon influence the Cherokees since the English
duties on furs prevent S.C. from trading with them. 8p.
[Enclosures to fol. 444b].

Fol. 433. 25 Jan. 1719/20, Williamsburg. Lt. Gov. Spotswood to Col. Schulyer (copy). Lt. Gov. Spotswood wants
peace with the Five Nations. During the Tuscarora war, the
Northern Indians on their way to fight against Southern
Indians attacked Va. traders. 9p.

*C.O. 5/1322   VIRGINIA, ORIGINAL CORRESPONDENCE, BD. OF TRADE: 1729-
             1732*

Fol. 68. 1730. Answer to Queries on the Situation of Virginia.
The nearest important Indian nation to the north are the Five

C.O. 5/1322 (CONT'D)

Nations and the Catawbas and Cherokees to the south. The two
Southern tribes are nearly 400 miles from Virginia. 13p.

C.O. 5/1324   VIRGINIA, ORIGINAL CORRESPONDENCE, BD. OF TRADE: 1736-
1740

Fol. 137. 20 Feb. 1738, [Williamsburg]. Lt. Gov. Gooche to
Bd. of Trade. The Six Nations have attacked the Cherokees
and Catawbas, both English friends. Gooche attempted to negotiate a peace with the Six Nations a year ago at the request
of the Cherokees and Catawbas. 5p.

Fol. 153. 15 Feb. 1739, [Williamsburg]. Lt. Gov. Gooche to
Bd. of Trade. N.Y. governor will hopefully force a peace
between the Six Nations and the Southern Indians or restrain
the former from passing through Va. to attack the latter. War
parties from the Six Nations travel 600 to 700 miles to attack
the Cherokees and Catawbas. 4p.

C.O. 5/1325   VIRGINIA, ORIGINAL CORRESPONDENCE, BD. OF TRADE: 1740-
1743

Fol. 42. Nov. 1740, Williamsburg. James Blair to Bd. of Trade.
Blair paid £100 sterling for presents to give the Five Nations
at Albany to conclude peace with the Cherokees and other Southern
Indians. Blair requested that the Southern Indians send deputies to Albany. 3p.

C.O. 5/1326   VIRGINIA, ORIGINAL CORRESPONDENCE, BD. OF TRADE: 1743-
1747

Fol. 6. 22 Aug. 1743, Virginia. Lt. Gov. Wm. Gooche to Bd.
of Trade. 2p. [Enclosures to fol. 19b].

Fol. 12. The Answer from William Gooche ... to Several
Queries Proposed by the Board of Trade. The Five Nations
are the closest important Northern tribe living under the N.Y.
jurisdiction. The Catawbas and Cherokees are the closest
Southern nations residing under the S.C. jurisdiction. Va.
befriends all Indians because they are a barrier against
the Western Indians who are allied with the French and
Spanish. 12p.

Fol. 44. 4 Sept. 1744, Williamsburg. *The Speech of ... William*
Gooche ... to the General Assembly. Gooche concluded peace with
the Northern Indians and obtained the Western lands claimed by
those nations. 3p.

Fol. 53. 21 Dec. 1744, Virginia. Lt. Gov. Gooche to Bd. of
Trade. 4p. [Enclosures to fol. 118b].

Fol. 55. June 1744. *Treaty Held with the Indians of the*
Six Nations at Lancaster in Pennsylvania. The Six Nations
and the Cherokees agree to peace. Catawbas refused to
attend the conference. Southern Indians and the Six
Nations claim the same land. 90p.

C.O. 5/1326 (CONT'D)

> Fol. 103. [ca. Dec. 1744]. The Answer of William Gooche
> ... to Queries Proposed by the Board of Trade. The Five
> Nations are the closest Northern nations and the Catawbas
> and Cherokees are the closest Southern tribes. 15p.

Fol. 120. 13 Jan. 1723/24, [London]. Richard West to Bd. of
Trade. West has no objections to the new acts being passed,
including the one enforcing existing treaties and regulating
treaties with foreign Indians. 2p.

Fol. 231. 10 June 1747, Williamsburg. Lt. Gov. Gooche to Bd.
of Trade. 4p. [Enclosures to fol. 268b].

> Fol. 234. [1747]. The Answer of William Gooche ... to
> Several Queries Proposed by the Board of Trade. The
> Five Nations are the nearest Northern tribes. Gooche
> sent presents to the young Cherokee King this spring. 20p.

*C.O. 5/1327   VIRGINIA, ORIGINAL CORRESPONDENCE, BD. OF TRADE: 1748-
1753*

Fol. 105. 29 Sept. 1750, Virginia. Col. Lee to Bd. of Trade.
The Catawbas are dependent upon Carolina. The Cherokees and
Chickasaws, two great nations with several thousand fighting
men each, are south and east of the Catawbas. 16p.

Fol. 166. 8 May 1751, Virginia. Joshua Fry to Lewis Burrell.
Fry reports on Virginia's boundaries and back settlements.
Cherokees sometimes intercept the French on the Mississippi.
Va. has been trading with the Cherokees for years and has never
warred against them or signed a peace treaty. 16p. [Enclosure
of Burrell's letter of 21 Aug. 1751].

Fol. 195. [Rec. 14 Apr. 1752], [Virginia]. Some Additions to
the Account of the Bounds of Virginia. A person who lived 15
years in Tennessee with the Cherokees reported that he had no
knowledge of settlers living between Kappa and Kaskaskia.
Cherokees live south of the back settlements. 12p.

Fol. 241. 10 Dec. 1752, Williamsburg. Lt. Gov. Dinwiddie to
Bd. of Trade. The Emperor and other Cherokees came to
Williamsburg to establish trade. Va. rejected their request
because the tribe lives too far away. Dinwiddie advised the
Emperor to end his dispute with S. Carolina. 5p.

Fol. 292. 16 June 1753, Williamsburg. Lt. Gov. Dinwiddie to
Bd. of Trade. Dinwiddie encloses his message to the Six Nations,
Catawbas, and Cherokees regarding the French. 5p. [Enclosures
to fol. 307b].

> Fol. 301. 31 May 1753, Williamsburg. Lt. Gov. Dinwiddie
> to the Cherokee Emperor, Sachems, and Warriors (copy).
> French threaten to attack all nations friendly to the
> English. Cherokees should conclude a peace with the
> Creeks. 2p.

C.O. 5/1327 (CONT'D)

> Fol. 304. 23 May 1753, Williamsburg. Lt. Gov. Dinwiddie
> to Gov. Glen (copy). Dinwiddie describes the French en-
> croachments. Peace is needed between the Creeks and
> Cherokees since Indian assistance against the French is
> essential. French Indians reportedly scalped the Cherokee
> emperor. 4p.

> Fol. 306. 22 May 1753, Williamsburg. Lt. Gov. Dinwiddie
> to Gov. Hamilton (copy). Dinwiddie has warned the
> Catawbas, Cherokees, and others about the French. The
> Mohawks, or the Praying Indians, scalped the Cherokee
> emperor and took his family prisoner to Canada. 4p.

C.O. 5/1328   VIRGINIA, ORIGINAL CORRESPONDENCE, BD. OF TRADE: 1753-
> *1756*

Fol. 8. 17 Nov. 1753, Williamsburg. Lt. Gov. Dinwiddie to Bd.
of Trade. Dinwiddie plans to invite the Cherokees, Catawbas,
and Chickasaws to meet with the Twightwees and the Six Nations.
All will hopefully reconcile their differences. 3p. [Enclo-
sures to fol. 31b].

> Fol. 11. 12 July - 24 Aug. 1753. Logstown. Wm. Trent to
> Lt. Gov. Dinwiddie (copy). Trent attaches an account of
> the meeting with the Six Nations and their allies. The
> Ottawas killed a Shawnee, and a party of Wyandots took two
> Cherokee prisoners from a Lower Shawnee town. Peace can
> hopefully be concluded with the Cherokees. There has been
> some reconciliation between the Creeks and Chickasaws and
> between the Wyandots and Cherokees. 17p.

> Fol. 20b. 22 Oct. 1753, Williamsburg. Wm. Fairfax to
> Lt. Gov. Dinwiddie. Fairfax attaches a narrative of the
> meetings with the Six Nations and allies (10-17 Sept.
> 1753). The Cherokees, Catawbas, and Chickasaws are ready
> to assist the Ohio Indians against the French. 23p.

Fol. 83. 12 Mar. 1754, Williamsburg. Lt. Gov. Dinwiddie to
Bd. of Trade. Dinwiddie asked the Catawbas and Cherokees for
assistance along the Ohio R. against the French. 3p.

Fol. 91. 10 May 1754, Williamsburg. Lt. Gov. Dinwiddie to Bd.
of Trade. Dinwiddie is traveling to Winchester to meet the
Indians. 4p. [Enclosures to fol. 102b].

> Fol. 97. 25 Apr. 1754, Will's Creek. Col. George
> Washington to Lt. Gov. Dinwiddie (copy). It may be advis-
> able to ask the Cherokees, Catawbas, and Chickasaws for
> aid since 600 Chippewas and Ottawas have reportedly joined
> the French. 4p.

Fol. 111. 23 Sept. 1754, Williamsburg. Lt. Gov. Dinwiddie to
Bd. of Trade. Allied Indians remain loyal and have fought some
encounters against the French and Indians. 4p.

C.O. 5/1328 (CONT'D)

Fol. 124. 25 Oct. 1754, Williamsburg. Lt. Gov. Dinwiddie to
Bd. of Trade. Dinwiddie has always tried to cultivate the
Catawbas and Cherokees. Many of them have visited Williamsburg.
Yet S.C. claims jurisdiction over those Indians and resents
Virginia's interference. 4p.

Fol. 140. 10 Feb. 1755, Williamsburg. Lt. Gov. Dinwiddie to
Bd. of Trade. 3p. [Enclosures to fol. 147b].

> Fol. 142. Jan. 1755. Lt. Gov. Dinwiddie. Present State
> of Virginia. Friendly Indians near Va. include the Six
> Nations (in the North), the Catawbas, Cherokees, Creeks,
> and Chickasaws (in the South), and the Picts, Twightwees
> and Shawnees (in the West). 11p.

Fol. 177. 24 Nov. 1755, Williamsburg. Lt. Gov. Dinwiddie to
Bd. of Trade. Since the French are courting the Southern
Indians, Dinwiddie plans to send some commissioners to those
Indians to reaffirm their friendship with the English. 2p.

Fol. 183. 23 Feb. 1756, Williamsburg. Lt. Gov. Dinwiddie to
Bd. of Trade (duplicate). Dinwiddie recommends some new forts
among the Upper Cherokees, Chickasaws, Creeks, and other tribes.
14p. [Enclosures to fol. 191b].

Fol. 201. 11 June 1756, Williamsburg. Lt. Gov. Dinwiddie to
Bd. of Trade. Because the French have sought Catawba and
Cherokee friendship, Dinwiddie has concluded a treaty with them.
He sent men to build a fort among the Upper Cherokees at their
request. 4p. [Enclosures to fol. 224b].

> Fol. 205. 20 Feb. and 13 Mar. 1756. *A Treaty Held with
> the Catawba and Cherokee Inidans at the Catawba Town and
> Broad River*. Signatories include Ammonscossittee, Chuchu,
> Willinawa, Oconostota, Oconago, Otterle-Cullougheulla
> [Attakullakulla?], Counnerculogo, Ukiyourough, Ammotoyouker,
> Kealkiruftkee, Telletchee, and Chunoyounkkee. 36p.

*C.O. 5/1329 VIRGINIA, ORIGINAL CORRESPONDENCE, BD. OF TRADE: 1756-
1760*

Fol. 1. 3 Jan. 1756 [1757], Whitehall. Wm. Pitt to Bd. of
Trade. 3p. [Enclosures to fol. 13b].

> Fol. 6. [1756]. Representation from the Council and
> Burgesses of Virginia to the King (copy). Assembly will
> carry out the agreement in the recent Cherokee treaty to
> build a fort protecting the tribe against the French. 12p.

Fol. 14. 12 Jan. 1757. James Abercromby. An Account of Mony
and Supplys Granted by the Province of Virginia for Carrying
on His Majesty's Service against the Enemy. Assembly has
provided money to build a fort among the Cherokees. 3p.

C.O. 5/1329 (CONT'D)

Fol. 16. 24 Sept. 1756, Williamsburg. Lt. Gov. Robt.
Dinwiddie to Earl of Halifax. An officer and 80 men will build
the Cherokee fort. Cherokees have promised 100 men to protect
the Va. frontiers. Cherokee friendhip is essential since the
French are busy courting the tribe. 3p. [Enclosures to fol.
20b].

Fol. 18. 20 Sept. 1756, Williamsburg. *The Speech of the
Honorable Robert Dinwiddie ... to the General Assembly.*
Cherokees have requested a garrison for the fort built in
their country. Dinwiddie expects 400 Cherokees to assist
in protecting Virginia's borders. 3p.

Fol. 21. 9 Nov. 1756, Williamsburg. Lt. Gov. Dinwiddie to Bd.
of Trade. French are trying to persuade the Creeks, Chickasaws,
and Choctaws to join them. Some Creeks persuaded the Cherokees
not to send assistance to Virginia. The Cherokee fort will not
be garrisoned until the Cherokee's intentions are known. 3p.

Fol. 23. 4 Jan. 1757, Williamsburg. Lt. Gov. Dinwiddie to Bd.
of Trade. Dinwiddie sent an officer to remind the Cherokees of
their promise to send warriors [to protect Virginia's frontiers].
3p. [Enclosures to fol. 28b].

Fol. 30. 16 May 1757, Williamsburg. Lt. Gov. Dinwiddie to Bd.
of Trade. Dinwiddie had almost 400 Catawbas, Cherokees, and
Tuscaroras protecting the frontiers, but many of the Catawbas
and Tuscaroras have already returned home. 3p. [Enclosures
to fol. 33b].

Fol. 35. 16 May 1757, Williamsburg. Lt. Gov. Dinwiddie to
Earl of Halifax. About 400 Catawbas, Cherokees, and Tuscaroras
have been protecting frontiers, but many of the Catawbas and
Tuscaroras have already returned home. 3p. [Enclosures to
fol. 39b].

Fol. 44. 12 Sept. 1757, Williamsburg. Lt. Gov. Dinwiddie to
Bd. of Trade. Mission to the Cherokees and Catawbas was
productive. Nearly 400 Indian warriors protected the frontiers.
Most Indians have gone home but promised to return in two moons.
3p.

Fol. 58. 4 July 1758, Treasury Chambers. Samuel Martin to Bd.
of Trade. Martin forwards a memorial from Wm. Byrd and Peter
Randolph, commissioners to the Cherokees. 1p. [Enclosures to
fol. 66b].

Fol. 59. [ca. 1758]. Memorial from Wm. Byrd and Peter
Randolph to Bd. of Trade (copy). Byrd and Randolph request
a reward for concluding a treaty with the Cherokees and
Catawbas, tribes which the French were trying to seduce.
5p.

Fol. 62. 1743-1756, Virginia. Copy of the minutes of
Council indicating that the Cherokee and Catawba treaty
was approved. Council also approved the treaty expenses. 9p.

C.O. 5/1329 (CONT'D)

Fol. 70. 20 June 1758, Williamsburg. John Blair to Bd. of
Trade. Va. paid for a fort in Cherokee country and sent Gov.
Glen £100 to build another. 5p. [Enclosures to fol. 74b].

Fol. 75. 11 June 1758, Williamsburg. Lt. Gov. Fauquier to
Bd. of Trade. A company of soldiers are resolving a frontier
scuffle involving some Cherokees. A party of 250 Cherokees
went to Winchester to join the English. Little Carpenter and
some other Cherokees are also expected. 4p.

Fol. 95. 20 Feb. 1759, Treasury Chambers. Samuel Martin to
John Pownall. Martin sends James Abercromby's memorial requesting that the same amount of money granted for buying
presents for Southern Indians also be granted for Western
Indians. 2p. [Enclosures to fol. 98b].

> Fol. 96. 22 Jan. 1759, Whitehall. Robert Wood to Samuel
> Martin. Pitt has ordered that Abercromby's memorial be
> sent to the Lords of Treasury. 2p.

> Fol. 97. 20 Jan. 1759, [London]. Memorial from James
> Abercromby to Wm. Pitt. Abercromby wants the same amount
> of money granted for Southern Indians to be also granted
> for Western Indians. 3p.

Fol. 100. 5 Jan. 1759, Williamsburg. Lt. Gov. Fauquier to
Bd. of Trade. The reward for Indian scalps has resulted in
Virginians killing friendly Indians for money. Cherokees are
angry. 8p. [Enclosures to fol. 108b].

Fol. 109. 30 Jan., 19 and 26 Feb. 1759, Williamsburg. Lt.
Gov. Fauquier to Bd. of Trade. At the suggestion of the
Indians, Forbes has reinforced Ft. Duquesne. 5p. [Enclosures
to fol. 115b].

Fol. 170. 30 Aug. 1759, Williamsburg. Lt. Gov. Fauquier to
Bd. of Trade. Cherokee war is settled. Two Cherokee deputies
recently visited Williamsburg requesting supplies. 4p.
[Enclosures to fol. 172b].

> Fol. 172. 15 Aug. 1759, Ft. Ligonier. Col. Wm. Byrd to
> Lt. Gov. Fauquier (copy). Cherokees have asked the Ohio
> Indians to join them against the English. 2p.

Fol. 176. 17 Dec. 1759, Williamsburg. Lt. Gov. Fauquier to
Bd. of Trade (duplicate). Lyttleton will not need Virginia's
assistance against the Cherokees. Lyttleton has gone to the
Cherokees to seek peace. 4p.

Fol. 178. 13 Mar. 1760, Williamsburg. Lt. Gov. Fauquier to Bd.
of Trade. Fauquier needs instructions about settling the western
lands. The English and Indians had agreed that forts were to
be built only for protection against the French. The land was
to remain Indian hunting ground. 6p.

C.O. 5/1330   VIRGINIA ORIGINAL CORRESPONDENCE, BD. OF TRADE: 1760-
*   1764*

Fol. 1.   17 Sept. 1760, Williamsburg. Lt. Gov. Fauquier to Bd.
of Trade. Fauquier has learned about the Ft. Loudoun massacre.
It is not wise to allow Col. Byrd to march into Cherokee country
with new troops since Montgomery and his regulars have retreated.
Amherst's assistance will be necessary if the war continues. 3p.
[Enclosures to fol. 3b].

> Fol. 3.   Copy of articles of capitulation of Ft. Loudoun.
> 2p.

Fol. 4a. 12 May 1760, Williamsburg. Lt. Gov. Fauquier to Bd.
of Trade. Cherokees have broken the peace made by Lyttleton.
Bull has asked Va. to aid Ft. Loudoun. 3p. [Enclosures to
fol. 7b].

Fol. 17.   2 June 1760, Williamsburg. Lt. Gov. Fauquier to Bd.
of Trade. Assembly has provided for 700 men to relieve Ft.
Loudoun or follow Bull's advice. 4p.

Fol. 19.   30 June 1760, Williamsburg. Lt. Gov. Fauquier to Bd.
of Trade. Fauquier is raising troops to assist Carolina against
the Cherokees. Troops will hopefully be ready to march when
the orders from Bull and Montgomery arrive. 5p.

Fol. 24.   1 Dec. 1759, Williamsburg. Lt. Gov. Fauquier to Bd.
of Trade (triplicate). A new government should be established
between the mountains and the Ohio and Miss. Rivers. 4p.
[Enclosures to fol. 27b].

> Fol. 26.   29 Oct. 1759, Camp at Pittsburg. Lt. Col. Stephen
> to Lt. Gov. Fauquier (copy). Stephen describes the Indian
> trade west of Pittsburg and argues that officers are en-
> titled to great amount of land. 3p.

Fol. 28.   1 Sept. 1760, Williamsburg. Lt. Gov. Fauquier to Bd.
of Trade. Fauquier has tried to get a copy of the treaty between
Forbes, Stanwix, and the Indians to settle questions about the
western settlements. 8p.

Fol. 32.   6 Dec. 1760, Williamsburg. Lt. Gov. Fauquier to Bd.
of Trade. Assembly had agreed to keep 1,000 men ready to assist
the Carolinas against the Cherokees in the spring. Amherst's
assistance will be necessary. 5p.

Fol. 35.   15 Dec. 1760, Williamsburg. Lt. Gov. Fauquier to
Bd. of Trade (duplicate). Fauquier delayed sending the acts
passed by the May Assembly because of the Cherokee danger. 3p.

Fol. 63.   12 May 1761, Williamsburg. Lt. Gov. Fauquier to Bd.
of Trade. Amherst has taken command of 1,000 man regiment to
make sure that the troops coordinate their actions against the
Cherokees with Col. Grant. The 500 men raised by Dobbs will
hopefully join Va. against the Upper Cherokees while Grant
attacks the Lower Cherokees. 8p.

Fol. 67.   27 Sept. 1761, New York. Lt. Gov. Fauquier to Bd. of
Trade. N.C. troops have not joined Virginia's forces to attack
the Upper Cherokee Towns. 4p.

Fol. 73.   29 Aug. 1761, Williamsburg. Lt. Gov. Fauquier to
Bd. of Trade. General Court will settle all Indian land claims
in October. 5p.

Fol. 77.   12 Oct. 1761, Williamsburg. Lt. Gov. Fauquier to
Bd. of Trade. Fauquier talked with Gov. Hamilton about the
Indian agreements on land settlements. 2p.

Fol. 89.   22 Jan. 1762, Lincoln's Inn. Matthew Lamb to Bd. of
Trade. Lamb reports on new Va. acts, including one raising
£32,000 to relieve Ft. Loudoun. 3p.

Fol. 93.   30 Nov. 1761, Williamsburg. Lt. Gov. Fauquier to Bd.
of Trade. Peter Randolph and Wm. Byrd persuaded the Cherokees
to join the King's troops near Ft. Duquesne. Cherokee insults,
the Virginians' revenge, and abuse of the scalping laws caused
the Cherokee war. 5p. [Enclosures to fol. 104b].

> Fol. 97.   7 Nov. 1761, Williamsburg. Minutes of Council
> considering the Six Nations' release of their land in Va.
> as required by the Treaty of Lancaster (1744). 4p.

> Fol. 99.   13 June 1752. Confirmation of a Deed of Release
> by the Ohio Indians Made at Logstown. 3p.

> Fol. 102.   A Narrative of What Hath Passed between the
> King's Generals, Governors, and the Indians in Relation
> to Land [since the Treaty of Easton]. 5p.

Fol. 108.   24 Feb. 1762, Williamsburg. Lt. Gov. Fauquier to
Bd. of Trade. Fauquier will disband the regiment as soon as
the Cherokee peace is officially confirmed. He recommends Lt.
Col. Stephen to succeed Atkin as Agent for Indian Affairs in
Southern District. 5p. [Enclosures to fol. 117b].

Fol. 121.   16 Apr. 1762, Williamsburg. Lt. Gov. Fauquier to
Bd. of Trade. Connetarke (Standing Turkey), chief warrior of
the Overhill Cherokees, will visit Williamsburg. 3p.

Fol. 123.   1 May 1762, Williamsburg. Lt. Gov. Fauquier to Bd.
of Trade. Skiagusta Oconesta [Ostenaco], the chief Overhill
warrior (not Connetarke who is old), came to confirm the recent
peace. Skiagusta seems more dependable than his rival (Little
Carpenter) and has requested permission to go to England.
Fauquier put Skiagusta, two followers, and an interpreter on
Capt. Blake's *Epreuve*. 4p.

Fol. 154.   10 July 1762, Williamsburg. Lt. Gov. Fauquier to
Bd. of Trade. Fauquier explains why he interpreted his instruc-
tions loosely when he sponsored the act to grant money for Ft.
Loudoun's relief. 7p. [Enclosures to fol. 163b].

C.O. 5/1330 (CONT'D)

Fol. 259. 7 Sept. 1763, Williamsburg. Lt. Gov. Fauquier to
Bd. of Trade. Indians on the southwestern frontiers are quiet
but Indians in the northwest are troublesome. 4p. [Enclosures
to fol. 284b].

> Fol. 261. [Rec. 1 Dec. 1763]. Lt. Gov. Fauquier. Answer
> to the Queries Sent ... by the [Board of Trade]. The
> nearest Indians are the Shawnees to the northwest with
> about 500 warriors and the Cherokees to the southwest
> with about 4,000 warriors. Virginia's Indian trade is
> insignificant. 47p.

Fol. 290. 22 Sept. 1763, Williamsburg. Lt. Gov. Fauquier to
Bd. of Trade. Fauquier sends the minutes of Council from May
1760 until the last Council before he left to attend the
Indian conference. 2p.

Fol. 292. 13 Feb. 1764, Williamsburg. Lt. Gov. Fauquier to
Bd. of Trade. Cherokees have renounced their claim to land
east of Holston R. at the recent Augusta congress. 8p.
[Enclosures to fol. 298b].

Fol. 299. 15 Feb. 1764, Williamsburg. Lt. Gov. Fauquier to
Bd. of Trade. After returning from the Southern Indian Congress
at Augusta, Fauquier received request for troops to fight the
Northern Indians. 3p. [Enclosures to fol. 305b].

> Fol. 301. 12 Jan. 1764. *The Speech of the Honorable
> Francis Fauquier ... to the General Assembly.* Fauquier
> requests troops to fight the Northern Indians. English
> should take precautions not to attack the Cherokees who
> will be fighting the Northern Indians this summer. 3p.

> Fol. 303. 14 Jan. 1764, *The Humble Address of the House of
> Burgesses* [to Fauquier]. Council congratulates Fauquier
> on the success of the Southern Indian Congress. 1p.

> Fol. 304. 16 Jan. 1764. *The Humble Address of the House
> of Burgesses* [to Fauquier]. House congratulates Fauquier
> on the treaty with the Southern Indians. 1p.

*C.O. 5/1331   VIRGINIA, ORIGINAL CORRESPONDENCE, BD. OF TRADE: 1764-
1767*

Fol. 5. [Rec. 20 Aug. 1765]. Copy of resolution from House of
Burgesses stating that the murderers of five Cherokees will be
punished. 2p. [Enclosure of Fauquier's letter of 26 May 1765].

Fol. 6. 8 May 1765, Staunton. Col. Andrew Lewis to Cherokee
Chiefs (copy). Nockonowe, the Pipe, and three other Cherokees
were killed in Staunton. Their murderers will be punished.
3p. [Enclosure of Fauquier's letter of 26 May 1765].

Fol. 8. 9 May 1765, Augusta County. Col. Lewis to Lt. Gov.
Fauquier (copy). Lewis reports that the five Cherokees were

murdered on their way to fight against the Ohio Indians. 3p.
[Enclosure of Fauquier's letter of 26 May 1765].

Fol. 10. 14 May 1765, Williamsburg. Lt. Gov. Fauquier to
Col. Lewis (copy). Fauquier orders Lewis to capture the
murderers of the Cherokees. Fauquier will inform the Cherokees about Lewis's action. 3p. [Enclosure of Fauquier's
letter of 26 May 1765].

Fol. 12. 14 May 1765, Williamsburg. Lt. Gov. Fauquier to Col.
Lewis (copy). Once the murderers are captured, Lewis must
secretly move them to a different site for trial. 2p.
[Enclosure of Fauquier's letter of 26 May 1765].

Fol. 13. 16 May 1765, [Williamsburg]. Lt. Gov. Fauquier to
Upper Cherokee Chiefs (copy). Fauquier reports the murder of
Cherokees and assures the tribe that justice will be done. 3p.
[Enclosure of Fauquier's letter of 26 May 1765].

Fol. 15. 13 May 1765, Williamsburg. Francis Fauquier. *A
Proclamation*. Fauquier offers a reward for the murderers of
five Cherokees. 2p. [Enclosure of Fauquier's letter of 26
May 1765].

Fol. 16. 14 June 1765, Williamsburg. Lt. Gov. Fauquier to
Bd. of Trade. Paxton Boys of Penn. vow to rescue any of their
party jailed for murdering the Cherokees. 3p. [Enclosures
to fol. 19b].

> Fol. 18. 3 June 1765, Augusta County. Col. Lewis to Lt.
> Gov. Fauquier (copy). Murderers of Cherokees escaped from
> jail. Choconante, Standing Turkey's son, was found dead
> near the place of the first murders. The Cherokees who
> escaped the murderers killed a blind man and his wife. 3p.

Fol. 20. 1 Aug. 1765, Williamsburg. Lt. Gov. Fauquier to Bd.
of Trade. Little Carpenter is satisfied with the assurances
that the Cherokee murderers will be punished. Little Carpenter
requests that Wm. Johnson mediate peace between the Cherokees
and Shawnees. Augusta men have left to destroy the presents
given to Little Carpenter to compensate the relatives of the
murdered Cherokees. 5p. [Enclosures to fol. 24b].

> Fol. 23. 16 and 29 July 1765, Williamsburg. Copy of
> Minutes of Council indicating that Little Carpenter
> presented strings of black and white beads to the English.
> Little Carpenter believes that the Cherokees will accept
> the promise to punish the murderers, and he requests that
> Wm. Johnson mediate peace with the Northern Indians. 4p.

Fol. 25. 5 June 1765, Augusta County. Col. Lewis to Lt. Gov.
Fauquier (copy). Augusta residents support the Cherokee
murders. 3p. [Enclosures to fol. 27b].

C.O. 5/1331 (CONT'D)

Fol. 27. [3-5 June 1765], Augusta County. Augusta Boys.
A Proclamation. The murdered Indians were Shawnees and
Delawares masquerading as Cherokees. 2p.

Fol. 28. 14 June 1765, Williamsburg. Lt. Gov. Fauquier to
Col. Lewis (copy). The reward for capturing the murderers will
hopefully be effective so that the Cherokees will not seek
revenge. 2p.

Fol. 29. 5 June 1765, Williamsburg. Lt. Gov. Fauquier to Bd.
of Trade. Va. recently passed an act to establish trade with
the Cherokees. There is no news from Augusta [County] about
the Cherokee murders. 5p. [Enclosures to fol. 32b].

Fol. 34. 3 Oct. 1765, Council Chambers, Whitehall. Order
from Committee of Council for Plantation Affairs requiring
that the Bd. prepare instructions for Va. and Penn. to evacuate
their settlements west of the Allegheny Mountains. 2p.

Fol. 35. 3 Oct. 1765, Council Chamber, Whitehall. Order from
Committee of Council for Plantation Affairs requiring the Bd.
to prepare instructions for Va. to use military force to
prevent future outrages similar to the murder of the Cherokees.
3p.

Fol. 148. 31 July 1766, Williamsburg. Francis Fauquier. *A
Proclamation.* Fauquier calls for the evacuation of settlements
on Indian lands west of the Allegheny Mountains. 2p. [Enclo-
sure of Fauquier's letter of 4 Sept. 1766].

Fol. 165. 18 Dec. 1766, Williamsburg. Lt. Gov. Fauqier to
Earl of Shelburne. Cherokees want their boundary line with
the Carolinas to continue north through Virginia. 4p.

Fol. 174. 2 Feb. 1767, Williamsburg. Lt. Gov. Fauquier to
Earl of Shelburne. Stuart has urged Fauquier to run the
Cherokee boundary line through Virginia. If the King orders
the line run, Fauquier needs instruction on where to run it. 3p.

Fol. 179. [Rec. 16 July 1765]. Memorial from George Mercer
on the behalf of the Ohio Company in Virginia to the King in
Council. Mercer requests a land grant or reimbursement for the
company's expenses incurred in following George II's orders.
7p.

Fol. 183. 21 June 1765. Ohio Company to King. Ohio Company
requests a land grant or reimbursement for its expenses. 7p.

*C.O. 5/1332   VIRGINIA, ORIGINAL CORRESPONDENCE, BD. OF TRADE: 1767-
          1770*

Fol. 42. 17 Oct. 1768, Hard Labor. John Stuart to President
John Blair (copy). Stuart concluded a treaty with the Upper
and Lower Cherokee chiefs ratifying land cessions and boundaries
in N.C., S.C., and Virginia. Chiefs will meet again on May 10.
4p. [Enclosure of Botetourt's letter of 12 Nov. 1768].

C.O. 5/1332 (CONT'D)

Fol. 44. 6 Nov. 1768, Williamsburg. Gov. Botetourt to John
Stuart (copy). Botetourt has postponed the meeting with the
Cherokees at Chiswell's Mine to 10 May. Va. sent goods to
Bedford for the Cherokees to compensate for the murders of
their tribesmen. 1p. [Enclosure of Botetourt's letter of
12 Nov. 1768].

Fol. 44. 6 Nov. 1768, Williamsburg. Gov. Botetourt to Col.
Andrew Lewis (copy). Indians request a postponement of the Nov.
10 meeting to May 10. 1p. [Enclosure to Botetourt's letter
of 12 Nov. 1768].

Fol. 45. 6 Nov. 1768, Williamsburg. Gov. Botetourt to Mr.
Calloway (copy). At the Indians' request, Botetourt postponed
the meeting to 10 May. 1p. [Enclosure of Botetourt's letter
of 12 Nov. 1768].

Fol. 45. 6 Nov. 1768, Williamsburg. Gov. Botetourt to Israel
Christian (copy). At the Indians' request, Botetourt postponed
the meeting to 10 May. 1p. [Enclosure of Botetourt's letter
of 12 Nov. 1768].

Fol. 54. 20 Dec. 1768, Williamsburg. Instructions from Gov.
Botetourt to Col. Lewis and Dr. Walker (copy). Commissioners
will explain to Stuart the necessity of new negotiations on the
boundary between Cherokees and Virginia. Cherokees have no
title to lands between the proposed line and the mouth of Cherokee R., lands which were sold by the Northern nations at Ft.
Stanwix. Goods intended for the relatives of the murdered
Cherokees are damaged and new goods are being sent to Toqueh.
4p. [Enclosure of Botetourt's letter of 20 Dec. 1768].

Fol. 56. 16 Dec. 1768, Williamsburg. Extract of minutes of
Council noting that Stuart's proposed boundary line would be
detrimental to Va. and Great Britain and give the Indians land
they never claimed. 2p. [Enclosure of Botetourt's letter
of 20 Dec. 1768].

Fol. 100. 19 Jan. 1769, Williamsburg. John Stuart to Gov.
Botetourt (copy). Fauquier's failure to consult with Stuart
has caused the inconveniences imposed upon Va. by the ratifica-
tion of the Cherokee boundary line. 4p. [Enclosure of
Botetourt's letter no. 8].

Fol. 102. 2 Feb. 1769. Report from Col. Andrew Lewis and Dr.
Walker to Gov. Botetourt (copy). Lewis and Walker, commissioners to negotiate the boundary with the Cherokees, describe
their work. Judd's Friend and Saluy agree to reopen boundary
negotiations. 9p. [Enclosure of Botetourt's letter no. 8].

Fol. 177. [Rec. 9 Mar. 1770], Virginia. Memorial from the
House of Burgesses to Gov. Botetourt (copy). Burgesses discuss
the Cherokee boundary line. 6p.

C.O. 5/1332 (CONT'D)

Fol. 197. 9 July 1770, London. Copy of letter to Thomas Walpole stating that the King's instructions concerning the Va. land grants have not been followed. Letter also discusses the Cherokee boundary line. 10p.

C.O. 5/1333   VIRGINIA, ORIGINAL CORRESPONDENCE, BD. OF TRADE: 1770-1772

Fol. 2a. 7 Nov. 1769, Williamsburg. *The Speech of ... Baron de Botetourt ... to the General Assembly.* Bd. of Trade approves the boundary extension between Va. and the Cherokees if Va. pays the expenses. 2p.

Fol. 3. 8 Nov. 1769. Gov. Botetourt to Earl of Hillsborough (duplicate). 2p. [Enclosures to fol. 5b].

    Fol. 5 7 Nov. 1769, Williamsburg. Speech from Botetourt to General Assembly. [Same as fol. 2a]. 2p.

Fol. 28. 31 May 1770, Williamsburg. Gov. Botetourt to Earl of Hillsborough. [Duplicate of C.O. 5/1348/107]. 2p. [Enclosures to fol. 29b].

    Fol. 29. [30 May 1770], [Williamsburg]. Address from House of Burgesses to Botetourt and Botetourt's answer. [Same as C.O. 5/1348/109]. 2p.

Fol. 31. 13 May 1769, Whitehall. Earl of Hillsborough to John Stuart. The King approves Stuart's suggestions for altering the boundary between Va. and Cherokees if Va. pays the expenses. 2p.

Fol. 32. 3 Aug. 1769, Charleston. John Stuart to [Gov. Botetourt]. (copy). Stuart describes the boundary line between Va. and the Cherokees approved by the King. 4p.

Fol. 34. [Rec. 5 Aug. 1769]. Alteration in the [Cherokee] Boundary Line as Proposed in Mr. Stuart's Letter No. 10. 2p.

Fol. 35. 16 June 1769. Copy of resolution from the House of Burgesses requesting that Botetourt settle the boundary with the Cherokees. 2p.

Fol. 37. 21 June 1770, [Williamsburg]. Gov. Botetourt to John Stuart (copy). Botetourt requests that Stuart obtain land cession from the Cherokees. Va. will pay the expenses. 2p.

Fol. 46. 24 June 1770, Williamsburg. Gov. Botetourt to Bd. of Trade. Botetourt requests information on land which may be granted immediately as result of the Treaty of Ft. Stanwix. 2p.

Fol. 47. 31 July 1770, Williamsburg. Gov. Botetourt to Bd. of Trade. 2p. [Enclosures to fol. 56].

Fol. 48. 6 Dec. 1769. A True and Full Account of All the
Orders of Council for Granting Lands ... Lying between the
Allegany Mountains and ... the Western Boundary of the
Carolina Line, to the Confluence of the River Ohio with
the Mississippi. 17p.

Fol. 57. 16 Nov. 1770. Memorial from Edward Bell to Earl of
Hillsborough and Bd. of Trade. Bell requests 80,000 acres in
western Va. free from the five shilling tax per 50 acres. 2p.

Fol. 59. [Rec. 5 Dec. 1770]. Memorial from Edward Bell to
Earl of Hillsborough and Bd. of Trade. Bell requests land in
western Virginia. 4p.

Fol. 77. 18 Oct. 1770, Virginia. Pres. Wm. Nelson to Earl of
Hillsborough. [Duplicate of C.O. 5/1348/160]. 11p. [Enclo-
sures to fol. 88b].

Fol. 83. 12 July 1749, Virginia. Copy of Council minutes
concerning land grants to the Ohio Company. 2p.

Fol. 84. 5 Oct. 1770, Mount Vernon. Geo. Washington to
Gov. Botetourt. [Same as C.O. 5/1348/177]. 4p.

Fol. 86. 12 Feb. 1755. Copy of proceedings of Council
concerning settlements west of the Alleghenies along the
Ohio River. 3p.

Fol. 88. Copy of proclamation from Gov. Dinwiddie promising land along the Ohio R. to army volunteers. 2p.

Fol. 90. 31 Oct. 1770, Virginia. Pres. Nelson to Earl of
Hillsborough. [Copy of C.O. 5/1349/9]. 2p.

Fol. 135. 18 Oct. 1770, Virginia. Pres. Nelson to Earl of
Hillsborough. [Copy of C.O. 5/1348/160]. 16p.

Fol. 143. 5 Mar. 1771, London. Thomas Walpole and Associates
to Earl of Hillsborough. Walpole discusses Nelson's letter of
18 Oct. 1770 referring to Virginia's purchase of Cherokee land
in 1769. 39p. [Enclosures to fol. 168b].

Fol. 154. 9 July 1770, London. Letter to Thomas Walpole.
[Same as C.O. 5/1332/197]. 10p.

Fol. 163. 24 Nov and 13 Dec. 1766. Extracts from Journal
of House of Burgesses stating that land between Pennsylvania (in the North), the Ohio River (to the West), and N.
Carolina (to the South) is not claimed or inhabited by
the Indians. Tribes would readily cede that land. 4p.

Fol. 165. 28 May 1770. [Thomas Walpole] to John Pownall.
[Walpole] thanks Pownall for sending memorial from the Va.
House of Burgesses proposing the purchase of all Cherokee
land. 3p.

C.O. 5/1333 (CONT'D)

       Fol. 167. Payton Randolph to the King. Randolph requests
that settlement of western lands be continued. 2p.

       Fol. 169. 10 Nov. 1770, New York. Lt. Gen. Gage to Earl of
Hillsborough (extract). Settlement of western land should end,
and the Indians should be left in peace. 6p.

       Fol. 176. 16 May 1772, Lincoln's Inn Field. Thomas Walpole
to [John Pownall]. Bd. of Trade objects to land request because
some land lies within territory claimed by the Six Nations,
their confederates, and the Cherokees. Walpole is willing to
send Pownall a copy of the Indian treaties since the Ft.
Stanwix cessions. 3p.

       Fol. 180. 11 Apr. 1772, Williamsburg. Earl of Dunmore to
Earl of Hillsborough (duplicate). Dunmore sends the plan for
the boundary between Va. and the Cherokees. This line deviates
from instructions because the proposed boundary would cross
mountains and would have been too expensive to run. 9p.

       Fol. 199. 14 Aug. 1772, St. James. Order in Council directing
the Bd. to give an opinion on the request by Thomas Walpole
and others for Indian land grants purchased by the government.
8p.

       Fol. 204. [Rec. 2 Nov. 1772]. Petition from Major Wm. Edmiston
et al to Bd. of Trade. Edmiston requests 80,000 acres of land
on the banks of the Ohio. 2p.

       Fol. 207. [Rec. 25 Nov. 1772]. Memorial from Lord Cathcart
et al to Bd. of Trade. Cathcart requests a land grant along
the Holston R. (called the Enemy R. by the Cherokees) and the
New River. 3p.

C.O. 5/1335   VIRGINIA, ORIGINAL CORRESPONDENCE, DRAFTS OF BD. OF
                TRADE: 1702-1752

       Fol. 92. 19 Dec. 1712, Whitehall. Bd. of Trade to Queen Anne.
Bd. asks that S.C. repeal its act preventing Virginia's Indian
traders from passing through S.C. to trade with the Western
Indians. 5p.

       Fol. 98. Apr. 1713, Whitehall. Bd. of Trade to Lt. Gov.
Spotswood. Bd. discusses Virginia's aid to S.C. against the
Tuscaroras. 7p.

       Fol. 160. 6 Dec. 1738, Whitehall. Bd. of Trade to Lt. Gov.
Gooche. Bd. praises Gooche's attempts to negotiate a peace
between the Cherokees, Catawbas, and the Five Nations. 7p.

       Fol. 239. 2 Sept. 1748, Whitehall. Report from Bd. of Trade
to Privy Council. Bd. reports on the grant applications for
land on the western side of Great Mountains. Settlement there
would increase commerce with the Indians. 11p.

C.O. 5/1336   VIRGINIA, ORGINAL CORRESPONDENCE, DRAFTS OF BD. OF TRADE:
1753-1774

Fol. 16.   21 Jan. 1757, Whitehall. Bd. of Trade to Wm. Pitt.
Bd. discusses the N.C. and Va. frontiers. Dobbs is building
a fort on the western frontier. 19p.

Fol. 27.   10 Mar. 1757, Whitehall. Bd. of Trade to Lt. Gov.
Dinwiddie. Cherokees are evidently friendlier to the French
than to the British. 4p.

Fol. 46.   1 Mar. 1765, Whitehall. Bd. of Trade to Lt. Gov.
Fauquier. Cherokees have been brought [to London] without
permission, risking the welfare of those Indians. Government
has ordered that they receive some small presents and expenses
for their passage. 3p.

Fol. 50.   27 Aug. 1765, Whitehall. Representation from Bd. of
Trade to the King. Frontiersmen killed a Cherokee chief and
four warriors who were travelling through Augusta County
[Virginia]. Murderers were arrested but their friends helped
them escape. The Cherokees have nearly 3,000 warriors. 10p.

Fol. 56.   27 Sept. 1765, Whitehall. Bd. of Trade to King.
Bd. describes actions taken due to the Cherokee murders. Little
Carpenter has asked Va. about its intentions to punish the
murderers of his people. 4p.

Fol. 62.   10 Oct. 1765, Whitehall. Bd. of Trade to Privy
Council for Plantations. The instructions to halt future
disturbances caused by the murder of several Cherokees are
ready to be sent to Virginia. 1p.

Fol. 63.   10 Oct. 1765, Whitehall. Additional instructions
from Bd. of Trade to Gen. Amherst. Amherst must stop future
outrages such as the Cherokee murders. 1p.

Fol. 64.   10 Oct. 1765, Whitehall. Bd. of Trade to Privy
Council for Plantation Affairs. Bd. sends a copy of the
instructions for the Va. and Penn. Governors to evacuate settlements in Indian territory along the Ohio River. 1p.

Fol. 67.   29 Nov. 1765, Whitehall. Bd. of Trade to Lt. Gov.
Fauquier. Bd. has prepared instructions to remove settlements
west of Allegheny Mtns. and to settle the question of the
Cherokee murders. 4p.

Fol. 162.   16 Mar. 1770, Whitehall. Bd. of Trade to Gov.
Botetourt (draft). Bd. will carefully consider the Va. memorial
about extending the province's western boundary. 5p.

Fol. 229.   29 Apr. 1772, Whitehall. Bd. of Trade to Lords of
Committee of Council (draft). Bd. sends a request from Ben.
Franklin and others for land tracts west of the line agreed
to by the Six Nations, their confederates, and the Cherokees.
70p.

C.O. 5/1336 (CONT'D)

>   Fol. 266.   6 May 1773, Whitehall.   Representation from Bd. of
>   Trade to the King.   Bd. wishes the King to make some land grants
>   along the Ohio and to establish a separate government there.
>   It is not necessary to consider the line agreed upon with the
>   Cherokees at Lochaber since the tribe has since agreed to accept
>   a natural boundary.   31p.

C.O. 5/1337   VIRGINIA, ORIGINAL CORRESPONDENCE, SEC. OF STATE: 1694-
>   *1745*

>   Fol. 128.   18 Sept. 1728, Cherokees Nayowee.   Report from
>   John Cary on the Cherokees.   The trader who lived with the
>   Cherokees believes they are the only Indians that Carolina can
>   depend upon and are the only barrier against the French.
>   Cherokees sent presents to the King and expressed a desire to
>   see him.   3p.

C.O. 5/1344   VIRGINIA, ORIGINAL CORRESPONDENCE, SEC. OF STATE: 1726-
>   *1783*

>   Fol. 19.   20 July 1732, Whitehall.   Bd. of Trade to Duke of
>   Newcastle.   Bd. requests that land petitions for tracts west of
>   the Va. mountains be submitted to the Queen.   3p.

>   Fol. 22.   20 July 1732, Whitehall.   Representation from Bd. of
>   Trade to the Queen.   The boundary between Va. and Maryland
>   should be surveyed before a decision is made on land west of
>   the Va. mountains.   4p.

>   Fol. 41.   18 Oct. 1739, Whitehall.   Bd. of Trade to Duke of
>   Newcastle.   Bd. sends an extract of a letter from the commis-
>   sioners of Indian Affairs about a French expedition against
>   the Southern Indians.   3p.   [Enclosures to fol. 53b].

>>   Fol. 52.   13 July 1739, Albany.   Commissioners for Indian
>>   Affairs to Lt. Gov. of New York (extract).   French have
>>   sent an army to attack the Indians friendly to Va. and
>>   Georgia.   Governors should warn their Indians.   3p.

>   Fol. 75.   28 June 1750, Whitehall.   Bd. of Trade to Duke of
>   Bedford.   The Six Nations and some French Indians plan to
>   destroy the Catawbas, and the French plan to settle 1,000
>   Indian families on the [New River], a branch of the Miss. River.
>   3p.   [Enclosures to fol. 79b].

>>   Fol. 78.   11 May 1750, Williamsburg.   Thomas Lee to Bd.
>>   of Trade (extract).   The Six Nations and the French Indians
>>   plan to settle 1,000 Indian families on the New River, a
>>   branch of the Miss. River.   3p.

>   Fol. 80.   1 Sept. 1750, Whitehall.   Bd. of Trade to Duke of
>   Bedford.   Bd. sends an extract of Thomas Lee's letter about
>   Virginia's fortifications against the Indians.   3p.   [Enclosures
>   to fol. 85b].

C.O. 5/1344 (CONT'D)

Fol. 83. 12 June 1750, Williamsburg. Col. Thomas Lee
to Bd. of Trade (extract). French are trying to incite
the English Indians to fight each other. 4p.

Fol. 115. 16 Mar. 1753, Whitehall. Bd. of Trade to Earl of
Holderness. 5p. [Enclosures to fol. 143b].

Fol. 120. June-July 1752. Wm. Trent to Lt. Gov. Dinwiddie
(copy). Trent describes his journey to the Twightwees
and Shawnees. Shawnees hoisted the French colors when
the Cherokees visited. 24p.

Fol. 228. 22 May 1754, Whitehall. Bd. of Trade to Thomas
Robinson. 2p. [Enclosures to fol. 232b].

Fol. 230. 12 Mar. 1754, [Williamsburg]. Lt. Gov. Dinwiddie
to Bd. of Trade (extract). Dinwiddie asked the Catawbas
and Cherokees to send as many warriors as possible to the
Ohio R. by mid-April. 4p.

Fol. 234. 3 July 1754, Whitehall. Bd. of Trade to Thomas
Robinson. 3p. [Enclosures to fol. 249b].

Fol. 240. 25 Apr. 1754, Wills Creek. Col. Geo. Washington
to Lt. Gov. Dinwiddie. [Same as C.O. 5/1328/97]. 10p.

Fol. 262. 6-18 Oct. 1760. Journal from House of Burgesses
(copy). Governor reports the Cherokee massacre of Ft. Loudoun's
garrison. Va. forces were fortunately delayed since they would
have been in the heart of Cherokee country when Montgomery
retreated. 26p.

*C.O. 5/1345   VIRGINIA, ORIGINAL CORRESPONDENCE, SEC. OF STATE: 1762-
1767*

Fol. 1. 1 May 1762, Williamsburg. Lt. Gov. Fauquier to Earl
of Egremont. Fauquier writes a letter of introduction for
Ensign Timberlake, who opened up a new route to Cherokee country.
Timberlake is accompanying the Cherokees [to London] at his own
expense. 3p.

Fol. 9. 10 July 1762, Whitehall. Earl of Egremont to Lt. Gov.
Fauquier (draft). Capt. Blake delivered Fauquier's letters
and the three Cherokees. Their visit is causing problems
because their interpreter died during the voyage and a replacement has not been found. 4p.

Fol. 11. 23 July 1762, Whitehall. Earl of Egremont to Lt.
Gov. Fauquier (draft). Egremont has recommended Timberlake to
fill the first vacancy for lieutenant that occurs. He will
also be rewarded financially. 3p.

Fol. 13. 27 Nov. 1762, Williamsburg. Lt. Gov. Fauquier to
Earl of Egremont. Fauquier is pleased that the King rewarded
Timberlake. 3p.

C.O. 5/1345 (CONT'D)

Fol. 40.   28 May 1763, Williamsburg. Lt. Gov. Fauquier to
Earl of Egremont. Fauquier informed Stuart and the governors
of N.C., S.C., and Ga. that he will attend the proposed Indian
meeting. 3p.

Fol. 44.   27 July 1763, Williamsburg. Lt. Gov. Fauquier to Earl
of Egremont. The Indian meeting will hopefully stop attacks
on the Va. frontier. 3p.

Fol. 46.   16 Aug. 1763, James River. Lt. Henry Timberlake to
Earl of Egremont. Timberlake was surprised when Amherst gave
him a commission at half pay. He hopes that Carrington will be
severely punished for overcharging the [Cherokee] Indians account
by £200. 2p.

Fol. 48.   19 Oct. 1763, St. James. Dunk Halifax to Lt. Gov.
Fauquier (draft). The King is pleased with Fauquier's actions
protecting the frontiers against the Indians. 3p.

Fol. 50.   7 Sept. 1763, Williamsburg. Lt. Gov. Fauquier to
Earl of Egremont. Northern Indians returning from attacking
the Cherokees probably caused the recent hostilities. 3p.

Fol. 52.   19 Oct. 1763, Whitehall. James Rivers to Edward
Sedgewick. Rivers was unaware of Timberlake's charges against
Carrington concerning the Cherokees' account and believes
Timberlake is mistaken. 4p.

Fol. 54.   20 Nov. 1763, Charleston. Lt. Gov. Fauquier to Earl
of Egremont. Augusta Indian congress went smoothly. 3p.

Fol. 58.   31 Jan. 1764, Williamsburg. Lt. Gov. Fauquier to
Earl of Halifax. A proclamation restricting western land
grants would give the French an opportunity to win over the
Indians. 4p.

Fol. 74.   28 Jan. 1765, Whitehall. Bd. of Trade to Earl of
Halifax. Bd. requests instructions concerning Timberlake's
petition to be reimbursed for the expenses of the three Cherokees. 2p. [Enclosure to fol. 77b].

     Fol. 76.   [ca. Jan. 1765], [London]. Petition from Lt.
     Timberlake to Bd. of Trade (copy). Timberlake requests
     reimbursement for maintaining the three Cherokees since
     the death of Aaron Trueheart. He also requests that the
     government pay for the Cherokees' return passage. 3p.

Fol. 78.   1 Feb. 1765, St. James. Earl **Halifax** to Bd. of Trade
(copy). The King will not reimburse Timberlake for the Cherokees' expenses since their visit is unauthorized. The King will
provide, however, for their passage home. 3p.

Fol. 80.   14 June 1765, Williamsburg. Lt. Gov. Fauquier to Earl
of Halifax. The murder of the Cherokees proves that Va. is
unable to control violations of treaties with neighboring
Indians. 4p.

C.O. 5/1345 (CONT'D)

Fol. 82.   14 Sept. 1765, St. James. Henry Conway to Lt. Gov.
Fauquier. Board will send advice on handling frontier
inhabitants. 6p.

Fol. 115.   24 Nov. 1765, Williamsburg. Lt. Gov. Fauquier to
Sec. Conway. 4p. [Enclosures to fol. 125b].

    Fol. 124.   14 June 1765, Williamsburg. Lt. Gov. Fauquier
    to Earl of Halifax. [Copy of fol. 80]. 3p.

Fol. 130.   26 July 1766, Williamsburg. Lt. Gov. Fauquier to Bd.
of Trade (copy). If the frontiersmen continue to break the law,
Va. will have more to fear from them than from the Cherokees. 5p.

Fol. 138.   4 Sept. 1766, Williamsburg. Lt. Gov. Fauquier to Bd.
of Trade (copy). Fauquier sends a copy of the proclamation
ordering settlers to leave Indian land. 3p. [Enclosures to
fol. 141b].

    Fol. 140.   31 July 1766, Williamsburg. Copy of proclama-
    tion from Lt. Gov. Fauquier requiring settlers to leave
    Indian land. 4p.

Fol. 154.   19 Feb. 1767, Whitehall. Earl of Shelburne to Lt.
Gov. Fauquier (draft). Government has hopefully punished the
violators of Indian treaties. A lasting peace with the Indians
cannot be established until the Indians know that the English
keep their promises. 5p.

Fol. 157.   18 Nov. 1766, Williamsburg. Lt. Gov. Fauquier to
Earl of Shelburne. Government has taken steps to remove
settlers from the Indian lands, but it is impossible to use
military force. 5p. [Enclosures to fol. 168b].

    Fol. 160.   13 Feb. 1764, Williamsburg. Lt. Gov. Fauquier
    to Bd. of Trade (copy). Cherokees at the Augusta congress
    renounced all claim to land east of the Holston River. 6p.

    Fol. 165.   4 Sept. 1766, Williamsburg. Lt. Gov. Fauquier
    to Bd. of Trade. [Same as fol. 138]. 3p.

    Fol. 167.   31 July 1766. Copy of proclamation from Lt.
    Gov. Fauquier. [Same as fol. 140]. 2p.

Fol. 169.   18 Dec. 1766, Williamsburg. Lt. Gov. Fauquier to
Earl of Shelburne. Fauquier wants an opinion on running the
boundary between Va. and the Cherokees. 5p. [Enclosures to
fol. 177b].

    Fol. 172.   22 June 1766, Redstone Creek. Copy of summons
    from Alex. Mackay requiring settlers to leave Indian land. 3p.

Fol. 178.   2 Feb. 1767. Lt. Gov. Fauquier to Earl of Shelburne.
Stuart has requested that the boundary be run between Va. and
the Cherokees. If the King decides to do so, Fauquier wants
instructions to be sent. 3p.

C.O. 5/1345 (CONT'D)

Fol. 186. 24 May 1767, Williamsburg. Lt. Gov. Fauquier to
Earl of Shelburne. Indian murderers cannot be punished. 4p.

Fol. 193. 8 Oct. 1767, Whitehall. Earl of Shelburne to Lt.
Gov. Fauquier (draft). Shelburne requests information on the
Ohio Company's claim to compensation for expenses incurred for
land cessions by the Indians to the company. 5p.

Fol. 196. 14 Nov. 1767, Whitehall. Earl of Shelburne to Lt.
Gov. Fauquier (draft). Shelburne explains how to run the
boundary between Va. and the Cherokees. 3p.

*C.O. 5/1347   VIRGINIA, ORIGINAL CORRESPONDENCE, SEC. OF STATE: 1768-
            1769*

Fol. 11. 10 Nov. 1768, Williamsburg. Gov. Botetourt to Earl
of Hillsborough. 2p. [Enclosures to fol. 20b].

> Fol. 13. 17 Oct. 1768, Hard Labor. John Stuart to Pres.
> Blair. [Same as C.O. 5/1332/42]. 4p.

> Fol. 15. 6 Nov. 1768, Williamsburg. Gov. Botetourt to
> John Stuart. [Same as C.O. 5/1332/44]. 1p.

> Fol. 15. 6 Nov. 1768, Williamsburg. Gov. Botetourt to
> Col. Andrew Lewis. [Same as C.O. 5/1332/44]. 1p.

> Fol. 16. 6 Nov. 1768, Williamsburg. Gov. Botetourt to
> Mr. Calloway. [Same as C.O. 5/1332/45]. 1p.

> Fol. 16. 6 Nov. 1768, Williamsburg. Gov. Botetourt to
> Israel Christian. [Same as C.O. 5/1332/45]. 1p.

Fol. 30. 24 Dec. 1768, Williamsburg. Gov. Botetourt to [Earl
of Hillsborough] (duplicate). Stuart's boundary line would
give to the Cherokees land recently purchased from the Six
Nations. 3p. [Enclosures to fol. 51b].

> Fol. 32. 14 Dec. 1768, Williamsburg. Dr. Thomas Walker
> and Col. Andrew Lewis to [Gov. Botetourt] (duplicate).
> Walker and Lewis are sending a report on the conferences
> at Ft. Stanwix with the Six Nations and at Chiswell's
> Mines with the Cherokees. 4p.

> Fol. 34. 24 Oct. - 5 Nov. 1768, Ft. Stanwix. Duplicate
> of minutes of conference at Ft. Stanwix in which the Six
> Nations cede to the English their land south to the
> Cherokee River. 12p.

> Fol. 40. 5 Nov. 1768, Ft. Stanwix. Duplicate of Treaty
> of Ft. Stanwix in which the Six Nations cede to the English
> their land to the Cherokee R., which is their boundary with
> the Southern Indians. 7p.

C.O. 5/1347 (CONT'D)

Fol. 44. 16 Dec. 1768, Williamsburg. Council Minutes. [Same as C.O. 5/1322/56]. 2p.

Fol. 46. 20 Dec. 1768, [Williamsburg]. Gov. Botetourt to John Stuart (duplicate). The proposed boundary would give the Cherokees land purchased from the Northern Indians at Ft. Stanwix. 3p.

Fol. 48. 20 Dec. 1768, Williamsburg. Instructions from Botetourt to Col. Lewis and Dr. Walker. [Same as C.O. 5/1332/54]. 4p.

Fol. 52. 24 Dec. 1768, Williamsburg. Gov. Botetourt to Earl of Hillsborough (duplicate). Cherokees can be easily persuaded to sell their land at a moderate rate. 2p.

Fol. 56. 1 Mar. 1769, Whitehall. Earl of Hillsborough to Gov. Botetourt (draft). Hillsborough describes the difficulties in continuing the Cherokee boundary line. 3p.

Fol. 58. 11 Feb. 1769, Williamsburg. Gov. Botetourt to Earl of Hillsborough (duplicate). Fauquier would probably have cooperated with Stuart [on the Cherokee boundary line] if he could have. 2p. [Enclosures to fol. 65b].

Fol. 60. 19 Jan. 1769, Charleston. John Stuart to Gov. Botetourt. [Same as C.O. 5/1332/100]. 4p.

Fol. 62. 2 Feb. 1769. Report from Col. Andrew Lewis and Dr. Thos. Walker to Gov. Botetourt. [Same as C.O. 5/1332/102]. 8p.

Fol. 68. 13 May 1769, Whitehall. Earl of Hillsborough to Gov. Botetourt (draft). Hillsborough is sending Stuart a copy of the directions altering the Cherokee boundary. 3p.

Fol. 83. 10 May 1769, Williamsburg. Gov. Botetourt to Earl of Hillsborough. Botetourt is pleased that the King approves his suggestions regarding the [Cherokee] boundary and that the Bd. of Trade will reconsider the issue. 2p. [Enclosures to fol. 88b].

Fol. 89. 12 May 1769, Williamsburg. Gov. Botetourt to Earl of Hillsborough. Botetourt awaits the Bd. of Trade's report on the [Cherokee] boundary. 2p.

Fol. 91. 16 May 1769, Williamsburg. Gov. Botetourt to Earl of Hillsborough. 2p. [Enclosures to fol. 108b].

Fol. 98. 16 Dec. 1768 - 20 May 1769, Williamsburg. Copy of minutes of Council stating that the Cherokee boundary line proposed by Stuart would injure Virginia. Stuart cannot reopen negotiations without authorization from the King. 14p.

C.O. 5/1347 (CONT'D)

Fol. 124. 14 July 1769, Williamsburg. Gov. Botetourt to Earl
of Hillsborough. 2p. [Enclosures to fol. 177b].

Fol. 130. 16 Dec. 1768 - 20 May 1769, Williamsburg.
Minutes of Council. [Same as fol. 98]. 13p.

Fol. 178. 9 Aug. 1769, Williamsburg. Gov. Botetourt to Earl
of Hillsborough. 2p. [Enclosures to fol. 183b].

Fol. 180. 29 July 1769, Frederick County. Adam Stephen
to Gov. Botetourt. Indians supposedly going to war against
the Cherokees received provisions at Ft. Pitt. The Indians
then drove off part of the garrison's cattle. 2p.

Fol. 182. 8 Aug. 1769, [Williamsburg]. Copy of minutes
of Council with news about Botetourt's plans to alter the
Cherokee boundary line. 3p.

Fol. 186. 8 Nov. 1769, Williamsburg. Gov. Botetourt to [Earl
of Hillsborough]. 2p. [Enclosures to fol. 189b].

Fol. 188. [7 Nov. 1769], Williamsburg. The Speech of ...
Baron de Botetourt ... to the General Assembly. [Copy of
C.O. 5/1333/2a.] 4p.

Fol. 190. 9 Nov. 1769, Williamsburg. Gov. Botetourt to Earl
of Hillsborough. 2p. [Enclosures to fol. 198b].

Fol. 192. [9 Nov. 1769], [Williamsburg]. Address from
Council to Botetourt. Botetourt's recommendation concerning the boundary line and other matters will be considered.
2p.

*C.O. 5/1348   VIRGINIA, ORIGINAL CORRESPONDENCE, SEC. OF STATE: 1769-
1770*

Fol. 3. 30 Sept. 1769, Williamsburg. Gov. Botetourt to Earl
of Hillsborough. Botetourt will be disappointed if the House
of Burgesses refuses to pay for the expenses to negotiate
alterations in the Cherokee boundary line. 2p. [Enclosures
to fol. 6b].

Fol. 5. 14 Sept. 1769, Frederick County. Col. Stephen to
Gov. Botetourt (extract). Stephen relates a speech from
White Mingo requesting that Virginians not kill Indians
going south to war. 4p.

Fol. 33. 18 Dec. 1769, Williamsburg. Gov. Botetourt to Earl
of Hillsborough. Hillsborough will hopefully persuade the King
to grant his requests [concerning salt and the boundary line].
2p. [Enclosures to fol. 48b].

Fol. 37. 7 Dec. 1769, Williamsburg. Resolution from House
of Burgesses to ask the governor to confirm any order of
Council to grant lands west of the Allegheny Mtns. between
the N.C. line and the juncture of the Ohio and Miss. Rivers.
2p.

C.O. 5/1348 (CONT'D)

Fol. 38. [Dec. 1769], [Williamsburg]. Memorial from
House of Burgesses to Botetourt. Burgesses suggest
alterations in the Cherokee boundary line. 3p.

Fol. 44. [Dec. 1769], Williamsburg. Address from House
of Burgesses to Botetourt. Burgesses will furnish £2,500
sterling to pay for expenses to alter the Cherokee boundary
line. Burgesses suggest a more extended boundary than that
recommended by the Bd. of Trade. 1p.

Fol. 44. [Dec. 1769], [Williamsburg]. Answer from
Botetourt to House of Burgesses. Botetourt will inform
Hillsborough why a more extended boundary than that recom-
mended by Bd. of Trade is needed. 1p.

Fol. 45. 18 Dec. 1769, Williamsburg. Gov. Botetourt to
John Stuart. House of Burgesses' request for a more
extended [Cherokee] boundary has been sent to Hillsborough.
2p.

Fol. 49. 17 Feb. 1770, Whitehall. Earl of Hillsborough to
Gov. Botetourt (draft). Hillsborough has submitted letters
[containing requests to extend the boundary line] to the King.
4p.

Fol. 73. 22 Feb. 1770, Williamsburg. Gov. Botetourt to Earl
of Hillsborough. Botetourt sends a copy of Stuart's letter and
an extract from Col. Stephen about the Indians' disposition.
2p. [Enclosures to fol. 82b].

Fol. 75. 13 Jan. 1770, Charleston. John Stuart to Gov.
Botetourt (copy). [Same as C.O. 5/71/61]. 4p.

Fol. 77. 8 Feb. 1770, Williamsburg. Gov. Botetourt to
John Stuart (copy). Stuart will probably be ordered to
assist in obtaining the boundary line [from the Cherokees]
that Va. wants. 2p.

Fol. 79. 29 July 1769, Toqueh. Talk from Cherokee
Headmen to John Stuart (abstract). [Same as C.O. 5/70/
295]. 2p.

Fol. 81. 9 Feb. 1770, Winchester. Col. Adam Stephen to
Gov. Botetourt (extract). A well-educated Indian, who
visited London two or three years ago, is explaining
Botetourt's proclamation to the Indians. 3p.

Fol. 99. 12 June 1770, Whitehall. Earl of Hillsborough to
Gov. Botetourt (draft). Bd. of Trade requests information on
the settlement between the mountains and the Great Kanawha R.
to aid in determining the boundary. 4p.

Fol. 107. 31 May 1770, Williamsburg. Gov. Botetourt to Earl
of Hillsborough. House of Burgesses is considering Stuart's
arguments against the Cherokee boundary sought by Virginia.
2p. [Enclosures to fol. 109b].

C.O. 5/1348 (CONT'D)

> Fol. 109. [30 May 1770], [Williamsburg]. Address from
> House of Burgesses to Botetourt and Botetourt's answer.
> Burgesses is more than willing to furnish more information
> concerning the request for a new boundary [with the Chero-
> kees]. 2p.

Fol. 110. 31 July 1770, Whitehall. Earl of Hillsborough to
Gov. Botetourt (draft). Hillsborough has submitted to Council
the address from the House of Burgesses [on salt imports, copper,
money, and the Cherokee boundary line]. 2p.

Fol. 112. 31 July 1770, Whitehall. Earl of Hillsborough to
Gov. Botetourt (draft). Va. government should stop land grants
that violate the Proclamation of 1763. 2p.

Fol. 114. 23 June 1770, Williamsburg. Gov. Botetourt to Earl
of Hillsborough (duplicate). 2p. [Enclosures to fol. 121b].

> Fol. 116. 21 June 1770, Williamsburg. Gov. Botetourt to
> John Stuart (copy). Stuart should begin negotiations with
> the Cherokees for the land cession approved by the King.
> Botetourt needs an itemized estimate of the expenses for
> completing the boundary line. 2p.

> Fol. 118. [16 June 1770], [Williamsburg]. Resolution
> from House of Burgesses. [Same as C.O. 5/1333/35]. 2p.

Fol. 131. 31 July 1770, Williamsburg. Gov. Botetourt to Earl
of Hillsborough. Since the King has entrusted management of
the Indian trade to the colonies, a meeting was held in N.Y. to
regulate the Indian trade; but nothing was decided. 2p.

Fol. 133. 10 Aug. 1770, Williamsburg. Gov. Botetourt to Earl
of Hillsborough. Stuart writes that the cost to purchase
[Cherokee] land will be £400 sterling more than his original
estimate. 2p. [Enclosures to fol. 139b].

> Fol. 135. 12 July 1770, Charleston. John Stuart to Earl
> of Hillsborough (copy). Stuart will meet with the Chero-
> kees in October at Lochaber. Meeting will cost about
> £2,884 sterling. Northern and Southern tribes have asked
> the Cherokees to join a confederacy to prevent encroach-
> ments on their land. 3p.

> Fol. 137. 9 Aug. 1770, Williamsburg. Gov. Botetourt to
> John Stuart (copy). Botetourt sends Stuart the authority
> to draw £2,900 sterling for the running of the boundary.
> Col. Donelson will meet Stuart at Lochaber to observe the
> Indian negotiations and to fix a time for running the
> boundary. 3p.

Fol. 140. 3 Oct. 1770, Whitehall. Earl of Hillsborough to
Gov. Botetourt (draft). Hillsborough is glad that the House of
Burgesses withdrew its request for a more extended boundary.
5p.

C.O. 5/1348 (CONT'D)

Fol. 160. 18 Oct. 1770, [Williamsburg]. Pres. [William]
Nelson to [Earl of Hillsborough]. Land grants west of
Allegheny Mtns. were made prior to 1763 and are thus not
in violation of the law. Cherokee boundary will be completed
in the spring. The new land will undoubtedly be subject to
quitrents. 11p. [Enclosures to fol. 180b].

> Fol. 169. 6 Dec. 1769, [Williamsburg]. Copy of grants
> of lands made since April 1745. Grants include lands
> along the New and Holston Rivers. 13p.

> Fol. 177. 5 Oct. 1770, Mount Vernon. Geo. Washington to
> Gov. Botetourt (copy). Land grant requested by Walpole
> and others will take up most of the land that Va. recently
> voted £2,500 to purchase and survey. 4p.

C.O. 5/1349   VIRGINIA, ORIGINAL CORRESPONDENCE, SEC. OF STATE: 1770-
*   1771*

Fol. 1. 2 Jan. 1771, Whitehall. Earl of Hillsborough to Pres.
Nelson (draft). Government will consider all claims from
bonafide settlers whose land came from grants to the Ohio Co.
or from Dinwiddie's proclamation. 4p.

Fol. 9. 31 Oct. 1770, Virginia. Pres. Nelson to [Earl of
Hillsborough]. Nelson denies that Va. violated the Proclamation
of 1763 by granting land between the Ohio R. and Allegheny
Mountains. 2p. [Enclosures to fol. 12b].

> Fol. 11. 12 Feb. 1755, Virginia. Copy of notice from
> Nathaniel Walthoe stating that grants west of [Alleghany]
> Mountains can be made if they do not exceed 1,000 acres.
> 3p.

Fol. 17. 15 Dec. 1770, Virginia. Pres. Nelson to [Earl of
Hillsborough]. Nelson sends a copy of the Cherokee cession
deed. Cherokee line is six miles further east of Long Island
on the Holston R. than planned. 3p. [Enclosures to fol. 23b].

> Fol. 19. 18 Oct. 1770, Lochaber. [Cherokee] Deed of
> Cession (copy). Signatories include Oconostota, Kittagusta,
> Attakullakulla, Keyaloy, Kennatitah, Ugey Yuley, Chukanunta,
> Skiagusta Tuechkee Wolf of Keowee, Skiagusta Tiftoy,
> Terrapin, Eury of Tugalo, Scalelosky and Chinistah of
> Sugar Town, Chinistah of Watoga, and Otasite of Hiwassee.
> 2p.

> Fol. 20. 25 Oct. 1770, Lochaber. John Stuart to Gov.
> Botetourt (copy). Cherokees would not give up Long Island.
> Cherokees added six miles to the line suggested by Hills-
> borough and offered compensation elsewhere. Stuart,
> however, had no authority to accept the offer. 3p.

> Fol. 22. 12 Dec. 1770, Williamsburg. Copy of minutes
> of Council reporting Col. John Donelson's return from the
> Cherokee Treaty meeting at Lochaber. 3p.

C.O. 5/1349 (CONT'D)

Fol. 24.   15 Dec. 1770, Virginia.   Pres. Nelson to Earl of
Hillsborough.   2p.   [Enclosures to fol. 37b].

> Fol. 29.   6 Aug. 1770, [Williamsburg].   Copy of minutes of
> Council containing Stuart's letter about the steps leading
> up to meeting the Cherokees at Lochaber for the land
> cession.   The meeting will cost £2,884 sterling.   2p.

> Fol. 29b.   17 Aug. 1770, [Williamsburg].   Copy of minutes
> of Council in which a letter (14 June 1770) from
> Oconostota was read.   Cherokees would like to give some
> land to Richard Pearis and Jacob Hite, but Stuart opposes
> this.   Cherokees would also like to meet at the Holston
> R. rather than in Carolina to discuss the sale of the
> Holston land.   Col. Lewis discussed the Cherokee meeting.
> 4p.

> Fol. 32.   20 Oct. 1770, [Williamsburg].   Copy of minutes
> of Council recording the decision not to give a further
> explanation to Bd. of Trade about grants west of Alleghany
> Mountains.   2p.

> Fol. 33b.   31 Oct. 1770, [Williamsburg].   Copy of minutes
> of Council in which a memorial from Thomas Bullitt was
> read about land promised to veterans for their military
> service.   2p.

Fol. 38.   19 Dec. 1770, Virginia.   Pres. Nelson to [Earl of
Hillsborough].   Nelson has no additional information regarding
the progress of the Cherokee boundary.   3p.

Fol. 44.   11 Feb. 1771, Whitehall.   Earl of Hillsborough to
Pres. Nelson (draft).   Hillsborough is pleased that Va. approved
Stuart's conduct in settling the Cherokee line.   New regulations
will hopefully be made to prevent future violations of the
treaty.   4p.

Fol. 56.   5 Feb. 1771.   Pres. Nelson to Earl of Hillsborough.
Nelson orders commissioners to establish new Indian trade
regulations.   3p.   [Enclosures to fol. 65b].

> Fol. 58.   5 Mar. 1770, Philadelphia.   Lt. Gov. Penn to
> Gov. Botetourt (copy).   All the colonies must agree to
> the new Indian trade regulations.   1p.

> Fol. 58.   24 Mar. 1770, Williamsburg.   Gov. Botetourt to
> Lt. Gov. Penn (copy).   Botetourt will submit plans to the
> Assembly for establishing new Indian trade regulations.
> 1p.

> Fol. 58b.   21 Apr. 1770, Philadelphia.   Lt. Gov. Penn to
> Gov. Botetourt (copy).   The meeting to establish new Indian
> trade regulations will be held in N. York.   1p.

C.O. 5/1349 (CONT'D)

Fol. 58b. 13 Mar. 1770, Quebec. Guy Carleton to Lt. Gov. Colden (copy). All the colonies must agree to the new Indian trade regulations. 2p.

Fol. 59. 16 Apr. 1770, N. York. Lt. Gov. Colden to Lt. Gov. Penn (copy). The meeting to establish the Indian trade regulations will be held in N. York in July. 1p.

Fol. 64. 21, 22, and 30 May 1770. Extracts from the Journal of the House of Burgesses recording that an act was passed to appoint commissioners for the meeting to regulate the Indian trade. 4p.

Fol. 72. 27 Feb. 1771, Virginia. Pres. Nelson to Earl of Hillsborough. Nelson has not heard when the next meeting to establish Indian trade regulations will be held. 2p. [Enclosures to fol. 79b].

Fol. 75. 11 July 1770, Spring Hill. Lt. Gov. Colden to Richard Bland and Patrick Henry (copy). Commissioners from Quebec cannot attend the meeting to establish new Indian trade regulations. 1p.

Fol. 76. 24 Mar. 1770, Williamsburg. Gov. Botetourt to Lt. Gov. Penn. [Same as fol. 58]. 1p.

Fol. 76b. 9 May 1770, Annapolis. Gov. Robt. Eden to Lt. Gov. Penn (copy). Eden has received no official word that the Indian trade is to be regulated by the colonies. 1p.

Fol. 77. 30 May 1770, Quebec. Guy Carleton to Lt. Gov. Colden (copy). Commissioners to establish the Indian trade regulations cannot meet before November. 1p.

Fol. 78. 28 June 1770, Philadelphia. Lt. Gov. Penn to Lt. Gov. Colden (copy). Penn. commissioners are not authorized to transact business on Indian affairs unless all the commissioners are present. 2p.

Fol. 87. 17 Apr. 1771, Virginia. Pres. Nelson to [Earl of Hillsborough]. Nelson is pleased that consideration will be given to bonafide settlers whose land came from Ohio Company grants. 4p.

Fol. 91. 18 May 1771, Virginia. Pres. Nelson to [Earl of Hillsborough]. Export taxes this summer will help the treasury unless expenses for running Cherokee line become too heavy. 2p. [Enclosures to fol. 93b].

Fol. 98. 27 May 1771, Virginia. Pres. Nelson to Earl of Hillsborough. The Cherokee-Va. line is hopefully progressing. 4p.

Fol. 107. 1 July 1771, Virginia. Pres. Nelson to Earl of Hillsborough. The meeting to draw up an Indian trade plan will be held in N.Y. in December. 2p.

C.O. 5/1349 (CONT'D)

Fol. 117. 26 July 1771, Virginia. Pres. Nelson to [Earl of Hillsborough]. 2p. [Enclosures to fol. 170b].

Fol. 122. 12 Dec. 1770, [Williamsburg]. Minutes of Council. [Same as fol. 22]. 2p.

Fol. 123. 14 Dec. 1770, [Williamsburg]. Copy of minutes of Council reporting that Col. Donelson should draw a payment for the purchase of provisions to mark the Cherokee line. 1p.

Fol. 123. 8 Jan. 1771, [Williamsburg]. Copy of minutes of Council reporting Hillsborough's belief that the Cherokees will not accept the line proposed by the House of Burgesses. 2p.

Fol. 124. 1 Feb. 1771, [Williamsburg]. Copy of minutes of Council stating that the colonies will meet to determine the Indian trade regulations. 2p.

Fol. 124b. 4 Mar. 1771, [Williamsburg]. Copy of minutes of Council reporting Stuart's claims that Va. still owes money for the Cherokee treaty. 3p.

Fol. 128. 12 Apr. 1771, [Williamsburg]. Copy of minutes of Council reporting that Hillsborough believes that bonafide settlers with grants from the Ohio Company will be granted compensation. 3p.

Fol. 129. 17 Apr. 1771, [Williamsburg]. Copy of minutes of Council reporting that Col. Donelson needs money to purchase goods for marking the Cherokee boundary. 3p.

Fol. 130b. 30 Apr. 1771, Williamsburg. Copy of minutes of Council recording the council's refusal to pay Alex. Cameron's bills from running the boundary line. 2p.

Fol. 140. 13 July 1771, Williamsburg. Copy of minutes of Council reporting that the young Cherokees are discontented with the Lochaber Treaty. 2p.

Fol. 173. 3 Oct. 1771, Williamsburg. Gov. Dunmore to Earl of Hillsborough. Plans for regulating the Indian trade will hopefully be made soon in order to end Indian discontent. 3p.

C.O. 5/1350   VIRGINIA, ORIGINAL CORRESPONDENCE, SEC. OF STATE: 1771-1772

Fol. 19. Mar. 1772, Williamsburg. Gov. Dunmore to Earl of Hillsborough. Dunmore describes the Cherokee boundary. The line includes more than Hillsborough wanted but less than what Va. desired. 8p. [Enclosures to fol. 40b].

C.O. 5/1350 (CONT'D)

Fol. 27. [ca. Nov. 1771 - Jan. 1772]. Talk from Attakullakulla and Chickasaw Mankiller to Col. Donelson.
Cherokees request trade with Virginia. 2p.

Fol. 28. 17 July 1771 - 8 Feb. 1772. Copy of journals
of Council containing Capt. Donelson's report on the
Cherokee boundary line and some bills. 13p.

Fol. 44. 6 June 1772, Whitehall. Earl of Hillsborough to
Gov. Dunmore (draft). Cherokee boundary changes are very
serious. 3p.

*C.O. 5/1351   VIRGINIA, ORIGINAL CORRESPONDENCE, SEC. OF STATE: 1772-
1773*

Fol. 1. 16 Nov. 1772, Williamsburg. Gov. Dunmore to Earl of
Dartmouth. Dunmore refers to a letter (20 Mar. 1772) containing
an account of running the Va. boundary line with the Cherokees.
He sends a map and a talk from the chiefs present at the marking.
13p.

C.O. 5/1352   ORIGINAL CORRESPONDENCE, SEC. OF STATE: 1774

Fol. 71. 16 May 1774, Williamsburg. Gov. Dunmore to Earl of
Dartmouth. Some settlers on the Va. border of Cherokee territory have set up their own government. 8p.

Fol. 116. 8 Sept. 1774, Whitehall. Earl of Dartmouth to Earl
of Dunmore (draft). Any attempt to acquire lands beyond the
Cherokee line will violate the Treaty of Lochaber with the
Cherokees. 8p.

Fol. 121. 9 June 1774, Williamsburg. Gov. Dunmore to Earl of
Dartmouth. No land survey has been allowed beyond the Cherokee
boundary. Dunmore discusses the request for an extension of
the boundary. 5p. [Enclosures to fol. 138b].

*C.O. 5/1353   VIRGINIA ORIGINAL CORRESPONDENCE, SEC. OF STATE: 1774-
1777.*

Fol. 7. 24 Dec. 1774, Williamsburg. Gov. Dunmore to Earl of
Dartmouth. Dunmore describes problems with the western
settlements. He has written Stuart that Cameron should stop
the Virginians from purchasing [Cherokee] land south and west
of the last boundary. 65p. [Enclosures to fol. 83b].

Fol. 40. 5 Apr. 1774, Williamsburg. Gov. Dunmore to
John Stuart (copy). Cameron should stop Virginians from
purchasing [Cherokee] land south and west of the last
boundary. 3p.

Fol. 42. 4 and 6 Nov. 1771, Williamsburg. Extract of
minutes of Council concerning the land grants to officers
and soldiers promised by Dinwiddie's proclamation of
19 Feb. 1754. 4p.

C.O. 5/1353 (CONT'D)

Fol. 87. 7 Feb. 1775. Gov. Dunmore to Earl of Dartmouth.
Dunmore encloses a letter concerning the attempts [by Henderson
and others] to purchase Cherokee land. 4p. [Enclosures to
fol. 100b].

Fol. 93. 23 Jan. 1775, Fincastle County. Col. Wm. Preston
to Gov. Dunmore (extract). Col. Henderson and other North
Carolinians are trying to purchase land between the Cherokee and Great Kanawha Rivers. Little Carpenter traveled
with Henderson to select goods to purchase this land.
Preston explains the history of claims to the Cherokee
land. 4p.

Fol. 95. 23 Jan. 1775. Gov. Dunmore. A Proclamation
(copy). Dunmore forbids attacks on the Indians and
encroachments on their land. 3p.

Fol. 103. 14 Mar. 1775, Williamsburg. Gov. Dunmore to Earl
of Dartmouth. Dunmore sends Henderson's proposals for settlement of land [purchased from the Cherokees]. If the Crown does
not ratify purchase, Henderson will set up an independent
government. 16p. [Enclosures to fol. 134b].

Fol. 126. 25 Dec. 1774 and 22 Feb. 1775. Proposals for
the Encouragement of Settling the Lands Purchased by ...
Richard Henderson ... from the Cherokees (copy). 6p.

Fol. 129. 21 Mar. 1775. Gov. Dunmore. *A Proclamation*.
Dunmore orders all officers to stop Henderson from
settling Indian lands. 2p.

Fol. 130. 23 Mar. 1775, Williamsburg. Talk from Gov.
Dunmore to Little Carpenter and Cherokee Chiefs (copy).
Land sale to Henderson will not be allowed and the Chero-
kees should ignore any agreements with Henderson. 4p.

C.O. 5/1364   VIRGINIA, ENTRY BOOK OF BD. OF TRADE CORRESPONDENCE:
1713-1717

Fol. 2b. 4 Dec. 1713. Wm. Lowndes to Wm. Popple. Lowndes
encloses a petition for settling the Va. and Carolina boundary.
2p.

Fol. 3. 14 Sept. 1713, Virginia. Lt. Gov. Spotswood to Bd.
of Trade. [Entry letter of C.O. 5/1316/426]. 10p.

Fol. 128b. 9 Aug. 1715, Virginia. Lt. Gov. Spotswood to Bd. of
Trade. Although two tribes have offered aid to Spotswood,
Carolina will still not be able (even with Va. aid) to subdue
all the enemy Indians in the South. 3p.

Fol. 171b. 4 June 1715, Virginia. Lt. Gov. Spotswood to Bd.
of Trade. S.C. had called for aid from many different tribes
to assist them against the Tuscaroras and French. The Indians
that assembled to aid S.C. eventually conspired against that
province. 9p.

C.O. 5/1364 (CONT'D)

Fol. 176. 24 Oct. 1715, Virginia. Lt. Gov. Spotswood to Bd. of Trade. Indians have not appeared along the N.C. frontiers since their last defeat. Northern Indians have ceased their hostilities and have sued for peace. Other Indians will probably soon follow their example. 11p.

Fol. 181b. 16 Feb. 1715/16, Virginia. Lt. Gov. Spotswood to Bd. of Trade. Indians at war with S.C. have asked Va. to mediate peace. Spotswood discusses the boundary between N.C. and Virginia. 10p.

Fol. 193. 9 May 1716, Virginia. Lt. Gov. Spotswood to Bd. of Trade. [Entry letter of C.O. 5/1317/185]. 15p.

C.O. 5/1366   VIRGINIA, ENTRY BOOK OF BD. OF TRADE CORRESPONDENCE: 1728-1752

Fol. 147. 6 Dec. 1738, Whitehall. Bd. of Trade to Lt. Gov. Gooche. Bd. praises Va. for mediating the peace between the Cherokees, Catawbas, and the Five Nations, even though the Cherokees and Catawbas do not live in Virginia. 4p.

Fol. 161b. 5 Sept. 1739, Whitehall. Bd. of Trade to Lt. Gov. Gooche. Bd. has sent a complaint about the Six Nations' hostilities towards the Cherokees to the Gov. of N. York. He has requested that the Commissioners of Indian Affairs investigate the situation. 4p.

Fol. 163b. 18 Oct. 1739, Whitehall. Bd. of Trade to Duke of Newcastle. Bd. sends an extract of a letter about the French expedition against the Southern Indians. 1p.

Fol. 165. 7 Aug. 1740, Whitehall. Bd. of Trade to Lt. Gov. Gooche. Bd. informed Newcastle about a French expedition against the Southern Indians and about the governor of N. York's plans to stop the Six Nations from attacking the Cherokees and other Indians. 3p.

Fol. 229. 1 Sept. 1750, Whitehall. Bd. of Trade to Col. Lee. Bd. fears that the Six Nations are trying to destroy the Catawbas. It is prudent to use Indian assistance in confirming the King's right to lands purchased in the Treaty of Lancaster (1744). 6p.

C.O. 5/1367   VIRGINIA, ENTRY BOOK OF INSTRUCTIONS AND BD. OF TRADE CORRESPONDENCE: 1752-1760

Fol. 3. 17 Jan. 1753, Whitehall. Bd. of Trade to Lt. Gov. Dinwiddie. Bd. has not received the acts, public papers, nor the report from the commissioners who delivered the Indian presents. 3p.

Fol. 10b. 16 Mar. 1753, Whitehall. Bd. of Trade to Earl of Holderness. Dinwiddie reports that the French and the Indian allies have attacked friendly tribes in western Virginia. 3p.

C.O. 5/1367 (CONT'D)

Fol. 12. 16 Mar. 1753, Whitehall. Representation from Bd. of Trade to the King. Bd. submits Dinwiddie's recommendation to build forts along the Ohio R. to protect the English and their Indians. 1p.

Fol. 16. 10 May 1753, Whitehall. Report from Bd. of Trade to Committee of Council for Plantation Affairs. Bd. approves a request to supply cannons for the forts on the Ohio River. 4p.

Fol. 18. 6 June 1753, Whitehall. Bd. of Trade to Lt. Gov. Dinwiddie. Bd. has recommended that cannons be provided for the small forts planned along the Ohio R. for protection against the French. It is important to maintain Indian friendship. 6p.

Fol. 22. 16 Aug. 1753, Whitehall. Bd. of Trade to the King. Dinwiddie reports that the French are building forts along the Ohio River. If they are allowed to continue, the English will lose friendship of the Indians. 4p.

Fol. 24b. 27 Aug. 1753, Whitehall. Sec. John Pownall to Lt. Gov. Dinwiddie. Bd. has warned the King about the French forts along the Ohio and has approved Dinwiddie's attention to Indian affairs. 3p.

Fol. 29b. 4 Apr. 1754, Whitehall. Bd. of Trade to Thomas Robinson. Maj. Washington has been sent to observe the French along the Ohio. 2p.

Fol. 35b. 20 June 1754, Whitehall. Bd. of Trade to Committee of Council. Bd. recommends that settlements be made west of the [Allegheny] Mtns. to protect against the French and to secure Indian friendship. 7p.

Fol. 39. 25 June 1754, Whitehall. Bd. of Trade to Committee of Council for Plantation Affairs. Bd. discusses the Ohio Company's request for more land along the Ohio and Great Kanawha Rivers. 12p.

Fol. 48. 3 July 1754, Whitehall. Bd. of Trade to Lt. Gov. Dinwiddie. No fee should be charged for land grants west of the Alleghenies. 7p.

Fol. 52b. 4 July 1754, Whitehall. Bd. of Trade to Lt. Gov. Dinwiddie. Although the Southern Indians should not be neglected, the Six Nations are the only dependable allies against the French. 7p.

Fol. 59. 6 Aug. 1754, Whitehall. Bd. of Trade to Committee of Council. Bd. has prepared instructions for Gov. Albemarle to remit quitrents on land grants west of the [Allegheny] Mountains. 2p.

C.O. 5/1367 (CONT'D)

Fol. 60. 27 Aug. 1754, Kensington. Instructions from the King
to Gov. Albemarle. The King orders the quitrents on land
grants west of [Allegheny] Mountains to be remitted. Grants
should not exceed 1,000 acres. 5p.

Fol. 65b. 18 Apr. 1755, Whitehall. Bd. of Trade to Lt. Gov.
Dinwiddie. Land grants west of Allegheny Mtns. are exempt from
quitrents and should also be fee exempt. 6p.

Fol. 83b. 17 Feb. 1756, Whitehall. Bd. of Trade to Lt. Gov.
Dinwiddie. The commissioners will hopefully persuade the
Southern Indians to join the English against the French. 4p.

Fol. 88b. 17 Mar. 1756, Whitehall. Bd. of Trade to the King. 3p.
[Enclosures to fol. 144b].

> Fol. 91. [ca. Mar.] 1756. Instructions from the King to
> the Earl of Loudoun. Loudoun should encourage trade with
> the Western Indians and prevent purchases of Indian land.
> 105p.

Fol. 147a. 21 Jan. 1757, Whitehall. Bd. of Trade to Wm. Pitt.
Va. assembly voted £2,000 to garrison a fort among the Cherokees and £3,000 more for presents to the Indians who defend
the frontiers. 18p.

Fol. 156b. 10 Mar. 1757, Whitehall. Bd. of Trade to Lt. Gov.
Dinwiddie. The officer sent to the Cherokees will hopefully gain
their assistance, but the Cherokees are probably more inclined
to join the French. 3p.

Fol. 170. 14 July 1758, Whitehall. John Pownall to Samuel
Martin. Bd. of Trade is unable to give an opinion on the
memorial from Byrd and Randolph, who negotiated a treaty with
the Cherokees. 2p.

Fol. 181. 1 Mar. 1759, Whitehall. Bd. of Trade to Lords of
Treasury. Abercromby requests £3,500 for the Western Indians,
the same amount granted for the Southern Indians. 5p.

Fol. 202. 13 June 1760, Whitehall. Bd. of Trade to Lt. Gov.
Fauquier. In the Treaty of Easton, the English relinquished
to the Indians all rights to the land west of great mountains.
As a result, why has Fauquier encouraged settlement there? 8p.

C.O. 5/1368   VIRGINIA, ENTRY BOOK OF INSTRUCTIONS AND BD. OF TRADE
*   CORRESPONDENCE: 1760-1768*

Fol. 127. 1 Mar. 1765, Whitehall. Bd. of Trade to Lt. Gov.
Fauquier. [Entry letter of C.O. 5/1336/46]. 2p.

Fol. 129. 27 Aug. 1765, Whitehall. Representation from Bd.
of Trade to the King. [Entry letter of C.O. 5/1336/50]. 10p.
[Enclosures to fol. 135b].

C.O. 5/1367 (CONT'D)

>   Fol. 134. Appendix containing a list of letters sent to
>   and about the Cherokees. 4p.

>   Fol. 136. 27 Sept. 1765, Whitehall. Bd. of Trade to the King.
>   [Entry letter of C.O. 5/1336/56]. 3p.

>   Fol. 144. 29 Nov. 1765, Whitehall. Bd. of Trade to Lt. Gov.
>   Fauquier. [Entry letter of C.O. 5/1336/67]. 4p.

*C.O. 5/1369   VIRGINIA, ENTRY BOOK OF INSTRUCTIONS AND BD. OF TRADE
            CORRESPONDENCE: 1769-1775*

>   Fol. 126. 29 Apr. 1772, Whitehall. Bd. of Trade to Lords of
>   Committee of Council. [Entry letter of C.O. 5/1336/229]. 45p.

*C.O. 5/1370   VIRGINIA, ABSTRACTS OF LETTERS TO BD. OF TRADE: 1704-
            1753*

>   Fol. 18b. 24 June 1708, [Virginia]. Col. Jennings to [Bd. of
>   Trade]. S.C. seized the Indian traders' goods from Virginia.
>   5p.

>   Fol. 21b. 27 Nov. 1708, [Virginia]. Col. Jennings to [Bd.
>   of Trade]. Jennings forwards a memorial from Wm. and Mary
>   College complaining about Carolina's seizure of the Indian
>   traders' goods. 3p.

>   Fol. 22b. 8 Oct. 1709, [Virginia]. Col. Jennings to [Bd. of
>   Trade]. [Abstract of C.O. 5/1316/113]. 2p.

>   Fol. 24. 24 Apr. 1710, [Virginia]. Col. Jennings to [Bd. of
>   Trade]. [Abstract of C.O. 5/1316/141]. 1p.

>   Fol. 24b. [1710], [Virginia]. Col. Jennings to [Bd. of Trade].
>   Jennings has appointed the commissioners for settling the
>   boundary [with Carolina]. 1p.

>   Fol. 27. 24 Oct. 1710, [Virginia]. Lt. Gov. Spotswood to
>   [Bd. of Trade]. Some Indian nations are requesting mediation
>   with Carolina over lands reserved for the Indians in 1677. 3p.

>   Fol. 28b. 6 Mar. 1710/11, [Virginia]. Lt. Gov. Spotswood to
>   [Bd. of Trade]. Spotswood justifies the delay in settling the
>   Virginia-Carolina boundary. 2p.

>   Fol. 30. 19 Dec. 1710, Virginia. Lt. Gov. Spotswood to [Bd.
>   of Trade]. Spotswood answers the Board's questions concerning
>   the boundaries with Carolina and concerning the Indian traders.
>   3p.

>   Fol. 33. 5 Sept. 1711, Virginia. Lt. Gov. Spotswood to [Bd.
>   of Trade]. [Abstract of C.O. 5/1316/326]. 1p.

>   Fol. 33b. 8 Feb. 1711, [Virginia]. Lt. Gov. Spotswood to Bd.
>   of Trade. While a prisoner, Baron de Graffenreid was forced to
>   agree to a peace with the Indians. 2p.

C.O. 5/1370 (CONT'D)

Fol. 35. 17 Nov. 1711, [Virginia]. Lt. Gov. Spotswood to
[Bd. of Trade]. Spotswood persuaded the tributary Indians to
send their children to college by remitting their tribute of
skins. 2p.

Fol. 35b. 8 May 1712, [Virginia]. Lt. Gov. Spotswood to
[Bd. of Trade]. [Abstract of C.O. 5/1316/341]. 3p.

Fol. 37. 15 May 1712, [Virginia]. Lt. Gov. Spotswood to
[Bd. of Trade]. Spotswood refers to his letter to N. Carolina's
governor about settling the boundaries. 1p.

Fol. 37b. 26 July 1712, [Virginia]. Lt. Gov. Spotswood to Bd.
of Trade. Trade with the Western Indians (closed since last
October) is now open. 3p.

Fol. 38b. 15 Oct. 1712, [Virginia]. Lt. Gov. Spotswood to Bd.
of Trade. [Abstract of C.O. 5/1316/384]. 2p.

Fol. 39. 11 Feb. 1712/13, [Virginia]. Lt. Gov. Spotswood to
[Bd. of Trade]. [Abstract of C.O. 5/1316/390]. 3p.

Fol. 40b. 2 June 1713, [Virginia]. Lt. Gov. Spotswood to Bd.
of Trade. Boundary negotiations with Carolina have stopped.
2p.

Fol. 42. 16 Nov. 1713, [Virginia]. Lt. Gov. Spotswood to
[Bd. of Trade]. Spotswood sent 50 tributary Indians to mediate
a peace with the Tuscaroras. 2p.

Fol. 43b. 25 Oct. 1714, [Virginia]. Lt. Gov. Spotswood to
[Bd. of Trade]. Spotswood went to settle the Indians and quiet
the frontier. 1p.

Fol. 44b. 28 Mar. 1715, [Virginia]. Lt. Gov. Spotswood to
[Bd. of Trade]. New method for guarding the frontier has
prevented mischief. Spotswood hopes to meet deputies from
some of the remote Indians. 1p.

Fol. 44b. 4 June 1715, [Virginia]. Lt. Gov. Spotswood to [Bd.
of Trade]. Spotswood has complied with the S.C. governor's
request for ammunition to fight the Indians. 2p.

Fol. 45. 15 July 1715 [Virginia]. Lt. Gov. Spotswood to [Bd.
of Trade]. Many powerful Indian nations have attacked S. Carolina. Va. is sending troops and supplies. 2p.

Fol. 46. 9 Aug. 1715, [Virginia]. Lt. Gov. Spotswood to
[Bd. of Trade]. Two Indian nations have offered their assistance
against Indian attacks in S. Carolina. 1p.

Fol. 46. 24 Oct. 1715, [Virginia]. Lt. Gov. Spotswood to Bd.
of Trade. Spotswood rejected the Indian overtures for peace.
2p.

C.O. 5/1370 (CONT'D)

Fol. 46b. 16 Feb. 1715/16, [Virginia]. Lt. Gov. Spotswood
to [Bd. of Trade]. Indians at war with Carolina have applied
to Va. for peace. Va. sells cheaper goods to those Indians
whose children are instructed in Christianity. 3p.

Fol. 48. 9 May 1716, [Virginia]. Lt. Gov. Spotswood to [Bd.
of Trade]. [Abstract of C.O. 5/1317/185]. 4p.

Fol. 49b. 23 May 1716, [Virginia]. Lt. Gov. Spotswood to
[Bd. of Trade]. S. Carolina's government mistreated the Va.
soldiers who aided S.C. in the recent Indian war. 3p.

Fol. 52b. [1717?], [Virginia]. Lt. Gov. Spotswood to [Bd. of
Trade]. Spotswood is pleased that measures for educating the
Indian children was approved. Frontiersmen are not likely to
improve Indian morals. Unlike the French, the English are not
inclined to marry Indians. 2p.

Fol. 53b. 6 Apr. 1717, [Virginia]. Lt. Gov. Spotswood to
[Bd. of Trade]. Spotswood comments on the Indian Trade Act. 2p.

Fol. 54b. 29 Aug. 1717, [Virginia]. Lt. Gov. Spotswood to
[Bd. of Trade]. Spotswood reports on negotiations with the
Western Indians to restore peace in Carolina. 3p.

Fol. 55b. 27 Feb. 1717/18, [Virginia]. Lt. Gov. Spotswood to
[Bd. of Trade]. Trade with the foreign Indians continues. 3p.

Fol. 66. 27 Sept. 1718, [Virginia]. Lt. Gov. Spotswood to
[Bd. of Trade]. There are new Indian hostilities in N. Carolina.
2p.

Fol. 66b. 22 Dec. 1718, [Virginia]. Lt. Gov. Spotswood to
[Bd. of Trade]. Spotswood denies rumors that the French plan
to cut off the Indians from the English. 4p.

Fol. 71b. 11 Aug. 1719, [Virginia]. Lt. Gov. Spotswood to
[Bd. of Trade]. The frontier militia has mobilized to stop
Indian hostility and to renew peace. 5p.

Fol. 73b. 1 Feb. 1719/20, [Virginia]. Lt. Gov. Spotswood to
[Bd. of Trade]. French are now trading with Coosatee [Cussita?]
Indians. French might even trade with the Cherokees since S.C.
stopped their Indian trade because of England's high duty on
furs. 3p.

Fol. 80b. 10 July 1724, [Virginia]. Maj. Drysdale to [Bd. of
Trade]. N. Carolina's governor insists on marking the boundary
according to the 1715 plans. 2p.

Fol. 81b. 31 May 1725, [Virginia]. Lt. Gov. Drysdale to
[Bd. of Trade]. Drysdale wants boundaries between Va. and
Carolina to be settled quickly. 2p.

Fol. 86b. [1727], [Virginia]. Col. Carter to [Bd. of Trade].
Western Indians threaten Virginia's frontier. 1p.

C.O. 5/1370 (CONT'D)

Fol. 86b. 21 Sept. 1727, [Virginia]. Lt. Gov. Gooche to [Bd. of Trade]. Gooche appointed commissioners to settle the boundary with N. Carolina. Col. Harrison has written about Indian hostilities along the frontiers. 1p.

Fol. 87. 12 Feb. 1727/28 [Virginia]. Lt. Gov. Gooche to [Bd. of Trade]. Commissioners were hopefully successful in settling the boundaries with Carolina. The misunderstanding with the Indians is over. 1p.

Fol. 87b. 8 June 1728, [Virginia]. Lt. Gov. Gooche to [Bd. of Trade]. Boundaries between N.C. and Va. should be completed in September. 1p.

Fol. 88b. 26 Mar. 1729, [Virginia]. Lt. Gov. Gooche to [Bd. of Trade]. A quarrel between tributary Indians would unfortunately result in an attack on the English. The boundary with Carolina has been completed. 2p.

Fol. 91b. 23 July 1730, [Virginia]. Lt. Gov. Gooche to Bd. of Trade. Gooche discusses the warrant to pay for running the Va. and N. C. boundary. 8p.

Fol. 102b. 15 July 1733, [Virginia]. Lt. Gov. Gooche to [Bd. of Trade]. The dispute with the tributary Indians has ended. 1p.

Fol. 109. 21 Feb. 1736/37, [Virginia]. Lt. Gov. Gooche to [Bd. of Trade]. Gooche will follow the Board's directions concerning settlements west of the Great Mountains. 2p.

Fol. 111b. 15 Feb. 1738/39, [Virginia]. Lt. Gov. Gooche to [Bd. of Trade]. Gooche reports Virginia's concern in an Indian quarrel. 1p.

Fol. 112. 1 Aug. 1739, [Virginia]. Lt. Gov. Gooche to [Bd. of Trade]. Gooche passes on information about a French expedition against the Southern Indians. 1p.

Fol. 114. 6 Nov. 1740, [Virginia]. Pres. Blair to [Bd. of Trade]. There is peace between the Northern and Southern Indians. 1p.

Fol. 116. 14 Feb. 1742/43, [Virginia]. Lt. Gov. Gooche to Bd. of Trade. Gooche reports a skirmish between the Indians, some whites (supposedly French), and Virginians. 1p.

Fol. 117b. 21 Dec. 1744, [Virginia]. Lt. Gov. Gooche to Bd. of Trade. Gooche sends a copy of the June Indian treaty about purchasing land. 1p.

Fol. 120b. 6 Nov. 1747, [Virginia]. Lt. Gov. Gooche to Bd. of Trade. There are advantages in granting land west of the Great Mountains. 1p.

C.O. 5/1370 (CONT'D)

Fol. 120b. 16 June 1748, [Virginia]. Lt. Gov. Gooche to Bd. of Trade. Gooche answers questions concerning the land grants west of the Great Mountains. 1p.

Fol. 122b. 12 June 1750, [Virginia]. Pres. Lee to Bd. of Trade. Catawbas will not meet the Six Nations at Fredericksburg. Lee believes that future Indian treaties should be made in Virginia. 2p.

Fol. 123. 12 July 1753, [Virginia]. Pres. Lee to [Bd. of Trade]. French have persuaded some tribes to destroy the English Indians. 1p.

Fol. 124b. 21 Aug. 1751, [Virginia]. Pres. Burwell to Bd. of Trade. Ambassador from the Cherokee Emperor has requested that trade be established and promises assistance against the French. 3p.

Fol. 125b. 10 Sept. 1751, London. Lt. Gov. Dinwiddie to Bd. of Trade. Dinwiddie encloses a memorial proposing additional instructions concerning Indian presents. 2p.

Fol. 126b. 5 June 1752, [Williamsburg]. Lt. Gov. Dinwiddie to Bd. of Trade. Dinwiddie has sent commissioners and presents to the Indians. 1p.

Fol. 127. 20 July 1752, [Virginia]. Lt. Gov. Dinwiddie to Bd. of Trade. Commissioners who were sent with presents for the Indians have returned. 1p.

Fol. 128. 10 Dec. 1752, Williamsburg. Lt. Gov. Dinwiddie to Bd. of Trade. Dinwiddie sends an account of the Logstown treaty. 1p.

C.O. 5/1372   VIRGINIA, ENTRY BOOK OF LETTERS TO SEC. OF STATE: 1766-1774

Fol. 1. 19 Feb. 1767, [Whitehall]. [Earl of Shelburne] to Lt. Gov. of Virginia. [Entry letter of C.O. 5/1345/154]. 1p.

Fol. 1. 18 Nov. 1766, Williamsburg. Lt. Gov. Fauquier to [Earl of Shelburne]. [Entry letter of C.O. 5/1345/157]. 1p.

Fol. 1b. 18 Dec. 1766, [Williamsburg]. Lt. Gov. Fauquier to [Earl of Shelburne]. [Entry letter of C.O. 5/1345/169]. 3p.

Fol. 2b. 2 Feb. 1767, [Williamsburg]. Lt. Gov. Fauquier to [Earl of Shelburne]. [Entry letter of C.O. 5/1345/178]. 2p.

Fol. 5. 24 May 1767, Williamsburg. Lt. Gov. Fauquier to Earl of Shelburne. [Entry letter of C.O. 5/1345/186]. 2p.

Fol. 6b. 8 Oct. 1767, [Whitehall]. [Earl of Shelburne] to Lt. Gov. Fauquier. [Entry letter of C.O. 5/1345/193]. 2p.

Fol. 8b. [1768]. Address from House of Burgesses to the King. [George II] authorized land settlements west of the Alleghenies.

Burgesses want to continue settling lands ceded by Indians at
Lancaster in 1744 and confirmed at Logstown in 1752. 3p.

Fol. 12. 21 Mar. 1768, [Williamsburg]. Pres. Blair to [Earl
of Hillsborough]. Blair has asked Wm. Johnson and John Stuart
to set a time for running the boundary. 3p.

Fol. 13b. 10 June 1768, Whitehall. Bd. of Trade to [Earl of
Hillsborough]. Board sends its opinion about an address from
House of Burgesses about settling west of the Great Mountains.
1p. [Enclosures to fol. 17].

    Fol. 13b. 10 June 1768, Whitehall. Bd. of Trade to the
    King. Superintendents of Indian Affairs have met with
    the tribes to run the boundary line. 8p.

Fol. 22. 12 July 1768, Williamsburg. Pres. Blair to [Earl of
Hillsborough]. Blair has sent the commissioners to Wm. Johnson
to discuss running the boundary line. Cameron writes that the
Cherokees wish to meet 25 Oct. at Chiswell's Mines. 3p.

Fol. 23. 20 Sept. 1768, Williamsburg. Pres. Blair to [Earl
of Hillsborough]. There are evidently no Virginians trading
with the Indians at the present. 6p.

Fol. 25b. 27 Sept. 1768, Williamsburg. Pres. Blair to [Earl
of Hillsborough]. Settlers west of the mountains refuse to
pay their taxes since their lands have been returned to the
Indians. Hopefully an agreement can be reached with the Indians
to include those returned lands within Virginia's borders. 8p.

Fol. 34b. 24 Dec. 1768, Williamsburg. Gov. Botetourt to [Earl
of Hillsborough]. [Entry letter of C.O. 5/1347/30]. 4p.

Fol. 36. 24 Dec. 1768, Williamsburg. Gov. Botetourt to [Earl
of Hillsborough]. [Entry letter of C.O. 5/1347/52]. 2p.

Fol. 37b. 11 Feb. 1769, Williamsburg. Gov. Botetourt to [Earl
of Hillsborough]. [Entry letter of C.O. 5/1347/58]. 2p.

Fol. 42. 10 May 1769, Virginia. Gov. Botetourt to [Earl of
Hillsborough]. [Entry of C.O. 5/1347/83]. 2p.

Fol. 42b. 12 May 1769, Williamsburg. Gov. Botetourt to [Earl
of Hillsborough]. [Entry letter of C.O. 5/1347/89]. 2p.

Fol. 43b. 5 Aug. 1769, Williamsburg. Gov. Botetourt to [Earl
of Hillsborough]. Botetourt will submit to the Assembly the
King's order to complete the [Cherokee] boundary. 1p.

Fol. 46. 30 Sept. 1769, Williamsburg. Gov. Botetourt to [Earl
of Hillsborough]. [Entry letter of C.O. 5/1348/3]. 2p.

Fol. 48b. 18 Dec. 1769, Williamsburg. Gov. Botetourt to [Earl
of Hillsborough]. [Entry letter of C.O. 5/1348/33]. 3p.

C.O. 5/1372 (CONT'D)

Fol. 54. 22 Feb. 1770, Williamsburg. Gov. Botetourt to [Earl of Hillsborough]. [Entry letter of C.O. 5/1348/73]. 1p.

Fol. 55b. 31 May 1770, Williamsburg. Gov. Botetourt to [Earl of Hillsborough]. [Entry letter of C.O. 5/1348/107]. 2p.

Fol. 57b. 31 July 1770, Williamsburg. Gov. Botetourt to [Earl of Hillsborough]. [Entry letter of C.O. 5/1348/131]. 2p.

Fol. 58. 10 Aug. 1770, Williamsburg. Gov. Botetourt to [Earl of Hillsborough]. [Entry letter of C.O. 5/1348/133]. 1p.

Fol. 62b. 18 Oct. 1770, Virginia. Pres. Nelson to [Earl of Hillsborough]. [Entry letter of C.O. 5/1333/77]. 13p.

Fol. 72b. 31 Oct. 1770, Virginia. Pres. Nelson to [Earl of Hillsborough]. [Entry letter of C.O. 5/1349/9]. 2p.

Fol. 77. 15 Dec. 1770, Virginia. Pres. Nelson to [Earl of Hillsborough]. [Entry letter of C.O. 5/1349/24]. 3p.

Fol. 78b. 19 Dec. 1770, Virginia. Pres. Nelson to [Earl of Hillsborough]. [Entry letter of C.O. 5/1349/38]. 3p.

Fol. 80. 5 Feb. 1771, Virginia. Pres. Nelson to [Earl of Hillsborough]. [Entry letter of C.O. 5/1349/56]. 4p.

Fol. 82. 27 Feb. 1771, Virginia. Pres. Nelson to [Earl of Hillsborough]. [Entry letter of C.O. 5/1349/72]. 3p.

Fol. 84b. 17 Apr. 1771, Virginia. Pres. Nelson to [Earl of Hillsborough]. Entry letter of C.O. 5/1349/87]. 3p.

Fol. 86. 18 May 1771, Virginia. Pres. Nelson to [Earl of Hillsborough]. [Entry litter of C.O. 5/1349/91]. 1p.

Fol. 87. 27 May 1771, Virginia. Pres. Nelson to Earl of Hillsborough. [Entry letter of C.O. 5/1349/98]. 4p.

Fol. 89. 1 July 1771, Virginia. Pres. Nelson to Earl of Hillsborough. [Entry letter of C.O. 5/1349/107]. 2p.

Fol. 93. 3 Oct. 1771, Williamsburg. Gov. Dunmore to Earl of Hillsborough. [Entry letter of C.O. 5/1349/173]. 3p.

Fol. 97. Mar. 1772, Williamsburg. Gov. Dunmore to Earl of Hillsborough. [Entry letter of C.O. 5/1350/19]. 7p.

Fol. 106. 16 Nov. 1772, Williamsburg. Gov. Dunmore to Earl of Dartmouth. [Entry letter of C.O. 5/1351/1]. 10p.

C.O. 1373   VIRGINIA, ENTRY BOOK OF LETTERS TO SEC. OF STATE: 1774-
1777

Fol. 5b. 16 May 1774, Williamsburg. Gov. Dunmore to [Earl of Dartmouth]. [Entry letter of C.O. 5/1352/71]. 5p.

C.O. 5/1373 (CONT'D)

Fol. 11. 9 June 1774, Williamsburg. Gov. Dunmore to [Earl
of Dartmouth]. [Entry letter of C.O. 5/1352/121]. 4p.

Fol. 15. 24 Dec. 1774, Williamsburg. Gov. Dunmore to [Earl
of Dartmouth]. [Entry letter of C.O. 5/1353/7]. 75p.

Fol. 52b. 7 Feb. 1775, Williamsburg. Gov. Dunmore to [Earl
of Dartmouth]. [Entry letter of C. O. 5/1353/87]. 4p.

Fol. 54b. 14 Mar. 1775, Williamsburg. Gov. Dunmore to [Earl
of Dartmouth]. [Entry letter of C.O. 5/1353/103]. 18p.

C.O. 1374   VIRGINIA, ENTRY BOOK OF LETTERS FROM SEC. OF STATE: 1767

Fol. 4. 14 Nov. 1767, Whitehall. Earl of Shelburne to Lt.
Gov. Fauquier. [Entry letter of C.O. 5/1345/196]. 2p.

*C.O. 5/1375   VIRGINIA, ENTRY BOOK OF LETTERS FROM SEC. OF STATE: 1768-
1776*

Fol. 37. 1 Mar. 1769, Whitehall. Earl of Hillsborough to Gov.
Botetourt. [Entry letter of C.O. 5/1347/56]. 3p.

Fol. 38. 13 May 1769, Whitehall. Earl of Hillsborough to Gov.
Botetourt. [Entry letter of C.O. 5/1347/68]. 2p.

Fol. 45b. 17 Feb. 1770, Whitehall. Earl of Hillsborough to
Gov. Botetourt. [Entry letter of C.O. 5/1348/49]. 3p.

Fol. 49b. 12 June 1770, Whitehall. Earl of Hillsborough to
Gov. Botetourt. [Entry letter of C.O. 5/1348/99]. 3p.

Fol. 51. 31 July 1770, Whitehall. Earl of Hillsborough to
Gov. Botetourt. [Entry letter of C.O. 5/1348/110]. 2p.

Fol. 51b. 31 July 1770, Whitehall. Earl of Hillsborough to
Gov. Botetourt. [Entry letter of C.O. 5/1348/112]. 2p.

Fol. 53b. 3 Oct. 1770, Whitehall. Earl of Hillsborough to
Gov. Botetourt. [Entry letter of C.O. 5/1348/140]. 4p.

Fol. 73b. 2 Jan. 1771, Whitehall. Earl of Hillsborough to
Gov. Botetourt. [Entry letter of C.O. 5/1349/1]. 4p.

Fol. 75. 11 Feb. 1771, Whitehall. Earl of Hillsborough to
Pres. Nelson. [Entry letter of C.O. 5/1349/44]. 3p.

Fol. 76. 11 Feb. 1771, Whitehall. Earl of Hillsborough to
Gov. Botetourt. [Entry letter of C.O. 5/1349/44]. 3p.

Fol. 85b. 6 June 1772, Whitehall. Earl of Hillsborough to
Gov. Dunmore. [Entry letter of C.O. 5/1350/44]. 2p.

Fol. 104b. 8 Sept. 1774, Whitehall. Earl of Dartmouth to Gov.
Dunmore. [Entry letter of C.O. 5/1352/116]. 5p.

C.O. 5/1429   VIRGINIA, SESSIONAL PAPERS, COUNCIL AND ASSEMBLY: 1752-
1760

Fol. 13. 11 Nov. 1752, Virginia. Minutes of Council containing
speech of the Cherokee Emperor (Ammonscossitte), who requests
more trade with Va. since S.C. has neglected the tribe. 5p.

Fol. 16. 12 Apr. 1751, Virginia. Minutes of Council recording
that the differences between the Cherokee Emperor and Samuel
Stalnaker have been settled. 2p.

Fol. 20b. 22 May 1753, Virginia. Minutes of Council recording
that the Governor was advised to warn the Cherokees and Catawbas
against the designs of the French and their Indian allies. 3p.

Fol. 29. 24 Aug. 1753, Virginia. Minutes of Council recording
that the Governor was advised to send Col. Fairfax a message
containing information from the Cherokees and Catawbas which
would convince the Winchester Indians that the Southern Indians
are firmly opposed to settlements along the Ohio River. 3p.

Fol. 30b. 17 Oct. 1753, Virginia. Minutes of Council recording
that Henry Morris will be paid £50 for his journey to the
Cherokees and Catawbas. The Cherokees and Catawbas were
requested to invite the Chickasaws to a Winchester meeting
next May. 2p.

Fol. 47b. 17 Apr. 1754, Virginia. Minutes of Council recording that the Governor has received letters from the Cherokees
and Catawbas indicating their willingness to fight the enemy
if they are given ammunition. 2p.

Fol. 48b. 24 Apr. 1754, Virginia. Minutes of Council recording
information from John Patten, a trader among the Indians west
of the Appalachian Mountains, about French forts along the Ohio
and the Lakes. 2p.

Fol. 93. 10 June 1756, Virginia. Minutes of Council recording
information from Maj. Andrew Lewis who writes that provisions
have arrived and that he will march to the Cherokee nation.
Cherokees have trespassed on Va. land and their conduct will
be investigated. 2p.

Fol. 93b. 28 June 1756. Minutes of Council recording the
auditor's report that the expense accounts for recent treaties
with the Catawbas and Cherokees are correct. 3p.

Fol. 96. 20 Sept. 1756, Virginia. Minutes of Council recording
information from Maj. Lewis who writes in July from Chote that
he expects to finish the fort within 12-15 days. Indians have
promised to send at least 100 men [to aid Va.], but Lewis expects
more. 1p.

Fol. 96b. 11 Oct. 1756, Virginia. Minutes of Council recording
the Earl of Loudoun's approval of securing a post in Cherokee
country. 1p.

C.O. 5/1429 (CONT'D)

Fol. 98b. 15 Dec. 1756, Virginia. Minutes of Council recording
information from Lyttleton who hopes that the talk he had with
Cherokees in Charleston will be productive. He will request
again that the Cherokees and Catawbas join the Virginians.
Capt. Demeré will act as English agent to the Cherokees. 1p.

Fol. 99b. 20 Jan. 1757, Virginia. Minutes of Council recording
information that the Cherokees' friendship towards the English
is doubtful. Governor wants advice on how to win the tribe
over and how to defeat the French designs. Troops should be
sent to garrison the fort built in Cherokee country. 2p.

Fol. 101. 18 Mar. 1757, Virginia. Minutes of Council containing talks from Keerarustikee and Second Yellowbird. Keerarustikee, a principal Cherokee Warrior, is returning home to raise
more men to assist the English. If he meets Swallow Warrior,
he will proceed immediately to war. Second Yellowbird with
another party of Cherokees is also returning home to recruit
more warriors. 3p.

Fol. 102b. 22 Mar. 1757, Virginia. Minutes of Council containing Council's opinion that Va. should jail the French prisoner
taken by the Cherokees if the Cherokees release him. 2p.

Fol. 103. 4 Apr. 1757, Virginia. Minutes of Council containing
agreement that Va. should send 100 men to garrison Ft. Loudoun,
50 men to Ft. Enoch to secure communications between Ft.
Loudoun and Ft. Cumberland, and 100 men to the new fort in
Cherokee country. The Tuscaroras have made peace with the
Cherokees, Catawbas, and Nottoways. 5p.

Fol. 105. 11 Apr. 1757, Virginia. Minutes of Council containing information from Col. Read who writes about the Cherokees'
misbehavior and the Catawbas' excellent conduct around Lunenburg.
1p.

Fol. 105b. 14 Apr. 1757, Virginia. Minutes of Council containing Council's advice that the wife of the murdered Chickasaw
(killed by the Cherokees) should be brought to Williamsburg
before going to S. Carolina. 1p.

Fol. 106. 3 May 1757, Virginia. Minutes of Council containing
information from Capt. Mercer who writes from Ft. Loudoun about
the Cherokees' conduct. 1p.

Fol. 106b. 7 May 1757, Virginia. Minutes of Council containing information that Edm. Atkin will visit Winchester with
presents needed to prevent future Indian misconduct. Col.
Read has sent some depositions concerning the Cherokee's rape
of Waller's daughter. 3p.

Fol. 108b. 24 May 1757, Virginia. Minutes of Council recording
that the Governor desires the Board's opinion on Atkin's proposals to encourage more Southern Indian assistance. 2p.

C.O. 5/1429 (CONT'D)

Fol. 112. 20 June 1757, Virginia. Minutes of Council containing information from Atkin who writes that Wauhatchee [Wawha-
hatchee?] and his party set off to war again. Atkin wants to
send for more Cherokees. Col. Washington reports that the
Cherokees killed a French prisoner in revenge for Swallow
Warrior's death. 1p.

Fol. 112b. 22 Sept. 1757, Virginia. Minutes of Council recording that the Cherokee Emperor complains about the lack of a
garrison for the Cherokee fort and the lack of promised trade.
Cherokees can be assured that goods and a sufficient garrison
will be there shortly. 2p.

Fol. 115. 14 Oct. 1757, Virginia. Minutes of Council containing information from Atkin who writes that he has established
the same regulations with the Cherokees as with the Catawbas.
Richard Smith has been apointed a Cherokee interpreter. 1p.

Fol. 117b. 12 Nov. 1757, Virginia. Minutes of Council containing information from Mr. Gist and Col. Washington. Gist reports
the presence in Winchester of 30 Chote and Tellico Cherokees
returning from pursuing the enemy. Gist has no interpreter
and needs supplies. Washington writes that the Cherokees are
sincere English supporters. 2p.

Fol. 158. 1 Nov. 1759, Virginia. Minutes of General Assembly
containing speech from Lt. Gov. Fauquier who states that Ft.
Loudoun is important as a storehouse depository for Indian goods
and a protection from the enemy. 4p.

Fol. 162. 19 Nov. 1759, Virginia. Minutes of General Assembly
containing protest from Philip Ludwell that the proposed bill
to protect Va. does not consider the Cherokee threats. 3p.

Fol. 163b. 21 Nov. 1759, Virginia. Minutes of General Assembly
containing speech from Fauquier who states that he will protect
the buildings now being erected at Pittsburg, assist Gov.
Lyttleton against the Cherokees in case of war, and secure
Virginia's frontiers. 3p.

Fol. 166. 24 Jan. 1758, Virginia. Minutes of Council recording
information that if Lord Loudoun approves garrisoning the Cherokee fort, Va. will appropriate money for that end. If Loudoun
turns down the fort, Va. will garrison the fort anyway with
60 men in the spring from revenues from goods (valued at
£5,000 sterling) being traded with the Cherokees. 2p.

Fol. 167b. 7 Mar. 1758, Virginia. Minutes of Council containing information that Lord Loudoun has sent Mr. Byrd to obtain
Cherokee aid in defending Virginia. 2p.

Fol. 171b. 19 May 1758, Virginia. Minutes of Council containing information from Col. Byrd who writes from Keowee that 400
Cherokees have gone to Virginia. Although he visited most of
the nation, Byrd has not been able to enlist their help. Byrd
has promised a reward to each warrior who goes to Winchester. 3p.

Fol. 173. 20 May 1758, Virginia. Minutes of Council containing information that on their return home, the Cherokees robbed
and plundered people in Bedford. Cherokees fought the militia,
and both whites and Indians were killed. The Indians may return
from Winchester and take revenge. 1p.

Fol. 173b. 25 May 1758, Virginia. Minutes of Council containing information from Col. Byrd who has arrived at Bedford's
Court House with 57 warriors. He expects Little Carpenter to
arrive with 200 Cherokees in a fortnight. The Cherokees threaten
to take revenge upon returning from Winchester. 2p.

Fol. 174. 2 June 1758, Virginia. Minutes of Council containing
information from Col. Washington who believes that it would be
useful to have 12 to 18 Virginians at Ft. Loudoun to help the
militia complete the fort and watch the stores. 4p.

Fol. 176b. 6 June 1758, Virginia. Minutes of Council containing information from Byrd who is convinced that the Indians he
brought to Winchester will be well behaved. He needs suitable
goods for his Indians, especially wampum and silver ornaments.
1p.

Fol. 179b. 17 Aug. 1758, Virginia. Minutes of Council recording that Lyttleton informed the commandants of the Cherokee
forts about the Indians' engagements with the militia of Halifax
and Bedford. 3p.

Fol. 181. 4 Oct. 1758, Virginia. Minutes of Council recording
that Mr. Martin's reception as a missionary to the Cherokees
was so successful that a second missionary, Rev. Richardson,
will be sent. 1p.

Fol. 182. 12 Oct. 1758, Virginia. Minutes of Council containing information that several parties of the Middle and Lower
Cherokees have vowed revenge against Virginia. Richard Smith
will take a letter to the Cherokees to try to prevent a
rupture. 2p.

Fol. 186. 11 Nov. 1758, Virginia. Minutes of Council recording
that Wade, capt. of a ranger company, will appear before the
governor and council to explain the recent murder of Cherokees
resulting from his orders. 1p.

Fol. 186. 13 Dec. 1758, Virginia. Minutes of Council containing information from Gen. Forbes who describes the infamous
behavior of Little Carpenter. 4p.

Fol. 188. 19 Jan. 1759, Virginia. Minutes of Council recording
that the Little Carpenter talked with the Council about settling
the differences between the Cherokees and Virginia. Little
Carpenter also asked about trade and garrisoning the Cherokee
fort. 3p.

C.O. 5/1429 (CONT'D)

Fol. 189. 20 Jan. 1759. Minutes of Council containing the
governor's speech to Little Carpenter and 14 other Cherokees
in which the governor assured the Indians of his attempts to
preserve their friendship. 3p.

Fol. 190. 23 Jan. 1759, Virginia. Minutes of Council recording that Little Carpenter received a copy of the governor's
speech. Little Carpenter blamed the Conjurer for persuading
him not to aid the English. 2p.

Fol. 190b. 23 Feb. 1759, Virginia. Minutes of Council recording that Lyttleton sent a copy of the minutes from November's
conferences with the Cherokees at Charleston. 2p.

Fol. 193. 17 Apr. 1759, Virginia. Minutes Council recording
that the Little Carpenter wrote on 15 Mar. that his people were
pleased to hear that the differences have been resolved. He
reminded the governor about the promised trade. 1p.

Fol. 194b. 15 June 1759, Virginia. Minutes of Council recording that the society for managing Indian missions and schools
has received Mr. Richardson's journal containing information
on the Cherokee's attitude. Cherokees should receive goods that
include presents for Old Hop and Little Carpenter. 2p.

Fol. 196b. 3 Sept. 1759, Virginia. Minutes of Council containing information from Gov. Lyttleton and Lt. Coytmore. Lyttleton
writes about the Cherokees scalping 19 people along the Yadkin
River. Coytmore reports that the Cherokees only promised some
future compensation for the murders. There was a meeting
between the Creeks and Cherokees. 3p.

Fol. 199b. 12 Dec. 1759, Virginia. Minutes of Council containing information from Lyttleton who writes that traders at
Salisbury will be informed immediately if matters are successfully concluded with the Cherokees. 3p.

Fol. 200b. 21 Feb. 1760, Virginia. Minutes of Council recording that Lyttleton transmits a copy of the peace concluded with
the Cherokees on 26 Dec. 1759. Lt. Coytmore describes the
Cherokees' behavior and asks for reinforcements at Ft. Loudoun.
2p.

Fol. 202b. 7 May 1760, Virginia. Minutes of Council containing information from Lt. Gov. Bull and Gov. Dobbs. Bull writes
about the Cherokee war and the size of Col. Montgomery's army.
Gov. Dobbs hopes that the assembly will raise the necessary
troops to fight the Cherokees. 2p.

Fol. 203. 8 May 1760, Virginia. Minutes of Council recording
that Lt. Gov. Bull stresses the necessity to send immediate
relief from Va. for Ft. Loudoun. 1p.

C.O. 5/1429 (CONT'D)

Fol. 223b. 7 Mar. 1760, Virginia. Minutes of Assembly containing a memorial from the officers of the Virginia regiment asking
for support in case the Cherokees prove unreliable. The militia
would be grateful for some guarantee of support. 4p.

CANADA
C.O. 42/15   ORIGINAL CORRESPONDENCE, SEC. OF STATE, QUEBEC: 1781-1783

Fol. 370. 2 Oct. 1783, Niagara. Copy of report of meeting with
the Six Nations, Shawnees, Delawares, and Cherokees deputized
to speak for the Western and Southern Indians. 4p.

C.O. 42/36   ORIGINAL CORRESPONDENCE, SEC. OF STATE, QUEBEC: 1776-1777

Fol. 69. 26 Mar. 1777, Whitehall. Geo. Germain to Guy Carleton
(draft). Lt. Gov. Hamilton met with the deputies from the
Ottawas, Chippewas, Wyandotts, Shawnees, Senecas, Delawares,
Cherokees, and Potawatomies. All the tribes were ready for war.
Hamilton will use the Indians against the Va. and Penn. frontiers.
9p.

C.O. 42/39   ORIGINAL CORRESPONDENCE, SEC. OF STATE, QUEBEC: 1778-1779

Fol. 91. 7 June 1779, Quebec. Gov. Frederick Haldimand to Geo.
Germain. 8p. [Enclosures to fol. 181b].

Fol. 105. 18 and 30 Dec. 1778, Ft. Vincennes. Lt. Gov.
Hamilton to Gen. Haldimand (copy). Shawnees, Delawares,
Ottawas, and Cherokees have assembled at the Cherokee R.
and plan to intercept rebel boats on the Ohio River. 7p.

Fol. 109. 24 and 30 Jan. 1779, Ft. Vincennes. Lt. Gov.
Hamilton to Gen. Haldimand (copy). Chickasaws, Cherokees,
Choctaws, and Alibamos plan to send out four parties this
spring -- one towards Kaskaskia to attack the rebels, one
to the Ohio to assist the Shawnees, one to visit Ft.
Vincennes and make peace with the Wabash Indians, and one
to the mouth of the Cherokee R. to intercept rebel boats.
5p.

Fol. 113. 26 Jan. 1779, Ft. Vincennes. Substance of a
Conference with the Indians (copy). Some Chickasaws and
Cherokees visited Detroit last spring. 4p.

Fol. 200. 3 Aug. 1779, Whitehall. Geo. Germain to Gen.
Haldimand (draft). English troops have been successful in Ga.
and Carolina. Rebels in West Fla. will find it difficult to
obtain supplies or reinforcements since Gen. Campbell is there
and since the Southern Indians support the English. 8p.

C.O. 42/40   ORIGINAL CORRESPONDENCE, SEC. OF STATE, QUEBEC: 1779-1780

Fol. 131. 25 Oct. 1780, Quebec. Gov. Haldimand to Geo. Germain
(duplicate). [Enclosures to fol. 161b]. 5p.

C.O. 42/40 (CONT'D)

>> Fol. 149. 30 Oct. 1779 - 14 May 1780, Detroit. Maj.
>> DePeyster. Accounts for the Indian Department (copy).
>> English paid £100 for a female slave claimed by the
>> Cherokee nation. 14p.

> Fol. 288. 25 Oct. 1780, Quebec. Gov. Haldimand to Wm. Knox
> (duplicate). Although the army and Indians were successful
> last August in Ky., they ultimately captured only a few rebel
> forts or houses. 2p.

C.O. 42/44 ORIGINAL CORRESPONDENCE, SEC. OF STATE, QUEBEC: 1782-
*   1783*

> Fol. 241. 20 Aug. 1783, Quebec. Gov. Haldimand to Lord North.
> [Enclosures to fol. 277b]. 9p.

>> Fol. 258. 17 July 1783, Detroit. Maj. DePeyster to Brig.
>> Gen. Maclean (copy). What should DePeyster do with the 70
>> Cherokees and 200 other Southern Indians coming to Detroit?
>> 3p.

C.O. 42/68 ORIGINAL CORRESPONDENCE, SEC. OF STATE, QUEBEC: 1790

> Fol. 279. 26 July 1790, Montreal. Lord Dorchester to Wm.
> Grenville. Creeks and Cherokees under Bowles who are on their
> way to England arrived in Montreal in July. They reported
> that the Americans plan to attack the upper posts and have
> asked for aid in going to London. [Enclosures to fol. 304b].
> 6p.

>> Fol. 282. 7 July 1790, [Quebec]. Wm. A. Bowles to Lord
>> Dorchester (copy). Bowles asks for aid to visit London
>> as a representative of the Creeks and Cherokees. 5p.

>> Fol. 286. 14 July 1790, Quebec. Wm. A. Bowles to Lord
>> Dorchester. Indians accompanying Bowles asked whether
>> Dorchester wishes them to visit England or to return home.
>> 3p.

>> Fol. 288. [July 1790], [Quebec]. Letter from Lord
>> Dorchester stating that he had no reason to stop Bowles
>> and the Indians from visiting England. 3p.

>> Fol. 290. 16 July 1790, Quebec. Wm. A. Bowles to Lord
>> Dorchester. Bowles encloses copies of some speeches from
>> the [Creeks and Cherokees] and hopes that Dorchester accepts
>> their reasons for coming to Quebec before going to England.
>> 4p.

>> Fol. 292. 7 May 1789, Cussita (Lower Creeks). Address
>> from Chiefs of Creek Nation to George III (copy). Creeks
>> request assistance in driving away the Americans who
>> usurped their lands. 7p.

C.O. 42/68 (CONT'D)

Fol. 296. 6 May 1789, Coweta Town. Address from Cherokee
Kings and Chiefs to George III (copy). Cherokees request
English assistance in punishing the usurpers of their land.
Virginians executed five Cherokee chiefs at Chilhowee.
Signatories include Little Turkey, Hanging Maw, Dragging
Canoe, Ishettechi, Unenegatee, Aguttahee, Nehenoatuah,
Skaantee, Catakish, Tekakolahan, Cheesguatelone, Chuleon,
and Richard Justice. 7p.

Fol. 300. July 1790, [Quebec]. Advice from Dorchester to
Creeks and Cherokees. Creeks and Cherokees were ill-
advised when they were told to contact the King in person
rather than by letter. They should return home and
Dorchester will forward their message to the King. 3p.

Fol. 302. 23 July 1790, Quebec. Wm. A. Bowles to Lord
Dorchester (copy). Chiefs do not have the authority to
deliver [to Dorchester] the message and belts intended for
His Majesty nor can they return home without a final answer
to their requests. 3p.

Fol. 304. July 1790, Quebec. Copy of decision from
Dorchester to give Bowles's party £100 to defray expenses
of trip. 3p.

Fol. 315. 5 Oct. 1790, Whitehall. Wm. W. Grenville to Lord
Dorchester. Grenville approves Dorchester's decision to furnish
the Creeks and Cherokees with the necessities to continue their
voyage to England. They have not yet arrived. 3p.

C.O. 43/8   ENTRY BOOK OF LETTERS FROM SEC. OF STATE: 1768-1787

Fol. 106b. 26 Mar. 1777, Whitehall. Geo. Germain to Guy
Carleton. [Entry letter of C.O. 42/36/69]. 11p.

Fol. 178. 3 Aug. 1779, Whitehall. Geo. Germain to Gen.
Haldimand. [Entry letter of C.O. 42/39/200]. 8p.

C.O. 43/14   ENTRY BOOK OF LETTERS TO SEC. OF STATE: 1776-1781

Fol. 145. 25 Oct. 1780, Quebec. Gov. Haldimand to Wm. Knox.
[Entry letter of C.O. 42/40/288]. 2p.

COLONIES GENERAL
C.O. 323/7   ORIGINAL CORRESPONDENCE, BD. OF TRADE: 1710-1719

Fol. 117. [Rec. 4 Dec. 1717]. Memorial from Richard Beresford
to Bd. of Trade. French have designs to extend their settlements from Canada to Mississippi. They plan to attack the
Cherokees and other friendly tribes along the Carolina frontier.
3p.

Fol. 161. [Rec. 18 Aug. 1719]. Memorial from Dr. Cox to Bd.
of Trade. Cox discusses Carolina and the boundaries between
the French and English in America. 3p.

C.O. 323/7 (CONT'D)

Fol. 166. 5 Dec. 1719, Paris. Mr. Pulteney to Bd. of Trade.
Pulteney includes a description of the French Miss. settlements
by an agent of John Law. Indians are staunch supporters of the
French. 4p.

C.O. 323/8   ORIGINAL CORRESPONDENCE, BD. OF TRADE: 1720-1729

Fol. 187. 20 and 26 Jan. 1725. Galfridous Grey to Bd. of
Trade. Grey makes suggestions for a barrier or boundary line
with the Indians and outlines the expenses involved. 3p.

C.O. 323/9   ORIGINAL CORRESPONDENCE, BD. OF TRADE: 1729-1733

Fol. 81. [Rec. 6 Apr. 1731], Peter Street [London?]. Petition
from John Slator to Bd. of Trade. Slator supports an alliance
between the British and Cherokees and asks for a land grant.
1p. [Enclosures to fol. 82b].

Fol. 82. Proposal from John Slator to Bd. of Trade.
Slator suggests that the Cherokees cultivate silk, an
activity which would be advantageous to the natives and
British alike. 2p.

C.O. 323/13   ORIGINAL CORRESPONDENCE, BD. OF TRADE: 1750-1757

Fol. 307. June 1756. Edmund Atkin to Bd. of Trade. Traders'
abuses are the principal reason peace is endangered. Atkin
requests a supply of presents to use whenever he visits the
Indians. 3p.

Fol. 351. 1 and 5 Mar. 1757, New York. Edmund Atkin to Mr.
Pownall. Atkin justifies the delay in executing his commission.
He has given Lord Loudoun a list of goods suitable for Indian
presents in the Southern District. 3p.

C.O. 323/15   ORIGINAL CORRESPONDENCE, BD. OF TRADE: 1760-1763

Fol. 101. 5 May 1763, Whitehall. Earl of Egremont to Bd. of
Trade. Egremont sent plans for protecting the Indian land to
the Southern governors and to the Agent for Indian Affairs in
the Southern Department. 14p.

C.O. 323/16   ORIGINAL CORRESPONDENCE, BD. OF TRADE: 1763

Fol. 84. [1763]. Plan of Forts and Garrisons Proposed for the
Security of North America (copy). Keowee and Augusta, two
forts near the Creeks and Cherokees, should be secured. 18p.

Fol. 101. 16 Mar. 1763, Whitehall. Earl of Egremont to
Southern Governors and John Stuart (copy). Governors and
Stuart should immediately explain to the Creek, Choctaw, Chero-
kee, Chickasaw, and Catawba Chiefs the new peace. 8p.

C.O. 323/17   ORIGINAL CORRESPONDENCE, BD. OF TRADE: 1763-1764

Fol. 34. 24 Aug. 1763, New York. Additional Orders from
Amherst to the Officers Commanding at Florida and Louisiana (copy).

C.O. 323/17 (CONT'D)

Commanding officers are ordered to exchange information with
the S.C. governor and Stuart about local Indian affairs. 4p.

Fol. 115. 10 Nov. 1763, Augusta. Governors of Southern Colonies and Agent to Earl of Halifax. Governors and Agent have met
with the Chickasaws, Creeks, Choctaws, Cherokees, and Catawbas.
Cherokees are on the verge of war with the Creeks. English need
to reestablish trade with the Indians. 4p.

Fol. 160. 1 Dec. 1763, Charleston. John Stuart to Bd. of Trade.
Stuart met with the Cherokees, Creeks, Chickasaws, Choctaws,
and Catawbas at Augusta. He includes the Indians' requests.
15p. [Enclosures to fol. 169b].

Fol. 168. 5 Nov. 1763, Ft. Augusta. Talk from Stuart and
Southern governors to Indians (copy). Governors and Stuart
promise the Indians peace, friendship, and trade. 4p.

Fol. 170. [Rec. 19 Apr. 1764], Charleston. John Stuart to Bd.
of Trade. Cherokees would like to see the Creeks humbled.
Oconostota is willing to send the Cherokees against the Northern
Indians. 4p. [Enclosures to fol. 177b].

Fol. 172. 26 Jan. 1764, Ft. Prince George. Talk from
Saluy to Gov. Boone (copy). Saluy denies the Creek charges
[concerning the murders at Long Canes]. Saluy was born and
raised in Tugaloo but is moving to Estatoy. 4p.

Fol. 174. 19 Jan. 1764, Chote. Copy of talk from Little
Carpenter requesting that goods be sent from Keowee to the
Overhill towns in trade for skins. 2p.

Fol. 176. 19 Jan. 1764, Chote. Talk from Great Warrior
to [John Stuart] (copy). Great Warrior will send the
Cherokees to fight [Northern Indians]. 2p.

Fol. 178. 16 Jan. 1764, Charleston. John Stuart to Bd. of
Trade. Creek murders have caused Stuart to write to the Creeks,
Cherokees, Choctaws, and Chickasaws. 4p. [Enclosures to 199b].

Fol. 180. [Dec. 1763]. Declaration from Arthur Cuddie
(Cherokee trader) and Lt. Patrick Colquohoun that Moytoy
of Hiwassee and Rabbit of Tugaloo advised Cuddie to flee
the approaching Creeks. The Creeks, not the Cherokees,
committed the murders at Long Canes. 4p.

Fol. 182. 6 Jan. 1764, Silver Bluff. Geo. Galphin to John
Stuart. Galphin believes that the Cherokees committed the
murders, although some Creeks might have been present. Two
families have settled on land claimed by the Cherokees. 3p.

Fol. 186. 8 Jan. [1764], [Silver Bluff]. Copy of talk
from Tugulkee (Young Twin). [Same as C.O. 5/648/286].

Fol. 187. 2 Jan. 1764, Charleston. John Stuart to Gov.
Wright (copy). Measures should be taken to prevent a
general defection by other Indian tribes. Message should

C.O. 323/17 (CONT'D)

be sent to the Cherokees reporting the friendship of
Moytoy and Rabbit towards the Long Canes' settlers and
thanking the tribe for their offer of assistance. 4p.

Fol. 189. 9 Jan. 1764. Savannah. Gov. Wright to John
Stuart (extract). Wright agrees with Stuart's proposals
to preserve friendship with the Indian tribes in case of
a rupture with the Creeks. 2p.

Fol. 191. 13 Jan. 1764, Charleston. Talk from Stuart to
Creeks (copy). News from Tugulkee indicates that the seven
Creeks who murdered the settlers used to live with the
Cherokees at Tugaloo. 2p.

Fol. 193. 14 Jan. 1764, [Charleston]. Talk from Stuart to
Saluy, Head Warrior of Estatoy and Tugaloo (copy). Stuart
does not believe the Creek charges that Saluy and other
Cherokees encouraged the Long Canes' murders. Creek
murderers should be executed if they return. 3p.

Fol. 195. [14-16 Jan. 1764], [Charleston]. Talk from
Stuart to Head Beloved Man and Principal Warriors of Chote
(copy). Stuart reports the Creek charges that the Cherokees encouraged the Long Canes' murders. He suggests that
the Creek murderers be killed if they return to Cherokee
country. 3p.

Fol. 196. [14-16 Jan. 1764], [Charleston]. Talk from
Stuart to Franchimastabe and Warriors of Choctaw Nation
(copy). Stuart tells the Choctaws about the murders committed by Creeks living in Cherokee country. 3p.

Fol. 198. [14-16 Jan. 1764], [Charleston]. Talk from
Stuart to Payamataha and Other Warriors of Chickasaw
Nation (copy). Stuart informs the Chickasaws of the [Long
Canes' murders] which insult all the Indians who signed
the Augusta treaty. 3p.

Fol. 200. 23 Feb. 1764. John Stuart to Bd. of Trade. Stuart
sends a copy of the proceedings of the [Augusta] Indian congress
and points out some errors in the copy. 3p. [Enclosures to
fol. 239b].

Fol. 203. Treaty of Peace and Friendship at the Congress
Held at Augusta 10 Nov. 1763 (copy). Signatories include
Attakullakulla, Kittagusta Chotis, Skyagunsta Ousteneca,
Ecuij, The Wolf, Tistoe, Amoytoy, and Willinawa. 3p.

Fol. 215. *Journal of the Congress of the Four Southern
Governors and the Superintendent of that District with
the Five Nations of Indians at Augusta, 1763.* 48p.

Fol. 240. 9 Mar. 1764, Charleston. John Stuart to Bd. of Trade.
Stuart reports information on the Cherokees, Creeks, Choctaws,
Chickasaws, and Catawbas. He gives the location of Cherokee

C.O. 323/17 (CONT'D)

country and lists the towns and warriors (Cherokees have 13,500 people, including 2,700 warriors). He describes the tribe's occupations, distribution of land, government, customs, and trade. Stuart includes his recommendation on the duties of the superintendent and the governors. 59p.

Fol. 274. 23 Mar. 1763, Savannah. John Stuart to Bd. of Trade. Cherokees have offered assistance against the Creeks if satisfaction is not given. Oconostota and some Cherokees have also agreed to aid Wm. Johnson against the Northern Indians. 5p. [Enclosures to fol. 282b].

> Fol. 281. 6 Feb. 1764. Talk from Coweta Headmen to [John Stuart]. Cowetas blame the Cherokees for the murders. 2p.

Fol. 283. 7 Feb. 1764, St. James. Dunk Halifax to Bd. of Trade. Halifax sends a copy of Stuart's account of intertribal relations. 2p. [Enclosures to fol. 290b].

> Fol. 285. 5 Dec. 1763, Charleston. John Stuart to Earl of Egremont. [Duplicate of C.O. 5/65/69 Part II]. 11p.

Fol. 291. 23 May 1764. St. James. Edw. Sedgewick to John Pownall. 2p. [Enclosures to fol. 349b].

> Fol. 293. 13 Apr. 1764, New York. Gen. Gage to Earl of Halifax (copy). Stuart's presence is necessary to regulate Indian affairs in Florida. He should buy Indian presents in Carolina to be distributed in Florida. 9p.

C.O. 323/18   ORIGINAL CORRESPONDENCE, BD. OF TRADE: 1764-1766

Fol. 1. 23 Mar. 1764, Savannah. John Stuart to Bd. of Trade (duplicate). Cherokees will try to aid the British if the Creeks refuse to give satisfaction [for the Long Canes' murders] and war erupts. 4p. [Enclosures to fol. 5b].

Fol. 6. 5 May 1764, Charleston. John Stuart to Bd. of Trade. At General Gage's request, Stuart will encourage conflict between the Creeks and Cherokees. Cameron has gone to manage Cherokee affairs. Cherokee friendship appears to be satisfactory. 7p. [Enclosures to fol. 19b].

> Fol. 10. 29 Apr. 1764, Augusta. Extract of letter to [John Stuart] reporting that the Mortar has changed his tone after returning from the Cherokee talks. 2p.

> Fol. 13. 28 Apr. 1764, Silver Bluff. Geo. Galphin to [John Stuart] (extract). [Creeks] have made peace with the Chickasaws, Choctaws, and Cherokees. 2p.

> Fol. 14. 26 Apr. 1764, Charleston. John Stuart to Alex. Cameron (copy). Cameron will reside with the Cherokees to strengthen their ties with the English and to prevent the Creeks and others from alienating the Cherokees. 4p.

C.O. 323/18 (CONT'D)

      Fol. 16. 26 Apr. 1764. Alex. Cameron to Kittagusta of Chote and Cherokee Head Warriors. Creeks have not yet provided satisfaction [for the murders at Long Canes] but Cameron hopes they will. 2p.

      Fol. 17. 18 Feb. 1764, Chote. Copy of talks from Great Warrior and Kittagusta reporting that the Creeks will not execute any of their people for murdering whites. 3p.

      Fol. 19. 22 Apr. 1764, Ft. Prince George. Extract of letter from Ensign George Price indicating that Saluy is ready to seek revenge for the murder of his eldest brothers. He hopes for English assistance. Tuskegetche brought in a Creek scalp. 2p.

Fol. 79. [Rec. Jan. 1765], [London]. Petition from Lt. Timberlake to Bd. of Trade. Timberlake requests that the Crown pay expenses for three Cherokees brought over by Aaron Trueheart. They want to return home since they could not obtain an audience. 2p.

Fol. 80. 1 Feb. 1765, St. James. Earl of Halifax to Bd. of Trade. Timberlake will not be reimbursed since he brought the Cherokees without permission and against the will of the Lt. Gov. of Virginia. Indians will be sent back safely and speedily. 3p.

Fol. 82. 7 Feb. 1765, [London]. Edward Montague to John Pownall. Montague encloses the estimated expenses for sending the three Cherokees home. 3p. [Enclosures to fol. 84b].

      Fol. 84. [Feb. 1765, London]. Edward Montague. An Estimate of the Expenses That Will Attend the Conveyance and Accomodation of Three Indians to Virginia. 2p.

Fol. 95. 4 Mar. 1765, [London]. Edward Montague. An Account of the Expenses Attending the Passage of Three Indians from England to Virginia and Providing a Few Presents for Them. 2p.

Fol. 226. 16 Aug. 1766, Whitehall. Earl of Shelburne to Bd. of Trade. Shelburne requests an estimate of the expenses to send home four Wappinger braves and three women, who came without permission like the Cherokees. 4p.

C.O. 323/20   ORIGINAL CORRESPONDENCE, BD. OF TRADE, INDIAN AFFAIRS: 1764

Fol. 2. 26 Oct. 1764. Gov. Murray. Notions for the Plan for the Management of Indian Affairs. 8p. [Enclosure of Gov. Murray's letter of 26 Oct. 1764].

Fol. 9. 26 Nov. 1764, Portsmouth, New Hampshire. Gov. Benj. Wentworth to Bd. of Trade (duplicate). Wentworth suggests changes in the plans sent to Johnson and Stuart for managing Indian affairs. 4p.

C.O. 323/20 (CONT'D)

Fol. 13. 17 Nov. 1764, Boston. Gov. Bernard to Bd. of Trade.
Plans for managing Indian affairs are intended for the remote
tribes and not for those tribes living near the English settlements. 11p.

Fol. 19. 12 Oct. 1764, New York. Lt. Gov. Colden to Bd. of
Trade. Colden suggests drawing a boundary to divide the
Northern and Southern Indian Districts. 12p.

Fol. 25. 30 Oct. 1764, Johnson Hall. Wm. Johnson to Bd. of
Trade. Johnson has already sent his recommendations for managing Indian affairs. 10p.

Fol. 31. 8 Oct. 1764, Johnson Hall. Wm. Johnson to Bd. of
Trade. 9p. [Enclosures to fol. 45b].

> Fol. 37. [Oct. 1764], [Johnson Hall]. Wm. Johnson.
> Sentiments on the Plan for the Future Management of
> Indian Affairs. 13p.

Fol. 46. [1764]. Col. Bradstreet. Thoughts on Indian Trade.
17p. [Enclosure of Mr. Sedgewick's letter of 23 Jan. 1765].

Fol. 55. 6 Oct. 1764, Burlington, New Jersey. Gov. Wm.
Franklin to Bd. of Trade. Franklin promises to send his ideas
on managing Indian affairs. 2p.

Fol. 57. 28 Oct. 1764, Burlington, New Jersey. Gov. Franklin
to Bd. of Trade. Franklin sends suggestions on managing Indian
affairs. 2p. [Enclosures to fol. 63b].

> Fol. 59. 27 Oct. 1764, [Burlington]. Gov. Franklin.
> Remarks on the Plan for the Future Management of Indian
> Affairs. Franklin suggests four Indian districts. The
> Southern District would include the Indians of N.C., S.C.,
> and Florida. 9p.

Fol. 64. 18 Oct. 1764, Annapolis. Lt. Gov. Horatio Sharpe to
Bd. of Trade. Sharpe makes suggestions for managing Indian
affairs. 5p.

Fol. 67. 24 Dec. 1764, Charleston. Lt. Gov. Bull to Bd. of
Trade. Bull makes suggestions on managing Indian affairs.
Cherokee trade is not very profitable, and the Creek and
Choctaw trade will probably decline. 5p.

Fol. 70. 10 Nov. 1764, Savannah. Gov. Wright to Bd. of Trade.
Wright makes suggestions on managing Indian affairs. 6p.

Fol. 73. 29 Dec. 1764, Savannah. Gov. Wright to Bd. of Trade.
2p. [Enclosures to fol. 83b].

> Fol. 75. [Nov. - Dec. 1764], Savannah. Gov. Wright.
> Report on the Plan for Regulating Indian Trade. One deputy
> for the Cherokee Nation and one for the Creeks and Choctaws
> will be sufficient. 13p.

C.O. 323/20 (CONT'D)

Fol. 84. 2 Jan. 1765, Mobile. Gov. Geo. Johnstone to Bd. of Trade (copy). Johnston makes suggestions for managing Indian affairs. By supplying the Creeks, Ga. provided the ammunition that the Cherokees used to kill Carolinians. 10p.

Fol. 87. 1 Dec. 1764, St. Augustine. Gov. James Grant to Bd. of Trade. Grant makes suggestions for managing Indian affairs. Commissary for the Cherokees should be located at Ft. Prince George. The amount of Creek and Cherokee trade cannot be determined since the French always shared in it. 7p.

Fol. 91. 29 Oct. 1764, Pensacola. John Stuart to Bd. of Trade. Stuart will send suggestions on managing Indian affairs. 2p. [Enclosures to fol. 94b].

Fol. 95. 8 Dec. 1764, Pensacola. John Stuart to John Pownall. Stuart sends suggestions on managing Indian affairs. 4p. [Enclosures to 107b].

> Fol. 97. 1 Dec. 1764, Pensacola. John Stuart. Observations on the Plan for the Future Management of Indians. Stuart estimates the annual expenses for the Upper and Lower Cherokees and lists the Indian tribes and number of warriors in Southern District (Cherokees have 2,800 warriors). 21p.

C.O. 323/23   ORIGINAL CORRESPONDENCE, BD. OF TRADE, INDIAN AFFAIRS: 1764-1768

Fol. 8. May 1765, Johnson Hall. Wm. Johnson to Bd. of Trade. 14p. [Enclosures to fol. 47b].

> Fol. 15. 29 Apr. - 11 May 1765, Johnson Hall. Proceedings of Conferences between Sir Wm. Johnson and the Six Nations and Delawares (copy). Boundary line should extend to the Cherokee River. 48p.

Fol. 48. [Rec. 29 Oct. 1765], Johnson Hall. Wm. Johnson to Bd. of Trade. Carolinians stopped Indians carrying a pass from Col. Lewis. 9p. [Enclosures to fol. 63b].

Fol. 66. 16 Nov. 1765, Johnson Hall. Wm. Johnson to Bd. of Trade. Fauquier has requested that Johnson mediate the disputes between the Cherokees, Six Nations, and Western Indians. Six Nations will listen to the [Cherokee] deputies but they do not want peace. Johnson requests that the Board consider his peace recommendation for the Northern and Southern Indians. 8p. [Enclosures to fol. 80b].

> Fol. 70. 15 May - 25 Sept. 1765, Journal of Transactions of Geo. Croghan with the Several Indian Nations on His Journey to the Illinois. French have told the Indians that the English will seize their land and send the Cherokees to enslave the tribes and settle their land. 17p.

C.O. 323/23 (CONT'D

Fol. 79. 7 June 1765, Ft. St. Vincent. J. Capucin to
B. Campeau (copy). A prisoner just released by the Cherokees arrived with a message that the English encouraged
the tribe to fight the French. Cherokees took a Canadian
prisoner and mistreated him because of his nationality.
4p. *French.*

Fol. 91. 1 Nov. - 1 Dec. 1764. Journal of Proceedings of John
Stuart. The Mortar considers the Cherokees his people. 65p.

Fol. 133. 24 Jan. 1764 [1765], Mobile. John Stuart to Secretary
[of Bd. of Trade]. Stuart sent some Chickasaw and Cherokee
parties to guard the Wabash and Ohio Rivers and to seize French
traders' goods. 5p. [Enclosures to fol. 167b].

    Fol. 161. 14 Jan. 1765, Mobile. John Stuart to d'Abbadie
    (copy). Cherokees and Chickasaws are concerned about am-
    munition sent to their Northern Indian enemies. 3p.

    Fol. 163. 13 Jan. 1765, Mobile. [John Stuart] to Mr.
    Aubrey (copy). Stuart advised the Cherokees and Chickasaws
    at the end of the war to regard the French as friends. 4p.

Fol. 168. 16 Apr. 1765, Mobile. John Stuart to John Pownall.
French in Illinois want the English government to become
established to prevent attacks from the Cherokees and Chickasaws.
8p. [Enclosures to fol. 175b].

Fol. 176. 24 Aug. 1765, Charleston. John Stuart to John Pownall.
Stuart wants gorgets and armplates for the Creeks, Cherokees,
and Catawbas. N. and S. Carolina have been encroaching on
Cherokee land. Terrapin, a Lower Cherokee, was jailed for
crossing the treaty line. Last May, Virginians killed five
Cherokees. Cherokee trade is in a state of confusion. 25p.
[Enclosures to fol. 267b].

    Fol. 189. List of papers enclosed in Stuart's letter of
    24 Aug. 1765. 3p.

    Fol. 216. 13 June 1765, Ft. Prince George. Geo. Price to
    John Stuart. Cherokees threatened traders when the tribe
    learned about the Va. murders. The sole Indian to escape
    blamed Col. Lewis for the murders. Great Warrior said that
    the Virginians, who hunt and steal in Cherokee territory,
    were responsible for the last war. 3p.

    Fol. 220. 6 June 1765, Toqueh. Alex. Cameron to John
    Stuart. Oconostota will not turn the Frenchmen over to
    Cameron. One Frenchman did not return after going out to
    a ball play. Kennititah [Kenoteta] of Hiwassee refused to
    attend the French talks. Great Warrior [Oconostota] blames
    the Virginians for the last war. 8p. [Letter continues at
    fol. 218].

C.O. 323/23 (CONT'D)

Fol. 222. 12 June 1765, Toqueh. Alex. Cameron to John
Stuart (copy). It is useless to stop guns from being
brought from Ga. when S.C. is allowed to send as many as
they desire. None of the five Cherokees who reportedly
escaped from Va. have returned home. Judd's Friend is
going to Ft. Prince George for presents from the Assembly.
3p.

Fol. 224. 26 June 1765, Ft. Prince George. Geo. Price to
John Stuart. Great Warrior appointed Judd's Friend to tell
the Middle and Valley Cherokees not to seek revenge for the
Va. murders. Young Warrior brought a string of white beads
with one black bead at the end. 4p.

Fol. 226. 29 June and 2 July 1765, Toqueh. Alex. Cameron
to John Stuart (copy). The Cherokee wounded in Va. has
just returned to Chilhowie with a report that two others
remain with the whites. Some suspect that the Chickasaws
murdered a Toqueh Indian and left a war hoop. Kennititah
[Kenoteta] of Hiwassee has gone north to war but [Little]
Carpenter's brother did not because a conjurer forecasts
bad success. Two Tawaw [Ottawa] prisoners have arrived.
4p.

Fol. 228. 6 July 1765, Toqueh. Alex. Cameron to John
Stuart (copy). Cherokees returned home with a Twightwee
scalp and a Cherokee boy taken from Chote. The enemy
wounded Black Dog of Tellico. Great Warrior's son became
deathly ill after visiting Augusta. Sealiloske of Great
Island is going to fight the Yachtanues. 4p.

Fol. 230. 19 July 1765, Ft. Prince George. Geo. Price to
John Stuart. Wilkinson has sent for the Overhill chiefs
to run the boundary. Chiefs at the fort say that the land
is theirs and that the Overhill people have no jurisdiction
over it. A Cherokee recaptured from the Twightwees reports
that the French have encouraged the Twightwees, Kaskaskias,
Shawnees, and three other tribes to attack the English. 3p.

Fol. 232. 9 and 12 Aug. 1765, Ft. Prince George. Geo.
Price to John Stuart. Some drunken Cherokees broke into
Cameron's house and threatened the traders. Old Warrior
of Estatoe and the Wolf went with Wilkinson to run the
boundary. Young Warrior and Tistoe complain that the land
belongs to the whole nation. 4p.

Fol. 234. 3 Feb. 1765. Alex. Cameron to John Stuart.
Only Judd's Friend agreed to stop the hunting to intercept
French supplies coming up the Ohio. Mortar is expected
in Chote with French talks. Attakullakulla has been in
Va. since last Fall. 4p.

Fol. 236. 5 Aug. 1765, Ft. Prince George. Geo. Price to
John Stuart. Price complains about traders bringing rum
for the Cherokees. Willinawa reports that the Cherokee war
parties are returning home. 5p.

C.O. 323/23 (CONT'D)

Fol. 241. 18 May 1765, Staunton. Talk from Maj. Lewis
to Upper Cherokees (copy). Lewis reports that five Cherokees have been murdered. 4p.

Fol. 243. 11 July 1765, Toqueh. Talk from Oconostota,
Willinawa, Ottassittie, Kittagusta, and others to Bull.
Cherokees want to wait until Stuart returns before settling
the boundary. If Brody's plantation is not accepted as
the boundary, whites will soon claim that the Twelve Mile
River is the boundary. 3p.

Fol. 245. 10 Aug. 1765, Charleston. [John Stuart] to
Lt. Gov. Bull (copy). Cameron complains about rum being
supplied to the Indians, especially the Cherokees. This
should be stopped immediately, particularly because the
Cherokees resent land encroachments and the murder of
their people. 7p.

Fol. 249. 18 Aug. 1765, Charleston. Lt. Gov. Bull to
John Stuart. Tugaloo and other Cherokee Towns receive
rum from Ga., N.C., Va., and S. Carolina. 4p.

Fol. [251]. 11 July 1764. Copy of John Nunn's license to
trade with the Cherokees in Econourste, Hiwassee, Little
Tellico, and other Valley Towns. 2p.

Fol. 254. 1 May 1765, Toqueh. Alex. Cameron. A Return
of Traders in the Cherokee Nation (copy). Cameron lists
Cherokee towns, traders, and provinces issuing licenses.
2p.

Fol. 255. [1765]. John Stuart. Calculation of Annual
Presents for the Southern Department. Stuart lists
presents given to the Cherokee, Creek, Catawbas, and other
Southern Indians. 2p.

Fol. 268. 10 July 1766, Charleston. John Stuart to Bd. of
Trade. Stuart sends a copy of the Cherokee land cession. Va.
has not punished the murderers of the Cherokees or sent compensation to their relatives. Va. is attempting to establish trade
with the Cherokees by selling cheaper goods. Cherokees have
blockaded the Illinois villages. 12p. [Enclosures to fol. 324b].

Fol. 274. Lists of papers enclosed in Stuart's letter of
10 July 1766. 2p.

Fol. 275. 19 Oct. 1765, Ft. Prince George. Cession of
Lands by Cherokees to the Province of South Carolina
(copy). Signatories include Kittagusta (Prince of Chote),
Judd's Friend, Saluy (Young Warrior), Ecuij (Good Warrior),
Skattihoske of Chilhowie, Tistoe of Keowee, Uqunecah (the
Wolf), Chinisto and Ottassatch of Sugar Town, Stocking
Head Man of Toxaway, Ottassatie of Qualatchie, and Johnnie
of Toxaway. 4p.

C.O. 323/23 (CONT'D)

Fol. 277. 10 May 1766, Ft. Prince George. Certificate
from Alex. Cameron of the Cherokee chiefs that they were
present for marking the boundary line between S.C. and the
Cherokees. Signatories include Kittagusta (Prince of Chote),
Ottassata Ustenecah [Judd's Friend], Ecuij (Good Warrior),
Tistoe of Keowee, Wolf of Keowee, and Keyhetake. 2p.

Fol. 278. 5 Feb. 1766, Charleston. John Stuart to [Gov.
Tryon]. Cherokees requested that their boundary be run
with N. Carolina. 2p.

Fol. 279. 9 Apr. 1765, Brunswick. Gov. Tryon to John
Stuart (copy). Tryon lacks the authorization to run the
Cherokee boundary. He is unaware of Cherokee complaints
about N.C. encroaching upon their land. 2p.

Fol. 280. 5 May 1765, Brunswick. Gov. Tryon to John Stuart
(copy). Tryon cannot direct Cameron on the boundary line
[with the Cherokees] since no one knows the location of
Dewise's Corner. 2p.

Fol. 281. 28 May 1765, Charleston. John Stuart to Gov.
Tryon (copy). Stuart describes the Cherokees' proposal
for a boundary with N. Carolina. Mortar has been encouraging the Cherokees to seek revenge for the murders in
Virginia. 4p.

Fol. 283. 10 Feb. 1766, Charleston. John Stuart to Gov.
Fauquier (copy). Stuart is upset to learn that the Cherokees were killed in Augusta County and that N.C. and S.C.
are encroaching on Indian hunting grounds. Boundary lines
will be run with the two Carolinas. 3p.

Fol. 285. 17 June 1766, Brunswick. Gov. Tryon to John
Stuart (copy). The best boundary with the Cherokees would
be the northern course from Reedy R. to the mountains and
then to Chiswell's Mines. Other proposed line would exclude
many N.C. residents. 4p.

Fol. 287. 3 June 1766, Ft. Prince George. Ensign Geo.
Price to [John Stuart]. [Same as C.O. 5/66/394]. 2p.

Fol. 288. 9 Apr. 1766, Ft. Prince George. Alex. Cameron
to [John Stuart]. [Same as C.O. 5/66/396]. 2p.

Fol. 289. 10 May 1766, Ft. Prince George. Alex. Cameron
to [John Stuart] (copy). Cameron reports on running the
boundary between N.C. and the Cherokees. He recommends
medals for Oconostota, Kittagusta, Attakullakulla, Willinawa,
Otassata among the Overhills, Moytoy and Man Killer of
Nucasse (now living in Little Chote south of the Valley
towns), Tistoe, Ecuij, Saluy, and the Wolf. Cherokees have
attacked the Northern Indians. 8p.

Fol. 293. 1 June 1766, Toqueh. Alex. Cameron to [John
Stuart]. [Same as C.O. 5/66/406]. 3p.

Fol. 295. 7 May 1766, Ft. Prince George. Ensign Geo. Price to [John Stuart] (extract). Overhill traders report that the Great Warrior and Man Killer of Settico almost killed two white men. Cherokees would have killed all the traders if the tribe had not been busy fighting the Northern Indians. 2p.

Fol. 296. 11 July 1765, Toqueh. Talk from Oconostota, Willinawa, Ottassattie and Kittagusta, and others to Lt. Gov. Bull. [Same as fol. 243]. 3p.

Fol. 298. 20 Oct. 1765, Ft. Prince George. Copy of talk from Cherokee Headmen and Warriors discussing boundary settlement and requesting lower prices for goods. 4p.

Fol. 300. 1 Feb. 1766, Charleston. Talk from John Stuart to Prince of Chote and other Cherokee Head Warriors (copy). Stuart thanks the Cherokees for agreeing to the boundary proposed by Bull. N.C. will run the line as the Cherokees wanted. Bull regrets that the Nottoways abducted two Cherokee women. Fauquier will give satisfaction for the murders in Augusta County. 3p.

Fol. 302. 8 May 1766, Ft. Prince George. Talk from Kittagusta (Prince of Chote) to Alex. Cameron and Ensign Price (copy). Kittagusta wants the boundary line continued from Reedy R. to Col. Chiswell's Mines. Cherokees want peace with the Northern Indians. 4p.

Fol. 304. 17 Sept. 1765, Johnson Hall. Wm. Johnson to [John Stuart]. [Same as C.O. 5/67/9]. 4p.

Fol. 306. 1 June 1766, Charleston. John Stuart to Lt. Gov. Bull. [Same as C.O. 5/67/13]. 2p.

Fol. 307. 16 May 1766, Oakchoys. Answer from Upper Creeks to talk of Gov. Johnstone. The government gave the Cherokees ammunition to fight the French Indians and asked the Creeks to remain neutral. Upper Creeks want to know whether the Cherokees received ammunition after the Cherokees visited England. 6p.

Fol. 311. 19 May 1766, Pensacola. Letter from Gov. Johnstone. [Same as C.O. 5/67/23]. 3p.

Fol. 317. 16 Dec. 1765, Ft. Cavendish, Illinois. Letter from Maj. Robert Farmer. [Same as C.O. 5/67/33]. 4p.

Fol. 321. 10 July 1766, Savannah. Gov. Wright to John Stuart. [Same as C.O. 5/67/39]. 4p.

Fol. 323. 29 Apr. 1766, Mucolassee. Answer from Wolf King to talk of Gov. Wright and John Stuart (copy). The only way to stop rebellious Indians is to curtail trade for two years. 3p.

C.O. 323/24 PART I   ORIGINAL CORRESPONDENCE, BD. OF TRADE: 1766-1768

Fol. 16. 20 Aug. 1766, Johnson Hall. Wm. Johnson to Bd. of Trade. 8p. [Enclosures to fol. 32b].

Fol. 19. 23 - 31 July 1766, [Lake Ontario]. Proceedings of a Congress with Pontiac and Chiefs of the Ottawas, Potawatamies, Hurons, and Chippawais (copy). An Onondaga reported a war party returning from the Cherokees with a scalp. 27p.

Fol. 57. 16 Nov. 1766, Charleston. John Stuart to Bd. of Trade. Stuart sent instructions to the Cherokee, Creek, and Choctaw commissaries to solicit help if war erupts between England and the Creeks. 4p. [Enclosures to fol. 62b].

Fol. 59. 30 Aug. 1766, New York. Gen. Gage to [John Stuart]. [Same as C.O. 5/67/114]. 3p.

Fol. 61. 1 Oct. 1766, Pensacola. Charles Stuart to [John Stuart]. [Abstract of C.O. 5/67/205]. 2p.

Fol. 62. 30 Sept. 1766, Pensacola. Geo. Johnstone to [John Stuart] (copy). Chickasaws and Choctaws (without the Cherokees) may be sufficient to punish the Creeks. 2p.

Fol. 65. 2 Dec. 1766, Charleston. John Stuart to Bd. of Trade. Cherokees postponed running the boundary because of sickness, death, and the approaching hunting season. Cherokees are uneasy about Fauquier's silence over continuing their boundary with Virginia. There may be 150-200 Natchez warriors residing among the Cherokees, Creeks, and Chickasaws who still retain their language, customs, and hatred of the French. 8p. [Enclosures to fol. 100b].

Fol. 69. List of papers enclosed in Stuart's letter of 2 Dec. 1766. 2p.

Fol. 70. 16 Nov. 1766, Charleston. John Stuart to Bd. of Trade. [Duplicate of fol. 57]. 2p.

Fol. 77a. 1 Oct. 1766, Pensacola. Charles Stuart to John Stuart. [Extract of C.O. 5/67/205]. 3p.

Fol. 78. 6 Nov. 1766, Ft. Prince George. Ensign Geo. Price to [John Stuart]. [Same as C.O. 5/67/220]. 2p.

Fol. 79. 27 Aug. 1766, Toqueh. Alex. Cameron to John Stuart. [Same as C.O. 5/67/218]. 2p.

Fol. 88. 22 Aug. 1766. Talk from Kittagusta and Upper Cherokee Headmen and Warriors to John Stuart. [Same as C.O. 5/67/244]. 3p.

Fol. 90. [1766], [Chote]. Talk from Oconostota, Atta-kullakulla, and other Head Warriors to John Stuart. [Same as C.O. 5/67/246]. 2p.

C.O. 323/24 PART I (CONT'D)

Fol. 95. 24 Nov. 1766, Charleston. John Stuart to Lt.
Gov. Fauquier. [Same as C.O. 5/67/212]. 6p.

Fol. 98. 22 Sept. 1766, Toqueh. Talk from Cherokee Chiefs
to John Stuart. [Copy of C.O. 5/67/240]. 4p.

C.O. 323/24 PART II   ORIGINAL CORRESPONDENCE, BD. OF TRADE: 1766-1768

Fol. 17. 30 Oct. 1767, London. Merchants trading with North
America to the Board of Trade. Each colony should regulate its
own Indian trade. 3p.

Fol. 18. 10 Oct. 1767, New York. Maj. Gen. Gage to Earl of
Shelburne (extract). Government captured several murderers
[of the Cherokees], but the country people freed them. Trials
should be held in provincial capitals where a jury could be
composed of civilized men. 8p.

Fol. 39. 3 Oct. 1767, Charleston. John Stuart to John Pownall
(copy). Stuart sends a journal of his proceedings with the
Creeks, Cherokees, and Indian traders. 2p. [Enclosures to 88b].

Fol. 44. 21 Apr. - 6 June 1767. John Stuart. Journal
of Proceedings with the Creek and Cherokee Deputies and
Traders to the Said Nations. Creek and Cherokee deputies
accepted the new regulations and prices of goods. Cherokees will not travel as far as Salisbury but will meet at
Reedy River. Stuart lists the Great and Small Medal Chiefs.
56p.

Fol. 185. 10 Feb. 1768, Charleston. John Stuart to Secretary
[of Bd. of Trade]. 2p. [Enclosures to fol. 195b].

Fol. 187. 10 Feb. 1768, Charleston. John Stuart to Earl
of Shelburne. [Copy of C.O. 5/69/128]. 6p.

Fol. 190. 17 Sept. 1767, Williamsburg. Lt. Gov. Fauquier
to John Stuart. [Same as C.O. 5/69/133]. 2p.

Fol. 192. 21 Nov. 1767, Williamsburg. Lt. Gov. Fauquier
to John Stuart. [Same as C.O. 5/69/131]. 2p.

Fol. 196. 14 Mar. 1768, Johnson Hall. Wm. Johnson to Bd. of
Trade. Cherokee deputies arrived last Dec. and peace has been
established with the Northern Indians. 4p.

C.O. 323/25   ORIGINAL CORRESPONDENCE, BD. OF TRADE: 1767

Fol. 1. 5 Oct. 1767, Whitehall. Earl of Shelburne to Bd. of
Trade. Bd. should consider the need for new regulations on
Indian trade and the new western governments. 12p. [Enclosures
to fol. 212b].

Fol. 7. List of papers enclosed in Shelburne's letter of
5 Oct. 1767. 7p.

Fol. 36. 17 Jan. 1767, [New York]. Maj. Gen. Gage to
Earl of Shelburne (extract). Indian traders and the French

receive large quantities of English goods from Mobile and
Pensacola merchants. Most skins and furs that are traded
for English goods, however, go to New Orleans. 3p.

Fol. 38. 22 Feb. 1767, New York. Maj. Gen. Gage to Earl
of Shelburne (extract). Indian traders take their peltry
to New Orleans since they receive higher prices there.
Regulations are needed for the Indian trade. 12p.

Fol. 44. 1766. Extracts from journal of Capt. Harry Gordon
reporting that the French garrisoned Ft. Massac to prevent
the Cherokees from harrassing the French trading with the
Wabash and Shawnee Indians. Gordon suggests that the
English garrison the fort to hold the balance of power
between the Cherokee and Wabash nations. 7p.

Fol. 48. 4 Apr. 1767, New York. Maj. Gen. Gage to Earl
of Shelburne (copy). Gage hopes that some of the past
Indian expenses will not recur. Bd. of Trade will determine
the annual number of Indian congresses and presents. The
colonies who benefit from the Indian trade should pay a
portion of the Indian expenses. 6p.

Fol. 88. 8 Aug. 1766, Charleston. John Stuart to Sec.
Conway (extract). Stuart discusses the problems of general
licenses for the traders. The only trading posts within
the Indian nations are at Ft. Prince George near the Cherokees and at Ft. Tombigbee near the Choctaws. Only Gov.
Johnstone forces the traders to work through the superintendent. 6p.

Fol. 91. 11 Apr. 1767, Port Royal. John Stuart to Earl
of Shelburne (extract). Montague and Gov. Wright will
recall the general licenses of Indian traders. In the
future traders will be restricted to certain districts.
2p.

Fol. 95. 28 July 1767, Charleston. John Stuart to Earl
of Shelburne. [Copy of C.O. 5/68/136]. 7p.

Fol. 102. 21 May 1767, Camp near Whitehall. Memorial from
S.C. Traders [with the Cherokees] to John Stuart. [Copy
of C.O. 5/68/140]. 6p.

Fol. 106. [1767]. Regulations for the Better Carrying on
Trade with the Indian Tribes in the Southern District
(copy). 10p.

Fol. 111. 21 May [1767], [Hard Labor]. Copy of affidavit
from James McCormick stating that he was attacked by
Cornelius Doharty and others while returning with a mulato
[from Chote]. 3p.

Fol. 113. 21 May [1767], Hard Labor. Affidavit from John
Bowie. [Same as C.O. 5/68/151]. 3p.

C.O. 323/25 (CONT'D)

Fol. 119. 23 Sept. 1765, New York. Maj. Gen. Gage to Sec.
Conway (extract). Gage sends a report on troop distribution
in North America, including Ft. Prince George. 2p.

Fol. 121. 24 Sept. 1765, New York. Maj. Gen. Gage.
General Distribution of His Majesty's Forces in North
America. [Same as C.O. 5/83/455]. 2p.

Fol. 127. 3 Apr. 1767, New York. Maj. Gen. Gage to Earl
of Shelburne. [Copy of C.O. 5/85/72]. 14p.

Fol. 155. [ca. 1766]. Memorial from Gen. Lyman to King
in Council (copy). Lyman requests a land grant to establish a colony in the territory from the mouth of the Ohio
R. to a line 300 miles south. 12p.

Fol. 161. [ca. 1766]. Gen. [Phineas] Lyman to Earl of
Shelburne (copy). Lyman explains the advantage in establishing a colony south of Ohio R., including greater security for the colony, a more efficient Indian trade, and
substantial benefits to the Indians. 24p.

Fol. 173. 28 Oct. 1766, London. Gen. Lyman to Earl of
Shelburne (copy). Lyman explains the reasons for a settlement south of the Ohio River. 8p.

Fol. 177. [1766]. Gen. Lyman. Plan for Settling Louisiana
and for Erecting New Colonies between West Florida and the
Falls of St. Anthony. 16p.

Fol. 194. [1766]. Some Thoughts on Indian Affairs.
English need a fort at the head of the Mobile R. which
would allow access to the interior almost to the Cherokees. 14p.

C.O. 323/26   ORIGINAL CORRESPONDENCE, BD. OF TRADE: 1769

Fol. 3. 13 Oct. 1769, Whitehall. Lachlin Maclean to John
Pownall. 2p. [Enclosures to fol. 21].

Fol. 5. 26 Aug. 1767, New York. Maj. Gen. Gage to Earl
of Shelburne (copy). Stuart describes problems with the
Southern Indians caused by competing traders from different
provinces. Substantial presents should not be given to
Indians except in the presence of superintendents or
deputies. 4p.

Fol. 8. 21 July 1767, Charleston. John Stuart to Maj.
Gen. Gage (extract). Presents sent to the governors for
distribution are expensive and increase Indian Department
expenses. 4p.

Fol. 10. May 1767. Speeches from Indian Chiefs to John
Stuart (extract). Saluy and two Creek chiefs complain
about the traders. 4p.

C.O. 323/26 (CONT'D)

>Fol. 12. 24 Aug. 1767, New York. Maj. Gen. Gage to Earl of Shelburne. [Extract of C.O. 5/85/155]. 7p.

C.O. 323/27   ORIGINAL CORRESPONDENCE, BD. OF TRADE: 1769-1773

Fol. 1. 6 Dec. 1769, Charleston. John Stuart to Earl of Hillsborough. [Duplicate of C.O. 5/71/9 Part I]. 5p.

Fol. 4. 20 Jan. 1770, Charleston. John Stuart to Earl of Hillsborough. [Duplicate of C.O. 5/71/52]. 3p. [Enclosures to fol. 21b].

>Fol. 6b. [ca. Nov. - Dec. 1769], [Williamsburg]. Memorial from House of Burgesses to Gov. Botetourt. [Same as C.O. 5/71/59 Part I]. 9p.

>Fol. 14. [ca. Nov. - Dec. 1769], [Williamsburg]. Address from House of Burgesses to Gov. Botetourt. [Same as C.O. 5/71/56 Part I]. 2p.

>Fol. 15. 18 Dec. 1769, Williamsburg. Gov. Botetourt to John Stuart. [Same as C.O. 5/71/54 Part I]. 2p.

>Fol. 17. 29 July 1769, Toqueh. Talk from Cherokee Headmen and Warriors to John Stuart. [Same as C.O. 5/70/295]. 2p.

>Fol. 19. 13 Jan. 1770, Charleston. John Stuart to Gov. Botetourt. [Same as C.O. 5/71/61 Part I]. 6p.

Fol. 22. 27 Jan. 1770, Charleston. John Stuart to Earl of Hillsborough. [Duplicate of C.O. 5/71/69 Part I]. 3p.

Fol. 26. 5 July 1770, Charleston. John Stuart to Earl of Hillsborough. [Duplicate of C.O. 5/71/21 Part II]. 3p.

Fol. 36. [Rec. 8 Mar. 1771]. Petition from John Evans to the King. Evans requests a grant to search for gold west of the Carolinas and east of the Miss. River. 2p.

Fol. 63. 10 Jan. 1772, Whitehall. Order in Council referring to the Bd. of Trade petition from Earl of Eglintoune, Wm. Taylor, and Montfort Browne on the expediency of settling along the Miss. River. 2p. [Enclosures to fol. 66b].

>Fol. 64. [Rec. 31 Jan. 1772]. Petition from Earl of Eglintoune, Wm. Taylor, and Montfort Browne to King in Council. Chief cause of the recent war was French influence over the Indians bordering the British settlements. Settlement along the Miss. will serve as barrier between the Indians and other European colonies. 5p.

Fol. 90. 29 Oct. - 2 Nov. 1771, Pensacola. Duplicate of minutes of a congress held with the Upper Creeks recording that Creeks and Cherokees must settle among themselves the dispute over land which the Cherokees propose to cede to the traders. 31p.

C.O. 323/27 (CONT'D)

Fol. 107. 31 Dec. 1771 - Jan. 1772, Mobile. Copy of minutes of
a congress held with the Chickasaws and Choctaws recording that
all Indians in the Southern Dept. have complained about whites
hunting on Indian land. 30p.

C.O. 323/28   ORIGINAL CORRESPONDENCE, BD. OF TRADE: 1768-1770

Fol. 10. 31 May 1768, Whitehall. Order in Council referring
to the Bd. of Trade the memorial of Gen. Phineas Lyman requesting
a land grant in western Virginia. 2p. [Enclosures to fol. 13b].

> Fol. 11. [1768]. Memorial from Gen. Phineas Lyman to
> King in Council. Lyman requests a land grant in western
> Va. (bounded in the north by the Great Kanawha and Ohio
> Rivers) for officers and soldiers. 3p.

Fol. 14. 23 and 25 Oct. 1768, Ft. Stanwix. Wm. Johnson to
Earl of Hillsborough (copy). Johnson has just opened the
conference with the Indians. The boundary line is not yet
settled. 11p.

Fol. 20. 18 Nov. 1768, Johnson Hall. Wm. Johnson to Earl of
Hillsborough. [Copy of C.O. 5/69/310]. 7p. [Enclosures to
fol. 55b].

> Fol. 24. Oct. and Nov. 1768, Ft. Stanwix. Proceedings at
> a Treaty Held by Wm. Johnson with the Six Nations, Shawnees,
> Delawares, Senecas of Ohio, and Other Dependent Tribes.
> [Copy of C.O. 5/69/314]. 60p.

> Fol. 54b. 5 Nov. 1768, Ft. Stanwix. Deed of the Six Nation
> land cession. [Same as C.O. 5/69/316]. 2p.

Fol. 56. 15 Sept. 1768, Charleston. John Stuart to Earl of
Hillsborough. [Same as C.O. 5/69/298]. 5p.

Fol. 59. 15 Sept. 1768, Charleston. John Stuart to Earl of
Hillsborough. [Same as C.O. 5/69/300]. 5p.

Fol. 64. 9 Mar. 1769, Whitehall. Order in Council referring
to the Bd. of Trade a petition requesting a land grant west of
the Allegheny Mountains. 2p. [Enclosures to fol. 69b].

> Fol. 65. [Rec. 1 May 1769]. Petition from Inhabitants
> of Great Britain's Virginia and Maryland to King in Council
> (copy). Petitioners request 2,500,000 acres from the
> Indian land obtained at Ft. Stanwix. 7p.

Fol. 81. 14 July 1768, Charleston. John Stuart to Earl of
Hillsborough. [Duplicate of C.O. 5/69/216]. 4p.

Fol. 83. 15 Sept. 1768, Charleston. John Stuart to Earl of
Hillsborough. [Duplicate of C.O. 5/69/260]. 4p. [Enclosures
to fol. 94b].

C.O. 323/28 (CONT'D)

Fol. 85. 25 June 1768, New York. Gen. Gage to John Stuart. [Same as C.O. 5/69/262]. 3p.

Fol. 87. 23 July 1768, Savannah. John Stuart to Capt. Fuser. [Same as C.O. 5/69/268]. 3p.

Fol. 89. 1 Aug. 1768, Savannah. John Stuart to Alex. Cameron. [Same as C.O. 5/69/272]. 3p.

Fol. 91. 1 Aug. 1768, Savannah. Talk from John Stuart to Oconostota, Attakullakulla, Ousteneka, Willinawa, and other Cherokee chiefs and warriors. [Same as C.O. 5/69/270]. 3p.

Fol. 93. 1 Aug. 1768, Savannah. John Stuart to Ensign Matthew Keough. Evacuation should be delayed until Stuart's talk is delivered to Chote. Cameron will assist with the evacuation of Ft. Prince George. 3p.

Fol. 95. 28 Dec. 1768, Charleston. John Stuart to Earl of Hillsborough. [Duplicate of C.O. 5/70/55]. 7p. [Enclosures to fol. 138b].

Fol. 114. 8-17 Oct. and 12-14 Nov. 1768. Journal of John Stuart. [Duplicate of C.O. 5/70/76]. 36p.

Fol. 134. 14 Oct. 1768, Hard Labor. Treaty with Cherokees. [Same as C.O. 5/70/95]. 4p.

Fol. 138. List of papers enclosed in Stuart's letter of 28 Dec. 1768. 2p.

Fol. 139. 3 Jan. 1769, Charleston. John Stuart to Earl of Hillsborough. [Duplicate of C.O. 5/70/105]. 4p.

Fol. 141. 3 Jan. 1769, Charleston. John Stuart to Earl of Hillsborough. [Duplicate of C.O. 5/70/110]. 3p.

Fol. 149. 30 July 1769, Charleston. John Stuart to Earl of Hillsborough (extract). Stuart requests appointment to provincial councils in order to assist in making Indian laws. 3p.

C.O. 323/29   ORIGINAL CORRESPONDENCE, BD. OF TRADE: 1773-1780

Fol. 48. 26 June 1776, Treasury Chambers. John Robinson to Richard Cumberland. Robinson asks for an opinion about the bills of Mr. Thomas, Deputy Superintendent, totaling £987. 2p.

Fol. 57. 26 Oct. 1776, Pensacola. John Stuart to Geo. Germain. [Same as C.O. 5/78/15]. 4p.

C.O. 323/33   ORIGINAL CORRESPONDENCE, BD. OF TRADE, ABSTRACTS: 1758-
            1759

Fol. 24. 5 Jan. 1759, Williamsburg. Lt. Gov. Fauquier to [Bd. of Trade]. [Abstract of C.O. 5/1329/100]. 3p.

C.O. 323/33 (CONT'D)

Fol. 33b. 30 Aug. 1759, Williamsburg. Lt. Gov. Fauquier to
[Bd. of Trade]. [Abstract of C.O. 5/1329/170]. 2p.

Fol. 37. 20 Dec. 1758, [Edenton]. Gov. Dobbs to [Bd. of Trade]
(abstract). Dobbs has received no orders since 1757 concerning
the boundary line between N. and S. Carolina. 1p.

Fol. 37b. 22 Jan. 1759. Gov. Dobbs to Bd. of Trade (abstract).
It is advisable to repeal Atkin's law prohibiting Indian trade
without a proper license. Problems concerning the boundary
between N. and S.C. are not being resolved. 2p.

Fol. 39. 11 Sept. 1759. Gov. Dobbs to [Bd. of Trade] (abstract).
Dobbs hopes Bd. will fix the boundary between N.C. and S.C. as
soon as possible. 5p.

Fol. 42b. 7 Aug. 1758, Charleston. Gov. Lyttleton to [Bd.
of Trade]. [Abstract of C.O. 5/376/41]. 6p.

Fol. 45. 2 Oct. 1758, [Charleston]. Gov. Lyttleton to [Bd.
of Trade]. [Abstract of C.O. 5/376/55]. 2p.

Fol. 45b. 1 Dec. 1758, [Charleston]. Gov. Lyttleton to [Bd.
of Trade]. [Abstract of C.O. 5/376/65]. 2p.

Fol. 46. 2 Dec. 1758, [Charleston]. Gov. Lyttleton to [Bd. of
Trade]. [Abstract of C.O. 5/376/71]. 2p.

Fol. 46b. 18 Feb. 1758 [1759], [Charleston]. Gov. Lyttleton
to [Bd. of Trade]. [Abstract of C.O. 5/376/77]. 2p.

Fol. 47. 21 Feb. 1759, [Charleston]. Gov. Lyttleton to [Bd.
of Trade]. [Abstract of C.O. 5/376/79]. 1p.

Fol. 47. 14 Apr. 1759, [Charleston]. Gov. Lyttleton to [Bd.
of Trade]. [Abstract of C.O. 5/376/81]. 5p.

Fol. 49b. 8 May 1759, Charleston. Gov. Lyttleton to [Bd. of
Trade]. [Abstract of C.O. 5/376/98]. 2p.

Fol. 50. 1 Sept. 1759, [Charleston]. Gov. Lyttleton to [Bd.
of Trade]. [Abstract of C.O. 5/376/105]. 8p.

Fol. 56. 25 Oct. 1758, Georgia. Gov. Ellis to [Bd. of Trade].
Virginians and Cherokees are close to quarreling.   3p.

Fol. 57. 9 Nov. 1759, [Georgia]. Gov. Ellis to [Bd. of Trade].
[Abstract of C.O. 5/646/199]. 2p.

Fol. 57b. 28 Jan. 1759, [Georgia]. Gov. Ellis to [Bd. of
Trade]. [Abstract of C.O. 5/646/201]. 4p.

Fol. 61. 24 Apr. 1759, [Georgia]. Gov. Ellis to [Bd. of Trade].
[Abstract of C.O. 5/646/234]. 6p.

Fol. 64. 26 July 1759, [Georgia]. Gov. Ellis to [Bd. of Trade].
[Abstract of C.O. 5/646/250]. 6p.

COLONIES GENERAL
C.O. 324/10   ENTRY BOOK OF COMMISSIONS, INSTRUCTIONS, BD. OF TRADE
*   CORRESPONDENCE: 1712-1722*

Fol. 148b. 8 Sept. 1721. Representation of His Majesty's
Plantations on the Continent of America. Cherokees are a
warlike nation with about 3,800 warriors inhabiting the Appalachian Mountains. Cherokee friendship can be easily won since
they dislike the French. 55p.

C.O. 324/16   ENTRY BOOK OF COMMISSIONS, INSTRUCTIONS, BD. OF TRADE
*   CORRESPONDENCE: 1756-1760*

Fol. 46. 13 May 1756, Whitehall. Bd. of Trade to Henry Fox.
Bd. proposes that Edmond Atkin be appointed Superintendent of
Indian Affairs for the Southern District. 2p.

Fol. 50. 1 July 1756, Whitehall. Bd. of Trade to Gov. Dinwiddie.
Circular letter to governors supporting Mr. Atkin for Superintendent of Indian Affairs in the South. 3p.

C.O. 324/17   ENTRY BOOK OF COMMISSIONS, INSTRUCTIONS, BD. OF TRADE
*   CORRESPONDENCE: 1760-1766*

Fol. 30b. 28 Apr. 1761, [Whitehall]. Bd. of Trade to Governors
in America. Bd. sends questionnaire for the governors in
America concerning the number of Indians, treaties, and trade.
10p.

Fol. 82. 2 Dec. 1761, Whitehall. Bd. of Trade to the King.
2p. [Enclosures to fol. 87b].

    Fol. 82b. 2 Dec. 1761, Whitehall. Draft of instructions
    for the Governors of Nova Scotia, N. Hampshire, N.Y., Va.,
    N.C., S.C., and Ga. forbidding land grants or settlements
    which might antagonize the Indians bordering these colonies.
    8p.

Fol. 107. 8 June 1763, Whitehall. [Bd. of Trade] to the King.
Indian fur and skin trade in North America will now be controlled by the English since the French are leaving. 50p.

Fol. 153b. 10 Oct. 1763, [Whitehall]. Bd. of Trade to Wm.
Johnson and John Stuart. Bd. sends a copy of the Proclamation
[of 1763]. 1p.

Fol. 208. 10 July 1764, [Whitehall]. Bd. of Trade to John
Stuart. Bd. sends a copy of the plan for the future management
of Indian Affairs. Bd. also includes its opinion of the proposal. 7p. [Enclosure at fol. 215].

Fol. 211b. 10 July 1764, Whitehall. Bd. of Trade to Governors
of American Colonies. Bd. sends copies of the plan for future
management of Indian Affairs. 2p.

Fol. 213. 13 July 1764, Whitehall. Bd. of Trade to Governors
of American Colonies. Government must notify the Bd. about
all land grants. 1p.

C.O. 324/17 (CONT'D)

Fol. 215. [1764]. Plan for the Future Management of Indian
Affairs. 17p. [Enclosure of fol. 208].

Fol. 225. 28 Jan. 1765, Whitehall. Bd. of Trade to Earl of
Halifax. Bd. submits Timberlake's petition requesting expenses
for maintaining three Cherokees and their passage home. 1p.

Fol. 225b. 13 Feb. 1765, Whitehall. Bd. of Trade to Earl of
Halifax. Arrangements have been made to send home the Cherokees
in England. 2p.

Fol. 235. 23 Aug. 1765, Whitehall. Bd. of Trade to Wm. Johnson
and John Stuart. Bd. should be informed about all events within
their districts. 1p.

*C.O. 324/18   ENTRY BOOK OF COMMISSIONS, INSTRUCTIONS, BD. OF TRADE
            CORRESPONDENCE: 1766-1780*

Fol. 12. 30 Aug. 1766, Whitehall. Bd. of Trade to King.
Indians in London should be treated well to avoid the disgraceful
treatment given the [Cherokees] Indians last year. 9p.

Fol. 21b. 10 Sept. 1766, [Whitehall]. S. Bradbury to Maurice
Morgan. Bradbury sends copies of papers from the Superintendents
of Indian Affairs. 1p. [Enclosures to fol. 25].

   Fol. 22. 10 Sept. 1766. List of papers from Wm. Johnson
   and John Stuart, several of which relate to Cherokees. 7p.

Fol. 33. 2 Jan. 1767, [Whitehall]. Bd. of Trade to Earl of
Shelburne. Bd. sends a copy of Stuart's letter relating to the
Indian war and the probability of English involvement. 2p.

Fol. 37. 10 Feb. 1767, Whitehall. Bd. of Trade to Lords of
Committee of Council. Proclamation of 1763 forbids the private
purchase of Indian land. 14p.

Fol. 91b. 22 Dec. 1767, [Whitehall]. Bd. of Trade to Earl of
Shelburne. Since the line is settled with the Cherokees, it is
not advisable that the border with the Six Nations be extended
below the mouth of Kanawha River. Land south of the mouth is
used by the Cherokees as hunting ground. 7p.

Fol. 102. 7 Mar. 1768, Whitehall. Bd. of Trade to the King.
Boundary line has been established with the Creeks, Cherokees,
and Choctaws. Cherokees and other independent tribes occupy
the land below the Kanawha River. 53p. [Enclosure at fol.
138b].

Fol. 138b. Appendix [to Bd. of Trade's letter of 7 Mar. 1768]
containing an extract of the Cherokee land cession to S.C. at
Ft. Prince George, 19 Oct. 1765, and letters from Cameron and
Tryon on the Cherokee boundary. 32p.

Fol. 154b. 25 Apr. 1769, Whitehall. Bd. of Trade to the King.
At Ft. Stanwix (Nov. 1768), the Northern Indians ceded land

C.O. 324/18 (CONT'D)

south to the Cherokee River. That boundary differs from the
King's instructions and from what Stuart and the Cherokees
agreed to. 28p.

Fol. 177. 22 Dec. 1769, Whitehall. Bd. of Trade to the King.
Bd. recommends that Stuart be appointed to the provincial
councils in the Southern District, thus allowing him to assist
in making Indian laws. 3p.

Fol. 244b. 18 July 1776, Whitehall. Richard Cumberland to
John Robinson. Cumberland recommends paying bills from Mr.
Thomas, Deputy Superintendent of Indian Affairs in the Southern
District. 4p.

C.O. 324/21   ENTRY BOOK OF REPORTS (1702-1782) AND LETTERS FROM BD.
             OF TRADE: 1744-1752

Fol. 243. 10 July 1764, Whitehall. Bd. of Trade to Wm. Johnson
and John Stuart. Bd. discusses plan for Indian commercial and
political regulations. 16p.

Fol. 271. [ca. 1768], Whitehall. Report from Bd. of Trade to
the King. Although the Six Nations may claim the country south
of the Ohio and Kanawha Rivers, the Cherokees and other independent tribes occupy that land. 51p.

Fol. 297. 15 Apr. 1768, Whitehall. Earl of Hillsborough to
Governors in North America. Regulation of Indian affairs will
be left to colonies. 6p.

Fol. 422. 18 July 1776, Whitehall. Richard Cumberland to John
Robinson. Cumberland discusses the expenses of Mr. Thomas,
Deputy Superintendent of Indian Affairs in the Southern District.
5p.

C.O. 324/40   ENTRY BOOK OF COMMISSIONS, WARRANTS, AND INSTRUCTIONS:
             1760-1764

Fol. 163. 9 Dec. 1761, St. James. Additional Instructions
from George III to Jeffrey Amherst. Amherst should issue a
proclamation prohibiting people from settling Indian lands. 5p.

Fol. 175. 5 Jan. 1762, St. James. Earl of Egremont to John
Stuart. Stuart is appointed Superintendent of Indian Affairs.
2p.

Fol. 204. 16 Aug. 1762, Whitehall. Certification that Skiagusta
Oconesta and two other Cherokees visited King George in London.
1p.

C.O. 324/44   ENTRY BOOK OF GRANTS AND WARRANTS: 1777-1783

Fol. 25. 21 Oct. 1777, St. James. Geo. Germain to John Stuart.
[Entry letter of C.O. 5/78/175.] 1p.

C.O. 324/44 (CONT'D)

Fol. 242.   24 June 1779, St. James. Geo. Germain to Alex.
Cameron. [Entry letter of C.O. 5/80/123.] 1p.

Fol. 243.   24 June 1779, St. James. Geo. Germain to Thomas
Brown. [Entry letter of C.O. 5/80/123.] 1p.

C.O. 324/53   ENTRY BOOK OF WARRANTS AND COMMISSIONS: 1773-1782

Fol. 35b.   24 June 1779, St. James. Geo. Germain to Thomas
Brown. [Entry letter of C.O. 5/80/123]. 1p.

MINUTES OF BOARD OF TRADE
C.O. 391/25   BD. OF TRADE, MINUTES: 1715-1716

Fol. 159.   8 July 1715, Whitehall. Minutes recording that
Stanhope sent the Bd. several letters from Va. and Carolina
governors about local Indian attacks. 2p.

Fol. 160.   12 July 1715, Whitehall. Minutes recording the
reading of a letter from the Carolina Proprietors about the
hostilities of Carolina Indians. 1p.

Fol. 162.   13 July 1715, Whitehall. Minutes recording a petition from the Carolina Proprietors for assistance against the
Carolina Indians. 4p.

Fol. 165.   14 July 1715, Whitehall. Minutes recording that the
Bd. has conferred with Stanhope about giving relief to Carolina
against the Indians. 2p.

Fol. 167.   15 July 1715, Whitehall. Minutes stating that it
would be impossible to prevent Carolina's destruction if the
Yamasees, Cherokees, and other Indians attack it. 8p.

Fol. 175.   16 July 1715, Whitehall. Minutes recording the
belief of the Carolina planters that the lack of good management among the Indian traders and the influence of the French
and Spanish caused the Indian attacks. There are no recent
reports about Indian enslavement. 4p.

Fol. 180.   19 July 1715, Whitehall. Minutes recording a letter
sent to Sec. Stanhope about the conditions in Carolina after
the Indian insurrection. 1p.

Fol. 189.   26 July 1715, Whitehall. Minutes recording that the
reason for the conflict in Carolina is the traders' abuse of
the Yamasees. Indian forces against Carolina could number
around 15,000 men. 4p.

Fol. 195.   28 July 1715, Whitehall. Minutes recording that the
Indians have destroyed most of Carolina's frontier settlements.
5p.

Fol. 206.   5 Aug. 1715, Whitehall. Minutes recording a request
from the House of Commons for papers on the Carolina Indian
hostilities. 3p.

C.O. 391/25 (CONT'D)

Fol. 211. 10 Aug. 1715, Whitehall. Minutes recording the
reading of a letter from Mr. Crawley to Mr. Byrd about the
Carolina Indian insurrection. 3p.

Fol. 252. 15 Sept. 1715, Whitehall. Minutes recording the
reading of a Lt. Gov. Spotswood describing Virginia's assistance
to Carolina against the Indians. 2p.

Fol. 254. 16 Sept. 1715, Whitehall. Minutes recording that
Mr. Kettleby is apprehensive about weapons from Va. going to
enemy Indians. Sec. Stanhope was advised about Virginia's
assistance to Carolina. 2p.

Fol. 306. 20 Dec. 1715, Whitehall. Minutes recording that
copies were made of letters relating to the Indian war in
Carolina. 3p.

Fol. 436. 15 May 1716, Whitehall. Minutes recording that
Mr. Offley requested to speak about a petition concerning
Virginia's Indian trade. 2p.

Fol. 437. 16 May 1716, Whitehall. Minutes recording that
Spotswood stopped Indian hostilities along the frontier.
Spotswood sent some proposals for settling the Va. and Carolina
boundary. 5p.

Fol. 442. 17 May 1716, Whitehall. Minutes recording Mr. Offley's
complaints that the Va. Indian Trade Act would limit the number
of traders to those appointed by the government. 3p.

Fol. 451. 24 May 1716, Whitehall. Minutes recording the reading of a memorial from Robert Carey supporting the Va. act
regulating the Indian trade. 1p.

C.O. 391/29　BD. OF TRADE, MINUTES: 1719-1720

Fol. 270. 28 July 1720, Whitehall. Minutes recording that the
Cherokees helped establish peace with the Yamasees. 6p.

Fol. 303. 16 Aug. 1720, Whitehall. Minutes recording that the
Carolinians have established trade with the Cherokees, whose
nearest town is 280 miles from Charleston. 6p.

C.O. 391/33　BD. OF TRADE, MINUTES: 1724

Fol. 271. 29 Oct. 1724, Whitehall. Minutes recording the
reading of talks between Gen. Nicholson, Outassatah, and the
Cherokees in Nov. 1723. 15p.

C.O. 391/34　BD. OF TRADE, MINUTES: 1725

Fol. 256. 18 Nov. 1725, Whitehall. Minutes recording the
reading of Gov. Nicholson's letters including several discussing
the Cherokee complaints against other Indians for thievery. 9p.

C.O. 391/39   BD. OF TRADE, MINUTES: 1730

Fol. 211. 18 Aug. 1730, Whitehall. Minutes recording that
Gov. Johnson talked with the Bd. about the Cherokee chiefs in
England. 2p.

Fol. 213. 19 Aug. 1730, Whitehall. Minutes recording a request
of Wm. Keith to prepare an Indian-style treaty to present to
the Cherokees in England. 2p.

Fol. 214. 20 Aug. 1730, Whitehall. Minutes recording that
Wm. Keith gave a preview of the forthcoming agreement between
the Cherokees in England and the King. 2p.

Fol. 215. 25 Aug. 1730, Whitehall. Minutes recording that
Wm. Keith, Gov. Johnson, and the interpreter for the Indian
chiefs talked with the Bd. concerning proper protocol with the
Indian chiefs. 1p.

Fol. 218. 1 Sept. 1730, Whitehall. Minutes recording the
approval of the King for making a treaty with the Cherokees,
who are scheduled to meet the Board on 7 September. 3p.

Fol. 226. 7 Sept. 1730, Whitehall. Minutes recording that the
treaty was explained to the Cherokees, who agreed to give a
reply within two days. 9p.

Fol. 237. 9 Sept. 1730, Whitehall. Minutes recording that the
Cherokees accepted the treaty. 5p.

Fol. 248. 29 Sept. 1730, Whitehall. Minutes recording the
reading of a memorial from Alex. Cuming about the Cherokee
Indians. Bd. will consider the memorial later. 4p.

Fol. 252. 30 Sept. 1730, Whitehall. Minutes recording the
reading of a letter from Cuming about a chief's desire to remain
in England. A copy of the Cherokee articles and their answer
was sent to Newcastle. 4p.

FOREIGN OFFICE, GENERAL CORRESPONDENCE
F.O. 4/4   UNITED STATES OF AMERICA, SERIES I: 1786

Fol. 310. New York. [P. Allairs?]. Occurences from 8 August
to 7 September 1786. Congress decided to divide the Indian
trade into two districts. Southern District will include all
Indians south of the Ohio River. Only American citizens can
trade with the Indians. 10p.

Fol. 325. 4 Oct. 1786, New York. John Temple to Marquis of
Carmarthen. 4p. [Enclosures to fol. 342b].

Fol. 335. 21 Sept. - 10 Oct. 1786. *Journals of Congress*.
James White of N.C. is appointed superintendent of Indian
Affairs for the Southern District. He will investigate
Indian problems in the Southern District. 16p.

Fol. 355. 3 Nov. 1786, New York. [P. Allairs?] to Geo. Yonge.
4p. [Enclosures to fol. 367b].

F.O. 4/4 (CONT'D)

Fol. 357. 3 Nov. 1786, New York. [P. Allairs?]. Occurrences from 5 October to 3 November 1786. Ga. army marched into Indian country to offer peace. 22p.

Fol. 387. 6 Dec. 1786. [P. Allairs?] to Geo. Yonge. 4p. [Enclosures to fol. 398b].

Fol. 389. 7 Dec. 1786, New York. [P. Allairs?]. Occurrences from 2 November to 6 December 1786. Southern Army under Clark has gone into Indian country to make peace. 20p.

Fol. 407. 11 Dec. 1786, Whitehall. Lord Carmarthen to John Adams (draft). Carmarthen requests information about the merchants' claim for payment stemming from the land cession by the Creeks and Cherokees in 1773. 4p.

Fol. 420. 21 Jan. 1786, London Tavern. *Memorial from the Committee of British Merchants Interested in Commerce with America to William Pitt and Marquis Carmarthen.* Merchants discuss their claims [from the Creek-Cherokee land cession]. 8p.

F.O. 4/5 UNITED STATES OF AMERICA, SERIES I: 1787

Fol. 22. 24 Jan. 1787. Grosvenor Square. John Adams to Marquis of Carmarthen. Adams has not received any information [about merchant claims resulting from the Creek-Cherokee land cessions]. 3p.

Fol. 89. 5 Apr. 1787, New York. [P. Allairs?]. Occurrences from 7 March to [5] April 1787. Indians have been warring in Kentucky. Congress is unable to raise money to send men against the Indians. 8p.

Fol. 123. 3 May 1787, New York. [P. Allairs?]. Occurrences from 5 April to 3 May 1787. All the tribes are in arms because an Indian king was killed while holding in his hands a peace treaty made with the [American] commissioners. 16p.

Fol. 210. 5 July 1787, New York. [P. Allairs?] to Geo. Yonge. 4p. [Enclosures to fol. 217b].

Fol. 212. 5 July 1787, New York. [P. Allairs?]. Occurrences from 7 June to [5] July 1787. Southern Indians have declared war against the United States since the Americans have not honored the treaties and have sent commissioners to take their hunting ground. 12p.

Fol. 319. 5 Oct. 1787, New York. [P. Allairs?]. Occurrences from 5 August to 5 October 1787. Indian war exists from Ga. to the Ohio River. Cherokees, Choctaws, and Chickasaws are now making peace with Congress, but they do not like the reception that they have been given. Franklin, Cumberland, and Kentucky are three new states within Indian territory. 16p.

F.O. 4/5 (CONT'D)

Fol. 339. 6 Nov. 1787, New York. [P. Allairs?]. Occurrences
from 5 October to 5 November 1787. All the frontier tribes in
Ga., N. and S. Carolina, and Va. have declared war against the
United States. The militia has been sent against them. 16p.

Fol. 377. 12 Nov. 1787, Philadelphia. *The Independent Gazetteer
or the Chronicle of Freedom.* A Cherokee from Chickamauga
reported seeing 500 Creeks at the mouth of the Hiwassee River.
4p.

Fol. 384. 6 Dec. 1787, New York. [P. Allairs?]. Occurrences
from 6 November to 6 December 1787. Congress has learned that
an Indian peace cannot be maintained without paying the tribes.
Southern Indians have declared war, and Ga. and N.C. have
asked for aid from the national government. 12p.

F.O. 4/6   UNITED STATES OF AMERICA, SERIES I: 1788

Fol. 47. 3 Jan. 1788, New York. [P. Allairs?]. Occurrences
from 6 December to 2 January 1788. Ga., the two Carolinas,
and Va. have raised 5,000 militia to fight the Southern Indians.
Franklin and Kentucky have asked the Spanish governor to discon-
tinue supplying the tribes. 19p.

Fol. 77. [Feb. 1788], [New York]. [P. Allairs?]. Occurrences
from 2 January to 27 February 1788. Indians have attacked the
frontiers of S.C. and Ga. and driven away the inhabitants. 14p.

Fol. 89. [Mar. 1788], New York. [P. Allairs?]. Occurrences
from 22 February to 5 March 1788. Ga. and the two Carolinas
have appointed commissioners to settle the Indian disputes. 4p.

Fol. 136. 3 Mar. [Apr.?] 1788, New York. [P. Allairs?].
Occurrences from 17 March to 2 April 1788. Ga. and the two
Carolinas have appointed commissioners to settle their Indian
problems and have invited the tribes to a Grand Indian Council
at Muskingum in May. 4p.

Fol. 138. 4 June 1788, New York. [P. Allairs?]. Occurrences
from 5 April to 6 May 1788. Ga. and the two Carolinas appointed
commissioners to settle Indian problems and to invite the tribes
to a Grand Indian Council in May. 11p.

Fol. 155. 6 May [June?] 1788, New York. [P. Allairs?]. Occurrences from 6 May to 5 June 1788. War with the Southern Indians
continues. Commissioners are unable to persuade the Indians to
meet. Money is the principal ingredient in making an Indian
peace last. 18p.

Fol. 209a. 4 July 1788, New York. [P. Allairs?]. Occurrences
from 4 June to 4 July 1788. Southern Indians have agreed to
meet with Gov. Sinclair in July. In June the tribes are holding
a Grand Council on the Canadian border. 6p.

F.O. 4/6 (CONT'D)

Fol. 227. 6 Aug. 1788, New York. [P. Allairs?]. Occurrences
from 6 July to 6 August 1788. Gov. Sinclair has asked Congress
for Indian presents to establish a permanent peace. English
successfully used this method earlier. 6p.

Fol. 291. 2 Oct. 1788, New York. [P. Allairs?]. Occurrences
from 5 September to 2 October 1788. Governors are meeting with
different tribes prior to the Indian meeting with Gov. Sinclair.
Cherokees have sent a representative to Congress seeking protection against Hodgston and Kentucky. 8p.

Fol. 307. 6 Nov. 1788, New York. [P. Allairs?]. Occurrences
from 4 October to 6 November 1788. Southern States have still
not made peace with the Indians. Gov. Sinclair's Indian treaty
is pending. 4p.

Fol. 309. 3 Dec. 1788, New York. [P. Allairs?]. Occurrences
from 6 November to 3 December 1788. S.C. has raised toops to
fight the Indians, violating Congressional orders. Sinclair's
treaty has not been concluded. 6p.

F.O. 4/7 UNITED STATES OF AMERICA, SERIES I: 1789

Fol. 6. 3-6 Jan. 1789, New York. [P. Allairs?]. Occurrences
from 3 December 1788 to 6 January 1789. Some 300 Indians said
to belong to McGillivray attacked Ft. Gulaspi [Gillespie?]. 8p.

Fol. 24. 18 Feb. 1789, New York. [P. Allairs?]. Occurrences
from 6 January to 4 February 1789. Indians are warring intense-
ly against the two Carolinas. Warriors unsuccessfully attacked
two forts. 6p.

Fol. 28. 21 Mar. 1789, New York. [P. Allairs?]. Occurrences
from 22 February to 4 March 1789. Carolinas and Kentucky
continue to war against the Indians. Many lives are lost
daily. 3p.

Fol. 90. 6 May 1789, Cowetas. Memorial from Cherokee Chiefs
(presented by Bowles) to George III. Cherokees are oppressed
by their neighbors. Under a white flag, Virginians killed
five Cherokee headmen. Cherokees request assistance. 4p.

Fol. 346. 1789. Situation of the Western and Other Frontier
Settlements. Franklin is doomed to fall due to frequent Indian
attacks and the settlement's weakness. 12p.

Fol. 368. [Dec. 1789]. [P. Affairs?]. Occurrences from
November to 3 December 1789. Indians continue war against the
Ga., S. and N. Carolina, and Va. frontiers. Recent raids from
Kentucky and Ohio have exasperated the Indians. 4p.

F.O. 4/8 UNITED STATES OF AMERICA, SERIES I: 1790

Fol. 232. [Apr. 1790]. [P. Allairs?]. Occurrences from
2 March to 7 April 1790. Indian Commissioners are preparing
to meet with the Southern Indians to try to settle Indian peace
proposals from last fall. 4p.

F.O. 4/8 (CONT'D)

Fol. 410. 8 Dec. 1790, Whitehall. [Lord Grenville?] to Wm. Bowles (draft). The King has denied Bowles's application for arms and ammunition for the Creeks and Cherokees. 4p.

Fol. 412. 15 Dec. 1790, Osborn's Hotel, Adelphi. Wm. Bowles to Lord Grenville. Creeks and Cherokees rely on Bowles. He did not cross the Atlantic merely for presents. Bowles requests a meeting. 3p.

F.O. 4/9   UNITED STATES OF AMERICA, SERIES I: JANUARY - APRIL 1791

Fol. 3. 3 Jan. 1791, Osborn's Hotel [London]. Wm. Bowles to Lord Grenville. Bowles hopes that he will be permitted to deliver the enclosed petition to the King. 2p. [Enclosures to fol. 17b].

> Fol. 5. [Jan. 1791.] Representation from Wm. Augustus Bowles, Unatoy, Kuahtekiske, Seponejah, Tuskeniah, and Wosseo to the King. Indians request an alliance and permission to trade with the British West Indies. 27p.

Fol. 69. 13 Jan. 1791, [Osborn's Hotel at] Adelphi [in the Strand-London]. Wm. Bowles to Lord Grenville. Indians will drive the Spanish from the Floridas and lower Louisiana if the Spanish do not grant him two ports along the Fla. Coast. Principal object of Bowles's trip is to secure a commercial treaty allowing the Creek and Cherokee ships to trade with the British free ports or Nassau, at least. 12p.

Fol. 81. 25 Jan. 1791, [Osborn's Hotel at] Adelphi [in the Strand-London]. Wm. Bowles to Lord Grenville. Bowles encloses a letter concerning his demand for the free ports from the Spanish. 2p.

> Fol. 82. 26 Jan. 1791, [Osborn's Hotel at] Adelphi [in the Strand-London]. Wm. Bowles to Spanish ambassador at London. Bowles needs an answer to his earlier letter to Floridablanca about free ports before leaving England. 2p.

F.O. 4/11   UNITED STATES OF AMERICA, SERIES I: SEPTEMBER - DECEMBER 1791

Fol. 260. 12 Dec. 1791. Philadelphia. Thomas Jefferson to Geo. Hammond (copy). Jefferson sends an extract of a letter about Bowles, who returned from England to incite the Creeks against the United States. 1p. [Enclosures to fol. 261].

> Fol. 260. [1791], Philadelphia. Geo. Hammond to Thomas Jefferson (extract). Hammond discusses Bowles's attempt to establish a post in East Fla. to maintain contact between England and the Indians. 3p.

Fol. 264. 14 Dec. 1791, Philadelphia. Geo. Hammond to Thomas Jefferson (copy). Hammond has no official knowledge of Bowles and cannot believe he is acting for Great Britain. 3p.

F.O. 4/76   UNITED STATES OF AMERICA, SERIES I: JULY - DECEMBER 1792

> Fol. 243. 6 Nov. 1792, Philadelphia. Geo. Hammond to Lord
> Grenville. Creek and Cherokee parties (one evidently as large
> as 400-500 men) have continued to attack the Ga. frontiers. 7p.

> Fol. 249. 6 Nov. 1792, Philadelphia. Geo. Hammond to Lord
> Grenville. [Duplicate of fol. 243]. 7p.

> Fol. 262. Nov. 1792, Norfolk. Col. Hamilton to Lord Grenville.
> Indians have been very troublesome along the frontiers. Whites
> are reportedly responsible by encroaching upon Indian lands. 4p.

> Fol. 266. 4 Dec. 1792, Philadelphia. Geo. Hammond to Lord
> Grenville. Spanish government is inciting the Creeks and
> Cherokees against the United States. 6p.

> Fol. 269. 4 Dec. 1792, Philadelphia. Geo. Hammond to Lord
> Grenville. [Duplicate of fol. 266]. 6p.

F.O. 5/141, PART I   UNITED STATES OF AMERICA, SERIES II: JANUARY -
APRIL 1819

> Fol. 26. 4 Jan. 1819, Washington. Charles Bagot to Viscount
> Castlereigh (duplicate). Bagot sends documents regarding
> Spanish and Seminole Indian relations with the United States.
> 6p. [Enclosures to fol. 101b].

>> Fol. 60. 23 July 1818, Washington. John Q. Adams to Don
>> Luis de Onís (printed). United States policy towards the
>> Indians is one of peace. This policy has been so successful
>> that for many years there has been no Indian hostility,
>> except that caused by foreign instigation. 6p.

>> Fol. 62b. 23 Apr. 1816, Washington. Andrew Jackson to
>> Gov. of Pensacola (printed). Banditti and hostile Creeks
>> continue secret attempts to entice slaves from Ga. as well
>> as from the Cherokees and Creeks. 2p.

F.O. 5/141, PART II   UNITED STATES OF AMERICA, SERIES II: JANUARY -
APRIL 1819

> Fol. 67. 4 Jan. 1819, Washington. Charles Bagot to Viscount
> Castlereigh (duplicate). 3p. [Enclosures to fol. 113b].

>> Fol. 69. 5 Dec. 1818, Washington. *Report of the Secretary*
>> *of War of a System Providing for the Abolition of the*
>> *Existing Indian Trade Establishments of the United States*
>> *and Providing for the Opening of the Trade with the Indians*
>> *to Individuals under Suitable Regulations.* 15p.

> Fol. 140. 1 Feb. 1819, Washington. Charles Bagot to Viscount
> Castereigh. 5p. [Enclosures to fol. 248b].

>> Fol. 169b. 23 Apr. 1816, Washington. Gen. Jackson to
>> Gov. of Pensacola. 2p. [Same as F.O. 5/141/62b, Part I].
>> 2p.

F.O. 5/146   UNITED STATES OF AMERICA, SERIES II: 1819

> Fol. 35. 9 Aug. 1814. Articles of Agreement and Capitulation
> ... between Maj. Gen. Jackson ... and the Creek Nation. All
> property taken from friendly Creeks, Cherokees, Chickasaws,
> and Choctaws will be returned. 10p.

F.O. 5/147   UNITED STATES OF AMERICA, SERIES II: 1819

> Fol. 21. 23 Mar. 1816 - 22 Feb. 1817. Gov. Cameron to Earl of
> Bathurst. Cameron forwards a memorial from the Creeks, Chero-
> kees, Choctaws, and Chickasaws. Indians complain about their
> inability to deal with the United States and have requested
> Great Britain's aid. 4p.

F.O. 5/166   UNITED STATES OF AMERICA, SERIES II: JANUARY - MARCH 1822

> Fol. 125. 8 Feb. 1822, Washington. Stratford Canning to
> Marquis of Londonderry. Canning encloses extracts from American
> newspapers about severe battle between the Osages and Cherokees.
> 2p. [Enclosures to fol. 127b].

> > Fol. 127. 1821. Two newspaper clippings (one from the
> > *Louisiana Herald*) about a fight between the Osages and
> > Cherokees. 2p.

PAYMASTER GENERAL, MISCELLANEOUS BOOKS
P.M.G. 14/2   DEPUTY PAYMASTER'S ACCOUNTS, AMERICA: 1761-1762

> Fol. 38. 17 Aug. 1761 - 1762. [Account of Expenses]. Account
> lists expenses for the campaign against the Cherokees. 79p.

P.M.G. 14/3   DEPUTY PAYMASTER'S ACCOUNTS, AMERICA: 1762-1769

> Fol. 37. 21 Mar. 1763 - 9 Dec. 1768. C. Burrell. [Account of
> Expenses]. Account lists some Cherokee expenditures. 146p.

P.M.G. 14/4   DEPUTY PAYMASTER'S ACCOUNTS, AMERICA: 1769-1773

> Fol. 8. 17 Mar. 1769 - 17 Aug. 1773. C. Burrell. [Account
> of Expenses]. Account lists some Cherokee expenditures. 81p.

DOCUMENTS ACQUIRED BY GIFT, DEPOSIT OR PURCHASE
P.R.O. 30 8/95   CHATHAM PAPERS, MISCELLANEOUS PAPERS RELATING TO
*   STATES OF NORTH AMERICA: 1742-1757*

> Fol. 90. Feb. 1756. Letter suggesting that a chain of forts
> be built from the western edge of the Allegheny Mountains to
> Lake Champlain, including some among the Cherokees. 7p.

> Fol. 96. 7 May 1756. Abstract of Loudoun's instructions and
> letters indicating that Mr. Atkin is appointed Agent and Super-
> intendent of the Southern Indians at same salary as Wm. Johnson
> (£600 a year). 7p.

> Fol. 138. 3 Dec. 1756. [Charles] Pinkney to Sec. of State.
> Pinkney describes the military strength of S.C., including plans

P.R.O. 30 8/95 (CONT'D)

for defense against the French. He refers to a fort at Keowee
(built about two years ago) and two forts proposed for the
Upper Creeks and Upper Cherokees. 6p.

Fol. 182. 28 May - 17 June 1757. Abstract of enclosures from
Earl of Loudoun's letter of 17 June 1757 that includes an
intercepted letter of Kerlerec concerning a Cherokee alliance.
6p.

Fol. 185. 17 June 1757. Abstract of letter from Earl of
Loudoun stating that Va. has not sent any troops to the Cherokee fort. 3p.

Fol. 213. 31 July - 16 Oct. 1757. Abstract of papers enclosed
in Loudoun's letter of 16 Oct. 1757 mentioning that the Cherokees remain friendly. Creeks are still neutral but probably
favor the French. The Va. fort among the Cherokees is not worth
maintaining. 7p.

Fol. 219. 19 Aug. 1756 - Sept. 1757. Abstract of Loudoun's
letters reporting that Va. sent only 200 men to S.C. and none
to the Cherokee fort. French made a treaty with the Cherokees
and are attempting to persuade the tribe to attack S. Carolina.
26p.

P.R.O. 30 8/96   CHATHAM PAPERS, MISCELLANEOUS PAPERS RELATING TO
STATES OF NORTH AMERICA: 1758-1763

Fol. 198. 2 Apr. 1759. Letter from [Ephraim Biggs?] describing
the French attempts to win over the Cherokees. A new colony
should be established among the Cherokees with its own government and treated as crown lands. 14p.

Fol. 230. 30 Oct. 1759. Considerations on a Future Peace as
it Relates to Great Britain. The Cherokees, Chickasaws, Creeks,
and other Indians have surrendered land and will continue their
trade unless the French turn them against the English. 16p.

Fol. 278. 6 Apr. 1761. Extract of a dispatch from Gen. Amherst
containing Virginia's act to raise troops in 1761. Virginia
has continued a regiment of 1,000 men to act against the Cherokees. 2p.

Fol. 280. 10 July 1760, Georgia. Henry Ellis to Gov. Ellis.
The success of Col. Montgomery's army against the Cherokees
might be the only way to prevent the tribe from receiving French
and Creek assistance. 4p.

Fol. 293. 9 Dec. 1761, Wilmington. Gov. Dobbs and Council to
William Pitt. Dobbs and Council recommend that Maj. Robert
Rogers replace the late Mr. Atkin as Superintendent of Southern
Indian Affairs. 1p.

*P.R.O. 30 8/97, PART I   CHATHAM PAPERS, MISCELLANEOUS PAPERS RELATING
                           TO STATES OF NORTH AMERICA: 1764-1774*

Fol. 50. 29 Mar. 1766. General Distribution of His Majesty's
Forces in North America. Report includes Ft. Prince George.
2p.

Fol. 53. May 1766. Statement on Indian trade and frontier
posts. 15p.

*P.R.O. 30 8/97, PART II   CHATHAM PAPERS, MISCELLANEOUS PAPERS RELATING
                           TO STATES OF NORTH AMERICA: 1764-1774*

Fol. 1. [2 Apr. 1774]. Mississippi Company papers [1763-1769]
sent to Wm. Pitt. Papers include memorial recommending the
construction of a small fort at the juncture of the Ohio and
Cherokee Rivers. 20p.

Fol. 30. Report concerning two intercepted letters to Duc de
Mirepoix. 4p. [Enclosures to fol. 38b].

    Fol. 32. Letter to [Duc de Mirepoix] stressing the neces-
    sity of having the Catawbas, Cherokees, and Chickasaws
    march to the Ohio. 14p.

Fol. 57. [1752-1753?]. Some Facts Stated Which Prove the
French to Be the Aggressors in North America. French have many
agreements with the Indians. Vaudeuil wrote (18 July 1743) that
their alliance with the Chickasaws and Cherokees was extremely
important. A fort should be built on the Cherokee River. 6p.

Fol. 61. America. Report from Mr. Abercromby describing the
military operations necessary in America. The English should
use the Catawbas to drive the French from their western Indian
posts. 5p.

*P.R.O. 30 8/344   CHATHAM PAPERS, MISCELLANEOUS PAPERS RELATING TO
                   STATES OF NORTH AMERICA: 1774-1804*

Fol. 10. 25 July 1784, St. Augustine. John Leslie to Thomas
Forbes (extracts). Company has negotiated the best possible
agreement on the Indian trade with the Spanish government for
the next three years. 1p.

Fol. 31. 8 Aug. 1793, York. Col. Simcoe to Capt. Brant
(extract). United States will not allow Simcoe to act as
mediator at Sandusky to determine boundary in spite of the
Indian's request. 2p.

Fol. 31b. 22 Aug. 1793, Foot of the Rapids. Col. McKee to
Col. Simcoe (extract). Six Nations disagreed with other nations
on their boundary. 3p.

Fol. 33. July 1794. Considerations on the Propriety of Great
Britain Abandoning the Indian Posts and Coming to a Good
Understanding with America. Great Britain should have considered the Southern Indians when the peace treaty was concluded
with America. 10p.

P.R.O. 30 8/344 (CONT'D)

Fol. 47. [1794]. Notes on the Indian Boundary Line. 4p.

Fol. 49. Sept. 1794. Precis of Negotiations between the United States and the Indians Relative to the Boundary line. 10p.

Fol. 136. 28 Feb. 1787, London. Petition from merchants (trading with South Carolina and Georgia) to Commons of Great Britain. Merchants complain they were never compensated for land ceded by the Cherokees and Creeks in payment for their debts. 4p. [Enclosures to fol. 145b].

    Fol. 138. 3 May 1782, [London]. Memorial from merchants (trading with South Carolina and Georgia) to Earl of Shelburne. Merchants request compensation for land ceded by the Cherokees and Creeks in payment for their debts. 4p.

    Fol. 140. 11 Feb. 1783, London. Memorial from merchants (trading with South Carolina and Georgia) to Sec. Fox. Merchants request compensation for land ceded by the Cherokees and Creeks and now possessed by Georgia. 2p.

    Fol. 142. May 1784, London. Memorial from merchants (trading with South Carolina and Georgia) to the King in Council. Merchants request compensation for land ceded by the Cherokees and Creeks. 2p.

    Fol. 144. 22 Apr. 1785, London. Memorial from merchants (who traded with South Carolina and Georgia) to Wm. Pitt. Merchants request compensation for land ceded by the Cherokees and Creeks. 3p.

Fol. 146. 1788, London. Petition from merchants trading with S. Carolina and Ga. to Commons of Great Britain. Merchants request compensation for land ceded by the Cherokees and Creeks in payment for debts. 5p.

Fol. 149. 23 Jan. 1788, London. John Nutt and Wm. Higginson to Wm. Pitt. Nutt and Higginson hope that the petition to Commons concerning land ceded by the Cherokees and Creeks will earn the government's support. 2p.

Fol. 151. [1788]. *Case of the Merchants and Others Interested in the Lands ... Ceded by the Cherokee and Creek Indian Nations to His Majesty for the Purpose of Discharging the Debts Due from Those Nations to the British Traders.* 8p.

Fol. 155. *Brief State of the Case of a Number of Merchants and Others Interested in Certain Lands in the Late Province of Georgia.* 2p.

Fol. 157. Report on the Claims for the Ceded Lands in Georgia (copy). 10p.

Fol. 223. 2 May 1789, Broad Street, [London]. John Nutt et al. to Wm. Pitt. Nutt requests that Pitt bring the report on Indian ceded lands before Parliament. 3p.

*P.R.O. 30 11/2   CORNWALLIS PAPERS, OFFICIAL CORRESPONDENCE RELATING
TO THE AMERICAN COLONIES: 1780*

Fol. 166. 18 June 1780, Augusta. Lt. Col. Brown to Gen.
Cornwallis. Brown plans to meet the Creeks and Cherokees at
Augusta to discourage their young warriors from seeking revenge
for losses they have sustained. 6p.

Fol. 173. 19 June 1780. John Cunningham. Account of Arms and
Stores Taken from the Rebels and Now in the Possession of the
Commissary at Ninety Six. 1p.

Fol. 191. 24 June 1780, Ninety Six. Nisbet Balfour to Gen.
Cornwallis. Brown will meet the principal Creeks and Cherokees at Augusta. 12p.

Fol. 208. 28 June 1780, Augusta. Lt. Col. Brown to Gen.
Cornwallis (duplicate). For 40 years Augusta has been the seat
of the Indian trade and the key to the Southern provinces
because of its proximity to the Creeks, Cherokees, and other
Indian tribes. Cherokees will probably renew their request to
get back their hunting grounds. 9p.

Fol. 307. 16 July 1780, Augusta. Lt. Col. Brown to Gen.
Cornwallis. Cherokees, who were driven from their towns and
reduced to misery by the rebels, will join the Creeks in Augusta.
It will be difficult to prevent Cherokee harrassment of the
rebels who are now in possession of tribe's hunting grounds.
10p.

*P.R.O. 30 11/3   CORNWALLIS PAPERS RELATING TO THE AMERICAN COLONIES:
1780*

Fol. 189. 5 Oct. 1780, Buffalo Creek. Major Pat. Ferguson to
Lt. Gen. Cornwallis (decoded duplicate). Ferguson is marching
towards Cornwallis by a road leading from the Cherokee ford
north of King's Mountain. 3p.

Fol. 212. 12 Oct. 1780, Camp at Col. Williams. Maj. Zachery
Gibbs to Gen. Cornwallis. Militia cannot hold the back country
as long as the Holston River, Nolachucky, and the Western Water
people remain unconquered. 3p.

Fol. 271. 24 Oct. 1780, near the Indians' land west of the
Catawba River. Lord Rawdon to Maj. Gen. Leslie. The enemy
from Nolachucky and other settlements beyond the mountains
killed Maj. Ferguson. 8p.

*P.R.O. 30 11/4   CORNWALLIS PAPERS RELATING TO THE AMERICAN COLONIES:
1780*

Fol. 345. 17 Dec. 1780, Augusta. Lt. Col. Brown to Gen.
Cornwallis. Cherokees have agreed to attack the usurpers of
their hunting grounds on the Watuga, Holston, Kentucky, Nolachucky, Cumberland, and Green Rivers. They have also attacked
boats going to New Orleans. 4p.

P.R.O. 30 11/4 (CONT'D)

Fol. 352. 5 Apr. 1780, Detroit. Maj. DePeyster to Commissary of Indian Affairs in the Upper Cherokees (extract). Cherokees will take the message (about the Northern Indians' aid to the English) to their nation, the Creeks, Chickasaws, and Choctaws. 2p.

P.R.O. 30 11/78   CORNWALLIS PAPERS RELATING TO THE AMERICAN COLONIES: 1780

Fol. 22. 17 July 1780, Charleston. Gen. Cornwallis to Lt. Col. Brown. Brown should not use the Indians for warfare under any circumstances. Cherokee claims are too complicated to consider at this time. 4p.

P.R.O. 30 47/14   EGREMONT PAPERS: 1761-1763

Fol. 47. 30-31 Aug. 1761. Col. Grant to Gen. Amherst. Journal of Conferences Held with the Cherokee Deputies (extract). Grant discusses the peace article that demands the death of four Cherokees. 4p. [Enclosure of Grant's letter to Amherst 3 Sept. 1761].

Fol. 61. 16 Mar. 1763, Whitehall. Earl of Egremont to Southern Governors and John Stuart. Governors and Stuart should invite the Creek, Choctaw, Cherokee, Chickasaw, and Catawba chiefs to a meeting at Augusta or another convenient place to inform them about changes resulting from the peace. 6p.

P.R.O. 30 55/5   CARLETON PAPERS: JANUARY - JUNE 1777

Doc. 472. 2 Apr. 1777, Whitehall. Geo. Germain to John Stuart. [Copy of C.O. 5/78/63]. 2p.

Doc. 498. 20 Apr. 1777, St. Augustine. Gov. Tonyn to David Taitt. [Same as C.O. 5/593/387]. 1p.

Doc. 506. 28 Apr. 1777, St. Augustine. Gov. Tonyn to Gen. Wm. Howe. [Same as C.O. 5/94/219]. 2p.   .

Doc. 512. 3 May 1777, New York. Gen. Howe to John Stuart (copy). Howe gives instructions for forming loyalist companies from refugees among the Indians. Hopefully these companies will contain men acquainted with the Ga. and Carolina frontiers. 4p.

Doc. 520. 9 May 1777, New York. Capt. Mackenzie to John Stuart (extract). Mackenzie encloses a talk for Stuart to deliver to the [Cherokee], Creek, Choctaw, and Chickasaw nations. 2p. [Enclosures to doc. 521(5)].

Doc. 521. 9 May 1777, New York. Talk from Gen. Howe to Cherokee, Creek, Choctaw, and Chickasaw Headmen and Warriors. [Same as C.O. 5/94/227]. 5p.

Doc. 525. 12 May 1777, New York. Gen. Howe to Gov. Tonyn (copy). Moses Kirkland, who is on his way to join Stuart in

P.R.O. 30 55/5 (CONT'D)

Pensacola, may be more usefully employed in East Florida.
Kirkland is ready to work with the Indians or do anything else
in his power. 2p.

Doc. 574. 10 June 1777, Pensacola. Elias Durnford to Gen.
Howe. Chickasaws and Choctaws are firmly tied to the English
and will not be led astray as easily as the Creeks or Cherokees.
Most of the Cherokees were forced to make peace with the
settlers. 2p.

Doc. 584. 14 June 1777, St. Augustine. Brig. Gen. Prevost to
Gen. Howe (extract). The rebels would find it difficult to
invade West Florida. After a several hundred mile march, they
would have to build boats and travel on a river leading to
Mobile. This would take them through hostile Chickasaw, Creek,
and Cherokee territory. 4p.

Doc. 585. 14 June 1777, St. Augustine. Brig. Gen. Prevost to
John Stuart. [Same as C.O. 5/78/191]. 4p.

Doc. 586. 16 June 1777, Pensacola. John Stuart to Gen. Howe.
Cherokee defeat keeps other Indians fearful that troops will
attack them. 4p.

Doc. 587. [June - July 1777?]. Joseph Vann to Alex. Cameron
(copy). Young warriors were ready to go to war when news
arrived that the Overhill Cherokees had made peace. Vann, the
Great Warrior, Little Carpenter, Willinawa, and Young Tassel
still persuaded warriors to go to war, but the Cherokees were
stopped by some new letters from Long Island. 4p.

P.R.O. 30 55/6   CARLETON PAPERS: JULY - OCTOBER 1777

Doc. 602. 11 July 1777, Pensacola. John Stuart to Alex.
Cameron. [Same as C.O. 5/78/195]. 4p.

Doc. 603. 12 July 1777, New York. Gen. Howe to Gov. Chester
(copy). If the King loses the Southern Indians, the consequences
will be serious. Chester should stop rum from reaching the
Indians. 4p.

Doc. 604. 12 July 1777, New York. Gen. Howe to John Stuart.
Indians should be employed offensively only when the principal
tribes can do so jointly. This will prevent one nation from being
singled out for retribution as happened to the Cherokees. 4p.

Doc. 606. 13 July 1777, New York. Gen. Howe to Lt. Col. Stiell.
Stiell should arrest anyone disregarding the rum regulations
with the Indians. 1p.

Doc. 608. 14 July 1777, New York. Gen. Howe to Brig. Gen.
Prevost (copy). Howe encloses letters explaining the liquor
trade restrictions with the Indians. Similar precautions should
be taken in East Florida. Howe is sending Indian presents. 7p.

Doc. 609. 14 July 1777, Headquarters, New York. Frederick G.
Mulcaster to [Alex. Skinner]. Mulcaster is sending a list of
the Indian presents on board the *Springfield* for Stuart. 2p.

P.R.O. 30 55/6 (CONT'D)

Doc. 611. 14 July 1777, Pensacola. John Stuart to David Taitt. [Same as C.O. 5/78/203]. 2p.

Doc. 629. 24 July 1777, Pensacola. John Stuart to Brig. Gen. Prevost. [Same as C.O. 5/78/205]. 8p.

Doc. 644. 13 Aug. 1777, Little Tallassee. David Taitt to John Stuart. [Same as C.O. 5/78/211]. 4p.

Doc. 649. 23 Aug. 1777, Pensacola. John Stuart to Gen. Howe. Choctaws attempted to strengthen their union with the Cherokees and Creeks. Howe's talk has been sent to the Choctaws, Chickasaws, Cherokees, and Lower Creeks. 4p.

Doc. 660. 3 Sept. 1777, Whitehall. Geo. Germain to Gen. Howe (duplicate). Germain regrets that the Southern Indians did not support the government. Since Howe understands the Indian attitude, Germain hopes to frustrate the rebel designs and secure the Indian's affection. 7p.

Doc. 695. 6 Oct. 1777, Pensacola. John Stuart to Gen. Howe (copy). The rebels have again attacked the Cherokees, destroying villages and crops. Creeks will surely join the strongest side to avoid the same fate. 7p. [Enclosures to doc. 696].

Doc. 710. 20 Oct. 1777, Pensacola. Talk from John Stuart to Philatouchy and Lower Creek deputies (copy). Rebel treatment of the Cherokees leaves no doubt that they intended to take the Creek lands. Rebels have already seized or forced the purchase of all the Cherokee country to the mountains. 4p.

P.R.O. 30 55/7   CARLETON PAPERS: NOVEMBER 1777 - JANUARY 1778

Doc. 728. 1 Nov. 1777, St. Augustine. Brig. Gen. Prevost to Gen. Howe (copy). Prevost did not want Stuart to act contrary to his own best judgement. He only wanted Stuart to protect the Cherokees threatened by destruction for their ties to England. 4p.

Doc. 859. 10 Jan. 1778, Pensacola. Proclamation from Gov. Chester. [Same as C.O. 5/79/122]. 4p.

P.R.O. 30 55/8   CARLETON PAPERS: FEBRUARY 1778

Doc. 925. 4 Feb. 1778, Pensacola. John Stuart to Gen. Howe (copy). Many Creeks remained in town all winter to get provisions. About 500 Cherokees have been in Pensacola since November. In spite of their defeat by the rebels, the Cherokees are ready to act when called upon. Cameron will accompany them to their nation and keep them ready. 6p. [Enclosures to doc. 926].

Doc. 926. Pensacola. Talk from John Stuart to Upper Creeks. Cherokees at Coosawaitee are uneasy because the trading path through the Creek nation will be blocked. 8p.

P.R.O. 30 55/8 (CONT'D)

Doc. 962. 24 Feb. 1778, St. Augustine. Gov. Tonyn to Gen. Howe (copy). Lack of support caused the Cherokees to be driven out of their country. 7p.

P.R.O. 30 55/9   CARLETON PAPERS: MARCH 1778

Doc. 996. 8 Mar. 1778, Whitehall. Geo. Germain to Henry Clinton (duplicate). Prevost is traveling with the Florida rangers and Indians, who will attack the southern frontier from St. Augustine while Stuart leads the other Indians toward Augusta. 20p.

Doc. 1025. 18 Mar. 1778, St. Augustine. Gen. Prevost to Gen. Howe. Using the Indians to invade Ga. might help secure the loyalty of some tribes which are vacillating. 2p.

Doc. 1030. 25 Mar. 1778, Pensacola. Gov. Chester to Brig. Gen. Prevost. [Copy of C.O. 5/594/341]. 4p.

Doc. 1058. 31 Mar. 1778, St. Augustine. Gov. Tonyn to Gen. Howe (copy). Brown, a party of rangers, and a few Indians have taken Ft. Barrington. 2p.

P.R.O. 30 55/10   CARLETON PAPERS: APRIL - MAY 1778

Doc. 1081. 10 Apr. 1778, Ft. Tonyn. Col. Brown to Brig. Gen. Prevost (copy). Several thousand loyalists who are camped at the Congarees (between the forks of the Saluda and Broad Rivers) are ready to help the English. Andrew Williamson, late commanding officer against the Cherokees, is dead. 3p.

Doc. 1100. 16 Apr. 1778 , Ft. Tonyn. Lt. Col. Brown to Gov. Tonyn (copy). Loyalists at the Congarees are ready to act. 5p.

Doc. 1133. 28 Apr. 1778, St. Augustine. Gov. Tonyn to Gen. Howe. Stuart discouraged the Indians from aiding the English by telling the tribes to plant their crops. 2p.

Doc. 1139. 1 May 1778, Philadelphia. Gen. Wm. Howe to John Stuart (copy). If Britain should go to war with France, Stuart's Indian difficulties will increase. 2p.

P.R.O. 30 55/16   CARLETON PAPERS: APRIL - MAY 1779

Doc. 1875. 1 Apr. 1779, Whitehall. Geo. Germain to Henry Clinton (duplicate). Indian Department expenses in the Southern District have increased tremendously since the superintendent was authorized to buy on credit. These expenses have been discussed in Parliament. 2p.

Doc. 1955. 29 Apr. 1779, Headquarters , New York. Henry Clinton to Alex. Cameron (copy). Clinton authorizes Cameron to act as superintendent due to Stuart's death. 1p.

P.R.O. 30 55/16 (CONT'D)

Doc. 1956.   29 Apr. 1779, New York. Henry Clinton to [Maj. Gen. Campbell] (copy). Clinton encloses Cameron's authorization to manage Indian affairs until further notice. 1p.

Doc. 1957.   29 Apr. 1779, Headquarters, New York. Henry Clinton to Gov. Chester (triplicate). Brown will replace Stuart to prevent trouble with the Indians. 2p.

Doc. 1958.   29 Apr. 1779, New York. [Henry Clinton to Gov. of Georgia?] (copy). Cameron's authorization to assume the superintendency of Indian affairs is enclosed. 1p.

Doc. 1969.   1 May 1779, St. Augustine. Gov. Tonyn to Henry Clinton. Tonyn hopes Clinton will use his influence to get Lt. Col. Thomas Brown appointed superintendent in Stuart's place. 4p.

Doc. 1970.   2 May 1779, New York. Henry Clinton to Maj. Gen. Prevost (copy). Clinton will consider Prevost's recommendation of Brown for Superintendent of Indian Affairs. 4p.

Doc. 1972.   3 May 1779, New York. Henry Clinton to George Germain. [Copy of C.O. 5/97/233]. 2p.

Doc. 2022.   28 May 1779, Pensacola. Commissioners for the Office of Indian Affairs to Brig. Gen. Campbell (copy). Commissioners cannot pay for or use the loyal refugee companies after June. They are unfit to serve among the Indians. 8p.

P.R.O. 30 55/17   CARLETON PAPERS: JUNE - JULY 1779

Doc. 2079.   25 June 1779, Whitehall. George Germain to Col. Brown and Alex. Cameron. [Copy of C.O. 5/80/123]. 4p.

Doc. 2118.   14 July 1779, Pensacola. John Campbell to Henry Clinton. Campbell has been forced to interfere with Indian affairs because of Capt. McIntosh and the loyalist refugees. 6p.

P.R.O. 30 55/19   CARLETON PAPERS: SEPTEMBER - OCTOBER 1779

Doc. 2281.   11 Sept. 1779, Red Cliffs at Pensacola Harbor. Maj. Gen. Cambell to Henry Clinton. Clinton is ordered to collect as many men and Indians as possible, without endangering Pensacola, to capture New Orleans. 16p.

Doc. 2289.   14 Sept. 1779, Pensacola. Gen. Campbell to [Henry Clinton]. Indians will not relieve Col. Dickson's troops unless they receive provisions and presents. Indian Department is confused since Cameron has not returned from the Cherokees. 8p.

Doc. 2372.   15 Oct. 1779, Little Tallassee (Creek nation). Alex. Cameron to Maj. Gen. Prevost. [Same as C.O. 5/182/207]. 4p.

P.R.O. 30 55/19 (CONT'D)

Doc. 2380.   22 Oct. 1779, New York.   Henry Clinton to Gen.
Haldimand (partially decoded copy).   Officials will hopefully
encourage the Indians to threaten the Va. frontiers.   8p.

P.R.O. 30 55/22   CARLETON PAPERS: MARCH - APRIL 1780

Doc. 2627.   9 Mar. 1780, Savannah.   Gen. Prevost to Henry
Clinton.   Prevost requests orders concerning Brown's memorial
and the accounts of extraordinary expenditures for the last two
months.   2p.

Doc. 2646.   18 Mar. 1780, Savannah.   Gov. James Wright to Henry
Clinton.   Cherokees will not stay in Savannah.   Wright hopes
they will not leave unhappy.   4p.

Doc. 2653.   24 Mar. 1780, Headquarters, James Island.   Henry
Clinton to [Gen. Prevost] (copy).   Clinton cannot judge the
propriety of the superintendent's accounts.   2p.

Doc. 2665.   1 Jan. - 31 Mar. 1780.   Alex. Cameron.   Account of
Extra Expenses Incurred by ... [the Indian Department].   1p.

Doc. 2681.   9 Apr. 1780.   Gov. Gálvez to Gen. Campbell (translation).   Gálvez proposes that the Indians not be employed in
national quarrels.   Arming Indians is very dangerous.   4p.

Doc. 2692.   20 Apr. 1780,   Headquarters, Pensacola.   Gen.
Campbell to Gov. Gálvez.   [Same as C.O. 5/587/209].   8p.

P.R.O. 30 55/27   CARLETON PAPERS: DECEMBER 1780 - JANUARY 1781

Doc. 3175.   3 Dec. 1780, Camp at Wynnesborough.   Gen. Cornwallis
to Henry Clinton (copy).   Wynnesborough is well situated to
protect most of the northern frontier and to assist Camden
and Ninety Six.   10p.

Doc. 3176.   4 Dec. 1780, South Carolina.   Gen. Cornwallis to
Henry Clinton (copy).   Cornwallis sends a copy of his letter to
Lt. Col. Cruger at Ninety Six in which someone (perhaps Gen.
Washington) changed the original meaning.   4p.

Doc. 3213.   17 Dec. 1780, Augusta.   Lt. Col. Brown to Gen.
Cornwallis.   [Copy of P.R.O. 30 11/4/345].   4p.

Doc. 3242.   [Dec. 1780?].   Alex Cameron.   Account of Extra
Expenses ... for Presents for Indians ... Employed on an
Expedition Against the Enemy and for Rewards to Indian Parties
Employed for the Protection of Mobile.   1p.

Doc. 3286.   18 Jan. 1781, Camp on Turkey Creek (Broad River).
Gen. Cornwallis to Henry Clinton.   Lt. Col. Tarleton will take
the 7th Regiment and one three pounder to reinforce Ninety Six.
8p.

P.R.O. 30 55/34   CARLETON PAPERS: DECEMBER 1781

Doc. 3930. 5 Dec. 1781, Savannah. Col. Brown to Col. Leslie
Clarke. Cherokees are exposed to invasions from the rebel
settlements. Because they are unable to hunt, the tribe must
receive clothing and ammunition. 4p.

Doc. 3955. 15 Dec. 1781, Savannah. John Graham to Henry
Clinton. Graham requests a position in the Department of Indian
Affairs when a vacancy occurs. Cameron has little or no hopes
of recovering from his illness. 2p.

Doc. 3994. 28 Dec. 1781, Charleston. Memorial from Joseph
Robinson to Geo. Germain. Robinson captured the courthouse at
Ninety Six from the rebels (22 Nov. 1775) but was later forced
to flee through the Creek and Cherokee territory. He requests
retirement with pay. 10p.

P.R.O. 30 55/45   CARLETON PAPERS: JULY 1782

Doc. 5108. 20 July 1782, Tyby in Georgia. John Graham to Guy
Carleton. As Cameron's replacement, Graham requests instructions concerning the different Indian nations. 4p.

P.R.O. 30 55/51   CARLETON PAPERS: OCTOBER 1782

Doc. 5822. 9 Oct. 1782, St. Augustine. Lt. Col. Brown to
Guy Carleton (duplicate). Since the evacuation of Savannah,
the Creeks and Cherokees have been very friendly towards the
government. Cherokees have given uncommon proof of their
fidelity. 3p.

P.R.O. 30 55/54   CARLETON PAPERS: NOVEMBER 1782

Doc. 6175. 15 Nov. 1782, Ft. Picolata. Lt. Col. Brown to
Guy Carleton. Creeks and Cherokees remain loyal in spite of
rebel and Spanish promises and presents. 8p.

P.R.O. 30 55/57   CARLETON PAPERS: DECEMBER 1782

Doc. 6476. 23 Dec. 1782, St. Augustine. Gov. Tonyn to Guy
Carleton. Recently arrived Indians include the Creeks, Choctaws,
Cherokees, and sundry Northern nations such as the Mohawks,
Senecas, Delawares, Shawnees, Manjoes, Tuscaroras, Yachtanues,
and other tribes from Ft. Detroit. 4p.

P.R.O. 30 55/60   CARLETON PAPERS: JANUARY 1783

Doc. 6728. 9 Jan. 1783, St. Augustine. Lt. Col. McArthur to
Guy Carleton (duplicate). Northern Indian deputies from
Detroit have arrived to confirm the Southern tribes' loyalty.
8p.

Doc. 6742. 12 Jan. 1783, St. Augustine. Lt. Col. Brown to
Guy Carleton. Northern Indians' deputies with 1,200 Cherokees
arrived last week to establish a confederacy among the different
Indian tribes. Brown has convinced the Cherokees to move their

P.R.O. 30 55/60 (CONT'D)

towns this winter. Brown includes a talk of Cherokee chief
at Picolata. 12p.

Doc. 6782. 20 Jan. 1783, St. Augustine. John Douglas to Guy
Carleton. Graham orders Douglas to humor the Indians in his
department to help secure their loyalty. 2p.

P.R.O. 30 55/62   CARLETON PAPERS: FEBRUARY 1783

Doc. 6920. 17 Feb. 1783, Quebec. Gen. Haldimand to Guy
Carleton. Haldimand has tried his best to prevent Indian
retaliation for the recent barbarity by Virginians. 2p.

P.R.O. 30 55/63   CARLETON PAPERS: FEBRUARY 1783

Doc. 6953. 23 Feb. 1783, St. Augustine. Lt. Col. Brown to
Sir Guy Carleton. Cherokees and the Northern deputies have
returned satisfied. Brown hopes the visit will be productive
since it was very expensive. 4p.

P.R.O. 30 55/68   CARLETON PAPERS: APRIL 1783

Doc. 7571. 28 Apr. 1783, St. Augustine. Lt. Col. Brown to
Guy Carleton. Brown has asked the officers, interpreters, and
traders among the Creeks and Cherokees to come to St. Augustine
as soon as possible. 4p.

Doc. 7587. 29 Apr. 1783, St. Augustine. Speaker of House of
Commons to Lt. Col. Brown (copy). Commons questions how long
the Indian friendship can be trusted considering the present
state of the province. 3p.

P.R.O. 30 55/69   CARLETON PAPERS: MAY 1783

Doc. 7564. 10 May 1783, St. Augustine. Copy of talk from the
head warrior of the Eufalees (Upper Creeks) stating that he
does not believe the rumor that the English will leave and
that the Indian lands would be divided between Va. and Spain.
2p.

Doc. 7688. 15 May 1783, St. Augustine. Lt. Col. Brown to
Brig. Gen. McArthur (copy). Cherokees are ignorant about
Florida being ceded [to Spain]. Germain had asked a large
number of Cherokees to meet Cornwallis in his march through
Carolina in July, 1780. 8p.

Doc. 7717. 19 May 1783, St. Augustine. Brig. Gen. McArthur
to Guy Carleton. Col. Brown has indicated that his credibility
might be ruined unless the method of delivering Indian presents
is changed. 4p.

P.R.O. 30 55/70   CARLETON PAPERS: MAY 1783

Doc. 7750. 23 May 1783, St. Augustine. Brig. Gen. McArthur
to Sir Guy Carleton. Indians have brought large quantities of
deer and bear skins. It would take a great amount of English
goods to exchange for these pelts. 5p.

P.R.O. 30 55/72   CARLETON PAPERS: JUNE 1783

Doc. 8084.   19 June 1783, New York. Sir Guy Carleton to Brig.
Gen. McArthur. Carleton is astonished that Col. Brown believes
that the new regulations concerning Indian presents would ruin
the Indians' opinion of him. Tribes should understand that
presents are from the King and not from the officers. 8p.

Doc. 8096.   [ca. 20 June 1783.] [Sir Guy Carleton] to Lt. Col.
McArthur. [Carleton] has requested the Superintendent of Indian
Affairs to send him all the receipts and accounts (old and new)
for Indian presents. 13p.

P.R.O. 30 55/74   CARLETON PAPERS: JULY 1783

Doc. 8334.   5 July 1783, St. Augustine. Brig. Gen. McArthur
to Sir Guy Carleton. McDonald, commissary for the Upper
Cherokees, reported that rebel troops were marching against the
Shawnees and Delawares. About 150 Cherokees and some Creeks
have gone north to aid Col. Brown. 3p.

P.R.O. 30 55/92   CARLETON PAPERS: JUNE 1783

Doc. 10116.   1 June 1783, St. Augustine. Lt. Col. Brown to Gen.
Guy Carleton. Brown has not received replies to his order for
the officers, interpreters, and traders among the Cherokees to
withdraw. 4p.

P.R.O. 30 55/93   CARLETON PAPERS: JULY 1783

Doc. 10139.   20 July 1783, St. Augustine. Lt. Col. Brown to
Guy Carleton. Because of their exposed situation, the Cherokees will probably be compelled to relinquish part of their
hunting grounds to the rebels. 4p. [Enclosures to doc. 10140].

Doc. 10140.   [20 July 1783], St. Augustine. Lt. Col. Brown.
A Return of Extra Officers, Interpreters, and War Conductors
Appointed by Earl Cornwallis and Sir Henry Clinton in the
Creek and Cherokee nation. 1p.

Doc. 10141.   20 July 1783, St. Augustine. Gen. McArthur to
Henry Clinton. McArthur sends an account of the Indian presents
in the Eastern Division of the Southern District. 2p.

TREASURY BOARD PAPERS
T.1/232   IN LETTERS: 1720

Fol. 110.   30 Sept. 1720, Whitehall. Charles Delafaye to Lords
of Treasury. Gov. Nicholson will be provided with Indian
presents in order to regain the friendship of tribes bordering
Carolina. 2p.

T.1/274   IN LETTERS: JULY-DECEMBER 1730

Fol. 113b.   [1730]. Payments Formerly Made on Account of Indian
Chiefs, with the Cravings [of the Georgia Trustees] on Account
of the Indian Chiefs Now Here. The Crown paid the expenses of
seven Cherokees in 1730. 3p.

T.1/286   IN LETTERS: JUNE - OCTOBER 1734

Fol. 120. 21 Aug. 1734. Memorial from Trustees of Georgia to
the King (copy). Trustees request reimbursement for £1,500 paid
the Creeks to consent to a new fort on the only river that the
French could use to invade Carolina. 2p.

T.1/304   IN LETTERS: SEPTEMBER - DECEMBER 1740

Fol. 77. 28 Oct. 1740, [Westminster]. Harmon Verelst to Lords
of Treasury. General Oglethorpe's bills incurred when using
the Cherokees and other Indians to attack St. Augustine should
be paid. 2p.

Fol. 102. 25 Nov. 1740, [Westminster]. Memorial from Harmon
Verelst to Lords of Treasury (copy). Verelst requests £5,735
for the expedition against St. Augustine and £1,750 for expenses
relating to the Creeks, Cherokees, and other Indians. 4p.

T.1/307   IN LETTERS: JANUARY - APRIL 1742

Fol. 202. 24 April 1742, Westminster. Harmon Verelst to Earl
of Wilmington. Verelst explains Oglethorpe's bills. 2p.
[Enclosures to fol. 210].

>   Fol. 203. 24 April 1742, [Westminster]. Harmon Verelst
>   to Lords of Treasury. Verelst reports Oglethorpe's
>   expenses. Creeks and Cherokees are being used to prevent
>   Spanish Indians and runaway slaves from Carolina from
>   harassing the country. If there is a war with France, it
>   will be necessary to keep the Creeks, Chickasaws, and
>   Cherokees armed. 9p.

>   Fol. 209. [Rec. Mar. 1742]. Gen. Oglethorpe to Harmon
>   Verelst (copy). Indian entertainment is expensive but
>   necessary. 4p.

T.1/308   IN LETTERS: MAY - SEPTEMBER 1742

Fol. 160. 5 Aug. 1742, [London]. Memorial from Harmon Verelst
to Lords of Treasury. Oglethorpe's orders concerning the
Spanish threat were the basis for drawing bills on the King.
3p. [Enclosures to fol. 163].

>   Fol. 162. [1741]. Proposals Relating to the War in
>   Georgia and Florida. If war erupts with France, it will
>   be necessary to arm the Creeks, Chickasaws, and Cherokees.
>   3p.

T.1/360   IN LETTERS: 1755

Fol. 86. 23 Dec. 1755, Williamsburg. Commission from Gov.
Dinwiddie to Peter Randolph and William Byrd (copy). Randolph
and Byrd will make a peace treaty with the Catawbas and Cherokees. 2p.

T.1/383   IN LETTERS: 1758

> Fol. 53. 14 July 1758, Whitehall. John Pownall to Samuel
> Martin. Lords of Treasury are unable to give an opinion on
> the memorial from Byrd and Randolph who were appointed to nego-
> tiate the Cherokee treaty. 3p.

T.1/416   IN LETTERS: 1762

> Fol. 163. 21 Sept. 1762, Inner Temple. Memorial from Charles
> Garth (Agent for S. Carolina) to Lords of Treasury. Garth asks
> for money to buy Indian presents. Indians between the Miss.,
> Ga., and S. Carolina are the provinces' chief barrier. French
> appear to have won over the Cherokees. 4p.

T.1/513   IN LETTERS: 1775

> Fol. 121. 28 Mar. 1775, Charleston. John Stuart to Earl of
> Dartmouth. Nothing disturbs the Indians more than losing their
> land through fraud. Gov. Martin has ordered the arrest of
> [Richard] Henderson in N. Carolina. 4p.

T.1/520   IN LETTERS: 1776

> Fol. 143. 19 Oct. 1776, Pensacola. Invoices from Wm. Knox of
> Indian presents sent to John Stuart. 7p.

> Fol. 212. 23 Aug. 1776, Pensacola. John Stuart to Lords of
> Treasury (duplicate). Stuart attaches an estimate of the
> Southern Department expenses during 1775-1776. 4p.

> Fol. 213. 12 Sept. 1775, Boston. Gen. Gage to [John Stuart]
> (copy). Stuart should persuade the Indians to fight the rebels.
> 2p.

T.1/535   IN LETTERS: 1777

> Fol. 269. 10 Mar. 1777, Pensacola. John Stuart to Geo. Germain.
> [Extract of C.O. 5/78/105]. 5p.

> Fol. 272. 10 Mar. 1777, Pensacola. John Stuart to Wm. Knox.
> [Extract of C.O. 5/78/116]. 4p.

T.1/552   IN LETTERS: 1779

> Fol. 57. 23 Oct. 1779. Commissioners for Indian Affairs to
> Lords of Treasury (quadruplicate). Cameron and Brown will
> succeed Stuart. Commissioners request payment for their earlier
> performance of the superintendent's duties. 4p.

> Fol. 59. 10 Dec. 1779, Pensacola. Commissioners for Indian
> Affairs to Lords of Treasury (triplicate). Commissioners ask
> for compensation for performing the duties of the Superintendent
> of Indian Affairs. 2p.

> Fol. 141. 1 June 1779, Pensacola. Commissioners for Indian
> Affairs to Lords of Treasury. Commissioners ask that loyal

T.1/552 (CONT'D)

refugees raised by Stuart and now on duty with Cameron among
the Cherokees be paid. Loyal refugees will accompany the
Cherokees to their Carolina frontiers. 3p.

T.1/553   IN LETTERS: 1779

N. fol. 31 Dec. 1778, Pensacola. John Stuart to John Robinson.
Stuart asks for payment of expenses. He supplied 700-800
Cherokees with food at Pensacola during the winter and most of
the spring. They were destitute until clothed by Stuart. 3p.

N. fol. [15 Dec. 1779.] Wm. Ogilvy. Account of Arrears of
Salary and Allowances Due the Officers of the Late Col. John
Stuart, Superintendent of Indian Affairs. 4p.

T.1/601   IN LETTERS: 1783-1784

Fol. 300. 3 Oct. 1783, St. Augustine. Brig. Gen. McArthur
to Lt. Col. Brown (copy). Brown should anticipate visits from
many Indians and be prepared to supply them. 3p.

Fol. 302. 4 Oct. 1783, New York. Guy Carleton to Lt. Col.
Brown. Carleton recommends again that Brown persuade the
Indians not to leave East Florida. 2p.

Fol. 304. [Jan. 1784], St. Augustine. Application from Lt.
Col. Brown to Gov. Tonyn and Gen. McArthur (copy). Brown
requests authorization to obtain Indian supplies. 2p.

Fol. 305. 10 Jan. 1784. Gov. Tonyn and Gen. McArthur to Lt.
Col. Brown (copy). Tonyn and McArthur grant authorization to
obtain Indian supplies. 3p.

Fol. 311. 15 Feb. 1784, St. Augustine. Thomas Brown to Lords
Commissioners of Treasury. General Account of Ordinary
[Expenses] Incurred in the Indian Department from 1 July to
31 December 1783. Account includes salary for a Cherokee interpreter and payment for ammunition given to the Cherokees. 24p.

T.1/608   IN LETTERS: 1784

Fol. 230. [ca. 1784]. Application from John Graham and others
of the Eastern and Western Divisions of the Southern Indian
District for half pay. 4p.

Fol. 247. [ca. 1784]. Application from Lt. Col. McGillivray
for half pay. McGillivray includes a brief account of his
actions since 1778. 11p.

Fol. 329b. [ca. 1784]. Application from Mrs. Sarah Stuart,
John Stuart's widow, for a pension. 5p.

T.1/620   IN LETTERS: 1785

Fol. 274. 11 Feb. 1783, London. Memorials from Merchants
(trading with South Carolina and Georgia) to Wm. Pitt and Lords

T.1/620 (CONT'D)

of Treasury. Merchants have not been reimbursed for losing
the land ceded by the Creeks and Cherokees to repay their
debts. 4p.

Fol. 276. 3 May 1782, London. Memorial from Merchants (trading
with South Carolina and Georgia) to Earl of Shelburne. [Same
as P.R.O. 30 8/344/138]. 5p.

Fol. 279. May 1784. Memorial from Merchants (trading with
South Carolina and Georgia) to the King in Council. [Same
as P.R.O. 30 8/344/142]. 2p.

Fol. 280. 22 Apr. 1785, London. Memorial from Merchants
(trading with South Carolina and Georgia) to Sec. Fox.
Merchants request reimbursement for losing the land ceded by
the Creeks and Cherokees in payment of their debts. 4p.

T.1/633   IN LETTERS: 1787

Fol. 337. 23 Jan. 1787, Dartmouth Street, Westminster.
Memorial from Helena Theresa Timberlake Ostenaco to Lords of
Treasury. Timberlake's widow requests assistance. 4p.

Fol. 338. 20 July 1786, Whitehall. Lord Amherst to [Geo.
Younge]. Amherst believes Timberlake's widow deserves
assistance. 2p.

Fol. 339. 21 July 1786, War Office. Geo. Younge to Geo. Rose.
Younge recommends the request from Timberlake's widow. 2p.

T.1/687   IN LETTERS: 1790

Fol. 127. 9-13 Sept. 1790, Charlotte Town, St. John. Memorial
from Creek and Cherokee Chiefs (Kooadiciska and Unatoy) to Bd.
of Customs. Chiefs request that Moses Whitley be given back
his schooner (the *Lord Dunmore*) since he assisted them. 4p.
[Enclosure of fol. 131].

Fol. 129. 14 Sept. 1790, Charlotte Town, St. John. Affidavit
from James Smith concerning the tobacco and hides paid by the
five Indians and Col. Bowles for their passage. 2p. [Enclo-
sure of fol. 131].

Fol. 131. 13 Nov. 1790, Halifax, Nova Scotia. Memorial from
Moses Whitley to Lords of Treasury. Whitley was paid 7,000
weight of tobacco and 83 rawhides for the passage of Moses Price
and Kooadiciska (Cherokee chiefs) and Lubyga and Thomas Lewis
(Creek chiefs). He asks for reimbursement for the losses
resulting from the confiscation of his ship and supplies. 4p.
[Enclosures at fols. 127 and 129].

T.1/692   IN LETTERS: 1791

Fol. 131. [1791]. Account of Expenditure for [William] Bowles
and Five Creek and Cherokee Indians. 3p. [Enclosure of fol.
133].

T.1/692 (CONT'D)

    Fol. 133. 2 Apr. 1791, Whitehall. Geo. Grenville to Lords
of Treasury. Grenville requests payment for the entertainment
and presents given to Bowles and the five Creeks and Cherokees.
3p. [Enclosure at fol. 131].

T.27/27   OUT LETTERS, GENERAL: 1751-1759

    Fol. 244. 5 Nov. 1756. [Nicholas] Hardinge to Mr. Pownall.
Lords of Treasury have agreed on the distribution of presents
to the Ga. frontier Indians. 1p.

    Fol. 354. 4 July 1758. Samuel Martin to Bd. of Trade. Lords
of the Treasury request a report on the memorial from Wm. Byrd
and Peter Randolph, commissioners to the Cherokees. 1p.

    Fol. 479. 27 July 1759. Samuel Martin to Bd. of Trade. Lords
of Treasury request a report on the memorial of Wm. Byrd and
Peter Randolph, commissioners to the Cherokees. 1p.

T.27/32   OUT LETTERS, GENERAL: 1777-1779

    Fol. 59. 22 Dec. 1777. John Robinson to Wm. Knox. Robinson
sends Stuart's bills for the Indian congress and presents at
Mobile. 1p.

    Fol. 532. 16 June 1779. John Robinson to Wm. Knox. Robinson
sends Stuart's bills for expenses in the Southern Department.
1p.

    Fol. 579. 20 Aug. 1779. John Robinson to Wm. Knox. Germain
has divided the superintendency of Indian Affairs in the South
into two districts. Cameron will handle the Miss. District
and Brown the Atlantic District. 1p.

T.27/35   OUT LETTERS, GENERAL: 1783-1784

    Fol. 74. 20 Mar. 1783. George Rose to Lords of Treasury.
Rose requests a report on the payment of Stuart's bills and
accounts. 1p.

T.29/26   TREASURY BOARD MINUTES: MAY 1727-FEBRUARY 1731

    Fol. 329. 20 July 1730, Windsor Castle, Treasury Chambers.
Treasury minutes recording that Gov. Johnson will be reimbursed
for maintaining in London and sending home the Carolina Indian
chiefs brought by Alex. Cuming. 1p.

    Fol. 330. 22 July 1730, Whitehall, Treasury Chambers. Treasury
Minutes recording that Cuming will be paid £42.13.0 for bills
concerning the Indian chiefs from N. Carolina. James Crowe
will receive £48.5 for providing food and lodging. 3p.

    Fol. 350. 1 Sept. 1730, Whitehall Treasury Chambers. Treasury
Minutes recording that Gov. Johnson will be paid £400 more for
expenses of the Cherokees. 1p.

T.52/52   MISCELLANEA, KING'S WARRANTS: 1761

Fol. 70.   7 Mar. 1761, St. James.   Order from King George to
Paymaster Forces.   Benjamin Martyn will be paid £1,500 to
purchase presents for the Ga. Indians.   2p.

Fol. 446.   30 July 1761, St. James.   Order from King George
that Wm. Byrd and Peter Randolph be rewarded for negotiating a
treaty with the Catawbas and Cherokees.   1p.

T.64/23   MISCELLANEA, VARIOUS: 1782

Fol. 38.   [1782].   List of officers from the Indian Department
in the Southern District on half pay in the King's Carolina
Rangers.   1p.

T.64/291   MISCELLANEA, VARIOUS

N. fol. 1761.   Order to pay Peter Randolph and Wm. Byrd for
their services in obtaining the Catawba and Cherokee treaty.
[Located in a bundle of the King's warrants].   3p.

WAR OFFICE
W.O. 1/6   IN LETTERS: 1764-1765

Fol. 132.   27 Apr. 1765, New York.   Gen. Gage to Sec. at War
Ellis.   Cherokees along the Ohio captured some Frenchmen who
were suspected of carrying supplies to the Shawnees.   8p.

W.O. 1/143   IN LETTERS, MISCELLANEOUS: 1814-1815

Fol. 80.   22 Nov. 1815, London.   Memorial from James Pott for
Forbes and Company to Earl of Bathurst.   During the recent war,
Forbes and Co. attempted to preserve the Southern Indians'
friendship toward the English.   Pott requests reimbursement for
property lost by Forbes and Company.   3p.

W.O. 1/144   IN LETTERS, MISCELLANEOUS: 1816-1817

Fol. 66.   1 Mar. 1816, Woolwich.   Lt. Col. Edward Nicolls to
Adm. Cochrane.   Except for the Cherokees, the Muskogees are
the most civilized of all North American Indians.   [Enclosures
to fol. 69b].   6p.

*W.O. 34/35   LETTERS FROM THE GOVERNORS OF NORTH AND SOUTH CAROLINA TO
THE COMMANDER-IN-CHIEF: 1756-1763*

Fol. 1.   6 Apr. 1758, New Bern.   Gov. Dobbs to Earl of Loudoun.
About 60 Catawbas and 500 Cherokees have gone to Virginia.
Byrd will try to persuade more Cherokees to go.   De Rossel is
empowered to supply Indians who pass through N.C. on their
way to assist the English.   3p.

Fol. 12.   2 Aug. 1760, Brunswick.   Gov. Dobbs to Gen. Amherst.
Dobbs has written Gen. Monckton for supplies in anticipation of
a Southern Indian war.   If such a war erupts, Ga. will be lost
and S.C. endangered.   Dobbs requests troops to end the Indian
war.   1p.

W.O. 34/35 (CONT'D)

Fol. 13. 25 Nov. 1760, Wilmington. Gov. Dobbs to Gen. Amherst.
Dobbs requests troops to crush the Cherokees. They should be
punished by demanding the execution of their head warriors who
began the war or by forcing the tribe to reside elsewhere. 3p.

Fol. 15. 20 Mar. 1761, Brunswick. Gov. Dobbs to Gen. Amherst.
Cherokee's fate will be decided before [N.C.] can raise troops.
1p.

Fol. 16. 24 Apr. 1761, Wilmington. Gov. Dobbs to Gen. Amherst.
Bill has passed to raise 500 men to protect the frontier for
seven months. 3p.

Fol. 19. 19 Jan. 1762, Brunswick. Gov. Dobbs to Gen. Amherst
(duplicate). [N.C.] troops joined the Va. provincials at
Chiswell's Fort in time to march to Ft. Attakullakulla and Great
Island on the Holston River. Cherokees sought an armistice
but Attakullakulla informed the chiefs that a peace had already
been signed. The chiefs were supposed to go to Charleston to
ratify the treaty. 2p.

Fol. 39. 4 and 6 Dec. 1762, New Bern. Gov. Dobbs to Gen.
Amherst. Dobbs recommends Lt. Thomas Howe to Amherst. Howe
served with the N.C. provincial troops during the Cherokee war
and wants to be attached to the British regulars. 2p.

Fol. 41. 4 Jan. 1763, Brunswick. Gov. Dobbs to Gen. Amherst.
N.C. raised 300 men in 1760 to defend the frontier and to repel
the Cherokees. In 1761, N.C. raised 500 men to join the Va.
forces. 2p. [Enclosures to fol. 46b].

>   Fol. 45. 10 Dec. 1762. John Ashe (Speaker of House) to
>   Gov. Dobbs. Amherst will verify the number of men in the
>   King's service from 1760 to 1761 so reimbursements can be
>   made. 1p.

Fol. 47. 23 Sept. 1763, Brunswick. Gov. Dobbs to Gen. Amherst.
Dobbs will meet with the Southern Indians at Augusta. 4p.

Fol. 54. 25 Aug. 1756, Charleston. Gov. Lyttleton to Earl of
Loudoun (duplicate). Little Carpenter is pleased that the
fort in Cherokee country will finally be built. Dinwiddie
believed that a new fort was necessary to obtain the Cherokees'
assistance for Virginia. Capt. Demeré reports that the Va.
fort at Chote is completed and located across the river from
where S.C. proposed to build its fort. 17p.

Fol. 62. 5 Nov. 1756, Charleston. Gov. Lyttleton to Earl of
Loudoun (duplicate). Capt. Demeré will request that the
Cherokees and Catawbas send more braves to Virginia. 4p.

Fol. 64. 15 July 1757, Charleston. Gov. Lyttleton to Earl of
Loudoun (duplicate). Money will be raised to pay the soldiers'
salaries at Ft. Loudoun. 2p.

W.O. 34/35 (CONT'D)

Fol. 81.   21 Mar. 1758, Charleston. Gov. Lyttleton to Earl of
Loudoun. Lyttleton has helped Byrd go to Keowee to obtain
Indian aid. S.C. is willing to provide funds (£20,000) for
raising an Indian party. 5p.

Fol. 90.   25 Mar. 1758, Charleston. Gov. Lyttleton to Earl
of Loudoun (copy). Col. Byrd has gone to Keowee with a message
from Atkin encouraging the [Cherokees] to [aid the English].
1p.

Fol. 91.   15 May 1758, Charleston. Gov. Lyttleton to Maj. Gen.
Abercromby. Col. Howarth reported that some 400-500 [Cherokees]
had gone to aid Virginia. An additional 60-70 from the Lower
Towns accompanied Col. Byrd to Winchester. Little Carpenter
promised to join Col. Byrd later. 3p. [Enclosures to fol.
94b].

   Fol. 93.   15 Apr. 1758, Charleston. Gov. Lyttleton to Maj.
   Gen. Abercromby (duplicate). Lyttleton has not learned
   whether Byrd or Howarth was successful in raising Cherokees
   for the operation along the Ohio. 4p.

Fol. 95.   3 Aug. 1758, Charleston. Gov. Lyttleton to Maj. Gen.
Abercromby (copy). Lyttleton recommends that Ensign Richard
Coytmore be promoted to Lieutenant. He served two years with
the Cherokees. 2p.

Fol. 96.   7 Feb. 1759, Charleston. Gov. Lyttleton to Maj. Gen.
Amherst. Chote is 500 miles from Charleston, making it difficult
to supply troops among the [Cherokees]. 9p.

Fol. 113.   3 July 1759, Charleston. Gov. Lyttleton to Maj.
Gen. Amherst. 2p. [Enclosures to fol. 116b].

   Fol. 115.   15 Sept. 1758, Charleston. Lt. Shaw and Ensign
   Coytmore to [Gov. Lyttleton] (copy). Shaw and Coytmore
   asked to be excused from serving under Lt. Charles Taylor,
   who reportedly embezzled money while Capt. Demeré was
   absent from the Cherokees. 2p.

Fol. 117.   9 Aug. 1759, Charleston. Gov. Lyttleton to Maj.
Gen. Amherst. 2p. [Enclosures to fol. 126b].

   Fol. 123.   [11-12 July 1759]. Message from Gov. Lyttleton
   to Assembly (copy). Cherokees, encouraged by the French,
   have slaughtered some inhabitants. Lyttleton cannot
   prevent these Cherokee atrocities unless S.C. raises a
   regiment. 2p.

   Fol. 125.   13 July 1759, [Charleston]. Message from Commons
   to Lyttleton (copy). Commons will make provision for two
   troops of rangers to patrol the back settlements and
   prevent Indian violence. 1p.

Fol. 127.   16 Oct. 1759, Charleston. Gov. Lyttleton to Maj.
Gen. Amherst. Council unanimously supported a declaration of

war against the Cherokees, but the Assembly unanimously voted
to defer such a declaration. Capt. Stewart has sent supplies
to Ft. Loudoun. 3p. [Enclosures to fol. 133b].

Fol. 129. 26 Sept. 1759, Ft. Prince George. Lt. Coytmore
to Gov. Lyttleton (copy). Lower Towns openly support war.
It is impossible to supply Ft. Prince George. Tiftoe and
the Wolf often come to the Fort. Great Warrior, Judd's
Friend, and eighteen other Cherokees brought a letter from
Capt. Demeré. 1p.

Fol. 131. 12 Oct. 1759, [Charleston]. Message from
Commons to Gov. Lyttleton (copy). Resolution from Commons
concerning money and supplies for the intended expedition
[against the Cherokees]. 3p.

Fol. 133. 16 Oct. 1759, Charleston. Lt. Gray to Gov.
Lyttleton (copy). Could Lyttleton recommend to Amherst
that all troops be paid the same? 1p.

Fol. 134. 23 Oct. 1759, Charleston. Gov. Lyttleton to Maj.
Gen. Amherst. Upper and Lower Cherokees came to Charleston.
Lyttleton explains why no agreement was reached with the tribe.
3p.

Fol. 136. 27 Dec. 1759, Ft. Prince George. Gov. Lyttleton to
Maj. Gen. Amherst. Lyttleton sends a copy of the treaty
concluded with the Cherokees. Indians left 22 principal warriors
as hostages, promising to deliver an equal number in the future.
2p. [Enclosures to fol. 139b].

Fol. 138. 26 Dec. 1759, Ft. Prince George. Treaty of
Peace and Friendship [between S.C. and the Cherokees]
(copy). Signatories include Attakullakulla, Oconostota,
Otassite, Kittagusta, Oconeca, and Kilcannokeh. 3p.

Fol. 144. 28 Dec. 1759, Ft. Prince George. Gov. Lyttleton to
Maj. Gen. Amherst. Lyttleton forwards a copy of the recent
Cherokee treaty. 2p.

Fol. 145. 25 Jan. 1760, Charleston. Gov. Lyttleton to Maj.
Gen. Amherst. Lyttleton returned from the Cherokee country
on Jan. 8. Cherokee expedition cost the Crown nothing. 1p.
[Enclosures to fol. 147b].

Fol. 148. 2 Feb. 1760, Charleston. Gov. Lyttleton to Maj.
Gen. Amherst. Cherokees have renewed hostilities and killed
a number of traders. Troops are needed to protect S.C. and to
secure Ft. Prince George and Ft. Loudon. 3p. [Enclosures to
fol. 154b].

Fol. 151. 31 Jan. 1760, Charleston. Col. Howarth. A
Return of the South Carolina Regiment of Foot. 2p.

Fol. 152. 1 Feb. 1760. Lt. Shaw. A Return of His
Majesty's Three Independent Company's Doing Duty in South
Carolina and Georgia. Report mentions Ft. Loudoun and
Ft. Prince George. 2p.

Fol. 153. 23 Jan. 1760, Ft. Prince George. Lt. Coytmore
to Gov. Lyttleton. Coytmore sends an extract of the daily
journal from 13-20 Jan. reporting renewed Cherokee hostilities. 4p.

Fol. 155. 9 Feb. 1760, Charleston. Gov. Lyttleton to Maj.
Gen. Amherst. Assembly has promised supplies but now requests
that Amherst send troops against the Cherokees. Lyttleton
asked Va. to send reinforcements to Ft. Loudoun. 2p.

Fol. 156. 18 Feb. 1760, Charleston. Gov. Lyttleton to Maj.
Gen. Amherst. Although Assembly has voted money to raise
1,525 men to fight against the Cherokees, Lyttleton believes the
levy will go slowly. He requests that Amherst send as many
men as planned. 3p.

Fol. 159. 22 Mar. 1760, Charleston. Gov. Lyttleton to Maj.
Gen. Amherst. Cherokees killed Lt. Coytmore, and Ensign Miln
now commands Ft. Prince George. Lyttleton has received news
that Col. Montgomery is coming to S.C. with 1,200 men. 2p.

Fol. 160. 31 Mar. 1760, Charleston. Gov. Lyttleton to Maj.
Gen. Amherst (duplicate). Montgomery will hopefully be successful [against the Cherokees]. Lyttleton brought only three
Cherokee murderers to Charleston. Cherokee hostages remained
at Ft. Prince George. 4p.

Fol. 163. 8 May 1760, Charleston. Lt. Gov. Bull to [Maj. Gen.
Amherst]. Col. Montgomery reached Congarees May 2 and awaits
provisions. Cherokees attacked Ft. Loudoun. Cherokees requested
aid from the Ottawas and sent deputies to New Orleans. Creeks
seem inclined towards neutrality. 4p.

Fol. 165. 16 May 1760, Charleston. Lt. Gov. Bull to Maj. Gen.
Amherst. Upper and Lower Creeks are divided between supporting
the French or the English. Some Creeks have threatened to
attack the English if the English successfully persuade other
Creeks to attack the Cherokees. 3p.

Fol. 167. 29 and 31 May 1760, Charleston. Lt. Gov. Bull to
Maj. Gen. Amherst. Upper Creeks have murdered English traders.
These Creek hostilities and the Cherokee war have caused great
distress. Creeks and Cherokees have 2,000 men each and the
Choctaws more than 5,000. Mortar plans to attack Ft. Loudoun
with some Creeks. 4p.

Fol. 170. 12 June 1760, Charleston. Lt. Gov. Bull to Maj. Gen.
Amherst. Col. Montgomery's success against the Cherokees
promises a happy and speedy end to the war. The zeal of Fauquier
and the Assembly to relieve Ft. Loudoun is commendable. 2p.

Fol. 171. 15 Aug. 1760, Charleston. Lt. Gov. Bull to Maj. Gen. Amherst. Montgomery destroyed the Cherokee Lower Towns and reached Echoe in the Middle Settlements. Virginia's troops did not leave until Aug. 10 to relieve Ft. Loudoun. Middle and Lower Cherokees request peace. 3p.

Fol. 173. 16 Oct. 1760, Charleston. Lt. Gov. Bull to Maj. Gen. Amherst. Bull recommends the promotion of Edward Wilkinson to ensign. Wilkinson went to Keowee with Lyttleton last Dec. and aided the officers there. 2p.

Fol. 174. 19, 24, and 29 Oct. 1760, Charleston. Lt. Gov. Bull to Maj. Gen. Amherst (duplicate). Bull reports the surrender of Ft. Loudoun and the massacre of part of the garrison in revenge for the murder of Cherokee hostages last February. Bull also reports the conditions at Ft. Prince George. 6p.

Fol. 182. 18 Nov. 1760, Charleston. Lt. Gov. Bull to Maj. Gen. Amherst. Lantagnac, a former member of an English Independent company and an ex-Cherokee trader, distributed presents at Chote and promised to assist the Indians with men and cannon against the English. Bull outlines his plans for attacking the Cherokees. 4p.

Fol. 184. 17 and 22 Dec. 1760, Charleston. Lt. Gov. Bull to Maj. Gen. Amherst. Bull is pleased that Amherst is sending Col. Grant and reinforcements to fight the Cherokees. French have supposedly built a fort on the Cherokee R. 10 days march below [above?] Ft. Loudoun. The Warrior of Settico has left with Lantagnac for the Alabama Fort and Great Warrior has gone to Fort l'Assomption. 3p.

Fol. 187. 27 Dec. 1760, Charleston. Lt. Gov. Bull to Maj. Gen. Amherst. Bull will wait for Grant to decide if the provincial troops should attack the Lower Towns in January. French have built a fort on Cherokee R. eight days northwest of Ft. Loudoun. 4p.

Fol. 189. 24 Jan. 1761, Charleston. Lt. Gov. Bull to Maj. Gen. Amherst. Great Warrior has returned from visiting the French with men and presents. Lower Creeks have offered provisions and protections to the Cherokees who came to their towns. Bull has informed Fauquier about his plans so Virginia's troops could arrive at Chote while the Cherokees are being attacked in the south. 2p.

Fol. 191. 13 and 14 Mar. 1761, Charleston. Lt. Gov. Bull to Maj. Gen. Amherst. Virginia's troops will have no provisions after 1 May. French and Cherokees are evidently making one last desperate effort to get the Creeks to fight the English. Grant's troops will move to Monk's Corner on 20 March. 3p.

Fol. 193. 3 Apr. 1761, Charleston. Lt. Gov. Bull to Maj. Gen. Amherst. Little Carpenter has delivered 20 English prisoners

to Ft. Prince George and promised to deliver more. Bull waits
for news from Va. about his request to send troops against the
Cherokees. 1p.

Fol. 194. 15 Apr. 1761, Charleston. Lt. Gov. Bull to Maj. Gen.
Amherst. Ft. Prince George has received 67 English prisoners,
21 of which belonged to Ft. Loudoun. Bull hopes that the rest
will be released before Grant approaches the Cherokees. Grant
should reach Ft. Prince George by 10 May. 3p.

Fol. 196. 20 Apr. 1761, Charleston. Lt. Gov. Bull to Maj. Gen.
Amherst. After receiving letters from Fauquier, Bull has no
hopes that Virginia's troops will be able to assist against the
Cherokees without reinforcements from Amherst. 2p.

Fol. 197. 26 Apr. 1761, Charleston. Lt. Gov. Bull to Maj. Gen.
Amherst. Assembly disagrees with Pitt that S.C. has failed in
its service to the King. S.C. has contributed much since the
first expedition against the Cherokees in 1759. 4p.

Fol. 199. 30 Apr. 1761, Charleston. Lt. Gov. Bull to Maj. Gen.
Amherst. Col. Grant expects to be at Ninety Six by 3 May.
Cherokees have returned 90 [English] prisoners. 2p.

Fol. 200. 6 June 1759 [1761?], Charleston. Lt. Gov. Bull to
Maj. Gen. Amherst. Hampered by the weather, Grant did not
arrive at Ft. Prince George until 27 May. Fauquier wants commissioners from N.C., S.C., and Va. to make peace with the
Cherokees. 3p.

Fol. 202. 17 June 1761, Charleston. Lt. Gov. Bull to Maj. Gen.
Amherst. Although the Creeks have agreed not to interfere in
the Cherokee war, the Creeks would immediately attack the Cherokees if the latter interrupted their trade from Augusta. 2p.

Fol. 203. 16 July 1761, Charleston. Lt. Gov. Bull to Maj.
Gen. Amherst. Bull congratulates Amherst on Grant's success.
Dobbs has ordered the N.C. regiment to meet the Va. troops at
Ft. Dobbs. 2p.

Fol. 204. 17 Aug. 1761, Charleston. Lt. Gov. Bull to Maj. Gen.
Amherst. Great Warrior and Standing Turkey sent Old Caesar to
ask for peace. Little Carpenter and others have asked Byrd for
peace. Bull has rewarded the Chickasaws who aided Grant in the
Cherokee expedition. 2p.

Fol. 206. 24 Sept. 1761, Charleston. Lt. Gov. Bull to Maj.
Gen. Amherst. Bull met with Little Carpenter and eight other
Cherokees at Ashley Ferry. Those Indians returned to inform
the Cherokees about the peace terms. 3p.

Fol. 208. 16 Nov. 1761, Charleston. Lt. Gov. Bull to Maj.
Gen. Amherst. Bull is grateful for Amherst's assistance during
the Cherokee war and hopes that Grant's success will bring an
honorable and lasting peace with the Indians. 2p.

Fol. 209. 5 Dec. 1761, Charleston. Lt. Gov. Bull to Maj. Gen.
Amherst. Four troops of rangers are still on the payroll since
peace with the Cherokees has not yet been concluded. 2p.

Fol. 210. 12 Jan. 1762, Charleston. Gov. Boone to Maj. Gen.
Amherst. Cherokee deputies who ratified the treaty have left
Charleston. 4p. [Enclosures to fol. 213b].

> Fol. 212. 18 Dec. 1761. Treaty of Peace and Friendship
> [between S.C. and the Cherokees] (copy). Signatories
> include Attakullakulla, Kittagusta, Old Warrior of Estatoe
> (Good Warrior), Cappy of Tomotly, Half Breed Will, Shalle-
> loski, Teetateloski, Anatoy, and Ottassite (the Man Killer
> of Keowee). 4p.

Fol. 214. 22 Feb. 1762, Charleston. Gov. Boone to [Maj. Gen.
Amherst]. S.C. has been quiet since the conclusion of the
Cherokee peace. 2p.

Fol. 215. 11 Mar. 1762, Charleston. Gov. Boone to Maj. Gen.
Amherst. Assembly will be informed of Amherst's expectations
concerning Ft. Loudoun. 1p.

Fol. 217. 25 Mar. 1762, Charleston. Gov. Boone to Maj. Gen.
Amherst. Two companies of rangers are being maintained to
secure communications with Ft. Prince George and to wait for
delivery of the remaining prisoners. 3p.

Fol. 219. 2 Apr. 1762, Charleston. Gov. Boone to Maj. Gen.
Amherst. 3p. [Enclosures to fol. 222b].

> Fol. 221. 30 Mar. 1762. Message from Commons to Gov.
> Boone. Commons believes it is impractical to raise
> additional troops because of the recent expenses during the
> Cherokee war and other events. 2p.

Fol. 232. 25 June 1762, Charleston. Gov. Boone to Maj. Gen.
Amherst. Cherokees have delivered most, if not all, of the
remaining [English] prisoners. 3p.

Fol. 237. 6 Aug. 1762, Charleston. Gov. Boone to Maj. Gen.
Amherst. Boone is happy that Amherst agrees with his ideas
concerning Indian treatment. 3p.

Fol. 253. 27 Jan. 1763, Charleston. Answer [from Smith and
Nutt] to Commissary Leake's Remarks on Provision Vouchers ...
of Ft. Prince George. 2p. [Enclosure of fol. 260].

Fol. 255. 17 Oct. 1761 - 2 Feb. 1762. A Return of Provisions
Left at Ft. Prince George by Col. Grant and What Has Arrived
Since (copy). 1p. [Enclosure of fol. 260].

Fol. 259. 1 Aug. 1762. Return of Provisions of the Garrison
at Ft. Prince George (copy). 1p. [Enclosure of fol. 260].

W.O. 34/35 (CONT'D)

Fol. 260.   28 Jan. 1763, Charleston.   Gov. Boone to Maj. Gen.
Amherst.   Boone sends contractor's answer to Leake's remarks
concerning provision vouchers [for Ft. Prince George].   2p.
[Enclosures from fol. 253-259b].

Fol. 263.   2 May 1763, Charleston.   Gov. Boone to Maj. Gen.
Amherst.   A Frenchman was captured in Cherokee country and
taken to Ft. Prince George.   2p.

Fol. 267.   29 July 1763, Charleston.   Gov. Boone to Maj. Gen.
Amherst.   The Southern Indians will probably follow the troops
which take possession of St. Augustine, Pensacola, and Mobile.
3p.

*W.O. 34/36   LETTERS FROM THE COMMANDER-IN-CHIEF TO THE GOVERNORS OF
             NORTH AND SOUTH CAROLINA: 1756-1763*

Fol. 2.   13 Feb. 1758, New York.   [Gen. Amherst] to [Gov. Dobbs]
(copy).   Dobbs should supply the 500-1,000 Cherokees who are
passing through N.C. to fight northern enemies.   2p.

Fol. 4.   1 Mar. 1760, New York.   [Gen. Amherst] to Gov. Dobbs
(copy).   Cherokees have broken the recent peace with S. Carolina.
[Amherst] is sending troops as Lyttleton requested.   Dobbs
should forward this information to Lyttleton.   1p.

Fol. 5.   27 Apr. 1760, New York.   [Gen. Amherst] to Gov. Dobbs
(copy).   [Amherst] thanks Dobbs for forwarding information
[about troops being sent to aid against the Cherokees.]   1p.

Fol. 6.   28 May 1760, Albany.   [Gen. Amherst] to Gov. Dobbs
(copy).   [Amherst] is gratified that N.C. will raise 500 men to
fight the Cherokees on the western frontiers.   2p.

Fol. 7.   3 Nov. 1760, Albany.   [Gen. Amherst] to Gov. Dobbs
(copy).   Loss of Ft. Loudoun is regrettable.   [Amherst] is
certain that troops will force the [Cherokees] to sue for peace.
1p.

Fol. 8.   19 Jan. 1761, New York.   [Gen. Amherst] to Gov. Dobbs
(copy).   N.C. troops have hopefully already joined the Va.
forces operating against the Cherokees while Grant attacks
from south.   2p.

Fol. 9.   29 May 1761, Albany.   [Gen. Amherst] to Gov. Dobbs.
[Same as C.O. 5/61/296].   2p.

Fol. 10.   17 Aug. 1761, Albany.   [Gen. Amherst] to Gov. Dobbs.
(copy).   Grant has undoubtedly forced the Cherokees to sue for
peace.   1p.

Fol. 11.   7 Feb. 1762, New York.   [Gen. Amherst] to Gov. Dobbs
(copy).   [Amherst] has received word that N.C. troops were
disbanded after returning from the frontier.   1p.

Fol. 20. 29 Oct. 1756, Ft. Edward. [Cmdr. in Chief] to Gov.
Lyttleton (copy). [Cmdr. in Chief] is pleased at the way S.C.
and Va. handled building a fort [in Cherokee country]. 2p.

Fol. 21. 24 Apr. 1757, New York. [Cmdr. in Chief] to Gov.
Lyttleton (copy). [Cmdr. in Chief] has ordered 160 Va. troops
to garrison Virginia's fort in Cherokee country. Since the
S.C. fort at Chote is nine miles away, S.C. troops should reinforce Virginia's fort. 6p.

Fol. 30. 13 Feb. 1758, New York. Lord Loudoun to Gov.
Lyttleton (copy). Loudoun has received accounts from Penn.
and Va. about the Cherokees' invaluable services last year.
Atkin has been ordered to assemble the Cherokees at Keowee for
the march to Winchester. 4p.

Fol. 32. 13 Feb. 1758, New York. Lord Loudoun to Gov.
Lyttleton (copy). Loudoun requests that Lyttleton prompt
Atkin to gather the Cherokees quickly. Capt. Bosomworth will
go to the Upper Towns with an interpreter. 4p.

Fol. 47. 21 Dec. 1759, New York. [Gen. Amherst] to Gov.
Lyttleton. [Same as C.O. 5/57/175]. 2p.

Fol. 48. 18 Jan. 1760, New York. [Gen. Amherst] to Gov.
Lyttleton (copy). [Amherst] awaits official word that the
Cherokees have given satisfaction for their misdeeds. 1p.

Fol. 49. 29 Jan. 1760, Ft. Herkhemier. [Gen. Amherst] to
Lt. Gov. Bull (copy). [Amherst] is happy to hear about
Montgomery's success over the Cherokees. 2p.

Fol. 50. 26 Feb. 1760, New York. [Gen. Amherst] to Gov.
Lyttleton. [Same as C.O. 5/57/320]. 4p.

Fol. 52. 1 Mar. 1760, New York. [Gen. Amherst] to Gov.
Lyttleton (copy). [Amherst] has obtained passage for the
troops being sent [against the Cherokees]. 2p.

Fol. 53. 1 Apr. 1760, New York. Gen. Amherst to Gov.
Lyttleton. [Same as C.O. 5/58/131]. 2p.

Fol. 54. 26 May 1760, Albany. [Gen. Amherst] to Lt. Gov. Bull
(copy). [Amherst] regrets that Montgomery has been delayed.
Montgomery will order the trial of Lt. Taylor if evidence can
be obtained before the troops leave. 4p.

Fol. 56. 3 June 1760, Albany. [Gen. Amherst] to Lt. Gov.
Bull. [Same as C.O. 5/58/391]. 4p.

Fol. 58. 18 June 1760, Albany. [Gen. Amherst] to Lt. Gov.
Bull. [Same as C.O. 5/58/397]. 4p.

Fol. 60. 29 June 1760, Ft. Herkhemier. Gen. Amherst to Lt.
Gov. Bull. [Same as C.O. 5/59/67]. 2p.

W.O. 34/36 (CONT'D)

Fol. 61. 24 July 1760, Camp at Oswego. Gen. Amherst to Lt.
Gov. Bull. [Same as C.O. 5/59/69]. 1p.

Fol. 62. 14 Oct. 1760, Lake Champlain. [Gen. Amherst] to Lt.
Gov. Bull. [Same as C.O. 5/59/291]. 2p.

Fol. 63. 27 Nov. 1760, New York. [Gen. Amherst] to Lt. Gov.
Bull. [Same as C.O. 5/60/72]. 7p.

Fol. 68. 12 Dec. 1760, New York. [Gen. Amherst] to Lt. Gov.
Bull (copy). [Amherst] requests that Bull aid Grant in preparing for the expedition [against the Cherokees]. Lantagnac's
actions prove that French deserters should not be employed in
King's service. 2p.

Fol. 69. 14 Jan. 1760. [Gen. Amherst] to Lt. Gov. Bull.
[Same as C.O. 5/60/203]. 4p.

Fol. 71. 15 Jan. 1761, New York. [Gen. Amherst] to Lt. Gov.
Bull (copy). [Amherst] promotes Lachlan McIntosh to the
lieutenancy left vacant by Coytmore. He also sends dispatches
for Grant. 1p.

Fol. 72. 13 Feb. 1761, New York. [Gen. Amherst] to Lt. Gov.
Bull (copy). [Amherst] commends Bull for using money to ransom
prisoners held by the Cherokees. He hopes that Virginia's
diversion will help. 1p.

Fol. 73. 6 Apr. 1761, New York. [Gen. Amherst] to Lt. Gov.
Bull (copy). Va. House of Burgesses agreed to continue a
1,000 man regiment for use against the Upper Cherokee Towns
while Grant strikes the Lower ones. Bull believes the Creeks
have not joined the Cherokees for the same reason they have
not joined the English. 4p.

Fol. 75. 7 May 1761, New York. [Gen. Amherst] to Lt. Gov.
Bull. [Same as C.O. 5/61/228]. 1p.

Fol. 76. 12 May 1761, New York. [Gen. Amherst] to Lt. Gov.
Bull. [Same as C.O. 5/61/279]. 2p.

Fol. 77. 2 July 1761, Albanany. [Gen. Amherst] to Lt. Gov.
Bull. [Same as C.O. 5/61/283]. 1p.

Fol. 78. 13 July 1761, Albany. [Gen. Amherst] to Lt. Gov.
Bull (copy). Col. Grant is scheduled to begin attacking the
Cherokee settlements in June. [Amherst] is pleased that the
escaped Cherokee prisoners were recaptured. 1p.

Fol. 79. 1 Aug. 1761, Albany. [Gen. Amherst] to Lt. Gov.
Bull. [Same as C.O. 5/61/290]. 2p.

Fol. 80. 1 Sept. 1761, Staten Island. [Gen. Amherst] to Lt.
Gov. Bull. [Same as C.O. 5/61/407]. 2p.

Fol. 81. 2 Oct. 1761, Staten Island (copy). [Gen. Amherst] to
Lt. Gov. Bull (copy). Grant wrote about the Cherokees going
to Charleston to discuss peace. 1p.

Fol. 82. 23 Oct. 1761, Staten Island. [Gen. Amherst] to Lt.
Gov. Bull. [Same as C.O. 5/61/528]. 1p.

Fol. 83. 18 Dec. 1761, New York. [Gen. Amherst] to Lt. Gov.
Bull (copy). [Amherst] acknowledges receipt of Bull's letter
thanking him for assistance in protecting S. Carolina. 1p.

Fol. 85. 4 Feb. 1762, New York. [Gen. Amherst] to Gov. Boone
(copy). Cherokee peace will hopefully establish a lasting
friendship. Ft. Loudoun should be garrisoned with provincial
troops. 2p.

Fol. 87. 13 Apr. 1762, New York. [Gen. Amherst] to Gov. Boone
(copy). [Amherst] has received the court-martial proceedings
against Ensign Alex. Miln for misconduct while commander at
Ft. Prince George. 1p.

Fol. 92. 8 July 1762, New York. [Gen. Amherst] to Gov. Boone
(copy). Cherokees have supposedly delivered all the English
prisoners because of the trade restrictions imposed on the
tribe. 2p.

Fol. 93. 23 Aug. 1762, New York. [Gen. Amherst] to Gov. Boone
(copy). Treatment and trade with Indians will hopefully improve.
Indian fears will soon end regardless of their discontent. 2p.

Fol. 97. 8 Dec. 1762, New York. [Gen. Amherst] to Gov. Boone
(copy). Robert Leake reports an error in the provision receipts.
2p. [Enclosures to fol. 99b].

Fol. 98. 27 Nov. 1762, New York. Robt. Leake to Gen.
Amherst (copy). It appears that the Crown was charged
twice for the provisions at Ft. Prince George. 2p.

Fol. 103. 18 Mar. 1762, New York. [Gen. Amherst] to Gov.
Boone (copy). [Amherst] thanks Boone for the information
allowing Leake to determine a mistake [in the receipts for
provisions at Ft. Prince George]. 1p.

Fol. 105. 15 June 1763, New York. [Gen. Amherst] to Gov.
Boone. [Same as C.O. 5/63/143]. 2p. [Enclosures to fol.
107b].

Fol. 106. 15 June 1763, New York. [Gen. Amherst] to Mr.
Smith and Mr. Nutt. [Amherst] orders supplies for the
meeting at Augusta between the governors and the Southern
Indians. 2p.

Fol. 109. 17 Aug. 1763, New York. Gen. Amherst to Gov. Boone.
Lands cannot be purchased too soon from the Indians. Peace cannot be certain as long as the Indians are trusted. 2p.

W.O. 34/36 (CONT'D)

Fol. 113. 16 Oct. 1763, New York. Gen. Amherst to [Gov. Boone]. Indian women will be sent to Charleston on the first available ship. 1p.

Fol. 115. Mar. 1757, Philadelphia. Minutes Taken at a Meeting of the Governors of North Carolina, Virginia, Maryland, and Pennsylvania with the Earl of Loudoun (copy). Troops (100) should be sent to the new Cherokee fort. Va. should garrison Ft. Loudoun near Winchester and Ft. Enoch. 8p.

Fol. 121. 20 Feb. 1762, St. Peters. Col. Grant to [Gen. Amherst]. Officers who served in S.C. have not received their pay. 2p.

Fol. 122. 30 Nov. 1762, Charleston. Raymond Demeré to [Gen. Amherst]. Demeré writes about Ft. Loudoun's debts while he commanded there. 4p.

Fol. 151. 16 Mar. 1758, New York. [Gen. Abercromby?] to Gov. Dobbs and Gov. Lyttleton (copy). [Abercromby?] requests assistance for Montgomery. 4p.

Fol. 166. 28 Mar. 1759, New York. [Gen. Amherst] to Governors of Va., Maryland, and Pennsylvania (copy). Amherst requests assistance for Gen. Stanwix to stop communications between Canada and the Western and Southern Indians. 2p.

Fol. 217. 4 May 1763, New York. [Gen. Amherst] to Southern Governors and John Stuart. [Same as C.O. 5/63/53]. 3p.

Fol. 222. 7 Sept. 1763, New York. [Gen. Amherst] to Gov. Sharpe and Lt. Gov. Fauquier (copy). Va. and Maryland should stop trade with all Indians. 2p.

Fol. 223. 5 Nov. 1763, New York. [Gen. Amherst] to Gov. Hamilton and Lt. Gov. Fauquier (copy). [Amherst] requests troops to crush the Indian insurrection. 4p.

W.O. 34/37   LETTERS OF THE GOVERNOR OF VIRGINIA AND THE COMMANDER-
*   IN-CHIEF: 1758-1763*

Fol. 3. 18 Feb. 1758, Williamsburg. John Blair to Earl of Loudoun. Blair received £800 for building the new Cherokee fort and for Indian presents. 3p.

Fol. 5. 8 Mar. 1758, Williamsburg. John Blair to Earl of Loudoun. Fresh provisions should be given to all friendly Indians visiting Augusta. Atkin complains that Indian goods are too cheap and are distributed without his permission. 6p.

Fol. 9. 1754-57. List of Acts. Ft. Loudoun provisions are listed. 2p. [Enclosure of fol. 10].

Fol. 10 [1758]. John Blair to [Gov. Fauquier] (copy). Except
for £800 set aside to build a Cherokee fort, Va. used the King's
money to pay for the English troops. 4p. [Enclosure at fol. 9].

Fol. 21.   17 Mar. 1759, Williamsburg. Lt. Gov. Fauquier to Gen.
Amherst. Fauquier has sent to N.Y. a young Canadian prisoner
to be exchanged. Cherokees captured him two years ago and Va.
bought him for £30 to save his life. 4p.

Fol. 25.   8 Apr. 1759, Williamsburg. Lt. Gov. Fauquier to
Gen. Amherst. Fauquier will be glad to meet with Amherst concerning adjustments to the Indian treaty. 4p.

Fol. 29.   10 Nov. 1759, Williamsburg. Lt. Gov. Fauquier to
Gen. Amherst. Fauquier called for an early session of the
Burgesses to approve regimental pay since he was warned that
the Cherokees might become hostile. 2p.

Fol. 33.   23 Feb. 1760, Williamsburg. Lt. Gov. Fauquier to
Gen. Amherst. Latest Cherokee treachery will probably persuade
the Assembly to continue regimental pay past May 1. 2p.

Fol. 37.   5 Apr. 1760, Williamsburg. Lt. Gov. Fauquier to Gen.
Amherst. Burgesses resolved to maintain the regiment until
November. Some 300 men will be needed to defend the south-
western frontier. 2p.

Fol. 42.   5 Oct. 1760, Williamsburg. Lt. Gov. Fauquier to Gen.
Amherst. Amherst should anticipate a request from the two
Carolinas and Va. concerning the Cherokees. Little Carpenter
has been sent to negotiate a peace. Fauquier wishes that the
Indians had been treated justly and humanely since this is the
only policy that could make the Indians friendly. 4p.

Fol. 44.   5 Dec. 1760, Williamsburg. Lt. Gov. Fauquier to Gen.
Amherst. Va. and the Crown were supposed to share expenses
for the Cherokees who joined Gen. Forbes. 2p.

Fol. 45.   15 Dec. 1760, Williamsburg. Lt. Gov. Fauquier to
Gen. Amherst. N.C. and S.C. want Va. to join them in asking
Amherst for troops to quell the Cherokees. Simultaneous attacks
should be made on the Lower and Upper Towns. Road from Va.
frontier to the Upper Towns is good. 2p.

Fol. 47.   13 Mar. 1761, Williamsburg. Lt. Gov. Fauquier to
Gen. Amherst. Lack of intelligence from Montgomery could
have resulted in the troops relieving Ft. Loudoun being
destroyed. Fauquier hopes that Grant will keep him constantly
informed. 4p. [Enclosures to fol. 50b].

> Fol. 49b. Address from Burgesses to Amherst. Burgesses
> thanks Amherst for his aid against the Cherokees and sug-
> gests that the Va. troops attack the Upper Towns while the
> British and the S.C. troops attack the Lower Towns. 3p.

W.O. 34/37 (CONT'D)

Fol. 51. 16 Mar. 1761, Williamsburg. Lt. Gov. Fauquier to Gen. Amherst. Fauquier forwards papers about the Cherokees and the preparations for Little Carpenter's return with the Upper Cherokee's answer to the peace proposals. 2p. [Enclosures to fol. 60b].

> Fol. 52. 16 Feb. 1761. Extract of letter from Col. Byrd describing new difficulties with the peace proposed to Little Carpenter. An attack now would be a breach of faith. If the Cherokees accept the peace, however, S.C. will feel deserted and accuse Va. of making a separate peace. 2p.

> Fol. 54. 17 Sept. 1760. Articles of Peace Proposed to the Cherokees. 2p.

> Fol. 56. 21 Feb. 1761, Williamsburg. Copy of letter to Richard Smith ordering that Little Carpenter and the Cherokees be told that no lasting peace can be made without an agreement from the Carolinas and without the acceptance of the Middle and Lower Cherokee Towns. 3p.

> Fol. 58. Williamsburg. Copy of letter to Capt. Bullitt ordering that Little Carpenter be told that there can be no peace without an agreement from the Carolinas and without the acceptance of the Middle and Lower Towns. 4p.

Fol. 63. 17 Apr. 1761, Williamsburg. Lt. Gov. Fauquier to Gen. Amherst. Byrd has requested more troops against the Cherokees. Virginia's efforts will be useless unless Grant is successful. 6p. [Enclosures to fol. 67].

> Fol. 66. [Mar. - Apr. 1761], [Williamsburg]. Lt. Gov. Fauquier. Instructions to the Commissioners Appointed to Purchase the Prisoners Brought In by the Cherokee Indians. 2p.

> Fol. 67. [Mar. - Apr. 1761], [Williamsburg]. Address from Burgesses to Fauquier (copy). Gen. Amherst has convinced the Burgesses that the present number of troops is sufficient for the Cherokee expedition. 1p.

Fol. 68. 22 Apr. 1761, Williamsburg. Lt. Gov. Fauquier to Gen. Amherst. Gov. Dobbs is positive that the Assembly will grant no troops without His Majesty's orders. Virginia's troops, consequently, will have to make the attack upon the Upper Cherokee Towns. 1p.

Fol. 69. 30 Apr. 1761, Williamsburg. Lt. Gov. Fauquier to Gen. Amherst. Fauquier has sent instructions to Byrd and an account of the distances from the frontier settlements to Chote and Ft. Loudoun. 2p. [Enclosures to fol. 70b].

> Fol. 70. 28 Apr. 1761. Lt. Gov. Fauquier. Instructions to ... Wm. Byrd ... Commander of the Forces of Virginia and of the Expedition into the Upper Cherokee Towns. (copy). 2p.

W.O. 34/37 (CONT'D)

Fol. 71. 6 May 1761, Williamsburg. Lt. Gov. Fauquier to Gen.
Amherst. N.C. has appropriated £20,000 to raise 500 men.
Amherst will hopefully order them to join the Va. forces. 2p.

Fol. 72. 27 May 1761, Williamsburg. Lt. Gov. Fauquier to Gen.
Amherst. Byrd has been told to proceed with the expedition.
Little Carpenter has been sent word that there can be no peace
without all Cherokees agreeing. Fauquier expects news daily
about Col. Grant's progress. 4p.

Fol. 74. 2 June 1761. Lt. Gov. Fauquier to Col. Byrd (copy).
Amherst will not postpone the expedition [against the Cherokees]
until he hears from Col. Grant. 4p. [Enclosure of fol. 76].

Fol. 76. 3 June 1761, Williamsburg. Lt. Gov. Fauquier to Maj.
Gen. Amherst. Col. Byrd has been unable to proceed [with
expedition against the Cherokees] because he lacks provisions.
Steps have been taken to remedy the situation. 2p. [Enclo-
sures at fol. 74 and to fol. 78b].

Fol. 77. 29 May 1761, Staunton. Col. Byrd to Lt. Gov.
Fauquier (copy). Col. Grant's fate must be determined
before Byrd's troops leave Staunton. Byrd will be unable
to draw the enemy away from Grant's army. 4p.

Fol. 79. 8 July 1761, Williamsburg. Lt. Gov. Fauquier to
Maj. Gen. Amherst. It is not known if the N.C. men are ready
to march. Col. Byrd's regiment suffers from desertion. 4p.

Fol. 81. 8 Aug. 1761, Williamsburg. Lt. Gov. Fauquier to Maj.
Gen. Amherst. Fauquier is greatly concerned about the numerous
delays of the Va. expedition against the Cherokees. 2p.

Fol. 82. 8 Aug. 1761, Williamsburg. Lt. Gov. Fauquier to
Maj. Gen. Amherst. In July Byrd was at Stalnakers, about 180
miles from Chote, but he had not received any reinforcements
from N. Carolina. Byrd fears that his small force will oblige
him to turn back. 2p.

Fol. 83. 15 Aug. 1761, Williamsburg. Lt. Gov. Fauquier to
Maj. Gen. Amherst. Fauquier has decided to let the Assembly
determine the number of troops needed this winter because of
the lack of success with the Cherokee expedition. 2p.

Fol. 84. 22 Aug. 1761, Williamsburg. Lt. Col. Fauquier to
Maj. Gen. Amherst. Fauquier has read about Grant's expedition
in the newspaper. Byrd has received no news from Bull or Grant
since 21 May. Moreover, Fauquier has no information about the
troops that N.C. plans to raise. 4p.

Fol. 87. 11 Oct. 1761, Williamsburg. Lt. Gov. Fauquier to
Maj. Gen. Amherst. N. Carolina's troops should be recalled if
they have not left to join the Va. troops. 4p. [Enclosures to
fol. 90b].

W.O. 34/37 (CONT'D)

Fol. 89.   7 Sept. 1761, Fort Chiswell.   Col. Stephen to
[Lt. Gov. Fauquier] (copy).   Stephen wonders why Grant
did not make peace at Chote.   Grant's troops at Ft. Prince
George, 250 miles away, cannot aid Virginia's operations.
4p.

Fol. 91.   26 Oct. 1761, Williamsburg.   Lt. Gov. Fauquier to
Maj. Gen. Amherst.   Col. Stephen has received letters from
Conocotocko (the present Cherokee Emperor) and Oconostota (the
Great Warrior), who have always opposed Little Carpenter in
making peace.   Cherokees report that Little Carpenter has gone
to Charleston to conclude peace.   2p.

Fol. 92.   9 Nov. 1761, Williamsburg.   Lt. Gov. Fauquier to Maj.
Gen. Amherst.   As soon as Fauquier receives word of peace from
Charleston, he will recall Virginia's troops.   2p.

Fol. 93.   17 Nov. 1761, Williamsburg.   Lt. Gov. Fauquier to
Maj. Gen. Amherst.   Assembly passed a law maintaining the
regiment until the Cherokee peace is confirmed.   Assembly hopes
that the Crown will pay for troops sent to relieve Ft. Loudoun
since it is not in Virginia.   2p.

Fol. 94.   11 Dec. 1761, Williamsburg.   Lt. Gov. Fauquier to
Maj. Gen. Amherst.   Assembly believes that the letter from Col.
Stephen reporting the Indians' interest in peace is sufficient
reason to disband the regiment.   Assembly hopes that the fort
built by Col. Stephen will not be garrisoned nor the cost
charged to Virginia.   2p.   [Enclosures to fol. 96b].

Fol. 96.   20 Nov. 1761, Great Island.   Articles of peace
with the Cherokees.   Signatories include Conocotocko,
Willinawa, Autassaty, Skiagunsta, and Connecaughte.   2p.

Fol. 97.   8 Jan. 1762, Williamsburg.   Lt. Gov. Fauquier to
Maj. Gen. Amherst.   Fauquier has not received news about the
peace from Bull.   Standing Turkey and some of his friends are
en route to Williamsburg.   2p.   [Enclosures to fol. 100b].

Fol. 98.   28 Nov. 1761.   A General Return of the Troops
Commanded by Col. Adam Stephen Encamp'd at the Great
Island.   2p.

Fol. 99.   Adam Stephen.   A Return of the Ammunition at the
Different Posts.   Report includes Great Island, Ft. Attacullaculla, and Ft. Chiswell.   2p.

Fol. 102.   19 Jan. 1762, Williamsburg.   Lt. Gov. Fauquier to
Maj. Gen. Amherst.   Fauquier has requested news from Bull about
whether peace has been concluded with the Cherokees.   2p.

Fol. 107.   1 Feb. 1762, Williamsburg.   Lt. Gov. Fauquier to
Maj. Gen. Amherst.   Burgesses has authorized maintaining a
regiment until Fauquier hears from S.C. [about peace with the
Cherokees].   4p.

Fol. 112. 12 Mar. 1762, Williamsburg. Lt. Gov. Fauquier to
Maj. Gen. Amherst. Provision delays have prevented the Va.
regiment from marching against the Cherokees. Carolinians'
belief that Va. wants Ft. Loudoun is not true. 4p.

Fol. 114. 1 Apr. 1762, Williamsburg. Lt. Gov. Fauquier to
Maj. Gen. Amherst. 4p. [Enclosures to fol. 119b].

> Fol. 116. [30-31 Mar. 1762], [Williamsburg]. Speech from
> Fauquier to Assembly (copy). Gov. Boone has advised
> Fauquier that the Cherokee peace has been ratified. 6p.

Fol. 120. 7 Apr. 1762. Lt. Gov. Fauquier to Maj. Gen. Amherst.
Capt. Bullitt sent a map of the rivers, mountains, and distances
from Virginia's back settlements to the Overhill Cherokee towns.
2p.

Fol. 152. 30 Oct. 1762, Williamsburg. Lt. Gov. Fauquier to
Gen. Amherst. Fauquier will send Timberlake to N.Y. as soon
as he arrives. 1p.

Fol. 177. 2 Aug. 1763, Williamsburg. Lt. Gov. Fauquier to
Gen. Amherst. Northern bands returning home from attacking
the Cherokees are apparently the Indians annoying Virginia. 2p.

Fol. 179. 29 Sept. 1763, Williamsburg. John Blair to [Gen.
Amherst]. A proclamation forbidding trade with the Indians
should not be issued at this time since the Lt. Gov. is on his
way to negotiate a lasting peace with the Cherokees and Southern
tribes. 2p.

Fol. 194. 13 Feb. 1758, New York. Letter to John Blair reporting that Byrd has been ordered to bring a number of Cherokees
to Winchester. Upper Towns' chiefs should attend the meeting
at Keowee and be prepared for an expedition. Dobbs has been
requested to provision the Cherokee march through N. Carolina.
6p.

Fol. 197. 14 Feb. 1758, New York. Letter to John Blair reporting that Byrd has been ordered to bring a number of Cherokees
to Winchester. Upper Town's chiefs should attend the meeting
at Keowee and be prepared for an expedition. 2p.

Fol. 198. 11 Feb. 1759, New York. [Gen. Amherst] to Lt. Gov.
Fauquier. The governors should meet to determine means of
gaining the Indians' friendship and to prevent them from supporting the enemy. 2p.

Fol. 208. 21 Dec. 1759, New York. [Gen. Amherst] to Lt. Gov.
Fauquier. Lyttleton's expedition will hopefully be successful
and he will not need more troops. 1p.

W.O. 34/37 (CONT'D)

Fol. 212. 17 Mar. 1760, New York. [Gen. Amherst] to Lt. Gov.
Fauquier. Troops have been sent to protect S.C. and to punish
the Cherokees. 1p.

Fol. 215. 20 Apr. 1760, New York. [Gen. Amherst] to Lt. Gov.
Fauquier. Troops sent to punish the Cherokees will certainly
allow Fauquier to stop worrying about Indian threats. 1p.

Fol. 218. 28 Dec. 1760, New York. [Gen. Amherst] to Lt. Gov.
Fauquier. [Amherst] has been assembling and embarking troops
for S.C. to help the Carolina and Virginia provincials chastise
the Cherokees. 2p.

Fol. 219. 19 Jan. 1761, New York. [Gen. Amherst] to Lt. Gov.
Fauquier. N. Carolina's Assembly will hopefully provide troops
to fight the Cherokees. 2p.

Fol. 220. 21 Jan. 1761, New York. [Gen. Amherst] to Lt. Gov.
Fauquier. The Va. troops should attack the Upper Towns while
Grant attacks the Lower ones. Indians would then be glad to
sue for peace and would be weakened for a long time. 2p.

Fol. 221. 13 Feb. 1761, New York. [Gen. Amherst] to Lt. Gov.
Fauquier. It is impractical for Grant to begin the expedition
before March. He does, however, plan to be at Ft. Prince
George by May. The Va. forces should then be at Chote. 1p.

Fol. 222. 25 Mar. 1761, New York. [Gen. Amherst] to Lt. Gov.
Fauquier. Byrd and Grant must maintain correspondence with
each other. Peace should not be granted to the Cherokees
until they are properly chastised and until the Southern governors approve the terms. 1p.

Fol. 223. 25 Mar. 1761, New York. [Gen. Amherst] to John
Robinson. Only the sword can bring peace with the misguided
people [Cherokees]. Assembly fears that Grant's success will
drive the Cherokees towards Col. Byrd, who will face their full
fury. 4p.

Fol. 226. 15 Apr. 1761, New York. [Gen. Amherst] to Lt. Gov.
Fauquier. [Amherst] has received papers outlining the necessary
preparations for the expected visit from Little Carpenter after
Byrd's peace proposals. 1p.

Fol. 227. 11 May 1761, New York. Gen. Amherst to Lt. Gov.
Fauquier. Amherst critizes Va. for not raising more than
1,000 men. 1p.

Fol. 228. 11 May 1761, New York. [Gen. Amherst] to Lt. Gov.
Fauquier. Col. Grant has left Congarees. Nothing can ensure
Grant's success more than a vigorous effort by Virginia. If
the troops are deligent, it would be impossible for the Cherokees to cut off 1,000 men. 4p.

W.O. 34/37 (CONT'D)

Fol. 230. 28 May 1761, Albany. [Gen. Amherst] to Lt. Gov.
Fauquier. Col. Byrd reports that he has not been able to
complete his regiment. 1p.

Fol. 231. 3 June 1761, Albany. [Gen. Amherst] to Lt. Gov.
Fauquier. Dobbs has certainly sent the portion of his troops
that were ready. They will hopefully arrive in time to join
the Va. regiment. 1p.

Fol. 232. 2 July 1761, Albany. [Gen. Amherst] to Lt. Gov.
Fauquier. Va. regiment can harrass the [Cherokees] and prevent
the tribe from concentrating against [Grant]. This is not the
time for Byrd to think of leaving his regiment. 1p.

Fol. 234. 2 Aug. 1761, Albany. [Gen. Amherst] to Lt. Gov.
Fauquier. Desertion has cut the strength of the Va. regiment.
Grant has chastized the Cherokees as severely as could be
expected. Cherokees will accept any terms offered by Grant to
prevent their destruction. The Va. and Carolina forces should
pursue their orders as if nothing has happened. 2p.

Fol. 235. 17 Aug. 1761, Albany. [Gen. Amherst] to Lt. Gov.
Fauquier. Although peace with the Cherokees has surely taken
place, no official word has been received. 1p.

Fol. 236. 28 Aug. 1761, Staten Island. [Gen. Amherst] to Lt.
Gov. Fauquier. [Amherst] is concerned about the numerous
delays in Col. Byrd's operations against the Cherokees. 1p.

Fol. 237. 28 Aug. 1761, Staten Island. [Gen. Amherst] to
Lt. Gov. Fauquier. Byrd is now well supplied and commands
sufficient troops. Byrd will hopefully not retire before the
designated date. 1p.

Fol. 238. 6 Sept. 1761, Staten Island. [Gen. Amherst] to Lt.
Gov. Fauquier. Va. should maintain its regiment until a solid
peace is concluded with the Cherokees and until Va. is free
from apprehension about any Indian disturbance. 2p.

Fol. 240. 15 Nov. 1761, New York. [Gen. Amherst] to Lt. Gov.
Fauquier. Fauquier has certainly recalled the Va. regiment
since peace has been settled with the Cherokees. 1p.

Fol. 241. 29 Nov. 1761, New York. [Gen. Amherst] to Lt. Gov.
Fauquier. [Amherst] approves Col. Stephen's advance into
Cherokee country. Bull and Grant, surprizingly, did not coop-
erate in concluding a peace with the Cherokees. 2p.

Fol. 242. 1 Dec. 1761, New York. [Gen. Amherst] to Lt. Gov.
Fauquier. [Amherst] disapproves of the assembly's plan to
disband the regiment once peace is confirmed with the Cherokees.
2p.

W.O. 34/37 (CONT'D)

Fol. 243. 16 Dec. 1761, New York. [Gen. Amherst] to Lt. Gov. Fauquier. [Amherst] is pleased to learn that nearly 100 Cherokees had turned themselves in. Boone has been ordered to communicate all the news about the Cherokee peace. 2p.

Fol. 245. 4 Feb. 1762, New York. [Gen. Amherst] to Lt. Gov. Fauquier. Legislature of S.C. has written the treaty [of peace with the Cherokees] so that the province is not responsible for Ft. Loudoun. Ft. Loudoun is still needed to protect Carolina. 1p.

Fol. 246. 12 Feb. 1762, New York. [Gen. Amherst] to Lt. Gov. Fauquier. [Amherst] approves the articles added to the Cherokee treaty by Col. Stephen since they agree with the rest of the treaty. 2p.

Fol. 248. 2 Mar. 1762, New York. [Gen. Amherst] to Lt. Gov. Fauquier. It is unfortunate that Fauquier was obliged to disband the Va. regiment after receiving news about the Cherokee peace. 2p.

Fol. 249. 2 Mar. 1762, New York. [Gen. Amherst] to Lt. Gov. Fauquier. [Amherst] disapproves the conduct of council members who pressed for the disbanding of the Va. regiment. 1p.

Fol. 252. 22 Apr. 1762, New York. [Gen. Amherst] to Lt. Gov. Fauquier. [Amherst] has been unable to send an engineer to work with the two provincial officers in making a map of the country beyond the Allegheny Mountains. 3p.

Fol. 269. 18 Oct. 1762, New York. [Gen. Amherst] to Lt. Gov. Fauquier. [Amherst] acknowledges receipt of the orders to reward Timberlake who went to England with the Indians. Timberlake is appointed lieutenant in the Royal Highland Regiment. 1p.

W.O. 34/38   LETTERS FROM THE COMMANDER-IN-CHIEF TO WILLIAM JOHNSON:
1757-1763

Fol. 12. 13 Dec. 1756, New Orleans. Kerlerec to French Ministry. [Translated extract of C.O. 5/375/193]. 4p.

Fol. 14. 30 Jan. 1757, New Orleans. Kerlerec to French Ministry. [Translated extract of C.O. 5/375/197]. 2p.

Fol. 18. 1 July 1757, Halifax. Letter to Wm. Johnson enclosing a copy of Kerlerec's letter and the preliminary articles of the peace treaty with the Cherokees. 3p.

Fol. 20. 1757. [Earl of Loudoun] to Wm. Johnson. [Loudoun] sends a copy of the intercepted letters and a treaty. [Enclosures to fol. 22b]. 2p.

Fol. 21. 23 Nov. 1756, New Orleans. Preliminary Articles
of Peace between the French and the Cherokee Nation. 4p.

Fol. 23. 25 Dec. 1757, New York. Earl of Loudoun to Wm. Johnson
(copy). Indian affairs seem unstable in spite of previous
treaties. Loudoun appointed Croghan to act as Johnson's deputy.
8p.

Fol. 30. 15 Feb. 1758, New York. [Cmdr. in Chief] to Capt.
Bosomworth. [Cmdr. in Chief] will visit Williamsburg to prepare
for a conference with the Upper Cherokee Towns at Keowee. 1p.

Fol. 35. 13 May 1758, Albany. [Cmdr. in Chief] to Wm. Johnson.
[Cmdr. in Chief] is forwarding a statement from Wawahatchee
(Cherokee chief) concerning an extraordinary speech by a Mohawk.
2p.

Fol. 44. 23 July 1758, Lake George. [Cmdr. in Chief] to Wm.
Johnson. Gen. Forbes has complained about Johnson's neglect
in not sending someone to manage the Cherokees. 1p.

Fol. 45. 20 Aug. 1758, Lake George. [Cmdr. in Chief] to Wm.
Johnson. Gen. Forbes reports that the Cherokees are friendly
towards the English. Forbes has been informed about the Cherokee relations. 1p.

Fol. 52. 13 Dec. 1758, New York. [Cmdr. in Chief] to Wm.
Johnson and Edm. Atkin. Johnson and Atkin should enlist as
many Northern and Southern Indians as possible to aid the
English. 1p.

Fol. 98. 24 Feb. 1760, New York. [Gen. Amherst] to Cmdr.
Jarvis. Cherokees have broken the peace concluded at Ft. Prince
George (26 Dec. 1759). Lyttleton requests sufficient troops to
protect S.C. and to secure Fts. Prince George and Loudoun. 2p.

Fol. 168. 20 Dec. 1761, New York. [Gen. Amherst] to Wm.
Johnson (copy). It is impossible to do anything about the
expense of clothing the Cherokees in 1757 without first
contacting Gen. Stanwix who held command at that time in the
South. 4p.

Fol. 173. 4 Jan. 1762, New York. [Gen. Amherst] to Wm. Johnson
(copy). [Amherst] is sending a list of the property of two
Indians who recently returned from Carolina. One died and the
other is in the interpreter's care. 1p.

Fol. 206. 17 Oct. 1762, New York. [Gen. Amherst] to Wm.
Johnson (copy). Intelligence from the French Indians about
new forts in Cherokee country may be accurate. 2p.

Fol. 216. 10 Dec. 1762, Ft. Pitt. Geo. Croghan to Col. Henry
Bouquet (copy). Senecas, Delawares, and Shawnees believe the
English are planning to attack them since otherwise the English
would be furnishing them with supplies to war against the
Southern Indians. 3p.

W.O. 34/38 (CONT'D)

Fol. 254. 14 Aug. 1763, New York. Intelligence from Capt.
Thomas Baugh (copy). People in Green Briar, Va., welcomed a
party of Indians after an Indian spokesman stated they were
going to war against the Cherokees. These same Indians later
committed hostilities around Green Briar. [Enclosure of
Johnson's letter of 14 Aug. 1763]. 3p.

Fol. 256. 20 Aug. 1763, New York. [Gen. Amherst] to Wm.
Johnson. Indians who have harrassed the Va. frontiers are
evidently Northern Indians returning from attacking the Cherokees. 2p.

Fol. 257. 27 Aug. 1763, New York. [Gen. Amherst] to Wm.
Johnson. Indians have attacked Bushy Run. Col. Stephen with
400 to 500 Va. militia has advanced as far as Fts. Cumberland
and Bedford, planning to cover the frontier and act offensively
against the savages. 6p.

*W.O. 34/39   LETTERS FROM WILLIAM JOHNSON TO THE COMMANDER-IN-CHIEF:
            1758-1763*

Fol. 18. 13 Apr. 1758, Ft. Johnson. Wm. Johnson to Maj. Gen.
Abercromby (copy). Peace is being settled with the Ohio and
Western Indians. Last fall at Ft. Johnson, the Cherokees
promised to join the English. A Cherokee alliance is especially important to the southern governments. 4p.

Fol. 20. 28 Apr. 1758, Ft. Johnson. Wm. Johnson to Maj. Gen.
Abercromby. Twightwees, Tenundadies, and Delawares are not
friendly with the Cherokees, Catawbas, and Creeks. The latter
will continue to fight the French on the Ohio if properly supported. Cherokees should not know about the negotiations with
the Delawares and Twightwees. 10p.

Fol. 43. 11 June 1758, Aughguaga. Extract of letter from Mr.
Croghan reporting that Tedyuskung told the Six Nations that
he had stopped the Cherokees from attacking the Six Nations.
1p.

Fol. 44. 22 June 1758, Ft. Johnson. Wm. Johnson to Maj. Gen.
Abercromby. A delegation of 23 Cherokees arrived at Albany on
their way to Ft. Johnson. 1p.

Fol. 45. 23 June 1758, Ft. Johnson. Wm. Johnson to John Appy.
The 23 [Cherokee] Indians camped near Ft. Ticonderoga saw no
signs of enemy Indians there. 1p.

Fol. 81. 30 Jan. 1759, Philadelphia. Geo. Croghan to Wm.
Johnson (extract). Virginians argued with some Indian parties
returning home last summer and killed about 40 Cherokees. Last
fall Gen. Forbes ordered that all guns and clothing be taken
from Little Carpenter and his party who were returning home.
4p. [Enclosure of Johnson's letter of 22 Feb. 1759].

Fol. 259. 10 May 1762, Ft. Pitt. Geo. Croghan to [Gen.
Amherst]. Many Six Nations' Indians pass Ft. Pitt when warring
against the Southern Indians. A party of 80 passed recently
with two Cherokee prisoners and eight scalps. 2p.

Fol. 260. 21 May 1762, Albany. Wm. Johnson to Gen. Amherst.
Johnson sends an extract of Croghan's journal regarding the
murders committed by the Shawnees who are at war with the
Cherokees. 2p. [Enclosures to fol. 261].

> Fol. 261. Ft. Pitt. Extract from Croghan's Journal
> reporting that a Shawnee party returning from attacking
> the Cherokees mistakenly murdered some whites. 1p.

Fol. 287. 24 Sept. 1762, Ft. Johnson. Wm. Johnson to Jeffrey
Amherst. Some Senecas report that the Miss. French are build-
ing forts on the banks of a large river running through the
Cherokee country. 4p.

Fol. 290. 5 Oct. 1762, Ft. Pitt. Letter from Geo. Croghan
noting his belief that three whites killed by Shawnees last
spring along the Carolina frontiers were half-breed Cherokees
and a mulato. 1p. [Enclosures to fol. 304b].

> Fol. 291. 4 Apr. 1762. Journal from Thomas Hutchins to
> Geo. Croghan (copy). Hutchins visited posts west of Ft.
> Pitt. Cherokees scalped two Shawnees and captured one
> Delaware boy. 15p.

> Fol. 299. Aug. 1762. Geo. Croghan. Minutes of the Treaty
> of Lancaster (extract). 3p.

> Fol. 301. 5 Oct. 1762. Instructions from Croghan to
> Alex. McKee (copy). McKee is ordered to find out why the
> Shawnees have not turned over the people guilty of killing
> three Englishmen along the Carolina frontier last spring
> [when returning from attacking the Cherokees]. 3p.

> Fol. 303. 28-30 Sept. 1762, Detroit. Intelligence from
> three Six Nations' Indians. A party of Ouiatanons [Weas]
> going to fight the Cherokees last spring passed a French
> fort at the forks of the Ohio River. 3p.

Fol. 334. 21 May 1763, Philadelphia. Geo. Croghan to Jeffrey
Amherst. Croghan doubts that any Indians living along the
Ohio or Miss. Rivers will attend the conference since they are
at war with the Southern Indians. 4p.

Fol. 336. 6 June 1763, Johnson Hall. Wm. Johnson to Jeffrey
Amherst. Johnson doubts the rumor that the French have ascended
the Miss. River, taken some English posts, and sent the Six
Nations (via the Southern Indians) a large belt of wampum with
English scalps to request assistance. 6p.

W.O. 34/39 (CONT'D)

Fol. 342.   19 June 1763, Albany. Wm. Johnson to Jeffrey
Amherst. Nothing could be more useful than turning the Chero-
kees, Catawbas, and other Indians against the Shawnees,
Chippewas, and Delawares. 1p.

Fol. 360.   8 July 1763, Johnson Hall. Wm. Johnson to Jeffrey
Amherst. If any troops are moved south, the Cherokees might
be persuaded to assist them once the tribe is told that the
English have stopped attacks from the Western Indians. 4p.

Fol. 394.   25 Aug. 1763, Johnson Hall. Wm. Johnson to Jeffrey
Amherst. Since the capture of Canada, the Six Nations and
Western tribes have busied themselves in attacking the Chero-
kees and others. 6p. [Enclosures to fol. 399b].

Fol. 400.   31 Aug. 1763, Johnson Hall. Wm. Johnson to Jeffrey
Amherst. Six Nations are not the likely source of hostilities
along the Va. frontiers. Both Northern and Western Indians
have sent many war parties against the Cherokees. 4p.

*W.O. 34/47   LETTERS FROM OFFICERS SERVING IN SOUTH CAROLINA AND
              VIRGINIA TO THE COMMANDER-IN-CHIEF: 1757-1763*

Fol. 1.   15 Oct. 1759. John Gray. A General Return of the
Strength of His Majesty's Three Independent Companies ... in
South Carolina and Georgia. Report includes Fts. Prince George
and Loudoun. 2p.

Fol. 2b.   1 Feb. 1760. Return of His Majesty's Three Independent Companies. Report includes Fts. Prince George and Loudoun.
1p.

Fol. 3.   31 Jan. 1760. Return of the South Regiment of Foot
Commanded by Lt. Col. Probart Howarth. Report includes Fts.
Prince George and Loudoun. 2p.

Fol. 4.   12 Apr. 1760, Charleston. Col. Montgomery to [Gen.
Amherst]. Preparations for the expedition were not made before
Montgomery's arrival. Indians will be more troublesome if they
have abandoned their Lower Towns. 4p.

Fol. 6.   17 Apr. 1760, Charleston. Col. Grant to [Gen. Amherst]
Grant doubts that the French support the [Cherokees]. The
Indians regret what has happened and will be glad to come to
terms. 2p.

Fol. 7.   22 Apr. 1760, Monk's Corner. Col. Montgomery to
[Gen. Amherst]. [Same as C.O. 5/58/401]. 1p.

Fol. 10.   16 May 1760, Charleston. Letter from Capt. Raymond
Demeré reporting that Lt. Taylor's trial is postponed until
Montgomery returns from the Cherokee expedition. 2p.

W.O. 34/47 (CONT'D)

Fol. 11.   28 Apr. 1760, S. Carolina. Gov. Glen to [Gen. Amherst].
Col. Montgomery has begun an expedition against the Cherokees.
Consequences may prove fatal if the Creeks or French assist the
Cherokees. 2p.

Fol. 12.   24 May 1760, Camp at Ninety Six. Col. Montgomery to
Gen. Amherst. [Same as C.O. 5/58/405]. 4p.

Fol. 14.   4 June 1760, Camp near Ft. Prince George. Col.
Montgomery to [Gen. Amherst]. [Same as C.O. 5/59/71]. 4p.

Fol. 16.   23 June 1760, Camp at Keowee Town. Col. Montgomery to
[Gen. Amherst]. [Same as C.O. 5/59/76]. 2p.

Fol. 17.   2 July 1760, Camp at Ft. Prince George. Col.
Montgomery to [Gen. Amherst]. [Same as C.O. 5/59/101]. 4p.
[Enclosures to fol. 19b].

> Fol. 19.   2 July 1760. Col. Montgomery. Return of the
> Killed and Wounded of the Detachment ... under Col.
> Archibald Montgomery. 2p.

Fol. 20.   11 Sept. 1760, Albany. Col. Montgomery to [Gen.
Amherst]. Although the war against the Cherokees has been
successful, the Indians have not made peace. Some troops
(four companies) remained in S.C. for protection against the
Indians. 4p. [Enclosures to fol. 24b].

> Fol. 22.   15 Aug. 1760, Charleston. Col. Montgomery to
> Maj. Frederick Hamilton (copy). Hamilton is ordered to
> remain with the four companies at Congarees until further
> notice. If the Cherokee war continues, troops may make
> their winter quarters in December. 4p.

> Fol. 24.   24 Aug. 1760. Col. Montgomery. Monthly Return
> of Eight Companies of the Detachment under Command of Col.
> Archibald Montgomery. 2p.

Fol. 25.   20 Sept. 1760, Ft. Hendrick. Col. Montgomery to
[Gen. Amherst]. Officers have not been paid for the Carolina
campaign against the Cherokees. 2p.

Fol. 26.   29 Sept. 1760, Albany. Col. Montgomery to Gen.
Amherst. Montgomery requests a leave of absence to visit
England. 2p. [Enclosures to fol. 28b].

> Fol. 27.   29 Sept. 1760, Albany. Certificate from Drs.
> Barr and Napier stating that Halifax's climate would be
> detrimental to Montgomery's health. 2p.

> Fol. 28.   24 Sept. 1760. Col. Montgomery. Monthly Return
> of Six Companies of the First Highland Battalion Commanded
> by ... Col. Archibald Montgomery. Monroe was left wounded
> in Charleston. 2p.

W.O. 34/47 (CONT'D)

Fol. 31.   20 Dec. 1760, New York.   Col. James Grant to [Gen.
Amherst].   Grant requests further instructions for the expedition against the Cherokees.   2p.

Fol. 36.   17 Jan. 1761, Charleston.   Col. Grant to [Gen.
Amherst].   Peace is not a fashionable topic in Charleston.
The war continues only in the imagination of officers at Ft.
Prince George.   Grant will attack the Lower Settlements while
the Va. troops attack the Upper Settlements.   6p.

Fol. 39.   13 Oct. 1760, Treasury Chambers.   Samuel Martin to
Commanding Officer in Carolina.   1p.   [Enclosures to fol. 41].

    Fol. 40.   8 Jan. 1761, Charleston.   Mr. Nutt and Mr. Smith
    to Col. Grant (copy).   Nutt and Smith regret Amherst's
    objection to the cost of their commission being charged
    to the account for Montgomery's expedition.   1p.

Fol. 42.   29 Jan. 1761, Charleston.   Col. Grant to [Gen.
Amherst].   McIntosh went to Ft. Prince George to gather intelligence on the Indians.   Expedition will begin in April.   4p.

Fol. 46.   3 Feb. 1761, Charleston.   Col. Grant to [Gen. Amherst].
Bull misinformed Amherst regarding preparations for the expedition [against the Cherokees].   Charleston is in a helpless state.
4p.

Fol. 48.   9 Feb. 1761, Charleston.   Col. Grant to [Gen. Amherst].
Grant explains his problems in preparing for the [Cherokee]
expedition.   2p.

Fol. 49.   22 Feb. 1761, Charleston.   Col. Grant to [Gen. Amherst].
Grant explains preparations [for the Cherokee] expedition.   4p.

Fol. 51.   9 Feb. 1761, Charleston.   Proceedings of a General
Court Martial Held in Charleston (copy).   Court-martial concerns
deserters during the expedition against the Cherokees.   5p.

Fol. 54.   15 Mar. 1761, Charleston.   Col. Grant to [Gen. Amherst].
Supplies have been sent to Ft. Prince George.   Rangers did not
see any Indians on their trip to and from the fort, but the
Indians did steal 29 horses during the night.   4p.

Fol. 57.   30 Mar. 1761, Camp at Monk's Corner.   Col. Grant to
Gen. Amherst.   Grant will proceed on the expedition [against
the Cherokees] around 10 April.   Little Carpenter has sent a
peace talk to Bull.   Tistoe and some 40 followers will settle
near [Ft Prince George] and deserve English protection.   4p.

Fol. 59.   12 Apr. 1761, Camp at Monk's Corner.   Col. Grant to
[Gen. Amherst.   Indians have delivered almost 100 prisoners.
Young Warrior of Estatoe blames mistreatment at the fort for
his fighting.   Rain has prevented the departure of troops.   4p.
[Enclosures to fol. 63b].

Fol. 61. Ft. Prince George. Talk from the Young Warrior of Estatoe to Mr. McIntosh (copy). Young Warrior is blamed for everything by both the whites and Indians. He initiated mischief only because of his mistreatment at the fort. 1p.

Fol. 64. 25 Apr. 1761, Camp at Congarees. Col. Grant to [Gen. Amherst]. Grant left Monk's Corner 12 Apr. and arrived at Congarees 22 April. Rangers are useless. 2p.

Fol. 65. 26 Apr. 1761, Camp Congarees. Col. Grant to [Gen. Amherst]. Grant has received Capt. Raymond Demeré's resignation. Several individuals wish to purchase Demeré's company or the lieutenancy. 1p.

Fol. 66. 5 May 1761, Camp at Mild Creek. Col. Grant to [Gen. Amherst]. Indians have delivered 113 prisoners and supplies to feed them. Great Warrior has reportedly brought ammunition, presents, and rum. 4p. [Enclosures to fol. 80b].

Fol. 68. [1761]. Memorial from Lt. Charles Forbes to Gen. Amherst. Forbes fought at Culloden and elsewhere. He requests a promotion to captain. 2p.

Fol. 69. 1761. Memorial from Ensign Richard Friend to Gen. Amherst. Friend requests promotion to lieutenant. 2p.

Fol. 70. 4 Apr. 1761, Frederica. Letter from Capt. Raymond Demeré resigning his commission. 1p.

Fol. 71. 6 Apr. 1761, Camp Congarees. A General Court Martial Held by Virtue of a Warrant from Col. James Grant, Commander-in-Chief of the Expedition against the Cherokee Indians (duplicate). 6p.

Fol. 75. 17 Apr. 1761, Camp near Sgt. Campbell's House. Proceedings of a General Court Martial (duplicate). Trial concerns deserters from the current expedition against the Cherokee Indians. 9p.

Fol. 81. 2 and 5 June 1761, Ft. Prince George. Col. Grant to [Gen. Amherst]. Bad weather has delayed the expedition. Assistance cannot be expected from Virginia. Little Carpenter requested that Grant remain at Ft. Prince George until his return. About 50-60 Indians have been given protection and allowed to settle near the fort. Grant has about 70 Mohawks, Stockbridges, Chickasaws, and Catawbas to assist in the expedition. 5p. [Enclosures to fol. 92b].

Fol. 85. 1 June 1761, Ft. Prince George. Return of His Majesty's Forces in South Carolina Commanded by Lt. Col. Grant. 2p.

W.O. 34/47 (CONT'D)

> Fol. 86. 4 June 1761, Camp near Keowee. Proceedings of
> a General Court Martial (copy). Trial concerns a murder
> [which took place during the Cherokee expedition]. 3p.
>
> Fol. 88. 23 May 1761, [Ft. Prince George]. Talk from
> Grant to Little Carpenter. Grant will not negotiate
> peace until the Ft. Loudoun garrison prisoners are return-
> ed. All Indians remaining in the towns will be regarded
> as friends. Those in the woods and mountains are enemies.
> 2p.
>
> Fol. 89. [ca. 23 May 1761], [Ft. Prince George]. Talk
> from Little Carpenter to Grant. Little Carpenter requests
> the opportunity to talk with his people before Grant
> advances any further. 2p.
>
> Fol. 90. 30 Mar. 1761, Charleston. Talk from Lt. Gov.
> Bull to Attakullakulla. Bull has ordered presents for
> the Cherokees who have treated the English well. He has
> received a token of friendship from Standing Turkey and
> Judd's Friend. Peaceful Cherokees will not be hurt. 4p.
>
> Fol. 92. 22 Apr. 1761, Williamsburg. Col. Byrd to Col.
> Grant (extract). Although Byrd was sent to attack the
> Upper Cherokees, he cannot march without supplies. Byrd
> claims that his army is too small to be successful. 2p.

Fol. 93. 10 July 1761, Camp at Ft. Prince George. Maj.
Monypenny to Gen. Amherst. Monypenny will follow Amherst's
orders to continue as a major under Col. Grant. 2p.

Fol. 94. 10 July 1761, Camp near Ft. Prince George. Col.
Grant to Gen. Amherst. Upper Chickasaws have been very helpful.
Grant will send for Great Warrior and Little Carpenter to negotiate a peace. Indians have moved too far away to be a threat.
4p. [Enclosures to fol. 98b].

> Fol. 96. [July 1761]. Names of the Towns in the Middle
> and Back Settlements Burnt by the Detachment under the
> Command of Col. Grant. Destroyed towns include Tassee,
> Newcasse, Neowee, Canuga, Waltoqui, Cowhee, Ayoree,
> Ussanah, Cowitchie, Burning Town, Alejoy, Sticoe, Kittoa,
> Tuckoritchie, and Tessantee. 2p.
>
> Fol. 97. 10 June 1761. Col. Grant. Return of the Killed
> and Wounded at Cowhowee. 2p.

Fol. 99. 3 Sept. 1761, Camp near Ft. Prince Geroge. Col.
Grant to [Gen. Amherst]. Little Carpenter and other headmen
begged for peace. A trader almost ruined the negotiations
by telling the Cherokees that the English wanted to kill them.
Grant will remain at Ninety Six until peace is settled. 4p.
[Enclosures to fol. 107b].

> Fol. 101. [1761]. Memorial of Ensign Richard Friend to
> Gen. Amherst. [Same as fol. 69]. 2p.

Fol. 102. [1761]. Memorial of Lt. Charles Forbes to Gen. Amherst. [Same as fol. 68]. 1p.

Fol. 103. 29 Aug. 1761, Camp near Ft. Prince George. Journal of conferences with the Cherokee deputies. Cherokees were told the peace terms. 6p.

Fol. 108. 6 Oct. 1761, Camp near Ft. Prince George. Col. Grant to [Gen. Amherst]. Grant was publicly attacked by the S.C. legislature. S.C. wants the war to continue in order to keep troops in the province. 4p.

Fol. 110. 19 Oct. 1761, Charleston. [Robert] Rogers to [Gen. Amherst]. Cherokees were arriving before Rogers left the army. Troops departed Ft. Prince George for Ninety Six about 13 October. 2p.

Fol. 111. 5 Nov. 1761, Camp at Ninety Six. Col. Grant to [Gen. Amherst]. Little Carpenter left Keowee to announce the peace. He promised to return to settle the Articles of Trade. Grant will proceed to New York when Little Carpenter returns. Lt. Col. Laurens was astonished to learn that the Article of Limits were omitted with Bull's permission. 4p.

Fol. 113. 18 Nov. 1761, Camp near Ninety Six. Col. Grant to [Gen. Amherst]. Grant expects Little Carpenter at any time. Grant will order the troop's return as soon as the Indians arrive. Cherokees have already returned to the Lower Towns. 4p. [Enclosures to fol. 115b].

Fol. 115. [Nov. 1761], [Charleston]. Lt. Gov. Bull to Lt. Col. Grant (extract). Bull apologizes for omitting the Article of Limits from the treaty. 1p.

Fol. 116. 19 Nov. 1761, Camp near Ninety Six. Col. Grant to [Gen. Amherst]. Little Carpenter and some headmen arrived at Ft. Prince George on 14 November. Grant will send them to Charleston when they arrive at Ninety Six. 2p.

Fol. 119. 24 Dec. 1761, Charleston. Col. Grant to [Gen. Amherst]. Col. Campbell escorted Little Carpenter and the other headmen to Charleston. Grant was insulted upon his arrival but people now treat him more favorably. 4p.

Fol. 146. 6 June 1757, Augusta Courthouse. Copies of original letters shown by Outassity Ostenaco, Chief Warrior of Tomatly, to [Edmund Atkin]. 1p. [Enclosures to fol. 155b].

Fol. 146. 28 Oct. 1756, Augusta Courthouse. Capt. John McNeil to Outassity Ostenaco (copy). McNeil is pleased that Ostenaco is taking the Cherokees to Virginia. McNeil will guard the women and children while the Cherokees are gone. 1p.

Fol. 146b. 30 Oct. 1756, Augusta. Maj. Andrew Lewis to Outassity Ostenaco (copy). Guns, ammunition, clothing,

and paint await the Cherokee arrival. Governor is preparing many men to garrison the fort that Lewis built at
Chote. 1p.

Fol. 147. 13 Nov. 1756, Williamsburg. Lt. Gov. Dinwiddie
to Upper and Lower Cherokee Sachems, Warriors, and Headmen
(copy). Va. built a fort in the Cherokee country as the
treaty stipulated. Cherokees have failed to live up to
their obligations by refusing to send many Cherokees to
Virginia. The French are attempting to win over the
Cherokees. 2p.

Fol. 147b. [ca. Nov. 1756], [Williamsburg]. Lt. Gov.
Dinwiddie to Outassity Ostenaco (copy). The French have
poisoned the Cherokees against the English. He will supply
a garrison for the fort built among the Cherokees when
their warriors arrive [in Williamsburg]. 2p.

Fol. 148. [ca. Nov. 1756]. Maj. Andrew Lewis to Outassity
Ostenaco (copy). Guns and goods await the Cherokee arrival.
Governor is preparing men to garrison the Chote fort. 2p.

Fol. 148b. 6 Nov. 1756, Roanoke. John McNeil to Outassity
[Ostenaco] (copy). McNeil awaits the arrival of Ostenaco
and the other Cherokees. 1p.

Fol. 149. 24 Dec. [1756], Ft. Loudoun. Lt. John Allen to
John Watts (copy). Watts will be rewarded if he brings
the Cherokees to Virginia. 1p.

Fol. 149. 9 Apr. 1757, Lunenburg. Clement Read to Lt.
Gov. Dinwiddie (copy). Read encloses letters from
Wawhahatchee (Head Warrior of all the southern Cherokee
towns) and Swallow Warrior of Estatoy. The 120 Cherokees
who are headed for Bedford Courthouse (to receive their
presents) are plundering plantations along the way. Little
Carpenter reports a new alliance between the French and the
Shawnees. 5p.

Fol. 151. 24 Apr. 1757, Ft. Loudoun. Capt. Geo. Mercer
to Geo. Washington (copy). Mercer informed Wawhahatchee
and the other Cherokees that he did not have time to
gather appropriate presents for them. Cherokees claimed
that the governor knew about their visit eighteen months
ago. French always gave the Cherokees the goods they
wanted. 4p.

Fol. 152b. [April 1757], [Ft. Loudoun]. Speech from
Swallow Warrior to Capt. Mercer (copy). Swallow Warrior
has visited the French and knows what presents they give
Indians. Overhill Cherokees will laugh at them when they
return without presents. 3p.

Fol. 153b. 26 Apr. 1757, Ft. Loudoun. Capt. Geo. Mercer
to Geo. Washington (copy). Cherokees told Mercer about
the presents the French give their Indians. Supplies are
needed for the Indians. 4p.

Fol. 156. 4 Aug. 1757, Winchester. Edmund Atkin to Cunnichtarky, Gov. of Cherokees (copy). Atkin has been appointed to
supervise the Indians living near Va., N.C., S.C., and Georgia.
The Six Nations request that the Southern Indians ignore the
French and maintain the English friendship. Atkin gave the
presents that Va. promised to Mankiller of Tomotly and the
Cherokees. 4p.

Fol. 158. 14 Dec. 1757, North Carolina. An Act for Preserving
Peace and Continuing a Good Correspondence with the Indians in
Alliance with His Majesty's Subjects (copy). 5p.

Fol. 161. 3 and 7 May 1757, [Williamsburg]. Copy of Council
Minutes recording that the Indians should be given the promised
presents. 3p.

Fol. 162. 14, 18, and 20 Oct. 1757, [Williamsburg]. Copy of
Council Minutes recording the reading of a letter from Atkin
concerning appointments to manage the Indians and concerning
an escort for those assisting Virginia. 4p.

Fol. 164. June - Oct. 1757. Account of Cash Paid at Winchester
by Edmond Atkin for Sundries Purchased for the Indians (copy).
Atkin lists individual Cherokees and presents. 4p.

Fol. 166. Oct. 1757. Reward and List of Goods Proposed by
Mr. Atkin to Be Provided by the Government of Virginia for the
[Cherokee, Catawba, and other] Indian Parties Coming to Its
Assistance (copy). 4p.

Fol. 168. 16 Nov. 1757, Smithfield, Virginia. Instructions
from Atkin to Christopher Gist (copy). Atkin outlines the
duties of the Cherokee and Catawba parties aiding Virginia. 17p.

Fol. 177. 25 July 1757, Winchester. Edmund Atkin's Deputation
of Christopher Gist for Managing and Transacting Whatever
Relates to the Parties of Indians Coming to the Assistance of
[Virginia] (copy). 3p.

Fol. 179. 1757. Representation from Edmund Atkin to Lt. Gov.,
Council and Assembly (copy). Atkin opposes Virginia's act
regulating trade with the allied Indians. Act was passed
primarily to establish trade with Cherokees. Atkin will propose uniform regulations. 11p.

Fol. 185. 8 June 1757, Virginia. An Act for Establishing a
Trade with the Indians in Alliance with His Majesty (copy). 4p.

Fol. 187. 26 Jan. 1758, New Bern. Edmund Atkin to Nathaniel
Walthoe (copy). Atkin hopes his representation opposing the
Va. Indian trade act will be given to Dinwiddie's successor. 6p.

W.O. 34/47 (CONT'D)

Fol. 190. 14 Feb. 1758, New York. [Lord Loudoun] to Edmund
Atkin. Atkin should send a large number of Cherokees to
Winchester. 2p.

Fol. 192. 21 Mar. 1758, Charleston. Wm. Byrd to Lord Loudoun
(copy). Atkin is ill and will be unable to accompany Byrd in
persuading the Cherokees to visit Winchester. Lt. Howarth will
invite the warriors from each town to meet at Keowee. 4p.

Fol. 194. 24 Mar. 1758, Charleston. Edm. Atkin to [Wm. Byrd]
(copy). Atkin encloses a letter to Cunnichtarky (called Hop
by the traders) to persuade the Cherokees to assist Loudoun's
expedition. 2p. [Enclosures to fol. 196b].

    Fol. 195. 24 Mar. 1758, Charleston. Edm. Atkin to
    Cunnichtarky and Cherokee Chiefs and Warriors (copy).
    Atkin requests the Cherokees' assistance at Winchester to
    attack the French. 3p.

Fol. 197. 25 Mar. and 1 Apr. 1758, Charleston. Edm. Atkin to
Earl of Loudoun. [Same as C.O. 5/50/39]. 4p.

Fol. 199. 12 Apr. 1758, Charleston. Gov. Lyttleton to Edm.
Atkin (copy). Lyttleton sends the names of individuals appointed
to inspect the Indian presents. 1p.

Fol. 199b. 9 May 1758, Charleston. Copy of an invoice for
Indian presents. 6p.

Fol. 203. 20 May 1758, Charleston. Edm. Atkin to Gen.
Abercromby (copy). Many Cherokees had already left to fight
the French in Va. before Byrd arrived in S. Carolina. French
are building a new fort between the Overhill towns and the
French fort at Chickasaw Landing. 8p.

Fol. 207. 7 Sept. 1759, Muccolossus, Upper Creeks. Edm.
Atkin. Injunction for Stopping Trade with the Albahma [Alibamos]
Indians (copy). Trade will cease with the Alibamos (commonly
called the Stinking Lingua Indians) or any other Indians who
trade with that tribe. 4p.

Fol. 209. 15 Nov. 1758 - 24 Dec. 1759, Charleston. Edm. Atkin.
Account of the Charge of a Small Troop of Light Horsemen ...
to Attend ... the Superintendent of Indian Affairs in His
Journey into Indian Country (copy). 3p.

Fol. 215. 25 Mar. 1760, Charleston. Edm. Atkin. Charges of
Carrying On the Indian Service in the Southern District ...
from 6 October 1756 to 24 March 1760. Atkin includes several
expenses concerning the Cherokees. 6p.

Fol. 218. 20 Nov. 1760, Charleston. Edm. Atkin to Gen.
Amherst. Hopes for peace with the Cherokees vanished with the
appearance of Lantagnac, who at one time served at the Alibamo
Ft. and later entered the English service. Atkin persuaded the

Creeks to remain neutral, but Ellis and Bull have bribed some
Creeks to fight the Cherokees. Atkin no longer desires to be
superintendent. 8p.

Fol. 222. 4 Apr. 1761, Orange Grove near Charleston. Edm.
Atkin to Gen. Amherst. In spite of their promises, Lantagnac
and the French are unable to support the Cherokees against the
English. Lasting peace with the Cherokees is impossible unless
they are humbled first. Atkin has warned the Creeks about the
fatal consequences in joining the Cherokees. Chickasaws are
fighting the Cherokees. 4p.

Fol. 224. 24 Oct. 1761, Charleston. Memorial from Robert
Rogers to Gen. Amherst. Rogers requests appointment as the
Superintendent of Southern Indians vacated after Atkin's death.
2p.

Fol. 226. 25 Feb. 1763, Charleston. John Stuart to Gen.
Amherst. Stuart has received his appointment as the Superintendent of Indian Affairs. 2p. [Enclosures to fol. 231b].

   Fol. 231. 5 Jan. 1762 [1763], St. James. Copy of the
   commission for John Stuart to be agent to the Southern
   Indians. 2p.

Fol. 232. 15 Mar. 1763, Charleston. Letter to Gen. Amherst
reporting Mr. Sumter's return after escorting home the Cherokees who went to England. Oconostota still resents his
imprisonment at Ft. Prince George by Lyttleton. Oconostota
met with the Creeks, Choctaws, and French at New Orleans and
talked about attacking the English settlements in spring. 8p.
[Enclosures to fol. 237b].

Fol. 238. 31 May 1763, Charleston. John Stuart to Gen.
Amherst. Stuart will attempt to prevent frauds in the Indian
trade and has written the southern governors concerning an
Indian congress. 4p.

Fol. 240. 2 June 1763, Charleston. John Stuart to Gen. Amherst.
Stuart will attempt to reconcile the Southern District Indians
at a future congress. Cherokees and Chickasaws have long been
at war with the Choctaws. 4p.

Fol. 242. 30 July 1763, Charleston. John Stuart to [Gen.
Amherst]. Stuart sent invitations to the Choctaws, Creeks,
Chickasaws, Cherokees, and Catawbas to attend a congress. An
escaped Catawba woman said that her captors were Shawnees and
a Mohawk, not Cherokees. 6p.

Fol. 246. 4 Oct. 1763, Charleston. John Stuart to Gen.
Amherst. Overhill Cherokees, Lower Creeks, and Catawbas have
accepted the invitation to hold a congress. Cherokees and
Creeks are being attacked by Northern Indians. Saluy has gone
to pursue the enemy. 4p. [Enclosures to fol. 253b].

W.O. 34/47 (CONT'D)

> Fol. 248. 4 Sept. 1763, Chote. Skiagunsta Ogunistoter, Little Carpenter, Willinawa, and Great Raven of Tellico to John Stuart (copy). It is not safe to travel to Augusta because the Creeks have killed several Cherokees. Ottawas captured a Cherokee last spring. Cherokees propose meeting at Saluda Old Town or Ninety Six. 3p.

> Fol. 250. 1 Aug. 1763, [Chote]. Little Carpenter to John Stuart (copy). Cherokees accepted the invitation to attend the congress. 2p.

> Fol. 251. 15 Aug. 1763. Talk from Little Carpenter to John Stuart (copy). Cherokees regard all the Northern Indians as enemies but will remain at peace with the Chickasaws and Catawbas. 2p.

Fol. 254. 6 Oct. 1763, Charleston. John Stuart to Gen. Amherst. Stuart informed Col. Robertson that Stuart's Indian presents are for the congress. Stuart is not authorized to send presents elsewhere. 2p.

Fol. 255. 26 Feb. 1761, Philadelphia. Wm. Byrd to [Gen. Amherst]. Byrd has ordered Lt. Irwin to report the transactions of the Va. troops with the Cherokees. 2p.

Fol. 256. 10 Mar. 1761, Philadelphia. Wm. Byrd to [Gen. Amherst]. Byrd does not expect any N.C. aid against the Cherokees. It is improbable that two armies sent against the Cherokees can attack at the same time. Virginia's regiment is not powerful enough to attack the Upper Towns and take Chote. 6p.

Fol. 259. 21 Mar. 1761, Philadelphia. Wm. Byrd to [Gen. Amherst]. Byrd needs instructions in case the Cherokees sue for peace. He hopes that Maj. Stuart and Capt. McKenzie will continue in the regiment until the expedition is over. 4p.

Fol. 262. 19 Apr. 1761, Williamsburg. Wm. Byrd to [Gen. Amherst]. Byrd will attempt to carry out Amherst's orders, but his regiment is too small to annoy the Cherokees. 4p.

Fol. 264. 9 May 1761, Virginia. Wm. Byrd to [Gen. Amherst]. Byrd was not successful in recruiting men for the Cherokee expedition. He will proceed with 500 men to Great Island. The remaining 200 soldiers will wait at Ft. Lewis for supplies and reinforcements. Byrd has had no intelligence from Grant or Bull. 2p.

Fol. 265. 30 May 1761, Camp in Augusta. Wm. Byrd to [Gen. Amherst]. Lack of supplies has prevented Byrd from moving troops beyond the frontier. Recruitment has been unsuccessful. 2p.

Fol. 266. 7 June 1761, Camp near Staunton. Wm. Byrd to Gen. Amherst. Byrd has not received provisions or money. It is too late to assist Grant. 2p. [Enclosures to fol. 267b].

Fol. 267. 6 June 1761, Camp near Staunton. Wm. Byrd.
General Return of the Virginia Regiment. 2p.

Fol. 268. 1 July 1761, Camp at Ft. Chiswell. Wm. Byrd to
[Gen. Amherst]. Since he has a month's provisions, Byrd will
march with 500 men to Stalnakers where he will remain until a
magazine is built. 2p. [Enclosures to fol. 270b].

Fol. 270. 30 June 1761, Ft. Chiswell. Wm. Byrd.
Return of the Virginia Regiment. 2p.

Fol. 271. 1 Aug. 1761, Camp at Stalnakers on the Holston
River. Wm. Byrd to [Gen. Amherst]. Army has been detained
at Stalnakers since 13 July from lack of provisions. Grant
evidently has completed his work. Byrd is still 200 miles
from the nearest Cherokee town and he has little chance of
success against the Cherokees. 4p. [Enclosures to fol. 274b].

Fol. 274. 31 July 1761, Stalnakers. Wm. Byrd.
General Return of the Virginia Regiment. 1p.

Fol. 275. 7 Sept. 1761, Philadelphia. Wm. Byrd to [Gen.
Amherst]. Contracters will be unable to supply troops in the
Cherokee country this season. Byrd resigned his regimental
command since he could make no progress without provisions. 2p.

Fol. 276. 13 Sept. 1761, Philadelphia. Wm. Byrd to [Gen.
Amherst]. Byrd regrets that Amherst still has some expectations
from the Va. regiment. Supplies cannot be sent to the Cherokee country this season. 2p.

Fol. 277. 5 Oct. 1761, Camp at Great Island. Lt. Col. Adam
Stephen to [Gen. Amherst]. Great Warrior and the other leading
Cherokees (stubborn English enemies and opposed to Little
Carpenter's action) have sent a letter to Stephen. Judd's
Friend also sent a message implying that the Cherokees are
ready for peace. 4p. [Enclosures to fol. 283b].

Fol. 279. Sept. 1761, Chote. Connetarke to Col. Byrd
(copy). Connetarke has sent Little Carpenter to Charleston
to make peace. 2p.

Fol. 280. [Sept. - Oct. 1761], Holston River. Col.
Stephen to Connetarke (copy). Connetarke should either
send a copy of the peace treaty made with Bull or Grant or
come himself to Williamsburg with Oconostota, Judd's Friend,
or other leading headmen. 2p.

Fol. 281b. Sept. 1761, Chote. Oconostota to [Col. Byrd?]
(copy). All Cherokees want peace. 1p.

Fol. 281b. Sept. - Oct. 1761, Holston River. Col. Stephen
to [Oconostota] (copy). [Oconostota] should send the peace
treaty made with Bull or Grant or come to Williamsburg
with Connetarke and the other Cherokee headmen. 2p.

W.O. 34/47 (CONT'D)

Fol. 282. 9 Oct. 1761, Great Island. Col. Stephen.
A Return of the Virginia Regiment of Foot Commanded by
the Honorable William Byrd. Stephen includes troops at
Great Island and Ft. Attakullakulla. 2p.

Fol. 284. 24 Oct. 1761, Camp at Great Island. Col. Stephen
to [Gen. Amherst]. Connetarke has been made Emperor through
the influence of Great Warrior and Judd's Friend. Little
Carpenter is unable to make peace until the [Cherokee] leaders
agree with him. Stephen has built a strong fort on the Holston
River. 4p. [Enclosures to fol. 288b].

Fol. 286. 23 Oct. 1761, Great Island. Return of Provisions in Store at Great Island. 2p.

Fol. 287. 23 Oct. 1761, Big [Great] Island. Col. Waddell.
A Return of a Detachment of the North Carolina Regiment
Encamped at Big Island on Holston's River. 2p.

Fol. 288. 17 Oct. 1761, Chote. Oconostota to [Col.
Stephen] (copy). Cherokees will stop their mischief. 1p.

Fol. 288. 17 Oct. 1761, Chote. Judd's Friend to [Col.
Stephen] (copy). Judd's Friend will come to Williamsburg
when the Cherokee King returns. 1p.

Fol. 289. 29 Nov. 1761, Philadelphia. Wm. Byrd to [Gen.
Amherst]. Assembly members have recommended to Fauquier that
the troops be disbanded after Bull proclaims a definite peace
with the Cherokees. 1p.

Fol. 291. 4 Mar. 1762, Philadelphia. Wm. Byrd to [Gen.
Amherst]. Virginia's troops were disbanded before Gov. Fauquier
received Egremont's letter. Byrd requests reimbursement for
his army expenses during the Cherokee expedition in 1760. 2p.

Fol. 292. 18 Sept. 1762, Philadelphia. Wm. Byrd to [Gen.
Amherst]. Byrd explains why the campaign expenses [against
the Cherokees] were so high. 4p.

*W.O. 34/48   LETTERS FROM THE COMMANDER-IN-CHIEF TO OFFICERS SERVING
             IN SOUTH CAROLINA AND VIRGINIA: 1760-1763*

Fol. 1. 24 Feb. 1760, New York. [Gen. Amherst] to Col.
Montgomery (copy). [Cherokees] have renewed hostilities and
killed a number of English. At Lyttleton's request, Montgomery
will proceed immediately to S. Carolina. 1p.

Fol. 2. 24 Feb. 1760, New York. [Gen. Amherst] to Col.
Montgomery (copy). Montgomery is ordered to ready a company
of grenadiers and one of light infantry together with four
other companies under Maj. Grant for embarkment. 1p.

Fol. 3. 3 Mar. 1760, New York. [Gen. Amherst] to Maj. Grant
(copy). Grant should be ready to embark with the troops for
Carolina on 7 Mar. 1p.

Fol. 4. 6 Mar. 1760, New York. [Gen. Amherst] to Col.
Montgomery. [Same as C.O. 5/57/364]. 8p.

Fol. 9. 7 Mar. 1760, New York. [Gen. Amherst] to Capt.
Dudgeon. [Same as C.O. 5/57/360]. 1p.

Fol. 10. 8 Mar. 1760, New York. [Gen. Amherst] to Maj.
Grant. [Same as C.O. 5/57/368]. 1p.

Fol. 11. 8 Mar. 1760, New York. Gen. Amherst to Maj.
Grant. Grant is appointed lieutenant colonel in the expedition to protect S.C. and punish the Cherokees. 1p.

Fol. 12. 14 Mar. 1760, New York. Jos. Allicocke. Account
of provisions shipped on the six transports for South Carolina.
1p.

Fol. 12b. [Mar. 1760], [New York]. Certificate from David
Wilson stating that the provisions were placed on transports
bound for S. Carolina. 1p.

Fol. 13. 13 Mar. 1760, New York. Receipt from Wm. Betton
acknowledging the provisions placed on board the *Albany* [bound
for S. Carolina]. 1p.

Fol. 14. 13 Mar. 1760, New York. Receipt from James Spelling
acknowledging the provisions placed on board the *Two Friends*
[bound for S. Carolina]. 1p.

Fol. 15. 13 Mar. 1760, New York. Receipt from James Nicholson
acknowledging the provisions placed on board the *Amherst* [bound
for S. Carolina]. 1p.

Fol. 16. 13 Mar. 1760, New York. Receipt from John Waddell
acknowledging the provisions placed on board the *Swan* [bound
for S. Carolina]. 1p.

Fol. 17. 13 Mar. 1760, New York. Receipt from Wm. Gilchrist
acknowledging the provisions placed on board the *Thornton*
[bound for S. Carolina]. 1p.

Fol. 18. 13 Mar. 1760, New York. Receipt from Robert Boyd
acknowledging the provisions placed on board the *Carolina*
[bound for S. Carolina]. 1p.

Fol. 19. 1 Apr. 1760, New York. [Gen. Amherst] to Lt. Maine
(copy). Maine should follow the instructions of Col. Montgomery, who is ordered to punish the Cherokees. 1p.

Fol. 20. 15 May 1760, Albany. [Gen. Amherst] to Col. Montgomery. Upon his return from S.C., Montgomery should proceed
with troops to Albany. 1p.

Fol. 22. 26 May 1760, Albany. [Gen. Amherst] to Lt. Charles
Taylor (copy). The court-martial will be held if Taylor and
Capt. Demeré can obtain the evidence before Montgomery leaves
[on the Cherokee expedition]. 1p.

W.O. 34/48 (CONT'D)

Fol. 23. 26 May 1760, Albany. [Gen. Amherst] to Col.
Montgomery. [Same as C.O. 5/58/403]. 4p.

Fol. 25. 31 May 1760, Albany. [Gen. Amherst] to James Glen.
Montgomery should follow his instructions until the [Cherokees]
are defeated or until S.C. makes a treaty with the tribe. 1p.

Fol. 26. 18 June 1760, Albany. [Gen. Amherst] to Col.
Montgomery. [Same as C.O. 5/58/408]. 4p.

Fol. 28. 29 June 1760, Ft. Herkhemier. [Gen. Amherst] to
Col. Montgomery. [Same as C.O. 5/59/74]. 2p.

Fol. 29. 29 June 1760. Ft. Herkhemier. Gen. Amherst to Col.
Montgomery. [Duplicate of fol. 28]. 4p.

Fol. 31. 24 July 1760, Camp at Oswego. Gen. Amherst to Col.
Montgomery [Same as C.O. 5/59/78]. 1p.

Fol. 33. 12 Sept. 1760, Camp at Montreal. [Gen. Amherst] to
Col. Montgomery (copy). Montgomery should proceed to Halifax
with troops returning from Carolina. 2p.

Fol. 34. 19 Sept. 1760, Camp at Montreal. [Gen. Amherst]
to Col. Montgomery (copy). [Amherst] received Montgomery's
account of operations in Carolina [against the Cherokees].
Montgomery ordered to proceed [to Halifax] upon arriving in
New York. 2p.

Fol. 35. 14 Oct. 1760, Lake Champlain. [Gen. Amherst] to
Col. Montgomery (copy). [Amherst] has no objection to Montgom-
ery [who is returning from the Cherokee expedition] visiting
England for the winter. 2p.

Fol. 36. 24 Oct. 1760, Crown Point. [Gen. Amherst] to Maj.
Hamilton (copy). [Amherst] approves the court-martial sentence
given to Lt. Charles Taylor who served under Lt. Col. Grant. 1p.

Fol. 37. 30 Nov. 1760. [Gen. Amherst] to Maj. Hamilton
[Same as C.O. 5/60/86]. 1p.

Fol. 38. 15 Dec. 1760, New York. [Gen. Amherst] to Maj.
Monypenny. [Same as C.O. 5/60/103]. 1p.

Fol. 39. 15 Dec. 1760, New York. Gen. Amherst to Lt. Col.
Grant. [Same as C.O. 5/60/88]. 13p.

Fol. 46. 15 Dec. 1760, New York. Account of the provisions
and troops on board each transport bound for Carolina. 4p.

Fol. 49. 15 Dec. 1760, New York. Instructions from Amherst
to Grant (copy). Grant is ordered to command the troops during
the Cherokee expedition. 1p.

Fol. 50. 21 Dec. 1760, New York. Lt. Col. Grant to Gen.
Amherst (copy). Questions from Grant about his instructions
and Amherst's answers. 7p.

Fol. 54. 21 Dec. 1760, New York. Instructions from Amherst
to Monypenny (copy). Monypenny is ordered to act as a major
under Grant's command. 1p.

Fol. 55. 22 Dec. 1760, New York. Gen. Amherst to Lt. Col.
Grant (copy). Grant should wait for the Indians sent by
Amherst. Capt. Kennedy will also wait for them. 1p.

Fol. 57. 10 Jan. 1761, New York. [Gen. Amherst] to Lt. Col.
Grant (copy). Certificates for [the Cherokee expedition's]
provisions should be signed by the Deputy Commissary of Stores
and by Grant. 1p.

Fol. 59. 14 Jan. 1761, New York. [Gen. Amherst] to Lt. Col.
Grant. [Same as C.O. 5/60/206]. 2p.

Fol. 60. 13 Feb. 1761, New York. [Gen. Amherst] to Lt. Col.
Grant. [Copy of C.O. 5/61/197]. 4p.

Fol. 62. 27 Feb. 1761, New York. [Gen. Amherst] to Lt. Col.
Grant (copy). Western Indians have not only refused to join
the Cherokees but threatened to fight against them. 6p.
[Enclosures to fol. 66b].

> Fol. 65. 27 Feb. 1761. Forage Money Payable to the
> Officers in Carolina for the Campaign, 1761 (copy). 1p.

> Fol. 66. 27 Feb. 1761. Return of the Number of Officers
> Belonging to the Corps in South Carolina (copy). 1p.

Fol. 68. 12 Mar. 1761, New York. [Gen. Amherst] to Lt. Col.
Grant (copy). [Amherst] approves Grant's proceedings with the
court-martial. There should be no dispute concerning the
two divisions of independents under Grant's command. 2p.

Fol. 69. 17 Mar. 1761, New York. Gen. Amherst to Jacob
Farrington. Amherst orders Farrington to deliver a packet and
follow Grant's orders. 1p.

Fol. 70. 17 Mar. 1761, New York. [Gen. Amherst] to Col.
Grant. [Amherst] is sending nine Indians and five whites to
work with Capt. Kennedy until Maj. Rogers arrives. 2p.
[Enclosures to fol. 71b].

> Fol. 71. [17 Mar. 1761]. Lists of Recruits Belonging
> to Major Rogers' Independent Company Embarked on Board
> the *Greyhound* Man of War for S. Carolina. Report lists
> nine Indians and five whites. 2p.

Fol. 72. 3 Apr. 1761. 1761, New York. [Gen. Amherst] to Lt.
Col. Grant. [Amherst] approves Grant's desire to begin the
expedition on 20 March. 4p.

W.O. 34/48 (CONT'D)

Fol. 74. 6 Apr. 1761, New York. [Gen. Amherst] to Lt. Col.
Grant. [Amherst] wrote Bull that Grant defended the Lt. Gov.
against the rangers' complaints. 1p.

Fol. 75. 6 May 1761, New York. [Gen. Amherst] to Maj.
Monypenny (copy). Monypenny should deliver his dispatches to
Lt. Col. Campbell, who has been assigned to Col. Burton's
regiment under Grant's command. 1p.

Fol. 76. 7 May 1761, New York. [Gen. Amherst] to Lt. Col.
Grant (copy). [Amherst] has no opinion about the talk [from
Little Carpenter]. He is glad that Grant kept women from
following the expedition. 1p.

Fol. 77. 12 and 18 May 1761, New York. [Gen. Amherst] to Lt.
Col. Grant (copy). Considering the number of Grant's deserters,
the court-martial was timely. Rangers may be useful watching
Grant's cattle. [Amherst] is pleased that [the Cherokees] have
delivered 100 prisoners. He has received Capt. Demeré's
resignation. 4p.

Fol. 79. 2 July 1761, Albany. [Gen. Amherst] to Lt. Col.
Grant (copy). [Amherst] is pleased that Lt. Mackintosh is
suitable to command at Ft. Prince George. French presents to
the Indians were small. He hopes [the expedition] is over
when this letter reaches Grant. 1p.

Fol. 80. 13 July 1761, Albany. [Gen. Amherst] to Lt. Col.
Grant (copy). Rain delays should aid the English in destroying
the [Cherokees'] corn. [Amherst] expects little help from Va.
but has renewed his instructions to Byrd and Fauquier. Little
Carpenter's talk seems calculated to gain time for the tribe
to harvest their crops. 4p.

Fol. 82. 24 July 1761, Albany. [Gen. Amherst] to Lt. Col.
Grant (copy). [Amherst] sends a duplicate of July 13 letter.
Robert Bell has been appointed surgeon to Col. Burton's regiment.
1p.

Fol. 83. 1 Aug. 1761, Albany. [Gen. Amherst] to Lt. Col. Grant
(copy). [Amherst] is satisfied with Grant's progress against
the Cherokees. [S.C.] will certainly reward the Upper Chick-
kasaws for their aid to Grant. Burning 15 towns and destroying
1400 acres of corn, beans, and peas will compell the Cherokees
to sue for peace. 4p.

Fol. 85. 11 Aug. 1761, Albany. [Gen. Amherst] to Lt. Col.
Grant (copy). [Amherst] sends a duplicate of the Aug. 1 letter
and informs Grant about the progress of the war in Europe. 1p.

Fol. 87. 2 Oct. 1761, Staten Island. [Gen. Amherst] to Lt.
Col. Grant (copy). [Amherst] has received Grant's report
about the conference with Little Carpenter and other headmen.
Grant had reason to expect the [Cherokees] to sue for peace
earlier. Grant will hopefully remain at Ninety Six until the
peace is settled. 2p.

Fol. 88. 9 Oct. 1761, Staten Island. [Gen. Amherst] to Major
Monypenny (copy). Grant has been directed to place two regiments
under Monypenny's command to sail for Dominica. 1p.

Fol. 89. 9 Oct. 1761, Staten Island. [Gen. Amherst] to Lt.
Col. Grant (copy). Grant should leave for New York as soon
as the Cherokee peace is concluded. 2p.

Fol. 90. 20 Oct. 1761, Staten Island. [Gen. Amherst] to Lt.
Col. Grant (copy). [Amherst] is sending the *Rachel* to carry
Grant's troops to New York [as soon as the Cherokee peace is
concluded]. 1p.

Fol. 91. 23 Oct. 1761, Staten Island. [Gen. Amherst] to Lt.
Col. Grant (copy). [Amherst] is pleased that the S.C. legislature has accepted the Grant's terms to Little Carpenter and
the other Cherokee headmen. Grant should proceed [to Charleston]
and sail to Dominica to join Lord Rollo. 2p.

Fol. 92. 28 Oct. 1761, Staten Island. [Gen. Amherst] to Lt.
Col. Grant (copy). [Amherst] sends a ship to carry Grant [to
Dominica]. 1p.

Fol. 94. 1 Jan. 1762, New York. [Gen. Amherst] to Lt. Col.
Grant (copy). Grant's conduct during the paper war was
satisfactory. [Amherst] does not wish to discuss [Bull's]
behavior. Boone will take steps to secure a future peace. 2p.

Fol. 95. 4 Feb. 1762, New York. [Gen. Amherst] to Lt. Col.
Grant (copy). [Amherst] learned from the newspapers that Grant
sailed January 10. Boone has sent a copy of the peace concluded
[with the Cherokees]. Grant's expenses in Carolina appear
reasonable. 2p.

Fol. 99. 24 Jan. 1758, Albany. [Gen. Amherst] to Edm. Atkin
(copy). Atkin should now contact Brig. Gen. Forbes about
Indian problems. 1p.

Fol. 100. 3 June 1760, Albany. [Gen. Amherst] to Edm. Atkin
(copy). [Amherst] has received the papers relating to the
Indians and presents. 1p.

Fol. 102. 18 Mar. 1763, New York. [Gen. Amherst] to John
Stuart (copy). Boone is responsible for Stuart's appointment.
Stuart will hopefully avoid unnecessary Indian expenses since
bribery is not necessary to keep them quiet. 1p.

Fol. 103. 16 Apr. 1763, New York. [Gen. Amherst] to John
Stuart (copy). Stuart should keep the tribes quiet until the
Indian trade is firmly established. Fraud in Indian trade
should be stopped. 2p.

Fol. 104. 15 June 1763, New York. [Gen. Amherst] to Joh Stuart.
[Same as C.O. 5/63/147]. 2p.

W.O. 34/48 (CONT'D)

Fol. 105. 17 June 1763, New York. [Gen. Amherst] to John
Stuart (copy). [Amherst] approves Stuart's plans for Indian
management. A congress will reconcile the inter-tribal problems
and hostilities toward England. 2p.

Fol. 106. 17 Aug. 1763, New York. [Gen. Amherst] to John
Stuart (copy). The Indian presents will hopefully arrive from
England in time for the congress. Certain precautions must be /
taken in the Indian trade. 1p.

Fol. 107. 17 Nov. 1763, New York. [Gen. Amherst] to John
Stuart (copy). Since Amherst is returning to England, Stuart
should inform Gage about Indian affairs. 1p.

Fol. 108. 17 Nov. 1763, New York. [Gen. Amherst] to John
Stuart. [Same as fol. 107]. 1p.

Fol. 111. 5 Mar. 1761, New York. [Gen. Amherst] to Col. Byrd
(copy). [Amherst] agrees with Fauquier's opposition to a
separate peace [with the Cherokees]. Any English promise to
Little Carpenter should not be broken without good reason. 2p.

Fol. 112. 16 Mar. 1761, New York. [Gen. Amherst] to Col.
Byrd (copy). [Amherst] appreciates Byrd's opinion on the
Cherokee expedition. There should be no dispute over rank with
Col. Grant. 2p.

Fol. 113. 24 Mar. 1761, New York. [Gen. Amherst] to Col. Byrd
(copy). While Grant attacks the Cherokees on one side, Byrd
should attack them on the other. Peace should not be granted
until the tribe has been properly chastised. 2p.

Fol. 115. 11 May 1761, New York. [Gen. Amherst] to Col. Byrd
(copy). Byrd will attack the Cherokees on one side while
Grant does the same on the other. After the Indians are properly
chastised, Bull and Fauquier should cooperate in determining
the peace terms. Indians cannot defeat a well-commanded force
of 1,000 men. 4p.

Fol. 117. 28 May 1761, Albany. [Gen. Amherst] to Col. Byrd
(copy). [Amherst] regrets Byrd's lack of success in recruiting
and laments his doubts about the effectiveness of the Cherokee
expedition. 1p.

Fol. 118. 2 July 1761, Albany. [Gen. Amherst] to Col. Byrd
(copy). Byrd should have known that the expedition would not
be stopped without Amherst's approval. [Amherst] is certain
that Byrd has already been sent provisions. 1p.

Fol. 119. 2 Aug. 1761, Albany. [Gen. Amherst] to Col. Byrd
(copy). If Grant's success does not produce peace, Byrd should
carry out the original instructions as if [the Cherokees] had
not been punished. 1p.

Fol. 120. 17 Aug. 1761, Albany. Gen. Amherst to Col. Byrd
(copy). Supplying Byrd's troops is so costly that Byrd must
return to Va. once news of the peace arrives. 2p.

W.O. 34/48 (CONT'D)

Fol. 121. 20 Aug. 1761, Albany. [Gen. Amherst] to Col. Byrd
(copy). Fauquier has hopefully recalled Byrd by now. If not,
Byrd should harrass the Upper Cherokees. 1p.

Fol. 122. 10 Sept. 1761, Staten Island. [Gen. Amherst] to Col.
Byrd (copy). [Amherst] regrets that Byrd had problems with the
contractors and resigned his command. Byrd undoubtedly gave the
command instructions to Lt. Col. Stephen. 1p.

Fol. 123. 17 Sept. 1761, Staten Island. [Gen. Amherst] to
Col. Byrd (copy). [Amherst] is pleased that Byrd ordered Stuart
and McKenzie to rejoin their regiments. 1p.

Fol. 124. 29 Nov. 1761, New York. [Gen. Amherst] to Lt. Col.
Stephen (copy). [Amherst] acknowledges the receipt of the
correspondence with the Cherokees. He approves marching towards
the Cherokees. 1p.

Fol. 125. 3 Dec. 1761, New York. [Gen. Amherst] to Col. Byrd
(copy). The regiment [on the Cherokee expedition] will hopefully
not be disbanded. 1p.

Fol. 127. 2 Mar. 1762, New York. [Gen. Amherst] to Col. Stephen
(copy). Stephen will hopefully have a better assignment than
to treat with the Cherokees now that they are quiet. 2p.

Fol. 128. 6 Mar. 1762, New York. [Gen. Amherst] to Col. Byrd
(copy). [Amherst] is surprised that the Va. regiment has been
disbanded. All legitimate charges for provisioning Virginia's
troops in 1760 will be paid. 1p.

Fol. 129. 5 June 1762, New York. [Gen. Amherst] to Col.
Stephen (copy). [Amherst] appreciates the sketch of the country
near the Cherokee territory and the Holston River. 2p.

*W.O. 34/59   CORRESPONDENCE BETWEEN THE COMMANDER-IN-CHIEF AND THE
              QUARTERMASTER'S DEPARTMENT: JANUARY 1758 - OCTOBER 1763*

Fol. 159. 19 Jan. 1761, New York. Letter to John St. Clair
concerning claims by Virginians to be reimbursed for presents
given to the Cherokees during Gen. Forbes' campaign. 2p.

Fol. 161. 2 Feb. 1761, New York. Letter to John St. Clair
concerning claims by Virginians to be reimbursed for presents
given to the Cherokees during Gen. Forbes' campaign. 2p.

Fol. 170. 18 Apr. 1761, New York. Letter to John St. Clair
concerning claims by Virginians to be reimbursed for presents
given to the Cherokees during Gen. Forbes' campaign. 2p.

SOCIETY OF FRIENDS LIBRARY

Greater London

MS. PORTFOLIO 34

Doc. 36. 29 June 1832. Minutes recording the committee's conclusion that in light of recent news about the North American Indians (particularly the Cherokees), the Friends should concentrate their attention on reservation Indians and consider what could be done for tribes living further west. 2p.

Doc. 140. 25 May 1758, Philadelphia. Letter to a Friend stating that many Cherokees have entered Va. and the tribe may have already commenced hostilities against the Delawares. 6p.

UNITED SOCIETY FOR THE PROPAGATION OF THE GOSPEL

Greater London

CONTEMPORARY COPIES OF LETTERS RECEIVED
SERIES A/7   LETTERS RECEIVED: 1711-1712

Fol. 390. 10 Jan. 1711/12, St. James Parish near Goose Creek, S. Carolina. Francis LeJau to Justice Chamberlain (copy). 2p. [Enclosures to fol. 395].

Fol. 391. 4 Jan. 1711/12, St. James Parish near Goose Creek, S. Carolina. Francis LeJau to Justice Chamberlain (copy). LeJau describes an Indian festival which apparently is related to the belief in Noah's Ark. 5p.

SERIES A/8   LETTERS RECEIVED: 1712-1713

Fol. 343. 17 Feb. 1712/13, Chowan, N. Carolina. Giles Rainsford to the Secretary (copy). S. Carolina's governor has sent 1,100 Indians to relieve N. Carolina. Col. Pollock is attempting to support the Ashley Indians. 3p.

Fol. 346. 23 Feb. 1712/13, St. James Parish near Goose Creek, S. Carolina. Dr. LeJau to the Secretary (copy). Missionaries should promote religion among the poor negro and Indian slaves living with white families. Missionaries should also promote good works among the Indians in the province until other means are available. 3p.

Fol. 360. 11 Apr. 1713, Charleston, S. Carolina. Dr. LeJau to the Secretary (copy). English defeated the Tuscaroras, killing or capturing some 800. English lost 26 white men and 58 Indians. 3p.

SERIES A/8 (CONT'D)

Fol. 362. 10 Aug. 1718, St. James Parish near Goose Creek, S. Carolina. Dr. LeJau to the Secretary (copy). Yamasees and other English Indian allies are greatly reduced in number because of their continuous Indian wars. The French or Spanish control the Yamasees. The Indians fight each other to obtain slaves to pay for goods since the skin trade has diminished. 4p.

SERIES A/10   LETTERS RECEIVED: 1714-1715

Fol. 83. 21 Mar. 1714, S. Carolina. Mr. Dennis to the Secretary (copy). Dennis has custody of a mustee or half-breed (Cherokee by origin), but he cannot persuade neighboring Indians to send him their children. 2p.

Fol. 105. 14 and 16 May 1715, St. James Parish near Goose Creek, S. Carolina. Dr. LeJau to the Secretary (copy). Col. Moore will hopefully establish peace with the Indians, especially the Cherokees. 4p.

Fol. 108. 21 May 1715, S. Carolina. Dr. Francis LeJau to the Secretary (copy). Indian war has erupted. The traditionally faithful Cherokees and Catawbas declared war against the English. 4p.

SERIES A/11   LETTERS RECEIVED: 1715-1716

Fol. 64. 3 Oct. 1715, S. Carolina. Dr. Francis LeJau to the Secretary (copy). Two white men friendly with the Cherokees have been sent to reconcile that tribe with the English. News of their success is expected in ten days. 4p.

Fol. 73. 28 Nov. 1715, St. James Parish near Goose Creek, S. Carolina. Dr. Francis LeJau to the Secretary [Wm. Taylor]. [Copy of B/4, doc. 32]. 4p.

Fol. 94. 31 Oct. 1715, St. Pauls, S. Carolina. Wm. Tredwell Bull to the Secretary. [Copy of B/4, doc. 31]. 3p.

Fol. 101. 19 Dec. 1715, Charleston. Gideon Johnson to the Secretary. [Copy of B/4, doc. 37]. 5p.

Fol. 106. 27 Jan. 1715, Charleston. Gideon Johnson to the Secretary. [Copy of B/4, doc. 21]. 12p.

Fol. 123. 18 Oct. 1715, S. Carolina. Clergy of S. Carolina to the Secretary (copy). Clergy hopes to obtain the Cherokees' assistance in restoring tranquility, which would allow missionary work to continue. 4p.

Fol. 127. 18 Feb. 1715/16, S. Carolina. Robert Maule to the Secretary (copy). Peace has been made with Cherokees. Maule expects the other Indians to accept the peace, thus preventing further mischief. 4p.

SERIES A/11 (CONT'D)

Fol. 130. 19 Mar. 1715/16, St. James Parish near Goose Creek, S. Carolina. Dr. Francis LeJau to the Secretary. [Copy of B/4, doc. 58]. 6p.

Fol. 135. 6 Feb. 1715/16, St. Pauls, S. Carolina. Wm. Tredwell Bull to the Secretary. [Copy of B/4, doc. 45]. 4p.

Fol. 138. 30 Mar. and 24 Apr. 1716, Parish of St. Thomas, S. Carolina. Rev. Thomas Hasell to the Secretary. [Copy of B/4, doc. 59]. 2p.

Fol. 147. 16 May 1716, St. Pauls, S. Carolina. Wm. Tredwell Bull to the Secretary. [Copy of B/4, Doc. 70]. 4p.

Fol. 158. 1 July 1716, St. James near Goose Creek, S. Carolina. Dr. Francis LeJau to the Secretary (copy). Peaceful Indians continue to be faithful. Indians will march against the enemy after their corn and provisions are gathered. 4p.

SERIES A/12   LETTERS RECEIVED: 1716-1717

Fol. 59. 12 Nov. 1716, Charleston. Wm. Guy to the Secretary (copy). Cherokees (2,500) left to attack the Creeks but the outcome is not known. Yamasees' and neighboring Indians' incursions have been very damaging. 2p.

ORIGINAL LETTERS RECEIVED FROM THE AMERICAS
SERIES B/4   LETTERS FROM THE CAROLINAS: 1715-1759

Doc. 21. 27 Jan. 1715, Charleston. Gideon Johnson to [the Secretary]. An Indian family and others have promised aid against the Yamasees and Creeks. Cherokee conjurer and others have received presents. 8p.

Dec. 23. 10 Aug. 1715, Charleston. Wm. T. Bull to the Secretary. Bull describes the Indian war and its causes. Several nations joined in the conspiracy and the Northern and Southern Indians killed the traders among them. 4p.

Dec. 25. 20 Sept. 1715, Charleston. Wm. Guy to [the Secretary]. Greatest Indian nation within the English trade circle is the Cherokee. Guy hopes to win them over for the English. 4p.

Doc. 31. 31 Oct. 1715, St. Pauls, S. Carolina. Wm. Tredwell Bull to Secretary of SPG. Cherokees, a powerful Indian nation 300 miles away, are the most numerous nation within the English trade circle. The Yamasses tried to persuade that tribe to kill their traders, but they did not. About 200 prominent Cherokee warriors arrived to renew the peace. 4p.

Doc. 32. 28 Nov. 1715, Parish of St. James, near Goose Creek, S. Carolina. Dr. Francis LeJau to Wm. Taylor, Secretary. The powerful Cherokees made peace and held some wild ceremonies. Exchanging clothes and smoking the same pipe is a Cherokee token of reconciliation and friendship. Eight chiefs and 120 other Indians were present at the ceremonies. 4p.

SERIES B/4 (CONT'D)

Doc. 37. 19 Dec. 1715, Charleston. Rev. Gideon Johnson to the [Secretary]. Johnson persuaded the Cherokee emperor to entrust Johnson with his eldest son. He did so willingly because the emperor saw how well the Yamasee youth fared. Johnson hopes his superiors will approve his scheme for converting the Yamasee and other neighboring Indians. Cherokees (500) have joined expedition that will end the Indian war in two months. 4p.

Doc. 45. 6 Feb. 1715/16, St. Pauls, S. Carolina. Wm. Tredwell Bull to [the Secretary]. Bull describes his losses in the Indian war. Cherokees have agreed to peace. There are hopes for peace with some Northern Indians but not with the Yamasees, Creeks, and smaller Southern nations. 3p.

Doc. 58. 19 Mar. 1715/16, St. James Parish near Goose Creek, S. Carolina. Rev. Francis LeJau to [the Secretary]. Only the Creeks, Yamasees, Savannahs, and Apalaches are still at war. Cherokees will declare war against the Creeks. LeJau's only son is with the English army in the Cherokee nation. LeJau has no choice but to send men to lead the Cherokees against the Creeks. 4p.

Doc. 59. 30 Mar. and 24 Apr. 1716, Parish of St. Thomas, S. Carolina. Rev. Thos. Hasell to Wm. Taylor, Sec. of S.P.G.. S. Carolina has discharged its regiments, except for 100 men who will join the Cherokees and others to carry on war against the Creeks, Yamasees, and other tribes. 2p.

Dec. 70. 16 May 1716, St. Pauls, S. Carolina. Wm. Tredwell Bull to the [Secretary]. Peace is not yet complete. Cherokee peace will probably be followed by another with most of the Northern Indians. Cherokees are supposed to punish the hostile Indians that fled toward the French settlement. 3p.

Doc. 132. 13 Jan. 1723, Dorchestor, S. Carolina. Letter from Francis Varnod stating that the Cherokees are the most populous tribe and that Christianity should be planted there first. The Cherokees are divided into ten tribes. Their language is gutteral and has Phoenecian words. 4p.

Doc. 173. 1 Apr. 1723/24, Dorchestor, S. Carolina. Letter from Francis Varnod containing Indian religious and social beliefs. Varnod lists the towns and population of the Cherokees in 1721, stating that the tribe had 53 towns with 10,379 people (3,510 men, 3,595 women, and 3,274 children). 4p.

Doc. 183. 21 July 1724, Dorchestor, S. Carolina. Letter from Francis Varnod reporting that he had sent town names and population statistics for the Cherokees. Varnod has been unable to get the same information about the Creeks. 5p.

Doc. 284. 31 Oct. 1759, Charleston, S. Carolina (copy). Alex. Garden to Rev. Dr. Philip Bearcroft, Sec. of S.P.G.. Although war exists throughout North America, S.C. has enjoyed peace. Garden fears, however, that S.C. might engage in a war. 2p.

UNBOUND MSS.: 1700-1850
C/A M8   SOUTHERN COLONIES: 1758-1784

> Doc. 35. 1 June 1765, Augusta. Samuel Frink to Dr. Burton
> (copy). Although Augusta has been repeatedly harassed by the
> the Upper and Lower Creeks and the Cherokees, the inhabitants
> hope for a better future. 4p.

BODLEIAN LIBRARY

Oxford

NORTH PAPERS: 1702-1778

> Fol. 327. [ca. 1762-1763]. Petition from Lt. Timberlake to
> Earl of Bute. Timberlake requests reimbursement for expenses
> of bringing three Cherokee chiefs to London. 2p.

WEDGEWOOD MUSEUM

Stoke on Trent

> Ref. 28415-39. 1767-1768. Thomas Griffith. Account of the
> Voyage to Ayoree in the United States in 1767 and 1768 (copy).
> Journal of Griffith's expedition to mine kaolin. He describes
> his meeting with some Cherokee chiefs (Prince of Chote, Old
> Wolf of Keowee, Little Carpenter, and others), purification
> rites for captured Cherokees, and tribal plans to send a peace
> commission to the Mohawks. 15p.

NATIONAL REGISTER OF ARCHIVES

Edinburgh

MACPHERSON-GRANT OF BALLINDALLOCH (0771)

> A. 1757-1759. Papers of Gen. James Grant which include an
> extract of his journal of the Cherokee expedition.

> B. 1760-1774. Papers of Gen. James Grant relating to his
> governorship of East Florida, his campaign against the Chero-
> kee Indians, and his correspondence with John Stuart and others.

ROBERTSON-AIKMAN OF THE ROSS (0174)

> A. [ca. 1757]. Partial letter from John Forbes reporting that
> the Cherokees and Catawbas have gone home.

Edinburgh

GIFTS AND DEPOSITS
GD 45/2/1   DALHOUSIE MUNIMENTS

> Fol. 1. Jan. 1749. [James Glen] to Board of Trade. Yellow
> Bird, his wife, the Prince of Tennessee's son, and many other
> Cherokees died during a visit to arrange peace with the Creeks.
> French Indians have attacked some other Overhill towns. Half-
> breed Johnie died from distemper caught in Charleston. The
> Emperor is expected to die also. 11p.

GD 45/2/44   DALHOUSIE MUNIMENTS

> Doc. 2. June [1758], Philadelphia. Letter from James Glen
> stating that the Creeks, Cherokees, and Chickasaws can warn
> the Choctaws to side either with England or face punishment.
> Cherokees have killed some members of the French garrison at
> a fort where the Tenn., Ohio, and Wabash Rivers flow into the
> Miss. River. 4p.

> Doc. 3a. 13 July 1758, Ft. Cumberland. James Glen to Gen.
> [Forbes?]. Glen has requested some 200-300 Indians from the
> Cherokees. Col. Byrd's failure to get Cherokee assistance
> made his expedition worthless. 4p.

> Doc. 3b. 23 June 1758, Winchester. Col. Byrd to [Gen.
> Forbes?]. Byrd has not heard from Little Carpenter. The
> 87 Cherokees with Byrd will probably leave him before the
> army is ready to depart Ft. Cumberland. 3p.

> Doc. 4. 13 July 1758, Ft. Cumberland. James Glen to [Gen.
> Forbes?]. Glen heard that Capt. Bosomworth is bringing
> supplies for the Indians. 2p.

GD 77/200   FERGUSSON OF CRAIGDARROCH MUNIMENTS

> Doc. 6. 18 Apr. 1759, Charleston. Philip Morison to James
> Ferguson. Little Carpenter and some Cherokees recently visited
> Charleston for presents and to apologize for abandoning the
> English expedition against Ft. Duquesne. Cherokees claim that
> they knew the French intended to blow up the fort and saw no
> reason to remain. 6p.

GD 219/287   MURRAY OF MURRAYTHWAITE MUNIMENTS

> Doc. 11a. 22 May 1756, Charleston. Wm. Murray to Mrs. Murray.
> John, William's brother, has gone with the governor to build
> a fort among the Cherokees to protect S.C. against the French. 2p.

> Doc. 11b. 23 May 1756, Charleston. Wm. Murray to Miss Aggie
> Murray. John Murray has gone with the governor to the Chero-
> kees where he will see emperors, empresses, kings, queens, and
> princesses. The Cherokees will be wearing bear or deer skins
> thrown over their shoulders. 2p.

GD 219/290   MURRAY OF MURRAYTHWAITE MUNIMENTS

Fol. 3.   31 Jan. 1756, Charleston.   [John Murray] to Mr. Oswald.
Cherokees formally surrendered their territory to the Crown.
Cherokees demanded that forts be built and garrisoned in their
country to prevent French encroachments.   Headman proposed
building a fort at the juncture of the Cherokee and Ohio Rivers
and another one at the Tennessee and Ogeechee Rivers.   5p.

MEXICO

ARCHIVO GENERAL DE LA NACIÓN

Mexico City

RAMO DE GOBERNACIÓN
GOBERNACIÓN TRAMO/75

Fol. 911. 1828. *Expediente* from First Sec. for Foreign Relations. 1p. [Enclosures to fol. 918b].

Fol. 917. 22 Nov. 1828, Mexico. Letter to Minister of Foreign Affairs quoting correspondence from the inspector gen. concerning the defense of Mexico and Spanish efforts to promote revolution. Indians in the North, who are probably provoked by foreign agents, are reportedly unhappy with the government. Tribes like the Cherokees, Kickapoos, Saguauahos, Dilahuas [Delawares?], Corates, Cadots [Caddos?], and others sent by the United States (as well as assassins, thieves, ruffians, and criminals) constantly augment the frontier population. 4p.

RAMO DE HISTORIA
HISTORIA/43   LOUISIANA-TEXAS PAPERS: 1756-1825

Doc. 21 (fol. 448). 1805. *Sacado de un mapa ynglés*. Description taken from an English map [not included] drawn by Lieux d'Anville and improved by Mr. Bolton. Map locates the North American tribes. Because of treaties with the Cherokees, Chickasaws, Natchez, and the Creek nations, England has legitimate claim to land between Lake Erie and the Chickasaws along the Mississippi. 5p. [Enclosures to fol. 454b]. *Spanish* and *English*.

Doc. 22 (fol. 451). [1805]. *Sacado de un mapa ynglés* (translation). Spanish version of the map description but containing additional information in French. 8p. *Spanish* and *French*.

HISTORIA/334   RIOTS AND DISORDERS: 1770-1799

Exp. 6 (fol. 189). 30 Oct. [?] 1799, Mexico. Letter to Andrés Álvarez Calderón. 2p. [Enclosures to fol. 192b].

Fol. 192. 9 Oct. 1799, Coweta [Tallassee?]. Benjamin Hawkins to Wm. Panton (translation). The leader of the bandits from [Tallassee?], Mankiller, has been punished by having his house burnt, his animals killed, his

HISTORIA 334 (CONT'D)

> personal belongings destroyed, and being nearly beaten to
> death. Some of his followers have fled to the Cherokees
> with many Creeks in pursuit. 2p.

HISTORIA/430   LIGHTLY POPULATED REGIONS: 1719-1800

Exp. 11 (fol. 168 *reservada*). 1795. *El gobernador de la
colonia del Nuevo Santander sobre haberse presentado al de
Texas 33 naciones de indios.* 1p. [Enclosures to fol. 251].

> Fol. 174. 10 July 1795, Mexico. Letter to el Conde de
> Sierra Gorda responding to a petition from the 33 Indian
> tribes seeking refuge in Texas from the Americans.
> Government needs to know their tribal name and reason
> for seeking sanctuary in each case. Government is aware
> that the states of Ky. and Cumberland have expelled the
> Talapooses and Alibamos from their territory. 4p.

HISTORIA/436   LETTERS FROM FLORIDA ET AL.: 1752-1755

Exp. 2 (fol. 23). 12 Dec. 1754, St. Augustine. Fulgencio
García de Solis to el Conde de Revilla Gigedo. 11p. [Enclo-
sures to fol. 41b].

> Fol. 29. 8 Nov. 1754, St. Augustine. Fulgencio García de
> Solis to el Conde de Revilla Gigedo. Talapooses and Yuchis
> always work together in their wars. Although less numerous
> than the Cherokees and other tribes friendly to the English,
> they are able to hold their own because of their unity and
> their aggressive spirit. Nevertheless, the English have
> encouraged the Talapooses, Cherokees, and Nactueques
> [Natchez?] to attack the Yuchis in hopes that the tribe
> could be exterminated. 5p.

Exp. 2 (fol. 51). 27 July 1754, St. Augustine. Fulgencio
García de Solis to el Conde de Revilla Gigedo. 10p. [Enclo-
sures to fol. 58].

> Fol. 56. 17 July 1754, Picolata. Raimundo Alonzo de
> Arrivas to Fulgencio García de Solis (copy). Spanish
> patrols have approached Picolata attempting to capture
> Yamasees. News from Coweta in June indicates that peace
> with the Mattuagues has been made and that some important
> Cherokee chiefs have arrived to negotiate peace as well.
> 5p.

RAMO DE MARINA
MARINA/17   FLORIDA AND ESPÍRITU SANTO: 1761-1781

> Fol. 288. 1761. *Testimonio de los autos ... del coronel dn.
> Miguel Ramón de Castilla y Lugo, gobernador del presidio de
> San Miguel de Panzacola.* 1p. [Enclosures to fol. 385].

MARINA/17 (CONT'D)

Fol. 329. [1762?]. Monberaut to Kerlerec (translation).
Monberaut reports conference with the Tchiahas [Chick-
asaws] who are demanding vengeance for the deaths of their
tribesmen. This is the tribe that contained the Talechis
[Cherokees?]. One Talechis reportedly killed the son of
Kiltanabe, an important member of the Chickasaws. 2p.

MARINA/139   VERACRUZ: 1799-1804

Fol. 119. 1800. *Llegada a Veracruz del bergantín San Cayetano
con pliegos de la Luisiana [que piden socorros]*. 1p. [Enclo-
sures to fol. 135].

Fol. 120. 6 Mar. 1800, Philadelphia. Carlos Martínez
de Yrujo to Commander Gen. of Louisiana. After having one
expedition against La. stopped in 1797, Blount has apparently approached the British to launch another. Since the
British were willing to help Bowles, Blount might have a
good chance of receiving their aid. 4p.

RAMO DE NOTAS DIPLOMÁTICAS
NOTAS DIPLOMÁTICAS/2   CORRESPONDENCE CONCERNING THE UNITED STATES:
1810-1820

Doc. 19 (fol. 62). 5 Aug. 1817, Natchitoches. Felix Trudeau
to Felipe Fatio. 2p. [Enclosures to fol. 78b].

Fol. 69. Copy of letter from [Felipe] Fatio reporting
continued American encroachment upon Indian hunting tribes.
Cherokees are an example of what has happened to many
tribes. Living once in Tennessee, half of the tribe has
now moved west, residing first around the St. Francis River,
next along the Arkansas, and lastly near the Red River. 20p.

Doc. 31 (fol. 107). 14 Nov. 1817. Letter to Felipe Fatio
(His Majesty's Consul in New Orleans) acknowledging receipt of
information on the Indian wars along the Spanish frontier. 1p.
[Enclosures to fol. 109].

Doc. 32 (fol. 108). 30 Aug. 1817, St. Louis. Translation
of a newspaper report [?] from the Ouachita R. indicating
that a number of Indians (the Cherokees, Choctaws, Shawnees,
and Delawares from the eastern bank of the Miss. R.; and
the Caddos, Cosbaltes, Comanches, and the Arkansas Cherokees from the western bank) met at the Cherokee village in
Arkansas to plan an attack on the Osages. The Indians
plan to employ artillery which they learned how to use
from Gen. Jackson in the last war. 1p.

Doc. 32 (fol. 109). 26 Sept. 1817, New Orleans. Felipe
Fatio to Viceroy of New Spain (duplicate). The *Gazeta de
la Luisiana* announced yesterday that the frontier Indians
were about to go to war. Viceroy should note that these
Indians reportedly will use artillery. 1p.

ARCHIVO HISTÓRICO DE LA SECRETARÍA DE RELACIONES EXTERIORES

Mexico City

H/200 (72:73)/1   L-E-1056(2)

Fol. 98. 1830. *Texas y la supuesta adquisición por los Estados Unidos de A.* 1p. [Enclosures to fol. 114].

Fol. 106. 20 Nov. 1830, Department of State, Washington. M[artin] Van Buren to Col. J.M. Fornet (copy). Col. Fornet claims that the Shawnees, Kickapoos, Delawares, and Cherokees have already crossed the Mexican frontier, but the American government questions the accuracy of these reports. It is well known that the Shawnees, Kickapoos, and Delawares have resided west of the Miss. since time immemorial. The Cherokees have lived there since 1803. The United States is not responsible for the actions of these tribes. 4p. *English.*

Fol. 108. 18 Dec. 1830, Baltimore. José María Fornet to Minister of Foreign Affairs. Fornet forwards Van Buren's reply to the inquiry about the incursions of barbaric Indians from the United States into Texas. 13p.

H/200 (72:73)/1   L-E-1057 (1ª PARTE)

Exp. 1 (fol. 101). 26 Aug. 1834, Philadelphia. F.M. de Castillo y Lanzas to Juan N. Almonte. 4p. [Enclosures to fol. 110].

Fol. 103. 2 Sept. 1834, Philadelphia. F. M. de Castillo y Lanzas to Minister of Foreign Affairs. Castillo received a letter from Juan N. Almonte reporting that the Choctaws and Cherokees have crossed into Mexican territory, violating Mexico's treaty with the United States. 2p.

Fol. 107. 29 Oct. 1834. Letter to the [Mexican] chargé d'affaires in the United States stating that the President has been informed about the frontier crossings by the Choctaws and Cherokees in violation of treaty with the United States. Mexican government will treat tribes who voluntarily enter the country to live under Mexican rules differently from those who are forced to flee the United States. 1p.

Fol. 108. 5 Mar. 1835, Philadelphia. F. M. de Castillo y Lanzas to Minister of Foreign Affairs. Castillo has forwarded the decision to the consul in New Orleans about Indians crossing the frontier from the United States. 3p.

Fol. 110. 25 Apr. 1835. Letter to the [Mexican] chargé d'affaires in the United States acknowledging receipt and instructions sent to the consul in New Orleans about Indians crossing the frontier. 1p.

H/200 (72:73)1   L-E-1076 (IV)

Fol. 38. 1828. *Tribus de indios salvajes de los Estados Unidos de A. que invaden Nuevo Mexico.* 1p. [Encloses to fol. 51b].

Fol. 39. 10 May 1828, Nacogdoches. Letter from Peter Ellis Bean reporting from the Kickapoo the news that some 600 warriors were about to cross the frontier into Mexico. Some 600 Moscobes are also crossing. 2p.

Fol. 40. 21 May 1828, Mexico. G. Pedraia to Minister of Foreign Affairs. Correspondence with the commander of the Eastern Interior Provinces has revealed that Indian immigration into Mexico territory continues from the United States. Eventually this immigration could pose a problem to Mexican settlements. Unlike the Cherokees, who are industrious farmers, the bulk of the new Indians are bellicose and vagabonds. 3p.

H/200 (72:73)1   L-E-1076 (V)

Fol. 52. 1828. *Invasiones de tribus indias del norte con perjuicio de las existentes en Texas.* 1p. [Enclosures to fol. 54].

Fol. 53. 5 July 1828, Nacogdoches. Manuel de Mier y Terán to Minister of Foreign Affairs. The introduction of savage tribes from the United States has made life hard for older nations in this area. The Navadachos [Nabedaches?], Texas, and other tribes have complained about this and they hope that the Mexicans will give them the agricultural tools and instruction to live like the Cherokees. 3p.

H/510 (73.0) "830"/1   5-2-7828

Fol. 27. 1 Sept. 1830, Baltimore. José María Fornet to Minister of Foreign Affairs. The atrocious policies of the American government towards the indigenous population of their country has come to a head with Ga. seizing Cherokee land and with the decision of the president to remove that tribe. These actions violate ancient and solemn treaties on the part of the United States. 3p.

IV/552 (73:72) "908"/1   27-3-122

Fol. 1. 6 Jan. 1909, Mexico. G. Martínez Baca to Minister of Foreign Affairs. Martínez Baca received the note concerning Cherokee intentions to migrate to Veracruz. 1p. [Enclosures to fol. 4].

Fol. 2. 30 Dec. 1908, Mexico. F. Gamboa to Minister of Development. The Mexican consul in Roma, Texas, sent a note about the Cherokees' intentions to migrate to the Veracruz region. 1p.

IV/552 (73:72) "908"/1   27-3-122 (CONT'D)

    Fol. 3.   30 Dec. 1908, Mexico.   F. Gamboa to Mexican Consul
in Roma, Texas.   The ministry received the clipping from
The San Antonio Daily Express referring to a Cherokee
migration to Mexico and to the conditions that the tribal
leader, J. Henry Dick, obtained from the Mexican government.   This information was forwarded to the Mininstry of
Development.   1p.

    Fol. 4.   18 Dec. 1908, Roma, Texas.   R. Gayón to Minister
of Foreign Affairs.   Gayón attaches a clipping from *The
San Antonio Daily Express* concerning Cherokee migration to
several spots in Veracruz and the concessions that their
leader, J. Henry Dick, had obtained from the Mexican
government.   1p.

15-5-100

    Fol. 1.   15 Apr. 1893, Washington.   [Matías] Romero to Minister
of Foreign Affairs.   The *Kansas City Times* reports from Tahlequah, Indian Territory, that the Cherokee Senate has approved
sending a delegation to Washington to collect the debt owed the
tribe by the American government.   Newspaper also reports that
the Mexican government has offered land to the tribe and that
it has assured them that they will be able to live as an independent nation.   2p.   [Enclosures to fol. 5].

    Fol. 2.   25 Apr. 1893, Mexico.   Mariscal to Minister of
Development.   Mariscal sends a note about the *Kansas City
Times* article.   1p.

    Fol. 3.   25 Apr. 1893, Mexico.   Mariscal to Mexican Repre-
sentative in Washington.   Mariscal sent information to the
Minister of Development about the Cherokees.   1p.

    Fol. 4.   28 Apr. 1893, Mexico.   Fernández Leal to Minister
of Foreign Affairs.   Fernández Leal acknowledges receipt
of information concerning the Cherokees contained in an
American newspaper.   His office had no previous knowledge
about Cherokee interest in buying Mexican land.   2p.

    Fol. 5.   4 May 1893, Mexico.   Mariscal to Mexican Repre-
sentative in Washington.   Material has been sent to the
Minister of Development.   1p.

15-8-66

    Fol. 1.   31 Jan. 1899, Washington.   José F. Godoy to Minister
of Foreign Affairs.   Godoy forwards two clippings concerning the
migration to Mexico of 10,000 Indians from Indian territory in
the United States.   1p.   [Enclosures to fol. 9].

    Fol. 2.   21 and 25 Jan. 1899.   Articles from the *Boston
Transcript* (21 Jan.) and from the *Baltimore Herald*
(25 Jan.) report an Indian migration to Mexico.   Purpose
of the migration is to establish Indian self-rule.   Cherokees, Creeks, and Delawares will take part.   1p.   *English.*

15-8-66 (CONT'D)

Fol. 3.   7 Feb. 1899, Washington.   José F. Godoy to
Minister of Foreign Affairs.   Godoy forwards a newspaper
copy of a telegram from Wm. Walker stating that an Indian
migration to Mexico in large numbers is not necessarily
true.   In spite of Walker's telegram, it is likely that
many Indians do plan to migrate to Mexico.   1p.

Fol. 4.   27 Jan. 1899, *Kansas City World*.   Wm. T. Walker,
a prominent Indian businessman, predicts that few Indians
will migrate to Mexico, although many are dissatisfied
with American treatment of Indians.   Most Choctaws and
Chickasaws approved the Dawes treaty.   The Seminoles have
already signed the treaty.   The Creeks, Cherokees, and
Delawares only narrowly voted the treaty down.   1p.
English.

Fol. 5.   15 Feb. 1899, Mexico.   Mariscal to Chargé d'
Affaires in Washington.   Mariscal acknowledges the receipt
of letters concerning a possible Indian migration to Mexico.
1p.

Fol. 6.   10 Feb. 1899, Mexico.   *Acuerdo* to ask the Minister
of Development whether the ministry has made concessions
to encourage Indian migration to Mexico as reported in the
Mexican Herald.   1p.

Fol. 7.   10 Feb. 1899, Mexico.   Mariscal to Minister of
Development.   Mariscal sends a clipping from the *Mexican
Herald* and asks whether the Ministry of Development has
made concessions to Indians planning to migrate to Mexico.
1p.

Fol. 8.   16 Feb. 1899, Mexico.   Fernández Leal to Minister
of Foreign Affairs.   Ministry of Development has made no
concessions to Indian representatives from the United
States.   1p.

Fol. 9.   24 Feb. 1899, Mexico.   Mariscal to Ministry of
Development.   Mariscal acknowledges receipt of a note
explaining that the Ministry of Development has made no
concession to the American Indians.   1p.

17-21-37

Fol. 1.   15 July 1897, Washington.   [Matías] Romero to Minister
of Foreign Affairs.   Many American newspapers have reported
that the Oklahoma Indians plan to migrate to Mexico because
Mexico permits polygamy.   The embassy has no previous information about this migration but will send more precise news once
it is available.   1p.   [Enclosures to Fol. 3].

17-21-37 (CONT'D)

>Fol. 2. 12 July 1897, *The Brooklyn Citizen.* Oklahoma
>tribes plan to migrate to Mexico because of tribal discon-
>tent with American bigamy laws and prejudice. Also
>Mexico is an Indian country where the tribes can live in
>a vast wilderness eating nature's fruits and vegetables.
>Tribes are also discontent with the Dawes Act. The leaders
>of the Choctaws, Cherokees, and Seminoles are scouting for
>land in Mexico. 2p. *English.*

>Fol. 3. 24 July [1897?], Mexico. Mariscal to Mexican
>Representative in Washington. Mariscal acknowledges
>receipt of information concerning the immigration of
>Oklahoma tribes to Mexico. 1p.

3737-13

>Fol. 20. 23 Mar. 1898, Washington. Letter to minister of
>foreign affairs noting that ex-Senator Call, Walter A. Duncan,
>and a third person visited the Mexican embassy as representa-
>tives of the Cherokees to find out whether recent statements
>by Senator A.B. Hulit are correct. Hulit has stated that he
>contracted with the Mexican government to buy millions of acres
>of land to settle the Five Civilized Tribes as independent
>countries. They believe that Hulit has made this claim in order
>to get the Cherokees to sell their land in the United States.
>2p. [Enclosures to fol. 49].

>Fol. 21. 22 Mar. 1898, National Hotel, Washington D.C..
>Walter A. Duncan to Don Matías Romero (copy). Duncan
>asks Romero four questions: 1) Has Hulit purchased land
>to settle the Five Civilized Tribes? 2) Would tribes be
>allowed to maintain an independent government? 3) What
>would be the rights and privileges of these tribes in
>Mexico? 4) What educational facilities would be provided
>the tribes? 2p. *English.*

>Fol. 22. 23 Mar. 1898, Washington. Matías Romero to
>Walter A. Duncan (copy). Neither the embassy nor the
>Mexican government has information about Hulit buying
>land in Mexico. Under Mexican law, tribes settling in
>the country could not maintain an independent government.
>They could form a separate municipal government but they
>would be under the jurisdiction of state and national laws.
>Schools in some parts of Mexico are as good as those in
>the United States. 2p.

>Fol. 23. 1 Apr. 1898, Mexico. [Ignacio?] Mariscal to
>Mexican Representative in Washington. Mariscal has
>received the report from Washington concerning the Chero-
>kee questions about Hulit's project. 1p.

>Fol. 24. 13 Apr. 1898, Mexico. Fernández Leal to Minister
>of Foreign Relation. If the Cherokees move to Mexico,
>they would have to live under Mexican laws. Cherokees

should be informed that the land in Sonora and Chihuahua
(the two states they seem to prefer) has not been divided
into lots for colonies nor is the soil fertile. 2p.

Fol. 25. 19 Apr. 1898, Mexico. Note from Mariscal reporting receipt of information from the Sec. of Development
about the Cherokees. 1p.

Fol. 26. 15 Apr. 1898, Washington. [Matías] Romero to
Minister of Foreign Affairs. Romero forwards an article
from the *Kansas City World* about the project of the Five
Civilized Tribes to immigrate to Mexico. Article states
that the idea is not very popular among the tribes because
most believe that they could not better themselves by the
move. Romero also includes a short article from the
St. Louis Globe Democrat on the same subject, indicating
that Sen. Hulit is involved in the project. 2p.

Fol. 27. 8 and 12 Apr. 1898. Two articles from the *St.
Louis Globe Democrat* and the *Kansas City World* report the
project to settle Indians in Mexico. 1p. *English.*

Fol. 28. 25 Apr. 1898, Mexico. Mariscal to Mexican Representative in Washington. Mariscal acknowledges receipt of
the newspapers clipping about Indian immigration to Mexico.
1p.

Fol. [29?]. 11 Dec. 1897, Mexico. Mariscal to Minister of
Development. Mariscal forwards note from the consul in San
Antonio about the Chickasaw colony. 1p.

Fol. 30. 11 Dec. 1897, Mexico. Mariscal to Mexican Consul
in San Antonio. Mariscal sent to the Minister of Development the consul's letter concerning correspondence from
A.B. Wyatt, leader of the Indians immigrating to Mexico,
asking for 320 acres per family. 1p.

Fol. 31. 25 Apr. 1898, Washington. [Matías] Romero to
Minister of Foreign Affairs. Romero forwards a copy of
the *Tahlequah Arrow*, an Indian newspaper. Newspaper
contains an article by W.A. Duncan, who contacted the
Mexican embassy about Indian migration to Mexico. 1p.

Fol. 32. 4 Apr. 1898, Washington. [Matías] Romero to
Minister of Foreign Affairs. Romero forwards a letter
from W.A. Duncan, chairman of Cherokee delegation. Romero
points out that the Cherokees cannot negotiate with a
foreign government without permission from the United
States. He asks whether James M. Tittle discussed Cherokee migration with Mexican officials. 2p.

Fol. 33. 2 Apr. 1898, National Hotel, City [Washington].
W.A. Duncan to Matías Romero (copy). Agents who are
trying to move the Five Civilized Tribes to Mexico are
self-appointed and sow seeds of discontent among the

tribes. A.B. Hulit is a white man who is not a citizen
of any tribe. According to the treaties of 1785 and
1791, legal representatives of the Cherokees could negotiate with Mexico without permission from the American
government. Have Cherokee agents contacted the Mexican
government? 4p. *English*.

Fol. 35. 4 Apr. 1898, Washington. [Matías] Romero to
W.A. Duncan. In reply to the inquiry about the accuracy
of James M. Tittle's article, the embassy has no informa-
tion on the subject except to say that no Cherokee or any
Indian representative has broached the subject with the
Mexican government as of 4 February. 1p. *English*.

Fol. 36. 24 Mar. 1898, Vinita, Indian Territory. James
M. Tittle sends a newspaper article from the *Vinita Leader
Supplement* describing the Cherokee project to move to
Mexico. 1p. *English*.

Fol. 37. 13 Apr. 1898, Mexico. Mariscal to Mexican
Representative. Mariscal has received copies of latest
correspondence with W.A. Duncan. 1p.

Fol. 38. 28 Mar. 1898, Washington. [Matías] Romero to
Minister of Foreign Relations. R.C. Adams, representative
of Cherokee faction opposed to the one headed by W.A.
Duncan, has visited Romero to see whether the Mexican
government would welcome Cherokee migration. Romero told
Adams that the Mexican government would probably accept
the Cherokees provided that they lived under Mexican law.
If Adams wants more precise information, he should visit
the government in Mexico City. 2p.

Fol. 39. 4 Apr. 1898, Mexico. Azpiroz to Mexican Representative in Washington. Azpiroz has forwarded the
correspondence concerning Mr. Adams to the Ministry of
Development. 1p.

Fol. 40. 4 Apr. 1898, Mexico. Azpiroz to Minister of
Development. Azpiroz forwards material about the Cherokees' wish to migrate to Mexico. 1p.

Fol. 41. 20 May 1898, Mexico. Fernández Leal to Minister
of Foreign Relations. Fernández Leal acknowledges receipt
of note concerning R.C. Adams's letter on behalf of the
Cherokees. 2p.

Fol. 42. 30 Apr. 1898, Washington. [Matías] Romero to
the Minister of Foreign Relations. Romero has received
a copy of the Development Minister's reply to the petition
of R.C. Adams on behalf of the Cherokees. At the same
time, Adams wrote that he had received permission from the
American Secretary of State to negotiate with Mexico.
Adams has meanwhile been sent the conditions stipulated
by the Minister of Development. 2p.

3737-13 (CONT'D)

Fol. 43. 26 Apr. 1898, The Oxford (Washington, D.C.).
R.C. Adams to [Matías] Romero. Adams encloses a copy of
the power of attorney that he holds on behalf of the
Cherokees. It is also on file with the American State
Department. A delegation has gone to Mexico and is
inspecting land for sale in Sonora and Chihuahua. If
the Mexican Government gives a favorable reply to the
Cherokee request, Adams will join the delegation and go
to Mexico City. 2p. *English.*

Fol. 44. 30 Apr. 1898, Washington. [Matías] Romero to
R.C. Adams. Romero has received the power of attorney
for Adams. Mexican government has decided that the Cherokees would be welcome in Mexico if the American government
does not oppose their migration. The tribe would be
subject to federal and state laws in Mexico. If the tribe
migrates as settlers, they will need a grant from the
Mexican government to pass their household goods free of
duty. There are federal lands for sale in Chihuahua and
Sonora but their quality is not very high. 2p. *English.*

Fol. 45. 26 Apr. 1898, The Oxford (Washington). R.C.
Adams to Mexican Legation to the United States in Washington. [Translation of fol. 43]. 2p.

Fol. 46. 30 Apr. 1898, Washington. [Matías] Romero to
R.C. Adams. [Translation of fol. 44]. 3p.

Fol. 48. 11 May 1898, Mexico. Mariscal to Minister of
Development. Mexican Minister in Washington has sent a
copy of the power of attorney [for Adams] and a translation of two letters. 1p.

Fol. 49. 11 May 1898, Mexico. Mariscal to Mexican Representative in Washington. Mariscal has forwarded the
latest materials sent from Washington to the Ministry of
Development. 1p.

Fol. 121. 7 June 1893, Washington. [Matías] Romero to Minister
of Foreign Relations. Romero reports that the *Globe Democrat*
of St. Louis published an article about a Cherokee delegation
visiting Mexico. Leader of the mission stated that Sonora was
unsuitable for Cherokees because it is too arid. The Society
of Keetowah evidently will decide against migration. The
expedition to Mexico might have been sent by opponents of Adams,
who will probably contact the embassy if such is the case.
The Senate has approved a proposal to eliminate the rights of
the Five Civilized Tribes acquired in previous treaties. This
will probably force the dissidents to migrate to Mexico or
accept American citizenship once and for all. 2p. [Enclosures
to fol. 124].

3737-13 (CONT'D)

Fol. 122. 29 [Apr. - May?] 1898, St. Louis. *Globe Democrat.* A delegation of full-blooded Cherokees has visited
Mexico. J. Henry Dick says that the country is not
suitable for farming. 1p. *English.*

Fol. 123. 16 June 1898, Mexico. Mariscal to Mexican
Representative in Washington. Mariscal acknowledges
receipt of recent news about Cherokee migration project.
1p.

Fol. 124. 14 Feb. 1898, Mexico. Mariscal to Mexican
Representative in Washington. Mariscal has sent information to the Minister of Development about the Indian plans
to migrate to Mexico. 1p.

ARCHIVO HISTÓRICO MILITAR DE MÉXICO

Mexico City

Exp. XI/481.3/738. 1828. Peter Ellis Bean to Manuel de Mier
y Terán. Bean discusses borders and friendship treaties with
the Cherokees, Kickapoos, and other tribes. 17p. [Although
cited in *Guía del Archivo Histórico Militar de México* (Mexico,
1948) 1:99, the archive reports that the document is not in
their collection].

INSTITUTO NACIONAL DE ANTROPOLOGÍA E HISTORIA
MUSEO DE ANTROPOLOGÍA

Mexico City

SERIE MONTERREY (3ª ÉPOCA): ARCHIVO DEL GENERAL FRANCISCO DE NARANJO

Rollo 17. 7 Dec. 1903, Washington. M. de Azpiroz to Francisco
Naranjo. In response to the question about whether the Delawares have enough funds to buy land, the embassy has learned
that the Delawares will acquire some funds from the division
of goods among each Cherokee (to which they now belong). As
a tribe, however, the Delawares have no money, only some
pending court settlements which they may or may not win. 1p.

ARCHIVO GENERAL DE LA NACIÓN

*NOTAS DIPLOMÁTICAS/2   CORRESPONDENCE CONCERNING THE UNITED STATES:
                        1810-1820*

    N. fol. A.L.L. [Lacarrière Latour]. *Mémoire* describing
Cherokee affairs. *French.* [Bolton, p. 65].

SECRETARÍA DE FORMENTO, CONLONIZACIÓN, É INDUSTRIA

COLONIZACIÓN/3: 1822-1835

    Exp. 6. 1823. Report from Foreign Minister that the Iroqueses
[Cherokees] have requested lands. 11p. [Bolton, p. 352].

COLONIZACIÓN/9: 1834-1836

    Exp. 57. 1835. Printed memorial from Chief Ross and the
Cherokees to the American Congress asking for land. 110p.
[Bolton, p. 359].

COLONIZACIÓN/10: 1836

    Exp. 59. 1836. *Expediente* discussing the Cherokees returning
to their lands. [Bolton, p. 360].

COLONIZACIÓN Y TERRENOS BALDÍOS/5: 1832-1835

    Exp. 118. 1824-1827. Report from Richard Fields giving
information on a Cherokee village. 78p. [Bolton, p. 362].

COLONIZACIÓN Y TERRENOS BALDÍOS/6: 1835-1841

    Exp. 194. 1841. *Expediente* concerning land concessions to
the Cherokees, Conchates, and Shawnees along the northern
frontiers. 13p. [Bolton, p. 362].

----

    *The following Cherokee material from Herbert E. Bolton's
*Guide to Materials for the History of the United States in the
Principal Archives of Mexico* (Washington, D.C., 1913) could not
be located during Dr. Lewis's research trip in 1979.

BOLTON (CONT'D)

SECRETARÍA DE GOBERNACIÓN

INDIOS BÁRBAROS: 1830-1834

> [1830-1834?], Monclova. Report from Veramendi that Chief
> Bowles [?] and other Cherokees intend to settle in Coahuila.
> [Bolton, p. 334].

TRANQUILIDAD PÚBLICA/133: 1821-1826

> No. 14. 1826. Report from the Gov. of Texas that the Chero-
> kees and other tribes are hostile. He asks for a military
> detachment to send to Nacogdoches. 16p. [Bolton, p. 342].

TRANQUILIDAD PÚBLICA: 1827

> No. 29. 1827. Recommendation from the Minister of War that
> the governors aid Nacogdoches. There is a report that the
> Cherokees killed Richard Fields and John Hunter. 7p. [Bolton,
> p. 343].

SECRETARÍA DE RELACIONES EXTERIORES

SERIE PRIMERA   COLONIZACIÓN/CAJA: 1824-1895

> N. fol. 1835. Petition from John Ross, Cherokee chief, to
> migrate to Mexican territory with his tribe. [Bolton, p. 237].

SERIE SEGUNDA   RESEÑAS POLÍTICAS/CAJA: 1820-1830

> N. fol. 1824. Washington. Political news from Minister
> Torrens about relations between the United States and the
> Cherokees. [Bolton, p. 266].

SECCIÓN III, SECRETARÍA DE ESTADO
ESTADO/3882   LOUISIANA: 1740-1773

Exp. 3 (no. 8). 1754 [1764]. *Discours sur la Luisiane.* 7p.
French. [Encloses 1 document].

N. fol. *Mémoire secret.* Several Indian nations from
Louisiana have united with the Cherokees to attack the
English in Carolina. 3p. *French.*

ESTADO/3884   AMERICAN REVOLUTION: 1777-1782

Exp. 1 (doc. 4). 26 Dec. 1777, Havana. Letter from [Juan
Bautista Bonet?] stating that a group of Yuchi Indians from
Coweta led by Tunapé [Funapé?] have arrived in Havana. These
Indians report that the English have attempted to unite the
Talapooses, Apizacas [Abekas], Chickasaws, Alibamos, and
Choctaws to fight with the royalists. Tunapé offers to turn
over St. Marks to the Spaniards. He also claims that the
Yuchis and Talapooses do not fear the English tribes such as
the Chalaques [Cherokees], Chickasaws, Chicasaos, Cunupuyas,
Chaschices, and Alojaas. 3p.

Exp. 1 (doc. 5, no. 167 *reservada*). 15 Jan. 1778, Havana.
Diego José Navarro to José de Gálvez. 3p. [Enclosures to
doc. 10].

Doc. 6 (no. 1). 22 Dec. 1777, Havana. Juan José Eligio
de la Puente to Navarro. *Declaraciones del patrón Joseph
Bermúdez y el cacique Tunapé.* Eligio de la Puente
discusses British-Indian relations in the Southeast. 7p.

Exp. 1 (doc. 12). 1 Apr. 1778, Havana. Juan José Eligio de
la Puente to Diego José Navarro. English boats have arrived
in Pensacola with weapons and goods for the Indians. But the
Chalaques [Cherokees] are the only tribe faithful to the
British at the moment. There are some 400 Cherokees in
Pensacola. The Yuchis, Talapooses, Apiscas [Abekas], Chickasaws,
Alibamos, and Choctaws have kept their distance from the
British. 3p.

ESTADO/3884BIS   AMERICAN AFFAIRS: 1777-1786

Exp. 7 (doc. 75). 8 Jan. 1788, New Orleans. *Estractos sovre el comercio de yndios de la Luysiana y Floridas.* Americans have sent five commissioners to deal with the Creeks, Cherokees, Choctaws, and Chickasaws with hopes of securing land from these tribes. Creek and Cherokee attack on Cumberland resulted in the death of ten Indians and a few Americans. 191p.

ESTADO/3885BIS   AMERICAN AFFAIRS: 1784-1793

Exp. 6 (doc. 20). 28 Apr. 1785, Havana. [Bernardo] de Gálvez to [Diego Gardoqui]. *Apuntes que convendrá tenga presentes ... el comisario ordenador dn. Diego Gardoqui.* Gálvez sets forth the Spanish position on the border between Fla. and the American states. He also discusses the problem of the Indian tribes along the border. 9p.

Exp. 7 (doc. 24, no. 3). 21 Mar. 1792, Natchez. Manuel Gayoso de Lemos to [Tascahetuca] King of the Chickasaw Nation. [Copy of AGI Cuba/2353/fol. 530]. 3p. [Enclosure of exp. 7, doc. 24, no. 5 *reservada*].

Exp. 7 (doc. 24, no. 4). 24 Mar. 1792, Natchez. Manuel Gayoso de Lemos to Esteban Minor. [Copy of AGI Cuba/2353/fol. 605]. 5p. [Enclosure of exp. 7, doc. 24, no. 5 *reservada*].

Exp. 7 (doc. 24, no. 5 *reservada*). 4 Apr. 1792, Natchez. Manuel Gayoso de Lemos to el Conde de Floridablanca. Gayoso sent a message to the Chickasaws via a Cherokee. The Americans plan to celebrate a peace with all the Cherokees and other tribes at the Great Bend of the Tennessee. 21p. [Enclosures at exp. 7, doc. 24, nos. 3 and 4].

Exp. 7 (doc. 28). 5 July 1792, Natchez. Manuel Gayoso de Lemos to [el Conde de Aranda]. *Indice de la carta [que remite Gayoso al exmo sr. Conde de Aranda]*. 1p. [Enclosures to doc. 30].

Doc. 29 (no. 1). 5 July 1792, Natchez. Manuel Gayoso de Lemos to el Conde de Aranda. 2p.

Doc. 30. 5 July 1792, Natchez. Manuel Gayoso de Lemos. *Estado político de ... Luisiana.* [Same as AGI Cuba/2353/fol. 508]. 19p.

Exp. 8 (doc. 21). 16 Nov. 1786, St. Augustine. Zéspedes. *Discursos preliminar sobre indios que el governador de San Agustín de la Florida cita en esta representación* (copy). Zéspedes discusses the history of recent European contact with the Indians of East Fla. and how to capture Indian loyalty for Spain. 15p.

ESTADO/3886   AMERICAN AFFAIRS: 1785-1796

Exp. 1 (doc. 41, no. 1). 31 Dec. 1795, Cherokee. John McDonald to el Barón de Carondelet. [Same as AGI Cuba/1447/no. 154 *reservada*/encl. no.1]. 3p. [Enclosure of exp. 1, doc. 43].

ESTADO/3886 (CONT'D)

Exp. 1 (doc. 43, no. 154 *reservada*). 30 Jan. 1796, New Orleans.
El Barón de Carondelet to Luis de las Casas. [Same as AGI
Cuba/1447/no. 154 *reservada*]. 11p. [Enclosure at exp. 1,
doc. 41].

Exp. 1 (doc. 49). *Descubrimiento, adquisición y establecimiento
del Kentucke.* Report discusses the history of European settlement of Ky. and the numerous conflicts with the Indians,
including the Cherokees. Cherokees are the most important
tribe that live near Ky., and the Chickamaugas (one branch of
the Cherokees) have numerous towns close to Kentucky. Ky. is
also interested in the Chickasaws, Choctaws, Yuchis, Catawbas,
Delawares, Mingoes, Wyandots, Six Nations, Shawnees, Gibbaways
[Chippewas], Hurons, Tawaws [Ottawas], Tawaas [Tawassa?],
Mawnees [Miamis], Piankashaws, Vermilions, Wabash, Kickapoos,
Ozaws [Osage], Kaskaskias, Illinois, Potowatamies, and the
Sioux. 49p.

ESTADO/3887 AMERICAN AFFAIRS: 1786-1790

Doc. 4 (no. 136 *reservada de preferencia*). 28 June 1786, New
Orleans. Esteban Miró to el Marqués de Sonora. [Same as AGI
SD/2551/fol. 223]. 2p. [Enclosures to doc. 7].

Doc. 7 (no. 1). 1 May 1786, Little Tallassee. Alex.
McGillivray to Esteban Miró. [Same as AGI SD/2551/fol.
231]. 18p.

Doc. 9 (no. 137 *reservada de preferencia*). 28 June 1786, New
Orleans. Esteban Miró to el Marqués de Sonora. [Same as AGI
SD/2551/fol. 240]. 2p. [Enclosures to doc. 14].

Doc. 11 (no. 2). 8 Jan. 1786, Seneca. Benjamin Hawkins
to Alex. McGillivray. [Translation of AGI Cuba/2360/n.
fol.]. 5p.

Doc. 12 (no. 3). 11 Jan. 1786, Seneca. Benjamin Hawkins
to Alex. McGillivray. [Translation of AGI Cuba/2360/n.
fol.]. 3p.

Doc. 13. 28 June 1786, New Orleans. Esteban Miró to el
Conde de Gálvez (copy). American efforts to secure tribes
along the frontier are important. The Americans continue
to press for a border between Spain and the United States
at the thirty-first parallel. 6p.

Doc. 14 (*reservada*). 12 Nov. 1786, San Lorenzo. *Real
orden* to Gov. of Louisiana approving the governor's
response to the American attempts to win over frontier
tribes. 1p.

Doc. 44 (no. 1 *reservada*). 25 Nov. 1786, New Orleans. Esteban
Miró to el Marqués de Sonora. 3p. [Enclosures to doc. 47].

ESTADO/3887 (CONT'D)

Doc. 45 (no. 1). 8 Oct. 1786, Little Tallassee. Alex.
McGillivray to Gov. O'Neill. [Translation of AGI Cuba/
2360/n. fol.]. 7p.

Doc. 48 (no. 2 *reservada*). 25 Nov. 1786, New Orleans. Esteban
Miró to el Marqués de Sonora. Georgia troops are marching
against the Creeks. McGillivray maintains that the Creeks will
be destroyed if the Georgians are joined by soldiers from
Cumberland. 2p. [Enclosures to doc. 49].

Doc. 49. 30 Oct. 1786. Alex. McGillivray to Gov. O'Neill.
[Translation of AGI Cuba/2360/n. fol.]. 3p.

Doc. 54 (nos. 12-13). 14 Nov. - 24 Dec. 1786, Florida. Summary
of correspondence from Zéspedes [to el Marqués de Sonora].
Some 100 Frenchmen are reportedly established along the Tenn.
R. with an escort of Delaware Indians. Franklin has promised
Ga. assistance against the Indians. Gov. of Franklin believes
that the Creeks have to be beaten in order for his state to
enjoy what it has won from the Cherokees and Chickasaws.
Cumberland wishes to be under Franklin's jurisdiction. 48p.

Doc. 60 (no. 13 *reservada*). 24 Dec. 1786, St. Augustine.
Vicente Manuel de Zéspedes to el Marqués de Sonora. Zéspedes
forwards some material explaining how Ga. attempted to get
Franklin's aid against the Indians. 6p. [Enclosures to doc.
63].

Doc. 61 (no. 1). 18 Sept. 1786, Mt. Pleasant. Gov. of
Franklin to [Gov. of Georgia] (extract of translation).
Gov. of Franklin expresses his expectation that the assembly will authorize sending forces from Franklin against
the Creeks. 1p.

Doc. 61 (no. 1). 18 Sept. 1786, Volachuchey [Nolichucky].
Robert Dijon and Stephen Fest to Gov. of Georgia (extract
of translation). Dijon and Fest presented the Ga. governor's letters to Gov. Sevier of Franklin. Gov. Sevier
predicted that Franklin would provide 1,000 - 1,500 men
against the Indians. 2p.

Doc. 61 (no. 1). 8 Feb. 1786, Franklin. Extract of
translated letter from George Elholm stating that the gov.
of Franklin had united the Cherokees and Chickasaws against
the Creeks. Southern tribes will be hard pressed to defend
themselves against Gen. Clark, who has 2,200 men in
Cumberland and is considering placing himself under the
command of the gov. of Franklin. 2p.

Doc. 61 (no. 1). 28 July 1786, Chickasaw Nation. Wm.
Davenport to John Sevier (extract of translation). Ga.
commissioned Davenport to secure peace with the Chickasaws
and Choctaws, which he has done. Since the Creeks have
pressured these tribes against Americans, Davenport has
decided to remain in Chickasaw territory to protect Ga.'s
interests. 2p.

ESTADO/3887 (CONT'D)

Doc. 80 (no. 11 *reservada*). 1 June [1787?], New Orleans. Esteban Miró to el Marqués de Sonora. 2p. [Enclosures to doc. 84].

   Doc. 83 (no. 3). 4 Mar. 1787, Little Tallassee. Alex. McGillivray to Gov. O'Neill. [Translation of AGI Cuba/ 177A/no. 11 *reservada*/encl. no. 3].

   Doc. 84 (no. 4). 4 Apr. 1787, Little Tallassee. Alex. McGillivray to Gov. O'Neill. [Translation of AGI Cuba/ 177A/no. 11 *reservada*/encl. no. 4]. 2p.

Doc. 93 (no. 21 *reservada*). 12 Oct. 1787, St. Augustine. Vicente Manuel de Zéspedes to el Marqués de Sonora. Zéspedes relays news from published accounts about the fight between the Americans and a group of Indians and Spaniards at Muscle Shoals along the Cherokee River. 6p. [Enclosures to doc. 94].

Doc. 95 (no. 22 *reservada*). 14 Oct. 1787, St. Augustine. Vicente Manuel de Zéspedes to el Marqués de Sonora. Zéspedes confirms the fight at Muscle Shoals between the Americans and a group of Indians and Spaniards. This post is not far from Cumberland. 5p.

Doc. 96 (no. 7 *reservada*). 24 Mar. 1787, New Orleans. Esteban Miró to el Marqués de Sonora. 2p. [Enclosures to doc. 98].

   Doc. 97 (no. 2 *reservada*). 24 Mar. 1787, New Orleans. Esteban Miró to Arturo O'Neill (copy). It is in Spain's interest to advise the Creeks not to attack the Americans this spring. A Creek attack could so exasperate the Americans that the tribe might be exposed to disastrous revenge from Cumberland and Georgia. 3p.

Doc. 109. 10 Aug. 1786, Pensacola. Arturo O'Neill to el Marqués de Sonora. Numerous parties of Upper Creeks and Cherokees have patrolled the frontier to expel Americans from Indian territory. They have forced Americans in Ga. and along the Cherokee R. to flee. Another party of Indians has attacked Cumberland, suffering ten deaths. Indians have requested that Spain establish forts in various strategic locations to help preserve their land. 4p.

Doc. 120 (no. 24 *reservada*). 9 Nov. 1787, St. Augustine. Vicente Manuel de Zéspedes to el Marqués de Sonora. Zéspedes discusses earlier letters informing the Marqués about Indian wars and attacks as far north as Va. against the Americans. Indians have particularly concentrated their efforts against Franklin and Cumberland. 5p.

Doc. 124 (no. 3 *reservada*). 10 Jan. 1788, St. Augustine. Vicente Manuel de Zéspedes to Antonio Valdés. 11p. [Enclosures to doc. 125].

   Doc. 125. 23 Oct. 1787, Assembly House, Georgia. *Acuerdo de la junta selecta* (translation). Having reviewed the Indian treaties [Creek and Cherokee] of Ga. since the Revolution, the committee believes that Ga. has permission to set the boundary lines for Indian hunting grounds. 12p.

ESTADO/3887   (CONT'D)

Doc. 129. 8 Jan. 1788, Havana. José de Ezpeleta to el Conde de Floridablanca. 2p. [Enclosures to doc. 131].

> Doc. 130 (no. 1). 12 Nov. 1787, New York. Diego de Gardoqui to José de Ezpeleta (copy). Gov. of Havana must be aware of the avaricious appetite of the Americans toward Spanish land in the West. The State of Franklin in N.C. has rebelled against the government. 4p.

Doc. 133. 3 Jan. 1789, Havana. Manuel Gayoso de Lemos to el Conde de Floridablanca. Gayoso reports on conversations with Diego White [alias Jacques Dubois] sent to Havana by the Spanish envoy in New York. White showed Gayoso his correspondence concerning Ky., Cumberland, and Franklin. Gayoso also saw an American document describing Cherokee boundaries. Spanish power has prevented Franklin residents from duplicating the feat of expelling Cherokees from Chote. 3p. [Enclosures to doc. 134].

> Doc. 134. 1 Sept. 1788, Congress. Cyrus Griffin. *Edicto por los Estados Unidos juntos en congreso* (translation). Document describes Cherokee boundaries. 2p.

Doc. 136 (no. 13 *reservada*). 1 Oct. 1788, St. Augustine. Vicente Manuel de Zéspedes to Antonio Valdés. 5p. [Enclosures to doc. 138].

> Doc. 137. *Extracto de ... cartas* (translation). Residents of Ky., Franklin, Cumberland, Kaskaskias, and Wabash have formed a secret association. 12p.

Doc. 148 (no. 47). 29 Nov. 1788, Havana. José de Ezpeleta to Antonio Valdés. 4p. [Enclosures to doc. 150].

> Doc. 149. 20 Sept. 1788, Little Tallassee. Alex. McGillivray to Gov. Miró. [Spanish version of AGI Cuba/2361/n. fol.]. 6p.

Doc. 176 (no. 38 *reservada*). 20 May 1789, New Orleans. Esteban Miró to Antonio Valdés. 7p. [Enclosures to doc. 182].

> Doc. 177 (no. 1). 22 Apr. 1789, Little Tallassee. Alex. McGillivray to Capt. Vicente Folch. [Same as AGI Cuba/2352/no. 38 *reservada*/encl. no. 1]. 4p.

ESTADO/3888   PANTON, LESLIE AND COMPANY: 1786-1809

Doc. 1. 1786-1806. *Expediente Estados Unidos 1786 a 1806. Expediente de la casa de Panton Leslie y Compañía de Penzacola.* 1p. [Encloses 212 folios].

> N. doc. 13 July [1788?], New Orleans. Summary of letter from Gov. Miró stating that McGillivray visited Pensacola and was told that the King wanted the Creeks to live in peace with the United States. McGillivray asked for a

copy of the King's order since peace with the United
States would ruin the Creeks if the tribe had to give up
land. McGillivray also passed along information about
Congress's efforts to solve the Indian problem between
N.C. and Ga. and the Cherokees and Creeks. 14p.

Doc. 28 (no. 10). 26 Feb. 1791, Pensacola. Alex. McGillivray
to Esteban Miró (summary). Americans want all the Southern
Indians' land. Although Congress seems moderate, it has the
same objectives as other American organizations. Ga. claims
the exclusive right to dispose of the land belonging to the
Creeks, Cherokees, Choctaws, and Chickasaws, even though
Congress wished to acquire title to the disputed land in the
West. 12p.

Doc. 35 (no. 41 *reservada).* 27 July 1794, New Orleans. El
Barón de Carondelet to el Duque de la Alcudia (duplicate).
Carondelet forwards a petition from Panton, Leslie and Company
(the firm which handles trade with the Creeks, Choctaws,
Chickasaws, and part of the Cherokees). Carondelet supports
the petition but recommends delaying its approval until it can
be determined if the Americans are successful in negotiating
exclusive trade rights with the Creeks. 21p. [Enclosures
to doc. 36].

> Doc. 36. Petition from [Panton, Leslie, and Company] to
> [the King]. Americans have tried to separate the Indians
> from Spain, something that would produce serious conse-
> quences for Spain. The company asks the Crown either to
> buy Panton and Leslie out or to grant the Company trade
> concessions that will allow them to stay in business. 9p.

Doc. 51 (no. 88 *reservada).* 9 Feb. 1797, New Orleans. El
Barón de Carondelet to el Príncipe de la Paz (duplicate). 6p.
[Enclosures to doc. 56].

> Doc. 56 (no. 5). *Palabra* [talk] from el Barón de Carondelet
> to Ugulayacabe, Payehouuna, and the Chickasaw Warriors.
> Carondelet reminds Ugulayacabe of Spain's efforts to unite
> all the Indians between the Ohio and the Great Lakes with
> the leaders of the Choctaws, Talapooses, Cherokees, and
> the Chickasaws. The border between Spanish and American
> territory should not affect the Indians since the tribes
> own their own land. 4p.

Doc. 57. 23 May 1797, New Orleans. El Barón de Carondelet to
el Príncipe de la Paz. *Indice de la representación [que dirige
el Mariscal de Campo, el Barón de Carondelet, al exmo sr.
Príncipe de la Paz].* 1p. [Enclosures to doc. 65].

> Doc. 58 (no. 95 *reservada).* 23 May 1797, New Orleans.
> El Barón de Carondelet to el Príncipe de la Paz. Carondelet
> forwards a representation from Panton and Leslie, who
> handle Indian trade. Wm. Panton is tired of the continued
> harassment by the interim intendent, Juan Ventura Morales,

ESTADO/3888 (CONT'D)

and threatens to withdraw his business from the area. If this commercial house stops trading with the Choctaws, Chickasaws, Creeks, and Cherokees, it would result in the devastation of these provinces. 8p.

Doc. 59. 6 May 1797, Pensacola. Vicente Folch to [el Barón de Carondelet]. Folch discusses the problems that Panton has had in continuing the Indian trade because of Spain's war with England and Panton's troubles with the Intendant Morales. 15p.

Doc. 66. 1 July 1797, New Orleans. El Barón de Carondelet to el Príncipe de la Paz (duplicate). *Indice de la representación que [el Barón de Carondelet manda al exmo sr. Príncipe de la Paz].* 2p. [Enclosures to doc. 71].

Doc. 67 (no. 98 *reservada*). 1 July 1797, New Orleans. El Barón de Carondelet to el Príncipe de la Paz (duplicate). Carondelet forwards a memorial from Wm. Panton, John Forbes, Leslie and Company (the commercial firm which trades with the Talapooses, Alibamos, Cherokees, Choctaws, and Chickasaws). The service of this firm merits royal favor. Because of the new treaty between the United States and Spain, it makes little difference to Spain whether the company stays or leaves. It does, however, make a difference to the Indians, and Spain still needs Indian friendship. 10p.

Doc. 68. 20 June 1797, New Orleans. Memorial from Panton, Leslie and Co. reminding the Crown that the Company offered to sell the firm to government in 1794 or to receive certain concessions that would allow the business to make a profit. Company asks the Crown to make a decision soon. 11p.

Doc. 69. Panton, Leslie and Company to el Barón de Carondelet. Americans have made efforts to win over the frontier tribes. Panton, Leslie and Company has managed to frustrate some of these efforts through its commercial ties with the Indians. Company asks for the Governor's help in convincing the government to choose between two alternatives. Either buy the company out or grant it generous concessions, including the prohibition of rival traders among the Choctaws, Chickasaws, Creeks, and Cherokees. 7p.

Doc. 72 (no. 15). 31 Mar. 1799, New Orleans. Juan Ventura Morales to Francisco [de] Saavedra (triplicate). 2p. [Enclosures to doc. 75].

Doc. 73. 12 Jan. 1799, New Orleans. Manuel Gayoso de Lemos to Juan Ventura Morales (copy). Gayoso is apprehensive because no Indian goods have arrived for the Talapooses, who may well return to the English scheme once sponsored by Bowles. Daniel McGillivray, nephew of the

late Creek chief, reported that the Cherokees have had to
cede land to the Americans because the tribe has no trade
with Pensacola. Government must issue passports to Panton
to obtain goods from Providence. 2p.

Doc. 73. 12 Jan. 1799, New Orleans. *Repuesta* (reply)
from Juan Ventura Morales to Manuel Gayoso de Lemos (copy).
Morales encloses passports but notes that Gayoso's actions
violate the King's instructions. 2p.

Doc. 76 (no. 16). 31 Mar. 1799, New Orleans. Juan Ventura
Morales to Francisco [de] Saavedra (duplicate). 7p. [Enclo-
sures to doc. 87].

Doc. 77 (no. 1). 7 Feb. 1799, New Orleans. Manuel Gayoso
de Lemos to Juan Ventura Morales. Boats have arrived from
Providence with goods for Panton. Panton has suffered
heavily in the Indian trade and is stuck with unpaid bills
from the Talapooses, Cherokees, Choctaws, and Chickasaws.
Yet Panton's Indian trade has kept these Indians friendly
to Spain. 10p.

Doc. 88 (no. 282). 31 Mar. 1799, New Orleans. Juan Ventura
Morales to Miguel Cayetano Soler (duplicate). 2p. [Enclosures
to doc. 90].

Doc. 89. 12 Jan. 1799, New Orleans. Manuel Gayoso de
Lemos to Juan Ventura Morales. [Same as doc. 73]. 2p.

Doc. 89. 12 Jan. 1799, New Orleans. *Repuesta* (reply)
from Juan Ventura Morales to Manuel Gayoso de Lemos.
[Same as doc. 73]. 5p.

Doc. 90. *Dictamen* recommending that passports be given to
[Panton]. 5p.

Doc. 100 (no. 8 *reservada*). 8 Oct. 1800, New Orleans. El
Marqués de Casa Calvo to Mariano Luis de Urquijo. Casa Calvo
discusses the merits of Panton's petitions for indemnities
earned by its trade with the border tribes between the Spanish
Floridas, Louisiana, and American territory. The new treaty
with the United States leaves only a few perverse Seminoles
within Spanish borders. The Choctaws, Chickasaws, Cherokees,
and the most intelligent part of the Creeks reside on the
American side. Yet Panton's Indian commerce is still important
for the security of the Spanish territory and the tribes are
still a barrier between Spanish territory and the Americans.
68p. [Enclosures to doc. 102].

Doc. 112 (no. 5 *reservada*). 20 Nov. 1800, New Orleans. Ramón
de López y Angulo to Secretary of State. 154p. [Enclosures
to doc. 113].

ESTADO/3888 (CONT'D)

>Doc. 113 (no. 11). 14 Feb. 1800, Aranjuez. *Real orden*
>to Gov. of Louisiana and West Florida. [Same as AHN
>Estado/3889bis/doc. 128]. 2p.

>Doc. 113 (no. 34). 27 Jan. 1799, Pensacola. Vincente
>Folch to Juan Ventura Morales (copy). Folch fears that
>the Talapooses will join Bowles since Folch has no Indian
>goods to give or trade with them. Daniel McGillivray
>reports that the Cherokees have had to sell land to the
>Americans because there are no trade goods for them in
>Pensacola. 2p.

ESTADO/3888BIS   POPULATION OF LOUSIANA AND THE FLORIDAS: 1785-1791

Doc. 56 (no. 4). 25 Sept. 1787, New Orleans. Esteban Miró.
*Relación de los establecimientos, que al occidente de los
montes Apalaches han poblado los vasallos de los Estados Unidos
en los ríos, o esteros, que vierten sus aguas en el Ohio.*
Miró lists several American settlements in Cherokee territory.
3p.

Doc. 136 (no. 21 *reservada*). 15 June 1788, New Orleans. Esteban
Miró to Antonio Valdés. There is political unrest in Cumberland
and Ky. among those who wish to separate from the United States.
Political divisions in Franklin result from personal differences
between two American leaders, differences which have caused
anarchy there. 5p. [Enclosures to doc. 137].

>Doc. 137. 25 Apr. 1788, Little Tallassee. Alex.
>McGillivray to Gov. O'Neill (translation). Several
>representatives from Cumberland have arrived in Little
>Tallassee with peace proposals. Creek warriors have
>reduced Cumberland to a state of misery. Some Cumberland
>residents said that they would be willing to become
>Spanish vassals. Col. Robertson, Bleduc [Bledsoe], Ewing,
>and two other men showed McGillivray proof that the Va.
>company purchased the Cumberland area forty years ago from
>the Northern Indians and the Cherokees. 2p.

Doc. 179 (no. 2 *reservada*). 29 Dec. 1788, Havana. José de
Ezpeleta to Antonio Valdés. Ezpeleta discusses the mission of
James White, a N.C. congressional representative. White claims
that N.C. will separate from the Confederation. In the areas
west of the Allegheny Mountains (called Ky., Cumberland, and
Franklin), more than 200,000 habitants reside. White really
represents only Franklin, but his ideas also exist in Cumberland
and Kentucky. Ezpeleta sends a map of Franklin. 11p. [Enclo-
sures to doc. 186].

>Doc. 180. 24 Dec. 1788, Havana. James White to Capt.
>General [of Louisiana] (translation). White describes
>Franklin, Cumberland, and Ky. and maintains that western
>areas have a natural economic tie to the Spaniards. Many
>residents of Franklin wish to be under Spanish protection.
>7p.

ESTADO/3888BIS (CONT'D)

Doc. 181. 1788-1790. Summary of documents from Capt. Gen. of Louisiana concerning James White's mission, including a discussion of Cumberland and Franklin. Ezpeleta sent a map of Franklin, which includes some boundaries for the Cherokees. 32p.

Doc. 182 *(muy reservada)*. 23 Mar. 1789, Madrid. *Real orden* to Capt. Gen. of Louisiana and Florida expressing the King's approval of James White's treatment by officials in Havana and Louisiana. Americans in the West must be encouraged to find another exit to the ocean than the Miss. R. for their goods. It will be very useful for Gayoso to secretly visit the Western states to discover the political situation there. 2p.

Doc. 183. 3 Jan. 1789, Havana. Manuel Gayoso de Lemos to Antonio Valdés y Bazán. Gayoso discusses his conversations with James White. After seeing White's information of the boundaries between the United States and the Cherokees, Gayoso plans to make a more detailed map of the area once he arrives in Louisiana. White received letters from Cumberland inquiring whether Spain claimed territory up to the Cherokee River. 2p.

Doc. 184. 1 Sept. 1788, Congress. Cyrus Griffin. *Edicto por los Estados Unidos juntos en congreso*. [Same as AHN Estado/3887/doc. 134]. 2p.

Doc. 185. 3 Jan. 1789, Havana. Manuel Gayoso de Lemos to Antonio Valdés y Bazán. James White has suggested that Gayoso take a trip to Cumberland, Franklin, and Kentucky. This would be the only way to verify the true situation there. 2p.

Doc. 186. 16 Mar. 1789, Supreme Council of State. *Dictamen* from Supreme Council of State that Gayoso make a trip to Cumberland, Franklin, and Ky. and that James White's friendship be maintained. (Marginal note: The King accepts the recommendation). 3p.

Doc. 187 (no. 31 *reservada*). 12 Feb. 1789, New Orleans. Esteban Miró to Antonio Valdés. Miró has allowed Pedro Wouves d'Arges to leave for Guarico in order that he not be in New Orleans when James White and Manuel Gayoso de Lemos arrive from Havana. 3p. [Enclosures to doc. 188].

Doc. 188. 10 Aug. 1789, Madrid. *Real orden* to Gov. of Louisiana acknowledging the receipt of letter concerning the trip of Pedro Wouves d'Arges to Guarico. 1p.

Doc. 189 (no 3 *reservada*). [3] Mar. 1789, Havana. José de Ezpeleta to Antonio Valdés. Manuel Gayoso de Memos and James White have left for New Orleans. 2p. [Enclosures to doc. 190].

ESTADO/3888BIS (CONT'D)

Doc. 190. 21 July 1789, Madrid. *Real orden* to interim Capt. Gen. of Florida and Louisiana acknowledging receipt of information on the departure of Manuel Gayoso de Lemos and James White for New Orleans. 1p.

Doc. 220 (no. 37 *reservada*). 30 Apr. 1789, New Orleans. Esteban Miró to Antonio Valdés. James White arrived in New Orleans eight days ago. Spanish ambassador in New York sent him to New Orleans because it was no longer safe or prudent for White to stay in New York. White has influence in Franklin, which is divided between those who want to remain part of N.C. and the Confederation and those who want something else. Cumberland has changed its name to Miró, in honor of the present Spanish governor of New Orleans. 9p. [Enclosures to doc. 227].

Doc. 221 (no. 1). 12 Sept. 1788, Franklin. John Sevier to Diego de Gardoqui (copy). Sevier assures Gardoqui that the Franklin residents want political and commercial ties with Spain. Since the United States has done what it could to stop progress here, Franklin also needs money. Nothing would cement friendship with Spain more than some sort of subsidy, no matter how small. 5p.

Doc. 222 (no. 2). 18 Apr. 1789, New Orleans. James White to Esteban Miró (copy). Gardoqui has authorized White to inform the Western states that Spain would grant them the King's protection in return for an alliance with Spain and separation from the United States. He has specifically given White letters for the leaders of Franklin containing this offer. Cumberland feels the same way Franklin does. 3p.

Doc. 223 (no. 3). 20 Apr. 1789, New Orleans. Gov. Miró to [James White]. Gov. Miró will permit American settlements in Louisiana and Natchez in response to a petition by James White representing Franklin and Miró [Cumberland]. Settlers can trade with New Orleans. Should these districts secure their independence, the King would do what he can to help them survive. 3p.

Doc. 224 (no. 4). [24 Apr. 1789], [New Orleans]. Esteban Miró to [Daniel Smith] (copy). Spanish government has attempted to influence the Creeks to make peace with Americans in the West. Spanish officials, however, have not communicated with the Cherokees or Mascoutens. Occasionally these tribes travel to Illinois. The Cherokees were there last May requesting permission to settle in that area. Miró has ordered officials to admit these tribes, which will be a great service to the Americans if it ever happens. 3p.

Doc. 225 (no. 5). 23 Apr. 1789, New Orleans. Esteban Miró to James Wilkinson (copy). Miró informs Wilkinson that Spain would like to see more immigration into Spanish territory. Gardoqui has recruited White, a member of

ESTADO/3888BIS (CONT'D)

Congress with land in Cumberland, to serve Spain's
interest in the West. Gardoqui has sent him to Franklin
to encourage independence from the United States. White
is now in New Orleans. 5p.

Doc. 226 (no. 6). 22 Apr. 1789, New Orleans. James White
to Esteban Miró (translation). White requests funds to
pay his expenses and cover debts. 1p.

Doc. 227. 25 Oct. 1789, San Lorenzo. *Real orden* to Gov.
of Louisiana approving agreements made with James White
and efforts to attract settlers from Cumberland and
Franklin. 1p.

ESTADO/3889BIS   AMERICAN AFFAIRS: 1790-1802

Exp. 10 (doc. 2). 30 Aug. 1789, New Providence, Bahama Islands.
Wm. A. [Bowles] to el Conde de Floridablanca. The Creeks and
Cherokees, numbering some 20,000 warriors, have united. These
nations need the same gifts that they were accustomed to under
British rule. Spain promised to provide these gifts through
Panton, Leslie and Company. Unfortunately, this company has
not lived up to its obligations. 3p.

Exp. 10 (doc. 3, no. 6). 15 Apr. 1791, London. El Marqués del
Campo to el Conde de Floridablanca. Six individuals have
arrived from Canada dressed as Indians, three claiming to be
Creek and the rest Cherokees. The leader is Wm. Bowles, whose
life sounds like a novel. In reality, he is a huckster attempting to extort as much money as possible. 13p.

Exp. 10 (doc. 4). 25 Mar. 1791, London. *Memorial a S.M.C. de
William Augustus Bowles, Unestoy, Kuaktekiske, Sepohejah,
Juskeneah, y Wossies.* On behalf of the united tribes of the
Creeks and Cherokees, Bowles seeks an alliance with Spain. 8p.

Exp. 10 (doc. 5). *Real orden* asking that Spanish officials
remain vigilant about Bowles's activities. 2p.

Exp. 10 (doc. 7). 30 Oct. 1791, Havana. Juan de Araoz to
Antonio Valdés (copy). Gov. of Havana informed Araoz that
Bowles and his Indian companions have returned from London and
are now in Providence. They hoped to secure British help to
wrestle the Floridas away from Spain and win over the tribes
in that region. 2p. [Enclosures to doc. 7].

Doc. 7. 26 Sept. 1791, Havana. Luis de las Casas to Juan
de Araoz. Bowles has returned from London with three
Indians. Bowles left Providence for the Florida coast,
where he can make trouble as he did in 1788. 3p.

Exp. 10 (doc. 8). 25 Apr. 1792, London. El Marqués del Campo
to el Conde de Aranda. Spanish ambassador wrote a report on
Bowles, the huckster who accompanied the Cherokees, when he

ESTADO/3889BIS (CONT'D)

departed from London. Ambassador now has learned about Bowles's criminal activities in Louisiana and Florida. Bowles is nothing more than a lazy Irishman. 2p.

Exp. 10 (doc. 14). 16 Dec. 1791, Pensacola. Arturo O'Neill to el Marqués de Bajamar (copy). It has been three and a half years since Bowles first appeared among the Creeks. Bowles went to Providence, London, and Halifax with some Cherokees and Creeks. 7p.

Exp. 10 (doc. 16, no. 2). 4 Dec. 1795, Coweta. Wm. A. Bowles to [Arturo O'Neill] (copy). Creeks and Cherokees are now united under a common council and leader to direct their affairs. Tribes look to Spain as a natural ally. These tribes request freedom of the seas for the coast line that corresponds to their dominion. 3p.

Exp. 10 (doc. 90, no. 65). Philadelphia. Carlos Martínez de Yrujo to el Príncipe de la Paz. Yrujo forwards a letter from Blount, a Tenn. senator, proving that some Americans are helping the English in their designs against Louisiana and the two Floridas. Yrujo also attaches a printed message of the American Secretary of State accusing Spain of inciting the Indians against the United States. 3p. [Enclosures to doc. 95].

Doc. 91. 21 Apr. 1797, Col. King's Foundary. Gov. Blount to Indian interpreter Carey (translation). Blount discusses the English plan to use Indians against Louisiana and the two Floridas. He asks Carey to contact Watts, the Creeks, and the Cherokees and to convince them that Blount is not responsible for the treaty that resulted in the border being surveyed between Spanish and American territory. 4p.

Doc. 92. 11 July 1797, Philadelphia. Carlos Martínez de Yrujo to Timothy Pickering (copy). Yrujo protests Pickering's published account about Spanish representatives carrying out the surveying of the border between Spanish and American territory. Spain has not stirred up the Indians against the United States. 16p.

[Doc. 93?]. 3 July 1797, State Department. *Informe* from Timothy Pickering to the President of the United States (translation). Pickering describes the Spanish forts inside American territory and the new border between Spanish and American territory. He charges that Spain has prepared the Indians to break with the United States. 6p.

Exp. 10 (doc. 125, no. 136). 7 Nov. 1799, Philadelphia. Carlos Martínez de Yrujo to Mariano Luis de Urquijo. Yrujo discusses Bowles's arrest and his subsequent release. Evidently England intends to send Bowles to the Creeks and Cherokees to turn them

ESTADO/3889BIS (CONT'D)

against Florida. Yrujo has kept the governors of the Floridas appraised of Bowles's arrival in Providence and of his plans to move to the Floridas. 2p. [Enclosures to doc. 128].

Doc. 126. 29 Nov. 1799, Philadelphia. Carlos Martínez de Yrujo to Timothy Pickering (copy). Bowles has arrived in Providence and exercises considerable influence over the Creeks and Cherokees. Bowles's purpose is to turn these tribes against Spain. 1p.

Doc. 127. 7 Nov. 1799, Philadelphia. Carlos Martínez de Yrujo to Timothy Pickering. Several months ago Bowles attempted to raise the Southern Indians against the Spanish possessions in Florida. He could not do this without entering American territory, but the American government has treaty obligations to prevent this. 2p.

Doc. 128. 14 Feb. 1800, Aranjuez. *Real orden* to Governor of Louisiana and W. Fla. reporting that Bowles has gone to W. Fla. with British gifts to stir up the Creeks and Cherokees against Spain and to attack Pensacola. 2p.

Doc. 128. [Aranjuez]. *Real orden* to American Envoy [in Spain] containing news that Bowles is attempting to turn the Creeks and Cherokees against Spanish West Florida. Spanish government requests American help in preventing this. 3p.

Doc. 128. [Aranjuez]. *Real orden* to Carlos Martínez de Yrujo noting that the King has taken measures that hopefully will result in Bowles's seizure. 3p.

Exp. 10 (doc. 142, no. 152). 6 Mar. 1800, Philadelphia. Carlos Martínez de Yrujo to Mariano Luis de Urquijo. Over the last couple of years, Yrujo has repeatedly stressed the dangers that Louisiana faces from the Americans and English. The unsuccessful expedition of Sen. Blount against Lousiana is just one example. English could easily wean away the Choctaws, Chickasaws, Creeks, and Cherokees with gifts. 11p. [Enclosures to doc. 144].

Doc. 144 (no. 2). Copy of letter discussing Blount's conspiracy in Knoxville against Spanish territory. 3p.

Exp. 10 (doc. 198, no. 1). 11 June 1803, New Orleans. Manuel de Salcedo to Pedro Cevallos. Bowles has been captured after attempting to attend a meeting of the Seminoles with the Talapooses, Cherokees, Chickasaws, and Choctaws. 13p.

ESTADO/3890   AMERICAN AFFAIRS: 1793-1798

Exp. 1 (doc. 6). 1 Oct. 1793, San Lorenzo. Letter from Wm. Short responding to the Spanish government's communication about Indian affairs. The United States has always attempted to keep the Indian tribes neutral, yet Spanish officials in the New

ESTADO/3890 (CONT'D)

World have incited the tribes against the United States. These
officials have called assemblies of Southern Indians and asked
them to disavow their treaties with the United States. Cherokees are one example of this. 10p. *English.*

ESTADO/3890BIS   AMERICAN AFFAIRS: 1796-1819

Exp. 5 (doc. 12, no. 2 confidential). 13 Mar. 1796, Aranjuez.
Wm. Tatham to Diego de Gardoqui. Tatham presents a description of his past activities, including participation in a
campaign against the Regulators of N.C. and against the Indians
at Watauga. Tatham was also active in the early history of
Franklin. 14p. *English.*

Exp. 5 (doc. 58). 19 Dec. 1787, Tarborough, N. Carolina.
Richard Caswell to Wm. Tatham. Tatham is appointed Lt. Col.
in the Robertson batallion of N. Carolina. 1p. [Encloses
3 documents].

   N. doc. 12 Dec. 1789, Richamond. *Testimonio* from Wm.
   Russell noting that Wm. Tatham served under Russell in
   the expedition against the Cherokees in 1776. 2p.

Exp. 11 (doc. 1). 4 Dec. 1797, St. Augustine. Enrique White
to el Príncipe de la Paz (duplicate). White opposes the King's
orders to eliminate Indian gifts. This would threaten the
security of the Floridas for the Indians would surely turn on
Spain. 7p.

Exp. 11 (doc. 2). 27 Nov. 1797, St. Augustine. Enrique White
et al. *Acuerdo* of war council discussing the royal order
curtailing distribution of Indian gifts in East Fla. because
the gifts duplicate those given elsewhere. If this order is
obeyed, it will cause the Indians to wreak vengeance upon East
Florida. The war council recommends that the royal order be
ignored until the King can consider the question again . 5p.

ESTADO/3893   AMERICAN AFFAIRS: 1784-1789

Ap. 3 (no. 19 *reservada*). Diego de Gardoqui to el Conde de
Floridablanca. Gardoqui discusses the situation in Franklin,
Cumberland, Ky., and other western areas. There have been
violent disturbances in Franklin. 19p. [Encloses 3 documents].

   N. fol. 18 Apr. 1788, New York. Diego de Gardoqui to
   Samuel Johnson (translation). In response to a letter
   delivered by Dr. James White concerning Indian violence
   along the N. C. frontiers, Spain is doing everything it
   can to prevent such attacks. 1p.

   N. fol. 18 Apr. 1788, New York. Diego de Gardoqui to
   Gov. Sevier (translation). Franklin can be assured that
   the King of Spain wishes to give that state all the
   protection that it can and that Spain does not encourage
   Indian attacks such as those suffered by Franklin. 1p.

N. fol. 18 Apr. 1788, New York. Diego de Gardoqui to
Elizah Robertson (translation). Mr. White has brought a
letter from Cumberland detailing Indian attacks. Spain
has had nothing to do with these incidents. The King only
wishes to help the western area. 1p.

Ap. 4 (no. 26). 21 Oct. 1785, New York. Diego de Gardoqui to
el Conde de Floridablanca. 2p. [Encloses 6 documents].

N. fol. 6 Aug. 1785, Savannah. Extract of translated
letter reporting the Southern states' fear that they will
be surrounded by Indian wars. Ga. has sworn testimony
from Indian traders and others explaining why the Cherokees and Creeks do not wish to cede land. 5p.

Ap. 6 (no. 75). 16 Apr. 1786, New York. Diego de Gardoqui
to el Conde de Floridablanca. Gardoqui encloses the Cherokee-
American treaty and notes that Indian friendship lasts only
as long as gifts are forthcoming. 23p. [Encloses 2 documents].

N. fol. 24 Mar. 1786, New York. Translation of newspaper
article from the *Gazeta de Nueva York* containing the Treaty
of Hopewell between the United States and the Cherokees.
4p.

Ap. 6 (no. 91). 18 June 1786, New York. Diego de Gardoqui to
el Conde de Floridablanca. Gardoqui already sent a copy of the
Cherokee treaty with the United States. He is now forwarding
copies of three other American treaties with the Chickasaws,
Choctaws, and Shawnees. 4p. [Encloses 3 documents].

Ap. 6 (no. 100). 19 June 1786, New York. Diego de Gardoqui
to el Conde de Floridablanca. 5p. [Encloses 10 documents].

Anexo 6. 19 Apr. 1786, Pensacola. Arturo O'Neill to
Diego de Gardoqui. Creeks, Choctaws, Chickasaws, and
part of the Cherokees are ready to resist any American
invasion designed to take Indian land. 3p.

Anexo 9. 28 Apr. 1786, Little Tallassee. Alex. McGillivray to Gen. Zéspedes (copy). Creeks dispute legality
of land cessions to the Americans and request Spanish help.
The Americans do not know whether Spain will agree to the
boundaries established by England and the United States.
As a result, the Americans sent commissioners last summer
to the Creeks, Cherokees, Choctaws, and Chickasaws to
acquire land, but the commissioners were unsuccessful. 9p.

Ap. 7 (no. 123). 28 Oct. 1786, New York. Diego de Gardoqui to
el Conde de Floridablanca. 2p. [Encloses 2 documents].

N. fol. 21 Oct. 1786, [New York]. *Gazeta de Nueva York*
(translation). Newspaper reprints letters and reports
containing information on Cherokee meetings with the
Shawnees and other tribes above the Ohio River. 8p.

ESTADO/3894   AMERICAN AFFAIRS: 1788-1791

Ap. 3 (no. 291). 24 Oct. 1788, New York. Diego de Gardoqui to
el Conde de Floridablanca. 3p. [Encloses 9 documents].

No. 2. 14 Nov. 1787. Secretary of War to Brig. Gen.
Harmar (extract of translated letter). There is a great
deal of discontent in the West, particularly in Cumberland
and Kentucky. The secretary wants specific information
on this discontent and orders that trusted individuals
be sent to Ky. and Franklin to report on situation. 4p.

No. 3. 15 June 1788, Ft. Harmar. Extract of translated
letter from Brig. Gen. Harmar stating that Lt. Armstrong
has been sent to Franklin to report on the news from that
area. 1p.

No. 4. 28 Apr. 1788, Garrison at the Ohio Rapids. Lt.
Armstrong to Maj. John Willis (translation). Armstrong
saw little evidence of unrest in Franklin and no evidence
that English agents were working in that area. Some
English agents have visited tribes in the area. Franklin
residents are divided into two political factions headed
by John Sevier and John [Fupton?]. A general Indian
conference in Mobile decided to wage war on American
frontiers. 3p.

Ap. 3 (no. 295). 21 Oct. 1788, New York. Diego de Gardoqui
to el Conde de Floridablanca. Gardoqui forwards some correspondence from Gov. Sevier. 4p. [Encloses 2 documents].

N. fol. 12 Sept. 1788, Franklin. John Sevier to James
Gardoqui (copy). Franklin's residents look forward to an
alliance with Spain. Sevier wants financial and material
aid from Spain. Now is the most favorable time to send
aid since N.C. has not yet approved the new national
constitution and is not a member of the union. 4p.
English.

N. fol. 12 Sept. 1788, Franklin. John Sevier to James
Gardoqui (copy). Franklin has completed a successful war
against the Cherokees, driving them out of Franklin's
territory. The Cherokees, however, might try to obtain
help from the Creeks, Choctaws, and Chickasaws. Sevier
would appreciate Spanish assistance in persuading other
tribes not to aid the Cherokees, who brought war upon
themselves. 2p. *English.*

Ap. 3 (no. 296). 24 Oct. 1788, New York. Diego de Gardoqui
to el Conde de Floridablanca. 4p. [Encloses 2 documents].

N. fol. 10 Oct. 1788, New York. Diego de Gardoqui to
Esteban Miró (copy). James Sevier, son of John Sevier in
Franklin, visited Gardoqui with two messages from his
father. Gardoqui informed Sevier that he could count on
Spain's protection and on aid from Louisiana. 2p.

Ap. 4 (no. 53). 4 Dec. 1791, Philadelphia. José de Jaudenes
and José Ignacio de Viar to el Conde de Floridablanca (duplicate).
American Senate and President ratified the treaty concluded with
the Cherokees in July. 2p. [Encloses 1 document].

N. fol. 2 July 1791, Holston River. *Tratado de paz y
amistad hecho ... entre [los Estados Unidos y la nación
Cherokee]* (translation). Signatories include William
Blount, Chuleoah, Squollecuttah, Occunna, Enoleh, Nontuaka,
Tekakiska, Chutloh, Tuckaseh, Kateh, Kunnochatutloh,
Cauguillehanah, Chesquotteleneh, Chickasawtehe, Tuskegatehe,
Kulsatehe, Tinkshalene, Sawutteh, Aukuah, Oosenaleh,
Kenotetah, Kanetetoka, Yonewatleh, Long Will, Kunoskeskie,
Nenetooyah, Chuquilatague, Koolaguah, Toowayelloh, Jah-
leoonoyehka, Kinnesah, Tullotehe, Kaalouske, Kulsatehe,
Auquotague, Talohteske, Cheakoneske, Keshukaune, Toonau-
nailoh, Teesteke, Robin McClemore, Skyuka, John Thompson,
and James Cery. 13p.

Ap. 5 (no. 72). 26 Mar. 1792, Philadelphia. José de Jaudenes
and José Ignacio de Viar to el Conde de Floridablanca. 8p.
[Encloses 1 document].

N. fol. 30 Jan. 1792, St. Augustine. Juan Nepomuceno de
Quesada to José de Jaudenes and José Ignacio de Viar (copy).
Quesada has received a newspaper with news about the
American-Cherokee treaty. 3p.

Ap. 4 (no. 245). 10 Aug. 1794, New York. José de Jaudenes to
el Duque de la Alcudia (coded). 4p. [Encloses 1 document].

No. 245. 10 Aug. 1794, New York. José de Jaudenes to
[el Duque de la Alcudia] (decoded). Through the use of
trickery and money, the Spanish envoy has influenced the
Cherokee delegation in Philadelphia to make a different
treaty with the United States from that which was intended.
Kentuckians are unhappy with this treaty and it will be
very easy to cause that state to break away from the
Confederation. 4p.

Ap. 4 (no. 248). 31 Oct. 1794, Philadelphia. José de Jaudenes
to el Duque de la Alcudia. A Cherokee delegation is visiting
Philadelphia to conclude a treaty with the United States. In
spite of American efforts to prevent a meeting, this delegation
met with Spanish diplomats and were advised on their negotiations with the United States. 7p. [Encloses 8 documents].

No. 2. 26 June 1794, New York. José de Jaudenes to John
Thompson (translation). Jaudenes applauds the Cherokee
decision in the new treaty with the United States to
reject American protection and to refuse granting the
United States exclusive trading rights with the tribe.
Jaudenes also approves postponing the question of tribal
borders until next spring. 2p.

ESTADO/3895BIS   (CONT'D)

No. 3. 26 June 1794, New York. José de Jaudenes and José
Ignacio de Viar to Little Turkey, Great Chief of the
Cherokee Nation. Spanish envoys are pleased that they had
the opportunity to meet some Cherokee leaders. Spain hopes
that the tribes will sign no agreement with the United
States contrary to earlier treaties made with Spain. If
the tribe places itself under American protection, the
Cherokees would separate themselves from Spain and violate
earlier treaties. 5p.

No. 4. 27 June 1794, Philadelphia. John Thompson to
José de Jaudenes (translation). Cherokees agreed to a
treaty with the United States before Jaudenes's letter
reached Thompson. The question of tribal borders will
not be decided until the tribe is consulted. The Cherokees
did not place themselves under American protection nor
did the tribe make any agreement concerning trade. 2p.

No. 5. 28 June 1794, Philadelphia. John Thompson to José
de Jaudenes (translation). Thompson thanks the Spanish
envoy for money sent him via Diego Morphy. 1p.

No. 6. 28 June 1794, Philadelphia. Receipt from John
Thompson to [José de Jaudenes] (translation). Thompson
received 500 *pesos fuertes en plata* [silver]. 1p.

N. fol. *Real orden* to [José de Jaudenes] with the King's
approval of Jaudenes's handling of the Cherokee delegation
in Philadelphia. The King orders Jaudenes to inform the
gov. of New Orleans about the affair. 1p.

Ap. 5 (no. 259). 31 Oct. 1794, Philadelphia. José de Jaudenes
to el Duque de la Alcudia. 3p. [Encloses 9 documents].

No. 8. 28 June 1794, New York. José de Jaudenes and José
Ignacio de Viar to Luis de las Casas. Jaudenes and Viar
have prevented the United States from placing the Cherokees
under American protection, acquiring exclusive trading
rights, and fixing boundaries with the tribe. 4p.

No. 9. 28 June 1794, New York. José de Jaudenes and José
Ignacio de Viar to Luis de las Casas. Thompson, a Cherokee
interpreter, has asked that the governors of Louisiana
and St. Augustine write to him in the future when they wish
to correspond with the Cherokees. 1p.

No. 1. 14 June 1794, Philadelphia. José Ignacio de Viar
and José de Jaudenes to Juan Nepomuceno de Quesada. Viar
and Jaudenes describe their efforts to keep the Americans
from winning over tribes friendly to Spain. A Cherokee
delegation arrived in Philadelphia recently in response
to the talks given to the tribe by Seagrove. Viar and
Jaudenes protested Seagrove's actions to the American
president and to the Cherokee leaders. Quesada should
pressure the tribe not to ratify any agreement forced
upon their leaders that is contrary to Spain's interests.
4p.

ESTADO/3895BIS (CONT'D)

No. 4. 2 July 1794, New York. José de Jaudenes and José
Ignacio de Viar to Juan Nepomuceno de Quesada. Jaudenes
and Viar explain their contacts with the Cherokee delegation that was in Philadelphia to negotiate a treaty with
the United States. It is very important that Quesada
send an agent to the Cherokees to counteract the influence
of the new American agent assigned to the tribe. The
Spanish envoys have managed to frustrate American intentions in Philadelphia. 3p.

Ap. 7 (no. 273). 30 Nov. 1794, Philadelphia. José de Jaudenes
to el Duque de la Alcudia. 5p. [Encloses 5 documents].

No. 7. 12 Aug. 1794, State Department. Edmund Randolph
to Commissioner of His Catholic Majesty (translation).
Seagrove has responded to the Spanish complaints about
his conduct. Randolph attaches Seagrove's letter. 1p.

N. fol. [James] Seagrove to Sec. of State (translation).
Seagrove denies the Spanish charges that he encouraged
the Indians against Spain. There is abundant proof that
Spanish representatives have urged the tribes to war on
the United States. Seagrove never made a talk to the
Cherokees since he does not speak their language. His
only contact with that tribe has been in Creek territory,
where he advised them to live in peace and to send a
delegation to visit the President of the United States.
5p.

No. 1. 11 June 1794, Philadelphia. José de Jaudenes and
José Ignacio de Viar to Edmund Randolph. The Cherokees
have been under Spanish protection since 1784. Seagrove
has tried to separate the tribe from its Spanish allegiance
and has incorrectly told the tribe that Spain and the
United States are negotiating the tribe's problems. 6p.

No. 10. 16 Aug. 1794, New York. José de Jaudenes to
Edmund Randolph. Jaudenes promises additional proof of
Seagrove's misconduct. Any treaty with Spanish Indians
which does not have the King's approval is invalid. 3p.

ESTADO/3896   AMERICAN AFFAIRS: 1795

Ap. 4 (no. 302). 29 July 1795, Philadelphia. José Ruiz de
Santayana to el Duque de la Alcudia (duplicate). Ruiz has
received the King's approval of actions taken towards the
Cherokee chiefs. 1p.

ESTADO/3897   AMERICAN AFFAIRS: 1798-1800

Ap. 1 (no. 95). 30 Jan. 1798, Philadelphia. Carlos Martínez
de Yrujo to el Príncipe de la Paz. American land speculators
are never happy with their country's borders. Speculators in
Ga. and the two Carolinas have bought land in the west that
belongs to the Creeks and Cherokees. These two tribes have

ESTADO/3897 (CONT'D)

    complained bitterly to the United States and have even signed
a treaty to protect their land. For political reasons, the
government does not wish to honor these treaties. Instead
the Americans wish to draw up new ones. 5p.

    Ap. 3 (no. 109). 11 Aug. 1798, Philadelphia. Carlos Martínez
de Yrujo to el Príncipe de la Paz. 6p. [Encloses 1 document].

        N. fol. 17 July 1798, Philadelphia. Extract from *La
Aurora* containing a report from Knoxville that the
Americans plan to erect a fort in an area claimed by the
Indians. The treaty negotiations in Tellico between the
United States and the Cherokees have been suspended, both
sides agreeing to meet again in September. 2p.

    Ap. 3 (n. fol.). 17 Sept. 1798, Philadelphia. Carlos Martínez
de Yrujo to el Príncipe de la Paz (duplicate). 5p. [Encloses
8 documents].

        No. 3. 1 Sept. 1798, Philadelphia. Carlos Martínez de
Yrujo to Timothy Pickering. Americans are suspicious that
Spain has encouraged the Indians to oppose running the
boundary line through their territory. These suspicions
are unfounded since the Indians always distrust those who
enter their land to divide it. Spanish correspondence
with the Cherokees proves Spain's good faith. 5p.

        No. 5. 5 Sept. 1798, Philadelphia. Carlos Martínez de
Yrujo to Timothy Pickering. Yrujo discusses treaty
obligations and the difficulties of running the boundary
line along the thirty-first parallel. Spain has done
all she could to see that the line is run without opposition from neighboring Indian tribes. 6p.

            N. fol. 1 July 1798, New Orleans. Manuel Gayoso de
Lemos to Carlos Martínez de Yrujo (extract). Gayoso
has sent a letter to Bloody Fellow. 1p.

            N. fol. 4 Nov. 1797, New Orleans. Manuel Gayoso de
Lemos to Chiefs and Warriors of the Cherokees.
Bloody Fellow has expressed his tribe's distress over
the new borders which favor the Americans. Although
Spain embraced the Cherokees, the tribe felt free to
make a treaty with the United States. Now the Cherokees must keep their word. They cannot expect to
receive hunting land west of the Miss. R. but Spain
would grant the tribe crop land there. 3p. *English.*

ESTADO/3898   LETTERS ABOUT LOUSIANA: 1785-1794

    Exp. 1 (no. 55 *de preferencia*). 27 Oct. 1785, Mexico. El
Conde de Gálvez to José de Gálvez. [Same as AGI SD/2550/fol.
152]. 8p. [Encloses 3 documents].

No. 2. 10 July 1785, Little Tallassee. Alex. McGillivray to [Miró]. [Same as AGI SD/2550/fol. 157]. 8p.

No. 1. 24 July 1785, Pensacola. Alex. McGillivray to Gov. O'Neill. [Same as AGI SD/2550/fol. 155]. 5p.

N. fol. 8 May 1786, Aranjuez. *Real orden* to Gov. Zéspedes and el Conde de Gálvez stating the King's concern over the Indians and guaranteeing protection for the tribes if they stay in Spanish territory. 2p.

Exp. 1 (no. 72). 26 Jan. 1786, Mexico. El Conde de Gálvez to el Marqués de la Sonora. 2p. [Encloses 5 documents].

No. 3. 23 July 1785, Greenwich. Andrew Pickens to Alex. McGillivray. [Translation of AGI Cuba/121/doc. 42]. 1p.

Exp. 4 (no. 2 *reservada*). 29 Nov. 1790, Havana. Luis de las Casas to el Conde de Campo de Alange (duplicate). 9p. [Encloses 9 documents].

No. 9 *reservada*. 7 Oct. 1790, New Orleans. Esteban Miró to Luis de las Casas (copy). Miró forwards letter from James O'Fallon, agent for the S.C. Yazoo Company. Gen. Wilkinson claims that O'Fallon was an Irish priest who formerly served in the American army and could not be trusted. 3p.

N. fol. 16 July 1790, Lexington. James O'Fallon to Esteban Miró (translation). O'Fallon discusses land cessions to the S.C. Yazoo Company, maintaining that all settlements would want to be under Spanish protection. At the beginning, the colony would obtain migrants from the two Carolinas, Georgia, and Franklin. Other western settlements like Kentucky, Franklin, and Cumberland would be forced to follow O'Fallon's example and ally themselves with Spain. 13p.

N. fol. 18 Oct. 1790, Pensacola. Arturo O'Neill to Luis de las Casas. [Duplicate of AGI Cuba/1445/no. 5]. 4p.

Exp. 5 (no. 8 *reservada*). 25 Feb. 1792, New Orleans. El Barón de Carondelet to el Conde de Floridablanca. 10p. [Encloses 2 documents].

N. fol. 4 Nov. 1791, Frankfort, Kentucky. James Wilkinson to Esteban Miró (translation). Wilkinson laments the lack of correspondence from Miró and suggests that the Indians, who have made the passage from Natchez to Cumberland very dangerous, have captured Miró's letters. The latest Indian attack in that area caused Mr. Walsh to drown in the Tenn. River. 2p.

ESTADO/3898 (CONT'D)

Exp. 5 (no. 9). 1791, Charleston. *Traducción en resumén de un librito yngles que contiene un extracto de los apuntes de la compañia de la Carolina del Sur en el Yazu* (translation). Pamphlet discusses the Carolina Company's claim to the Yazoo territory, mentioning legal title to such areas as Muscle Shoals and other Cherokee territory. 52p.

Exp. 5 (no. 14 *reservada*). 22 Mar. 1792, New Orleans. El Barón de Carondelet to el Conde de Floridablanca. Some 500 Americans have descended the Chickasaw R. to build an establishment between Muscle Shoals and the old French Fort. 2p. [Encloses 3 documents].

Exp. 5 (no. 17 *reservada*). 29 Mar. 1792, New Orleans. El Barón de Carondelet to el Conde de Floridablanca. 3p. [Encloses 2 documents].

> No. 1 *reservada*. 29 Mar. 1792, New Orleans. El Barón de Carondelet to Manuel Gayoso de Lemos (copy). The King has decided to keep the fort at Nogales, making it imperative to complete arrangements rapidly with the Choctaws. Americans are presently busy trying to implement their 1790 treaty with the Creeks, an agreement very detrimental to the King's interest since it places both the Creeks and Cherokees completely within the American borders. Gayoso should convince the Choctaws to join a defensive alliance with the Chickasaws, Creeks, Cherokees, and Shawnees to protect their land from the Americans. 5p.

> No. 2. 23 Mar. 1792, New Orleans. El Barón de Carondelet to Franchimastabe and all the rest of the Choctaw Chiefs and Warriors. [Copy of AGI Cuba/2362/no. 9]. 3p.

Exp. 5 (no. 19 *reservada*). 4 Apr. 1792, New Orleans. El Barón to el Conde de Floridablanca. Carondelet forwards materials concerning American efforts to implement the 1790 Creek treaty. If the Americans attack the Creeks, Spain will aid the tribe with arms and ammunition. It is probable that the Cherokees, Choctaws, and Chickasaws will also assist the tribe. As long as Spain has the Five Southern Tribes in her favor and as long as Havana is ready to send 2,000 troops at a moment's notice, Lousiana can resist whatever hostilities the Americans might plan in this area. 5p. [Encloses 4 documents].

> No. 1. 30 Mar. 1792, New Orleans. El Barón de Carondelet to Arturo O'Neill. [Copy of AGI Cuba/18/doc. 291]. 4p.

> No. 4. 30 Mar. 1792, New Orleans. El Barón de Carondelet to Pedro Olivier. [Same as AGI Cuba/2352/fol. 861]. 5p.

Exp. 5 (no. 21 *reservada*). 14 Apr. 1792, New Orleans. El Barón de Carondelet to el Conde de Floridablanca. 2p. [Encloses 5 documents].

ESTADO/3898 (CONT'D)

N. fol. 14 Apr. 1792, New Orleans. El Barón de Carondelet
to Luis de las Casas (copy). The critical situation in La.
demands that reinforcements be allowed to stay rather than
return to Havana. The colony is constantly threatened by
the new settlements of Ky., Cumberland, and Franklin.
Louisiana also has to contend with French efforts to return
the province to its former owners as well as the danger of
a slave uprising. 9p.

Exp. 5 (no. 23 *reservada*). 17 Apr. 1792, New Orleans. El
Barón de Carondelet to el Conde de Floridablanca. Having learned
that the Americans sent a commissioner to Madrid and London to
negotiate the question of borders, Carondelet wishes the court
to know that the Choctaws have ceded Nogales to Spain. The
Cherokees, Chickasaws, Choctaws, and Creeks have concluded an
alliance making the tribes one nation. 4p. [Encloses 1
document].

Exp. 5 (no. 25 *reservada*). 29 Apr. 1792, New Orleans. El
Barón de Carondelet to el Conde de Floridablanca. 1p.
[Encloses 3 documents].

No. 26 *reservada*. 29 Apr. 1792, New Orleans. El Barón
de Carondelet to Luis de las Casas (copy). The Americans
have made unusually large levies of troops in the West.
War is likely between the Americans and Creeks. If a war
erupts, Carondelet expects that the Cherokees, Choctaws,
Chickasaws, and Shawnees will participate. 3p.

Exp. 5 (no. 26 *reservada*). 4 May 1792, New Orleans. El Barón
de Carondelet to el Conde de Floridablanca. As long as Spanish
commerce with the tribes is carried out by English companies,
Spain faces possible Indian hostilities if war breaks out with
Great Britain. Free trade, however, would encourage many
Spanish companies to trade with the Choctaws, Chickasaws,
Creeks, and Cherokees. If the Crown chooses not to grant free
trade, it is indispensable that Panton be allowed to establish
a post at Nogales to trade with the Choctaws and Chickasaws.
If Panton is not given this permission, these tribes will take
their furs to the Americans living in the Cherokee and Cumberland
areas. 6p. [Encloses 5 documents].

N. fol. 3 Apr. 1792, Natchez. Esteban Minor. *Diario
del teniente dn. Esteban Minor ... comisionado [para ir
a la nación chacta].* Diary covers a trip from 13 Mar. to
3 Apr. 1792 and reports a visit of a Creek and Cherokee
delegation to the Choctaws. 14p.

Exp. 5 (no. 28 *reservada*). 22 May 1792, New Orleans. El Barón
de Carondelet to el Conde de Floridablanca. Carondelet forwards
documents concerning the treaty with the Choctaws and Chickasaws
over Nogales. A war between the Creeks and Americans will
probably bring the Cherokees, Chickasaws, and Choctaws into
the fray. The Americans would be fighting the four most powerful tribes on the continent. 4p. [Encloses 2 documents].

ESTADO/3898 (CONT'D)

Exp. 5 (no. 1 *reservada*). 10 June 1792, New Orleans. El
Barón de Carondelet to el Conde de Aranda. [Same as AGI Cuba/
2362/no. 1 *reservada*]. 10p.

Exp. 5 (no. 2 *reservada*). 11 June 1792, New Orleans. El
Barón de Carondelet to el Conde de Aranda. 4p. [Encloses 8
documents].

> N. fol. 12 May 1792, Little Tallassee. Alex. McGillivray
> to Arturo O'Neill. [Translation of AGI Cuba/205/fol. 699].
> 1p.

Exp. 5 (no. 3 *reservada*). 11 June 1792, New Orleans. El
Barón de Carondelet to el Conde de Aranda. 4p. [Encloses 21
documents].

> No. 86. 29 May 1792, Natchez. *Relación* from Manuel
> Gayoso de Lemos to el Barón de Carondelet (copy). Gayoso
> describes the informal congress at Natchez with the
> Chickasaws. Franchimastabe [Chickasaw Chief] claimed that
> the Cherokees, Talapooses, Choctaws, and Chickasaws had
> made an alliance and were now one nation. The head of
> this alliance was the King of the Chickasaws. This is why
> the Cherokees sent him strings of beads (*las sartas de
> avalorios*) to distribute among the tribes. 54p.

Exp. 5 (no. 4 *reservada*). 7 July 1792, New Orleans. El Barón
de Carondelet to el Conde de Aranda (duplicate). Carondelet
forwards an agreement recently made with Alex. McGillivray,
supplementing the 1784 treaty with the Creeks. Spanish provinces
have taken precautions because of the American military build-
up in the West and because of the continued hostilities by
Cumberland against New Madrid. 15p. [Encloses 2 documents].

Exp. 5 (no. 5 *reservada*). 25 July 1792, New Orleans. El
Barón de Carondelet to el Conde de Aranda. Americans have
threatened the Chickasaws and Choctaws. Gov. Blount supports
efforts to break these two tribes away from Spain. 10p.
[Encloses 6 documents].

> N. fol. 17 Feb. 1792, Philadelphia. Henry Knox to Chiefs
> and Warriors of the Choctaw Nation (translation). Gen.
> Washington is satisfied with the talk sent by the Cherokees
> last fall. Although the United States is at peace with the
> Creeks, Cherokees, Chickasaws, and Choctaws, it is fighting
> the Northern Indians, like the Kickapoos, who have misbe-
> haved. For this reason, the Americans have raised an
> army in the West. 5p.

> N. fol. 27 Apr. 1792, Knoxville. Wm. Blount to Chiefs
> and Warriors of the Choctaw Nation (translation). The
> letter from the Sec. of War was originally meant to be
> delivered to the Choctaws by Mr. Shaw, who has been
> detained in working with the Cherokees. Blount, therefore,
> sent the letter to the Choctaws via Cumberland. 3p.

N. fol. 10 May 1792, Knoxville. Wm. Blount to Chiefs and
Captains of the Choctaw Nation (translation). Blount asks
the Choctaws to visit Nashville to celebrate a friendship
treaty. Americans have no intention of asking for more
land. Chickasaws will also be invited. 4p.

N. fol. 5 June 1792. Translated letter from Thomas
James extending an invitation to come to [Nashville] to
celebrate a treaty of friendship. 2p.

N. fol. Translated letter to Franchimastabe and the
Englishman Wel [Welbank?] among the Choctaws asking that
Franchimastabe send a representative to the Cumberland
meeting if he cannot attend himself. 2p.

Exp. 5 (no. 6 *reservada*). 31 July 1792, New Orleans. El
Barón de Carondelet to el Conde de Aranda. Carondelet forwards
copies of some letters to McGillivray in which the Americans
try to win the tribe over. The Americans are doing the same
with the Choctaws and Chickasaws at Cumberland. The Indians
will follow the nation that provides them with goods. American
pretensions that they are not interested in Indian land is
belied by their usurpation of two-thirds of the Creek land and
even a larger part of Cherokee territory. 8p. [Encloses
4 documents].

Exp. 5 (no. 7 *reservada*). 31 July 1792, New Orleans. El
Barón de Carondelet to el Conde de Aranda. 3p. [Encloses 2
documents].

No. 2. 22 July 1792, Mobile. Alex. McGillivray to el
Barón de Carondelet. [Translation of AGI Cuba/2371/
doc. 40]. 4p.

Exp. 5 (no. 10 *reservada*). 15 Aug. 1792, New Orleans. El
Barón de Carondelet to el Conde de Aranda. The Creek Treaty
of 1790 with the United States is undesirable and violates
earlier treaties with Spain. It will be impossible to keep
tribes united under Spanish guidance if the 1790 Treaty is
put into effect. Americans claim that the Talapooses, Choctaws,
Chickasaws, Shawnees, and Cherokees are all within their borders,
leaving none to Spain. 16p. [Encloses 5 documents].

No. 1. 5 July 1792, Havana. Luis de las Casas to el
Barón de Carondelet (copy). Carondelet's desire to
publicly proclaim Spain's intention to maintain the Indians
in their present homes is already the King's policy, but
he must restrain the tribes from hostilities against the
Americans. Only if tribes are attacked can Spain help
them. It is important to keep tribes united. 3p.

No. 3. 1 May 1786, Little Tallassee. Alex. McGillivray
to Esteban Miró. [Translation of AGI Cuba/2352/no. 14/
encl.]. 12p.

ESTADO/3898 (CONT'D)

Exp. 5 (no. 13 *reservada*). 10 Sept. 1792, New Orleans. El Barón de Carondelet to el Conde de Aranda. 2p. [Encloses 8 documents].

> N. fol. 30 Aug. 1792, Pensacola. *Declaración* from Thomas Young that he knew Wm. Augustus Bowles when Bowles was in Halifax, Nova Scotia, in 1790 traveling with some Creeks and Cherokees. Bowles and the Indians were preparing to leave for England. In 1791, in Providence, Bowles asked Young to carry him and his followers to the Florida, which Young did. 7p.

Exp. 5 (no. 14 *reservada*, no.1). 10 Sept. 1792, House of Simón Favre, interpreter. Juan de la Villebeuvre to Manuel Gayoso de Lemos. [Same as AGI Cuba/177B/no. 14 *reservada*/encl. no. 1]. 5p. [Cover letter no. 14 *reservada* missing].

> No. 2. 12 Sept. 1792, Boukfouka. Juan de la Villebeuvre to el Barón de Carondelet. [Same as AGI Cuba/177B/no. 14 *reservada*/encl. no. 2].

Exp. 5. 1 Oct. 1792, New Orleans. El Barón de Carondelet. *Indice de las cartas reservadas que ... dirige el Barón de Carondelet[al exmo sr. Conde de Aranda]*. Index includes a summary of letter no. 14 [10 Sept. 1792] concerning a meeting between the Chickasaws, Choctaws, and the Americans at Cumberland. 2p.

Exp. 5 (no. 20 *reservada*). 8 Nov. 1792, New Orleans. El Barón de Carondelet to el Conde de Aranda. Carondelet has tried to form a defensive confederation among tribes in the south and in the north to contain the Americans within their borders and to protect Mexico. If these tribes unite, Spain will have nothing to fear from the Americans since it will be many years before they could contest these tribes. Carondelet rejects the American claims to such Spanish territory as Nogales, Natchez, Tombigbee, and the navigation of the Mississippi. He also rejects their claim to exclusive rights to treat with the Creeks, Cherokees, Shawnees, Choctaws, and Chickasaws. 10p. [Encloses 2 documents].

> N. fol. 12 Oct. 1792, Boukfouka. Juan de la Villebeuvre to el Barón de Carondelet (translation). Villebeuvre felt at first that a league of Indian nations would be very hard to form, especially with the Northern tribes who live so far away and are always fighting among themselves. Yet it might be possible. Villebeuvre wrote Carondelet earlier about the visit of a Chickasaw chief with talk and strings of beads *(sartas de avalorios)* from the Talapooses, Shawnees, Cherokees, Abnakis, Houis, Ouyatanons [Weas], Masentens [Mascoutens], Hauas, Chippewas, Sacs, Kickapoos, Theaquies, Pauates [Paiutes?], and Chipcas for the Chickasaws and Choctaws. The messages warned the tribes not to let happen to them what had happened to the Cherokees. 7p.

ESTADO/3898 (CONT'D)

Exp. 5 (no. 22 *reservada*). 13 Nov. 1792, New Orleans. El
Barón de Carondelet to el Conde de Aranda. Cherokee leaders
have just arrived to negotiate the defensive alliance of tribes
that Carondelet had been advocating. Carondelet is expecting
at any moment the King of the Chickasaws with word from the
Creeks, Cherokees, Lower Shawnees, and various Northern tribes
accepting the alliance. Chickasaws seem to be holding back,
but the Creeks and Cherokees have threatened them if they do
not join. The Cherokees have begun a war against Cumberland.
Bloody Fellow persuaded the Americans to agree to return some
Cherokee land, but it is not enough for the tribe. 9p.
[Encloses 4 documents].

>   No. 1. 5 Nov. 1792, Pensacola. Arturo O'Neill to el
>   Barón de Carondelet (copy). McDonald, six chiefs, twenty-
>   five additional Cherokees, and two whites have arrived in
>   Pensacola. Some of these have been sent on to New Orleans.
>   Bloody Fellow is the most feared leader of his nation and
>   the one who expects the most gifts. Cherokees, Creeks,
>   and Chanes have attacked an American fort. 3p.

>   No. 2. 6 Oct. 1792, Cherokees. John McDonald to Wm.
>   Panton. [Translation of AGI Cuba/177B/no. 22 *reservada/*
>   encl. no. 2]. 4p.

>   No. 3. 6 Nov. 1792, Pensacola. Wm. Panton to el Barón
>   de Carondelet. [Same as AGI Cuba/177B/no. 22 *reservada/*
>   encl. no. 3]. 2p.

Exp. 5 (no. 23 *reservada*). 20 Nov. 1792, New Orleans. El
Barón de Carondelet to el Conde de Aranda. Led by Bloody
Fellow, the Cherokee chiefs in New Orleans have petitioned
Spain to reestablish two forts occupied by the French -- the
first at Tombigbee and the second at Muscle Shoals. These two
forts would allow Spain to dominate both banks of the Miss. R.
up to the Ohio River. The Americans also realize the importance
of these posts and have been trying for years to rebuild them.
8p. [Encloses 2 documents].

Exp. 5 (no. 24 *reservada*). 28 Nov. 1792, New Orleans. El Barón
de Carondelet to el Conde de Aranda. Franchimastabe, the King of
the Chickasaws, Kilikaski (leader of the Creeks at Cussitas),
26 Choctaw chiefs, and 1,094 warriors and captains met in New
Orleans. The Cherokees already in the city participated also.
Carondelet spoke for his version of an Indian confederation to
protect Indian land and for forming a permanent congress in
the spring. The Cherokees led by Bloody Fellow spoke eloquently
about the American intentions to take all Indian land. Carondelet thought that the Northern tribes could be brought into
the confederation through the influence of the Creeks and
Cherokees. 9p. [Encloses 2 documents].

>   No. 2. 24 Nov. 1792, New Orleans. El Barón de Carondelet
>   to Chiefs, Warriors, and the rest of the Cherokee Nation.
>   [Same as AGI Cuba/2353/fol. 752]. 2p.

ESTADO/3898 (CONT'D)

Exp. 5 (no. 25 *reservada*). 15 Dec. 1792, New Orleans. El
Barón de Carondelet to el Conde de Aranda. [Same as AGI Cuba/
177B/no. 25 *reservada*]. 5p. [Encloses 3 documents].

No. 1. 15 Nov. 1792, Little Tallassee. Alex. McGillivray
to el Barón de Carondelet. [Same as AGI Cuba/177B/no. 25
reservada/encl. no. 1]. 5p.

Exp. 5 (no. 26 *reservada*). 8 Jan. 1793, New Orleans. El Barón
de Carondelet to el Conde de Aranda. An American army in Ky.
is preparing for an expedition to expel the Cherokees from the
Tenn. and Cumberland River area. Other information suggests
the purpose of the American army is to build a fort at Muscle
Shoals. Carondelet has made defense plans if the Americans
attempt either. 12p. [Encloses 3 documents].

N. fol. 30 Mar. 1793, Aranjuez. *Real orden* to the Gov.
of New Orleans approving Carondelet's preparations in
case the Americans attempt to occupy Muscle Shoals. 2p.

Exp. 5 (no. 27 *reservada*). 8 Jan. 1793, New Orleans. El Barón
de Carondelet to el Conde de Aranda. 3p. [Encloses 1 document].

N. fol. 3 Dec. 1792, New Madrid. Thomas Portell to el
Barón de Carondelet. [Same as AGI Cuba 1447/no. 62
reservada/encl. no. 1]. 3p.

Exp. 5 (no. 1). 28 Feb. 1793, New Orleans. El Barón de
Carondelet to el Duque de Alcudia. [Same as AGI Cuba/178A/no. 1
reservada]. 7p. [Encloses 3 documents].

Exp. 5 (no. 2 *reservada*). 9 Mar. 1793, New Orleans. El Barón
de Carondelet to el Duque de Alcudia. The death of McGillivray
could help the Americans in their designs against Muscle Shoals
and other Spanish positions. Moreover, the Chickasaws may now
ask for help from Cumberland in their dispute with the Creeks.
6p. [Encloses 5 documents].

No. 2. 5 Mar. 1793, New Orleans. El Barón de Carondelet
to Manuel Gayoso de Lemos. [Copy of AGI Cuba/2353/fol.
801]. 4p.

No. 3. 26 Feb. 1793, New Orleans. El Barón de Carondelet
to [Manuel Gayoso de Lemos] (copy). *Puntos sobre los
quales se deberá tratar en el congreso de los indios.*
Carondelet lists eleven points to consider with the Creeks,
Cherokees, Choctaws, and Chickasaws. Borders between the
Cherokees and Americans set in Treaty of 1785 will be
strictly obeyed. 6p.

Exp. 5 (no. 5 *reservada*). 14 Jan. 1794, Madrid. El Conde del
Campo de Alange to el Duque de la Alcudia. King has been
informed about the representation from the gov. of New Orleans
concerning defense of province. The Count asks for information
concerning the congress of Choctaws, Chickasaws, Creeks, and
Cherokees. 9p. [Enclosure of no. 5 *reservada*].

ESTADO/3898 (CONT'D)

Exp. 5 (no. 8 *reservada*). 24 May 1793, New Orleans. El Barón de Carondelet to el Duque de la Alcudia. Carondelet forwards a representation from the Cherokees, who are presently at war with the Americans. The Americans are attempting to take what hunting land the tribe has left between the Cumberland and Tenn. Rivers. Cumberland inhabitants and the Philadelphia newspapers have falsely blamed Carondelet for this conflict with the Cherokees. 5p. [Encloses 2 documents].

    N. fol. 5 Apr. 1793, Cherokee Nation. John McDonald, Spider of Lookout Mountain, Water Hunter, Richard Justice, Badgers Mother Warrior, Wm. Shawney to el Barón de Carondelet (translation). Cherokees protest American seizure of Cherokee land and ask for Spanish help. Cumberland has been a great source of trouble for the Cherokees. 3p.

Exp. 5 (no. 9 *reservada*). 24 May 1793, New Orleans. El Barón de Carondelet to el Duque de la Alcudia. [Same as AGI Cuba/ 2363/no. 9 *reservada*]. 7p. [Encloses 4 documents].

    No. 1. 7 May 1793, New Madrid. Thomas Portell to el Barón de Carondelet (copy). Boat has arrived from Cumberland carrying the son of Gen. Robertson and destined for the Chickasaws with a cargo of corn. Americans plan to build an establishment in Barrancas de Margot. 4p.

    N. fol. 23 Apr. 1793, Nashville. James Robertson to Thomas Portell (translation). Robertson asks Portell to pass along letter to the Delawares. A group of Chickasaws are now in Nashville. 2p.

    No. 2. 21 May 1793, New Orleans. El Barón de Carondelet to James Robertson. [Same as AGI Cuba/2363/no. 8 *reservada/* encl.]. 3p.

    N. fol. 31 Aug. 1793, San Ildefonso. *Real orden* to el Barón de Carondelet approving his zeal in dealing with problems of the Chickasaws and Cherokees. 1p.

Exp. 5 (no. 10 *reservada*). 11 June 1793, New Orleans. El Barón de Carondelet to el Duque de la Alcudia. Carondelet forwards a copy of a small land cession by the Choctaws to build a Spanish fort. Among other things, this fort will help maintain contact with the Cherokees. The Chickasaws, because of the efforts of Gov. Blount, generally favor the United States, but they are unhappy with the prospects of this new fort. 6p. [Encloses 2 documents].

Exp. 5 (no. 13). 31 July 1793, New Orleans. El Barón de Carondelet to el Duque de la Alcudia (duplicate). Since the death of McGillivray, the Creeks have been confused about their attitude towards the Americans and towards the proposed permanent congress of tribes allied to Spain. 5p. [Encloses 4 documents].

ESTADO/3898 (CONT'D)

No. 1. 14 June 1793, Mongulacha. Pedro Olivier to el
Barón de Carondelet (copy). Olivier discusses a meeting
to consider the Spanish plan of confederation. Kilikaski
could have been a great leader of the Cussitas had he not
left some ten years ago to live with the Cherokees. 17p.

Exp. 5 (no. 15 *reservada*). 27 Aug. 1793, New Orleans. El Barón
de Carondelet to el Duque de la Alcudia. Carondelet explains
the latest developments on negotiations with the Indians to
form a defensive alliance and on efforts to frustrate Gov.
Blount and Brig. Robertson who want to build an establishment
at Barrancas de Margot. Carondelet fears that the American
army will strike at the Cherokees once the Northern Indians are
defeated. Spain should help this tribe because of its strategic
location. 5p. [Encloses 3 documents].

No. 1. 25 July 1793, Nogales. Manuel Gayoso de Lemos to el
Barón de Carondelet. [Same as AGI Cuba/178A/no. 7 *sobre
la asamblea de indios*]. 8p.

No. 2. 15 Aug. 1793, New Orleans. El Barón de Carondelet
to Manuel Gayoso de Lemos. [Same as AGI Cuba/2353/fol.
834]. 6p.

Exp. 5 (no. 18 *reservada*). 27 Sept. 1793, New Orleans. El
Barón de Carondelet to el Duque de la Alcudia. Carondelet
reports all the news since Apr. 11 concerning the Creeks, Choctaws, Chickasaws, Cherokees, and the Indian alliance. Carondelet
fears that the Cherokees are about to begin a war because of the
assassination of tribal leaders inspired by Gen. Blount. It
has been confirmed that part of the American army has marched
towards the Great Bend in the Tenn. R. in order to build an
establishment at Muscle Shoals and to attack the Cherokees from
behind. This would cut that tribe off from Spanish territory
and from assistance by other tribes. 18p. [Encloses 2
documents].

No. 10. 12 Sept. 1793, Natchez. Manuel Gayoso de Lemos
to el Barón de Carondelet (copy). Gayoso acknowledges
receiving news from Carondelet about the relations between
the Americans, Creeks, and Cherokees. The commandant at
Nogales notified Gayoso that the Talapooses have arrived
and were surprised that the assembly has been postponed
because the Creeks and Cherokees are exposed to attacks
from the Americans. 11p.

Exp. 5 (no. 21 *reservada*). 6 Nov. 1793, New Orleans. El Barón
de Carondelet to el Duque de la Alcudia. 3p. [Encloses 7
documents].

No. 6. 29 Oct. 1793, New Orleans. El Barón de Carondelet
to Manuel Gayoso de Lemos (copy). Carondelet sends a
message to be forwarded to Gen. Wilkinson about the Spanish
need for information from Ky. and Cumberland. 5p.

ESTADO/3898 (CONT'D)

Exp. 5 (no. 22 *reservada*). 5 Dec. 1793, New Orleans. El Barón
de Carondelet to el Duque de la Alcudia. [Same as AGI Cuba/
2353/fol. 730]. 8p. [Encloses 2 documents].

    N. fol. 28 Oct. 1793, Nogales. Manuel Gayoso de Lemos
    et al. Treaty of Nogales. [Same as AGI SD/2563/fol. 8].
    8p.

ESTADO/3899   LETTERS FROM LOUISIANA: 1794-1795

Exp. 1 (no. 26 *reservada*). 24 Jan. 1794, New Orleans. El
Barón de Carondelet to el Duque de la Alcudia. Carondelet
discusses the Treaty of Nogales. Spain needs the Indian tribes
[Cherokees, Creeks, Choctaws, and Chickasaws] to counteract
hostile American activities against Spanish Louisiana and
Florida. 4p. [Encloses 1 document].

    No. 1 (no. 13). 6 Dec. 1793, Natchez. *Relación* from
    Manuel Gayoso to el Barón de Carondelet (copy). Gayoso
    describes the treaty negotiations. The Creek chiefs
    represented the Cherokees. All the tribes attending the
    assembly discussed the Cherokee desire to receive Spanish
    protection. 78p.

Exp. 1 (no. 31 *reservada*). 9 Apr. 1794, New Orleans. El Barón
de Carondelet to el Duque de la Alcudia. The continued hostility of the American western settlements has caused many
difficulties for Spanish possessions. Americans rarely try to
restrain groups like the French, who are plotting against
Spain. Spanish officials, however, have continually refused
to support tribes like the Cherokees, who have many grievances
against the United States. 10p. [Encloses 2 documents].

    N. fol. 20 Mar. 1794, Cloaly. [Louis de] Milfort to el
    Barón de Carondelet. [Same as AGI Cuba/2354/fol. 24].
    17p.

Exp. 1 (no. 44 *reservada*). 18 Aug. 1794, New Orleans. El
Barón de Carondelet to el Duque de la Alcudia. 3p. [Encloses
3 documents].

    N. fol. 8 May 1794, Augusta. James Seagrove to [Creek
    Nation] (translation). Indians have committed a robbery
    along the upper Oconee R. that resulted in the death of
    several Americans. Seagrove hopes that these Indians were
    Cherokees because it means war if they were Creeks. If
    these Indians were Cherokees, the Creeks should punish
    them severely since those actions could be disastrous
    for the Creeks. A Cherokee delegation is in Philadelphia.
    6p.

Exp. 1 (no. 46 *reservada*). 17 Sept. 1794, New Orleans. El
Barón de Carondelet to el Duque de la Alcudia. 3p. [Encloses
4 documents].

ESTADO/3899 (CONT'D)

> N. fol. El Barón de Carondelet to [Commandant of
> Pensacola]. Col. Montgomery from Cumberland has stationed
> himself at the mouth of the Ohio R. with 200 men and has
> detained all the boats destined for New Orleans with
> provisions. An invasion from the Ohio R. would be ex-
> tremely dangerous for posts like St. Louis and Arkansas.
> 1p.

> Exp. 1 (no. 129). 24 Nov. 1794, New Orleans. Report from el
> Barón de Carondelet to el Duque de la Alcudia. The rapid
> increase of Americans west of the Appalachians in areas like
> Cumberland is a grave threat to Spain. One of Spain's best
> weapons against these Americans is the Indian tribes [Choctaws,
> Chickasaws, Creeks, and Cherokees], who bitterly resent the loss
> of land to the Americans and who will always be willing to wage
> the cruelest type of war if rewarded with gifts and weapons.
> Cherokees are important for the defense of the west bank of
> the Mississippi. 97p. [Encloses 5 documents].

> Exp. 2 (no. 56 *reservada*). 12 July 1795, New Orleans. El
> Barón de Carondelet to el Duque de la Alcudia. [Same as AGI
> Cuba/2354/fol. 291]. 2p. [Encloses 7 documents].

> Exp. 2 (no. 58 *reservada*). 1 Sept. 1795, New Orleans. El
> Barón de Carondelet to el Duque de la Alcudia. 4p. [Encloses
> 4 documents].

>> No. 142 *reservada*. 1 Sept. 1795, New Orleans. El Barón
>> de Carondelet to Luis de las Casas (copy). 7p.

>>> No. 1. Daniel McGillivray to el Barón de Carondelet.
>>> [Same as AGI Cuba/2354/fol. 228]. 6p.

> Exp. 2 (no. 60 *reservada*). 25 Sept. 1795, New Orleans. El
> Barón de Carondelet to el Duque de la Alcudia (duplicate).
> 8p. [Encloses 1 document].

>> No. 15 *reservada*. 12 Aug. 1795, San Fernando de las
>> Barrancas. Manuel Gayoso de Lemos to el Barón de
>> Carondelet. [Copy of AGI Cuba/2354/fol. 69]. 24p.

> Exp. 2 (no. 134 *reservada*). 1 May 1795, New Orleans. El
> Barón de Carondlet to Luis de las Casas. [Duplicate of AGI
> Cuba/2354/fol. 397]. 9p.

ESTADO/3900   LETTERS FROM LOUISIANA AND WEST FLORIDA: 1796-1798

> Ap. 3 (no. 6). 20 Oct. 1797, New Orleans. Manuel Gayoso de
> Lemos to el Príncipe de la Paz. 2p. [Encloses 8 documents].

>> N. fol. 20 Oct. 1797, New Orleans. Manuel Gayoso de
>> Lemos to Carlos Martínez de Yrujo. There is unrest among
>> Americans in the Natchez district. Dr. White, congressional
>> representative for Cumberland and Blount's friend, is one
>> of the Americans responsible for the sedition. Gayoso has

known Dr. White for many years, dating back to the efforts
to link Franklin, Cumberland, and the rest of the west with
Spain. 10p.

Ap. 3 (no. 7 *reservada*). 30 Nov. 1797, New Orleans. Manuel
Gayoso de Lemos to el Príncipe de la Paz. Gayoso opposes
measures to economize the exchequer by cutting costs in dealing
with Indian tribes because Spain needs their friendship. The
Ga. frontier Indians, those in the Western and Northwestern
states, the nations of the Upper Louisiana, and the Talapooses,
Choctaws, Chickasaws, and Cherokees form a natural barrier
against the Americans. Bloody Fellow, a Cherokee chief, is now
in New Orleans seeking Spanish help against the Americans, who
have completely cut his tribe off from contact with Spain and
other Indians. 14p.

Ap. 4 (no. 29 *reservada*). 26 Sept. 1798, New Orleans. Manuel
Gayoso de Lemos to el Príncipe de la Paz. 2p. [Encloses 2
documents].

N. fol. 16 Aug. 1798, Pensacola. Carlos Howard to [Manuel
Gayoso de Lemos] (translation). James McQueen reported a
general assembly of Indian leaders (Choctaw, Cherokees,
Creeks, and Chickasaws) near Tuckabatchee. All the tribes
agreed to defend one another against attacks by the whites
and to oppose the surveying of the new border between
Spanish and American territory. 2p.

No. 169. 20 Aug. 1798, Pensacola. Vicente Folch to
Manuel Gayoso de Lemos. Indians oppose the surveying of a
new border between Spanish and American territory. Folch
pointed out to the Creek leaders that those surveying the
line would be both Spaniards and Americans and that they
could not kill the Americans without endangering the
Spaniards. Indians have met in Tuckabatchee and decided
to oppose surveying the line. 4p.

ESTADO/3901   LETTERS FROM LOUISIANA AND WEST FLORIDA 1784-1800

Ap. 1 (no. 7 *reservada*). 1 May 1799, New Orleans. Manuel
Gayoso de Lemos to Francisco de Saavedra. Gayoso complains
about the obstructions that the Intendant Juan Ventura Morales
has placed in Gayoso's way. Among the Intendant's harmful
activities has been his attack on Panton, whose business is
the major reason Spain has the loyalty of the Talapooses,
Choctaws, Chickasaws, and the Cherokees. 20p.

Ap. 3 (no. 22 *reservada*). 13 July 1788, New Orleans. Esteban
Miró to Antonio Valdés. Miró encloses information about the
committee of the American Congress appointed to conduct Indian
affairs. 11p. [Encloses 9 documents].

ESTADO/3901 (CONT'D)

No. 1. 12 June 1788, Little Tallassee. Alex. McGillivray
to Esteban Miró (translation). George Whitefield from S.C.
brought the Creeks news about an American commission
composed of representatives from Ga., N.C., S.C., and an
agent of Congress to negotiate with the Southern tribes.
Congress has a committee in charge of Indian affairs. 7p.

No. 2. *Junta ... a quienes se cometió el conocimiento* [*de
los negocios de los yndios del departamento del sur*]
(translation). There has been some seizures of land belonging to the Talapooses and Cherokees by residents of Ga.
and N. Carolina. This question needs the serious attention
of Congress since it could provoke a general Indian war.
15p.

No. 3. 29 Mar. 1788, Ft. Charlotte. Andrew Pickins and
George Matthews [Mathews] to Alex. McGillivray et al.
[Translation of AGI Cuba/121/doc. 45]. 3p.

No. 4. 4 June 1788, Little Tallassee. Alex. McGillivray
to Gen. Pickins and Mathews (translation). Creeks want
the Americans to withdraw from land that was granted to
the tribe when Ga. was British. The Creeks attacked
various Americans last summer in retaliation for numerous
deaths suffered at the hands of the Georgians. This was
done before the meeting with Dr. White. 9p.

No. 5. 8 July 1788, New Orleans. Esteban Miró to Alex.
McGillivray (copy). Miró has received the documents sent
by McGillivray concerning the negotiations between the
Creeks and the United States. Miró instructs McGillivray
on what can be negotiated with the Americans and reminds
him that Spain has exclusive rights to trade with the
Southern tribes who signed the Treaty of 1784. 6p.

No. 6. 4 June 1788, Pensacola. Arturo O'Neill to Esteban
Miró (copy). O'Neill questions the loyalty of Wm. Panton
and Alex. McGillivray. Both would prefer British rule.
Spanish officials need to keep close watch over McGillivray
who is now trying to conduct a war with Ga. while making
peace with the Americans in Cumberland. 6p.

Ap. 3 (no. 50 *reservada*). 22 May 1790, New Orleans. Esteban
Miró to Antonio Valdés. 9p. [Encloses 6 documents].

No. 1. 26 Jan. 1790, Lexington. James Wilkinson to Esteban
Miró (translation). Wilkinson discusses political situation
in Kentucky. Wilkinson has not seen Dr. White since he
passed through the District of Miró [Cumberland], where he
made some preparations to settle and where he took measures
to keep the promise made to Miró by Brig. Smith of Cumberland. 6p.

ESTADO/3901 (CONT'D)

Ap. 3 (no. 52 *reservada*). 10 Aug. 1790, New Orleans. Esteban Miró to Antonio Valdés. Creeks have complained that Spain does not have paid officials to handle Indian affairs. Creeks have attacked several American flatboats in order to prevent settlements by the Tenn. Company. It is important that Spain maintain a commissioner among the Creeks. The Americans appointed Dr. White to be their superintendent of the Talapooses, Choctaws, and Chickasaws. 11p. [Encloses 3 documents].

> N. fol. 8 May 1790, Little Tallassee. Alex. McGillivray to Esteban Miró (translation). Americans have decided to establish three new settlements along the Miss. River. The Creeks will oppose the one sponsored by the Tenn. Company since this establishment is in Creek territory along the southwestern bank of the Cherokee River. Creek party, accompanied by some Cherokees and Shawnees, attacked a group of Americans in Creek territory. 8p.

ESTADO/3902   LETTERS FROM LOUISIANA: 1789-1799

Ap. 2[3?] (no. 110). 31 Mar. 1797, New Orleans. Juan Ventura Morales to Pedro Varela y Ulloa. Although the Americans have not occupied the sites that they received in the recent treaty with Spain, Indian distrust of the United States has already surfaced. Sixty Cherokees visited New Madrid asking for land in Spanish territory. The Alibamos have made the same request in New Orleans. 4p.

Ap. 6[4?] (no. 2). 20 Jan. 1798, New Orleans. Juan Ventura Morales to el Príncipe de la Paz (duplicate). Without the assistance of Spanish military authorities (who feel that Indian affairs belong exclusively to them), it is impossible for Morales to carry out his responsibilities. Gov. Gayoso asked Morales to send 500 pesos to Pensacola to pay for the customary subsidy to John McDonald, Spanish Commissioner among the Chero-kees. Gayoso noted that his would be the last payment since the Cherokees are now under American rule according to the last treaty. Morales not only ordered McDonald paid but also issued instructions to assist Bloody Fellow. 6p. [Encloses 4 documents].

> No. 1. 18 Oct. 1797, New Orleans. Juan Ventura Morales to Manuel Gayoso de Lemos. Once funds arrive for Pensacola, Morales will issue 500 pesos to Wm. Panton, McDonald's representative in that city. 1p.

> No. 1. 20 Oct. 1797, New Orleans. Juan Ventura Morales to Manuel Gayoso de Lemos. Morales asks whether money for McDonald this year violates the King's directive. 2p.

> No. 2. 19 Oct. 1797, New Orleans. Manuel Gayoso de Lemos to Juan Morales. The 500 pesos requested for McDonald are the payment for this year. 1p.

ESTADO/3902 (CONT'D)

No. 2. 24 Oct. 1797, New Orleans. Manuel Gayoso de Lemos
to Juan Ventura Morales. Gayoso examined the royal orders
concerning Indian gifts that Morales sent the governor.
All possible measures should be taken to reduce Indian
expenses, but Spain must maintain good relations with the
Indians until the Americans take over the area assigned
them in treaty. 3p.

No. 2. 25 Oct. 1797, New Orleans. Manuel Gayoso de Lemos
to Juan Morales. Gayoso will do his best to meet the
King's directives [to cut in Indian expenses], but circumstances are such that Spain cannot afford to have
discontented Indians. It would not be appropriate to cut
Indian subsidies all at once. This would expose Spanish
civilians to Indian retaliation. 2p.

No. 2. 16 Nov. 1797, Pointe Coupée. Manuel Gayoso de
Lemos to Juan Morales. The question of economizing Indian
costs is one that the Gov. takes seriously. Yet it will
take time to do so, especially since there is a delay in
carrying out the treaty provisions with the United States
giving them responsibility over the Indians. Once these
matters are concluded, Spain can cut Indian gifts by a
third or a half. 3p.

No. 3. 4 Nov. 1797, New Orleans. Manuel Gayoso de Lemos
to Juan Ventura Morales (duplicate). Bloody Fellow has
just visited the gov. to discuss the recent treaty between
the Cherokees and Mr. Blount (American representative).
According to Bloody Fellow, the Americans tricked the
tribe and plan to seize their hunting grounds near Muscle
Shoals. Even though the King has directed that no more
Indian gifts be made, it is in Spain's interest to reward
this Cherokee chief who has been so loyal to His Majesty
and who could do substantial damage to Upper La. if he
went over to the Americans. 3p.

N. fol. 4 Nov. 1797, New Orleans. *Noticia del regalo que
he considerado a dos grandes gefes, dos yd. considerados,
siete guerreros, y quinze mugeres de la nación cheroquis*
(copy). 2p.

Ap. 6[4?] (no. 3). 20 Jan. 1798, New Orleans. Juan Ventura
Morales to el Príncipe de la Paz (duplicate). Morales attaches
the list of Indian gifts distributed in New Orleans and elsewhere during the previous year. 2p.

N. fol. 20 Jan. 1798, New Orleans. [Juan Ventura] Morales.
*Relación de los efectos de yndios consumidos en todo el
año de 1797* (duplicate). 5p.

Ap. 6[4?] (no. 19 *reservada*). 20 Jan. 1798, New Orleans. Juan
Ventura Morales to el Marqués de las Hormazas (duplicate). 2p.
[Encloses 2 documents].

No. 1 *muy reservada*. 5 Nov. 1797, New Orleans. Manuel
Gayoso de Lemos to Juan Ventura Morales (duplicate).
Americans evidently plan some action against Spanish
possessions. They are determined to seize the land around
Muscle Shoals in spite of Cherokee opposition. Gayoso asks
Morales to do everything he can to raise enough money for
the government to send armed boats to the area. 2p.

Ap. 6[4?] (no. 4). 30 Apr. 1798, New Orleans. Juan Ventura
Morales to el Príncipe de la Paz (duplicate). Morales
attaches a report concerning the proper approach to funding
Indian expenses. 2p. [Encloses 4 documents].

N. fol. 19 Apr. 1798, New Orleans. *Informe* from Juan
Ventura Morales to Manuel Gayoso de Lemos. Gayoso has
decided to continue gifts to certain tribes because some
Indians might retaliate against Spanish citizens if the
gifts were stopped. Although this is against the King's
orders, there is no doubt that stopping gifts suddenly
would bring unfortunate results. In general, however, the
Cherokees should be ignored. Morales recommends that the
suppression of Indian gifts not be publicized, that gifts
no longer be sent to their villages, that gifts only be
distributed once a year, that only Pensacola and Mobile
should have ·freedom to spend money on Indian gifts, and
that Indians be discouraged from coming to New Orleans by
saying that the capital is experiencing epidemics. 9p.

N. fol. 23 Apr. 1798, New Orlans. Manuel Gayoso de Lemos
to Juan Morales (duplicate). Gayoso will follow Morales's
suggestions whenever they can be implemented. The Cherokee gifts can be stopped completely since Spain no longer
has contact with the tribe. This also applies to John
McDonald, Spanish agent to the tribe. 3p.

Ap. 7[5?] (no. 12). 31 Mar. 1799, New Orleans. Juan Ventura
Morales to Francisco Saavedra (triplicate). Morales attaches
a list of Indian gifts in 1798, the total differing little from
the year before. 2p. [Encloses 4 documents].

N. fol. 31 Dec. 1798, New Orleans. Juan Ventura Morales.
*Relación de los efectos de indios consumidos en el año de
1798* (duplicate). 3p.

Ap. 7[6?] (no. 1 *reservada*). 8 May 1789, New Orleans. Manuel
Gayoso de Lemos to Antonio Valdés y Bazán. Gayoso traveled to
New Orleans with Dr. White, who represented Franklin to the
American congress. Gov. in New Orleans informed Gayoso of
developments concerning Gayoso's new post in Natchez as well as
the latest news about Cumberland, Franklin, and Kentucky.
Gayoso believes that White is far more interested in the inde-
pendence of Franklin than in linking the area to Spain. 5p.
[Encloses 1 document].

ESTADO/3902 (CONT'D)

N. fol. 8 May 1789, New Orleans. Manuel Gayoso de Lemos
to el Conde de Floridablanca. Gayoso describes his trip
to New Orleans from Havana in the company of Dr. White.
Gov. in New Orleans discussed the latest news about Ky.,
Cumberland, and Franklin. Franklin is divided into two
factions -- one favoring N.C. and the other supporting
independence. 16p.

Ap. 7[6?] (no. 4 *reservada*). 26 Jan. 1792, New Orleans. Manuel
Gayoso de Lemos to el Conde de Floridablanca. Gayoso describes
the province of Natchez. Many transients from Ky., Cumberland,
and Franklin spend some time in the Natchez area and many remain
to settle. Although a fickle people, most Americans find no
problem in being Spanish subjects. Gayoso discusses American
land seizures from the Indians, especially those involving land
companies from the Atlantic states. 22p.

Ap. 7 (no. 1 *reservada*). 19 Sept. 1793, Natchez. Manuel Gayoso
de Lemos to el Duque de la Alcudia. If Kentuckians conclude
that Spain encouraged Chickasaw, Creek, and Cherokee hostility
along the Ohio, relations with that state will change radically.
13p.

ESTADO/5639-1   CORRESPONDENCE FROM LUIS DE ONÍS: 1813-1814

Libro 6 (doc. 10). 23 Dec. 1813, Philadelphia. [Luis de Onís]
to Antonio Cano Manuel (duplicate). American invasion of the
Floridas seems less likely now. A number of American officials
believe that Spain has incited and armed the Creeks against the
Americans. Sensible officials do not believe this, but they
do acknowledge that the Americans have incited the Cherokees
against the Creeks. 3p.

ESTADO/5641   CORRESPONDENCE FROM LUIS DE ONÍS: 1816

Libro 4 (doc. 31). 29[?] Apr. 1816, Headquarters, Southern
Department. Andrew Jackson to Gov. of Pensacola. Jackson
protests the creation of a fort manned by blacks, many of whom
are escaped slaves. Hostile bands of Creeks and bandits
continue to steal slaves from Ga. as well as from the Cherokees
and Creeks. Jackson threatens to destroy the fort if Spanish
officials do not take action. 2p. [Encloses 1 document].

Doc. 31. 26 May 1816, Pensacola. Mauricio de Zuñiga to
Andrew Jackson. Zuñiga has reported Jackson's protest to
the capt. gen. and awaits his instructions on what to do
about the black fort. Although Zuñiga agrees with Jackson
that action must be taken against this establishment, he
cannot destroy it until authorized by superiors. 4p.

ESTADO/5642-2   CORRESPONDENCE FROM LUIS DE ONÍS: 1817

Libro 1 (doc. 26). 2 Sept. 1817, Philadelphia. *Nota* from Luis
de Onís to Richard Rush (copy). Onís protests the presence of

ESTADO/5642-2 (CONT'D)

Americans from Ky. and Tenn. trying to settle in Spanish
territory along the frontier. Onís also protests that 2,000
more Americans are ready to settle there once an agreement is
reached with neighboring Indians. 1p.

Libro 7 (doc. 25). 12 Sept. 1817, Philadelphia. Luis de Onís
to José Pizarro. Onís passes on information about 300 settlers
from Ky. and Tenn. who have established themselves along the
frontier and plan to live in Spanish territory. Americans
reportedly plan to bring 2,000 more settlers with permission
of the Indians into the region. 1p.

ESTADO/5643-2   CORRESPONDENCE FROM LUIS DE ONÍS: 1818

Libro 7 (doc. 3, no. 84). 19 May 1818, Washington. Luis de
Onís to José Pizarro. Jackson still hopes to seize both Floridas and exterminate the local Indians. He has declared that
all Indians who do not fight against the Seminoles will be
considered enemies. A large portion of the Creeks, Cherokees,
Choctaws, and other tribes form Jackson's vanguard and are
fighting against their brothers, the Seminoles, thus destroying
one another in the process. 5p.

Libro 9 (doc. 29). 23 July 1818, Washington. John Quincy
Adams to Luis de Onís (copy). In response to Spain's complaint
against Jackson's activities, it is the responsibility of every
power to restrain the Indians under their control from committing
robbery and butchery upon their neighbors, something Spain has
been unable to do. 8p. *English.* [Encloses 2 documents].

   N. fol. 23 Apr. 1816, Headquarters, Division of the South.
   Andrew Jackson to Gov. of Pensacola. The Negro fort
   erected during the War of 1812 near the junction of the
   Chattahoochee and Flint Rivers has been reinforced by
   escaped slaves from Ga. as well as from the Cherokees and
   Creeks. This activity cannot continue. 2p. *English.*

   N. fol. 26 May 1816, Pensacola. Mauricio de Zuñiga to
   Andrew Jackson. [Copy of AHN Estado/5641/libro 4/doc. 31/
   encl.]. 5p.

ESTADO/5660   CORRESPONDENCE: 1817

Libro 2 (doc. 2) 1 Apr. 1817, United States. Letter reporting
on relations with the United States and the instruction that
should be given to the Spanish envoy in the United States.
American leaders want to acquire the two Floridas. England,
however, has an interest in Florida since she could exercise
her control over the Southern and Northern Indians to hold back
American expansion towards Canada. 25p.

BIBLIOTECA NACIONAL

Madrid

SECCIÓN DE MANUSCRITOS
MS./19248

> Fol. 239 (no. 37). 1 Oct. 1792, New Orleans. El Barón de
> Carondelet to el Conde de Aranda. Carondelet attaches news
> [not included] about the Choctaws and Chickasaws, both of which
> had recently visited Cumberland to attend a congress called by
> Gov. Blount. Americans plan to wean these nations and other
> Indian tribes away from Spain. 6p.

MS./19508

> Fol. 89 (no. 5). [1777], [New Orleans]. Bernardo de Gálvez.
> *Noticias de Panzacola.* Gálvez, Governor of Louisiana, reports
> on an Indian congress in Mobile attended by the Creeks,
> Choctaws, and a few Chickasaws. Indians are determined to
> resist any attempt by the Americans to pass through their
> territory because these tribes know what disasters happened
> to the Cherokees and do not want the same for their people.
> All the tribes at the congress wish to remain neutral during
> the present conflict. 8p.

ARCHIVO GENERAL DE INDIAS

Seville

SECCIÓN V.   GOBIERNO.   AUDIENCIA DE SANTO DOMINGO
SD/224   FLORIDA, SECULAR PAPERS

Fol. 1 (doc. 9). 1 Apr. 1569[?], Santo Domingo. *Relación* of
Juan Pardo's expedition from St. Helena to the interior of
S. Carolina. 70p.

SD/1598   LETTERS FROM THE GOVERNORS OF HAVANA: 1776-1779

No. 231 *reservada*. 1 Apr. 1778, Havana. Diego José Navarro to
José de Gálvez. 3p. [Encloses 1 document].

N. fol. 1 Apr. 1778, Havana. Juan José Elijio de la
Puente to Diego José Navarro (copy). The loyalists can
only count on the Cherokees among all the Indian tribes.
The relations of the loyalists with the Yuchi, Talapoose,
Apiscai [Abeka?], Chickasaw, Alibamo, and Choctaw are
not secure. There are persistent Indian rumors about an
impending attack on Spanish St. Augustine. Most tribes
feel that the Cherokees will not put up much resistance
against the Americans. 7p.

SD/2082   LETTERS FROM NAVARRO TO GÁLVEZ: 1779-1780

No. 76 *reservada*. 26 July 1779, Havana. Diego José Navarro
to José de Gálvez. 2p. [Encloses 2 documents].

No. 1. 20 July 1779, Havana. Instructions from Diego
José Navarro to Francisco Ruiz del Canto (copy). Navarro,
Governor of Havana, orders Ruiz to visit St. Marks and
report on the loyalties of all the southern tribes,
including the Cherokees. 7p.

No. 103 *reservada*. 20 Feb. 1780, Havana. Diego José Navarro
to José de Gálvez. 4p. [Encloses 4 documents].

No. 1. 14 Feb. 1780, Havana. Francisco Ruiz del Canto
Relación de lo acaecido desde ... 16 de diciembre. During
his visit with the Yuchi Indians near St. Marks, Ruiz
learned that the Yuchis, Talapooses, Chickasaws, and
Cherokees would support a Spanish attack on Pensacola.
6p.

SD/2531   CONSULTAS FROM THE COUNCIL OF THE INDIES: 1787-1796

No. 24 *reservada*. 18 Jan. 1791, New Orleans. El Barón de
Carondelet to el Duque de la Alcudia. Carondelet explains the

SD/2531 (CONT'D)

latest news from Louisiana, including the recent treaty with the Cherokees (a tribe that will help the Spanish build an invincible barrier against American expansion). 18p.

SD/2541   LETTERS TO FLORIDA'S GOVERNORS: 1717-1752

Exp. 39. 2 Mar. 1738. Copy of *real orden* to Gov. of Florida, Manuel de Montiano. 1p. [Encloses 4 documents].

N. fol. 11 Nov. 1737, St. Augustine. Letter from Manuel de Montiano reporting news from the English colonies. Oglethorpe has attempted to convince Parliament to seize Spanish Florida. Chief Sacafaca reports from Chalacarliche that the Indians agreed with the English plan to send war parties against Spanish possessions. 11p.

N. fol. 11 Nov. 1737, Florida. Letter from Manuel de Montiano. [Abstract of preceding letter]. 6p.

N. fol. 2 Mar. 1738, Madrid. *Real orden* to Manuel de Montiano reporting that his information about Florida has reached Spain, including news from Chief Sacafaca in Chalacarliche that the English Indians plan to attack Spanish possessions. Indians are scheduled to meet soon to discuss various problems. 12p.

Exp. 42. 19 Dec. 1737, St. Augustine. Duplicate of letter from Manuel de Montiano with news from 2 English informants. Chief Sacafaca of Chalacarliche reports that the English Indians have moved south to attack Spanish possessions. English ordered those Indians to meet with them to discuss various matters. 15p.

Exp. 81. 16 Mar. 1748. Copy of summary of Montiano's report. 2p. [Encloses 1 document].

N. fol. 15 Mar. 1748, St. Augustine. *Informe* from Manuel de Montiano reporting the latest news from Florida. The Yuchis are at war with the Cherokees. 43p.

Exp. 101. 15 Nov. 1742, St. Augustine. Letter from Melchor de Navarrete describing efforts to christianize Indians. Priests have baptized several Yuchis and one Cherokee. 9p.

SD/2543   LETTERS: 1769-1787

No. 86 *de preferencia*. 20 June 1785, St. Augustine. Vicente Manuel de Zéspedes to José de Gálvez. 9p. [Encloses 3 documents].

No. 2. 13 June 1785, St. Augustine. Vicente Manuel de Zéspedes to Alexander McGillivray (copy). Creeks should be aware that the Americans have begun hostilities against Spanish frontiers, particularly against a Spanish fort called Muscle Shoals along the Cherokee River. Zéspedes, however, has never heard of a Spanish settlement on that site. 4p.

SD/2543 (CONT'D)

No. 91 *de preferencia*. 16 Sept. 1785, St. Augustine. Vicente Manuel de Zéspedes to José de Gálvez (duplicate). 4p. [Encloses 1 document].

N. fol. 22 Aug. 1785, Little Tallassee. Alexander McGillivray to Gov. Zéspedes (translation). Zéspedes's news about American hostilities is false. There have been no attacks yet and there is no Spanish fort along the Cherokee River. 4p.

SD/2544   LETTERS FROM GOV. MIRÓ AND INTENDANT NAVARRO: 1788

Fol. 608 (no. 21 *reservada*). 15 June 1788, New Orleans. Esteban Miró to Antonio Valdés. [Duplicate of AHN Estado/3888 bis/doc. 136]. 6p. [Enclosures to fol. 611b].

Fol. 611. 25 Apr. 1788, Little Tallassee. Alexander McGillivray to Gov. O'Neill. [Same as AHN/Estado/3888bis/ doc. 137]. 2p.

Fol. 613 (no. 22 *reservada*). 13 July 1788, New Orleans. Esteban Miró to Antonio Valdés. [Duplicate of AHN Estado/3901/ ap. 3/no. 22 *reservada*]. 11p. [Enclosures to fol. 650].

Fol. 622 (no. 2). 29 Mar. 1788, Ft. Charlotte. Translation of a report from a committee composed of Messrs. Kearney, Carrington, Bengham, [Bingham?], Smith, and Dane appointed [by the Confederation] to negotiate with Indians in the Southern Department. There is evidence that some residents of Ga. and N.C. have usurped land from the Talapooses and Cherokees. These tribes need to establish commercial trade with the United States to obtain vital goods. 15p.

Fol. 641 (no. 6). 4 June 1788, Pensacola. Arturo O'Neill to Esteban Miró. [Copy of AHN Estado/3901/ap. 3/no. 22 *reservada*/enc. no. 6]. 7p.

Fol. 657 (no. 24 *reservada*). 28 Aug. 1788, New Orleans. Esteban Miró to Antonio Valdés. 13p. [Enclosures to fol. 685b].

Fol. 669 (no. 2). 28 June 1787, Philadelphia. V. [sic] Knox to James White (translation). White is instructed on how to manage commercial relations with the Choctaws and Chickasaws. Mr. Drumgoole has asked the government for employment with the Cherokees [as a trader?]. White should decide whether to honor Drumgoole's request. 3p.

SD/2547   LETTERS FROM THE LOUISIANA GOVERNORS: 1776-1780

Fol. 602 (no. 200 *reservada*). 24 Oct. 1778, New Orleans. Bernardo de Galvéz to José de Galvéz. 1p. [Enclosures to fol. 610b].

SD/2547 (CONT'D)

> Fol. 609. 17 Sept. 1778, New Orleans. Bernardo de Gálvez
> to Peter Chester. Spain will never authorize expeditions
> against English territory in spite of such English prov-
> ocations as encouraging the Choctaws, Cherokees, and
> Chickasaws to attack Spanish possessions. 4p.

SD/2548   DUPLICATE CORRESPONDENCE FROM THE GOVERNORS: 1781-1782

Fol. 22 (no. 29). 26 May 1781, Pensacola. Bernardo de Gálvez
to José de Gálvez (triplicate). Gálvez explains his efforts
to cultivate friendship with the Louisiana Indians, the need
for Indian gifts, and Gilberto Antonio Maxent's mission to
Europe to secure Indian presents. 3p.

Fol. 100 (no. 17). 26 Oct. 1781, Havana. Bernardo de Gálvez
to José de Gálvez (duplicate). 3p. [Enclosures to fol. 103b].

> Fol. 102. 4 Sept. 1781, Havana. José de Ezpeleta to
> Bernardo de Gálvez. Ezpeleta describes the attack on
> Mobile and role that the Indians played in defending the
> city. Indians reportedly had two hundred horses. 4p.

Fol. 107 (no. 22). 26 Oct. 1781, Havana. Bernardo de Gálvez
to José de Gálvez (duplicate). There is an urgent need for
presents to prevent Indian hostility. Juan Macarty from
New Orleans has left for London under a flag of truce to
purchase Indian goods. On his return trip, a Spanish corsair
captured and took him to Cuba. 7p. [Enclosures to fol. 116b].

> Fol. 111 (no. 1). 22 Aug. 1781, Havana. Bernardo de
> Gálvez to José Solano (copy). Indian gifts are needed in
> Louisiana and Pensacola, and Macarty's mission was de-
> signed to supply these. Could Solano assist in releasing
> Macarty's cargo? 2p.

> Fol. 112 (no. 2). 18 Oct. 1781, Havana. José Solano to
> Bernardo de Gálvez (copy). Solano discusses the seizure
> of Macarty's ship loaded with Indian gifts. 1p.

> Fol. 113 (no. 3). 13 Oct. 1781, Havana. Bernardo de
> Gálvez to José Solano. Gálvez discusses seizure of
> Macarty's ship loaded with Indian gifts. 1p.

> Fol. 114. 13 Oct. 1781, Havana. Petition from Juan
> Bautista Macarty to the Commander General. Macarty asks
> for assistance in releasing boat with Indian goods. 2p.

> Fol. 115. 29 Aug. 1781, Havana. *Auto* from the *junta de
> marina* concerning Juan Macarty and his ship of Indian
> goods. 2p.

> Fol. 115b. 11 Sept. 1781, Havana. *Auto* from the *junta de
> marina* concerning Juan Macarty and his ship of Indian
> gifts. 3p.

SD/2549   DUPLICATE CORRESPONDENCE FROM THE GOVERNORS: 1783-1784

Fol. 633. 2 Feb. 1783, New Orleans. Esteban Miró to Martín
Navarro (copy). Mexican gunpowder is necessary for Indian
gifts in order to help defend area. 2p.

Fol. 634. 3 Dec. 1787, Pensacola. Arturo O'Neill to Antonio
Valdés y Bazán (duplicate). Indian allegiance has switched
from the English to the Spanish during the rule of O'Neill.
3p.

SD/2550   DUPLICATE CORRESPONDENCE FROM THE GOVERNORS: 1785

Fol. 36 (no. 19). 22 Apr. 1785, Havana. El Conde de Gálvez
to José de Gálvez (duplicate). Intendant Martín Navarro should
be promoted because of his actions at the recent Indian congresses in Pensacola and Mobile and because of other services.
2p.

Fol. 39 (no. 21). 23 Apr. 1785, Havana. El Conde de Gálvez
to José de Gálvez (duplicate). Governor Martín Navarro has
taken a number of measures to cut expenses in Louisiana,
including reducing the costs of the *ramo de indios*. 9p.
[Enclosures to fol. 61b].

>   Fol. 44. 20 Mar. 1785, Havana. Martín de Navarro and
>   el Conde de Gálvez. *Reglamento general de empleados y
>   mas obligaciones de ... Luisiana [y Mobila y Pensacola]*.
>   Document lists expenses for the *ramo de indios* in Loui-
>   siana, Mobile, and Pensacola. 36p.

Fol. 92 (no. 46 *de preferencia*). 25 Sept. 1785, Mexico. El
Conde de Gálvez to José de Gálvez. 4p. [Enclosures to fol.
131b].

>   Fol. 105. 24 July 1785, Ft. Panmure de Natchez. Francisco
>   Bouligny to Esteban Miró. [Wm.] Davenport, a Ga. com-
>   missioner in charge of setting that state's boundary with
>   Spain, is in Natchez. There has been some activity along
>   the Cherokee River. 10p.

Fol. 142 (no. 53). 25 Oct. 1785, Mexico. El Conde de Gálvez
to José de Gálvez (duplicate). There are some 300 Americans
now along the Cherokee and Cumberland Rivers. 3p. [Enclosures
to fol. 148b].

>   Fol. 144. 4 Aug. 1785, Ft. Panmure de Natchez. Francisco
>   Bouligny to Esteban Miró. Bouligny mentions Cumberland
>   and Cherokee territory. 10p.

Fol. 152 (no. 55). 27 Oct. 1785, Mexico. El Conde de Gálvez
to José de Gálvez. Gov. of Pensacola has received petitions
from the Creeks, Chickasaws, Cherokees, and Alex. McGillivray
asking for Spain's protection of their land from the Americans
and for the continuation of Spanish trade. 5p. [Enclosures
to fol. 159].

SD/2550 (CONT'D)

Fol. 155. 24 July 1785, Pensacola. Alex. McGillivray
to Gov. O'Neill (translation). McGillivray mentions
recent congress of Creeks, Chickasaws, and Cherokees.
Indians are satisfied with Panton's goods and hope that
Spanish commerce will continue. 3p.

Fol. 157. 10 July 1785, Tallassee among the Upper Talapooses. *Representación* from McGillivray to [Miró]
(translation). The Creeks, Chickasaws, and Cherokees
protest that the Americans have no claim to Indian territory in the forthcoming discussions between Spain and the
Americans over their borders. 5p.

No. 2 *reservada*. 24 Aug. 1785, St. Augustine. Vicente Manuel
de Zéspedes to José de Gálvez. Ga. wants to capture Indian
trade in La. and West Florida. 4p. [Encloses 3 documents].

No. 1. 18 Aug. 1785, St. Mary's River. Thomas Brown to
[Zéspedes] (translation). Brown discusses the intentions
of Continental Congress and Ga. towards the Floridas and
the Indians. 6p.

No. 1. [sic] 6 Aug. 1785. Gov. of St. Augustine to Col.
Thomas Brown. [Brown's?] Indian friends have arrived in
Savannah. Governor discusses the possibility of war
between Ga. and the Indians and the relations between the
Creeks and Cherokees. 6p.

No. 3. 1 June [1785?], East Florida. Important resident
of East Florida to Lt. Gov. of Bermuda (translation).
Well-armed Indians [Cherokees?] have visited a plantation
in Florida. 8p.

No. 84 *de preferencia*. 12 June 1785, St. Augustine. Vicente
Manuel de Zéspedes to José de Gálvez (duplicate). Zéspedes
discusses the British governor's request for a Spanish ship
to take an Indian envoy to England. These Indians seek an
alliance of all Indians from Canada to Mississippi to resist
American land pressure. 6p.

SD/2551   DUPLICATE CORRESPONDENCE FROM THE GOVERNORS: 1786

Fol. 21 (no. 72). 26 Jan. 1786, Mexico. El Conde de Gálvez to
el Marqués de la Sonora (duplicate). Americans are trying to
win over the Louisiana tribes. 2p. [Enclosures to fol. 25b].

Fol. 24 (no. 3). 23 July 1785, Greenwich. Andrew Pickens
to Alex. McGillivray. [Translation of AGI Cuba/121/doc.
42]. 1p.

Fol. 99 (no. 103). 26 Aug. 1786, Mexico. El Conde de Gálvez
to el Marqués de la Sonora (duplicate). Gálvez has received
the King's decision to allow Panton, Leslie, and Co. to continue the Indian trade with the Floridas. This company can
also supply the Louisiana Indians according to the agreements
made at various Pensacola Indian congresses. 2p.

SD/2551 (CONT'D)

Fol. 223 (no. 136 *reservada*). 28 June 1786, New Orleans.
Esteban Miró to el Marqués de Sonora. Miró forwards materials
concerning Creek hostilities towards the Americans because of
their encroachment on Indian hunting grounds. 3p. [Enclosures
to fol. 239b].

> Fol. 231. 1 May 1786, Little Tallassee. *Relación* from
> Alex. McGillivray to Esteban Miró. [Translation of AGI
> Cuba/2352/no. 14/encl.]. 18p.

Fol. 240 (no. 137 *reservada*). 28 June 1786, New Orleans.
Esteban Miró to el Marqués de Sonora (duplicate). If the
border question is settled in favor of the Americans, they will
win over the Indians. This has serious implications for Spain.
2p. [Enclosures to fol. 254b].

> Fol. 241 (no. 311 *reservada*). 28 June 1786, New Orleans.
> Esteban Miró to el Conde de Gálvez (copy). American
> commissioners called a meeting at Hopewell along the
> Keowee R. for the Chickasaws, Choctaws, and Talapooses
> but had little success. 7p.

> Fol. 245 (no. 1). 13 Jan. 1786, Hopewell along the
> Keowee. *Traducción de los artículos del tratado [con]* ...
> *toda la nación chacta*. 10p.

> Fol. 250 (no. 2). 8 Jan. 1786, Seneca. Ben Hawkins to
> Alex. McGillivray. [Translation of AGI Cuba/2360/n. fol.].
> 6p.

> Fol. 253 (no. 3). 11 Jan. 1786, Seneca. Ben Hawkins to
> Alex. McGillivray. [Translation of AGI Cuba/2360/n. fol.].
> 4p.

Fol. 433 (no. 1 *reservada*). 25 Nov. 1786, New Orleans. Esteban
Miró to [el Marqués de Sonora?] (duplicate). 2p. [Enclosures
to fol. 440].

> Fol. 434 (no. 1). 8 Oct. 1786, Little Tallassee. Alex.
> McGillivray to Arturo O'Neill. [Translation of AGI Cuba/
> 2360/n. fol.]. 5p.

> Fol. 439 (no. 3). 18 Sept. 1786, Little Tallassee. Alex.
> McGillivray to John Habersham and the Committee of Ga.
> Indian Commissioners (translation). Georgians have usurped
> Indian land and the state has failed to do anything about
> it. 3p.

Fol. 441 (no. 2 *reservada*). 25 Nov. 1786, New Orleans.
Esteban Miró to el Marqués de Sonora. [Duplicate of AHN Estado/
3887/doc. 48]. 2p. [Enclosures to fol. 443].

> Fol. 442. 30 Oct. 1786, Little Tallassee. Alex.
> McGillivray to O'Neill. [Translation of AGI Cuba/2360/
> n. fol.]. 3p.

SD/2551 (CONT'D)

Fol. 444 (no. 3 *reservada*).   25 Nov. 1786, New Orleans.
Esteban Miró to el Marqués de Sonora (duplicate). 2p.
[Enclosures to fol. 450b].

> Fol. 445 [1786?], Charleston. Fabius to Messrs. Bowen
> and Mark Land (translation). Letter [in *La Gazeta de la
> Carolina del Sur*] complaining that Cumberland residents
> and other Americans would be affected if Spain denied
> them the right to use the Miss. River. 4p.

> Fol. 447. [1786?], [Charleston]. Fabius to Messrs. Bowen
> and Mark Land (translation). Letter [in the *La Gazeta de
> la Carolina del Sur*] noting the growth of American estab-
> lishments along the Cumberland River. 8p.

No. 5 *reservada*. 25 May 1786, St. Augustine. Vicente Manuel
de Zéspedes to el Marqués de Sonora (duplicate). 4p. [Encloses
3 documents].

> [No. 1]. 25 Apr. 1786, Little Tallassee. Alex. McGillivray
> to Gov. of St. Augustine (copy). Americans tried to reach
> agreements with the Southern tribes (Creeks, Cherokees,
> Choctaws, and Chickasaws). 8p.

> No. 3. 24 May 1786, St. Augustine. Vicente Manuel de
> Zéspedes to Diego de Guardoqui (copy). Zéspedes discusses
> McGillivray's life and Spanish aid to the Indians. 4p.

No. 13 *reservada*. 24 Dec. 1786, St. Augustine. Vicente Manuel
de Zéspedes to el Marqués de Sonora. [Duplicate of AHN Estado/
3887/doc. 60]. 4p. [Encloses 3 documents].

> No. 1. 18 Sept. 1786, Mount Pleasant, Franklin. Gov.
> of the New State of Franklin to Gov. of Georgia. [Same
> as AHN Estado/3887/doc. 61]. 1p.

> No. 1. 18 Sept. 1786, Notachuchey [Nolichucky?]. Robert
> Dijon and Steven Fest to Gov. of Georgia. [Same as AHN
> Estado/3887/doc. 61]. 1p.

> No. 1. 8 Feb. 1786, Georgia. Extract of translated letter
> from George Elholm. [Same as AHN Estado/3887/doc. 61]. 2p.

> No. 1. 28 July 1786, Chickasaw Nation. Wm. Davenport to
> John Sevier. [Same as AHN Estado/3887/doc. 61]. 2p.

No. 167. 31 Aug. 1786, St. Augustine. Vicente Manuel de
Zéspedes to el Marqués de Sonora (duplicate). Zéspedes acknowledges the King's approval of his reply to the Indians
concerning Spain's position should war break out between the
Indians and Americans. Gov. will forward a copy of the agreement reached with the Indians during the Congress of 1784. 2p.

SD/2552   DUPLICATE CORRESPONDENCE FROM THE GOVERNORS: 1787

Fol. 5 (no. 168). 11 Jan. 1787, New Orleans. Esteban Miró to el Marqués de Sonora (duplicate). Miró lists his services to the Crown, including his activities with Indian tribes. 12p.

Fol. 543 (no. 11 *reservada*). 1 June 1787, New Orleans. Esteban Miró to el Marqués de Sonora. 2p. [Enclosures to fol. 548b].

> Fol. 546 (no. 3). 4 Mar. 1787, Little Tallassee. Alex. McGillivray to Gov. O'Neill (translation). Lower Creeks were asked to find someone to assassinate McGillivray. Creek parties have attacked Cumberland. 3p.

> Fol. 548 (no. 4). 4 Apr. 1787, Little Tallassee. Alex. McGillivray to Gov. O'Neill (translation). McGillivray has corresponded with Col. White, American commissioner, and has learned that the Canadian Indians are waging a general war against the western American settlements. Some assistants of Hutchins, the surveyor, have been killed and their papers have been turned over to Cherokee traders. 2p.

Fol. 775 (no. 7). 6 Dec. 1787, Havana. José de Ezpeleta to Antonio Valdés (duplicate). Ezpeleta reports on the latest tensions between the Louisiana Indians and the Americans and notes developments in Indian commerce. 2p.

No. 15 *reservada*. 22 Mar. 1787, St. Augustine. Vicente Manuel de Zéspedes to el Marqués de Sonora (duplicate). Zéspedes reports on the latest news about the Indians and Georgians. Americans continue their efforts to win over the Indians. 4p. [Encloses 5 documents].

> No. 3. 8 Jan. 1787. Charles MacLatchy to John Leslie (translation). Ga. Commissioner is trying to win the Indians away from Spain. By next summer, Ga. will require that all Indians above the 31° parallel support the Americans or face expulsion. 2p.

No. 21 *reservada*. 12 Oct. 1787, St. Augustine. Vicente Manuel de Zéspedes to el Marqués de Sonora. [Duplicate of AHN Estado/ 3887/doc. 93]. 4p. [Encloses 1 document].

> [No.1] 1 Aug. 1787, New York. Diego de Gardoqui to Vicente Manuel de Zéspedes (copy). Entire Spanish frontier needs to be alert against American actions. 3p.

No. 22 *reservada*. 14 Oct. 1787, St. Augustine. Vicente Manuel de Zéspedes to el Marqués de Sonora. [Duplicate of AHN Estado/3887/doc. 95]. 3p.

No. 23 *reservada*. 27 Oct. 1787, St. Augustine. Vicente Manuel de Zéspedes to el Marqués de Sonora (duplicate). Indian troubles extend all the way from Ga. to Va. and war will soon break out. 3p. [Encloses 2 documents].

SD/2553   DUPLICATE CORRESPONDENCE FROM THE GOVERNORS: 1788-1789

Fol. 73 (no. 47). 29 Nov. 1788, Havana. José de Ezpeleta to
Antonio Valdés (duplicate). 3p. [Enclosures to fol. 79b].

Fol. 77. 20 Sept. 1788, Little Tallassee. Alex. McGillivray to Esteban Miró. [Translation of AGI Cuba/2361/n.
fol.]. 6p.

Fol. 158 (no. 2 *reservada*). 29 Dec. 1788, Havana. José de
Ezpeleta to Antonio Valdés. [Duplicate of AHN Estado/3888bis/
doc. 179]. 11p. [Enclosures to fol. 167].

Fol. 164. 24 Dec. 1788, Havana. James White to José de
Ezpeleta. [Same as AHN Estado/3888bis/doc. 180]. 7p.

Fol. 169 (no. 3 *reservada*). 3 Mar. 1789, Havana. José de
Ezpeleta to Antonio Valdés. [Duplicate of AHN Estado/3888bis/
doc. 189]. 2p.

Fol. 233 (no. 1 *muy reservada*). 6 June 1789, Havana. Domingo
Cabello to Antonio Valdés (duplicate). Cabello discusses
James White and the need to keep Franklin and Cumberland from
using the Miss. River. 2p.

Fol. 234 (no. 2 *reservada*). 6 June 1789, Havana. Domingo
Cabello to Antonio Valdés (duplicate). Merchants involved
in Indian trade are exempt from the 6% tax on imports and
exports. The King wants to reassure the Indians that Spain
will protect and aid the tribes. 3p.

Fol. 236 (no. 3 *reservada*). 28 June 1789, Havana. Domingo
Cabello to Antonio Valdes. Cabello acknowledges the royal
order that only Indian chiefs and important followers should
attend congresses in Louisiana since the treasury needs to
conserve its funds. 1p.

Fol. 237 (no. 4). 26 Feb. 1790, Havana. Doming Cabello to
Antonio Valdés (duplicate). Lt. Col. Manuel Gayoso de Lemos
has not visited Franklin and Cumberland as ordered for numerous
reasons. 1p. [Enclosures to fol. 238b].

Fol. 238. 18 Jan. 1790, New Orleans. Esteban Miró to
Domingo Cabello (copy). Health, danger, and expenses
have prevented Gayoso from visiting Franklin and Cumberland. 2p.

Fol. 426 (no. 37 *reservada*). 30 Apr. 1789, New Orleans.
Esteban Miró to Antonio Valdés. [Duplicate of AHN Estado/3888
bis/doc. 220]. 8p. [Enclosures to fol. 442].

Fol. 430 (no. 1). 12 Sept. 1788, Franklin. John Sevier
to Gardoqui. [Copy of AHN Estado/3888bis/doc. 221]. 5p.

Fol. 433 (no. 2). 18 Apr. 1789, New Orleans. James White
to Esteban Miró. [Same as AHN Estado/3888bis/doc. 222].
3p.

Fol. 435 (no. 3). 20 Apr. 1789, New Orleans. Esteban
Miró to [James White]. [Copy of AHN Estado/3888bis/doc.
223]. 3p.

Fol. 437 (no. 4). 24 Apr. 1789, New Orleans. Esteban
Miró to Daniel Smith. [Copy of AHN Estado/3888bis/doc.
224]. 3p.

Fol. 439 (no. 5). 23 Apr. 1789, New Orleans. Esteban
Miró to James Wilkinson. [Copy of AHN Estado/3888bis/
doc. 225]. 5p.

Fol. 442 (no. 6). 22 Apr. 1789, New Orleans. James White
to Esteban Miró. [Same as AHN Estado/3888bis/doc. 226].
1p.

No. 3 *reservada*. 10 Jan. 1788, St. Augustine. Vicente Manuel
de Zéspedes to Antonio Valdés (duplicate). 10p. [Encloses
1 document].

[No. 1?] 23 Oct. 1787, Legislative Capitol. James
Simmons (notary for the General Assembly). *Acuerdo de la
junta selecta ... de Georgia.* [Same as AHN Estado/3887/
doc. 125]. 12p.

No. 4 *reservada*. 16 Jan. 1788, St. Augustine. Vicente Manuel
de Zéspedes to Antonio Valdés (duplicate). Zéspedes reports
a conspiracy involving Col. Tate, Thomas Brown, Capt. Farragutt,
and others who now live somewhere along the Tennessee, Shawnee,
and Ohio Rivers. 7p. [Encloses 3 documents].

No. 2. 26 Nov. 1787, New York. Diego de Gardoqui to
Vicente Manuel de Zéspedes (copy). Gardoqui describes a
conspiracy of adventurers in Franklin. 3p.

No. 3. Davidson County, N. Carolina. Extract of translated letter sent to Benjamin Hawkins stating that
western N.C. is unhappy with the Spanish refusal to allow
use of the Miss. River. 11p.

No. 7 *reservada*. 24 Mar. 1788, St. Augustine. Vicente Manuel
de Zéspedes to Antonio Valdés (duplicate). Northern and
Southern Indians, supported by England, are trying to form a
confederation against the Americans. 19p. [Encloses 4
documents].

No. 1. 6 Feb. 1788, St. Augustine. *Representación* from
Vicente Manuel de Zéspedes to José de Ezpeleta (duplicate).
Zéspedes keeps the capt. general abreast of the latest
developments between the Southern Indians and Spain. 6p.

No. 2. 5 Jan. 1788, Apalache. Alex. McGillivray to
General Zéspedes (translation). McGillivray discusses the
recent attack on Cumberland and the Creek's need for
Spanish gunpowder and ammunition. 5p.

SD/2553 (CONT'D)

No. 2.   4 Oct. 1787, Pensacola. Alex. McGillivray to
Gov. Col. Miró (translation). McGillivray discusses
Indian affairs and the attack on Cumberland. Former
inhabitants of Cumberland are now assembling in N.C. and
Va. along the Holston R. and plan to move into the area
around the Cherokee River. Carolina has sent a letter
asking for peace between the Creeks and Cumberland. 6p.

No. 4.   30 [20?] Oct. 1787, Little Tallassee. Alex.
McGillivray to a resident of the Bahamas (extract of
translation). McGillivray's letter appeared in the *La
Gazeta de las Yslas Bahamas* and discusses White's mission
to the Creeks, new hostilities by the Georgians, and the
mission of the Northern Indians to the Creeks. 18p.

SD/2554   DUPLICATE CORRESPONDENCE FROM THE GOVERNORS: 1790

Fol. 37 (no. 51 *reservada*). 10 Aug. 1790, New Orleans. Esteban
Miró to Antonio Valdés (duplicate). Miró discusses some land
formerly held by Cherokees in connection with the Yazoo land
claims. 24p.

Fol. 49 (no. 52 *reservada*). 10 Aug. 1790, New Orleans. Esteban
Miró to Antonio Valdés. [Same as AHN Estado/3901/ap. 3/no. 52
reservada]. 11p. [Enclosures to fol. 65b].

Fol. 55. 8 May 1790, Little Tallassee. Alex. McGillivray
to Gov. Esteban Miró. [Same as AHN Estado/3901/ap. 3/no. 52
reservada/encl.]. 7p.

Fol. 541 (no. 9). 14 Aug. 1790, Havana. Luis de las Casas to
el Conde del Campo de Alange (duplicate). Three Indians [Chero-
kees with Bowles?] and one interpreter from Florida arrived in
Providence. British officials arrested the Indians and sent
them on to London. 2p.

Fol. 544 (no. 11). 24 Sept. 1790, Havana. Luis de las Casas
to el Conde del Campo de Alange (duplicate). Las Casas elab-
orates on earlier report about the three Indians and an
American interpreter in Providence. Gov. Miró reports that
those Indians were merely attempting to obtain gifts. One of
the Indians was probably *Perro Rabioso* [Mad Dog]. 2p.

SD/2556   DUPLICATE CORRESPONDENCE FROM THE GOVERNORS: 1791

Fol. 30 (no. 29). 30 Dec. 1790, Havana. Luis de las Casas to
el Conde del Campo de Alange (duplicate). Three Indians and
one interpreter who recently arrived in Providence are connected
with an Englishman in East Fla. named Woules [Bowles?]. 2p.
[Enclosures to fol. 32b].

Fol. 31. 13 Nov. 1790, Pensacola. Arthur O'Neill to Luis
de las Casas (copy). O'Neill describes the latest news
from the Creeks after having learned that Bowles offered
to turn St. Augustine over to the British. Bowles and his
three Indians have gone to Nova Scotia. 2p.

Fol. 93 (no. 61). 26 Mar. 1791, Havana. Luis de las Casas to
el Conde del Campo de Alange (duplicate). 3p. [Enclosures
to fol. 105].

Fol. 95 (no. 1). 16 Nov. 1790, Pensacola. Arthur O'Neill
to Esteban Miró (copy). Antonio Garzon has returned from
the Creeks where he had been sent to investigate the
Indians that recently visited Providence. 2p.

Fol. 227 (no. 87). 3 Aug. 1791, Havana. Luis de las Casas to
el Conde del Campo de Alange (duplicate). 2p. [Enclosures to
fol. 267b].

Fol. 243 (no. 206). 15 July 1791, New Orleans. Esteban
Miró to Luis de las Casas (copy). Choctaws and Chickasaws
oppose a fort at Nogales. 3p.

Fol. 245 (no. 1). 1 July 1791, Natchez. Manuel
Gayoso de Lemos to Esteban Miró (copy). Choctaws
and Chickasaws oppose Ft. Nogales. Without the
Spanish present, the Indians fear that the Americans
will move in and destroy the tribes as they have done
at Franklin, Cumberland, and Tennessee. 20p.

Fol. 423 (no. 118). 27 Oct. 1791, Havana. Luis de las Casas
to el Conde del Campo de Alange (duplicate). Las Casas reports
the latest news from Cumberland. 1p. [Enclosures to fol. 424b].

Fol. 424 (no. 83). 9 May 1791, Natchez. Manuel Gayoso
de Lemos to Esteban Miró (copy). Indians have attacked
Cumberland residents. Blount notified the Cherokees and
Chickasaws that Cumberland plans to establish settlements
at Muscle Shoals. 2p.

Fol. 429 (no. 120). 27 Oct. 1791, Havana. Luis de las Casas
to el Conde del Campo de Alange (duplicate). Bowles and the
Indians have returned to Spanish territory and officials are
ordered to apprehend them. 4p. [Enclosures to fol. 432].

Fol. 431 (no. 1). 12 Aug. 1791, [East Florida]. John
McQueen. *Copia de parrajo del diario de dn. Juan MacQueen
encargado ... para prender el aventurero Guillermo Bowles*
(translation). MacQueen's diary describes an expedition
to capture Bowles. 3p.

Fol. 433 (no. 121). 21 Oct. 1791, Havana. Luis de las Casas
to el Conde del Campo de Alange (duplicate). Las Casas reports
the news from New Orleans, including developments between the
Americans and the Cherokees. 1p. [Enclosures to fol. 439].

Fol. 436. 23 Sept. 1791, New Orleans. Esteban Miró to
Luis de las Casas (copy). Treaty between the Cherokees
and Gov. [Blount] could be advantageous to the Creeks by
fixing Cherokee borders and prohibiting American settlements within that area. 2p.

SD/2556 (CONT'D)

> Fol. 436b. 28 Aug. 1791, Little Tallassee. Alex. McGilli-
> vray to Esteban Miro. Two Cherokees asked McGillivray's
> opinion about a possible treaty with the Americans. Follow-
> ing McGillivray's advice, the Cherokees made peace with the
> Americans. The treaty prohibits the erection of military
> posts along any part of the Cherokee R. or at the mouth of
> the Ohio. 6p.

Fol. 522 (no. 8 *reservada*). 4 May 1791, Havana. Luis de las
Casas to el Conde del Campo de Alange (duplicate). Las Casas
reports recent news concerning the Americans, the Yazoo area,
and the Spanish borders west of the mountains. 4p. [Enclosures
to fol. 575b].

> Fol. 524 (no. 1). Nov. 1790, New Orleans. Esteban Miró
> to Luis de las Casas (copy). Miró discusses the activities
> of S. Carolina's Yazoo Company. 2p.

> > Fol. 524b (no. 1). 24 Jan. 1790, Charleston. Alex.
> > Moultrie to [Dr. Farar] (translation). Moultrie
> > discusses the Yazoo territory and outlines the land
> > belonging to the three companies involved -- the
> > companies of S.C., Va., and N. Carolina. N. Carolina's
> > group is called the Tennessee Company. 13p.

> Fol. 531 (no. 2 *reservada).* 24 Feb. 1791, New Orleans.
> Esteban Miró to Luis de las Casas (copy). Miró sends Las
> Casas a copy of Gayoso's instructions concerning activities
> of S.C. Yazoo Company. 1p.

> Fol. 532 (no. 3 *reservada*). 8 Apr. 1791, New Orleans.
> Esteban Miró to Luis de las Casas (copy). Miró requests
> the capt. general's approval for his replies to the letters
> from Dr. O'Fallon (Yazoo Company). 1p.

> > Fol. 533 (no. 1). 15 Jan. 1791, Harrodsburg, Kentucky.
> > James O'Fallon to Miró (translation). O'Fallon ex-
> > plains why people in Franklin and Cumberland want to
> > migrate to the Yazoo area and tells how many settlers
> > are planning to move. O'Fallon wants peace with the
> > Indians along the way and with those living in the
> > Yazoo territory. 17p.

> > Fol. 542 (no. 2). 18 Feb. 1791, Crab Orchard,
> > Kentucky. James O'Fallon to Brigadier Miró (transla-
> > tion). O'Fallon explains the intentions of the S.C.
> > Company in the Yazoo area. O'Fallon found support
> > for his project during his visits to Cumberland and
> > Franklin. 7p.

> > Fol. 546 (no. 3). 26 Mar. 1791, New Orleans. Esteban
> > Miró to James O'Fallon (copy). O'Fallon is misin-
> > formed about the Spanish reaction to his Yazoo Company.
> > 6p.

Fol. 549 (no. 4 *reservada*). 8 Apr. 1791, New Orleans.
Esteban Miró to Luis de las Casas (copy). Miró is not
certain what Spanish territory lies in the Yazoo region.
That territory really belongs to the Choctaws and Chickasaws. The Tennessee part belongs to the Creeks. Miró
can urge these tribes not to cede their lands or allow
settlements. 4p.

> Fol. 550b (no. 1). 25 Dec. 1790, Madrid. *Real orden
> reservada* from el Conde de Floridablanca to Esteban
> Miró (copy). The King approved Miró's refusal to
> allow the land companies to settle in Spanish terri-
> tory between the Yazoo and Tennessee Rivers. He also
> approved the idea of stalling O'Fallon by letting
> him think that he might obtain permission to settle
> if he goes to Spain. 5p.

> Fol. 552b (no. 2). 25 Dec. 1790, Madrid. *Real orden
> reservada* from [El Conde de] Lerena to the Gov. and
> Intendant of Louisiana (copy). The King approved
> the governor's refusal to allow land companies to
> settle in Spanish territory between the Yazoo and
> Tennessee Rivers. 3p.

Fol. 554 (no. 5 *reservada*). 13 Apr. 1791, Havana. [Capt.
General of Cuba] to [Esteban] Miró (copy). La. needs to
prepare its defenses against the designs of the Carolina
Company until the company desists in its settlement plans
or until the Spanish are able to negotiate an agreement
with the United States over the territory. Miró should
get O'Fallon to make a trip to Spain. Spanish borders go
up to the Cherokee River. 4p.

Fol. 556 (no. 6 *reservada*). 4 Apr. 1791, Havana. [Luis
de las Casas] to Esteban Miró (copy). Las Casas instructs
Miró on what to do if attacked by the S.C. Yazoo Company.
2p.

Fol. 557 (no. 7 *reservada*). 20 Apr. 1791, Havana. [Luis
de las Casas] to Esteban Miró (copy). There might be
several ways to get O'Fallon to Spain. 3p.

Fol. 559 (no. 8 *reservada*). 29 Apr. 1791, Havana. [Luis
de las Casas] to Esteban Miró (copy). Las Casas discusses
Spanish borders and the land that the S.C. Yazoo Company
claims. He approves using the Indians to defend Spanish
territory. He also approves direct correspondence between
the governor and officials in Spain about Indian matters
in order to speed up decisions. 6p.

Fol. 571 (no. 10). 26 Feb. 1791, Pensacola. Alex. McGillivray to Brig. Esteban Miró (copy). McGillivray draws
Miró's attention to Georgia's pretentions of having exclusive right to dispense with the Creek, Cherokee, Choctaws,
and Chickasaw land. American Congress also wishes to
acquire Indian land. 10p.

SD/2556 (CONT'D)

Fol. 576 (no. 9 *reservada*). 10 June 1791, Havana. Luis de las Casas to el Conde del Campo de Alange (copy). Las Casas passes on information from James Wilkinson about Dr. O'Fallon and the S.C. Yazoo Company. 1p. [Enclosures to fol. 594].

Fol. 577 (no. 23 *reservada*). 30 Apr. 1791, New Orleans. Esteban Miró to Luis de las Casas (copy). O'Fallon's claims are usually exaggerated and there is little reason to fear him. The reported settlement at Muscle Shoals is in Cherokee territory and there is nothing for Spain to worry about there. 4p.

Fol. 578. 14 Feb. 1791, Frankfort, Kentucky. James Wilkinson to Brig. Esteban Miró (translation). Wilkinson discusses the activities of McGillivray and O'Fallon. Georgia's Yazoo Company, called the Tennessee Company, is preparing a settlement at Muscle Shoals along the Tennessee River. 9p.

Fol. 601 (no. 12 *reservada*). 3 Aug. 1791, Havana. Luis de las Casas to el Conde del Campo de Alange (duplicate). 2p. [Enclosures to fol. 610].

Fol. 606b (no.1). 8 June 1791, Little Tallassee. Alex. McGillivray to Esteban Miró. [Translation of AGI Cuba/ 2371/doc. 23]. 5p.

SD/2559   DUPLICATE CORRESPONDENCE FROM THE GOVERNORS: 1792

No. 1. *Testimonio de varios documentos relativos a los servicios hechos a S.M. (Q.D.G.) don Francisco Ruiz del Canto* (duplicate). 1p. [Enclosures to fol. 35].

Fol. 14b. 20 July 1779, Havana. Diego José Navarro to [Francisco Ruiz del Canto] (copy). *Instrucción de lo que ha de observar y effectuar don Francisco Ruiz del Canto.* During his trip to St. Marks to determine conditions among the Yuchis, Ruiz will also seek news about the Choctaws, Alibamos, Cherokees, and Chickasaws. 14p.

Fol. 23. 14 Feb. 1780, Havana. Francisco Ruiz del Canto. *Relación de lo acaecido desde la tarde del 16 de diciembre último.* Cherokees, Chickasws, and other tribes are unhappy with the English and are not likely to support them if the Spanish besiege Pensacola. 13p.

SD/2560   DUPLICATE CORRESPONDENCE FROM THE GOVERNORS: 1792

Fol. 486 (no. 206). 2 July 1792, Havana. Luis de las Casas to el Conde del Campo de Alange (duplicate). La. is concerned about the new army raised by the United States since its objective is not clear. La. is also concerned about McGillivray's efforts to reach a border agreement with Georgia. 2p. [Enclosures to fol. 488b].

Fol. 487 (no. 26 *reservada*). 29 Apr. 1792, New Orleans.
El Barón de Carondelet to Luis de las Casas (copy).
Carondelet confirms the report about Americans organizing
an army in the west. This army is too large for operations
against the Indians. Carondelet has sent Wm. Panton to
disuade McGillivray from reaching a border agreement with
the Americans. If war breaks out between the Creeks and
Americans, Carondelet hopes that the Cherokees, Choctaws,
Chickasaws, and Shawnees will support the Creeks. 2p.

Fol. 490 (no. 207). 30 July 1792, Havana. Luis de las Casas
to el Conde del Campo de Alange (duplicate). Las Casas reports
the latest news from La. about American hostility. 2p.
[Enclosures to fol. 495].

Fol. 491 (no. 31 *reservada*). 24 May 1792, New Orleans.
El Barón de Carondelet to Luis de las Casas (copy).
Americans have a systematic plan to usurp Indian territory
and to destroy the tribes along their borders. If Spain
does not take advantage of the present moment to unite
the Choctaws, Chickasaws, Creeks, and Cherokees against the
United States, Spain will lose these invaluable allies
forever. At the same time, Spain will be unable to keep
her possessions any longer. 3p.

Fol. 492b (no. 2). 2 May 1792, Little Tallassee.
Pedro Olivier to el Barón de Carondelet (copy).
Olivier has dissuaded McGillivray from reaching a
border agreement with the Americans. McGillivray
thinks that the proposed meeting between the Creek
and Cherokee leaders should take place in Pensacola.
Wm. Panton is visiting the Cherokees on business. 4p.

Fol. 494. 5 July 1792, Havana. Luis de las Casas to
el Barón de Carondelet (copy). The King's policy is
to keep the Spanish Indian allies in the territory that
they now possess, but it is also the King's wish to
dissuade them from all hostile acts against the Americans. Spanish officials can aid the Indians if they
are attacked, but officials must not encourage the
tribes to start a war. 3p.

SD/2562   DUPLICATE CORRESPONDENCE FROM THE GOVERNORS: 1793

Fol. 370 (no. 319). 9 July 1793, Havana. Luis de las Casas
to el Conde del Campo de Alange (duplicate). Las Casas reports
on the latest activities of the Americans affecting Louisiana.
He encloses a letter from the Cherokees and news concerning
Cumberland and the Chickasaws. 3p. [Enclosures· to fol. 396].

Fol. 372 (no. 76 *reservada*). 13 May 1793, New Orleans.
El Barón de Carondelet to Luis de las Casas (copy). The
intrigues of Gov. Blount of Cumberland and other American
agents have set one tribe against the other, perhaps with
the objective of taking advantage of situation to plant
settlements at Margot [Chickasaw Bluffs], Muscle Shoals,
and other sites. 9p.

SD/2562 (CONT'D)

Fol. 377 (no. 78 *reservada*). 22 May 1793, New Orleans.
El Barón de Carondelet to Luis de las Casas (copy).
Cherokee representatives visited New Orleans November 10
to ask for Spanish assistance. It is to Spain's advantage
that the Cumberland R. be considered the Cherokee border.
Spain needs the Cherokees to control the eastern bank of
the Miss. River. 4p.

Fol. 378b. 5 Apr. 1793, Cherokee Nation. John
McDonald, Bloody Fellow, Glass, Charles of Chickamauga, Spider, Water Hunter, Richard Justice, Badgers
Mother Warrior, and Wm. Shawney to el Barón de Carondelet. [Same as AHN Estado/3898/exp. 5/no. 8 *reservada*/encl.]. 5p.

Fol. 381 (no. 79 *reservada*). 22 May 1793, New Orleans.
El Barón de Carondelet to Luis de las Casas (copy).
Carondelet has written Robertson in Cumberland and the
Spanish diplomatic representative in Philadelphia asking
that they make sure that the Americans stay out of the
Barrancas de Margot area and out of Chickasaw affairs.
5p.

Fol. 383 (no. 1). 7 May 1793, New Orleans. Thomas
Portell to el Barón de Carondelet (copy). Gen.
Robertson's son has arrived from Cumberland with a
letter. He is on his way to help the Chickasaws
against the Creeks. 6p.

Fol. 385b. 23 Apr. 1793, Nashville. James Robertson
to Capt. Thomas Portell (translation). Robertson
acknowledges earlier correspondence and notes that
this is his son's first trip to New Orleans. Chickasaw party is presently in Nashville. 2p.

Fol. 386 (no.2). 21 May 1793, New Orleans. El
Barón de Carondelet to Brig. Gen. James Robertson
(copy). Carondelet approves the trip of Robertson's
son, but he cautions Robertson against sending weapons
to the Chickasaws. Spaniards have restrained themselves from doing so with the Cherokees in spite of
numerous petitions. In fact, the Spaniards have
persuaded the Cherokees to stop hostilities against
Cumberland and have persuaded the Creeks not to attack
the Georgians. Just recently, the Cherokees asked
Spain to dissuade the Creeks from using Cherokee
territory to war on Cumberland. 4p.

Fol. 388 (no. 80 *reservada*). 23 May 1793, New Orleans.
El Barón de Carondelet to Luis de las Casas (copy). The
letter from the Cherokee leaders [AGI SD/2562/fol. 378b]
shows how false the charges in the American newspapers
were against Brig. O'Neill and Capt. Gen. Las Casas.
Carondelet has sent a copy of the letter to Spanish
diplomats in Philadelphia so that it could be used to
disprove Gov. Blount's charges. 2p.

SD/2562 (CONT'D)

Fol. 388b. 16 May 1793, Natchez. Manuel Gayoso de
Lemos to el Barón de Carondelet (copy). Cumberland
has raised a small detachment to guard against the
Creeks and Shawnees. Gen. Robertson has encouraged
American newspapers to accuse Spain of prompting the
Creeks to attack Americans. 8p.

Fol. 605. 1791, Charleston. *Resumen de un librito ynglés,
que contiene un extracto de los apuntes de la compañia de la
Carolina del Sur en el Yasu* (translation). The best way to
supply Franklin and other western areas is to send goods up
the Alabama and Hiwassee Rivers, then travel overland a short
distance to the headwaters of the Tennessee River. This means
going through Spanish, Creek, and Cherokee territory. 3p.

SD/2563   DUPLICATE CORRESPONDENCE FROM THE GOVERNORS: 1794

Fol. 6 (no. 364), 9 Jan. 1794, Havana. Luis de las Casas to el
Conde del Campo de Alange (duplicate). Las Casas announces the
treaty of Nogales with the Creeks, Cherokees, Choctaws, and
Chickasaws. This is an offensive and defensive alliance, and
these tribes serve as a powerful shield in protecting Spanish
possessions. 2p. [Enclosures to fol. 11b].

Fol. 7 (no. 97 *reservada*). 5 Dec. 1793, New Orleans. El
Barón de Carondelet to Luis de las Casas (copy). Carondelet attaches the Treaty of Nogales. 1p.

Fol. 8. 28 Oct. 1793, Nogales. Manuel Gayoso de
Lemos et al.. Copy of the Treaty of Nogales between
Spain and the Chickasaws, Creeks, Talapooses, Alibamos,
Cherokees, and Choctaws. Other tribes represented
the Cherokees. Spain granted the Cherokees Spanish
protection and will distribute the tribe's annual
gifts in Pensacola. 8p.

Fol. 336 (no. 398), 18 May 1794, Havana. Luis de las Casas
to el Conde del Campo de Alange (duplicate. 7p. [Enclosures
to fol. 353b].

Fol. 343 (no. 2). 1794, [St. Augustine]. John Hambly.
*Diario de don Juan Hambley en su último viage a las tierras
de los yndios.* [Copy of AGS GM/7235/no. 398/encl. no. 3].
18p.

Fol. 353. 7 Feb. 1794, Cocha Tuna. John Kinnard to James
Seagrove. [Same as AGS GM/7235/no. 398/encl.]. 2p.

Fol. 359 (no. 401). 12 May 1794, Havana. Luis de las Casas to
el Conde del Campo de Alange (duplicate). 9p. [Enclosures to
fol. 421b].

Fol. 365 (no. 1). 8 and 10 Mar. 1794, Ft. Nogales. Copy
of *declaración* from John [Peter?] Pisgignous stating that
300 soldiers have gathered in Cumberland with hostile
intentions against the Spaniards. 25p.

SD/2563 (CONT'D)

>   Fol. 409 (no. 6). 20 Mar. 1794, Cloaly. Report from
>   Milfort to el Barón de Carondelet (translation). Chero-
>   kees (130) visited the Creeks on March 16. Cherokees
>   asked the American agents among the Creeks for the same
>   treaty granted the Creeks. Americans evidently killed
>   twelve Creeks and captured two women along the Cherokee
>   River. 21p.

>   Fol. 669 (no. 101). 24 Feb. 1794, New Orleans. El Barón de
>   Carondelet to Diego de Gardoqui (duplicate). Carondelet
>   discusses the exchequer of La. and West Fla. and the annual
>   Indian gifts. 34p. [Enclosures to fol. 769b].

>   Fol. 721 (no. 7). 28 Oct. 1793, Nogales. Manuel Gayoso
>   de Lemos et al. Copy of the Treaty of Nogales between
>   Spain and the Chickasaws, Creeks, Talapooses, Alibamos,
>   Cherokees, and Choctaws. 6p. [Same as fol. 8].

>   Fol. 724 (no. 8). 8 Dec. 1793, Old Village of Wetonka.
>   Pedro Olivier to el Barón de Carondelet. [Same as AGI
>   SD/2580/fol. 231]. 6p.

>   Fol. 726 (no. 9). 24 Feb. 1794, New Orleans. El Barón
>   de Carondelet. *Relación de los gastos [del] ... ramo de
>   yndios.* [copy of AGI SD/2580/fol. 234]. 4p.

SD/2564   DUPLICATE CORRESPONDENCE FROM THE GOVERNORS: 1796

>   Fol. 2 (no. 455). 11 Jan. 1795, Havana. Luis de las Casas
>   to el Conde del Campo de Alange (duplicate). 4p. [Enclosures
>   to fol. 4].

>   Fol. 3. 30 Sept. 1794, Pensacola. *Instancia* (petition)
>   from Enrique White asking for promotion to Colonel.
>   White's present duties include handling some Creek and
>   Cherokee affairs. 3p.

>   Fol. 62 (no. 465). 22 Jan. 1795, Havana. Luis de las Casas
>   to el Conde del Campo de Alange (duplicate). 4p. [Enclosures
>   to fol. 89b].

>   Fol. 64 (no. 126 *reservada*). 30 Oct. 1794, New Orleans.
>   El Barón de Carondelet to Luis de las Casas (copy).
>   Carondelet reports that hostilities are likely between the
>   Creeks and Gen. Clark. Carondelet has received a letter
>   from John McDonald, Spanish commissioner among the Chero-
>   kees. 4p.

>   Fol. 68b (no. 1). 18 Sept. 1794, [Creek Nation].
>   John Galphin to James Burges (translation). Galphin
>   claims that the Choctaws, Chickasaws, and Cherokees
>   will join the Creeks against the Americans, who have
>   built a fort along the Oconee River. 6p.

Fol. 71 (no. 2). 2 Oct. 1794, St. Marks. Diego de
Vegas to James Burges (copy). Indians have lost all
faith in Mr. Seagrove, the American Indian agent.
The Cowetas and Cherokees have reportedly ambushed
a party of Americans. 8p.

Fol. 74b (no. 2 *muy reservada*). 31 Oct. 1794, New
Orleans. El Barón de Carondelet to Diego de Vegas
(copy). Carondelet acknowledges the critical situation between the Spanish Indians (the Creeks and
Cherokees) and the Americans. 4p.

Fol. 77 (no. 4). 20 Sept. 1794, Cherokees. John
McDonald to el Barón de Carondelet (translation).
Cherokees have maintained the peace but Gov. Blount's
actions have created great discontent. Cumberland
attacked the Cherokee villages of Necofacky [Nicka-
jak?] and Running Water. Cherokees are divided on
how to respond, but the Lower Cherokees remain firm
Spanish friends. 5p.

Fol. 149 (no. 492). 6 May 1795, Havana. Luis de las Casas to
el Conde del Campo de Alange (duplicate). Las Casas describes
the sale by Ga. of land that belongs to Spain and her Indian
allies. 6p. [Enclosures to fol. 181b].

Fol. 152b (no. 51 *reservada*). 4 Mar. 1795, New Orleans.
El Barón de Carondelet to el Duque de la Alcudia (copy).
Ga. has sold 30,000 *arpanes* of land which belong to Spain's
Indian allies. If the Georgians actually occupy this land,
Spain will have to provide refuge for her allies west of
the Miss., as she has already done with some Shawnees and
Cherokees. Unfortunately, shifting the tribes westward
will expose other Spanish possessions to Indians accustomed
to robbery, cattle rustling, and other crimes. 4p.

Fol. 156 (no. 132 *reservada*). 30 Mar. 1795, New Orleans.
El Barón de Carondelet to Luis de las Casas (copy).
Carondelet recommends armed resistance to American encroach-
ment. Otherwise, the tribes will migrate west across the
Miss., as have the Shawnees and Cherokees. Once there,
these tribes will engage in many undesirable activities. 5p.

Fol. 159b (no. 2). Dec. 1794 - Jan. 1795, Augusta.
Thomas Napier et al. *Actos del estado de Georgia*
(translation). Ga. passed acts which established
borders for land sold by the state [part of which
includes Cherokee territory]. 31p.

Fol. 182 (no. 493). 7 May 1795, Havana. Luis de las Casas to
el Conde del Campo de Alange (duplicate). 4p. [Enclosures to
fol. 189b].

Fol. 183 (no. 133 *reservada*). 30 Mar. 1795, New Orleans.
El Barón de Carondelet to Luis de las Casas (copy).

SD/2564 (CONT'D)

Because of the Chickasaw-Talapoose war, the Chickasaws
gave the Americans permission to build a fort at Muscle
Shoals. 7p.

Fol. 323 (no. 508). 20 June 1795, Havana. Luis de las Casas
to el Conde del Campo de Alange (duplicate). Americans are
building a fort at Muscle Shoals in order to seize Barrancas
de Margot. 6p. [Enclosures to fol. 365b].

Fol. 326 (no. 134 *reservada*). 1 May 1795, New Orleans.
El Barón de Carondelet to Luis de las Casas (copy).
Americans have evidently begun to build a fort at Muscle
Shoals. Carondelet will prevent this if possible. 10p.

Fol. 330b. 30 Mar. 1793, Aranjuez. *Real orden* from
el Duque de la Alcudia to el Barón de Carondelet
(copy). The King approves Carondelet's decisions
against allowing the Americans to remain at Muscle
Shoals. 2p.

Fol. 429 (no. 514). 16 July 1795, Havana. Luis de las Casas
to el Conde del Campo de Alange (duplicate). 1p. [Enclosures
to fol. 441].

Fol. 430 (no. 136 *reservada*). 13 June 1795, New Orleans.
El Barón de Carondelet to Luis de las Casas (copy).
Carondelet continues his effort to frustrate the proposed
American settlement at Muscle Shoals aimed at seizing
Barrancas de Margot. Cumberland has taken steps to favor
the Chickasaws against the Creeks, although there are
Americans supporting both sides. Cherokees have recently
signed another treaty with the Americans ceding more ter-
ritory. 7p.

Fol. 438 (no. 2). 27 Apr. 1795, Ft. Massac. Maj.
Doyle to Thomas Portell (copy). Some militia have
left Cumberland to aid the Chickasaws and are headed
for Barrancas de Margot. 2p.

Fol. 690 (no. 570). 25 Jan. 1795, Havana. Luis de las Casas
to el Conde del Campo de Alange (duplicate). 2p. [Enclosures
to fol. 720].

Fol. 694 (no. 25 *reservada*). 3 Dec. 1795, New Madrid.
Manuel Gayoso de Lemos to el Barón de Carondelet (copy).
Cumberland is reportedly planning an attack against San
Fernando de las Barrancas. 2p.

Fol. 695 (no. 153 *reservada*). 9 Jan. 1796, New Orleans.
El Barón de Carondelet to Luis de las Casas (copy).
Carondelet discusses the exposure of Ft. San Fernando de
las Barrancas to an attack from Cumberland. 3p.

SD/2569   DUPLICATE CORRESPONDENCE FROM THE GOVERNORS: 1802-1803

Fol. 152 (no. 4). 26 Mar. 1795, New Orleans. El Barón de Carondelet to Antonio Palao. Americans are taking advantage of the war between the Chickasaws and Creeks to fortify Muscle Shoals. 2p.

Fol. 153 (no. 5). 9 July 1795, New Orleans. El Barón de Carondelet to Antonio Palao (copy). Gov. orders Palao to tell the Indians that the Americans are the real enemy. Americans will treat other tribes as they have the Cherokees, conclude one treaty only to return later to ask for more land. 2p.

SD/2571   DUPLICATE CORRESPONDENCE FROM THE GOVERNORS: 1805-1818

Fol. 297 (no. 609). 17 Mar. 1806, Havana. El Marqués de Someruelos to José Antonio Cavallero (copy). 2p. [Enclosures to fol. 299b].

Fol. 298. 20 Jan. 1806, Pensacola. Vicente Folch to el Marqués de Someruelos (copy). Folch recommends measures to be taken in case of war with the United States. Cumberland is one of the American possessions in which the Spanish should sponsor a revolt. 4p.

SD/2576   LETTERS AND EXPEDIENTES: 1787-1789

Fol. 264 (no. 503). 7 June 1787, New Orleans. Martín Navarro to el Marqués de Sonora. *Ocurrencias de la provincia de la Luisiana en los seis primeros meses de este año*. The Cherokees and Creeks are constantly alarmed at American activities. 16p. [Enclosures to fol. 279].

Fol. 272 (no. 503). 7 June 1787, New Orleans. [Martín Navarro to el Marqués de Sonora]. [Copy of fol. 264]. 13p.

SD/2578   LETTERS AND EXPEDIENTES: 1793-1794

Fol. 783 (exp. 8). 6 Feb. 1794, Natchez. Manuel Gayoso de Lemos to Diego de Gardoqui. Gayoso has asked for the King's approval of the 2,000 pesos spent in the latest treaty negotiations with the Chickasaws, Creeks, Talapooses, Alibamos, Cherokees, and Choctaws. 4p. [Enclosures to fol. 788].

Fol. 788. 9 July 1794, Madrid. Copy of *real orden* to the Gov. of Louisiana approving Gayoso's expenses in making the treaty with the Chickasaws, Creeks, Talapooses, Alibamos, Cherokees, and Choctaws. 1p.

SD/2580   LETTERS AND EXPEDIENTES: 1798-1822

Fol. 56 [exp. 2]. 1794-1799, Louisiana. El Barón de Carondelet. *Expediente promovido por el yntendente de la Luisiana [el] Barón de Carondelet sobre reformar el antiguo plan de dotación y gastos de provincias: Ynformes de la contaduría general*. 1p. [Enclosures to fol. 324].

SD/2580 (CONT'D)

Fol. 113 (no. 123). 18 Apr. 1796, New Orleans. Summary
of report from Intendant Francisco Rendon on reforms proposed for the exchequer. Rendon mentions commerce with
Cumberland. 63p.

Fol. 171. 3 Jan. 1793, New Orleans. José de Orúe.
*Relación que forma la contaduría principal de exército
y real hacienda de la provincia de la Luisiana* (copy).
Orúe examines the exchequer, which includes the expenses
of the Treaty of Nogales within the expenditures of the
ramo de población y amistad de indios. 14p.

Fol. 227. 28 Oct. 1793, Nogales. Manuel Gayoso de Lemos
et al. Treaty of Nogales. [Same as AGI SD/2563/fol. 8].

Fol. 231. 8 Dec. 1793, Old Village of Wetonka. Pedro
Olivier to el Barón de Carondelet (copy). American agent
has arrived among the Creeks to negotiate a peace treaty.
Creeks have a treaty (Nogales) with the Chickasaws, Choctaws, and Cherokees. 6p.

Fol. 234. 24 Feb. 1794, New Orleans. El Barón de Carondelet. *Relación de los gastos [del] ... ramo de yndios*.
Annual appropriations for the Cherokees and other tribes
in Louisiana. Cherokees number 6,000 people. 3p.

Fol. 549 (no. 123). 18 Apr. 1796, New Orleans. Francisco
Rendon to Diego de Gardoqui. 17p. [Enclosures to fol. 600].

Fol. 558. 7 Apr. 1796, New Orleans. *Presupuesto* (budget)
from Juan Ventura Morales of the principal expenditures in
the La. exchequer. Budget includes the Cherokees subsidy.
33p.

Fol. 576. 7 Apr. 1796, New Orleans. *Informe* from Juan
Ventura Morales to Francisco Rendon. Morales recommends
changes in the exchequer and includes a reference to
commerce with Cumberland. 49p.

SD/2591   EXPEDIENTES ABOUT THE EXPULSION OF THE ENGLISH: 1733-1736

N. fol. 20 Oct. 1735, St. Augustine. Francisco del Moral
Sánchez to José Patiño. Moral Sánchez describes Indian relations in N. Carolina. All [Florida] Indian tribes are devoted
to the English, except the Tuscaroras, who are so weak and
persecuted that they pose no threat. English have posted a
bounty for each Tuscarora brought to them dead or alive. 5p.

SD/2593   EXPEDIENTES ABOUT THE EXPULSION OF THE ENGLISH: 1738-1743

N. fol. [exp. 48?]. 28 May 1738, Havana. Juan Francisco de
Guëmes y Horcasitas to el Marqués de Thorren. 3p. [Encloses
8 documents].

SD/2593 (CONT'D)

N. fol. 14 Apr. 1738, St. Mark. *Acuerdo* between the Yuchis and Spain. The Natiri, Cabaxquia, Cherokee, Chickasaw, and Choctaw are accustomed to receiving English goods. 6p.

N. fol. [exp. 65?]. 12 July 1742. Draft of letter to the Gov. of Havana. 1p. [Encloses 1 document].

N. fol. 20 Mar. 1742, Havana. [Antonio Arredondo]. *Demonstración historiográphica del derecho que tiene el rey cathólico a el territorio que oy posee el rey británico con el nombre de Nueva Georgia* (copy). [Arredondo] discusses DeSoto's trip through Indian territory, including his visit to the Cherokees. 203p.

SD/2596   EXPEDIENTES ABOUT THE ENGLISH AND AMERICANS: 1776-1779

Fol. 50 (no. 63). 10 July 1777, New Orleans. Bernardo de Gálvez to José de Gálvez. 4p. [Enclosures to fol. 58b].

Fol. 52. [1777]. *Noticias de Penzacola.* [Copy of BN MS./19508]. 11p.

Fol. 373 (no. 178 *reservada*). 28 July 1778, New Orleans. Bernardo de Gálvez to José de Gálvez (duplicate). 4p. [Enclosures to fol. 384b].

Fol. 378b. 6 July 1778, San Gabriel de Manchak. Juan de la Villebeuvre to Bernardo de Gálvez (copy). The English plan to attack New Orleans using the Choctaws, Chickasaws, Cherokees, and a few English soldiers. Cherokees and Chickasaws, however, refuse to participate because they fear the Americans. 3p.

Fol. 410 (no. 200 *reservada*). 24 Oct. 1778, New Orleans. Bernardo de Gálvez to José de Gálvez. 1p. [Enclosures to fol. 419].

Fol. 411. 17 Sept. 1778, New Orleans. Bernardo de Gálvez to Pedro Cherer [Peter Chester?] (copy). Gálvez mentions reports that the Choctaws, Cherokees, and Chickasaws are marching against New Orleans. 4p.

SD/2597   LETTERS FROM MIRALLES AND RENDON: 1779-1784

Fol. 316 (no. 88). 12 Oct. 1783, Philadelphia. Francisco Rendon to José de Gálvez (duplicate). 3p. [Enclosures to fol. 318b].

Fol. 318. 27 Sept. 1783, Richmond, Virginia. [A resident of Richmond to a resident of Philadelphia] (copy). N. Carolinians who settled along the Cumberland or Shawnee Rivers were not justified in attacking a Spanish outpost. Spaniards repulsed the attack. 2p.

SD/2598   LETTERS FROM MIRALLES AND RENDON: 1779-1784

Fol. 13. 6 Sept. 1779, Philadelphia. Juan de Miralles to José
de Gálvez (duplicate). The Americans have concluded a peace
treaty with the Cherokees. 3p.

Fol. 379. 5 Mar. 1781, Philadelphia. Francisco Rendon to José
de Gálvez (triplicate). 4p. [Enclosures to fol. 414b].

Fol. 403b. 14 Feb. 1781, Philadelphia. *Noticias de
Philadelphia* (copy). Cherokees have decided to fight the
Americans and have sent war parties against the Va. and
N.C. frontiers. Col. Campbell and the militia from
Washington County attacked the Cherokees and destroyed
some of their villages. 2p.

Fol. 408. 12 Feb. 1781, Richmond. Extract of letter from
Mr. Jefferson, Gov. of Virginia, giving news from the
southern war zone. Since efforts to prevent war with the
Cherokees have failed, Americans have decided to carry the
war to the Cherokees rather than wait to be attacked. 4p.

SD/2599   EXPEDIENTES ABOUT BORDERS: 1802-1804

Fol. 129 (no. 426). 24 June 1804, Philadelphia. [Irujo?] to
Pedro Cevallos (copy). 2p. [Enclosures to fol. 148].

Fol. 133. [Apr. 1804?]. *Relación* from [John Forbes]
about Spanish Florida, including the Cherokee and general
Indian debt owed to Panton, Leslie, and Company. 30p.

SD/2604   DOCUMENTS FROM THE ROYAL EXCHEQUER: 1752-1800

N. fol. 5 May 1759, St. Augustine. Lucas de Palazio to [Julian
de Arriaga]. 9p. [Encloses 11 documents].

N. fol. 10 Feb. 1759, Tolomato. Fr. Agustín Trujillo.
Padrón del pueblo de yndios, nombrado Tolomato (copy).
Census listing some residents of Tolomato as Chiluques
[Cherokees?]. 5p.

N. fol. 10 Feb. 1759, Pueblo Nra. Señora de la Leche.
[Fray Alonzo Ruiz]. *Padrón del pueblo de yndios Nra.
Señora de la Leche* (copy). Census listing some residents
as Chiluques [Cherokees?]. 7p.

SD/2612   DUPLICATE CORRESPONDENCE FROM THE INTENDANTS: 1788-1795

Fol. 710 (no. 4 *reservada*). 25 Apr. 1795, New Orleans.
Francisco Rendon to Diego de Gardoqui (duplicate). A party
of 400 men from Ga. is on its way to seize Muscle Shoals. 15p.
[Enclosures to fol. 745].

Fol. 732 (no. 2). 23 Mar. 1795, New Orleans. El Barón
de Carondelet to Francisco Rendon (copy). Americans are
reportedly helping the Chickasaws against the Creeks
because the Chickasaws promised them permission to erect
a fort along the Cherokee R. at Muscle Shoals. 4p.

SD/2612 (CONT'D)

Fol. 737 (no. 5). 27 July 1794, New Orleans. El Barón
de Carondelet to el Duque de la Alcudia (copy). Carondelet
forwards a proposal from Panton, Leslie and Company, who
have the responsibility of furnishing treaty goods to the
Creeks, Choctaws, Chickasaws, and part of the Cherokees.
He recommends that the King accept their offer to sell
their company to the Crown. 7p.

Fol. 741 (no. 6). [1794]. Panton, Leslie and Company to
el Barón de Carondelet (copy). Panton, Leslie and Company
has been so successful with the Indians that the United
States has felt it necessary to use public funds to combat
their achievements. Now the Americans threaten to provide
goods at a cheaper rate. Panton, Leslie and Company offers
either to sell the firm to the Spanish government or continue operating if the Crown grants the company a 400,000
peso loan for ten years. If Spain chooses the latter,
the company must have a monopoly of the trade among the
Choctaws, Chickasaws, Creeks, and Cherokees. 9p.

SD/2613   DUPLICATE CORRESPONDENCE FROM THE INTENDANTS: 1796

Fol. 155 (no. 123). 18 Apr. 1796, New Orleans. Francisco
Rendon to Diego de Gardoqui (duplicate). 15p. [Enclosures to
fol. 200].

Fol. 163. 7 Apr. 1796, New Orleans. Juan Ventura Morales.
*Presupuesto ... en que pueden quedar arregladas la mayor
parte de las erogaciones de la real hacienda.* Budget
includes annual gifts for the Cherokees. 35p.

Fol. 181. 7 Apr. 1796, New Orleans. Juan Ventura Morales
to Francisco Rendon. Morales examines the budget proposal
and discusses tax rates for goods from Cumberland and
Kentucky. 39p.

SD/2614   DUPLICATE CORRESPONDENCE FROM THE INTENDANTS: 1797

Fol. 66 (no. 83). 21 Jan. 1797, New Orleans. Juan Ventura
Morales to Diego de Gardoqui (duplicate). Goods are being sent
to Pensacola , Mobile, Apalache [St. Marks], and Barrancas de
Margot to give to the Choctaws, Chickasaws, Creeks, Cherokees,
and Alibamos. 3p. [Enclosures to fol. 69b].

Fol. 68. 31 Dec. 1796, New Orleans. Juan Ventura Morales.
*Relación que manifiesta los efectos consumidos en los
regalos de yndios en todo este presente año* (duplicate).
Lists Indian goods for 1796. 4p.

Fol. 241 (no. 110). 21 Mar. 1797, New Orleans. Juan Ventura
Morales to Pedro Varela y Ulloa. [Duplicate of AHN Estado/
3902/ap. 2/no. 110]. 4p.

SD/2615   DUPLICATE CORRESPONDENCE FROM THE INTENDANTS: 1798-1799

Fol. 663 (no. 282). 31 Mar. 1799, New Orleans. Juan Ventura
Morales to Miguel Cayetano Soler (triplicate). 2p. [Enclo-
sures to fol. 665b].

Fol. 664. 12 Jan. 1799, New Orleans. Manuel Gayoso de
Lemos to Juan Ventura Morales. [Copy of AHN Estado/3888/
doc. 73]. 2p.

SD/2619   DUPLICATE CORRESPONDENCE FROM THE INTENDANTS: 1802

Fol. 335 (no. 163). 30 Nov. 1802, New Orleans. Juan Ventura
Morales to Miguel Cayetano Soler (duplicate). 2p. [Enclo-
sures to fol. 352].

Fol. 338 (no. 2). 9 Nov. 1802, New Orleans. Manuel de
Salcedo to Juan Ventura Morales (copy). There is a large
party of Osages at the Arkansas Post. Spanish commander
talked with the Osage leaders in the presence of many
Choctaws, Chickasaws, and Cherokees who live around the
post. Spanish commander asked the Osages to seek peace
with the Arkansas, Choctaws, Chickasaws, and Cherokees.
5p.

Fol. 346 (no. 4). 11 Nov. 1802, New Orleans. Juan
Ventura Morales et al. *Acuerdo de la junta de real
hacienda* (copy). The exchequer approves the commandant's
actions and funds spent in Arkansas to obtain peace between
the Osages and the Arkansas, Chickasaws, Choctaws, and
Cherokees. 13p.

SD/2640   EXPEDIENTES FROM THE ROYAL EXCHEQUER: 1803-1804

Fol. 560 (no. 163). 30 Nov. 1802, New Orleans. Juan Ventura
Morales to Miguel Cayetano Soler. [Same as AGI SD/2619/fol.
335]. 2p. [Enclosures to fol. 579].

Fol. 563 (no. 2). 9 Nov. 1802, New Orleans. Manuel de
Salcedo to Juan Ventura Morales. [Same as AGI SD/2619/
fol. 338]. 4p.

Fol. 569 (no. 4). 11 Nov. 1802, New Orleans. Juan
Ventura Morales et al. *Acuerdo de la junta de real
hacienda*. [Same as AGI SD/2619/fol. 346]. 13p.

SD/2670   EXPEDIENTES ABOUT COMMERCE: 1805-1817

Fol. 275. [Exp. 3]. 1807. Expediente concerning the English
merchant Forbes. 1p. [Enclosures to fol. 498b].

Fol. 442 (no. 64). 6 Apr. 1805, Pensacola. *Petición*
from James Ynnerarity to the Gov. General (copy).
Ynnerarity, an associate of John Forbes and Company,
requests that Spain honor earlier agreements made with
the company because the war with England has begun again.
John Forbes and Company was established to trade with the
Choctaws, Chickasaws, Cherokees, and Talapooses. 4p.

SD/2670 (CONT'D)

Fol. 563 (exp. 5, no. 407). 31 Mar. 1806, Pensacola. Juan
Ventura Morales to Miguel Cayetano Soler (duplicate). 4p.
[Enclosures to fol. 579].

Fol. 565 (no. 1). 18 Apr. 1805, Pensacola. James Ynnerarity to the Governor General (copy). Ynnerarity (an
associate of John Forbes's Company which is in charge of
the trade with the Choctaws, Chickasaws, Cherokees, and
Talapooses) reminds the governor about permission granted
to the company to remove its property, debts, and goods
in case war erupted with Great Britain. Spain and the
company have handled this problem in various ways since
1789. 3p.

N. fol. (no. 41 *reservada*). 27 July 1794, New Orleans. El
Barón de Carondelet to el Duque de la Alcudia. [Copy of AGI
SD/2612/fol. 737]. 5p. [Encloses 2 documents].

N. fol. [1794?] *Representación* from Panton, Leslie and
Company to el Barón de Carondelet. [Copy of AGI SD/2612/
fol. 741]. 6p.

SECCIÓN IX   SECRETARÍA DE ESTADO
ESTADO/9   SERIES 1: LOUISIANA AND FLORIDA

Doc. 27. 3 Dec. 1792, Havana. Luis de las Casas to [el Conde
de Aranda] (triplicate). Las Casas explains his approval of
the request by the governor of Louisiana to rebuild two French
forts at the instigation of the Cherokees. 1p. [Encloses 2
documents].

Doc. 27 (*reservada*). 3 Dec. 1792, Havana. Luis de las
Casas to el Conde de Aranda. Cherokees have requested
the rebuilding of two French forts near Tombigbee and
Muscle Shoals. Las Casas has approved the request because
it will aid in building alliance of Southern tribes against
the United States. 8p.

Doc. 27 (no. 57 *reservada*). 20 Nov. 1793, New Orleans.
El Barón de Carondelet to Luis de las Casa (copy).
Bloody Fellow and the other Cherokees in New Orleans have
requested that Spain reestablish two old French forts --
one at Tombigbee and the other at Muscle Shoals. This
would allow Spain to dominate both sides of the Miss. R.
up to the Ohio. Cherokees can cede this land with no
problem. Secrecy is important in order to prevent the
Americans from seizing these two sites. 6p.

ESTADO/14   SERIES 1: LOUISIANA AND FLORIDA

Doc. 100. 5 Mar. 1794, Aranjuez. *Real orden* to Luis de las
Casas. 1p. [Encloses 4 documents].

ESTADO/14 (CONT'D)

Doc. 100. 5 Mar. 1794, Aranjuez. *Real orden* to the
governor of New Orleans stating that the capt. gen. had
been told how to treat the request for assistance from the
Lower Creeks and Cherokees, two tribes which have provoked
the Americans' desire for vengeance because of the cruelties committed against the residents of Ga. and Carolina.
In spite of the Nogales treaty with these tribes, Spain
should not aid them since they have started a war with the
United States without first informing Spanish officials.
3p.

Doc. 100. 20 June 1794, Havana. Luis de las Casas to el
Duque de la Alcudia. Las Casas has forwarded a royal order
to Carondelet concerning the Spanish conduct towards the
Creeks, Cherokees, and others. Las Casas also explained
the content of the order to the governors of St. Augustine
and Pensacola. 1p.

Doc. 100. 20 June 1794, Havana. Letter from Luis de las
Casas stating he has sent the royal order concerning
Spanish treatment of the Creeks, Cherokees, and other
tribes to the Gov. of Louisiana. 1p.

SECCIÓN XI   CAPITANÍA GENERAL DE LA ISLA DE CUBA
CUBA/2   CORRESPONDENCE OF BERNADO DE GÁLVEZ: 1780-1786

Doc. 193. 6 Apr. 1780, New Orleans. Pedro Piernas to Bernardo
de Gálvez. A party of 800 Chickasaws, Cherokees, Creeks, and
Choctaws (with some English) are expected to attack Spanish
outposts along the river. 6p.

Doc. 221. 25 Apr. 1780, Ft. Panmure. Commandant at Natchez
to [Bernardo de Gálvez?] (copy). Indian attacks on those
fleeing Spanish at Mobile have influenced settlers around
Natchez not to leave. A party of Cherokees and Shawnees
attacked a group of Carolina immigrants as they traveled down
the Ohio River. The immigrants suffered many casualties. 3p.

CUBA/3B   CORRESPONDENCE OF ESTEBAN MIRÓ: 1781-1785

Doc. 911. 3 Sept. 1785, New Orleans. Esteban Miró to Arturo
O'Neill (copy). Miró acknowledges the receipt of a memorial
from the Creeks, Chickasaws, and Cherokees and a letter
forwarded by O'Neill from Alex. McGillivray. 1p.

Doc. 918. 9 Sept. 1785, New Orleans. Esteban Miró to Francisco
Bouligny (copy). Miró received a memorial from the Creeks and
Cherokees that resulted from a meeting between the tribes
sponsored by McGillivray. These tribes protested against the
lands that Great Britain granted the Americans and against
recent American settlements. Indians have asked for Spain's
protection. 2p.

CUBA/3B (CONT'D)

Doc. 929. 10 Sept. 1785, Chickasaws. Thomas Green to Col.
Blide. Green is worried about Spanish relations with the
Indians who attacked the Cumberland area last year. 4p.

Doc. 1092 (no. 258). 10 Dec. 1785, New Orleans. Esteban Miró
to el Conde de Gálvez. Miró forwards a letter from Luis
Cacheré concerning Francisco Bouligny's commission to learn
the truth about the reported war preparations in Cumberland
and Ohio. Gen. Clark is recruiting an army to be used against
the Indians, but it is possible that troops might be employed
against Natchez. Several Cumberland residents have sought land
around Barrancas de Margot to set up a colony. 3p. [Enclosures
to doc. 1092a].

> Doc. 1092a (no. 1). [1785]. Luis Chaceré to Francisco
> Bouligny (translation). Chaceré reports on his visit to
> Cumberland, describing the agriculture, rivers in the
> area (including the Cherokee R.), Muscle Shoals, the
> population, and Gen. Clark's activities against the
> Indians. 11p.

[Siles 456] (no. 101). 11 Nov. 1785, New Orleans. Esteban
Miró to Francisco Bouligny. Nicholas Long has arrived in New
Orleans with a party from Cumberland. 1p.

CUBA/4A   CORRESPONDENCE OF ESTEBAN MIRÓ: 1786-1787

[Siles 532](no. 54). 19 May 1786, New Orleans. Esteban Miró
to Carlos de Grand-Pré. Miró acknowledges receipt of Cumberland
news. Grand-Pré should maintain harmony with Cumberland inhabitants. 1p.

CUBA/4B   CORRESPONDENCE OF ESTEBAN MIRÓ: 1786-1787

Doc. 591 *muy reservada*. 24 Mar. 1787, New Orleans. Esteban
Miró to Arturo O'Neill. O'Neill should advise McGillivray
that if Creeks attack Americans in the spring they might be
confronted with Americans from Ga. and Cumberland. Spain
should restrain the Creeks by limiting the number of guns
supplied them. 6p.

Doc. 661. 18 May 1787, New Orleans. Esteban Miró to Arturo
O'Neill. Miró wants to know if O'Neill has received the
Cherokee king, chiefs, and warriors that McGillivray[?]
informed O'Neill about. 1p.

[Siles 578]. 3 Aug. 1787, New Orleans. Esteban Miró to
Arturo O'Neill. Miró reports news about the Talapooses and
Cumberland residents. 1p.

[Siles 580]. 12 Aug. 1787, New Orleans. Esteban Miró to
Arturo O'Neill. Miró has been notified about the death of
Davenport (the American commissioner), the ruin of an American
trading venture, and the recent hostilities of the Talapooses
against Cumberland. 1p.

CUBA/5A   CORRESPONDENCE OF ESTEBAN MIRÓ: 1788

Doc. 189 *muy reservada*. 24 Feb. 1788, New Orleans. Esteban
Miró to Arturo O'Neill. Diego Gardoqui, Spanish envoy in New
York, reports that Franklin has decided to raise 1,500 militia
in response to Spanish hostilities. Cumberland will assist them
with 500 men. If they attack, the Spanish will have to use the
Indians in defense, especially the Creeks. 8p.

Doc. 248 *reservada*. 1 Apr. 1788, New Orleans. Esteban Miró
to Arturo O'Neill. The capt. general of Cuba and Miró believe
that Spanish officials should encourage the Creeks to maintain
peace with Americans. There is no recent news that Franklin
and Cumberland have attacked the Creeks. Even if they have,
this is still not enough provocation to break the peace. 4p.

Doc. 798. 5 Sept. 1788, New Orleans. Esteban Miró to Manuel
Pérez. [Copy of doc. 798a]. 4p. [Enclosures to doc. 798a].

> Doc. 798a. 5 Sept. 1788, New Orleans. Esteban Miró to
> Manuel Pérez. Miró has received Pérez's proposal to allow
> the Cherokees to settle in Spanish territory. Government
> has no objection to the proposal but cannot grant a gift
> to the Cherokees without the King's permission. 4p.

[Siles 600] (no. 572). 10 Apr. 1788, New Orleans. Esteban
Miró to Carlos de Grand-Pré. Miró acknowledges receipt of
information about the arrival in Natchez of Americans from
Cumberland and the Tennessee River. 2p.

CUBA/6   CORRESPONDENCE OF ESTEBAN MIRÓ: 1789

Doc. 706. 19 Sept. 1789, New Orleans. Esteban Miró to Manuel
Pérez. Miró approves Pérez's decision to grant part of Vilpocha
to the group of Indians [Cherokees?] who crossed the Mississippi.
2p.

[Siles 680] (no. 530). 20 Apr. 1789, New Orleans. Esteban
Miró to Carlos de Grand-Pré. Miró instructs Grand-Pré on the
response he can make to a petition from two Ky. and Cumberland
settlers to immigrate to Spanish territory. 2p.

CUBA/7   CORRESPONDENCE OF ESTEBAN MIRÓ: 1790

[Siles 737]. 25 Jan. 1790, New Orleans. Esteban Miró to
Carlos de Grand-Pré. Miró is aware that families from Ky. and
Cumberland are immigrating to Spanish territory. 1p.

CUBA/8   CORRESPONDENCE OF ESTEBAN MIRÓ: 1791-1792

[Siles 767]. 8 July 1790, New Orleans. *Minuta de oficio* from
Carlos de Grand-Pré reporting that Davis Deadrick of Cumberland
paid his taxes. 1p.

[Siles 772]. 7 Oct. 1790, New Orleans. Esteban Miró to Manuel
Pérez. Miró acknowledges receipt of news that an army had
left Cumberland. 1p.

CUBA/9B   CORRESPONDENCE FROM THE FLORIDAS: 1781-1783

[Siles 909]. 27 Aug. 1783, Natchez. Francisco Collell to
Esteban Miró. Georgia and the Cherokees have reached an
agreement as have Cumberland and the Chiis. 2p.

CUBA/11   CORRESPONDENCE TO ESTEBAN MIRÓ: 1785

[Siles 945]. 2 Aug. 1785. *Minuta de oficio* to Arturo O'Neill
reporting that Cumberland intends to attack Natchez. 4p.

CUBA/12   CORRESPONDENCE TO ESTEBAN MIRÓ: 1786

[Siles 995] (no. 28). 3 Apr. 1786, Ft. Panmure at Natchez.
Carlos de Grand-Pré to Esteban Miró. Cherokees have decided
on war against the United States. 2p.

[Siles 1012] (no. 26). 28 May 1786, Mobile. Pedro Favrot to
Esteban Miró. Talapooses are reportedly marching on Cumberland.
1p.

[Siles 1022] (no. 67). 19 July 1786, St. Louis, Illinois.
Francisco Cruzat to Esteban Miró. The Talapooses, Cherokees,
and Chickasaws have decided to remain loyal to Spain. 2p.

[Siles 1023], 25 July 1786. Smith to Col. Gaillard. Davenport
is heading towards Natchez with troops and a party of Indians.
Smith requests information about Green's victory over the
Cherokees and Creeks. 1p. *French.*

CUBA/13   CORRESPONDENCE TO ESTEBAN MIRÓ: 1787

[Siles 1048] (no. 341). 13 May 1787, Ft. Panmure at Natchez.
Carlos de Grand-Pré to Esteban Miró. Four Americans from
Cumberland have taken a loyalty oath to Spain. 2p.

CUBA/14   CORRESPONDENCE TO ESTEBAN MIRÓ: 1788

[Siles 1061] (no. 554). 4 Mar. 1788, Natchez. Carlos de
Grand-Pré to Esteban Miró. Natchez is preparing to defend
itself against an expedition from Franklin. 4p.

[Siles 1065] (no. 604). 30 Apr. 1788, Natchez. Carlos de
Grand-Pré to Esteban Miró. There is no reason to fear developments in Cumberland and Kentucky. 2p.

CUBA/15A   CORRESPONDENCE TO ESTEBAN MIRÓ: 1789

Doc. 129 (no. 792). 22 Mar. 1789, Natchez. Carlos de Grand-
Pré to Esteban Miró. Grand-Pré is sending a list of settlers
from Ky. and Cumberland. 3p. [Enclosures to doc. 129a].

Doc. 129a. 22 Mar. 1789, Natchez. Carlos de Grand-Pré.
*Relación de los Americanos y efectos que han traido en
cinco chalanes de la pertenencia de Jon Yivvins.* Grand-
Pré lists settlers from Cumberland. 1p.

CUBA/15A (CONT'D)

Doc. 178 (no. 802). 4 Apr. 1789, Natchez. Carlos de Grand-Pré to Esteban Miró. Grand-Pré has received letters from Cumberland and Ky. asking for permission to immigrate to Spanish territory. Among the petitioners are a noted colonel in Ky. and a judge in Cumberland. 5p.

Doc. 255 (no. 73). 1 May 1789, St. Louis, Illinois. Manuel Pérez to Esteban Miró. Pérez has learned that the Cherokees will settle at St. Louis this spring. 2p.

Doc. 314 (no. 839). 22 May 1789, Natchez. Carlos de Grand-Pré to Esteban Miró. Grand-Pré attaches a list of recent immigrants to Natchez. 2p. [Enclosures to doc. 314a].

> Doc. 314a. 22 May 1789. Natchez. Carlos de Grand-Pré. *Relación de los individuos últimamente venidos de los puestos americanos de arriva.* List includes immigrants from Cumberland. 1p.

CUBA/17   CORRESPONDENCE TO ESTEBAN MIRÓ: 1791-1793

[Siles 1172] (no. 165). 4 Dec. 1790, St. Louis. Manuel Pérez to Esteban Miró. Various Indian tribes have attacked and defeated Cumberland. 3p. [Encloses 1 document].

[Siles 1184] (no. 49). 19 Apr. 1792, New Orleans. Thomas Portell to Esteban Miró. Portell accepted a petition from a Cherokee chief to settle in Spanish territory. 2p.

CUBA/18   CORRESPONDENCE OF EL BARÓN DE CARONDELET: 1791-1792

Doc. 2. El Barón de Carondelet to [Juan] de la Villebeuvre. Carondelet discusses Indian affairs and American relations with the Creeks and Cherokees. 3p. *French.*

Doc. 158. 21 Feb. 1792, New Orleans. El Barón de Carondelet to Manuel Gayoso de Lemos. In order to pacify the Cherokee chief in New Orleans, Gayoso is authorized to give him liquor, powder, and shot. 2p.

Doc. 286. 29 Mar. 1792, New Orleans. El Barón de Carondelet to Manuel Gayoso. The King and capt. general have decided to keep the fort at Nogales, and Gayoso is ordered to make the appropriate arrangements with the Choctaws. If the Creeks and Cherokees end up under American control, only the Choctaws would be left to act as a barrier against American expansion. Gayoso should try to convince the Choctaws that the only way to protect their territory is to form a defensive alliance with the Creeks, Chickasaws, Cherokees, and Shawnees. 9p. [Enclosures to doc. 286a].

Doc. 289. 29 Mar. 1792, New Orleans. El Barón de Carondelet to Juan de la Villebeuvre (duplicate). Villebeuvre is authorized to act as the Spanish commissioner to the congress that the Creeks, Choctaws, Chickasaws, and Cherokees are holding at Natchez and Muscle Shoals. He should leave for the congress immediately. 2p.

Doc. 291. 30 Mar. 1792, New Orleans. El Barón de Carondelet to
to Arturo O'Neill. Carondelet is sending O'Neill a copy of
instructions given to Pedro Olivier to delay execution of the
treaty between the Americans and the Creeks. This treaty is
not in the interest of Spain and violates the Spanish treaty
with the Creeks in 1784. The American treaty will place the
Creeks and, by necessity, the Cherokees under American control.
10p.

Doc. 299 *reservada*. 31 Mar. 1792, New Orleans. El Barón de
Carondelet to Enrique White. White will receive 400 muskets
to give the Creeks if that tribe happens to go to war with the
United States. White must convince the Creeks that their
survival depends upon Spanish protection and the tribe's ability
to reach an agreement with the Cherokees, Choctaws, Chickasaws,
and Shawnees. 5p.

Doc. 306 *muy reservada*. 11 Apr. 1792, New Orleans. El Barón
de Carondelet to Manuel Gayoso de Lemos. Wm. Bowles has
notified Natchez residents that he will soon take up arms to
protect Ky. and Cumberland. He assumes that Natchez residents
will help him. 3p.

Doc. 320. 13 Apr. 1792, New Orleans. El Barón de Carondelet to
Manuel Gayoso de Lemos. Carondelet acknowledges receiving
news about the dispute between the Cherokees and Choctaws
resulting in the death of a Cherokee horse. 1p.

Doc. 322. 4 Apr. 1792, New Orleans. El Barón de Carondelet
to Manuel Gayoso de Lemos. Carondelet received Gayoso's
message concerning the American Indian congress planned at
Muscle Shoals for the Creeks, Choctaws, Chickasaws, and Cherokees. 2p. [Enclosures to doc. 322c].

Doc. 322a (no. 2). 23 Mar. 1792, New Orleans. El Barón
de Carondelet to Franchimastabe, Head Chief. Carondelet
has learned that the Choctaws are at war with the Kickapoos
and Abnakis. Spanish Indian allies (the Choctaws, Chickasaws, Creeks, and Cherokees) must meet to plan a common
response to losing land to the Americans. 3p. *French.*

Doc. 322b. 3 Apr. 1792, New Orleans. El Barón de
Carondelet. *Ynstrucción para el capitán ... dn. Juan de
la Villebeuvre, nombrado comisario de S.M.C. en el congreso
de Muscle Shoals.* Carondelet orders Villebeuvre to
frustrate American efforts to win over the Indians.
Carondelet wants the tribes to realize that friendship
with the Americans means war, loss of their land and
property, and extermination -- as happened to the Cherokees.
3p.

Doc. 322c. 4 Apr. 1792, New Orleans. *Comisión* from el
Barón de Carondelet to Juan de la Villebeuvre. Because
of the American congress with the Creeks, Choctaws,
Chickasaws, and Cherokees at Muscle Shoals, Carondelet

ordered Juan de la Villebeuvre to attend the meeting
as the Spanish commissioner so that Spain's interests
could be defended. 2p.

Doc. 385. 18 Apr. 1792, New Orleans. El Barón de Carondelet
to Manuel Lanzos. Carondelet discusses a complaint about
a slave purchased by a Cumberland resident among the Chickasaws and never delivered. 3p.

Doc. 627. 19 June 1792, New Orleans. El Barón de Carondelet
to Arturo O'Neill. John Mills, who accompanied Wm. Panton to
Cherokee territory, reported that the Cherokees and Creeks
returned with 15 or 16 captives (women and children) from
Cumberland. 2p.

Doc. 631. 20 June 1792, New Orleans. El Barón de Carondelet
to Manuel Gayoso de Lemos. Carondelet received a report about
the Creeks attacking Wm. Cerne's property and attacking a fort
along the Cumberland River. 2p.

Doc. 685. 10 July 1792, New Orleans. El Barón de Carondelet
to Manuel Gayoso de Lemos. The Northern tribes sent an
Iroquoian chief named Foammy [Toammy?] to talk with the Creeks
some time ago to encourage a general Indian alliance. Carondelet would like to talk with Foammy since the governor also
wants to unite all tribes. 7p.

Doc. 944. 18 Oct. 1792, New Orleans. El Barón de Carondelet
to Manuel Gayoso de Lemos. The Anglo-Americans have reportedly
made a large gift to the Indians in Cumberland. The Americans
are obviously trying to seduce the Indians away from Spain. 3p.

Doc. 956. 19 Oct. 1792, New Orleans. El Barón de Carondelet
to Manuel Gayoso de Lemos. Carondelet has received Gayoso's
news about the number of Choctaws and Chickasaws that went to
Cumberland. 2p.

Doc. 957. 19 Oct. 1792, New Orleans. El Barón de Carondelet
to Manuel Gayoso de Lemos. Carondelet has received intelligence
about Cumberland from some Indians who visited there. 2p.

Doc. 1045. 24 Nov. 1792, New Orleans. El Barón de Carondelet
to Manuel Lanzos. Carondelet complains about the number of
Chickasaws (1000) and Cherokees visiting New Orleans. 2p.

Doc. 1046. [1792]. *Nota de regalos que se ha subministrado a
los yndios de la nación cheraquies.* Lists goods given to
Cherokees. 4p.

Doc. 1047. 24 Nov. 1792, New Orleans. *Palabra* (talk) from
el Barón de Carondelet to the Breath, Charles of Chickamauga,
and Bloody Fellow. Spain loves the Indians, but the tribes
must keep the peace with the United States. Spanish King will
try to protect their land. 2p. [Enclosures to doc. 1048].

Doc. 1048. 24 Nov. 1792, New Orleans. El Barón de
Carondelet to the chiefs, warriors, and other Cherokees.
[Copy of doc. 1047]. 2p.

Doc. 1076. 13 Dec. 1792, New Orleans. El Barón de Carondelet
to Arturo O'Neill. Carondelet received O'Neill's report about
the supplies given to the Cherokees, including those who visited
New Orleans. 2p.

Doc. 1128 reservada. 22 Dec. 1792, New Orleans. El Barón de
Carondelet to Manuel Gayoso de Lemos. Carondelet has learned
from New Madrid that Cumberland residents plan some hostilities
against Natchez. Carondelet is sending reinforcements to
Natchez. 7p.

[Siles 1264] (no. 3). 3 Nov. 1792, Mobile. José Deville
Degoutin to el Barón de Carondelet. Deville reports the
latest news about the Talapooses and Cherokees. 2p.

[Siles 1269](reservada). 22 Dec. 1792, New Orleans. El Barón
de Carondelet to Thomas Portell. Carondelet gives instructions
concerning the Cherokee-American war. 8p. [Encloses 1
document].

CUBA/19   CORRESPONDENCE OF EL BARÓN DE CARONDELET: 1793

[Siles 1279]. 29 Jan. 1793, New Orleans. El Barón de Carondelet to Zenón Trudeau. Carondelet denies the rumor that he
instructed the Indians to attack Cumberland. 5p.

[Siles 1281]. 30 Jan. 1793, New Orleans. El Barón de Carondelet to Thomas Portell. Carondelet acknowledges receipt of
letter concerning the American army and the American desire to
set up an establishment in Cumberland. 1p.

CUBA/20   CORRESPONDENCE OF EL BARÓN DE CARONDELET: 1793

Doc. 590. 9 Nov. 1793, New Orleans. El Barón de Carondelet to
Manuel Gayoso de Lemos. Carondelet acknowledges receipt of a
certified copy of the Nogales treaty with the Chickasaws, Creeks,
Talapooses, Alibamos, Cherokees, and Choctaws. 2p.

Doc. 653. 20 Dec. 1793, Old Village of Wetonka. Pedro Olivier
to el Barón de Carondelet. Some Cherokees (160) are here whose
village was destroyed by Americans. They wish to visit the
commandant in Pensacola and Olivier cannot dissuade them from
doing so. One of their leaders wants to go to New Orleans. 3p.

Doc. 693. 30 Nov. 1793, New Orleans. El Barón de Carondelet
to Enrique White. Carondelet is forwarding the section of
the Nogales treaty that directly affects White. 1p.

Doc. 762. 20 Dec. 1793, New Orleans. El Barón de Carondelet
to Manuel Gayoso de Lemos. Carondelet has received confirmation
of the Treaty of Nogales and noted Gayoso's decision to supplement gifts given to Little Turkey. 3p.

CUBA/21   CORRESPONDENCE OF EL BARÓN DE CARONDELET: 1794

Doc. 92 *reservada*. 22 Jan. 1792, New Orleans. El Barón de
Carondelet to Manuel Gayoso de Lemos. Carondelet has learned
that Col. Montgomery in Cumberland is prepared to stop traffic
at the mouth of the Ohio in order to impede trade with La. in
spite of the fact that the Americans owe the Spanish 3,000
barrels of flour. Gayoso should do his best to secure corn
for the Indians, who can be substituted for Spanish soldiers
in an emergency. 3p.

Doc. 189 *reservada*. 3 Mar. 1794, New Orleans. El Barón de
Carondelet to Thomas Portell. Carondelet acknowledges
Portell's report that he found nothing disturbing in his trip
to the Cumberland R. and Redbanks, although Col. Montgomery
did have 500 men under arms. 2p.

Doc. 223. 21 Mar. 1794, New Orleans. El Barón de Carondelet
to Manuel Gayoso de Lemos. Carondelet has received Gayoso's
letter about the arrival of Bloody Fellow and Watts with
40 warriors. These Indians have obtained 150 rifles from an
unknown source. 2p.

Doc. 282. 9 Apr. 1790, New Orleans. El Barón de Carondelet
to Enrique White. White can give liquor to the Cherokees
traveling with Pedro la Valle since they received none in
New Orleans. White, however, should give them nothing else
since they have already received their gifts. They are
supposed to share their gifts with McDonald. 2p.

Doc. 284. 9 Apr. 1794, New Orleans. El Barón de Carondelet
to Enrique White. The Cherokees' annual gift should be
rationed out to those who customarily visit White's post
rather than turning it over to one group. 11p.

Doc. 296. 12 Apr. 1794, New Orleans. El Barón de Carondelet
to Manuel Gayoso de Lemos. Cherokee leaders Volate and Tetage
and 52 members of their tribe have arrived in New Orleans with
Gayoso's letter. The French interpreter who accompanied them
is not trustworthy. Carondelet approves of Gayoso's ideas
concerning the rifles that Bloody Fellow found. 2p.

Doc. 373 [*reservada*]. 12 May 1794, New Orleans. [El Barón
de Caronelet] to Thomas Portell (copy). [Carondelet] acknowledges Portell's information about Col. Montgomery reestablishing
a post at the mouth of the Cumberland R. that will interfere
with Indian traffic. 2p. [Enclosures to doc. 373a].

> Doc. 373a *reservada*. 12 May 1794, New Orleans. El Barón
> de Carondelet to Thomas Portell. [Same as doc. 373]. 2p.

Doc. 458. 1 June 1794, New Orleans. El Barón de Carondelet to
Manuel Gayoso. Carondelet has received a copy of Little
Turkey's letter and Gayoso's reply. Governor approves the
decision to give the Cherokees a canoe and he has granted
generous gifts to the tribe. The government, however, cannot
afford to appoint an interpreter for them. 4p.

CUBA/21 (CONT'D)

Doc. 528 reservada. 26 June 1794, New Orleans. El Barón de
Carondelet to Manuel Gayoso de Lemos. Carondelet has received
the latest news about the mouth of the Cumberland River. A
detachment of Gen. Wayne's army is on their way to Ft. Cherokee.
3p.

Doc. 531. 29 Aug. 1794, New Orleans. El Barón de Carondelet to
Enrique White. Carondelet forwards a copy of a letter from
the Spanish envoys in Philadelphia to Little Turkey, a Cherokee
chief. 2p. [Enclosures to doc. 532].

> Doc. 532. 26 June 1794, New York. José de Jaudenes and
> José Ignacio de Viar to Little Turkey (copy). Spanish
> envoys ask the Cherokees to consult with them before
> negotiating with the Americans. Cherokees should not put
> themselves under American protection since Spain has
> protected them for so many years. 3p.

Doc. 655. 5 Aug. 1794, New Orleans. [El Barón de Carondelet]
to Thomas Portell. [Copy of doc. 655a]. 2p. [Enclosures to
doc. 655a].

> Doc. 655a. 5 Aug. 1794, New Orleans. El Barón de Caron-
> delet to Thomas Portell. Carondelet orders Portell to
> have a Cherokee or Shawnee accompany Henry Owen to Ohio.
> 3p.

Doc. 719 reservada. 20 Aug. 1794, New Orleans. El Barón de
Carondelet to Manuel Gayoso de Lemos. Capt. general in Havana
has ordered Gayoso to encourage the Chickasaws to reclaim the
land that the Americans have usurped to build Ft. Massac. The
real American objective is Muscle Shoals and Ecores à Margot.
Gayoso should also attempt to get the Cherokees and Creeks to
attack the American post since those two tribes know what
happens when the Americans move in as they have at Cumberland.
6p.

Doc. 777 reservada. 28 Sept. 1794, New Orleans. El Barón de
Carondelet to Manuel Gayoso de Lemos. Carondelet has received
Gayoso's ideas about the capt. general's order to expel the
Americans from Ft. Massac. 7p.

Doc. 898. 15 Nov. 1794, New Orleans. El Barón de Carondelet
to Enrique White. Carondelet is sending White a letter for
John McDonald, the Spanish representative among the Cherokees.
1p.

Doc. 931. [1795], [New Orleans?]. John Milton. Actos del
estado de Georgia celebrados en Augusta (translation). Extract
of land acts passed by Georgia assembly [dealing in part with
Cherokee land]. 23p.

CUBA/22   CORRESPONDENCE OF EL BARÓN DE CARONDELET: 1795

Doc. 129. 17 Feb. 1795, New Orleans. El Barón de Carondelet
to [Juan] de la Villebeuvre. Carondelet discusses relations
between the Indian tribes and the distribution of Indian gifts.
Indians might turn Ecores à Margot and Muscle Shoals over to the
Americans. 4p. *French.*

Doc. 195. 18 Mar. 1795, New Orleans. El Barón de Carondelet
to Manuel Gayoso de Lemos. Since taking over the government,
Carondelet has gone to great lengths to convince the Indians
of Spain's good intentions and to unite the four nations
(Cherokees, Creeks, Chickasaws, and Choctaws) together in a
defensive alliance to protect their territory. It is hard to
understand, consequently, why Gayoso can claim that Spain does
not have one Indian nation securely under its control. 12p.

Doc. 203. 22 Mar. 1795, New Orleans. El Barón de Carondelet
to Manuel Gayoso de Lemos. Carondelet had been working before
the Creek-Chickasaw hostilities with Red Shoes and other Creeks
to prevent Ga. from seizing land belonging to the Four Nations
[including the Cherokees]. The Creeks were convinced that
the Four Nations should meet to discuss how to stop the land
seizures. 21p.

Doc. 206. 24 Mar. 1795, New Orleans. El Barón de Carondelet
to Manuel Gayoso de Lemos. Americans will take advantage of
war between the Talapooses and Chickasaws to erect a fort at
Muscle Shoals along the Tennessee. 10p.

Doc. 219. 26 Mar. 1795, New Orleans. El Barón de Carondelet
to Juan de la Villebeuvre. [Copy of doc. 219a]. 2p. [Enclo-
sures to doc. 219a].

    Doc. 219a. 26 Mar. 1795, New Orleans. El Barón de
    Carondelet to Juan de la Villebeuvre. Villebeuvre must
    keep the Choctaws out of the Creek-Chickasaw conflict
    since they must be available to force the Americans from
    Muscle Shoals. 4p.

Doc. 247. 8 Apr. 1795, New Orleans. [El Barón de Carondelet]
to Enrique White. [Incomplete draft of doc. 247a]. 1p.
[Enclosures to doc. 247a].

    Doc. 247a. 8 Apr. 1795, New Orleans. El Barón de
    Carondelet to Enrique White. Spanish officials want to
    know the results of negotiations between the Cherokees
    and Americans. 3p.

Doc. 277. 29 Apr. 1795, Pensacola. Enrique White to el Barón
de Carondelet. White has requested that John McDonald send a
copy of the Cherokee treaty with the Americans. 1p.

Doc. 518. 4 July 1795, New Orleans. Letter from el Barón de
Carondelet stating that Manuel Gayoso has finished the fort
at Ecores, which will help the Creeks against the Americans
and enable the tribe to sell goods after hunting in Cumberland.
4p.

CUBA/22 (CONT'D)

Doc. 619. 8 July 1795, [New Orleans?]. El Barón de Carondelet
to [Juan] de la Villebeuvre. Carondelet explains how the
Americans reached peace agreements with the Creeks and Cherokees,
causing those two tribes to lose land. 6p. *French*.

Doc. 854 *muy reservada*. 31 Oct. 1795, New Orleans. El Barón
de Carondelet to Diego de Vegas. Carondelet has received
Vegas's reports concerning the critical situation between the
Americans and the Cherokees. 6p.

[Siles 1455]. 29 June 1795, New Orleans. El Barón de Carondelet to Carlos de Grand-Pré. Carondelet gives instructions on
the course of action if the militia from Cumberland or other
Americans should attack the fort at Barrancas. 2p. [Encloses
1 document].

[Siles 1461]. 9 July 1795, New Orleans. El Barón de Carondelet
to Manuel Gayoso de Lemos. Carondelet acknowledges receipt of
information about Cumberland's intentions to attack Natchez. 2p.

CUBA/24   CORRESPONDENCE OF EL BARÓN DE CARONDELET: 1797

Doc. 19. 8 Jan. 1796, New Orleans. El Barón de Carondelet to
Manuel Gayoso de Lemos. Carondelet acknowledges Gayoso's
warning about Cumberland's decision to attack San Fernando de
la Barrancas. 2p.

[Siles 1603]. 29 June 1797, New Orleans. El Barón de Carondelet to Juan de la Villebeuvre. Americans are reportedly
building a fort at Muscle Shoals and another one at Ecores à
Margot. 1p.

CUBA/25A   CORRESPONDENCE TO EL BARÓN DE CARONDELET: 1792

Doc. 117 *reservada*. 11 Mar. 1792, Pensacola. Enrique White
to el Barón de Carondelet. Although the Upper Creeks know
nothing about Bowles's recent activities, they do report that
some 500 Americans have set up an establishment at Muscle
Shoals. 3p.

Doc. 176 *reservada*. 1 Apr. 1792, [New Orleans?]. [El Barón
de Carondelet?] to Enrique White. White will receive 600
treaty muskets to aid the Creeks in case of war with the United
States. White must persuade the Creeks and their neighbors
(the Cherokees, Choctaws, Chickasaws, and Lower Shawnees) that
their survival depends upon a confederation of tribes and the
protection of Spain. 2p.

Doc. 117 (no. 2). 10 Apr. 1792, Little Tallassee. Pedro
Olivier to el Barón de Carondelet. Olivier has arrived in
Little Tallassee. He does not know whether the Creeks are
preparing for war against the Americans, although a Creek
party from Oconee and some Shawnees did kill a few Americans
along the Cherokee River. Panton informed Olivier that Bowles's
brother, called Welbank, is trying to flee to the Cherokees.
Panton asked the Creeks to detain him. 6p.

CUBA/25A (CONT'D)

Doc. 386. 11 June 1792, Pensacola. Arturo O'Neill to el Barón
de Carondelet. John Mills, Wm. Panton's companion on his visit
to the Cherokees, has returned. He talked to some [Cumberland]
women and children taken prisoner by the Cherokees and Creeks.
4p. [Enclosures to doc. 386a].

    Doc. 386a. 19 [June?] 1792, New Orleans. [El Barón de
    Carondelet] to Arturo O'Neill. Carondelet received
    O'Neill's letter about John Mills and the Cumberland
    captives. 1p.

Doc. 438 (no. 62). 28 June 1792, New Madrid. Thomas Portell
to el Barón de Carondelet. Portell has learned that Andrés
Fagaut has just arrived from Cumberland with information about
American military preparations. 3p. [Enclosures to doc. 438a].

Doc. 465 (no. 6). 5 July 1792, Little Tallassee. Pedro Olivier
to el Barón de Carondelet. Olivier discusses the various
Spanish Indian interpreters. He has received news from the
Cherokees, via John Beng (a trader who lives among the tribe),
that the Americans have built an establishment at Muscle Shoals.
The Cherokees dislike this. Panton, who is returning from
visiting the Cherokees, will be able to give more information
about the matter. 5p.

Doc. 466. 6 July 1792, Little Tallassee. Pedro Olivier to el
Barón de Carondelet. Olivier mentions efforts to earn the
Creek's confidence. He has taken every opportunity to encourage
the Creek chiefs to save their land by forming an alliance with
the Cherokees, Chickasaws, and Choctaws under Spanish protection.
6p.

CUBA/25B   CORRESPONDENCE TO EL BARÓN DE CARONDELET: 1792

Doc. 713. 10 Sept. 1792, Little Tallassee. Pedro Olivier to
el Barón de Carondelet. Olivier has received the treaty supplement signed by Carondelet and McGillivray. A party of Cherokees,
Shawnees, and Choctaws hope to intercept the American commissioners to the Chickasaws and Choctaws returning from Cumberland.
Those Indians will no doubt destroy Muscle Shoals if an American
post has been established there. 5p.

Doc. 794 (no. 79). 7 Oct. 1792, New Madrid. Thomas Portell to
el Barón de Carondelet. Two Cherokee companions of John
Macormek, a resident of New Madrid, evidently killed him on
a trip to Cumberland. Since this news has not been confirmed,
Portell has sent two men to Cumberland to investigate. 3p.

Doc. 847. 15 Oct. 1792, Little Tallassee. Pedro Olivier to el
Barón de Carondelet. Creeks held a meeting to decide how to
deal with Ga. and Cumberland. 10p.

Doc. 848. 15 Oct. 1792, Little Tallassee. Pedro Olivier to
el Barón de Carondelet. Creeks will evidently suspend their
hostilities against the Ga. frontier. The latest news from
Cumberland indicates that the Americans met with the Chickasaws

along the Cherokee R. to persuade the tribe to cede land. The
Chickasaws have asked that their gifts from Spain be doubled,
a concession which would cause resentment among the Creeks and
Cherokees. 8p.

Doc. 955 (no. 96). 15 Nov. 1792, New Madrid. Thomas Portell
to el Barón de Carondelet. The two men sent to Cumberland to
see if the [Cherokees] had killed John Macormek [McCormick?]
have returned. There is considerable concern in Cumberland
about the Indians, particularly the Cherokees. Cumberland
residents might attack the Indians in this area. 7p.

Doc. 1065. 17 Dec. 1792, Little Tallassee. Pedro Olivier to
el Barón de Carondelet. Olivier describes Spain's relations
with the Creek leader Alex. McGillivray. The Chickasaws
reportedly attacked a Creek party near Cumberland. Mr. Bellew
has information that Gen. Sevier plans to attack the Cherokees.
7p.

Doc. 1070 (no. 46). 18 Dec. 1792, St. Louis. Zenón Trudeau to
el Barón de Carondelet. Trudeau sends a copy of a letter
reporting an attack by the Creeks and Cherokees on Cumberland.
4p. [Enclosures to doc. 1070a].

> 1070a. 29 Jan. 1793, New Orleans. [El Barón de Carondelet]
> to Zenón Trudeau (copy). [Carondelet] believes that the
> report of an attack by the Creeks and Cherokees on Cumber-
> land is false. 8p.

Doc. 1109. 28 Dec. 1792, Little Tallassee. Pedro Olivier to
el Barón de Carondelet. Various Creek parties had left to
support the Cherokees and Shawnees in their attacks against
Cumberland. It was those parties that stole the horses belonging to the Chickasaws who had gone to a meeting in Cumberland.
5p.

Doc. 1147. 3 May 1794, Pensacola. Enrique White to el Barón
de Carondelet. A number of Cherokees have arrived in Pensacola
aboard the schooner *Ventura*. They will transport the tribe's
annual gift to McDonald, who will distribute it. 2p.

Doc. 1148. 3 May 1794, Pensacola. Enrique White to el Barón
de Carondelet. White has followed Carondelet's instructions
in distributing muskets to the Cherokees. 1p.

Doc. 1200 (no. 14 *reservada*). 18 July 1795, San Fernando de las
Barrancas. Manuel Gayoso de Lemos to el Barón de Carondelet.
Spain has been successful in forcing the Americans among the
Chickasaws to return to Cumberland. 8p.

CUBA/26   CORRESPONDENCE TO EL BARÓN DE CARONDELET: 1793

[Siles 1694](no. 248). 27 Feb. 1793, Natchez. Blas de Bouchet
to el Barón de Carondelet. Bouchet attaches a list of the
cargo on a flat boat from Cumberland. 2p. [Encloses 1 document].

CUBA/26 (CONT'D)

[Siles 1700](no. 160). 7 May 1793, New Madrid. Thomas Portell to el Barón de Carondelet. A flat boat from Cumberland has arrived carrying corn for the Chickasaws. 6p.

CUBA/27A   CORRESPONDENCE TO EL BARÓN DE CARONDELET: 1793

[Siles 1706](no. 3). 7 Aug. 1793, Mongulassa. Pedro Olivier to el Barón de Carondelet. Olivier reports a Cumberland attack on the Cherokees. 2p.

CUBA/28   CORRESPONDENCE TO EL BARÓN DE CARONDELET: 1794

Doc. 14. 1 Jan. 1794, New Madrid. Thomas Portell et al. *Ynstrucción para dn. Luis Lorimier* (copy). When the Loups and Shawnees leave New Madrid to meet with the Cherokees, Lorimier must find out what the Spanish enemies who are planning to attack New Madrid are doing. 4p.

Doc. 27. 4 Jan. 1794, Pensacola. Enrique White to el Barón de Carondelet. 2p. [Enclosures to doc. 27a].

> Doc. 27a. 1 Dec. 1793, Old Village at Wetonka. Pedro Olivier to Enrique White (copy). The carrier of this letter is a Cherokee from one of the villages recently destroyed by the Americans and has been forced to seek refuge. He wishes to go to New Orleans and ask for help from the governor. 2p.

Doc. 263 (no. 427). 27 Feb. 1794, Natchez. Manuel Gayoso de Lemos to el Barón de Carondelet. Gayoso forwards a letter from Bloody Fellow, who will visit New Orleans to see his son Carlos and Gov. Carondelet. Bloody Fellow is accompanied by Watts, a Cherokee. They also wish to acquire arms and ammunition. 6p.

Doc. 271 (no. 509). 28 Feb. 1794, Mobile. Manuel de Lanzos to el Barón de Carondelet. Lanzos has received a copy of the Nogales treaty with the Talapooses, Choctaws, and Cherokees. 1p.

Doc. 417 (no. 442). 26 Mar. 1794, Natchez. Manuel Gayoso de Lemos to el Barón de Carondelet. About 50 Cherokees, led by Volate and Fetahe, have arrived in Natchez. They have brought a French interpreter with them who is untrustworthy. This group has split with Bloody Fellow. 7p. [Enclosures to doc. 417a].

> Doc. 417a. 12 Apr. 1794, New Orleans. [El Barón de Carondelet] to Manuel Gayoso de Lemos. [Copy of AGI Cuba/21/doc. 296]. 2p.

Doc. 429. 28 Mar. 1794, Pensacola. Enrique White to el Barón de Carondelet. The Cherokees arrived here on the 26 of [March?] and Spanish officials attended the funeral of the chief's wife. Although some of the Cherokees have left, others might stay for at least two months, a problem since there are no supplies to maintain them. 3p.

CUBA/28 (CONT'D)

Doc. 460. 2 Apr. 1794, Cowetas. James Durouzeaux to Henry White (copy). Indians were warned about a group of Georgians near the fork of the Oconee and about an army of Carolinians marching to Muscle Shoals. 2p. *English.*

Doc. 483. 2 Apr. 1794, Pensacola. Enrique White to el Barón de Carondelet. White has received several letters from Milfort discussing the plans of Cumberland and Ky. towards the Miss. River. Panton believes that the Cherokees should receive their annual gift in one payment because they live so far from Pensacola. There are about 100 Cherokees in Pensacola. 6p. *Spanish* and *French.*

Doc. 485. 9 Apr. 1794, New Orleans. [El Barón de Carondelet?] to Enrique White. [Same as AGI Cuba/21/doc. 284]. 4p.

Doc. 501. 2 Apr. 1794, New Orleans. [El Barón de Carondelet] to Enrique White. 3p. [Enclosures to doc. 501i].

> Doc. 501a. *Regalo que se remite a Panzacola por la goleta S.M. San Marcos para la nación Cheroquies.* Lists the annual gifts for the Cherokees. 2p.

Doc. 524. 18 Apr. 1794, Natchez. Manuel Gayoso de Lemos to el Barón de Carondelet. Gayoso talked with John Turnbull about the guns that Bloody Fellow brought to Natchez. 3p.

Doc. 555 (no. 171). 24 Apr. 1794, St. Louis. Zenón Trudeau to el Barón de Carondelet. Trudeau reports the latest news about the military preparations in Cumberland and Ky. that might threaten the Spanish possessions. 2p.

Doc. 594. [1794?]. Copy of letter stating that the bearer is a Cherokee chief and requesting that the recipient reward the chief and his followers. 2p. *French.*

Doc. 629. 2 May 1794, Pensacola. Enrique White to el Barón de Carondelet. White has just met with the Cherokee chiefs and told them that the governor ordered their annual gifts to be delivered to McDonald for distribution. 2p.

Doc. 633 (no. 252). 3 May 1794, New Madrid. Thomas Portell to el Barón de Carondelet. There was a fight between Cumberland troops and the Indians. 2p.

Doc. 697. 11 May 1794, Pensacola. Enrique White to el Barón de Carondelet. The Cherokees are still in Pensacola. White has just received a letter from McDonald. 2p.

Doc. 728. 21 May 1794, Pensacola. Enrique White to el Barón de Carondelet. Cherokees under Tom Watts and Bloody Fellow have asked for their gifts. White refused their request because he learned that they plan to sell some of the goods and not give the rest to McDonald. Another group of Cherokees is in Pensacola and they will escort the goods to McDonald. 2p.

CUBA/28 (CONT'D)

Doc. 745 (no. 487). 24 May 1794, Natchez. Manuel Gayoso de
Lemos to el Barón de Carondelet. Gayoso forwards a letter from
Little Turkey, principal chief of the Cherokees, and recommends
that Spanish officials satisfy Little Turkey's request. The
governor should allow the white man who is traveling with this
group to become Spain's interpreter with the tribe. 3p.
[Enclosures to doc. 745a].

> Doc. 745a. 1 June 1794, New Orleans. El Barón de Caron-
> delet to Manuel Gayoso (copy). Governor has rewarded those
> Cherokees who came here with Little Turkey. It is not
> possible at the moment to name an interpreter for the
> Cherokees because the treasury lacks the money and because
> a Cherokee among that group also speaks Choctaw and
> Chickasaw. 4p.

[Siles 1716](no. 224). 3 Jan. 1794, New Madrid. Thomas Portell
to el Barón de Carondelet. New Madrid is prepared if Cumberland
attacks. 1p. [Encloses 1 document].

[Siles 1728](no. 426). 26 Feb. 1794, Natchez. Manuel Gayoso
de Lemos to el Barón de Carondelet. Bloody Fellow has arrived
with 150 rifles that he found hidden at Barrancas de Margot.
They belong to Payemingo, who received them from Pres.
Washington. 3p.

CUBA/29   CORRESPONDENCE TO EL BARÓN DE CARONDELET: 1794

[Siles 1755]. 2 June 1794, New Madrid. Thomas Portell to
el Barón de Carondelet. Portell has sent a confidential agent
to Cumberland. 2p.

[Siles 1756](no. 283). 17 June 1794. New Madrid. Thomas
Portell to el Barón de Carondelet. Portell reports news from
his confidential agent in Cumberland. 2p.

[Siles 1759]. 5 July 1794, New Madrid. Thomas Portell to el
Barón de Carondelet. Portell reports again that he has sent
a confidential agent to Cumberland. 4p. [Encloses 2 documents].

[Siles 1761](no. 530). 16 July 1794, Natchez. Manuel Gayoso
de Lemos to el Barón de Carondelet. Gayoso reports that the
Americans are taking possession of the old Cherokee fort and
that there is a possibility of a split between the Creeks and
the [Chickasaws?]. 13p. [Encloses 1 document].

[Siles 1762]. 29 July 1794, Pensacola. Enrique White to el
Barón de Carondelet. King has approved the Nogales treaty with
the Creeks, Cherokees, Chickasaws, and Choctaws. 2p.

[Siles 1763]. 11 June 1795, San Fernando de las Barrancas.
Manuel Gayoso de Lemos to el Barón de Carondelet. Gayoso
describes his plan of action if bandits from Cumberland attack
the fort. 2p.

CUBA/30   CORRESPONDENCE TO EL BARÓN DE CARONDELET: 1794

[Siles 1772](no. 35). 4 Nov. 1794, Confederation. Juan de la
Villebeuvre to el Barón de Carondelet. Americans have attacked
the Cherokee villages. 3p.

[Siles 1776]. 5 Dec. 1794, New Madrid. Thomas Portell to el
Barón de Carondelet. Montgomery died during a fight with the
Cherokees. 2p.

CUBA/31   CORRESPONDENCE TO EL BARÓN DE CARONDELET: 1795

[Siles 1779]. 14 Feb. 1795, Confederation. Juan de la
Villebeuvre to el Barón de Carondelet. Payemingo (Chickasaw
chief) has ceded Muscle Shoals to the Americans to build a fort
and store. Americans will declare war against the Spanish if
they oppose these developments. 2p. *French.*

[Siles 1780]. 18 Mar. 1795, Confederation. Juan de la Villebeuvre to el Barón de Carondelet. The Americans at Muscle
Shoals intend to ask the Choctaws for part of their hunting
grounds. 3p. *French.*

[Siles 1786]. 4 Apr. 1795, Pensacola. Enrique White to el
Barón de Carondelet. White discusses the American establishment
at Muscle Shoals. 1p. [Encloses 2 documents].

    N. doc. 29 Mar. 1795, Mobile. Extract of letter from
    John Forbes stating that the Americans at Muscle Shoals
    are backed by Payemingo and the Chickasaws. 1p. *English.*

    N. doc. 12 Feb. 1795, Choctaw Nation. Copy of letter
    from Benjamin James stating that hostilities exist between
    the Creeks and the Chickasaws and the Americans at Muscle
    Shoals. 1p. *English.*

[Siles 1814](no. 25). 3 Dec. 1795, New Madrid. [Manuel Gayoso
de Lemos] to el Barón de Carondelet. *Minuta de oficio* explaining the Spanish reaction to rumors of an impending attack by
Cumberland against San Fernando de las Barrancas. 2p.

CUBA/32   CORRESPONDENCE TO EL BARÓN DE CARONDELET: 1795

[Siles 1815](no. 26). 6 Dec. 1795, New Madrid. [Manuel Gayoso
de Lemos] to el Barón de Carondelet. *Minuta de oficio* explaining the latest news concerning a rumored attack by Americans at
Cumberland on Barrancas. 3p.

[Siles 1818](no. 21). 22 Dec. 1795, San Fernando de las
Barrancas. Vincente Folch to el Barón de Carondelet. Col.
McKee has asked permission from the Chickasaws to build a fort
at Muscle Shoals, but the Chickasaw leaders refused. 2p.

CUBA/34   CORRESPONDENCE TO EL BARÓN DE CARONDELET: 1796

[Siles 1837]. [El Barón de Carondelet] to John McDonald.
Minuta de oficio accompanying the Treaty of Nogales (not
attached). [Carondelet] has written the Spanish envoys in the
the United States to urge Congress to suspend the American
hostilities against the Cherokees. 1p.

CUBA/35   CORRESPONDENCE TO EL BARÓN DE CARONDELET: 1797-1798

[Siles 1848](no. 45). 6 Mar. 1797, New Madrid. Carlos Dehault
Delassus to el Barón de Carondelet. Capt. John Taylor has
arrived with a Cherokee leader and 150 followers asking for
Spanish protection. 1p.

CUBA/36   CORRESPONDENCE OF ARTURO O'NEILL: 1781-1784

Doc. 129 (no. 85). 9 July 1783, Pensacola. Arturo O'Neill to
el Conde de Gálvez. Two Cherokee chiefs and an Irish trader
arrived in Pensacola last month. They asked for Spanish
assistance in arranging peace with the Americans. If peace
cannot be arranged, the Cherokees asked for permission to
settle in Spanish territory. The Cherokees maintained that
they were an industrious tribe which tilled the soil for a
living. 3p.

Doc. 190. 27 June 1783, Pensacola. Arturo O'Neill to Esteban
Miró. Two Cherokees and an Irishman have arrived in Pensacola
seeking Spanish assistance to end the American hostility towards
the tribe. They mentioned that the tribe might have to abandon
their territory and move to Spanish territory. O'Neill told
them that he would talk to Talapooses about granting land to
the Cherokees. 2p.

Doc. 215. 16 Apr. 1784, Pensacola. Arturo O'Neill to Esteban
Miró. O'Neill has learned that Miró now exercises the authority that Col. Gilberto Antonio Maxent formerly did as head of
the *ramo de indios*. O'Neill also learned that Juan Morales
(treasury auditor) will supply the food and goods needed for
the Creeks, Alibamos, Shawnees, Ochayas, and Cherokees who will
soon visit Pensacola for the Indian congress. 7p.

Doc. 340 (no. 102). 19 Oct. 1783, Pensacola. Arturo O'Neill
to José [de] Ezpeleta. If the Cherokees return and ask to
settle in the Pensacola area, O'Neill will follow Ezpeleta's
instructions on the matter. 1p.

Doc. 379 (no. 14). 30 June 1784, Pensacola. Arturo O'Neill to
José de Ezpeleta. The Cherokees did not attend the recent
congress because they live too far away and because they would
have to travel through Creek territory. Nevertheless, the
Cherokees have traded skins here through an interpreter of
their nation. Should they come in person, O'Neill will let
them settle in Pensacola. 2p.

Doc. 19. 17 Aug. 1785, Pensacola. Arturo O'Neill to Esteban
Miró. O'Neill forwards a copy of a letter from Alex. McGillivray concerning the Creeks, Chickasaws, and Cherokees. 1p.

Doc. 130. 16 Nov. 1786, Pensacola. Arturo O'Neill to Esteban
Miró. McGillivray reports that the Americans are ready to
attack the Creeks and that the Indians have made peace with
Cumberland. Brig. [Gen.] Twigs and Col. Clark have 1,500
Georgians ready to attack the Creeks. Marten [Martin?], an
American, has 200 men to prevent the Cherokees from aiding
the Creeks. 3p. [Enclosures to doc. 130-1].

Doc. 153. 17 Feb. 1787, Pensacola. Arturo O'Neill to Esteban
Miró. O'Neill forwards a petition from residents along Tenn.
R. concerning Charles Wetherford. He was married to the
mestiza sister of Alex. McGillivray, but he separated from
his wife because of differences with McGillivray. Wetherford
evidently wants to retire with his goods to Cumberland. 3p.
[Enclosures to doc. 153-4].

> Doc. 153-3. 24 Mar. 1787, Pensacola. Arturo O'Neill to
> Esteban Miró. O'Neill has received Miró's reply to a
> petition from residents along the Tenn. R. concerning the
> imprisonment of Carlos Wetbrerfor [Charles Wetherford?].
> Miró refuses to reduce the sentence because [Wetherford],
> who has some influence among the Indian traders, plans to
> retire to Cumberland with his goods. 6p.

Doc. 158 (no. 1). 1 Mar. 1787, Pensacola. Arturo O'Neill to
Esteban Miró. 2p. [Enclosures to doc. 158-1].

> Doc. 158-1 (no. 2 *reservada*). [1787], [New Orleans?].
> [Esteban Miró to Arturo O'Neill] (copy). O'Neill should
> advise the Creeks not to attack the Americans. Since the
> Creeks are already afraid that Georgia and Cumberland
> could destroy them, adding the rest of the Americans to
> the tribe's enemies would irreversibly tilt the odds. 2p.

Doc. 188. 5 Mar. 1787, Pensacola. Arturo O'Neill to Esteban
Miró. O'Neill has received Miró's recommendation that he treat
kindly the visiting Cherokees who favor Spain. 2p.

Doc. 207. 2 June 1787, Pensacola. Arturo O'Neill to Esteban
Miró. O'Neill decided to reward some visiting Cherokees by
granting them considerable time to talk with him. 1p.

Doc. 221 *reservada*. 16 Juen 1787, Pensacola. Arturo O'Neill
to Esteban Miró. Alex. McGillivray remains firmly opposed to
American expansion and continues to follow Spain's direction,
although he obviously still has an affection for Great Britain.
The Indians killed three Americans on the road to Cumberland.
4p.

Doc. 244. 3 Aug. 1787, Pensacola. Arturo O'Neill to Esteban
Miró. Some 100 Creeks carrying a Spanish flag have left to
attack Cumberland. 6p.

CUBA/37 (CONT'D)

Doc. 253. 8 Aug. 1787, Pensacola. Arturo O'Neill to Esteban Miró. 1p. [Enclosures to doc. 253-1].

Doc. 253-1. 10 July 1787, Little Tallassee. [Alex. McGillivray] to Gov. O'Neill (copy). [McGillivray] received another report that Cumberland residents killed some French traders along the Cherokee River. They also killed some Cherokees. The tribe sent 500-600 braves to revenge this act. 1p. English.

Doc. 264 reservada. 17 Sept. 1787, Pensacola. Arturo O'Neill to Esteban Miró. Poismeco, a Creek leader who favored the Americans, has turned on his former friends because the Americans killed some Creeks from Casista [Cussita?] and from the Cherokee River area. 3p.

Doc. 274 reservada. 19 Oct. 1787, Pensacola. Arturo O'Neill to Esteban Miró. A Creek war party reports that the Americans have abandoned Cumberland and retired to the Holston River, which flows into the Cherokee River. 3p.

Doc. 337. 21 July 1785, Pensacola. Arturo O'Neill to el Conde de Gálvez. The Chiis [Chickasaws?] and the Cherokees report that the Americans have moderated their activities around Natchez. 2p. [Enclosures to doc. 337-1].

[Doc. 337-1]. 22 Sept. 1785, Mexico. [El Conde de Gálvez] to Arturo O'Neill (copy). Gálvez acknowledges receipt of a letter containing news from the Chiis and Cherokees about the American activities around Natchez. 1p.

Doc. 343. 7 Aug. 1785, Pensacola. Arturo O'Neill to el Conde de Gálvez. Creeks report that some Americans are being recruited in Ga. and Carolina to go to Cumberland and Natchez. The Creeks are determined not to give them passage through their territory. O'Neill hopes to instill the same attitude in the Cherokees and Chiis. 2p.

Doc. 344. 4 Sept. 1785, Pensacola. Arturo O'Neill to el Conde de Gálvez. [Duplicate of enclosed document]. 2p. [Enclosures to doc. 344].

Doc. 344. 4 Sept. 1785, Pensacola. Arturo O'Neill to el Conde de Gálvez. O'Neill forwards an agreement reached by the Chiis, Choctaws, Cherokees, and Creeks. 2p.

Doc. 364. 8 Nov. 1786, Pensacola. Arturo O'Neill to el Conde de Gálvez. 2p. [Enclosures to doc. 364-1].

Doc. 364-1. 20 May 1786, Pensacola. Arturo O'Neill to Diego de Gardoqui (copy). Alex. McGillivray reported that several Creek and Cherokee parties are patrolling the frontier to expell the Americans. A Chickasaw chief has illegally ceded land around Muscle Shoals to the Americans. The Cherokees under Bloody Fellow are presently attacking Cumberland. The Americans killed Bloody Fellow's son. 2p.

CUBA/38   CORRESPONDENCE OF ARTURO O'NEILL: 1788-1790

[Siles 1992]. 29 June 1792. Chiefs of the Cherokee Nation
to Governor of Mobile. Cherokee chiefs present a plan to form
a united front against the Americans and to ask for Spanish
help. 6p. *English*. [Encloses 2 documents].

CUBA/39   CORRESPONDENCE OF ARTURO O'NEILL: 1791-1793

Doc. 292. 20 July 1792, Pensacola. Arturo O'Neill to el Barón
de Carondelet. O'Neill has received a copy of the Creek treaty
concluded by Carondelet. O'Neill has urged several Indian
leaders to contact the Northern tribes to make a common cause
against the Americans, but he doubts whether the messages will
be sent since the bearers would have to pass through the
American settlements and up the Cherokee and Ohio Rivers. 5p.

Doc. 319. 5 Aug. 1792, Pensacola. Arturo O'Neill to el Barón
de Carondelet. O'Neill includes correspondence with a Cherokee leader. The Cherokee leader assures O'Neill that he will
follow the Creeks against the Americans. 2p. [Enclosures to
doc. 319-3].

> Doc. 319-1. 1 July 1792, Cherokees. Bloody Fellow to Gov.
> O'Neill (copy). Bloody Fellow expresses his friendship
> for the Spaniards and lists services that the Cherokees
> could provide Spain. The Cherokee need many things. 2p.
> *English*.

> Doc. 319-2. 20 July 1792, Pensacola. O'Neill to Bloody
> Fellow (copy). O'Neill is pleased by the presence of the
> Cherokee warrior John Watts and will do everything possible
> to aid the Cherokees. 1p. *English*.

> Doc. 319-3. 6 Aug. 1792, Pensacola. [O'Neill?]. *Noticia
> del regalo ... a los Cheroquies*. 2p.

Doc. 324. 6 Aug. 1792, Pensacola. Arturo O'Neill to el Barón
de Carondelet. The Cherokee *mestizo* chief Richard Finleson
[Finnelston] arrived yesterday. He was in Pensacola four years
earlier as part of Bowles's group and at one time worked for
Panton. He complained about how much Americans oppress the
Cherokees. Other Cherokee chiefs are expected shortly in
Pensacola to make an alliance. 4p.

Doc. 325. 6 Aug. 1792, Pensacola. Arturo O'Neill to el Barón
de Carondelet. The Cherokees in Pensacola report that there
is no American establishment at Muscle Shoals yet. 5p.

Doc. 332. 8 Aug. 1792, Pensacola. Arturo O'Neill to el Barón
de Carondelet. A Frenchman and a Cherokee *mestizo* called
Finnelston returned with Panton. 3p.

Doc. 342. 31 Aug. 1792, Pensacola. Arturo O'Neill to el Barón
de Carondelet. An Indian party left for Cumberland. Other
Creeks are rumored ready to leave for Muscle Shoals and the
Cherokee R. to stop the Americans from running the boundary in
that area. 8p.

CUBA/39 (CONT'D)

Doc. 409 (no. 1). 5 Nov. 1792, Pensacola. Arturo O'Neill to
el Barón de Carondelet. O'Neill sends a letter received from
a Cherokee trader [McDonald?]. He arrived in Pensacola with
six Cherokee leaders and 25 followers, all of whom O'Neill
rewarded handsomely. Some of those Indians offered to persuade
the Chickasaws not to cede land to the Americans. Those Cherokees, led by Bloody Fellow and including the Breath, attacked
some Americans not long ago. 7p.

Doc. 410. 5 Nov. 1792, Pensacola. Arturo O'Neill to el Barón
de Carondelet. Mapelle (a Creek) and Moses Price (a Cherokee
mestizo) arrived in Pensacola. Price is a trader who accompanied Bowles to London. He knows the Lower Creeks well. Some
Creeks have left to attack the Americans along the Cherokee R.
and in Cumberland. 7p. [Enclosures to doc. 410-2].

> Doc. 410-2. 13 Nov. 1792, [New Orleans]. [El Barón de
> Carondelet] to Arturo O'Neill (copy). [Carondelet]
> acknowledges receipt of the letter concerning Moses Price.
> 1p.

Doc. 418. 7 Nov. 1792, Pensacola. Arturo O'Neill to el Barón
de Carondelet. O'Neill has sent a list of goods given to the
Cherokees, including supplies given to those who visited New
Orleans. 3p. [Enclosures to doc. 418-2].

> Doc. 418-1. 21 Oct. 1792, Pensacola. [Arturo O'Neill?].
> *Relación del regalo subministrado a los ... Chiroquies*
> (copy). 2p.

> Doc. 418-2. 6 Nov. 1792, Pensacola. [Arturo O'Neill?].
> *Relación de viveres, y demás efectos dado a los ...
> Chiroquies* (copy). 1p.

Doc. 445. 4 Dec. 1792, Pensacola. Arturo O'Neill to el Barón
de Carondelet. Another group of Cherokees arrived today. The
Creeks from Pequeño Oxfosque[?], who live with the Cherokees,
are also in Pensacola. 8p.

Doc. 456. 12 Dec. 1792, Pensacola. Arturo O'Neill to el Barón
de Carondelet. 2p. [Enclosures to doc. 456-1].

> Doc. 456-1. 12 Dec. 1792, Pensacola. Arturo O'Neill to
> el Barón de Carondelet. O'Neill received a copy of
> Carondelet's talk with the Cherokees and the list of
> presents given the tribe. O'Neill approves of Carondelet's
> idea to treat with the Cherokees on an annual basis. The
> Cherokees have already received the arms and powder that
> Carondelet ordered. In the future, it would be better
> to give the Cherokees their gifts in Mobile. Cherokee
> chief Towaytorlow from Hiwassee will explain this decision
> to Carondelet in New Orleans. 4p.

CUBA/39 (CONT'D)

Doc. 465. 28 Dec. 1792, Pensacola. Arturo O'Neill to el Barón
de Carondelet. It is clear that the Creeks will take revenge
on the Chickasaws for some recent murders, and the Cherokees will
undoubtedly side with the Creeks if the Chickasaws continue
their alliance with Cumberland. The best way to supply the
Cherokees is by river. 6p.

Doc. 475. [5?] Jan. 1793, Pensacola. O'Neill to el Barón de
Carondelet. American newspapers complain about the involvement
of Carondelet, O'Neill, and Panton in the Cherokee war. 3p.

Doc. 478. 30 Jan. 1793, Pensacola. Arturo O'Neill to el Barón
de Carondelet. Americans are exasperated with the Spanish
willingness to give munitions to the Indians, and there is no
doubt that Americans are preparing for war in Ky. and Cumberland. Americans under Gov. Blount burnt a Cherokee village
but lost nine soldiers. The Indians burned one prisoner at
the stake. A group of Northern Indians have come to urge the
Lower Creeks to unite against the Americans. 10p.

Doc. 479. 15 Feb. 1793, Pensacola. Arturo O'Neill to el
Barón de Carondelet. A Cherokee chief brought a letter and
a list of presents received in New Orleans. The Cherokees
are not as happy with gifts as the governor thinks. 3p.

Doc. 497. 19 May 1793, Pensacola. Arturo O'Neill to el Barón
de Carondelet. Indians are more content than ever. Lower
Creeks are quiet since Welbank left to visit the Cherokees.
3p.

[Siles 2000]. 13 July 1792, Pensacola. Arturo O'Neill to
el Barón de Carondelet. O'Neill acknowledges receipt of
letters concerning the Americans at Ft. Washington. Panton
believes that the Creeks and Cherokees should be told that
Spain will supply them with ammunition. 3p.

[Siles 2007]. 16 Aug. 1792, Pensacola. Arturo O'Neill to
el Barón de Carondelet. Creeks asked for more munitions
and have attacked the Americans in Cumberland. 2p.

CUBA/40   CORRESPONDENCE OF ARTURO O'NEILL: 1781-1793

Doc. 16. 3 Sept. 1785, New Orleans. Copy of letter to
[Arturo O'Neill?] forwarding a memorial from the Creeks,
Chickasaws, and Cherokees. 1p.

Doc. 443. 13 Dec. [1790?], [New Orleans?]. Letter to Arturo
O'Neill acknowledging receipt of a list of gifts and food
given to the Cherokees, including that given to the nine who
came to [New Orleans?]. 1p.

CUBA/40 (CONT'D)

Doc. 1033 (no. 23). 25 Aug. 1792, Mobile. Manuel de Lanzos
to Arturo O'Neill. Carondelet is worried that the new
American fort near Tombigbee will soon be as large as Franklin
or Cumberland and will threaten the Spanish Indians. 14p.

Doc. 1039. 4 July 1792, Little Tallassee. Pedro Olivier to
Arturo O'Neill. Olivier informed Carondelet that a [Cherokee?]
trader confirmed the presence of an American establishment
at Muscle Shoals along the Cherokee River. Furthermore, the
Cherokees sent two chiefs before Congress to protest this establishment. Since Wm. Panton has just made a trip to the Cherokees, he can give additional information on the matter. 2p.

CUBA/42   CORRESPONDENCE OF MANUEL GAYOSO DE LEMOS: 1793-1794

Fol. 150. 10 July 1794, Natchez. Manuel Gayoso de Lemos to
Elias Beauregard. John Stowers has complained that Beauregard
failed to reimburse him for the canoe *(pirogue)*, rent of a
mule, and supplies given to the Cherokees at Natchez.
Beauregard must pay this debt. 4p.

Fol. 185 (no. 235). 8 Jan. 1793, Natchez. Manuel Gayoso de
Lemos to el Barón de Carondelet. Bloody Fellow (Cherokee
leader), Chickamauga Charlie, John Taylor (tribe's interpreter),
and the rest of the Cherokees have left. The Cherokees had
asked for the King's help in recovering their land from the
Americans and they requested that Spain erect a fort at Muscle
Shoals. The Americans tricked the Cherokees in the Treaty of
Hopewell. Carlos, Bloody Fellow's son, has remained with the
Spaniards. 37p. [Enclosures to fol. 218].

> Fol. 204 (no. 1). 28 Dec. 1792, Natchez. Manuel Gayoso
> de Lemos to Juan de la Villebeuvre (copy). The bearer
> of this letter is Bloody Fellow. Cherokees have visited
> New Orleans to solicit the King's protection. They have
> agreed to enter into alliance with the Talapooses,
> Choctaws, and Chickasaws to defend their land. Villebeuvre
> must encourage the Choctaws and Chickasaws to cooperate.
> Bloody Fellow will visit those tribes to encourage their
> participation. 4p.

> Fol. 206 [no. 1]. 28 Dec. 1792, Natchez. [Gayoso] to
> Juan de la Villebeuvre. [Same as fol. 204]. 4p.

> Fol. 208 (no. 2). 29 Dec. 1792, Natchez. Manuel Gayoso
> de Lemos to Franchimastabe (copy). Gayoso is pleased to
> hear about Franchimastabe's visit to the governor in
> New Orleans. Franchimastabe already knows Bloody Fellow
> and his companions and should treat them well. 2p.
> *English.*

Fol. 209 (no.3). 29 Dec. 1792, Natchez. [Manuel Gayoso de Lemos] to Fascaoutuca (copy). [Gayoso] is pleased to hear about Fascaoutuca's visit to the governor in New Orleans. Fascaoutuca already knows Bloody Fellow and his companions and should treat them well. 2p. *English*.

Fol. 210 (no. 4). 29 Dec. 1792, Natchez. Manuel Gayoso de Lemos to Payemingo and Ugulayacabe (copy). Gayoso expresses his desire to see the two chiefs and show them Spanish friendship. The bearer of this letter is Bloody Fellow, a Cherokee, who brings good news. Ugulayacabe is urged to treat him kindly. 3p. *English*.

Fol. 212 [no. 4]. 29 Dec. 1792, Natchez. [Manuel Gayoso de Lemos] to Payemingo and Ugulayacabe. [Same as fol. 210]. 2p. *English*.

Fol. 213 (no. 5). 29 Dec. 1792, Natchez. Manuel Gayoso de Lemos to Hardy Perry (copy). Gayoso will shortly send the mulatto women to Perry and hopes to have the friendliest relations with the Cherokees. The bearer of this letter is Bloody Fellow, a Cherokee, who is on his way home. Gayoso recommends him highly to Perry. 3p.

Fol. 215 [no. 5]. 29 Dec. 1792, Natchez. [Manuel Gayoso de Lemos] to Hardy Perry. [Same as fol. 213]. 3p.

Fol. 217 (no. 7). 8 Jan. 1792, Natchez. Francisco Gutiérrez de Arroyo. *Relación de los regalos hechos a los ... Cherokees*. List of gifts given to the Cherokees in December, 1791, including a description of goods given to the Choctaws accompanying the Cherokees. 3p.

Fol. 401 (no. 7). 31 May 1793, Natchez. Manuel Gayoso de Lemos to Gov. Carondelet. Cumberland officials have seized a load of corn being sent to the [Spanish possessions]. The Creeks and Cherokees have annoyed Cumberland a great deal and Cumberland has formed two cavalry companies to defend the frontier. 7p.

Fol. 430 (no. 299). 3 June 1793, Natchez. Manuel Gayoso de Lemos to el Barón de Carondelet. Gayoso forwards a memorial from John Hinds asking to bring his family from the United States. Hinds, who recently passed through Cumberland, has assured Gayoso that it was impossible to send goods from Cumberland to Spanish territory by land for fear of being attacked by the Cherokees and Creeks. 11p. [Enclosures to fol. 437].

Fol. 634 (no. 367). 1 Nov. 1793, Natchez. Manuel Gayoso de Lemos to el Barón de Carondelet. Gayoso sends a copy of the Nogales treaty concluded with the Chickasaws, Creeks, Talapooses, Alibamos, Cherokees, and Choctaws. 2p.

CUBA/42 (CONT'D)

Fol. 636 (no. 369). 6 Nov. 1793, Natchez. [Manuel Gayoso de Lemos] to el Barón de Carondelet. [Duplicate of fol. 637]. 2p. [Enclosures to fol. 637b].

Fol. 637 (no. 369). 6 Nov. 1793, Natchez. Manuel Gayoso de Lemos to el Barón de Carondelet. Gayoso forwards a copy of the treaty with the Creeks, Talapooses, Alibamos, Cherokees, Chickasaws, and Choctaws. 2p.

Fol. 646 (no. 375). 10 Nov. 1793, Natchez. Manuel Gayoso de Lemos to el Barón de Carondelet. The bearer of this letter is Little Turkey. Kauytamingo, Fachale, Kaeita Chacche, Chuleua, and Ulave (all Cherokee chiefs) arrived yesterday in Nogales. They were told that the treaty was already concluded and that a copy had been sent to the Cherokees. Two of the chiefs sought an interview with Gayoso to explain the hardship they went through to travel this far. Those Indians presented letters from John Thompson and John McDonald. Bloody Fellow would have come but he was fighting the Americans. 12p.

Fol. 665 (no. 380). 12 Nov. 1793, Natchez. Manuel Gayoso de Lemos to el Barón de Carondelet. Since no one in Natchez understood Cherokee, Gayoso sent the two Cherokee chiefs back to Nogales. He ordered that an excellent rifle (*carabina*) be given to them to demonstrate Spanish esteem for the tribe. 3p. [Enclosures to fol. 669].

Fol. 667. 11 Nov. 1793, Natchez. Manuel Gayoso de Lemos to Elias Beauregard (copy). The two Cherokees have arrived from Nogales. Beauregard should have sent an interpreter with them . Little Turkey is evidently their leader. Beauregard should tell the Cherokees that they will be rewarded if they go to New Orleans since all the Indian supplies at Natchez have been exhausted. 4p.

Fol. 669. [1793?], [Nogales?]. [Beauregard?] to [Gayoso?]. [Beauregard?] could get more cooperation from the Chero-kees if [Gayoso?] would give more than just a gun to Little Turkey. Bloody Fellow is very interested in an alliance of the four major Indian nations against the Americans. 1p.

Fol. 685 (no. 13). 6 Dec. 1793, Natchez. Manuel Gayoso de Lemos to el Barón de Carondelet. Gayoso describes the negotia-tions, which were attended by more than 1,000 Indians, resulting in the Treaty of Nogales. Tasquenisia and Sulusmas represented the Cherokees and also spoke for Creeks, Talapooses, and Alibamos. The Cherokees petitioned for Spanish protection. 82p. [Enclosures to fol. 727b].

Fol. 726. 28 Oct. 1793, Nogales. Manuel Gayoso de Lemos et al. Treaty of Nogales. [Same as AGI SD/2563/fol. 8]. 4p.

Fol. 748 (no. 6 *reservada*). 10 Jan. 1793, Natchez. Manuel Gayoso de Lemos to el Barón de Carondelet. News from Illinois

CUBA/42 (CONT'D)

indicates that Cumberland and the United States still blame
Carondelet for turning the Indians against them. Spanish
officials must be careful that the Americans cannot prove
these charges. 3p. [Enclosures to fol. 755].

Fol. 750. 16 [Nov.?] 1792, [Kaskaskia]. Copy of a letter
to [el Barón de Carondelet] stating that 600 Creeks and
Cherokees have reportedly invaded Cumberland. 4p. *French*.

Fol. 752 (no. 100). 27 Dec. 1792, New Madrid. Thomas
Portell to el Barón de Carondelet (copy). Reports from
the Ohio R. indicate that Cumberland residents plan some
hostilities against Spanish territory because they are
convinced that Spain encourages the Cherokees and the
Talapooses. Cumberland claims to have documents proving
this. 2p.

Fol. 752b. 28 Nov. 1792, Louisville. Extract of a letter
from R.J.[?] Waters reporting that the residents of
Philadelphia blame Spain for inciting the Creeks and
Cherokees against the United States. 2p. *English*.

Fol. 754. 21 Jan. 1793, New Orleans. [El Barón de
Carondelet] to Manuel Gayoso de Lemos. Carondelet assures
Gayoso that Spain has done nothing to incite the tribes
against the Americans. Indians have allied themselves
with Spain because the Spaniards understand how the
Americans have taken the Indian land. 3p.

Fol. 805 (no. 12). 5 Dec. 1792, Natchez. Manuel Gayoso de
Lemos to el Barón de Carondelet. Little Turkey (Cauitamico),
principal chief of the Cherokees, is in Nogales with 103
followers. Since the Cherokees missed the treaty negotiations,
Gayoso has decided to hold a special ceremony in which the
tribe can ratify the treaty. Some Cherokees are going on to
New Orleans and Gayoso is sending Antonio Villeverde to interpret for them. 9p.

Fol. 948 (no. 49 *reservada*). 19 July, 1794, Natchez. Manuel
Gayoso de Lemos to el Barón de Carondelet. 2p. [Enclosures
to fol. 958b].

Fol. 949. 17 July 1794, Natchez. [Manuel Gayoso de Lemos
to Benjamin Fooy] (copy). The presence of Americans near
the Old Cherokee or French Fort makes Ugulayacabe uneasy.
[Gayoso] wants the Chickasaws to do something about the
situation. 7p. *English*.

Fol. 954. 17 July 1793, Natchez. [Manuel Gayoso de Lemos]
to Ugulayacabe (copy). News about the Americans in the
French Fort is not unexpected. Chickasaws would not find
Americans there had they followed Spanish advice. 9p.
English.

CUBA/42 (CONT'D)

Fol. 1019 (no. 1). 18 Oct. 1793, Nogales. Manuel Gayoso de
Lemos to el Barón de Carondelet. Gayoso discusses the forthcoming assembly with Indians. It is not possible to decide
where the Cherokees should receive their annual gifts since
that tribe has not expressed a preference. Pensacola would
be the most likely place although Old Tombigbee would also be
acceptable. 15p.

Fol. 1205. 12 Sept. 1793, Natchez. Manuel Gayoso de Lemos
to Mistilebek Chaty (Soulier Rouge), Faskihiniha, Famchacho,
and Yaticahacho (Creek Great Medal Chiefs). Gayoso is pleased
that the chiefs have arrived in Natchez for the assembly which
the Chickasaws, Choctaws, and the Cherokees (reportedly) will
also attend. 3p. [Enclosures to fol. 1207b].

> Fol. 1207. [12 Sept. 1793], [Natchez]. [Manuel Gayoso
> de Lemos] to Mistilebek Chaty et al. [Draft of fol. 1205].
> 2p.

Fol. 1232. 9 July 1794, Madrid. *Real orden* from Gardoqui to
Governor of Louisiana. The King wants to know why the
governor authorized Gayoso to spend 2,000 pesos on the Treaty
of Nogales concluded with the Chickasaws, Creeks, Talapooses,
Alibamos, Cherokees, and Choctaws. 1p.

CUBA/43   CORRESPONDENCE OF MANUEL GAYOSO DE LEMOS: 1795-1797

Doc. 69 (no. 234). 8 Jan. 1793, Natchez. Manuel Gayoso de
Lemos to el Barón de Carondelet. Creeks have threatened to kill
all the whites in Chickasaw territory. These same Creeks have
done much harm to the residents of Cumberland. 4p.

Doc. 100 (no. 612). 14 Mar. 1795, Natchez. Manuel Gayoso de
Lemos to el Barón de Carondelet. Chickasaws report that a war
with the Creeks is inevitable and that one group of the Chickasaws has given the Americans permission to establish a fort
at Muscle Shoals. 6p. [Enclosures to doc. 100i].

> Doc. 100a (no. 1). 1 Feb. 1795, Talkey [?]. Benjamin
> Fooy to Manuel Gayoso de Lemos. Fooy discusses events
> along the Cherokee River. 5p. *English*.

> Doc. 100c (no. 3). 17 Feb. 1795, Chickataza [?]. Letter
> from Ouglsayaekabee [Ugulayacabe?] discussing a fort along
> the Cherokee River. 5p. *English*.

> Doc. 100i. 24 Mar. 1795, [New Orleans?]. [El Barón de
> Carondelet?] to Manuel Gayoso de Lemos. [Carondelet?]
> acknowledges news that the Americans have taken advantage
> of the Chickasaw-Creek war to get permission to build a
> fort at Muscle Shoals. 10p.

Doc. 133 (no. 7). 25 Aug. 1795, New Madrid. Manuel Gayoso de
Lemos to el Barón de Carondelet. Gayoso has learned that Ga.,
N. Carolina, and Cumberland have raised three companies of
soldiers to march against Barrancas de San Fernando in Chickasaw territory. 5p.

CUBA/43 (CONT'D)

Doc. 143 (no. 23 *reservada*). 9 Oct. 1795, on board the galley
(galeota) La Vigilante. Manuel Gayoso de Lemos to el Barón
de Carondelet. Chickasaws under Payemingo expect a gift from
Cumberland. 4p. [Enclosures to doc. 143a].

> Doc. 143a (no. 23 *reservada*). 9 Oct. 1795, on board the
> galley *(galeota) La Vigilante*. [Manuel Gayoso de Lemos]
> to el Barón de Carondelet. [Same as doc. 143]. 5p.

Doc. 297. 13 May 1797, Natchez. Manuel Gayoso de Lemos to el
Barón de Carondelet. American hunters have killed several
Cherokee hunters, which will surely cause some hostility. 4p.

Doc. 326. 5 Apr. 1797, Natchez. Manuel Gayoso de Lemos to
Commandant of Camp Hope. 1p. [Enclosures to doc. 326i].

> Doc. 326d (no. 4). 19 Dec. 1796, Philadelphia. James
> McHenry to Chiefs and Warriors of the Chickasaws (copy).
> In last year's talk with the Chickasaws, the chiefs
> complained that they found the road to Cumberland crowded
> with people and that they wanted a border established to
> keep people away. Americans understand that the Chickasaws
> are retaining property taken from the Cherokees. If the
> tribe does not settle its obligations with the Cherokees,
> the Americans will deduct the amount owed from the Chick-
> asaws' annual gifts. 4p. *English*.

CUBA/48   CORRESPONDENCE TO MANUEL GAYOSO DE LEMOS: 1795-1797

Doc. 414. 25 Aug. 1797, Camp Hope. *Relación* from José Meville
Deyoutin [Deville Degoutin?] to Commandant General. An
inebriated Chickasaw chief reported that 500 mounted whites
were on their way to Natchez, but it was not clear if they
were coming from Cumberland, Holston, or Tennessee. 27p.

Doc. 414. 17 Dec. 1796, Camp Hope. Manuel García to Manuel
Gayoso de Lemos. Ugulayacabe is unhappy with the treaty and
claims that the Choctaws, Talapooses, and Cherokees are also
discontent with it. 16p.

CUBA/67   CORRESPONDENCE TO MANUEL LANZOS: 1792-1806

Fol. 122. 24 Nov. 1792, New Orleans. Letter to Manuel de
Lanzos reporting that there are over a thousand Indians
(including a few Cherokees) in New Orleans with the King of
the Chickasaws. 1p.

CUBA/103   CORRESPONDENCE FROM VARIOUS OFFICIALS: 1783-1814

No. 2. 10 July 1793, Boukfouka. Juan de la Villebeuvre to
[Manuel] Gayoso de Lemos. Three Cherokees have complained
that their nation had no knowledge about the forthcoming
assembly of Indians at Nogales. 4p. *French*.

CUBA/103 (CONT'D)

No. 5.   23 July 1793, Nogales. Manuel Gayoso de Lemos to
Ugulayacabe-Mingo. Gayoso is pleased that the conflict with
the Creeks has ended. He discusses the timing of the upcoming
Indian assembly and the need to notify the Cherokees in advance.
Gayoso asks Ugulayacabe-Mingo to forward some letters to Bloody
Fellow and the other Cherokees. 5p. *English*.

No. 8.   23 July 1793, Natchez. Manuel Gayoso de Lemos to
Souloushemastabe, Chief of the Creek Nation (copy). Gayoso
discusses the forthcoming assembly of the Four Nations
[including the Cherokees]. 3p. *English*.

No. 9.   23 July 1793, Nogales or Walnut Hills. Manuel Gayoso
de Lemos to Bloody Fellow, Chief of the Cherokees. Gayoso has
sent messages to the Cherokees via Mr. Turnbull and the Chickasaws. Cherokees are invited to the forthcoming congress of
the Choctaws, Creeks, and Chickasaws. Because of the war
between the Creeks and Chickasaws, the weather, and the corn
dance festivals, the meeting was postponed until October.
Bloody Fellow should bring Taylor or someone else to interpret
for the Cherokees. 4p. *English*.

No. 11.   8 July 1793, Boukfouka. Talk from Ougela Xyachabee
and Paye Wakio to Talapooses. Ougela discusses peace with the
Talapooses. Chiefs are sending rations [of alcohol] to
Kaouita-Mingo, Chief of Cherokees. 4p. *French*. [Encloses 1
document].

CUBA/121   CORRESPONDENCE TO THE GOVERNOR OF LOUISIANA: 1790

N. doc. Incomplete report discussing the unjustified war by
the Chickasaws against the Creeks. The author has worked with
the Creeks to stop Ga. from illegally occupying land belonging
to the Four Nations. He has also been planning an assembly
of the Four Nations (including the Cherokees) to consider
various problems. Rumors persist that the Americans are now
fortifying Muscle Shoals. 4p.

Doc. 38 [Congress]. Report of Congressional Committee. In
response to the numerous complaints and charges that Ga. and
N.C. are encroaching upon Creek and Cherokee land, the committee
believes that a strict investigation should be made. There is
no doubt that Cherokee land has been violated by American
settlements. 7p. *English*.

Doc. 42.   23 July 1785, Greenwich. Andrew Pickens to Alex.
McGillivray. Congress has appointed five commissioners to hold
talks with the Creeks, Cherokees, Choctaws, Chickasaws, and
all other nations within the boundaries of the United States.
Among many topics, Pickens would like to discuss the question
of the Creeks and Cumberland. 2p. *English*.

Doc. 44.   [Henry] Knox to James White. Knox, the Sec. of War,
discusses problems concerning the Chickasaws and Choctaws, with
a brief reference to the Cherokees. 2p. *English*.

CUBA/121 (CONT'D)

Doc. 45. 29 Mar. 1788, Ft. Charlotte. Andrew Pickens and George Mathews to Alex. McGillivray and the Creeks. Congress sent Mr. White to negotiate with the Creeks last year because of the tribe's dispute with Georgia. N.C., S.C., and Ga. have appointed commissioners this year to negotiate a firmer peace with the Creeks. These men can meet with tribal representatives whenever McGillivray desires. 2p. *English*.

Doc. 46. 1 Sept. 1788, Congress in session. Cyrus Griffin (President). *A Proclamation by the United States in Congress*. Proclamation lists Indian borders in the American Southeast (including the Cherokees). 2p. *English*.

N. doc. 28 Oct. 1793, Nogales. Manuel Gayoso de Lemos et al. Treaty of Nogales. [Same as AGI SD/2563/fol. 8]. 10p.

CUBA/123   CORRESPONDENCE TO THE GOVERNOR OF LOUISIANA: 1793

Doc. 4. 20 Apr. 1793, New Orleans. [El Barón de Carondelet] to Wm. Panton. Carondelet received a duplicate of McDonald's letter. The Cherokees are so divided that it is difficult to respond to them. 4p.

Doc. 5. 14 June 1793, Pensacola. Wm. Panton to el Barón de Carondelet. Panton's illness has kept him away from the Creeks. McDonald's Cherokees have been waiting in Panton's house for a month for Carondelet's reply. The president of Congress has invited the Cherokees to visit Philadelphia. 3p. *English*.

Doc. 152 (no. 110). 17 Dec. 1793, Pensacola. Enrique White to Francisco Montreuil. White forwards a copy of the Treaty of Nogales. 1p. [Enclosures to doc. 152-1].

    Doc. 152-1. 28 Oct. 1793, Nogales. Manuel Gayoso de Lemos
    et al. Treaty of Nogales. [Same as AGI SD/2563/fol.8]. 5p.

Doc. 207. 10 Sept. 1793, New Orleans. [El Barón de Carondelet] to Enrique White. White is ordered to inform the Creeks and Cherokees that they will receive the munitions necessary for hunting and defense. 2p.

Doc. 245. 16 July 1793, New Orleans. [El Barón de Carondelet?] to Pedro Olivier. Creeks want the assembly of the Four Nations to take place at Old Tombigbee or Mobile. 3p. [Enclosures to doc. 245-3].

Doc. 256. 1 July 1794, New Orleans. Answer [from el Barón de Carondelet] to the talk of Ouolettays and Detenhee, Chiefs of the Cherokee Nation. The Indian war with the Americans goes back many years and it is difficult to know whom to blame. At the request of the Cherokees, the King is in the process of discussing all disputes between the Creeks and Cherokees and the Americans. Meanwhile, he asks that the Cherokees remain on their land and take no action beyond defending themselves. 4p. *English*.

CUBA/123 (CONT'D)

N. doc. 28 Oct. 1793, Nogales. Manuel Gayoso de Lemos et al.
Treaty of Nogales. [Same as AGI SD/2563/fol. 8]. 7p.

N. doc. 30 Nov. 1793, Natchez. Manuel Gayoso de Lemos et al.
*Confirmación del tratado celebrado en los Nogales ... por lo
respectivo a la nación Cherokee.* Cherokees in attendance,
including Cauitamico (Little Turkey), Cayetehe [Gayetechy],
Chache [Chachoy], Cholehua [Cholehoova], Skahihoka, Conchanabe
[Conchanawley], and Chinabe [Chinacoby] confirm the Treaty of
Nogales. [Spanish version of AGI Cuba/188C/fol. 96]. 1p.

N. doc. 15 Feb. 1793, New Orleans. [El Barón de Carondelet?]
to Thomas Portell. [Carondelet?] approves the decision to
send someone to spy on Cumberland, especially since Cumberland
blames Spain for the recent Cherokee and Creek attacks. 2p.

CUBA/125   CORRESPONDENCE OF THE GOVERNOR OF LOUISIANA: 1793-1802

N. fol. 22 July 1794, New Orleans. Letter to Mr. Simcoe with
news that the Spanish can mobilize the Cherokees, Creeks,
Choctaws, and Chickasaws in case of war. 2p. *French.*

N. fol. 26 Apr. 1794, Pensacola. Enrique White to Diego de
Vegas. Carondelet has ordered that the Cherokee gifts be
distributed at different times, rather than all at once, to
those who come to Pensacola to collect them. 10p.

No. 1. 27 May 1794, St. Marks. Diego de Vegas to Enrique
White. Seagrove (the American Indian agent) held talks with
the Creeks in April seeking, among many things, permission to
establish a trading post near the Cherokees. 5p.

CUBA/177A   DRAFTS OF LETTERS TO THE MINISTERS: 1790-1792

N. fol. 10 Aug. 1786, Pensacola. [Governor?] to el Marqués
de Sonora. Creeks will resist any American efforts to settle
their land. Various parties of the Upper Creeks and Cherokees
are patrolling the frontiers, forcing settlers along the Oconee,
Altamaha, and Cherokee Rivers (at a place called Hoghego or
Muscle Shoals) to leave. One group of Indians attacked Cumberland. The banks of the Ohio belong to the Creeks and Cherokees.
4p.

N. fol. 1 June 1787, New Orleans. *Indice de las representa-
ciones reservadas ... [del governador de Luisiana] al exmo.
sr. Marqués de Sonora.* 2p. [Encloses 12 documents].

No. 11 *reservada.* 1 June 1787, [New Orleans]. [Governor
of Louisiana] to el Marqués de Sonora (copy). 2p.

No. 3. 4 Mar. 1787, Little Tallassee. Alex. McGillivray to Gov. O'Neill. [Translation of following
letter]. 3p.

[No. 3]. 4 Mar. 1787, Little Tallassee. [Alex.
McGillivray] to Gov. O'Neill. The Tallassees,
Oakfuskees, Shawnees, and Savannahs have attacked
Cumberland. 2p. *English*.

No. 4. 4 Apr. 1787, Little Tallassee. Alex.
McGillivray to Gov. O'Neill. [Translation of the
English copy below].

[No. 4]. 4 Apr. 1787, Little Tallassee. Alex.
McGillivray to Gov. O'Neill. [Translation of
English copy below]. 3p.

[No. 4]. 4 Apr. 1787, Little Tallassee. Mr.
McGillivray to Gov. O'Neill (copy). McGillivray
confirms the existence of a general war by the Great
Lakes Indians against all American settlements,
including Cumberland. The mission of the surveyor
Hutchins has probably failed since some of his
assistants have been killed along the Ohio and their
papers given to some Cherokee traders. 2p. *English*.

No. 12 *reservada*. 1 June 1787, New Orleans. [Gov. of
Louisiana] to el Marqués de Sonora. 5p.

N. fol. 18 Apr. 1787, Little Tallassee. Alex.
McGillivray to Gov. O'Neill. Some Creeks have left
to attack Cumberland. 3p. *English*.

N. fol. 18 Apr. 1787, Little Tallassee. Alex.
McGillivray to Gov. O'Neill. [Translation of the
previous letter]. 5p.

No. 6 *reservada*. 4 June 1788, Pensacola. Arturo O'Neill to
Esteban Miró. Spain needs to control the amount of powder
given to McGillivray since he plans hostilities against
Georgia. At the same time, McGillivray proposes peace with
Cumberland. 11p. [Encloses 1 document].

No. 21. 15 June 1788, New Orleans. [Esteban Miró?] to Antonio
Valdés. [Miró?] encloses information about the desire of
Cumberland and Ky. to leave the union. Franklin is politically
divided, a split that has led to actual fighting. Franklin
had not reunited with N.C. nor has part of it returned to
Cherokee control. 4p. [Encloses 1 document].

N. fol. 25 Apr. 1788, Little Tallassee. Alex. McGillivray
to Gov. O'Neill (translated). Cumberland representatives
have arrived in Little Tallassee with peace proposals.
The new state of Franklin has split apart, one part re-
joining N. Carolina and the other merging with the
Cherokees who had lost the land to Franklin originally.
McGillivray has seen proof that the Va. Company bought
Cumberland from the Cherokees and Northern Indians forty
years ago. 3p.

CUBA/177A (CONT'D)

No. 37. 30 Apr. 1789, [New Orleans?]. [Esteban Miró?] to
Antonio Valdés. James White has arrived in [New Orleans?]
from Franklin, which is now an independent nation. Antonio
Fagot has arrived from Cumberland, a N.C. district. 7p.
[Encloses 7 documents].

   No. 1. 12 Sept. 1788, Franklin. John Sevier to [Esteban
   Miró?] (translation). Franlin's inhabitants definitely
   want an alliance and commercial connections with Spain.
   They are ready to break away from N. Carolina. 5p.

   No. 2. 18 Apr. 1789, New Orleans. James White to Esteban
   Miró (translation). Gardoqui gave White some letters for
   the leaders of Franklin promising them Spanish protection
   if they wished it. The circumstances in Cumberland are
   similar. 3p.

   No. 3. 20 Apr. 1789, [New Orleans?]. Letter to Esteban
   Miró stating that Miró is authorized to offer the residents
   of Franklin and Cumberland permission to settle in La. and
   to trade with New Orleans. At present Spain cannot
   encourage the two areas to join its empire and separate
   from the United States. Should they obtain independence,
   however, the King would treat them favorably. 4p.

   No. 4. [New Orleans?]. Esteban Miró to Brig. Gen. Samuel
   Smith. Miró assures Smith that Spain will do everything
   possible to assist [Cumberland?]. Miró, however, has had
   no communication with the Cherokees. Nevertheless, some
   Cherokees will visit Illinois next year to ask permission
   to settle on the west bank of the Mississippi. Miró has
   ordered that such permission be granted, which will be a
   great service to [Cumberland?]. 4p.

   No. 5. 23 Apr. 1789, New Orleans. Letter from [Esteban
   Miró] stating that Don Diego Gardoqui has engaged James
   White, a member of congress and property owner in Franklin
   and Cumberland, to work for Spain. Gardoqui sent White
   to Franklin to encourage the inhabitants to separate from
   the United States and form a tie with Spain. [Miró] has
   learned that Cumberland will separate form N.C. and send
   delegates to New Orleans to place that province under
   Spanish protection. 8p.

   No. 6. 22 Apr. 1789, New Orleans. James White to Gov.
   [Miró]. [Translation of English original below]. 1p.

   [No. 6]. 22 Apr. 1789, New Orleans. James White to Gov.
   Miró. White needs money. 1p. *English*.

N. fol. 17 Feb. 1792, Philadelphia. Henry Knox to Choctaw
Chiefs and Warriors (translation). President Washington has
received the Cherokees' message via the Choctaws and is very
pleased with it. The United States is at peace with the Creeks,
Cherokees, Choctaws, and Chickasaws. 5p. [Encloses 4 documents].

N. fol. 27 Apr. 1792, Knoxville. Wm. Blount to Choctaw
Chiefs and Warriors (translation). Cherokee negotiations
have delayed Blount's reply to the Choctaw letters. 3p.

N. fol. Translation of letter to Franchimastabe, King
of the Choctaw nation, and to the Englishman Wells [?]
stating that Franchimastabe should send a representative
if he cannot personally visit Cumberland. 2p.

CUBA/177B   DRAFTS OF LETTERS TO THE MINISTERS: 1780-1792

N. fol. 4 June 1792, Cumberland. Jane Brown to Gen. Alex.
McGillivray. Brown presently lives at Cumberland with her
four children. 1p. *English*. [Encloses 1 document].

N. fol. 25 May 1792, Cumberland. James Hoggath to Col.
Alex. McGillivray. The Indians wounded a mutual friend,
Gen. Robertson, and he will likely die. Indians have
attacked numerous families in Cumberland. Hoggath would
like McGillivray to have some captives taken by the
Indians returned. 1p. *English*.

N. Fol. 25 Feb. 1792, New Orleans. *Indice de las cartas
reservadas que ... [remite el Barón de Carondelet] al exmo.
sr. Conde de Floridablanca.* 2p. [Encloses 3 documents].

No. 9 *reservada*. 25 Feb. 1792, [New Orleans]. [El Barón
de Carondelet] to el Conde de Floridablanca. The attached
information demonstrates how badly the Americans are
trying to seize the land bordered by the Appalachians,
the Gulf of Mexico, and the Ohio and Miss. Rivers. The
settlements in Ky., Cumberland, and Franklin are clear
indications of the American intentions. Americans are
raising troops as fast as they can to attack the Cherokees,
and Carondelet is doing his best to convince the four
Southern tribes that their survival depends upon Spanish
protection. 9p.

N. fol. 1791, Charleston. *Librito ynglés que
contiene un extracto de los apuntes de la compañia
de la Carolina del Sur en el Yazu* (translation).
The South Carolina Company has a justifiable claim
to the Yazoo territory. This claim directly and
indirectly includes the Cherokee, Creek, Franklin,
Cumberland, N. and S. Carolina, Virginia, and Georgia
borders. 64p.

N. fol. 22 Mar. 1792, New Orleans. *Indice de las cartas
reservadas que ... [remite el Barón de Carondelet] al exmo.
sr. Conde de Floridablanca.* 3p. [Encloses 15 documents].

No. 11 *reservada*. New Orleans. El Barón de Carondelet
to el Conde de Floridablanca [doc. missing].

CUBA/177B (CONT'D)

No. 3. 4 Dec. 1791, Coweta. Translation of letters
from Wm. Augustus Bowles stating that the Creeks and
Cherokees have formed a common government headed by
a council. Bowles has been appointed director. It
would be very useful to [Spain?] and Bowles to form
an alliance. 4p.

No. 5. 13 Mar. 1792, New Orleans. Wm. Augustus
Bowles to el Barón de Carondelet (translation). It
is not true that Bowles planned hostilities against
Spanish subjects. In 1788 Cumberland and Ky. residents secretly asked Bowles to attack the Spanish
possessions, but he persuaded the Creeks not to do
so. 7p.

No. 12 *reservada*. 22 March 1792. New Orleans. [El
Barón de Carondelet] to el Conde de Floridablanca. 2p.

No. 3. 14 Mar. 1792, New Orleans. Wm. A. Bowles to
el Barón de Carondelet (translation). Bowles came
to New Orleans to correct all the misinformation that
existed between Spaniards and Creeks. The Creeks are
the original inhabitants of Florida up to the 36°
latitude. The Cherokees are the original inhabitants
of land north of that latitude to the Ohio. These
two countries united some time ago and have proposed
an alliance to the Northern tribes. 3p.

No. 14 *reservada*. 22 Mar. 1792, [New Orleans]. [El Barón de
Carondelet] to el Conde de Floridablanca. [Same as AHN Estado/
3898/exp. 5/ no. 14 *reservada*]. 1p.

N. fol. 28 Mar. 1792, New Orleans. *Indice de las cartas
reservadas que escribe [el Barón de Carondelet] ... al exmo.
sr. Conde de Floridablanca.* 1p. [Encloses 6 documents].

No. 15 *reservada*. 28 Mar. 1792, New Orleans. [El Barón
de Carondelet] to el Conde de Floridablanca (duplicate).
4p.

[No. 2]. [1792?], [New Orleans?]. Translated
declaración from William Cunningham stating that he
traveled to Franklin in 1790 and lived there some 60
days. At one time, he taught school in Franklin.
Later, he visited the Cherokees for five to six weeks.
He saw McDonald visit the Creeks. 17p.

No. 16 *reservada*. 28 Mar. 1792, New Orleans. [El Barón
de Carondelet] to el Conde de Floridablanca. 1p.

N. fol. 4 Jan. 1792. Translated *declaración* from
Gen. Wm. Augustus Bowles announcing the free entry
by all nations to the rivers, ports, and coasts of
[Florida?]. Bowles grants this privilege as Director
of the United Nations of Creeks and Cherokees. 1p.

N. fol. 7 Apr. 1792, [New Orleans]. *Indice de las cartas reservadas que remite el Barón de Carondelet ... al exmo. sr. Conde de Floridablanca.* [Encloses 8 documents].

No. 17 *reservada.* 29 Mar. 1792, New Orleans. [El Barón de Carondelet] to el Conde de Floridablanca. 2p.

N. fol. 29 Mar. 1792, [New Orleans]. [El Barón de Carondelet] to Manuel Gayoso de Lemos. Gayoso must negotiate with the Choctaws with as much secrecy and speed as possible since the Americans will use every trick to frustrate it. Gayoso must try to convince the Choctaws that their only protection is an alliance of the four Southern tribes under Spanish guidance. 2p.

N. fol. 23 Mar. 1792, New Orleans. [El Barón de Carondelet] to Franchimastabe. All Indian friends (particularly the Choctaws, Chickasaws, Creeks, and the Cherokees) must maintain a close alliance to defend their lands against the Americans. The Cherokees, which have lost so much land after having many of their people killed, should serve as an example to all Indians. 3p.

No. 18 *reservada.* 4 Apr. 1792, New Orleans. [El Barón de Carondelet] to el Conde de Floridablanca. The declaration of Wm. Cunningham indicates that individuals from Franklin and elsewhere have formed a secret agreement against Spain. 2p.

N. fol. 17 Apr. 1792, New Orleans. *Indice de la carta reservada que [dirige el Barón de Carondelet] ... al exmo. sr. Conde de Floridablanca.* 1p. [Encloses 2 documents].

N. 23 *reservada.* 17 Apr. 1792, [New Orleans]. [El Barón de Carondelet] to el Conde de Floridablanca. [Same as AHN Estado 3898/exp. 5/no. 23 *reservada*]. 3p.

N. fol. 4 May 1792, New Orleans. *Indice de la carta reservada [que remite el Barón de Carondelet] ... al exmo. sr. Conde de Floridablanca (duplicate).* 1p. [Encloses 5 documents].

No. 26 *reservada.* 4 May 1792, New Orleans. [El Barón de Carondelet] to el Conde de Floridablanca. [Duplicate of AHN Estado 3898/exp. 5/ no. 26 *reservada*]. 4p.

N. fol. 11 June 1792, New Orleans. *Indice de las cartas reservadas que [remite el Barón de Carondelet] ... al exmo. sr. Conde de Aranda.* 2p. [Encloses 6 documents].

No. 2 *reservada.* 11 June 1792, New Orleans. [El Barón de Carondelet] to el Conde de Aranda. 2p.

CUBA/177B (CONT'D)

N. fol. 12 May 1792, Little Tallassee. Alex.
McGillivray to Brig. Gen. O'Neill. [Same as AGI
Cuba/205/fol. 699]. 2p. *English.*

N. fol. 12 May 1792. Little Tallassee. Alex.
McGillivray to Brig. Gen. Arturo O'Neill. [Transla-
tion of the previous letter]. 1p.

No. 3 *reservada.* 11 June 1792, New Orleans. El Barón de
Carondelet to el Conde de Aranda. 4p.

No. 2. 30 June 1792, Mobile. Manuel de Panzos [Lan-
zos?] to el Barón de Carondelet (copy). An Irishman who
was looking for work in Mobile used to live among the
Choctaws and reported that there were American commissioners there. These commissioners influenced the
Indians to go to Cumberland for a meeting where
considerable gifts were distributed. 2p.

N. fol. 5 July 1792, Natchez. *Indice de la carta [que remite
el Coronel dn. Manuel Gayoso de Lemos] ... al exmo. señor Conde
de Aranda.* 1p. [Encloses 5 documents].

No. 1. 5 July 1792, Natchez. [Manuel Gayoso de Lemos to
el Conde de Aranda]. 1p.

N. fol. 5 July 1792, Natchez. Manuel Gayoso de Lemos.
Estado político de la provincia de la Luisiana (copy).
The Spanish must watch the American settlements in Ky.,
Cumberland, and Franklin very closely. 42p.

N. fol. 7 July 1792, New Orleans. *Indice de la carta reservada [que dirige el Barón de Carondelet] ... al exmo. sr. Conde
de Aranda.* 1p. [Encloses 2 documents].

No. 4 *reservada.* 7 July 1792, New Orleans. [El Barón de
Carondelet to el Conde de Aranda]. [Copy of AHN Estado/
3898/exp. 5/no. 4 *reservada*]. 5p.

N. fol. 25 July 1792, New Orleans. *Indice de la carta reservada que [remite el Barón de Carondelet] ... al exmo. sr. Conde
de Aranda.* 2p. [Encloses 3 documents].

No. 5 *reservada.* 25 July 1792, New Orleans. [El Barón
de Carondelet] to el Conde de Aranda. 3p.

No. 2. [1792?]. *Relación* from Messrs. Kearney,
Carrington, Bengham [Bingham], Smith, and Dane[s?].
[Translation of following documents]. 15p.

[No. 2]. [1792?]. Congressional Committee report
from Mr. Kearney, Mr. Carrington, Mr. Bingham, Mr.
Smyth, and Mr. Danes. Ga. and N.C. have usurped land
from the Creeks and the Cherokees. Congress must take
steps to solve these disputes. 5p. *English.*

N. fol. 31 July 1792, New Orleans. *Indice de las cartas reservadas que [remite el Barón de Carondelet] ... al exmo. sr. Conde de Aranda.* 2p. [Encloses 16 documents].

> No. 6 *reservada.* 31 July 1792, [New Orleans]. [El Barón de Carondelet] to el Conde de Aranda. [Same as AHN Estado/ 3898/exp. 5/no. 6 *reservada*]. 3p.

>> N. fol. 1 Aug. 1792, New Orleans. [Carondelet to McGillivray]. Americans are about to establish themselves at Muscle Shoals and the Creeks must oppose this. Creeks may combine their activities with the Cherokees, three of whom are presently in Pensacola. 2p. *English.*

>> N. fol. 1 Aug. 1792, New Orleans. [El Barón de Carondelet] to Alex. McGillivray. [Translation of the previous letter]. 2p.

>> No. 3. 4 June 1792, Natchez. Manuel Gayoso de Lemos to el Barón de Carondelet (copy). Gayoso acknowledges Carondelet's orders to impede the land companies from settling in Spanish and Indian territory and to encourage the Indians to push out American settlements near the Barrancas de Margot and the Yazoo River. Gayoso does not believe that the Americans plan immediate settlements in those areas. 10p.

> No. 7 *reservada.* 31 July 1792. [New Orleans]. [El Barón de Carondelet] to el Conde de Aranda. 2p.

>> No. 2. 22 July 1792, Mobile. Alex. McGillivray to el Barón de Carondelet. [Translation of AGI Cuba/ 2371/doc. 40]. 7p.

N. fol. 1 Oct. 1792, New Orleans. *Indice de las cartas reservadas que [dirige el Barón de Carondelet] ... al exmo. sr. Conde de Aranda.* 2p. [Encloses 5 documents].

> No. 14 *reservada.* 1 Oct. 1792, New Orleans. [El Barón de Carondelet] to el Conde de Aranda. Carondelet attaches two documents concerning the Choctaws who recently met the Americans in Cumberland. 3p.

>> No. 1. 10 Sept. 1792, [House of Simon Favre, interpreter]. Juan de la Villebeuvre to Manuel de Gayoso de Lemos (translation). Villebeuvre reports that some 100 Choctaws received gifts at Cumberland. The 500 Chickasaws, who also went to Cumberland, were more enthusiastic about the Americans than the Choctaws. 10p.

>> [No. 2]. 12 Sept. 1792, Boukfouka. Juan de la Villebeuvre to el Barón de Carondelet [translation]. Some 550 Chickasaws and 107 Choctaws met Gen. Blount in Cumberland. Gov. Blount appointed four Chickasaw

CUBA/177B (CONT'D)

   chiefs to visit Philadelphia during the coming spring.
The Creeks have warned the Choctaws not to be misled
by the Americans, who will take their lands, enslave
their women, and mistreat them like they did the
Cherokees. 10p.

N. fol. 18 Oct. 1792, New Orleans. *Indice de las cartas
reservadas [que remite el Barón de Carondelet]* ... *al exmo
sr. Conde de Aranda.* 2p. [Encloses 2 documents].

  No. 17 *reservada.* 18 Oct. 1792, New Orleans. [El Barón
  de Carondelet] to Conde de Aranda. [Same as AGS GM/6916/
  no. 17 *reservada*]. 3p.

N. fol. 8 Nov. 1792, New Orleans. *Indice de las cartas
reservadas [que remite el Barón de Carondelet]* ... *al exmo. sr.
Conde de Aranda.* 2p. [Encloses 4 documents].

  No. 20 *reservada.* 8 Nov. 1792, New Orleans. [El Barón
  de Carondelet] to el Conde de Aranda. [Same as AHN Estado/
  3898/exp. 5/ no. 20 *reservada*]. 3p.

    N. fol. 12 Oct. 1792, Boukfouka. Juan de la Ville-
    beuvre to el Barón de Carondelet. [Same as AHN
    Estado/3898/exp. 5/no. 20 *reservada*/encl.]. 9p.

N. fol. 13 Nov. 1792, New Orleans. *Indice de la carta reservada [que remite el Barón de Carondelet]* ... *al exmo. sr. Conde
de Aranda.* 1p. [Encloses 5 documents].

  No. 22 *reservada.* 13 Nov. 1792, New Orleans. [El Barón
  de Carondelet] to el Conde de Aranda. [Same as AHN Estado/
  3898/exp. 5/no. 22 *reservada*]. 3p.

    [No. 2]. 6 Oct. 1792, Cherokees. Mr. McDonald to
    Wm. Panton. There has been a noticeable change among
    the Cherokees in favor of Spain. Bloody Fellow
    returned from Congress inclined towards the Americans,
    but McDonald persuaded him to change his way of think-
    ing. A war party has left for Cumberland to destroy
    Nashville. McDonald, (accompanied by Bloody Warrior,
    the Breath, the Glass, Charles of Chickamauga, John
    Taylor, Wm. Shawney, the Hair, and others) will visit
    Panton on Oct. 25. 3p. *English.*

    No. 2. 6 Oct. 1792, Cherokees. John McDonald to
    Wm. Panton. [Translation of the preceding letter].
    7p.

    No. 3. 6 Nov. 1792, Pensacola. Wm. Panton to [el
    Barón de Carondelet](extract). The Cherokees and
    McDonald arrived recently. The tribe has renewed its
    war against the Americans by joining the Upper Creeks
    in attacking Cumberland. Nevertheless, the Cherokees
    and Creeks are not unanimous in desiring war with the

Americans. There is a peace party in both tribes,
but those favoring war have more prestige. Moses
Price, a *mestizo* who visited England with Bowles,
has accompanied the tribe to Pensacola. 8p.

N. fol. 20 Nov. 1792, New Orleans. *Indice de la carta reservada [que remite el Barón de Carondelet] ... al exmo sr. Conde
de Aranda.* 1p. [Encloses 2 documents].

No. 23 *reservada*. 20 Nov. 1792, New Orleans. [El Barón
de Carondelet] to el Conde de Aranda. [Same as AHN Estado/
3898/exp. 5/no.23 *reservada*]. 2p.

N. fol. 28 Nov. 1792, New Orleans. *Indice de las cartas
reservadas [que remite el Barón de Carondelet] ... al exmo.
sr. Conde de Aranda.* 1p. [Encloses 1 document].

No. 24 *reservada*. 28 Nov. 1792, New Orleans. [El Barón
de Carondelet] to el Conde de Aranda. [Same as AHN Estado/
3898/exp. 5/no. 24 *reservada*]. 3p.

N. fol. 20 Dec. 1792, New Orleans. *Indice de la carta reservada [que remite el Barón de Carondelet] ... al exmo. sr. Conde
de Aranda.* 2p. [Encloses 3 documents].

No. 25 *reservada*. 20 Dec. 1792, New Orleans. [El Barón
de Carondelet] to el Conde de Aranda. The Creeks have
obviously been successful in keeping the Americans from
surveying the border. McGillivray agrees that only an
alliance of the Creeks, Cherokees, Choctaws, and Chickasaws can prevent the Americans from seizing the western
land. 2p.

No. 1. 15 Nov. 1792, Little Tallassee. Alex. McGillivray to el Barón de Carondelet (translation). The
Americans pretended to demonstrate their moderation
in the last Cumberland treaty by asking the Choctaws
and Chickasaws to agree to be friendly and to remain
neutral in the American conflicts with other nations.
5p.

N. fol. 24 Nov. 1792, New Orleans. *Palabra* (talk)
from el Barón de Carondelet to the chiefs, warriors,
and the rest of the Cherokee Nation (copy).
Cherokee leaders such as the Breath, Charles of
Chickamagua, and Bloody Fellow have talked with Carondelet about the tribe's misfortunes and what Spain
can do to help. The King will do his best to arrange
a peace for the tribe and protect its territory. 2p.

N. fol. 14 May 1793, Natchez. *Indice de dos cartas que ...
escrive el governador de Natchez al exmo. senor Duque de la
Alcudia.* 2p. [Encloses 9 documents].

CUBA/177B (CONT'D)

No. 2. 14 May 1793, Natchez. [Gov. of Natchez] to el
Duque de la Alcudia. The Americans invited the Chickasaws and Choctaws to a meeting in Cumberland to turn their
friendship away from Spain. Spanish officials have done
their best to prevent contact between their Indian allies
and the United States. Yet these officials have always
operated on the assumption that the Creeks, Chickasaws, and
Choctaws were free nations and that Spain could not use
force to prohibit their meeting with the United States.
The only peaceful way to achieve this is through gifts,
the amount of which will always rise since the Americans
are doing the same. 7p.

> N. fol. 28 Oct. 1793, Nogales. Manuel Gayoso de
> Lemos et al. Treaty of Nogales. [Copy of AGI SD/
> 2563/fol. 8]. 3p.

> N. fol. 19 [July?] 1794, Natchez. *Indice de una carta
> que ... escribe el gobernador de Natchez al exmo. Duque
> de la Alcudia.* [Enclosures are missing but index describes
> the Chickasaw, Creek, and Cherokee hostilities against
> the Americans]. 1p.

CUBA/178A   DRAFTS OF LETTERS TO THE MINISTERS: 1793-1798

N. fol. 8 Jan. 1793, New Orleans. *Indice de las cartas
reservadas que dirige el Barón de Carondelet ... al exmo.
dn. Conde de Aranda.* 2p. [Encloses 1 document].

> No. 26 *reservada.* 8 Jan. 1793, New Orleans. [El Barón
> de Carondelet] to el Conde de Aranda. [Same as AHN Estado/
> 3898/exp. 5/no. 26 *reservada*]. 4p.

N. fol. 28 Feb. 1793, New Orleans. *Indice de la carta reservada [que remite el Barón de Carondelet] ... al exmo. sr. Duque
de Alcudia.* 1p. [Encloses 4 documents].

> [No. 1 *reservada.*] 28 Feb. 1793, New Orleans. El Barón
> de Carondelet to el Duque de Alcudia (copy). Alex.
> McGillivray's death (17 Feb.) in Pensacola is a serious
> blow to Spanish interests. Carondelet had hoped that the
> Choctaws, Chickasaws, Cherokees, and Creeks would hold a
> congress to solve the disputes between the Creeks and
> Chickasaws. This congress would cost considerable money.
> 3p.

>> N. fol. 5 Mar. 1793, [New Orleans]. [El Barón de
>> Carondelet] to Manuel Gayoso de Lemos. Gayoso must
>> arrange for an Indian congress [of the Creeks, Chero-
>> kees, Chickasaws, and Choctaws]. He will receive
>> 2,000 pesos to cover expenses. It is important that
>> the Great Chief of the Chickasaws, Payemingo, be won
>> over and helped to settle his differences with the
>> Creeks. [Carondelet] fears that Payemingo would ask
>> Cumberland for help if the war against the Creeks
>> goes badly. 3p.

N. fol. 28 Jan. 1793, New Orleans. El Barón de
Carondelet to Manuel Gayoso de Lemos. *Puntos sobre
los quales se deberá tratar en el congreso de los
indios.* Gayoso should encourage a defensive confederation of the Creeks, Cherokees, Choctaws, and
Chickasaws under Spanish supervision. These tribes
should hold an annual session and be represented by
three chiefs from each nation. No tribe would be
able to start a war or conclude a peace without
previous permission of the confederation. Negotiations would begin between the confederation and the
United States to make sure that the Americans respect
the 1784 Cherokee borders. 6p.

No. 7 *sobre la asamblea de indios.* 25 July 1793, Nogales.
Manuel Gayoso de Lemos to el Barón de Carondelet. Gayoso has
tried to convince all the Indians to attend the assembly but
it is difficult to coordinate four tribes. The Cherokees
evidently never received their invitation. Gayoso sent a new
invitation to Bloody Fellow via Ugulayacabe and Pedro Olivier.
30p.

No. 15 *reservada.* 27 Aug. 1793, New Orleans. [El Barón de
Carondelet] to el Duque de la Alcudia. [Duplicate of AHN
Estado/3898/exp. 5/no. 15 *reservada*]. 5p. [Encloses 6 docu-
ments].

   N. fol. 25 July 1793, Nogales. Manuel Gayoso de Lemos to
   el Barón de Carondelet. [Same as no. 7 *sobre la asamblea
   de indios*]. 10p.

   N. fol. 15 Aug. 1793, New Orleans. El Barón de Carondelet
   to Manuel Gayoso de Lemos. [Same as AGI Cuba/2353/fol.
   834]. 4p.

No. 10 *sobre la asamblea proyectada.* 12 Sept. 1793, Natchez.
Manuel Gayoso de Lemos to el Barón de Carondelet. Gayoso
acknowledges the news about the relations between the Americans
and the Creeks and Cherokees. Creeks have indicated that the
assembly date is inconvenient for them and for the Cherokees.
28p. [Encloses 2 documents].

N. fol. 27 Sept. 1793, New Orleans. *Indice de la carta
reservada [que dirige el Barón de Carondelet]* ... *al exño. sr.
Duque de la Alcudia.* 1p. [Encloses 1 document].

   No. 18 *reservada.* 27 Sept. 1793, New Orleans. [El Barón
   de Carondelet] to el Duque de la Alcudia. [Same as AHN
   Estado/3898/exp. 5/no. 18 *reservada*]. 7p.

N. fol. 5 Dec. 1793, New Orleans. *Indice de la carta reservada
[que escribe el Barón de Carondelet]* ... *al exño sr. Duque de
la Alcudia.* 1p. [Encloses 1 document].

CUBA/178A (CONT'D)

No. 22 *reservada*. 5 Dec. 1793, New Orleans. [El Barón
de Carondelet] to el Duque de la Alcudia. [Same as AGI
Cuba/2353/fol. 730]. 4p.

N. fol. 7 Dec. 1793, New Orleans. *Indice de la carta reservada
[que remite el Barón de Carondelet] ... al exmo. sr. dn. Diego
de Gardoqui.* 1p. [Encloses 1 document].

No. 90 *reservada*. 7 Dec. 1793, New Orleans. [El Barón de
Carondelet] to Diego de Gardoqui. [Carondelet] has
received a royal order concerning the taxation rates for
foreign goods coming down the Ohio to New Orleans. He
has suspended the royal order until the threat of an
attack by French, Irish, and Americans disappears. Spanish
representatives in the United States have told Carondelet
that Cumberland and Ky. have supplied money to the leaders
of these hostile bands. 2p.

No. 16. 23 Dec. 1793, Natchez. Manuel Gayoso de Lemos to el
Barón de Carondelet. The American West favors the French,
particularly the regions of Illinois and Cumberland which
would gladly break away from the union. Cumberland's militia
would be reluctant to leave home from fear that the Indians
would attack while they are away. 31p.

No. 26 *reservada*. 24 Jan. 1794, [New Orleans?]. [El Barón de
Carondelet to el Duque de la Alcudia]. [Same as AHN Estado/
3899/exp. 1/no. 26 *reservada*]. 2p. [Encloses 2 documents].

No. 3. Puesto de los Nogales. Manuel Gayoso de Lemos to
Mistilebek Chaty et al. (Creek Grand Medal Chiefs) (copy).
Gayoso is pleased that the Creeks have come to attend the
assembly with the Choctaws, Chickasaws, and Cherokees. 2p.

No. 32 *reservada*. 9 Apr. 1794, New Orleans. [El Barón de
Carondelet] to el Duque de la Alcudia. Cherokees have petitioned numerous times for a Spanish flag and have been turned
down. The Americans, however, permit their colors to fly in
Cherokee territory. 4p. [Encloses 1 document].

N. fol. 20 Mar. 1794, Cloaly. Milford to el Barón de
Carondelet (translation). Creek leaders met with the
Americans under Seagrove at Tuckabatchee. The Americans
evidently brought along extra gifts in case the Cherokees
and Choctaws attended. Some 130 Cherokees eventually did
arrive. 16p.

No. 34 *reservada*. 1 May 1794, New Orleans. [El Barón de
Carondelet] to Duque de la Alcudia. [Carondelet] attaches a
description [missing] of the destruction of the French fort
near the Shawnee and Cumberland Rivers by Spanish Indians. 8p.

No. 41 *reservada*. 27 July 1794, New Orleans. [El Barón de Carondelet] to el Duque de la Alcudia. [Carondelet] encloses a petition [missing] from Panton, Leslie and Company who are in charge of trade with the Creeks, Choctaws, Chickasaws, and part of the Cherokees. [Carondelet] recommends delaying action on petition until the success of American negotiations with the Creeks is known. 4p.

No. 51 *reservada*. 4 Mar. 1795, [New Orleans]. [El Barón de Carondelet] to el Duque de la Alcudia. The Americans may well cause a massive Indian migration to Spanish territory west of the Mississippi when they run the new border. Spain will be forced to accept the tribes since she already has done so with some Shawnees and Cherokees fleeing the hostile actions of Ky. and Cumberland. The only way to prevent this migration is to support the Spanish Indian allies where they are now and to form a defensive confederation. 4p. [Encloses 1 document] .

N. fol. 20 Oct. 1797, New Orleans. *Indice de la carta [que remite el Brigadier dn. Manuel Gayoso de Lemos] ... al exmo. sr. Príncipe de la Paz.* 1p. [Encloses 12 documents].

    No. 6. 20 Oct. 1797. [New Orleans]. [Manuel Gayoso de Lemos] to el Príncipe de la Paz. 1p.

        N. fol. 20 Oct. 1797, New Orleans. Manuel Gayoso de Lemos to Carlos Martínez de Yrujo. Dr. White, who represented Cumberland in the American Congress, arrived in Natchez last year. White is a suspicious person who is familiar to Gayoso from the days when White represented Franklin and Cumberland to Spain as areas wishing independence. 11p.

N. fol. 30 Apr. 1798, Philadelphia. Carlos Martínez de Yrujo to Manuel Gayoso de Lemos. In order to show Spain's good faith in keeping the border quiet, Yrujo showed the American Sec. of State Gayoso's reply to Bloody Fellow, who represents the Creeks [sic]. 5p. [Encloses 1 document].

No. 189. 26 Sept. 1798, New Orleans. [Manuel Gayoso de Lemos] to el Conde de Santa Clara. 1p. [Encloses 2 documents].

    N. fol. 16 Aug. 1798, Pensacola. Carlos Howard to [Manuel Gayoso de Lemos?] (translation). James McQueen arrived yesterday and said that an Indian meeting was held at Tuckabatchee a month ago attended by Choctaw, Cherokee, and Chickasaw chiefs. The tribes evidently agreed that they would defend each other in case of an attack by whites. 2p.

N. fol. 1 July 1797, New Orleans. *Indice de la representación reservada [que hace el Barón de Carondelet] ... al exmo. sr. Príncipe de la Paz.* 2p. [Encloses 2 documents].

CUBA/178B (CONT'D)

No. 98. 1 July 1797, [New Orleans]. [El Barón de Caron-
delet] to el Príncipe de la Paz. [Carondelet] forwards a
report from Panton, Forbes, Leslie and Company (merchants
licensed to trade with Talapooses, Alibamos, Cherokees,
Choctaws, and Chickasaws). 5p.

N. fol. [1797?]. *Representación* from Panton, Forbes,
Leslie and Co. stating that their company is licensed
by Spain to trade with the Talapooses, Alibamos, Chero-
kees, Choctaws, and Chickasaws. Company asked the
Crown in 1794 to choose one of two means to keep the
Indian trade -- either buy the company out or grant it
an interest free loan of 400,000 pesos for ten years.
Company requests that the Crown make a decision. 12p.

N. fol. 30 Nov. 1797, New Orleans. *Indice de las cartas reser-*
vadas [que dirige el Brigadier dn. Manuel Gayoso de Lemos] ...
al exmo. sr. Príncipe de la Paz. 1p. [Encloses 1 document].

No. 7 *reservada.* 30 Nov. 1797, New Orleans. [Manuel
Gayoso de Lemos] to el Príncipe de la Paz. It would be a
mistake to cut the allowances used for Indian friendship.
The Americans will take advantage of this false economy to
win over the Indians and their lands. The Talapooses,
Choctaws, Chickasaws, Cherokees, and the Western and North-
western tribes are a natural barrier against the Americans.
Bloody Fellow just arrived to ask Spanish advice about the
American seizure of his lands. Blount is secretly gather-
ing people to build an establishment along the Tenn. River
which would effectively surround the Cherokees with
Americans on all sides. 17p.

CUBA/188C CORRESPONDENCE OF THE GOVERNOR OF LOUISIANA: 1757-1807

Fol. 8. 19 Mar. 1794, Tuckabatchee. Talk from the Chiefs of
the Creek Nation to el Barón de Carondelet. The Creeks wish
to make peace with the United States as Carondelet has recommended. Yet they have been asked to send warriors to help Spain
fight the French and bad Americans. The Creeks have listened
to Carondelet's bad advice too long. Some 37 Cherokee chiefs
attended a recent Creek meeting and have joined the Creeks in
desiring peace with United States. 3p. *English.*

Fol. 96. 30 Nov. 1793, Natchez. Confirmation of the Part of
Treaty of Nogales Which ... Concerns the Cherokee Nation.
[English version of AGI Cuba/123/n. doc.]. 2p. *English.*

CUBA/205 MISCELLANEOUS CORRESPONDENCE: 1792-1794

Fol. 16. 28 May 1793, New Orleans. [El Barón de Carondelet?]
to Brig. General James Robertson. [Carondelet?] has approved
the courtesies shown Robertson's son and companions at New
Madrid. Spain, however, does not approve shipping weapons
such as small cannons to the Chickasaws. Spanish officials

do not send their Indian allies such weapons or interfere in
the Indians' internal affairs. Spain's policy toward the
Indians can be seen by Carondelet's dealings with the Cherokees,
who requested aid against the United States. Carondelet
persuaded the tribe to stop its hostilities against Cumberland
and has done the same with the Creeks. 3p. *English*.

Fol. 367. 31 Dec. 1792, Natchez. Incomplete letter from
Manuel Gayoso de Lemos stating that the Natchez authorities
have begun defensive preparations in response to Dr. O'Fallon's
schemes. Spain confirmed her good will towards the United
States by restraining Indian hostility against Cumberland.
Col. Robertson's threat to destroy the Cherokees at the first
sign of hostility against Cumberland has influenced many young
Cherokees at a Corn Danil [Dance?] to strike first since their
young people would be blamed anyway. 8p. *English*.

Fol. 680. 22 Dec. 1792, [New Orleans?]. [El Barón de Carondelet?] to Thomas Portell. [Carondelet?] has decided to
reinforce the fort under Portell's command. He approves
Portell's efforts to keep the tribes near his fort in order
to harass potential enemies coming down the river. He may
assist the Cherokees in their war against the Americans, and
he can give the tribe asylum in Spanish territory if they
request it. 2p.

Fol. 696. 6 May 1792, Little Tallassee. Alex. McGillivray
to Lt. Col. Henry White. Panton paid McGillivray a surprise
visit on his way to the Cherokees. 2p. *English*.

Fol. 699. 12 May 1792, Little Tallassee. Alex. McGillivray
to Brig. [Gen.] O'Neill. Panton has gone to visit the Cherokees and is expected back in ten days. 1p. *English*.

Fol. 706. [18 July 1792]. [New Orleans]. [El Barón de Carondelet to Gen. McGillivray]. [Translation of fol. 707]. 1p.
[Enclosures to fol. 707b].

> Fol. 707. 18 July 1792, New Orleans. [El Barón de Caron-
> delet] to Gen. McGillivray. McGillivray will see from
> Gen. Washington's talk to the Choctaws how fearful the
> United States is that Spain's Indians might join the
> Northern tribes. Carondelet will do his best to warn
> the tribes about the American intentions in inviting them
> to make a treaty at Cumberland. If the Creeks warned the
> Choctaws and Chickasaws about the meeting, they would be
> even more hesitant to attend. 2p. *English*.

Fol. 717. 3 Sept. 1792, Pensacola. Alex. McGillivray to el
Barón de Carondelet. Americans have been trying to encourage
the Chickasaws and Choctaws to go to a congress in Cumberland.
Some have gone and the Americans have offered to build a post
along the Cherokee R. to trade with the Choctaws and Chickasaws.
4p. *English*.

CUBA/205 (CONT'D)

Fol. 719. 21 Apr. 1788, Pensacola. Gov. O'Neill to Alex. McGillivray (copy). Spain has asked its envoy to the American Congress to use his influence to aid Spain's Indian allies. As McGillivray knows, the people of Franklin and other westerners consider themselves independent of Congress. 1p. *English.*

Fol. 729. 11 Nov. 1792, New Orleans. [El Barón de Carondelet] to Gen. McGillivray. [Carondelet] protests the Creek murder of a blacksmith in Choctaw territory. Chickasaw King Taskaetowkawus has arrived in New Orleans with a message from the Creeks, Cherokees, Shawnees, and several Northern nations. 4p. *English.*

Fol. 733. 11 Nov. 1792, New Orleans. [El Barón de Carondelet] to Alex. McGillivray. [Spanish copy of fol. 729]. 2p.

Fol. 735. 20 Nov. 1792, Little Tallassee. Alex. McGillivray to Brig. Gen. O'Neill. The Chickasaws have killed some Creeks near Cumberland. The Creek chief who lost his son in this skirmish has called his warriors home from hunting to seek revenge on the Chickasaws. 2p. *English.*

Fol. 739. 21 Nov. 1792, New Orleans. [El Barón de Carondelet?] to [Wm. Panton?]. [Carondelet] gave permission to Turnbull to set up a store at Mobile to trade with the Choctaws and Chickasaws. Otherwise these tribes would have turned to the Americans, who still hope for a trading post at Muscle Shoals. 2p. *English.* [Enclosures to fol. 740].

Fol. 741. 14 Dec. 1792, New Orleans. [El Barón de Carondelet] to Alex. McGillivray. In an attempt to contain the Americans in the West, [Carondelet] has tried to unite the Cherokees, Creeks, Choctaws, and Chickasaws in a defensive alliance under Spanish protection. [Carondelet] has met in New Orleans with the Chickasaws, Chief Franchimastabe, Coweta Chief Kaskilikasky, six Cherokee chiefs led by Bloody Fellow, and numerous Choctaws. They have all accepted Carondelet's plan and promised to discuss it with their tribes. 4p. *English.*

Fol. 743. 15 Nov. 1792, Little Tallassee. Alex. McGillivray to el Barón de Carondelet. McGillivray believes that nothing can restrain the Americans from seizing land, even though they professed moderation in the recent Cumberland treaty. McGillivray expects a Northern Indian delegation in the spring to ask the Southern tribes to unite against the Americans. 4p. *English.*

Fol. 749. 12 Oct. 1792, Boukfouka. Jean de la Villebeuvre to el Barón de Carondelet. [Same as AGI Cuba/177B/no. 20 *reservada*/encl.]. 7p. *French.*

Fol. 767. 11 Nov. 1792, Boukfouka. Juan de la Villebeuvre to Manuel Gayoso de Lemos. The Choctaws are leading a party to kill the Americans in Cumberland. 8p. *French.*

Fol. 775. 18 Nov. 1792, Boukfouka. Juan de la Villebeuvre to Manuel Gayoso de Lemos. News from Cumberland indicates that

CUBA/205 (CONT'D)

the Americans are sending 1,500 men to attack the Cherokees.
The Chiis lost 17 horses in Cumberland. 5p. *French.*

Fol. 778. 18 [Oct.?] 1792, Boukfouka. Juan de la Villebeuvre
to el Barón de Carondelet. Cumberland news indicates that the
Northern Indians have made peace with the Americans. 5p.
French.

Fol. 781. 30 Nov. 1792, Boukfouka. Juan de la Villebeuvre to
el Barón de Carondelet. A group of Choctaws are preparing to
visit Cumberland. 6p. *French.*

Fol. 789. Letter describing the Chickasaws' trip to Cumberland.
Chickasaws brought a message from the Talapooses, Cherokees,
and Shawnees. The Choctaws are forming a league with other
tribes under Spanish protection. 12p. *French.*

Fol. 809. 1 Sept. 1788, Congress. Cyrus Griffin et al. Copy
of a proclamation of Congress approving the Treaty of Hopewell
with the Cherokees. 3p. *English.*

Fol. 811. 4 Dec. 1795, Coweta. Letter from Wm. Bowles stating
that the Creeks and Cherokees are now united and Bowles has
formed a council composed of chiefs from both nations. Bowles
has been appointed director of their affairs. 3p. *English.*

Fol. 838 (no. 3). 27 Apr. 1792, Knoxville. Wm. Blount to
Chiefs and Warriors of the Choctaw Nation (duplicate). Sec.
of War originally ordered Mr. Shaw to deliver this letter.
Unfortunately, Shaw has been detained by business with the
Cherokees. As a result, Blount has sent the message to the
tribe via several residents of Cumberland (Anthony Foster and
James Randolph). 2p. *English.* [Enclosures to fol. 840].

Fol. 839 (no. 5). 27 May 1792, [Knoxville?]. Wm. Blount
to Chiefs and Warriors of the Choctaw Nation. Levy Perry
will deliver the documents that Blount sent with Foster
and Robertson. These two individuals have evidently been
detained in Cumberland. Blount would like to meet the
Choctaws in Nashville as soon as possible. The Americans
do not wish to buy land or anything else from the tribe.
2p. *English.*

Fol. 839b (no. 6). 16 May 1792, Knoxville. Wm. Blount to
Chiefs and Warriors of the Choctaws. The President of the
United States would like the Choctaws to meet Blount in
Nashville to sign a treaty. The purpose of this meeting
is to strengthen the friendship begun at the Treaty of
Hopewell. Blount has also invited the Chickasaws. 2p.
English.

Fol. 857. 9 Aug. 1792, Cumberland. David Smith to John Pitch-
land. Smith reports the arrival of some Virginians. They
do not want the Indians' land, only their friendship. The
Americans do not wish the Indians to favor Spain. 3p. *English.*

CUBA/205 (CONT'D)

Fol. 891. 22 Sept. 1792, Chickasaw Nation. Hardy Perry to [el Barón de Carondelet?]. There are no bad people among the Indians at the moment. Mountain Leader (Hopoyemingo) has started to hunt around Cumberland. 1p. *English*. [Enclosures to fol. 892b].

Fol. 895. 4 Sept. 1792, [Natchez?]. [Gayoso?] to Turner Brathears. [Gayoso?] regrets that so many Lower Town [Choctaws?] have gone to Cumberland. No people depend more upon Spanish trade than do the Lower Towns. 3p. *English*.

Fol. 902. 28 Nov. 1792, Louisville. Letter from R. J. Waters stating that the Americans believe that Spain has encouraged Creek and Cherokee hostilities against the United States. 2p. *English*.

Fol. 904. 14 Dec. 1792, New Orleans. Letter from [el Barón de Carondelet] stating that no treaty can deter the Americans from taking land. Nevertheless, [Carondelet] has formed a plan to unite the Cherokees, Creeks, Choctaws, and Chickasaws in a defensive confederation under Spain's guidance to protect Indian territory. Bloody Fellow and other Indian leaders in New Orleans have agreed to this proposal and have promised to discuss it with their tribe. 2p.

Fol. 911. 5 Jan. 1794, New Orleans. [El Barón de Carondelet?] to Wm. Panton. Louisiana faces the prospect of being invaded and [Carondelet?] has dedicated his efforts towards defense. [Carondelet?] wrote Panton that Spain should compensate McDonald for his services. 4p.

Fol. 924. [New Orleans?]. Letter from [el Barón de Carondelet?] stating that the gazette article sent to New Orleans will only serve to arouse Cumberland's residents against Spain. [Carondelet?] has denied all the charges in the paper and has shown how Spain restrained the Cherokees and Creeks from attacking the Georgians, Blount, and Robertson, who wrongly seized the Indian's land. 3p.

Fol. 953. Letter to the Chickasaw Nation stating that a great assembly has been held of the Indian nations friendly to Spain. The delegates promised to support one another. Chickasaws are in danger of being forced from their land by the actions of one chief who wants the Chickasaws to fight the Creeks. Creeks have been told that the Creek, Cherokee, and Choctaw lands have been sold and they wish to make peace with the Chickasaws to defend their lands. Ga. has sold part of the Chickasaw land. 6p. *English*.

CUBA/208A   MISCELLANEOUS CORRESPONDENCE: 1777-1816

Fol. 296 (no. 1). 4 Nov. 1793, Natchez. Manuel Gayoso de Lemos to Gen. Wilkinson (copy). Gayoso informs Wilkinson about the recent treaty at Walnut Hills (Nogales) with the Chickasaws,

Creeks, Cherokees, and Choctaws. The Cherokees begged for
Spanish protection, which was granted since they had no
connection with the United States. 5p. *English*.

Fol. 303 (no. 1). 4 Nov. 1793, Natchez. Manuel Gayoso de
Lemos to Brig. James Wilkinson. [Translation of fol. 296]. 4p.

Fol. 306 [no. 1]. 4 Nov. 1793, Natchez. Manuel Gayoso de
Lemos to Brig. James Wilkinson. [Translation of fol. 296].
4p.

Fol. 505. 28 May 1793, New Orleans. Letter to Milfort
discussing the conflict between the Creeks and Chickasaws and
the possibility that the Chickasaws might ask Cumberland for
aid. The Cherokees and Chickasaws will suffer if the Americans
settle Ecores à Margot. 4p. *French*.

Fol. 511b. [May 1793], [Pensacola]. *Relación de los
papeles ... que trajó un gefe cherokqui al governador de Pan-
zacola*. Gov. of Pensacola received two letters [not included]
from John McDonald which inquired about Bloody Fellow's son
in New Orleans and discussed the Cherokee boundaries along
the Green and Ohio Rivers. 2p.

Fol. 574. 3 Mar. 1795, Coweta. James Durouzeaux to Henry
White. Most Lower Town warriors have returned from hunting
and reported no clashes with the Georgians. Chickasaws have
killed some Upper Town Creeks. The Tusques have brought in
some scalps from Cumberland. 1p. *English*.

Fol. 595. Coweta. James Durouzeaux to Milfort. Many Cowetas
are planning to join the Upper Towns in crossing the Cherokee
R. and taking revenge for recent insults. 1p. *English*.

Fol. 599. Juan de la Villebeuvre to Manuel de Lanzos.
Villebeuvre convinced the chiefs not to continue their visits
to Cumberland but rather to rely upon the Spaniards. 3p.

Fol. 609 (no. 3). 1793. *Jounal des voyages de l'Amérique
Septentrionale en 1793*. Author expresses his fear that some
Americans might attack his party near Cumberland. He also
mentions a Cherokee town near Cumberland. 38p. *French*.

Fol. 654. 19 Jan. 1794, Tuckabatchee. Talk from White
Lieutenant and Mad Dog to Chiefs of the Choctaw Nation. There
has been much turmoil recently due to evil men among the
Choctaws. Creeks are determined to establish peace with all
people and have asked the Chickasaws and the Cherokees to meet
this spring. 2p. *English*.

Fol. 656. 19 Mar. 1794, Tuckabatchee. Talk from White Lieutenant et al. to el Barón de Carondelet. In a general meeting
the Creek chiefs decided to seek peace with the United States.
Chiefs do not agree that the tribal boundary can be decided
by the Spanish court. Some 37 Cherokee chiefs attended Creek
meeting. 3p. *English*.

CUBA/208B   MISCELLANEOUS CORRESPONDENCE: 1777-1816

Fol. 329. 28 Jan. 1793. Letter to Juan de la Villebeuvre stating that the Chickasaw leader Uguluya [Ugulayacabe?] is convinced that the security of the Chickasaws, Choctaws, Creeks, and Cherokees depends upon an alliance. A meeting of tribal leaders from these nations in Choctaw territory will help promote such an alliance. The United States is not as generous with the tribes as Spain is. Last year the Americans offered the Cherokees less than 1,500 pesos annually (and the Creeks 2,000) to cede land in Georgia. Spain spent more than 80,000 pesos last year on Indian affairs. 2p.

Fol. 367. 21 July 1793, Nogales. Manuel Gayoso de Lemos to Gov. Blount. Peace has been concluded between the Chickasaws and Creeks. After the last war, Spain assumed protection over the Creeks, Choctaws, and Chickasaws. Yet Blount has called the Choctaws and Chickasaws to Cumberland to negotiate a treaty. Any trouble the Americans have with these nations can easily be solved through the Spanish governor. 7p. *English.*

Fol. 452. 16 Jan. 1793, Boukfouka. Juan de la Villebeuvre to el Barón de Carondelet. Villebeuvre is saving supplies for the Cherokees. Payemingo, a Chickasaw chief, has declared war on the Cherokees and Talapooses. Piclhem[?] has offered to spy on Cumberland. 6p. *French.*

Fol. 455. 16 Jan. 1793, Boukfouka. Juan de la Villebeuvre to el Barón de Carondelet. Bloody Fellow delivered Carondelet's letter. 5p. *French.*

Fol. 458. 21 Jan. 1793, Boukfouka. Juan de la Villebeuvre to el Barón de Carondelet. An army under Gov. Blount, who is on his way to destroy the Cherokees, will join with a S.C. army to attack the Talapooses. 4p. *French.*

Fol. 460. 4 Feb. 1793, Boukfouka. Juan de la Villebeuvre to el Barón de Carondelet. Cherokees have left to meet with the Chickasaws. Bloody Fellow has been instructed to reconcile the Chiis and Payemingo. 7p. *French.*

Fol. 464. 5 Feb. 1793, Boukfouka. Juan de la Villebeuvre to Manuel Gayoso de Lemos. Cherokees have been treated properly. They deserve good treatment since Villebeuvre has not seen any Indian group as civilized, especially their leader Bloody Fellow. 4p. *French.*

Fol. 466. 7 Feb. 1793, Boukfouka. Juan de la Villebeuvre to el Barón de Carondelet. Cherokees and Bloody Fellow spent a pleasant visit with Villebeuvre. Bloody Fellow is better than other Indians and most whites. 4p. *French.*

Fol. 472. 12 Feb. 1793. Letter to Juan de la Villebeuvre stating the author's disbelief in a rumor that the S.C. militia has joined with Gen. Blount to destroy the Cherokees and Creeks. Nevertheless, Villebeuvre should forward all possible information

CUBA/208B   (CONT'D)

on the matter. It is unfortunate that Bloody Fellow had trouble
with his mission, but the arrival of a Northern Indian commission
should allow Spain to conclude the alliance. 2p.

Fol. 473. 12 Feb. 1793, New Orleans. [Carondelet?] to Juan
de la Villebeuvre. Villebeuvre's letters about the need for an
establishment in Ecores à Margot has reached New Orleans. It
would be possible to handle Cherokee trade from a store there.
[Carondelet?] approves Villebeuvre's measures regarding Bloody
Fellow and the other Cherokee chiefs. 13p.

Fol. 487. 27 Feb. 1793, Boukfouka. Juan de la Villebeuvre to
el Barón de Carondelet. Villebeuvre forwards a letter from
Payemingo and Bloody Fellow. Cherokees killed a Spaniard
(mistaken for an American) on his way to Cumberland. 3p.
French.

Fol. 489. 27 Feb. 1793, Boukfouka. Juan de la Villebeuvre to
el Barón de Carondelet. Cherokees killed a Spaniard going to
Cumberland. 3p. *French.*

Fol. 499. 30 Mar. 1793, Boukfouka. Juan de la Villebeuvre to
el Barón de Carondelet. Poucha Houman, appointed to meet the
Cherokees, has left. Cherokees have postponed their visit.
3p. *French.*

Fol. 518. 10 Apr. 1792, Cherokees. [John] McDonald to Arthur
O'Neill. Eight Cherokees are going to [Pensacola?]. Bold
Hunter, who visited New Orleans, reported that he had letters
for McDonald, but McDonald has not received them. 2p.
English.

Fol. 521. 11 Feb. 1793, Village de Tchoukafals [Chukafalaya?].
Letter from Bloody Fellow describing his visit to Natchez and
to the Choctaws and Chickasaws. He was well treated and those
tribes want peace. 2p. *French.*

Fol. 522. 11 Feb. 1793, Chickasaw. Letter from Payemingo et
al. stating that Mr. Farre, who came with the Cherokees,
delivered a letter. 2p. *French.*

Fol. 526. 5 Apr. 1793, Cherokees. John McDonald to el Barón
de Carondelet. For nearly a year McDonald has exerted his
influence to convince the Indians to give their allegiance to
Spain. He was promised a handsome reward if successful. Gov.
Blount, however, is pushing hard for another treaty with the
Cherokees. McDonald will try to delay it until he hears from
Spanish officials. Bloody Fellow wants news about his son.
3p. *English.*

Fol. 528. 5 Apr. 1793, Cherokees. John McDonald to Arthur
O'Neill. McDonald has not received instructions from New
Orleans on how the Cherokees should proceed. Nor has he been
notified that he is superintendent of the Cherokee nation.

CUBA/208B (CONT'D)

The Creeks will unfortunately involve themselves in trouble despite the governor's advice to Bloody Fellow against such activity. 3p. *English.*

Fol. 551. 28 May 1793, New Orleans. Letter to Pedro Olivier urging him to do everything in his power to reestablish peace between the Creeks and Chickasaws (who have requested Cumberland's aid). It is convenient for Spain, nevertheless, that the Creeks and Cherokees send war parties to Muscle Shoals and Ecores to keep the Americans from settling there under the pretext of aiding the Chickasaws. Cherokees have asked for help in restraining the Creeks from sending war parties through Cherokee territory to war on Cumberland. 4p.

Fol. 562. 22 June [1793?], [Cherokee Territory?]. John McDonald to [Wm.] Panton (extract). Cherokees are disorganized because the Americans have invaded the frontier. An American party killed seven Cherokees and mortally wounded five more, including Charles of Chickamauga. Cherokees are holding a general congress at Assonallie, one of the Lower Towns. 2p. *English.*

Fol. 588. 26 Oct. 1793, New Orleans. Letter to Milfort reporting Georgia's incursions against the Creeks. The court in Madrid will handle the affairs of Spain's four allies -- the Creeks, Cherokees, Choctaws, and Chickasaws. 7p. *French.*

Fol. 609. [1793?]. *Receuilles en forme de journal des différentes missions auxquels Louis Lorimier à été employé depuis l'année 1787 jusqu'à celle de 1793.* Lorimier's responsibilities include serving as an interpreter for the Shawnees, Osages, and Cherokees. 13p. *French.*

Fol. 618. Bloody Fellow to el Barón de Carondelet. Bloody Fellow has arrived safely among the Choctaws and is now visiting the Gov. of Natchez. He also went to the Chickasaws to talk to his old friend Payemingo, who speaks Cherokee. Bloody Fellow urges Carondelet to inform the Cherokees about the next meeting with the Spaniards. 3p. *English.* [Enclosures to fol. 621].

> Fol. 621. 8 [Feb.?] 1793, Holkey. List of food and expenses, some of which were provided for Bloody Fellow. 1p. *English.*

Fol. 622. *Notte donnée par le sieur Bargelot au sujet de la Rivière Tenésé ou Cheraqui.* Note describes the land around the Cherokee River. 2p. *French.*

CUBA/211A   MISCELLANEOUS CORRESPONDENCE: 1788-1797

Fol. 20. 25 Mar. 1795, New Orleans. Letter to Yta Acho, Chief of Taukebache [Tuckabatchee?], concerning Georgia and the selling of land belonging to [the Tuckabatchees], Cherokees, Choctaws, and the Chickasaws. 2p. [Enclosures to fol. 21b].

CUBA/211A (CONT'D)

Fol. 21. [25 Mar. 1795], [New Orleans]. Letter to Yta
Acho, Chief of Taukebache. [Copy of fol. 20]. 2p.
French.

Fol. 121. 18 Sept. 1793, New Orleans. Letter to Pedro Olivier
noting that it is not clear whether the Americans really plan
to destroy the Cherokees once peace has been achieved with the
Northern tribes. Bloody Fellow wrote that the Americans have
beheaded a number of Cherokee women and children who were
surprised while planting crops. Cherokees plan an expedition
under Watts [to take revenge?]. 3p.

Fol. 657 (no. 4). 14 Mar. 1795, Natchez. Letter from [Gayoso?
to Chickasaws?]. [Chickasaws] and the Creeks are at war.
[Gayoso] regrets that the tribe began the war without consulting
Spain or the Choctaws and Cherokees. If [the Chickasaws] had
requested help, they would have received it. Creeks are only
angry at those [Chickasaws] who favor the Americans. 2p.
English.

Fol. 688. 13 June 1796, Natchez. Grand-Pré. *Instruction
adressée aux alcades et officiers commandant les compagnies
de volontaires du gouvernement des Natchez.* The war between
the Talapooses and Chickasaws has provoked Cumberland to
intervene, and Spanish officials must be vigilant. 7p.
French.

CUBA/211B   MISCELLANEOUS CORRESPONDENCE: 1788-1797

Fol. 125. 17 Oct. 1793, Pensacola. Henry White to John
McDonald. Mr. Ross, not Little Turkey, delivered McDonald's
letter. White ordered that Ross be given four horse loads of
munitions. 1p. *English.* [Enclosures to fol. 126b].

Fol. 125. 5 May 1794, Pensacola. [Henry White?] to John
McDonald. [White?] encloses a list of presents ordered
by Gov. Carondelet for the Cherokees. 1p. *English.*

Fol. 125. 19 June 1794, Pensacola. Henry White to John
McDonald. Oliolate [Breath?], chief of Niroche [Nicoche?],
has returned to Pensacola and reported that McDonald's
lack of interest in the Spanish gifts stems from the
opinion of Tom Watts and Bloody Fellow that the gifts
were not worth sending for. Yet the gifts are valuable.
Teoain of Cocain and Oliolate received gifts to deliver
to McDonald. 2p. *English.*

Fol. 125b. 11 Aug. 1794, Pensacola. [Henry White] to
John McDonald. Cottehatoye [Cotteahtoye] brought McDonald's
latest letter. He told [White] that Bloody Fellow and
Tom Watts did not intend to deliver the Cherokee gifts
to McDonald. If White cannot depend upon the chiefs to be
honest with each other, he would appreciate a list from
McDonald of the Cherokee districts so the gifts could be
assigned directly in Pensacola. Oweleata [Breath?] has
left for Cherokee territory with almost all the gifts. 1p.
English.

CUBA/211B (CONT'D)

Fol. 125b. 24 Sept. 1794, Pensacola. [Henry White to
John McDonald]. White forwarded McDonald's letters to the
governor in New Orleans. Spanish are doing everything they
can to promote harmony between the Cherokees and Creeks.
Mad Dog has indicated that he wishes the same. 1p.
English.

Fol. 125b. 1 Feb. 1795, Pensacola. [Henry White to John
McDonald]. White received McDonald's letter and a copy
of the *Knoxville Gazette*, which he gave to Mr. Panton.
White would like to know if the Frenchman Chayser [?] still
lives in Cherokee territory since the Spanish authorities
wish to apprehend him. 2p. *English.*

Fol. 126. 16 Apr. 1795. Pensacola. [Henry White to John
McDonald]. White encloses a list of Cherokee presents from
New Orleans. 1p. *English.*

Fol. 126. 2 July 1795, Pensacola. [Henry White to John
McDonald]. McDonald should maintain peace with all the
Cherokee's neighbors. He should also follow the advice of
the Spanish envoy in Philadelphia and not permit the border
to be run. 1p. *English.*

Fol. 126. 16 Sept. 1795, Pensacola. [Henry White to John
McDonald]. White has received McDonald's list of presents
to be given to Wellstown, Lookout Mountain, and Running
Water. McDonald mentioned that a few guns should be given
to Watt's [?] Town. 2p. *English.*

Fol. 126b. 3 Oct. 1795, Pensacola. [Henry White to John
McDonald]. White followed McDonald's recommendations in
distributing gifts to Little Turkey's gang and to Turner's
Mountain. 1p. *English.*

Fol. 126b. 16 Jan. 1796, Pensacola. [Henry White to John
McDonald]. White received McDonald's warning about the
American plans against the port at St. Ferdinand. McDonald
should tell Bloody Fellow that the governor was told about
Bloody Fellow's wish to have his son sent to Pensacola.
1p. *English.*

Fol. 127. 30 July 1794, Pensacola. Oulethia [Oliolate?],
Cherokee Chief, and Tetin Nay [Teoain?], Great Cherokee Chief,
to the eldest of all our brothers among the Cherokee Chiefs
and our commissioner. Some 50 Americans have been killed.
Cherokee villages are worried because there are many American
parties nearby. Cherokees will continue to war against the
Americans. 3p. *French.*

Fol. 131. 1 Apr. 1795, Pensacola. H[enry] White. Presents
for the Cherokee Nation Corresponding to the Year 1795. 1p.
English.

Fol. 132. 19 Oct. 1795, Pensacola. John McDonald to Henry
White. McDonald explained to the chiefs that representatives
from each town should visit Pensacola for their gifts. Cherokee leaders, however, cannot prevent others from coming. Gov.
Blount has urged the Cherokees, Choctaws, Chickasaws, and Creeks
to attend the treaty negotiations at Knoxville. Although the
Spanish presents are liberal, they are not enough to divide
among all the Cherokees. It would be best to have half of the
towns receive gifts on alternating years. 3p. *English.*

Fol. 182. [Ft. Confederation?]. Juan de la Villebeuvre to Gov.
of [New Orleans?]. Payemingo has granted land to the Americans
near the Cherokee River. 4p. *French.*

Fol. 189 (no. 27). 21 Apr. 1794, Ft. Confederation. [Juan de
la Villebeuvre to Mr. le Baron]. 5p. *French.* [Enclosures to
fol. 257b].

> Fol. 191b. 9 June 1794, Ft. Confederation. [Juan de la
> Villebeuvre to Mr. le Baron]. Payemingo has gone to
> Cumberland for some gifts. 3p. *French.*

> Fol. 197 (no. 16). 22 July 1794, Boukfouka. [Juan de la
> Villebeuvre] to Mr. le Baron. [Villebeuvre] has received
> a letter about the chiefs in Cumberland. Chickasaws
> believe that the Americans will prevent the Spaniards from
> helping the Cherokees. 3p. *French.*

> Fol. 209b. 30 Apr. 1795, Yanabece. [Juan de la Villebeuvre]
> to Mr. le Baron. Talapooses are planning to attack the
> Americans who are building a fort along the Cherokee River.
> Choctaws are visiting Cumberland and think highly of the
> Americans. Chiis have killed five Cherokees. 7p.
> *French.*

> Fol. 224. 8 Aug. 1795, Ft. Confederation. [Juan de la
> Villebeuvre to Carondelet]. Pitchillin [Pitchlynn] has
> left for Cumberland with some warriors and will return with
> news. 6p. *French.*

> Fol. 230b. 18 Sept. 1795, Fort [Confederation]. [Juan de
> la Villebeuvre] to Mr. le Baron Carondelet. Choctaws in
> Cumberland were warned that they will receive no more
> Spanish presents. 8p. *French.*

Fol. 358. 17 Feb. 1795, Chickasaw. Copy of letter from
Ugulayacabe stating that the Creeks are such troublemakers that
even the Cherokees have killed three of them. Creeks have
forced Ugulayacabe to agree to the Americans' request to build
fort along the Cherokee River. 4p. *English.*

Fol. 375. 16 Sept. 1795, San Fernando. Incomplete letter to
the governor stating that the Spaniards have spread rumors in
Cumberland that Ugulayacabe has permitted a settlement at
Ecores à Margot. 4p. *French.*

CUBA/211B (CONT'D)

Fol. 380. *Correspondencia en Inglés de dn. Henrique White con el comisario de la nación Cheroqui dn. Juan McDonald.* 1p. [Enclosures to fol. 403b].

Fol. 381. 12 Sept. 1793, Cherokees. John McDonald to Gov. White. The bearer of this letter is Little Turkey, a Cherokee chief. He is authorized to receive the ammunition promised Bloody Fellow in New Orleans. The governor is undoubtedly acquainted with the murder of the Cherokees who assembled at Hangingman at Gov. Blount's invitation. 3p. *English.*

Fol. 383. 18 July 1794, Cherokees. John McDonald to Gov. White. Colteahtoye is the bearer of this letter. McDonald is exasperated at the actions of Owholeata (Breath), chief of Nickajack. In 20 days, some parties under Little Turkey will be going to Pensacola. Tribe would appreciate more ammunition. It is dangerous to travel on the Cherokee R. since both the Indians and whites are hostile there. Indians destroyed a party on the river last summer and the whites attacked a group of Cherokee women and children who were on their way to S.C. to buy corn. 4p. *English.*

Fol. 385. 22 Dec. 1794, Lower Cherokees. John McDonald to Gov. White. Whatever Gov. Blount professes concerning peace, his intentions are certainly not peaceful towards the Creeks and Cherokees. He has offered the Indians a $100 reward for Creek scalps. Two men have just returned from the Shawnees and fought in the engagement of 20 August [against the Americans?]. 3p. *English.*

Fol. 387. 17 Apr. 1795, Pensacola. *Noticia del regalo que ha venido de la Nueva Orleans para regalar a la nación Chiroqui.* Notice lists the Cherokee gifts recently arrived from New Orleans. 2p.

Fol. 388. June 1795, Cherokees. John McDonald to Gov. White. Bearer of the letter is Cheelagiskie. Cherokees have had a generally peaceful winter. McDonald stopped a group of Cherokees who wanted to leave the nation last winter. Tribe had a general meeting with American officials at Estanacilie not long ago. Gov. Blount wanted to erect a fort along the Creek paths leading north. When the Cherokees were in Philadelphia, some visited the Spanish minister. Chiefs blame the Chickasaws for recent disturbances along the frontier. The Frenchmen whom White wants captured are still in Cherokee territory. 4p. *English.*

Fol. 390. Aug. 25, 1795, Cherokees. John McDonald to Gov. White. Altahiskie (Wood Carrier) is the bearer of this letter. McDonald has just toured the towns near Wellstown and has told them to keep the peace. He plans

CUBA/211B (CONT'D)

to be in Pensacola around October. Each party going to
Pensacola will have a list of goods allotted them for their
annual gifts. 3p. *English*.

Fol. 392. Presents for Wells Town. 2p. *English*

Fol. 393. 26 Aug. 1795, Cherokees. John McDonald to Gov.
White. McDonald replied to White's letter via Wood Carrier,
leader of party from Wellstown. The bearer of this letter
is Chiswanoshie (Reed Eye) from Lookout Mountain, who heads
a party from that town. 1p. *English*.

Fol. 394. 28 Aug. 1795, Cherokees. John McDonald to
Governor White. McDonald has sent a list of presents to
be given to Wellstown and Lookout Mountain. He also sent
a list for a party from Running Water headed by Cheenowie
and Sour Mush. He was unable to limit the size of the
parties. 2p. *English*.

Fol. 395. Presents for the Look Out Mountain. 1p.
English.

Fol. 396. 2 Sept. 1795, Cherokees. John McDonald to Gov.
White. McDonald encloses a list of presents for Turners
Mountain. 1p. *English*.

Fol. 397. 3 Sept. 1795, Cherokees. John McDonald to Gov.
White. McDonald encloses a gift list for Little Turkey
and his party. 2p. *English*.

Fol. [398]. J.D. [?]. For the Little Turkey and His Gang.
A list of presents for Little Turkey. 1p. *English*.

Fol. 399. *Noticia de los efectos que existen para la
nación cheroquies*. List of Cherokee gifts to be distributed in Pensacola. 2p.

Fol. 400. 16 Oct. 1795, Pensacola. *Noticia de los efectos
existentes para la nación cheroqui*. List of goods for
the Cherokees. 2p.

Fol. 401. 31 Dec. 1795, Cherokees. John McDonald to Gov.
White. McDonald heard from Capt. Chisolm, who had
returned from Tuckabatchee, that the Americans plan to
attack Louisiana. Gov. Blount has asked Little Turkey
and Bloody Fellow why they love the Spaniards. They
replied that Spain never asked for anything from them.
Bloody Fellow is anxious about his son. The bearer of
this letter is Uboashata. 4p. *English*.

Fol. 403. Report from John McDonald listing the Cherokee
towns and warriors. 2p. *English*.

Fol. 404. 12 May 1795, New Orleans. Le Baron de Carondelet to
Chiefs and Warriors of the Choctaw Nation. Talapooses will

CUBA/211B (CONT'D)

keep all from hunting around Muscle Shoals. Georgians have sold
land belonging to the Creeks, Choctaws, Chickasaws, and Cherokees. Spanish want peace among the four tribes. 3p. *French.*

Fol. 406. 23 Nov. 1795, New Orleans. Talk from el Barón de
Carondelet to Great Chief Yta Acho et al. Carondelet is hopeful that the Creeks, Chickasaws, Choctaws, and Cherokees will
settle their differences in a friendly fashion. The Chickasaws
are willing to make peace. 3p. *English.*

Fol. 433. [1795]. Heads [?] of an Act of ... Georgia Passed
at Augusta in December 1794. Report details Georgia's claim to
land in the west, including some Cherokee territory. 5p.
English. [Enclosures to fol. 437b].

Fol. 443. 18 Feb. 1795, Holkey. Benjamin Fooy to Manuel Gayoso
de Lemos. Long Town Indians killed five Creeks traveling to
Cumberland. The American Roberson [?] wrote to the Chickasaws
that the tribe should allow the Americans to build a fort along
the Cherokee River, probably at Muscle Shoals. 6p. *English.*

Fol. 451. 24 Jan. 1795, Bayou Pierre [?]. Bryan Bruin.
Declaration from Jack (alias Smart), a negro slave who now
belongs to Robert Ashley. Jack spent part of his life in
Cumberland. 1p. *English.* [Enclosures to fol. 452b].

Fol. 511. 20 Sept. 1795, Bougtugla. Letter from John
Ptehlym [?] stating that Forier [?] had returned to the Chickasaws from Cumberland. 1p. *English.*

Fol. 559. [Fort Wayne?]. Letter from F. Doyse [?] stating that
Capt. Portell informed him some time ago about a Cumberland party
planning to help the Chickasaws against the Creeks. Would the
Spanish permit such help? 2p. *English.* [Enclosures to fol.
560].

Fol. 579. Presents for Wasatú['s] 16 Indians. 2p. *English.*
[Enclosures to fol. 583].

> Fol. 581. Presents for the Runing [Running] Water. 2p.
> *English.*

> Fol. 583. [Presents] for the Turnip Mountain by the Broom.
> 1p. *English.*

Fol. 593. *Observaciones* mentioning the English plan to exclude
Spaniards and Americans from the Southeastern Indian trade,
especially that with the Talapooses, Choctaws, Chickasaws,
Cherokees east of the Miss. and with the Caudadahos [Caddos],
Osages, Padaicas [Paducas], and Laytanes west of the river. 6p.

CUBA/213   MISCELLANEOUS CORRESPONDENCE: 1768-1801

Fol. 818. 30 Apr. 1797, Pensacola. Panton, Leslie and Co.
List of Outstanding Indian Debts Owing to Messrs. Panton,
Leslie and Co. of Pensacola. Bloody Fellow and Moses Price
owe money to Panton, Leslie and Company. 2p. *English.*

CUBA/213 (CONT'D)

Fol. 846. 5 Nov. 1789, Hopefield. Benjamin Fooy to Manuel
Gayoso de Lemos. Moses Price and a group of Cherokees passed
through Hopefield coming from the Arkansas. They inquired
whether they could join the Shawnee and Delaware parties on this
side of the river under Spanish protection. John Taylor was
with the Cherokee group. 4p. *English*.

Fol. 877. 26 Sept. 1797, Hopefield. Benjamin Fooy to Manuel
Gayoso de Lemos. Some Cherokees are now living up the St.
Francis River. 4p. *English*.

Fol. 885. 12 Nov. 1798, New Madrid. Letter from Carlos Dehault
de la Juis [Delassus] reporting that the Cherokees received an
order demanding that the tribe withdraw from Spanish territory.
These Cherokees are part of Taylor's group and have settled
with Spanish permission along the St. Francis River. Is this
expulsion order valid? 2p. *English*.

Fol. 886. Benjamin Fooy to Manuel Gayoso de Lemos. Some
Indians from the Cumberland area were asked to guide a group of
soldiers and cattle to the Bluffs. 3p. *English*.

Fol. 922. 14 Mar. 1796, St. Ferdinand of the Bluffs. Benjamin
Fooy to Manuel Gayoso de Lemos. 3p. *English*. [Enclosures to
fol. 925b].

> Fol. 924. 26 Aug. 1795, Philadelphia. Talk from Secretary
> of War to Maj. Wm. Colbert, John Brown [the Younger), and
> Wm. McGillivray. The President has refused the Chickasaw
> request for aid to fight the Creeks. Just like the Chero-
> kees, the Chickasaws are under American protection. 4p.
> *English*.

Fol. 1000. 12 Sept. 1768, Augusta, Georgia. John Stuart et al.
At a Congress of the ... Creek Nation. New treaty sets limits
for the Creek nation and discusses land cession of 1763 by the
Creeks, Cherokees, Choctaws, Chickasaws, and Catawbas. 5p.
English.

Fol. 1008 (no. 4). 19 Nov. 1796. Talk from James McHenry [?]
to Chiefs and Warriors of the Chickasaws. President has
considered the Chickasaw talk of Nov. 24, 1795, in which the
tribe complained about the number of people traveling back and
forth between tribal land and Cumberland. He has taken note
of the Chickasaw complaint that the Cherokees have retained
some Chickasaw slaves. The reverse also seems true. If
Chickasaws wish to communicate with the United States, there
are numerous ways, including the use of Mr. Dansmoor who resides
with the Cherokees. 4p. *English*.

Fol. 1019. 4 June 1797, Village Oteyoiquinthin. Namatogoqué,
Thinaoué, Thelaqui, Tethéquelachqui, and Chocelaux to Our
Spanish Father. Cherokees will be pleased to visit their
Spanish Father. 3p. *French*.

CUBA/213 (CONT'D)

Fol. 1028. 30 Sept. 1797, Cherokees. John McDonald to Gov. Folch. Bloody Warrior is on his way to New Orleans where he plans to discuss the Cherokee gifts. A large party of Cherokees are considering settling at Muscle Shoals this spring, unless the Georgians beat them to it. 2p. *English.*

CUBA/215A   MISCELLANEOUS CORRESPONDENCE: 1780-1800

Fol. 267. 15 June 1798, Arkansas. Carlos de Villemont to [Gov. of New Orleans]. Villemont reports 40 Loups and Cherokees along the White River. 2p. *French.* [Enclosures to fol. 268].

> Fol. 268. 14 July 1798, New Orleans. [Gov. of New Orleans] to Carlos de Villemont. Villemont has exclusive right to continue trading with the village of 40 Loups and Cherokees living along the White River. 1p.

CUBA/215B   MISCELLANEOUS CORRESPONDENCE: 1780-1800

Fol. 191. 9 Nov. 1793, Nogales. Pie Beauregard to [Manuel] Gayoso. Cherokees are going to attend Gayoso's assembly. 2p. *French.*

Fol. 599. 5 Feb. [?] 1795, Hope Field [?]. Benjamin Fooy to Manuel Gayoso de Lemos. Cherokees are hunting in Hope Field [?] this winter. 4p.

Fol. 720. 1 Sept. 1798, Coweta. [James] Durouzeaux to Vicente Folch. Cherokees are having a dispute with the whites over settlements within Indian territory. These settlements have petitioned congress to allow them to make a treaty with the tribe. Durouzeaux told the Cherokees not to cede any land. 2p. *English.*

Fol. 724. 15 Feb. 1798, Cherokees. John McDonald to Wm. Panton. Little Turkey's complaints against McDonald are surprising. Little Turkey was at McDonald's house when McDonald learned what Little Turkey said. Little Turkey blamed a French vagabond for the rumor that Little Turkey and the Cherokees did not receive their goods. Cushatee is the bearer of this matter. 2p. *English.* [Enclosures to fol. 730].

> Fol. 725. 15 Feb. 1798, Cherokees. John McDonald to Gov. Folch. Refutation of the Charge the Bloody Fellow Made against Me to the Governor General. Bloody Fellow and John Watts asked Gov. White for the delivery of Cherokee goods. Governor refused their request unless they agreed to deliver the goods to McDonald. Tentenhay and Ouoletay (Breath) agreed to deliver the gifts to McDonald, but McDonald never received the entire amount and had to go to Pensacola himself. 3p. *English.*

> Fol. 727. 16 Feb. 1798, Cherokees. Little Turkey to Gov. Folch. McDonald called a meeting of the chiefs to confront Bloody Fellow who had complained about McDonald in New

CUBA/215B (CONT'D)

Orleans. Little Turkey declared in front of the chiefs (Bloody Fellow, Water Hunter, and Cheenowie) that he had received goods in Pensacola, which clears McDonald of Bloody Fellow's charge. Since Bloody Fellow and McDonald are good friends, Little Turkey thinks that this whole matter resulted from an interpreter's malice. 2p. *English.*

Fol. 727b. [16 Feb. 1798], [Cherokees]. Bloody Fellow to Gov. Folch. When Bloody Fellow arrived in Pensacola, he was fearful that Cox from Georgia would settle at Muscle Shoals. Bloody Fellow is determined to take up the hatchet and call upon his northern brothers for help. Since Cox did not settle at Muscle Shoals, Bloody Fellow returned home in peace. 1p. *English.*

Fol. 728. 16 Feb. 1798, Cherokee. Pavo Chico (Little Turkey) to Gov. Folch. [Translation of fol. 727]. 2p.

Fol. 728b. 15 Feb. 1798, Cherokees. John McDonald to Gov. Folch. *Refutación de la acusación que hizo contra mí el Bloody Fellow a sr. governador general.* [Translation of fol. 725]. 3p.

Fol. 729b. 15 Feb. 1798, Cherokee. John McDonald to Wm. Panton. [Translation of fol. 724]. 2p.

CUBA/224A CORRESPONDENCE FROM LOUISIANA: 1770-1819

No. 258. 10 Dec. 1785, New Orleans. Letter to el Conde de Gálvez reporting that Francisco Bouligny has been commissioned to determine if the Americans are preparing for war along the Ohio and Cumberland Rivers. Several residents of Cumberland have been surveying land around Barrancas de Margot for a settlement. 3p. [Enclosures to no. 2].

No. 1. Luis Chaceré to Francisco Bouligny (translation). Chaceré traveled to Cumberland and learned that Robertson had left to survey land around Barrancas de Margot. There are about 4,000 people living in Cumberland, 2,000 of which can bear arms. Their major crops are tobacco and corn. Chaceré describes the Cherokee, Cumberland, and Chickasaw Rivers. 13p.

No. 2. 10 Sept. 1785, Chickasaws. Thomas Green to Col. Blide in Cumberland (translation). Green has learned that it was the Talapooses who invaded Cumberland and Kentucky las spring. 4p.

CUBA/224B CORRESPONDENCE FROM LOUISIANA: 1770-1819

N. fol. [16 Dec. 1791], [Pensacola]. Letter to Antonio Porlier stating that Bowles first arrived among the Lower Creek three and a half years ago. He lived with some Cherokees for a while. Later he took a group to London and received gifts for the Cherokees and Creeks. 10p. [Encloses 2 documents].

CUBA/224B (CONT'D)

No. 23. 20 Aug. 1792, New Orleans. El Barón de Carondelet to Manuel de Lanzos. The Americans plan to create another settlement as large as Franklin and Cumberland in Indian territory. 4p.

No. 59. 20 Aug. 1792, New Orleans. El Barón de Carondelet to Manuel de Lanzos. The Americans are about ready to build a new establishment as big as Franklin and Cumberland. 3p.

No. 1. 3 Oct. 1794, St. Marks. Diego de Vegas to Juan Nepomuceno de Quesada. There was a fight between the Americans, Cowetas, and Cherokees at the headwaters of the Apalachicola River. Americans fled, leaving four dead, 30 horses with saddles, and 40 rifles. 3p.

No. 3. 13 July 1795, St. Marks. Diego de Vegas to Bartolomé Morales. Vegas read a copy of a talk from the Indian chiefs meeting with the Americans to discuss peace. It contains many falsehoods. Vegas has explained these mistaken ideas to the Indians at St. Marks and forwards the proper answers to el Barón de Carondelet, Enrique White, Luis de Villiers, Juan de la Villebeuvre, and to the interpreters Benjamin Fooy and John McDonald so they can do the same with Indians in their areas. 2p.

CUBA/271   ACCOUNTS AND REPORTS: 1784-1811

No. 12. 24 June 1784, Mobile. [Esteban] Miró. *Relación de los efectos que se necesitan para el regalo de un indio de la nación chiraqui, que concurrió al presente congreso.* Spanish presents for one Cherokee who attended the congress. 2p.

CUBA/1375   ROYAL ORDERS AND MISCELLANEOUS DOCUMENTS: 1781-1786

N. fol. 2 May 1784, Aranjuez. José de Gálvez to el Conde de Gálvez. 2p. [Encloses 2 documents].

N. fol. 1 Jan. 1784, Little Tallassee, Upper Cherokee [sic] Nation. Alex. McGillivray (chief of the Cherokees) to [Arturo O'Neill] (translation). McGillivray solicits peace with Spain on behalf of the Cherokees. 4p.

No. 26. 31 Dec. 1783, Palace. *Real orden* indicating the King's approval of the decision to let the Cherokees settle near Pensacola. 1p. [Encloses 2 documents].

N. fol. 31 Dec. 1783, Palace. *Real orden* from José de Gálvez to el Conde de Gálvez. The King has seen the Cherokees' petition asking for Spain's help in the restitution of their lands taken by the Americans, or for permission to settle near Pensacola, or that the Creeks be prevailed upon to cede some land. The King agrees with the decision to allow the Cherokees to settle near Pensacola. 3p.

CUBA/1375 (CONT'D)

N. fol. 22 Dec. 1783, Madrid. [El Conde de Gálvez?] to
José de Gálvez. Gálvez discusses the petition from two
Cherokee chiefs, who represent 1,800 warriors, asking the
King's mediation to establish peace, restoration of their
land taken by the Americans, and the intercession with
Talapooses to allow the Cherokees to settle in Spanish
territory. It is in Spain's interest to allow these
Indians to settle in Spanish territory. 3p.

CUBA/1377 CORRESPONDENCE OF BERNARDO DE GÁLVEZ AND OTHERS: 1783-1784

No. 13. 8 Feb. 1784, Havana. José de Ezpeleta to el Conde de
Gálvez (duplicate). 6p. [Encloses 7 documents].

No. 13. 1 Sept. 1783, Havana. [El Conde de Gálvez? to
José de Gálvez?] José de Ezpeleta has forwarded a petition
from 1,800 Cherokees (an agricultural and industrious
nation) to settle in Spanish territory. 1p.

No. 4. 1 Sept. 1783, Havana. José de Ezpeleta to el Conde
de Gálvez. Ezpeleta forwards a request from two Cherokees
and his reply. Gilberto Maxent, supervisor of the *ramo de
indios,* has been informed about the matter. 3p.

No. 1. 9 July 1783, Pensacola. Arturo O'Neill to el
Conde de Gálvez (copy). Two Cherokee chiefs and one
Irish trader arrived here last month. They reported
that the Cherokees had been reduced by the Americans to
1,800 braves hiding out in the mountains. Chiefs
requested the King's help in securing peace or permission to settle in Spanish territory. O'Neill offered
to help them. 2p.

No. 2. 21 Aug. 1783, Havana. José de Ezpeleta to
Arturo O'Neill (copy). Ezpeleta approves O'Neill's
reaction to the Cherokee requests. Obviously, the
court will have to decide this issue. 3p.

N. fol. 16 Jan. 1784, Madrid. Letter to José de
Ezpeleta reporting the content of the King's Royal
Order of Dec. 31, 1783. [See AGI Cuba/1375/no. 26].
1p.

N. fol. 24 Dec. 1783, Madrid. Letter to José de
Ezpeleta informing him that the King will decide the
Cherokee problem. 1p.

No. 27. 13 Apr. 1784, Havana. José de Ezpeleta to el Conde de
Gálvez. Ezpeleta has received the royal order favoring the
Cherokee request. 2p.

*CUBA/1393   CORRESPONDENCE OF THE ARMY OF OPERATIONS AND MISCELLANEOUS
            DOCUMENTS: 1780-1791*

> Fol. 178 (no. 14). 10 Nov. 1787, Pensacola. Arturo O'Neill
> to José de Ezpeleta. Chief Spanahagn, King of the Abeka Creeks,
> led a party against Cumberland, burning two homes and seizing
> two horses. Since then, there has been violence along the Creek
> and Cherokee borders. 3p.

> Fol. 483. *Correspondencia con Mr. Maxent seguida por el Brig.
> dn. José de Ezpeleta.* 1p. [Enclosures to fol. 486].

>> Fol. 484. 29 Aug. 1783, Havana. [José de Ezpeleta to
>> Gilberto Maxent]. Cherokees have petitioned to settle in
>> Spanish territory and to receive the King's assistance. 3p.

CUBA/1394   CORRESPONDENCE OF ESTEBAN MIRÓ: 1783-1789

> N. fol. *Indice de la correspondencia reservada remitido por
> el governador de Luisiana de 1787, 88, 89, y 90.* 3p.
> [Encloses 314 pages].

>> No. 1½ *reservada*. 24 Sept. 1787, New Orleans. Esteban
>> Miró to José Ezpeleta. 3p.

>>> No. 1. 25 July 1787, Little Tallassee. Alex. McGil-
>>> livray to Miró (translation). A group from Cumberland
>>> attacked a party of Creeks and traders near Muscle
>>> Shoals. Creeks have sent some 600 warriors to revenge
>>> this and to make sure that the Americans do not settle
>>> in the Muscle Shoals area. Creeks recently killed
>>> the Americans Wm. Davenport and Allen. 4p.

>> No. 3 *reservada*. 13 Oct. 1787, New Orleans. Esteban Miró
>> to José de Ezpeleta. 2p.

>>> N. fol. 4 Oct. 1787, Pensacola. Alex. McGillivray
>>> to Esteban Miró (translation). Warriors sent to
>>> attack Cumberland have returned. The inhabitants of
>>> that area fled before the Creeks, abandoning their
>>> homes and crops. Many of these Cumberland residents
>>> reportedly sought refuge in the mountains of N.C. and
>>> Va. near the Holston River. 6p.

>> No. 8 *reservada*. 2 Nov. 1788, New Orleans. Esteban Miró
>> to José de Ezpeleta. 2p.

>>> N. fol. 20 Sept. 1788, Little Tallassee. Alex.
>>> McGillivray to Esteban Miró (translation). McGillivray
>>> will send Mr. Nowlan on to Cumberland when he is well,
>>> but it is best for the moment to travel via Mobile
>>> and the Chickasaws since the Cherokees are at war with
>>> the Americans. 7p.

>> No. 11 *reservada*. 1 Apr. 1788, New Orleans. Esteban Miró
>> to José de Ezpeleta. 10p.

CUBA/1394 (CONT'D)

No. 2. 28 June 1787, Philadelphia. Knox to James
White (translation). White is instructed to do his
best to increase trade with the tribes. White should
use Mr. Woods to negotiate with the Choctaws and Mr.
Drumgoole with the Cherokees. 3p.

No. 12 *reservada*. 16 Sept. 1788, New Orleans. Esteban
Miró to José de Ezpeleta. 4p.

No. 2. 22 Aug. 1788, Pensacola. Arturo O'Neill to
Esteban Miró (copy). O'Neill believes that the Creeks
under McGillivray are sympathetic to the English.
He also tries to implicate McGillivray in the uprising
of Franklin residents under Sevier against the American
Congress. 3p.

No. 13 *reservada*. 15 July 1788, New Orleans. Esteban Miró
to José de Ezpeleta. 1p.

No. 2. Kearney, Carrington, Bingham, Smith. *Junta
... a quienes se sometió [varios papeles relativos a
los negocios de los yndios del departamento del sur]*
(translation). Residents of Ga. and N.C. have usurped
land belonging to the Creeks and Cherokees. 15p.

No. 6. 4 June 1788, Pensacola. Arturo O'Neill to
Esteban Miró (copy). O'Neill expresses his distrust
of Panton and McGillivray who would not act in the
interest of Spain if war breaks out with Great Britain.
McGillivray is willing to continue the war with Ga.,
although he is trying at the same time to obtain peace
with Cumberland. 7p.

CUBA/1409   MISCELLANEOUS DOCUMENTS: 1785-1789

N. fol. 22 June 1787, New York. Diego de Gardoqui to Esteban
Miró (duplicate). The Cherokee Chief Sconetoyah has arrived in
Philadelphia. Gardoqui discusses some other Indians in Philadel-
phia and the Treaty of Hopewell. 4p.

N. fol. 22 June 1787, New York. Diego de Gardoqui to Arturo
O'Neill. O'Neill should ignore the claims of independence by
New Cumberland and Kentucky. American newspapers report the
arrival of the Cherokee Chief Sconetoyah in Philadelphia. 6p.

N. fol. 24 Sept. 1787, Charleston. John Sullivan to Maj. Wm.
Brown (copy). Sullivan plans to return to Franklin soon.
Franklin is the best spot to live on the continent. Brown
should come south and secure some land along the Tenn. River.
8p. *English*. [Encloses 9 documents].

No. fol. 24 Sept. [1787], [Charleston]. John Sullivan to
Maj. Wm. Brown. [Translation of the preceding letter].
2p.

CUBA/1409 (CONT'D)

N. fol. 12 Nov. 1787, New York. Diego de Gardoqui to José
de Ezpeleta. Ezpeleta can see from the attached documents
how the Americans covet Spanish territory. There are rumors
that Franklin has risen in revolt, which partly explains
the excesses reported there. 8p.

N. fol. 26 Nov. 1787, New York. Diego de Gardoqui to José
de Ezpeleta. Gardoqui has learned that Sullivan planned
to travel from Charleston to Franklin, a district presently
in turmoil. Sullivan then plans to leave Franklin for New
Orleans via the Tennessee, Ohio, and Miss. Rivers. 3p.

CUBA/1425   CORRESPONDENCE OF THE GOVERNOR OF LOUISIANA: 1788-1790

No. 2 *reservada*. 10 Mar. 1789, New Orleans. Esteban Miró to
José de Ezpeleta. 5p. [Encloses 7 documents].

No. 1. 1 Feb. 1789, Little Tallassee. Alex. McGillivray
to Wm. Panton (translation). McGillivray has received an
express from the [American] commissioners which was brought
by Terrapin, a Cherokee. 11p.

No. 4. 26 Jan. 1789, Little Tallassee. Alex. McGillivray
to Thomas Pinckney (translation). Cherokee warrior Terrapin
has delivered Pinckney's letter of Nov. 6. Creeks cannot
cede Ga. any more land since the tribe is bordered by that
state on the east and northeast; by Spanish Florida to
the south, southeast, and southwest; by the Choctaws and
Chickasaws to the west; and by the Cherokees and Cumberland
to the north and northwest. 8p.

No. 5. 28 Nov. 1788, Hopewell along the Keowee. Richard
Winn et al. to Chiefs and Warriors of the Creek Nation
(translation). Americans would like to advise the Creeks
about a number of treaty violations, including the stealing
of 16 to 20 horses and a murder in Franklin County. They
also wish the tribe to note the theft of two excellent
horses belonging to Gen. Martin, who was working as agent
of the congress to the Creeks and Cherokees. 7p.

No. 6. 26 Jan. 1789, Little Tallassee. Alex. McGillivray
to Richard Winn et al. (translation). Terrapin, a Cherokee,
delivered Winn's letters of Nov. 28. 11p.

No. 15 *reservada*. 28 Nov. 1789, *Real orden* to Gov. of Louisiana
concerning the lack of news about Col. Manuel Gayoso de Lemos's
trip to Franklin and Cumberland. 2p. [Encloses 1 document].

N. fol. 18 Jan. 1790, New Orleans. Esteban Miró to
Domingo Cabello. Gayoso's health prevented him initially
from going to Franklin and Cumberland. Later, after living
in Natchez, he found it impossible to travel to Franklin and
Cumberland because he was too well known in those areas.
Nevertheless, he has taken every opportunity to collect
news about those places. 3p.

CUBA/1425 (CONT'D)

No. 122. 19 May 1790, New Orleans. Esteban Miró to Domingo Cabello. Miró reports the latest Indian hostilities along the Cherokee River. 1p. [Encloses 2 documents].

> N. fol. 27 Mar. 1790, New Madrid. Pedro Foucher to Esteban Miró (copy). Many wounded American soldiers have arrived from the Cherokee River. 3p.

> N. fol. 19 July 1790, Havana. Letter to Gov. of New Orleans acknowledging the receipt of information about the Indian attack on the Americans along the Cherokee River. 2p.

N. fol. 21 Aug. 1789, New Providence, Bahama Islands. Wm. Bowles to Gov. of Havana. [Translation of the following letter]. 3p. [Encloses 3 documents].

> N. fol. 21 Aug. 1789, New Providence, Bahama Islands. Wm. Bowles to [Gov. of Havana]. Bowles has recently arrived from the Creek and Cherokee nations and has brought some of their leaders. These two nations have been greatly oppressed in Florida by Panton, Leslie and Company. 2p. *English*.

No. 3 *reservada*. 10 Jan. 1788, St. Augustine. Vicente Manuel de Zéspedes to José de Ezpeleta. 8p. [Encloses 5 documents].

> N. fol. 23 Oct. 1787, Assembly House. Wm. Gibbons. *Acuerdo de la junta selecta ... de Georgia* (translation). Resolution discussing Indian treaties, including the Cherokee treaty of 1783. 12p.

No. 6 *reservada*. 1 June 1790, St. Augustine. Vicente Manuel Zéspedes to Domingo Cabello. 3p. [Encloses 1 document].

> N. fol. 20 May 1790, Coweta. Alex. McGillivray to John Leslie (translation). McGillivray reports a squadron of armed boats on the Cherokee River. 9p.

CUBA/1440A   CORRESPONDENCE OF THE GOVERNOR OF LOUISIANA: 1790-1791

No. 2. 12 Aug. 1790, New Orleans. Esteban Miró to Luis de la Casas. The Americans continue their efforts to win over the Chickasaws and Choctaws. Americans were attacked along the Cherokee River. 6p. [Encloses 6 documents].

> No. 3. 16 July 1790, New Orleans. Talk from Esteban Miró to Chiefs and Warriors of the Choctaw Nation. Miró opposes granting land to the Americans for a trading post. This would open Indian territory to American vagrants, as happened in Cumberland, and no one could stop them. 6p.

No. 39. 6 Oct. 1790, New Orleans. Esteban Miró to Luis de las Casas. A Creek party from Coweta told Miró about three Cherokees and a white man who were in Providence this past spring.

CUBA/1440A (CONT'D)

Miró is persuaded that these Cherokees could have no other
motive than the acquisition of gifts since their tribe lives
so far from St. Augustine. 3p. [Encloses 1 document].

> N. fol. 3 Nov. 1790, Havana. [Luis de las Casas] to
> Governor of Louisiana. The three Cherokees who were in
> Providence requested that they be allowed to settle in
> Louisiana. This migration would violate the King's
> regulations. 1p.

No. 141. 15 Mar. 1791, New Orleans. Esteban Miró to Luis de
las Casas. 3p. [Encloses 1 document].

> N. fol. 26 Feb. 1791, Pensacola. Alex. McGillivray to
> Brig. Esteban Miró (translation). McGillivray discusses
> his difficulties with Georgia, which claims the right to
> sell land belonging to the Creeks, Choctaws, and Chick-
> asaws. 11p.

CUBA/1440B   CORRESPONDENCE OF THE GOVERNOR OF LOUISIANA: 1790-1791

No. 206. 15 July 1791, New Orleans. Esteban Miró to Luis de
las Casas. 4p. [Encloses 4 documents].

> No. 136. 1 July 1791, Natchez. Manuel Gayoso de Lemos
> to Esteban Miró (copy). Gayoso examines the Choctaw and
> Chickasaw opposition to a Spanish establishment at Nogales.
> If the Americans get this land, they will destroy the
> Indians as they have done around Cumberland and Franklin.
> 23p.

No. 259. 23 Sept. 1791, New Orleans. Esteban Miró to Luis de
las Casas. The new treaty between the Americans and Cherokees
is advantageous since it prohibits the establishment of land
companies within Cherokee territory. 3p. [Encloses 4 docu-
ments].

> N. fol. 28 Aug. 1791, Little Tallassee. Alex. McGilli-
> vray to Brig. Esteban Miró (translation). The Cherokees
> and Col. Blount signed a new treaty during the spring.
> McGillivray pointed out to the Cherokees the advantages
> of the treaty, which sets fair boundaries with the Americans
> and which prohibits renegade Chickasaws and Choctaws from
> signing treaties that give away Cherokee land as happened
> at Muscle Shoals and other sites along the Cherokee River.
> 3p.

> N. fol. 2 Dec. 1791, Havana. Letter to [Gov. of Louisiana]
> stating that the King has been notified about the Cherokee
> treaty. 1p.

No. 288. 15 Oct. 1791, New Orleans. Esteban Miró to Luis de
las Casas. Bowles is the same man who went to London with
three Cherokees and who is now in Florida. 3p. [Encloses 5
documents].

CUBA/1440B (CONT'D)

No. 303. 28 Oct. 1791, New Orleans. Esteban Miró to Luis de
las Casas. 1p. [Encloses 4 documents].

N. fol. 8 Oct. 1791, Pensacola. Wm. Panton to Esteban
Miró (translation). Wm. Bowles and his Indian companions
convinced the English that they were important members of
the Creek and Cherokee nations. 4p.

N. fol. 1 Aug. 1791, New Providence. Thomas Forbes to
John Leslie (extract). Forbes discusses Wm. Bowles, who
convinced British officials that he was an important member
of the Southern tribes. 3p.

CUBA/1445   CORRESPONDENCE OF THE GOVERNOR OF PENSACOLA: 1790-1796

No. 3. 2 Oct. 1790, Pensacola. Arturo O'Neill to Luis de las
Casas. O'Neill has heard rumors that three Indians and an
American interpreter have offered to seize St. Augustine for
the Gov. of Providence. O'Neill has sent Antonio Garzon to
investigate these rumors. Alex. McGillivray really favors the
British and is capable of formenting support for England among
the American settlers along the Cherokee and Cumberland Rivers
and in Kentucky. 3p.

No. 5. 18 Oct. 1790, Pensacola. Arturo O'Neill to Luis de las
Casas. O'Neill attaches information concerning the Americans
who are interested in buying western land. McGillivray is
trying to reconcile the American residents along the Ohio,
Cherokee, Cumberland, and Miss. Rivers with Great Britain. 3p.

CUBA/1447   CORRESPONDENCE OF THE GOVERNOR OF LOUISIANA: 1793-1796

No. 62 *reservada*. 9 Jan. 1793, New Orleans. El Barón de
Carondelet to Luis de las Casas. [Same as AGI Cuba 2353/fol.
767]. 2p. [Encloses 3 documents].

No. 26 *reservada*. 8 Jan. 1793, New Orleans. El Barón de
Carondelet to el Conde de Aranda. [Copy of AHN Estado/
3898/exp. 5/no. 26 *reservada*]. 8p.

[No. 1]. 3 Dec. 1792, New Madrid. Thomas Portell to
el Barón de Carondelet. Cherokees and Creeks have
done much damage at Cumberland. 3p.

No. 78 *reservada*. 22 May 1793, New Orleans. El Barón de Carondelet to Luis de las Casas. Carondelet forwards a petition from
the Cherokees, who are presently at war with the Americans.
Cherokee leaders were in New Orleans last November asking for
Spanish aid against the American seizure of their land. The
Americans now want to take the tribe's last hunting grounds
between the Cumberland and Tenn. Rivers. 4p. [Encloses 1
document].

N. fol. 5 Apr. 1793, Cherokee Nation. John McDonald,
Bloody Fellow, Glass, Charles of Chickamaugua, Water Hunter,

CUBA/1447 (CONT'D)

Spider of Lookout Mountain, Richard Justice, Badgers Mother
Warrior, and Wm. Shawney to el Barón de Carondelet. [Same
as AHN Estado/3898/exp. 5/no. 8 *reservada*/encl.]. 3p.

No. 79 *reservada*. 22 May 1793, New Orleans. El Barón de
Carondelet to Luis de las Casas. Americans intend to establish
a post at Barrancas de Margot on the Miss. River. Carondelet
has written to Brig. Robertson in Cumberland. 6p. [Encloses
3 documents].

No. 1. 7 May 1793, New Madrid. Thomas Portell to el
Barón de Carondelet. [Same as AHN Estado/3898/exp. 5/
no. 9 *reservada*/encl. no. 1]. 4p.

No. 2. 21 May 1793, New Orleans. El Barón de Carondelet
to James Robertson. [Copy of AGI Cuba/2363/no. 8
reservada/encl.]. 3p.

N. fol. 23 Apr. 1793, Nashville. James Robertson to
Thomas Portell. [Same as AHN Estado/3898/exp. 5/ no. 9
reservada/encl.]. 2p.

No. 81 *reservada*. 23 May 1793, New Orleans. El Barón de
Carondelet to Luis de las Casas. Carondelet reports the latest
news from Cumberland. The American gazetteers have falsely
charged Carondelet and O'Neill of stirring up the Indians.
Carondelet's letter to the Cherokees demonstrates his interest
in peace. He has sent word to the King's representative in
Philadelphia that the charges against him are false. 2p.

N. fol. 16 May 1793, Natchez. Manuel Gayoso de Lemos to
el Barón de Carondelet. Gayoso reports on news from
Cumberland. 6p.

No. 82 *reservada*. 6 July 1793, New Orleans. El Barón de
Carondelet to Luis de las Casas. The Duque de la Alcudia was
informed that the Choctaws ceded a small piece of land around
Old Tombigbee to Spain. This will help Spain's contact with
the Cherokees, who are very important. The Chickasaws are
upset about the Choctaw concession since Gov. Blount has won
over many Chickasaws for the United States. 5p. [Encloses 2
documents].

No. 89 *reservada*. 3 Aug. 1793, New Orleans. El Barón de Carondelet to Luis de las Casas. 8p. [Encloses 2 documents].

N. fol. 30 Mar. 1793, Aranjuez. *Real orden* from el Duque
de la Alcudia to el Barón de Carondelet. The King approves
Carondelet's measures to prevent the Americans from establishing themselves at Barrancas de Margot and Muscle
Shoals. 1p.

No. 91 *reservada*. 27 Aug. 1793, New Orleans. El Barón de
Carondelet to Luis de las Casas. El Duque de la Alcudia has
been informed that the American army along the Ohio intends to

destroy the Cherokees once the Americans achieve peace with
the Northern tribes. All the land that stretches from the Ohio
to the Barrancas de Margot belongs to the Cherokees. It is in
Spain's interest to prevent the destruction of the Cherokees.
4p. [Encloses 2 documents].

> N. fol. 25 July 1793, Nogales. Manuel Gayoso de Lemos to
> el Barón de Carondelet. [Copy of AGI Cuba/178A/no. 7
> *sobre la asamblea de indios*]. 9p.

> N. fol. 15 Aug. 1793, New Orleans. El Barón de Carondelet
> to Manuel Gayoso de Lemos. [Same as AGI Cuba/2353/
> fol. 834]. 6p.

No. 93 *reservada*. 27 Sept. 1793, New Orleans. El Barón de
Carondelet to Luis de las Casas. Carondelet forwards a copy of
the letter sent to the ministry of foreign affairs concerning
Spain's Indian allies and the American establishments in the
West. Carondelet has ordered officials stationed in the upper
[Miss.] to prevent the immigration of all Frenchmen coming
from Ky. and Cumberland since they may be Jacobins trying to
stir up a revolt. 4p. [Encloses 4 documents].

> No. 18 *reservada*. 27 Sept. 1793, New Orleans. El Barón
> de Carondelet to el Duque de la Alcudia. [Copy of AHN
> Estado 3898/exp. 5/no. 18 *reservada*]. 10p.

> No. 10. 12 Sept. 1793, Natchez. Manuel Gayoso de Lemos
> to el Barón de Carondelet. [Same as AHN Estado/3898/exp.5/
> no. 18 *reservada*/encl. no. 10]. 12p.

No. 103 *reservada*. 8 Feb. 1794, New Orleans. El Barón de
Carondelet to Luis de las Casas. 6p. [Encloses 17 documents].

> No. 1 (no. 224). 3 Jan. 1794, New Madrid. Thomas Portell
> to el Barón de Carondelet (copy). Foraging troops from
> Cumberland and Ky. plan to attack Portell. 1p.

> No. 2 (no. 325?) 3 Jan. 1794, New Madrid. Thomas Portell
> to el Barón de Carondelet (copy). Last December the
> Cherokees with several Shawnees and Loups expressed their
> support for the Spaniards. Louis Lorimier is traveling
> with the Cherokees in order to unite all three tribes to
> guard Spanish territory against American hostilities. 3p.

> No. 3. 1 Jan. 1794, Ft. Celeste, New Madrid. Thomas
> Portell et al. to Louis Lorimier (copy). *Instrucción para
> dn. Luis Lorimie*. Once the Loups and Shawnees are united
> with the Cherokees, Lorimier is ordered to discover the
> true intentions of the French revolutionaries who are
> coming from Vincennes and Ohio. 5p.

> No. 4 *reservada*. 7 Feb. 1794, New Orleans. El Barón de
> Carondelet to Manuel Gayoso de Lemos (copy). 4p.

CUBA/1447 (CONT'D)

> No. 398. 17 Jan. 1794, Natchez. Manuel Gayoso de
> Lemos to el Barón de Carondelet (copy). Gayoso
> forwards information about the New Madrid Commandant's
> fear of being attacked and his use of Indian allies.
> 2p.

No. 112 *reservada*. 30 Apr. 1794, New Orleans. El Barón de
Carondelet to Luis de las Casas. Shawnees attacked a French
fort along the Ohio near the Shawnee and Cumberland Rivers.
3p. [Encloses 1 document].

> N. fol. 2 Apr. 1794, New Madrid. Thomas Portell to el
> Barón de Carondelet (extract). Portell reports an Indian
> attack along the Cumberland River. 2p.

No. 118 *reservada*. 28 June 1794, New Orleans. El Barón de
Carondelet to Luis de las Casas. A detachment of Gen. Wayne's
army is planning to fortify the Old Cherokee Fort. This
detachment will supposedly check the unruly residents of
Cumberland. The Chickasaws, Creeks, Choctaws, and Cherokees
will undoubtedly stop any American effort to push South. 4p.

No. 154 *reservada*. 30 Jan. 1796, New Orleans. El Barón de
Carondelet to Luis de las Casas. Carondelet forwards a letter
from John McDonald, commissioner to the Cherokees. With the
help of Indian allies, Spain could stop any American expedition.
The Cherokees and Creeks will gladly aid Spain in the defense
of the Ohio and Mississippi if given money and weapons. 13p.
[Encloses 2 documents].

> No. 1. 31 Dec. 1795, Cherokees. John McDonald to el
> Barón de Carondlet. Americans will probably attack
> Louisiana in the spring. Americans also plan to seize the
> fort at San Fernando de Barrancas. Little Turkey and
> Bloody Fellow have learned that the Americans have decided
> to use numerous boats on the Cherokee and Ohio Rivers.
> 3p.

[No. 158 *reservada*]. 15 Apr. 1796, New Orleans. El Barón de
Carondelet to Luis de las Casas. 8p. [Encloses 2 documents].

> No. 1. 26 Aug. 1795, Philadelphia. Sec. of War to Maj.
> Wm. Colbert, John Brown Jr., and Wm. McGillivray.
> Cherokees are under American protection. United States
> cannot help the Chickasaws if they fight against tribes
> under American protection. 7p.

CUBA/1469   MISCELLANEOUS CORRESPONDENCE: 1790-1796

N. fol. 16 July 1792, Philadelphia. José de Jaundenes and
José Ignacio de Viar to Luis de las Casas. Spanish envoys can
find no accurate map showing the proper boundaries between the
colonies in N. America. Nor have they been able to find copies
of the English concessions to the Indians. Jaudenes and Viar
have attempted to forward copies of all the Indian treaties

signed by the Americans. They would like copies of the Spanish treaties with the Indians to determine if they antedate the American ones. 4p. [Encloses 1 document].

N. fol. 10 Apr. 1792, Havana. [Luis de las Casas] to the Envoys in New York. Since the government lacks information of the precise borders between Florida, Louisiana, and the United States and since it also lacks copies of the English treaties with the Indians, [Las Casas] would appreciate receiving such information. 1p.

N. fol. 28 June 1794, New York. José de Jaudenes and José Ignacio de Viar to Luis de las Casas. [Same as AHN Estado/ 3895bis/ap. 5/no. 259/encl. no. 8]. 4p. [Encloses 3 documents].

No. 1. 11 June 1794, Philadelphia. José de Jaudenes and José Ignacio de Viar to Edmund Randolph. [Copy of AHN Estado/3895bis/ap. 7/no. 273/encl. no. 1]. 6p.

No. 3. 26 June 1794, New York. José de Jaudenes and José Ignacio de Viar to Little Turkey. [Copy of AHN Estado/ 3895bis/ap. 4/no. 248/encl. no. 3]. 5p.

N. fol. 6 Sept. 1794, Havana. [Luis de las Casas] to José de Jaudenes y José Ignacio de Viar. [Las Casas] received the information concerning negotiations between the Cherokees and Americans. Since the Spanish envoys probably have not seen the treaty of 28 Oct. 1793 between Spain and the Indians (Chickasaws, Creeks, Talapooses, Alibamos, Choctaws, and the Cherokees), they should know it clearly antedates any agreement between the Americans and Cherokees. 2p.

N. fol. 7 Jan. 1795, Philadelphia. José de Jaudenes to Luis de las Casas. Jaudenes gave copies of the Spanish treaty with the Cherokees to the American government. 2p.

N. fol. 7 Jan. 1795, Philadelphia. José de Jaudenes to Luis de las Casas. Jaudenes has forwarded his correspondence with the Cherokee interpreter to Juan Nepomuceno de Quesada and to Las Casas. Jaudenes, however, has not been able to acquire a copy of the American treaty. Nevertheless, the Indian agent Thompson among the Cherokees could tell Spain what the contents of the treaty are. 2p. [Encloses 7 documents].

N. fol. 2 July 1794, New York. José de Jaudenes and José Ignacio de Viar to Juan Nepomuceno de Quesada. [Copy of AHN Estado/3895bis/ap. 5/no. 259/encl. no. 4]. 3p.

No. 1. 23 June 1794, Philadelphia. John Thompson to José de Jaudenes (translation). Cherokees plan to conclude a treaty of friendship and peace with the Americans without placing the tribe under American protection. Cherokees view themselves as a free people and will not be placed under anyone's protection. 2p.

CUBA/1469 (CONT'D)

         No. 2.   26 June 1794, New York. José de Jaudenes to John Thompson. [Same as AHN Estado/3895bis/ap. 4/ no. 248/encl. no. 2].   2p.

         No. 3.   26 June 1794, New York. José de Jaudenes and José Ignacio de Viar to Little Turkey. [Same as AHN Estado/3895bis/ap. 4/no. 248/encl. no. 3].   7p.

         No. 4.   27 June 1794, Philadelphia.   John Thompson to José de Jaudenes. [Same as AHN Estado/3895bis/ap. 4/no. 248/encl. no. 4].   2p.

         No. 5.   28 June 1794.   Philadelphia.   John Thompson to José de Jaudenes. [Same as AHN Estado/3895bis/ ap. 4/no. 248/encl. no. 5].   2p.

         No. 6.   28 June 1794, Philadelphia.   Translated receipt from John Thompson. [Same as AHN Estado/ 3895bis/ap. 4/no. 248/encl. no. 6].   1p.

N. fol.   19 Feb. 1795, Havana.   Letter to charges d'affaires in Philadelphia acknowledging receipt of information about the Cherokee negotiations in Philadelphia.   2p.

N. fol.   Instructions that the Cherokee materials should be sent to Carondelet and that the Spanish commissioners among the Cherokees should be ordered to forward a copy of the tribe's treaty with the Americans.   1p.

N. fol.   26 May 1794, Havana.   Letter to Dunmore.   3p.   [Encloses 6 documents].

         N. fol.   15 Aug. 1789, New Providence.   *Declaración de Guillermo A. Bowles* (translation).   Bowles has visited the Creeks and Cherokees many times.   6p.

         N. fol.   19 Aug. 1789, New Providence.   *The Lucayan Royal Herald and the Weekly Advertiser.*   Several articles discuss Bowles (who visited the Cherokees), Indian relations with Franklin, and the antipathy of the Creeks and Cherokees towards the United States.   4p.   *English.*

CUBA/1573   CORRESPONDENCE OF THE GOVERNORS OF THE FLORIDAS: 1790-1806

No. 8 *reservada*.   1 June 1804, Pensacola.   Vicente Folch to el Marqués de Someruelos.   Ten Talapooses and Cherokees, led by Opayochicco's son and the King of Cussita, came to Pensacola four days ago.   They wanted to know if Spain was really granting Louisiana to the Americans.   They also wanted to know what Spain considered Lousiana's borders to be.   4p.   [Encloses 10 documents].

CUBA/1573   (CONT'D)

No. 1. 6 May 1804, [Pensacola]. Opoyomico to Gov. Folch
(copy). Cherokee chiefs (Black Fox and Path Killer) have
sent some warriors to hear the governor's talks. When the
Four Nations gathered at Hickory Ground to hear the
governor, some Cherokees were absent. They wish to hear
the governor now. Tribes have heard that the Spanish and
French have sold Louisiana. 4p. *English.*

No. 2. 18 May 1804, Pensacola. Vizente Folch to Opoyomico
(copy). Folch has received the talk from Opoyomico and
the Cherokees. The Indians should keep peace with the
white man and not enter into his quarrels. The Spanish
gave Louisiana to the French who in turn handed it over
to the Americans. The borders have not yet been fixed.
3p. *English.*

CUBA/2351   WEST FLORIDA: 1746-1784

Doc. 7 (no. 91 *reservada*). 13 July 1778, New Orleans. Bernardo
de Gálvez to Diego José Navarro. 2p. [Encloses 2 documents].

Doc. 7a. 6 July 1778, Manchac. Juan de la Villebeuvre
to Gov. of Louisiana (*capítulo*). English had planned to
seize New Orleans, attacking with the two frigates already
there and 1,500 Choctaws, 400 Chickasaws, 300 Cherokees,
and 250 Englishmen. The project did not materialize
because the Cherokees and Chickasaws feared what the
Americans might do. 3p.

Doc. 7b. 8 July 1778, Pointe Coupée. Carlos de Grand-Pré
to Gov. of Louisiana (*capítulo*). There are no rumors in
Pointe Coupée about the supposed plans of the Choctaws,
Cherokees, and Chickasaws to attack Spanish possessions.
This does not mean that the English do not have other
devilish plans concerning the Indians and Spain. 2p.

Doc. 9. 15 July 1778, [New Orleans]. Bernardo de Gálvez.
*Copias de los documentos presentados, en la junta de guerra que
el sr. dn. Bernardo de Gálvez ... mandó celebrar.* 1p.
[Encloses 4 documents].

N. doc. 6 July 1778, Manchac. Juan de la Villebeuvre to
Bernardo de Gálvez (copy). English had plans to entice
the Choctaws, Chickasaws, and Cherokees to assist them in
an attack upon New Orleans. Although the Choctaws showed
up, the Cherokees and Chickasaws did not, fearing hostile
actions by the Americans. 3p.

N. doc. 8 July 1778, Pointe Coupée. Carlos de Grand-Pré
to Bernardo de Gálvez (copy). There is no news in Pointe
Coupée about the hostile intentions of the Choctaws, Chickasaws, and Cherokees. The English probably have other
plans with these tribes. 2p.

CUBA/2351 (CONT'D)

N. doc. 13 July 1778, Pointe Coupée. Carlos de Grand-Pré
to Bernardo de Gálvez (copy). There are various ways to
defend Spanish territory against the English plan to use
hostile Indians. 3p.

N. doc. 13 July 1778, Manchac. Juan de la Villebeuvre to
Bernardo de Gálvez (copy). Villebeuvre discusses preparations in case the Indians attack Spanish provinces. 2p.

Doc. 34 (no. 228 *reservada*). 16 Oct. 1779, New Orleans.
Bernardo de Gálvez to [Diego José Navarro?] (duplicate). It is
still not clear whether the Chickasaws, Choctaws, and Cherokees
plan to attack Spanish possessions. 8p.

Doc. 53. 29 June 1781, St. Louis. Francisco Cruzat to Pedro
Piernas. 8p. [Encloses 6 documents].

Doc. 53bis/a. [1781]. Talk from Governor in Georgia to the
Fat King, the Tallassee King, and [other Creeks]. Peace
will be coming soon with the defeat of the British. Chiefs
know that the Cherokees and many Creeks fought against the
Americans. Cherokees now regret their actions and have
been invited to discuss many issues with the Americans.
Creeks are also invited to discuss their problems since
the land ceded by the Cherokees to the Americans is
adjacent to Creek territory. 3p. *English*.

Doc. 68 (no. 192). 15 Apr. 1784, New Orleans. Esteban Miró
to el Conde de Gálvez. Miró attaches a Cherokee petition
seeking Spanish protection. Because of the petition's importance,
Miró will attend a Talapoose and Creek congress scheduled for May
in Pensacola. He will also attend the congress for the Choctaws,
Alibamos, and Chickasaws in June at Mobile. 10p. [Encloses 1
document].

Doc. 70. 16 Apr. 1784, Pensacola. Arturo O'Neill to Juan
Ventura Morales. O'Neill acknowledges the receipt of a list
enumerating supplies and gifts for the Creeks, Alibamos,
Cherokees, Sabanoques [Savannahs?], and Ochayas [Oakchoys?]
at the congress. 7p. [Enclosures to doc. 70a].

CUBA/2352 WEST FLORIDA: 1785-1791

N. fol. 29 Dec. 1792, New Orleans. Interrogation of David
McCleish [McClish?]. McCleish, a sailor, testified that he met
Bowles in Halifax when the Indian leader was there with two
Talapooses, two Cherokees, and one mestizo. In conversations
with Moses Price (a Cherokee mestizo) and Thomas Lewis (a
Talapoose mestizo), he learned that the British had not given
Bowles permission to set up a store among the Creeks. 11p.

N. fol. 20 Oct. 1785, Mexico. El Conde de Gálvez to Esteban
Miró (duplicate). Gálvez has received copies of McGillivray's
petition representing the Chickasaws and the Cherokees. This
is a good opportunity to bring both tribes under Spanish
protection. 4p. [Encloses 4 documents].

No. 125. 21 Dec. 1785, New Orleans. Esteban Miró to
Francisco Bouligny. Miró discusses McGillivray's memorial
representing the Chickasaws, Cherokees, and Talapooses.
5p.

N. fol. 20 Oct. 1785, Mexico. El Conde de Gálvez to Esteban
Miró (duplicate). Gálvez received Miró's letter describing
those Americans along the Cherokee and Cumberland Rivers who
are preparing boats to attack Spanish possessions. 2p.

N. fol. 12 May 1786, Little Tallassee. Alex. McGillivray to
Arturo O'Neill. Georgia claims not only the Creek's land
within their state but also all the land stretching to the
Mississippi. This includes Creek territory along the Chero-
kee R. and Muscle Shoals. Americans have tricked some
Cherokees into ceding land. 3p.

N. fol. 8 Nov. 1785, Little Tallassee. Alex. McGillivray to
Gov. O'Neill (copy). Indian traders among the Choctaws and
Chickasaws have solicited permission to settle above Mobile.
They plan to set up an American colony aided by vagabonds
from Cumberland. 3p.

N. fol. 1 May 1786, Little Tallassee. Alex. McGillivray to
Esteban Miró. [Same as AHN Estado/3887/doc. 7]. 2p.

N. fol. 10 July 1785, Little Tallassee. Translation of
petition from Alex. McGillivray protesting that the Americans
have no title to Creek, Talapoose, Chickasaw, and Cherokee
land. Americans have illegally established settlements, like
Cumberland, in Indian hunting grounds. Since Spain has sent
an envoy to negotiate borders with the Americans, McGillivray
insists the Indian land be respected. 6p.

N. fol. 29 Dec. 1791, New Orleans. Interrogation of David
McCleish [McClish?]. [Same as AGI Cuba/2352/n. fol.]. 8p.

No. 16. 4 Aug. 1785, Ft. Panmure at Natchez. Francisco
Bouligny to Esteban Miró. The settlements at Cumberland,
Cherokee, Chute, and Ky. can place 40,000 men under arms.
Much of this population comes from English army deserters.
13p.

No. 225. 14 Aug. 1785, New Orleans. Esteban Miró to el Conde
de Gálvez (duplicate). Indians have reported some 300 men
building boats along the Cherokee and Cumberland Rivers. These
boats are presumably designed to aid an attack against Spanish
territory. 7p.

No. 229. 5 Sept. 1785, New Orleans. [Esteban Miró to el Conde
de Gálvez] (abstract). 1p. [Encloses 3 documents].

No. 229. 5 Sept. 1785, New Orleans. Esteban Miró to el
Conde de Gálvez. Miró attaches McGillivray's petition
from the Creeks, Chickasaws, and Cherokees. 8p.

CUBA/2352 (CONT'D)

> No. 1. 24 July 1785, Pensacola. Alex. McGillivray
> to Gov. O'Neill. [Same as AHN Estado/3898/exp. 1/
> no. 55 *de preferencia*/encl. no. 1]. 3p.

> No. 2. 10 July 1785, [Little Tallassee]. Alex.
> McGillivray to Gov. Miró. [Same as AHN Estado/3898/
> exp. 1/no. 55 *de preferencia*/encl. no. 2]. 5p.

No. 311 *reservada*. 28 June 1786, New Orleans. Esteban Miró
to el Conde de Gálvez. [Same as AGI SD/2551/fol. 241]. 10p.
[Encloses 2 documents].

> No. 2. 8 Jan. 1786, Seneca. Benjamin Hawkins to [Alex.
> McGillivray]. [Translation of AGI Cuba/2360/n. fol.]. 6p.

No. 14. 4 May 1786, Pensacola. Arturo O'Neill to el Conde de
Gálvez. 3p. [Encloses 4 documents].

> No. 4. 19 Apr. 1786, Pensacola. Arturo O'Neill to Diego
> de Gardoqui (copy). The Creeks, Choctaws, Chickasaws,
> and some Cherokees have decided to resist the Americans
> invading their lands. 3p.

> N. fol. 1 May 1786, Little Tallassee. Alex. McGillivray
> to Stephen Miró. Creeks have decided to defend their land
> and one party left for Muscle Shoals. The party sent to
> Cumberland could not drive the Americans off that land
> because they were too numerous. Americans held a meeting
> of Indian nations in Cherokee territory last October and
> requested that the tribes cede land. 10p. *English*.

No. 17. 20 May 1786, Pensacola. Arturo O'Neill to el Conde
de Gálvez. McGillivray reports that several Cherokee and Creek
parties are patrolling the frontier in hopes of expelling all
Americans. The parties have patrolled the Oconee R. and Muscle
Shoals, a site illegally granted to Americans by a Chickasaw
chief. The Cherokees under Bloody Fellow are attacking Cumberland. 3p.

No. 18. 30 May 1786, Pensacola. Arturo O'Neill to el Conde de
Gálvez. 3p. [Encloses 2 documents].

> N. fol. 21 May 1786, Little Tallassee. Alex. McGillivray
> to Arthur O'Neill. Since the Creeks have not been able to
> remove the Americans peacefully from their hunting ground,
> the tribe must use force. Muscle Shoals, which belongs
> to the Creeks and not the Chickasaws, is one of the places
> that the Americans have settled. McGillivray will personal-
> ly visit the Cherokees to get their cooperation against the
> Americans. 3p. *English*.

No. 23. 11 Oct. 1786, Pensacola. Arturo O'Neill to el Conde
de Gálvez. Indian traders report that the Americans have
established a new site in Cumberland. 4p. [Encloses 1 docu-
ment].

   N. fol. 30 Oct. 1786, Little Tallassee. Alex. McGillivray
   to Gov. O'Neill. [Same as AGI Cuba/2360/n. fol.]. 2p.
   English.

No. 28. 16 Nov. 1786, Pensacola. Arturo O'Neill to el Conde
de Gálvez. Brig. Twiggs and Col. Clark have some 1500 militia
in Ga. ready to attack the Creeks. Martin, another American,
commands some 200 men whose mission is to prevent the Cherokees from aiding Creeks. 2p. [Encloses 2 documents].

   No. [74?]. 13 Oct. 1786, Pensacola. Arturo O'Neill to
   Esteban Miró. Indian traders report that Americans in
   Cumberland have begun negotiations with the Creeks. 11p.

N. fol. 4 Oct. 1787, Pensacola. Translation of a letter from
Alex. McGillivray reporting that two weeks ago a large Creek
party returned from attacking Cumberland. Most Cumberland
residents fled, seeking refuge in the mountains of Carolina
and Virginia. N. Carolina's governor has requested peace
between the Creeks and Cumberland. 6p.

N. fol. 1 Dec. 1786, Pensacola. Arturo O'Neill to Pedro
Favrot. Some 1,500 American soldiers have advanced against
the Creeks in Ga. and nearly 200 more under Martin have
fortified themselves in Cherokee territory. Indians have made
peace with Cumberland and have returned to protect their
villages against the Americans. 5p.

N. fol. 3 Jan. 1788, Havana. José de Ezpeleta to Esteban
Miró. 1p. [Encloses 3 documents].

   N. fol. 12 Nov. 1787, New York. Diego de Gardoqui to José
   de Ezpeleta (copy). Franklin, a new country in S. Carolina
   [sic], has revolted against the government. 4p.

   N. fol. 24 Sept. 1787, Charleston. John Sullivan to Maj.
   Wm. Brown. [Translation of AGI Cuba/1409/n. fol.]. 2p.

No. 38 *reservada*. 20 May 1789, New Orleans. Esteban Miró to
Antonio Valdés. 6p. [Encloses 4 documents].

   No. 1. 23 Apr. 1789, Little Tallassee. Alex. McGillivray
   to Vicente Folch (translation). Indians fear that
   residents in Cumberland plan to settle on their land. 5p.

No. 21 *reservada*. 8 Apr. 1791, New Orleans. [Esteban Miró] to
Luis de las Casas. 2p. [Encloses 3 documents].

   No. 1. 15 Jan. 1791, Harrodsburg, Kentucky. Translation
   of letter from [Doctor O'Fallon] stating he has just
   visited Franklin and Cumberland where many people wish
   to emigrate. 37p.

CUBA/2352 (CONT'D)

    No. 2. 18 Feb. 1791, Crab Orchard, Kentucky. James
O'Fallon to Esteban Miró (translation). O'Fallon discusses
es land around Yazoo and the company that he represents.
O'Fallon plans to keep his troops and followers in Cumberland or Franklin until following fall. The western states
will become independent from the United States and the
eastern states will not be able to prevent it. 8p.

N. fol. 10 July 1785, Little Tallassee. Alex. McGillivray to
[Miró]. [Same as AHN Estado/3898/exp. 1/no. 55 *de preferencia/*
encl. no. 2]. 6p.

No. 3. 11 Jan. 1786, Seneca. Benjamin Hawkins to Alex.
McGillivray. [Translation of AGI Cuba/2360/n. fol.]. 4p.

N. fol. 25 Mar. 1791, London. *Memorial de Guillermo Augusto
Bowles, director de la nación Talapuche*. In the name of the
Creeks and Cherokees, Bowles petitions the Spanish King.
Creeks and Cherokees are the original inhabitants of the land
they live on. These two tribes have recently united and Bowles
is their director. 14p.

CUBA/2353   WEST FLORIDA: 1792-1793

    Fol. 5 (no. 30). 24 Nov. 1792, St. Marks. Francisco Montreuil
to Arturo O'Neill. Panton, Leslie and Co. lack sufficient
funds to supply treaty Indians such as the Choctaws, Chickasaws,
and Cherokees. 8p. [Enclosures to fol. 10b].

Fol. 56. 30 Aug. 1793, Boukfouka. Letter to Manuel Gayoso
de Lemos stating that the Cherokees wish to delay the meeting
since they fear an American attack. 5p. *French*.

Fol. 111 (no. 12). 24 Mar. 1792, Natchez. Manuel Gayoso de
Lemos to el Barón de Carondelet. [Same as fol. 481]. 6p.

Fol. 118 (no. 27). 2 Apr. 1792, Natchez. Manuel Gayoso de
Lemos to el Barón de Carondelet. Spain must be aware of American
efforts to win over the Indians. Americans signed a treaty in
1790 with the Creeks and have been working to win over the
Cherokees. This would leave Spain with only the Choctaws as
allies. 28p.

Fol. 259 (no. 176). 27 Sept. 1792, Natchez. Manuel Gayoso de
Lemos to el Barón de Carondelet. Americans in Cumberland have
given Indians abundant gifts. 14p.

Fol. 283 (no. 189). 10 Nov. 1792, Natchez. Manuel Gayoso de
Lemos to el Barón de Carondelet. The possibility of Creek
raids in Natchez against Americans must be eliminated. Except
for a few people from Cumberland, all people in Natchez are
Spanish vassals. 28p.

Fol. 303 (no. 1). 11 Apr. 1793, Natchez. Manuel Gayoso de
Lemos to el Barón de Carondelet. Gayoso reports on the Indian
assembly at Nogales and attaches a letter sent to Bloody
Fellow, the Cherokee representative. Gayoso asks for approval
of his efforts to assemble the Choctaw, Chickasaw, Cherokee,
and northern tribal representatives. 13p.

Fol. 310 (no. 2). 10 May 1793, Natchez. Manuel Gayoso de Lemos
to el Barón de Carondelet. Miss. boats can stop the Americans
if they try a river invasion from Ky. and Cumberland. 18p.

Fol. 319 (no. 3). 8 June 1793, Natchez. Manuel Gayoso de Lemos
to el Barón de Carondelet. Gayoso could not send a letter to
Bloody Fellow earlier because no one wished to risk a trip to
the Cherokees. 44p.

Fol. 372 (no. 8). 19 Aug. 1793, Natchez. Manuel Gayoso de
Lemos to el Barón de Carondelet. Mad Dog, a Creek leader, has
called for a junta to approve Carondelet's efforts to hold a
meeting of the Creeks, Cherokees, Choctaws, and Chickasaws.
Choctaw leaders have expressed some reluctance to meet with
the Creeks and Cherokees because both nations steal horses,
even from their allies. 50p.

Fol. 400 (no. 10). [1793], [Natchez]. [Manuel Gayoso de Lemos]
to el Barón de Carondelet. Gayoso acknowledges receipt of
recent news about the Americans, Cherokees, and Creeks. Creeks
and Cherokees have asked that the assembly be delayed because
they expect an American attack. 12p.

Fol. 406 (no. 11). 18 Oct. 1793, Nogales. [Manuel Gayoso de
Lemos] to el Barón de Carondelet. Since the Cherokees are not
present, the best location for the future distribution of their
gifts is uncertain. 14p.

Fol. 413 (no. 12). 5 Dec. 1793, Natchez. [Manuel Gayoso de
Lemos] to el Barón de Carondelet. Cauitamico (Little Turkey)
is in Nogales with three other Cherokees. Since the Creeks
represented the Cherokees at the treaty, Gayoso proposed to
the visiting Cherokees that they ratify the part of the treaty
affecting their tribe, which they did. A large number of
Cherokees will proceed to New Orleans. 7p.

Fol. 419 (no. 12). 6 Dec. 1793, Natchez. [Manuel Gayoso de
Lemos] to el Barón de Carondelet. At the Indian assembly in
Nogales, the Creeks held the Cherokee proxy. Cherokees
petitioned protection from Spain. Cherokees want their annual
gifts to be distributed in Pensacola. 62p.

Fol. 481 (no. 12). 24 Mar. 1794, Natchez. [Manuel Gayoso de
Lemos] to el Barón de Carondelet. Choctaws, Chickasaws,
Talapooses, Cherokees, and other tribes are planning to sign
a treaty with the Americans at the great bend in the Tennessee
River. 4p. [Encloses to fol. 498b].

CUBA/2353 (CONT'D)

Fol. 484 (no. 2). 13 Mar. 1792, Natchez. *Instrucciones* from Manuel Gayoso de Lemos to Esteban Minor. Minor should tell the Choctaws that Spain will protect them and not allow the tribe to lose its possessions as other Indians have to Cumberland, Franklin, and Kentucky. 15p.

Fol. 491 (no. 3). 2 Mar. 1792, Natchez. Manuel Gayoso de Lemos to the King of the Chickasaw Nation. Gayoso is a friend of all Indians and asks that the Chickasaws remain united with the Choctaws, Talapooses, Cherokees, and other neighboring tribes. 3p.

Fol. 492 (no. 4). *Instrucciones* from [Gayoso? to Minor?] Americans are planning to sign a treaty with the Choctaws, Chickasaws, Talapooses, Cherokees, and other tribes. [Gayoso?] wants to be kept informed about the matter. 6p.

Fol. 495 (no. 3). 9 Aug. 1793, Natchez. Manuel Gayoso de Lemos to Payamataha and Yteleghana, chiefs of the Choctaws (copy). Gayoso is surprised that the chiefs are now at the Yazoo since the meeting is scheduled for later. Officials postponed the meeting because the Creeks and Cherokees could not attend earlier. 3p. *English.*

Fol. 508. 5 July 1792, Natchez. Manuel Gayoso de Lemos. *Estado político de la provincia de la Luisiana.* Ky., Cumberland, and Franklin threaten Spanish interests. Indian tribes play an important role in the competition between the United States and Spain. 8p.

Fol. 513 (no. 1). 7 Apr. 1793, Natchez. Instructions from Manuel Gayoso to John Turnbull (copy). Government will attempt to hold a meeting of the Cherokees, Chickasaws, Choctaws, and Creeks at the ball ground in Yazoo. Turnbull should inform the tribes about this meeting. Gayoso has sent Turnbull a number of letters for Indian leaders, including Bloody Fellow. 8p. *English.*

Fol. 517 (no. 21). 7 Apr. 1793, Natchez. Manuel Gayoso de Lemos to Tascaotupa, King of the Chickasaws (copy). There will be a meeting of the tribes near the end of June at the ball ground. It will be attended by the Chickasaws, Choctaws, Creeks, and Cherokees. 2p. *English.*

Fol. 522 (no. 7). 7 Apr. 1793, Natchez. Manuel Gayoso de Lemos to Bloody Fellow (copy). Cherokees, Choctaws, Creeks, and Chickasaws will meet at the ball ground at the mouth of the Yazoo. Gayoso asks Bloody Fellow to bring as many Cherokees and representatives as possible from the northern tribes. Bloody Fellow should also bring an interpreter who speaks either Spanish, French, or English. Bloody Fellow's son is well in New Orleans. 2p. *English.*

Fol. 530 (no. 3). 21 Mar. 1792, Natchez. Manuel Gayoso de
Lemos to Tascahetuca, King of the Chickasaws. If the Choctaws,
Chickasaws, Talapooses, and Cherokees can stay united under
Spanish protection, there will be no need to fear the Americans.
3p. [Enclosures to fol. 532].

> Fol. 532. 21 Mar. 1792, Natchez. [Manuel Gayoso de Lemos
> to Tascahetuca]. [English version of fol. 530]. 2p.

Fol. 542 (no. 1). 31 July 1792, Natchez. Manuel Gayoso de
Lemos to Juan de la Villebeuvre (copy). Spain's objective is
to preserve peace with the Indian nations that surround Louisiana,
particularly those that are under Spanish jurisdiction like the
Creeks, Talapooses, Alibamos, Choctaws, and Chickasaws. The
Americans are doing everything they can to win over the
Indians, including calling a meeting soon at Cumberland to sign
treaties with the various Indian nations. 14p.

Fol. 552 (no. 3). 28 Sept. 1792, Natchez. Manuel Gayoso de
Lemos to Juan de la Villebeuvre (copy). Villebeuvre can demonstrate that the Americans do want Indian land. The Indians
can be told that Spain has given and will continue to give
many more gifts than the tribes have been receiving at Cumberland. Moreover, the Indians will not have to go so far to
receive them. 9p.

Fol. 557 (no. 4). 23 July 1792, Choctaw Nation. Benjamin James
to [Manuel Gayoso de Lemos]. Creeks have petitioned the Choctaws
for permission to pass through their territory to kill Americans.
James does not know whether the Choctaws will grant permission,
but the Creeks would probably attack the Americans around
Natchez. Some Choctaws have gone to Cumberland. 2p. *English*.

Fol. 582 (no. 4). 23 July 1793, Nogales. Manuel Gayoso de
Lemos to Juan de la Villebeuvre (copy). Gayoso does not object
to Indian desire to postpone the assembly since the season will
be more favorable, but officials cannot change the site just
because the Creeks think it is too far. The Cherokees have to
travel a long distance also. 8p.

Fol. 597 (no. 2). 13 Mar. 1792, Natchez. [Manuel Gayoso de
Lemos]. *Instrucciones para el Teniente Minor*. Spain always
recommends peace for the Choctaws, but the tribe should be very
careful not to cede land to people who will usurp tribal territory as has happened in Ky., Cumberland, and Franklin. 15p.

Fol. 605 (no. 4). 24 Mar. 1792, Natchez. [Manuel Gayoso de
Lemos] to Esteban Minor. Gayoso has received Minor's news
about the American intentions to celebrate a treaty with the
Choctaws, Chickasaw, Talapooses, Cherokees, and others at the
bend in the Tennessee River. Minor should keep [Gayoso] posted.
5p.

Fol. 665. 28 Oct. 1793, Nogales. Manuel Gayoso de Lemos et al.
Treaty of Nogales. [Same as AGI SD/2563/fol. 8]. 8p.

CUBA/2353 (CONT'D)

Fol. 673. 26 Feb. 1793, New Orleans. El Barón de Carondelet.
*Puntos sobre los quales se deberá tratar en el congreso de los
indios.* Creeks, Cherokees, Choctaws, and Chickasaws should be
brought together in a defensive alliance under Spain's protection. Indians must respect the borders between the Cherokees
and the United States negotiated in 1785. 6p.

Fol. 680. 16 Feb. 1794, Nogales. *Diario* from Juan Barno y
Ferrusola describing his trip from Natchez to New Madrid and
reporting the arrival of men from Cumberland in New Madrid.
42p.

Fol. 724 (no. 10 *reservada*). 11 June 1793, New Orleans. [El
Barón de Carondelet] to el Duque de Alcudia. [Same as AHN
Estado/3898/exp. 5/no. 10 *reservada*]. 2p. [Enclosures to fol.
727].

> Fol. 725 (no. 1 *reservada*). 28 Feb. 1793, New Orleans.
> El Barón de Carondelet to el Duque de Alcudia. [Copy of
> AHN Estado/3898/exp. 5/no. 1]. 5p.

Fol. 730. 5 Dec. 1793, New Orleans. El Barón de Carondelet to
el Duque de Alcudia. Carondelet forwards the treaty with the
Creeks, Cherokees, Choctaws, and Chickasaws at Nogales. This
alliance gives Spain 18,000 warriors to use against the United
States. It is almost the only means Spain has to contain states
like Ky. and Vermont. The Americans will almost surely object
to placing the Cherokees under Spanish protection, but the
Cherokee and Chickasaw territory is a perfect shield to keep
the Americans away from Spanish possessions. 4p.

Fol. 741 (no. 3). 18 Apr. 1793, New Orleans. El Barón de
Carondelet. *Relación del estado de las plazas, fuertes y
puestos de ... Luisiana y Florida Occidental.* New Madrid needs
to be fortified to help curtail Cumberland. 15p.

Fol. 749. *Palabra del Barón de Carondelet a los Cheroquis.*
1p. [Enclosures to fol. 756b].

> Fol. 752. 24 Nov. 1792, New Orleans. Talk from el Barón
> de Carondelet to Chiefs, Warriors, and the rest of the
> Cherokee Nation. Carondelet has listened with pleasure to
> the Breath, Charles of Chickamaugua, and Bloody Fellow.
> The King of Spain will be informed of the tribe's problems
> and will do his best to insure peace between the tribe and
> the Americans. The King will try to acquire the hunting
> grounds that the Cherokees need from the Americans. 2p.

> Fol. 756. 27 May 1793, New Orleans. Talk to the Chiefs,
> Headmen, and Warriors of the Cherokee Nation reassuring
> them that the King of Spain will help the Cherokees. He
> will make the United States know the just claim of the
> war-like Cherokees. The Creeks will be advised that the
> Cherokees wish to live in peace with the Americans and
> that the Creeks should not pass through their land to
> raid Cumberland. 2p. *English.*

Fol. 762. 20 Nov. 1792, New Orleans. *Indice de la carta reservada que ... remite el Barón de Carondelet [al exmo sr. dn. Luis de las Casas].* 1p. [Enclosures to fol. 765].

> Fol. 763 (no. 57 *reservada*). 20 Nov. 1792, New Orleans. [El Barón de Carondelet to Luis de las Casas]. Cherokees led by Bloody Fellow are in New Orleans. They have petitioned Spain to garrison two old French forts (Tombigbee and Muscle Shoals). Spain would thus dominate both sides of the Miss. R. up to the Ohio R. and would be able to contain the Americans in the West. Spain must move rapidly to prevent the Americans from destroying the Cherokees. 5p.

Fol. 766. 9 Jan. 1793, New Orleans. *Indice de las cartas reservadas que ... dirige el Barón de Carondelet [al exmo sr. dn. Luis de las Casas].* 1 p. [Enclosures to fol. 768].

> Fol. 767 (no. 62 *reservada*). 9 Jan. 1793, New Orleans. [El Barón de Carondelet] to Luis de las Casas. [Carondelet] forwards information concerning the American moves to build establishments at Barrancas de Margot and Muscle Shoals. 1p.

Fol. 769 (no. 66). 24 Jan. 1793, New Orleans. [El Barón de Carondelet] to Luis de las Casas. A possible French invasion increases the likelihood that the Americans will be able to occupy Muscle Shoals. Officials are attempting to prevent the Chickasaws from signing a treaty in Cumberland with the Americans that would be contrary to tribal and Spanish interests. The Chickasaws' future rests upon their alliance with the Creeks, Choctaws, and Cherokees. 3p. [Enclosures to fol. 770b].

Fol. 771 (no. 69 *reservada*). 3 Mar. 1793, New Orleans. El Barón de Carondelet to Luis de las Casas. Americans will take advantage of the Creek and Chickasaw war to realize their hopes of building a fort at Muscle Shoals and Ecores à Margot. Chickasaws will certainly ask for aid from Cumberland if the Creeks begin to win. 5p.

Fol. 777 (no. 97). 5 Dec. 1793, New Orleans. [El Barón de Carondelet] to Luis de las Casas. Carondelet sends a copy of the treaty with the Creeks, Cherokees, Choctaws, and Chickasaws. 1p. [Enclosures to fol. 778].

Fol. 789 (no. 1). 11 Apr. 1792, New Orleans. Translated testimony from Wm. Cunningham reporting some conversations with Wm. Bowles. Bowles received no aid in Canada, only a minor offer of arms and munitions to supplement what Bowles planned to get from residents in Ky. and Cumberland. The Americans concluded a treaty with the Cherokees at a time when Cunningham was a teacher in Franklin. 3p.

Fol. 795 (no. 19). 4 Apr. 1792. Letter to el Conde de Floridablanca stating that the Americans will be faced with a difficult situation if they make war upon the Creeks. The Americans would be even worse off if Spain, the Cherokees, Choctaws, and Chickasaws aid the Creeks. 2p.

CUBA/2353 (CONT'D)

Fol. 796 (no. 18 *reservada*). 4 Apr. 1792, New Orleans. Letter to el Conde de Floridablanca stating that the second declaration of Wm. Cunningham, Bowles's so-called Major General, makes it obvious that some sort of secret agreement against Louisiana exists among Lord Dunmore (Gov. of Providence), Gen. Clark of Ga., Gov. Wm. Blount, Col. Ross of Washington County (Virginia), the lawyers Cock (Franklin) and Hancock (Boltuto County), the surveyor John, the adventurer Bowles, the merchant Miler [Miller] of Providence, and some British firms. 5p.

Fol. 799. 22 May 1792, New Orleans. *Indice de la carta reservada que ... remite el Barón de Carondelet [al Conde de Floridablanca].* 1p. [Enclosures to fol. 801].

    Fol. 800 (no. 28 *reservada*). 22 May 1792, New Orleans. [El Barón de Carondelet] to el Conde de Floridablanca. [Same as AHN Estado/3898/exp. 5/no. 28 *reservada*]. 2p.

Fol. 801. 5 Mar. 1793, New Orleans. El Barón de Carondelet to Manuel Gayoso de Lemos. The King will be well-served by preventing the war between the Creeks and Chickasaws formented by Gov. Blount. Spain will also benefit by taking advantage of the spring meeting between the Creeks, Cherokees, Choctaws, Chickasaws, and Northern tribes to establish a permanent Indian congress. 5p. [Enclosures to fol. 806].

Fol. 808. 17 June 1793, New Orleans. Letter insisting that the recipient should do everything possible to aid Bloody Fellow and the other Cherokees to attend the assembly. This tribe is ready to break with the United States and place itself under Spanish protection. Since the Americans concluded the treaty of Hopewell without consulting the rest of the Chickasaws, Choctaws, or Spain, officials can sign a treaty with the Cherokees that contradicts the agreement that Blount made with the Cherokees. The Americans are so upset about the possibility of a treaty between the Cherokees and Spaniards that Gov. Blount has offered $500 for McDonald's head. 2p.

Fol. 817. 11 July 1793, New Orleans. El Barón de Carondelet to Manuel Gayoso de Lemos. Creeks are very interested in allying with the Cherokees, Choctaws, and Chickasaws. 5p.

Fol. 822. 31 Aug. 1793, New Orleans. Letter to Manuel Gayoso de Lemos instructing him not to wait for the Cherokees if they fail to arrive after the other nations show up. Nevertheless, Gayoso should request that the other tribes help the Cherokees keep their land. If the Americans destroy the Cherokees and Creeks, it is unlikely that the Chickasaws could survive very long. 12p. [Enclosures to fol. 833].

Fol. 834. 15 Aug. 1793, New Orleans. El Barón de Carondelet to Manuel Gayoso de Lemos. Louisiana has little to fear from the Americans at the moment. The residents of Cumberland are the only ones Spain needs to watch, and they can be controlled through their fear of the Creeks and Cherokees. 13p.

Fol. 856. 29 May 1793. Letter to John McDonald advising him
how the Cherokees should conduct themselves with the Americans.
Tribe should remain at peace with Americans, but the Cherokees
should not permit the Americans to take territory or to establish
a post at Muscle Shoals and Ecores à Margot. These posts would
separate the tribe from their neighbors. McDonald should assure
Bloody Fellow that his son is healthy. 1p. [Enclosures to
fol. 858b].

Fol. 856b. 27 May 1793, New Orleans. *Palabra* (talk) to
the Cherokees reporting that the tribe's messages have
been sent to the King. The King will protect and help the
Cherokees in their complaints against the Americans.
Spanish government will ask the Creeks not to cross Cherokee land to attack Cumberland. 2p.

Fol. 858. 29 May 1793, New Orleans. Letter to Thomas
[sic] McDonald. [English version of fol. 856]. 2p.

Fol. 861 (no. 4). 30 Mar. 1792. [El Barón de Carondelet] to
Pedro Olivier. Olivier should persuade the Creeks about the
necessity of an alliance with the Cherokees, Choctaws, and
Chickasaws under Spanish protection to save their lands. He
should also convince the Creeks and Cherokees to attend the
Indian congress sponsored by Spain rather than one proposed
by Americans at Muscle Shoals. 2p.

Fol. 865 (no. 1). 31 Mar. 1792, New Orleans. Copy of letter
to Arturo O'Neill stating that Pedro Olivier has been instructed
to impede the implementation of treaty between the Creeks and
the United States. If the Creeks join with the Americans, it
will force the Cherokees to do the same. It is absolutely
vital that the American Indian congress scheduled for Muscle
Shoals be stopped. 2p.

Fol. 867. 6 Aug. 1793, New Orleans. El Barón de Carondelet to
Thomas Portell (*reservada*). Spain opposes Cumberland's efforts
to send arms to Ecores à Margot. Consequently, Spanish officials
will stop American boats shipping weapons to that area and to
the Chickasaws. If the inhabitants of Cumberland threaten New
Madrid, Spanish commanders have been ordered to use the Cherokees and Creeks against Cumberland. Portell must keep the good
graces of Lorimier and his Cherokees since they are useful to
Spain. 7p.

Fol. 871. 17 Sept. 1793, New Orleans. El Barón de Carondelet
to Juan de la Villebeuvre. The sole hope for the Four Indian
Nation's survival is to remain united. The Cherokees are now
in open war and Carondelet fears that they might be destroyed
before the King can aid them. Bloody Fellow will be in New
Orleans in October. 3p. [Enclosures to fol. 876].

Fol. 903 (no. 11). 22 Mar. 1793, New Orleans. Letter to el
Conde de Floridablanca reporting that Bowles's desire for a
defensive alliance among the Creeks, Cherokees, Choctaws, and

CUBA/2353 (CONT'D)

Chickasaws under Spanish protection is Spain's wish also. It appears that the Cherokees have joined the Creeks to impede American progress between the Miss. and the Apalachicola Rivers. 13p.

Fol. 912. 21 May 1793, Philadelphia. Mr. Jefferson to José de Jaudenes and José Ignacio de Viar (copy). 2p. *English.* [Enclosures to fol. 921b].

> Fol. 913. 25 May 1793, Philadelphia. José Jaudenes and José Ignacio de Viar to Mr. Jefferson (copy). Jefferson will see from the attached materials that Carondelet has urged the Indians to practice peace with the United States. This is certainly different from what the Americans at Cumberland under Gov. Blount have been attempting to do with the tribes. 3p.

> Fol. 915. 5 June 1793, Philadelphia. Mr. Jefferson to José Ignacio de Viar (translation). The American government assures Spain that the United States has always wanted the tribes to live in peace with Spain. Any efforts to turn the Cherokees against Spain was done without American knowledge or approval. 2p.

> Fol. 916. 12 June 1793, Philadelphia. José de Jaudenes and José Ignacio de Viar to Thomas Jefferson. Spanish government wishes to emphasize that American representatives have incited the Indians against Spain. Gov. Blount invited the Indians to Cumberland and urged them to be hostile towards the Spanish possessions. 3p.

CUBA/2354   WEST FLORIDA: 1794-1798

Fol. 1 (no. 2). 2 Oct. 1794, St. Marks. Diego de Vegas to James Burges. The Cherokees and Cowetas ambushed in the mountains a group of Americans, killing four and capturing 30 horses, 30 saddles, and 40 rifles. 5p.

Fol. 4 (no. 1). 18 Sept. 1794, [New Orleans?]. John Galphin to James Burges (translation). The Creeks, Choctaws, Chickasaws, and Cherokees plan to unite and attack the Americans who want to strip the Indians of their rights. 4p.

Fol. 24. 20 Mar. 1794, Cloaly. [Louis de] Milfort to el Barón de Carondelet (translation). A group of 130 Cherokees arrived in Cloaly to inform the Creeks about the Cherokee's intention. Once there, however, they petitioned Seagrove, the American representative, for gifts. Seagrove and Milfort addressed the assembled Indians. 12p.

Fol. 56 (no. 588). 8 Jan. 1795, Natchez. Letter from Manuel Gayoso de Lemos stating that the Chickasaws were warned about the unfortunate consequences if the Americans build a fort at Muscle Shoals. Bloody Fellow has discovered a cachet of arms [destined for Chickasaws?]. 26p.

CUBA/2354 (CONT'D)

Fol. 69 (no. 15 *reservada*). 12 Aug. 1795, San Fernando de las Barrancas. Manuel Gayoso de Lemos to el Barón de Carondelet. Gayoso reminds Carondelet that he was told to build forts in Indian territory after learning that Ga. had sold large chunks of land belonging to the Chickasaws, Choctaws, Cherokees, and Creeks. These forts were to keep land speculators from occupying their purchases. 21p.

Fol. 113 (no. 1 *reservada*). 19 Sept. 1794, Natchez. Letter to el Duque de Alcudia protesting the order to encourage the Chickasaws to attack Ft. Massac. If Ky. residents ever believe that Spain is responsible for the Chickasaw, Creek, and Cherokee hostilities in their area, they will present some very difficult problems for the Spanish government. 16p.

Fol. 121. 31 Mar. 1795, Natchez. Letter indicating that Ga. has recently sold all the land belonging to the Chickasaws, Choctaws, and a good part of the land belonging to the Creeks and Cherokees. They have even sold land that belongs to Spain. 17p.

Fol. 192. Panton, Leslie and Company to el Barón de Carondelet. The company reports on American efforts to win over frontier tribes and difficulties that Panton, Leslie and Company have had in continuing the Indian trade. The government should prohibit all commercial rivals of the company from trading with the Choctaws, Chickasaws, Creeks, and Cherokees. 9p.

Fol. 228. Daniel McGillivray to el Barón de Carondelet (translation). The Americans have asked the Hickory Ground Creeks to return Col. Fitzworth's daughter and slave captured by the tribe in Cumberland. 5p.

Fol. 231. 20 June 1795, St. Augustine. Bartolomé Morales to Diego de Vegas (copy). Morales discusses the need to watch the frontier. Seagrove, the American commissioner, talked to the Creeks and spread many falsehoods against Spain. A reply to Seagrove's talk should be sent to Carondelet, Enrique White, Luis Villiers, Juan de la Villebeuvre, Benjamin Fooy, and John McDonald. 4p. [Enclosures to fol. 234b].

Fol. 279. 9 Apr. 1794, New Orleans. El Barón de Carondelet to el Duque de la Alcudia (copy). [Copy of AHN Estado/3899/exp. 1, no. 31 *reservada*]. 6p.

Fol. 282. 1 Dec. 1794, New Orleans. *Indice de la carta reservada que ... [remite el Barón de Carondelet] al exmo sr. Duque de la Alcudia.* 1p. [Enclosures to 287b].

> Fol. 283 (no. 48 *reservada*). 1 Dec. 1794, New Orleans. [El Barón de Carondelet] to el Duque de la Alcudia. [Carondelet] forwards a map of La. and West Fla. and a report. The map is the most precise one to date of the region, showing the political realities of the area. 3p.

CUBA/2354 (CONT'D)

Fol. 285. 4 Mar. 1795, New Orleans. Relación from el Barón de Carondelet to el Duque de la Alcudia (copy). The consequences for Spain are unpleasant if the Americans seize all the Indian land east of the Mississippi. Such a seizure would result in the migration of 30,000 Indians to Spanish territory west of the river, a situation that has already happened with some Shawnees and Cherokees. 6p.

Fol. 288. 10 June 1795, New Orleans. Indice de la representación reservada ... [que remite el Barón de Carondelet] al exmo sr. Duque de la Alcudia. 1p. [Enclosures to fol. 290].

Fol. 289 (no. 53 reservada). 10 June 1795, New Orleans. [El Barón de Carondelet] to el Duque de la Alcudia. Since the Americans have fortified Muscle Shoals and planned to do the same at Barrancas à Margot, Carondelet sent troops to prevent the occupation of Barrancas à Margot. Brig. Robertson in Cumberland has initiated contact with the Choctaws in an attempt to win them over to the Americans. 3p.

Fol. 291 (no. 56 reservada). 12 July 1795, New Orleans. El Barón de Carondelet to el Duque de la Alcudia. Carondelet forwards information concerning Barrancas à Margot, which the Chickasaws have ceded to Spain. The inhabitants of Cumberland still are attempting to win over the Chickasaws under the pretext of aiding them against the Talapooses. 2p. [Enclosures to fol. 293].

Fol. 368 (no. 126 reservada). 30 Oct. 1794, New Orleans. El Barón de Carondelet to Luis de las Casas. Carondelet attaches a letter from John McDonald, who is the Spanish commissioner among the Cherokees. 4p.

Fol. 340 (no. 129). 24 Nov. 1794, New Orleans. Report from el Barón de Carondelet to Luis de las Casas. Americans can build their establishments almost overnight, as they did eight years ago at Cumberland. Spanish defense of Louisiana against the Americans relies heavily upon the Choctaws, Chickasaws, Creeks, and Cherokees. The Cherokees, Shawnees, Abnakis, and the Osages are also important in the defense of Spanish posts such as St. Louis and New Madrid. 95p.

Fol. 393 (no. 133 reservada). 30 Mar. 1795, New Orleans. El Barón de Carondelet to Luis de las Casas. Americans have encouraged the war between the Chickasaws and Talapooses and have secured the Chickasaws' approval to build a fort at Muscle Shoals. 8p.

Fol. 397 (no. 134 reservada). 1 May 1795, New Orelans. El Barón de Carondelet to Luis de las Casas. Americans have begun building a fort at Muscle Shoals with Chickasaw approval. 10p.

CUBA 2354 (CONT'D)

Fol. 415. 18 Mar. 1795, New Orleans. Letter to Manuel Gayoso de Lemos stating that the Cherokees, Creeks, Chickasaws, and Choctaws must remain united and at peace with one another. 4p.

Fol. 485. 20 Sept. 1794, Lower Cherokees. John McDonald to el Barón de Carondelet. [Same as AGI SD/2564/fol. 77]. 4p.

Fol. 499 (no. 2). 10 Jan. 1795, Georgia. *Actos del estado de Georgia celebrados en Augusta.* Lists bills passed by Ga. assembly detailing limits and amounts of land sold in the West. Some land belonged to the Cherokees. 21p.

Fol. 510. 18 Mar. 1795, New Orleans. Andrés López Armesto. *Extracto de las actas del estado de Georgia celebrados en Augusta.* Document describes limits and amount of land sold by Ga. in the West. Some land belonged to the Cherokees. 3p.

CUBA/2355   WEST FLORIDA: 1799-1803

Fol. 163. 9 Nov. 1799, Coweta. Ja[mes] Durouzeaux to Vicente Folch (copy). Durouzeaux discusses Bowles's proclamation ordering Spanish and American officials to leave Indian territory. Bowles must be stopped before he gets too far into Indian territory where he will receive a great deal of support. Bowles might soon reach Cherokee territory, where he can expect ample help. 3p.

Fol. 175b. 18 Apr. 1793. *Parafo de una carta [escrita al Carondelet].* The war between the Chickasaws and Creeks will not detour Spanish attempts to hold an Indian assembly. There is no doubt that Gov. Blount supports the Chickasaws because the Creeks have been a thorn in the side of Cumberland for some time. Yet it would be playing into the hands of the Americans to send the Creeks and Cherokees against the Chickasaws. 1p.

Fol. 261. 1 May 1803, Pensacola. *Ynstrucciones a que deve ceñirse ... dn. Esteban Folch.* Folch is instructed on how to obtain Bowles's removal from Spanish territory. One method would be to convince the Creek assembly that all Indians oppose what Bowles is trying to do. 11p. [Enclosures to fol. 271].

Fol. 288. 4 Nov. 1799, Coweta Tallahassee. Report from Tushimnue[?] Hays and Robert Walton to Agent of Indian Affairs (extract). Several Creek thieves have been punished, but a few fled to the Cherokees. 2p. *English.*

Fol. 302. 31 Dec. 1799, Wekiva, Head Quarters. Copy of proclamation from Wm. Bowles. 2p. *English.* [Enclosures to fol. 323b].

Fol. 304. 31 Oct. 1799, Wekiva, Head Quarters. Letter from [Wm. Bowles] discussing the Treaty of Ft. Stanwix (Nov. 1768) and Indian territory, including Cherokee land. 16p.

CUBA/2355 (CONT'D)

Fol. 320. 1 Oct. 1799, Wekiva, Head Quarters. Letter from Wm. Bowles stating that in Treaty of Ft. Stanwix (Nov. 1768) the Six Nations claimed territory to the Cherokee R. and ceded that land to Great Britain. Crown agreed that no land would be ceded beyond the treaty boundaries. Now the United States and Spain are violating this old agreement by granting lands that belong to the Six Nations, Cherokees, Chickasaws, Choctaws, and the Muskogees. 8p. *English.*

Fol. 516 (no. 8 *reservada*). 8 Oct. 1800, New Orleans. El Marqués de Casa-Calvo to Mariano Luis de Urquijo. Panton has suffered financial losses in his Indian trade. Except for some perverse Seminoles, all of Spain's Indian allies (Talapooses, Choctaws, Chickasaws, and Cherokees) are now within American territory. Cherokee trade with Panton is almost nonexistent. 42p. [Enclosures to fol. 578].

Fol. 562 (no. 2). [New Orleans?]. Vicente Folch. *Reflexiones producidas de resultas de la retrocesión de la ... Luisiana [a los Estados Unidos de América]* (triplicate). Among the defensive measures Spain should take against the United States is the encouragement of tribes west of the Miss. R. (such as the Cherokees, Creeks, Choctaws, and Chickasaws who hate the Americans because they forced them to leave their homelands) to serve as a barrier against further American expansion. 33p.

CUBA/2360   SPANISH LOUISIANA: 1783-1786

N. fol. 1784, Mobile. *Original del congreso celebrado en la Mobila con la nación chicacha.* 1p. [Encloses 5 documents].

N. fol. [1784?]. Address to Indians discussing peace with the Cherokees. 21p.

N. fol. 8 Nov. 1785, Little Tallassee. Alex. McGillivray to Gov. O'Neill (copy). McGillivray notices that the Americans wish to meet with the Creeks. He has heard that the Choctaws or Chickasaw traders have received permission to establish themselves above Mobile. These traders plan to introduce American control, aided by seditious settlers from Natchez and vagabonds from Cumberland. 3p.

N. fol. 8 Jan. 1786, Seneca. Benjamin Hawkins to Alex. McGillivray. Some 918 Cherokees met Hawkins in Seneca and signed a treaty. The Cherokee treaty became the basis for a similar agreement with the Choctaws. 4p. *English.*

N. fol. 11 Jan. 1786, Seneca. Benjamin Hawkins to Alex. McGillivray. Hawkins reports on the progress of the commission to Southern Indians and on Creek hostility in Cumberland. The Six Nations, Wyandots, Delawares, Chippewas, Ottawas, Cherokees, Choctaws, and Chickasaws have all accepted treaties with the United States. Only the Creeks have refused. 3p. *English.*

CUBA/2360 (CONT'D)

N. fol. 24 Mar. 1786, New York. Translation from the *Gazeta de Nueva York* containing the Treaty of Hopewell with the Cherokees. 7p.

N. fol. 8 Oct. 1786, Little Tallassee. McGillivray [to Gov. O'Neill] (copy). Hallowing King has returned with a supply of ammunition. McGillivray regrets the misbehavior of the pack-horsemen and has ordered their arrest. There is a good chance, however, that they have fled to the Cherokees. 3p. *English.*

N. fol. 30 Oct. 1786, Little Tallassee. Alex. McGillivray to Gov. O'Neill. John McDonald received a letter confirming the reports that the Americans plan to attack the Indians. The Creeks, consequently, have sought peace with Cumberland in order to avoid fighting on two fronts. 2p. *English.*

N. fol. *Relaciones de regalos a yndios y un padrón de diferentes naciones.* 1p. [Encloses 3 documents].

    No. 2. 8 Jan. 1786, Seneca. Benjamin Hawkins to Alex. McGillivray. [Translation of AGI Cuba/2360/n. fol.]. 6p.

    No. 3. 11 Jan. 1786, Seneca. Benjamin Hawkins to Alex. McGillivray. [Translation of AGI Cuba/2360/n. fol.]. 4p.

    N. fol. 8 Oct. 1786, Little Tallassee. Alex. McGillivray to Gov. O'Neill. [Translation of AGI Cuba/2360/n. fol.]. 4p.

N. fol. 30 Oct. 1786, Little Tallassee. Alex. McGillivray to Gov. O'Neill. [Translation of AGI Cuba/2360/n. fol.]. 3p.

No. 375. 15 Apr. 1786. *Informe* to el Marqués de Sonora regarding an offer from Buffet Duquayla, a Burdeos merchant, to begin trade with the Indians of Louisiana. Choctaws, Alibamos, Chickasaws, Cherokees [?], Creeks (Talapooses), and Apalaches have traditionally been supplied from Mobile or Pensacola. 40p.

CUBA/2361   SPANISH LOUISIANA: 1780-1789

N. fol. 5 Nov. 1787, Havana. José de Ezpeleta to Esteban Miró. 2p. [Encloses 4 documents].

    N. fol. 12 Oct. 1787, St. Augustine. Vicente Manuel de Zéspedes to José de Ezpeleta (copy). Americans attacked a party of Indians and Spanish (or French) along the Cherokee R. near Muscle Shoals, resulting in forty deaths. 3p.

N. fol. 28 Mar. 1788, Little Tallassee. Alex. McGillivray to Gov. O'Neill. One of the four Creek parties scouting the Cherokee R. area attacked some settlers between the Cumberland and Ohio Rivers. 3p. *English.*

CUBA/2361 (CONT'D)

N. fol. 16 Apr. 1788, New Orleans. Letter to [Alex.]
McGillivray stating that Spanish policy is to accept American
immigrants who wish to settle in Louisiana. Several have
recently arrived in Natchez from Cumberland. 11p. *English.*

    N. fol. 16 Apr. 1788, New Orleans. Letter to [Alex.]
McGillivray. [Translation of the above entry]. 10p.

N. fol. Letter to Alex. McGillivray expressing satisfaction at
hearing that Barby from Ky. has arrived in Cumberland. 2p.

N. fol. 1 Sept. 1788, Congress. Cyrus Griffin. *Edicto por
los Estados Unidos juntos en congreso.* [Same as AHN Estado/
3887/doc. 134. 2p.

N. fol. 20 Sept. 1788, Little Tallassee. Alex. McGillivray to
Gov. Miró. It is best not to travel to Cumberland via Cherokee
territory at the moment since that tribe and others are at war
with the Americans. Congress tries to appease tribes like the
Cherokees, but states like Ga. and S.C. plan to destroy them.
A large Creek war party helped defeat a number of Americans
recently in Cherokee territory. 3p. *English.*

No. 1. 1 Feb. 1789, Little Tallassee. Alex. McGillivray to
Wm. Panton (translation). Cherokee warrior Terrapin, who was
Whitefield's companion last year, has brought news from the
Americans. 15p.

[No. 3?]. 26 Jan. 1789, Little Tallassee. Alex. McGillivray
to Richard Winn (translation). Cherokee warrior Terrapin brought
Winn's letter of Nov. 28. 2p.

No. 4. 16 Jan. 1789, Little Tallassee. Alex. McGillivray to
Richard Winn (translation). Cherokee warrior Terrapin brought
Winn's letter of Nov. 6. 6p.

No. 5. 28 Nov. 1788, Hopewell at Keowee. Richard Winn, Andrew
Pickins, and Geo. Strothers [?] to Alex. McGillivray et al.
Creeks are guilty of numerous misdeeds against the Americans
-- including the robbery of horses in Franklin. McGillivray
should be aware of Congress's latest law affecting the Cherokees.
5p.

N. fol. 28 Mar. 1788, Little Tallassee. Alex. McGillivray to
Gov. O'Neill. [Translation of AGI Cuba/2361/n. fol.]. 4p.

No. 3. 12 Aug. 1788, Little Tallassee. Alex. McGillivray to
Gov. O'Neill (translation). Creeks have made peace with Amer-
icans to the Northwest. Gov. of Franklin, called Secres
[Sevier], has led a rebellion against the American congress. 7p.

N. fol. 20 Sept. 1788, Little Tallassee. Alex. McGillivray to
[Gov. Miró]. [Translation of AGI Cuba/2361/n. fol.]. 8p.

CUBA/2362   SPANISH LOUISIANA: 1790-1792

N. fol. 10 June 1792, New Orleans. *Indice de la carta reservada que ... [remite el Barón de Caronaelet al exmo señor Conde
de Aranda]* (duplicate). 1p. [Encloses 1 document].

No. 1 *reservada*. 10 June 1792, New Orleans. [El Barón
de Carondelet] to el Conde de Aranda. The American army
has been campaigning along the Ohio against the Northern
Indians. Now is an ideal time to encourage the Creeks to
regain their lost territory from the Americans. Such an
effort would probably involve the Choctaws, Chickasaws,
Cherokees, and Shawnees since they all have similar
problems with the Americans. An Indian war in the South
would force the Americans to be fighting from Florida to
Canada and would ruin such establishments as Cumberland
and Franklin. 9p.

N. fol. 18 [17?] Dec. 1790, Gen. Clark's Residence in Louisville.
James O'Fallon to Esteban Miró (translation). O'Fallon discuss-
es an alliance with Spain. Gen. Sevier is O'Fallon's agent for
Franklin and Col. James Robertson performs that role for
Cumberland. O'Fallon's trip to recruit soldiers in Franklin,
Cumberland, and N.C. has delayed his visit to New Orleans. 9p.

No. 1 *reservada*. 8 Feb. 1791, Natchez. Manuel Gayoso de Lemos
to Esteban Miró. O'Fallon claims to be recruiting soldiers in
Cumberland, Franklin, and N. Carolina. Those soldiers will
join other groups coming from different parts of the South.
27p.

N. fol. 12 Apr. 1790, Choctaw Nation. Translation of letter
from Simón Fabre reporting that the [Shawnees?], Cherokees, and
Talapooses killed four Americans along the Cherokee River. 1p.

N. fol. 10 June 1792, New Orleans. *Indice de la carta reservada que ... [remite el Coronel Barón de Carondelet al exmo sr.
Conde de Aranda]*. 1p. [Encloses 7 documents].

No. 1 [*reservada*]. 10 June 1792, New Orleans. El Barón
de Carondelet to el Conde de Aranda. [Same as AGI Cuba/
2362/no. 1 *reservada*]. 3p.

No. 2. 3 Apr. 1792, New Orleans. El Barón de Carondelet. *Instrucción para el comandante del fuerte de
Tombecbe*. The commandant must maintain good relations
with tribes around the fort who will be very useful
if the Americans attack. Commandant must make sure
that the Americans do not erect an establishment near
Tombigbee and he must convince the neighboring Indians
that the Americans would take their land as they have
done with the Northern tribes, Shawnees, Cherokees,
and lately the Creeks. 5p.

N. fol. [New Orleans]. Talk from el Barón de Carondelet to
Chief Yta-acho and other Creeks. Spain seeks an alliance and
peace between the Creeks, Chickasaws, Cherokees, and Choctaws.

CUBA/2362 (CONT'D)

Unfortunately, the Creeks and Chickasaws have warred against each other, but now is the time to end this conflict. 4p. *English.* [Encloses 1 document].

> N. fol. [New Orleans]. *Palabra* (talk) from [El Barón de Carondelet to Chief Yta-acho and other Creeks]. [Spanish translation of the above letter]. 3p.

N. fol. 24 Nov. 1792, New Orleans. Talk to Chiefs, Headmen, and Warriors of the Cherokee Nation expressing Spanish pleasure at the presence in New Orleans of the Breath, Charles of Chickamauga, and Bloody Fellow. The Cherokee misfortunes greatly disturb Spain. The tribe should suspend hostilities with the United States until the King can resolve the tribe's difficulties with the Americans. 3p. *English.*

N. fol. *Palabra en frances para el rey de los chicachas.* 1p. [Encloses 3 documents].

> N. fol. 10 Sept. 1792, Boukfouka. *Harrangue* (talk) from Jean de la Villebeuvre to small Indian parties in the village of Boukfouka. Villebeuvre recommends a confederation with the Choctaws, Cherokees, and Talapooses. 4p. *French.*

> N. fol. 10 Sept. 1792, Boukfouka. Jean de la Villebeuvre to Manuel Gayoso de Lemos. Americans did not ask the Choctaws visiting Cumberland for land. 4p. *French.*

N. fol. 12 June 1792, New Orleans. *Declaración* from Henry Smith, an American and a follower of Wm. Bowles, claiming to have lived four years among the Cherokees and six years with the Creeks. Bowles's followers and relatives routinely sent letters to the Cherokees. 14p.

No. 2. 20 Apr. 1792, New Orleans. Letter to Juan de la Villebeuvre noting that the government cannot permit Turnbull to erect a store on the Yazoo because it would be too close to Panton's business. The only site where someone could legally compete with Panton would be Ecores à Margot. If the court permitted a store there, it could handle the treaty trade with the Chickasaws, Cherokees, Abnakis, and other tribes. 3p.

No. 9. 23 Mar. 1792, New Orleans. *Palabra* (talk) from [El Barón de Carondelet] to the Choctaw Nation (translation). Carondelet disapproves of the Choctaw war with the Abnakis and Kickapoos. All of Spain's allies -- especially the Choctaws, Chickasaws, Creeks, and Cherokees -- need to remain at peace with one another in order to better resist the Americans. The Cherokees have learned this sad lesson after the Americans took much of their land and killed many of their warriors. 3p.

N. fol. 22 Oct. 1791, Havana. Luis de las Casas to Arturo O'Neill (duplicate). 1p. [Encloses 3 documents].

CUBA/2362 (CONT'D)

N. fol. 9 Aug. 1791, St. Augustine. *Traducción de declaración [de Eduardo Landres]*. Landres, who recently arrived from Providence, saw Bowles and the mestizo Moses Prices there. 3p.

N. fol. 1 Aug. 1791, Providence. Thomas Forbes to John Leslie (translated extract). Forbes saw Moses Price several times in Providence. 3p.

N. fol. 27 July 1790, New Orleans. Talk to Taske Etoka, King, Chiefmen, and Warriors of the Chickasaw Nation discussing Indian relations with the United States. Chickasaws are warned not to cede any land to the United States and are asked to reject the Hopewell Treaty with the United States. Americans will always encroach upon Indian land as they did at Cumberland. 7p. *English*. [Encloses 1 document].

N. fol. 16 July 1790, New Orleans. Talk to Chiefmen and Warriors of the Choctaws discussing Indian relations with the United States. Choctaws are warned not to cede land to the United States and asked to reject the Hopewell Treaty with the United States. Americans will always encroach upon Indian land as they did at Cumberland. 8p. *English*.

N. fol. 25 Mar. 1791, Pensacola. Wm. Panton to Gov. Miró. Panton's company lost its Cherokee trade in 1789 and has not received payment for the Cherokee debts since then. 3p. *English*.

N. fol. 8 May 1790, Little Tallassee. Alex. McGillivray to Esteban Miró (translation). Ga. and the other American states are determined to settle in the West no matter what the risks, but the Creeks will oppose some of these efforts. A party of Creeks (with some Cherokees and Shawnees) attacked a group of Americans traveling to Chickasaw territory. 6p.

N. fol. 29 May 1792, Little Tallassee. Pedro Olivier to el Barón de Carondelet. Olivier told the Creeks that their recent treaty with the Americans was disastrous for the tribe. The Creeks should form a defensive alliance with the Cherokees, Chickasaws, and Choctaws. Creeks have agreed to hold a congress in Pensacola with the Cherokees. 7p.

N. fol. 13 Dec. 1792, New Orleans. Letter to Wm. Panton noting that Arturo O'Neill will keep Panton informed about the Cherokee chiefs in New Orleans. The Choctaws have accepted an alliance with the Cherokees. Nevertheless, a number of problems could frustrate Panton's efforts to unify the four Southeastern tribes. The English cession of land to the Americans, for example, could cut communications between the Cherokees, Iroquois, and other Canadian tribes. 2p.

CUBA/2363   SPANISH LOUISIANA: 1787-1794

N. fol. 24 May 1793, New Orleans. *Indice de las cartas reservadas [que remite el Barón de Carondelet al exмo. sr. Duque de
la Alcudia]* (duplicate). 1p. [Encloses 10 documents].

> No. 8 *reservada*. 24 May 1793, New Orleans. [El Barón de
> Carondelet] to el Duque de la Alcudia. [Same as AHN
> Estado/3898/exp. 5/no. 8 *reservada*]. 9p.

> > N. fol. 21 May 1793, New Orleans. El Barón de Caron-
> > delet to James Robertson. Carondelet protests the
> > American decision to arm the Chickasaws with cannons.
> > It is in the interest of the United States and Spain
> > to discourage the Indians from attacking other European
> > powers. Spain has practiced considerable restraint in
> > this area, as evidenced by her response to the Chero-
> > kee request for assistance against the United States
> > and Cumberland. 3p.

> > N. fol. 5 Apr. 1793, Cherokee Nation. Petition from
> > John McDonald, Bloody Fellow, Glass, Charles of
> > Chickamaugua, Water Hunter, Spider, Richard Justice,
> > Badgers Mother, and Wm. Shawney to el Barón de Caron-
> > delet. [Same as AHN Estado/3898/exp.5/no. 8 *reser-
> > vada/encl.*]. *4p.*

> No. 9 *reservada*. 24 May 1793, New Orleans. El Barón de
> Carondelet to el Duque de la Alcudia. Carondelet forwards
> some correspondence with Cumberland. 7p.

> > N. fol. 7 May 1793, New Madrid. Thomas Portell to
> > el Barón de Carondelet. [Same as AHN Estado/3898/
> > exp. 5/no. 9. *reservada*/encl. no. 1]. 4p.

N. fol. 17 Jan. 1795, Cape Girardeau. *Journal a L. Lorimier
Cap Girardeau du 27 dbre. 1793 et 1794.* Lorimier had frequent
contact with the Cherokees. Cherokee hunters traveled with the
Maskoux [Mascoutens?] and Loups. On occasions, they assembled
in the Spanish commandant's house. 69p. *French.*

N. fol. *Copie des lettres d'offices et instructions par messrs.
les commandants.* 1p. *French.* [Encloses 57 pages].

> N. fol. 18 Jan. 1794, New Madrid. Thomas Portell to Louis
> Lorimier (copy). Spanish spy in Cumberland is returning,
> hopefully with some interesting news. 2p. *French.*

N. fol. 1794. *Lettres écrittes par L. Lorimier a messrs. les
commandants.* 1p. *French.* [Encloses 100 pages].

> No. 1. 13 Jan. 1794, Cape Girardeau. [Louis Lorimier]
> to Thomas Portell. Lorimier wishes to use the Cherokees
> to scout the Cumberland River. 5p. *French.*

> No. 21. 13 Apr. 1794, Cape Girardeau. [Louis Lorimier] to
> Thomas Portell. Point du Jour (chief of the Abnakis) and the

Shawnees, Ottawas, and Miamis are leaving to meet with the
Choctaws, Chickasaws, Maskous [Mascoutens?], Cherokees,
and other Southern nations to renew alliances. 4p.
French.

No. 23. 15 Apr. 1794, Cape Girardeau. [Louis Lorimier]
to Thomas Portell. Chief of the Loups has been waiting
for the Cherokees. 2p. *French*.

No. 25. 28 Apr. 1794, Cape Girardeau. [Louis Lorimier]
to Thomas Portell. Cherokees will meet at the commandant's
house to find out why the Shawnees plan to stay behind.
3p. *French*.

No. 27. 7 May 1794, Cape Girardeau. [Louis Lorimier]
to Thomas Portell. Lorimier has asked the Cherokees to
scout the Cumberland River, and they have agreed to do so.
4p.

No. 31. 9 June 1794, Cape Girardeau. [Louis Lorimier]
to Thomas Portell. George Wilson arrived from the
territory between the Cherokee and Cumberland Rivers.
1p. *French*.

N. fol. 1793. *Lettres de messrs. les commandants des différents
postes des Illinois ... à Louis Lorimier*. 1p. *French*.
[Encloses 35 pages].

N. fol. 4 May 1789, St. Louis. [Henri?] Peyrous to Louis
Lorimier. Lorimier will be in St. Louis to interpret for
the Shawnees and Cherokees. 1p. *French*.

N. fol. 11 June 1793, New Orleans. Letter to Luis de las
Casas reporting that the intrigues of Gov. Blount of Cumberland
have won over most of the Chickasaws to the American side. 4p.

N. fol. 4 Aug. 1793, Pensacola. Wm. Panton to el Barón de
Carondelet. Panton forwarded Carondelet's letter to McDonald
and the Cherokees. Although the American government might
wish friendly relations with Spain and her Indian allies, the
Americans that reside along the frontier do not. Gov. Blount's
cruel treatment of the Cherokees illustrates this. 2p.
English.

N. fol. 14 Aug. 1793, Cherokees. John McDonald to Wm. Panton.
The Hair, a Cherokee warrior, delivered Panton's letter. The
present situation with the United States is alarming. Capt.
John Beard carried out the Hanging Maw affair, evidently without
the knowledge of Gov. Blount. Beard also slaughtered some
Cherokee women around Tellico. Cherokees have invited the
Creeks to aid them. 2p. *English*.

N. fol. 19 Sept. 1793, New Orleans. Letter to Wm. Panton
stating that Spaniards are aware of how inhumanely the Americans

CUBA/2363 (CONT'D)

have treated the Cherokees in killing defenseless women and
children. The Court will make a vigorous protest to the United
States about these events. The Indians need to be armed to
resist similar atrocities. 2p.

N. fol. 5 Apr. 1793, Cherokee Nation. Petition from John
McDonald, Bloody Fellow, Glass, Charles of Chickamauga, Water
Hunter, Spider, Richard Justice, Badgers Mother, and Wm.
Shawney to el Barón de Carondelet. [Same as AHN Estado/3898/
exp. 5/no. 8 *reservada*/encl.]. 4p.

N. fol. 14 Aug. 1793. John McDonald to Wm. Panton. [Spanish
translation of AGI Cuba/2363/n. fol.]. 3p.

N. fol. 11 Aug. 1793, Cherokee. Bloody Fellow to Gov. Gen. of
Louisiana (translation). Gov. has undoubtedly heard about the
massacre at Hanging Maw. Whites have invaded Cherokee country
three times since this atrocity. Tribe has held a meeting to
see how the Cherokees can revenge these cruelties and has
decided to send an expedition across the white frontier. Turpen
[Terrapin?], Kitagiska, and John Watts will lead expedition,
but the Cherokees need arms and munitions from the Spanish. 4p.

N. fol. 28 Oct. 1793, Nogales. Manuel Gayoso de Lemos et al.
Treaty of Nogales. [English version of AGI SD/2563/fol. 8].
7p. [Encloses 5 documents].

    N. fol. 28 Oct. 1793, Nogales. Manuel Gayoso de Lemos et
    al. [Same as AGI SD/2563/fol. 8]. 4p.

N. 1. 11 June 1794, Philadelphia. José de Jaudenes and José
Ignacio de Viar to Edmund Randolph. [Copy of AHN Estado/3895bis/
ap. 7/no. 273/encl. no. 1]. 6p. [Encloses 4 documents].

N. fol. 28 June 1794, New York. José de Jaudenes and José
Ignacio de Viar to Luis de las Casas. [Copy of AHN Estado/
3895bis/ap. 5/no. 259/encl. no. 8]. 4p.

No. 4. 20 Sept. 1794, Lower Cherokees. John McDonald to el
Barón de Carondelet. [Same as AGI SD/2564/fol. 77]. 4p.

No. 1. 3 July 1794. Benjamin Fooy to Manuel Gayoso de Lemos.
Groups of whites are returning to Cumberland. Cherokee hunters
have reported Americans building a fort. 12p. *English*.

N. fol. 23 Apr. 1793, Nashville. James Robertson to Thomas
Portell (translation). Robertson's son is carrying corn that
the Spaniards requested. He sends along letters to forward to
the Delawares and Shawnees. There are Chickasaws in Nashville
who wish peace. 2p.

No. 3. 10 Jan. 1794, Tuckabatchee. Talk from White Lieutenant
to Chickasaws. White Lieutenant wants peace, which he has also
proposed to the Choctaws and Cherokees. 2p. *English*.

N. fol. 8 May 1794, Augusta, Georgia. James Seagrove to Creeks. Americans are pleased at the news about peace with the Creeks. Yet some Indians (perhaps the Cherokees) have stolen a few horses and killed their white owners. If the Cherokees are guilty of some of this mischief, the Creeks should call them to account because the Creeks will be blamed for it. 4p. *English*. [Encloses 1 document].

   N. fol. 8 May 1794, Augusta. James Seagrove to [Creeks]. [Spanish copy of preceding letter]. 6p.

N. fol. 15 January [1793], Mobile. Alex. McGillivray to el Barón de Carondelet. McGillivray has learned about the good advice that Carondelet gave the Cherokee chiefs in New Orleans. The threat of the Americans in Muscle Shoals trading with the Indians has been exaggerated. American merchants who have attempted to trade with Indians have failed. 8p. *English*.

N. fol. 22 July 1794, Boukfouka. [Juan] de la Villebeuvre to Manuel Gayoso de Lemos. Gov. Blount attempted to negotiate a treaty with the Cherokees in Knoxville, but most of the tribe opposed his effort and burned their gifts. Blount sent a Cherokee delegation to New York to negotiate with Congress. Reports from Cumberland indicate that 1,500 Indians and 400 English are threatening the Americans. 3p. *French*.

N. fol. 14[?] Nov. 1794, New Orleans. Letter to John McDonald stating that Spain is pleased that the Cherokees have decided to live in peace with the Americans. Spanish officials, however, deplore Gov. Blount's behavior. Cherokees should never be the aggressors but should always be ready to defend themselves. Spain will provide the arms to do so. The Spanish King has declared that the Cherokees are his vassals and is negotiating with the United States to protect them. Bloody Fellow's son, Charles, is doing fine. 4p. *English*. [Encloses 1 document].

   N. fol. 15 Nov. 1794, [New Orleans]. Letter to John McDonald. [Spanish copy of the preceding letter]. 3p.

No. 119 *reservada*. 16 July 1794, New Orleans. El Barón de Carondelet to Luis de las Casas. Carondelet has correspondence from Canada concerning the American threat to British and Spanish possessions. 2p. [Encloses 6 documents].

   N. fol. 9 July 1794, New Orleans. El Barón de Carondelet to el Duque de la Alcudia (copy). Carondelet discusses correspondence from the governor of Lower Canada and newspaper reports that the Americans are planning a city in Spanish territory where the Mo. and Miss. Rivers come together. Like Spain, the British are using Indians to check American threats. 6p.

CUBA/2363 (CONT'D)

> No. 1. 11 Apr. 1794, Miami River Falls at Lake Erie.
> J. Graves Simcoe to el Barón de Carondelet (translation).
> The position of the American army now could prevent the
> British from aiding St. Louis if it were attacked. Indian
> nations are a useful tool against the Americans trying to
> seize land. The British government regrets the situation
> with Mr. Bowles, whose influence over the Creeks and
> Cherokees is designed to form a barrier against Ga. and
> Carolina and not against Spain or Great Britain. 4p.

N. fol. Dec. 1794 and Jan. 1795, Augusta. Acts of the State
of Georgia, Passed at Augusta. Documents list western land
[some of which belongs to the Cherokees] sold to the Georgia
Company. 5p. *English.*

CUBA/2367   SPANISH LOUISIANA: 1780-1802

N. fol. 6 June 1801, Augusta, Georgia. *Augusta Chronicle and
Gazette of the State.* Bids are solicited for supplying army
troops at Knoxville, Tellico, South West Point, and many other
places. 4p. *English.*

No. 17. 29 May 1801, St. Marks. Jacobo Dubreuil to el Marqués
de Casa Calvo. Upper and Lower Creeks, Choctaws, and Cherokees
did not hold a congress to consider their relations with Bowles.
10p.

Fol. 161. 9 Dec. 1801, Mackesucke. Report from John DeLacy
to Wm. Augustus Bowles. DeLacy gives village census for the
Creeks and lists the total number of Choctaw (12,000), Chickasaw (3,000), and Cherokee (5,000) warriors. DeLacy estimates
the commercial value of trade with the Southern tribes, including the Cherokees. 19p. *English.* [Enclosures to fol. 172b].

CUBA/2370   SPANISH LOUISIANA: 1769-1789

N. fol. 20 Apr. 1789, New Orleans. Letter to James Robertson
indicating pleasure at hearing about the pacific intentions of
the residents of Robertson's district towards Spanish territory.
Spain has convinced the Creeks to seek peace with Robertson's
district, but Spanish officials have little contact with the
Cherokees. This tribe goes now and then to the Illinois
territory and Spanish authorities there will ask them to
respect Robertson's district. 3p. *English.*

N. fol. 23 Apr. 1789, New Orleans. Letter reporting that
Diego Gardoqui (Spanish envoy to the United States) has won
over James White, a member of Congress with property in Cumberland, to Spain's side. He has been sent to Franklin to encourage
the residents there to break with the United States. 7p.
English.

N. fol. 12 Sept. 1788, Franklin. John S[evier?] to Gardoqui
(copy). Franklin residents have a favorable opinion of Spain.
4p. *English.*

CUBA/2370 (CONT'D)

N. fol. 18 Apr. 1789, New Orleans. James White to Gov. Miró. Gardoqui has sent White to inform the western settlements that Spain would grant them protection if they chose to separate from the other states. Gardoqui gave White letters to give to the principal men of Franklin. Cumberland evidently has the same views as Franklin. 3p. *English*.

N. fol. 2 Sept. 1789, Nashville. James Robertson to Gov. [of Louisiana?]. Robertson thanks the governor for letter via Mr. White. Cumberland has decided to separate from N. Carolina. This district needs protection from the Cherokees and Creeks, something that the United States does not do but hopefully Spain will. 2p. *English*.

N. fol. 24 Apr. 1789, New Orleans. [Esteban Miró] to Brig. Daniel Smith. Spain is very interested in promoting the welfare of the residents of Cumberland [now called Miró]. Mr. White will carry the Spanish proposals. Miró has convinced the Creeks to maintain peace with Smith's area. Spanish officials, however, have no connection with the Cherokees and Mascoutens but might be able to contact them in Illinois to encourage them to maintain the peace also. 4p. *English*.

N. fol. 23 Jan. 1778, Charleston. John Rutledge to Bernardo de Gálvez. Spain can begin commerce with the Cherokees via New Orleans while Spain, England, and France remain at peace with one another. Rutledge requests a response to the inquiry about whether the Americans can establish a commercial house in New Orleans to carry on foreign trade. 1p. [Encloses 3 documents].

> N. fol. 23 Jan. 1778, Charleston. John Rutledge to Bernardo de Gálvez. [English copy of preceding letter]. 2p.

N. fol. 1783, [New Orleans]. Gilberto Antonio de Maxente. *Instrucciones dadas a los interpretes de las diferentes naciones de yndios.* 1p. [Encloses 3 documents].

> N. fol. 20 Sept. 1783, New Orleans. *Instructions que nous, dn. Gilbert Antoine de Maxente ... donnons au sr. Louis Fourneret, interprète des nations Chactaw, Alibamons et Chicahas à Pansacola.* Gov. of Pensacola has approved the Cherokee request to settle as close as possible to Spanish territory. 4p. *French*.

> N. fol. 20 Sept. 1783, New Orleans. *Instructions que nous dn. Gilberto Antoine de Maxent ... donnons au sieur Antoine Garçon interprète de la nation Talapouches à Pansacola.* Pensacola governor approves the Cherokee request to settle as close as possible to Spanish territory. 4p. *French*.

CUBA/2371   SPANISH LOUISIANA: 1790-1799

Doc. 23. 8 June 1791, Little Tallassee. Alex. McGillivray to Stephen Miró. In April the Tennessee Company assembled 150 armed men along the French Broad R. to go to Muscle Shoals to build a fort. Creeks sent a party to destroy them but could not find the group. 4p. *English.*

Doc. 27. 4 [Dec.?] 1791, Cawetabo [?]. Letter from Wm. Bowles stating that the Creeks and Cherokees have united, formed a council, and appointed a director (Bowles). 4p. *English.*

Doc. 29 (no. 2). 4 Jan. 1792. Copy of decree from Gen. Wm. A. Bowles declaring that vessels and goods of all nations may freely trade with the Indian tribes. Bowles's authority to order this rests upon his position as director of the United Nation of Creek and Cherokees. 1p. *English.*

Doc. 34. 13 Mar. 1792, New Orleans. Wm. Bowles to el Barón de Carondelet. Bowles denies the charges that he planned to attack Spanish possessions. The residents of Cain Tuke [Kentucky?] and Cumberland petitioned him to have the Creeks protect the area and to attack the Spaniards along the Mississippi. Bowles, however, refused. 4p. *English.*

Doc. 35. 14 Mar. 1792, New Orleans. Wm. Bowles to el Barón de Carondelet. Bowles reviews earlier correspondence concerning the misunderstanding between Spain and the Creeks. Creeks are the original inhabitants of East and West Florida up to the 36° north. The Cherokees are the original inhabitants of all country north of this parallel to the Ohio. These two nations have united to form a single government containing 20,000 warriors. 2p. *English.*

Doc. 36. 29 Apr. 1792, Barracks, New Orleans. Declaration from Wm. Cunningham discussing his residency in Franklin and Cherokee territory [1790-1791?]. Cunningham received a passport to visit Creek territory from John McDonald, who lives with the Cherokees. Cunningham reports a conspiracy to seize Spanish territory by Lord Dunmore, Gen. Clark, Gov. Wm. Blount and John Sevier (in Franklin). 9p. *English.*

Doc. 40. 22 July 1792, Mobile. Alex. McGillivray to el Barón de Carondelet. Americans invited the Choctaws to Cumberland but the important chiefs did not attend. Creeks evidently forced the American envoys who issued these invitations to flee for their lives to Cumberland. 3p. *English.*

Doc. 41. Letter from [Gov. of Louisiana?] stating that many Americans believe that the Spaniards encourage the Indians to attack American settlements. Cumberland residents publicly acknowledge that they could not exist without Spanish help and protection. Indeed, they have renamed their district Miró. Travelers who had been in Cumberland told the Cherokees that Col. Robertson threatened to destroy them. Cherokees learned about this during their new corn dance and took matters into their own hands. 8p. *English.*

CUBA/2371 (CONT'D)

Doc. 42.   25 Jan. 1793, New Orleans. *Punto sobre los quales se deven tratar en el congreso de los indios.* The Creeks, Cherokees, Choctaws, and Chickasaws must form a defensive alliance under Spanish protection. If the Americans reject the pacific proposals of the Cherokees and Creeks, all four allied nations and the Northern tribes would fight together. 2p.

Doc. 101.   Letter maintaining that, in light of the war between the Choctaws on one hand and the Abnakis and Kickapoos on the other, officials should remind Spanish Indian allies (such as the Choctaws, Chickasaws, Creeks, and Cherokees) that they should live in peace with one another since the Americans are their biggest threat. The Cherokees, for example, have lost a considerable part of their territory to the Americans. 2p.

Doc. 151.   25 Jan. 1798, Cherokees. Bloody Fellow to Manuel Gayoso de Lemos. After returning home 20 days ago, it was reported that two Cherokees were killed in Cumberland. Although the Americans have offered $700 reward to capture the guilty party, the Cherokees have seen the results of these rewards before. Moses Price has been sent to Spanish territory to buy horses, but officials seized his goods and sent him in irons to New Orleans. 2p. *English.*

Doc. 151.   12 May 1798, New Orleans. Letter to Bloody Fellow expressing regret at the Cherokees being killed in Cumberland and apologizing for the misadventures of Moses Price. Author promises to supply a letter of recommendation for Price and to ask officials to restore his goods. 2p. *English.*

Doc. 163.   2 Aug. 1798, Tuckabatchee. Richard Thomas to James Burges. Mad Dog requested that Burges give a speech to the Seminoles and others. Only the Creeks and Chickasaws appeared at the latest assembly. The Choctaws and Cherokees were absent. The Cherokees and others are needed to guard the frontiers. 3p. *English.*

ARCHIVO GENERAL DE SIMANCAS

Simancas

SECCIÓN VI   SECRETARÍA DE ESTADO
ESTADO/6849   NEGOTIATIONS WITH ENGLAND: 1721

> N. fol. 17 Apr. 1721, London. Jazinto de la Pozobueno to el
> Marqués de Grimaldo. Pozobueno, Spanish diplomatic represent-
> ative in London, has complained to Lord Carteret about the
> hostilities of the Carolina English and Indians towards Spanish
> subjects in Florida. 2p. [Encloses 2 documents].

>> N. fol. 13 Apr. 1721, London. El Marqués de Pozobueno
>> to Lord Carteret (copy). Pozobueno protests against the
>> hostilities of the Carolina Indians towards Florida and
>> its Spanish residents. 3p. *French.*

>> N. fol. [13 Apr. 1721], [London]. [El Marqués de Pozo-
>> bueno to Lord Carteret]. [Spanish copy of the preceding
>> letter]. 2p.

ESTADO/6995   NEGOTIATIONS WITH ENGLAND: 1776

> Doc. 37 (no. 367). 18 Oct. 1776, London. El Príncipe de
> Masserano to el Marqués de Grimaldi. S.C. Indians have sided
> with the British and have destroyed a party of S.C. militia
> whom they scalped. British are unhappy about these new
> hostilities for fear that some day the Indians might repeat
> these same acts against the British. 2p.

ESTADO/6996   NEGOTIATIONS WITH ENGLAND: 1777

> Doc. 10 (no. 430). 17 Jan. 1777, London. El Príncipe de
> Masserano to el Marqués de Grimaldi. The Americans have
> encouraged the Indians to rebel. As a result, the Indian
> tribes have attacked Carolina and committed numerous atrocities.
> 10p.

ESTADO/7000   NEGOTIATIONS WITH ENGLAND: 1778

> Doc. 1. 12 June 1777, Charleston. *The South-Carolina and
> American General Gazette.* A Cherokee Indian delegation has
> arrived at Ft. Henry, Virginia, led by Oconostota and Little
> Carpenter. Tribal leaders have ceded about three million acres
> of land to Virginia. 8p. *English.*

ESTADO/7020   NEGOTIATIONS WITH ENGLAND: 1779

> Atado 3°-15. Letter stating that the Choctaws, Cherokees, and
> Chickasaws have been incited to attack Louisiana residents.
> 4p. *French.*

ESTADO/7620   COMMERCE AND FOREIGNERS.

N. fol. 1726, Florida. *Testimonio de los autos y declaraziones que sean ... [por los límites y jurisdicción de este govierno].* 1p. [Encloses 8 documents].

N. fol. 30 Mar. 1727, Madrid. *Acordado* from the Council of the Indies concerning English hostilities against the Yamassees, a tribe loyal to Spain. Two other tribes, the Yguaja and the Chilucus [Cherokees?], are also involved in this affair. 24p.

No. 14. [7?] Oct. 1682, Florida. Letter from Gov. Juan Marquéz Cabrera responding to a *real cedula* to count the population of Florida. 2p. [Encloses 6 documents].

N. fol. 14 July 1681, San Pedro. Solana [?]. *Certificazión de los tenientes de la provincia de Apalache, Timucua, y Guale de los naturales que tiene cada una.* Document mentions northern posts at Zapala and Tupiqui along the frontier with English Chichimecos, Chiluques [Cherokees?], Chalaques [Cherokees?], and other hostile Indians. 11p.

ESTADO/8137   SPANISH EMBASSY IN ENGLAND: 1789-1795

Atado 2°-63. 18 Feb. 1793, St. Mary's River. Copy of letter from John Foraster stating that the Shawnees and Creeks have discussed whether to war against the Americans. Creeks return daily with horses, slaves, and scalps from their raids against Cumberland and Kentucky. 3p.

ESTADO/8143   SPANISH EMBASSY IN ENGLAND: 1786

Doc. 51. [5 Sept. 1786], [London]. Letter to [el Conde de Floridablanca]. 1p. [Encloses 3 documents].

N. doc. 12 Aug. [1786], [London]. Fabius to editor (translation). Fabius emphasizes American hostility towards the Spanish colonies. Ky. and Cumberland alone could seize the Spanish possessions if they were provided with the right supplies. 8p.

Doc. 64. 17 Dec. [?], Kingston, Jamaica. Translation of [newspaper article] indicating that the Spanish have worked hard to earn the friendship of the Chickasaws, Creeks, Choctaws, and Cherokees. 4p.

ESTADO/8148   SPANISH EMBASSY IN ENGLAND: 1790-1792

Doc. 15. 15 Apr. 1791, London. Letter to el Conde de Floridablanca reporting the arrival from Canada of a group of Indians (three Creeks and three Cherokees) led by Wm. Bowles. 10p. [Encloses 2 documents].

N. doc. 25 Mar. 1791, London. Memorial from Wm. Bowles, Unatoy, Kuahtekiske, Seponejah, Tuskeniah, and Wosseo (deputies of the United Nation of the Creek and Cherokee Indians) to [His] Catholic Majesty. Deputies seek an

ESTADO/8148 (CONT'D)

alliance with the Spaniards and explain the Creek and
Cherokee claim to territory in the Southeast. Creeks
and Cherokees have a defensive alliance with the Chickasaws and Choctaws. 12p. *English.*

N. doc. 25 Mar. 1791, London. Memorial from Wm. Bowles
to [His Catholic Majesty]. [Spanish copy of the preceding
entry]. 7p.

Doc. 21. 25 Apr. 1792, London. Letter to el Conde de Aranda
discussing the departure of Bowles and the Cherokees from
London. Bowles is a disreputable character who is nothing
more than an Irishman, in spite of pretentions to being something else. 2p.

ESTADO/8154   SPANISH EMBASSY IN ENGLAND: 1791-1797

Doc. 7. 26 June 1792, London. [El Marqués del Campo to Lord
Grenville]. Campo reports the hostile actions of Bowles in
East Florida. Bowles claims to be operating with British
approval and has offered the tribes British protection, but
British possessions do not include Creek and Cherokee territory.
6p. *French.*

ESTADO/8168   SPANISH EMBASSY IN ENGLAND: 1802-1804

Doc. 2. 16 May 1803, London. Thomas Powell to Chevalier
D'Anguado. 2p. *English.* [Encloses 3 documents].

N. doc. 14 May 1803, London. Thomas Powell to Chevalier
D'Anguado. Powell describes his visit to Knoxville and
his acquaintance with the Blount family. 9p. *English.*

SECCIÓN IX   SECRETARÍA DE GUERRA: GUERRA MODERNA
GM/6916   THE FLORIDAS AND LOUISIANA

No. 120. 27 Oct. 1791, Havana. Luis de las Casas to el Conde
del Campo de Alange. 4p. [Encloses 4 documents].

No. 3. 31 Jan. 1792, Ft. St. Marks. Robert Leslie to
John Leslie (copy). Bowles has given Geo. Welbank the
title of sergeant major. Welbank was formerly an overseer
for Stuart in the Bahamas and has recently arrived from the
Cherokees. 6p.

No. 157. 1 Mar. 1792, Havana. Letter from Capt. Gen. of
Florida discussing Wm. Bowles's activities in Florida. Bowles
claims to be the director of the united Creek and Cherokee
nations. 3p.

No. 171. 20 Oct. 1792, San Lorenzo. *Real orden* to Capt. Gen.
of Louisiana denying Carondelet's request for a salary increase.
Moreover, he is not relieved of his traditional obligation to
entertain Indian representatives when they visit New Orleans.
The King wants to know if Carondelet still wished to continue
his position under these conditions. 3p. [Encloses 9 documents].

N. fol. 30 Mar. 1792, Havana. Letter from Capt. Gen. of
Louisiana who forwards Carondelet's petition for a salary
raise because of the enormous personal expense of entertaining visiting Indian delegations. Capt. gen. reports
that the custom of feeding Indian delegations comes from
the British and he supports the request for a salary increase. He also favors returning the military command of
Louisiana to the gov. of Louisiana. 10p.

No. 257. 15 Feb. 1793, Havana. Letter from Capt. Gen. of
Louisiana forwarding the King's decision not to increase
Carondelet's salary. The capt. gen. still feels it is
best to make the gov. of Louisiana responsible for military
and civilian affairs within Louisiana. 6p.

No. 2. 18 Jan. 1792, New Orleans. El Barón de Carondelet
to el Conde de Floridablanca. Carondelet petitions that
his salary be augmented because of the enormous expenses
of his position, including the cost of feeding Indian
delegations arriving in New Orleans. 4p.

N. fol. 18 Jan. 1792, New Orleans. Letter from el Barón
de Carondelet noting the inadequacy of his salary due to
the large number of Indian delegations who come to New
Orleans and must be fed by the governor. 3p.

No. 171. 30 Mar. 1792, Havana. Luis de las Casas to el
Conde del Campo de Alange. Las Casas supports the petition
of gov. of Louisiana for salary raise and wants to unite
military and civilian functions in the hands of Carondelet.
6p.

N. fol. Copy of petition in the name of La. residents
asking that the Crown unite the military and civilian
control of the government in the hands of the governor
of Louisiana. 4p. *French.*

No. 257. 15 Feb. 1793, Havana. Luis de las Casas to el
Conde del Campo de Alange. Las Casas explains his support
for augmenting governor's salary and for combining civilian
and military powers in the hands of the governor of New
Orleans. 7p.

No. 270. 23 Mar. 1793, Havana. Luis de las Casas to el
Conde del Campo de Alange. Las Casas has sent on to the
gov. of Louisiana the decision concerning his petition
for increase in salary. 1p.

N. fol. 8 Feb. 1793, New Orleans. El Barón de Carondelet
to Luis de las Casas (copy). In reply to the Crown's
request whether Carondelet wishes to continue as governor
at the same salary and maintain the custom of entertaining
Indians, Carondelet will serve as long as the King wishes.
3p.

No. 202. 27 June 1792, Havana. Luis de las Casas to el Conde del Campo de Alange. 1p. [Encloses 3 documents].

> No. 30 *reservada*. 22 May 1792, New Orleans. El Barón de Carondelet to Luis de las Casas (copy). Carondelet reports successful conclusion of efforts to secure Nogales for Spain from the Choctaws and Chickasaws. This step will facilitate Spain's alliance with the four major Indian nations needed to defend Spanish territory against the Americans. 1p.

No. 319. 9 July 1793, Havana. Luis de las Casas to el Conde del Campo de Alange. [Same as AGI SD/2562/fol. 370]. 3p.

N. fol. 25 Apr. 1792, London. El Marqués del Campo to el Conde de Aranda. Bowles has left London where he represented himself as an envoy from the Cherokees and other tribes. 3p.

N. fol. 26 May 1792, Aboard the frigate *The Mississippi*. Wm. Augustus Bowles to Esteban Miró (translation). Bowles explains certain facts about his life, including his trip in 1789 with two Creeks and three Cherokees to form an alliance against the Americans. 15p.

No. 79 *reservada*. 22 May 1793, New Orleans. El Barón de Carondelet to [Luis de las Casas]. [Copy of AGI Cuba/1447/ no. 79 *reservada*]. 4p. [Encloses 2 documents].

> No. 1. 7 May 1793, New Madrid. Thomas Portell to el Barón de Carondelet. [Copy of AHN Estado/3898/exp. 5/ no. 9 *reservada*/encl. no. 1]. 5p.

> N. fol. 23 Apr. 1793, Nashville. James Robertson to [Thomas Portell]. [Same as AHN Estado/3898/exp. 5/no. 9 *reservada*/encl.]. 3p.

No. 80 *reservada*. 23 May 1793, New Orleans. El Barón de Carondelet to Luis de las Casas. Carondelet passes along the latest news from Cumberland. He denies the allegations in American newspapers that he or Brig. O'Neill have stirred up the Cherokees against the Americans. Carondelet sent copies to the Spanish envoys in Philadelphia of his recent talks with the Cherokees in order to dispose of this charge. 2p. [Encloses 1 document].

> N. fol. 16 May 1793. Manuel Gayoso de Lemos to el Barón de Carondelet (copy). James Pike has arrived from Cumberland. Blount has warned the residents of Cumberland that the Talapooses and Shawnees are planning to attack the area. Blount has also circulated newspapers charging that Carondelet and O'Neill have encouraged the Talapooses to attack the Americans. 7p.

GM/6916 (CONT'D)

No. 97 *reservada*. 5 Dec. 1793, New Orleans. El Barón de
Carondelet to Luis de las Casas (copy). Carondelet reminds
the capt. gen. that he sent him a copy of the treaty with the
Creeks, Cherokees, Choctaws, and Chickasaws. 1p. [Encloses
2 documents].

> No. 364. 3 Jan. 1794, Havana. Luis de las Casas to el
> Conde del Campo de Alange. Las Casas forwards a copy of
> the Nogales treaty with the Creeks, Cherokees, Choctaws,
> and Chickasaws. He considers this an important step
> towards preserving Spanish possessions from the Americans
> 2p.

> N. fol. 28 Oct. 1793, Camp at Nogales. Manuel Gayoso de
> Lemos et al. Treaty of Nogales. 8p. [Same as AGI SD/
> 2563/fol. 8].

No. 17 *reservada*. 18 Oct. 1792, New Orleans. El Barón de
Carondelet to el Conde de Aranda. Treaty of Mobile in 1784
placed the Choctaws, Chickasaws, Creeks, and Cherokees under
Spanish protection. Later tribal treaties with the United
States could not legally include provisions fobidden in the
earlier ones with Spain. The United States is too weak to
declare war against Spain. The Creeks only await the King's
permission to attack the southern states. Their braves have
already devastated Cumberland and the Cherokees have sought
Spain's assistance. 11p.

GM/6918   THE FLORIDAS AND LOUISIANA

No. 465. 27 May 1795, Aranjuez. *Real orden* to Capt. Gen. of
Louisiana. 3p. [Encloses 5 documents].

> No. 126 *reservada*. 30 Oct. 1794, New Orleans. El Barón
> de Carondelet to Luis de las Casas. [Copy of AGI Cuba/
> 2354/fol. 368]. 4p.

> > No. 1. 18 Sept. 1794, [New Orleans?]. John Galphin
> > to James Burges. [Same as AGI Cuba/2354/fol. 4]. 7p.

> > No. 2. 2 Oct. 1794, St. Marks. Diego de Vegas to
> > James Burges. [Same as AGI Cuba/2354/fol. 1]. 8p.

> > No. 2 *muy reservada*. 31 Oct. 1794, New Orleans.
> > El Barón de Carondelet to Diego de Vegas. Carondelet
> > has received Vegas's letter concerning the critical
> > situation that the Creeks and Cherokees find them-
> > selves in with the Americans. He outlines what
> > military strategy should be followed if the Americans
> > defeat these two tribes and then proceed to attack
> > St. Marks. 5p.

> > No. 4. 20 Sept. 1794, Lower Cherokees. John McDonald
> > to el Barón de Carondelet. [Same as AGI SD/2564/
> > fol. 77]. 4p.

GM/6928   THE FLORIDAS AND LOUISIANA

No. 12 *reservada*. 3 Aug. 1791, Havana. Luis de las Casas to
el Conde del Campo de Alange. 1p. [Encloses 4 documents].

No. 1. 8 June 1791, Little Tallassee. Alex. McGillivray
to Esteban Miró (copy). [Spanish copy of AGI Cuba/2371/
doc. 23]. 5p.

No. 118. 27 Oct. 1791, Havana. Luis de las Casas to el Conde
del Campo de Alange. Las Casas forwards the latest news about
Cumberland. 1p. [Encloses 1 document].

No. 83. 9 May 1791, Natchez. Manuel Gayoso de Lemos to
Esteban Miró (copy). John Hinds has arrived in Natchez
from Cumberland and reports that the Indians continue to
attack that state and have killed several important people
recently. The Cherokees and Chickasaws have been notified
about the American desire to build a fort at Muscle Shoals.
1p.

No. 121. 31 Oct. 1791, Havana. Luis de las Casas to el Conde
del Campo de Alange. 1p. [Encloses 4 documents].

[No. 259]. 23 Sept. 1791, New Orleans. Esteban Miró to
Luis de las Casas. [Copy of AGI Cuba/1440B/no. 259]. 2p.

N. fol. 28 Aug. 1791, Little Tallassee. Alex.
McGillivray to Esteban Miró. [Same as AGI Cuba/
1440B/no. 259/encl.]. 4p.

No. 206. 2 July 1792, Havana. Luis de las Casas to el Conde
del Campo de Alange. 2p. [Encloses 8 documents].

No. 26 *reservada*. 29 Apr. 1792, New Orleans. El Barón
de Carondelet to Luis de las Casas (copy). Americans have
made efforts to raise a large army to combat the Northern
Indians. Carondelet is trying to dissuade McGillivray
from meeting with the Americans and from following through
with the border agreement with Georgia. Should war break
out between the Creeks and Americans, the Governor expects
the Cherokees, Choctaws, Chickasaws, and Shawnees to assist
the Creeks. 2p.

No. 31 *reservada*. 24 May 1792, New Orleans. El Barón de
Carondelet to Luis de las Casas (copy). Americans have
systematically usurped and destroyed the Indian nations
along their borders. They plan to continue with this
pattern until all tribes are exterminated or pushed to the
other side of the Mississippi. If Spain does not soon
unite the Choctaws, Chickasaws, Creeks, and Cherokees
against the United States, the Americans will win these
tribes over. Without such allies, Spain could not resist
the United States alone. 4p.

GM/6928 (CONT'D)

No. 132 *reservada*. 30 Mar. 1795, New Orleans. El Barón de
Carondelet to Luis de las Casas (copy). Spanish government
has spent 35,000 pesos in Indian gifts to prevent Genet's
projected invasion of the Upper Mississippi. Indian costs
surpass 55,000 pesos if the efforts to unite the four Southern
tribes are taken into account. Expenses will rise even higher
since the Americans are attempting to sell more Indian land.
A number of Cherokees and Shawnees have already been forced to
seek asylum on the other side of the Mississippi. 5p.
[Encloses 2 documents].

> No. 2. Dec. 1794 and Jan. 1795, Augusta. Benjamin
> Taliaferro et al.. *Actos del estado de Georgia celebrados
> en Augusta* (translation). Act describes land grants and
> territory sold by Georgia, including some Cherokee land.
> 27p.

No. 364. 3 Jan. 1794, Havana. Letter from Capt. Gen. of
Louisiana sending a copy of Treaty of Nogales in which Spain
grants the Cherokees her protection. Cherokees will receive
their annual gifts in Pensacola during the spring. 9p.

GM/6929   THE FLORIDAS AND LOUISIANA

Doc. 53. 31 Aug. 1795, San Ildefonso. *Real orden* to Capt.
Gen. of Louisiana reporting that the Council of State informed
the King about American efforts to establish themselves along
the Tenn. R. [Muscle Shoals]. The King approved Carondelet's
measures taken to prevent it. 1p. [Encloses 15 documents].

> Doc. 54 (no. 508). 20 June 1795, Havana. Luis de las
> Casas to el Conde del Campo de Alange. Las Casas passes
> on information concerning American interests in estab-
> lishing a fort at Muscle Shoals, territory that Spain
> considers under her jurisdiction. 4p.

>> Doc. 55 (no. 134 *reservada*). 1 May 1795, New Orleans.
>> El Barón de Carondelet to Luis de las Casas (copy).
>> Americans are intent on fortifying Muscle Shoals
>> with the permission of the Chickasaws. Chickasaws are
>> involved in hostilities with the Creeks and depend
>> upon the Americans to help them. 8p.

>> N. doc. 30 Mar. 1793, Aranjuez. *Real orden* from
>> el Duque de la Alcudia to el Barón de Carondelet
>> (copy). In response to letters concerning American
>> intentions to establish fort at Muscle Shoals, the
>> King approves Carondelet's measures to prevent it.
>> 2p.

GM/7235   THE INDIES: MISCELLANEOUS.

Nos. 397, 398, 400, and 401. Nov. 1794, Havana. Capt. Gen. of
Louisiana to [el Conde del Campo de Alange]. Summary of four
letters [nos. 397, 398, 400, and 401] which contain a report

GM/7235 (CONT'D)

of a Shawnee attack on a fort held by French revolutionaries near the Cumberland and Shawnee Rivers. The Upper Creeks and Cherokees met with the Americans. 43p.

No. 398. 18 May 1794, Havana. Luis de las Casas to el Conde del Campo de Alange. 9p. [Encloses 3 documents].

N. fol. 7 Feb. 1794, Cocha Funa. John Kinnard to James Seagrove (translation). A number of Georgians have assembled to invade East Florida. Another large group has gathered at Muscle Shoals with the intention of attacking West Fla. and Louisiana. Kinnard warns that the Indians will oppose these invasions. 2p.

No. 3. 10 Apr. 1794, St. Augustine. John Hambly. *Diario de dn. Juan Hambley en su último viage a ... los yndios* (copy). Hambly traveled through Creek territory from Jan. through Apr. 1794. Upper Creeks planned a general Indian meeting in March. There is a need for several congresses since it was decided at the last general assembly that the Choctaws, Chickasaws, Cherokees, Creeks, and Seminoles would meet in the presence of Pedro Olivier and James Seagrove. 12p.

No. 401. 19 May 1794, Havana. Luis de las Casas to el Conde del Campo de Alange. 8p. [Encloses 7 documents].

No. 6. 20 Mar. 1794, Cloaly. [Louis] Milfort to el Barón de Carondelet. [Same as AGI Cuba/2354/fol. 24]. 17p.

Nos. 409 and 415. 27 Sept. 1794, San Ildefonso. [*Real orden*] to the Capt. Gen. of Louisiana. 1p. [Encloses 1 document].

N. fol. 26 Sept. 1794, Council of State. José de Anduaga (D'Anguado). *Acordada* from the Council of State in which the capt. general's letter on Gen. Wilkinson's actions to contain Cumberland hostilities were discussed. Council also heard about the possibility that the Chickasaws -- aided by the Cherokees, Creeks, and Choctaws -- might keep the Americans from establishing themselves in Spanish territory. 13p.

No. 409. 5 July 1794, Havana. Luis de las Casas to el Conde del Campo del Alange. 6p. [Encloses 2 documents].

No. 118 *reservada*. 28 June 1794, New Orleans. El Barón de Carondelet to Luis de las Casas (copy). Gen. Wayne intends to use the American army to reoccupy an old site called Ft. Cherokee, but Carondelet believes that the Chickasaws will stop that as well as contain Cumberland's hostile activities. 3p.

N. fol. 26 Feb. 1794, Ft. Jefferson. W[ilkinson]
to el Barón de Carondelet (translation). Wilkinson
informs the Spanish officials about the political
turmoil in Ky. and suggests ways that Spain can defend
the Upper Mississippi. Americans plan to station
troops at the mouth of the Ohio R. to intercept groups
seeking to attack Spanish territory. This will help
impede the English who travel easily to Vincennes,
Cumberland, and Louisville. 8p.

No. 453. 12 Nov. 1794, Havana. Luis de las Casas to el Conde
del Campo de Alange. 2p. [Encloses 7 documents].

No. 599. 11 Sept. 1794, St. Augustine. Juan Nepomuceno
de Quesada to Luis de las Casas. Quesada announces John
Hambly's arrival and forwards some of his documents.
Quesada laments the lack of Indian commissioners and
reports that Hambly does not speak Cherokee and has only
worked with the Cherokees on a few occasions. Hopefully,
there are people in Pensacola who can interpret for the
Cherokees. 6p.

No. 1. 11 Sept. 1794, St. Augustine. John Hambly.
*Traducción del diario que don Juan Hambly formó en su
viaje a las naciones yndias.* Hambly's diary of a trip
through Creek territory during June and July, 1794.
Hambly reports Creek attitudes towards the Americans
and the efforts of the American commissioner to win
the Creeks away from Spain. There is a possibility
that a congress composed of Cherokees, Creeks,
Choctaws, and Chickasaws will meet. Hambly speculates
that Bowles's second in command, George Welbank, came
from Cherokee territory. 15p.

Nos. 453 and 454. Nov. 1794, Havana. Capt. Gen. of Louisiana
and the Floridas to [el Conde del Campo de Alange]. [Summary
of letters nos. 453 and 454 and attachments]. 18p. [Encloses
8 documents].

No. 454. 29 Nov. 1794, Havana. Luis de las Casas to el
Conde del Campo de Alange. 2p.

No. 126 *reservada.* 30 Oct. 1794, New Orleans. El
Barón de Carondelet to Luis de las Casas. [Copy of
AGI Cuba/2354/fol. 368]. 4p.

No. 1. 18 Sept. 1794, [New Orleans?]. John Galphin
to James Burges (translation). [Same as AGI Cuba/
2354/fol. 4]. 6p.

No. 2. 2 Oct. 1794, St. Marks. Diego de Vegas to
James Burges. [Copy of AGI Cuba/2354/fol. 1]. 7p.

GM/7235 (CONT'D)

No. 2 *muy reservada*.   31 Oct. 1794, New Orleans.
El Barón de Carondelet to Diego de Vegas.   [Copy of
AGS GM/6918/no. 465/encl. no. 2 *muy reservada*].   4p.

No. 4.   20 Sept. 1794, Lower Cherokees.   John McDonald
to el Barón de Carondelet.   [Same as AGI SD/2564/
fol. 77].   5p.

No. 488.   18 Jan. 1794, St. Augustine.   Juan Nepomuceno
de Quesada to Luis de las Casas (copy).   10p.   [Encloses
5 documents].

No. 3.   15 Jan. 1794, St. Augustine.   *Plática* (talk)
from Juan Nepomuceno de Quesada to Juan Canard
[Kinnard?], Chief of the Lower Creeks (copy).   A
large number of Georgians are preparing to invade
East Fla. under the French banner.   Another group
is collecting in S.C. to move to Muscle Shoals to
invade West Fla. and Louisiana.   6p.

INDEX